SIPRI Yearbook 2008
Armaments, Disarmament and International Security

sipri
Stockholm International Peace Research Institute

SIPRI is an independent international institute for research into problems of peace and conflict, especially those of arms control and disarmament. It was established in 1966 to commemorate Sweden's 150 years of unbroken peace.

The Institute is financed mainly by a grant proposed by the Swedish Government and subsequently approved by the Swedish Parliament. The staff and the Governing Board are international. The Institute also has an Advisory Committee as an international consultative body.

The Governing Board is not responsible for the views expressed in the publications of the Institute.

sipri
Stockholm International Peace Research Institute
Signalistgatan 9, SE-169 70 Solna, Sweden
Telephone: 46 8/655 97 00
Fax: 46 8/655 97 33
Email: sipri@sipri.org
Internet URL: http://www.sipri.org

SIPRI Yearbook 2008

Armaments, Disarmament and International Security

Stockholm International Peace Research Institute

OXFORD UNIVERSITY PRESS
2008

OXFORD

UNIVERSITY PRESS

Great Clarendon Street, Oxford OX2 6DP

Oxford University Press is a department of the University of Oxford.
It furthers the University's objective of excellence in research, scholarship,
and education by publishing worldwide in

Oxford   New York

Auckland   Cape Town   Dar es Salaam   Hong Kong   Karachi
Kuala Lumpur   Madrid   Melbourne   Mexico City   Nairobi
New Delhi   Shanghai   Taipei   Toronto

With offices in

Argentina   Austria   Brazil   Chile   Czech Republic   France   Greece
Guatemala   Hungary   Italy   Japan   Poland   Portugal   Singapore
South Korea   Switzerland   Thailand   Turkey   Ukraine   Vietnam

Oxford is a registered trade mark of Oxford University Press
in the UK and in certain other countries

Published in the United States
by Oxford University Press Inc., New York

© SIPRI 2008

Before 1987 the Yearbook was published under the title
'World Armaments and Disarmament:
SIPRI Yearbook [year of publication]'

British Library Cataloguing in Publication Data
Data available

Library of Congress Cataloging in Publication Data
Data available

Typeset and originated by Stockholm International Peace Research Institute
Printed and bound in Great Britain
on acid-free paper by
Clays Ltd, St Ives plc

ISSN 0953–0282
ISBN 978–0–19–954895–8

Contents

Part II. Military spending and armaments, 2007

Part III. Non-proliferation, arms control and disarmament, 2007

Appendix 8A. World nuclear forces, 2008 366

Shannon N. Kile, Vitaly Fedchenko and Hans M. Kristensen

Appendix 8B. Global stocks of fissile materials, 2007 399

Harold Feiveson, Alexander Glaser, Zia Mian and Frank von Hippel

Appendix 8C. A survey of US ballistic missile defence programmes 402

Shannon N. Kile

Annexes

Preface

It is with great pleasure that we publish *SIPRI Yearbook 2008*, the 39th edition of SIPRI's iconic flagship. This year's edition, like those before it, maintains the highest standards for authoritativeness in its research and analysis. The SIPRI Yearbook remains the single most extensive and in-depth publication available covering the spectrum of international and regional security and conflict, peacekeeping operations, military spending, defence production, arms transfers, weapons of mass destruction, and arms control, disarmament, and non-proliferation.

In taking up this important work, the contributors to this edition of the Yearbook look back on 2007 and consider what lies ahead in 2008 and beyond. Some consistent and important themes emerge. As in recent years, the authors point to the continuing fragmentation of violence in regional conflicts and the continuing and growing role of non-state actors, including those acting on behalf of states. Global military spending and arms trade continue to expand, while the technologies relevant to both conventional and unconventional weaponry have become more diffuse and accessible. At the same time, the contributors note a continuation in the weakening of the institutions and mechanisms—multilateral, bilateral and unilateral—that states can employ to alleviate these potential threats to security and stability. In the face of these developments, and in many ways *because* of them, SIPRI also sees a growing sense—albeit constrained by a cautious realism—that the world is moving into a period in which arms control and non-proliferation will be more hotly debated in the international community—and possibly strengthened—than at any time in the past decade.

While the SIPRI Yearbook is rightly valued for its bedrock constancy, SIPRI itself has seen a year of change. After five years of outstanding service, Alyson J. K. Bailes stepped down from the SIPRI directorship in August 2007 to take up a post as a Visiting Professor at the University of Iceland. Alyson's tenure will be remembered for her work in strengthening the rigorous analysis of SIPRI's research; expanding SIPRI's networks with policymakers in Europe, Asia and beyond; developing SIPRI's interest and expertise in global and regional security affairs; and diversifying SIPRI's funding base. Before departing, Alyson also oversaw the early stages of preparation for this volume, and laid the groundwork for a smooth transition to the new Director of SIPRI.

Another important figure at SIPRI, Connie Wall, also departed from the institute. For 37 years at SIPRI—the majority of which she headed the Editorial and Publications Department—Connie more than anyone else assured the institute's global reputation for outstanding publications with the highest standards of editorial, scientific and academic integrity.

These two remarkable colleagues left SIPRI in a strong position to continue its transformation to the next level. Over the latter half of 2007 and into 2008, SIPRI launched several new initiatives—including a monthly email newsletter, *SIPRI Update: Global Security & Arms Control*, a SIPRI weblog (blog) on Afghanistan, the development of a new website to be launched in the autumn of 2008, and the redesign of our publications—all aimed at engaging a broader audience of partners, supporters and interested readers. Throughout the year, SIPRI's international staff continued their excellent research and practical work, travelling to more than 50 countries—from Australia to Iran, from Malaysia to Ukraine, from Colombia to Egypt, and across Europe and North America. SIPRI was especially proud in 2007 to be named one of the 'Top 30 Global Go-To Think Tanks' based on a survey conducted by the US Foreign Policy Research Institute of more than 5000 think tanks and policy research institutes worldwide.

Such an ambitious undertaking as the Yearbook is simply not possible without the dedicated efforts of a host of exceptional people. The hard-working editorial team for this volume—David Cruickshank, Joey Fox, Jetta Gilligan Borg and Caspar Trimmer—deserves particular thanks. I also gratefully thank the authors of this volume, both those from SIPRI and outside contributors, as well as Peter Rea, who has done his usual excellent indexing of the volume. The outstanding work of others at SIPRI, including their staffs, calls for further special appreciation: Daniel Nord, Deputy Director (who also served as Acting Director between August and October 2007); Ian Anthony, Research Coordinator; Anna Helleday, Head of the Finance and Administration Department; Nenne Bodell, Head of the Library and Documentation Department; Gerd Hagmeyer, Head of the Information Technology Department; and Cynthia Loo, Special Assistant to the Director.

In publishing *SIPRI Yearbook 2008*, the first under my directorship, I thank the SIPRI Governing Board, the entire SIPRI staff and our many partners and friends around the world, and look forward to continuing our important work together in the years ahead.

Dr Bates Gill
SIPRI Director
May 2008

Abstracts

SIPRI Yearbook 2008: Armaments, Disarmament and International Security

Oxford University Press, Oxford, 2008, 604 pp.
(Stockholm International Peace Research Institute)
ISSN 0953–0282
ISBN 978–0–19–954895–8

GILL, B., 'Introduction. A call to arms control', in *SIPRI Yearbook 2008*, pp. 1–12.

The coming years will see more high-level discussion and debate on the merits of arms control and disarmament. This emerges from a broadening consensus that more serious and effective arms control and disarmament measures should be implemented. Disarmament and related confidence- and security-building measures by Russia and the USA will be especially important. However, a broader, global effort will also be needed which includes both nuclear and non-nuclear weapon states and which crosses political divides. Three caveats are in order. First, the priorities of the next US Administration will play a critical role. Second, progress on existing and new multilateral treaties should not overshadow other mechanisms. Finally, arms control and disarmament cannot solve all the world's problems. The traditional meaning of 'arms control' should be broadened to encompass non-treaty- and non-state-based approaches. Voices from across the political spectrum are coming to recognize again the value of arms control. It is clearly in the interest of citizens and governments alike to take steps in the right direction.

HAINE, J.-Y., HEROLF, G. and LACHOWSKI, Z., 'Euro-Atlantic security institutions and relationships', in *SIPRI Yearbook 2008*, pp. 15–41.

During 2007 the main Euro-Atlantic actors sought to manage old and renewed estrangements. The most significant development in Euro-Atlantic relations was Russia's restored self-confidence and aspirations to equal status in security matters with its Western partners. Nevertheless, Russia appears willing to maintain cooperative relations with the West and is unlikely to risk challenging it too forcefully. The European Union adopted the Lisbon Treaty, but the Constitutional Treaty debacle of 2005 continued to hamper its programmes for the European neighbourhood, external relations and foreign and security policies. NATO remained uncertain about its sense of purpose, although France's overtures to NATO raised modest hopes for the alliance's rejuvenation. The European–US rapprochement that emerged in 2007 reflected more acknowledged weaknesses than projected strengths. The USA's policies that had diminished its influence have largely been replaced by a more pragmatic approach to world affairs.

STEPANOVA, E., 'Trends in armed conflicts', in *SIPRI Yearbook 2008*, pp. 43–71.

In 2007 the fragmentation of violence and diversification of armed actors continued in some of the world's deadliest armed conflicts, including Iraq and Darfur (Sudan). This trend is associated with lower levels of battle-related deaths, but high costs for civilians in terms of casualties, displacement and other less direct impacts. The trend has been accompanied by further erosion of the boundaries between different forms of violence (including terrorism and sectarian and other inter-communal strife) and actors (including state-affiliated actors, private security contractors, criminals and local-level power-brokers). This violence may occur in the context of—and be triggered by—an armed conflict, but often acquires its own dynamics, becomes self-perpetuating and may not necessarily end or decline even if the conflict's main incompatibility is more or less effectively addressed.

SCHNABEL, A., 'The human security approach to direct and structural violence', in *SIPRI Yearbook 2008*, pp. 87–95.

In human security analysis and provision, using direct and structural violence as interdependent core variables offers opportunities to address the most crucial threats to populations and to prepare for the most effective mitigation mechanisms. The mitigation of human insecurity requires: (*a*) population- and context-specific threat and violence identification and analysis; (*b*) threat-, context- and actor-specific designs of preventive and response measures; (*c*) multi-actor strategies for the targeted prevention of direct and structural violence; and (*d*) monitoring and assessment of threat levels and implemented mitigation and adaptation measures. Such a systematic approach is particularly relevant in the presence of structural violence, which is not always easy to recognize, and the identification of responsible causes and actors is a challenge at best. Moreover, special attention must be paid to the role of armed violence and its potential for escalating existing and creating new waves of direct and structural violence.

WIHARTA, S., 'Planning and deploying peace operations', in *SIPRI Yearbook 2008*, pp. 97–112.

With eight new operations launched in 2007, pre-deployment planning became a focus for the peacekeeping community. The United Nations sought to fully implement its Integrated Mission Planning Process. Advance planning is a complex process that is integral to the success of a peace operation. An initial coherent strategy is key to developing a peace operation that has clearly defined objectives and mandates and is equipped with the necessary human, material and financial resources. Peace operations are likely to be more effective if they are conceived, planned and evaluated based on a critical analysis of the needs of the affected country. In recent years the peacekeeping community has sought to widen participation in the planning process to include national stakeholders. The cases of UNAMID in Sudan and of MINURCAT and EUFOR Tchad/RCA in Chad and the Central African Republic illustrate the challenges in striking the balance between inclusivity and getting a mission on the ground.

BASTICK, M., 'Integrating gender in post-conflict security sector reform', in *SIPRI Yearbook 2008*, pp. 149–71.

While there is wide recognition of the importance of women's participation and gender equality in post-conflict peacebuilding, security sector reform (SSR) processes often fail to include women, and fail to address the security needs of the entire population—including women and children. Experiences in Afghanistan, Kosovo, Liberia, Peru, Rwanda, Sierra Leone and Timor-Leste demonstrate the value of measures to integrate gender in SSR. Efforts include involving women in civil society and government, increasing women's participation in security services, and transitional justice processes. SSR has much to gain by integrating gender; doing so increases responsiveness to the security needs and roles of all parts of the community, strengthens local ownership of the reform process and enhances security sector oversight.

STÅLENHEIM, P., PERDOMO, C. and SKÖNS, E., 'Military expenditure', in *SIPRI Yearbook 2008*, pp. 175–206.

World military expenditure is estimated to have been $1339 billion in 2007—a real-terms increase of 6 per cent over 2006 and of 45 per cent since 1998. This spending was equivalent to 2.5 per cent of world gross domestic production and $202 per capita. In 2007 the USA had the highest military expenditure—with 45 per cent of the total—followed by the UK, China, France and Japan, with 4–5 per cent each. Since 2001 US military spending has increased by 59 per cent in real terms and is now higher than at any time since World War II. The factors driving increases in world military spending include countries' foreign policy objectives, real or perceived threats, armed conflict and policies to contribute to multilateral peacekeeping operations, combined with the availability of economic resources.

PERLO-FREEMAN, S. and SKÖNS, E., 'Arms production', in *SIPRI Yearbook 2008*, pp. 255–77.

Arms sales by the world's 100 largest arms-producing companies (outside China)—the SIPRI Top 100—totalled $315 billion in 2006, a 9 per cent nominal increase over 2005. The increase was led by US companies, benefiting from continuing increases in US military spending. Generally, companies specializing in armoured vehicles—in demand by the USA for the conflict in Iraq—and in expanding sectors, such as military services and high-technology electronics and communications, had the biggest increases in arms sales in 2006. There were seven mergers and acquisitions worth over $1 billion in the North American and West European arms industry in 2007. Six involved the acquisition of a US company by either a US or a British buyer. The European Defence Agency and the European Commission proposed further measures in 2007 aimed at creating a more integrated arms industry and market in the European Union, while the Russian Government continued moves to consolidate the Russian arms industry into large state-owned conglomerates.

HOLTOM, P., BROMLEY, M. and WEZEMAN, P. D., 'International arms transfers' in *SIPRI Yearbook 2008*, pp. 293–317.

More than 80 per cent of the volume of exports of major conventional weapons for the period 2003–2007 was accounted for by the five largest suppliers—the USA, Russia, Germany, France and the UK. With decreased deliveries to and orders by China—the single largest recipient for the period 2003–2007—2007 gave the first signs of a potentially significant change among the major recipients. Despite attention-grabbing headlines and an increased volume of imports by Chile and Venezuela in the period 2003–2007 compared to 1998–2002, it seems unlikely that South America is in the midst of an arms race. Arms transfers to armed non-state actors, national armed forces and peacekeeping missions in the conflict-zones of Afghanistan and Sudan were also highlighted in 2007.

KILE, S. N., 'Nuclear arms control and non-proliferation' in *SIPRI Yearbook 2008*, pp. 337–65.

Iran's nuclear programme remained in the spotlight as the United Nations Security Council Resolution 1747 imposed additional sanctions on Iran over its refusal to halt its uranium enrichment activities. The US intelligence community concluded that Iran had halted its nuclear weapon programme in 2003 and had not resumed it. The Six-Party Talks on North Korea produced an agreement on a two-phase Action Plan under which North Korea agreed to shut down and then disable its nuclear facilities. North Korea failed to meet the year-end deadline for implementing the plan's steps. Elsewhere, there was controversy over the terms of a draft agreement governing the resumption of trade in nuclear material and technology envisaged in the 2005 Indian–US Civil Nuclear Cooperation Initiative. The Conference on Disarmament failed again to open negotiations on a global fissile material cut-off treaty.

KILE, S. N., 'A survey of US ballistic missile defence programmes', in *SIPRI Yearbook 2008*, pp. 402–14

The USA continues to pursue an expansive array of weapon and sensor programmes for active defences against short-, medium- and long-range ballistic missiles. It has given high priority to deploying an integrated, multi-layer defence system designed to protect US territory and allies from perceived emerging threats posed by adversaries with missiles potentially armed with nuclear weapons. Under a controversial US plan, key elements of the system will be deployed in the Czech Republic and Poland. There remain concerns about the technological readiness of the system as well as about its cost and likely effectiveness in realistic missile engagement scenarios. The USA has bilateral ballistic missile defence development programmes under way with Israel and Japan, which involve significant defence-industrial cooperation.

FEDCHENKO, V., 'Nuclear forensic analysis', in *SIPRI Yearbook 2008*, pp. 415–27.

Many international treaties and national laws require mechanisms to verify compliance, which, in turn, rely on technology. As technology advances, it provides better means for verification. Nuclear forensic analysis (nuclear forensics) is a newly emerging scientific discipline with direct applications in treaty verification and law enforcement. Nuclear forensic techniques were first developed in the 1940s and have since been used in the verification of bilateral arms control treaties. Recent technological advances provide an opportunity for nuclear forensics to be successfully applied in (*a*) combating nuclear smuggling, (*b*) International Atomic Energy Agency safeguards, (*c*) identifying nuclear explosions and verifying the 1996 Comprehensive Nuclear Test-Ban Treaty, and (*d*) the proposed fissile material cut-off treaty. The amount of information that can be obtained from application of nuclear forensic techniques depends on access to relevant sites and samples, which is often limited by legal or political considerations.

HART, J. and CLEVESTIG, P., 'Reducing security threats from chemical and biological materials' in *SIPRI Yearbook 2008*, pp. 429–55.

In 2007 threat perceptions and chemical and biological warfare (CBW) prevention and response measures continued to evolve away from state-based programmes to include more diffuse, less quantifiable, non-state and even speculative threat scenarios. The parties to the 1972 Biological and Toxin Weapons Convention exchanged information related to effective national implementation of the convention. Albania completed destruction of its chemical weapon stockpile as part of its obligations under the 1993 Chemical Weapons Convention. The United Nations Special Commission on Iraq was disbanded while a number of attacks using chlorine were carried out by insurgents in Iraq. The increasing involvement of the security sector in scientific research in order to prevent CBW has continued to raise concern about the free pursuit and dissemination of peaceful research. Increasing bio-preparedness research in some states may also pose an inherent threat because it increases potentially sensitive data and expertise.

RAVECHÉ, B., 'International public health diplomacy and the global surveillance of avian influenza', in *SIPRI Yearbook 2008*, pp. 456–69.

Security rhetoric has been used increasingly to discuss global public health. This is reflected in the changing role of the World Health Organization in governing global health as evidenced by the revised International Health Regulations (IHR) that began to be implemented in June 2007. Because of the IHR's long history of ineffectiveness and non-compliance by some member states, the revised IHR uses a legal framework giving the WHO unprecedented legal authority over the global disease surveillance and reporting requirements of the member states. The looming threat of an avian influenza pandemic and Indonesia's reluctance to send the WHO timely samples of influenza virus represents the tension between developed and developing countries and the challenges facing the revised IHR.

LACHOWSKI, Z., 'Conventional arms control', in *SIPRI Yearbook 2008*, pp. 471–91.

In 2007 the biggest challenge yet to the 1990 Treaty on Conventional Armed Forces in Europe occurred when Russia 'suspended' its participation in the regime. Reconciliation over this and related issues seemed unlikely. While the deadlock over the Russian military presence in Moldova persisted, in contrast, the 2005 agreement on Russia's withdrawal from Georgia was implemented. Subregional arms control in the Balkans operated smoothly. The Organization for Security and Co-operation in Europe (OSCE) Code of Conduct on Politico-Military Aspects of Security retains its relevance, and other confidence-building steps among OSCE participants continue to focus on the multiple dangers created by surplus stockpiles of small arms, ammunition and toxic rocket fuel. The number of states adhering to the 1997 Anti-Personnel Mines Convention rose to 156, taking it further towards universalization. More and more countries are participating in the 'Oslo process' to ban the use of cluster munitions.

ANTHONY, I., BAUER, S. and WETTER, A., 'Controls on security-related international transfers', in *SIPRI Yearbook 2008*, pp. 493–513.

Export controls are preventive measures intended to help ensure that exported goods do not contribute to activities in other countries that are either illegal or undesirable from the perspective of the exporting state. The role of export controls in supporting the main multilateral non-proliferation treaties is now supplemented by the role that they play in implementing decisions of the United Nations Security Council focused on particular countries (e.g. Iran and North Korea). The effective enforcement of export controls laws and non-proliferation sanctions requires adapting legal bases, rethinking institutional set-ups and procedures, and the involvement of a range of national actors—including customs, police, intelligence and prosecution services. An international debate about what constitutes dissuasive, effective and proportionate sanctions in response to violations of export control law has been initiated, in particular within the European Union.

Abbreviations and conventions

ABM	Anti-ballistic missile	CFSP	Common Foreign and Security Policy
ACV	Armoured combat vehicle		
AG	Australia Group	CICA	Conference on Interaction and Confidence-building Measures in Asia
ALCM	Air-launched cruise missile		
APC	Armoured personnel carrier	CIS	Commonwealth of Independent States
APEC	Asia–Pacific Economic Cooperation		
		CSBM	Confidence- and security-building measure
APM	Anti-personnel mine		
APT	ASEAN Plus Three	CSCAP	Council for Security Cooperation in the Asia Pacific
ARF	ASEAN Regional Forum		
ASAT	Anti-satellite		
ASEAN	Association of Southeast Asian Nations	CSTO	Collective Security Treaty Organization
ATT	Arms trade treaty	CTBT	Comprehensive Nuclear Test-Ban Treaty
ATTU	Atlantic-to-the Urals (zone)		
AU	African Union	CTBTO	Comprehensive Nuclear-Test-Ban Treaty Organization
BMD	Ballistic missile defence		
BSEC	Organization of the Black Sea Economic Cooperation	CTR	Co-operative Threat Reduction
BTWC	Biological and Toxin Weapons Convention	CW	Chemical weapon/warfare
		CWC	Chemical Weapons Convention
BW	Biological weapon/warfare		
CADSP	Common African Defence and Security Policy	D-8	Developing Eight (countries)
CAR	Central African Republic	DDR	Disarmament, demobilization and reintegration
CBM	Confidence-building measure		
CBSS	Council of the Baltic Sea States	DPKO	UN Department of Peacekeeping Operations
CBW	Chemical and biological weapon/warfare	DPRK	Democratic People's Republic of Korea (North Korea)
CCW	Certain Conventional Weapons (Convention)		
		DRC	Democratic Republic of the Congo
CD	Conference on Disarmament		
		EAEC	European Atomic Energy Community (Euratom)
CEI	Central European Initiative		
CEMAC	Communauté Economique et Monétaire d'Afrique Centrale (Economic and Monetary Community of Central Africa)	EAPC	Euro-Atlantic Partnership Council
		ECOWAS	Economic Community of West African States
		EDA	European Defence Agency
CFE	Conventional Armed Forces in Europe (Treaty)	ENP	European Neighbourhood Policy

ERW	Explosive remnants of war	IMF	International Monetary Fund
ESDP	European Security and Defence Policy	INDA	International non-proliferation and disarmament assistance
EU	European Union		
FMCT	Fissile material cut-off treaty	INF	Intermediate-range Nuclear Forces (Treaty)
FSC	Forum for Security Co-operation	IRBM	Intermediate-range ballistic missile
FY	Financial year	ISAF	International Security Assistance Force
FYROM	Former Yugoslav Republic of Macedonia	IST	Iraqi Special Tribunal
G8	Group of Eight (industrialized states)	JCG	Joint Consultative Group
		JCIC	Joint Compliance and Inspection Commission
GAERC	General Affairs and External Relations Council	JHA	Justice and Home Affairs
GCC	Gulf Cooperation Council	LEU	Low-enriched uranium
GDP	Gross domestic product	MANPADS	Man-portable air defence system
GLCM	Ground-launched cruise missile	MDGs	Millennium Development Goals
GNEP	Global Nuclear Energy Partnership	MER	Market exchange rate
GNI	Gross national income	MERCOSUR	Mercado Común del Sur (Southern Common Market)
GNP	Gross national product		
GTRI	Global Threat Reduction Initiative	MIRV	Multiple independently targetable re-entry vehicle
GUAM	Georgia, Ukraine, Azerbaijan and Moldova	MOTAPM	Mines other than anti-personnel mines
HCOC	Hague Code of Conduct	MTCR	Missile Technology Control Regime
HEU	Highly enriched uranium	NAM	Non-Aligned Movement
IAEA	International Atomic Energy Agency	NATO	North Atlantic Treaty Organization
ICBM	Intercontinental ballistic missile	NBC	Nuclear, biological and chemical (weapons)
ICC	International Criminal Court	NGO	Non-governmental organization
ICJ	International Court of Justice	NNWS	Non-nuclear weapon state
ICTY	International Criminal Tribunal for the former Yugoslavia	NPT	Non-Proliferation Treaty
		NRF	NATO Response Force
IED	Improvised explosive device	NSG	Nuclear Suppliers Group
IGAD	Intergovernmental Authority on Development	NWS	Nuclear weapon state
		OAS	Organization of American States
IGC	Intergovernmental Conference		

OCCAR	Organisation Conjointe de Coopération en matière d'Armement (Organisation for Joint Armament Cooperation)
ODA	Official development assistance
ODA	UN Office for Disarmament Affairs
OECD	Organisation for Economic Co-operation and Development
OIC	Organization of the Islamic Conference
OPANAL	Organismo para la Proscripción de las Armas Nucleares en la América Latina y el Caribe (Agency for the Prohibition of Nuclear Weapons in Latin America and the Caribbean)
OPCW	Organisation for the Prohibition of Chemical Weapons
OPEC	Organization of the Petroleum Exporting Countries
OSCC	Open Skies Consultative Commission
OSCE	Organization for Security and Co-operation in Europe
PFP	Partnership for Peace
PPP	Purchasing power parity
PRT	Provincial reconstruction team
PSC	Private security company
PSI	Proliferation Security Initiative
R&D	Research and development
SAARC	South Asian Association for Regional Co-operation
SADC	Southern African Development Community
SALW	Small arms and light weapons
SAM	Surface-to-air missile
SCO	Shanghai Cooperation Organization
SECI	Southeast European Cooperative Initiative
SLBM	Submarine-launched ballistic missile
SLCM	Sea-launched cruise missile
SORT	Strategic Offensive Reductions Treaty
SRBM	Short-range ballistic missile
SRCC	Sub-Regional Consultative Commission
SSM	Surface-to-surface missile
SSR	Security sector reform
START	Strategic Arms Reduction Treaty
TLE	Treaty-limited equipment
UAE	United Arab Emirates
UAV	Unmanned aerial vehicle
UCAV	Unmanned combat air vehicle
USAID	US Agency for International Development
UN	United Nations
UNDP	UN Development Programme
UNHCR	UN High Commissioner for Refugees
UNMOVIC	UN Monitoring, Verification and Inspection Commission
UNROCA	UN Register of Conventional Arms
UNSCOM	UN Special Commission on Iraq
WA	Wassenaar Arrangement
WEU	Western European Union
WMD	Weapon(s) of mass destruction

Conventions

..	Data not available or not applicable
–	Nil or a negligible figure
( )	Uncertain data
b.	Billion (thousand million)
kg	Kilogram
km	Kilometre (1000 metres)
kt	Kiloton (1000 tons)
m.	Million
Mt	Megaton (1 million tons)
th.	Thousand
tr.	Trillion (million million)
$	US dollars, unless otherwise indicated
€	Euros

Introduction
A call to arms control

BATES GILL

I. A widening window of opportunity

As this edition of the SIPRI Yearbook so amply shows, the world faces some very difficult security challenges in the years ahead, not least regarding a fragile security environment in certain regions, continuing build-ups of conventional and unconventional arms around the world, and uneven progress for arms control, non-proliferation and disarmament. Moreover, numerous structural challenges—including tightened supplies of energy and other natural resources; a lack of consensus on global governance of security challenges; inadequate regional capacity for conflict management, peacekeeping, and post-conflict reconstruction and reconciliation; weakening state structures; and the fragmentation of violence—will continue to undermine security in societies around the globe and especially in the developing world.

However, there are some potentially brighter spots on the horizon. The next 12 months promise the beginnings of the first serious discussions of arms control and disarmament in more than a decade. This fortuitous opportunity emerges from a broadening consensus around the world—both among women and men on the street and among elites—that more serious and effective arms control and disarmament measures should be implemented.

This would not be the first time in the post-World War II era that arms control and disarmament have risen to the forefront of international consciousness. But in recent years two critical trends have converged in ways that raise the arms control policy debate to new and interesting levels. One trend points to increasing concerns about, threats to and the potential collapse of long-standing agreements and understandings on arms control and non-proliferation. The other, more encouraging, trend points to new and emergent opportunities for more effective arms control, non-proliferation and disarmament steps in the coming years. On the one hand, these developments—both threatening and encouraging—have begun to energize some long-standing, but flagging, arms control and disarmament efforts around the world. On the other hand, these efforts face powerful and continuing obstacles and will demand redoubled energies to take fuller advantage of a widening window of opportunity.

Looking ahead, it is becoming clearer than ever that the next one to two years will see far more high-level discussion and debate, both globally and in leading capitals around the world, on the merits of arms control and disarmament. Less clear at this stage is how successful this renewed effort will be.

II. Growing concerns

At least four important areas of concern regarding arms control and disarmament have gained prominence in recent years to drive more progressive
and urgent thinking on these issues.

The diffusion of sensitive goods, technologies and know-how

There is intensifying awareness around the world of the need to balance the
obvious advantages of globalization with its increasingly apparent disadvan-
tages. Regarding arms control, this is demonstrated by a growing need to
balance the benefits of greater and more diffuse flows of people, goods, technologies and knowledge—including those relevant to developing weapons of
mass destruction (WMD)—with a greater ability to monitor and prevent their
misuse towards illicit and violent ends.

This conundrum applies across a widening spectrum of current and emergent technologies—such as nuclear technologies, but especially in the biological sciences, including genetic engineering, synthetic biology and nano-
technologies—and, as discussed in this volume, raises new and vexing questions about the appropriate balance between the greater diffusion and the
appropriate control of such technological advancements.[1] This is not only a
'North–South' problem, or a contest between the world's 'haves' and 'have
nots'. Within the developed world there are also difficult contradictions and
concerns between those who wish to use such technologies for legitimate professional purposes—scientists, researchers and medical personnel, for
example—and national authorities concerned with domestic security, emergency preparedness and law enforcement which may wish to see greater safety
and security restrictions placed on their use.

More specifically, this concern relates to the growing demands that, for the
benefit of humankind, both mature and emergent technologies should be
spread more widely and equitably in order to expand access to energy, health,
education and other public goods. Perhaps the best understood example of this
challenge concerns the development and diffusion of nuclear technology.

On the one hand, the demand for nuclear energy seems to be on the rise.
Energy demand on the whole continues to rise as the world's leading economies continue to grow and as newly burgeoning economies, such as China,
India, and Russia, emerge more prominently. As the world's demand for and
dependence on carbon-based energy sources has an impact on and exacerbates
climate change, and as the price of oil edged over $100 a barrel in early 2008,
there is a glaring need for energy alternatives. Hence, there is a growing sense
of a nuclear energy 'renaissance' across the globe, and particularly in the
developing world. Moreover, nuclear technology also provides numerous cur-

---

[1] See chapters 8, 9 and 11 in this volume.

rent and potential future benefits in a wide range of medical, health and scientific fields.

On the other hand, nuclear technology and materials—designed for both military and civilian purposes—pose considerable risks. Russia and the United States—which, as documented in this volume, together account for more than 90 per cent of the approximately 10 200 deployed nuclear weapons in the world today[2]—continue to maintain thousands of nuclear weapons capable of being launched against each other and virtually any corner of the globe in a matter of minutes. Even if the possibility of an intentional nuclear exchange among such states is remote, the accidental or unauthorized use of nuclear weapons and, in some cases, their vulnerability to diversion and theft, remains an ongoing and dangerous problem. The political instability witnessed in Pakistan in 2007 raised questions about the safety and security of nuclear arsenals.

Having access to certain parts of the nuclear fuel cycle, particularly uranium enrichment and spent fuel reprocessing technologies, also provides the means to pursue a nuclear weapon programme: North Korea's detonation of a nuclear device in 2006 and suspicions about Iran's nuclear intentions are only the most current cases in point. Meanwhile, concerns are increasing that poorly protected fissile and other radioactive materials will ultimately be malignly used—perhaps in a nuclear explosive device or radiological weapon—not by states, but in a terrorist act with catastrophic consequences. In addition, both civilian and military nuclear facilities pose potential risks resulting from deliberate attack or an accident. The risk of such an accident is not inherently less in the military than the civilian sector and may actually be greater given that military facilities are not subject to international safeguards regimes.

These challenges concern not only nuclear-related technologies but apply also to current and emergent technologies in other fields such as the biosciences, chemistry and genetics. Chemical and biological technologies and capacities are far more widespread than their nuclear counterparts, but far less attention has been given to grappling with the threats that this situation may pose. With these challenges in mind, many argue that, rather than allowing for continuing and growing access to nuclear and other potentially dangerous technologies—whether WMD-related, dual-use or otherwise sensitive—much more needs to be done to manage their role and availability and prevent their illicit, accidental or unauthorized use.

Complex conventional conflict and increased conventional spending

Conventional armed conflict in the world is also taking on a far more complex and intractable character than generally presumed. As discussed in the chapter on armed conflicts, forms of violence that are more diversified and fragmented—and hence more difficult to address and resolve—are becoming a greater threat to human security. While the number of state-based major armed

---

[2] See appendix 8A in this volume.

conflicts has fallen from 20 to 14 over the past decade, the number of non-state conflicts is both higher, at 21 in 2006, and varies more erratically.[3]

In addition, the world as a whole continues to devote larger and larger sums of money to military spending. As discussed and documented in the chapter on military expenditure, military spending globally was approximately $1339 billion in 2007, an increase of 6 per cent over 2006; over the 10-year period 1998–2007, global military spending increased by 45 per cent in real terms. At the level of individual countries and subregions, the increases are even more striking. Over the period 1998–2007, military spending in Eastern Europe (Armenia, Azerbaijan, Belarus, Georgia, Moldova, Russia and Ukraine) increased by 162 per cent, with Russia accounting for 61 per cent of that increase. North America increased its military spending by 63 per cent over that same period, dominated by increases in US military spending; the USA alone accounted for 45 per cent of the world's total military spending in 2007.[4]

Similarly, arms production and international arms transfers are also on the rise, as detailed in the chapters on these activities.[5] The arms sales of the SIPRI Top 100 arms-producing companies (outside China) in 2006 were $315 billion, an increase of $23 billion, or 8 per cent, over the arms sales of the Top 100 for 2005. The volume of transfers of major conventional weapons over the period 2003–2007 was 7 per cent higher than over the period 2002–2006.

Weakened institutions

A third concern relates to the mechanisms, both currently in place and under consideration, which are intended to address the kinds of problems outlined above. The 1968 Non-Proliferation Treaty (NPT) is a good case in point.[6] The NPT faces some serious questions over the next two years in the run-up to its next quinquennial review conference, in 2010. The previous NPT review conference, in 2005, for a variety of reasons ended in deadlock, resulting in no substantive recommendations or decisions for further promoting the operations and aims of the treaty.[7] As preparations are under way for the 2010 review conference, many observers question the ability of the NPT and its related inspection regimes to successfully address the treaty's long-term goals of non-proliferation and disarmament. At a minimum, some argue, these mutually reinforcing goals cannot be achieved within the confines of the NPT when several nuclear-armed states—such as India, Israel and Pakistan—are not parties to the treaty and when North Korea, which is believed to have detonated a nuclear device in 2006, has suspended its membership.

---

[3] See appendix 2A in this volume.

[4] See chapter 5 in this volume.

[5] See chapters 6 and 7 in this volume.

[6] For a summary of the 1968 Treaty on the Non-Proliferation of Nuclear Weapons see annex A in this volume.

[7] See Kile, S. N., 'Nuclear arms control and non-proliferation', *SIPRI Yearbook 2006: Armaments, Disarmament and International Security* (Oxford University Press: Oxford, 2006), pp. 608–18.

As described in the chapters on nuclear and conventional arms control, other major arms control and disarmament mechanisms—such as the 1990 Treaty on Conventional Armed Forces in Europe (CFE Treaty), the 1991 Strategic Arms Reduction Treaty (START I Treaty), the 1996 Comprehensive Nuclear Test-Ban Treaty (CTBT) and a proposed fissile material cut-off treaty—are all faltering or making little progress.[8] Moreover, these arms control and disarmament treaties and agreements aim to bring states within their ambit, when the greatest threat of WMD use—not to mention growing threats to human security from conventionally armed actors—may well emanate from non-state actors, such as terrorist or criminal groups.

The lack of consensus among major actors

A fourth set of concerns arises among and within states in the international system—the very players that are currently in the best position to counteract and alleviate the growing concerns noted above. The standing of the USA in the international system is at a low ebb, weakening its ability to mobilize support and forge consensus on matters of global security. In its last year, and with a sceptical approach to arms control, the US Administration of President George W. Bush is unlikely to take a more proactive stance on arms control and disarmament in any event. Moreover, as developed in this volume, rather than de-emphasizing the role of nuclear weapons, those countries possessing a nuclear weapon capability—the USA, Russia, the United Kingdom, France, China, India, Pakistan, Israel and North Korea—continue to place a strong reliance on these weapons in their national security strategies.[9]

In addition—as discussed in the chapter on Euro-Atlantic security—an undercurrent of mistrust and estrangement continues to characterize security relations among many of the world's major powers on issues of arms control and disarmament—including between Russia and the USA, between China and the USA, and between Russia and Western Europe.[10] Even within well-established multilateral institutions among 'like-minded' countries, such as the European Union (EU) and the North Atlantic Treaty Organization (NATO), stark differences exist among member states over questions of the future role of nuclear weapons, the deployment of strategic defences and the desirability of disarmament. Many non-nuclear weapon states are highly sceptical of the sincerity of nuclear weapon states' pursuit of disarmament according to their NPT commitments, and will understandably assume a 'wait-and-see' approach towards new disarmament and non-proliferation initiatives.

These points all add up to a difficult and ominous situation whereby potential threats—such as accidental, unauthorized or intentional use of nuclear and other dangerous weapons and technologies—increase, while the means and

---

[8] See chapters 8 and 10 in this volume. For summaries of the START I Treaty, the CFE Treaty and the CTBT see annex A in this volume.

[9] See appendix 8A in this volume.

[10] See chapter 1 in this volume.

mechanisms to prevent or diminish the likelihood of such a catastrophic event face growing challenges.

III. Emerging opportunities

In response to these challenges, there is growing urgency across the globe to bring new life and a mainstream momentum to arms control. This seems particularly promising in the near term in relation to nuclear arms control and disarmament. Two important and encouraging developments should be noted and strengthened in this regard.

A new political space

First, there is a growing expectation that governments will actually find it politically possible to take concrete action on the arms control and disarmament front. Much of that anticipation reflects a political changing of the guard around the world. There is new leadership in the United Nations and newly elected leaders in France, Germany, Japan, Russia and the UK. There will be a new US President in 2009. The EU, which has been developing a more coherent position on arms control since the early-2000s, expects to emerge as a greater political force on the global scene in the coming years. Even in China, leaders installed in 2002 are now solidifying their confidence and position in their second term in office. In major surveys, citizens throughout the world strongly support verifiable steps towards a world free of nuclear weapons.[11] However, progress remains a political challenge for governments around the globe, despite the widespread sentiments in favour of disarmament amongst their citizenries. Responding to the real threat posed by nuclear weapons, and building on the growing public concern with the threat, these leaders, more so than their predecessors, can take action in the increasingly favourable political space around disarmament issues.

Some interesting and new political space around arms control has been generated by high-profile calls for disarmament coming out of the USA and other Western powers. This includes the two *Wall Street Journal* opinion pieces by George Schultz, Sam Nunn, Henry Kissinger and William Perry, who in January 2007 and again in January 2008 forcefully called for steps aimed at eliminating nuclear weapons.[12] In 2007 US Democratic Party presidential hopeful Barack Obama said that as president he would cooperate with Russia to 'dramatically reduce the stockpiles of our nuclear weapons' and 'update and scale back our dangerously outdated Cold War nuclear postures and de-emphasize the role of nuclear weapons', and that the USA would seek

---

[11] See e.g. Angus Reid Strategies, *Global Public Opinion on Nuclear Weapons* (Simons Foundation: New York, 2007), <http://www.angusreidstrategies.com/index.cfm?page=6>.

[12] Schultz, G. P. et al., 'A world free of nuclear weapons', *Wall Street Journal*, 4 Jan. 2007; and Schultz, G. P. et al., 'Toward a nuclear-free world', *Wall Street Journal*, 15 Jan. 2008.

'a world in which there are no nuclear weapons'.[13] US Republican Party presidential candidate John McCain said in early 2008, 'We should work to reduce nuclear arsenals all around the world, starting with our own. . . . We do not need all the weapons currently in our arsenal. The United States should lead a global effort at nuclear disarmament consistent with our vital interests and the cause of peace.'[14]

In the UK, a January 2008 editorial in *The Guardian* called on the UK to 'lead the way' in getting rid of nuclear weapons,[15] and in 2007 the British Foreign Secretary, Margaret Beckett, called for both 'vision' and 'action' which could lead to 'a world free of nuclear weapons'.[16] In another high-profile step in favour of arms control, Warren Buffett, one of the world's wealthiest entrepreneurs and philanthropists, donated $50 million—which was then matched by the US Government—in 2006 to promote progress towards creation of a multilateral nuclear fuel bank under the auspices of the International Atomic Energy Agency.[17] A range of other high-level appeals and activities are planned for 2008 and 2009 in the USA, in Europe and around the world, promising to keep issues of arms control and disarmament politically front and centre.[18]

Advances in technological tools

Second, there are also encouraging developments on the technical front, offering greater certainty on questions of monitoring and verification for arms control treaties and other forms of arms control agreements. For example, advances in nuclear forensics analysis—a tool most often associated with helping to prevent illicit trafficking of nuclear materials—now hold out greater promise of strengthening the monitoring and verification regimes of the NPT, the CTBT (when it enters into force) and a prospective fissile material cut-off treaty, not to mention its uses in investigations following nuclear or radiological attacks.[19] The monitoring system put in place under the auspices of the CTBT was able to help detect and assess the low-level nuclear explo-

[13] Obama, B., 'A new beginning', Remarks made at DePaul University, Chicago, Ill., 2 Oct. 2007, <http://www.barackobama.com/2007/10/02/remarks_of_senator_barack_obam_27.php>; and Obama, B., 'Renewing American leadership', *Foreign Affairs*, vol. 86, no. 4 (July/Aug. 2007).

[14] McCain, J., Remarks to the Los Angeles World Affairs Council, 26 Mar. 2008, <http://www.johnmccain.com/Informing/News/Speeches/>.

[15] 'Disarmament still matters', *The Guardian*, 7 Jan. 2008.

[16] Beckett, M., 'A world free of nuclear weapons?', Keynote address, Carnegie International Nonproliferation Conference, Washington, DC, 25 June 2007, <http://www.carnegieendowment.org/events/index.cfm?fa=eventDetail&id=1004>.

[17] International Atomic Energy Agency (IAEA), 'IAEA welcomes US contribution of $50 million to Nuclear Fuel Bank', News release, 9 Jan. 2008, <http://www.iaea.org/NewsCenter/News/2008/usdonation.html>.

[18] E.g. George Schultz, a former US Secretary of State, leads the work of the 'Hoover Plan' and Bruce Blair and the World Security Institute are promoting a 'Compact for the Elimination of Nuclear Weapons'. Hoover Institution, 'No more nukes', Issues in Focus, 24 Oct. 2007, <http://www.hoover.org/research/focusonissues/focus/10609912.html>.

[19] On nuclear forensic analysis see appendix 8D in this volume.

sion conducted by North Korea in 2006. This and the recent review by US scientists of the past decade's developments in CTBT verification both suggest that the CTBT is effectively verifiable by available technologies.[20] As discussed in more detail in the chapter on chemical and biological weapons, another field of technological promise is the use of microbial forensics for biological weapon arms control.[21]

In another development, considerable scientific research and policy discussion is under way to determine the feasibility and effectiveness of an international, multilateral uranium enrichment facility and nuclear fuel bank as a means to prevent the diversion to military purposes of enriched uranium meant for civilian use, while ensuring the security of fuel supply. Proliferation-resistant nuclear fuel cycle technologies are also under active consideration.[22]

IV. Much work to be done

Current and future steps

Even as the convergence of threatening and encouraging developments opens new opportunities for arms control, much work will need to be done. To begin, it is well worth noting that, despite many challenges, arms control has not lain dormant and continues to make important progress, albeit out of day-to-day headlines. For example, as of the end of 2007, 159 states had ratified or acceded to the 1972 Biological and Toxin Weapons Convention (BTWC) and 183 states had ratified or acceded to the 1993 Chemical Weapons Convention (CWC).[23] Similarly, regarding conventional weapons, encouraging progress has been made in recent years in addressing the problem of 'inhumane weapons' such as landmines and the 'Oslo process' on cluster munitions, launched in 2006, has also taken important steps forward: more than 80 states have joined the process, with the stated aim of finalizing a treaty to ban cluster munitions by 2008.[24]

Looking ahead, the effective implementation—and possibly the survival—of the NPT will demand a demonstrable recommitment by all parties to the treaty's central bargain. This means earnest and transparent disarmament steps by nuclear weapon states, especially and initially through unilateral and bilateral measures by Russia and the USA, but also through greater positive

[20] Jeanloz, R., 'Comprehensive nuclear test-ban treaty and the US security', eds G. P. Schultz, S. D. Drell and J. E. Goodby, *Reykjavik Revisited: Steps Toward a World Free of Nuclear Weapons* (Hoover Institution Press: Stanford, Calif., 2008).

[21] See chapter 9 in this volume.

[22] International Atomic Energy Agency (IAEA), *Multilateral Approaches to the Nuclear Fuel Cycle: Expert Group Report to the Director General of the International Atomic Energy Agency*, INFCIRC/640 (IAEA: Vienna, 22 Feb. 2005). See also Fedchenko, V., 'Multilateral control of the nuclear fuel cycle', *SIPRI Yearbook 2006* (note 7), pp. 698–704; and Forden, G. and Thomson, J., 'Iran as a pioneer case for multilateral nuclear arrangements', SIPRI Special Research Report, 24 May 2007, <http://www.sipri.org/contents/expcon/iranmna.html>.

[23] See annex A in this volume for full list of signatories to the BTWC and the CWC.

[24] See chapter 10 in this volume.

involvement of non-nuclear middle-ranking powers. It also requires strengthened protocols to allow the dissemination of civil nuclear technologies but
prevent additional states from acquiring nuclear weapons. Another stalemate
at the 2010 NPT Review Conference would further undermine the security of
the international community.

Furthermore, political leaders need to know of the technologies developed
over the past decade which enhance the ability to verify compliance with and
enforce arms control and disarmament agreements. Many of the criticisms of
arms control put forward in the late-1990s and early-2000s were valid, particularly where effective compliance and verification measures were lacking.
'Arms control' alone is not enough; there needs also to be a focus on 'arming
the controllers' with the tools necessary to ensure verification and enforcement and to substantively demonstrate the confidence that political leaders
should have in these tools. Such measures will be critical to gaining the technical confidence and political will of nuclear and non-nuclear weapon states
alike to genuinely pursue arms control, non-proliferation and disarmament.

Understandably, much of the focus on disarmament will be on specific steps
that the five NPT-defined nuclear weapon states should take to reduce the role
of nuclear weapons in their overall security postures. The times call for
governments, and especially nuclear weapon states, to invest anew in beginning negotiations for a fissile material cut-off treaty. The Comprehensive Test
Ban Treaty now has 35 of the necessary 44 ratifications for entry into force.
France, Russia and the UK have ratified the CTBT; ratification by China and
the USA will be critical to seeing the treaty move forward.[25]

Disarmament by the two principal nuclear weapon powers—Russia and the
USA—will be especially important, and these two states should take a number
of critical steps forward in the near term. These include ensuring the smooth
continuation of the 1991 START I Treaty, which is set to expire in December
2009; a decision by the two parties to extend it for five more years should be
taken by December 2008. The coming year should also see forward movement
in the realization of goals of the 2002 Russian–US Treaty on Strategic Offensive Reductions (SORT), which envisages the number of deployed strategic
nuclear warheads being reduced to between 1700 and 2200 on each side by
2012.

Additional disarmament-related confidence- and security-building measures
should be negotiated between Russia and the USA in the coming years,
including reducing the threat of unintentional, accidental or unauthorized
nuclear attacks, accounting for and securing nuclear weapons and related-
materials, accounting for and phasing out forward-deployed short-range
nuclear weapons across Europe, and finding common ground on the deployment of missile defences.[26] These important objectives will need to be realized

[25] For a complete list of signatories and ratifications of the CTBT as of 1 Jan. 2008 see annex A in
this volume.

[26] See e.g. Drell, S. D., 'Oslo talk', Opening keynote address to the conference on Achieving the
Vision of a World Free of Nuclear Weapons, Oslo, 26 Feb. 2008, <http://disarmament.nrpa.no/>; Blair,
B. G., 'De-alerting nuclear forces' and Gottemoeller, R., 'Eliminating short-range nuclear weapons

in a way that is transparent and verifiable, not only to reassure the two parties to the treaty, but also to reassure the rest of the international community, and to highlight the fact that Russia and the USA comply with their NPT obligations in addition to meeting more narrow bilateral interests in confidence- and security-building between themselves.

However, a broader, global effort will also be needed which includes but reaches beyond Russia and the USA, which pulls in both nuclear and non-nuclear weapon states, and which—very importantly—firmly stakes out expansive, mainstream common ground across political divides of right and left, 'doves' and 'hawks', nationalists and internationalists, hope and fear. Given the threats that have emerged in the past decade, there is a clear case to be made for the merits of arms control and disarmament on realistic, hard-nosed, national security grounds, in addition to normative, moral and legal grounds. In this regard, there is a need to continue and reinvigorate investment in securing the existing but poorly protected stocks of fissile and other radio-active material in the civilian sector around the world.

This broad consensus has to be built across key countries as well as across key constituencies. The positions of such countries as China, India, Iran, Israel, North Korea and Pakistan must be sought and built in to an emerging global consensus on arms control and disarmament. Forward movement with a fissile material cut-off treaty would be a useful mechanism by which to draw key non-NPT states such as India, Israel, and Pakistan into the non-proliferation regime.

Senior military leaders and their staffs will need to be consulted and their views included in this arms control and disarmament process. Governmental and non-governmental scientists will need to be integrated into the consensus-building process as well. Think tanks and other non-governmental organizations will need to play a constructive role—especially when official government relations are constrained from doing so—in generating the kind of awareness raising, information sharing and consensus building that will real-ize, sustain and verify concrete disarmament results.

Caveats and looking ahead

We are entering an important period for arms control, and there are a number of reasons to see a widening window of opportunity for important gains on this front. However, three caveats are in order which should cast a more real-istic light on coming prospects for arms control.

First, in many respects, the priorities of the next US Administration will play a critical role in shaping the progress of arms control. This is true not only in the USA's approach to bilateral and multilateral arms control dis-cussions, but also in its overall approach in the years ahead to security build-ing at the global and regional levels. A rather clear path for arms control and

designed to be forward deployed', eds Schultz, Drell and Goodby (note 20). On recent Russian–US mis-sile defence developments see chapter 1 and appendix 8C in this volume.

disarmament was outlined and initially followed over the period 1995–2000. For most of the time since, the USA chose not to move down this path, or to divert from it all together. Today, there is some tendency to return to a path of diplomacy and negotiation, including agreements related to arms control and non-proliferation. That trend will probably continue and could increase under the next US president and Congress. But narrowly defined, traditional arms control—including new, lengthily negotiated treaties—will probably not be an uppermost priority in the first years of the new presidency. Other priorities on the international security agenda—including global financial stability, a framework of rules for world trade, climate issues, energy and other resource policy, and infectious diseases[27]—will be higher priorities than some traditional security concerns. Even among the 'harder' security issues it is not clear that arms control would be a higher priority than counterterrorism, Iraq, Afghanistan, other regional stability matters and reforms in the US military. Hard-headed and strong political leadership, from both inside and outside the government, will be needed if the USA is to move again down a pragmatic path of arms control.

Second, while progress on existing and potentially new multilateral treaties might garner most international attention, these approaches should not overshadow other mechanisms which hold out good prospects in the near- to medium-term for concrete progress in arms control and disarmament. For example, important progress can be made through other mechanisms, such as the Six-Party Talks to address, among other issues, North Korea's nuclear weapon programme. Important non-proliferation and disarmament assistance programmes, such as the 1993 Russian–US Highly Enriched Uranium Purchase Agreement, continue apace; as of September 2007, more than 300 tonnes of highly enriched uranium, equivalent to 12 600 nuclear warheads, had been converted under the agreement for use in fuel civil nuclear reactors.[28] The United Nations Security Council has made use of resolutions, such as Resolution 1540, to introduce arms control and non-proliferation measures related to weapons of mass destruction that member states must implement at the national level.

Finally, arms control and disarmament cannot solve all the world's problems. Indeed, there are many challenges to global and regional security—from financial uncertainty and chaos, via resource accessibility, to climate change—where arms control may have little or no relevance. If anything, for 'arms control' to have greater relevance, the traditional meaning of the term should—and in many respects must—undergo some broadened redefinition. Such a broadening should encompass, at a minimum, non-treaty- and non-state-based approaches to security building which can also effectively lower the threat of unnecessary and indiscriminate violence with both conventional and non-conventional weapons, while building confidence among security actors at the international, national and sub-state levels.

[27] On the global surveillance of infection diseases see appendix 9A in this volume.

[28] See chapter 8 in this volume.

Looking ahead, it is interesting how voices from across the political spectrum are coming to recognize again the value of arms control in the face of looming threats to humankind. Yet, as the pages which follow explain, moving ahead faces tremendous obstacles. Arms control and disarmament is far more complicated today and will only become more so, particularly with the more prominent role in recent years of China, India, Russia, the EU and major European states, and the emergence of other new actors—states and non-states—that can have a strategic effect at regional and global levels. However, in the coming year, a new window of opportunity will open even wider to realize constructive progress on arms control and disarmament. It is clearly in the interest of citizens and governments alike to take pragmatic and positive steps in the right direction.

Part I. Security and conflicts, 2007

Chapter 1. Euro-Atlantic security institutions and relationships

Chapter 2. Trends in armed conflicts

Chapter 3. Planning and deploying peace operations

Chapter 4. Integrating gender in post-conflict security sector reform

1. Euro-Atlantic security institutions and relationships

JEAN-YVES HAINE, GUNILLA HEROLF and
ZDZISLAW LACHOWSKI

I. Introduction

During 2007 the main Euro-Atlantic actors confronted renewed estrangements and overcame old ones. A number of sharpened differences between Russia and other states of the Euro-Atlantic community were among the outstanding features of this dynamic. Russia's conduct has left the West divided, unable to form a united response. The European Union (EU), despite the adoption of a new treaty in December 2007, has not yet fully recovered from the Constitutional Treaty debacle of 2005; this has considerably hampered its programme for the wider European neighbourhood, external relations and common foreign and security policies. Greater pragmatism and realism characterized the United States' security policy, resulting in a partial, yet real, readiness for engagement and dialogue.

This chapter analyses key security challenges and policies in the Euro-Atlantic region, with an emphasis on institutional developments. Section II presents an overview of the challenges of 'managing estrangement', with subsequent sections examining at these challenges in more detail. Section III looks at Russia's new assertiveness, focusing on the key sticking points of the USA's missile defence programme, energy security issues, the Kosovo crisis and important developments in the post-Soviet area. Section IV reviews the EU's choices concerning enlargement and its ambition to wield more influence in foreign, security and defence policies. Section V addresses the Atlantic community's problems with security cooperation including counterterrorism, collective defence and other security endeavours. Section VI presents conclusions.

II. Managing estrangement

Russia's new assertiveness, based on a few, but crucial, instruments of power, has raised significant problems for other European countries, the USA and multilateral institutions on a spectrum of issues. Compared to the recent past, Russia has tended to be a less cooperative partner with the rest of Europe, opposing a wide range of Western preferences, from enlargement of the North Atlantic Treaty Organization (NATO) and missile defence to energy supplies. Analogies with the cold war period are, however, misplaced. So far, confrontations remain largely rhetorical, even if some moves and pronouncements by Russia give rise to major concerns. For the most part Russia's alienation, in some measure provoked by US policies, has a regional rather than a global dimension.

National interests and specific security concerns have hampered a common EU approach to Russia. This was particularly so in the case of energy security, where embedded trade relations and different dependencies have made concerted action in this area difficult for the EU. The challenge of EU unity was even more acute over the issue of Kosovo. More broadly, the EU tends to be reactive and divided when dealing with Russia; instead it needs to engage it more effectively.

Beyond the Russian challenge, the EU had numerous problems of its own during 2007. Much attention was devoted to settling the constitutional dispute that has deeply divided Europeans in recent years. The Treaty of Lisbon was agreed, but the treaty negotiations were more about members managing differences, opt-outs and 'red lines' than unifying diverse interests.[1] In this process, the central EU institutions seem to have lost momentum vis-à-vis the more sceptical member states. With such an inward-looking agenda, the EU's foreign policy coherence could only suffer.

In the Western Balkans, where the EU has massively invested diplomatic and economic resources, the outcomes have been mixed. While the region's future is said to 'lie in the EU', this aim is not easily achievable. There have been positive developments in progress towards membership by the interested countries, but the process is uneven, hampered by insufficient domestic reforms and unsatisfactory governance. The EU wavers between imposing strict conditions that may encourage nationalist reaction in these countries and offering them a clearer prospect of accession, which has so far been insufficient to overcome political inertia. In its wider neighbourhood, conflicting plans about a Mediterranean Union, divergent interests in Asia and fundamental disagreements about Turkey continue to weaken the EU's clout.

A similar absence of cohesion affects its defence and security policies. The lack of deployable military capabilities constrains the scope and range of its humanitarian interventions. EU battle groups are now on standby, but there is no consensus on how and when to use them. National deployments in Lebanon under the United Nations and in Afghanistan under NATO take precedence over common EU missions, the majority of which are civilian operations, most importantly in Kosovo. To speak with a more influential voice and to act more decisively remains an unfulfilled ambition for the EU.

In this context of fragmentation, relationships with the United States remain critical. After years of estrangement between Europe and the USA following the split over the 2003 US–British-led invasion of Iraq, a genuine willingness to place the transatlantic relationship in a more constructive framework was apparent on both sides in 2007. While public perceptions in Europe of the

---

[1] The Treaty of Lisbon amending the Treaty on European Union and the Treaty establishing the European Community was signed on 13 Dec. 2007. Its text is available at <http://europa.eu/lisbon_treaty/>.

USA have continued to deteriorate,[2] there have been real improvements in transatlantic relationships at official levels. This was especially noticeable in the case of France: President Nicolas Sarkozy seems keen to restore a friendly relationship with the USA and a constructive approach towards NATO. Highly symbolic gestures, such as Sarkozy's speech before the US Congress in November, were followed by convergence in the French and US positions on Iran, Kosovo and Syria.[3] In contrast, the new British Prime Minister, Gordon Brown, while reasserting the United Kingdom's status as the USA's best friend, in practice distanced himself from Tony Blair's embrace of the US agenda, starting with the partial withdrawal of British troops from Al-Basra, Iraq. Between these two reversals in position, German Chancellor Angela Merkel has so far succeeded in sticking to the middle ground with considerable influence, especially on climate change issues.

In this landscape of Euro-Atlantic relationships, multilateral security institutions do not effectively reinforce cooperation and rapprochement or mitigate crises and conflicts. The Organization for Security and Co-operation in Europe (OSCE), the institution that is most suitably designed to deal with regional challenges, has thus far been helpless in the face of Russia's new assertiveness, on the one hand, and the EU's encroachment on the OSCE's competence, on the other. Meanwhile, the EU itself lacks a coherent and proactive strategy towards Russia. NATO has yet to regain its central significance to Euro-Atlantic security, and its relationship with Russia remains uncertain. The second half of 2007 saw the USA more actively engaging in intra-NATO cooperation regarding conventional arms control in Europe and pushing for NATO enlargement. However, the main bone of contention between Russia and the West at present—the US missile defence plan—is for the most part being addressed bilaterally between the USA, the Czech Republic and Poland and with NATO following rather than shaping the process.

III. Russia's policy

Russia's changed approach to the West

During the last full year of his presidency, Vladimir Putin embarked on a forceful course in security and political relations with Russia's Euro-Atlantic partners. This assertiveness in 2007 seems to have been motivated by a number of factors—a restored sense of international power based on Russia's growing wealth and influence in energy markets; domestic political calcu-

[2] A 2007 opinion survey in the 5 largest EU states—France, Germany, Italy, Spain and the United Kingdom—shows that a large portion of the public sees the USA as the greatest threat to world stability. According to the FT/Harris Poll, 32% of respondents labelled the USA 'a bigger threat than any other state'. The view of younger generations is particularly negative: e.g. 57% of Germans aged 18–29 years consider the USA as more dangerous than the regime in Iran. Dombey, D. and Pignal, S., 'Europeans see US as threat to peace', *Financial Times*, 1 July 2007. See also Malzahn C. C., 'Evil Americans, poor mullahs', *Der Spiegel*, 29 Mar. 2007.

[3] 'Bush and Sarkozy declare Iran aim', BBC News, 7 Nov. 2007, <http://news.bbc.co.uk/2/hi/americas/7083339.stm>.

lations (including the search to secure the current leadership's grip on the country); and Russia's genuine disenchantment with the USA.

In light of Russia's lack of an officially articulated defence and security policy, there were a number of noteworthy security developments in 2007.[4] In February the Russian Defence Minister, Sergei Ivanov, announced a new armament programme for the years 2007–2015.[5] The programme budgets nearly 5 trillion roubles ($189 billion) to replace 45 per cent of the Russian arsenal with modernized weapon systems, including intercontinental missiles, long-range strategic bombers, early-warning stations and possibly aircraft carriers.[6] In August Russian strategic bombers began to fly long-range missions in the North Atlantic, the North Sea and the Pacific. In December the aircraft carrier *Admiral Kuznetsov* set sail to patrol strategic lanes in the Atlantic and the Mediterranean.[7] The year also saw successful tests of new Russian intercontinental multiple-warhead ballistic missiles.

Russia launched a political counteroffensive in the face of growing Western criticism about Russia's perceived anti-democratic conduct domestically. Russia also reacted to what it saw as the USA's dismissal of its desire to be treated as an equal partner and player in global politics. At the annual Munich Conference on Security Policy in February, President Putin surprised the audience with a confrontational speech.[8] He accused the USA of attempting to force its will on the world and provided a catalogue of complaints regarding the superpower and its allies, from NATO's progressive enlargement via foreign interventions to a new arms race. During the year the rhetoric charging the USA with 'imperialism', 'diktat', 'containment' and the like was ratcheted up in successive pronouncements by Putin and other prominent Russian political and military leaders.[9] All this led some observers to portend a 'new cold war'.[10]

---

[4] In Jan. 2007 a special joint meeting of the Russian Academy of Military Sciences and the command of the Russian Armed Forces was held to discuss the shape of a new military doctrine. The discussion lacked any substantial result, while the unchanged role of nuclear weapons in Russia's security policy was confirmed. Korobyshin, V, 'Al'ternativy poka net' [No alternative for the time being], *Nezavisimoe voennoe obozreniye*, 2 Feb. 2007.

[5] For discussion of Russia's armaments modernization programme see e.g. Saradzhyan, S., 'Russia prepares for "wars of the future"', ISN Security Watch, 12 Feb. 2007, <http://www.isn.ethz.ch/news/sw/details.cfm?ID=17240>.

[6] For more on Russia's military expenditure see chapter 5 in this volume.

[7] Nevertheless, many analysts see a continuing decline in the Russian armed forces. See e.g. Rostopshin, M., 'Strategicheskaya poterya tempa' [The strategic loss of the tempo], *Nezavisimoe voennoe obozreniye*, 9 Feb. 2007; and Associated Press, 'Experts see decline in Russia's military', *International Herald Tribune*, 13 Nov. 2007.

[8] Russian President Vladimir V. Putin, Speech at the 43rd Munich Conference on Security Policy, Munich, 10 Feb. 2007, <http://www.securityconference.de/konferenzen/rede.php?sprache=en&id=179>.

[9] See e.g. Lavrov, S. 'Containing Russia: back to the future?', Ministry of Foreign Affairs of the Russian Federation, 19 July 2007, <http://www.ln.mid.ru/brp_4.nsf/sps/8F8005F0C5CA3710C325731D0022E227>. In May Putin referred to Nazi Germany while criticizing an 'aspiration' (of the USA) to dominate the world. Vladimir Putin, Speech at the Military Parade Celebrating the 62nd Anniversary of Victory in the Great Patriotic War, Moscow, 9 May 2007, <http://www.kremlin.ru/eng/speeches/2007/05/09/1432_type82912type127286_127675.shtml>.

[10] For a Russian analysis of the strain in Russian–Western relations see Arbatov, A, 'Is a new cold war imminent?', *Russia in Global Affairs*, vol. 5, no. 3 (July–Sep. 2007), pp. 84–97.

During the year the Russian–Western security disputes and clashes centred on four prominent issues: missile defence, the 1990 Treaty on Conventional Armed Forces in Europe (CFE Treaty) regime, energy security and Kosovo.[11]

Missile defence[12]

From the Russian political perspective, the issue of missile defence constituted the yardstick of Western goodwill and credibility in 2007. Russia has concerns about the effectiveness of the US plans in their stated objective of intercepting missiles launched in the Middle East (specifically, by Iran). Apart from these concerns, other motives have been suspected behind the Russian campaign. Russia sees US military bases and presence close to Russia's European borders as a breach of an understanding that Western military resources will not be deployed into the territories of new NATO members. The charge that Russia is trying to drive a wedge between NATO members has also been levied again.[13]

In early 2007 the Czech and Polish governments agreed to start formal talks with the USA on the deployment of a radar system and associated 10 missile interceptors on their respective territories. The future deployments are strongly contested in both Central European countries. Russia's response was sharp: suspecting the USA of dubious intentions to counteract Russia's nuclear deterrent rather than defend against a rogue actor, President Putin and his top military commanders warned of possible 'asymmetrical responses', including targeting future installations.[14] In the Russian view, the USA's missile dialogues with the Czech Republic and Poland notably coincided with the USA's military basing plans in Bulgaria and Romania. Moreover, despite US assurances, Russia believes that the modest facilities in Central Europe forewarn of an expanded system with a strategic purpose.

In June, President Putin offered the USA joint operation of the Russian-leased Gabala radar station in Azerbaijan.[15] While not rejecting the proposal, the US Defense Secretary, Robert Gates, made clear that Gabala could be an 'additional capability' but not a replacement or alternative to other US plans in Central Europe.[16] At the Bush–Putin meeting in early July, Putin offered more suggestions aimed at closer cooperation (e.g. another radar site in southern Russia), but the USA remained committed to developing its presence in Eastern Europe. Following the meeting, Russia hinted at the possibility of deploy-

---

[11] On developments in the CFE Treaty in 2007 see chapter 10 in this volume.

[12] The military aspects of the US ballistic missile defence programmes are elaborated in detail in appendix 8C in this volume.

[13] For analysis of Russian motives in this regard see e.g. Buckley, N., 'Why the Kremlin is making a stand over missile defence', *Financial Times*, 7 June 2007.

[14] Abdullaev, N., 'Russia pushes back against U.S. missile plans', *Defense News*, 26 Feb. 2007, p. 12.

[15] US experts argue that the Azerbaijani facilities are outdated, lack reliable tracking ability and are too close to potential Iranian launch sites. Hildreth, S. A. and Ek, C., *Long-Range Ballistic Missile Defense in Europe*, CRS Report for Congress no. RL34051 (Congressional Research Service: Washington, DC, 25 July 2007), p. 10.

[16] Shanker, T., 'US to keep Europe as site for missile defense', *New York Times*, 15 June 2007.

ing medium-range missiles in Kaliningrad, close to the Lithuanian and Polish borders.[17]

On 12 October Gates and the US Secretary of State, Condoleezza Rice, while meeting their counterparts in Moscow, offered Russia a 'joint regional missile defence architecture' under which Russia would join the USA and NATO as a full partner in designing and operating a missile defence system guarding all of Europe.[18] The US proposals would allow each country to retain exclusive command and control over its missiles and decide when they should be launched. Moreover, the US negotiators suggested that Russia could station monitors at the US bases if the Czech Republic and Poland agreed to house the US missiles. Gates further suggested that the USA could delay activating the missile sites until it had 'definitive proof' of a missile threat from Iran.[19]

The change of government in Poland in the autumn resulted in its more persistent demands for stronger military cooperation with, and security protection from, the USA—primarily the USA's bolstering of Polish air defences and coming to agreement on missile defence.[20] In December Russia and Poland agreed to enter bilateral consultations on missile defence.[21] Meanwhile, in November the US Government apparently backed down on most of its initial informal proposals from October, including those concerning constant Russian monitoring of planned US facilities in Central Europe and joint evaluations of threats. Instead the USA proposed a set of transparency measures.[22]

Energy security

As one of the largest exporters of natural gas and oil, Russia has become a major player in world energy markets. Since 2000 the Putin Administration has consistently encouraged the renationalization of Russia's energy industry. Consequently, the state has taken control of the country's energy supplies and

[17] The Russian First Deputy Prime Minister, Sergei Ivanov, stated: 'If our proposals are accepted, Russia will find it unnecessary to deploy new missile armaments in the European part of the country, including the Kaliningrad region, aimed at fending off the threats that would emerge in case of the deployment of missile defence elements in the Czech [Republic] and Poland. . . . If our proposals are not accepted, we will adopt adequate measures. An asymmetric and effective response will be found.' Cited in Sukhov, P., 'Rossiya nashla "asimmetrichnyi" otvet stranam NATO' [Russia found an 'asymmetric' response to the NATO countries], *Nezavisimaya gazeta*, 4 July 2007.

[18] Shanker, T. and Myers, S. L., 'Putin derides US antimissile plans', *International Herald Tribune*, 12 Oct. 2007.

[19] Burns, R., 'Gates: US may delay missile shield', *Washington Times*, 23 Oct. 2007.

[20] Cienski, J. and Sevastopulo, D., 'Poland demands US air defence system', *Financial Times*, 19 Nov. 2007.

[21] Dempsey, J., 'Russia and Poland to hold discussions on proposed U.S. missile shield', *International Herald Tribune*, 18 Dec. 2007.

[22] Associated Press, 'Russia complains about US proposals on missile shield', *International Herald Tribune*, 5 Dec. 2007. See also Russian Ministry of Defence, 'Tezisy vystupleniya nachalnika Generalnogo shtaba Vooruzhennykh Sil Rossiyskoi Federatsii na press-konferentsii 15 dekabrya 2007 g.: Otsenki rossiysko-amerikanskikh konsultatsii po PRO' [Theses of the address by the chief of the General Staff of the Armed Forces of the Russian Federation at the press conference of 15 Dec. 2007: assessments of the Russian–US consultations on anti-missile defence], 15 Dec. 2007, <http://www.mil.ru/info/1069/details/index.shtml?id=35200>. In this speech General Yuriy Baluevskiy hinted at the risk of delivering an 'automatic' counterstrike by Russian strategic missiles if an anti-missile missile were launched from Polish territory.

production, pipelines and long-term contracts with European customers.[23] Russia's natural resources have become a tool with which to influence its allies and client states as well as to reassert itself vis-à-vis the West, especially the EU. Russia's energy policy has evoked concerns, among them that supplies to the rest of Europe could become unreliable (some see Russia's recent cut-offs to some of its neighbours as a precedent[24]); that Russia's aims are incongruous with the EU's (i.e. state control versus privatization); and that EU–Russian energy relations are unbalanced (i.e. there is no 'strategic partnership' between the EU and Russia). It is questionable whether energy serves Russia's offensive or defensive purposes. Its commercial aims notwithstanding, Russia's purported energy-related political aims can be summarized as follows: (*a*) bringing the 'near abroad' countries in Central Asia and Eastern Europe under stricter control; (*b*) neutralizing the new EU members in Central Europe; and (*c*) constraining the other EU and Western partners.

Russia's energy ambitions are not without complications. Russia has not invested enough in the development of its domestic gas reserves to meet future demands and apparently faces shortages in the coming years. The first signs of possibly adverse energy trends emerged in 2007 (including growing inflation and Gazprom's declining profits) At the same time, Russia has invested heavily in pipelines and downstream assets in Europe.[25] A strategic battle has started over the rich gas resources of Central Asia. Thus far Russia has trumped the EU's belated attempts since 2006 to institute a policy of direct access to the Central Asian resources by ensuring that pipelines run through and to Russia. Such control would eliminate Western competition, bind the Central Asian governments to Russia and satisfy Russia's internal demand for energy. Given the volatility of the situation in Central Asia, however, Russia's future monopoly cannot be presumed.

In May and December 2007 Russia signed agreements with Kazakhstan and Turkmenistan to build a natural gas pipeline along the Caspian Sea coast. This frustrated Western hopes of diversifying its supplies from Central Asia and apparently foiled the EU plan for a trans-Caspian gas pipeline. Compounding this frustration, the EU-backed Nabucco gas pipeline project, intended as the EU's main alternative to Russian supplies, remained in limbo during the year.[26] Furthermore, Western Europe failed to make progress in persuading

[23] E.g. in 2000 only 15% of Russian domestic oil production was national; in 2007, 50% was under state control, mainly through the renationalization of Yukos in 2003. The Russian Parliament voted to give Gazprom, the state-controlled natural gas monopoly, an exclusive right to export natural gas. On European energy security see e.g. 'A bear at the throat', *The Economist*, 12 Apr. 2007.

[24] In Eastern Europe oil and gas serve as tools for curbing the real and potential political leanings of the countries in the region towards the West. Following energy shut-offs in Georgia, Lithuania and Ukraine, Belarus and Latvia were similarly 'punished' for their respective behaviours during 2007.

[25] Javier Solana has questioned Russia's political use of its energy: 'There is a justified concern across Europe about Russia seeming more interested in investing in future leverage than in future production. Contrast Gazprom's strategic spending spree abroad with the lack of investment at home.' Solana, J., Speech at the 44th Munich Conference on Security Policy, 10 Feb. 2008, <http://www.securityconference.de/konferenzen/rede.php?sprache=en&id=221>.

[26] This concerned Austria, Bulgaria, Hungary and other countries. During 2007 Hungary switched sides from the EU's Nabucco gas pipeline project (a southern corridor from the Caspian Sea to Turkey to

Russia to ratify the 1991 Energy Charter Treaty, which would require Russia to allow foreign access to its energy resources. Meanwhile, European and US companies (e.g. BP and Shell) had problems with their stakes in Russia's infrastructure.[27]

Kosovo

Administered by the UN and protected by a NATO peace operation (KFOR) since 1999, Kosovo has become a proving ground for post-conflict peace-building and conflict prevention for the EU, Russia, the USA and the broader international community. In January 2007 the UN special envoy, Martti Ahtisaari, unveiled his proposals on the province's future. The proposals sought to overcome the apparently irreconcilable differences between the Serbian and Kosovar positions.[28] His plan offered all the main elements of sovereignty to Kosovo without naming it a sovereign state.[29] This wide auton-omy would involve EU supervision for at least two years. Overwhelmingly accepted by Kosovo's Albanians, the Ahtisaari plan was rejected almost immediately by Russia and Serbia. Russia claimed that diplomacy needed more time; moreover, it warned against possible repercussions elsewhere—in such 'frozen conflict' areas as the South Caucasus and Trans-Dniester. The situation became a double impasse at the international and Serbia–Kosovo levels.

The following months witnessed a tug-of-war between the Western powers, which circulated several Kosovo-related draft UN Security Council reso-lutions, and Russia, which rejected each draft, standing firmly by Serbia. Con-sequently the frustrated US Government unilaterally declared uncompromis-ing support of Kosovo's independence.[30] The EU had a tough choice: either recognize Kosovo's independence without a UN mandate or hold back, thus allowing its Common Foreign and Security Policy (CFSP) to be taken hostage by Russia. Both options ran the risk of fomenting further unrest in the

Central Europe, aimed at bypassing Russia) to Gazprom's gas pipeline Blue Stream, then recommitted itself to the former project, and in another turn at the end of 2007 agreed with Gazprom to be linked to the latter's South Stream gas pipeline project. In Jan. 2008 Bulgaria and Serbia signed an agreement with Russia regarding the South Stream gas pipeline project further undermining the Nabucco. 'The planned South Stream gas pipeline and Hungary', Budapest Analyses, no. 180 (11 Feb. 2008), <http://www.budapestanalyses.hu/docs/En/Analyses_Archive/analysys_180_en.html>.

[27] On the links between energy and security see Prońinska, K., 'Energy and security: regional and global dimensions', *SIPRI Yearbook 2007: Armaments, Disarmament and International Security* (Oxford University Press: Oxford, 2007), pp. 215–40.

[28] On developments in and around Kosovo see Dunay, P., 'Status and statehood in the Western Balkans', *SIPRI Yearbook 2006: Armaments, Disarmament and International Security* (Oxford University Press: Oxford, 2006), pp. 65–72; and Dunay, P. and Lachowski, Z., 'Euro-Atlantic security and institutions', *SIPRI Yearbook 2007* (note 27), pp. 44–48.

[29] In Mar. 2007, in a letter to the UN Secretary-General, Ban Ki-moon, Ahtisaari wrote that 'I have come to the conclusion that the only viable option for Kosovo is independence, to be supervised for an initial period by the international community'. United Nations, Report of the Special Envoy of the Sec-retary-General on Kosovo's future status, S/2007/168, 26 Mar. 2007, p. 2.

[30] During his visit to Albania in June, President Bush asserted: 'At some point, sooner rather than later, you've got to say, "Enough is enough—Kosovo is independent"'. Associated Press, 'Bush says Kosovo needs to be independent "sooner rather than later"', *International Herald Tribune*, 10 June 2007.

Balkans. Facing Russia's indirect threat of vetoing a UN Security Council resolution, several major EU countries considered recognizing Kosovo without a resolution. This, however, would have jeopardized EU cohesion, as members with real or potential secessionist problems or national minority protection concerns—Cyprus, Hungary, Romania, Slovakia and Spain—would have been reluctant to go along without a UN directive.

With the decision delayed and UN authority being worn down, the EU brought more pressure to bear on Kosovo and Serbia to reach a solution.[31] The EU threatened to withdraw the possibility of early EU membership for both actors and suggested, for the first time, partitioning Kosovo along ethnic lines if both sides agreed.[32] In August, the UN Secretary-General, Ban Ki-moon, ordered a new round of Kosovar–Serbian talks with a troika of high-ranking mediators from the EU, Russia and the USA. The talks were due to end on 10 December, the date on which Kosovo vowed to declare independence. Meanwhile, the USA reiterated its readiness to unilaterally recognize Kosovo by the end of the year, thus potentially aggravating its relations with the EU, which again was enticing Serbia with a fast track to membership. In response, a top Serbian official threatened to use force in the event of Kosovo's independence, but he was soon disavowed by Serbian President Boris Tadić and the foreign and defence ministers.[33] In the autumn the USA renewed diplomatic efforts with Russia to find an amenable Kosovo solution in a 'package deal' that also addressed the CFE regime and missile defence problems—once again, to no avail. On 8 December, the troika informed the UN Secretary-General that they had failed to broker an agreement on Kosovo's status.[34] The end of the year saw no denouement; the UN signalled that it was unable to resolve the status of Kosovo and the EU prioritized unity and delayed its decision until after the presidential election in Serbia in early 2008. On 17 February 2008 Kosovo unilaterally declared independence followed by a controversy among the states concerned.

The post-Soviet area

In 2007 the former Soviet states continued to cope with a variety of problems and challenges related to the democratization process. For all its troubles with illiberal democracy, multi-year efforts by Kazakhstan to be granted the OSCE's chairmanship bore fruit at the end of 2007. The OSCE participating

---

[31] Wood, N., 'Kosovo independence will probably face delay', *International Herald Tribune*, 8 July 2007.

[32] This suggestion was soon dropped as both Kosovo and Serbia firmly rejected it. See e.g. 'EU puts pressure on Kosovo rivals to reach deal', *International Herald Tribune*, 12 Aug. 2007; and Bilefsky, D., 'Top EU mediator warns against partition of Kosovo', *International Herald Tribune*, 6 Sep. 2007.

[33] Wood, N., 'Serbia threatens to use force if West recognizes Kosovo', *International Herald Tribune*, 5 Sep. 2007.

[34] In parallel, NATO foreign ministers decided to keep KFOR troops in the region at least at the current level of 17 000. 'NATO/Ministerial: in Kosovo, NATO hopes for best but prepares for worst', *Europe Diplomacy & Defence*, 8 Dec. 2007, p. 3.

states conditionally agreed to Kazakhstan's candidacy for the year 2010.[35] Given its poor record on human rights and political freedoms, Kazakhstan's appointment as the first post-Soviet state to chair the OSCE was based less on merit than other relevant considerations, such as the insistence of Russia and its Collective Security Treaty Organization (CSTO) partners, Western geo-political calculations regarding Russia, the OSCE's viability and other political contexts as well as Kazakhstan's role as a major political player and oil-rich country in Central Asia.[36]

Parliamentary or presidential elections were scheduled in a number of coun-tries in the post-Soviet area in 2007. The record was mixed, with the ruling governments, except for one (in Ukraine), retaining power. In May in Armenia the parliamentary elections improved from previous ones and were held largely in accordance with international commitments.[37] The local elections in Moldova in June showed that key problems persisted, particularly media bias and the intimidation of candidates.[38] The August parliamentary elections in Kazakhstan reflected progress but a number of international standards were not met, specifically regarding the new legal framework and the vote count.[39] In contrast, the September parliamentary elections in Ukraine were conducted mostly in line with international commitments and standards for democratic elections;[40] the election led to a narrow victory of pro-Western parties that formed a government under Yuliya Tymoshenko at the year's end. In Novem-ber, the OSCE Office for Democratic Institutions and Human Rights (ODIHR) announced that it would not be able to observe the December elections to the Russian State Duma (the lower house of the Russian Parliament).[41] The December parliamentary elections in Kyrgyzstan failed to meet a number of OSCE commitments, including those relating to transparency and account-ability.[42] Also in December, the presidential election in Uzbekistan was held in

[35] To meet certain conditions in the run-up to the 2010 chairmanship, Kazakhstan amended its laws on the media and elections and promised to create a better model of public dialogue. It also vowed not to seek to weaken the ODIHR mandate. Originally the Kazakh Government aimed at gaining OSCE chairmanship for 2009. See Government of the Republic of Kazakhstan, Address of H. E. Dr. Marat Tazhin, Minister of Foreign Affairs of the Republic of Kazakhstan, at the OSCE Ministerial Meeting, Madrid, 29 Nov. 2007, <http://en.government.kz/documents/publications/page09>.

[36] The CSTO is a collective security arrangement founded in 2002 by the presidents of Armenia, Belarus, Kazakhstan, Kyrgyzstan, Russia and Tajikistan. Uzbekistan joined in 2006.

[37] OSCE, 'Armenian poll demonstrates progress, observers say', Press release, 13 May 2007, <http://www.osce.org/item/24421.html>.

[38] OSCE, 'Polling in second round of Moldova's local elections slightly improved, but serious short-comings remain', Press release, 18 June 2007, <http://www.osce.org/item/25168.html>.

[39] OSCE, 'Kazakh elections: progress and problems', Press release, 19 Aug. 2007, <http://osce.org/item/25959.html>.

[40] OSCE, 'Ukraine's elections open and competitive but amendments to law of some concern, inter-national observers say', Press release, 1 Oct. 2007, <http://www.osce.org/odihr-elections/item_1_26824.html>.

[41] ODIHR experts and observers have been denied entry visas for a long time into the Russian Feder-ation. OSCE, 'ODIHR unable to observe Russian Duma elections', Press release, 16 Nov. 2007, <http://www.osce.org/odihr-elections/item_1_27967.html>.

[42] OSCE, 'Kyrgyz elections fail to meet a number of OSCE commitments in missed opportunity', Press release, 17 Dec. 2007, <http://www.osce.org/item/28914.html>. The US State Department released a statement on 20 Dec. 2007 criticizing some aspects of the elections, including 'uncertainty over elec-

a clearly dictatorial environment which left no room for real opposition and 'generally failed to meet many OSCE commitments for democratic election'.[43] The international outrage following the 2005 Andijon massacre, however, did not prevent the EU from taking steps towards easing the sanctions imposed on Uzbekistan in October 2007.[44] Turkmenistan, which did not hold elections in 2007, has slowly been overcoming the legacy of late President Saparmurat Niyazov's reclusive regime.

Progress in frozen conflict areas remained stalled. Despite hopes for a breakthrough, no headway was made in the Armenian–Azerbaijan conflict in 2007. In fact both countries accelerated their military build-ups, reinforcing the growing instability in the region.[45] Nevertheless both sides declared their will to continue the ongoing negotiations on the settlement of the Nagorno-Karabakh conflict.[46] Moldova seeks to balance its policy between the Eastern and Western orientations, streamline relations with Russia and other neighbours, get closer to the EU and, above all, solve the frozen conflict in Trans-Dniester.[47]

Georgia and Russia continued to face a wide spectrum of issues, such as Russia's support of secessionists in Abkhazia and South Ossetia, Russia's energy-related punitive sanctions and Georgia's desire to join NATO. The most publicized incident of 2007 took place in August when a Russian military aircraft allegedly dropped a missile on Georgian territory, near South Ossetia. Russia denied the incident and the OSCE chose not to act further. These issues notwithstanding, the pullout of Russian armaments and troops from Georgia continued uninterrupted in 2007, with the one exception of the Russian presence at the base in Gudauta in Abkhazia. Acclaimed by Western countries as a model democracy-building state, Georgia faced a domestic crisis and international concern in November when President Mikheil Saakashvili briefly imposed a state of emergency in response to anti-government protests. In an early presidential election held in January 2008, Saakashvili won against a divided opposition.

In August 2007 the Shanghai Cooperation Organization (SCO)—which brings together China, Russia, Kazakhstan, Kyrgyzstan, Tajikistan and

tion rules, widespread vote count irregularities and exaggerations in voter turnout, [and] late exclusions from voter lists'. US State Department, 'The Kyrgyz Republic's December 16 parliamentary elections', Press statement, 20 Dec. 2007, <http://www.state.gov/r/pa/prs/ps/2007/dec/97906.htm>.

[43] OSCE, 'Strictly controlled Uzbek elections did not offer a genuine choice, ODIHR observers conclude', Press release, 24 Dec. 2007, <http://www.osce.org/odihr-elections/item_1_29125.html>; and 'Uzbek incumbent wins presidential poll without "genuine choice"', Radio Free Europe/Radio Liberty, 24 Dec. 2007, <http://www.rferl.org/featuresarticle/2007/12/66C01656-B3BF-4DF6-BE9D-8DE161C30 9DD.html>.

[44] In Nov. 2007 Human Rights Watch accused Uzbekistan of employing a wide range of torture methods on detainees. Human Rights Watch, 'Uzbekistan: UN body finds torture "routine"', 23 Nov. 2007, <http://hrw.org/english/docs/200711/23/uzbeki17406.htm>.

[45] See e.g. Pugliese, D., 'Baku builds up, warns Armenia, warms NATO ties', Defense News, 3 Sep. 2007, p. 21; and Mamedov, S., Litovkin, V. and Simonyan, Y., 'Baku zhdet ob'yasneniy Moskvy [Baku awaits clarification from Moscow], Nezavisimaya gazeta, 12 Sep. 2007.

[46] OSCE Ministerial Council, Adoption of Ministerial Council documents, MC15EJ02, 30 Nov. 2007, p. 2.

[47] On the conflict in Trans-Dniester see chapter 10 in this volume.

Uzbekistan—held a counterterrorism 'Peace Mission 2007' exercise in China and Russia, officially aimed at cooperation in combating 'terrorism, separatism and extremism'.[48] The exercise fuelled speculation that the SCO was laying the groundwork for a military bloc to rival NATO and minimize Western influence in Central Asia. While the predictions turned out to be unfounded, it cannot be ruled out that future SCO operations may be used for quelling rebellion or managing political instability.[49] Also, the agreement signed on 6 October between the SCO and the CSTO was not intended to confront NATO. The agreement was interpreted as a sign of Chinese and Russian determination to strengthen security links with each other and energy-rich Central Asia.[50]

IV. The European Union

For the EU, 2007 was not a year of much celebration. The Lisbon Treaty, when finally agreed to and signed, was accompanied by sighs of relief rather than fanfare. Enlargement fatigue dominated. Efficiency versus cohesion was the theme for many deliberations on the working of the enlarged Union. At the same time it was obvious that cooperation in the EU was primarily led by states rather than EU institutions and was centred on protecting national interests rather than those of Europe as a whole. Still, the foreign, security and defence policies showed both activity by the European institutions and determination among the member states to continue to play a role in the stabilization of the EU's neighbourhood and on a global level.[51]

The Treaty of Lisbon

During 2007, after two years of stalemate with the 2004 Constitutional Treaty, a solution was finally achieved.[52] In June, after overcoming many hurdles from various quarters (with Poland and the UK among the staunchest sceptics) a draft reform treaty text was agreed. EU heads of state and government signed the Treaty of Lisbon on 13 December.[53]

If ratified, the treaty will be implemented starting in 2009. It contains several reforms related to institutions, leadership and decision making, aiming at

[48] Daly, J. C. K., 'SCO to host "peace mission 2007" anti-terrorist drill in August', *Eurasia Daily Monitor*, 27 July 2007.

[49] McDermott, R. N., *The Rising Dragon: SCO Peace Mission 2007*, Occasional Paper (Jamestown Foundation: Washington, DC, Oct. 2007). On the development of the SCO see Bailes, A. J. K. et al., *The Shanghai Cooperation Organization*, SIPRI Policy Paper no. 17 (SIPRI: Stockholm, May 2007).

[50] 'CIS: Dushanbe summit discusses labor migration, free-trade zone', Radio Free Europe/Radio Liberty, 5 Oct. 2007, <http://www.rferl.org/featuresarticle/2007/10/2773A2EB-AB89-42AB-A0BA-E5867 88A40B0.html>.

[51] On the structure and membership of the EU see annex B in this volume.

[52] The Treaty Establishing a Constitution for Europe was signed on 29 Oct. 2004 but has not been fully ratified. Its text is published in *Official Journal of the European Union*, C310 (16 Dec. 2004).

[53] For analysis of individual states' positions before the June summit see e.g. Peel, Q., 'Why a Europe of opposites needs to break its constitutional deadlock?', *Financial Times*, 10 June 2007.

increased efficiency. The European Council will have a full-time president, elected for a two-and-a-half year term, renewable once. From 2014 qualified majority voting will be extended into new areas and the European Commission will no longer include members from all countries.

In foreign and security matters the posts of High Representative for the CFSP and the European Commissioner for External Relations are to be merged under the title High Representative of the Union for Foreign Affairs and Security Policy, assuming a position of Vice-President of the Commission. This merged post will be supported by another innovation, the External Action Service.[54] A mutual defence clause (from which non-aligned states are excluded) and a solidarity clause, which is similar in kind but concerns assistance in case of a natural catastrophe or terrorist attack, were among the steps taken to strengthen the EU defence policy. Furthermore, permanent structured defence cooperation was included, allowing states that are willing and able to cooperate on the development of military capabilities. How relations will develop between the President of the European Council, the President of the European Commission, and the High Representative of the Union for Foreign Affairs and Security Policy remains to be seen. However, for all the progress achieved, the treaty has not fully succeeded in its stated ambition to give European citizens a more effective, more accountable and more comprehensible EU.

Enlargement and neighbourhood policies

With the recent accessions creating a Union of 27 members, enlargement fatigue is prevalent especially among older EU states. The poor performance of Bulgaria and Romania—which joined the EU on 1 January 2007—in fulfilling the promised post-accession reforms is a case in point.[55] In 2007 Nicolas Sarkozy proposed a committee of experts—dubbed the 'wise men group'—to focus on defining the EU's final borders. However, the idea met with opposition from enlargement-friendly states, such as the UK. Instead the group, later renamed the 'reflection group', is to help the EU anticipate and meet challenges more effectively for the period 2020–2030.[56]

The countries of the Western Balkans are seen by the EU as future members. First in line for membership is the candidate state Croatia, whose accession negotiations are advancing well. A number of deficiencies in the

[54] Treaty of Lisbon (note 1), Article 30. The service will comprise members from the EU Council, the Commission and the national diplomatic services of the member states.

[55] Faced with their problems, the Commission, which sees corruption as one of the most severe problems, has taken some safeguard measures and will follow up during 2008 on the critical reports of June 2007. European Commission, Report from the Commission to the European Parliament and the Council on Bulgaria's progress on accompanying measures following accession, COM(2007) 377 final, Brussels, 27 June 2007; and European Commission, Report from the Commission to the European Parliament and the Council on Romania's progress on accompanying measures following accession, COM(2007) 378 final, Brussels, 27 June 2007.

[56] Barber, T., 'EU reins in Sarkozy "wise men" plan', Financial Times, 5 Dec. 2007; and European Council, Presidency Conclusions, 16616/1/07 REV 1, 14 Dec. 2007, p. 2.

reform processes for the Former Yugoslav Republic of Macedonia (a candidate country) and Albania, Bosnia and Herzegovina, Montenegro and Serbia
(potential candidate states) will delay their memberships.[57]

The acrimonious controversy over the accession to the EU of Turkey, the
third candidate state, continued. Concerns included freedom of expression,
rights of non-Muslim religious communities and the Kurdish population, corruption, judicial reform, trade union and human rights, and the normalization
of relations with Cyprus.[58] Despite French attempts to block Turkish accession
and tensions between EU members on this issue, two new chapters were
opened for negotiation in December 2007. However, a consequence of this
was that Turkish enthusiasm for the EU dampened.[59]

The EU's European Neighbourhood Policy (ENP)—established to foster
positive relationships with EU neighbours—continues to be a set of disparate
endeavours. Without offering the hope of membership, the goal of coming to
terms with security and societal problems in partner states remains elusive.
There is, furthermore, an ambivalence among EU states' attitudes to the EU
neighbours. This has been demonstrated by the EU members' timid market
openings and their reluctance to take full advantage of some of the provisions
of the agreements, such as those regarding mobility.[60]

The Common Foreign and Security Policy

French President Sarkozy has proposed that the 2003 European Security
Strategy (ESS) be revised with a common vision on the threats facing Europe
and the means of response. Following this the European Council of 14 December 2007 invited the High Representative for the CFSP, Javier Solana, 'in full
association with the Commission and in close cooperation with the Member
States', to propose ways in which the ESS could be improved as well as
complemented with the aim of adoption by the European Council in December
2008.[61] Further development of the ESS will, however, not be unproblematic

[57] European Commission, Communication from the Commission to the European Parliament and the
Council, Enlargement Strategy and Main Challenges 2007–2008, Brussels, 6 Nov. 2007. In Dec. 2007
Bosnia and Herzegovina concluded a Stabilization and Association Agreement with the EU. See
'Bosnia–Herzegovina signs stabilization deal with EU', EUX.TV, 4 Dec. 2007, <http://eux.tv/article.
aspx?articleId=18688>.

[58] European Commission, (note 57), pp. 8–9; and Council of the European Union, 2839th Council
meeting, Press release, 16326/07, 10 Dec. 2007, p. 9–10.

[59] In the spring of 2007 62% of the Turkish population endorsed EU membership. This figure had
gone down to 53% at the end of the year. European Commission, Eurobarometer 68: Public Opinion in
the European Union (First Results), Dec. 2007, p. 27; 'Turkey's EU membership talks move forward',
EurActiv.com, 20 Dec. 2007, <http://www.euractiv.com/en/enlargement/turkey-eu-membership-talks-
move-forward/article-169296>; and 'EU to open new chapters with Turkey', European Voice, 6–12 Dec.
2007, p. 2. The chapters concern trans-European networks and consumer and health protection. According to French statements, Turkey can participate in these EU policies whether it is a member state or not.
Each chapter corresponds to an area of the acquis communautaire (EU common rights and obligations).

[60] European Commission, Communication from the Commission: A Strong European Neighbourhood
Policy, COM (2007) 774 final, Brussels, 5 Dec. 2007, pp. 4–6.

[61] Council of the European Union, 'A secure Europe in a better world', The European Security Strategy, Brussels, 12 Dec. 2003; Sarkozy, N., Speech, Fifteenth Ambassadors' Conference, Paris, 27 Aug.

considering the divergence of views among EU countries, as evidenced in the Lisbon Treaty provisions to the effect that the ESDP

shall not prejudice the specific character of the security and defence policy of certain Member States and shall respect the obligations of certain Member States, which see their common defence realised in the North Atlantic Treaty Organisation (NATO), under the North Atlantic Treaty and be compatible with the common security and defence policy established within that framework.[62]

Some EU countries' dependence on Russian energy supplies has been a major impediment in forming a united policy towards Russia. In September 2007 the European Commission, striving for an integrated EU-wide market for gas and electricity, unveiled a radical liberalization package that would break up Europe's national energy companies to open the markets to greater competition and to promote diversification.[63] The Commission also proposed limitations on foreign ownership of European power assets, aimed at Russian energy giants such as Gazprom and Rosneft. Due to strong French and German opposition, the Commission's energy liberalization plan will face a long legislative battle in the years to come.

Immigration, climate change and counterterrorism were among a host of pressing issues involving the Council, the Commission and the European Parliament in 2007.

The need for a common European immigration and asylum system became even more urgent as illegal immigration led to great difficulties for some EU states, especially in southern Europe.[64] The EU's 'Global Approach to Migration' of December 2005 and 2006, which focused on Africa and the Mediterranean region, was extended during the year to include the regions to the east and south-east of the EU.[65] A joint EU–Africa strategy and action plan that contained a number of concrete measures related to migration was endorsed in December.[66] However, border control remains difficult and there is still no implementation of the agreed external border controls for the Schengen area, which was extended to include nine more states in December 2007.[67]

2007, <http://www.ambafrance-uk.org/President-Sarkozy-s-speech.html>; Solana, J., Speech, Annual Conference of the EU Institute for Security Studies, Paris, 22 Nov. 2007, <http://iss.europa.eu/fileadmin/fichiers/pdf/seminars/annual_2007/ac07-02.pdf>; and European Council (note 56), p. 24.

[62] Treaty of Lisbon (note 1), Article 28A.

[63] For analysis and links to documentation see 'EU unveils plan to dismantle big energy firms', EurActive.com, 20 Sep. 2007, <http://www.euractiv.com/en/energy/eu-unveils-plan-dismantle-big-energy-firms/article-166890?_print>; and Barysch, K., 'Russia, realism and EU unity', Policy Brief, Centre for European Reform, July 2007, <http://www.cer.org.uk/russia_new/index_russia_new.html>.

[64] Bilefsky, D., 'EU Nations refuse to split up the refugee burden', International Herald Tribune, 12 June 2007.

[65] Council of the European Union, EU Council Conclusions on coherence between EU migration and development policies, Brussels, 20 Nov. 2007, <http://www.europa-eu-un.org/articles/en/article_7537_en.htm>.

[66] European Commission, The Africa–EU strategic partnership: a joint Africa–EU strategy, 9 Dec. 2007, <http://www.ue2007.pt/NR/rdonlyres/D449546C-BF42-4CB3-B566-407591845C43/0/071206jsapenlogos_formatado.pdf>.

[67] The Schengen area was extended to cover the Czech Republic, Estonia, Hungary, Latvia, Lithuania, Malta, Poland, Slovenia and Slovakia. European Council (note 56). Schengen is a body of Euro-

The need for an integrated climate and energy policy was another important issue during 2007. This issue took a step forward with the March 2007 agreement to achieve at least a 20 per cent reduction of greenhouse gas emissions by 2020 as compared to 1990 levels.[68]

A crucial area for both the EU and its citizens is the fight against terrorism.[69] Its saliency has increased owing to several foiled attacks during the year.[70] The November 2007 biannual review of the EU Counter-Terrorism Strategy of 2005 described existing problems among states in coordinating activities in terms of insufficient capabilities.[71] Corrective action taken in 2007 included the EU Council agreement of June 2007 on the Visa Information System (VIS) aimed at preventing, detecting and investigating terrorist offences. The VIS will be used by designated authorities and Europol (the European Police Office). Another is an agreement with the USA on processing of passenger name record (PNR) data.[72] After the six-month vacancy following the stepping-down of Gijs de Vries, Gilles de Kerchove was appointed the EU Counterterrorism Coordinator in September. The vacancy has been interpreted as a sign of disagreement over the mandate and capabilities of this position, with some countries resisting a strengthening of them.[73] The European Commissioner for Justice, Freedom and Security, Franco Frattini, has put forward a number of proposals, the reactions to some of them demonstrating the sensitive nature of measures dealing with personal privacy.[74]

As security threats cross borders easily, solutions often require a variety of means and cooperation among several countries and organizations. Efforts under the CFSP and the Justice and Home Affairs (JHA) pillars address both internal and external dimensions of security. The JHA pillar is complemented by the 2005 Prüm Convention on a number of security objectives such as the exchange of DNA information.[75] A number of EU countries are in the process

pean Union Law ('the Schengen acquis') that enables greater freedom of movement for persons, while at the same time introducing compensatory measures to maintain and reinforce the level of security.

[68] European Council, Presidency Conclusions, 7224/1/07 REV, 2 May 2007, p.13.

[69] According to Eurobarometer of Dec. 2007, 81% of the EU population see the fight against terrorism as the most important task for the Union. European Commission (note 59), p. 28.

[70] See e.g. Dempsey, J. and Bennhold, K., 'Germany building case in foiled terrorist plot', *International Herald Tribune*; and '3 sought after 2nd car bomb found in London', MSNBC and NBC News, 29 June 2007, <http://www.msnbc.msn.com/id/19495826>.

[71] Council of the European Union, 'Implementation of the Strategy and Action Plan to Combat Terrorism', Brussels, 28 Nov. 2007, In the document (pp. 1–3) the problems are described as relying on lack of platforms bringing together the different agencies, such as police, customs and financial intelligence units (FIU) and on insufficient links between the agencies' databases.

[72] Council of the European Union (note 71), pp. 5–6.

[73] See Oxford Analytica, 'European Union, counter-terror tsar', *International Herald Tribune*, 26 Sep. 2007.

[74] See e.g. European Commission, Communication from the Commission to the European Parliament and the Council: Stepping up the fight against terrorism, COM (2007) 649 final, Brussels, 6 Nov. 2007; and Council of the European Union, Amendment of the Framework Decision on combating terrorism and Evaluation report on the implementation of the Framework Decision on combating terrorism, MEMO/07/448, Brussels, 6 Nov. 2007. For reactions against Frattini's proposals see Fay, J., 'MEP slate EU's terror assault on our data rights', *The Register*, 13 Dec. 2007.

[75] The Prüm Convention (Schengen III Agreement) was signed on 27 May 2005. Its text is available at <http://www.libertysecurity.org/IMG/rtf/Prum_Convention.rtf>. Originally only 7 countries were

of ratifying the Prüm Convention, which was included in EU law in 2007.[76] Furthermore, JHA issues are dealt with in the 'EU G6'—the unofficial grouping of the interior ministers of France, Germany, Italy, Poland, Spain, and the UK. While this signifies the great importance given to the particular area, unavoidably there are overlaps and complications.[77]

Africa, Central Asia and the Middle East are all areas of vital importance for CFSP policies. In Africa, the EU is concerned by the lack of cooperation from the Sudanese Government in deploying the African Union/UN Hybrid Operation in Darfur (UNAMID). Nevertheless, there is some hope in the political talks about Darfur that started in Sirte, Libya, in October.[78] Central Asia is of crucial importance to the EU because of its strategic location and energy resources. However, the EU strategy for future collaboration in Central Asia as officially adopted by the European Council has been hampered by human rights concerns in the region.[79] The Middle East peace process—in which EU participation is pursued along with the UN, the USA and Russia in the Quartet—is seen more positively than before in light of the Annapolis Conference and the understanding between the Israeli Prime Minister, Ehud Olmert, and the President of the Palestinian Authority, Mahmoud Abbas.[80]

The variable geometry of EU cooperation acknowledges that not every country needs to be part of every policy and some countries can cooperate together more closely than others. The cooperation initiated by France, Germany and the UK (the E3), on behalf of the EU and including Javier Solana, to address the issue of the Iranian uranium programme offers one example of variable geometry.[81] Another example of this approach relates to the role of the Contact Group—which brings together France, Germany, Italy and the UK with Russia and the USA—in the search for a solution to the Kosovo issue.[82]

party to the Prüm Convention: Austria, Belgium, France, Germany, Luxembourg, the Netherlands and Spain.

[76] European Council, Presidency Conclusions, 11177/1/07 REV 1, 20 July 2007, p. 6.

[77] For a critical evaluation see Justice, 'Comments for the House of Lords EU Sub-Committee F on the conclusions of the meeting of the G6 Interior Ministers at Heiligendamm on 22–23 March 2006', London, May 2006, <http://www.justice.org.uk/parliamentpress/parliamentarybriefings/>, p. 4.

[78] Council of the European Union, Press Release 2840th meeting, General Affairs and External Relations, External Relations, 16327/07, Brussels, 10 Dec. 2007, p. 9. On the establishment of UNAMID see chapter 3 in this volume.

[79] European Council (note 76), p. 12; and Council of the European Union, General Secretariat, *The European Union and Central Asia: Strategy for a New Partnership* (General Secretariat of the Council: Brussels, Oct. 2007). Sanctions imposed on Uzbekistan in 2005 after the ruthless suppression of a demonstration were partially lifted by the EU Council on 15–16 Oct. 2007 to encourage improved human rights and maintained cooperation with the West in combating terrorism in Afghanistan.

[80] Council of the European Union (note 78), p. 16. The Annapolis Conference took place between the Israeli Prime Minister, Ehud Olmert, and the President of the Palestinian Authority, Mahmoud Abbas. The White House, Office of the Press Secretary Joint Understanding read by President Bush at Annapolis Conference, 27 Nov. 2007, <http://www.whitehouse.gov/news/releases/2007/11/20071127.html>.

[81] This delegation has been accepted by all EU members. When the 3 largest powers—France, Germany and the UK—took the initiative in 2003 and spoke in the name of the EU without involving it, there was strong criticism by others, leading to the involvement of the organization and Solana personally. See Crowe, B., *Foreign Minister of Europe* (Foreign Policy Centre: London, Feb. 2005), p. 15.

[82] See e.g. 'Ban Ki-moon receives Contact Group report on Kosovo', UN News Service, 7 Dec. 2007, <http://www.un.org/apps/news/story.asp?NewsID=24977&Cr=kosovo&Cr1>.

More problematic is when countries cooperate without connection to and in competition with the EU. Sarkozy's plan for a Mediterranean Union, which would exclude countries without a Mediterranean coast, has been criticized by many EU countries for serving French interests and, if implemented, potentially weakening the EU.[83]

The European Security and Defence Policy

As in previous years, the ESDP managed a variety of issues in 2007, including conflict prevention and crisis management, training, military and civilian capabilities, adequate financing, European Defence Agency (EDA) progress, civil–military coordination and cooperation with other international organizations and states.[84] The 1992 Petersberg Tasks, whose scope and range were extended by the June 2004 European Council, have been given an anti-terrorism emphasis in the Lisbon Treaty.[85] By the end of 2007 the EU was carrying out 10 peace operations, most of them outside Europe.[86]

The large number and variety of missions reflects the EU's interest in stabilizing both its neighbourhood and conflict zones around the globe. In 2007 and early 2008 the EU initiated a police mission in Afghanistan (EUPOL Afghanistan) and was preparing a military operation in Chad and the Central African Republic (EUFOR Tchad/RCA) and a police mission in Kosovo (EULEX Kosovo).[87] In January 2007 the first two battle groups became operational, to be replaced by two others on 1 July, but as yet none has been used in an operation.[88] In October the European Gendarmerie Force became operational and sent a contingent of 140 gendarmes to Sarajevo, Bosnia and Herzegovina.[89] As a result of the improved situation in that country, forces supporting the largest EU mission, EUFOR ALTHEA, were cut down to 2500.[90]

---

[83] See e.g. Bennhold, K., 'Sarkozy's proposal for Mediterranean bloc makes waves', *International Herald Tribune*, 10 May 2007; Longherst, K., 'A new Mediterranean Union will mean a weaker Europe', *European Voice*, 31 Oct.–7 Nov. 2007, p. 12; and 'Sarkozy's Mediterranean Union plans irk Merkel', EurActiv.com, 13 Dec. 2007, <http://www.euractiv.com/en/future-eu/sarkozy-mediterranean-union-plans-irk-merkel/article-169080>.

[84] On EDA activities see chapter 6 in this volume; and European Council, Presidency report on ESDP, 16426/07, 11 Dec. 2007.

[85] According to Article 28b of the Lisbon Treaty (note 1), the Petersberg Tasks include 'joint disarmament operations, humanitarian and rescue tasks, military advice and assistance tasks, conflict prevention and peace-keeping tasks, tasks of combat forces in crisis management, including peace-making and post-conflict stabilization'. The Petersberg Tasks were introduced in the 1997 Amsterdam Treaty.

[86] See appendix 3A in this volume.

[87] On the preparations for EUFOR Tchad/RCA see chapter 3 in this volume.

[88] For a general description of the battle groups see Lindström, G., *Enter the EU Battle Groups*, Chaillot Papers no. 97 (European Union Institute for Security Studies: Paris, Feb. 2007).

[89] The force is composed of Dutch, French, Italian, Portuguese and Spanish gendarmerie and is based in Vicenza, Italy. It could have up to 2300 men, with an 800-strong rapid reaction force. In addition to the missions sent out for specific and sometimes urgent tasks, the EU has special representatives in key areas of the world promoting EU policies and seeking to maintain peace and stability in the area. 'EU/Gendarmerie: gendarmie unit in Sarajevo shortly', *Europe Diplomacy & Defence*, 23 Oct. 2007, p. 3.

[90] EU Council Secretariat, EU military operation in Bosnia and Herzegovina (Operation EUFOR–Althea), Fact sheet, Dec. 2007.

However, the events in Kosovo were a reminder that all is not going well in the Western Balkans.

Both Middle East missions have encountered obstacles related to the Israeli–Palestinian conflict. Aimed at contributing to sustainable and effective policing under Palestinian ownership, the EU Police Mission in the Palestinian Territories had a long wait for Israeli accreditation.[91] The European Union Border Assistance Mission in Rafah (EUBAM Rafah) suspended operations after the closure of the Rafah crossing point in June 2007.[92]

Africa is a region of special interest and a constant source of concern for the EU. For example, EUFOR Tchad/RCA, anticipated to start in January 2008 and to be operational in April, suffered from slow force generation and insufficient capabilities (e.g. helicopters).[93] EUSEC DRC, which assists in security sector reform in the Democratic Republic of the Congo, is at an impasse, chiefly over the disarmament, demobilization and reintegration (DDR) programme and the creation of a secure payment procedure.[94] Missions are often small and short-term and are therefore inadequate to secure long-term progress. For example, the area of eastern Congo where Operation ARTEMIS was launched in 2003 is troubled again.[95]

The EU grapples with other challenges as well. First, on a more general level, it faces overstretch. In this context, US demands for increased forces in Afghanistan have created problems for European countries related to the competing prioritization of EU and NATO missions.[96] Second, the battle group concept proved to be an imperfect solution. Although the battle groups were formed in order to give the EU access to standby troops, none of the ongoing conflicts fit all the criteria put on battle group missions during their first year. Third, there is the issue of operation headquarters. While some would prefer that EU operations rely on NATO (under the 2003 Berlin Plus Agreement[97]),

[91] The official name for the mission is EU Police Co-ordinating Office for Palestinian Police Support, (EUPOL COPPS). Council of the European Union, European Union Police Mission for the Palestinian Territories (EUPOL COPPS), Fact sheet, Jan. 2008.

[92] The suspension is seen as temporary and formally EUBAM is therefore still operational. EUBAM Rafah, 'EUBAM still operational', Fact sheet, Dec. 2007.

[93] Taylor, S., 'Chad mission to test Union's will and power', *European Voice*, 2–29 Aug. 2007, p. 7; 'EU/Chad: timid progress on way to forming European force for deployment in Sudan/Darfur border regions', *Europe Diplomacy & Defence*, 27 Sep. 2007, p. 2; 'EU/AFRICA: General Nash describes for ambassadors difficult conditions in which EUFOR Chad-DRC will be deployed', *Europe Diplomacy & Defence*, 1 Nov. 2007, p. 1; and 'EU/AFRICA: CONOPS for EUFOR Chad-DRC to be finalised soon', *Europe Diplomacy & Defence*, 6 Nov. 2007, p. 2.

[94] EUSEC DRC is the EU security sector reform mission in the Democratic Republic of the Congo. DDR of former combatants plays a critical role in order to make the transition from war to peace. See 'EU/DRC: EUSEC is in impasse', *Europe Diplomacy & Defence*, 20 Dec. 2007, p. 2.

[95] Polgreen, L., 'A battered Congo again in convulsions', *International Herald Tribune*, 13 Dec. 2007.

[96] The US Defense Secretary, Robert Gates, has called for 'a greater role for the UN and the European Union in economic development and the training of the Afghan police'. See 'NATO/Defence: first day of informal meeting in Noordwijk dominated by Afghanistan', *Europe Diplomacy & Defence*, 26 Oct. 2007, p. 3.

[97] The Berlin Plus Agreement gives the EU the possibility to make use of NATO planning support or NATO capabilities and assets for the execution of any operations. NATO, 'Berlin Plus Agreement', 17 Mar. 2003, <http://www.nato.int/shape/news/2003/shape_eu/se030822a.htm>.

others strive towards an autonomous EU military headquarters. The ESDP is now dependent on a number of national headquarters for many of its missions.[98] If the EU is to assume a major role in the area of defence policy, it needs to deal with the lack of consensus on this vital issue.

V. Atlantic community security cooperation

At the heart of NATO's difficulties is its relative marginalization in the transatlantic dialogue. For the USA, the greater Middle East theatre and combating terrorism remain the most important security challenges, and in this regard NATO does not necessarily offer an obvious added value. NATO urgently needs a new Strategic Concept to give it a clear sense of purpose, whether alliance-related or global. France's possible full return to NATO, much publicized in 2007, looks hopeful, but much will depend on whether the USA and other Atlanticist governments (the UK in particular) are prepared to adopt a more favourable view of the ESDP. At the end of 2007 and in the run-up to the April 2008 Bucharest Summit, the prospects for NATO enlargement with the entry of Balkan states seemed to be brighter, with Croatia in the lead.

The European–US rapprochement

The overall rapprochement between the USA and its European allies and partners has limitations. The USA is now less a 'European' power than it used to be.[99] The USA considers the greater Middle East its main strategic theatre, and it remains heavily engaged there, both diplomatically and militarily, with its ongoing conflict in Iraq as the highest priority.[100] Despite the hope that US troop numbers in Iraq could be reduced after the 'surge' of 2007, the Iraqi Government appears to require a continuing US presence.[101] In December 2007 the legal basis for the US presence in Iraq was renewed until 31 December 2008 by UN Security Council Resolution 1790, but this is to be the last such renewal.[102] After that date, a bilateral agreement will have to be negotiated between the two countries, one of the first tasks awaiting the new US Administration in 2009.

The US Administration of President George W. Bush took a more pragmatic approach to the Israeli–Palestinian conflict, allowing for more constructive

[98] See Lindström (note 88), pp. 22–23.

[99] As the US Under Secretary of State for Political Affairs, Nicholas Burns, succinctly put it, 'The United States' policy towards Europe is no longer about Europe. It's about the rest of the world.' Beatty, A., 'America and Europe go their separate ways', *European Voice*, 7 Apr. 2007.

[100] See e.g. Hollis, R., 'The greater Middle East', *SIPRI Yearbook 2005: Armaments, Disarmament and International Security* (Oxford University Press: Oxford, 2005), pp. 232–34.

[101] For a detailed account of the conflict in Iraq see chapter 2 in this volume, section III.

[102] UN Security Council Resolution 1790, 18 Dec. 2007. On 26 Nov. 2007 the Iraqi Prime Minister, Nouri al-Maliki, and US President George W. Bush signed the Declaration of Principles for a Long-Term Relationship of Cooperation and Friendship between the Republic of Iraq and the United States of America. The text of the declaration is available at <http://www.whitehouse.gov/news/releases/2007/11/20071126-11.html>.

cooperation with the EU, which has long regarded the peace process as a key prerequisite for a stable Middle East. The revival of the 'road map' for peace and the negotiations launched at the November 2007 Annapolis Conference marked a clear departure from President Bush's past choices.[103] Transatlantic rapprochement was also noticeable regarding the other crucial issue in the Middle East: the Iranian proliferation problem.[104] However, Western cohesion in Afghanistan suffered from strategic divergences, national constraints and the resurgence of the Taliban.

EU–NATO cooperation

In recent years, despite their declared commitment to closer collaboration and consultation in security matters, the EU and NATO—the two main Euro-Atlantic institutions—have remained entangled in rivalry. In January 2007 the NATO Secretary General, Jaap de Hoop Scheffer, called for 'strategic partnership' between the two organizations, with a special emphasis on Kosovo's final status, Afghanistan, military capabilities and political dialogue.[105] Along with Darfur, these shared challenges should result in more effective collaboration and 2007 saw promising progress in these areas.[106] For example, France's overtures to NATO during the year and its engagement in the Afghanistan mission raised modest hopes for agreement on a more effective division of labour. In practical terms, however, high-level EU–NATO cooperation continues to be uneven. For instance, in Afghanistan—where there appears to be solid cooperation on the ground—the dispute between the EU and Turkey (a NATO member) over EU access to NATO intelligence and logistics hampered their joint Afghan police training plans. A number of possibly formidable issues could block the EU–NATO collaboration deal, among them forthcoming reviews of the European Security Strategy and NATO's Strategic Concept, avoiding the competition between the EU battle groups and the NATO Response Force (NRF), and resolving the Cyprus–Turkey stalemate.

Combating terrorism

Differences between US and European approaches to international terrorism have continued to rise difficulties for the transatlantic community, despite a change in tone and tactics in the USA. The USA's 'global war on terrorism' has proven far more complex and expensive than anticipated. Constantly reinventing itself, al-Qaeda has changed its leadership, diversified its bases and recruitment tactics, and expanded its Internet activities.[107] According to a

[103] White House (note 80).

[104] See chapter 8 in this volume, section II.

[105] de Hoop Scheffer, J., 'NATO and the EU: time for a new chapter', Keynote speech, 29 Jan. 2007, <http://www.nato.int/docu/speech/2007/s070129b.html>.

[106] Tigner, B., 'NATO, EU working harder to coordinate efforts', *Defense News*, 23 Apr. 2007, p. 22.

[107] B. Riedel, a former senior CIA counterterrorism official, stated 'what we are seeing is the reconstitution of Al-Qaeda's capabilities to strike targets in Western Europe and ultimately North America on

US Government report, al-Qaeda 'is driven by an undiminished strategic intent to attack the [US] homeland' and is expected to 'enhance' its capability to attack the USA through cooperation with US-based terrorist groups. The report also underlines al-Qaeda's 'persistent desire for weapons of mass destruction, as the group continues to try to acquire and use chemical, biological, radiological or nuclear material'.[108] Six years after the terrorist attacks on 11 September 2001 the USA remained vulnerable. A unclassified summary of the July 2007 US National Intelligence Estimate on terrorism threats concludes that the USA found itself in a 'heightened threat environment', underlining the 'rejuvenating effect' the conflict in Iraq has had on al-Qaeda and pointing to the failure to counter extremism in Pakistan's tribal areas. Even if al-Qaeda perceives the USA as a more difficult target to strike, and despite several US successes against its leaders, al-Qaeda has been able 'to recruit and indoctrinate operatives, including for [US] Homeland attacks'.[109] The USA is increasingly concerned about Europe being used as a base for attacks against the USA; this led to reinforced measures to better control the flow of passenger airline traffic crossing the Atlantic. Since the terrorist attacks in Madrid in 2004 and London in 2005, European intelligence services have focused on domestic radicalization.

The USA's reputation across Europe and beyond continues to suffer. Even if the USA's sole superpower status fuels resentment and suspicion, US foreign policy choices have contributed to its isolation.[110] In this context, the 'jihadist' movement seems to have gained ground in Pakistan, the Maghreb is increasingly embattled, Sunni extremism is on the rise in Lebanon and Hamas has maintained its power in the Gaza Strip. The deteriorating strategic environment affects Europe too. Not only have the risks of attacks in the UK as well as against US assets in Europe increased (e.g. in Germany), but the further radicalization of Muslim extremists against an undifferentiated West threatens Europe as a whole.[111] In a move favoured by Europe, in 2007 the Bush Administration aimed to regain its strategic initiative by adopting a more comprehensive approach in the 'global war on terrorism', advocating engagement and negotiation in addition to coercion and containment. This was evidenced by the emergence of a more congruent framework of internal and external measures, and of hard and soft policies.

a scale identical or bigger than Sep. 11, creating franchises and buying franchises, offering expertise, networks, money. Al-Qaeda leaders have rebuilt a network of field commanders that was largely decimated in the post-Sep. 11 attacks on its bases in Afghanistan'. Cited in Meyer, J., 'Al Qaeda co-opts new affiliates', *Los Angeles Times*, 16 Sep. 2007.

[108] US Homeland Security Council, *US National Strategy for Homeland Security* (White House: Washington, DC, Oct. 2007), <http://www.whitehouse.gov/infocus/homeland/nshs/2007/index.html>.

[109] US National Intelligence Council, 'National Intelligence Estimate: the terrorist threat to the US homeland', July 2007, <http://www.dni.gov/press_releases/20070717_release.pdf>.

[110] For a more in-depth discussion about the sources and types of anti-US perceptions see Katzenstein, P. J. and Keohane, R. O. (eds.), *Anti-Americanisms in World Politics* (Cornell University Press: Ithaca, N.Y., 2007).

[111] Dempsey and Bennhold (note 70); and MSNBC and NBC News (note 70).

Collective defence and rapid response issues

The novelty of 2007 was the reopening of 'cold war'-style issues with Russia (see section III). The Russian–US brinkmanship over the CFE Treaty and missile defence reflected the wide spectrum of strategic, political, military issues that divide the Euro-Atlantic community. There has long been an unease among the members of NATO over the right approach to relations with Russia. For the sake of NATO cohesion as well as the viability of the CFE regime, NATO states—including the USA—have belatedly acknowledged the need to pay more serious attention to Russia's CFE-related concerns. Given the growing tension and Russian demands, the autumn of 2007 saw the USA shift towards enhanced diplomatic efforts with Russia, undertaken in consultation with NATO allies. A challenge for the USA was to find creative ways to persuade Russia to not react adversely to the new developments in the European security environment and also maintain NATO unity.[112]

NATO suffers from a lack of consensus about its threat assessment and the scope of cooperation over the related US plan for missile defence in Central Europe. Pending the Bucharest Summit in April 2008, the North Atlantic Council has so far 'taken note' of progress in its 'ongoing work' on the political and military implications of missile defence for NATO and has offered Russia consultations in the NATO–Russia Council as a cooperative transparency measure.[113]

Meanwhile NATO, as part of its 1999 Strategic Concept, has elaborated a plan for a theatre missile defence system, the Active Layered Theatre Ballistic Missile Defence (ALTBMD) programme. This 'system of systems' will be integrated into a single NATO command and control network.[114] ALTBMD is scheduled to achieve an initial operational capability by 2010 and to be fully operational by 2016. Its goal is to protect NATO-deployed forces inside or outside NATO territory against short- and medium-range ballistic missiles. However, there have been discussions at NATO Headquarters about making ALTBMD complementary with the USA's missile defence plan for long-range missiles.

Little headway has been made on missile defence cooperation since the 2006 Riga Summit's confirmation that the defence of NATO forces and territory from the entire range of ballistic missile threats was feasible. The USA's missile defence plan, bilaterally negotiated with the Czech Republic and Poland, does not cover the whole of NATO's European territory, leaving the south east exposed. On 14 June 2007 NATO defence ministers agreed to assess the possibility of 'bolting' the ALTBMD system on to the US system to ensure that all of NATO territory would be protected from missile threats and that the two systems would be interoperable.[115] US officials have apparently

---

[112] See chapter 10 in this volume, section II.

[113] NATO, Final communiqué—Ministerial meeting of the North Atlantic Council held at NATO headquarters, Press Release (2007)130, 7 Dec. 2007, <http://www.nato.int/docu/pr/2007/p07-130e.html>.

[114] For more detail see appendix 8C in this volume, section III.

[115] 'NATO agrees on missile defence way forward', *NATO News*, 14 June 2007.

interpreted this decision as NATO's implied endorsement of the US missile defence plan, although this is debatable.

The NATO Response Force is capable of performing missions worldwide across a spectrum of operations, including evacuations, disaster management, counterterrorism, and acting as 'an initial entry force' for larger, follow-on forces.[116] The NRF, which so far has been deployed twice—in the aftermath of Hurricane Katrina and after the Pakistani earthquake, both in 2005—is to have about 25 000 troops on standby. While the NRF remains an important tool for the transformation, improvement and interoperability of NATO forces, the perennial problem of members' asymmetrical sharing of the costs and military burden has effectively stymied its operability. As NATO's engagement in various theatres around the world has strained NATO members' capabilities, NATO defence ministers meeting in Noordwijk, the Netherlands, in October decided, as an interim measure, to reduce the core number of troops in a state of readiness while retaining the ability to rapidly reinforce the NRF to its full complement of 25 000.[117]

Afghanistan

Although the much-feared Taliban spring offensive did not materialize and the Taliban leadership appeared to be divided and unable to control their provincial factions, the security situation in Afghanistan deteriorated throughout 2007. After six years, progress in stabilization and reconstruction remains limited.[118] Almost half of Afghanistan, primarily in the south, is too dangerous for aid workers to operate due to Taliban presence.[119] This deteriorating situation exacerbated the pre-existing tensions among NATO allies and raised serious questions about the sustainability of the NATO-led International Security Assistance Force (ISAF).

As a result of NATO members' continuing to frame the mission in different and exclusive terms and limiting their involvement to specific and restricted tasks (e.g. only a limited number of countries have accepted combat missions), the flexibility and efficiency of NATO's efforts have been reduced. For example, the different approaches have led to different strategies, and not all units under NATO command are using the same tactics: the Dutch forces in Uruzgan province have opted for developing relationships with tribal leaders

[116] NATO, 'The NATO Response Force', <http://www.nato.int/issues/nrf/index.html>.

[117] 'NATO/Defence: Changes planned to make NATO better able to respond to new challenges', *Europe, Diplomacy & Defence*, 26 Oct. 2007, p. 2.

[118] The UN noted that 'the numbers of incidents are higher than comparable periods in 2006 . . . The nature of the incidents has however changed considerably, with high numbers of armed clashes in the field giving way to a combination of armed clashes and asymmetric attacks countrywide'. Harrison, C. S., 'Half-year review of the security situation in Afghanistan', UN Department of Safety and Security, 13 Aug. 2007. Terrorist attacks targeting visible and symbolic assets increased significantly in 2007.

[119] A Senlis Report added that 'The insurgency exercises a significant amount of psychological control, gaining more and more political legitimacy in the minds of the Afghan people who have a long history of shifting alliances and regime change'. Senlis Afghanistan, *Stumbling into Chaos: Afghanistan on the Brink* (Senlis Council: London, Nov. 2007).

while other forces have chosen to actively confront the leaders. The UK and Denmark are pushing for greater use of tribal militias to strengthen efforts against Taliban and al-Qaeda forces, while General Dan McNeill, the commander of ISAF, and the USA more generally question this approach.

Despite the urgent need for a common, comprehensive strategic vision that involves both military and civilian aspects of the mission, 'the coalition does not have a coherent strategy' and the consensus-based nature of NATO is increasingly at risk.[120] The provincial reconstruction teams (PRTs) and the reconstruction efforts experienced incoherence similar to that of ISAF. Since ISAF's chain of command only covers the military components of PRTs, civilians working in PRTs only reported to their national governments, each with different frameworks and objectives. With limited budgets, frequent rotations, increased insecurity and without a specific mandate, the PRTs' activities continued to amount to short-term crisis management.

Force generation problems have also plagued the mission. NATO members' varying security concerns have strained NATO solidarity and fuelled disgruntlement about the mission among NATO member governments—Canada, Germany, Italy, the Netherlands and others—which had serious difficulties convincing their public to continue their deployments.[121] According to NATO experts, ISAF needs at least four more battalions, including one to patrol Afghanistan's Pakistani border, and suffers persistent shortages of helicopters and other heavy equipment.[122] As a result, ISAF can clear territory but is

[120] See Center for the Study of the Presidency (CSP), *Afghan Study Group Report: Revitalizing Our Efforts, Rethinking Our Strategies* (CSP: Washington, DC, 30 Jan. 2008). US Defense Secretary Robert Gates had openly criticized this lack of strategic coherence, thereby infuriating NATO members that are engaged in combat operations. See Spiegel, P., 'Gates says NATO force unable to fight guerrillas', *Los Angeles Times*, 16 Jan. 2008; and 'Gates faults NATO force in southern Afghanistan', Reuters, 16 Jan. 2008. For Ali Jalali, the former Interior Minister of Afghanistan, 'NATO is conducting strategic combat but without strategy. Until there is a unified vision, adding to troop numbers will not make much difference.' 'NATO/Afghanistan: major US reinforcement for Afghanistan—NATO Secretary General calls for patience', *Europe Diplomacy & Defence*, 15 Jan. 2008, p. 3.

[121] E.g. 71 Canadian soldiers and 1 diplomat have been killed in Afghanistan and approximately 243 Canadian Forces personnel have been wounded, while other national forces did not suffer any casualties. Canada has regularly complained about the lack of solidarity. See Cox, J., *Afghanistan: The Canadian Military Mission*, Infoseries publication PRB 07-19E (Parliamentary Information and Research Service: Ottawa, 6 Nov. 2007). In Canada 61% of the population disagrees with extending the Afghan mission beyond Feb. 2009. In Germany 29% of the population supports the deployment of German armed forces in Afghanistan, in contrast to 51% of the population 5 years ago. In the Netherlands 34% of the population agrees that the military mission in Uruzgan should be extended. In the UK 62% of the population favours withdrawal with 27% wanting an immediate withdrawal and 35% favour withdrawal in 1 year. 'Canadians reject extending Afghan mission', Angus Reid Global Monitor, 1 Jan. 2008, <http://www.angus-reid.com/polls/view/canadians_reject_extending_afghan_mission/>; Harsch, M., 'Germany's growing Afghan dilemma', ISN Security Watch, 3 Dec. 2007, <http://www.isn.ethz.ch/news/sw/details.cfm?ID=18423>; 'Dutch grow hostile to Afghan mission', Angus Reid Global Monitor, 9 July 2007, <http://www.angus-reid.com/polls/view/16427/dutch_grow_hostile_to_afghan_mission>; and YouGov, Sunday Times survey results, 17 Dec. 2007 <http://www.yougov.com/uk/archives/pdf/2007 12 17 ST toplines.pdf>. Overall, according to a German Marshall Fund poll, European support for combat operations in Afghanistan is about 31%. Cited in Binnendijk, H., 'Finishing the job in Afghanistan', *Wall Street Journal*, 10 Nov. 2007, p. A11.

[122] Cordesman, A. H., 'Open letter on Afghanistan to the House Committee on Armed Services', Center for Strategic and International Studies, 16 Jan. 2008, <http://www.csis.org/component/option,com_csis_pubs/task,view/id,4293/type,1/>.

unable to hold it. The USA, after repeated but largely fruitless appeals to other NATO members to expand their commitments, has decided to send an additional 3200 marines by the spring of 2008.[123]

In addition to NATO's efforts, the wider international community's attempts to build internal security capacity have also been fraught. Although the Afghan National Army (ANA) plays an increasingly active role alongside ISAF, the ANA comprises fewer than 35 000 men, well below the goal of 70 000 by 2010. The Joint Coordination and Monitoring Board (JCMB), which oversees the 2006 Afghanistan Compact, set a goal of recruiting 82 000 policemen, including 18 500 border police.[124] The new EU and US effort to provide nearly 2500 personnel to train and equip the police force has not so far achieved significant results.[125] Corruption is rife in the police force, especially regarding the booming opium trade, and the local population sees the police force as part of the problem rather than the solution. Moreover, repeatedly targeted by the Taliban, it remains weak and dysfunctional.[126]

Towards a new transatlantic bargain

The troubles in Afghanistan underscore the profound challenge that NATO faces in transforming from a regional collective defence organization to a global collective security alliance. It is possible that intrinsically multifaceted and long-lasting operations like Afghanistan, which demand a high level of unity and harmony in commitments, capabilities and strategic choices, are beyond the consensus-based culture of NATO—particularly because these types of security operations are a matter of national choice, not collective necessity. Stabilization and reconstruction efforts must be given a real chance to succeed. If state building is a responsibility that the USA is 'utterly unable, for material, political and cultural reasons, to shoulder alone',[127] and if humanitarian operations remain the cornerstone of the EU's ambitions in defence and security, then such tasks are an inescapable subject for transatlantic cooperation and the collective responsibility of NATO. To carry them out, fundamental institutional, strategic and operational changes must be add-

---

[123] Scott Tyson , A., '3,200 marines to deploy to Afghanistan in spring', *Washington Post*, 16 Jan. 2008, p. A11.

[124] The London Conference on Afghanistan in 2006 resulted in the Afghanistan Compact. The Compact, considered a political commitment on the part of the participants, sets forth 'specific and achievable goals in security, governance, economic and social development, and counter-narcotics.' The Afghan Government and the international community established the JCMB for the 'overall strategic coordination of the implementation' of the Compact. US Department of State, 'The London Conference and the Afghanistan Compact', Fact sheet, Office of the Spokesman, Washington, DC, 31 Jan. 2006; and JCMB, 'Joint Coordiantion & Monitoring Board (JCMB)—facts for journalists', United Nations Assistance Mission in Afghanistan, April 2006, <http://www.unama-afg.org/news/_publications/fact%20 sheets/2006/FactSheet-onJCMB.pdf>.

[125] See International Crisis Group (ICG), *Reforming Afghanistan's Police*, Asia Report no. 138 (ICG: Brussels, 30 Aug. 2007). See also section IV this chapter and appendix 3A in this volume.

[126] Rohde, D., 'Afghan police suffer setbacks as Taliban adapt', *New York Times*, 2 Sep. 2007.

[127] Allin, D. H. et al., *Repairing the Damage, Possibilities and Limits of Transatlantic Consensus*, Adelphi Paper no. 389 (Routledge: London, 2007), p. 84.

ressed—chief among them are the poor cooperation between the EU and NATO, the persistent failures to meet European capabilities targets, the opportunities for common funding and an updated Strategic Concept. The 2007 rapprochement between France and NATO was a potentially significant step toward achieving these reforms. At the same time, Turkey's further alienation may render the effort ineffective. The NATO Bucharest Summit in April 2008 has a broad agenda with many outstanding issues. Given NATO's apparent lack of consensus about its future relevance, a significant breakthrough is unlikely.

VI. Conclusions

The most significant development in Euro-Atlantic relations in 2007 was Russia's restored self-confidence and aspirations to equal status in security matters with its Western partners. Russia in the coming years will remain under the influence of the Putin-era leadership. Increasingly self-assured by the lucrative exploitation of its natural resources and emboldened by their use as a successful political weapon, Russia has returned to its traditional policy of playing its European partners against each other, seeking to weaken the transatlantic ties and to reassert influence over the former Soviet states. At the same time, Russia appears eager to maintain cooperative relations with the West and it is unlikely to risk challenging it too forcefully. In particular, the question of Kosovo, if not managed, is likely to be the source of increasing security tensions in South Eastern Europe and among the EU, Russia and the USA.

The challenges of the transatlantic partnership are increasingly global. Consensus and commitment are difficult to achieve and sustain. When acting together—for example, in the Middle East peace process or over Iran, Kosovo or Afghanistan—the partnership still suffers from self-imposed constraints, divergent approaches or insufficient leverage. The European–US rapprochement that emerged in 2007 was based more on acknowledged weaknesses than projected strengths. For both Europe and the USA, 2007 has been a year of reckoning. The EU has taken an important step by adopting the Lisbon Treaty, which broadly maintains the main elements of the rejected Constitutional Treaty, especially in foreign and security policy areas. The EU can now harness its considerable potential by translating this legal framework into political action. However, the treaty ratification processes may absorb the EU's energies by emphasizing once again national preferences and opt-outs rather than genuine foreign agendas. In the USA, the policies that had diminished the country's influence and prestige at home and abroad have largely been abandoned in favour of a more pragmatic approach to world affairs. Yet the USA remains heavily involved in Iraq and its diplomatic impact has shrunk globally. With a pending election, no foreseeable exit from Iraq and a worsening economy, the USA may become more inward-looking. Thus, transition will be the Euro-Atlantic community's theme in 2008 and 2009.

2. Trends in armed conflicts

EKATERINA STEPANOVA

I. Introduction

In 2007 there was a clear trend towards the further fragmentation of violence in the locations of some of the world's deadliest armed conflicts and other conflict-prone areas. This has been accompanied by the diversification of armed groups and the further erosion of the boundaries between different forms of violence. Much of this 'fragmented' violence is difficult to measure and categorize. While it often occurs in areas of major armed conflict, it may not be directly related to the conflict's main incompatibility.[1] Rather, the larger conflict provides a favourable environment for other forms of violence, both organized and unorganized, and may even trigger them. This fragmented violence often acquires its own dynamics and becomes self-perpetuating. While it is generally carried out on a lower scale in terms of battle-related deaths, it has high costs for civilians in terms of casualties, displacement and less direct impacts.

Section II introduces the chapter's thematic focus on the diversity of armed violence and the erosion of the boundaries between, for example, insurgency, terrorism, sectarian violence and one-sided violence against civilians. Sections III–V, respectively, address the mix of forms of violence in the context of a major armed conflict in Iraq; in the Darfur region of Sudan, where the fighting in 2007 fell short of a major armed conflict;[2] and in Pakistan, which in 2007 suffered multiple forms of violence and instability—only some linked to local armed conflicts—that threatened human, national, regional and international security. The first two cases demonstrate a general fragmentation of armed violence, while all three show the diversification of armed actors and the erosion of boundaries between forms of violence. The conclusions are offered in section VI.

Appendix 2A presents data on major armed conflicts in the period 1998–2007 from the Uppsala Conflict Data Program (UCDP), along with a brief survey of trends in lower-intensity conflicts, particularly those fought between non-state actors. Appendix 2B provides the definitions, sources and methods for the UCDP data and explains some significant changes made to the coding of major armed conflicts in 2007. Appendix 2C discusses the human security approach to direct and structural violence.

---

[1] I.e. the incompatible positions being contested by the conflict parties. See appendix 2B.
[2] See appendix 2A.

II. The fragmentation and diversification of armed violence

A variety of forms of armed violence perpetrated by non-state and state-affiliated actors are becoming widespread and increasingly interconnected in both
conflict and post-conflict settings. In different combinations, these forms often
account for much of the ongoing violence in areas affected by armed conflicts.[3] They are carried out in the same locations, often by the same actors and
may be integrated to the point where they are indistinguishable from one
another.

The diversity of violence reflects the range of motivations, identities and
levels of activity of armed actors. Predatory groups that engage in criminal
violence and exploit opportunities offered by a war economy continue to pro-
liferate in conflict zones. Increasingly, states engaged in counter-insurgency
are trying to mount symmetrical responses to asymmetrical challenges from
non-state actors by relying on paramilitary groups, including ethnic, sectarian
or tribal militias. The merging of insurgent, inter-communal, tribal and criminal violence with counter-insurgency operations can easily acquire cross-
border or broader transnational dimensions.[4] In addition, 99 per cent of one-
sided violence—that is, violence that directly and intentionally targets civilians—takes place in countries where an armed conflict is active.[5] While states
can cause many civilian casualties, especially in the course of conflicts over
governmental authority, in conflicts over territory more civilians are killed by
non-state actors.

Weak or dysfunctional state capacity appears to be the main condition for
the fragmentation of armed violence. One symptom of state failure is the loss
of the state's monopoly on violence. This is accompanied by the proliferation
of armed non-state actors, hinders conflict management and may keep violence at a relatively high level even after a conflict has ended. All three countries that serve as case studies for this chapter—Iraq, Sudan and Pakistan—are
among the top 20 in the 2007 Failed States Index.[6] The involvement of neighbouring states, regional powers and other international actors—in the form of
military interventions, support to groups in conflict, or political and economic
pressure—may also contribute to the fragmentation of violence and erosion of
the boundaries between its different forms. While this involvement may in
part be a response to the weakness of state capacity, it can itself be destabilizing if it fails to promote effective post-conflict state building.

For decades, non-state actors engaged in armed conflicts have often combined traditional insurgent tactics—attacks against government military and

---

[3] On the definitions of major and minor armed conflict see appendices 2A and 2B.

[4] See Lindberg, S. and Melvin, N. J., 'Major armed conflicts', *SIPRI Yearbook 2007: Armaments, Disarmament and International Security* (Oxford University Press: Oxford, 2007), pp. 55–78.

[5] On 1-sided violence see Eck, K. and Hultman, L., 'One-sided violence against civilians in war: insights from new fatality data', *Journal of Peace Research*, vol. 44, no. 2 (Mar. 2007), pp. 233–46.

[6] Sudan and Iraq are ranked as the most unstable states and Pakistan is ranked number 12. Fund for Peace and *Foreign Policy* magazine, 'Failed States Index 2007', *Foreign Policy*, vol. 86, no. 4 (July/ Aug. 2007), p. 57.

security targets—with terrorism—the politically motivated use or threat of violence against non-combatants.[7] Other manifestations of armed violence have become more widespread and increasingly intertwined with one-sided violence and with criminal violence. Three of these—the combination of terrorism with sectarian strife, violence by state-aligned actors ranging from tribal militias to private security companies (PSCs), and violent local power play—are discussed below.

Terrorism and sectarian strife. Traditionally, sectarian violence implies a symmetrical confrontation between two or more non-state actors representing different population groups.[8] While terrorist acts may sometimes be aimed at fomenting broader sectarian strife, the state has traditionally been terrorism's ultimate target, making it an asymmetrical tactic. This has made it possible to distinguish between terrorism and sectarian violence. However, the close association of some sectarian groups with the state may reach a point, as it has in Iraq, when the state becomes a semi-sectarian entity. In such cases, the distinctions between sectarian violence and terrorism—and between the groups that carry them out—may become increasingly blurred. When a state that is perceived as having a strong sectarian bias is confronted with insurgent forces representing other sectarian groups, the transformation of anti-government terrorism into an instrument of sectarian strife is almost inevitable. For such a state, counter-insurgency may also blend with sectarian violence.

The blending of terrorism with sectarian violence was one of the main trends in patterns of violence in Iraq in 2007 and may also explain why such a large proportion of global terrorist activity is taking place there. In January–November 2007 Iraq accounted for over 69 per cent of the world's terrorist incidents and for 85.8 per cent of fatalities from such incidents.[9] While there have been peaks of conflict-related terrorist activity before, the dynamics of global terrorism have never been so dominated by one major armed conflict.

State-aligned militias and private contractors. States' use of armed groups other than their security forces is not a new phenomenon. However, it acquires a new dimension when coupled with a general pattern of fragmentation of violence, further eroding the boundary between state-aligned and non-state violence, as is clearly demonstrated by the activities of pro-state militias in Darfur and Iraq.

Another aspect of the problem is the growing presence of PSCs in conflict areas, particularly Iraq, which in 2007 was the site of the largest private

---

[7] This definition distinguishes terrorism from the broader notion of using terror to intimidate a population, which may be employed by states. See Stepanova, E., *Terrorism in Asymmetrical Conflict: Ideological and Structural Aspects*, SIPRI Research Report no. 23 (Oxford University Press: Oxford, 2008), pp. 5–15.

[8] Sectarian violence here refers to violence both between members of different sects (inter-sectarian violence) and between different groups in the same sect (intra-sectarian violence).

[9] In 2003 only 7.7% of terrorist incidents and 23% of fatalities took place in Iraq. Terrorism Knowledge Base, Memorial Institute for the Prevention of Terrorism (MIPT), <http://www.tkb.org/>. In May 2008 the Terrorism Knowledge Base was merged with the Global Terrorism Database managed by the National Consortium for the Study of Terrorism and Responses to Terrorism (START) at the University of Maryland, <http://www.start.umd.edu/data/gtd/>.

military deployment in modern history. While these forces have a role to play as security providers, their participation in counter-insurgency operations and their use of force against civilians remains highly controversial.[10]

Violent power play at the local level. Many conflict and post-conflict zones are experiencing a proliferation of militias engaged in localized acts of violence. Although this violence may take an ethnic, tribal, sectarian, criminal or other form—or several forms at once—it could often be more accurately characterized as violent local power play. Many of the militias involved are essentially opportunistic, frequently changing alliances and even including members of ethnic, sectarian, tribal or other groups that are otherwise in conflict with each other. They fight for power, resources and control at the local level, rather than for a nationalist, religious, sectarian or socio-political agenda. This localized violence inevitably includes predatory and parasitical activities related to the informal economy (e.g. smuggling by tribal networks), taking advantage of the formal economy's weakness or limited reach. It thrives when state control is weak or non-existent, as is often the case when the state is mired in multiple conflicts at the sub-national and national levels.

III. Iraq

The context: the insurgency and the surge

Insurgency aimed largely at the United States-led Multinational Force in Iraq (MNF-I) and the Iraqi security forces (ISF), reached a new peak in early 2007, resulting in over 5700 battle-related deaths by the end of the year.[11] In June, 73 per cent of attacks were directed against the MNF-I, the highest level since 2005, although the ISF and Iraqi civilians suffered the most casualties.[12] Even though the insurgent groups were not united, they shared some common goals, which could be summarized as enhancing their control over the population, driving out foreign forces and undermining the Iraqi Government.[13]

While some Shia forces, such as the Jaish al-Mahdi (JAM, or Mahdi Army), fought against the US-led coalition in 2004, most of them had ceased their insurgent activities before 2007. The strongly nationalist Sunni part of the insurgency took on a more radical Islamist and sectarian profile from 2006, with al-Qaeda in Iraq (AQI) becoming one of its deadliest elements. However, while AQI has been responsible for many mass-casualty terrorist incidents and large-scale attacks against the MNF-I and the ISF, most sources suggest that

---

[10] See Holmquist, C., *Private Security Companies: The Case for Regulation*, SIPRI Policy Paper no. 9 (SIPRI: Stockholm, 2005); and Perlo-Freeman, S. and Sköns, S., 'The private military services industry', SIPRI Research Paper, June 2008, <http://books.sipri.org/product_info?c_product_id=361>.

[11] See appendix 2A. The term 'insurgency' is used here for the sake of consistency with the Uppsala Conflict Data Program's coding of this conflict as being between the Iraqi Government, the multinational coalition and 'Iraqi insurgents'. However, most insurgent groups in Iraq see themselves as engaged in resistance against foreign occupation.

[12] US Department of Defense (DOD), *Measuring Stability and Security in Iraq*, Report to Congress (DOD: Washington, DC, Sep. 2007), pp. 19–20.

[13] US Department of Defense (note 12), p. 16.

AQI and allied groups comprise no more than 15 per cent of the insurgency's total strength.[14] Foreign fighters make up an even smaller proportion of the insurgency, between 4 and 10 per cent.[15]

Since early 2006 the Sunni-dominated insurgency had become increasingly intertwined with Sunni sectarianism directed at Shias perceived as being pro-MNF-I, pro-government or pro-Iranian. At the same time, several Shia militias—including some, like the Badr Corps, that are affiliated with political forces that are part of the Iraqi Government—started to engage in sectarian violence against the Sunnis. At the end of 2006 US officials and commanders in Iraq suggested a substantial increase in US military presence in response to the sharp rise in sectarian violence. On 10 January 2007 President George W. Bush announced a change of US strategy in Iraq and a plan to commit over 20 000 additional US troops to support 18 Iraqi Army and National Police brigades in Baghdad.[16]

The US military build-up—commonly referred to as the surge—started with a major offensive in early February. The first phase of the surge, which lasted until early June, was dominated by intense counter-insurgency operations, including the bombing of parts of Baghdad in February and June. It met heavy resistance and even led to an increase in some types of violence, but produced few security dividends. US troop fatalities peaked at 123 in May, close to the all-time highs of April 2004 (135) and November 2004 (137). The surge did not change the main causes of US military fatalities since occupation. Between January and September, half of US troop deaths were caused by improvised explosive devices.[17] The average number of US military helicopters brought down every month during the same period was slightly higher than in 2006.[18] Non-state actors in Baghdad systematically struck at well-protected strategic targets, including the best-protected area in Iraq—the international zone—which suffered over 80 attacks between March and May.[19] The high frequency of suicide attacks remained unchecked: between July 2006 and

[14] Cordesman, A. H., *The Tenuous Case for Strategic Patience in Iraq: A Trip Report* (CSIS: Washington, DC, 6 Aug. 2007), p. 11. AQI's role in the resistance and sectarian killings and its links to transnational Islamist networks seem to have been exaggerated by US Government sources.

[15] Estimates of the size of the insurgency range between 5000–15 000 and 30 000 in 2006 and up to 70 000 in 2007, while estimates of foreign fighters range from 800 to 2000. International Crisis Group (ICG), *In Their Own Words: Reading the Iraqi Insurgency*, Middle East Report no. 50 (ICG: Brussels, 15 Feb. 2006), p. 1; and O'Hanlon, M. E. and Campbell, J. H., 'Iraq index: tracking variables of reconstruction and security in Iraq', Brookings Institution, Washington, DC, 1 Oct. 2007, <http://www.brookings.edu/iraqindex/>, pp. 26–27. The US bipartisan Iraq Study Group estimated the number of foreign 'jihadists' in Iraq in 2006 to be 1300. Baker, J. A. and Hamilton, J. H. (co-chairs), 'The Iraq Study Group report', 6 Dec. 2006, <http://www.usip.org/isg/iraq_study_group_report/report/1206/>, p. 10.

[16] The White House, Office of the Press Secretary, 'President's address to the nation', 10 Jan. 2007, <http://www.whitehouse.gov/news/releases/2007/01/20070110-7.html>. Up to 28 000 extra troops were eventually dispatched to Iraq—21 500 troops in 5 combat brigades and 7000–8000 support personnel. Garamone, J., 'Support troops put surge total at 28,000 U.S. servicemembers', US Department of Defense, American Forces Press Service, 16 Mar. 2007, <http://www.defenselink.mil/news/newsarticle.aspx?id=32483>.

[17] For US DOD daily casualty reports see O'Hanlon and Campbell (note 15), pp. 17–18.

[18] O'Hanlon and Campbell (note 15), p. 33.

[19] UN Security Council, Report of the Secretary-General pursuant to Paragraph 30 of Resolution 1546 (2004), S/2007/330, 5 June 2007, p. 11.

June 2007 there were at least 540 such attacks, compared with just 300 between the 2003 invasion and June 2006.[20] Suicide bombings—which often resulted in over 100 deaths—and the monthly totals for all multiple-fatality bombings both peaked in February–April 2007.[21] The most spectacular terrorist acts targeted crowded places in Baghdad's Shia neighbourhoods, provoking new sectarian revenge attacks. Iraqi officials continued to be targeted. In June US commanders acknowledged that despite the deployment of 18 000 additional troops in Baghdad, US forces controlled fewer than a third of the city's neighbourhoods.[22]

The MNF-I was forced to change tactics once again. From mid-June a new series of offensives, collectively known as Operation Phantom Thunder, were launched in key Baghdad districts, in the so-called 'belts' around Baghdad, in Diyala governorate and its capital, Ba'quba, and in Babil and Al-Anbar governorates.[23] An important new feature of this second phase of the surge was the MNF-I's arming and financing of selected Sunni tribal militias to fight their former allies, the more radical Islamist insurgent groups, particularly AQI.[24] In 2007 dissatisfaction with the Islamists' radical agenda and violent practices—reinforced by 'turf wars' over smuggling, illicit road taxing and similar activities—grew among some Sunni Arab tribes, especially in Al-Anbar governorate, leading to violent clashes between Sunni groups. US military and financial support to the dissatisfied tribes contributed to the rise of new Sunni tribal militias—a phenomenon that was dubbed 'tribal awakening' in US sources—and the fragmentation and, thus, weakening of the Sunni armed resistance in the centre of the country. Another characteristic of the second phase of the surge was a new emphasis on making the troop presence much more visible.[25]

Stage two of the surge appeared to have a stabilizing effect on the security situation in some central governorates, including Baghdad and Al-Anbar. The Commanding General of the MNF-I, David Petraeus, stated on 10 September that the military objectives of the surge were, 'in large measure, being met' and the level of 'security incidents' had significantly decreased since mid-

---

[20] Nordland, R. and Dehghanpisheh, B., 'Surge of suicide bombers', *Newsweek*, 13 Aug. 2007.

[21] O'Hanlon and Campbell (note 15), pp. 10–11.

[22] 'Security plan only able to protect 146 of the 457 Baghdad neighbourhoods despite surge', Associated Press, 4 June 2007.

[23] US Central Command, Headquarters, 'MNC-I conducts Operation Phantom Thunder', Press release, 20 June 2007.

[24] The US military insisted that the 'tribal awakening' among the more moderate Sunni tribes was the result of a well-prepared strategy on the part of the MNF-I, but some civilian experts have argued that it had local origins and 'had not been the function of the surge strategy'. Petraeus, D. H., Report to Congress on the situation in Iraq, 10–11 Sep. 2007, <http://foreignaffairs.house.gov/110/pet091007. pdf>, pp. 2, 4; and Cordesman (note 14), p. 9.

[25] A similar strategy was used by British forces in southern Iraq (Operation Sinbad, Sep. 2006–Mar. 2007). At first it had some stabilizing effect but was unsustainable as long as it was not matched by significant progress in building legitimate and functional Iraqi authorities. See e.g. International Crisis Group (ICG), *Where is Iraq Heading? Lessons from Basra*, Middle East Report no. 67 (ICG: Brussels, 25 June 2007), pp. 16–17.

June. He also cited a considerable decline in civilian casualties since December 2006, by 45 per cent across Iraq and by 70 per cent in Baghdad.[26]

However, Petraeus admitted that the overall security situation was 'complex, difficult, and sometimes downright frustrating'.[27] US intelligence estimates pointed at 'uneven improvements' in preventing 'the steep escalation of rates of violence'.[28] Other US military sources showed that there had been a more modest decline in civilian casualties over the summer than the figures cited by Petraeus and hesitated to claim that the trend was sustainable.[29] The US Government Accountability Office (GAO) stated that 'measures of population security show differing trends' and average numbers of daily attacks against civilians remained unchanged between February and July 2007.[30] The new series of offensives also did not help to decrease suicide attacks. The number of suicidal mass-casualty bombings in September, 12, was the same as that in January or in June 2007.[31] Car bomb incidents remained at 80 per month from May through September, the highest level since July 2005.[32] Terrorist violence increasingly targeted ethnic and religious minorities. The worst terrorist attack since 2003 was directed against Yazidi Kurds in August,[33] while on 7 July a suicide bombing in the Shia Turkoman-populated village of Amerli in Salah ad-Din governorate, killed around 150 people.[34] Overall, the surge had not decisively weakened the insurgency by the end of 2007. AQI and allied groups retreated from some areas but showed considerable resilience and remained active in other areas. Other Sunni rebel groups, such as Jaysh Ansar al-Sunna, did not suffer major losses and remained active.

Another notable trend in 2007 was a renewal of activity by Shia insurgents, even as sectarian tensions prevented coordination between Sunni and Shia elements of the insurgency. New Shia insurgent groups, along with some splinter groups and the most radical factions of JAM, targeted the MNF-I, the ISF and government-affiliated Shia groups, such as the Islamic Supreme Council of Iraq (ISCI) and its militia, the Badr Corps.[35] Shia insurgent activity started in January with heavy fighting between the ISF (backed by US forces) and a Shia

---

[26] Petraeus (note 24), p. 3.

[27] Petraeus (note 24), pp. 1–3.

[28] US National Intelligence Council, 'Prospects for Iraq's stability: some security progress but political reconciliation elusive', National Intelligence Estimate, Washington, DC, Aug. 2007, p. 1.

[29] US Department of Defense (note 12), p. 20.

[30] US Government Accountability Office (GAO), *Securing, Stabilizing, and Rebuilding Iraq: Iraqi Government Has Not Met Most Legislative, Security, and Economic Benchmarks*, Statement of David M. Walker before the US Senate Committee on Foreign Relations, GAO-07-1220T (GAO: Washington, DC, 4 Sep. 2007), pp. 1–2, 9. Official information on violence in Iraq rarely includes data on lower-scale but widespread inter-tribal and intra-sectarian clashes.

[31] O'Hanlon and Campbell (note 15), p. 11.

[32] O'Hanlon and Campbell (note 15), p. 21.

[33] On 14 Aug. 2007 suicide bombers drove 4 trucks into 2 houses in Shaam, an area near the Syrian border populated by Yazidis (an Iraq-based Kurdish group), killing over 250 people and injuring 350. Glanz, J., 'Iraqi toll reaches 250 in multiple bombing', *International Herald Tribune*, 15 Aug. 2007.

[34] Farrel S., 'Around 150, death toll in Iraq attack among war's worst', *New York Times*, 8 July 2007.

[35] ISCI was known as the Supreme Council for Islamic Revolution in Iraq (SCIRI) until May 2007. International Crisis Group (ICG), *Shiite Politics in Iraq: The Role of the Supreme Council*, Middle East Report no. 70 (ICG: Brussels, 15 Nov. 2007), p. 15.

militia in Zarqa near An-Najaf, ahead of the Shia Ashura celebrations.[36] For the MNF-I and the ISF, Shia insurgent groups began to 'emerge as a more serious threat in many of the disputed areas in Iraq than Al Qa'ida and Sunni Islamist threats'.[37]

Overall, the security situation was uneven across Iraq in 2007 and the differences between regions grew. The reach of the MNF-I in many parts of the country was limited; intelligence assessments primarily focused on the central governorates and claims about a decline in incidents elsewhere could not be verified.[38] The MNF-I and Iraqi Government's control of Baghdad and the areas around it remained limited, despite the surge, while violence shifted to new areas, including the previously relatively stable south.[39]

The fragmentation of violence

Sunni–Shia sectarian violence

Sectarian strife remained the main form of inter-communal violence in Iraq in 2007. Sectarian violence had not been prevalent at the earlier stages of the invasion but intensified following mass-casualty terrorist attacks against Shia targets that were blamed on Sunni insurgents, especially after the bombing of a Shia shrine in Samarra's Golden Mosque in February 2006. Shia sectarian violence combined reprisal attacks by pro-government militias against Sunni insurgents with one-sided violence against Sunni civilians. Sectarian violence on both sides mainly took the forms of 'sectarian cleansing' (i.e. killing the members of one sectarian group or driving them out of a community) and revenge attacks by squads affiliated with either Sunni or Shia militias, rather than involving the larger populations or mass violence. Areas with mixed populations, such as Baghdad, the northern city of Tel Afar and Diyala governorate, were the worst affected.

The sharp rise in sectarian clashes was one of the main reasons cited for the surge in 2007.[40] However, the US military's claims that MNF-I and Iraqi operations reduced 'ethno-sectarian' deaths by 55 per cent across Iraq and by 80 per cent in Baghdad since their peak in December 2006 should be treated with caution.[41] Estimates of the dynamics of sectarian violence are complicated by the difficulty of establishing 'whether the perpetrators' intents were sectarian in nature'.[42] Also, stage two of the surge achieved success in areas

[36] 200 people were killed and a US helicopter was shot down in the fighting. '"Hundreds" killed in Iraq battles', BBC News, 29 Jan. 2007, <http://news.bbc.co.uk/2/6308821.stm>.

[37] Cordesman (note 14), p. 12.

[38] US National Intelligence Council (note 28).

[39] Three central governorates—Baghdad, Salah ad-Din and Diyala—and the northern governatorate of Ninawa have 42% of the Iraqi population but accounted for 78% of attacks in May–July 2007. US Department of Defense (note 12), p. 17.

[40] The White House (note 16).

[41] Petraeus (note 24), pp. 1, 3. The term 'ethno-sectarian' is used in Petraeus's report to denote both the prevailing sectarian violence and comparatively marginal inter-ethnic violence.

[42] See US Government Accountability Office (note 30), p. 2.

where there was minimal inter-sectarian conflict.[43] Even General Petraeus acknowledged that the confessionally and ethnically homogenous Al-Anbar was 'unique' and that the US strategy of arming and financing Sunni tribal militias in Sunni-populated regions like Al-Anbar and Diyala might not be easy to replicate elsewhere.[44] If applied in more mixed areas, the marriage of convenience between the MNF-I and some Sunni tribes may indirectly stimulate further sectarian tensions. Furthermore, the Shia-dominated Iraqi Government has become increasingly suspicious of the MNF-I's reliance on Sunni tribes and could in response step up its support to Shia militias. In the long run, the possibility of the 'tribalization' of sectarian violence and its spread to non-urban areas cannot be excluded.[45]

A modest decline in inter-sectarian violence in mixed areas such as Baghdad in 2007 can be more directly attributed to the impact of 'sectarian cleansing' and a sharp increase in population displacement. In 2003–2004 the number of newly internally displaced persons (IDPs) in Iraq was growing by 100 000 people per year. It grew by 50 000 in 2005, and the total number of IDPs reached 250 000. In 2006, as inter-sectarian violence increased, the number of new IDPs rose sharply, by 435 000, reaching a total of 685 000. During the surge, in January–August 2007, there were over 520 000 new IDPs, almost doubling the previous total in just eight months.[46] The displacement involved the forced creation of mono-sectarian enclaves that were more difficult for enemy militants to penetrate.[47] The polarization of communities was most evident in Baghdad.

Operation Fardh al-Qanoon, the Baghdad component of Operation Phantom Thunder, contributed to this process both indirectly by tolerating sectarian separation and directly through the construction of barriers to separate Sunni enclaves such as Azamia from Shia-dominated areas. In addition, while stage one of the surge provoked new terrorist attacks that primarily resulted in Shia deaths, stage two refocused some of the Sunni groups from anti-Shia violence back to fighting the MNF-I and the ISF. From June on, much of the inter-sectarian violence in Baghdad area was perpetrated by Shia militias who took advantage of the withdrawal of the Sunni groups in order to push Sunni residents out, especially from the city's north-western districts.[48] This was largely tolerated by the Shia-dominated ISF.

While no major armed actors in Iraq, including Shia groups both inside and outside the Iraqi Government, stayed immune from sectarian strife, Shia-

---

[43] US National Intelligence Council (note 28), p. 2.

[44] Petraeus (note 24), p. 5.

[45] Al-Khalidi, A. and Tanner, V., 'Sectarian violence: radical groups drive internal displacement in Iraq', Brookings Institution–University of Bern Project on Internal Displacement Occasional Paper, Oct. 2006, <http://www.brookings.edu/papers/2006/1018iraq_al-khalidi.aspx>, p. 1.

[46] O'Hanlon and Campbell (note 15), p. 33. With those displaced prior to 2003, the number of IDPs in Iraq may have reached 2 256 000 in Sep. 2007. Internal Displacement Monitoring Centre, 'Total internally displaced population is estimated to be more then 2 million (as of September 2007)', <http://www.internal-displacement.org/>.

[47] US National Intelligence Council (note 28), p. 3.

[48] Cordesman (note 14), p. 10.

generated sectarian violence seemed to come as much from militias associated with political forces inside the government as from the few Shia insurgent groups.[49] The role of state-affiliated and state-aligned actors in sectarian and one-sided violence against civilians had been growing since the formation of the Iraqi Government, which was largely along sectarian and ethnic lines. The association of some key Shia militias with the state and sectarian tendencies and mixed loyalties within the ISF continued to play a highly destabilizing role in 2007.[50] This 'sectarian creep' into state power also blurred the lines between sectarian violence, terrorism and insurgency.

Intra-Sunni and intra-Shia violence

The dynamics of violence in Iraq in 2007 were also characterized by a rise in both intra-Sunni and intra-Shia clashes. The widening divisions between the Arab Sunni 'tribal awakening' movement and the main Sunni insurgent groups were primarily driven by competition for power rather than by confessional imperatives. Even so, the growing religious extremism of parts of the Sunni insurgency played a role in aggravating intra-Sunni tensions. In October 2006 the Mujahideen Shura Council, the AQI-led coalition of Sunni insurgent groups formed earlier that year,[51] jointly declared with some tribal militias 'the foundation of the righteous state, the Islamic state' in Iraq, based on Islamic law (sharia).[52] Council forces went beyond Islamist statements and started to impose strict regulations and norms in areas under their control. This radical version of Islamism was rejected by some tribal groups, who were also attracted by the possibility of support offered by the new US strategy.[53] Nevertheless, the 'tribal awakening' has not 'translated into Sunni Arab support for the Iraqi Government or widespread willingness to work with the Shia'.[54] Abdul al-Rishawi, the USA's main Sunni tribal ally in Al-Anbar, was killed in a bomb attack on 13 September, allegedly by insurgents, only 10 days after he shook hands with President Bush during the latter's surprise visit to the area.[55]

In 2007 intra-Shia clashes intensified in the south of Iraq. In the summer, tensions between JAM and the ISCI-affiliated Badr Corps escalated into fighting between Shia groups in all the main southern cities. Advisers and supporters of the ISCI's spiritual leader, Grand Ayatollah Ali al-Sistani, were regularly attacked by rival Shia groups. In mid-August, the Badr-affiliated governors of Al-Qadisiyah and Al-Muthanna were killed, possibly by units

---

[49] The SCIRI-led United Iraqi Alliance entered government after the Jan. 2005 parliamentary elections.

[50] Petraeus (note 24), p. 1; and US National Intelligence Council (note 28), p. 3.

[51] The Mujahideen Shura Council included AQI and 5 smaller groups: Jaish al-Taifa al-Mansoura, al-Ahwal Brigades, Islamic Jihad Brigades, al-Ghuraba Brigades and Saraya Ansar al-Tawhid. It was later joined by the Army of al-Sunnah Wal Jama'a. See MIPT Terrorism Knowledge Base (note 9).

[52] Mujahideen Shura Council in Iraq, 'The announcement of the establishment of the Islamic State of Iraq', Video statement, 15 Oct. 2006. A partial transcript in English, produced by the Al-Boraq Workshop, is available at <http://www.e-prism.org/>.

[53] Knights, M., 'Struggle for control', Jane's Intelligence Review, vol. 19, no. 1 (Jan. 2007).

[54] US National Intelligence Council (note 28), p. 1.

[55] Rubin, A. J., 'Sunni sheik who backed U.S. in Iraq is killed', New York Times, 14 Sep. 2007.

close to JAM. At the end of August, more than 50 people were killed in intra-Shia fighting in Karbala, leading JAM's leader, Muqtada al-Sadr, to announce a six-month suspension of militant operations. The increase in both Shia insurgent activity and intra-Shia fighting in the south was facilitated by the withdrawal of some JAM militants from Baghdad during the surge. Violent competition for power and resources between Shia factions is likely to intensify as Iraqis assume control of provincial security—in Al-Basrah, violence escalated with the drawdown of British forces, which started in September 2007.[56] However, despite violent clashes between rival Shia militias, for much of 2007 al-Sadr's movement and the ISCI remained the main components of the United Iraqi Alliance, the Shia political coalition supported by al-Sistani.

Other armed actors

In 2007 violence by non-state actors in Iraq went beyond insurgency and sectarianism, continued to fragment, took more localized forms and was carried out by a growing number of armed actors of different types.

Important armed actors on the MNF-I side included private security companies. At least 180 PSCs, with about 30 000 employees (at least 170 of whom had been killed by early 2007), augmented the number of foreign troops in Iraq by 20 per cent. The range of tasks given to the PSCs is unprecedented and they work in the most dangerous areas, often as stand-ins for MNF-I troops. The status of PSCs, their chains of command, operating guidelines and role in security operations that may result in civilian deaths have not so far been subject to any formal control.[57] There was a major international scandal after 17 Iraqi civilians were killed by employees of the PSC Blackwater USA who were escorting a diplomatic convoy on 16 September 2007.[58]

Armed Iraqi non-state actors other than insurgents and sectarian squads included in 2007 (*a*) tribal groups not associated with insurgency or counter-insurgency; (*b*) ethno-nationalist, primarily Kurdish, groups ranging from the Kurdistan Workers' Party (Partiya Karkeren Kurdistan, PKK) to the Kurdish Peshmerga militias that are only partly integrated into the ISF; and (*c*) violent actors at the local level, ranging from predatory gangs, sometimes reinforced by ethnic or tribal links, to 'neighbourhood security groups'. While this power-brokering is often driven by a natural impulse to create some degree of

---

[56] US National Intelligence Council (note 28), p. 2. The second largest force contributor, the UK, cut its contingent in Al-Basrah by 1600 troops down to 5250—10% of the peak strength in 2003—and announced further major cuts. Walker, S., 'Brown sees more troops home by end 2007', Reuters, 3 Oct. 2007; and Smyth, P., 'UK troop withdrawals', Commentary, Royal United Services Institute, 11 Oct. 2007, <http://www.rusi.org/research/hsr/intro/commentary/ref:C470E091E6C335/>. Denmark withdrew its 460 troops from southern Iraq by Aug. 2007.

[57] Some PSCs are paid directly by the US Government while others work as subcontractors of foreign companies in Iraq. Project for Excellence in Journalism, 'A media mystery: private security in Iraq', 21 June 2007, <http://www.journalism.org/node/6153>.

[58] Blackwater is the largest PSC in Iraq, with about 1000 contractors. Glanz, J. and Tavernise, S., 'Security firm faces criminal charges in Iraq', *New York Times*, 23 Sep. 2007. On other incidents involving PSCs see e.g. 'Iraq arrests foreign contractors', Al Jazeera, 19 Nov. 2007, <http://english.aljazeera.net/NR/exeres/BCD517FD-B1F3-41EB-8CFA-B28ABC40AAFC.htm>.

order and fill the security vacuum, it also promotes the further fragmentation of violence and proliferation of armed actors.

Criminal violence, exacerbated by the release en masse of criminals from Iraqi prisons on the eve of the US-led invasion and the security vacuum that followed it—accounted for 36 per cent of all civilian deaths in Iraq in 2003–2005 and has continued to rise since then.[59] Public opinion surveys show that Iraqis often see criminal violence as the greatest security concern.[60] In addition to violence by urban street gangs, criminal groups engaged in black market activities such as the smuggling of oil, gasoline, arms and other commodities, and kidnapping for ransom continued to be responsible for a large share of local-level violence in Iraq in 2007. It is increasingly difficult to distinguish 'purely' criminal violence from other armed violence in Iraq, as rival sectarian, insurgent and anti-insurgent groups, as well as corrupt officials, often share the profits from these activities with criminal gangs.[61]

Underlying factors and implications

Of the broad range of factors that affect the dynamics of violence, the most critical are (a) the weakness of the state and (b) the influence and policies of external actors. These factors are closely interrelated; for instance, the post-invasion state-building agenda promoted by the US-led coalition emphasized sectarian and ethnic mobilization over national platforms and thus contributed to the structural weakness of the new Iraqi state.

State weakness

Of all three cases reviewed in this chapter, the state in Iraq appears to suffer most from a lack of domestic legitimacy and functionality. The sectarian leanings of the government of Nuri al-Maliki and its lack of interest in national reconciliation were underscored by its reluctance to adopt de-Baathification legislation that could promote Sunni political involvement and to pass legislation that would guarantee fairer distribution of Iraq's oil funds.[62] The large size of the Iraqi security forces, coupled with sectarianism in their ranks and the USA's selective support for militias may have long-term destabilizing effects, with or without the presence of the foreign forces.[63] Growing regional factionalism in the Kurdish north and the Shia-dominated south of the country

---

[59] Approximately 40 000 criminals were released. Burke, J., 'Iraq: an audit of war', *The Observer*, 6 July 2003. On civilian deaths see Iraq Body Count, 'A dossier of civilian casualties in Iraq 2003–2005', 19 July 2005, <http://www.iraqbodycount.org>; and Overseas Security Advisory Council, 'Iraq 2007 crime & safety report', 18 Dec. 2006, <https://www.osac.gov/Reports/>.

[60] See e.g. Perito, R., 'Policing Iraq: protecting Iraqis from criminal violence', USIPeace Brief, United States Institute of Peace, June 2006, <http://www.usip.org/pubs/usipeace_briefings/>.

[61] It has been claimed that as much as 300 000 barrels a day of oil were smuggled from southern Iraq to Iran alone in 2007. 'Oil and corruption in Iraq part II: smuggling thrives in Basra', Environmental News Service, 11 Sep. 2007.

[62] US Government Accountability Office (note 30), pp. 2, 13.

[63] As of Sep. 2007, estimates of the ISF's strength ranged from 359 700 to 445 000. O'Hanlon and Campbell (note 15), p. 34; and Petraeus (note 24), p. 5.

make the prospects for effective power-sharing and national-level reconciliation questionable in the foreseeable future.

Although political processes in Iraq are tending to erode, rather than consolidate, the state, simplistic solutions such as the division of Iraq into ethno-sectarian quasi-states do not seem realistic precisely because of the complex interplay of multiple forms and levels of violence. The same is true for a highly centralized state based on secular Iraqi nationalism, an idea compromised by Baathism. However, it may be premature to write off populist cross-sectarian Iraqi nationalism as a potential unifying force to serve as a basis for at least a minimally functional and legitimate system of governance. Very few politico-militant forces have kept their nationalist credentials untainted, address social and governance issues and can reach across sectarian divisions. Nevertheless, some elements of this approach can, for instance, be traced in the mass-based Sadrist movement.[64] Any lasting solution to state weakness in Iraq would also require full, rather than symbolic, Sunni political participation, but this is unlikely as long as the US-led forces remain in Iraq and the Sunni-dominated insurgency continues.

The role of regional and international actors

While the USA, through its military presence, exercises the main direct external influence on the dynamics of violence in Iraq, there are several other significant external actors, from transnational extremist networks to neighbouring states with interests in Iraq—such as Iran and Syria—and other international actors and organizations.[65] In February the USA said it was ready to hold talks with Iran and Syria on the situation in Iraq, although official US sources still presented both countries as major destabilizing influences in Iraq.[66] Nevertheless, Iran and Syria took part in the Iraqi 'neighbours conference' on security and political matters in Sharm el-Sheikh, Egypt, on 4 May,[67] and their deputy foreign ministers attended a follow-up conference in Baghdad in September.[68] Unlike most of the other external developments in 2007, the neighbours dialogue initiative had at least some positive impact on the

[64] While JAM, especially its radical offshoots, was involved in sectarian clashes in 2007, it officially declared in Apr. that it had ceased terrorist activity. On 26 May al-Sadr delivered a Friday sermon calling for US troops to withdraw and for Shias and Sunnis to unite in confronting the occupying forces and offering reconciliation to the Sunni Arabs 'on all issues'. 'Sadr uses dramatic reappearance to deliver blast of anti-US rhetoric', *The Independent*, 26 May 2007.

[65] The influence of transnational terrorist networks on the overall dynamics of violence in Iraq appears to have been exaggerated. More disturbing is the role of the conflict in Iraq as a symbol and rallying point for transnational violent Islamism.

[66] While Syria was mainly accused of letting foreign militants heading to Iraq cross its territory, Iran was blamed for intensifying its financial, training and arms support for Shia militants since 2006. US National Intelligence Council (note 28), p. 4.

[67] LaFranchi, H., 'Iraq's neighbors weigh next steps after regional conference', *Christian Science Monitor*, 7 May 2007.

[68] Associated Press, 'Iraq tells neighbors violence could spill over borders', *International Herald Tribune*, 9 Sep. 2007.

dynamics of violence in Iraq.[69] The reluctance of other Arab and Muslim governments to offer major support to Iraq might be due to suspicion of al-Maliki's alleged Iranian sympathies and reflect his government's lack of legitimacy in the Arab world.[70]

Turkey, a major regional actor, was threatened by violence originating in Iraq. In October PKK militants stepped up their incursions from Iraq's semi-independent Kurdish north into Turkish territory. On 17 October the Turkish Parliament voted to allow the government to launch military operations against the PKK in Iraq.[71] On 1 December the Turkish Army fired on PKK forces based inside Iraqi territory.[72] Further Turkish artillery and air attacks followed from 16 December.

One of the broader international developments was the launch of the International Compact with Iraq on 3 May in Sharm-el-Sheikh. This joint UN–Iraqi plan, backed by the World Bank, was initiated in 2006 in response to requests from the USA and the Iraqi Government. It established a five-year road map for economic reform, reconciliation and peacebuilding and pledged debt reduction of around $30 billion.[73] A related development was the adoption of UN Security Council Resolution 1770 on 10 August. Resolution 1770 extended the mandate of the UN Assistance Mission to Iraq (UNAMI) for another year.[74] For the first time since 2003 the Security Council did not simultaneously extend the MNF-I's mandate.[75] While Resolution 1770 also expanded the UN's role to include strengthening of the neighbours dialogue process, donor coordination and implementation of the International Compact, this had no tangible effect on developments in Iraq during 2007. A qualitative upgrade of the UN's role will be needed to assist state building and the future national unity government in Iraq. It will depend on many interrelated factors, including the levels of violence and the pace of a gradual and planned—but imminent—reduction of the USA's military role.[76] To maintain its credibility in Iraq, the UN will need to further distance itself from the US military presence.

[69] E.g. after Nov. 2007 even US sources acknowledged that Iran had stemmed the flow of weapons to Iraq. Reid, R. H., 'US general: Iran sticking by pledge to stem flows of weapons, explosives to Iraq', Associated Press, 14 Nov. 2007.

[70] US National Intelligence Council (note 28), p. 3. In Apr. 2007 Saudi King Abdullah declared that the US military presence in Iraq was an 'illegal foreign occupation'. MacLeod, S., 'Will Iraq's neighbors help?', Time, 3 May 2007.

[71] These issues dominated the third Iraq neighbours conference held in Istanbul in Nov. 2007. 'Other regional crises steal spotlight at Iraq neighbors conference', Daily Star (Beirut), 5 Nov. 2007.

[72] 'Turkey attacks PKK fighters in Iraq', Al Jazeera, 1 Dec. 2007, <http://english.aljazeera.net/NR/exeres/79EAF5B4-B2C6-47E4-903B-FBE65BD439B4.htm>.

[73] On the International Compact with Iraq see <http://www.iraqcompact.org>; and 'Conference adopts Iraq plan', Al Jazeera, 3 May 2007, <http://english.aljazeera.net/NR/exeres/C841C9B9-BB77-44 67-B8CE-28AE2935F8D5.htm>.

[74] UN Security Council Resolution 1770, 10 Aug. 2007.

[75] The Security Council's agreement to the continuation of the MNF-I's mandate was announced in a press statement. UN Security Council, 'Security Council press statement on Iraq', SC/9042, 13 June 2007, <http://www.un.org/News/Press/docs/2007/sc9042.doc.htm>.

[76] On 26 Nov. Iraq and the USA signed a 'declaration of principles' for further bilateral negotiations on the long-term US military presence. 'Iraq deal eyes long US presence', Al Jazeera, 27 Nov. 2007, <http://english.aljazeera.net/NR/exeres/817CBD8C-DBCF-40E5-857C-C50E8B0F41E0.htm>.

IV. Darfur, Sudan

The context

Violence in Sudan's most conflict-affected region, Darfur, did not cease after the signing of the Darfur Peace Agreement (DPA) in May 2006 between the Sudanese Government and a faction of the Sudan Liberation Movement/Army (SLM/A) led by Minni Minawi (SLA/MM).[77] In 2007 the main patterns of violence continued a shift from state-based armed confrontation to a complex mix of less intensive but numerous mini-conflicts, with shifting allegiances and unabated violence against civilians.

The armed conflict between the government and the SLM/A in Darfur dates back to 2003. Rebels in Darfur were encouraged by the success of the Sudan People's Liberation Movement/Army (SPLM/A) insurgency in the south of the country.[78] At the same time, the Government of Sudan was able to redeploy forces from the south due to progress in peace negotiations with the SPLM. Unwilling to be forced to make concessions to yet another insurgency and fearing international involvement, the government launched a harsh counter-insurgency campaign in Darfur, also involving some local Arab nomadic groups.

Darfur is one of the least developed parts of Sudan. The region's north is badly affected by the desertification of the Sahel, while the populations of ecologically more stable areas such as Jebel Marra are expanding rapidly.[79] Most of the Arab tribes in the region are either cattle nomads, such as the Rezeigat, or camel nomads, such as the Mahariya. Some non-Arabs, such as the Zaghawa, are also camel nomads, but most non-Arab tribes, including the Fur and Massalit, are settled farmers. Livelihood patterns and social factors have traditionally been the most important factors in the tribal identities of the almost entirely Muslim population than Arab or non-Arab ethnicity.

A systematic drive by the nomads—who traditionally have better military organization—to seize land from settled tribes, especially in Jebel Marra, started with the droughts and famine of the mid-1980s. Inter-tribal tensions over land and water were exacerbated by a policy implemented by the second Sadiq al-Mahdi government (1986–89) of arming Arab nomads from Darfur against the SPLA and mobilizing members of the Zaghawa tribe to support their kin in the civil war in Chad.[80] In response, the Chadian Government armed the Fur in Darfur. In 1987, 27 Arab tribes formed an alliance—the

---

[77] The Darfur Peace Agreement was signed by the Government of Sudan and the SLA/MM on 5 May 2006. Its text is available at <http://www.unmis.org/english/dpa.htm>. The SLA/MM split from the SLA in Nov. 2005.

[78] The SPLM/A managed to gain major concessions from the Sudanese Government under the 2005 Comprehensive Peace Agreement (CPA) after a protracted peace process. The text of the CPA is available at <http://www.unmis.org/english/cpa.htm>.

[79] The Sahel is a strip of arid savannah running south of the Sahara desert, stretching from Eritrea and Sudan in the east to Senegal in the west.

[80] The al-Mahdi clan is part of the Arab elite that is now in opposition to the government of President Omar Hassan Ahmad al-Bashir, who came to power in 1989.

Janjaweed (or 'hordes')—against the Fur, who formed militias to defend themselves. From the mid-1990s, the Janjaweed were increasingly supported by the Sudanese Government to fight against the Fur and other non-Arabs, while the Fur started to be supported by the SPLM/A and established ties with the Zaghawa against the Arabs. The Fur–Zaghawa alliance formed the backbone of the 2003 insurgency by the Darfur Liberation Movement (renamed SLM/A in March 2003)—which included Fur, Massalit and Zaghawa—and of the Zaghawa-dominated Justice and Equality Movement (JEM)—which was supported by the Popular National Congress Party of Hassan al-Turabi.[81]

While the conflict in Darfur had local roots, it was exacerbated by political struggles at the national level and by Chad and Sudan's policies of supporting the other's rebels. The broader dimensions of the conflict include sharp disparities in socio-economic development between the Sudanese capital, Khartoum, and the peripheral areas and the failure of the north Sudanese Arab elites to build a more representative system of governance in a socially and culturally diverse country.[82]

The fragmentation of violence

In 2007 small-scale conflicts in and around Darfur continued to multiply and featured several interconnected forms of violence. A lull in the fighting between the government and the main rebel factions—JEM, the SLA faction led by Abdel Wahid al-Nur (SLA/AW) and another SLA splinter group, G19[83]—in early 2007 was short-lived. However, even though aerial bombardment of rebel positions and clashes between the military and the insurgents continued in some areas throughout the year, state-based fighting declined considerably.[84] This did not, however, lead to a marked improvement in security conditions, which continued to deteriorate—especially for the civilian population—mainly due to a marked increase in non-state violence. The main clashes were no longer those between the rebels and the Janjaweed but those between the splintering rebel groups. The integration of the SLA/MM into the political process was slow and weakened the group's local support. Furthermore, a pattern of generalized violence became embedded in Darfur, with armed groups shifting alliances depending on the circumstances and engaging in predatory violence, local power play and cross-border incursions.[85]

---

[81] Al-Turabi was removed from power in 2001 by more moderate Islamists led by the current president, Omar Hassan Ahmad al-Bashir, and Vice-president Ali Osman Mohamed Taha.

[82] The 'Black Book', a pamphlet authored by rebel leaders Khalil Ibrahim of JEM, complains about regional disparities in Sudan and the predominance of Arabs in positions of power and wealth. Ibrahim, K., [The Black Book: imbalance of power and wealth in Sudan], 2000, <http://www.sakanab.wtcsites.com/black_book.htm> (in Arabic).

[83] The G19 is named for 19 commanders originally aligned with Wahid Nur who walked out of peace negotiations in Abuja in 2006.

[84] For this reason the conflict in Darfur was removed from the table of major armed conflicts for 2007. See appendix 2A.

[85] Natsios, A. S., US President's Special Envoy to Sudan, Statement before the US Senate Committee on Foreign Relations, 11 Apr. 2007, <http://www.senate.gov/~foreign/hearings/2007/hrg070411a.html>,

Both defecting groups, like the SLA/MM, and rebel factions continued to fragment. With its leader in exile in Paris since 2006, the SLA/AW had less military clout on the ground but still enjoyed popular support, particularly among the IDPs. However, the SLA/AW, which first splintered in 2006 into G19 and several other factions, continued to divide in 2007. The National Redemption Front, an alliance formed by G19, JEM and several other groups in Eritrea in June 2006 failed to form an executive body and was on the verge of disintegration by mid-2007.[86] JEM was also torn by internal rivalries (e.g. between JEM leader Khalil Ibrahim and Idris Azraq) and split into several factions. Thus, in 2007 the rebels were more divided than ever and their key leaders were absent from the talks brokered by the UN and the African Union (AU) at Sirte, Libya, in October.[87] More representative talks among rebel factions were held in Juba, southern Sudan, in November. However, there were indications that at least half a year may be required for the rebels to agree even on the basic terms of a ceasefire, the first item on the agenda.[88]

In 2007 more rebel factions from Darfur were based in—and received support from—Chad (and, to a lesser extent, from Eritrea).[89] An agreement between Chad and Sudan to improve security along the border, brokered by Libya in February 2007, did not significantly reduce the support that both countries provided to each other's rebels.[90] While bases in neighbouring states allowed rebels to regroup, long stays abroad made them increasingly detached from the developments in Darfur and deprived them of local support.

The fragmentation of rebel groups was accompanied by their growing involvement in criminal activities, ranging from cattle looting and banditry to assaults on international peacekeepers and aid workers, usually to hijack vehicles and supplies.[91] While attacks against peacekeepers and humanitarian workers, primarily by the rebels,[92] represented only a tiny proportion of the violence in Darfur, they markedly increased in 2007, when AU peacekeepers suffered the deadliest attacks since 2004.[93]

p. 1; and Human Rights Watch, 'Darfur 2007: chaos by design', Sep. 2007, <http://hrw.org/reports/2007/sudan0907/sudan0907web.pdf>, p. 5.

[86] 'Founding declaration of Darfur's National Redemption Front', *Sudan Tribune*, 20 June 2006.

[87] Associated Press, 'Mediators brace to reboot Darfur peace talks after rebel no-show', *International Herald Tribune*, 28 Oct. 2007.

[88] McDoom, O., 'Darfur rebels may unite but talks still tough', Reuters, 12 Nov. 2007.

[89] On military support to armed non-state actors in Darfur by Chad and Eritrea see chapter 7 in this volume, section V.

[90] Since 2006, rebels from Chad, such as the Union of Forces for Democracy and Development, and the Central African Republic have been based in and have operated from Darfur.

[91] In the first half of 2007, 70 UN and NGO humanitarian vehicles were hijacked or stolen. UN Office for Coordination of Humanitarian Assistance (OCHA), 'Humanitarian news from Sudan: monthly digest—Jun 2007', Reliefweb, 7 Aug. 2007, <http://wwww.reliefweb.int/rw/rwb.nsf/db900sid/SHES-75UR5H?OpenDocument>.

[92] The signatory faction SLA/MM also engaged in fighting with AU peacekeepers. The government applied more indirect pressure on international humanitarian personnel, especially through delays in issuing visas and travel permits.

[93] The deadliest attack was carried out on 30–31 Sep. allegedly by SLA/Unity (G19) rebels who for the first time overran an AU peacekeeping outpost, killing 10 Nigerian and Sengalese peacekeepers and seizing military vehicles, arms, ammunition and fuel. According to the chief of the AU mission in

There were more defections by rebel factions, such as a Massalit-dominated group led by the former governor of West Darfur, Ibrahim Yahia, which joined the DPA in June.[94] Clashes between splintering factions overlapped with inter- and intra-tribal violence, including violence between Arab groups.[95] Some Arab groups started fighting against the government.[96] An Arab rebel group led by members of the Rezeigat tribe—the Popular Forces Army—established contact with G19 in Chad. Some of the Janjaweed fighters also joined forces with the rebels against the government or against other Arab tribes.

Nevertheless, most of the semi-autonomous, government-affiliated Janjaweed militias continued to attack tribes from which the rebels draw their support, especially the Fur and Zaghawa.[97] Like the rebels, the Janjaweed are very mobile and have been actively engaged in cross-border raids.[98] Attempts to dismiss the Janjaweed as either plain criminals or government-controlled militia driven by a combination of greed and Arab supremacism are both inadequate. The Janjaweed are mainly from north Darfurian camel nomad tribes, without traditional land rights, who have been the most heavily affected by environmental problems. These tribes have for decades been armed and subcontracted by the Sudanese Government to guard the border with Chad. The origin of these tribal militias helps to explain why only relatively few Arab tribes in Darfur joined the Janjaweed. The rest—cattle herders and farmers with traditional land rights, primarily in South Darfur—tried to remain on the sidelines of the conflict.[99] No more than 20 000 Arabs are thought to have joined the government's counter-insurgency campaign since 2003.[100]

Darfur, Rodolphe Adada, the incident 'has no political rationality', while SLM/A leaders blamed it on 'rogue elements'. Associated Press, 'African peacekeepers surprised by rebel attack that came as they sat to break Ramadan fast', *International Herald Tribune*, 1 Oct. 2007. The second deadliest was the killing of 5 Sengalese peacekeepers by unidentified gunmen on 2 Apr., for which the theft of a truck was the likely motive. Polgree, L., 'Rebel attack on African Union force in Darfur is deadliest', *International Herald Tribune*, 3 Apr. 2007. See also Shahine, A., 'African Union says Darfur militias acting with impunity', Reuters, 25 Apr. 2007, <http://www.alertnet.org/thenews/newsdesk/L25725561.htm>.

[94] 'Darfur rebel faction signs peace agreement with Khartoum', *Sudan Tribune*, 8 June 2007. The impact of such defections on the events on the ground in Darfur has been minimal.

[95] Examples include the clashes between the formerly allied tribes the Mahria and the Terjem, the Habanniya and the Salamat, the Habanniya and the Rizeigat, and the Hotya and the Rizeigat.

[96] Since the signing of the DPA, it is estimated that up to 4000 Arab fighters may have joined rebel forces in Jebel Marra by May 2007. Crilly, R., 'In Darfur, some Arabs now fight alongside rebels', *Christian Science Monitor*, 22 May 2007.

[97] In May the International Criminal Court issued an arrest warrant for Janjaweed commander Ali Kushayb, an alias of Ali Muhammad Ali Abd-al-Rahman, who was already in custody in Sudan on other charges. International Criminal Court, 'Warrants of arrest for the Minister of State for Humanitarian Affairs of Sudan, and a leader of the militia/Janjaweed', Press release, 2 May 2007, <http://www.icc-cpi.int/press/pressreleases/241.html>; and Human Rights Watch, 'Sudan: hand over war crimes suspects to ICC', 2 May 2007, <http://hrw.org/english/docs/2007/05/02/sudan15822.htm>.

[98] Associated Press, 'Janjaweed fighters kill 400 on Chad border with Sudan', *International Herald Tribune*, 10 Apr. 2007.

[99] Arabs comprise up to one-third of Darfur's population of 7 million and have long provided the local support base for al-Mahdi's Umma Party, which is in opposition to the present government.

[100] Flint, J., 'The Arab lion bares its head in Darfur's ongoing war', *Daily Star* (Beirut), 22 Dec. 2006; and Polgreen, L., 'Militia talks could reshape Darfur violence', *International Herald Tribune*, 15 Apr. 2007.

While the Sudanese Government continued to arm the Janjaweed and appeared to exercise more control over them at the outset of the Darfur conflict, it did not fully control them even at the peak of the counter-insurgency campaign in 2003–2004.[101] It was much less able—and probably less willing—to do so after the DPA. While the Janjaweed's origin and structure mean that their full disarmament is impossible, the government had not made any seriously attempt to disarm them, as required by the DPA, by the end of 2007.[102] Anger at the failure to provide them with promised land, privileges or funds was one reason why some Janjaweed turned their arms against the government in 2007. The accommodation between the rebels and some Janjaweed militias underscores the eroding distinction between non-state and state-aligned actors, who may often switch alliances.

Fragmenting violence in and around Darfur had high human costs and dramatic humanitarian consequences in 2007. Despite a decrease in civilian casualties in January–April 2007, overall one-sided violence against civilians continued unabated.[103] The main change in casualty patterns was that tribal and factional violence started killing more people than battles between government and the rebels.[104] Fatality figures in the Darfur conflict are often exaggerated.[105] The most accurate estimates, according to an expert panel convened by the GAO and the US National Academy of Sciences in April 2006, have been made by the Center for Research on the Epidemiology of Disasters (CRED).[106] According to CRED, by mid-2007 the total death toll for Darfur from direct violence and conflict-related disease and malnutrition was around 200 000.[107]

While fewer people were dying in Darfur from hunger and disease in 2006–2007 than at the peak of the fighting in 2003–2004, over 2 million remained displaced, making Darfur the site of the largest humanitarian operation in the world. In 2007, up to 2.5 million IDPs and refugees were living in camps in Darfur and eastern Chad. Some 250 000 were newly displaced in January–September 2007, mainly as a result of factional and tribal clashes.[108] The population of IDP camps continued to grow, and nearly all camps around

---

[101] On the arming of the Janjaweed see chapter 7 in this volume.

[102] The AU commander in Nyala, southern Darfur, Col. James Oladipo, quoted in Gettleman, J., 'Chaos in Darfur on rise as Arabs fight with Arabs', *International Herald Tribune*, 2 Sep. 2007.

[103] Natsios (note 85), p. 2.

[104] Gettleman (note 102).

[105] An estimate of 'close to 400 000' deaths in Darfur between Feb. 2003 and Apr. 2005, first made by the Coalition for International Justice and 2 US experts and cited by several advocacy groups in 2007, was criticized as being inflated. See British Advertising Standards Authority, Adjudication on complaint by the European Sudanese Public Affairs Council against Save Darfur Coalition t/a Globe for Darfur and the Aegis Trust, 8 Aug 2007, <http://www.asa.org.uk/asa/adjudications/Public/TF_ADJ_42993.htm>.

[106] US Government Accountability Office (GAO), *Darfur Crisis: Death Estimates Demonstrate Severity of Crisis, but Their Accuracy and Credibility Could be Enhanced*, GAO-07-24 (GAO: Washington, DC, Nov. 2006), p. 3.

[107] Guha-Sapir, D. and Degomme, O., *Darfur: Counting the Deaths—Mortality Estimates from Multiple Survey Data* (Center for Research on the Epidemiology of Disasters: Brussels, 26 May 2005), p. 6; and Dealey, S., 'An atrocity that needs no exaggeration', *International Herald Tribune*, 12 Aug. 2007.

[108] 'Funding shortfall may force UNHCR to scale down operations in Darfur', *UNHCR News*, 25 Sep. 2007, <http://www.unhcr.org/news/NEWS/46f9313b2.html>.

El-Fasher, the capital of northern Darfur, and Nyala, the capital of southern Darfur were at full capacity by mid-2007. Tensions in the camps mounted during the year, with armed elements among the IDPs assaulting humanitarian workers and damaging facilities.[109] Despite an agreement reached between the UN and the government in March 2007 to improve humanitarian access, the proliferation of armed actors in Darfur threatened the security of humanitarian personnel and made it more difficult to negotiate the safe passage of workers and supplies.[110]

Underlying factors and implications

The most common explanations offered for the further fragmentation of violence and diversification of armed actors in Darfur are that it is 'chaos by design'—that is, an intended outcome of government policies—and that it is due to the destabilizing activities of Chad and other neighbouring states. The dynamic interaction of 'force and talks' typical of many complex peace processes—when armed actors try to make gains on the ground when the peace process is already under way in order to strengthen their negotiating position so that they can demand larger concessions—may be an additional explanation, in view of the hasty and unrepresentative DPA. Militias may have intensified their violent power play in an attempt to improve their positions before deployment of the AU/UN Hybrid Operation in Darfur (UNAMID), which eventually took place in December 2007.[111]

While continuing violence in Darfur is not a product of the Sudanese Government's counter-insurgency strategy alone, government policy is central to addressing the problem. The government is unlikely to revise its position significantly as long as it thinks it is threatened by what it sees as open or creeping separatism in many peripheral regions that is backed by international involvement. From the government's perspective, the costs of chaos in Darfur are smaller than the costs of an internationally imposed solution. While Sudan may be considered a fragile state in terms of the chronic inability of its elites—both those in power and those in opposition—to build a more representative power-sharing system and to develop its marginalized peripheral regions, the government is not in danger of collapse but is firmly in power. It may resist external pressure and be unwilling to accept international standards in the area of human rights, but it actively engages in economic cooperation with Arab, Asian and other partners and maintains security contacts on anti-terrorism with the USA. With real gross domestic product (GDP) growing by 12.8 per cent and revenues growing by 11 per cent up to 17.5 billion Sudanese pounds ($8.7 billion in 2007), mainly due to oil exports, the government can mobilize enough resources to rule most of the country effectively.[112] Unable to

---

[109] See UN Office for Coordination of Humanitarian Assistance (note 91).

[110] Natsios (note 85), p. 3.

[111] On the long planning process for UNAMID see chapter 3 in this volume.

[112] GDP growth is expected to slow in 2008–2009 but will still remain high at 8.9% in 2008 and 7.2% in 2009. Economist Intelligence Unit (EIU), *Country Report: Sudan* (EIU: London, Jan. 2008), pp. 4, 14.

defeat the rebels militarily, the government actively combined divide-and-rule and stick-and-carrot approaches in Darfur and successfully manipulated the DPA to weaken the then most powerful faction, the SLA/MM. An internal regime change in Khartoum would only lead to the replacement of one group of traditional elites with another, without solving most of the country's underlying problems.

Another important issue is how the current dynamic of fragmenting violence in Darfur can be addressed if neither the unification of the rebels nor the disarmament of the Janjaweed is likely to occur in the near future. UNAMID can be expected to establish at least basic security in Darfur's urban centres and IDP camps and, in concert with the European Union deployments in Chad and the Central African Republic, to limit chaos along Sudan's western borders.[113] In Darfur, greater emphasis should be placed on inter-tribal peacebuilding initiatives that are largely overlooked by the international community. The SPLM/A will remain a credible mediator on Darfur, even as this role is complicated by the crisis in relations between Sudan's north and south that occurred in late 2007.[114] Limited external pressure could be put on the government by China, Sudan's main economic investor and trading partner, and, to some extent, by the USA, through its role as the largest humanitarian donor and anti-terrorism ties.

Much as the fragmentation of violence and the diversification of armed actors complicate the situation in Darfur, the relative ease with which former foes have become allies across tribal and ethnic divisions demonstrates that these divisions are surmountable. Many Arab tribes have the same grievances about the region's marginalization as the rest of the population of Darfur. While this may not be enough to reinforce the ambitious political demands of the rebel factions, it can facilitate indigenous inter-communal peacebuilding initiatives at the local level.

The underlying factors behind the Darfur conflict—deep political and socio-economic imbalances and the long-term effects of environmental degradation—are structural problems, and thus require a structural developmental solution as much as a political one. Key international actors should encourage the continuing gradual transformation of Sudan's rentier state economy and the enhancement of its development strategies in the peripheral regions. As such, the irreversible effects of Darfur's 'traumatic' conflict-accelerated modernization, such as rapid urbanization and the breakdown of traditional ways of life, often viewed only as problems, could also be mobilized as resources for development.

---

[113] See chapter 3 in this volume.

[114] Dissatisfaction with the CPA implementation led the SPLM to suspend its participation in the government in Oct. Agence France-Presse, 'SPLM withdraw from Sudan national unity government', *Sudan Tribune*, 11 Oct. 2007.

V. Pakistan

In contrast to Iraq and Darfur, in 2007 Pakistan experienced neither a major armed conflict nor the fragmentation of a structured armed confrontation that qualified as major prior to 2007. Nevertheless, the proliferation and integration of various forms of violence—some of which have significant cross-border and transnational implications—could also be observed in Pakistan in 2007. While much of the violence in the major armed conflict in neighbouring Afghanistan was linked to instability in Pakistan's border areas, it would be wrong to view the complex web of tribal, Islamist, inter- and intra-sectarian and other armed violence in Pakistan only in the context of the situation in Afghanistan.[115] The political and religious violence in Pakistan has its own sources and dynamics.

'Talibanization' and cross-border violence

While the Taliban originated in Deobandi madrasas in areas of Pakistan along the border with Afghanistan,[116] in the 1990s the movement mainly spread in Afghanistan, where it became the de facto government in 1996. Following the US-led intervention in 2001 and the disintegration of the Taliban regime, many Taliban fighters found refuge in the Pashtun-populated border areas of Pakistan. However, the Taliban's recent revival in Pakistan has gone beyond the regrouping of the remnants of the Afghan Taliban. In 2007 a new generation of Pashtun Islamists, often referred to as 'neo-Taliban', were active in Pakistan's Federally Administered Tribal Areas (FATA), where they controlled North and South Waziristan, and were expanding their influence into North-West Frontier Province (NWFP).[117] 'Talibanization'—the spread of Taliban presence and influence—was as much a domestic problem for Pakistan in 2007 as the Taliban insurgency was for Afghanistan.

The neo-Taliban movement is rooted in radical Islamism merged with Pashtun tribalism. This combination filled a vacuum created by the erosion of traditional tribal structures and has stimulated their further transformation. From

[115] Rubin, B. R., 'Saving Afghanistan', *Foreign Affairs*, vol. 86, no. 1 (Jan./Feb. 2007), pp. 57–79; and Jones, S., 'Pakistan's dangerous game', *Survival*, vol. 49, no. 1 (spring 2007), pp. 15–32. The Uppsala Conflict Data Program records 2 ongoing minor armed conflicts in Pakistan in 2007: (*a*) between the government and the Baluchistan Liberation Army and Baluch Ittehad (Baluch Unity); and (*b*) between the government and Tehreek-e-Nafaz-e-Shari'at-e-Mohammad (Movement for the Enforcement of Islamic Laws, a neo-Taliban organization in Swat, North-West Frontier Province), with unclear involvement of other groups.

[116] Deobandi is a conservative strand of Islam in Afghanistan, India and Pakistan that advocates strict adherence to the teachings of the Prophet Muhammad and rejects the possibility of reinterpretation of Islamic texts to accommodate changing times or other religious traditions. The Afghanistan–Pakistan border, established by the 1893 Durand Line Treaty, is not recognized by Pashtun tribes. Afghan governments, including the Taliban regime, have refused to renew the treaty since it expired in 1993.

[117] Talibanization mostly affected the southern areas of NWFP in 2007 but was increasing in the north, particularly in Charssada, Dir, Kohat, Mardan, Swat and the provincial capital, Peshawar. Siddique, A., 'The pace of talibanization appears to accelerate in Pakistani tribal areas', EurasiaNet, 26 Mar. 2007, <http://www.eurasianet.org/departments/insight/articles/eav042607.shtml>.

the end of the 1980s, a social system based on power-sharing between tribal leaders (*maliks*), landowning and merchant clans, and religious leaders started to give way to one dominated by Deobandi clerics supported by semi-tribal militias who were mostly trained in local madrasas.[118] While the neo-Taliban militias support the original Taliban of Mullah Mohammad Omar, they were in 2007 not a consolidated force and did not necessarily coordinate their actions.[119] The most influential neo-Taliban figure in 2007 was Sirajuddin Haqqani, leader of one of the strongest militias and based in Miram Shah.[120] As both a tribal leader and a senior Deobandi cleric, Haqqani was able to build alliances using both tribal and religious links. He supported military operations with funds raised from cross-border opium, arms and timber smuggling, semi-legitimate businesses, and the diversion of religious donations. Despite similarities and links between the Taliban-style groups in Afghanistan and Pakistan—and the futility of distinctions between 'Afghan' and 'Pakistani' in the Pashtun 'tribal belt'—the movements have distinct local roots.

The main cause of the erosion of traditional tribal structures and the rise of Islamist tribalism in the region has been the Pakistani Government's long-standing policy of sponsoring Islamist–tribal militancy—and its lack of control over the militias involved. Decades of conflict in Afghanistan have also contributed, for example, through refugee flows and increasing cross-border smuggling.[121] Pakistan's long-term strategic interest in maintaining a Pashtun 'buffer zone' between the two countries and in supporting Pashtuns in Afghanistan is partly driven by the need to mitigate problems with Pashtun nationalism among Pakistan's sizeable Pashtun population both in and outside the tribal belt, including in large cities such as Karachi. This was reinforced by concerns that the Taliban regime's defeat in 2001 would allow growing Indian influence in Afghanistan. These long-term interests conflict with the government's official goal of integrating the tribal areas into Pakistan's political and economic system.[122]

The resulting inconsistency in Pakistani policy in the border areas has been exacerbated since 2001 by a third factor. There may be between 85 000 and

[118] Rubin, B. R. and Siddique, A., 'Resolving the Pakistan–Afghanistan stalemate', US Institute of Peace Special Report no. 176, Oct. 2006, <http://www.usip.org/pubs/specialreports/sr176.html>; and 'Pakistan's military drift: Taliban all over', *The Economist*, 12 Apr. 2007.

[119] There may be 15–20 such militias operating in South Waziristan and 10–12 in North Waziristan.

[120] Sirajuddin Haqqani builds on the influence of his father, Jalaluddin Haqqani, who carried out anti-Soviet guerrilla operations in Afghanistan in the 1980s. Shahzad, S. S., 'Revolution in the mountains, part 3: through the eyes of the Taliban', *Asia Times*, 5 May 2004. Mullah Omar is highly respected by militias on both sides of the border, but the overall influence of the Taliban's older generation of commanders based in Quetta, Pakistan, is diminishing.

[121] Afghanistan has been racked by internal armed conflict since a communist revolution in 1978. In the wars of resistance against Soviet occupation and then the Soviet-backed regime of President Mohammad Najibullah, which was ousted in 1992, Pakistan supported, and provided a base for, Mujahideen insurgents. The Pakistani Government backed the Taliban until the 2001 US-led intervention.

[122] Currently, the FATA are under direct presidential authority, administered through a political agent in each tribal agency. The tribal agencies are represented in the national assembly. Basic services (health and education) are operated from the NWFP. 'FATA at a glance: administrative system', <http://www.fata.gov.pk/index.php?link=3>. The tribal areas have the worst socio-economic indicators in Pakistan and lack police and formal justice or tax-collection systems.

101 000 Pakistani troops deployed along the Afghan border, with much of their equipment and training provided by the USA.[123] Under US pressure, the Pakistani Government undertakes military operations against the neo-Taliban, while also trying to persuade some of the militias to come over to its side and promising broader reforms. However, the Pakistani Army is increasingly reluctant to fight in the FATA—where it suffers heavy casualties—in pursuit of what is widely dismissed in Pakistan as a US-imposed anti-terrorism agenda.[124] Another highly controversial issue is the covert support given to the neo-Taliban in Pakistan and to the insurgency in Afghanistan by parts of the Pakistani military and security forces.[125]

Militant activity other than clashes between government forces and the neo-Taliban groups also continued in the tribal areas in 2007. There was sectarian violence between Shias and Sunnis, especially in the Kurram tribal agency, the large Shia population of which is seen by the neo-Taliban as supportive of the Northern Alliance in Afghanistan.[126] In March and April, violent clashes in Wana, South Waziristan, between local Pashtun groups and the FATA-based militants of the Islamic Movement of Uzbekistan killed at least 250 people.[127] Also in April, approximately 100 people were killed in sectarian fighting around Kurram.[128]

A ceasefire between the Pakistani Government and pro-Taliban militants—part of the agreement signed with tribal and neo-Taliban leaders in Miram Shah, North Waziristan, on 5 September 2006—held until the middle of 2007.[129] Under the agreement, the government was also to withdraw its military checkpoints and troops, release militants captured since 2001, return their weapons and vehicles, pay compensation to tribe members for their losses, and allow them to carry small arms in exchange for a pledge to stop incursions into Afghanistan and attacks against the Pakistani military.[130] However, on 22 May Pakistani special forces attacked a compound in the village of Zargarkhel in North Waziristan, claiming that it was a training facility for for-

[123] Boucher, R. A., Statement before the US House of Representatives Committee on Oversight and Government Reform, Subcommittee on National Security and Foreign Affairs, 12 July 2007, <http://nationalsecurity.oversight.house.gov/story.asp?ID=1389>, p. 5; and Burke, J., 'The new Taliban', *The Observer*, 14 Oct. 2007.

[124] Abbas, H., 'Pakistan's grip on tribal areas is slipping', *Asia Times*, 4 Oct. 2007.

[125] See Jones (note 115); and United Nations Assistance Mission to Afghanistan (UNAMA), 'Suicide attacks in Afghanistan (2001–2007)', 1 Sep. 2007, pp. 85–89.

[126] The United Islamic Front for the Salvation of Afghanistan (Northern Alliance) was the main armed opposition to the Taliban regime. It is composed mainly of ethnic Tajiks and Uzbeks.

[127] Siddique (note 117); 'Pakistan's military drift: Taliban all over' (note 118); and 'Timeline: Pakistan', BBC News, 26 Mar. 2008 <http://news.bbc.co.uk/2/1156716.stm>.

[128] Abbas (note 124); and Hoodbhoy, P., 'Pakistan: the threat from within', University of Bradford, Pakistan Security Research Unit (PSRU) Brief no. 13, 23 May 2007, <http://spaces.brad.ac.uk:8080/display/ssispsru/Publications/>, p. 4.

[129] Khan, I. and Gall, C., 'Pakistan lets tribal chiefs keep control along border', *New York Times*, 6 Sep. 2007.

[130] The agreement followed the declaration of the establishment of the 'Islamic Emirate of Waziristan' on 14 Feb. 2006. Zissis, C. and Bajoria, J., 'Pakistan's tribal areas', Council on Foreign Relations Backgrounder, 26 Oct. 2007, <http://www.cfr.org/publication/11973>; and Hoodbhoy (note 128), p. 13. The Miram Shah agreement was just one in a series of controversial pacts between the Pakistani Government and pro-Taliban militias and tribal leaders in the FATA.

eign militants. A 'peace committee' of tribal leaders claimed that the raid violated the Miram Shah agreement. The neo-Taliban declared an end to the ceasefire on 15 July, after which incursions into Afghanistan surged and attacks on government forces and terrorist acts against civilians became daily occurrences. On 9–11 October the fiercest fighting in the area for several years, involving air strikes and artillery fire as the army confronted local and, reportedly, foreign militants in the Mir Ali area of North Waziristan, left over 200 people dead.[131]

Militants based in Pakistan's tribal areas also played a major role in the violence in Afghanistan. In addition to launching cross-border incursions, much of the training for suicide attacks in south-eastern Afghanistan took place in Pakistani madrasas, according to the UN.[132] In an attempt to counter this problem, the Afghan Government hosted about 650 tribal leaders from both sides of the border for a tribal summit, the 'peace *jirga*', in Kabul on 9–12 August. However, the participants were chiefly government-affiliated leaders, while major militant and radical political actors, including the Taliban and the Hezbe-Islami group led by Gulbiddin Hekmatyar, were either not invited or boycotted the gathering.[133] The *jirga* produced little practical result apart from President Pervez Musharraf's first public acknowledgement that the Taliban in Afghanistan received support from groups in Pakistan.[134]

In 2007 cross-border violence also involved the Afghan and Pakistani armed forces and often resulted indirectly from international pressure to step up anti-terrorist activity. For instance, Pakistan's decision, under pressure from the USA, to erect a 35-kilometre fence along a section of its border with Afghanistan provoked clashes between the two countries' armies in Afghanistan's Paktia province in May 2007.[135]

Islamist violence beyond the tribal areas

Prior to 2007 the impact of Islamist militancy on Pakistan's own politics and security was often dismissed as marginal by government officials and analysts. The problem in the tribal areas, however, is paralleled by Islamist radicalization, violence and sectarianism across Pakistan, including in large cities such as Islamabad and Karachi.

---

[131] Khan, I. and Gall, C., 'Tribesmen urge Pakistan to halt air raids', *New York Times*, 11 Oct. 2007; Burke (note 123); and 'Timeline: Pakistan' (note 127).

[132] Equipment and explosives for suicide operations are mainly prepared in Pakistan's border areas, where the targets are also selected and funds raised. United Nations Assistance Mission to Afghanistan (note 125), pp. 86, 89.

[133] The *jirga* was boycotted by tribal leaders from North and South Waziristan and representatives of the Jamiat ulema-e-Islam—a prominent party in the hard-line Islamist coalition Muttahida Majlis-e-Amal (United Action Front) that rules in NWFP and is in opposition to the government.

[134] Swisspeace, 'Pakistan: trends in conflict and cooperation', FAST Update, July–Aug. 2007, p. 1.

[135] Thirteen Afghan civilians were killed in the fighting on 13 May. Grare, F., 'Choosing sides: Afghan–Pakistani cross-border tensions rise', *Jane's Intelligence Review*, vol. 19, no. 7 (July 2007), pp. 28–29.

In mid-2007 Pakistan became a focus of international attention due to events at the Lal Masjid (Red Mosque) in Islamabad. This state-funded mosque was home to radical Islamists, led by brothers Abdul Aziz and Abdur Rashid Ghazi,[136] who openly supported the Taliban. Many of the students at nearby madrasas came from the FATA and the NWFP. The Islamists were known for their attempts to advocate and impose a strict Deobandi code of behaviour on the population and called for the rebuilding of illegally constructed mosques demolished by the city administration. On 6 April a sharia court was established at Lal Masjid and about 100 clerics from across the country gathered to call for enforcement of sharia in Pakistan.[137] On 18–19 May, four police officers were taken hostage at the mosque and Abdul Aziz threatened suicide attacks in response to any security operation. The stand-off escalated into street violence and ended on 10–11 July, when security forces stormed the mosque, where about 150 hostages were held. At least 102 people died in the attack, which provoked public demonstrations across the country and further Islamist political activism and violence.[138] The mosque reopened in October, broadcasting a recorded sermon by the incarcerated Abdul Aziz.[139]

The Lal Masjid crisis was the most evident manifestation of a broader process of Islamist radicalization in Pakistan. Musharraf's relatively secular policy of 'enlightened moderation' was increasingly compromised by his administration's support of the US-led 'global war on terrorism'—seen by many Pakistanis as submitting to US pressure—the high civilian death toll in the government's crackdown on Islamist militants, and the regime's growing authoritarianism. Sympathy with the neo-Taliban's support for Afghan insurgency—if not for the social and religious order that the movement advocated—spread even among urban middle class Pakistanis. Musharraf's government acquiesced to gradual Islamicization, trying to co-opt or channel it to the administration's advantage.[140] Musharraf had to tread carefully in order preserve the political dominance of the military, defend the interests of non-Islamist elites, avoid full-scale confrontation with radical Islamists and prevent their consolidation at the national level.

However, the potential for Islamicization in Pakistan has limits, and comparisons drawn by some observers between contemporary Pakistan and pre-revolutionary Iran are unjustified.[141] Radical Islamists consistently fail in national elections in Pakistan and are not a united movement.[142] Sectarian

---

[136] Their father, chief cleric Maulana Abdullah, was close to former Pakistani president Zia-ul-Haq.

[137] On 9 Apr. the sharia court issued its first edict, against the Minister of Tourism, Nilofar Bakhtiar.

[138] 'A chronology of Lal Masjid saga', *Dawn* (Karachi), 11 July 2007; Hasan, S. S., 'Profile: Islamabad's Red Mosque', BBC News, 27 July 2007, <http://news.bbc.co.uk/2/6503477.stm>; and Hoodbhoy (note 128), pp. 4–5.

[139] 'Pakistan's Red Mosque open again', BBC News, 3 Oct. 2007, <http://news.bbc.co.uk/2/7025 477.stm>.

[140] E.g. the government's declared anti-terrorism campaign in practice had a limited impact on most of the armed Islamist groups active in Kashmir.

[141] E.g. Dalrymple, W., 'A friend of feudalism', *The Guardian*, 1 Sep. 2007.

[142] The success of the Islamist Muttahida Majlis-e-Amal (United Action Front) in the NWFP and Baluchistan can be attributed to factors more specific to these regions: Islamist–tribal violence and ethno-confessional separatism, respectively.

intolerance among groups such as the anti-Shia Sipah e-Sahaba, the Shia Tehreek-e-Jaferia Pakistan and madrasas engaged in intra-Sunni violence is no less potent than Islamist dissatisfaction with the secular state.[143] In 2007 sectarian violence, in addition to ethnic tensions and regional divisions, continued to limit the prospects for radical Islamists to rise to power at the national level.[144]

Terrorism and anti-terrorism

The diversity of violent actors and the overlapping of four dimensions of political and religious violence in Pakistan—local, national, regional and transnational—is best demonstrated by the dynamics of terrorism and counterterrorism. While much of the low-scale terrorism in tribal areas is carried out by local militias, most of the large-scale attacks, especially suicide bombings, are organized by foreign militants. Suicide bombings were rare in Pakistan until 2005–2006 but became more frequent in the country's tribal areas and urban centres in 2007,[145] even as terrorism incidents declined overall.[146] Statements issued in July and September 2007 that were attributed to the al-Qaeda leaders Ayman al-Zawahiri and Osama bin Laden called for revenge on Musharraf's regime for the Lal Masjid operation and addressed the 'friends of Allah' in the tribal agencies.[147] In 2007 the USA did not rule out carrying out its own military strikes in Pakistan's tribal areas against the neo-Taliban and foreign militants.[148] Nevertheless, the presence of foreign Islamist militants affected security beyond the tribal areas primarily by galvanizing external pressure on Pakistan, mainly from the USA, to intensify action against Islamist militants in general. It also guarantees the continued flow of US aid to Pakistan and a degree of US tolerance towards the Musharraf Administration's authoritarian practices.

At the level of national politics, President Musharraf was accused of using counterterrorism for political ends when he cited terrorist attacks as one of the

[143] International Crisis Group (ICG), *The State of Sectarianism in Pakistan*, Asia Report no 95 (ICG: Brussels, 18 Apr. 2005); and Riikonen, K., 'Sectarianism in Pakistan: a destructive way of dealing with difference', University of Bradford, Pakistan Security Research Unit (PSRU) Brief no. 2, 1 Mar. 2007, <http://spaces.brad.ac.uk:8080/display/ssispsru/Publications/>,

[144] Ethnic violence in Pakistan included Muhajir–Pashtun and Muhajir–Punjabi clashes in May 2007 during days of street battles between supporters of the pro-government, Muhajir-dominated Muttahida Qaumi Movement (MQM) and opposition groups over MQM attempts to prevent the ousted supreme court chief justice, Muhammad Chaudry, from delivering a speech in the city. UN Integrated Regional Information Network (IRIN), 'Pakistan: Karachi violence stokes renewed ethnic tensions', 16 May 2007, <http://www.irinnews.org/Report.aspx?ReportId=72145>.

[145] Hoodbhoy (note 128), p. 3. Suicide attacks directly targeting the military are not terrorist attacks.

[146] Terrorist incidents in Pakistan declined from 254 in 2006 to 104 in Jan.–Nov. 2007 and fatalities from these incidents dropped from 243 in 2006 to 86 in Jan.–Nov. 2007. In Kashmir, terrorism by Pakistan-based Islamist militants also declined. Terrorism Knowledge Base (note 9).

[147] SITE Intelligence Group, '"The aggression against Lal Masjid [Red Mosque]": an audio speech by Dr Ayman al-Zawahiri produced by as-Sahab Media', 11 July 2007; and SITE Intelligence Group, '"Come to Jihad": an audio speech from Usama bin Laden addressing the people of Pakistan, declaring war on the Pakistani Government', 20 Sep. 2007, <http://www.siteinstitute.org/>.

[148] See Boucher (note 123), p. 3.

main pretexts for declaring a state of emergency on 3 November 2007.[149] An overall decline in terrorist attacks in the country during 2007 was interrupted by the year's two largest terrorist bombings in Pakistan, which targeted the procession of former prime minister Benazir Bhutto, the leader of the opposition Pakistan People's Party, in Karachi on 18 October. While the attacks were blamed on unidentified 'Islamist militants', they also appeared to be tied to political struggle at the national level.[150] On 27 December, Bhutto was killed in Rawalpindi in a sniper attack combined with a suicide bombing. The assassination provoked violent anti-government protests throughout Pakistan, particularly in Sindh province, and national elections were postponed until February 2008. While the government blamed the attacks on pro-Taliban and al-Qaeda elements, Bhutto's supporters accused the authorities of a security lapse and complicity in the attack.[151]

VI. Conclusions

The diversification of militant actors and blurring of boundaries between different forms and levels of violence in and beyond the sites of major armed conflicts reflect a general trend of fragmentation of violence. They may partly explain the high civilian costs of violence and why so many countries relapse into violence when well into peace processes and post-conflict stages: armed violence becomes self-perpetuating and so deeply embedded in a society that it may not end, or even significantly decline, with the resolution of a conflict's main incompatibility.

The two most critical factors stimulating the fragmentation of armed violence and erosion of the boundaries between its various forms appear to be (a) state weakness, in terms of lack of functionality and legitimacy, and (b) external involvement, which can range from political and economic pressure backed by the threat of military power to actual military intervention and occupation. These two factors are often interconnected: state failure may be one of the reasons why external forces intervene, but, as in the case of Iraq, it may result from the dismantling of the state by the foreign intervention and the failure to replace it with a functional and legitimate system. Counter-insurgency strategies may also contribute to fragmentation of violence when the interveners or the government encourage internecine tensions in order to weaken the armed opposition.

---

[149] 'Proclamation of emergency issued by General Pervez Musharraf', *International Herald Tribune*, 4 Nov. 2007. Musharraf also cited judicial 'interference' in various spheres. Musharraf had met strong resistance from lawyers in his attempts to remove legal obstacles to a third presidential term, and his re-election in controversial elections in Oct. was contested in the Supreme Court.

[150] Gall, C. and Masood, S., 'After bombing, Bhutto assails officials' ties', *New York Times*, 20 Oct. 2007.

[151] At least 20 other people were killed in the attack. 'Violent protests rock Pakistan', Al Jazeera, 28 Dec. 2007, <http://english.aljazeera.net/NR/exeres/D804F355-D988-4EA9-9476-E049D6106BC6.htm>; and Khan, M. I., 'Bhutto murder: key questions', BBC News, 31 Dec. 2007, <http://news.bbc.co.uk/2/7165892.stm>.

In contexts where violence has fragmented in this way, even a minimal degree of state functionality and legitimacy can help to reduce the violence. However, this combination of functionality and legitimacy can only be provided by a domestically generated movement that has an appeal beyond its own ethnic or sectarian group, enjoys considerable popular support and whose activities embrace social, political, security and justice issues. Such political forces cannot be artificially constructed from outside. In some cases, the groups best prepared to play this role may be radical movements of a nationalist, religious or socio-political form, or a combination of these forms.

It is in the vital interest of international peace and security that external actors correctly identify these groups and encourage their further politicization and integration into political processes, rather than trying to marginalize or antagonize them. In weak, conflict-torn states, support to state building that combines functionality with local legitimacy should be a priority—even if the agendas and ideologies of the local groups most capable of moving the process forward are different from those promoted by the leading international actors.

Appendix 2A. Patterns of major armed conflicts, 1998–2007

LOTTA HARBOM and PETER WALLENSTEEN*

I. Major armed conflicts in a wider context

This appendix reports on trends in major armed conflicts in the past 10 years. These include some of the deadliest conflicts on our planet and consequently have significant implications for international peace and security.[1] There were 14 major armed conflicts in 2007, based on new criteria for defining major armed conflicts that were introduced by the Uppsala Conflict Data Program (UCDP) in 2007.[2] This is the same number as in 2006, although only 11 of the conflicts in 2007 were also active in 2006.

Section II of this appendix describes global trends in major armed conflicts over the decade 1998–2007. Section III describes trends at the regional level in the same period. Section IV discusses changes to the list of major armed conflicts between 2006 and 2007. Table 2A.3 presents data on the major armed conflicts that were active in 2007. Appendix 2B provides details of the definitions, sources and methods used in compiling the major armed conflict data.

While the focus of this appendix remains on major armed conflicts, other armed conflicts are taking place. These others include conflicts in which at least one conflict party is the government of a state that have not reached the level of intensity required to be classified as major armed conflicts[3] and non-state conflicts (conflicts waged between non-state groups)[4]. Non-state conflicts include violence between, for

---

[1] The Uppsala Conflict Data Program (UCDP) defines a major armed conflict as a contested incompatibility concerning government and/or territory over which the use of armed force between the military forces of 2 parties—of which at least 1 is the government of a state—has resulted in at least 1000 battle-related deaths in a single calendar year. After a conflict reaches this threshold, it reappears in the data set on major armed conflicts if it results in at least 25 battle-related deaths in a single year. For more detail see section II, and for a definition of the separate elements see appendix 2B. Elsewhere, the UCDP uses the category war rather than major armed conflict. War is defined by the same criteria except that the conflict must cause 1000 battle-related deaths every year. Thus, major armed conflicts listed in the SIPRI Yearbook may in some years be classified as minor armed conflicts (see note 3) in other UCDP lists, publications and databases.

[2] For discussion of the revised criteria see appendix 2B.

[3] Most of these lower-scale conflicts fall under the broader UCDP category of minor armed conflict, defined as a contested incompatibility concerning government and/or territory over which the use of armed force between the military forces of 2 parties—of which at least 1 is the government of a state—has resulted in at least 25 battle-related deaths in a single calendar year. The UCDP has data on all state-based conflicts in the forms of a data set from 1946 and of an online database, containing a wide range of variables, from 1989.

[4] The UCDP defines a non-state conflict as the use of armed force between 2 organized groups—neither of which is the government of a state—which results in at least 25 battle-related deaths in a single calendar year. The UCDP has collected data on non-state conflicts since 2002, making global

---

* Uppsala Conflict Data Program (UCDP), Department of Peace and Conflict Research, Uppsala University. For Table 2A3, Kristine Eck was responsible for the conflict location India; Hanne Fjelde for Sri Lanka; Helena Grusell for Colombia and Peru; Joakim Kreutz for Iraq and Myanmar (Burma); Ralph Sundberg for Afghanistan, Israel and the USA; Hannah Tsadik for the Philippines and Somalia; and Nina von Uexküll for Russia and Turkey.

example, rebel organizations or different ethnic groups. In the years since 1998, major armed conflicts have, on average, comprised about half of all state-based conflicts. In order to shed light on the broader context in which major armed conflicts take place, section V of this appendix includes information on non-state conflicts in 2002–2006.

II. Global patterns in major armed conflict

In recording the major armed conflicts active in 2007 some revisions have been made to the definition of major armed conflict. The main criterion for classifying an armed conflict as major remains: that fighting between two parties, one or both of which is a state, has resulted in 1000 battle-related deaths during at least one calendar year of the conflict. In previous editions of the SIPRI Yearbook such conflicts were still recorded as major armed conflicts if there was at least one battle-related death in a year due to fighting between the same two parties. The new rule raises the minimum to 25 battle-related deaths. The tables, figures and data set for all years in the period 1990–2007 have been revised accordingly.[5]

In 2007, 14 major armed conflicts were active in 13 locations around the world. Over the past decade the global number of active major armed conflicts has declined overall. However, as can be seen in table 2A.1, the revised data reveal a very uneven decline, with major drops in 2002 and 2004—the year with the lowest number of active conflicts during the period—and an increase of three in 2005.

For the fourth consecutive year no interstate conflict was recorded in 2007. Only three major armed conflicts were fought between states during the entire period 1998–2007: Eritrea–Ethiopia (1998–2000); India–Pakistan (1998–2003); and Iraq versus the United States and its allies (2003). The first two conflicts concerned territory while the third was fought over governmental power. The remaining 30 major armed conflicts recorded for this period were all fought within states, with 9 concerning territory and 21 governmental power.

In 2007 four conflicts were categorized as internationalized—that is, they included troops from a state that was not a primary party to the conflict but was aiding one of the conflict parties. This is an increase of one over the number in 2006. Interestingly, just as in 2006, all the internationalized conflicts in 2007 were in some way linked to the US-led 'global war on terrorism'. Those most clearly connected to it were the conflict between the US Government and al-Qaeda; the conflict between the Afghan Government and the Taliban; and the conflict between the Iraqi Government and the numerous insurgent groups operating there. The fourth internationalized major armed conflict recorded in 2007 was between the Government of Somalia and the Supreme Islamic Council of Somalia (SICS).[6] Here, however, its link to the 'global war on

information about this type of conflict available for the first time. The UCDP also collects information on one-sided violence—the use, by the government of a state or by a formally organized group, of armed force deliberately targeting civilians that results in at least 25 deaths in a calendar year. There data are available from 1989, both as a data set and in the UCDP online database. All data can be found at the UCDP webpage <http://www.ucdp.uu.se>. They are presented annually in the Human Security Report and the *Journal of Peace Research*.

[5] The revised list of major armed conflicts for the period 1990–2007 is available at <http://www.pcr. uu.se/research/UCDP/data_and_publications/datasets.htm>.

[6] For the states contributing troops to these conflicts see table 2A.3. On the conflict between the USA and al-Qaeda, and the complex issues affecting its coding, see Eriksson, M., Sollenberg, M. and Wallen-

Table 2A.1. Regional distribution, number and type of major armed conflict, 1998–2007

Region	1998 G	1998 T	1999 G	1999 T	2000 G	2000 T	2001 G	2001 T	2002 G	2002 T	2003 G	2003 T	2004 G	2004 T	2005 G	2005 T	2006 G	2006 T	2007 G	2007 T
Africa	9	1	8	1	7	1	7	0	6	0	5	0	3	0	3	0	3	0	1	0
Americas	1	0	1	0	0	0	2	0	2	0	1	0	2	0	2	0	2	0	3	0
Asia	2	5	2	4	2	5	2	5	1	4	1	5	1	2	2	4	2	3	2	4
Europe	0	1	0	2	0	1	0	1	0	1	0	1	0	1	0	1	0	1	0	1
Middle East	0	1	1	1	1	2	1	2	0	2	1	2	1	2	1	2	1	2	1	2
Total	**12**	**8**	**12**	**8**	**10**	**9**	**12**	**8**	**9**	**7**	**8**	**8**	**7**	**5**	**8**	**7**	**8**	**6**	**7**	**7**
Total	**20**		**20**		**19**		**20**		**16**		**16**		**12**		**15**		**14**		**14**	

G = Government and T = Territory, the two types of incompatibility

terrorism' is more tenuous. As Ethiopian troops aiding the Somali Government fought to push the militia of the SICS out of the country, the USA carried out air strikes against al-Qaeda operatives who had sought refuge among the Somali Islamists. Thus, US military action was not directly a part of the Somali conflict.

III. Regional patterns

In 2007 six major armed conflicts were recorded for Asia, making it the region with the highest number of major armed conflicts for the third year running. Three major armed conflicts each were recorded for the Americas and the Middle East. The lowest incidence of major armed conflicts was recorded for Europe and Africa, where only one major armed conflict was recorded for each region in 2007. The regional distributions of major armed conflicts and of conflict locations for the period 1998–2007 are shown in tables 2A.1 and 2A.2, respectively. Figure 2A.1 shows the total number and regional distribution of major armed conflicts in each year of this period.

Thirteen major armed conflicts were recorded for Africa between 1998 and 2007.[7] While this makes Africa the region with the highest total figure, there was a dramatic decrease in major armed conflicts there over the period. From 1998 until 2000, and again in 2002, Africa had the highest annual totals of major armed conflicts of any region.[8] However, the number of conflicts recorded for Africa started to fall slightly in 1999. This decline continued steadily until 2004, when only three conflicts were active in the region, and remained at that level until 2006. In 2007 only one major armed conflict in Africa was recorded. Between 1998 and 2007, only one major

steen, P., 'Patterns of major armed conflict, 1990–2001', *SIPRI Yearbook 2002: Armaments, Disarmament and International Security* (Oxford University Press: Oxford, 2002), pp. 67–68. Prior to its renaming on 25 June 2006, the SICS was referred to by several names, including the Supreme Council of Islamic Courts and the Union of Islamic Courts.

[7] The 13 major armed conflicts recorded in Africa for the period 1998–2007 are Algeria, Angola, Burundi, Democratic Republic of the Congo, Republic of the Congo, Eritrea–Ethiopia, Guinea-Bissau, Liberia, Rwanda, Sierra Leone, Somalia, Sudan and Uganda. When only the name of a country is given, the conflict is over governmental power. The name of the contested territory appears in parenthesis after the country name in the case of conflicts over territory.

[8] In 2001 and 2004 equally high totals were recorded for Asia.

Table 2A.2. Regional distribution of locations with at least one major armed conflict, 1998–2007

Region	1998	1999	2000	2001	2002	2003	2004	2005	2006	2007
Africa	10	9	8	7	6	5	3	3	3	1
Americas	1	1	0	2	2	1	2	2	2	3
Asia	7	6	6	6	4	5	2	5	5	5
Europe	1	2	1	1	1	1	1	1	1	1
Middle East	1	2	3	3	2	3	3	3	3	3
Total	**20**	**20**	**18**	**19**	**15**	**15**	**11**	**14**	**14**	**13**

armed conflict in Africa was fought between states: Eritrea–Ethiopia. A distinctive characteristic of major armed conflicts in Africa during this period is the large proportion that were internationalized: of the 12 intrastate conflicts, seven were internationalized at some point. All but one of the major armed conflicts recorded in this region were fought over governmental power.

For the Americas three conflicts were recorded in the past decade.[9] The annual number of major armed conflicts recorded as active for the region ranged from zero (in 2000) to three (in 2007). All three conflicts recorded for the period were intrastate and concerned governmental power.

Ten major armed conflicts were recorded for Asia in 1998–2007.[10] The annual number of conflicts ranged between five and seven, except in 2004, when the number fell to three. In 2003 and again in 2005–2007 the highest annual totals of active major armed conflicts were recorded for Asia.[11] Two of the major armed conflicts in Asia were active in all years of the period 1998–2007: India (Kashmir) and the Philippines. Only one of the conflicts recorded for Asia, India–Pakistan, was fought between states. Five intrastate conflicts were fought over territory, while the remaining four concerned governmental power.

Only two of the major armed conflicts recorded between 1998 and 2007 had their location in Europe, making it the region with the lowest total. The intrastate conflict in Yugoslavia over the territory of Kosovo was active in 1998 and 1999. Russia (Chechnya) was active from 1999 and continued until 2007.

In the 10-year period, five major armed conflicts were recorded for the Middle East.[12] In 1998 only one conflict was recorded for the region. Thereafter, the annual totals fluctuated between two and three. The same three conflicts have been active since 2004: the conflict in Iraq, Israel (Palestinian territories) and Turkey (Kurdistan). Turkey (Kurdistan) was active in all years of the period. One conflict recorded for the region was fought between states: Iraq–USA and its allies. The remaining four were fought within states, two over governmental power and two over territory.

[9] The 3 major armed conflicts in the Americas recorded for the period 1998–2007 are Colombia, Peru and the USA (the conflict between the US Government and al-Qaeda).

[10] The 10 major armed conflicts recorded for Asia in the period 1998–2007 are Afghanistan, Cambodia, India (Kashmir), India–Pakistan, Indonesia (East Timor), Myanmar (Karen State), Nepal, the Philippines, the Philippines (Mindanao) and Sri Lanka ('Tamil Eelam').

[11] In 2001 and 2004 equally high totals were recorded for Africa.

[12] The 5 major armed conflicts in the Middle East recorded for the period 1998–2007 are Iran, Iraq, Iraq–USA and its allies, Israel (Palestinian territories) and Turkey (Kurdistan).

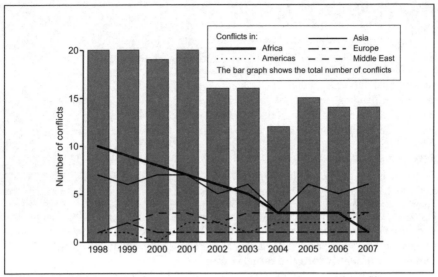

Figure 2A.1. Regional distribution and total number of major armed conflicts, 1998–2007

IV. Changes in the list of major armed conflicts for 2007

Conflicts added to the table in 2007

Three conflicts appear in the table for 2007 that were not registered for 2006: Peru, the Philippines (Mindanao) and Somalia.[13]

Conflict-related violence in Peru escalated in 2007 to a level not recorded since 1999. The Maoist rebel group Sendero Luminoso (Shining Path) launched an armed campaign against the Peruvian Government in 1980 that continued throughout the 1980s. The group's leader, Abimael Guzmán, was captured in 1992. This major set-back, compounded by internal divisions, weakened Sendero Luminoso and conflict activity subsequently declined. While some attacks were carried out between 2000 and 2006, the violence did not reach the threshold for inclusion in the list of major armed conflicts. In 2007 the same pattern of irregular ambushes and attacks continued, but their frequency increased somewhat, pushing the toll of battle-related deaths over 25.

The conflict between the Philippine Government and the Moro Islamic Liberation Front (MILF) separatist group escalated in 2007 and once again passed the threshold of 25 battle-related deaths. Fighting between these parties was first registered as a major armed conflict in 2000. Intermittent fighting has continued since then, although there was a brief de-escalation in 2006. During most of 2007 MILF members

---

[13] Peru and Philippines (Mindanao) both appeared in the table published in *SIPRI Yearbook 2007*, but they are no longer in the UCDP data set for 2006 due to the new coding rule. All comparisons in this section relate to the current UCDP list (note 5) not the tables published in previous editions of the SIPRI Yearbook.

appeared frustrated by the continual stalling of negotiations. However, in mid-November exploratory talks took place and were deemed successful by both parties.[14]

A major armed conflict was last recorded for Somalia in 1996. After some chaotic years when no central government could be identified, a transitional government was established in 2001, only to collapse two years later. A new transitional government was established in December 2004. This government soon suffered infighting and faced an expanding network of local Islamic courts in Mogadishu that refused to recognize its authority. From 2006, the SICS took over large swathes of land in the south of the country. Government forces, together with Ethiopian troops, launched an offensive against the SICS in late 2006 that resulted in hundreds of deaths.[15] By early 2007 the Ethiopian troops had seized control of Mogadishu and attempted to push the SICS forces out of the country. Fighting persisted in southern Somalia and by April violence had returned to Mogadishu, as the SICS launched long-distance mortar attacks on Ethiopian targets. Civilians bore the brunt of the violence. In 2007 the fighting in Somalia was of an intensity not recorded in many years.

Conflicts removed from the table in 2007

Three conflicts were removed from the list of major armed conflicts in 2007: Burundi, Sudan and Uganda.

In Burundi the last active rebel group, Parti pour la libération du peuple Hutu–Forces nationales de libération (Palipehutu–FNL, Party for the Liberation of the Hutu People–National Liberation Forces) signed a ceasefire accord in September 2006. The agreement was largely respected in 2007 and the conflict was subsequently inactive for the first time since 2001. However, neither the country nor the peace process was stable during the year. In July senior rebel figures quit the truce-monitoring team and throughout the rest of the year there were fears that war would return. While this did not happen, violence did break out between rival factions of the Palipehutu–FNL, causing many civilians to flee.

In the Darfur region of Sudan the situation continued to be chaotic in 2007. However, there was an overall decline in organized violence, especially in fighting between rebels and government forces. Thus, for the first time since this conflict erupted, fighting between the government and the Sudan Liberation Movement/Army (SLM/A) did not reach the threshold required for inclusion in the table of major armed conflicts. The decline in fighting can be attributed to two factors. First, the rebels were weakened as a result of splits within the movement. Second, infighting in the Janjaweed militia, which had been extensively used by the government against the SLM/A, reduced its capacity to fight.[16]

In 2007 the conflict between the Government of Uganda and the Lord's Resistance Army (LRA) rebel group was inactive for the first time since 1994. Negotiations between the two parties were initiated in southern Sudan in mid-2006 and a ceasefire

[14] Xinhua, 'Philippine gov't, rebel group to hold formal talks early 2008', *People's Daily*, 16 Nov. 2007.

[15] On the situation in Somalia see Lindberg, S. and Melvin, N. J., 'Major armed conflicts', *SIPRI Yearbook 2007: Armaments, Disarmament and International Security* (Oxford University Press: Oxford, 2007), pp. 72–78.

[16] While the violence between government, pro-government and rebel forces declined in 2007, fighting between non-state groups in Darfur increased as various Arab groups competed for large areas of land abandoned by populations displaced by the main conflict. See chapter 2, section IV.

was signed in August of that year. Even though the talks have been slow and marred by frequent walkouts, the ceasefire was largely respected in 2007 and most observers agreed that this offered the best chance for peace in Uganda in many years.

Changes in intensity of conflict

Four of the 14 major armed conflicts that were active in 2007 increased in intensity compared to 2006: Sri Lanka ('Tamil Eelam'), Afghanistan, Myanmar (Karen State) and Turkey (Kurdistan). In the latter three, battle-related deaths increased by more than 50 per cent.

In Afghanistan 2007 was the most violent year so far in the conflict between the Taliban rebels and the government in Kabul, supported by troops from the North Atlantic Treaty Organization (NATO)-led International Security Assistance Force (ISAF). The intensification was partly due to the Taliban's effort to establish stable footholds in the country. Another factor was the more aggressive and offensive tactics employed by ISAF and US-led forces. Afghan President Hamid Karzai invited Taliban leaders to talks several times during the year. However, the rebels refused to negotiate until the foreign troops had left the country.

In eastern Myanmar (Burma) the conflict between the government and the Karen National Union (KNU) rebel group escalated in 2007. This was the result of a government offensive into Karen areas, launched in 2006, which brought about the most violent fighting there in a decade.

In Turkey the protracted conflict between the government and the Partiya Karkerên Kurdistan (PKK, Kurdistan Workers' Party) escalated markedly after a period of relative calm in 2006. PKK leader Abdullah Öcalan called for negotiations in 2007, but the Turkish Government stated that it would not negotiate with terrorists. On the military front, fighting continued unabated throughout the year, mainly in the PKK strongholds of south-eastern Turkey. In October, the Turkish Parliament authorized an attack on the PKK headquarters in northern Iraq and Turkish forces carried out several cross-border air strikes.

Six major armed conflicts decreased in intensity between 2006 and 2007: Colombia, India (Kashmir), Israel (Palestinian Territories), Russia (Chechnya), the Philippines and the USA—the Philippines by more than 50 per cent. Philippine President Gloria Macapagal-Arroyo vowed in early 2007 to crush the Communist Party of the Philippines (CPP) militarily, but this hard-line strategy apparently failed to achieve its end and between July and September Macapagal-Arroyo made at least three overtures to the rebels in an attempt to draw them back to the negotiating table. The rebels responded that they would not negotiate until they had been removed from the USA's list of foreign terrorist organizations.

Only one major armed conflict did not change in intensity between 2006 and 2007: that between the Government of Iraq and the numerous Iraqi insurgency groups. While the overall level of violence was the same as in 2006, marked changes in intensity could be discerned during the year. There was a dramatic increase in violence in the first half of 2007 compared to 2006, but the rest of 2007 was much calmer.[17] There were also changes in the geographical pattern of the fighting, with the violence spreading in 2007 to northern Iraq, an area that had been relatively unaffected by the conflict. Meanwhile, the situation in the Iraqi capital, Baghdad, improved.

[17] On developments in Iraq in 2007 see chapter 2, section III.

In four of the major armed conflicts active in 2007 there were more than 1000 battle-related deaths: Afghanistan (over 5800), Iraq (over 5700), Sri Lanka (*c.* 2500) and Somalia (almost 1400).

V. Patterns in non-state conflict, 2002–2006

The recent general decline registered in the number of major armed conflicts has been paralleled in non-state conflicts. In 2002, the first year covered by the UCDP data on this phenomenon, 32 non-state conflicts were active around the world. After climbing to 35 in 2003, the number dropped to 23 in 2004 and 2005 and then to 21 in 2006. However, although the overall trend in the numbers of non-state conflicts is downward, there is considerable fluctuation.

The great majority of the non-state conflicts in the period were in Africa. The region accounted for over 80 per cent of the non-state conflicts recorded in 2002 and 2003, falling to 66 per cent in 2006. Furthermore, the non-state conflicts were concentrated in a handful of countries. The countries with the most non-state conflicts during the period 2002–2006 were Somalia (24), Nigeria (15), Ethiopia (14) and Sudan (11).

The region with the second highest number of non-state conflicts was Asia, accounting for between 8 per cent of all non-state conflicts recorded (in 2003 and 2004) and 23 per cent (in 2006). The Americas accounted for between 3 per cent (in 2002) and 13 per cent (in 2004 and 2005) of recorded non-state conflicts between 2002 and 2005. No non-state conflict was registered for the Americas in 2006. The rest of the non-state conflicts took place in the Middle East, which accounted for between 0 and 9.5 per cent of the world totals annually. No non-state conflict was registered for Europe in the period 2002–2006.

From the first five years' data it is possible to identify some characteristics that seem to be prevalent among non-state conflicts.[18] One characteristic is that they are significantly less deadly than state-based conflicts. While the average death toll of state-based conflicts in 2005 was 388,[19] the corresponding figure for non-state conflicts was 82.[20] Another characteristic is that non-state conflicts tend to be relatively brief, lasting only one or two years. No non-state conflict was registered as being active throughout the period 2002–2006. The non-state conflicts of the longest duration, both recorded for four consecutive years, were those between the Colombian rebel group Fuerzas Armadas Revolucionarias Colombianas (FARC, the Revolutionary Armed Forces of Colombia) and the militia Autodefensas Unidas de Colombia (AUC, United Self-Defense Forces of Colombia) and between the Ivorian Dioulas and Krou ethnic groups. The short duration of most non-state conflicts may be, in large part, due to the parties having smaller resources. State-based armed conflicts, in contrast, involve the resources of at least one government, making them potentially longer, more deadly and more costly.

---

[18] For a more detailed overview of non-state conflicts see Kreutz, J., 'Conflicts without borders? A brief overview of non-state conflicts', ed. L. Harbom, *States in Armed Conflict 2006*, Research Report no. 79 (Uppsala University, Department of Peace and Conflict Research: Uppsala, 2007), pp. 155–67.

[19] This average includes both major and minor armed conflicts. See note 3.

[20] Human Security Centre, *Human Security Brief 2006* (University of British Columbia, Liu Institute for Global Issues, Human Security Centre: Vancouver, 2006), p. 9

Table 2A.3. Major armed conflicts, 2007

Location	Incompatibility[a]	Year formed/year stated/ year joined/year entered[b]	Warring parties[c]	Total deaths (including 2007)[d]	Deaths in 2007[e]	Change from 2006[f]
Africa						
Somalia	Government	1981/2006/2006/2007	Government of Somalia, Ethiopia vs Supreme Islamic Council of Somalia (SICS)	. .	<1 400	n.a.
Americas						
Colombia	Government	1964/1966/1966/. .	Government of Colombia vs FARC	>45 100*	>300	–
Peru	Government	1980/1980/1980/1981	Government of Peru vs Sendero Luminoso (Shining Path)	>28 000	25–100	n.a.
USA*	Government	2001/2001/2001/2001	Government of USA, Multinational coalition** vs al-Qaeda	<3 100	<200	–

FARC: Fuerzas Armadas Revolucionarias de Colombia (Revolutionary Armed Forces of Colombia)

* This figure includes deaths involving parties other than FARC in the fighting since 1964, although the vast majority of the deaths can be attributed to FARC and, to a lesser extent, the Ejército de Liberación Nacional de Colombia (ELN, National Liberation Army of Colombia).

* 'Location' refers to the government of the state that is being challenged by an opposition organization. Thus, location refers to the incompatibility and is not necessarily the geographical location of the fighting. For background and the origins of this intrastate conflict see *SIPRI Yearbook 2002*, pp. 67–68.

** In 2007 the US-led multinational coalition included troops from Afghanistan, Australia, Canada, Czech Republic, Denmark, France, Germany, Italy, the Netherlands, New Zealand, Pakistan, Poland, Romania, Saudi Arabia and the UK. Note that reliable information on states contributing troops is sensitive and hard to find, so this list should be seen as preliminary.

Asia

Afghanistan	Government	1990/1994/1994/2005	Government of Afghanistan, ISAF* vs Taliban	..	>5 800	+ +
India	Territory (Kashmir)	1977/1977/1989/1990	Government of India vs Kashmiri insurgents	>29 300	>500	–
Myanmar	Territory (Karen State)	1948/1948/1948/1949	Government of Myanmar vs Karen National Union (KNU)	>20 100	>100	+ +
Philippines	Government	1946/1968/1969/1982	Government of the Philippines vs Communist Party of the Philippines (CPP)	20 000–27 000	>100	– –
	Territory (Mindanao)	1968/1981/1986/2000	Government of the Philippines vs Moro Islamic Liberation Front (MILF)	>38 600	25–100	n.a.
Sri Lanka	Territory ('Tamil Eelam')	1976/1976/1975/1989	Government of Sri Lanka vs Liberation Tigers of Tamil Eelam (LTTE)	>64 400	<2 500	+

Europe

Russia	Territory (Chechnya*)	1991/1991/1991/1995	Government of Russia vs Chechen insurgents	40 000–70 000	<200	–

* The following countries contributed troops to the NATO-led International Security Assistance Force (ISAF) in 2007: Albania, Australia, Austria, Azerbaijan, Belgium, Bulgaria, Canada, Croatia, Czech Republic, Denmark, Estonia, Finland, France, Germany, Greece, Hungary, Iceland, Ireland, Italy, Jordan, Latvia, Lithuania, Luxembourg, Macedonia (Former Yugoslav Republic of), the Netherlands, New Zealand, Norway, Poland, Portugal, Romania, Slovakia, Slovenia, Spain, Sweden, Switzerland, Turkey, the UK and the USA. While all these countries contributed troops to ISAF, some did not have a mandate to fight. All the countries are listed here because information on the mandates of individual states' troops is often sensitive and hard to find.

* Most of the violence in 2007 took place in the neighbouring Russian republics of Dagestan and Ingushetia.

Location	Incompatibility[a]	Year formed/year stated[b]/ year joined/year entered[b]	Warring parties[c]	Total deaths (including 2007)[d]	Deaths in 2007[e]	Change from 2006[f]
Middle East						
Iraq	Government	2003/2003/2003/2004	Government of Iraq, Multinational coalition* vs Iraqi insurgents**	>24 300	>5 700	0
Israel	Territory (Palestinian territories)	1964/1964/1964/..	Government of Israel vs Palestinian organizations*	>15 100	>300	–
Turkey	Territory (Kurdistan)	1974/1974/1984/1992	Government of Turkey vs Partiya Karkerên Kurdistan (PKK)*	<31 000	>400	+ +

* The US-led multinational coalition in Iraq included combat troops from Albania, Armenia, Australia, Azerbaijan, Bosnia and Herzegovina, Bulgaria, the Czech Republic, Denmark, El Salvador, Estonia, Georgia, Kazakhstan, Latvia, Lithuania, Macedonia (Former Yugoslav Republic of), Moldova, Mongolia, Poland, Romania, Slovakia, South Korea, the UK and the USA.

** These included e.g. the ISI (Islamic State of Iraq, Dawlat al-'Iraq al-Islamiyya)—the successor to al-Qaeda in Iraq (AQI)—the Reformation and Jihad Front (RJF, Ansar al-Islam) and the Mahdi Army (Jaish al-Mahdi). The ISI was previously called Tanzim Qa'idat al-Jihad fi Bilad al-Rafidayn (Organization of Jihad's Base in the Country of the Two Rivers), the RJF was previously called al Jaysh al-Islami fi Iraq (Islamic Army of Iraq) and Ansar al-Islam was previously called Jaish Ansar al-Sunna (Army of Ansar al-Sunna).

* These included Fatah (Movement for the National Liberation of Palestine), Hamas (Islamic Resistance Movement) and Palestinian Islamic Jihad (Jihad).

* The Partiya Karkerên Kurdistan (PKK, Kurdistan Workers' Party) has changed names several times in recent years: in 2002 to the Kurdish Freedom and Democracy Congress (KADEK), in Nov. 2003 to the Conference of the People's Congress of Kurdistan (Kongra-Gel) and in Apr. 2005 back to its previous name, PKK.

Notes: Although some countries are also the location of minor armed conflicts, the table lists only the major armed conflicts in those countries. For the definitions, methods and sources used see appendix 2B.

The conflicts in table 2A.3 are listed by location, in alphabetical order, within 5 geographical regions: Africa—excluding Egypt; the Americas—including North, Central and South America and the Caribbean; Asia—including Oceania, Australia and New Zealand; Europe—including the Caucasus; and the Middle East—Egypt, Iran, Iraq, Israel, Jordan, Kuwait, Lebanon, Syria, Turkey and the states of the Arabian peninsula.

a The stated general incompatible positions—'Government' and 'Territory'—refer to contested incompatibilities concerning *governmental power* (type of political system or a change of central government or its composition) and *territory* (control of territory, secession or autonomy), respectively. A location may have incompatibilities over several different territories, but only 1 incompatibility over government.

b 'Year formed' is the year in which a warring party first stated the incompatibility. In conflicts where several parties have fought over the same incompatibility, the year that the incompatibility was first stated is given, even if the party that stated it is no longer active in the conflict. 'Year stated' is the first year in which 1 of the currently active opposition parties (see note c) stated its incompatibility. 'Year joined' is the first year in which armed force was used in the conflict by at least 1 of the active opposition parties. 'Year entered' is the first year in which fighting between the government and 1 or more of the active opposition parties led to 1000 or more battle-related deaths in a single calendar year and was therefore classified as a major armed conflict. Thus, 'year formed' refers to the start of the armed conflict itself, while the other 3 years listed in the table ('year stated', 'year joined' and 'year entered') refer to the involvement of least 1 active opposition party.

c The government party and its allies are listed first, followed by the opposition parties, which may be organizations or other states. Opposition parties are only listed in the table if fighting between them and the government over the declared incompatibility has passed the threshold of 1000 battle-related deaths in a calendar year. An opposition organization is any non-governmental group that has publicly announced a name for itself as well as its political goals and has used armed force to achieve its goals. Only those parties and alliances that were active during 2007 are listed in this column. A comma between 2 warring parties indicates an alliance. In cases where 2 governments have both stated incompatible positions, e.g. over a shared border, they are listed in alphabetical order.

d The figures for total battle-related deaths refer to those deaths caused by the warring parties since the start of the conflict that can be directly connected to the incompatibility. This figure thus relates to the 'Year formed' variable. In the case of intrastate conflicts, it should be noted that the figures include only battle-related deaths that can be attributed to fighting between the government and opposition parties that have at some point been listed in the table. Information that covers a calendar year is necessarily more tentative for the last months of the year. Experience has also shown that the reliability of figures improves over time; they are therefore revised each year.

e Numbers over 100 are, as far as possible, rounded to the nearest hundred. Thus, figures ranging between 101 and 150 are presented as >100, while figures ranging between 151 and 199 are presented as <200. Figures between 25 and 100 are presented as 25–100.

f The 'Change from 2006' is measured as the increase or decrease in the number of battle-related deaths in 2007 compared with the number of battle-related deaths in 2006. Although the symbols are based on data that cannot be considered totally reliable, they represent the following changes:

++   increase in battle deaths of >50%
+   increase in battle deaths of >10–50%
0   stable rate of battle deaths (± 10%)
–   decrease in battle deaths of >10–50%
– –   decrease in battle deaths of >50%
n.a. not applicable, since the major armed conflict is not recorded for 2006.

Appendix 2B. Definitions, sources and methods for the conflict data

UPPSALA CONFLICT DATA PROGRAM

This appendix clarifies the definitions and methods used in the compilation of data on major armed conflicts and explains the treatment of the sources consulted. The armed conflict records presented in appendix 2A are compiled by the Uppsala Conflict Data Program (UCDP) of the Department of Peace and Conflict Research, Uppsala University.[1]

I. Definitions

The UCDP defines a major armed conflict as a contested incompatibility concerning government or territory over which the use of armed force between the military forces of two parties, of which at least one is the government of a state, has resulted in at least 1000 battle-related deaths in at least one calendar year.[2] The separate elements are defined as follows:

1. *Incompatibility that concerns government or territory.* This refers to the stated generally incompatible positions of the parties to the conflict. An *incompatibility that concerns government* refers to incompatible positions regarding the state's type of political system or the composition of the government. It may also involve an aim to replace the current government. An *incompatibility that concerns territory* refers to incompatible positions regarding the status of a territory and may involve demands for secession or autonomy (intrastate conflict) or aims to change the state in control of a certain territory (interstate conflict).

2. *Use of armed force.* This refers to the use of armed force by the military forces of the parties to the conflict in order to promote the parties' general position in the conflict. Arms are defined as any material means of combat, including anything from manufactured weapons to sticks, stones, fire or water.

3. *Party.* This refers to the government of a state, any of its allies, an opposition organization or an alliance of opposition organizations. The *government of a state* is the party that is generally regarded as being in central control, even by those organizations seeking to seize power. If this criterion is not applicable, the party controlling the capital of the state is regarded as the government. An *opposition organization* is any non-governmental group that has announced a name for itself as well as its political goals and that has used armed force to achieve them. Opposition organizations operating from bases in neighbouring states are listed as parties to the conflict in the location (country) where the government is challenged. Apart from these primary parties to the conflict, one other type of actor may be included in the table: a state or a

---

[1] See the UCDP Internet site at <http://www.ucdp.uu.se/>.

[2] This definition of major armed conflicts differs slightly from that used by the UCDP in *SIPRI Yearbooks 1988–1999* (Oxford University Press: Oxford, 1988–99). The requirement that a conflict must cause at least 1000 battle-related deaths in a single year, rather than over the entire course of the conflict, ensures that only conflicts which reach a high level of intensity, as measured by the number of battle-related deaths, are included. Tables 2A.1 and 2A.2 have been retroactively revised accordingly.

multinational organization that supports one of the primary parties with regular troops. In order to be listed in the table, this secondary party must share the position of one of the warring parties. In contrast, a traditional peacekeeping operation is not considered to be a party to the conflict but is rather seen as an impartial part of a consensual peace process.

4. *State.* A state is an internationally recognized sovereign government controlling a specific territory or an internationally non-recognized government controlling a specific territory whose sovereignty is not disputed by an internationally recognized sovereign state that previously controlled the territory in question.

5. *Battle-related deaths.* This refers to deaths caused by the warring parties that can be directly related to combat over the contested incompatibility. Once a conflict has reached the threshold of 1000 battle-related deaths in a calendar year, it reappears in the annual list of major armed conflicts in any year that there are 25 or more battle-related deaths in fighting between the same parties and concerning the same incompatibility.[3] The focus is thus not on political violence per se but on incompatibilities that are contested by the use of armed force. Thus, in appendix 2A the UCDP registers one major type of political violence—battle-related deaths—which serves as a measure of the magnitude of a conflict. Other types of political violence are excluded, such as the unilateral use of armed force (e.g. massacres); unorganized or spontaneous public violence; and violence that is not directed at the state (e.g. rebel groups fighting each other).[4]

The period analysed in appendix 2A is 1998–2007, but the conflicts in the annual table can have reached the required threshold of 1000 battle-related deaths in any calendar year since 1946 and need not have done so during the analysed period.

II. Sources

The data presented in appendix 2A are based on information taken from a wide selection of publicly available sources, both printed and electronic. The sources include news agencies, newspapers, academic journals, research reports, and documents from international and multinational organizations and non-governmental organizations (NGOs). In order to collect information on the aims and goals of the parties to the conflict, documents of the warring parties (governments, allies and opposition organizations) and, for example, the Internet sites of rebel groups are often consulted.

Independent news sources, carefully selected over a number of years, constitute the basis of the data collection. The Factiva news database (previously known as the Reuters Business Briefing) is indispensable for the collection of general news reports. It contains 8000 sources in 22 languages from 118 countries and thus provides sources from all three crucial levels of the news media: international (e.g. Agence France-Presse and Reuters), regional and local. However, it is worth noting that the availability of the regional and national news sources varies. This means that for some countries several sources are consulted, whereas for other countries and regions only a few high-quality region- or country-specific sources are used.

---

[3] In previous editions of the SIPRI Yearbook the threshold was 1 battle-related death. It has been raised to 25 in order to ensure that only those conflicts are included in which fighting did indeed occur in the year. This is in line with other UCDP data sets, in all of which a fundamental part of the definition of an active conflict is that it has led to at least 25 battle-related deaths in a year.

[4] The UCDP collects information on 2 of these types of violence: non-state conflicts and 1-sided violence. Data on these additional categories can be found at the UCDP website, <http://www.ucdp.uu.se/>.

The UCDP regularly scrutinizes and revises the selection and combination of sources in order to maintain a high level of reliability and comparability between regions and countries. One important priority is to arrive at a balanced combination of sources of different origin with a view to avoiding bias. The reliability of the sources is judged using the expertise of the UCDP together with advice from a global network of experts (academics and policymakers). Both the independence of the source and the transparency of its origins are crucial. The latter is important because most sources are secondary, which means that the primary source also needs to be analysed in order to establish the reliability of a report. Each source is judged in relation to the context in which it is published. The potential interest of either the primary or secondary source in misrepresenting an event is taken into account, as are the general climate and extent of media censorship. Reports from NGOs and international organizations are particularly useful in this context, complementing media reporting and facilitating cross-checking. The criterion that a source should be independent does not, of course, apply to sources that are consulted precisely because they *are* biased, such as government documents or rebel groups' Internet sites. The UCDP is aware of the high level of scrutiny required and makes great effort to ensure the authenticity of the material used.

III. Methods

The data on major armed conflicts are compiled by calendar year. They include data on conflict location, type of incompatibility, onset of the armed conflict, warring parties, total number of battle-related deaths, number of battle-related deaths in a given year and change in battle-related deaths from the previous year.[5]

The data on battle-related deaths are given the most attention in coding for the conflict database. Information on, for example, the date, news source, primary source, location and death toll is recorded for every event. Ideally, these individual events and figures are corroborated by two or more independent sources. The figures are then aggregated for the entire year of each conflict. The aggregated figures are compared to total figures given in official documents, in special reports and in the news media. Regional experts such as researchers, diplomats and journalists are often consulted during the data collection. Their role is mainly to clarify the contexts in which the events occur, thus facilitating proper interpretation of the published sources.

Because very little precise information is publicly available on death figures in armed conflicts, the numbers presented by the UCDP are best viewed as estimates. Rather than always providing exact numbers, ranges are sometimes given. The UCDP is generally conservative when estimating the number of battle-related deaths. As more in-depth information on an armed conflict becomes available, the conservative, event-based estimates often prove more correct than others widely cited in the news media. If no figures are available or if the numbers given are unreliable, the UCDP does not provide a figure. Figures are revised retroactively each year as new information becomes available.

[5] See also the notes for table 2A.3 in appendix 2A.

Appendix 2C. The human security approach to direct and structural violence

ALBRECHT SCHNABEL

I. Introduction

In *SIPRI Yearbook 2007* Elisabeth Sköns argues that there is a clear disconnection between the intended objective of security provision and its current focus on the prevention of collective violence, which leads to much human death and suffering.[1] In the same edition of the Yearbook, Michael Brzoska calls for the traditional categories of collective violence and armed conflict to be augmented.[2] This appendix builds on their arguments. In exploring the causes and consequences of violence and insecurity, consideration must also be given to those threats that are the main causes of death and injury of humans and affect the stability of a society—many of which do not fit into either the category of armed conflict or that of collective violence. Many such threats are the consequence of 'structural violence'. A human security approach can encompass these threats and direct violence for both analysis and mitigation.

If individuals and communities feel secure and protected from the threats that emanate from direct and structural violence—that is, if their basic human security is guaranteed—then human suffering on an individual level and conflict and violence on communal, regional and international levels can be significantly reduced.[3] In contrast, violation of the basic human needs of individuals and communities leads to human suffering and social and communal deterioration, and therefore to more violence in its direct and structural manifestations. This, in turn, perpetuates the frustration of human needs.[4] Breaking this cyclical relationship hinges on the ability to reduce or avoid violence and thus provide human security.

Section II of this appendix defines 'direct' and 'structural' violence and explores the utility of the human security concept in addressing both. Section III identifies armed violence as a unique catalyst of both types of violence. Section IV suggests how to design human security-driven threat and mitigation analyses that help identify and respond to both direct and structural violence more appropriately and effectively. The conclusions are presented in section V.

---

[1] Sköns, E., 'Analysing risks to human lives', *SIPRI Yearbook 2007: Armaments, Disarmament and International Security* (Oxford University Press: Oxford, 2007), p. 243.

[2] Brzoska, M., 'Collective violence beyond the standard definition of armed conflict', *SIPRI Yearbook 2007* (note 1), pp. 94–106.

[3] Specific examples of structural violence include e.g. civilian grievances as a result of economic blockades or the discriminatory practices of global trade regimes; unequal access to political power, resources, health care, education, or legal standing causing significantly higher risk for people from particular segments of society to suffer and prematurely die from communicable and non-communicable diseases or extreme poverty; and institutionalized race segregation (e.g. apartheid in South Africa), which can kill slowly by preventing people from meeting their basic needs.

[4] Burton, J. (ed.), *Conflict: Human Needs Theory* (St. Martin's Press: New York, 1990).

II. Human security provision as a response to direct and structural violence in society

Defining direct and structural violence

Johan Galtung refers to 'the type of violence where there is an actor that commits the violence as *personal* or *direct*, and to violence where there is no such actor as *structural* or *indirect*'.[5]

In both cases individuals may be killed or mutilated, hit or hurt in both senses of these words, and manipulated by means of stick or carrot strategies. But whereas in the first case these consequences can be traced back to concrete persons as actors, in the second case this is no longer meaningful. There may not be any person who directly harms another person in the structure. The violence is built into the structure and shows up as unequal power and consequently as unequal life chances.[6]

According to Galtung, both direct and structural violence can be expressed through physical and psychological violence, whether directed at specific objects or not, with acts that are intended or unintended, and expressed in manifest or latent terms. Direct and structural violence are interdependent forces and, although direct violence tends to be more visible and easily perceived, 'there is no reason to assume that structural violence amounts to less suffering than personal [direct] violence'.[7] As a particular expression of direct violence, armed violence causes damage and promotes conditions for structural violence. It also weakens a society's capacity to resist or adapt to other life-threatening harm. Thus, armed violence and its debilitating direct and structural effects threaten peace—both negative peace, which is characterized by the absence of direct violence, and positive peace, which is characterized by the absence of structural violence.[8]

Galtung's differentiation between direct and structural violence is not an undisputed approach, but it makes sense in the context of human security analysis. If human security generally means 'the security of people—their physical safety, their economic well-being, respect for their dignity and worth as human beings, and the protection of their human rights and fundamental freedoms',[9] then threats experienced by individuals and communities that are part of specific social, cultural, economic and political communities are not limited to direct armed violence. Such threats may be overt expressions of violence committed by specific and identifiable actors or covert expressions of violence inherent in the disadvantaged position of individuals and communities in a social, political or economic system that is upheld by power structures beyond their control. Without violence there is greater potential to provide and meet at least basic human needs, and to develop possibilities to satisfy needs that determine not only survival but also well-being and quality of life. Galtung seems to have sensed the need to give greater consideration to the structural aspects

---

[5] Galtung, J., 'Violence, peace, and peace research', *Journal of Peace Research*, vol. 6, no. 3 (1969), p. 170 (emphasis in original).

[6] Galtung (note 5), pp. 170–71.

[7] Galtung (note 5), p. 173; on the interrelationship between direct and structural violence see pp. 177–83.

[8] Galtung (note 5), p. 183.

[9] International Commission on Intervention and State Sovereignty, *The Responsibility to Protect* (International Development Research Centre: Ottawa, 2001), p. 15, para. 2.21.

and sources of violence and to shift exclusive (or primary) focus, particularly by governments, from the prevention of direct violence to the prevention of structural violence. Whether done voluntarily due to a sense of national and international responsibility or forced by others promoting such norms, such a shift would lower violence and increase human security.

Galtung argues that 'there is no reason to believe that the future will not bring us richer concepts and more forms of social action that combine absence of personal violence with [the] fight against social injustice [i.e. negative and positive peace] once sufficient activity is put into research and practice'.[10] This appendix suggests that human security may well be the concept that offers this opportunity. Focusing on the impact that both types of violence have on the human security of individuals and communities, without prejudicing one over the other in terms of strategic, political or economic significance, allows a more effective focus on the basic needs of individuals, compared to the security needs of states as expressed in more traditional national security thinking. This approach responds to one of the original components of the human security concept: that national and international political and security structures should consider human security equally important to national security. At this juncture, the human security concept is able to advance the distinctions between direct and structural violence and between negative and positive peace. In combination with a heightened sense of (or a moral and legal call for) responsibility by human security providers—those who govern individuals and communities, the referent objects of human security—both accountability and responsibility for the prevention of human insecurity might eventually enter the theory and practice of international law and custom.

The contribution of human security in responding to direct and structural violence is discussed below, following a brief outline of the concept.

The human security concept

The concept of human security is much debated and has been given varying definitions by scholars and governments alike.[11] For the purpose of this appendix 'human security threats' are identified as those that threaten the lives of individuals and communities through both direct and structural violence. This approach is manageable both in research and in practice. Although it covers threats posed by both direct and structural violence, the approach applies an impact threshold requiring violence

---

[10] Galtung (note 5), p. 186.

[11] See e.g. UN Development Programme, *Human Development Report 1994* (Oxford University Press: Oxford, 1994); Commission on Human Security, *Human Security Now* (Commission on Human Security: New York, 2003), <http://www.humansecurity-chs.org/finalreport/index.html>; Thakur, R., 'From national to human security', eds S. Harris and A. Mack, *Asia–Pacific Security: The Economics–Politics Nexus* (Allen & Unwin: St Leonards, 1997), pp. 53–54; and International Commission on Intervention and State Sovereignty (note 9), p. 15, para 2.21. On human security as a foreign policy tool see Debiel, T. and Werthes, S. (eds), *Human Security on Foreign Policy Agendas: Changes, Concepts and Cases*, INEF Report 80/2006 (Institute for Development and Peace: Duisburg, 2006). See also Oberleitner, G., 'Human security: a challenge to international law?', *Global Governance*, vol. 11, no. 2 (2005), pp. 185–203; Human Security Centre, *Human Security Report 2005: War and Peace in the 21st Century* (Oxford University Press: New York, 2005); and International Commission on Intervention and State Sovereignty (note 9), p. xii. See also Glasius, M. and Kaldor, M. (eds), *A Human Security Doctrine for Europe: Project, Principles, Possibilities* (Routledge: London, 2005); Kaldor, M., 'What is human security?', eds D. Held et al., *Debating Globalization* (Polity Press: Cambridge, 2005), pp. 175–90; and Kaldor, M., *Human Security: Reflections on Globalization and Intervention* (Polity Press: Cambridge, 2007).

to be life threatening to individuals and communities. The mere avoidance of direct and structural violence does not satisfy the full range of requirements for positive peace, broad human security provision and the satisfaction of the complete hierarchy of human needs.[12] It does, however, offer a manageable definition that links population security with national security, structural violence with direct violence, and accountability for human insecurity with responsibility for the provision of human security.

III. Violence and human insecurity

From the literature cited above, three main streams of thought define the source, meaning and impact of human insecurity. Broad definitions focus on 'freedom from fear' and 'freedom from want'; narrow definitions focus on the impact of direct, armed violence. The approach suggested in this appendix focuses on a combination of direct and structural violence in so far as they threaten the lives of individuals and communities. If the rationale for such an approach is pursued further, at least two critical questions arise. First, why does direct violence still figure so prominently in human security and insecurity analysis when its contribution to the overall numbers of people killed as a result of preventable violence is comparably low? Second, why work with structural violence, where the origins of threats are already difficult to trace and the responsibility for their occurrence, impact and alleviation are even more difficult to assign? Instead, focus could be placed separately on direct, armed violence on the one hand and various other forms of harm on the other. As is argued below, opting for direct and structural violence as interdependent core variables in human security analysis and provision offers opportunities to address the most crucial threats to populations and to prepare the grounds for the most effective mitigation mechanisms.

Direct violence as a catalyst of human insecurity

Among the causes of insecurity, armed violence is a factor of unique significance because it: (*a*) causes human insecurity and prevents the adequate provision of human security through its debilitating direct and indirect effects; (*b*) acts as an accelerator of human insecurity, with knock-on effects that increase the negative impact of existing levels of violence and harm; and (*c*) is often the articulation of underlying, protracted and unresolved structural violence and thus an indicator of societal and political instability. Armed violence is a highly visible pointer to the long overdue necessity of addressing structural violence and its manifestations.

In order to assess the impact of armed violence on prevailing stress levels and human insecurity potential, the type of armed violence must be determined (e.g. state-based or non-state violence). Furthermore, the existing and potential—increasing or decreasing—levels of armed violence must be ascertained in addition to its internal and external costs. (Internal costs include the probable number of victims of violence, infrastructural damage, and political, economic and social costs. External costs include, among others, impact on regional peace and stability through conflict spillover or refugee movements.) The psychological effects of armed violence (such as

---

[12] Maslow, A. H., 'A theory of human motivation', *Psychological Review*, vol. 50 (1943), pp. 370–96.

fear and terror) on populations and on opinion and decision makers are also significant, with definite yet difficult to estimate implications for peace and stability. If the 11 September 2001 attacks on the United States were an attempt to destabilize the political, economic, social and cultural foundations of Western civilization, they may at least have shaken those foundations. The attacks created a sense of fear and terror that was powerful enough to persuade political decision makers and populations in numerous (primarily) Western societies to significantly limit some long-held and protected values and norms (such as civil freedoms) in an effort to deter future terrorist activity of a similar kind. The structural and direct violence emanating from the 'global war on terrorism', triggered by the September 2001 attacks on (presumed) Western stability and security, turned out to be significant threats to human security in countries such as Afghanistan, Iraq and Pakistan, and to the civil rights and freedoms of Western societies.[13]

Although the 2004 Indian Ocean tsunami did not cause major political or social breakdown in any of the affected countries, armed violence that results in far fewer victims can easily have this effect. Depending on the impact on the society where it occurs, armed violence can be considered an 'extraordinary disaster' causing infra-structural, political, economic, psychological, environmental and socio-cultural damage. Environmental crises cause localized destruction (which can be repaired) and instability (which can usually be corrected fairly quickly), while an armed crisis can easily cause significant irreparable inter-communal damage and instability, affecting political and social relations for years or decades to come.[14] Thus, armed violence can trigger protracted structural violence with extraordinary long-term consequences. In a 2007 study, the International Action Network on Small Arms (IANSA), Oxfam and Saferworld estimate the economic cost of armed conflict to Africa's development.

On average, armed conflict shrinks an African nation's economy by 15 per cent, and this is probably a conservative estimate. . . . There are the obvious direct costs of armed violence—medical costs, military expenditure, the destruction of infrastructure, and the care for displaced people—which divert money from more productive uses. The indirect costs from lost opportunities are even higher. Economic activity falters or grinds to a halt. Income from valuable natural resources ends up lining individual pockets rather than benefiting the country. The country suffers from inflation, debt, and reduced investment, while people suffer from unemployment, lack of public services, and trauma.[15]

Preventing the outbreak of armed violence, or at least curtailing its scope and duration, is an important contribution to the combating of the unwieldy spread of structural and direct violence with compounded human security consequences. One of the first major attempts to address direct violence from the human security perspective emerged from the debate on the responsibility to prevent and mitigate grave vio-

[13] For an interesting study of the costs of the conflict in Iraq to the USA, Iraq and the world see Bennis, P. et al., *A Failed 'Transition': The Mounting Costs of the Iraq War* (Institute for Policy Studies and Foreign Policy in Focus: Washington, DC, Sep. 2004). The study reports and estimates the costs to the USA (human, security, economic and social costs); to Iraq (human, security, economic, social, human rights and sovereignty costs); and to the world (human costs, the costs of disregarding international law and undermining the UN as well as global security and disarmament, the costs of US-led ad hoc military coalitions, the costs to the global economy and global environmental costs).

[14] See e.g. Pouligny, B. et al. (eds), *After Mass Crime: Rebuilding States and Communities* (United Nations University Press: Tokyo, 2007).

[15] Hillier, D., 'Africa's missing billions: international arms flows and the cost of conflict', Briefing Paper 107 (IANSA, Oxfam, and Saferworld: Oxford, Oct. 2007).

lations of human security in the form of genocide, ethnic cleansing and other mass atrocities. This debate led to the United Nations General Assembly's endorsement of the 'responsibility to protect' concept at the 2005 UN World Summit, the establishment of the Global Centre for the Responsibility to Protect in New York and the creation of the position of a Special Advisor on the Responsibility to Protect in December 2007 to work closely with the office of the UN Secretary-General's Special Representative for the Prevention of Genocide and Mass Atrocities.[16]

Structural violence and human insecurity

Structural violence can be expressed in various ways. One such way is as suffering by all or part of society as a consequence of local, national and international exploitive and unjust political, economic and social systems and structures that prevent people from meeting their basic needs. Structural violence impinges on the basic survival needs of individuals and communities and is thus a source of human insecurity. Many effects of structural violence are devastating in human terms as well as destabilizing in political terms. Economically or politically marginalized populations that suffer from structural violence may breed extremist violence (insurgency or terrorism). In this case structural violence feeds direct violence. Structural violence matters in terms of its immediate impact on human security and its correlation with increasing direct violence.

In *SIPRI Yearbook 2007*, Elisabeth Sköns appears to state the obvious when she notes that 'If the ultimate objective of security is to save human beings from preventable premature death and disability, then the appropriate security policy would focus on prevention instruments and risk reduction strategies for their causes.' The point is well taken since the occurrence and scope of armed violence—and directly related casualties—are often used to inform general analyses of trends in peace and conflict worldwide. The *Human Security Report 2005* is an example of such thinking, although it is widely criticized for this approach.[17] Sköns further asserts that 'While collective violence causes a great many premature deaths and disabilities, other types of injury cause an even greater number.'[18] She cites relevant statistics prepared by the World Health Organization, according to which worldwide 17 million people died of communicable diseases in 2005, while 184 000 deaths occurred as a result of collective violence. (Although the latter figure is a highly uncertain estimate, it nevertheless captures the relative magnitude of such causes of death.) Thus, approximately 100 times more individuals died of preventable diseases than perished as a result of direct collective violence. The data cited by Sköns also show that almost five times as many individuals committed suicide and three times as many were killed in interpersonal violence than those who fell victim to collective violence.[19] However, in the light of those figures, an important caveat, which is likely to increase the reported levels of indirect victims of armed violence, should be considered. Recent Uppsala Conflict

---

[16] The responsibility to protect concept focuses on states' obligations to protect their populations and those of other states against genocide and other large-scale atrocities. United Nations, 'World Summit Outcome', UN General Assembly Resolution 60/1, 24 Oct. 2005, <http://www.un.org/summit2005 documents.html>, paras 138 and 139. On the Global Centre for the Responsibility to Protect see <http://www.globalcentrer2p.org/>.

[17] Human Security Centre (note 11).

[18] Sköns (note 1), p. 243.

[19] Sköns (note 1), p. 250.

Data Program (UCDP) data suggest that the promising decline in the number of state-based conflicts that began in the 1990s has ceased, and the annual number of such conflicts has remained constant at 32 for three years (2004–2006).[20] The annual totals for 'major armed conflicts', as defined by the UCDP and SIPRI, have also remained relatively stable in the past three years (at 14–15 conflicts in 2005–2007). Furthermore, since 2004, all of the major armed conflicts recorded have been intrastate conflicts.[21]

While it is likely that damage from armed violence contributes greatly to years or decades of post-violence suffering, from a human security perspective deadly harm that is not caused by armed violence deserves at least as much attention. There is a need to rethink security analysis and provision by moving from analysing 'conflict potential', which focuses on direct violence, to 'human insecurity potential', which focuses on both direct and structural violence and its mitigation.

Structural violence matters in the analysis of both violence and possible mitigation efforts. It is both a source and a result of direct violence. Structural violence manifests itself in marginalization and repression, and in the intentional and the unintentional creation of obstacles to the development or maintenance of individual and community-based strategies for managing harm. Based on the human security and human needs perspectives, both direct and structural violence are unacceptable burdens on human development and social justice and order—whether they are committed intentionally or not. The prevailing preoccupation in many quarters with the prevention of primarily direct violence (and of the outbreak of violent conflict or its recurrence in the post-conflict reconstruction phase) should give way to a more thorough focus on the detection and mitigation of structural violence. The latter is the source of great human suffering and societal tension, with the potential to destabilize societies to the point where armed violence becomes unavoidable.

IV. The human security approach as an analytical framework to address violence

Alleviating, mitigating and coping with direct and structural violence are essential requirements for sustainable and positive peace—and for assuring that fragile post-conflict societies in particular do not relapse into collective violence. The priorities and responsibilities for preventive and restorative engagement need to be clarified. The human security approach to structural and direct violence is a method to assist in identifying such priorities and responsibilities. It selects threats in a specific geographic context with a focus on the needs of the affected population, identifies sources of direct and structural violence and develops and communicates mitigation strategies to the actors in charge of human security provision.

A number of issues are thus necessary components of a framework for effective human insecurity mitigation: (*a*) population- and context-specific threat and violence identification and analysis; (*b*) threat-, context- and actor-specific designs of preventive and response measures; (*c*) targeted prevention of direct and structural violence through multi-actor strategies; and (*d*) monitoring and assessment of threat levels and of the implementation of mitigation and adaptation measures. Particular attention

---

[20] Harbom, L. and Wallensteen, P., 'Armed conflict, 1989–2006', *Journal of Peace Research*, vol. 44, no. 5 (2007), p. 623.

[21] For more detail see appendix 2A.

must be paid to the role of armed violence and its potential for escalating existing and creating new waves of direct and structural violence; and to the sources and impacts of structural violence. Using this framework as the basis for human security threats will help identify priority threats and entry points for effective preventive measures. However, the response side of this equation will remain a challenge, although not a difficult one. Desirable outcomes include: (*a*) observable and measurable reduction of direct and structural violence and threat levels; (*b*) decreasing vulnerability to direct violence and other life-threatening harm; (*c*) increasing levels of human security; (*d*) the reduced likelihood of conflict; and (*e*) improvements in social and political stability.[22]

Such a systematic approach to the analysis of violence is particularly relevant in the presence of structural violence, which is not always easy to recognize and where the identification of responsible causes and actors are a challenge at best. In Galtung's words, 'Personal violence represents change and dynamism—not only ripples on waves, but waves on otherwise tranquil waters. Structural violence is silent, it does not show—it is essentially static, it *is* the tranquil waters.'[23]

The human security approach is concerned with the needs of, and threats affecting, individuals and communities, and violence has to be analysed and mitigated primarily at the levels of their social, political and economic interactions. Thus, a human security approach to identifying and alleviating direct and structural violence must be able to identify sources of, and remedies to, violence that are realistically attributable to affected individuals and communities. Analysis of the sources of human insecurity and of the responsibilities for human security provision has to be undertaken in the context in which such analysis delivers relevant information to identify accountabilities and responsibilities, and where remedial or preventive strategies become feasible. In many instances, this will result in a multi-tiered approach to human security analysis and provision. Both direct and structural violence can be traced back to local, national, regional and international sources (i.e. structures and actors). Responsibilities for action lie with different actors at each of those levels. Sometimes remedial or preventive strategies can be pursued at all levels from the local to the global (with the greatest potential for effective and sustainable human security provision), while most often less ambitious (and possibly less effective) strategies will have to focus on measures at those levels where actors, structures and processes are most agreeable towards cooperation in the reduction of violence. For instance, financial or ideological support for an insurgency from local populations and external governments may be targeted at either or both of those levels. Global structural inequalities (such or globalization pressures or unfair trade patterns) might be identified as sources of structural violence at the local level, but would need to be addressed at the international level.

---

[22] This approach was developed by the present author in the context of the research project 'Operationalizing human security for livelihood protection: analysis, monitoring and mitigation of existential threats by and for local communities', jointly sponsored by swisspeace (HUSEC) and the National Center of Competence in Research (NCCR) North–South: Research Partnerships for Mitigating Syndromes of Global Change, <http://www.swisspeace.ch/typo3/en/peace-conflict-research/human-security/index.html>.

[23] Galtung (note 5), p. 173.

V. Conclusions

As discussed in the previous section, the human security concept implies that the provision of human security requirements is largely the responsibility of states. Many states need to rethink and refocus their security policies and systems in order to provide effective human security for their population and—in cooperation with other states and coordinated by intergovernmental organizations—assist or encourage states that lack the necessary capacities to follow suit. The 'responsibility to protect' concept seems a suitable response to these calls for the provision of universal human security. Yet it is for this very reason that scepticism prevails about the legality of a new norm that considers human security as an innate right and the provision of human security as the responsibility of states. Such expectations seem to be at odds with states' rights to sovereignty and non-intervention. Protagonists of the concept point out that their work—and the accompanying evolving global norm—applies only to direct violence and, in that context, the extreme action of military intervention under the responsibility to protect concept is concerned only with the most grievous crimes: mass atrocities and genocide. However, the basic assumptions of the concept justifying measures short of military intervention are applicable to direct violence in more general terms and to structural violence 'committed' by national and international cultural, social, economic and political structures—a major paradigm shift in international norms and values.

Depending on one's reading of *The Responsibility to Protect*,[24] there seems to have been a struggle within the International Commission on Intervention and State Sovereignty over the inclusion of some types of violence at the expense of other similarly destructive yet politically and legally less practicable ones. The responsibility to protect concept focuses on conflict and violence prevention and on post-conflict and post-violence rebuilding as the main tools of international responsibility towards disadvantaged and threatened populations worldwide. Direct violence short of mass atrocities and structural violence are gradually being recognized as viable and legitimate justifications for triggering international concern and pressure on states that are not able or willing to meet their populations' human security needs.

Using existing means and instruments to address state-based conflicts and—although more challenging—other forms of collective violence might be easier, less expensive and under current international law more likely to occur. From a human security perspective, such an approach reflects concerns mainly with the impact that tensions or crises have on national, regional and international order and stability. The fate and survival of affected populations are not primary considerations despite the destructive impact of both direct and structural violence on the stability and fabric of societies and their political systems. Moreover, such narrow approaches to addressing collective violence ignore opportunities to become involved in dealing with major suffering that is short of direct violence, and in checking its escalation to armed violence. Focusing threat analysis and mitigation on an approach that applies human security to identifying and reducing direct and structural violence offers promising opportunities for creating the normative, legal and eventually political conditions for the consolidation of positive and sustainable peace in threatened societies.

---

[24] International Commission on Intervention and State Sovereignty (note 9).

3. Planning and deploying peace operations

SHARON WIHARTA

I. Introduction

Mission planning was a crucial issue for the peacekeeping community in 2007, a year in which eight new peace operations were launched and the United Nations and the European Union (EU) both prepared to deploy their largest new peace operations to date.[1] The continued surge in demand for new peace operations over the past decade and the complex multidimensional nature of many of the operations that have been deployed have underlined the need for a more nuanced approach to mission planning. While mission planning in organizations such as the African Union (AU), the EU and the UN has previously been carried out largely by one or two departments, the integration of political, humanitarian, development and military dimensions requires much more internal coordination. Similarly, there is a need for better cooperation between the numerous external actors with whom the operations must interact.

Planning for any peace operation is a complex process with several distinct phases, each of which has its own priorities and potential pitfalls. This chapter focuses on pre-mission planning, the earliest stage of planning that culminates in the operation's deployment. Some of the most significant developments in—and criticisms of—peace operations in recent years have concerned this stage of planning. It is recognized that a coherent mission strategy, defined early in planning, is crucial not only to developing a peace operation with clear objectives and mandates but also to identifying and obtaining the necessary human, material and financial resources. Weaknesses in pre-mission planning have been identified as causing poor coordination and leading to the deployment of peace operations that do not meet the needs of the host country and the affected groups, thus compromising the sustainability of progress in several major peace operations, such as the UN operations in East Timor, Kosovo and Liberia.[2]

There have been two main criticisms of past UN pre-mission planning exercises. The first is that the process has been overly—even exclusively—based in UN Headquarters, far removed from the country and the communities

---

[1] The EU Military Operation in Chad and the Central African Republic (EUFOR Tchad/RCA), launched on 28 Jan. 2008, has an authorized strength of 3500 troops. The EU Military Operation in Bosnia and Herzegovina, EUFOR ALTHEA, which was launched in 2004, included over 6000 troops but was largely a 'rehatting' of the NATO Stabilization Force (SFOR) and so required less planning than an entirely new mission. On multilateral peace operations ongoing in 2007 see appendix 3A.

[2] These are the UN Transitional Administration in East Timor (UNTAET, 1999–2002); the UN Interim Administration in Kosovo (UNMIK, 1999–present); and the UN Mission in Liberia (UNMIL, 2003–present).

where the operation will be deployed. The second is that there has been too little consultation and coordination among UN departments and agencies, between UN Headquarters and the UN in-country presence, and between the UN and other relevant stakeholders, which range from other peacekeeping operations to the host government, civil society, rebels and affected communities.

In 2007 the UN began full implementation of its Integrated Missions Planning Process (IMPP) as part of its wider 'Peacekeeping 2010' reform strategy.[3] The IMPP, which attempts to create a sequential, coherent and unified framework for the planning of all UN multidimensional operations, includes substantial elements of in-country planning and consultation.[4]

The planning processes for several operations in 2007 illustrated both attempts to address the problems of pre-mission planning—and the difficulties that can be encountered. Section II of this chapter examines in more detail some of the recent attempts that have been made to address problems in UN peace operation planning, particularly pre-mission planning, and thus create operations that better address the needs and realities of the host country. It summarizes the IMPP and, for comparison, gives a brief overview of the EU's mission planning process. Section III examines the pre-mission planning in 2007 for three new peace operations: the AU/UN Hybrid Operation in Darfur (UNAMID), the UN Mission in the Central African Republic and Chad (MINURCAT) and the EU Military Operation in Chad and the Central African Republic (EUFOR Tchad/RCA). Section IV offers conclusions. Appendix 3A gives details of all multilateral peace operations ongoing, launched or terminated in 2007.

II. Efforts to improve pre-mission planning

The imperative for needs-driven operations

There is a growing recognition that the needs of the affected country must be better reflected in the planning of UN peace operations.[5] Academics and practitioners argue that, as the UN continues to move towards ambitious, multidimensional deployments, the 'one size fits all' approach that has often been taken in the past is less and less likely to result in operations that are genuinely 'needs-driven'.

---

[3] United Nations, 'Overview of the financing of the United Nations peacekeeping operations: budget performance for the period from 1 July 2004 to 30 June 2005 and budget for the period from 1 July 2006 to 30 June 2007', Report of the Secretary-General, A/60/696, 24 Feb. 2006, pp. 6–21.

[4] United Nations, Report of the Special Committee on Peacekeeping Operations and its Working Group on the 2007 Substantive Session, A/61/19 (part II), 5 June 2007, p. 17.

[5] Eide, E. B. et al., 'Report on integrated missions: practical perspectives and recommendations', Independent study for the Expanded UN Executive Committee on Humanitarian Affairs Core Group, May 2005, <http://www.reliefweb.int/rw/lib.nsf/db900SID/SODA-6CK7SK>; and United Nations, Department of Peacekeeping Operation (DPKO), United Nations Peacekeeping Operations: Principles and Guidelines (Capstone Doctrine) (DPKO: New York, 18 Jan. 2008), <http://pbpu.unlb.org/pbps/Pages/Public/viewdocument.aspx?docid=895>.

Pre-mission planning has traditionally been done at the headquarters level—and crucial decisions have been made after only minimal attempts to find out the realities of the affected country. It has thus been suggested that field-based fact-finding and needs-assessment exercises should become integral elements of the planning process for any peace operation—whether conducted by the UN or by a regional security organization. In response, the UN increasingly carries out fact-finding and needs-assessment exercises prior to mission deployment—such as the one that prepared a detailed plan for the implementation of the 2005 Comprehensive Peace Agreement in Sudan[6]—although they are often criticized for being too short. In 2006 the EU went as far as to establish a large in-country planning mission, the EU Planning Team for Kosovo (EUPT Kosovo). During the whole of 2007 EUPT Kosovo planned and prepared for the possible handover of certain responsibilities of the UN Interim Administration Mission in Kosovo (UNMIK) to an EU crisis-management mission as well as drawing up detailed plans for the EU Rule of Law Mission in Kosovo (EULEX Kosovo), which started deployment in February 2008.[7]

Fact-finding and needs-assessment teams in the past have often comprised mainly military planners but are gradually expanding to comprise multi-disciplinary expertise, including existing in-country development and humanitarian staff, anthropologists, members of expatriate and diaspora communities, and other local experts. Nevertheless, these teams—and peace operation planning processes in general—are frequently accused of not adequately consulting and involving local stakeholders. However, as the experiences in Chad and Sudan in 2007 discussed below illustrate, there are inherent difficulties in and limitations to increasing local involvement. The status quo at the outset of pre-mission planning, the conflict situation, the local political context and international political will all affect the practicalities of local involvement.

In addition, any attempt to move towards more needs-driven peace operations must eventually confront the fundamental question of whose needs to prioritize. Different stakeholders—local and external—will have different priorities. For instance, in its initial decision to deploy a robust multidimensional operation in Chad, the UN was responding to the needs of the refugees and internally displaced persons (IDPs) in the eastern part of the country. However these needs directly conflicted with those of the rebel groups there.

It has been observed that consultations undertaken under pressure, for example during rapid needs assessments, may serve to reinforce the planners' preconceptions rather than generate independent and objective analysis. They thus fail in their stated goal of identifying the true needs and priorities of the affected populations. Also, local non-government stakeholders may feel pres-

---

[6] Joint Assessment Mission (JAM) Sudan, *Framework for Sustained Peace, Development and Poverty Eradication* (JAM: 18 Mar. 2005). On the conflict in Southern Sudan see Holmqvist, C., 'Major armed conflicts', *SIPRI Yearbook 2006: Armaments, Disarmament and International Security* (Oxford University Press: Oxford, 2006), pp. 87–89.

[7] See EUPT Kosovo, 'Preparations for EULEX Kosovo: a European Union rule of law mission', <http://www.eupt-kosovo.eu/new/index.php?id=10&news=1>.

sured to say what they believe the international community wants to hear, rather than expressing their real priorities.[8] In contrast, powerful local stakeholders can manipulate consultation processes to their own advantage, as the Government of Sudan clearly did in 2007.

Reforming UN mission planning

Integrated mission task forces

Until the turn of the 21st century, it was normal for the planning of UN peace operations to begin in earnest only after the UN Security Council had passed a resolution authorizing the mission. Important decisions had thus already been made and planning consisted mainly of operationalizing the resolution. Mission planning was done only by the UN's departments of Peacekeeping Operations (DPKO), Humanitarian Affairs (DHA) and Political Affairs (DPA). Poor planning capabilities led to a lack of detailed pre-mission planning for complex operations such as the UN Transitional Authority in Cambodia (UNTAC, 1992–1993), the UN Operation in Somalia (UNOSOM I and II, 1992–1995), the UN Transitional Administration in East Timor (UNTAET, 1999–2002) and UNMIK (1999–present).[9] A seminal 2000 report by the independent Panel on United Nations Peace Operations—known as the Brahimi Report—articulated the need for coordination between the development and peace and security elements of the UN system to allow the emergence of an integrated approach to peacekeeping and peacebuilding.[10] It called for all pre-mission planning to take place through mission-specific integrated task forces, with the active participation of the UN Secretariat (DPKO and DPA) and UN agencies such as the Office for the Coordination of Humanitarian Affairs (OCHA), the Office of the UN High Commissioner for Refugees (UNHCR), the Office of the High Commissioner for Human Rights (OHCHR) and the UN Development Programme (UNDP).[11]

The integrated mission task force (IMTF) concept was first put into practice during planning for the UN Assistance Mission in Afghanistan (UNAMA).[12] The IMTF established for UNAMA comprised representatives of 13 UN departments and agencies. It operated full time for four months before UNAMA was deployed in March 2002. An internal evaluation by the UN

[8] De Coning, C., *Coherence and Coordination in United Nations Peacebuilding and Integrated Missions: A Norwegian Perspective*, Security in Practice no. 5 (Norwegian Institute of International Affairs: Oslo, 2007), p. 17.

[9] US General Accounting Office (GAO), *U.N. Peacekeeping: Issues Related to Effectiveness, Cost, and Reform*, Statement of Harold J. Johnson, Associate Director, International Relations and Trade Issues, National Security and International Affairs Division before the US House of Representatives Committee on International Relations, GAO/T-NSIAD-97-139 (GAO: Washington, DC, 9 Apr. 1997).

[10] United Nations, Report of the Panel on United Nations Peacekeeping Operations (Brahimi Report), attached to A/55/305–S/2000/809, 21 Aug. 2000, <http://www.un.org/peace/reports/peace_operations/>.

[11] United Nations (note 10), pp. 34–36.

[12] A prototype IMTF was established to plan the UN Mission of Support in East Timor (UNMISET, 2002–2005), the successor to UNTAET. Caplan, R., *International Governance of War-Torn Territories: Rule and Reconstruction* (Oxford University Press: New York, 2005), p. 235.

found that the IMTF was successful in ensuring that all relevant UN agencies and departments were centrally involved in pre-mission planning.[13] However, an external report noted that the IMTF for UNAMA played a largely advisory, rather than decision-making, role and had little direct contact with the pre-existing country team based in Islamabad, Pakistan.[14] A UN assessment in 2007 found that: 'the IMTF functions well only as an information exchange and has been less successful as a strategic planning and management mechanism'.[15]

The 2006 IMPP guidelines (see below) expanded the composition of IMTFs to include at a minimum representatives from the political, military, police, security, logistics, humanitarian, development and human rights sections of the UN Secretariat along with representatives of the UN country team, if there is one.

In April 2007 UN Secretary-General, Ban Ki-moon, proposed the establishment of seven integrated operational teams (IOTs), which would support UN peace operations, including forming the core of future IMTFs.[16] The IOTs will consist of military, police, support and political experts and are to be situated in the regional divisions of the DPKO's Office of Operations. The IOTs are designed to make integrated mission planning, management and support more effective by serving as information and liaison hubs. They should ensure a much higher level of continuity during planning and implementation. The first IOT was formed to help in the planning of UNAMID. The others were expected to be operational in January 2008.[17]

The Integrated Mission Planning Process

Following the Brahimi Report, and building on lessons learned in UNAMA, the UN Mission in Liberia (UNMIL) and others, the DPKO made further efforts to improve and develop its operational planning capacity by creating new structures, plans and standard procedures. The IMPP was developed to ensure a transparent and inclusive approach in the planning of multidimensional operations. The IMPP includes consultations with key external partners and stakeholders, including national actors when appropriate.

In June 2006 guidelines setting out the IMPP, which had been in development for several years, were endorsed by the UN Secretary-General, Kofi

[13] Griffin, M., 'The helmet and the hoe: linkages between United Nations development assistance and conflict management', *Global Governance*, vol. 9 (2003), pp. 199–217.

[14] Durch, W. J. et al., *The Brahimi Report and the Future of UN Peace Operations* (Henry L. Stimson Center: Washington, DC, 2003), p. 49. The UN Special Mission in Afghanistan (UNSMA) was forced to relocate to Pakistan following the US invasion of Afghanistan in Oct. 2001. Caplan (note 12).

[15] United Nations, 'Report of the Office of Internal Oversight Services on the audit of the management structures of the Department of Peacekeeping Operations', A/61/743, 14 Feb. 2007.

[16] United Nations, 'Comprehensive report on strengthening the capacity of the United Nations to manage and sustain peace operations', Report of the Secretary-General, A/61/858, 13 Apr. 2007.

[17] United Nations, 'Momentous year for United Nations peacekeeping as it mounts two unique operations in Africa, sustains 18 more, restructures department, Fourth Committee told', GA/SPD/382, 31 Oct. 2007. In the same announcement, the UN Under-Secretary-General for Peacekeeping, Jean-Marie Guéhenno, said that the number of IOTs would be cut to 6.

Annan.[18] This policy document details the steps involved in establishing, maintaining and terminating a UN integrated peace operation. It sets out priorities and establishes a clear delineation of responsibilities within the UN system.

The guidelines divide planning for an integrated mission into three stages. Stage one, advance planning, consists of pre-mission planning, including developing strategic options for an enhanced UN engagement. It is the basis for developing a concept of operations. Stage two consists of operational planning and occurs when the mission has been authorized by the UN Security Council. The final stage is review and transition planning, which includes continual assessment and updating of the mission plan and planning for the closure of the mission.[19] The rest of this section looks at the planning processes in the IMPP leading up to deployment.

In the advance planning stage, the IMTF gathers information from a wide variety of sources, including the national and regional stakeholders. It draws up a range of strategies, options and scenarios for the scope of the operation and identifies factors and risks that could affect the operation's deployment or functioning. For example, it assesses the security situation in the country to prevent the operation being deployed in an inhospitable environment. The guidelines recommend a time frame of six weeks for this initial assessment.

The assessment is followed by the drafting of the UN Under-Secretary-General for Peacekeeping's planning directive, which outlines the strategic objectives for UN engagement, the priorities of the mission, and the timing and sequencing of further planning activities. This directive is then translated into a draft concept of operations. At this stage, a technical review or assessment team is sent to the affected country to see what adjustments are needed to the concept of operations, based on the local situation. The IMPP guidelines stress the importance in this process of properly consulting local stakeholders and other external actors who would be engaged in the region. The team also makes a preliminary assessment of resource requirements and prepares an initial estimate of the funding required to carry out the concept of operations. In the cases reviewed in this chapter, it is evident that the time frame of two weeks for the technical review was barely sufficient, not least because of geographical constraints, which added to the travel time.

If the proposed operation receives authorization from the UN Security Council, detailed operational planning then takes place. This involves refinement of the concept of operations into a mission plan. The core elements of the mission plan include a comprehensive results framework, which indicates the objectives of the operation, the desired outputs and activities, and the key benchmarks of the operation. The plan also outlines the operation's structure, including a detailed elaboration of its thematic and functional components. According to the IMPP guidelines, this process should take six weeks. How-

[18] United Nations, 'Integrated Missions Planning Process (IMPP)', Guidelines endorsed by the Secretary-General on 13 June 2006.

[19] United Nations (note 18).

ever, owing to the operation's complexity and the political difficulties it encountered, operational planning for UNAMID took several months. Human and material resources needed for the operation are also gathered at this stage.

The final stage of pre-deployment planning—referred to as implementation planning—concerns the handover of planning responsibilities from the IMTF to the operation's leadership. A 2006 study commissioned by the DPKO's Best Practices Section, which looked at management issues during the start-up phase of a peace operation, found that this handover is often problematic.[20] Because the planning team and the operation leadership are almost never the same people, there is a danger of losing continuity and valuable insight gained during the earlier planning processes. The study recommends that more time be devoted to pre-deployment briefing and there should be greater focus on substantive and planning issues. Most notably, it recommended that the briefings be centred on meetings with the various substantive and support units involved in the advance planning process. This would allow the incoming head of mission—a Special Representative of the UN Secretary-General (SRSG)—and the senior leadership of the operation to obtain an over-view of the mission planning processes. More importantly, it would give them the opportunity to discuss the plan in depth with the people who drafted it, including their assumptions and the challenges they anticipate. This would supplement the SRSG's normal bilateral meetings with senior UN Secretariat officials and key member states. The establishment of the IOTs should also improve continuity.

The study also stresses the importance of the mission's senior leadership—in particular the SRSG, the deputy SRSG, the force commander and the police commissioner—establishing contacts with key local people, including opposition leaders and civil society figures, as quickly as possible. A number of this study's recommendations were taken up in planning for UNAMID.

The IMPP entered its first year of full implementation in 2007. The planning processes for MINURCAT and UNAMID, which are discussed in section III, were the first in which the IMPP was tested.

Launching an EU peace operation

Compared to the UN, the EU has little experience of planning and conducting peace operations, having deployed its first missions only in 2003.[21] The EU typically deploys smaller missions in support of the UN. It does not deploy multidimensional operations. While the main aspects of the EU and UN planning processes are similar, the biggest difference is that the EU process is led

---

[20] Gilmore, S., Wilcock, G. and MacKinnon, M., 'Mission management/start up scoping project: final report', Final report, Peace Dividend Trust, 24 Apr. 2006. The study was based on 200 interviews with current and past senior peace operation leaders.

[21] The EU deployed its first civilian mission, the EU Police Mission in Bosnia and Herzegovina (EUPM), in Jan. 2003 and its first military mission, the EU Military Operation in the Former Yugoslav Republic of Macedonia (EUFOR Concordia), in Mar. 2003.

by the Political and Security Committee (PSC), which comprises national diplomats. This can unduly politicize mission planning.

The decision to launch an EU peace operation, under the framework of the European Security and Defence Policy—whether military or civilian—lies with the Council of the European Union and therefore requires consensus.[22] There are four phases in the decision-making process: development of the draft 'crisis-management concept' (CMC); approval of the CMC and development of strategic options; adoption of a Council joint action (CJA) and development of planning documents; and implementation.[23]

In the first phase, a crisis-response coordinating team comprising representatives of the 'key entities'—the EU Military Staff, the High Representative for the Common Foreign and Security Policy, the Police Unit, the Policy Unit and the European Commission—is set up to draft the CMC. The team carries out a field-based assessment of the situation in the affected country and identifies the options for an EU operation. The PSC may also choose to appoint an EU special representative to the affected country to heighten diplomatic engagement. The draft CMC is presented to the PSC, which then submits it to the Council for approval.

Upon approval of the CMC, the mission's senior leadership is identified and strategic options—military, police or civilian—are elaborated. The CJA—the legal basis for the operation—is drafted based on these options and goes through several bodies within the Council Secretariat for review before submission to the Council for approval. Like a UN Security Council resolution, the CJA is a document that specifies the mission's mandate, objective, duration, structure, including the chain of command, and financial costs. The CJA also specifies the start date of the mission. However, in the case of a military mission, a separate Council decision is necessary.

The time frame for the adoption of the CJA varies according to the urgency of the deployment and how long it takes to reach political consensus among the member states. Adoption has previously taken between 4 and 19 weeks. Once the CJA is adopted, the concept of operation (CONOPS) and the plan of operation (OPLAN) are drafted. During this stage, necessary personnel and equipment and the countries that will provide them are identified. In recent experience, this stage has been prone to the greatest delays, hindering rapid deployment of the mission. When the OPLAN and the CONOPS documents have been adopted by the General Affairs and External Relations Council the mission is formally launched.

---

[22] The European Commission is more actively involved in civilian peace operations than those with a military component.

[23] This description of the EU planning process is based on Born, H. et al., *Parliamentary Oversight of Civilian and Military ESDP Missions: the European and National Levels* (European Parliament: Brussels, Oct. 2007).

III. Mission planning in practice

UNAMID

Efforts to revitalize the Darfur peace process and to deploy the AU/UN hybrid operation UNAMID attracted international attention throughout 2007. [24] UNAMID's planning and deployment illustrate strikingly the disconnect between policy and practice as well as the fact that even a well-planned operation may suffer from implementation challenges. Several features distinguish UNAMID. It was the first hybrid peace operation—an operation jointly conducted by two or more security organizations but under a single chain of command—ever deployed. While the operation's planners attempted to follow the IMPP guidelines, this unique aspect of the operation tested the IMPP's flexibility. In few past peace operations has there been such a long gap between the initial discussions and deployment. The planning process was also unusually intensive. Among other things, there was a high level of consultation with local stakeholders, in line with the IMPP guidelines. Besides complicating the planning process, this also allowed it to be held hostage to political developments. The fact that planning was taking place simultaneously at the AU Headquarters in Addis Ababa and the UN Headquarters in New York also created difficulties.

UNAMID assumed full authority from the African Union Mission in Sudan (AMIS) on 31 December 2007, after a protracted planning process that began in 2006 and went through numerous amendments.[25] The operation was authorized by UN Security Council Resolution 1769, adopted on 31 July 2007. This resolution was unique in that it set out a deployment schedule for the operation. UNAMID's headquarters was to reach initial operating capability, including command-and-control structures, by October 2007. In the same month it was to complete preparations to assume operational command over the 'light support package', all AMIS personnel, and any 'heavy support package' and newly deployed UNAMID personnel.[26]

Resolution 1769 was welcomed as a major step towards stability in the region. Following the IMPP guidelines, the advance planning stage had included substantial consultations with the Government of Sudan and others. In June 2007 the AU and the UN held high-level technical talks with the government, leading to the latter's acceptance of UNAMID and the key ele-

---

[24] On the conflict in Darfur, Sudan, see chapter 2 in this volume, section IV.

[25] On the background to UNAMID see Wiharta, S., 'Peacekeeping: keeping pace with changes in conflict', *SIPRI Yearbook 2007: Armaments, Disarmament and International Security* (Oxford University Press: Oxford, 2007), pp.107–128.

[26] The light support package consisted of human and material resources from the UN to help AMIS to fulfil its expanded mandate. The heavy support package included more personnel and substantial air and other military assets. It was agreed to by the Sudanese Government in Nov. 2006 but was still only partially deployed in Dec. 2007. United Nations, Letter dated 28 Sep. 2006 from the Secretary-General addressed to the President of the Security Council, UN document S/2006/779, 29 Sep. 2006; and United Nations, Monthly report of the Secretary-General on Darfur, S/2006/1041, 28 Dec. 2006.

ments of Resolution 1769.[27] This high-level meeting was the culmination of several rounds of negotiations. The resolution thus represented a firm commitment from the Sudanese Government that it would cooperate with the UN in the three-phased peacekeeping plan leading to the deployment of UNAMID. In marked contrast, the government had strongly opposed UN Security Council Resolution 1706, adopted on 31 August 2006, evidently because it had had little input. Resolution 1706 authorized the existing UN Mission in Sudan (UNMIS) to deploy in Darfur, which the Sudanese Government had never agreed to.

The idea for a hybrid operation had initially been developed and agreed to in principle by all three parties at the November 2006 meeting of the AU's Peace and Security Council.[28] A tripartite mechanism consisting of the AU, the UN and the Sudanese Government was established to ensure transparency and facilitate the deployment of the light and heavy support packages and the establishment of the hybrid operation. In February 2007 the AU and UN sent in a review team to undertake a quick assessment of whether an evaluation carried out by a UN technical team in June 2006 was still relevant and, more critically, whether the conditions in Darfur were still appropriate for deployment of the new operation. An AU–UN multidisciplinary planning team— composed of experts in the fields of human rights, humanitarian affairs, refugee return and reintegration, disarmament, demobilization and reintegration, military and police planning and mission support—was subsequently formed to elaborate on the findings of the review and technical assessment missions. The fact that the team was split between Addis Ababa and New York created coordination challenges. More substantial issues included balancing the respective organizations' standards and interests.[29]

The first of several joint AU–UN planning exercises took place in March 2007 in Addis Ababa to decide the broad tasks for the various mission components and identify personnel requirements.[30] At a subsequent joint planning session it was determined that it would be necessary to deploy an advance police and military contingent—an 'early-effect capability'—which would already be operational on the day of the transfer of authority.[31] The credibility of UNAMID hinged on gaining the confidence of the local population in Darfur through an early and visible improvement in the security situation.

[27] African Union, Communiqué on the situation in Darfur, 79th Meeting of the Peace and Security Council of the African Union, PSC/PR/Comm.(LXXIX), 22 June 2007.

[28] African Union, High-level consultation on the situation in Darfur: conclusions, 16 Nov. 2006, <http://www.amis-sudan.org/psccommunique.html>; and African Union, Communiqué of the 66th Meeting of the Peace and Security Council of the African Union, PSC/AHG/Comm.(LXVI), 30 Nov. 2006.

[29] Heller Chu, M., Darfur Integrated Operational Team, UN Department of Peacekeeping Operations, Interview with the author, 30 Nov. 2007.

[30] African Union, Report of the Chairperson of the Commission and the Secretary-General of the United Nations on the hybrid operation in Darfur, PSC/PR/2(LXXIX), 22 June 2007.

[31] The early-effect capability consisted of 1 formed police unit, 40 more police officers, 1 infantry battalion, 4 reserve companies, up to 60 liaison officers and military aviation capability. United Nations, Report of the Secretary-General on the deployment of the African Union–United Nations Hybrid Operation in Darfur, S/2007/517, 30 Aug. 2007.

Following Resolution 1769, the planning team entered the operational planning stage and focused on force generation. Normally an arduous process in itself, force generation became even more complicated because of the multiple criteria that had been imposed. For example, the Sudanese Government had insisted that the force had to be predominantly African. However, from the UN's perspective the force also had to be able to implement UNAMID's robust mandate effectively. On 2 and 3 August 2007 the AU and the UN held meetings with potential contributors of troops and police in Addis Ababa and New York, respectively. Five countries agreed to make up the early-effect deployment. Offers for regular troops for UNAMID exceeded the requested numbers. However, some of the countries that pledged the troops indicated that they lacked the equipment necessary to implement the required tasks. More critical military capabilities, such as aviation, and transport and multi-role logistical units were not pledged.[32] With respect to the police component, although the overall requested numbers were met, these came from a small number of countries and did not satisfy a broad enough geographic representation.[33]

Force generation problems continued throughout the rest of the year and into 2008, greatly exacerbated by the attitude of the Sudanese Government (see below). By the end of August 2007 the AU and the UN had not been able to finalize an agreement on troop generation and the configuration of the UNAMID military and police components. There was concern that UNAMID would not be ready to take over full authority from AMIS by the 31 December deadline.[34] A third meeting with potential contributing countries on 19 September did not obtain any more pledges.[35] When UNAMID assumed full authority at the end of the year, the final force composition had still not been agreed and several force-enabling assets, including ground transport units, transport helicopters and attack helicopters, had still not been pledged.[36]

In September 2007, in keeping with the IMPP guidelines, a joint AU–UN multidisciplinary transition team had been established in El Fasher, Darfur. The team, headed by the UNAMID deputy joint special representative, was responsible for implementing the deployment plans on the ground.

The Sudanese Government insisted on being centrally involved in all major decisions relating to UNAMID. In no other peace operation in recent history was the host government given so much influence. However, while the UN has embraced the principle of inclusiveness as a way of making peace operations more needs-driven, the Sudanese Government's main aim was apparently to weaken UNAMID. For instance, the government ruled out UNAMID

---

[32] On the supply of military equipment to UNAMID see chapter 7 in this volume, section V.

[33] United Nations (note 31), p. 3.

[34] 'Darfur deadlines', *Africa Confidential*, vol. 48, no. 18 (7 Sep. 2007), p. 9.

[35] United Nations, Report of the Secretary-General on the deployment of the African Union–United Nations Hybrid Operation in Darfur, S/2007/596, 8 Oct. 2007.

[36] United Nations, 'Peacekeeping head, briefing Security Council, reports "dramatic deterioration" in Darfur security, UN hybrid mission many month from full deployment', UN Press Briefing SC/9222, 9 Jan. 2008, <http://www.un.org/News/Press/docs/2008/sc9222.doc.htm>.

using force to disarm the militias, making it much harder for the peacekeepers to carry out one of their key mandated tasks.[37] The government also demanded veto rights on the composition of the mission, to which the AU and UN reluctantly consented. An initial list of pledged troop and police contributions was given to the government on 18 September and a final list submitted on 2 October. The government did not respond for several weeks, preventing the AU and UN from carrying out predeployment assessments of each pledged unit to establish whether it met the required standards. The government finally responded in November with objections to the inclusion of Nepalese, Thai and joint Norwegian–Swedish units, despite the fact that the list of troop contributing countries was 80 per cent African.[38] The exclusion of these units would significantly weaken UNAMID. At the same time, the Justice and Equality Movement, one of the main rebel groups, had earlier objected to the possible participation of Chinese engineering units—China is widely seen as partisan in the Darfur conflict.[39]

Besides manipulating the principles of host country consent and inclusiveness to its advantage, the Sudanese Government took other measures that openly obstructed the deployment and functioning of UNAMID. These include refusing to provide suitable land for the operation's secondary bases, proposing that the government be allowed to disable the operation's communications network when necessary for security reasons, requiring UNAMID to notify the government in advance of any troop movements, denying night-time flying rights and, in the final moments before the transfer of authority, objecting to the 're-hatting' ceremony.[40]

Some other external factors influenced UNAMID's fraught planning process. In April and May 2007 the International Criminal Court issued arrest warrants for two men— Ahmed Mohamed Harun, the Sudanese State Minister for Humanitarian Affairs, and Ali Mohamed Ali Abdel Rahman, a commander of the government-aligned Janjaweed militia—for crimes against humanity and war crimes. This created tension in Khartoum and raised fears that UNAMID would be given the authority to carry out the arrests.[41]

Two months after adopting Resolution 1769, the UN Security Council authorized a multidimensional peace operation in the neighbouring Central African Republic and Chad—MINURCAT—aimed at containing the violence spilling over from Darfur and protecting civilians. It also requested the EU to deploy a military operation in support of MINURCAT.[42] The simultaneous

[37] Caffrey, C., 'Darfur mission is facing tough task', *Jane's Defence Weekly*, 22 Aug. 2007, p. 22.

[38] Joint NGO report, *UNAMID Deployment on the Brink: The Road to Security in Darfur Blocked by Government Obstructions* (Americans Against the Darfur Genocide et al.: Dec. 2007).

[39] 'Darfur rebels spurn Chinese force', BBC News, 24 Nov. 2007, <http://news.bbc.co.uk/2/7111206. stm>.

[40] Hoge, W., 'U.N. official warns of Darfur failure', *New York Times*, 10 Jan. 2008.

[41] Saeed, S., '"UNAMID" troops' obligation to apprehend ICC suspects in Darfur', *Sudan Tribune*, 12 Feb. 2008; and Glassborow, K. and Eichstaedt, P., 'Sudan seeks to thwart UN force', Institute for War & Peace Reporting, ICC–Africa Update no. 153, 29 Jan. 2008, <http://www.iwpr.net/?p=acr&s=f& o=342303>.

[42] UN Security Council Resolution 1778, 25 Sep. 2007.

deployment of these operations and the involvement of another regional security organization had a significant impact on the planning of all three operations.

MINURCAT and EUFOR Tchad/RCA

Responding to concerns that the conflict in Darfur had extended into eastern Chad and north-eastern Central African Republic (CAR), at the request of the African Union and as called for in the IMPP guidelines, the UN dispatched a multidisciplinary assessment team to Chad and the CAR at the end of 2006 to explore the feasibility of a UN peace operation.[43]

Hostilities in the affected areas limited the team's ability to conduct its assessment, and the concept of operations the team proposed for a UN deployment was consequently set out in broad terms. The assessment team proposed that the UN could deploy either a monitoring mission or a monitoring and protection mission. Although both options would include political and civil affairs, police, human rights and humanitarian components, the second would entail a significantly larger, robust military component able to deter potential attacks on civilians and stabilize the border area. The assessment team also noted that support for the proposed UN peace operation was uneven—the Government of the CAR was considerably more positive about the idea than the Government of Chad. Based on the team's findings, Ban Ki-moon recommended that the Security Council authorize a monitoring and protection operation.[44]

A second technical assessment team was deployed in January 2007. The mission took two and a half weeks to produce detailed recommendations for the Security Council. Unlike the earlier assessment team, the technical assessment team was able to visit areas outside Bangui and N'Djamena, the capitals of the CAR and Chad, including the Wadi Fira and Ouaddai departments of eastern Chad and Vakaga prefecture in north-eastern CAR, where many Sudanese had taken refuge. More importantly, the team was able to hold consultations with a wider group of stakeholders. These included refugees and IDPs, representatives of rebel groups and local authorities in eastern Chad; security actors in the CAR; and international diplomats and humanitarian organizations in both Bangui and N'Djamena. During the discussions rebel groups in Chad warned that a UN operation could—depending on its structure and mandate—be seen as supporting the Chadian Government and hence as partisan.[45] To promote greater transparency in the planning process and ensure that any resulting UN operation should have legitimacy, the technical assessment team shared its findings and its recommendations for the make-up of the

[43] On the subregional dimensions of the conflict in Darfur see chapter 2 in this volume, section IV.

[44] United Nations, Report of the Secretary-General on Chad and the Central African Republic pursuant to paragraphs 9(d) and 13 of Security Council Resolution 1706 (2006), S/2006/1019, 22 Dec. 2006. p. 17.

[45] United Nations, Report of the Secretary-General on Chad and the Central African Republic, S/2007/97, 23 Feb. 2007.

operation with the CAR and Chadian governments and other stakeholders. Interestingly, the Security Council requested the deployment of a sizeable advance mission that could prepare the ground for an eventual multidimensional UN operation.[46]

During the ensuing discussions, the Chadian Government indicated that it would agree to the deployment of a civilian police operation but not to a UN operation with a military component.[47] Negotiations with the Chadian Government regarding the operation's structure continued into mid-2007, where with the intervention of newly appointed French Foreign Minister Bernard Kouchner, the government softened its position and agreed in principle to an EU military force in support of the UN multidimensional operation.[48] A revised proposal for the UN multidimensional operation was drawn up, with three significant changes to reflect the demands of the host countries. First, the tasks and functions of the military component would be carried out by an EU force for the first year. Second, the UN operation would not be directly involved in the border area between the CAR, Chad and Sudan. Third, Chadian police and gendarmes maintaining law and order in refugee and IDP camps inside Chad would remain under national authority and not be placed under UN command, as had been suggested in the earlier concept. However, they would be vetted, selected, trained, monitored and mentored by the UN police component and would be paid by the UN.[49]

The revised plan raised many concerns among the international humanitarian community. For example, UN humanitarian officials said that the mandate would have to be carefully drafted in order to prevent rebels being suspicious of the EU force. The EU force was associated with France, the former colonial power and perceived by some Chadian rebels as a government ally. If the rebels decided to attack the EU force, humanitarian workers in the area could be at risk. They also argued that the lack of direct involvement in the border area diminished MINURCAT's ability to provide security for people living there, including refugees and IDPs. The displaced people may even move again en masse when they realized that they were not in an internationally protected area. Finally, the decision to allow Chadian police and gendarmes to maintain law and order in the refugee and IDP camps was seen to be flawed because the population in eastern Chad had lost trust in the Chadian security forces.[50]

It was hoped that the EU planning process would be fast-tracked, with the CMC and CJA approved simultaneously in mid-September 2007, thus allow-

---

[46] United Nations, Statement by the President of the Security Council, S/PRST/2007/2, 16 Jan. 2007.

[47] Amnesty International, 'Chad: government must accept UN forces to protect civilians in East', Press release, 4 Apr. 2007; Integrated Regional Information Networks (IRIN), 'Revised plan for peacekeeping raises concern', 23 Aug. 2007, <http://www.irinnews.org/Report.aspx?ReportId=73893>; and United Nations, Report of the Secretary-General on Chad and the Central African Republic, S/2007/488, 10 Aug. 2007, p. 4.

[48] Miarom, B., 'Chad opens door to possible foreign military force', Reuters, 10 June 2007.

[49] United Nations (note 47).

[50] Integrated Regional Information Networks (note 47).

ing for possible deployment of the force by the end of October.[51] However, no agreement on the CMC or force composition had been reached by early September. The EU was struggling to obtain the necessary troop commitments from member states. One suggestion was that the bulk of the force could come from the 2400-strong Nordic Battlegroup, even though it was not due to start operational duties for the EU until January 2008. EU member states wanted guarantees that the EU force would be replaced after a year, as originally planned.[52]

When both MINURCAT and the EU force, EUFOR Tchad/RCA, received UN Security Council authorization on 25 September 2007, MINURCAT was able to deploy almost immediately. However, planning for EUFOR Tchad/RCA was still not finalized and there had been no CJA. One of the obstacles to approval of the CJA related to cost: there was disagreement as to whether the costs of airlift and the use of satellite images—which had not been used before in an EU mission—should be common costs, and thus be shared by all member states, regardless of their participation.[53] Disagreement on the concept of operations and the plan of operations also delayed deployment, as did continuing problems with force generation. By mid-December, four force-generation meetings had been held, but with little success.[54] The plans and concept were finally completed in January 2008 and deployment scheduled for mid-February.

MINURCAT's final authorized strength of 300 civilian police, 50 military liaison officers and 135 civilian staff, and the 3500 troops envisaged for EUFOR Tchad/RCA, are a far cry from the UN's initial plan to deploy up to 10 900 military and civilian personnel in the CAR and Chad.[55] The revisions to MINURCAT were made in order to obtain consent from the host governments, a necessary precondition for deployment. However, the revised plans arguably do not meet the needs on the ground, nor do they take into account the demands of the civilian population for a robust force that could offer them genuine protection.

IV. Conclusions

The case of UNAMID clearly illustrates some of the inherent difficulties in trying to make the planning and design of peace operations more needs-driven. An inclusive and transparent planning process may succeed in fostering a sense of local ownership and in satisfying some local stakeholders. How-

[51] Leopold, E., 'U.N. Council backs EU–U.N. force in Chad and CAR', Reuters, 27 Aug. 2007.

[52] Taylor, S., 'Political dissent could delay EU military mission to Chad', European Voice, 6–12 Sep. 2007, p. 2.

[53] 'EU/NATO: France seeks to forge trust between EU and NATO', Europe Diplomacy & Defence, 11 Oct. 2007.

[54] 'EU/Chad: Member States still show little interest for fate of refugees in Eastern Chad', Europe Diplomacy & Defence, 20 Dec. 2007.

[55] 'EU/Chad/CAR: EUFOR deployment continues according to schedule', Europe Diplomacy & Defence, 27 Feb. 2008.

ever, UNAMID demonstrates that such an approach can dangerously delay deployment and result in an operation that is barely capable of meeting the needs of the affected population. Inclusiveness involves listening to several stakeholders, each with their own agendas, and some—particularly governments and armed groups—able to exert greater leverage than others. Trade-offs and compromises are inevitable. The challenge is to negotiate for an operation that can fulfil its core purpose of supporting sustainable peace. The UN Under-Secretary-General for Peacekeeping, Jean-Marie Guéhenno, accurately captured the difficult question facing the UN in Darfur: 'Do we move ahead with the deployment of a force that will not make a difference, that will not have the capability to defend itself, and that carries the risk of humiliation of the Security Council and the United Nations, and tragic failure for the people of Darfur?'[56]

Similarly, the UN assessment team that visited the CAR and Chad early in the planning process, after consulting with a range of local stakeholders, found that IDPs and refugees in the border areas wanted protection by an international force, leading to Ban Ki-moon's recommendation that a robust military mission be deployed for the purpose. However, after accommodating the Chadian Government's objections, the final deployment—MINURCAT and EUFOR Tchad/RCA, unable to operate in the border area of Chad—is arguably too weak to be effective, while security for IDPs and refugees in Chad is supposed to be provided by the Chadian police and gendarmes, whose commitment to the task is questionable.

Another factor common to all three missions is the struggle to find the necessary equipment and skilled personnel. Shortfalls in expertise, tools, manpower and resources are likely to increase as the demand for peace operations grows. This raises the question of whether further adjustments are needed to planning processes, so that supply factors are also taken into account.

[56] Quoted in Hoge, W, 'U.N. official criticizes Sudan for resisting peace force in Darfur', *New York Times*, 28 Nov. 2007.

Appendix 3A. Multilateral peace operations in 2007

KIRSTEN SODER

I. Global developments

A total of 61 peace operations were conducted in 2007, two more than in 2006 and the highest number since 1999.[1] This continues a rising trend since 2002, when 48 operations were carried out (see figure 3A.1). The known costs of peace operations also continued to rise in 2007 and the number of personnel deployed to such operations reached an all-time high of 169 467.[2] This appendix draws on data collected in the SIPRI Multilateral Peace Missions Database to analyse the trends in peace operations in 2007.[3]

The number of personnel deployed to peace operations in 2007 was 2.5 per cent more than in 2006 and 60 per cent more than in 2003 (see figure 3A.2). Of the deployed personnel, 150 651 were military and 18 816 were civilian. The United Nations remained the largest actor in peacekeeping, conducting 22 operations—its largest number since 2000—deploying 90 305 personnel during 2007. The UN's police deployment reached an unprecedented high of 11 077 officers at the end of 2007. In addition, a new record of participating countries was established during 2007: 119 countries contributed troops, military observers or police. While Timor-Leste and Vanuatu withdrew their contributions, Burundi, the Democratic Republic of the Congo, Cyprus, Kazakhstan, Libya, Mauritania and Palau started to deploy personnel to UN peace operations. The North Atlantic Treaty Organization (NATO) deployed the second highest number of personnel—57 930—in three operations. NATO-led operations were supported by all member countries and by 16 non-member countries, which were responsible for about 7.5 per cent of personnel assigned to the three operations.[4] Together, UN and NATO operations accounted for more than 85 per cent of personnel deployed. The African Union (AU), with 7371 personnel in three operations, rose to third place in terms of personnel deployed. All three of these organizations increased their total personnel deployments during 2007. In contrast, at 2819 in 10 operations, the number of personnel deployed by the European Union (EU) was 5900 fewer than in 2006 and the lowest number since the EU

---

[1] In previous editions of the SIPRI Yearbook, the Multinational Force in Iraq (MNF-I) was classified as a peace operation (although its activities included counter-insurgency) and it appeared in the tables of peace operations for 2003–2006. After a review, the MNF-I has been excluded from the lists of multilateral peace operations for 2006 and 2007 because its focus has largely shifted from peacekeeping to counter-insurgency. It thus no longer met SIPRI's definition of a peace operation (see section III below). The figures for 2006 and 2007 in this appendix take account of this change.

[2] The figures for personnel deployments given in this appendix are generally estimates as of 31 Dec. 2007 or the date on which a mission closed. They do not represent maximum numbers deployed or the total of personnel deployed during the year.

[3] The SIPRI Multilateral Peace Missions Database can be accessed at <http://www.sipri.org/contents/conflict/database-Intro/>.

[4] Non-NATO member countries that contributed to NATO-led operations during 2007 were Albania, Armenia, Australia, Austria, Azerbaijan, Croatia, Finland, Georgia, Ireland, Jordan, Macedonia (Former Yugoslav Republic of), Morocco, New Zealand, Sweden, Switzerland and Ukraine .

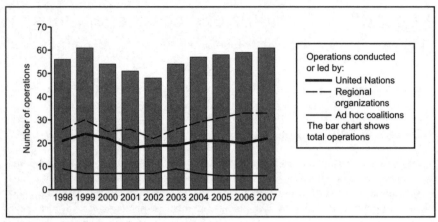

Figure 3A.1. Number of peace operations, 1998–2007

Source: SIPRI Multilateral Peace Missions Database.

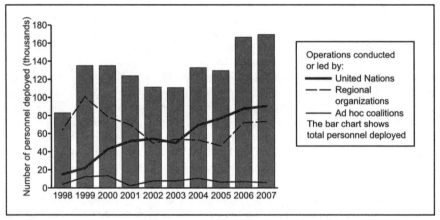

Figure 3A.2. Personnel deployments to peace operations, 1998–2007

Note: The figures for 1998 do not include civilians deployed by the United Nations.

Source: SIPRI Multilateral Peace Missions Database.

started conducting peace operations under the European Security and Defence Policy in 2003. Seven of the 10 EU operations were conducted outside Europe.

The great majority of personnel were deployed to a handful of large operations. With 41 741 troops deployed during 2007—8200 more than in 2006 and 32 800 more than in 2005—the NATO-led International Security Assistance Force (ISAF) in Afghanistan remained the largest operation in terms of personnel. The second largest, the UN Organization Mission in the Democratic Republic of the Congo (Mission des Nations Unies en République Démocratique du Congo, MONUC), deployed 19 307 personnel. The five largest operations together accounted for 62 per cent of personnel deployed in 2007; these were ISAF, MONUC, NATO's Kosovo Force (KFOR, with 16 017 personnel), the UN Mission in Liberia (UNMIL, with 15 219 personnel) and the UN Interim Force in Lebanon (UNIFIL, with 13 572 personnel).

Even greater numbers of personnel might have been deployed in 2007 had not several operations encountered significant delays and difficulties in force generation. The AU/UN Hybrid Operation in Darfur (UNAMID), which gradually incorporated the AU Mission in Sudan (AMIS) between October and the end of the year, had an authorized strength of 27 566 personnel but, due to delays in its deployment, had only reached a strength of 7008 at the end of December, including the AMIS personnel. At 1792 troops, the AU Mission in Somalia (AMISOM) also fell far short of its authorized strength of 7650, making it unable to replace Ethiopian troops in Somalia as planned. Two planned EU operations did not open in 2007 due to delays: the Rule of Law Mission in Kosovo (EULEX Kosovo) and EUFOR Tchad/RCA, a protection force in eastern Chad and north-eastern Central African Republic, which was to support UN operations in the region.[5]

In addition to difficulties in reaching their planned personnel strengths, some missions encountered shortfalls in critical equipment in 2007. For example, UNAMID sought an additional 24 helicopters and NATO considering hiring helicopters from the private sector for ISAF. The EU held five force generation conferences to obtain the necessary equipment, such as helicopters for EUFOR Tchad/RCA.[6]

The total known cost of peace operations in 2007 reached $7.1 billion (at constant (2005) prices and exchange rates). The UN, NATO and the EU accounted for $5.7 billion of this total, compared to $5.5 billion in 2006.[7]

Eight peace operations started and five ended in 2007. The UN launched four new operations. Two of these are special political and peacebuilding missions: the UN Integrated Office in Burundi (Bureau Intégré des Nations Unies au Burundi, BINUB)—a follow-on mission to the UN Operation in Burundi (Opération des Nations Unies au Burundi, ONUB)—and the UN Mission in Nepal (UNMIN). The other two are the UN Mission in the Central African Republic and Chad (Mission des Nations Unies en République centrafricaine et au Tchad, MINURCAT) and, jointly with the AU, UNAMID.

Besides UNAMID, the AU launched two new operations. The AU sent troops to Somalia under AMISOM and to the Comoros under the AU Electoral and Security Assistance Mission to the Comoros (Mission d'assistance électorale et securité, MAES). The EU launched the EU Police Mission in Afghanistan (EUPOL Afghanistan) and transformed its police mission in the Democratic Republic of the Congo, EUPOL Kinshasa, into EUPOL RD Congo, signalling the extension of the mission's mandate beyond the country's capital city.

In addition to AMIS and EUPOL Kinshasa, three operations terminated in 2007. After 16 years, the EU closed its observer mission in the Western Balkans, the EU Monitoring Mission (EUMM). The Organization of American States (OAS) closed its Special Mission for Strengthening Democracy in Haiti in 2007 and the Organization for Security and Co-operation in Europe (OSCE) closed its Mission to Croatia at the end of December 2007.

[5] EUFOR Tchad/RCA was launched on 28 Jan. 2008.

[6] United Nations, Security Council, 'Peacekeeping head, briefing Security Council, reports "dramatic deterioration" in Darfur security, UN hybrid mission many months from full deployment', Press release SC/9222, 9 Jan. 2008; 'EU/Chad: member states still show little interest for fate of refugees in eastern Chad', *Europe Diplomacy & Defense*, 20 Dec. 2007; and Jennings, G., 'Nato considers civilian helicopter solution for ISAF lift', *Jane's Defence Weekly*, 31 Oct. 2007.

[7] These figures greatly underestimate the true costs of peace operations because of gaps in the available data and the wide variety of budgetary and cost-sharing practices used in different missions. See section III below.

Table 3A.1. Number of peace operations and personnel deployed, by region, 2007

Conducting organization	Africa	Americas	Asia	Europe	Middle East	World
United Nations[a]	10	1	4	3	4	22
Regional organiza-tions or alliances	7	2	3	17	4	33
Ad hoc coalitions	1	–	3	–	2	6
Total operations	**18**	**3**	**10**	**20**	**10**	**61**
Total personnel deployed	**69 335**	**9 406**	**46 019**	**27 018**	**17 689**	**169 467**

[a] These figures comprise peace operations led by the UN Department of Peacekeeping Operations and those led by the UN Department of Political Affairs. They include the AU/UN Hybrid Operation in Darfur.

Source: SIPRI Multilateral Peace Missions Database.

II. Regional developments

Six of the eight new peace operations in 2007 were in Africa, taking the overall number of peace operations in the region to 18 (see table 3A.1), three more than in 2006. The other two were in Asia. Europe continues to be the region with the highest number of peace operations, at 20.

Most of the peace operations in Europe were conducted by regional organizations and alliances, principally the OSCE. The UN continues to be the main actor in Africa, with 10 operations—the highest number of UN peace operations in one region—and 58 076 personnel, 85 per cent of all personnel deployed in the region.

In 2007, 41 per cent of all personnel were deployed to operations in Africa. Another 27 per cent were deployed in Asia, the great majority of whom were the 41 741 troops participating in ISAF. The third largest number of personnel was deployed in Europe.

The rest of this section briefly discusses some of the significant developments in the area of peacekeeping in each world region during 2007.

Africa

The Darfur region of Sudan and the neighbouring areas of eastern Chad and north-eastern Central African Republic were the focus of attention in 2007, with the launches of UNAMID and MINURCAT and the delayed launch of EUFOR Tchad/RCA.[8] Two operations conducted by the AU elsewhere in Africa—AMISOM and MAES—had difficulty fulfilling their mandates.

AMISOM, which was tasked to support the reconciliation process and contribute to overall security in Somalia, was supposed to replace Ethiopian troops backing the Somali Transitional Federal Government in December 2006 but was unable to do so

---

[8] On the conflict in Darfur see chapter 2 in this volume, section IV. On EUFOR Tchad/RCA see chapter 3, section III.

due to the shortfall in personnel.[9] AMISOM's initial six-month mandate was renewed in August 2007, with the expectation that the operation would later be replaced by a UN operation. Like the operations in Darfur and Chad, AMISOM had to operate in a context of ongoing violence.[10]

MAES was the second AU operation deployed to the Comoros within a year. Like its predecessor, the AU Mission for Support to the Elections in the Comoros (AMISEC), MAES consisted of troops sent to monitor elections. MAES was launched in response to violence that erupted in April 2007 following the refusal of Mohamed Bacar to step down as president of the island of Anjouan despite a Comoran Supreme Court ruling that his mandate had expired. Presidential elections were held on Anjouan in June 2007, even though the AU and the Supreme Court demanded a postponement. Bacar claimed to have won 90 per cent of the votes cast, but the election was declared null and void.[11] In October 2007 MAES's mandate was expanded to include supporting the implementation of sanctions against Bacar's illegal government and disarming Anjouan's gendarmerie, along with facilitating a new round of free and fair elections. At the end of 2007 MAES troops had still not been deployed on Anjouan.

The Americas

During 2007 the OAS incorporated its Special Mission for Strengthening Democracy in Haiti into the OAS Haiti country office as part of a drive to consolidate the organization's activities in the country. The OAS Mission to Support the Peace Process in Colombia (Misión de Apoyo al Proceso de Paz de la Organización de Estados Americanos, MAPP/OEA) opened three new field offices and increased its contingent of observers in 2007. This continued a process of extending the mission's geographic coverage that began in 2006. MAPP/OEA, which is mandated to monitor and verify the demobilization, disarmament and reintegration process and law and order, now covers the whole of Colombia.

Asia

In response to continuing instability in Afghanistan, the international community redoubled its efforts to strengthen the rule of law in the country. In June 2007 the EU launched EUPOL Afghanistan, which took over from a German police reform project.[12] The mission has a three-year mandate to advise, monitor, mentor and train the Afghan National Police, and to contribute to an overall strategy on police reform. It is deployed in Kabul and alongside the regional commands and provincial reconstruction teams of ISAF. However, in its first few months the operation encountered difficulties typical of the international engagement in Afghanistan in 2007: a shortfall of

[9] On the presence of Ethiopian troops in Somalia see Lindberg, S. and Melvin, N. J., 'Major armed conflicts', *SIPRI Yearbook 2007: Armaments, Disarmament and International Security* (Oxford University Press: Oxford, 2007), pp. 72–78.

[10] See appendix 2A in this volume, section IV.

[11] Integrated Regional Information Networks (IRIN), 'Comoros: political crisis overshadows smooth elections', 25 June 2007, <http://www.irinnews.org/Report.aspx?ReportId=72917 >.

[12] In July 2007 'approximately 25 countries and several international organisations' were engaged in police reform in Afghanistan. Wilder, A., *Cops or Robbers? The Struggle to Reform the Afghan National Police* (Afghanistan Research and Evaluation Unit: Kabul, July 2007).

personnel—by the end of 2007 EUPOL Afghanistan had not reached half of its authorized strength of 195—and tensions due to the lack of a common strategy among different countries.[13]

The second new operation in Asia was UNMIN. The mission was established at the invitation of the Nepalese Government and the Communist Party of Nepal (Maoist) after the signing of the Comprehensive Peace Agreement (CPA) in November 2006.[14] It was initially given a one-year mandate and deployment began in January 2007. UNMIN's tasks include: to assist in monitoring the ceasefire agreement and in implementing and monitoring the agreement on the management of arms and armed personnel; and to support the election of an assembly to draft a new national constitution. In the first half of the year, UNMIN started to register weapons and monitor their storage. Later it oversaw the destruction of improvised explosive devices and completed the registration of Maoist personnel. The elections for the assembly had to be postponed twice due to political tensions between the parties to the CPA. They were rescheduled for April 2008. During 2007 the peace process was accompanied by rising violence among marginalized groups throughout Nepal.[15]

Europe

In 2007, 11 of the 20 peace operations in Europe were carried out in the former Yugoslavia. The EU Planning Team in Kosovo (EUPT Kosovo), established in April 2006 in preparation for an eventual EU crisis management operation in the area, was active in 2007.[16] The team, which consisted of about 80 personnel, consulted with representatives of the international community, Kosovar institutions and other local stakeholders to ensure a smooth handover of responsibilities from the UN Interim Administration Mission in Kosovo (UNMIK) to EULEX Kosovo and local institutions. This mission started at the beginning of 2008 (and hence is not included in table 3A.2), has an authorized strength of 1900 and will comprise international police, judges, prosecutors and customs officials.[17] As such, it will be the largest civilian peace operation ever conducted by the EU.

With the improved security situation in Bosnia and Herzegovina, the EU approved the reduction in EUFOR ALTHEA's troop numbers from around 6000 to about 2500 in early 2007.

---

[13] On how national attitudes affect EU deployment see Giegerich, B., 'Europe: near and far', eds D. C. F. Daniel, P. Taft and S. Wiharta, *Peace Operations: Trends, Progress, and Prospects* (Georgetown University Press: Washington, DC, forthcoming 2008).

[14] The Comprehensive Peace Agreement was signed on 21 Nov. 2006. An English translation of its text is available at <http://www.parliament.gov.np/downloads.htm>.

[15] United Nations, Report of the Secretary-General on the request of Nepal for UN assistance in support of its peace process, S/2008/5, 3 Jan. 2008.

[16] SIPRI does not classify EUPT Kosova as a peace operation and is thus not included in table 3A.2.

[17] International Civilian Office/EU Special Representative Preparation Team, EUPT Kosovo and European Commission, *European Union: Preparing for a Future International and EU Presence in Kosovo* (EU in Kosovo: [Jan. 2008]), <http://www.eupt-kosovo.eu/new/home/docs/EU_booklet ENG_ Jan 2008.pdf>.

The Middle East

The Rafah border crossing point between Egypt and the Gaza Strip was closed after Hamas took control of the Gaza Strip in June 2007. The EU Border Assistance Mission Rafah (EU BAM Rafah)—which is mandated to monitor, verify and evaluate the performance of Palestinian Authority border control, security and customs officials at the Rafah crossing point—was suspended from 13 June and its personnel contingent cut from 72 to 33. However, the EU confirmed its commitment to further supporting the Palestinian Authority by maintaining the mission's capacity to redeploy and proceed with its mandate. After 13 June EU BAM Rafah personnel worked on capacity building projects, partly in support of the EU Police Mission in the Palestinian Territories (EUPOL COPPS). EUPOL COPPS came close to reaching its authorized strength of 33 during 2007, and continued to assist the Palestinian Civil Police to establish sustainable policing arrangements.

III. Table of multilateral peace operations

Table 3A.2 provides data on the 61 multilateral peace operations that were active during 2007, including operations that terminated during the year. The table lists missions that were conducted under the authority of the United Nations and operations conducted by regional organizations and alliances or by non-standing (ad hoc) coalitions of states that were sanctioned by the UN or authorized by a UN Security Council resolution, with the stated intention to: (a) serve as an instrument to facilitate the implementation of peace agreements already in place, (b) support a peace process, or (c) assist conflict-prevention or peacebuilding efforts.

SIPRI uses the UN Department of Peacekeeping Operations (DPKO) description of peacekeeping as a mechanism to assist conflict-ridden countries to create conditions for sustainable peace. It may include monitoring and observing ceasefire agreements; serving as confidence-building measures; protecting the delivery of humanitarian assistance; assisting with the demobilization and reintegration processes; strengthening institutional capacities in the areas of judiciary and the rule of law (including penal institutions), policing, and human rights; electoral support; and economic and social development. The table thus covers a broad range of peace operations, reflecting the growing complexity of operation mandates and the potential for operations to change over time. The table does not include good offices, fact-finding or electoral assistance operations, nor does it include peace operations comprising non-resident individuals or teams of negotiators, or operations not sanctioned by the UN.[18]

The operations are grouped by the entity conducting them and listed chronologically by launch date within these groups. UN operations are divided into three groups. The first includes 16 observer and multidimensional peace operations run by the DPKO. The second includes five special political missions and peacebuilding missions. The AU/UN Hybrid Operation in Darfur is given its own group. The next seven groups include operations conducted or led by regional organizations or alliances: three by the AU; one by the Economic and Monetary Community of Central African States (Communauté Economique et Monétaire d'Afrique Centrale,

---

[18] E.g. as mediator in the conflicts in the Philippines, Malaysia has led an observer mission to monitor the ceasefire agreements between the warring parties since 2003, which is not sanctioned by the UN and is thus not included in the table.

CEMAC); three by the Commonwealth of Independent States (CIS), including two carried out by Russia under bilateral arrangements; 10 by the EU; three by NATO; two by the OAS; and 11 by the OSCE. The final group includes six UN-sanctioned operations conducted by ad hoc coalitions of states.

Missions that were initiated in 2007 and new states joining an existing mission are shown in bold type. Operations and individual state participation that ended in 2007 are shown in italic type. Designated lead states (those that either have operational control or contribute the most personnel) in missions with a military or police component are underlined.

The legal instruments underlying the establishment of an operation—UN Security Council resolutions or formal decisions by regional organizations—and the start dates for the operations (the dates of the first deployments) are given in the first column.

The figures for approved personnel numbers listed are those most recently authorized. Numbers of volunteers and locally recruited support staff are not included in the table but, where available, are given in the notes. Data on national breakdowns of civilian staff are only partially available for UN missions. Complete information on national contributions to the missions can be found in the SIPRI Multilateral Peace Missions Database.[19]

Mission fatalities since the beginning of the mission and in 2007 are reported. Causes of death—whether accidental, by hostile act or through illness—as reported during 2007 are also recorded. Causes of death have not been reported for all deaths in 2007, so these figures do not always add up to the total number of deaths in 2007.

Cost figures are presented in millions of US dollars at current prices. The budget figures given are for the calendar year of 2007, rather than for financial years, in order to allow comparison of operations. Costs for the calendar year are calculated on the assumption of an even rate of spending throughout the financial year. Budgets set in currencies other than the US dollar are converted based on the International Monetary Fund's aggregated market exchange rates for 2007.[20]

The cost figures provided for UN and OSCE operations are the amounts budgeted for the year. The figures provided for other operations represent actual spending. The cost figures presented for UN operations are the core operational costs, which include the cost of deploying personnel, per diems for deployed personnel and direct non-field support costs (e.g. requirements for the support account for peacekeeping operations and the UN logistics base in Brindisi, Italy). The costs of UN peacekeeping operations are shared by all UN member states through a specially derived scale of assessed contributions that takes no account of their participation in the missions. Special political and peacebuilding missions are funded through regular budget assessments. UN peacekeeping budgets do not cover programmatic costs, such as those for disarmament, demobilization and reintegration, which are financed by voluntary contributions.

The cost figures given for operations conducted by regional organizations and alliances, such as the EU and NATO, refer only to common costs. These include mainly the running costs of the EU and NATO headquarters (i.e. the costs for civilian personnel and operation and maintenance costs) and investment in the infrastructure necessary to support the mission. The costs of deploying personnel are borne by indi-

---

[19] SIPRI Multilateral Peace Missions Database (note 3). The database also gives full lists of mandated tasks, heads of missions and details of documentation relevant to individual missions.

[20] Details of the budgets of peace missions are available from the SIPRI Multilateral Peace Missions Database (note 3).

vidual contributing states and are not reflected in the figures given here. Most EU missions are financed in one of two ways: civilian missions are funded through the Community Budget, while military missions or missions with military components are funded through the Athena mechanism, to which only the participating member states contribute.[21]

For CIS missions there is no designated common budget and countries participating in the missions bear the costs of troop deployments. In operations conducted or led by other organizations, such as by the OAS or ad hoc coalitions, budget figures for missions may include programme implementation.

For all these reasons, budget figures presented in table 3A.2 should be viewed as estimates and the budgets for different operations should not be compared.

Unless otherwise stated, all figures in the table are as of 31 December 2007 or, in the case of operations that were terminated in 2007, the date of closure.

Data on multilateral peace operations are obtained from the following categories of open source: (a) official information provided by the secretariat of the organization concerned; (b) information provided by missions themselves, either in official publications or in written responses to annual SIPRI questionnaires; and (c) information from national governments contributing to the mission in question.[22] These primary sources are supplemented with a wide selection of publicly available secondary sources consisting of specialist journals; research reports; news agencies; and international, regional and local newspapers.

[21] The Athena mechanism is an instrument for the administration of costs that are defined as common costs. The mechanism was agreed in Council Decision 2004/197/CFSP of 23 Feb. 2004 establishing a mechanism to administer the financing of the common costs of European Union operations having military or defence implications, *Official Journal of the European Union*, L63 (28 Feb. 2004).

[22] In some instances additional information on the mission is obtained through telephone interviews by SIPRI staff.

Table 3A.2. Multilateral peace operations, 2007

Acronym/ (Legal instrument)/ Start date	Name/ Location	Countries contributing troops, military observers (Mil. obs), civilian police (Civ. pol.) or civilian staff (Civ. staff) in 2007 (bold text = new in 2007; italic text = ended in 2007; underlined text = designated lead states)	Troops/ Military observers/ Civilian police/ Civilian staff		Total deaths: to date/in 2007/ (due to hostilities, accidents, illness)	Cost ($ m.): 2007/ Unpaid
			Approved	Actual		
United Nations						
Total: 16 operations		**117 contributing countries**	**73 241** / **2 660** / **10 048** / **6 113**	**70 273** / **2 528** / **9 424** / **4 888**	**961** / **76**	**5 135.3** / **1 959.9**
UNTSO (SCR 50)[1] June 1948	UN Truce Supervision Organization / Egypt, Israel, Lebanon, Syria	Mil. obs: Argentina, Australia, Austria, Belgium, Canada, Chile, China, Denmark, Estonia, Finland, France, Ireland, Italy, Nepal, Netherlands, New Zealand, Norway, Russia, Slovakia, Slovenia, Sweden, Switzerland, USA	– / – / – / 126	– / 153 / – / 106[2]	49 / 1 / (–, –, –)	31.1 / –
UNMOGIP (SCR 91)[3] Jan. 1949	UN Military Observer Group in India and Pakistan / India, Pakistan (Kashmir)	Mil. obs: Chile, Croatia, Denmark, Finland, Italy, Korea (South), Sweden, Uruguay	– / 45 / – / 26	– / 44 / – / 254	11 / –	7.9 / –
UNFICYP (SCR 186)[5] Mar. 1964	UN Peacekeeping Force in Cyprus / Cyprus	Troops: Argentina, Austria, Canada, Croatia, Hungary, Slovakia, UK[6] Civ. pol.: Argentina, Australia, Bosnia and Herzegovina, Croatia, El Salvador, India, Ireland, Italy, Netherlands	860 / – / 69 / 41	857 / – / 66 / 37	177 / 1 / (–, 1, –)	47.2 / 22.2
UNDOF (SCR 350)[7] June 1974	UN Disengagement Observer Force / Syria	Troops: Austria, Canada, India, Japan, Nepal, Poland, Slovakia	1 047 / – / – / 44	1 047 / – / – / 40[8]	42 / –	39.8 / 24.0

Mission (SCR, start)	Full name / Location	Contributing countries	Approved	Actual	Deaths	Cost ($m.)
UNIFIL (SCR 425 and 426)[9] Mar. 1978	UN Interim Force in Lebanon — Lebanon	**Troops:** Belgium, China, **Croatia, Cyprus**, *Denmark*, Finland, France, Germany, Ghana, Greece, Guatemala, Hungary, India, Indonesia, Ireland, *Italy*, **Korea (South)**, Luxembourg, **FYROM**, Malaysia, Nepal, Netherlands, *Norway*, Poland, Portugal, Qatar, *Slovenia*, Spain, *Sweden*, **Tanzania**, Turkey **Civ. pol.:** Egypt, El Salvador	14 382; –; –; 417	13 264; –; –; 308[10]	268; 10; (6, 3, 1)	605.1; 71.0
MINURSO (SCR 690)[11] Sep. 1991	UN Mission for the Referendum in Western Sahara — Western Sahara	**Troops:** *Denmark*, Ghana, Malaysia **Mil. obs:** Argentina, Austria, Bangladesh, **Brazil**, China, Croatia, *Denmark*, **Djibouti**, Egypt, El Salvador, France, Ghana, Greece, Guinea, Honduras, Hungary, Ireland, Italy, Kenya, Malaysia, Mongolia, Nigeria, Pakistan, Poland, *Russia*, Sri Lanka, Uruguay, **Yemen**	27; 203; 6; 115	27; 183; 6; 96[12]	15; 1; (–, –, 1)	46.8; 47.3
UNOMIG (SCR 849 and 858)[13] Aug. 1993	UN Observer Mission to Georgia — Georgia (Abkhazia)	**Mil. obs:** Albania, Austria, Bangladesh, Croatia, Czech Republic, Denmark, Egypt, France, **Germany**, Greece, Hungary, Indonesia, Jordan, Korea (South), **Lithuania, Moldova, Mongolia, Nepal, Nigeria**, Pakistan, Poland, Romania, Russia, Sweden, Switzerland, Turkey, UK, Ukraine, Uruguay, USA, **Yemen** **Civ. pol.: Czech Republic**, Germany, Ghana, **Philippines**, Poland, Russia, **Sweden**, Switzerland, **Ukraine**	–; 135; 20; 116	–; 132; 18; 99[14]	11; –	34.2; 8.6
UNMIK (SCR 1244)[15] June 1999	UN Interim Administration Mission in Kosovo — Serbia (Kosovo)	**Mil. obs:** Argentina, Bangladesh, Bolivia, Bulgaria, Chile, Czech Republic, Denmark, Finland, Hungary, Ireland, *Italy*, Jordan, **Kenya**, Malawi, Malaysia, Nepal, New Zealand, Norway, Pakistan, Poland, Portugal, Romania, Russia, Spain, UK, Ukraine, Zambia **Civ. pol.:** Argentina, Austria, Bangladesh, Brazil, Bulgaria, China, Croatia, Czech Republic, Denmark, *Egypt*, Finland, France, Germany, Ghana, Greece, Hungary, India, Italy, Jordan, Kenya, Kyrgyzstan, Lithuania, **Malawi**, Nepal, *Netherlands*, Nigeria, Norway, Pakistan, Philippines, Poland, Portugal, Romania, Russia, Slovenia, Spain, Sweden, Switzerland, *Timor-Leste*, Turkey, **Uganda**, UK, Ukraine, <u>USA</u>, Zambia, Zimbabwe	–; 38; 2 078; 608	–; 39; 1 996; 468[16]	49; 3; (–, –, 3)	214.3; 126.0

Acronym/ (Legal instrument)/ Start date	Name/ Location	Countries contributing troops, military observers (Mil. obs), civilian police (Civ. pol.) or civilian staff (Civ. staff) in 2007; (bold text = new in 2007; italic text = ended in 2007; underlined text = designated lead states)	Troops/ Military observers/ Civilian police/ Civilian staff		Total deaths: to date/in 2007/ (due to hostilities, accidents, illness)	Cost ($ m.): 2007/ Unpaid
			Approved	Actual		
MONUC (SCR 1279)[17] Oct. 1999	UN Organization Mission in the Democratic Republic of the Congo / Democratic Republic of the Congo	Troops: Bangladesh, Benin, Bolivia, China, Ghana, Guatemala, _India_, Indonesia, Jordan, Malawi, Morocco, Nepal, Pakistan, Senegal, Serbia, South Africa, Tunisia, Uruguay Mil. obs: Algeria, Bangladesh, Belgium, Benin, Bolivia, Bosnia and Herzegovina, Burkina Faso, **Cameroon**, Canada, China, Czech Republic, Denmark, Egypt, France, Ghana, Guatemala, India, Indonesia, Ireland, Jordan, Kenya, Malawi, Malaysia, Mali, Mongolia, Morocco, Nepal, _Netherlands_, Niger, Nigeria, _Pakistan_, Paraguay, Peru, Poland, Romania, Russia, Senegal, South Africa, Spain, Sri Lanka, Sweden, Switzerland, Tunisia, UK, Ukraine, Uruguay, Yemen, Zambia Civ. pol.: _Argentina_, Bangladesh, Benin, Burkina Faso, Cameroon, Central African Republic, Chad, Côte d'Ivoire, Egypt, France, Guinea, India, Jordan, **Kenya**, Madagascar, Mali, Niger, Romania, Russia, Senegal, Sweden, Turkey, Ukraine, _Vanuatu_, Yemen	17 030 760 1 141 1 121	16 614 733 1 036 924[18]	117 12 (1, 2, 5)	1 105.0 683.7
UNMEE (SCR 1312)[19] July 2000	UN Mission in Ethiopia and Eritrea / Eritrea, Ethiopia	Troops: Bangladesh, _Gambia_, Ghana, India, Jordan, Kenya, Malaysia, Namibia, Nigeria, Tanzania, Tunisia, Uruguay, Zambia Mil. obs: Algeria, Austria, Bangladesh, Bolivia, Bosnia and Herzegovina, Brazil, Bulgaria, China, Croatia, Czech Republic, Denmark, Finland, France, Gambia, Germany, Greece, Guatemala, India, Iran, Jordan, Kenya, Kyrgyzstan, Malaysia, Mongolia, Namibia, Nepal, Nigeria, Norway, Pakistan, Paraguay, Peru, Poland, Romania, Russia, South Africa, Spain, **Sri Lanka**, Sweden, _Switzerland_, Tanzania, Tunisia, Ukraine, Uruguay, USA, Zambia	1 470 230 – 177	1 465 218 – 147[20]	20 3 (–, –, 1)	125.4 47.6

UNMIL (SCR 1509)[21] Nov. 2003	UN Mission in Liberia — Liberia	14 060 215 1 240 570	13 310 199 1 203 50722	101 14 (–, 1, 9)	701.6 251.6

Troops: Bangladesh, Benin, *Bolivia*, Brazil, China, Croatia, Ecuador, Ethiopia, Finland, France, *Germany*, Ghana, Ireland, Jordan, Kenya, Korea (South), *Malawi*, **Mali**, *Moldova*, Mongolia, Namibia, Nepal, Nigeria, Pakistan, **Paraguay**, **Peru**, Philippines, Senegal, *Sweden*, Togo, UK, Ukraine, USA

Mil. obs: Bangladesh, Benin, Bolivia, Bulgaria, China, Czech Republic, Denmark, Ecuador, Egypt, El Salvador, Ethiopia, Gambia, Ghana, Indonesia, Jordan, Kenya, Korea (South), Kyrgyzstan, Malaysia, Mali, Moldova, Montenegro, Namibia, Nepal, Niger, Nigeria, Pakistan, Paraguay, Peru, **Philippines**, Poland, **Romania**, Russia, Senegal, Serbia, Togo, Ukraine, USA, Zambia, **Zimbabwe**

Civ. pol.: Argentina, Bangladesh, Bosnia and Herzegovina, China, Czech Republic, **Egypt**, El Salvador, Fiji, Gambia, Germany, Ghana, **India**, Jamaica, Jordan, Kenya, Kyrgyzstan, FYROM, Malawi, Namibia, Nepal, Nigeria, Norway, Pakistan, Philippines, Poland, Russia, Rwanda, Samoa, Serbia, Sri Lanka, Sweden, Turkey, Uganda, Ukraine, Uruguay, USA, Yemen, Zambia, Zimbabwe

UNOCI (SCR 1528)[23] Apr. 2004	UN Operation in Côte d'Ivoire — Côte d'Ivoire	7 915 200 1 200 485	7 838 195 1 127 40724	36 8 (–, 4, 1)	471.9 166.8

Troops: Bangladesh, Benin, Brazil, France, Ghana, Jordan, Kenya, Morocco, Niger, Pakistan, Paraguay, Philippines, Senegal, Tanzania, Togo, Tunisia, Uganda, *Uruguay*

Mil. obs: Bangladesh, Benin, Bolivia, Brazil, Chad, China, Croatia, Dominican Republic, Ecuador, El Salvador, Ethiopia, France, Gambia, Ghana, Guatemala, Guinea, India, Ireland, Jordan, Kenya, Moldova, *Morocco*, Namibia, Nepal, Niger, Nigeria, Pakistan, Paraguay, Peru, Philippines, Poland, Romania, **Russia**, Senegal, Serbia, Tanzania, Togo, Tunisia, Uganda, Uruguay, Yemen, Zambia, Zimbabwe

Civ. pol.: Argentina, Bangladesh, Benin, **Burundi**, Cameroon, Canada, Central African Republic, Chad, **Congo (Dem. Rep. of)**, Djibouti, France, Ghana, *India*, Jordan, **Libya**, Madagascar, Niger, Nigeria, Pakistan, *Philippines*, Rwanda, Senegal, Switzerland, Togo, Turkey, Uruguay, *Vanuatu*, Yemen

Acronym/ (Legal instrument/ Start date)	Name/ Location	Countries contributing troops, military observers (Mil. obs), civilian police (Civ. pol.) or civilian staff (Civ. staff) in 2007 (bold text = new in 2007; italic text = ended in 2007; underlined text = designated lead states)	Troops/ Military observers/ Civilian police/ Civilian staff — Approved	Actual	Total deaths: to date/in 2007/ (due to hostilities, accidents, illness)	Cost ($ m.): 2007/ Unpaid
MINUSTAH (SCR 1542)25 June 2004	UN Stabilization Mission in Haiti Haiti	Troops: Argentina, Bolivia, Brazil, Canada, Chile, Croatia, Ecuador, France, Guatemala, Jordan, *Morocco*, Nepal, Pakistan, Paraguay, Peru, Philippines, Sri Lanka, Uruguay, USA Civ. pol.: Argentina, Benin, **Brazil**, Burkina Faso, Cameroon, Canada, **Central African Republic**, Chad, Chile, China, Colombia, **Congo (Dem. Rep. of)**, **Côte d'Ivoire**, **Croatia**, Egypt, El Salvador, France, **Grenada**, Guinea, Jordan, Madagascar, Mali, *Mauritius*, Nepal, Niger, Nigeria, Pakistan, Philippines, Romania, Russia, Rwanda, Senegal, *Sierra Leone*, Spain, **Sri Lanka**, Togo, Turkey, Uruguay, USA, *Vanuatu*, *Yemen*, *Zambia*	7 200 — 1 951 540	7 047 — 1 826 49826	33 8 (–, 2, 2)	512.3 164.8
UNMIS (SCR 1590)27 Mar. 2005	UN Mission in Sudan Sudan	Troops: Australia, Bangladesh, **Bolivia**, Cambodia, Canada, China, Croatia, Denmark, Egypt, Finland, **France**, **Gambia**, Germany, *Ghana*, Greece, **Guatemala**, India, **Italy**, Jordan, Kenya, Korea (South), Malawi, Malaysia, Nepal, Netherlands, New Zealand, Niger, Nigeria, Norway, Pakistan, Russia, Rwanda, **Senegal**, South Africa, Sweden, Tanzania, **Thailand**, Turkey, UK, **Yemen**, Zambia, Zimbabwe Mil. obs: Australia, Bangladesh, Belgium, Benin, Bolivia, Botswana, Brazil, Burkina Faso, Cambodia, Canada, China, Denmark, Ecuador, Egypt, El Salvador, Fiji, Gabon, Germany, Greece, Guatemala, Guinea, India, Indonesia, Jordan, Kenya, Korea (South), Kyrgyzstan, Malawi, Malaysia, Mali, Moldova, Mongolia, Mozambique, Namibia, Nepal, Netherlands, New Zealand, Nigeria, Norway, Pakistan, Paraguay, Peru, Philippines, Poland, Romania, Russia, Rwanda, **Sri Lanka**, Sweden, Tanzania, Thailand, Uganda, Ukraine, Yemen, Zambia, Zimbabwe	9 250 750 715 1 130	8 804 596 637 86428	30 14 (2, 2, 6)	962.9 283.0

UNMIT (SCR 1704)[29] Aug. 2006	UN Integrated Mission in Timor-Leste Timor-Leste	Civ. pol.: Argentina, Australia, Bangladesh, Bosnia and Herzegovina, **Botswana**, Brazil, Canada, China, Denmark, Egypt, El Salvador, Fiji, Finland, Gambia, Germany, Ghana, India, **Indonesia**, Jamaica, Jordan, *Kenya*, Kyrgyzstan, Malaysia, **Mali**, Namibia, Nepal, Netherlands, **New Zealand**, Nigeria, Norway, Pakistan, Philippines, Russia, Rwanda, Samoa, Sri Lanka, Sweden, *Tanzania*, Turkey, Uganda, **UK**, Ukraine, Uruguay, USA, *Vanuatu*, Yemen, Zambia, Zimbabwe	– 34 1 328 462	–[30] 33 1 480 336[31]	2 1 (–, –, –)	169.0 63.3
		Mil. obs: Australia, Bangladesh, Brazil, China, Fiji, Malaysia, New Zealand, Pakistan, Philippines, Portugal, **Sierra Leone,** Singapore				
		Civ. pol.: Australia, Bangladesh, Brazil, Canada, **China**, Croatia, **Egypt,** El Salvador, Gambia, India, **Jamaica, Japan,** *Jordan,* Korea (South), Kyrgyzstan, Malaysia, **Namibia,** Nepal, New Zealand, **Nigeria,** Pakistan, **Palau,** Philippines, Portugal, Romania, Russia, Samoa, **Senegal,** Singapore, Spain, Sri Lanka, Sweden, Thailand, Turkey, **Uganda, Ukraine,** Uruguay, *USA, Vanuatu,* Yemen, **Zambia,** Zimbabwe				
MINURCAT (SCR 1778)[32] Sep. 2007	UN Mission in the Central African Republic and Chad Central African Republic/Chad	**Mil. obs: France, Senegal, Sweden** **Civ. pol.: Cameroon, Côte d'Ivoire, France, Madagascar, Mali, Niger, Senegal, Togo**	– 50 300 135	– 3 29 26	– –	60.8 –

Acronym/ (Legal instrument)/ Start date	Name/ Location	Countries contributing troops, military observers (Mil. obs), civilian police (Civ. pol.) or civilian staff (Civ. staff) in 2007 (bold text = new in 2007; italic text = ended in 2007; underlined text = designated lead states)	Troops/ Military observers/ Civilian police/ Civilian staff — Approved	Actual	Total deaths: to date/in 2007/ (due to hostilities, accidents, illness)	Cost ($ m.): 2007
United Nations political and peacebuilding missions						
Total: 5 operations	**133 contributing countries**		**298** **202** **53** **1 246**	**223** **196** **36** **1 108**	**21** **9**	**416.8**
UNAMA (SCR 1401)[33] Mar. 2002	UN Assistance Mission in Afghanistan — Afghanistan	Mil. obs: Australia, *Austria*, Bangladesh, **Bolivia**, Denmark, Germany, Korea (South), **Lithuania**, New Zealand, **Norway**, **Paraguay**, *Poland*, Romania, **Sweden**, **UK**, Uruguay Civ. pol.: Nepal, Nigeria, Philippines Civ. staff: Argentina, Australia, Austria, **Bahamas**, Bangladesh, **Barbados**, **Belarus**, **Bhutan**, Bosnia and Herzegovina, Brazil, Bulgaria, **Cameroon**, Canada, China, **Colombia**, Congo (Dem. Rep. of), Croatia, Czech Republic, Denmark, Egypt, El Salvador, **Ethiopia**, Fiji, Finland, France, **Gambia**, Germany, Ghana, *Guatemala*, Honduras, India, Iran, Iraq, Ireland, Italy, Jamaica, Japan, *Jordan*, **Kazakhstan**, Kenya, Korea (South), Kyrgyzstan, Laos, **Latvia**, Liberia, FYROM, Malaysia, Myanmar, Nepal, Netherlands, New Zealand, **Nigeria**, Norway, Pakistan, Peru, Philippines, Poland, Romania, Russia, Rwanda, Serbia, Sierra Leone, South Africa, Spain, Sri Lanka, Sudan, Sweden, Tajikistan, **Tanzania**, Thailand, Trinidad and Tobago, Tunisia, Uganda, UK, Ukraine, USA, Uzbekistan, Zimbabwe	– 18 3 283	– 15 3 234[34]	10 5 (–, 1, 1)	74.2
UNAMI (SCR 1500)[35] Aug. 2003	UN Assistance Mission in Iraq — Iraq	Troops: Fiji Mil. obs: Australia, Canada, Denmark, New Zealand, UK Civ. staff: Afghanistan, **Angola**, **Argentina**, Australia, Austria, Bangladesh, Barbados, Bosnia and Herzegovina, **Bulgaria**, Canada, Congo (Dem. Rep. of), Croatia, Czech Republic, Denmark, Ecuador, Egypt, Estonia, Ethiopia, Fiji, Finland, France, Germany, Ghana,	298 8 – 463	223 7 – 454[36]	7 3 (–, –, 1)	176.5

Greece, **Hungary**, India, **Indonesia**, Iran, Ireland, Israel, Italy, Jamaica, Japan, Jordan, Kenya, Korea (South), Kuwait, Kyrgyzstan, Lebanon, **Liberia**, FYROM, Morocco, *Myanmar*, Nepal, Netherlands, New Zealand, Nigeria, Pakistan, Palestinian Territory, Peru, Philippines, Poland, **Romania**, Russia, **Rwanda**, Senegal, **Serbia**, Sierra Leone, Singapore, Somalia, South Africa, Spain, Sri Lanka, Sudan, Sweden, Syria, Tajikistan, Tanzania, Thailand, Trinidad and Tobago, Tunisia, Uganda, UK, Uruguay, USA, **Uzbekistan**

UNIOSIL[37] Jan. 2006	UN Integrated Office in Sierra Leone		–	–	4	32.3
	Sierra Leone		14	14	1	
			29	21	(–, –, –)	
			89	76[38]		

Mil. obs: Bangladesh, **China**, **Croatia**, **Egypt**, Ghana, Kenya, Nepal, Nigeria, Pakistan, *Russia*, **Sweden**, UK, Zambia

Civ. pol.: Gambia, Ghana, India, Kenya, *Malaysia*, Nepal, <u>Nigeria</u>, *Norway*, Portugal, **Spain**, Sweden, Turkey, UK

Civ. staff: *Afghanistan*, Angola, Barbados, **Belgium**, *Bhutan*, Bulgaria, **Burkina Faso**, Burundi, Cameroon, Canada, China, Congo (Dem. Rep. of), Croatia, *Egypt*, Ethiopia, Fiji, Finland, **France**, Germany, Ghana, *Honduras*, India, *Italy*, Jamaica, *Japan*, Kenya, **Lebanon**, Liberia, **FYROM**, Malawi, Nepal, Nigeria, Pakistan, Palestinian Territory, Philippines, Poland, Portugal, *Rwanda*, Senegal, **Serbia**, **Spain**, Sudan, *Swaziland*, Sweden, Trinidad and Tobago, **Turkey**, *Uganda*, UK, USA, Zimbabwe

BINUB (SCR 1719)[39] Jan. 2007	**UN Integrated Office in Burundi**		–	–	–	38.2
	Burundi		7	8	–	
			14	12		
			141	122[40]		

Mil. obs: Bangladesh, Croatia, Netherlands, Niger, Pakistan, South Africa, Switzerland, Tunisia

Civ. pol.: Benin, Burkina Faso, Cameroon, Côte d'Ivoire, Madagascar, Turkey

Civ. staff: Albania, Angola, Austria, Bahamas, Barbados, Belgium, Benin, Bosnia and Herzegovina, Burkina Faso, Cambodia, Cameroon, Canada, Congo (Dem. Rep. of), Congo (Rep. of), Côte d'Ivoire, Croatia, Djibouti, Dominican Republic, Egypt, Eritrea, Ethiopia, Fiji, France, Germany, Ghana, Guatemala, Guinea, Haiti, Honduras, India, Italy, Kenya, Lebanon, Liberia, Mauritania, Mauritius, Morocco, Niger, Nigeria, Pakistan, Peru, Philippines, Portugal, Russia, Rwanda, Senegal, Sierra Leone, Switzerland, Tanzania, Togo, Trinidad and Tobago, Tunisia, UK, Ukraine, USA, Zambia, Zimbabwe

Acronym/ (Legal instrument)/ Start date	Name/ Location	Countries contributing troops, military observers (Mil. obs), civilian police (Civ. pol.) or civilian staff (Civ. staff) in 2007 (bold text = new in 2007; italic text = ended in 2007; underlined text = designated lead states)	Troops/ Military observers/ Civilian police/ Civilian staff		Total deaths: to date/in 2007/ (due to hostilities, accidents, illness)	Cost ($ m.): 2007
			Approved	Actual		
UNMIN (SCR 1740)[41] Jan. 2007	United Nations Mission in Nepal Nepal	Mil. obs: Austria, Bolivia, Brazil, Croatia, Denmark, Ecuador, Egypt, Finland, Gambia, Ghana, Guatemala, Indonesia, Japan, Jordan, Kazakhstan, Korea (South), Malaysia, Nigeria, Norway, Paraguay, Romania, Russia, Sierra Leone, Singapore, South Africa, Sweden, Switzerland, Thailand, UK, Uruguay, Yemen, Zambia, Zimbabwe Civ. pol.: *Malaysia, Philippines, Singapore, Switzerland* Civ. staff: Afghanistan, Algeria, Argentina, Australia, Austria, Barbados, Benin, Bolivia, Bosnia and Herzegovina, Cambodia, Cameroon, Canada, Chile, Côte d'Ivoire, Croatia, Cuba, Denmark, El Salvador, Eritrea, Ethiopia, Fiji, Finland, France, Germany, Ghana, Guatemala, Guyana, Haiti, Honduras, Hungary, Iceland, India, Indonesia, Iran, Iraq, Ireland, Israel, Italy, Jamaica, Japan, Jordan, Kenya, Liberia, Lithuania, FYROM, Madagascar, Malaysia, Mali, Moldova, Morocco, Myanmar, Netherlands, New Zealand, Nigeria, Norway, Pakistan, Palestinian Territory, Peru, Philippines, Portugal, Romania, Russia, Rwanda, San Marino, Serbia, Sierra Leone, Slovakia, South Africa, Spain, Sri Lanka, Sudan, Sweden, Switzerland, Syria, Tajikistan, Thailand, Trinidad and Tobago, Turkey, Uganda, UK, Ukraine, Uruguay, USA, Venezuela, Zambia	155 7 270	– 152 222[42]	– –	95.6
African Union–United Nations						
Total: 1 mission		34 contributing countries	19 315 240 6 432 1 579	12 – 1 617 –	– –	318.9

UNAMID (AU, 22 June 2007/ SCR 1769)[43] Oct. 2007[44]	African Union/UN Hybrid Operation in Darfur Sudan (Darfur)	**Troops: China, Egypt, France, Nigeria, Rwanda, Senegal, UK** **Civ. pol.: Bangladesh, Botswana, Burkina Faso, Cameroon, Canada, Egypt, Finland, Gambia, Germany, Ghana, Jordan, Kenya, Madagascar, Malaysia, Mali, Mauritania, Mauritius, Nepal, Niger, Nigeria, Rwanda, Senegal, Sierra Leone, South Africa, Sweden, Tanzania, Turkey, Uganda, Uruguay, Zambia**	**19 315** **240** **6 432** **1 579**	**12** **–** **1 617**[45] **–**	**–** **–**	**492.6**
African Union **Total: 3 operations**		**31 contributing countries**	**13 821** **450** **1 560** **–**	**6 675** **636** **–** **60**	**65** **5**	**312.8**
AMIS (AU, 28 May 2004)[46] June 2004	*African Union Mission in Sudan* *Sudan*	*Troops: Chad, Gambia, Kenya, Nigeria, Rwanda, Senegal, South Africa* *Mil. obs: Algeria, Benin, Botswana, Burkina Faso, Burundi, Cameroon, Chad, Congo (Rep. of), Egypt, Gabon, Gambia, Ghana, Kenya, Lesotho, Libya, Madagascar, Malawi, Mali, Mauritania, Mozambique, Namibia, Nigeria, Rwanda, Senegal, South Africa, Togo, Uganda, Zambia* *Civ. pol.: Botswana, Burkina Faso, Cameroon, Egypt, Gambia, Ghana, Kenya, Lesotho, Madagascar, Mali, Mauritania, Niger, Nigeria, Rwanda, Senegal, South Africa, Uganda, Zambia[47]*	*6 171* *450* *1 560* *–*	*4 683* *636* *–* *60*	*60* *>21* *(21, –, –)*	*280.8*[48]
AMISOM (AU, 19 Jan. 2007)[49] Mar. 2007	African Union Mission in Somalia Somalia	**Troops: Burundi, Uganda**	**7 650** **–** **–** **–**	**1 792**[50] **–** **–** **–**	**5** **5** **(4, 1, –)**	**32.0**[51]
MAES (AU, 9 May 2007)[52] May 2007	*AU Electoral and Security Assistance Mission to the Comoros* *Comoros*	*Troops: Sudan, Tanzania[53]*	*200* *–* *–* *–*	*–* *–* *–* *–*	*–* *–*	*..*

Acronym/ (Legal instrument)/ Start date	Name/ Location	Countries contributing troops, military observers (Mil. obs), civilian police (Civ. pol.) or civilian staff (Civ. staff) in 2007 (bold text = new in 2007; italic text = ended in 2007; underlined text = designated lead states)	Troops/ Military observers/ Civilian police/ Civilian staff		Total deaths: to date/in 2007/ (due to hostilities, accidents, illness)	Cost ($ m.): 2007
			Approved	Actual		
Economic and Monetary Community of Central African States (CEMAC)						
Total: 1 mission		**3 contributing countries**	**500**	**379**	**8**	**18.5**
			–	–	–	
			–	–		
			–	–		
FOMUC (Libreville Summit, 2 Oct. 2002)[54] Jan. 2003	CEMAC Multinational Force in the Central African Republic / Central African Republic	Troops: Chad, Congo (Rep. of), Gabon[55]	500	379[56]	8	18.5
			–	–	–	
			–	–		
			–	–		
Commonwealth of Independent States (CIS)						
Total: 3 operations		**4 contributing countries**	**6 000**	**4 274**	..	..
			–	–	..	
			–	–		
			–	–		
(Bilateral, 21 July 1992)[57] July 1992	Joint Control Commission Peacekeeping Force / Moldova (Trans-Dniester)	Troops: Moldova, Russia, (Trans-Dniester) Mil. obs: Ukraine	1 500	1 174	..	..
			–	–	..	
			–	–		
(Bilateral, 24 June 1992)[58] July 1992	South Ossetia Joint Force / Georgia (South Ossetia)	Troops: Georgia, Russia, (South Ossetia)	1 500	1 500	..	..
			–	–	..	
			–	–		

Name / Legal instrument / Start date	Location	Contributing countries	Troops	Mil. obs. / Civ. pol. / Civ. staff	No. of deaths	Cost (US$ m.)
— (CIS, 15 Oct, 1994)[59] June 1994	CIS Peacekeeping Forces in Georgia, Georgia (Abkhazia)	Troops: Russia	3 000	1 600	..	..
Total: 10 operations	**European Union (EU)**	**41 contributing countries**	**2 500** **120** **372** **28**	**2 261** **48** **355** **155**	**21** **2**	**147.7**
EUMM (Brioni Agreement, 7 July 1991)[60] July 1991	*EU Monitoring Mission Western Balkans*	*Mil. obs: Austria, Finland, France, Germany, Greece, Ireland, Netherlands, Norway, Slovakia, Spain, Sweden, UK*	*120*	*–* *48* *–61*	*11* *–*	*3.2*
EUPM (CJA 2002/ 210/CFSP)[62] Jan. 2003	EU Police Mission in Bosnia and Herzegovina Bosnia and Herzegovina	Civ. pol.: Austria, Belgium, Bulgaria, Canada, *Cyprus*, Czech Republic, Denmark, Estonia, Finland, France, <u>Germany</u>, **Greece**, Hungary, **Iceland**, Ireland, Italy, Latvia, Lithuania, Luxembourg, Malta, Netherlands, Norway, *Poland*, Portugal, Romania, Slovakia, Slovenia, Spain, Sweden, Switzerland, Turkey, UK, Ukraine Civ. staff: Belgium, Bulgaria, France, Germany, Ireland, Italy, *Netherlands*, Norway, Portugal, Spain, **Sweden**, Turkey, UK, Ukraine	– – –	– – 173 2863	3 –	16.7
EUFOR ALTHEA (CJA 2004/ 570/CFSP)[64] Dec. 2004	EU Military Operation in Bosnia and Herzegovina Bosnia and Herzegovina	Troops: Albania, Austria, Belgium, Bulgaria, *Canada*, Chile, Czech Republic, Estonia, Finland, France, Germany, Greece, Hungary, Ireland, Italy, Latvia, Lithuania, Luxembourg, FYROM, *Morocco*, Netherlands, *New Zealand*, Norway, Poland, Portugal, Romania, Slovakia, Slovenia, <u>Spain</u>, Sweden, Switzerland, Turkey, UK[65]	2 500 – –	2 261 – 3066	6 1 (–, –, 1)	45.2

Acronym/ (Legal instrument)/ Start date	Name/ Location	Countries contributing troops, military observers (Mil. obs), civilian police (Civ. pol.) or civilian staff (Civ. staff) in 2007 (bold text = new in 2007; italic text = ended in 2007; underlined text = designated lead states)	Troops/ Military observers/ Civilian police/ Civilian staff		Total deaths: to date/in 2007/ (due to hostilities, accidents, illness)	Cost ($ m.): 2007
			Approved	Actual		
EUPOL Kinshasa (CJA 2004/ 847/CFSP)[67] Apr. 2005	EU Police Mission in Kinshasa (DRC) Democratic Republic of the Congo	Civ. pol.: Angola, **Belgium**, Canada, Denmark, _France_, Italy, Mali, Portugal, Romania, **Spain**, Sweden, Turkey Civ. staff: Belgium, France, Portugal, **Sweden**	– / 30 / –	– / 25 / 468	– / –	2.8
EUSEC DR Congo (CJA 2005/ 355/CFSP)[69] June 2005	EU Advisory and Assistance Mission for DRC Security Reform Democratic Republic of the Congo	Civ. staff: Austria, _Belgium_, **Cyprus**, _France_, Germany, Hungary, **Italy**, Luxembourg, Netherlands, Portugal, Sweden, UK	– / – / –	– / – / 46[70]	1 / 1 / (–, –, 1)	9.4
EUJUST LEX (CJA 2005/ 190/CFSP)[71] July 2005[72]	EU Integrated Rule of Law Mission for Iraq Iraq	Civ. staff: **Belgium**, **Bulgaria**, Denmark, **Finland**, France, Germany, **Hungary**, **Ireland**, Italy, Lithuania, **Luxembourg**, Netherlands, Poland, _Portugal_, **Romania**, Spain, **Sweden**, UK[73]	– / – / 28	– / – / 26	– / –	8.1
EU BAM Rafah (CJA 2005/ 889/CFSP)[74] Oct. 2005	EU Border Assistance Mission for the Rafah Crossing Point Rafah Crossing Point	Civ. pol.: Belgium, Denmark, Finland, France, Germany, Greece, Italy, _Luxembourg_, Netherlands, _Portugal_, Romania, Spain, _Sweden_ Civ. staff: _Estonia_, **Germany**, Italy, _Portugal_, Spain, UK	– / 75 / –	– / 28 / 575	– / –	14.3
EUPOL COPPS (CJA 2005/ 797/CFSP)[76] Jan. 2006	EU Police Mission in the Palestinian Territories Palestinian territories	Civ. pol.: **Austria**, Belgium, **Czech Republic**, Denmark, Finland, France, Germany, **Greece**, _Ireland_, Italy, Portugal, Sweden, UK Civ. staff: **Austria**, Estonia, **Italy**, **Spain**, Sweden, UK	– / 33 / –	– / 19 / 7	– / –	3.3

Acronym / Legal instrument / Start date	Name / Location	Contributing countries				Cost
EUPOL Afghanistan (CJA 2007/369/CFSP)[77] June 2007	EU Police Mission in Afghanistan[78]	Civ. pol.: Belgium, *Bulgaria*, Canada, Croatia, Czech Republic, Denmark, Estonia, Finland, France, **Germany**, Ireland, Italy, Latvia, Lithuania, Netherlands, *Norway*, Romania, Spain, Sweden, UK	– / 195 / –	– / 85[79] / –	– / –	40.9
EUPOL RD Congo (CJA 2007/405/CFSP)[80] July 2007	EU Police Mission in the Democratic Republic of the Congo Democratic Republic of the Congo	Civ. pol.: Belgium, France, Italy, **Portugal**, Romania, Spain Civ. staff: Belgium, Finland, France, Germany, Portugal, Sweden	– / 39 / –	– / 25 / 9[81]	– / –	3.8
North Atlantic Treaty Organization (NATO) and NATO-led						
Total: 3 operations	44 contributing countries		17 300 / – / – / –	57 868 / – / – / 62	456 / 173	263.7
KFOR (SCR 1244)[82] June 1999	NATO Kosovo Force Serbia (Kosovo)	Troops: *Argentina*, Armenia, Austria, Azerbaijan, Belgium, Bulgaria, Czech Republic, Denmark, Estonia, Finland, France, Georgia, Germany, Greece, Hungary, Ireland, Italy, Latvia, Lithuania, Luxembourg, *Mongolia*, Morocco, Netherlands, Norway, Poland, Portugal, Romania, Slovakia, Slovenia, Spain, Sweden, Switzerland, Turkey, UK, **Ukraine**, USA	17 000 / – / – / –	15 967[83] / – / 50	127 / 14 / (–, 8, 3)	37.1
ISAF (SCR 1386)[84] Dec. 2001	International Security Assistance Force Afghanistan	Troops: Albania, Australia, Austria, Azerbaijan, Belgium, Bulgaria, Canada, Croatia, Czech Republic, Denmark, Estonia, Finland, France, **Germany**, Greece, Hungary, Iceland, Ireland, Italy, **Jordan**, Latvia, Lithuania, Luxembourg, FYROM, Netherlands, New Zealand, Norway, Poland, Portugal, Romania, Slovakia, Slovenia, Spain, Sweden, Switzerland, Turkey, UK, USA[85]	– / – / –	41 741[86] / – / –	329 / 159 / (144, –, –)[87]	203.2
NTM-I (SCR 1546)[88] Aug. 2004	NATO Training Mission in Iraq Iraq	Troops: Bulgaria, Czech Republic, Denmark, Estonia, Hungary, *Iceland*, Italy, Lithuania, Netherlands, *Norway*, Poland, Portugal, Romania, *Slovakia*, Slovenia, Turkey, UK, Ukraine, USA[89]	300 / – / –	160 / – / 12	– / –	23.4

Acronym/ (Legal instrument)/ Start date	Name/ Location	Countries contributing troops, military observers (Mil. obs), civilian police (Civ. pol.) or civilian staff (Civ. staff) in 2007 (bold text = new in 2007; italic text = ended in 2007; underlined text = designated lead states)	Troops/ Military observers/ Civilian police/ Civilian staff — Approved	Actual	Total deaths: to date/in 2007/ (due to hostilities, accidents, illness)	Cost ($ m.): 2007
Organization of American States (OAS)						
Total: 2 operations		**20 contributing countries**	– 6 22	– – 35	**1** **–**	**9.4**
MAPP/OEA (CP/RES. 859)90 Feb. 2004	Mission to Support the Peace Process in Colombia / Colombia	Civ. staff: **Argentina, Bolivia, Brazil, Chile, Costa Rica, Ecuador, Guatemala, Italy, Lithuania,** Mexico, **Nicaragua, Peru, Spain,** Sweden, **Uruguay**	– – –	– – 3591	– –	9.4
– (CP/RES. 806)92 June 2004	*OAS Special Mission for Strengthening Democracy in Haiti* / *Haiti*	*Civ. pol.: Benin, France* *Civ. staff: Argentina, Benin, Bolivia, Canada, Dominica, Ecuador, France, Grenada, Mexico, Peru*	– 6 22	–	*1* –	..
Organization for Security and Co-operation in Europe (OSCE)						
Total: 11 operations		**46 contributing countries**	– – 226	– – 531	**12** **5**	**130.4**
– (CSO 18 Sep. 1992)93 Sep. 1992	OSCE Spillover Monitor Mission to Skopje / Former Yugoslav Republic of Macedonia	Civ. staff: Austria, Azerbaijan, Belarus, *Belgium*, Bosnia and Herzegovina, Canada, Croatia, France, Georgia, Germany, Hungary, Ireland, Italy, Japan, *Netherlands*, Norway, *Poland*, **Portugal**, Romania, Russia, Slovenia, Spain, Sweden, Turkey, UK, Ukraine, USA, *Uzbekistan*	– – 92	– – 6894	1 1 (–, –, 1)	13.4

Legislative authority / Dates	Name / Location	Civ. staff (contributing states)			Deaths	Cost
— (CSO 6 Nov. 1992)[95] Dec. 1992	OSCE Mission to Georgia Georgia	Civ. staff: Austria, **Belarus**, Bosnia and Herzegovina, Bulgaria, Canada, Czech Republic, Estonia, Finland, France, Germany, Hungary, *Ireland, Lithuania, FYROM*, Poland, Romania, Russia, Slovakia, **Spain**, *Turkey*, UK, Ukraine, USA	64	39[96] —	—	13.9
— (CSO 4 Feb. 1993)[97] Apr. 1993	OSCE Mission to Moldova Moldova	Civ. staff: *Belarus*, **Bulgaria**, **Czech Republic**, **Estonia**, France, Germany, *Italy*, Norway, Poland, *Slovakia*, UK, USA	10	13[98] —	—	2.6
— (Rome MC Decision, no. 4.1, 1 Dec. 1993)[99] Feb. 1994	OSCE Centre in Dushanbe Tajikistan	Civ. staff: *Belarus*, Bulgaria, Denmark, Germany, Italy, Lithuania, *Moldova*, Norway, **Romania**, Russia, UK, Ukraine, USA	17	16[100] —	2 2 (–, 2, –)	5.4 –
— (10 Aug. 1995)[101] Aug. 1995	Personal Representative of the Chairman-in-Office on the Conflict Dealt with by the OSCE Minsk Conference Azerbaijan (Nagorno-Karabakh)	Civ. staff: Czech Republic, *Germany*, Hungary, Kazakhstan, Poland, UK	6	6[102] —	—	1.4 –
— (MC, 8 Dec. 1995)[103] Dec. 1995	OSCE Mission to Bosnia and Herzegovina Bosnia and Herzegovina	Civ. staff: Armenia, Austria, Azerbaijan, *Belgium*, Bulgaria, Canada, Croatia, Czech Republic, Finland, France, Germany, Greece, Hungary, Ireland, Italy, Kyrgyzstan, Netherlands, Norway, Romania, Russia, Slovakia, Slovenia, Spain, Sweden, Switzerland, Tajikistan, Turkey, UK, USA	—	75[104] —	—	22.7
(PC.DEC 112, 18 Apr. 1996)[105] July 1996	*OSCE Mission to Croatia Croatia*	*Civ. staff: Austria, Czech Republic, Estonia, France, Germany, Greece, Italy, Lithuania, Moldova, Netherlands, Poland, Romania, Slovakia, Spain, Sweden, UK, USA, Uzbekistan*	—	10[106] —	—	9.8

Acronym/ (Legal instrument)/ Start date	Name/ Location	Countries contributing troops, military observers (Mil. obs), civilian police (Civ. pol.) or civilian staff (Civ. staff) in 2007 (bold text = new in 2007; italic text = ended in 2007; underlined text = designated lead states)	Troops/ Military observers/ Civilian police/ Civilian staff		Total deaths: to date/in 2007/ (due to hostilities, accidents, illness)	Cost ($ m.): 2007
			Approved	Actual		
— (PC.DEC 160, 27 Mar. 1997)[107] Apr. 1997	OSCE Presence in Albania Albania	Civ. staff: Austria, Bulgaria, Czech Republic, Finland, France, **Germany**, *Ireland*, Italy, Latvia, Lithuania, Netherlands, **Poland**, Romania, **Spain**, Turkey, UK, USA	— — —	— — 32[108]	— —	5.1
OMIK (PC.DEC 305, 1 July 1999)[109] July 1999	OSCE Mission in Kosovo Serbia (Kosovo)	Civ. staff: *Albania*, Armenia, Austria, Azerbaijan, Belgium, Bosnia and Herzegovina, Bulgaria, Canada, Croatia, Czech Republic, Denmark, **Estonia**, **Finland**, France, *Georgia*, Germany, Greece, Hungary, Ireland, Italy, *Japan*, Lithuania, **FYROM**, Moldova, Netherlands, Norway, Poland, Portugal, Romania, Russia, **Montenegro**, Slovakia, Spain, Sweden, Switzerland, Tajikistan, Turkey, UK, **Ukraine**, USA, Uzbekistan	— — —	— — 219[110]	9 2 (–, 1, 1)	42.9
— (PC.DEC 401, 11 Jan. 2001)[111] Mar. 2001	OSCE Mission to Serbia Serbia	Civ. staff: **Austria**, *Belgium, Bosnia and Herzegovina, Bulgaria,* Canada, Croatia, Czech Republic, *Denmark,* Estonia, Georgia, Germany, *Hungary,* Ireland, Italy, Moldova, Netherlands, Norway, Portugal, *Slovakia,* **Slovenia**, Sweden, Turkey, UK, USA	— — 37	— — 39[112]	— —	10.3
— (PC.DEC 732, 29 June 2006)[113] June 2006	OSCE Mission to Montenegro Montenegro	Civ. staff: **Austria**, *Bosnia and Herzegovina*, Bulgaria, Germany, *Ireland*, Italy, *Netherlands*, Norway, Romania, **Slovenia**, Sweden, Turkey, UK, USA	— — —	— — 14[114]	— —	3.0

Ad-hoc coalitions

Total: 6 operations	27 contributing countries	3 000 / 2 000 / – / 15	3 564 / 1 704 / 327 / 218	89 / 13	550.8–619.3
NNSC (Armistice Agreement, 27 July 1953)[15] North Korea, South Korea; July 1953	Neutral Nations Supervisory Commission. Mil. obs: Sweden, Switzerland	– / – / –	– / 10 / –	– / –	2.4
MFO (Protocol to Treaty of Peace, 3 Aug. 1981)[16] Egypt (Sinai); Apr. 1982	Multinational Force and Observers. Mil. obs: Australia, Canada, Colombia, Fiji, France, Hungary, Italy, New Zealand, Norway, Uruguay, USA; Civ. staff: USA	2 000 / 15[117]	1 691 / 15[118]	59 / 10 / (–, 10, –)	66.8
TIPH 2 (Hebron Protocol, 21 Jan. 1997)[119] Hebron; Jan. 1997	Temporary International Presence in Hebron. Mil. obs: Turkey; Civ. pol.: Denmark, Italy, Norway; Civ. staff: Denmark, Norway, Sweden, Switzerland, Turkey[120]		– / 3 / 21 / 34[121]	2 / –	2.4
Operation Licorne (SCR 1464)[122] Côte d'Ivoire; Feb. 2003	Troops: France	3 000 / – / – / –	2 400[123] / – / – / –	24 / 1 / (–, 1, –)	205.7–274.2

Acronym/ (Legal instrument)/ Start date	Name/ Location	Countries contributing troops, military observers (Mil. obs), civilian police (Civ. pol.) or civilian staff (Civ. staff) in 2007; (bold text = new in 2007; italic text = ended in 2007; underlined text = designated lead states)	Troops/ Military observers/ Civilian police/ Civilian staff		Total deaths: to date/in 2007/ (due to hostilities, accidents, illness)	Cost ($ m.): 2007
			Approved	Actual		
RAMSI (Multilateral agreement, 24 July 2003)124 July 2003	Regional Assistance Mission in the Solomon Islands Solomon Islands	Troops: <u>Australia</u>, *Fiji*, New Zealand, Papua New Guinea, Tonga Civ. pol.: <u>Australia</u>, Cook Islands, Fiji, Kiribati, Marshall Islands, Micronesia, Nauru, New Zealand, **Niue**, Palau, Papua New Guinea, **Samoa**, Tonga, Tuvalu, Vanuatu Civ. staff: Australia, Fiji, New Zealand, Papua New Guinea, **Samoa**, Tonga	– – –	214 306 169	3 1 (–, –, 1)	152.1
ISF (25 May 2006 and SCR 1690)125 May 2006	International Security Forces Timor-Leste	Troops: <u>Australia</u>, New Zealand	– – –	950 – –	1 1 (–, –, –)	121.4

CJA = EU Council Joint Action; CP/RES = OAS Permanent Council Resolution; CSO = OSCE Committee of Senior Officials (now the Senior Council); DDR = disarmament, demobilization and reintegration; FYROM = Former Yugoslav Republic of Macedonia; MC = OSCE Ministerial Council; PC.DEC = OSCE Permanent Council Decision; SCR = UN Security Council Resolution; SSR = security sector reform; UNV = UN volunteer.

1 UNTSO was established by SCR 50 (29 May 1948) and mandated to assist the Mediator and the Truce Commission in supervising the truce in Palestine after the 1948 Arab–Israeli War. In the following years it also assisted in observing the General Armistice Agreement of 1949 and the ceasefires in the aftermath of the 1967 6-Day Arab–Israeli War. UNTSO cooperates closely with UNDOF and UNIFIL. A positive decision by the UN Security Council is required to terminate the mission.

2 The mission is supported by 120 locally recruited staff.

3 UNMOGIP was established by SCR 91 (30 Mar. 1951) to replace the UN Commission for India and Pakistan. It is mandated to supervise the ceasefire in Kashmir under the Karachi Agreement (July 1949). A positive decision by the UN Security Council is required to terminate the mission.

4 The mission is also supported by 49 locally recruited staff.

5 UNFICYP was established by SCR 186 (4 Mar. 1964), and mandated to prevent fighting between the Greek Cypriot and Turkish Cypriot communities and to contribute to the maintenance and restoration of law and order. Since the end of hostilities in 1974, the mandate has included monitoring the de facto ceasefire (Aug. 1974) and maintaining a buffer zone between the 2 sides. SCR 1789 (14 Dec. 2007) extended the mandate until 15 June 2008.

6 The Argentinean contingent included soldiers from Brazil (1), Chile (15) and Paraguay (14). The mission is supported by 106 locally recruited staff.

7 UNDOF was established by SCR 350 (31 May 1974), in the wake of the 1973 Middle East War, in accordance with the Agreement on Disengagement. It is mandated to observe the ceasefire and the disengagement of Israeli and Syrian forces as well as to maintain an area of limitation and separation. SCR 1788 (14 Dec. 2007) extended the mandate until 30 June 2008.

8 The mission is supported by 105 locally recruited staff.

9 UNIFIL was established by SCR 425 and SCR 426 (19 Mar. 1978), with a mandate to confirm the withdrawal of Israeli forces from southern Lebanon and to assist the Government of Lebanon in ensuring the return of its effective authority in the area. Following the conflict between Hezbollah and Israel in 2006, SCR 1701 (11 Aug. 2006) revised the mission's mandate to include assisting in the establishment of a permanent ceasefire. SCR 1773 (14 Aug. 2007) extended the mandate until 31 Aug. 2008.

10 The mission is supported by 602 locally recruited staff.

11 MINURSO was established by SCR 690 (29 Apr. 1991) to monitor the ceasefire between the Frente Polisario and the Moroccan Government, to observe the reduction of troops and to prepare for a referendum concerning the integration of Western Sahara into Morocco. The mandate was renewed until 30 Apr. 2008 by SCR 1783 (31 Oct. 2007).

12 The mission is supported by 148 locally recruited staff and 23 UNVs.

13 UNOMIG was established by SCR 849 (9 July 1993) and SCR 858 (24 Aug. 1993). Its mandate of verifying the ceasefire between the Georgian Government and the Abkhazian authorities was invalidated by resumed fighting in Sep. 1993. It was given an interim mandate to maintain contacts with both sides to the conflict and with the Russian military contingents and to monitor and report on the situation. Following the signing of the 1994 Agreement on a Ceasefire and Separation of Forces, SCR 937 (27 July 1994) expanded the mandate to include monitoring and verification of the implementation of the agreement. SCR 1781 (15 Oct. 2007) extended the mandate until 15 Apr. 2008.

14 The mission is supported by 182 locally recruited staff and 1 UNV.

15 UNMIK was established by SCR 1244 (10 June 1999). Its mandate includes, among others, promoting the establishment of substantial autonomy and self-government in Kosovo, performing civilian administrative functions, maintaining law and order, promoting human rights, and ensuring the safe return of all refugees and displaced persons. It cooperates with the EU and the OSCE, which are responsible for the 'reconstruction and economic development' and 'democratization and institution building' pillars, respectively. A positive decision by the UN Security Council is required to terminate the mission.

16 The mission is supported by 1953 locally recruited staff and 137 UNVs.

17 MONUC was established by SCR 1279 (30 Nov. 1999). It was mandated by SCR 1291 (24 Feb. 2000) to monitor the implementation of the Ceasefire Agreement between the Democratic Republic of the Congo (DRC), Angola, Namibia, Rwanda, Uganda and Zimbabwe, to supervise and verify the disengagement of forces, to monitor human rights violations, and to facilitate the provision of humanitarian assistance. The mission was given UN Charter Chapter VII powers by SCR 1493 (28 July 2003). Currently, the mission is mandated to protect civilians, humanitarian personnel, and UN personnel and facilities; to contribute to the territorial security of the DRC; to assist disarming and demobilizing foreign and Congolese armed groups; to assist SSR; and to promote human rights, national reconciliation and good governance. SCR 1794 (21 Dec. 2007) extended the mandate until 31 Dec. 2008.

18 The mission is supported by 2088 locally recruited staff and 592 UNVs.

19 UNMEE was established by SCR 1312 (31 July 2000). It was expanded by SCR 1320 (15 Sep. 2000) and mandated to monitor the ceasefire; to repatriate Ethiopian troops and supervise the position of Ethiopian and Eritrean troops outside a 25-km temporary security zone; to chair the Military Coordination Commission of the UN and the AU; and to assist in mine clearance. SCR 1767 (30 July 2007) extended the mandate until 31 Jan. 2008 due to delays in the demarcation of the Eritrea–Ethiopia border.

20 The mission is supported by 203 locally recruited staff and 66 UNVs.

21 UNMIL was established by SCR 1509 (19 Sep. 2003) under UN Charter Chapter VII. It is mandated to support the implementation of the 2003 Comprehensive Peace Agreement, to provide assistance in matters of humanitarian and human rights, to assist in SSR and to protect civilians. It cooperates with UNOCI and UNIOSIL. SCR 1777 (20 Sep. 2007) renewed the mandate until 30 Sep. 2008.

22 The mission is supported by 944 locally recruited staff and 245 UNVs.

23 UNOCI was established by SCR 1528 (27 Feb. 2004) under UN Charter Chapter VII. It is mandated to monitor the cessation of hostilities, movements of armed groups and of the arms embargo; to implement a programme of disarmament, demobilization, repatriation, resettlement and reintegration; to support security sector reform; to assist in the fields of law and order, human rights and public information; to facilitate humanitarian assistance and the redeployment of state administration; and to assist in the holding of free elections. In 2007 the mandate was expanded to include supporting the full implementation of the Ouagadougou Political Agreement (4 Mar. 2007) and of the Supplementary Agreements (28 Nov. 2007), restoring peace and security. The mission cooperates with UNMIL and Operation Licorne. SCR 1765 (15 Jan. 2008) extended the mandate until 30 July 2008.

24 The mission is supported by 573 locally recruited staff and 292 UNVs.

25 MINUSTAH was established by SCR 1542 (30 Apr. 2004) under UN Charter Chapter VII and mandated to maintain a secure and stable environment to ensure that the peace process is carried forward; to assist the Haitian Government's efforts in SSR, including a comprehensive DDR programme, building the capacity of the national police and re-establishing the rule of law; to support humanitarian and human rights activities; and to protect civilians. SCR 1780 (15 Oct. 2007) extended the mandate until 15 Oct. 2008.

26 The mission is supported by 1140 locally recruited staff and 203 UNVs.

27 UNMIS was established by SCR 1590 (24 Mar. 2005) following the 2005 Comprehensive Peace Agreement. It is mandated to monitor the implementation of the peace agreement, to protect and promote human rights, and to facilitate the DDR process. SCR 1706 (31 Aug. 2006) expanded the mandate to include deployment to the Darfur region, where UNMIS is tasked to monitor implementation of the 2006 Darfur Peace Agreement and the 2006 N'Djamena Agreement on Humanitarian Cease-fire on the Conflict in Darfur, to maintain a presence in key areas, to monitor border activities, to protect civilians, and to promote and protect human rights. SCR 1784 (31 Oct. 2007) extended the mandate until 30 Apr. 2008.

28 The mission is supported by 2400 locally recruited staff and 251 UNVs.

29 UNMIT was established by SCR 1704 (25 Aug. 2006) following the outbreak of violence in May 2006. It is mandated to support the Government of Timor-Leste in post-conflict peacebuilding; and in capacity building, support and training of the East Timorese national police; and in the organization and holding of presidential and parliamentary elections in 2007. SCR 1745 (22 Feb. 2007) extended the mandate until 26 Feb. 2008.

30 SCR 1704 (25 Aug. 2006) leaves the Australian-led Joint Task Force Timor-Leste (930 troops) in place.

31 The mission is supported by 791 locally recruited staff and 122 UNVs.

32 MINURCAT was established by SCR 1778 (25 Sep. 2007) as part of a multidimensional presence in concert with the EU (EUFOR Tchad/RCA). The mission, which is located in eastern Chad and north-eastern Central African Republic, is mandated to provide security and protection of civilians by advising the Chadian Police and liaising with parties involved and to monitor and promote human rights and the rule of law. The mandate is for an initial period of 12 months.

33 UNAMA was established by SCR 1401 (28 Mar. 2002). It is mandated to provide political and strategic advice; to fulfil the tasks and responsibilities entrusted to the UN in the 2001 Bonn Agreement and support the implementation of the Afghanistan Compact; to manage all UN humanitarian, relief, recovery and reconstruction activities in Afghanistan in coordination with the Afghan Government; promote human rights; and provide technical assistance. It cooperates with ISAF in carrying out its mandate. SRC 1776 (19 Sep. 2007) extended the mandate for 12 months from 31 Oct. 2007.

34 The mission is supported by 1057 locally recruited staff and 32 UNVs.

35 UNAMI was established by SCR 1500 (14 Aug. 2003). In coordination with the Government of Iraq, the mission is mandated to support dialogue and national reconciliation; assist in the processes for holding elections, referendums and the implementation of constitutional provisions; facilitate humanitarian assistance and the safe return of refugees and displaced persons; support the implementation of the International Compact with Iraq; coordinate reconstruction and assistance programmes; assist in economic reform, capacity building and sustainable development; and promote the protection of human rights, judicial and legal reform and the strengthening of the rule of law. In carrying out its mandate, UNAMI cooperates with the Multinational Force in Iraq (MNF-I), NTM-I and EUJUST LEX. SCR 1770 (10 Aug. 2007) extended the current mandate until 10 Aug. 2008.

36 The mission is supported by 183 locally recruited staff.

37 UNIOSIL was established by SCR 1620 (31 Aug. 2005) to assist the Government of Sierra Leone in capacity building of state institutions, democratization, good governance, rule of law, human rights promotion, strengthening the security sector, and preparation for free and fair elections in 2008; to monitor security; to address cross-border challenges; and to coordinate with the Special Court for Sierra Leone. SCR 1793 (31 Dec. 2007) extended the mandate until 30 Sep. 2008, when the mission will end.

38 The mission is supported by 198 locally recruited staff and 23 UNVs.

39 BINUB was established by SCR 1719 (25 Oct. 2006) to succeed the UN Operation in Burundi (ONUB), which terminated on 31 Dec. 2006. It is mandated to assist the Burundian Government in the areas of peace consolidation and democratic governance, DDR and security sector reform, promotion and protection of human rights and ending impunity, and coordinating donors and UN agencies. BINUB cooperates with MONUC. SCR 1791 (19 Dec. 2007) extended the mandate until 31 Dec. 2008.

40 The mission is supported by 225 locally recruited staff and 46 UNVs.

41 UNMIN was established by SCR 1740 (23 Jan. 2007) and tasked to monitor and assist in implementing the management of arms and armed personnel of the Seven Party Alliance-led government and the Communist Party of Nepal (Maoist) in line with the provisions of the Nov. 2006 Comprehensive Peace Agreement, assist in monitoring ceasefire arrangements, and support electoral processes. SCR 1796 (23 Jan. 2008) extended the mandate until 23 June 2008.

42 The mission is supported by 226 locally recruited staff and 156 UNVs.

43 UNAMID was established by a decision of the AU Peace and Security Council (PSC/PR/Comm.(LXXIX), 22 June 2007) and by SCR 1769 (31 July 2007). The mission was endorsed and given UN Charter Chapter VII powers. UNAMID is mandated to contribute to the restoration of a secure environment, protect the civilian population, facilitate humanitarian assistance, monitor the implementation of related ceasefire agreements, and promote the rule of law and human rights, among other tasks. The initial mandate is for 12 months.

44 Preparations for UNAMID to assume operational command of personnel deployed under AMIS and of the UN Light Support Package (LSP) and Heavy Support Package (HSP) to AMIS (see note 46), were completed by 31 Oct. 2007. The formal handover of authority took place on 31 Dec. 2007.

45 The mission is supported by 66 UNVs.

46 AMIS was originally established as an observer mission by the Agreement with the Sudanese Parties on the Modalities for the Establishment of the Ceasefire Commission and the Deployment of Observers in the Darfur on 28 May 2004 and was endorsed by SCR 1556 (30 July 2004) under UN Charter Chapter VII. Its mandate was expanded by AU Peace and Security Council (PSC/PR/Comm.(XVII), 20 Oct. 2004) and now includes monitoring the N'Djamena ceasefire agreement, assisting in confidence building between the parties and contributing to a secure environment in Darfur. On 22 June 2007 the AU Peace and Security Council extended the mandate until 31 Dec. 2007. At the end of 2007 AMIS was incorporated into UNAMID.

47 Military observers were also contributed by unspecified states listed as 'EU/US', the Government of Sudan, the Justice and Equality Movement and the Sudan Liberation Movement/Army. During 2007 the UN supported the mission by deploying the LSP (105 military officers, 33 police advisers and 48 civilians) and the HSP (135 troops, 87 police officers, 1 formed police unit and 285 international staff deployed as of Dec. 2007).

48 The figure represents the sum of the major financial contributions in 2007 by the USA ($50 million), the EU (including bilateral contributions, €137 million) and Canada (C$48 million). Technical and logistical assistance was also provided. The AU estimates that a monthly budget of $23–25 million is needed to sustain operations.

49 AMISOM was established by a decision of the AU Peace and Security Council (AU PSC/PR/Comm.(LXIX), 19 Jan. 2007) and was endorsed by SCR 1744 (21 Feb. 2007) under UN Charter Chapter VII. The mission was mandated to support the dialogue and reconciliation process in Somalia by supporting the Transitional Federal Institutions, facilitating the provision of humanitarian assistance and contributing to the overall security situation. On 18 July 2007 the Peace and Security Council extended the mission's mandate for an additional 6 months. This was endorsed by SCR 1772 (20 Aug. 2007).

50 A Burundian advance team was deployed on 23 and 24 Dec. 2007; the rest of the 2 pledged Burundian battalions are still outstanding. The deployment of troops from Ghana (350) and Nigeria (850) is not scheduled yet. Logistical and personnel support is provided by the UN, the USA, NATO, Kenya and Algeria.

51 About $32 million had been contributed by the end of 2007; a total of up to $622 million will be needed.

52 MAES was established by a decision of the AU Peace and Security Council (AU PSC/MIN/Comm.1 (LXXVII), 9 May 2007). It is mandated to contribute to a secure environment for free and fair presidential elections on the 3 islands of the Comoros. The mandate was revised to support the implementation of sanctions imposed against the illegal authorities of Anjouan, disarm the Anjouan gendarmerie and guarantee fair and free elections on the island.

53 Sudan and Tanzania are mentioned as troop contributors in AU documents. According to information received from the Tanzanian Ministry of Foreign Affairs, Tanzania is currently the only contributor, with c. 200 troops in the Comoros, including an unspecified number of police officers.

54 FOMUC was established by a decision of the CEMAC Libreville Summit (2 Oct. 2002) to secure the border between Chad and the Central African Republic (CAR) and to guarantee the safety of former President Ange-Félix Patassé. Following the 15 Mar. 2003 coup, its mandate was expanded by a decision of the Libreville Summit (21 Mar. 2003) to include contributing to the overall security environment, assisting in the restructuring of CAR's armed forces and supporting the transition process. The mandate was maintained during 2007.

55 FOMUC will be reinforced with an attachment of 121 Cameroonian troops in 2008.

56 FOMUC is supported by and co-located with a detachment of c. 400 French soldiers (Opération Boali). The mission is supported by 82 locally recruited staff.

57 The mission was established pursuant to the Agreement on the Principles Governing the Peaceful Settlement of the Armed Conflict in the Trans-Dniester region, signed in Moscow by the presidents of Moldova and Russia (21 July 1992). A monitoring commission with representatives of Russia, Moldova and Trans-Dniester was established to coordinate the activities of the joint peacekeeping contingent.

58 The South Ossetia Joint Force was established by the Agreement on the Principles Governing the Peaceful Settlement of the Conflict in South Ossetia (24 June 1992). A monitoring commission with representatives of Russia, Georgia, and the North and South Ossetia authorities was established to oversee implementation of the agreement.

59 The CIS Peacekeeping Forces in Georgia was established by the Georgian–Abkhazian Agreement on a Ceasefire and Separation of Forces (14 May 1994). The operation's mandate was approved by heads of state of the members of the CIS Council of Collective Security (21 Oct. 1994) and endorsed by the UN through SCR 937 (21 July 1994). Its mandate was extended indefinitely from Jan. 2004.

60 The EUMM (known as the European Community Monitoring Mission until 2000) was established by the Brioni Agreement (7 July 1991) between representatives of the European Community (EC), the Yugoslav Government and Croatia and Slovenia. The mission was originally tasked to monitor developments in Slovenia and then to monitor the withdrawal of Yugoslav troops from Croatia and Slovenia. The mission's mandate was later expanded to cover the entire Western Balkans, including Albania. The EUMM's mandate covered monitoring political and security developments in the Western Balkans, borders, inter-ethnic issues and refugee returns; contributing to the early warning mechanism of the European Council; and contributing to confidence building and stabilization in the region (CJA 2000/811/CFSP, 22 Dec. 2000). CJA 2006/867/CFSP (30 Nov. 2006) narrowed the mission's geographical focus to Serbia, including Kosovo. In 2007 the mission also operated in Bosnia and Herzegovina, in FYROM, and in Montenegro (from which it withdrew in the middle of the year). The mission closed on 31 Dec. 2007 (CJA 2006/867/CFSP, 30 Nov. 2006). A team of 4 international and 7 local staff will remain in the region until Mar. 2008.

61 The mission was supported by 53 locally recruited staff.

62 The EUPM was established by the CJA 2002/210/CFSP (11 Mar. 2002) to ensure sustainable policing arrangements in Bosnia and Herzegovina under Bosnian ownership, in accordance with European and international standards. It is mandated to monitor, mentor and inspect the establishment of a sustainable, professional and multi-ethnic police. CJA 2007/749/CFSP (19 Nov. 2007) extended the mandate until 31 Dec. 2009.

63 The mission is supported by 219 locally recruited staff.

64 EUFOR ALTHEA was established by CJA 2004/570/CFSP (12 July 2004) and was endorsed and given UN Charter Chapter VII powers by SCR 1551 (9 July 2004). It is mandated to maintain a secure environment for the implementation of the 1995 Dayton Agreement, to assist in the strengthening of local capacity, and to support Bosnia and Herzegovina's progress towards EU integration. SCR 1785 (21 Nov. 2007) extended the mandate until 21 Nov. 2008.

65 Along with the transition plan EUFOR ALTHEA's troops strength was reduced from around 6000 to 2500 in 2007. From 28 Mar., the 3 multinational task forces were replaced by a single multinational manoeuvre battalion comprising Hungarian, Polish, Spanish and Turkish troops, stationed in Sarajevo. Liaison and observation teams remain in place throughout Bosnia and Herzegovina.

66 The mission is supported by 247 locally recruited staff located at the EUFOR headquarters.

67 EUPOL Kinshasa was established by CJA 2004/847/CFSP (9 Dec. 2004) and was mandated to monitor, mentor and advise the Congolese police force. EUPOL Kinshasa closely collaborated with EUSEC DR Congo. The mission closed on 30 June 2007 and was succeeded by EUPOL DR Congo.

68 The mission was supported by 9 locally recruited staff.

69 EUSEC DR Congo was established by CJA 2005/355/CFSP (2 May 2005). It is mandated to advise and assist the Congolese authorities, specifically the Ministry of Defence, on security matters, ensuring that policies are congruent with international humanitarian law, the standards of democratic governance and the principles of rule of law. The mission also closely coordinates with MONUC and EUPOL RD Congo. The mandate runs until 30 June 2008 (CJA/406/CFSP, 12 June 2007).

70 The majority of the deployed personnel are military advisers. Of the 46, 26 are based in Kinshasa while 20 are located in the east of DR Congo. In addition, the mission is supported by 36 locally recruited staff.

71 EUJUST LEX was established by CJA 2005/190/CFSP (7 Mar. 2005) and works in accordance with SCR 1546 (8 June 2004) as an integrated civilian rule-of-law mission to strengthen Iraq's criminal justice system through the training of magistrates, senior police officers and senior penitentiary staff. EUJUST LEX cooperates with and complements NTM-I and UNAMI. CJA 2007/760/CFSP (22 Nov. 2007) extended the mandate until 30 June 2009.

72 The EU Council reached political agreement on the mission on 21 Feb. 2005. On 7 Mar. 2005 it adopted a Joint Action on the EU Integrated Rule of Law Mission for Iraq. After a 3-month planning phase, the operational phase of the mission began on 1 July 2005 (CJA 2005/190/CFSP, 7 Mar. 2005). An official request was made from the new Iraqi Transitional Government in early June 2005.

73 Listed are the host states providing training courses in 2007. The operation's staff includes national police, judicial experts, political advisers, mission security officers and information technology experts. A total of 25 EU member states contribute to the operation by providing training, trainers, staff or financial resources.

74 EU BAM Rafah was established pursuant to CJA 2005/889/CFSP (12 Dec. 2005) and on the basis of the Agreement on Movement and Access between Israel and the Palestinian Authority (15 Nov. 2005). It is mandated to monitor, verify and evaluate the performance of Palestinian Authority border control, security and customs officials at the Rafah crossing point with regard to the 2005 Agreed Principles for Rafah Crossing; and support the Palestinian Authority's capacity building in the field of border control. CJA/ 2007/359/CFSP (23 May 2007) extended the mandate until 24 May 2008. On 9 June 2007 the Rafah crossing point was closed following riots in the Gaza Strip. The mission was suspended but maintained full operational capability. It currently focuses on capacity building and is supporting EUPOL COPPS.

75 The mission is supported by 8 locally recruited staff.

76 EUPOL COPPS was established by CJA 2005/797/CFSP (14 Nov. 2005). It is mandated to provide a framework for and advise Palestinian criminal justice and police officials and coordinate EU aid to the Palestinian Authority. The mission's mandate runs until 31 Dec. 2008.

77 EUPOL Afghanistan was established by CJA 2007/369/CFSP (30 May 2007) and is tasked to support the government in strengthening the rule of law, particularly improving civil policing and law enforcement capacity. The mandate runs until 30 May 2010.

78 The mission's personnel are deployed at the central level (in Kabul) and at regional and provincial levels alongside the regional commands and provincial reconstruction teams of ISAF.

79 Included are an unspecific number of administrative and logistics staff. The mission is supported by 25 locally recruited staff.

80 EUPOL RD Congo was established by CJA 2007/405/CFSP (12 June 2007) to succeed EUPOL Kinshasa. The mission is tasked to assist the Congolese authorities in reforming the National Police and in improving the criminal justice system. EUPOL RD Congo closely cooperates with EUSEC DR Congo. The mandate runs until 30 June 2008 (CJA 2007/405/CFSP, 12 June 2007).

81 The mission is supported by 8 locally recruited staff.

82 KFOR was established by SCR 1244 (10 June 1999). Its mandated tasks include deterring renewed hostilities, establishing a secure environment, supporting UNMIK and monitoring borders. Along with KFOR headquarters in Pristina, KFOR contingents are grouped into 6 task forces: Multinational Task Force (MNTF) Centre located in Lipljan is led by Sweden; MNTF North located in Novo Selo is led by France; MNTF South located in Prizren is led by Turkey; MNFT West located in Peje/Pec is led by Italy; MNTF East located in Urosevac is led by the USA; and the Multinational Specialized Unit (MSU) in Pristina is led by Italy.

83 The total number of troops continuously changes due to troop rotation. The mission is supported by 140 locally recruited staff.

84 ISAF was established by SCR 1386 (20 Dec. 2001) under UN Charter Chapter VII as a multinational force mandated to assist the Afghan Interim Authority to maintain security, as envisaged in Annex I of the 2001 Bonn Agreement. NATO took on command and control of ISAF in Aug. 2003. ISAF also has control of all 25 provincial reconstruction teams (PRTs). The territory of Afghanistan is divided in 5 areas of responsibility: Regional Command (RC) Capital in Kabul, led by Italy; RC North in Mazar-e Sharif, led by Germany; RC West in Herat, led by Italy; RC South in Kandahar, led by the UK; and RC East in Bagram, led by the USA. SCR 1776 (19 Sep. 2007) extended the mandate for 12 months from 13 Oct. 2007.

85 The following countries have contributed military or civilian personnel to the 25 PRTs: Australia, Belgium, Canada, Croatia, Czech Republic, Denmark, Estonia, Finland, France, Germany, Hungary, Iceland, Italy, Latvia, Lithuania, the Netherlands, New Zealand, Norway, Poland, Romania, South Korea, Spain, Sweden, Switzerland, Turkey, the UK and the USA.

86 The USA will deploy c. 3200 additional troops in the spring of 2008.

87 The 15 reported non-battle deaths resulted from accidents, accidental firing of weapons, suicide or other causes.

88 NTM-I was established pursuant to SCR 1546 (8 June 2004) and approved by the North Atlantic Council on 17 Nov. 2004. It is mandated to assist in the development of Iraq's security institutions through training and equipment of, in particular, middle- and senior-level personnel from the Iraqi security forces. In 2007 the mandate was revised to focus on mentoring and advising Iraqi-led institutional training programmes.

89 No data on national breakdowns were available and therefore no lead state could be identified.

90 MAPP/OEA was established by OAS Permanent Council resolution CP/RES 859 (1397/04) of 6 Feb. 2004 to support the efforts of the Colombian Government to engage in political dialogue with the National Liberation Army (ELN). It is mandated to facilitate the DDR process.

91 Mexican verification officers are seconded while the other international observers are contracted to the mission. The mission is supported by 18 national professionals, 41 local administrative staff and 9 information officers.

92 The OAS Special Mission for Strengthening Democracy in Haiti was established by OAS Permanent Council Resolution CP/RES 806 (1303/02, 16 Jan. 2002). It is mandated to contribute to resolution of the political crisis in Haiti, including by assisting the Government of Haiti to strengthen its democratic processes and institutions. OAS General Assembly Resolution A/RES 2058 (XXXIV-O/04, 8 June 2004) amended the mandate to include assistance in the holding of elections, promoting and protecting human rights, and the professionalization of the Haitian National Police. In 2007 the Special Mission was incorporated into the OAS Country Office.

93 The OSCE Spillover Monitor Mission to Skopje was established following a decision of the 16th meeting of the OSCE Committee of Senior Officials (CSO) (18 Sep. 1993). It was authorized by the FYROM Government through Articles of Understanding agreed by an exchange of letters on 7 Nov. 1992. Its tasks include monitoring, police training, development and other activities related to the 1992 Ohrid Framework Agreement. PC.DEC/822 (6 Dec. 2007) extended the mandate until 31 Dec. 2008.

94 The mission is supported by 183 locally recruited staff.

95 The OSCE Mission to Georgia was established at the 17th CSO meeting (6 Nov. 1992). It was authorized by the Government of Georgia through a memorandum of understanding on 23 Jan. 1993 and by South Ossetia's leaders through an exchange of letters on 1 Mar. 1993. Its initial objective was to promote negotiations between the conflicting parties. The mandate was expanded at the 14th Permanent Council Meeting (29 Mar. 1994) to include monitoring the Joint Peacekeeping Forces in South Ossetia. PC.DEC/450 (13 Dec. 1999) expanded the mandate to include monitoring Georgia's borders with Russian Republic of Ingushetia. PC.DEC/522, 19 Dec. 2002 expanded the mandate to include

observing and reporting on cross-border movement between Georgia and the Russian Republic of Dagestan. PC.DEC/831 (21 Dec. 2007) extended the mandate until 31 Dec. 2008.

96 The mission is support by 154 locally recruited staff

97 The OSCE Mission to Moldova was established at the 19th CSO meeting (4 Feb. 1993) and authorized by the Government of Moldova through a memorandum of understanding (7 May 1993). Its tasks include assisting the conflicting parties in pursuing negotiations on a lasting political settlement and gathering and providing information on the situation. PC.DEC/832 (21 Dec. 2007) extended the mandate until 31 Dec. 2008.

98 The mission is supported by 34 locally recruited staff.

99 The OSCE Centre in Dushanbe was established by a decision taken at the 4th meeting of the OSCE Ministerial Council, CSCE/4-C/Dec.1, Decision I.4 (1 Dec. 1993). No bilateral memorandum of understanding has been signed. The mission's mandate includes facilitating dialogue, promoting human rights and informing the OSCE about further developments. This was expanded in 2002 to include economic and environmental dimensions. PC.DEC/826 (13 Dec. 2007) extended the mandate until 30 June 2008.

100 The mission is supported by 74 locally recruited staff.

101 A Personal Representative on the Conflict Dealt with by the OSCE Minsk Conference was appointed by the OSCE Chairman-in-Office (CIO) on 10 Aug. 1995. The Minsk Conference seeks a peaceful settlement to the Nagorno-Karabakh conflict. The Personal Representative's mandate consists of assisting the CIO in planning possible peacekeeping operations, assisting the parties in confidence-building measures and in humanitarian matters, and monitoring the ceasefire between the parties. A positive decision is required to terminate the mission.

102 The mission is supported by 11 locally recruited staff.

103 The OSCE Mission to Bosnia and Herzegovina was established by a decision of the 5th meeting of the Ministerial Council (MC(5).DEC/1, 8 Dec. 1995), in accordance with Annex 6 of the 1995 Dayton Agreement. The mission is mandated to assist the parties in regional stabilization measures and democracy building. PC.DEC/818 (6 Dec. 2007) extended the mandate until 31 Dec. 2008.

104 The mission is supported by 507 locally recruited staff.

105 The OSCE Mission to Croatia was established by PC.DEC/112 (18 Apr. 1996), PC.DEC/176 (26 June 1997) and C/DEC/239 (25 June 1998) revised its mandate. Its mandate included assisting and monitoring the return of refugees and displaced persons and protecting national minorities. The mission closed on 31 Dec. 2007 and was replaced by the OSCE Office in Zagreb.

106 The mission is supported by 94 locally recruited staff.

107 The OSCE Presence in Albania was established by PC.DEC/160 (27 Mar. 1997). In 2003 the mission's mandate was revised to include assisting in legislative, judicial and electoral reform, capacity building, anti-trafficking and anti-corruption activities, police assistance, and good governance. PC.DEC/819 (6 Dec. 2007) extended the mandate until 31 Dec. 2008.

108 The mission is supported by 84 locally recruited staff.

109 The OSCE Mission in Kosovo was established by the PC.DEC/305 (1 July 1999). Its mandate includes training police, judicial personnel and civil administrators and monitoring and promoting human rights. The mission is a component (pillar III) of UNMIK. PC.DEC/835 (21 Dec. 2007) extended the mandate until 31 Jan. 2008, after which the mandate will be renewed monthly unless a participating state objects.

110 The mission is supported by 688 locally recruited staff.

111 The OSCE Mission to Serbia is the new name given to the OSCE Mission to Serbia and Montenegro in June 2006. The mission was originally established by PC.DEC/401 (11 Jan. 2001) as the OSCE Mission to the Federal Republic of Yugoslavia. Its mandate is to advise on the implementation of laws and monitor the proper functioning and development of democratic institutions and processes in Serbia. It assists in the training and restructuring of law enforcement bodies and the judiciary. PC.DEC/816 (6 Dec. 2007) extended the mandate until 31 Dec. 2008.

112 The mission is supported 138 locally recruited staff.

113 The OSCE Mission to Montenegro was established by PC.DEC/732 (29 June 2006) following Montenegro's declaration of independence (3 June 2006). Prior to independence, the current mission was part of the OSCE Mission to Serbia and Montenegro. Its mandate is to assist in institution building and reform of law enforcement bodies and the judiciary and to support local and central governance structures. PC.DEC/821 (6 Dec. 2007) extended the mandate until 31 Dec. 2008.

114 The mission is supported by 32 locally recruited staff.

115 The NNSC was established by the agreement concerning a military armistice in Korea signed at Panmunjom on 27 July 1953. It is mandated with the functions of supervision, observation, inspection and investigation implementation of the armistice agreement.

116 The MFO was established on 3 Aug. 1981 by the Protocol to the Treaty of Peace between Egypt and Israel, signed 26 Mar. 1979. Deployment began on 20 Mar. 1982 following the withdrawal of Israeli forces from the Sinai but the mission was not operational until 25 Apr. 1982, the day that Israel returned the Sinai to Egyptian sovereignty.

117 A large part of the MFO's basic mission in the Sinai is performed by the Civilian Observer Unit (COU). The COU has its origins in the US Sinai Field Mission, which came into existence with the Sinai II Agreement (4 Sep. 1975). The COU currently has 15 personnel, all US nationals.

118 The mission is supported by 38 expatriate and 34 Egyptian nationals.

119 TIPH 2 was established by the Protocol Concerning the Redeployment in Hebron (17 Jan. 1997) and the Agreement on the Temporary International Presence in Hebron (21 Jan. 1997). Its mandate is to provide by its presence a secure and stable environment and monitor and report breaches of international humanitarian law. The mandate is renewed every 6 months pending approval from both the Palestinian and Israeli parties.

120 Due to rotations the figures given might vary from the fixed number of 58 that are allocated.

121 The mission is supported by 6 locally recruited staff.

122 Operation Licorne, consisting entirely of French troops, was deployed under the authority of SCR 1464 (4 Feb. 2003) under UN Charter Chapter VII and UN Charter Chapter VIII, to support the ECOWAS mission in contributing to a secure environment and, in particular, to facilitate implementation of the 2003 Linas-Marcoussis Agreement. SCR 1528 (27 Feb. 2004) provides its current authorization and revised the mandate to working in support of UNOCI. SCR 1795 (15 Jan. 2008) expanded the mandate to assist in the preparation of free and fair elections in accordance with the Ouagadougou political Agreement (4 Mar. 2007) and the Supplementary Agreements (28 Nov. 2007), and extended the mission's mandate until 30 July 2008.

123 Following the signing of the Ouagadougou Agreement in Mar. 2007, French troops started to withdraw c. 1100 troops during 2007. The remaining troops are stationed in Abidjan, and around Bouake and Toumbokro, supported by mobile units. The mission is supported by a naval attachment in the Gulf of Guinea (Mission Corymbe, 100 personnel).

124 Under the framework of the 2000 Biketawa Declaration, members of the Pacific Islands Forum agreed to mount a collective response to crises, usually at the request of the host government. RAMSI was established by the Agreement between Solomon Islands, Australia, New Zealand, Fiji, Papua New Guinea, Samoa and Tonga concerning the operations and status of the police and armed forces and other personnel deployed to Solomon Islands to assist in the restoration of law and order and security, signed on 24 July 2003. It is mandated to assist the Solomon Islands Government in restoring law and order and in building up the capacity of the police force.

125 The ISF was deployed at the request of the Government of Timor-Leste to assist in stabilizing the security environment in the county and endorsed by SCR 1690 (20 June 2006). The ISF cooperates closely with UNMIT.

4. Integrating gender in post-conflict security sector reform

MEGAN BASTICK*

I. Introduction

The importance of security sector reform (SSR) has increasingly been emphasized in international engagement with post-conflict countries.[1] In February 2007 the United Nations Security Council stressed that 'reforming the security sector in post-conflict environments is critical to the consolidation of peace and stability, promoting poverty reduction, rule of law and good governance, extending legitimate state authority, and preventing countries from relapsing into conflict'.[2] National governments also identify SSR as a key tool in consolidating their authority and healing divisions of the past.

In parallel, many governments and UN and donor agencies have emphasized women's participation and efforts to achieve gender equality as crucial elements of post-conflict reconstruction. In 2000 the UN Security Council adopted Resolution 1325 on 'Women, peace and security',[3] highlighting the interdependence of post-conflict gender equality, peacebuilding and security. Women are acknowledged as playing important roles in peacebuilding and in sustaining security on a communal level. Gender inequality is understood to inhibit development and violence against women to be a pervasive form of

---

[1] The term 'security sector reform' has been in general public use since 1998 when it featured in a speech by Clare Short, then British Secretary of State for International Development; there is, however, no single accepted definition. See Brzoska, M., *Development Donors and the Concept of Security Sector Reform*, Geneva Centre for the Democratic Control of Armed Forces (DCAF) Occasional Paper no. 4 (DCAF: Geneva, 2003), p. 3. The Development Aid Committee (DAC) of the Organisation for Economic Co-operation and Development (OECD) prefers the term 'security *system* reform'. OECD, *Security System Reform and Governance*, DAC Guidelines and Reference Series (OECD: Paris, 2005), <http://www.oecd.org/dataoecd/8/39/31785288.pdf>, p. 20. Under most accepted definitions and as further explained in this chapter, the term covers a reform and renewal process—with both normative and efficiency goals—covering all state institutions and agencies of defence, security, law and justice and any non-state actors with important roles or influence in these fields. On SSR see also Hendrickson, D. and Karkoszka, A., 'The challenges of security sector reform', *SIPRI Yearbook 2002: Armaments, Disarmament and International Security* (Oxford University Press: Oxford, 2002), pp. 175–201; Caparini, M., 'Security sector reform and NATO and EU enlargement', *SIPRI Yearbook 2003: Armaments, Disarmament and International Security* (Oxford University Press: Oxford, 2003), pp. 237–60; and Caparini, M., 'Security sector reform in the Western Balkans, *SIPRI Yearbook 2004: Armaments, Disarmament and International Security* (Oxford University Press: Oxford, 2004), pp. 251–82.

[2] UN Security Council, Statement by the President of the Security Council, UN document S/PRST/2007/3, 21 Feb. 2007. The UN documents cited here are available from <http://documents.un.org/>.

[3] UN Security Council Resolution 1325, 31 Oct. 2000.

* The author thanks Alyson J. K. Bailes and, at the Geneva Centre for the Democratic Control of Armed Forces (DCAF), colleagues Alan Bryden, Anja Ebnöther, David Law and Kristin Valasek for their comments on the draft of this chapter.

insecurity with widespread ill-effects across society. There is also growing awareness of the need to address the particular experiences of men and boys, both as victims and as sources of insecurity.

SSR is a process of transformation: sometimes rapid, sometimes gradual and incremental. It brings opportunities—and responsibilities—to create more inclusive and less discriminatory security sector institutions. One relevant issue is ethnic representation within security services: in a multiethnic state security services need to reflect the composition of society if the population is to have confidence in them, and if they are to be able to fulfil their mission.[4] Equally, for security services to be representative, trusted and effective, they must include women as well as men. SSR strategies that promote the recruitment of women in security services, and ensure that women participate equally in security decision making, contribute to creating an efficient and legitimate security sector. More broadly, the integration of gender issues into SSR processes increases responsiveness to the security needs and roles of all parts of the community, strengthens local ownership of the reform process and enhances security sector oversight. It is a key condition for achieving successful and sustainable SSR through a legitimate and locally owned process.[5]

This chapter explores the case and methods for addressing gender issues in post-conflict SSR processes, drawing upon experiences in Afghanistan, Kosovo, Liberia, Peru, Rwanda, Sierra Leone and Timor-Leste, and potential models from Serbia and South Africa. Section II further defines the concepts of SSR and gender, as well as their relationship to each other. The rationale for and experiences of gender mainstreaming in SSR and promoting the full and equal participation of men and women in SSR processes are discussed in section III, with practical examples from post-conflict settings. Section IV focuses on promoting women's participation in post-conflict security services. Section V examines some challenges for key post-conflict SSR and SSR-related activities, including gender dimensions in disarmament, demobilization and reintegration (DDR) processes, transitional justice and justice reform. Section VI summarizes the case for integrating gender into future SSR programming and policymaking and outlines the key opportunities and challenges.

II. Gender and security sector reform

While SSR can be defined in broader or narrower terms, there is an emerging consensus on a governance-based approach that defines the security sector as comprising all state institutions and other entities with a role in ensuring the

---

[4] DCAF, 'Backgrounder: multiethnic armed forces', Mar. 2006, <http://www.dcaf.ch/publications/kms/details.cfm?id=18416>.

[5] In 2006 the Council of the European Union (EU) emphasized that gender perspectives should be incorporated in all the EU's policies and activities on SSR. Council of the EU, 2760th Council Meeting, General Affairs and External Relations, General Affairs, Brussels, 13 Nov. 2006, Press release, <http://europa.eu/rapid/pressReleasesAction.do?reference=PRES/06/302>. Similarly, in its Feb. 2007 debate on SSR, the UN Security Council recognized 'inter-linkages' between SSR and 'other important factors of stabilisation and reconstruction, such as . . . gender equality'. UN Security Council (note 2).

security of the state and its people, including justice and penal institutions, non-state armed groups and civil society organizations providing security services or engaged in oversight activities.[6] By keeping the focus on individuals and communities, distinct from the state, as the ultimate benefic-iaries, and by stressing the potentially important roles of civil society groups in both oversight and security provision, SSR allies itself with the aims of a 'human security' approach.[7] Anchoring SSR in the values of human security in turn helps to ensure that SSR does in fact address the needs of the entire population, including women, girls and boys.

In the aftermath of armed conflict, SSR is an essential part of peacebuilding: to prevent the reoccurrence of conflict and to enhance public security, which in turn creates the conditions for reconstruction and development work. In such contexts, SSR has some features that are less present or even absent in non-conflict affected settings.[8] Provision of physical security is likely to be heavily prioritized, with SSR commencing while some parts of the country are still experiencing violence. Post-conflict SSR may thus prioritize security sector capacity building over community-level security initiatives and judicial and legislative reform. Immediate SSR efforts may have to proceed before a functioning national government is in place and before the results can be legit-imated through an electoral process, which reinforces the need to include opposition political groupings, civil society organizations and other commun-ity representatives.

In post-conflict contexts, local and donor agendas may need to include spe-cial features. Transitional justice mechanisms, such as truth and reconciliation commissions (TRCs) and special judicial processes to address crimes com-mitted in the conflict, are increasingly seen as a necessity to promote national reconciliation and cohesion. SSR can only succeed as a long-term process, sustained by local stakeholders and external supporters alike.

'Gender' and security

The concept of 'gender' was developed during the 1970s to mean the roles and relationships, personality traits, attitudes, behaviours, values, relative power and influence that society ascribes to men and women. Generally speaking, 'gender' is understood as referring to learned differences between men and women, while 'sex' refers to the biological differences between females and males. Gender differences—or 'gender roles'—are not static; they vary across cultures and within cultures according to such factors as class, sexual orienta-

---

[6] On SSR see Hänggi, H., 'Making sense of security sector governance', eds H. Hänggi and T. H. Winkler, *Challenges of Security Sector Governance* (DCAF: Geneva, 2003), pp. 17–18.

[7] For a discussion of the human security concept vis-à-vis SSR see Law, D, M., 'Human security and security sector reform: contrasts and commonalities', *Sicherheit und Frieden*, vol. 23, no. 1 (2005).

[8] The analysis here draws on Law, D. M., *The Post-Conflict Security Sector*, DCAF Policy Paper no. 14 (DCAF: Geneva, 2006), <http://www.dcaf.ch/publications/kms/details.cfm?id=25252>, pp. 2–3, which, in turn, is based on case studies of Afghanistan, Bosnia and Herzegovina, Haiti, Kosovo, Sierra Leone and Timor-Leste.

tion and age. The concept of gender has been widely adopted within academic literature and development programming as a way to understand the different roles and behaviours of men and women within their particular social context. Using gender as a point of reference highlights that differences between the sexes are not immutable and may change, for example during periods of armed conflict or as a result of development interventions.

In SSR, attention to gender highlights the fact that forms of insecurity experienced by men and women are not only different, but different because of the social processes and structures within which men and women live. Although there are significant numbers of exceptions, the overwhelming majority of the victims of rape are women and of armed violence are men.[9] These vulnerabilities result from a range of differences in the way that lives of men and women are shaped, including their relative access to power and resources. Likewise, the roles that men and women perform as security providers, in security forces and institutions or as perpetrators of violence, reflect social processes and can be subject to change.

Gender and (in)security in post-conflict settings

In post-conflict settings, the incidence of violence against women and children is often higher than preceding the conflict. The UN's group of independent experts on the impact of armed conflict on women observed that during armed conflict 'violence against women comes to be an accepted norm'.[10] Sexual and domestic violence continues and increases in the post-conflict period, fuelled by the availability of weapons, trauma among male family members, and lack of jobs, shelter and basic services.[11] Lack of livelihood opportunities and the post-conflict influx of mostly male international personnel make women and girls particularly vulnerable to sexual exploitation and to being trafficked.[12]

---

[9] A World Health Organization (WHO) study of 52 countries notes that 90.4% of firearms deaths are male. WHO, World Health Report database, cited in WHO, *Small Arms and Global Health* (WHO: Geneva, 2001, p. 3. As none of the countries included in this survey was engaged in civil conflict, these estimates exclude deaths due to armed conflict.

[10] Rehn, E. and Johnson Sirleaf, E., *Women, War and Peace: The Independent Experts' Assessment on the Impact of Armed Conflict on Women and Women's Role in Peace-Building (Progress of the World's Women 2002, vol. 1)* (UN Development Fund for Women: New York, 2002), p. 13. There is an extensive literature on violence against women in conflict. See e.g. Bastick, M., Grimm, K. and Kunz, R., *Sexual Violence in Armed Conflict: Global Overview and Implications for the Security Sector* (DCAF: Geneva, 2007); UN Office for the Coordination of Humanitarian Affairs (OCHA) and Integrated Regional Information Networks (IRIN), *The Shame of War: Sexual Violence against Women and Girls in Conflict* (OCHA/IRIN: Nairobi, Mar. 2007); and Ward, J., *If Not Now, When? Addressing Gender-Based Violence in Refugee, Internally Displaced, and Post-conflict Settings: A Global Overview* (Reproductive Health for Refugees Consortium: New York, 2002). For analysis of gender-based violence against men and boys in armed conflict see Sivakumaran, S., 'Sexual violence against men in armed conflict', *European Journal of International Law*, vol. 18, no. 2 (2007); and Carpenter, C. R., 'Recognizing gender-based violence against civilian men and boys in conflict situations', *Security Dialogue*, vol. 37, no. 1 (2006), pp. 83–103.

[11] Rehn and Johnson Sirleaf (note 10), p. 16.

[12] See e.g. UN Department of Peacekeeping Operations (DPKO), 'Human trafficking and United Nations peacekeeping', DPKO Policy Paper, Mar. 2004, <http://www.unmikonline.org/civpol/gender/doc/Human_trafficking.pdf>.

Not only do women, men, boys and girls experience security differently, but key challenges to state security in post-conflict contexts are also linked to gender and require gender-responsive SSR. The linkages between masculinities, youth and gun violence are well documented.[13] The Small Arms Survey observes that 'gender ideologies—particularly those that associate masculinity with power—offer crucial insight into why many marginalized young men see violence as an attractive means of achieving manhood and respect'.[14] SSR efforts should, however, not treat young men primarily as a security risk and women and girls primarily as victims. To do so risks ignoring the vast majority of men who are not violent and undermining women as providers of security.[15] Brigadier General Karl Engelbrektson, Force Commander of the Nordic Battlegroup, has emphasized the importance of women's everyday roles for an armed force tasked to create security: 'Understanding the role of women is important when building stability in an area . . . If women are the daily bread-winners and provide food and water for their families, patrolling the areas where the women work will increase security and allow them to continue. This is a tactical assessment . . . Creating conditions for a functioning everyday life is vital from a security perspective.'[16]

A gender-sensitive SSR approach needs to address the patterns of vulnerabilities of women, men, girls and boys as well as the resources available to them and the strategies that they employ for their own security. SSR programmes based on such understanding will be more targeted and responsive, and thus more effective and sustainable. Moreover, security institutions that are seen to listen and respond to the needs of all parts of the community will be perceived as more legitimate and accountable.

Principles for integrating gender in security sector reform

'Gender mainstreaming' is a holistic approach to ensuring that gender issues as they affect both men and women are comprehensively addressed in SSR. In 1997 the UN Economic and Social Council (ECOSOC) adopted gender mainstreaming as a strategy to be systematically used in all areas of work through-

[13] E.g. Dowdney, L., Children and Youth in Organised Armed Violence (COAV), 'Neither war nor peace: international comparisons of children and youth in organised armed violence', COAV Report, 2005, <http://www.coav.org.br/>. The term 'masculinities' indicates that 'there are many socially constructed definitions for being a man and that these can change over time and from place to place. The term relates to perceived notions and ideals about how men should or are expected to behave in a given setting.' Women's Commission for Refugee Women and Children, *Masculinities: Male Roles and Male Involvement in the Promotion of Gender Equality, A Resource Packet* (Women's Commission for Refugee Women and Children: New York, Sep. 2005), p. 5.

[14] Small Arms Survey, 'Few options but the gun: angry young men', *Small Arms Survey 2006: Unfinished Business* (Oxford University Press: New York, 2006), p. 295.

[15] The Centre for Humanitarian Dialogue stresses that 'attention has to be given to men's resiliency, i.e. the factors that lead the majority of men, even in settings where armed violence is prevalent, to resist resorting to gun violence'. Widmer, M., Barker, G. and Buchanan, C., 'Hitting the target: men and guns', Revcon Policy Brief, June 2006, <http://www.hdcentre.org/files/MenandGuns.pdf>, p. 3.

[16] Engelbrektson, K., 'Resolution 1325 increases efficiency', *Good and Bad Examples: Lessons Learned from Working with United Nations Resolution 1325 in International Missions* (Genderforce: Uppsala, 2007), p. 29.

out the UN system, in particular in development, poverty eradication, human rights, humanitarian assistance, budgeting, disarmament, peace and security, and legal and political matters. ECOSOC defined gender mainstreaming in this context as:

the process of assessing the implications for women and men of any planned action, including legislation, policies or programmes, in all areas and at all levels. It is a strategy for making women's as well as men's concerns and experiences an integral dimension of the design, implementation, monitoring and evaluation of policies and programmes in all political, economic and societal spheres so that women and men benefit equally and inequality is not perpetuated. The ultimate goal is to achieve gender equality.[17]

Gender mainstreaming has since been adopted by other international and regional organizations and institutions (such as the Organization for Security and Co-operation in Europe, the World Bank and the Economic Community of West African States) and by individual governments, to be applied in their overseas development work and in domestic programmes. As gender main-streaming has evolved, it has become better understood that other factors—such as race, ethnicity, sexual orientation and age—interact with gender in any society, and that gender mainstreaming must take these other factors into account to be effective. The UN High Commissioner for Refugees, for example, implements 'age, gender and diversity mainstreaming' as an integrated approach.

In SSR, gender mainstreaming means assessing the impact of all SSR policies and activities on women, men, boys and girls at every stage of the process. For example, in an SSR assessment, gender mainstreaming would lead to inclusion of questions and mechanisms to identify the different insecurities facing men, women, girls and boys.

A second approach to ensuring that SSR programmes take account of the different needs and roles of men and women is to ensure that both men and women participate and are represented. As women continue to be under-represented in SSR processes, efforts should be made both to increase women's presence and representation in public institutions concerned with security and to give women's civil society organizations a voice in SSR.

III. Gender mainstreaming and promoting women's participation in post-conflict security sector reform

Gender mainstreaming in security sector reform

In order for SSR to recognize and respond to the particular needs of men and women, those designing SSR processes must be alert to gender issues and

---

[17] UN Economic and Social Council, 'Agreed conclusions 1997/2', UN document A/52/3, 18 Sep. 1997, p. 3.

willing and competent to undertake gender mainstreaming.[18] Gender insights can then be applied to the analysis of security deficits, the content of SSR policies and the design of implementation processes.

Gender mainstreaming in SSR requires mechanisms to ensure that a broad range of men and women are consulted and participate in SSR, so that the particular concerns of women and men may be identified. The content of 'gender issues' and the means to address them can be identified only by the men and women who are the beneficiaries of SSR, not assumed or imported from outside. Thus the substance of SSR programmes should address the concerns raised by both men and women. The resulting requirements could range from initiatives to improve street lighting to the establishment of community policing forums to technical training for police on interviewing male and female victims of sexual assault. A wider range of such possible prescriptions is given in table 4.1. Monitoring and evaluation of SSR results must focus on how gender issues are being addressed and the degree to which men and women are participating in the SSR process and the reformed security institutions.

The challenge of women's participation in security sector reform

The Development Assistance Committee (DAC) of the Organisation for Economic Co-operation and Development (OECD) has identified the 'core values' for SSR as 'to be people-centred, locally-owned and based on democratic norms and human rights principles and on the rule of law'.[19] Each of these values represents an imperative for both men and women to fully and equally participate in SSR. A process cannot be people-centred if the needs of half the people are not represented, or democratic if half the population has no voice in it. Local ownership, described by Laurie Nathan as 'both a matter of respect and a pragmatic necessity' can be deepened and strengthened by including women as owners.[20] The OECD's SSR guidelines state that 'Ensuring women's participation beyond the grass-roots enhances the legitimacy of the [SSR] process by making it more democratic and responsive to all parts of the affected population.'[21] Human rights principles require that states ensure that women are not excluded from public processes, including in security decision making.[22]

---

[18] A key resource in this regard is Bastick, M. and Valasek K. (eds), *Gender and Security Sector Reform Toolkit* (DCAF, Organization for Security and Co-operation in Europe/Office for Democratic Institutions and Human Rights and UN International Research and Training Institute for the Advancement of Women: Geneva, 2008).

[19] OECD (note 1), p. 22.

[20] Nathan, L., *No Ownership, No Commitment: A Guide to Local Ownership of Security Sector Reform* (University of Birmingham: Birmingham, May 2007), p. 3.

[21] OECD (note 1), p. 42.

[22] Article 7 of the Convention on the Elimination of All Forms of Discrimination against Women (opened for signature on 18 Dec. 1979 and entered into force on 3 Sep. 1981), which has been ratified by 185 states, requires state parties to ensure to women, on equal terms with men, the right to participate in the formulation and implementation of government policy, to hold public office and to perform all public func-

Table 4.1. Examples of gender activities within security sector reform programmes

Internal activities	External activities
Gender mainstreaming within security institutions	
Gender awareness training	Initiatives to prevent and respond to
Sexual harassment training	gender-based violence
Codes of conduct	Training on interviewing victims of rape,
Gender advisers	human trafficking etc.
Resources, such as manuals, on	Training on gender for civil society
how to integrate gender issues	organizations involved in oversight of
	security institutions
Promoting participation of women within security institutions	
Measures to increase female recruitment,	Collaboration with women's organizations
retention and advancement	for information gathering, referral of
Family friendly human resources policies	victims, drafting security policy etc.
Support for female staff associations and	Training for women's organizations on
women's caucuses	security sector oversight

Source: Adapted from Valasek, K., 'Security sector reform and gender', eds M. Bastick and K. Valasek, *Gender and Security Sector Reform Toolkit* (DCAF, Organization for Security and Co-operation in Europe/Office for Democratic Institutions and Human Rights and UN International Research and Training Institute for the Advancement of Women: Geneva, 2008).

However, post-conflict SSR processes tend to be planned, agreed and implemented by men. This is true both as regards the personnel of donors and institutions supporting SSR and the individuals involved in countries undergoing SSR processes.[23] While the reasons for this vary from case to case, a number of common factors conspire to ensure that women are rarely in decision-making positions. The first is women's comparative lack of participation in government security agencies, in particular at the highest levels—whether in SSR donor states or states undergoing SSR. As of January 2008, women ministers in 185 countries held 1022 portfolios. Only 6 of these were portfolios for defence and veteran affairs.[24] Few countries emerging from conflict have women in senior ranks in the security services. When SSR is heavily weighted towards security sector capacity building, as it tends to be in the wake of con-

tions at all levels of government. UN Security Council Resolution 1325 (note 3) reaffirms 'the important role of women in the prevention and resolution of conflicts and in peace-building' and urges states 'to ensure increased representation of women at all decision-making levels in national, regional and international institutions and mechanisms for the prevention, management, and resolution of conflict'.

[23] That the overwhelming majority of personnel in international and other agencies who work on SSR programming is male is often remarked on, by both women and men, in discussions around gender and SSR. This chapter focuses on the participation of the *women of countries* undergoing SSR. However, analysis of women's participation in SSR agencies, barriers thereto and how it impacts on the gender responsiveness of programming would be of interest.

[24] Inter-Parliamentary Union (IPU) and the UN Division for the Advancement of Women, 'Women in politics: 2008' (map poster), Feb. 2008, available at <http://www.ipu.org/pdf/publications/wmnmap08_en.pdf>. Taking an example from national security institutions: in Serbia in 2005 women constituted 19.68% of the total number of employees of the Ministry of Interior, but only 15.81% of authorized officers and 7.83% of executives. Novovic, S. and Petrovic, D., *Women in Policing* (Republic of Serbia Ministry of Interior Police College: Belgrade, Apr. 2006), pp. 35–36.

flict, women are less likely to be involved through the external and internal agencies engaged in reform or from inside the security services. Second, while the proportion of women in parliament has greatly increased in many post-conflict states, women rarely chair the defence and security committees or take part in special commissions appointed to deal with security issues.[25] Third, all too often SSR is planned and implemented in a manner that excludes meaningful civil society input. When civil society organizations are given a voice in SSR this can be a means for strong participation and representation of women.

A gender-aware SSR design will both devise measures to involve women from all sectors of the community and be welcoming to such initiatives taken by women themselves. Planning and implementation should include actions that promote broad participation in SSR: national dialogue and consultation, public hearings and discussion in the media, and including civil society representatives in bodies planning and executing SSR. This may require efforts to convene focus groups and other meetings at times and locations and in languages that are accessible for women and men who might otherwise be marginalized from the process. Special steps to ensure women's participation may include sessions dedicated to addressing women's security concerns, ensuring that the ministry of gender or women's affairs is formally involved in SSR at a decision-making level and a caucus within parliament to develop a shared platform on gender and security issues.

Involvement of civil society organizations in security sector oversight, and empowering parliamentarians to be sensitive to gender in their oversight functions, can help to ensure that SSR processes mainstream gender issues.[26] In order to allow women parliamentarians to be engaged in SSR there must of course be enhanced women's participation in parliament itself—an illustration of how SSR requirements go hand in hand with improving women's access to public decision making and policy formulation more generally.[27]

Women's civil society groups in security sector reform

The roles that women play in provision of security within their communities should be recognized and supported in SSR. Women's groups often provide a range of services to victims of violence, such as shelter, legal advice, and medical and psychological assistance. They can work with formal security ser-

[25] Inter-Parliamentary Union (IPU) world surveys on women in politics over 25 years have shown that women are still largely absent from, or under-represented in, parliamentary defence committees and rarely occupy the function of presiding or deputy presiding officer or rapporteur in such committees. Of 97 parliaments that provided data on women in parliamentary committees for the 1997 IPU survey, only 3% had a woman chairing their defence committee. DCAF and IPU, *Parliamentary Oversight of the Security Sector: Principles, Mechanisms and Practices* (DCAF and IPU: Geneva, 2003), p. 47.

[26] For detailed guidance on integrating gender in civil society and parliamentary oversight of the security sector see eds Bastick and Valasek (note 18); and DCAF and IPU (note 25).

[27] Strategies to promote the participation of women in parliaments are available from the IPU, <http://www.ipu.org/>; International IDEA, <http://www.idea.int/>; and the International Knowledge Network of Women in Politics, <http://www.iknowpolitics.org/>.

vices in providing information about local-level security threats and in implementing security initiatives. For example, in a 2004 study of reintegrated former combatants in Sierra Leone, 55 per cent of the respondents indicated that women in the community played a significant role in helping them reintegrate, compared to 20 per cent who were helped by traditional leaders and 32 per cent by international aid workers.[28]

Women's civil society organizations can be important partners in ensuring local ownership of post-conflict SSR. In Liberia, for example, women's groups that throughout the 1989–2003 civil wars worked for peace continue to work on post-conflict reconstruction, reconciliation and promotion of women's rights. In December 2006 Liberian women's civil society groups called on their government and the international community to 'increase the role of women in security sector reform by engaging women-led civil society organizations in: transforming public perception of the military and police, strengthening disarmament, and recruiting women for the armed forces and police'.[29] In February 2007 a joint delegation of female government officials and civil society leaders addressed donors to Liberia at the World Bank. The women's input stressed the interconnectedness of security, economic development, health and education. They urged that Liberia's SSR process embrace a broader view of human security in the light of the increasing incidence of gender-based violence and insecurity in local communities. They made concrete recommendations as to how the SSR process could be more effective and responsive to gender issues, including that: (a) penal reform address the needs of male, female and youth prisoners; (b) training for the security forces include trauma counselling; and (c) anti-corruption measures combat requests for sex as well as for money. They urged that women be full partners in the creation of the national security policy and defence strategy and recommended that the Governance Reform Commission, responsible for SSR, involve gender experts in its planning. They underlined that women should be recognized and more extensively involved in 'managing security risks', given their skills, for example, in advancing local reconciliation, connecting local communities with national government and reaching out to youth.[30]

The energy and focus of Liberian women's civil society in demanding full access to the SSR process has produced some results and signs that, in reforming its security sector, Liberia is responding to women's security needs. A Women and Children Protection Section of the Liberian National Police has been established, with officers specially trained in the handling and manage-

---

[28] Cited in Association of European Parliamentarians for Africa (AWEPA), *The Role of Parliaments in Conflict Management and Peacebuilding*, Occasional Paper Series no. 13 (AWEPA: Amsterdam, Sep. 2006), <http://www.awepa.org/index.php?option=com_content&task=view&id=338>, p. 70.

[29] Hunt Alternatives Fund, Initiative for Inclusive Security, 'The initiative for inclusive security civil society consultation: women civil society leaders' recommendations for the Government of Liberia and the international community', Washington, DC, 12 Dec. 2006, <http://www.huntalternatives.org/down load/333_microsoft_word_12_12_06_civil_society_recommendations_for_ejs.pdf>.

[30] Hunt Alternatives Fund, Initiative for Inclusive Security, 'Priorities for reconstruction: input to the Liberian Interim Poverty Reduction Strategy (IPRS)', Washington, DC, Feb. 2007, <http://www.huntalter natives.org/download/380_microsoft_word_preparatory_conference_iprs_recommendations_final.pdf>.

ment of cases of sexual and other forms of gender-based violence.[31] A Women and Children's unit has been formed in the Liberian prisons, and prison officers receive training on gender and sexual and gender-based violence.[32] Liberia has adopted a 20 per cent quota for women's inclusion in the police and armed forces. A boost to recruitment of women in the Liberian police has come from India. In January 2007 the UN's first all-female peacekeeping contingent, made up of 103 Indian policewomen, was deployed in Liberia. The Liberian National Police received three times the usual number of female applicants in the month following their deployment.[33]

The Liberian women's movement, where women's activists work with government officials, demonstrates how gender can be a shared platform for vertical cooperation between government, political party and local levels; and how women's networks can operationalize the linkages between local security and justice concerns and SSR. These networks allow women's groups to facilitate dialogue between local communities and SSR policymakers and practitioners and help SSR processes respond to the communities' own needs, dynamics and resources. The participation of women in Liberia's new security services helps to imbue them with public trust and legitimacy.

The participation of women's organizations in the 1996–98 South African Defence Review could be used as a model for promoting civil society involvement in SSR in countries emerging from conflict.[34] At the insistence of women parliamentarians, among others, the Parliamentary Joint Standing Committee on Defence called for a national consultation as part of the defence review process. A variety of measures were taken to ensure public participation, including using military aircraft and buses to transport religious and community leaders, non-governmental organization (NGO) activists and representatives of women's organizations to regional meetings and workshops. Grassroots women's organizations drew attention to previously ignored security issues, such as the plight of dispossessed communities whose land had been seized for military use and the sexual harassment of women by military personnel. The participatory defence review helped to build national consensus around defence issues in South Africa and generate legitimacy for the new security structures. The South African National Defence Force introduced a number of initiatives and mechanisms to promote gender equality, in accordance with the defence review's explicit commitment to the constitutional principles of non-discrimination on the basis of sex, race or sexual orientation.

[31] UN Children's Fund (UNICEF), 'New women and children protection section for Liberia's police', Press release, 1 Sep. 2005, <http://www.unicef.org/media/media_28159.html>.

[32] UN Mission in Liberia (UNMIL), 'Outcomes of gender mainstreaming by the Office of the Gender Adviser: UNMIL, 2004–2006', <http://www.unmil.org/documents/OGA_Achievement_2004_2006.pdf>.

[33] Guéhenno, J. M., Statement to the UN Security Council, Debate on Women, Peace and Security, UN document S/PV.5766, 23 Oct. 2007, p. 5.

[34] Anderlini, S. N., *Negotiating the Transition to Democracy and Reforming the Security Sector: The Vital Contributions of South African Women* (Hunt Alternatives Fund, Initiative for Inclusive Security: Washington DC, Aug. 2004), pp. ix, 23–25.

Women parliamentarians in security sector reform

Women in parliament also have distinctive contributions to make to SSR. Female parliamentarians, being as diverse as their male counterparts, will not necessarily advocate any one particular approach to SSR. However, as pointed out by Gertrude Mongella, President of the Pan-African Parliament, 'the participation of women not only provides equal opportunity on a practical level, but also offers a new perspective and diversity of contributions to policy-making and priorities for development'.[35] After the Rwandan genocide, electoral reforms introducing legislative quotas helped to make Rwanda the world leader in terms of women's representation in parliament, with 48.8 per cent of parliamentarians being women.[36] Female parliamentarians established the first parliamentary caucus that reached across party lines and included both Hutus and Tutsis. It addressed issues of women's security, regardless of their ethnic or party affiliation, initiating laws on women's right to inherit property and widows' right to claim property from their deceased husband's male relatives, and on gender-based violence.[37] A 1999 survey of 187 women politicians from 65 countries, including conflict-affected countries in Africa, Europe, Latin America and the Caribbean, recorded their perceptions of how women's involvement in politics makes a difference. Women pointed to tangible achievements in the areas of social security, gender equality, fighting violence against women and children, employment, services, the environment and—although to a lesser extent as yet—arms control and conflict resolution.[38]

Serbia has developed capacity-building programmes that might usefully be replicated in post-conflict countries to support the full participation of women in SSR.[39] In Serbia, women in the ministries of defence and interior, and female parliamentarians, political and NGO activists and journalists are trying to insert their particular perspectives on security into the SSR process. In 2007 the Belgrade Fund for Political Excellence initiated a programme to increase the visibility of women in the security sector and strengthen their engagement in its reform. Women are brought together in a series of seminars to discuss human and global security, multinational security organizations, peacebuilding, and the role and contribution of women. In a second phase, the women more specifically examine the role of women in reforming security agencies,

[35] Cited in AWEPA (note 28), p. 61.

[36] Inter-Parliamentary Union, 'Women in national parliaments', 31 Dec. 2007, <http://www.ipu.org/wmn-e/world.htm>.

[37] In many post-conflict contexts, where male heads of household are dead or missing and displaced populations are returning home, reform of land laws and procedures for demonstrating land ownership are urgently needed. See Luciak, I. A., 'Conflict and a gendered parliamentary response', UN Development Programme (UNDP), Apr. 2006, <http://www.parlcpr.undp.org/docs/conference/Luciak.pdf>, p. 39; AWEPA (note 28), p. 66; and Powley, E., 'Rwanda: the impact of women legislators on policy outcomes affecting children and families', UNICEF, Dec. 2006, <http://www.unicef.org/sowc07/docs/powley.pdf>, p. 11.

[38] Inter-Parliamentary Union, *Politics: Women's Insight* (IPU: Geneva, Jan. 2000), p. 5.

[39] Whether Serbia is a 'post-conflict country' is debatable, but the relevance of the Belgrade Fund for Political Excellence's programme stands regardless.

with an emphasis on the implementation of UN Security Council Resolution 1325 in Serbia and the Western Balkans.[40]

IV. Promoting women's full and equal participation in post-conflict security services

The challenge of women's participation in security services

The under-representation of women in SSR, as noted above, is related to the
scarcity of women in the senior ranks of the security services in post-conflict
countries (see table 4.2, which includes figures from some other transitional,
developing and developed countries for comparison). In some cases, women
are formally barred from working in the police and other security services, but
most often they are under-represented because of informal barriers to
recruitment and an internal culture that makes it difficult for women to
advance or unlikely that they will stay.

In a democratic state women have a right to participate in security sector
institutions as an aspect of their citizenship. In principle, all positions within
the security services should be open to all citizens, regardless of gender, political affiliation, class, race or religion. The UN Committee on the Elimination
of All Forms of Discrimination against Women affirmed this in its comment
on participation of women in the military: 'The military is important to
women in their role as citizens . . . Since the military constitutes an important
element of State order, decision-making and governance, all citizens should be
concerned about the kind of military they have.'[41] Security Council Resolution 1325 calls for women's participation in mechanisms for the management and resolution of conflict, of which participation in security services is
an aspect. More broadly, the composition of security forces should be a mirror
of society at large: women's participation is crucial to creating structures that
are representative, and thus trusted and legitimate.

Women are also an important human resource pool of skills that are increasingly needed in security institutions. The very positive experiences of involving women in peacekeeping have underscored the operational benefits of
women's inclusion in such military tasks.[42] Engelbrektson describes women's

---

[40] Petrovic, N., Program Coordinator, Belgrade Fund for Political Excellence, Personal correspond-
ence with the author, 7 Nov. 2007.

[41] UN Committee on the Elimination of All Forms of Discrimination against Women (CEDAW),
Implementation of Article 21 of the Convention on the Elimination of All Forms of Discrimination
against Women: analysis of articles 7 and 8 of the convention, CEDAW/C/1994/1, 30 Nov. 1993,
<http://www.un.org/documents/ga/cedaw/13/cedawc1994-4.htm>. See also Klein, U., 'The gender per-
spective of civil–military relations in Israeli society', *Current Sociology*, vol. 50, no. 5 (Sep. 2002),
pp. 669–86. Klein suggests that without the experience of participation in the military, women are less
able to raise their voices in security discourse.

[42] The practical benefits of women as peacekeepers are discussed in e.g. Vlachová, M. and Biason, L.
(eds), *Women in an Insecure World: Violence against Women—Facts, Figures and Analysis* (DCAF:
Geneva, 2005); GenderForce: Sweden, 'From words to action', 2005, <http://www.genderforce.se/>;
Valenius, J., *Gender Mainstreaming in ESDP Missions*, Chaillot Paper no. 101 (EU Institute for Security

Table 4.2. Percentage of female officers in the police force of select countries

Country	Year	Percentage of female police officers
Post-conflict		
South Africa	2006	*29*
Cyprus	2006	*16*
Sierra Leone	2006	*15*
Kosovo[a]	2006	*14*
Transitional and developing		
Jamaica	2001	*18*
Czech Republic	2001	*12*
Venezuela	2002	*10*
Romania	2005	*8*
India	2006	*2*
Developed		
Australia	2002	*29*
Canada	2006	*18*
Sweden	2001	*18*
United States	2006	*12–14*
Finland	2004	*10*

[a] Although listed among independent countries here, Kosovo did not declare its independence until 17 Feb. 2008.

Source: Denham, T., 'Police reform and gender', eds M. Bastick and K. Valasek, *Gender and Security Sector Reform Toolkit* (DCAF, Organization for Security and Co-operation in Europe/Office for Democratic Institutions and Human Rights and UN International Research and Training Institute for the Advancement of Women: Geneva, 2008).

participation in peacekeeping operations as 'a key to success' in overcoming certain operational limitations of purely male forces, such as the searching and interrogation of women.[43] The UN Department of Peacekeeping Operations has set a target of ensuring that 10 per cent of peacekeeping police and military personnel are women.[44]

The benefits of increased participation of women in policing are also well documented. Research conducted both in the United States and internationally clearly demonstrates that women officers' style of policing uses less physical force, is less likely to use it to excess and is better at defusing and de-escalating potentially violent confrontations with citizens. Additionally, women officers often possess better communication skills than their male counterparts and are better able to earn the cooperation and trust needed for a community

Studies: Paris, May 2007), p. 28; and Pillay, A., *Gender, Peace and Peace-keeping: Lessons from Southern Africa*, Institute for Security Studies (ISS) Occasional Paper no. 128 (ISS: Pretoria, Oct. 2006).

[43] Engelbrektson, K., quoted in GenderForce: Sweden (note 42).

[44] UN Department of Peacekeeping Operations, 'Implementation of Security Council Resolution 1325 (2000) on women, peace and security in peacekeeping contexts: final report', A Strategy Workshop with Women's Consistencies from Troop and Police Contributing Countries, Pretoria, 7–9 Feb. 2007, p. 8.

policing model.[45] Where women are victims of sexual or domestic violence, there is overwhelming evidence—including from the Democratic Republic of the Congo, India and Sierra Leone—that they are more likely to report this to a female police officer or to a women's police station or family unit than to a male officer within a traditional police structure.[46] The UN's Model Strategies and Practical Measures on the Elimination of Violence against Women in the Field of Crime Prevention and Criminal Justice, endorsed by the General Assembly, urge states: 'To encourage women to join police services, including at the operational level'.[47]

Women's participation within post-conflict security services

A number of countries emerging from conflict, like Liberia (discussed above), have prioritized the recruitment of women in their security services. The high incidence of violence against women, in particular domestic violence and rape, in post-conflict settings has in some cases created strong demand for police services that meet women's particular security needs inter alia by employing female officers. Addressing family violence has been prioritized in reform of the security sector in Afghanistan, Kosovo, Liberia and Sierra Leone, each of which has established specialized police units for the purpose.

Many post-conflict countries have little tradition of women in uniform, and social attitudes are the major barrier to women's full and equal participation in security services. However, the post-conflict period can be one of opportunity for women. Changes in gender roles during armed conflict, when women often take on new responsibilities for ensuring their family's safety or themselves join armed groups, can contribute to a new recognition of the contributions women make to security. Living through a conflict offers women new skills, knowledge and leadership regarding security issues and new insight into the armed forces' relationship with the community.[48] SSR processes can build on and support any such positive changes in women's status during the conflict. In rebuilding security institutions, SSR should include a range of measures to increase the recruitment and retention of women and to create a work environment that is supportive of women not only in police and defence forces, but also in intelligence services, penal services, border authorities, the judiciary and the institutions that manage them. These include setting targets for

[45] Lonsway, K. et al., National Center for Women & Policing, 'Hiring & retaining more women: the advantages to law enforcement agencies', spring 2003, <http://www.womenandpolicing.org/pdf/New AdvantagesReport.pdf>, p. 2.

[46] See e.g. Suddle, M. S., 'Reforming the police forces of South Asia', *Strengthening the Criminal Justice System: From the ADB Regional Workshop in Dhaka, Bangladesh, 30–31 May 2006* (Asian Development Bank: Manila, Jan. 2007), p. 56; Rehn and Johnson Sirleaf (note 10), p. 73; Kandaswamy, D., 'Indian policewomen practice policing and politicking', *Ms. Magazine*, winter 2004; and Fakondo, K., Personal interview, 17 Sep. 2007, quoted in Denham, T., 'Police reform and gender', eds Bastick and Valasek (note 18).

[47] UN General Assembly Resolution 52/86, UN document A/RES/52/86, 2 Feb. 1998, annex 8.

[48] Anderlini, S. N. and Conaway, C. P., 'Security sector reform', *Inclusive Security, Sustainable Peace: A Toolkit for Advocacy and Action* (Hunt Alternatives Fund and International Alert: Washington, DC, 2004), p. 35.

women's recruitment and recruitment strategies designed to attract women. Linkages with DDR programmes (see section V) may facilitate integration of female former combatants into new security services.

Such strategies have been implemented in Kosovo, with mixed success. In the immediate aftermath of the March–June 1999 NATO military operations significant efforts were made to recruit women as cadets in the new basic policing programme. There had been no female police in Kosovo before the conflict.[49] In the first years of the new police training courses, as many as a third of the graduates were female, and currently some 14 per cent of the Kosovo Police are women. Efforts to persuade women to join Kosovo's Border and Boundary Police Training Unit failed. Women's stated reasons for not joining included that their family or husband would not permit them to work so far from home—giving some insight into the social barriers to women's full and equal participation in all arms of the security services.[50]

In Afghanistan also, efforts are being made to attract more women to the police. Given the separation of the sexes in Afghanistan, women are uniquely qualified to handle female victims of crime and female suspects. Persistent sexual violence against women is considered to be a cause of the sharp increase in recent years in the number of Afghan women attempting suicide by setting fire to themselves, or being murdered in so-called honour killings.[51] This situation adds grave urgency to the need to ensure women's access to appropriate police services. Women are also required for day-to-day policing activities. Male recruits for the Afghan National Police in Uruzgan have complained that they are unable to perform body searches of persons wearing burkas at checkpoints due to the lack of female colleagues, and security is as a result jeopardized by men passing disguised as women.[52]

So far, however, success in recruiting women to the Afghan police has been limited: by July 2007, 71 147 rank-and-file police had received training, of which only 118 were women, and there were only 232 female police in the whole country. Recruitment and training strategies specifically for women are necessary if women are to attain leadership positions. Efforts to attract more women now include a women's dormitory at the Kabul Police Academy and a pilot project offering regional training so that women are not required to live away from their families for long periods of time.[53] The United Nations Population Fund is supporting the establishment of Family Response Units in the Afghan National Police. These units are staffed by female police officers, who receive training to enable them to react to violence against women, children in

[49] Novovic and Petrovic (note 24), p. 35.

[50] Mackay, A., 'Border management and gender', eds Bastick and Valasek (note 18).

[51] Amnesty International, *Afghanistan: Women Still Under Attack—A Systematic Failure to Protect* (Amnesty International: London, May 2005), pp. 23–25; and Integrated Regional Information Networks, 'Afghanistan: honour killings on the rise', 15 Sep. 2006, <http://www.irinnews.org/report.aspx?report id=61698>.

[52] Interview reported by Verwijk, M., Senior Policy Officer, Dutch Ministry of Foreign Affairs, quoted in Valasek, K., 'Security sector reform and gender', eds Bastick and Valasek (note 18).

[53] International Crisis Group (ICG), *Reforming Afghanistan's Police*, Asia Report no. 138 (ICG: Brussels, 30 Aug. 2007), pp. 10–12.

trouble and kidnappings; to provide support to female victims of crime; and to interrogate, detain and investigate female suspects.[54]

However, women's participation alone is not enough. As an NGO has reported from Sierra Leone, 'although female police officers have been hired, and the lower ranks of the [Sierra Leone Police] have been trained in gender sensitivity, the commanders have not. Female police officers are sometimes expected to do little more than cook lunch for the male police officers.'[55] This underlines the need for recruitment measures to be supported by women-friendly cultural change throughout security institutions, and from the highest levels. This itself demands gender mainstreaming measures. Training for all staff on human rights and gender issues, internal codes prohibiting discrimination and sexual harassment, and transparent and non-discriminatory promotional structures are necessary conditions for successfully integrating women into security services and benefiting from their integration.

V. Gender and specific post-conflict security sector reform issues

Integrating gender in disarmament, demobilization and reintegration

There are strong linkages between SSR and DDR within the framework of post-conflict peacebuilding, such that the OECD DAC affirms that 'the two issues are often best considered together as part of a comprehensive security and justice development programme'.[56] In recent years, greater awareness of the magnitude and various forms of women's and girls' participation in armed conflicts has led to a realization that DDR plans have often failed to cover them.[57] An estimated 88 per cent of girl soldiers were denied access to DDR programmes in Sierra Leone between 1998 and 2002.[58] The need for gender-sensitive DDR programmes was affirmed in UN Security Council Resolution 1325, which encouraged 'all those involved in the planning for disarmament, demobilisation and reintegration to consider the different needs of female and male ex-combatants and to take into account the needs of their dependants'.[59] The UN Development Fund for Women (UNIFEM) checklist

[54] UN Population Fund, 'Afghanistan's first family response unit open for business', 24 Jan. 2006, <http://www.unfpa.org/news/news.cfm?ID=740>.

[55] Refugees International, 'Sierra Leone: promotion of human rights and protection for women still required', 18 Mar. 2004, <http://www.refugeesinternational.org/content/article/detail/949/>.

[56] OECD, *OECD DAC Handbook on Security System Reform: Supporting Security and Justice* (OECD: Paris, 2007), p. 105. See discussion in Bryden, A., 'Understanding the DDR–SSR nexus: building sustainable peace in Africa', Issue Paper, Second International Conference on DDR and Stability in Africa, Kinshasa, 2–14 July 2007, <http://www.dcaf.ch/publications/kms/details.cfm?id=34308>, p. 5.

[57] McKay, S. and Mazurana, D., *Where are the Girls? Girls in Fighting Forces in Northern Uganda, Sierra Leone and Mozambique: Their Lives During and After War* (Rights & Democracy: Quebec, 2004), p. 14.

[58] Statement by Paterson, M., Senior Advisor, Gender Equality Division, CIDA, 'Forum report', Women and Leadership: Voices for Security and Development, Ottawa, 28–29 Nov. 2002, p. 20.

[59] UN Security Council Resolution 1325 (note 3).

Box 4.1. Gender is also for men and boys

Masculinity and violence

Notions of masculinity are often linked with possession of weapons. In order to transform a violent masculine identity into a non-violent one, it is important to consider men's gender identities, roles and relations, and how these link to the perpetration of sexual and gender-based violence.

Male victims of sexual and gender-based violence

Men and boys are vulnerable to sexual violence inflicted by other men during military conscription or abduction into paramilitary forces, sometimes as part of initiation and integration rituals. It is essential to pay special attention to male victims of sexual and gender-based violence. Male victims are more unlikely to report incidents, as such issues are taboo in most societies.

Men's traditional roles

Male ex-combatants who are unable to fulfil their traditional role (i.e. as breadwinner of the household) often face an identity crisis. This can lead to an increase in domestic violence and alcohol and drug abuse. Disarmament, demobilization and reintegration programmes should not reinforce stereotypical men's roles, but rather encourage proper counselling mechanisms and flexible socioeconomic support. This is an important aspect of preventing further perpetration of sexual and gender-based violence.

Source: Adapted from United Nations, Integrated Disarmament, Demobilization and Reintegration Standards (IDDRS) Operational Guide, <http://www.unddr.org/iddrs/og/OG_5_10.pdf>, p. 195.

---

on Gender-aware Disarmament, Demobilization and Reintegration and the UN's Integrated DDR Standards (IDDRS) now provide detailed guidelines on addressing the particular needs of women and girls during demobilization and reintegration.[60]

Women and girls have often had difficulties in meeting the traditional selection criterion for DDR programmes, namely that they should surrender a weapon or be able to prove their military rank or recruitment. While some women were combatants, many more were deprived of their social support systems through the demobilization of male combatants upon whom they depended. As stated in the IDDRS: 'If the aim of DDR is to provide broad-based community security, it cannot create insecurity for this group of women by ignoring their special needs.'[61] Recognition of the extra categories of female beneficiaries proposed in the IDDRS, 'female supporters/females associated with armed forces and groups' and 'female dependants', is designed to ensure that women and girls are not overlooked.

---

[60] UN Development Fund for Women (UNIFEM), 'Gender-aware disarmament, demobilization and reintegration (DDR): a checklist', 2004, <http://www.undp.org/cpr/cpr_all/4_cross_cutting/4.1_gender/1_UNIFEM_DDR_Checklist.pdf>; and UN Disarmament, Demobilization and Reintegration Resource Centre, 'Integrated disarmament, demobilization and reintegration standards: women, gender and DDR', 2006, <http://www.unddr.org/iddrs/05/index.php?search_phrase=Women_gender_and_DDR>.

[61] UN Disarmament, Demobilization and Reintegration Resource Centre (note 60) p. 11.

Even when women and girls are included in such schemes on paper, experience from the DDR programmes in Liberia and Sierra Leone suggests that they may fail to enrol in DDR programmes for various gender-related reasons, such as fear for their safety—including risks of sexual violence—owing to the presence of large numbers of male ex-combatants at the encampment site, and fear of the social stigma attached to women who participated in armed conflict or who were associated with armed groups.[62] This underscores the need for DDR programmes to include specific information addressing women's concerns and communication methods that reach female combatants and supporters directly.

In Liberia, local women's organizations were a key partner in designing and distributing DDR information. An initial needs assessment estimated that some 2000 female combatants would undergo DDR. In 2003 women's groups organized under the banner Concerned Women of Liberia and became involved in DDR. Working with the UN mission and the Ministry of Gender and Development, they helped to design an awareness campaign using print media and radio to encourage women and girls to participate in the DDR process.[63] By February 2005, 22 370 women and 2440 girls had been disarmed and demobilized, of a total of 101 495 persons in the DDR programme. Women associated with fighting forces as well as female combatants were recognized.[64] By the end of 2006, 13 223 of these women had been 'reinserted', mainly into agriculture, formal education or vocational training.[65]

Gender-sensitive DDR is also about recognizing and meeting the particular needs of men and boys, and responding to their roles and available choices in their community. The IDDRS Operational Guide highlights three areas in which 'Gender is also for men and boys' (see box 4.1). For disarmament to be effective, it may be necessary to provide incentives that replace the prestige and power of owning a weapon for a man.[66] Involving communities in weapon-collection processes can be a way to shift social pressures from approval to disapproval of men's possession of weapons. In the demobilization of male combatants, support should be provided that addresses the likelihood that they have suffered or perpetrated sexual violence. Nathalie de Watteville notes that 'unemployed, demobilized young men, socialized to vio-

[62] McKay and Mazurana (note 57), p. 101. See also Mazurana, D. and Carlson, K., *From Combat to Community: Women and Girls of Sierra Leone* (Hunt Alternatives Fund, Initiative for Inclusive Security: Washington, DC, Jan. 2004), p. 3; Coulter, C., '"Bush wives" marginalized in rehabilitation programme', *New Routes*, vol. 11, no. 4 (2006), pp. 4, 10; and Bouta, T., Frerks, G. and Bannon, I., *Gender, Conflict, and Development* (World Bank: Washington, DC, 2005), p. 18.

[63] UN Department of Peacekeeping Operations, *Gender Mainstreaming in Peacekeeping Operations: Progress Report* (United Nations: New York, 2005), pp. 31–32.

[64] UN Disarmament, Demobilization and Reintegration Resource Centre, Country programme: Liberia, 1 June 2007, <http://www.unddr.org/countryprogrammes.php?c=52>; and UNMIL, Disarmament, demobilization, reintegration and rehabilitation, 1 June 2007, <http://www.unmil.org/content.asp?ccat=ddrr>.

[65] UN Mission in Liberia (note 32).

[66] United Nations, Integrated Disarmament, Demobilization and Reintegration Standards (IDDRS), Module 5.10 Women, gender and DDR, <http://www.unddr.org/iddrs/05/download/IDDRS_510.pdf>, p. 18.

lence and brutality during war, are more likely than others to form gangs, particularly in urban areas, and can pose a constant threat to the security of women and children'.[67] In addition to economic reintegration programmes for male ex-combatants that provide an alternative base for living, psychosocial services for them must continue during the reintegration phase.

Integrating gender in transitional justice and justice reform

'Transitional justice' is increasingly seen as essential for post-conflict states, to set the scene for eventual reconciliation by establishing a process of accountability and acknowledgement, and to deter the reoccurrence of violence and thus ensure sustainable peace.[68] Transitional justice may be pursued through temporary, specifically created bodies—such as ad hoc criminal tribunals, truth and reconciliation commissions and reparations programmes—or a state's permanent justice mechanisms. In post-conflict contexts, transitional justice mechanisms are often part of a broader process of justice reform (discussed below) and are closely linked to wider reforms of the security sector.[69]

Transitional justice has come to play a role of particular importance in addressing wartime sexual and gender-based violence against women. The International Criminal Tribunal for the former Yugoslavia (ICTY) and the International Criminal Tribunal for Rwanda (ICTR) broke new ground in securing the first convictions for rape and other forms of sexual violence as war crimes, crimes against humanity and acts of genocide. The jurisprudence of the ICTY and ICTR has been crucial in developing recognition and understanding of different forms of sexual violence in conflict as crimes under international law. However, the international tribunals have been less successful in protecting and supporting victims of sexual violence. A number of witnesses for the ICTR, for example, were threatened or killed before or after testifying at the tribunal.[70] Witnesses are reported to have received inadequate preparation and to have experienced aggressive cross-examination during the trials, which left them feeling re-victimized and humiliated. A decision by a survivor to testify sometimes led to her abandonment by her spouse or expulsion from her com-

---

[67] De Watteville, N., *Addressing Gender Issues in Demobilization and Reintegration Programs*, Africa Region Working Paper Series, no. 33 (World Bank: Washington, DC, May 2002), p. 20.

[68] Mobekk, E., *Transitional Justice and Security Sector Reform: Enabling Sustainable Peace*, DCAF Occasional Paper no. 13 (DCAF: Geneva, Nov. 2006), p. 2. See also Wiharta, S., 'Post-conflict justice: developments in international courts', *SIPRI Yearbook 2004* (note 1), pp. 197–98; and Dwan, R. and Wiharta, S., 'Multilateral peace missions: the challenges of peace-building', *SIPRI Yearbook 2005: Armaments, Disarmament and International Security* (Oxford University Press: Oxford, 2005), pp. 139–98.

[69] Mobekk e.g. notes that: 'Transitional justice mechanisms such as truth commissions can provide recommendations for what changes and reform need to take place within government institutions that perpetrated violations against its citizens. Domestic and hybrid courts can potentially enhance and reform the judicial system whilst ensuring accountability.' Mobekk (note 68), pp. 2–3. See also van Zyl, P., 'Promoting transitional justice in post-conflict societies', eds A. Bryden and H. Hänggi, *Security Governance in Post-Conflict Peacebuilding* (DCAF: Geneva, 2005), pp. 209–31.

[70] Walsh, C., 'Witness protection, gender and the ICTR', Rights & Democracy, International Centre for Human Rights and Democratic Development, July 1997, <http://www.ichrdd.ca/english/commdoc/publications/women/womtrirw.html>.

munity. Women who contracted HIV/AIDS as a result of rape were not always provided with adequate treatment.[71]

Some progress in addressing these problems has been demonstrated by the Special Court for Sierra Leone, which, for example, dedicated experienced women investigators to investigate crimes of sexual violence, adopted a gender-sensitive interviewing method to ensure that victims of sexual violence felt comfortable reporting crimes, and emphasized witness preparation.[72] Nonetheless, the risk remains that a prosecution process leaves victims stigmatized within their communities and feeling that they did not have an opportunity to fully tell their story, or that justice was not delivered (especially when a conviction is not secured). There has been a growing acknowledgement that 'gender justice' cannot be achieved through judicial processes of accountability alone.

Truth-telling bodies seek to provide a space for victims to tell their stories by officially recognizing and condemning the wrongdoings, and to prevent abuses from reoccurring by confronting impunity. Their comparative flexibility and informality give them the potential to be more sensitive than are criminal legal processes to gender issues. The more recent TRCs, including those in Peru, Sierra Leone and Timor-Leste, demonstrate how TRCs can take steps to address the particular experiences and justice needs of women. Thematic hearings dedicated to women, according to Ruth Rubio-Marín, 'have offered wonderful opportunities to give women voice, but also to ensure that this voice transcends and reaches the public . . . and to render women's sexual violence explicit'.[73] Other mechanisms used to activate gender mainstreaming in TRC work include the formation of special research teams dedicated to women (in Timor-Leste) and the dedication of some of the chapters in the final reports of commissions to recording violence against women and its diverse impact on their lives (in Peru and Sierra Leone).[74] In Sierra Leone, the TRC reached out to women's organizations to include them in the process. As a result, women's groups were very active in raising awareness about the TRC's work, testifying in the hearings, assisting victims of sexual violence, making recommendations for a reparations programme and pressuring the government to implement it.[75]

A glaring absence in much analysis of transitional justice and gender is understanding of the particular needs of men and boys. The Sierra Leone TRC did prioritize male survivors of sexual violence as a category of victim in its

---

[71] Human Rights Watch, 'Struggling to survive: barriers to justice for rape victims in Rwanda', *Human Rights Watch*, vol. 16, no. 10 (Sep. 2004), <http://www.hrw.org/reports/2004/rwanda0904/>, pp. 9–10, 27–29; and Nowrojee, B., *'Your Justice is Too Slow': Will the ICTR Fail Rwanda's Rape Victims?*, UN Research Institute for Social Development (UNRISD) Occasional Paper no. 10 (UNRISD: Geneva, Nov. 2005), <http://www.womensrightscoalition.org/pdf/binaifer_paper.pdf>, p. 4.

[72] Bastick, Grimm and Kunz (note 10).

[73] Rubio-Marín, R., University of Seville, cited in Bastick, Grimm and Kunz (note 10).

[74] Rubio-Marín, R., University of Seville, cited in Bastick, Grimm and Kunz (note 10).

[75] King, J., 'Gender and reparations in Sierra Leone: the wounds of war remain open', ed. R. Rubio-Marín, *What Happened to the Women? Gender and Reparations for Human Rights Violations* (International Center for Transitional Justice, Social Science Research Council: New York, 2006), pp. 256–57.

recommendations for reparations.[76] However, given that all the incidents of rape and sexual slavery reported to the TRC were committed against women and girls, it might be concluded that insufficient effort was made to encourage men and boys who suffered sexual violence to come forward.[77]

Simultaneously, in recognizing the particular impact of armed conflict on women and girls it is necessary to go beyond sexual violence. Peruvian women, while welcoming the work on sexual violence by their TRC, have expressed concern that this focus has led to deprioritization of other women's experiences, such as those of refugee and internally displaced women, women who became sole breadwinners as a result of human rights abuse against spouses, and women prisoners.[78] These points illuminate at least two challenges: how to ensure that gender justice also delivers justice to male victims; and how to ensure that mandates and mechanisms for transitional justice are developed in a participatory manner, so that they address the local communities' own priorities for justice and reparation.

Beyond transitional justice, countries emerging from conflict tend to be in urgent need of reforms across the justice sector. If the reformed justice sector is to have credibility and legitimacy in the eyes of the community, including those of women, the reform process must include the participation, and address the needs, of all segments of society with emphasis placed on identifying laws and practices that discriminate against particular men or women.

Laws to punish gender-based violence are also often inadequate and lagging behind international human rights standards. Some of the first legislation passed in post-conflict Rwanda and Liberia were new laws addressing rape.[79] The process for educating and appointing judicial personnel should also be scrutinized and measures put in place to encourage equal participation and ethnic and religious diversity of men and women within the judiciary and legal profession.

VI. Conclusions

Gender has been recognized as a crucial factor in development for over 20 years but is making rather a late entry into discourse and policymaking on SSR. While many donors that support SSR also do extensive work to support gender equality in post-conflict contexts, the two areas of work are often planned and implemented independently of each other.

The main challenges to successfully integrating gender are to some extent those that have hampered SSR in so many post-conflict contexts: an impa-

[76] Truth and Reconciliation Commission, Sierra Leone, 'Chapter 4: reparations', *The Final Report of the Truth and Reconciliation Commission of Sierra Leone*, vol. 2 (Truth and Reconciliation Commission, Sierra Leone: Freetown, 2004), p. 250.

[77] King (note 75), p. 252.

[78] International Center for Transitional Justice (ICTJ), *Truth Commissions and Gender: Principles, Policies and Procedures* (ICTJ: New York, 2006), p. 9.

[79] On Rwanda see Luciak (note 37); AWEPA (note 28); and Powley (note 37). On Liberia see Rehn and Johnson Sirleaf (note 10), p. 163.

tience to complete programmes, leading to insufficient local ownership; and assumptions that models that have been used elsewhere can be replicated without due regard to context. Consultation and dialogue with a larger range of stakeholders do not necessarily demand large financial resources, but they do take time and a personal commitment by many individuals. Gender issues are often of great cultural sensitivity, so while external actors can encourage and support, initiatives must be led by local stakeholders.

It is these local stakeholders who represent the most important resource and opportunity for integrating gender in post-conflict SSR. In many countries that are emerging from conflict, parliamentarians, women working in security services, civil society organizations and others are voicing demands for gender-responsive SSR. As policies and approaches to SSR are increasingly codified by international organizations and donors, steps to ensure the integration of gender should be embedded in standard operating, monitoring and reporting procedures and training.

SSR has much to gain by integrating the gender dimension. By drawing on the full participation of both men and women it can become more responsive to local needs, more legitimate and better able to address the range of security and justice priorities that coexist in communities. In post-conflict contexts, working with women's groups and others marginalized from pre-existing power structures can build public trust, help to ground SSR in inclusiveness and improve provision of security and justice across all parts of the community. Conversely, SSR approaches that ignore gender will fall short of achieving their goal of effective and accountable delivery of security to all.

Part II. Military spending and armaments, 2007

Chapter 5. Military expenditure

Chapter 6. Arms production

Chapter 7. International arms transfers

5. Military expenditure

PETTER STÅLENHEIM, CATALINA PERDOMO and
ELISABETH SKÖNS

I. Introduction

World military expenditure in 2007 is estimated to have been $1339 billion, a real-terms increase over 2006 of 6.0 per cent.[1] Over the 10-year period 1998–2007, world military spending has increased by 45 per cent in real terms. Military spending in 2007 corresponded to 2.5 per cent of world gross domestic product (GDP) and $202 per capita.[2]

Based on data from the SIPRI Military Expenditure Database, this chapter provides information on military expenditure trends over the period 1998–2007 and analyses these trends for selected countries in each region.[3] Section II presents the statistics on regional trends in military spending and data on the 15 largest spenders. Section III is devoted to US military expenditure since the United States accounts for the overwhelming share—45 per cent—of global spending. The rest of the chapter focuses on the countries that have increased military spending most rapidly in recent years. Section IV discusses the factors driving and facilitating the particularly rapid increases in military expenditure in the South Caucasus. Section V provides information on regional trends. The concluding section VI summarizes the main factors driving the increase in military spending in 2007.

Appendix 5A presents SIPRI data on military expenditure for 168 countries for 1998–2007. As well as world and regional totals, data for individual countries are provided in local currency at current prices for 1998–2007, in constant US dollars for 1998–2007, in current US dollars for 2007 and as a share of GDP for 1998–2006. Appendix 5B presents the military expenditure of members of the North Atlantic Treaty Organization (NATO) devoted to equip-

---

[1] The figure for world military expenditure in 2007 is in current US dollars. The real-terms increase is based on expenditure in US dollars at constant (2005) prices and exchange rates. Figures in constant dollars are used to assess the trends in spending, while figures in current dollars are used for analysing shares of spending, such as country shares of regional totals and country or regional shares of the world total. All figures in US dollars are calculated using the average annual market exchange rates. On the choice of exchange rate see appendix 5C, section V. SIPRI provides figures in current dollars only for the most recent year. See tables 5A.1 and 5A.3 in appendix 5A.

[2] The share of GDP is based on a projected figure for world GDP in 2007 of $53 352 billion at market exchange rates. International Monetary Fund (IMF), *World Economic Outlook, October 2007: Globalization and Inequality* (IMF: Washington, DC, 2007), p. 215. The per capita spending figure is calculated by dividing world military spending by world population, estimated at 6616 million in 2007, with no national weighting. United Nations Population Fund (UNFPA), *State of the World Population 2007: Unleashing the Potential of Urban Growth* (UNFPA: New York, 2007), p. 99.

[3] The SIPRI Military Expenditure Database can be accessed at <http://www.sipri.org/contents/milap/milex/mex_database1.html>.

Table 5.1. World and regional military expenditure estimates, 1998–2007

Figures are in US$ b., at constant (2005) prices and exchange rates. Figures in italics are percentages. Figures may not add up because of the conventions of rounding.

Region[a]	1998	1999	2000	2001	2002	2003	2004	2005	2006	2007	% change, 1998–07
Africa	11.1	11.9	12.3	13.5	14.3	14.1	15.8	16.0	15.8	16.8	*+51*
North	4.3	4.0	4.1	5.2	5.2	5.4	5.9	6.2	6.0	6.6	*+53*
Sub-Saharan	6.8	7.9	8.3	8.4	9.1	8.7	9.9	9.8	(9.7)	(10.1)	*+49*
Americas	367	367	382	388	431	481	522	548	559	598	*+63*
North	340	341	354	357	399	453	493	516	525	562	*+65*
Central	3.6	3.7	3.9	3.8	3.6	3.6	3.4	3.4	3.6	4.0	*+14*
South	23.3	22.1	23.9	26.7	27.5	24.6	25.8	28.1	30.1	32.0	*+38*
Caribbean	..	..	..	..	..	..	..	..	..	..	..
Asia, Oceania	132	135	139	146	153	160	166	176	186	200	*+52*
Central	(0.6)	0.5	..	(0.6)	..	(0.8)	..	..	..	..	..
East	100	101	104	110	116	122	127	132	140	152	*+51*
Oceania	11.4	11.9	11.8	12.2	12.7	13.2	13.8	14.3	15.1	16.4	*+45*
South	19.6	21.9	22.8	23.5	23.6	24.2	25.0	28.2	29.7	30.7	*+57*
Europe	276	280	287	288	295	302	306	306	311	319	*+16*
Central	15.1	14.7	14.8	15.5	15.8	16.2	16.3	16.8	17.1	18.0	*+19*
Eastern	15.6	15.9	21.4	23.3	25.8	27.6	28.9	32.0	35.6	40.8	*+162*
Western	245	250	251	249	253	258	261	257	258	261	*+6*
Middle East	48.8	48.1	54.3	56.7	54.3	56.0	60.3	67.2	73.9	79.0	*+62*
World	**834**	**843**	**875**	**892**	**947**	**1013**	**1071**	**1113**	**1145**	**1214**	***+45***
Change (%)		*1.0*	*3.8*	*2.0*	*6.2*	*7.0*	*5.7*	*4.0*	*2.9*	*6.0*	

( ) = total based on country data accounting for less than 90 per cent of the regional total; .. = available data account for less than 60 per cent of the regional total.

[a] For the country coverage of the regions, see appendix 5A, table 5A.1. Some countries are excluded because of lack of data or of consistent time series data—Africa excludes Angola, Equatorial Guinea and Somalia; the Americas excludes Cuba, Guyana, Haiti and Trinidad and Tobago; Asia excludes North Korea, Myanmar (Burma) and Viet Nam; and the Middle East excludes Qatar. World totals exclude all these countries.

Source: Appendix 5A, tables 5A.1 and 5A.3.

ment and personnel. Appendix 5C describes the sources and methods used for SIPRI's military expenditure data and appendix 5D provides statistics on the reporting by governments of their military spending to SIPRI and the United Nations.

II. Regional trends and major spenders

SIPRI estimates on military expenditure by region and subregion are presented in table 5.1. These data reflect what is available in open sources and in particular in official government sources. They understate the true level of spending for three reasons: (*a*) data are not available for all countries; (*b*) the data on some countries are underestimates, since the SIPRI figures are based on official government data which do not always cover all military-related expenditure; and (*c*) some countries finance military activities outside the budget, through extra-budgetary revenues or other off-budget sources. In addition, the division between military and other security spending—accounted for in internal security expenditure—is often blurred, since some countries' internal security forces have military functions. With these qualifications, the SIPRI data broadly capture overall levels of and trends in military expenditure.[4]

The subregion with by far the highest rate of increase in military expenditure during the 10-year period 1998–2007 is Eastern Europe, at 162 per cent.[5] Russia accounted for 86 per cent of this increase. Other subregions with 10-year real-term growth rates exceeding 50 per cent are North America, entirely due to the trend in US military spending; the Middle East, with strong increases in all Gulf Cooperation Council (GCC) member states apart from the United Arab Emirates (UAE), and in Iran, Jordan and Lebanon;[6] South Asia, where the trend is dominated by a real-terms increase of 64 per cent in Indian military spending; North Africa, because of Algeria's 97 per cent increase; and East Asia. In East Asia, three countries increased their military spending by more than 50 per cent over the period 1998–2007: China with a 202 per cent increase, Indonesia with a 100 per cent increase and Malaysia with a 153 per cent increase. Other countries in East Asia reduced their military spending, including Cambodia and Taiwan.[7] The subregions with the lowest rates of increase in military expenditure over the 10-year period were Western Europe and Central America.

The pattern of increases in 2007 over 2006 was slightly different. The subregions with the strongest increases included not only Eastern Europe (15 per cent), North Africa (10 per cent) and the Middle East (6.8 per cent), but also Central America (13 per cent). Military spending in Oceania is also picking up, with growth of 8.6 per cent in 2007, the same rate as in East Asia. The subregions with the lowest rates of increase in 2007 were Western Europe (0.9 per cent) and South Asia (3.1 per cent).

Table 5.2 lists the countries with the highest military spending in 2007. On the left-hand side of the table, countries are ranked according to their military spending converted into constant US dollars using market exchange rates. The top 15 military spenders accounted for 83 per cent of world military spending and the top 5 spenders accounted for 63 per cent, the same proportions as in 2006. The USA accounted for 45 per cent of the world total, with the next-largest spenders—the United Kingdom, China, France and Japan—far behind, at 4–5 per cent each. The levels of military spending per capita and as a share of GDP vary significantly among the top 5. The countries among the top 15 with the highest economic burden of military expenditure ('military burden')

---

[4] See also appendix 5C.

[5] Eastern Europe includes Armenia, Azerbaijan, Belarus, Georgia, Moldova, Russia and Ukraine. See appendix 5A.

[6] The GCC member states are Bahrain, Kuwait, Oman, Qatar, Saudi Arabia and the UAE. See annex B in this volume. The SIPRI Military Expenditure Database does not have data for Qatar, and the data series for Iraq and the UAE do not cover the full 10-year period 1998–2007. See appendix 5A.

[7] No data were available for Myanmar (Burma), North Korea and Viet Nam.

Table 5.2. The 15 countries with the highest military expenditure in 2007 in market exchange rate terms and purchasing power parity terms

Spending figures are in US$, at constant (2005) prices and exchange rates.

Military expenditure in MER dollar terms					Military expenditure in PPP dollar terms[a]		
Rank	Country	Spending ($ b.)	World share (%)	Spending per capita ($)	% of GDP, 2006[b]	Rank	Country	Spending ($ b.)
1	USA	547	45	1 799	4.0	1	USA	547
2	UK	59.7	5	995	2.6	2	China	[140]
3	China	[58.3]	[5]	[44]	2.1	3	Russia	[78.8]
4	France	53.6	4	880	2.4	4	India	72.7
5	Japan	43.6	4	339	1.0	5	UK	54.7
Sub-total top 5		**762**	**63**			**Sub-total top 5**		**893**
6	Germany	36.9	3	447	1.3	6	Saudi Arabia[c]	52.8
7	Russia	[35.4]	[3]	[249]	3.6	7	France	47.9
8	Saudi Arabia[c]	33.8	3	1310	8.5	8	Japan	37.0
9	Italy	33.1	3	568	1.8	9	Germany	33.0
10	India	24.2	2	21	2.7	10	Italy	29.6
Sub-total top 10		**925**	**76**			**Sub-total top 10**		**1 094**
11	South Korea	22.6	2	470	2.5	11	South Korea	29.4
12	Brazil	15.3	1	80	1.5	12	Brazil	26.7
13	Canada	15.2	1	461	1.2	13	Iran[d]	22.1
14	Australia	15.1	1	733	1.9	14	Turkey	16.5
15	Spain	14.6	1	336	1.2	15	Taiwan	15.8
Sub-total top 15		**1 008**	**83**			**Sub-total top 15**		**1 204**
World		**1 214**	**100**	**183**	**2.5**			

GDP = gross domestic product; MER = market exchange rate; PPP = purchasing power parity; [ ] = estimated figure.

[a] The figures in PPP dollar terms are converted at PPP rates (for 2005), based on price comparisons of the components of GDP.

[b] The figures for national military expenditure as a share of GDP are for 2006, the most recent year for which GDP data are available.

[c] The figures for Saudi Arabia include expenditure for public order and safety and might be slight overestimates.

[d] The figure for Iran is for national defence and does not include spending on the Islamic Revolutionary Guards Corps, which constitutes a considerable part of Iran's total military expenditure.

Sources: *Military expenditure*: Appendix 5A; *PPP rates*: International Comparison Program, *2005 International Comparison Program: Preliminary Results* (World Bank: Washington, DC, Dec. 2007), pp. 21–24.

in 2006 are Saudi Arabia, the USA and Russia, while seven of the countries had a military burden below 2 per cent.

Although SIPRI uses market exchange rates for its analysis of military expenditure, for the purpose of comparison on the right-hand side of table 5.2 countries are ranked according to their military spending converted using

GDP-based purchasing power parity (PPP) rates.[8] The PPP-based ranking is significantly different, primarily for developing countries and, to a lesser extent, transition economies, largely due to the higher domestic purchasing power of such countries' currencies. This leads to the higher ranking of, in particular, China, India, Russia and Saudi Arabia and to the presence of Iran, Taiwan and Turkey in the list. However, interpreting military expenditure converted to dollars using GDP-based PPP rates—the only PPP rates available for most countries—is highly problematic because they primarily reflect the price ratios of civilian goods and services. International comparison of expenditure data is a problematic task in general, and no ideal method for comparisons of military expenditure is available today.[9]

III. The United States

US military expenditure has increased considerably since September 2001. By 2007 the level was higher than at any point since the end of World War II. However, the growth of the US economy and the total budget mean that military spending as a share of GDP and as a share of total US Government outlays is lower than during previous periods.[10] This section provides details of these trends, the budget request for financial year (FY) 2008, and the distribution of military spending between allocations for the annual base budget for defence and emergency supplemental funding under the heading of the 'global war on terrorism'.[11]

Military expenditure trends

During FYs 2001–2007, US military expenditure increased by 85 per cent in nominal terms and by 59 per cent in real terms according to SIPRI data.[12] Official US data for the same period show an increase in US outlays for national

---

[8] The PPP rates are estimates made by the International Comparison Program (ICP) for the World Bank. On the ICP PPP rates and on the problems involved in interpreting military expenditure in PPP terms see appendix 5C, section V.

[9] See appendix 5C.

[10] In US budget terminology, an *outlay* is a payment made. An outlay may be for payment of obligations incurred in previous financial years. In contrast, a *budget authority* is the authority to incur legally binding financial obligations on the US Government. A budget authority may result in immediate or future outlays. Funds are provided to US Government agencies for specified purposes through an annual *appropriations* act or a permanent law. A *supplemental appropriation* may provide additional budget authority. See e.g. the glossary in US Congress, Congressional Budget Office, *The Budget and Economic Outlook: Fiscal Years 2008 to 2018* (US Congress: Washington, DC, Jan. 2008), pp. 165–81.

[11] In budget documents published by the US Department of Defense (DOD) and the White House Office of Management and Budget, funding under the heading 'global war on terrorism' (or 'global war on terror' or GWOT) includes allocations to the DOD and other departments for Operation Iraqi Freedom, for Operation Enduring Freedom (in Afghanistan, the Philippines, the Horn of Africa and elsewhere) and for Operation Noble Eagle (which covers enhanced security in the USA). Most of the 'global war on terrorism' funding (94% during the period FYs 2001–2007) is allocated to the DOD.

[12] See appendix 5A. SIPRI data for US military expenditure are based on NATO data for all years but the most recent. Figures for 2007 are obtained by applying the percentage change in US official estimates, including Department of Defense outlays for the 'global war on terrorism'.

Table 5.3. US outlays for the Department of Defense and total national defence, 2001–2008

Figures are in US$ b. Years are financial years. Figures may not add up to totals because of the conventions of rounding.

	2001	2002	2003	2004	2005	2006	2007[a]	2008[b]
Outlays[c] at current prices								
DOD, military	290.2	331.9	387.2	436.5	474.1	499.3	548.9	583.3
Military personnel	74.0	86.8	106.7	113.6	127.5	127.5	128.8	135.7
O&M	112.0	130.0	151.4	174.0	188.1	203.8	224.8	248.6
Procurement	55.0	62.5	67.9	76.2	82.3	89.8	104.3	110.8
RDT&E	40.5	44.4	53.1	60.8	65.7	68.6	71.1	69.6
Military construction	5.0	5.1	5.9	6.3	5.3	6.3	8.8	10.1
Family housing	3.5	3.7	3.8	3.9	3.7	3.7	4.3	4.0
Other[d]	0.3	–0.6	–1.6	1.6	1.5	–0.3	6.8	4.5
DOE, military	12.9	14.8	16.0	16.6	18.0	17.5	17.9	18.0
Other, military	1.6	1.8	1.6	2.8	3.2	5.1	5.1	5.3
Total national defence	**304.7**	**348.5**	**404.8**	**455.8**	**495.3**	**521.8**	**571.9**	**606.5**
Military expenditure (SIPRI)	**312.7**	**356.7**	**415.2**	**464.7**	**503.4**	**527.7**	**578.3**	**..**
Outlays at constant prices								
Total national defence (FY 2000 prices)	297.2	329.3	364.4	394.3	407.8	417.2	446.7	461.3
Military expenditure (SIPRI, 2005 prices)	344.9	387.3	440.8	480.5	503.4	511.2	546.8	..
Outlays as a share of gross domestic product (%)								
Total national defence	3.0	3.4	3.7	4.0	4.0	4.0	4.2	4.2
Military expenditure (SIPRI)	3.1	3.4	3.8	4.0	4.0	4.0	..	..
Outlays as a share of total US Government outlays (%)								
Total national defence	16.4	17.3	18.7	19.9	20.0	19.7	20.5	20.9

DOD = Department of Defense; DOE = Department of Energy; FY = financial year; O&M = operations and maintenance; RDT&E = research, development, test and evaluation.

[a] The figures for FY 2007 are estimates that include outlays derived from the emergency supplemental request in Feb. 2007 for $93.4 billion in budget authority for FY 2007.

[b] The figures for FY 2008 are the estimated future outlays to be generated from requested budget authority. In addition to the annual base budget, they include outlays from the initial FY 2008 'global war on terrorism' request (for $141.7 billion). They do not include estimated outlays from the 'global war on terrorism' requests submitted in July and Oct. 2007 for additional budget authority of $5.3 billion and $42.3 billion, respectively, and are thus underestimates.

[c] Outlays are the amount of money spent in a given year (i.e. expenditure), as a result of budget authority provided.

[d] A negative number in this category is the result of difficulties of classifying budget activities according to function rather than to spending agency or organization.

Sources: US Office of Management and Budget, *Budget of the United States Government, Fiscal Year 2008: Historical Tables* (Government Printing Office: Washington, DC, 2007), <http://www.budget.gov/budget/fy2008/>, pp. 59–60, 124–25; and appendix 5A.

defence of 88 per cent in nominal terms and 50 per cent in real terms (see table 5.3).[13] The increase has been high across all spending categories, although with some variation. The category of spending that has increased most rapidly is operations and maintenance, which doubled in nominal terms between 2001 and 2007. The increase in nominal terms in procurement was 90 per cent, in military construction 76 per cent, in research, development, test and evaluation 76 per cent, and in military personnel 74 per cent.

The level of US military expenditure (total outlays on national defence) in FY 2007 was 7.4 per cent higher in real terms than the spending peak during the Korean War (FY 1953), 6.3 per cent higher than at the peak of Viet Nam War spending (FY 1968) and 12 per cent higher than at the third peak of cold war spending (FY 1989). However, due to the growth of the US economy, military expenditure as a share of GDP and as a share of total US Government outlays was lower in FY 2007 than during all previous peak spending years since World War II (see figure 5.1).

The budget request for financial year 2008

The defence budget request for FY 2008 was submitted to the US Congress by the Administration of President George W. Bush on 5 February 2007.[14] It consists of two separate requests for budget authority: one for the Department of Defense (DOD) of $481.4 billion—a nominal increase of 11.3 per cent over FY 2007 and a real-terms increase of 8.6 per cent—and one for the 'global war on terrorism' of $141.7 billion.[15] The request also includes $22.5 billion for Department of Energy and other non-DOD military activities, giving a total budget authority request for national defence of $645.6 billion.[16] An emergency supplemental request for an additional $93.4 billion in 'global war on terrorism' funding for FY 2007 was presented at the same time.[17]

---

[13] The difference between SIPRI and US official data in real terms depends on the use of different deflation methods. While SIPRI uses the consumer price index, the US Department of Defense uses defence-specific deflators (which are not available for most countries), which indicate a faster rate of inflation in the prices of military goods than in consumer prices.

[14] The request of the US Administration is always for budget authority. Most defence budget authority is provided in the form of annually enacted appropriations. See also note 10. The budget authority figures here differ from the figures in table 5.3, which are for outlays.

[15] US Department of Defense, 'Fiscal 2008 Department of Defense budget released', News Release no. 129-07, 5 Feb. 2007, <http://www.defenselink.mil/releases/release.aspx?releaseid=10476>. In addition to the $481.4 billion, there was a small mandatory authority for the DOD, giving a total DOD budget authority of $483.2 billion. Office of the Under Secretary of Defense (Comptroller), *National Defense Budget Estimates for FY 2008* (Department of Defense: Washington, DC, Mar. 2007). This and other FY 2008 defence budget materials are available at <http://www.defenselink.mil/comptroller/defbudget/fy2008/>.

[16] Kosiak, S. M., *Analysis of the FY2008 Defense Budget Request* (Center for Strategic and Budgetary Assessments: Washington, DC, 2007), p. 1. Total US military (national defence) expenditure consists of the military spending of the DOD and of other departments, primarily the Department of Energy, for nuclear weapon-related activities.

[17] US Department of Defense (note 15).

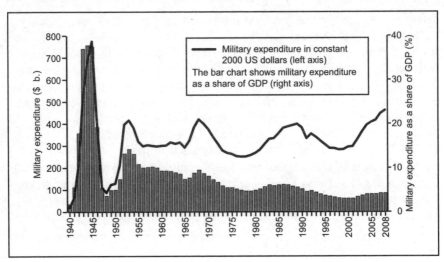

Figure 5.1. Trends in US military expenditure, financial years 1940–2008

Source: US Office of Management and Budget, *Budget of the United States Government, Fiscal Year 2008: Historical Tables* (Government Printing Office: Washington, DC, 2007), <http://www.budget.gov/budget/fy2008/>, pp. 118–25.

While in previous years the Bush Administration had used emergency supplemental appropriations throughout the year and outside the annual base budget to request funding for 'global war on terrorism' activities, the FY 2008 budget request was the first to include a separate budget request under this heading in addition to the base budget. However, this was based on the DOD's best estimate of war funding needs as of February 2007, and two supplementary 'global war on terrorism' funding requests for FY 2008 followed later in the year. In July $5.3 billion was requested to maximize the production and deployment of mine-resistant ambush-protected (MRAP) vehicles for US troops in Afghanistan and Iraq. In October a request for $45.9 billion was submitted for military and intelligence operations in support of the 'global war on terrorism', of which $42.3 billion was for the DOD.[18]

The justifications given for the growth in the FY 2008 base budget request were: 'to ensure a high state of military readiness and ground force strength; to enhance the combat capabilities of the United States Armed Forces; to . . . maintain traditional U.S. superiority against potential threats; and to continue the [DOD's] strong support for service members and their families'.[19] The FY 2008 base budget request includes funding to increase the size of the US Army and the Marine Corps: 'Recognizing that threats to U.S. security exist beyond the war on terror in Iraq and Afghanistan', the DOD plans to increase the size of the army by 65 000 troops to 547 000 active personnel by FY 2012 and the

[18] US Office of Management and Budget, 'FY 2008 revised emergency proposal', Estimate no. 5, 31 July 2007; and Estimate no. 6, 22 Oct. 2007, <http://www.whitehouse.gov/omb/budget/07amendments.htm>.

[19] US Department of Defense (note 15), p. 1.

Marine Corps by 27 000 to 202 000 active personnel by FY 2011.[20] The FY 2008 budget also included funding to continue a broad range of weapon programmes, including $27 billion to fund the acquisition of unmanned aerial vehicles and combat aircraft—including 20 F-22, 18 EA-18G, 24 F/A-18 and 26 V-22 aircraft—the continued development and procurement of 12 Joint Strike Fighter (F-35) combat aircraft, and the upgrading of existing aircraft.[21]

Funding the 'global war on terrorism'

It has proven difficult to keep track of the appropriations and actual expenditure incurred for the 'global war on terrorism'. Since the attacks on the USA of 11 September 2001, three operations have been initiated under this heading: Operation Iraqi Freedom; Operation Enduring Freedom, covering operations in Afghanistan, the Philippines, the Horn of Africa and elsewhere; and Operation Noble Eagle, covering enhanced security in the USA. According to estimates by the US Congressional Research Service (CRS), by late December 2007 a total of $699.9 billion had been approved by the US Congress for FYs 2001–2007 for these three operations.[22] Of this total, the CRS report estimates that the DOD has received $655.0 billion (94 per cent), the Department of State and the US Agency for International Development (USAID) $42.4 billion—for reconstruction, embassy operation and construction, and foreign aid programmes for Afghanistan and Iraq—and the Department of Veterans Affairs $2.5 billion. The CRS report estimates total US appropriations for the 'global war on terrorism' at $805.1 billion for the period FYs 2001–2008.

In October 2007 the DOD presented data showing the distribution of defence budget authority between the base budget and 'global war on terrorism' operations (see table 5.4). These show that, while overall DOD appropriations have increased by 110 per cent in nominal terms over the period FYs 2001–2008, the base budget has also increased—albeit at a lower rate—by 59 per cent.[23]

The US Government Accountability Office (GAO), which has the authority to conduct evaluations on its own initiative, has conducted a series of reviews of the funding of military operations in support of the 'global war on terrorism'. In particular, it has criticized the use of emergency supplemental appropriation requests. In a November 2007 report the GAO describes how the

---

[20] US Department of Defense (note 15), p. 2. This refers to 'active permanent end strength'.

[21] US Department of Defense (note 15), p. 3.

[22] Belasco, A., *The Cost of Iraq, Afghanistan, and Other Global War on Terror Operations Since 9/11*, Congressional Research Service (CRS) Report for Congress RL33110 (US Congress, CRS: Washington, DC, 8 Feb. 2008), pp. 6–7. The US Congressional Budget Office provides figures based on funds already obligated. According to a Jan. 2008 report, the US Congress and the US President had provided a total of $691 billion 'in budget authority for military and diplomatic operations in Iraq, Afghanistan and other regions in support of the war on terrorism and for related veteran's benefits and services'. US Congress (note 10), p. 6.

[23] The increase in overall appropriations does not take account of the full amount of supplemental appropriations for FY 2008. US Department of Defence (DOD), *FY2008 Global War on Terror Amendment* (DOD: Washington, DC, Oct. 2007), <http://www.defenselink.mil/comptroller/defbudget/fy 2008/>, p. 1.

Table 5.4. US appropriations for the Department of Defense base budget and the 'global war on terrorism', 2001–2008

Figures are for budget appropriations,[a] in US$ b. at current prices. Years are financial years.

	2001	2002	2003	2004	2005	2006	2007	2008
Base budget[b]	302	328	375	377	403	421	438	481
'Global war on terrorism'[c]	17	14	69	66	103	115	169	189
Total Department of Defense appropriations	**319**	**342**	**444**	**443**	**506**	**536**	**607**	**670**

[a] The figures for 2001–2007 are from defence appropriation acts. The figures for 2008 are from the initial and supplemental budget requests submitted up to Oct. 2007.

[b] The base budget is for the regular defence budget during peacetime.

[c] These appropriations are for budget authority requested and appropriated under the heading 'global war on terrorism'.

Source: US Department of Defense (DOD), *FY2008 Global War on Terror Amendment* (DOD: Washington, DC, Oct. 2007), <http://www.defenselink.mil/comptroller/defbudget/fy2008/>, p. 1.

DOD's emergency funding requests for most contingency operations have historically been limited to funding the initial incremental costs—defined as additional costs 'that would not have been incurred if a contingency operation . . . had not been supported'.[24] As soon as a limited and partial projection of costs could be made, previous administrations had requested funding for ongoing military operations in the base budget requests. However, despite this past practice and the recommendations of several GAO reports, the GAO notes that current US Administration policy dictates that funding for military operations in support of the 'global war on terrorism', such as operations Enduring Freedom and Iraqi Freedom, should be requested as emergency funding, and that this has been the practice since September 2001.

There have also been claims that the practice of in effect running two parallel budget processes—one for the annual base defence budget and another for the 'global war on terrorism', based on emergency supplemental appropriations—has had an impact on the integrity of the defence budget process at the DOD. For example, Gordon Adams, the senior national security budget official in the US Administration of President Bill Clinton, has argued that the fact that emergency and supplemental funding requests are not processed through the normal mechanisms of the DOD's Planning, Programming, Budgeting and Execution System (PPBES) has resulted in a tendency at the DOD to treat the base and 'global war on terrorism' budgets as mutually interchangeable.[25] Given that by FY 2008 about a quarter of all the resources avail-

[24] US Government Accountability Office (GAO), *Global War on Terrorism: DOD Needs to Take Action to Encourage Fiscal Discipline and Optimize the Use of Tools Intended to Improve GWOT Cost Reporting*, GAO-08-68 (GAO: Washington, DC, Nov. 2007), pp. 6, 19–20.

[25] Adams, G., 'Budgeting for Iraq and the GWOT', Testimony before the US Senate Committee on the Budget, 6 Feb. 2007, <http://budget.senate.gov/republican/NewHearings&Testi2007.htm>.

able to the DOD were provided through the emergency funding mechanism, Adams saw the impact as considerable.

In October 2006 (with effect from FY 2007) the DOD revised the funding guidance for the 'global war on terrorism' to allow for the inclusion of funding for what it calls the 'longer war against terror' in addition to the specific operations in Afghanistan and Iraq. However, the DOD has not clearly defined the 'longer war' and the new guidance has resulted in billions of dollars being added to 'global war on terrorism' funding requests. The DOD now includes funding for items generally found in the base budget request—such as future weapon systems, transformation and general increases in military personnel—in the budget request for the 'global war on terrorism'. The GAO notes that this has blurred the line between longer-term costs—that have traditionally been requested and funded from the base budget—and additional costs of contingency operations.[26] It argues that 'if the administration believes that the nature of the security challenges facing the United States has changed such that [the USA is] engaged in a long-term conflict, the implications—for example, in terms of force structure, investment priorities, and long-term versus short-term costs—should be the focus of discussion with Congress'. The GAO concludes that continuing to fund the 'global war on terrorism' through emergency funding requests 'reduces transparency and avoids the necessary reexamination and discussion of defense commitments', and since the Bush Administration defines the 'global war on terrorism' as long term, more of its costs should be included in the base budget to allow it to be transparent and subject to debate.

IV. Rapidly rising military expenditure in the South Caucasus

The South Caucasus is a region with a host of different security concerns, the most salient being the more or less dormant conflicts in Abkhazia and South Ossetia (both secessionist regions in Georgia) and in Nagorno-Karabakh (a de facto independent Azerbaijani region largely controlled from Armenia; see figure 5.2). A significant factor in the region's security situation is the involvement of external actors. Russia, the United States and, increasingly, the European Union (EU) compete for access to and control over the region's energy resources and transit routes. The international interest is also due to the region's important geographical location for the USA's 'global war on terrorism'.[27]

The combined military expenditure of the three South Caucasian countries—Armenia, Azerbaijan and Georgia—has increased by more than 500 per cent in real terms over the 10-year period 1998–2007 and by 285 per cent over the five years 2003–2007 (see table 5.5). By 2006 all these countries spent a greater share of their GDPs on their militaries than the world average of

---

[26] US Government Accountability Office (note 24), pp. 6–8.

[27] de Haas, M., 'Current geostrategy in the South Caucasus', Eurasia Insight, Eurasianet, 7 Jan. 2007, <http://www.eurasianet.org/departments/insight/articles/pp010707.shtml>.

Figure 5.2. Map of the South Caucasus

2.5 per cent; Georgia in particular had a very high level of military spending in comparison to the size of its economy. Since these figures do not include spending by non-state actors, they underestimate the economic burden that military spending constitutes for these countries. These figures also under-represent the military build-up in the South Caucasus, since they do not take account of the vast amounts of military aid that have flowed into the region over recent years.[28]

The driving factors behind the upward trend in military expenditure in the South Caucasus are: the unresolved conflicts in Abkhazia, Nagorno-Karabakh and South Ossetia; the aspirations of the three countries to join NATO and the high cost associated with the related need for transformation and modernization; the states' respective relationships with, or perceived threat from, neighbouring states; and efforts to secure energy resources and transport routes. The effect of these driving factors has been facilitated by the three countries' increasing economic resources, which have been generated by economic reforms and high and rising oil revenues.

While the driving forces—especially the probability of resumed conflict in the region—work in favour of continued increases in military spending in all the South Caucasian states, the economic factors have a more diverse impact. In Azerbaijan the oil-driven economy is booming, resulting in a windfall of revenues, which the government has chosen to use for increased spending on military expenditure. The more moderate economic growth in Armenia and Georgia has given less leeway for increased spending on both the military and the non-military sectors. Thus, unless the immediate security situation deteriorates, Armenia and, to a lesser degree, Georgia are likely to keep military expenditure increases at a more moderate level than Azerbaijan.

---

[28] Foreign military aid is included in the military expenditure of the donor country, not the recipient. On military expenditure and foreign military aid in the South Caucasus for the period up to 2002 see Perlo-Freeman, S. and Stålenheim, P., 'Military expenditure in the South Caucasus and Central Asia', A. J. K. Bailes et al., *Armament and Disarmament in the Caucasus and Central Asia*, SIPRI Policy Paper no. 3 (SIPRI: Stockholm, July 2003), <http://books.sipri.org/>.

Table 5.5. Military expenditure in the South Caucasus, 1998–2007

Figures are in US$ m., at constant (2005) prices and exchange rates and as share of gross domestic product (GDP).

Country	1998	1999	2000	2001	2002	2003	2004	2005	2006	2007	% change, 2003–07
Military expenditure ($ m.)											
Armenia	86.4	93.0	94.3	91.5	90.5	104	115	141	157	194	*87*
Azerbaijan	[102]	[133]	[141]	[160]	[172]	[215]	[260]	305	625	667	*210*
Georgia	[51.7]	[39.8]	[27.2]	[34.5]	49.3	57.7	80.6	214	362	592	*921*
Total	**240**	**266**	**262**	**286**	**312**	**377**	**456**	**660**	**1144**	**1453**	*285*
Military expenditure as a share of GDP (%)											
Armenia	*3.5*	*3.7*	*3.6*	*3.2*	*2.7*	*2.7*	*2.7*	*2.9*	*2.8*	..	
Azerbaijan	*[2.4]*	*[2.6]*	*[2.3]*	*[2.3]*	*[2.2]*	*[2.4]*	*[2.6]*	*2.3*	*3.6*	..	
Georgia	*[1.1]*	*[0.9]*	*[0.6]*	*[0.7]*	*1.0*	*1.1*	*1.4*	*3.3*	*5.2*	..	

[ ] = SIPRI estimate.

Source: Appendix 5A, tables 5A.2 and 5A.4.

Armenia and Azerbaijan

The major reason for the rapid increases in military spending in Armenia and Azerbaijan has been the unresolved conflict over Nagorno-Karabakh.[29] Military expenditure in Armenia has increased by 125 per cent in real terms between 1998 and 2007. Azerbaijani military spending has increased much faster over the decade: by 554 per cent in real terms. The increase was particularly high in 2006, when spending more than doubled. The official justification for this increase was Russia's transfer of military equipment from its base in Batumi, Georgia, to its 102nd Military Base in Gyumri, Armenia, which the Azerbaijani Government sees as Russian military aid to Armenia.[30] Despite Russia asserting that the move would not change the balance of forces in the South Caucasus and that the military equipment would not be available for Armenian forces, Azerbaijani President Ilham Aliyev argued that such a move could spur an arms race in the South Caucasus.[31] Another significant increase in Azerbaijan's military spending has been budgeted for 2008 with the explicit goal of 'creating a powerful army' to be able to 'liberate its lands by any means'.[32] One interpretation is that 'The goal of the Azeri leadership is

[29] According to the Azerbaijani Foreign Minister, Elmar Mammadyarov, the issue of Nagorno-Karabakh is the most serious challenge to the region's security. UN News Centre, 'Armenia and Azerbaijan offer views on Nagorno-Karabakh during UN debate', 30 Oct. 2007 <http://www.un.org/apps/news/story.asp?NewsID=24169>.

[30] Matirosyan, S. and Mir Ismail, A., 'Armenia and Azerbaijan differ over Russian base pull-out', Eurasia Instight, Eurasianet, 28 June 2005, <http://www.eurasianet.org/departments/insight/articles/eav062805.shtml>.

[31] Matirosyan and Mir Ismail (note 30).

[32] 'Azerbaijan boosts defence budget, warns Armenia', Reuters, 22 Oct. 2007, <http://www.alertnet.org/thenews/newsdesk/L22373221.htm>.

to drive defense spending upward to the point where it will break the back of Armenia's will to continue the impasse between the two countries over territorial issues'.[33] Azerbaijan has clearly stated that it aims to spend more on its armed forces than Armenia does on its total state budget.[34]

According to the Armenian Defence Minister, Serge Sarkisian, Armenia's 24 per cent increase in military expenditure in 2007 would suffice to sustain its combat readiness and to match Azerbaijani forces if the conflict between the two countries resumes.[35] The official military budget does not fully reflect Armenia's military capabilities. Armenia reportedly has a higher combat capability than Azerbaijan, which is reinforced by the geostrategic advantage of holding strategic heights on the frontline.[36] In addition, Armenia has received considerable amounts of military aid from Russia and, allegedly, from Iran.[37] However, lack of information about the size of these extra resources makes it difficult to assess the overall level of spending on Armenia's military.

Both Armenia and Azerbaijan hope for closer cooperation with NATO, and ultimately NATO membership. The aim of achieving NATO standards throughout their security sectors and to be able to participate in NATO and Partnership for Peace exercises and peacekeeping operations has pushed their military expenditures up.[38] For Azerbaijan, the need to secure energy interests in the Caspian Sea and energy transport routes has also added to the upward trend in military expenditure.

During the late 1990s both Armenia and Azerbaijan went through fundamental economic reforms that laid the ground for sound economic growth. For Azerbaijan, these reforms along with windfall revenues from gas and oil exports have been the basis for a rapidly improved economic situation. GDP growth rates in recent years have been among the highest in the world, which has facilitated Azerbaijan's rapidly increasing military spending.[39] Armenia's economic reforms have resulted in a rapidly growing economy.[40] However,

---

[33] Darling. D., 'Azerbaijan boosting military spending', Forecast International, 9 May 2007, <http://www.forecastinternational.com/press/release.cfm?article=110>.

[34] 'Azeri military budget to equal total Armenian state budget—Aliyev', Central Asia–Caucasus Analyst, 22 Mar. 2006, p. 21.

[35] 'Armenian defense chief unfazed by bigger military spending in Azerbaijan', Arminfo, Yerevan, 6 Nov. 2006, Translation from Russian, World News Connection, National Technical Information Service, (NTIS), US Department of Commerce; and Darling (note 33).

[36] Darling (note 33); and International Crisis Group (ICG), Nagorno-Karabakh: Risking War, Europe Report no. 187 (ICG: Brussels, 14 Nov. 2007), <http://www.crisisgroup.org/home/index.cfm?id=5157>, p. 13.

[37] Haeri, S., 'Islamic Iran, Orthodox Armenia, strange bedfellows', Iran Press Service, 9 Sep. 2004, <http://www.iran-press-service.com/ips/articles-2004/september/khatami_armenia_9904.shtml>.

[38] NATO Parliamentary Assembly, Sub-committee on Future Security and Defence Capabilities, 'Viewing NATO from the South Caucasus: Armenia, Azerbaijan and Georgia', 167 DSCFC 07 E bis, 6 Oct. 2007, <http://www.nato-pa.int/default.asp?SHORTCUT=1161>.

[39] According to the International Monetary Fund, Azerbaijan's GDP growth was among the 5 largest in 2006. International Financial Statistics database, Sep. 2007, <http://www.imfstatistics.org/imf/>.

[40] International Monetary Fund (IMF), Republic of Armenia: Fifth Review under the Three-Year Arrangement under the Poverty Reduction and Growth Facility and Request for Modification of Performance Criteria, IMF Country Report no. 07/377 (IMF: Washington, DC, 9 Nov. 2007).

with its geostrategically advantageous position and without Azerbaijan's energy revenues, Armenia has not been willing or able to fully respond to the challenge of Azerbaijan's spending.

Georgia

Georgia's military expenditure has increased more than tenfold in real terms since 2003. This fast growth came after a period of continuously declining military expenditure. Since its low point of 0.6 per cent of GDP in 2000, Georgian military expenditure has increased to 5.2 per cent of GDP in 2006.

When Georgian President Mikhail Saakashvili took office in January 2004, following the November 2003 'Rose Revolution', he inherited a country close to state failure. The economy and many state functions were in ruins and the government did not have full control over all Georgian territory. Abkhazia and South Ossetia were de facto independent republics, and the renegade region of Adjaria was also outside Tbilisi's control.[41] During the presidency of Eduard Shevardnadze, constant underfunding, fraud and corruption had made the armed forces non-functional.[42]

Saakashvili's government faced the seemingly impossible tasks of rebuilding society, reforming the economy, rejuvenating the armed forces and restoring the country's territorial integrity. To achieve these, the government decided to establish closer ties with the West rather than with Russia and it made serious moves towards starting the intensified process for NATO membership. The hope was that NATO would act as a counterweight to Russia's strong position in Abkhazia and South Ossetia and its friendly relations with the Adjarian leader, Aslan Abashidze.

Georgia now receives military aid from several NATO members, with the bulk coming from the USA.[43] In 2002 the USA provided more than $34 million in military aid, equal to 70 per cent of Georgia's domestic military spending. Of this, $20 million was given specifically to enable the Georgian armed forces to deal with Chechen rebels in the Pankisi Gorge.[44] In 2006 and 2007 US military aid amounted to approximately $10 million.[45]

After Saakashvili took power, military expenditure increased at a very high rate: 40, 166, 69 and 64 per cent, respectively, for each of the years 2004–

---

[41] Lynch, D., *Why Georgia Matters*, Chaillot Paper no. 86 (EU Institute for Security Studies: Paris, Feb. 2006), pp. 24–31.

[42] Perlo-Freeman and Stålenheim (note 28), pp. 13–14; and Lynch (note 41), pp. 17–22.

[43] US Department of State, Bureau of Political–Military Affairs, 'Georgia: security assistance', 2 July 2007, <http://www.state.gov/t/pm/64766.htm>; and Darling, D., 'Onward, upward, Georgia defense spending continues to swell', Forecast International, 4 May 2007.

[44] Perlo-Freeman and Stålenheim (note 28), p. 15.

[45] In addition, the USA has provided Georgia with other security-related aid under the US 1992 Freedom Support Act (FSA) to improve export controls, border security and law enforcement. FSA-related aid was $97 million in 2002 and $55 million in 2007. US Department of State, *Congressional Budget Justification, Foreign Operations, Fiscal Year 2004* (US Department of State: Washington, DC, Feb. 2003), pp. 340–42; US Department of State, *Congressional Budget Justification, Foreign Operations, Fiscal Year 2009* (US Department of State: Washington, DC, Feb. 2008), pp. 462–65; US Department of State (note 43); and Darling (note 43).

2007. The most common official justification for the big increase in Georgian military spending is its aim of NATO membership. NATO accession enjoys wide popular support and is seen as a legitimate reason for increased military spending, both domestically and by many of Georgia's Western partners.[46] Georgia joined NATO's Partnership for Peace in March 1994 and negotiated an individual Partnership Action Plan in 2006. In February 2007, President Saakashvili was confident that Georgia would join NATO in 2009.[47] However, the Georgian Government's declaration of a state of emergency and the forced closure of an opposition television station and other media in November 2007 might have decreased the likelihood of an early accession. The NATO declaration issued following these events clearly indicated disapproval of these decisions. It stated that 'The imposition of Emergency Rule, and the closure of media outlets in Georgia ... are of particular concern and not in line with Euro-Atlantic values.'[48]

The other major reason for the increase in Georgia's military expenditure is its ambition to re-establish control over Abkhazia and South Ossetia, as had already been done, in a largely peaceful manner, with Adjaria in May 2004. More recently, the Georgian Government has adopted a more peaceful approach to resuming control over its territory, especially South Ossetia. The Georgian Government intends to decrease Georgia's military budget over a number of years: the budget for 2008 is 27 per cent lower than in 2007.[49] This policy, which is necessary for balancing the budget, is dependent on the peaceful resolution of the South Ossetian and Abkhaz conflicts, but the option of resorting to force has not been abandoned.

V. Regional trends

Africa

Military expenditure in Africa was $18.5 billion in 2007, 1.4 per cent of the world total.[50] During the period 2004–2006, military expenditure in the region was relatively flat, following average annual growth of 6 per cent in 1998–2004. This changed in 2007: African military expenditure increased again by 6 per cent in real terms over 2006. Over the 10-year period 1998–2007 the real-terms growth was 51 per cent.

These figures show the broad trends for Africa. However military expenditure statistics for Africa are problematic and in some countries they tend to

---

[46] '77% Georgians voted for NATO membership—Central Election Commission', Regnum News Agency, 18 Jan 2008, <http://www.regnum.ru/english/944417.html>.

[47] Fiorenza, N., 'Georgia aims to start NATO membership talks by early 2008', *Jane's Defence Weekly*, 7 Mar. 2007, p. 6.

[48] NATO, 'Statement by the Secretary General on the situation in Georgia', Press Release (2007)114, 8 Nov. 2007, <http://www.nato.int/docu/pr/2007/p07-114e.html>.

[49] Brunnstrom, D., 'Georgia PM vows to cut defense spending', *Defense News*, 5 Dec. 2007; and 'Georgian parliament approves 2008 state budget', Kavkaz-Press, Tbilisi, 28 Dec. 2007, Translation from Russian, World News Connection, NTIS.

[50] See appendix 5A, table 5A.1.

understate the true level of spending.[51] Several countries in Africa are involved in armed conflict, which makes access to reliable data difficult.[52] Furthermore, SIPRI data cover only the military expenditure of governments, not spending by non-state actors.

The 2007 increase in African military expenditure can be explained by a number of factors, some of which generate the demand for increased spending and some of which facilitate the increase. Demand-side factors include increased participation in peacekeeping operations; ongoing demobilization, disarmament and reintegration (DDR) processes; military reform and modernization programmes; and internal security problems. Strong economic growth, in some cases reinforced by increased oil revenues, has allowed these demand factors to be translated into increased military spending. For three consecutive years (2004–2006), sub-Saharan Africa had annual economic growth rates of 5–6 per cent, and this is projected to increase to 6–7 per cent in 2007.[53]

To a great extent, three major spenders—Algeria, Morocco and South Africa—determine the trend for Africa's military expenditure since they account for 58 per cent of the total. Of these, Algeria had the highest real-terms growth over the period 2003–2007: 45 per cent. Mid-level spenders also increased their military expenditure in 2003–2007. In particular, Ghana, Nigeria and Angola—among the top 10 spenders in the region—accelerated their military spending in real terms.

Ghana's military budget increased sharply in 2007, by 71 per cent—the highest increase globally—to 106 million cedis ($114 million).[54] While part of the 2007 military budget is for human resource development and housing projects, a major part is for the military equipment and logistics required by Ghana's provision of troops to United Nations and African Union peacekeeping operations. To meet this need the Ghanaian Government has agreed to provide the Ministry of Defence with a loan of $73 million. This money is to be raised through a private financing initiative, which the government says will be serviced and repaid by the anticipated future annual revenues of

---

[51] For an analysis of the quality of official military expenditure data for select African countries see Omitoogun, W., *Military Expenditure Data in Africa: A Survey of Cameroon, Ethiopia, Ghana, Kenya, Nigeria and Uganda*, SIPRI Research Report no. 17 (Oxford University Press: Oxford, 2003).

[52] In 2005 there were 5 state-based armed conflicts (including 3 major armed conflicts) and 14 non-state armed conflicts in sub-Saharan Africa, according to data from the Uppsala Conflict Data Program (UCDP), Uppsala University. See Human Security Centre, *Human Security Brief 2006* (University of British Columbia, Liu Institute for Global Issues, Human Security Centre: Vancouver, 2006), pp. 7, 10; and appendix 2A in this volume.

[53] 'Sub-Saharan Africa economic outlook: growth outlook is positive, but more reforms are needed', *IMF Survey*, vol. 36, no. 7 (23 Apr. 2007), p. 110.

[54] Judging from the past record of relatively good defence budget implementation in Ghana, it is likely that the increase in the 2007 defence budget will be translated into actual expenditure. However, in 2005 the budget for administration of the Ministry of Defence, which represented 13% of the total budget, was overspent by more than 400%—it ultimately represented 50% of total spending. World Bank, *Ghana: 2006 External Review of Public Financial Management*, Report no. 36384-GH, vol. 1 (World Bank: Washington, DC, June 2006), p. 39.

$26 million from UN peacekeeping operations.[55] Ghana's participation in peacekeeping missions serves as a way of creating a more professional military force.[56] Previously, the substantial revenues from international peacekeeping were excluded from the official Ghanaian defence budget, which was a major source of unreliability in its military expenditure data.[57]

Ghana has established close ties with China and Russia for the acquisition of new military equipment and the rebuilding of facilities. The defence budget for 2007 includes funding for the procurement of K-8 trainer aircraft and a simulator from China, as well as for refurbishment of Ghana's Fokker aircraft. A Chinese construction company has been contracted to build a new Ministry of Defence office complex, starting in 2007. This project has an estimated cost of $6.75 million, of which $5 million is to be provided by the Chinese Government.[58]

Nigeria's military spending amounted to 122 billion naira ($960 million) in 2007, an increase of 17 per cent in real terms over 2006. The combination of rising internal security demands, Nigeria's role in regional peacekeeping missions and high oil revenues could partly explain the growth in spending on defence in Nigeria, particularly for 2007.

The oil-rich Niger Delta region has increasingly been the scene of armed violence from non-state actors.[59] This is one of the reasons for the Nigerian Government's investment in maritime capabilities, which are intended particularly for the surveillance of the Niger Delta region. Construction began in 2006 on a naval surveillance system, intended to protect Nigeria's coastline and offshore oil platforms.[60] This programme was complemented in 2007 with the acquisition of equipment such as modern patrol boats, to provide security for the oil companies operating in the region.[61] The Nigerian Government allocated 2 billion naira ($16 million) for this purpose in 2007, a decision that attracted strong domestic criticism.[62]

[55] Republic of Ghana, *The Budget Statement and Economic Policy of the Government of Ghana for the 2007 Financial Year* (Ministry of Finance and Economic Planning: Accra, 16 Nov. 2006), <http://www.mofep.gov.gh/budget2007.cfm>, p. 370.

[56] E.g. in Oct. 2005 more than 1000 soldiers from the Ghanaian Armed Forces and NATO engaged in joint training exercises. 'Security sector reform in Ghana', Inventory of security sector reform (SSR) efforts in partner countries of German development assistance, Bonn International Center for Conversion (BICC), [n.d.], <http://www.bicc.de/ssr_gtz/>, pp. 2–3.

[57] Omitoogun (note 51), pp. 57, 61.

[58] Maslov, A., 'Gana mozhet stat' klyuchevym pokupatelem rossiiskogo oruzhiya v Zapadnoi Afrike [Ghana can become a key customer of Russian weapons in Western Africa], *Eksport Vooruzheniy*, no. 4/ 2006 (July–Aug. 2006), pp. 4–5; 'Re-equipping our air force', *Accra Daily Mail*, 6 June 2006; and 'China to build Ghana Defence Ministry offices', Ghana Broadcasting Corporation Radio 1, 20 Apr. 2007, Transcript from World News Connection, NTIS.

[59] According to the US Department of State, there were 54 attacks on oil installations during which 11 hostages were taken during 2006. Fisher-Thompson, J., 'US partners with Nigeria on security for oil-rich Delta region', US Department of State, USINFO, 15 Mar. 2007.

[60] Ben-David, A., 'Nigeria develops unmanned coastal capability', *Jane's Defence Weekly*, 12 Apr. 2006.

[61] 'FG procures gun boats to battle N/Delta Militants', *Daily Champion* (Lagos), 6 Mar. 2007.

[62] Buhari, R., 'Nigerian government spending of $16.3 million on security enhancements attracts criticism', *This Day*, 7 Feb. 2007.

The USA has been supporting Nigeria with training and equipment programmes to protect oil facilities and their workers because the violence in the region threatens the daily delivery of more than 1 million barrels to the USA (8 per cent of total US oil imports).[63] In the 2008 budget the government of President Umaru Yar'Adua, who took office in May 2007, clearly prioritized spending on infrastructure in the Niger Delta and on security in the Niger Delta and elsewhere in Nigeria.[64]

Improvement of the Nigerian Air Force was another important area in 2007. However, while the government pursued negotiations in 2007 with Italy and the Czech Republic, among others, for the purchase and refurbishment of aircraft,[65] a lack of funding meant that the acquisition of 14 F-7 combat aircraft from China, agreed in 2000, was suspended in late 2007.[66]

Angolan military expenditure has increased considerably over the decade 1998–2007. However, it is impossible to make reliable estimates of the precise increase because of the uncertainty of data on military expenditure during and immediately after the 1975–2002 civil war and, even more so, because of deficient and unreliable macroeconomic data, which are the basis for assessments of real-terms trends. The best estimates suggest that Angola's military spending increased by 500–800 per cent in real terms between 1998 and 2007.

Most of this growth can be explained by the 1975–2002 civil war with UNITA (União Nacional para a Independência Total de Angola, National Union for the Total Independence of Angola) and the 1975–2006 conflict with the Front for the Liberation of the Enclave of Cabinda (FLEC). In more recent years, significant spending has been required for DDR programmes and a modernization plan for the Angolan Armed Forces (Forças Armadas de Angolanas, FAA) to be completed by 2015.[67] In 2007 the process of integrating FLEC soldiers into the FAA and, to a lesser extent, the National Police began. A large part of the DDR costs have been covered by domestic spending because of problems with the donor involvement in Angola's post-war rebuilding efforts.[68]

Asia

Military expenditure in Asia increased by 7.9 per cent in real terms in 2007 and reached $200 billion.[69] Asian military spending has increased by 25 per

---

[63] Fisher-Thompson (note 59).

[64] 'FY08 budget to reach $19 billion', Agence France-Presse, 3 Oct. 2007.

[65] 'Possible Czech L-159 sales to Georgia and Nigeria', *Air Forces Monthly*, July 2007; and Cini, M., 'New Nigerian Air Force G.222', *Air Forces Monthly*, Dec. 2007.

[66] Egua, H., 'N50 billion abandoned defence projects for review', *Business Day* (Lagos), 7 Feb. 2008.

[67] 'Minister highlights head of state's engagement in modernisation of armed forces', Angola Press Agency, Luanda, 9 Oct. 2007; and 'Armed forces modernisation ends by 2015', Angola Press Agency, Luanda, 28 Sep. 2007.

[68] 'Roundup: reporting on incorporation of FLEC soldiers to Angolan Armed Forces', 11 Jan. 2007, World News Connection, NTIS; and Ruigrok, I., 'Whose justice? Contextualising Angola's reintegration process', *African Security Review*, vol. 16 no. 1 (Mar. 2007), p. 2.

[69] See appendix 5A, table 5A.1.

cent since 2003 and by 53 per cent since 1998. Over the past decade, the average annual rate of increase has been 4.8 per cent. Historically, military expenditure in this region, and especially in East Asia, has risen steeply. The trend over the 10-year period 1998–2007 was affected by two major events: the Asian financial crisis in 1997–98—which led to a reduction from even higher growth rates before 1997—and the Indian Ocean tsunami of December 2004, which led to some reallocation of budgetary resources from the military to reconstruction. The four major spenders in the region—China, India, Japan and South Korea, with expenditures in 2007 of $66 billion, $28 billion, $40 billion and $26 billion, respectively—together account for 80 per cent of the regional total.

South Asia

India's military expenditure, which accounts for 80 per cent of South Asia's total, increased by 3 per cent in real terms in 2007. The average annual growth rate over 1998–2007 was 6 per cent. Afghanistan is the South Asian country with the highest increase in military expenditure in 2007, at 52 per cent. This was an increase from a low level as the Afghan National Army (ANA) is being rebuilt virtually from scratch. Even though the ANA is not expected to be a well-equipped force in the short term, the build-up of new armed forces requires a large amount of resources, large parts of which come from foreign military aid.[70]

Over a longer time period, most South Asian states have had high rates of increase in their military expenditure. Over the period 2003–2007, Pakistan's expenditure increased by 11 per cent in real terms, Nepal's by 8 per cent, India's by 30 per cent and Sri Lanka's by 43 per cent. Over the decade since 1998, Nepal had by far the greatest rate of increase—at 150 per cent—followed by India and Pakistan—at 64 per cent and 38 per cent, respectively.

Mutual accusations over high military expenditure are still a significant element in relations between India and Pakistan. Even if Pakistan's increase since 1998 can be largely explained by the armed conflict with India in Kashmir, other factors—such as military operations in the regions bordering on Afghanistan[71]—also play a role. India's increase has paralleled its economic growth and rise as a regional power.[72]

In Sri Lanka the intensified fighting between the government and the Liberation Tigers of Tamil Eelam (LTTE) since July 2006 has resulted in an increase in military spending by 13 per cent in real terms in 2007 and plans for

---

[70] On arms acquisitions for the ANA see chapter 7 in this volume, section V. According to SIPRI's definition of military expenditure foreign military aid is not included in the recipient country's military expenditure. To the extent possible, SIPRI has deducted military aid received from the figures for Afghanistan's military expenditure. Afghanistan also received foreign general budget support. This has not been deducted.

[71] See chapter 2 in this volume, section V.

[72] Raghuvanshi, V., 'India may increase defense spending as percent of GDP', *Defense News*, 24 Sep. 2007, p. 25.

a further increase of 20 per cent in nominal terms in the 2008 budget.[73] Sri Lanka's military spending has fluctuated considerably in the past decade, reflecting the security and economic situations in the country.

In contrast to the large increases elsewhere in South Asia in 2007, Nepal's military spending decreased by 8 per cent in real terms following the 2006 peace agreement between the government and Maoist insurgents.[74]

East Asia

In 2007 Chinese military expenditure increased by 12 per cent while Japan's spending was stable in real terms. In combination with sharp increases in the mid-level spenders Taiwan, South Korea and Singapore—with increases of 28, 10 and 5 per cent, respectively—the subregion saw a total increase of 9 per cent in real terms in 2007. The countries with the highest real-terms increases in 2007 were Thailand and Taiwan—32 and 28 per cent, respectively. Over the five-year period 2003–2007, China had the highest increase—59 per cent—while over the past decade, China, Malaysia and Indonesia had the highest increases—202, 153 and 100 per cent, respectively.

Transparency in Chinese military spending has increased over recent years. Each of the biannual Chinese Defence White Papers provides more disaggregated data.[75] In 2007 China reported its military expenditure to the UN for the first time using the Instrument for Reporting Military Expenditures.[76] However, large parts of Chinese military expenditure remain undisclosed.

China has increased its military spending rapidly over the past decade, in some years at a higher rate than the country's already impressive rate of economic growth. The Chinese military burden increased from 1.7 to 2.1 per cent of GDP between 1998 and 2006. While the rapid rate of increase is widely acknowledged, the actual level of Chinese military spending is contested. SIPRI's estimate of Chinese military expenditure in 2007 is 506 billion yuan, which is 46 per cent higher than the official figure of 347 billion yuan.[77] Most other external analysts do not provide estimates in local currency and there are major differences between their estimates in dollar terms. While SIPRI uses market exchange rates for conversion from local currency into dollars, others use various purchasing power parity rates, which generate much higher dollar estimates of Chinese military spending.[78]

---

[73] Athas, I., 'Sri Lanka records 20% rise', *Jane's Defence Weekly*, 7 Nov. 2007, p. 16.

[74] The Comprehensive Peace Agreement was signed on 21 Nov. 2006. An English translation of its text is available at <http://www.parliament.gov.np/downloads.htm>.

[75] Chinese State Council, *China's National Defense*, 1998–2006 (Information Office of the State Council of the People's Republic of China: Beijing, 1998–2006), all available at <http://www.china.org.cn/e-white/>.

[76] On the reporting of military expenditure to the UN see appendix 5D.

[77] The SIPRI estimate is based on a method developed in Wang, S., 'The military expenditure of China, 1989–98', *SIPRI Yearbook 1999: Armaments, Disarmament and International Security* (Oxford University Press: Oxford, 1999), pp. 334–49.

[78] On the use of PPP rates in international comparisons of military expenditure see appendix 5C, section V.

The rapidly increasing Chinese military expenditure since 1997 has been directed primarily towards (a) a major pay raise for military personnel,[79] (b) long-term investment to transform the People's Liberation Army (PLA) into a high-technology force and (c) a build-up of military capabilities for a potential war over Taiwan. The military reform process, which began in the late 1990s, was largely a reaction to the high level of technology demonstrated by the USA in the 1991 Gulf War.[80] The aim is to transform the PLA from a mass army trained and equipped for protracted wars on the Chinese mainland into a 'slim but strong' force able to engage in local high-tech wars by 2010 and a high-tech force able to project power globally by 2050.[81]

One reason for the very rapid increases in some East Asian countries—in particular Indonesia and Malaysia—over the 10 years since 1998 is the effect of the 1997–98 Asian financial crisis. In the first years following the crisis these countries reduced their military spending by postponing or cutting procurement programmes. These have since been resumed.

Indonesia, and especially the conflict-riven Aceh province, was also severely affected by the 2004 tsunami. The Indonesian Government decided to decrease its 2005 military budget in order to reallocate funds to the reconstruction of the catastrophe-hit areas. Despite almost a decade of military reform, the Indonesian armed forces and their finances are still largely outside the control of the Indonesian Parliament and Department of Defence. Vast commercial activities are a source of considerable extra-budgetary funding for the military.[82]

Although Malaysia's current five-year plan envisages a decrease in total military spending over the years 2006–10, the country increased its military spending by 13 per cent in real terms in 2007 according to SIPRI data. The Malaysian armed forces are currently undergoing reform, with the aim of transforming a counter-insurgency force into a more conventional territorial defence force.[83] As the planned budgets have proven to be insufficient, several of the largest procurement deals have been paid for from accounts other than the defence budget. It is not clear whether these external contingency funds will eventually be included in the official total military spending figure.[84]

[79] In the second half of 2006 many low- and middle-rank officers received a salary increase of 80–100%. Chinese State Council, *China's National Defense in 2006* (note 75); and Xu G., 'What's behind increase in the military budget?', *China Daily*, 15 Mar. 2007, p. 9.

[80] Scobell, A., *Chinese Army Building in the Era of Jiang Zemin* (US Army War College, Strategic Studies Institute: Carlisle, Pa., Aug. 2000), <http://www.strategicstudiesinstitute.army.mil/pubs/display.cfm?PubID=69>, p. 11; 'Chinese army commander warns military reform threatened', BBC News, 15 Mar. 1998, <http://news.bbc.co.uk/2/hi/65750.stm>; and 'Jiang calls for military reform of Chinese army', *People's Daily*, 11 Mar. 2003.

[81] Jacobs, K., 'China's military modernisation', *Asia–Pacific Defence Reporter*, Sep. 2007, pp. 46–48; and 'China to "gradually" increase defense budget: president', Xinhua, Beijing, 1 Aug. 2007.

[82] Mietzner, M., *The Politics of Military Reform in Post-Suharto Indonesia: Elite Conflict, Nationalism, and Institutional Resistance*, Policy Studies no. 23 (East–West Center: Washington, DC, 2006), pp. 62–63.

[83] Mahadzir, D., 'Modernising Malaysia's armed forces', *Asia–Pacific Defence Reporter*, Nov. 2007, pp. 42–45.

[84] Mahadzhir, D., 'Malaysia's defence budget shows strong boost for RMAF', *Asia–Pacific Defence Reporter*, Mar. 2007, pp. 54–56.

In the wake of the military coup in Thailand in September 2006, the new government proposed a budget for 2007 that included a 34 per cent nominal increase in military spending.[85] The 2008 budget includes a continued increase in military spending, by 24 per cent in nominal terms.[86] The Prime Minister, Surayud Chulanont, gained broad support for the massive increases by referring to misspending and depletion of military resources under the previous government, led by Thaksin Shinawatra, and to the armed forces' additional internal security tasks, primarily due to the ongoing insurgency in the south of the country.[87]

In Taiwan the six-year-long parliamentarian feud over the procurement of a large package of military equipment from the USA, which had blocked any major procurement, was finally resolved in 2007.[88] After two years of declining military spending, the defence budget increased by 28 per cent in real terms in 2007.

Europe

Military expenditure in Europe in 2007 amounted to $370 billion, a real-terms increase of 3 per cent over the previous year.[89] The subregion with the highest rate of increase globally in 2007 was Eastern Europe, at 15 per cent. Central and Western Europe increased by 6 and 0.9 per cent, respectively. The trend over the 10-year period 1998–2007 shows similar patterns. While the regional total increased by 16 per cent in real terms, Eastern Europe increased by 162 per cent and Central and Western Europe by 19 and 6 per cent, respectively. While Western Europe accounts for 80 per cent of the 2007 European total, this share is shrinking as the spending of Central and Eastern European states is increasing faster. Meanwhile, of the 27 European countries that increased their spending in 2007, 17 were Central or East European states; and seven of the 10 Central European states that joined NATO in 1999 and 2004 increased their spending.

In contrast with the pattern elsewhere in Western Europe, Austria (which is not a member of NATO) increased its military spending by 23 per cent in real terms in 2007. The reasons given for the increase were (*a*) participation in international operations, (*b*) the 2005–12 military reform programme and (*c*) the purchase of 15 Eurofighter Typhoon combat aircraft.[90]

[85] Cropley, E., 'Thai military draws fire for post-coup budget hike', Reuters, 4 July 2007, <http://www.reuters.com/article/idUSBKK277720>; and Matthews, R., 'Fighter purchase: heralding Thai military modernisation programme?', *The Nation* (Bangkok), 21 Feb. 2008.

[86] 'Bt115-bn budget for defence as transport takes a Bt622m cut', *The Nation* (Bangkok), 12 Dec. 2006.

[87] 'Military now has to shape up', *The Nation* (Bangkok), 8 Dec. 2006. On the conflict in southern Thailand see Melvin, N. J., *Conflict in Southern Thailand: Islamism, Violence and the State in the Patani Insurgency*, SIPRI Policy Paper no. 20 (SIPRI: Stockholm, Sep. 2007), <http://books.sipri.org/>.

[88] Black, S., 'Arms sales to Taiwan: a means to what end?', Center for Defence Information, Washington, DC, 25 July 2007, <http://www.cdi.org/program/document.cfm?documentid=4031>.

[89] See appendix 5A, table 5A.1.

[90] Austrian Ministry of Finance, *Bericht der Bundesregierung: Budgetbericht 2007/2008* [Report of the Federal Government: budget report 2007/2008] (Ministry of Finance: Vienna, 2007), <http://www.

Estonia, which joined NATO in 2004, increased its military spending by 31 per cent in 2007. This is the second highest growth rate in Europe (after Georgia). Estonia is trying to increase its military spending to 2 per cent of GDP, the target set by NATO.[91] It aims to reach this target by 2010 and since 1998 has increased its military expenditure by 283 per cent in real terms. By 2006 the military burden had reached 1.6 per cent of GDP, up from 1.1 per cent in 1998. Spending is set to increase by 21 per cent in nominal terms in 2008.[92]

In 2006 only six of the 24 European NATO member states reached or exceeded the target of 2 per cent of GDP—Bulgaria, France, Greece, Poland, Turkey and the UK. Several other members intend to increase their spending in line with the NATO requirement but for other countries this is not an option that they even consider. During 2007 the NATO Secretary General, Jaap de Hoop Scheffer, continued to express concern about the unwillingness of member states—especially the pre-1999 members—to shoulder the common defence burden.[93] The discussion of whether military expenditure as a share of GDP is a good measure of a member state's contribution to the alliance is not new and many countries consider their niche capabilities and contribution of troops to international operations as relevant factors. For example, the Czech Republic points to the fact that, despite spending only 1.8 per cent of its GDP on the military in 2006, it managed to implement military reforms and to participate in military exercises while nearly 1900 of its personnel were deployed in Afghanistan, the Balkans and Iraq.[94]

A factor that can push up the military spending of several Central and Eastern European states is their ambitions to transform their armed forces into fully professional forces. Albania plans to have a small professional force by 2010 and Bulgaria ended conscription in favour of a fully professional force by 1 January 2008.[95] Modernization, professionalization and adaptation to NATO standards have pushed up military expenditure since 1998 by 182 per cent in Albania—which signed a NATO membership action plan in 1999— and 32 per cent in Bulgaria—which joined NATO in 2004.[96]

bmf.gv.at/budget/budget20072008/>, p. 16; and Mader, G., 'Austria stays with Typhoon—to a point', *Military Technology*, vol. 31, no. 8 (2007), pp. 6–7.

[91] E.g. De Hoop Scheffer, J., Speech at the NATO Parliamentary Assembly's Annual Session, Reykjavík, 9 Oct. 2007, <http://www.nato.int/docu/speech/2007/s071009a.html>.

[92] 'Defense spending to make up 1.69 pct of Estonia's GDP in 2008', Baltic News Services, Tallin, 20 Sep. 2007.

[93] De Hoop Scheffer (note 91).

[94] 'Czech military completes stage 1 of reform in '06, faces budget slip in '07', CTK, Prague, 25 Jan. 2007.

[95] Agence France-Presse, 'Bulgaria to reduce army size', *Defence News*, 1 Feb. 2008; and 'Defense minister expects Albania to have "small professional army" by 2010', *Rilindja Demokratike* (Tirana), 13 Nov. 2006, Translation from Albanian, World News Connection, NTIS.

[96] 'Defense minister Bliznakov: 2997 [*sic*] budget jeopardizes Bulgarian army modernization', BGNES, Sofia, 7 Nov. 2006, Translation from Bulgarian, World News Connection, NTIS; and NATO, 'NATO's relations with Albania', 11 Apr. 2008, <http://www.nato.int/issues/nato_albania/>.

Russia

Russian military expenditure increased by 13 per cent in 2007, a somewhat higher growth rate than the 11 per cent annual average over the past 10 years. Russia's spending has increased by 41 per cent since 2003 and by 160 per cent since 1998, the year of the Russian financial crisis. Due to the large resource-driven increase in the overall economy, military spending as a share of GDP declined from 4.3 per cent in 2003 to 3.6 per cent in 2006.

Russia is now the seventh biggest spender in the world. With its national defence budget for 2008–10 projecting increases of 16 per cent in 2008, 11 per cent in 2009 and 12 per cent in 2010, Russia is set to continue climbing the ranks.[97]

As oil revenues have increased, the Russian Ministry of Finance has repeatedly revised the original budgets upwards by raising spending in different government sectors, in particular national security. This makes the military budget highly opaque.[98] The particular focus on security in the budget is said to reflect the Russian leadership's ambitions for the country to reassert itself in the international arena by improving the capability of its conventional forces and maintaining its nuclear forces.[99] It also reflects President Vladimir Putin's determination to reform and modernize the Russian armed forces, which still are in a poor state. The reform process currently focuses on the transformation of the Russian armed forces from a large, conscripted force into a smaller, professional force. However, a lack of suitable recruits means that this process will become increasingly expensive.[100] The modernization process has not yielded the expected results, despite the increase in the state defence order by 81 per cent over the period 2003–2007.[101] One reason for this is mismanagement; according to Sergey Stepashin, head of the Russian Accounts Chamber (the national audit office), the Ministry of Defence's main problem is not a shortage of funds but a lack of financial management and quality control.[102]

Latin America

Total military expenditure in Latin America (Central and South America) amounted to $43.9 billion in 2007, a 7 per cent increase in real terms over

[97] Cooper, J., 'Military expenditure in the three-year federal budget of the Russian Federation, 2008–10', Research working paper, Oct. 2007, <http://www.sipri.org/contents/milap/milex/publications/unpublished.html>.

[98] On the trend towards less transparency in the Russian military budget see Cooper (note 97).

[99] Sardzhyan, S., 'Russia prepares for "wars of the future"', ISN Security Watch, 12 Feb. 2007, <http://www.isn.ethz.ch/news/sw/details.cfm?id=17240>; and Liaropoulos, A., 'The Russian defense reform and its limitations', *Caucasian Review of International Affairs*, vol. 2, no. 1 (winter 2008). See also chapter 1 in this volume, section III.

[100] Tsimbal, V. and Zatsepin, V., 'Army accounting', *Kommersant*, 5 Apr. 2007.

[101] The state defence order is the state plan for the procurement and modernization of all state armaments, not only for the Ministry of Defence. Lashkina, E., 'Son v novogodiyuyu noch'' [Dream in new year's night], *Rossiiskaya gazeta*, 31 Dec. 2004; Gavrilov, Y., '300 milliardov oborony' [300 billion defence], *Rossiiskaya gazeta*, 1 Sep. 2006; and Tsimbal and Zatsepin (note 100).

[102] Kukol, E., 'Stepashin post prinyal' [Stepashin assumed office], *Rossiiskaya gazeta*, 22 June 2007.

2006.[103] Following a drop in 2003, annual growth has averaged 6 per cent in real terms. Over the 10-year period 1998–2007 the real-terms increase was 34 per cent, which is low compared to other regions.

Significant arms purchases by Brazil, Chile and Venezuela in recent years have given rise to speculation about an arms race in Latin America. While it is doubtful that these are signs of an arms race in the sense of an action–reaction pattern,[104] nonetheless there have been big increases in the military spending of some countries in the region.[105]

Over the five-year period 2003–2007, Venezuela, Ecuador and Chile had the highest increases in military spending in South America, with real-terms increases of 78, 53 and 49 per cent, respectively. In Central America, Honduras (20 per cent) and Mexico (16 per cent) had the highest increases over this period. In absolute terms, Brazil is by far the largest spender in the region, accounting for 46 per cent of the Latin American total. Other significant spenders are Colombia (15 per cent of the regional total) and Chile (13 per cent of the total).

Some of the main factors that have led to increased military expenditure in Latin America are exemplified by the cases of Ecuador and Mexico. Both countries have had significant growth in military spending in recent years, and in neither case is there evidence of an action–reaction cycle in relation to their neighbours.

While Ecuador increased its military spending in 2007 by 30 per cent, there were considerable cuts during the 10-year period 1998–2007. An economic crisis meant that military expenditure decreased by nearly 50 per cent in real terms between 1998 and 1999.[106] Spending returned to the pre-crisis level in 2003, and since then military expenditure has been growing almost continuously, following the recovery of the economy. The rise in spending in recent years can be partly attributed to an increase in military salaries. In 2006 salaries for military personnel increased by 10 per cent, and an additional increase of 22.5 per cent was budgeted for 2007.[107] These salary increases are part of a process to integrate the defence establishment's salary system with that of the rest of the central government.[108]

---

[103] See appendix 5A, table 5A.1.

[104] See chapter 7 in this volume, section IV.

[105] It should be noted that it is not clear whether the most recent arms acquisitions by some Latin American countries are fully reflected in military expenditure figures, since payments for the acquisition of major weapon systems are often spread out over a number of years.

[106] Ecuadorean Ministry of National Defence, *Política de la Defensa Nacional del Ecuador* [National defence policy of Ecuador], White Paper 2006 (Ministry of National Defence: Quito, 2006), <http://midena.gov.ec/content/section/10/135/>. Ecuador's military expenditure was $688 million in 1998 and $353 million in 1999, at constant (2005) prices and exchange rates. See appendix 5A.

[107] 'Ejecutivo aprobó aumento de sueldo para militares' [Executive approves salary increase for the military], *Ecuador News*, 23 Jan. 2008; and Baranauskas, T., 'Ecuadoran military asking for $918m for 2007', Forecast International Government & Industry Group, 12 Feb. 2007.

[108] Celi, P., 'Ecuador: transformación de la defensa y reestructuración de las Fuerzas Armadas' [Ecuador: defence transformation and armed forces restructuring], *Atlas comparativo de la defensa en América Latina* [Comparative atlas of defence in Latin America], 2007 edn (Red de Seguridad y Defensa de América Latina: Buenos Aires, 2007), p. 180.

There is a strong link between political power and the armed forces in Ecuador. The military has intervened directly and openly in the country's political processes by removing elected presidents.[109] This has led to suggestions that President Rafael Correa supports high military budgets as a way to establish friendly relations with the military.[110]

Soon after taking office in January 2007, the government of President Correa started to implement a plan for new priorities and military acquisitions for the Ecuadorean armed forces, which would involve substantial increases in military spending.[111] The plan prioritizes improving security along the northern border with Colombia. Outposts on the border with Peru have been closed and 15 army detachments have been redeployed to the northern border and given better transport capabilities.[112] The proposed defence budget for 2008 represents a further increase of 50 per cent in nominal terms, including $149 million to boost capabilities on the northern border.[113]

Mexico has the fourth largest military budget in Latin America, and by far the largest in Central America.[114] In 2007 military expenditure in Mexico amounted to 43 152 million pesos ($3941 million), a 13 per cent increase in real terms. Mexico's main security challenges are internal, such as drug trafficking or the conflict in the southern state of Chiapas, and the Mexican military has always been involved in the provision of internal security.[115] This role has expanded since the mid-1990s as a result of the Azteca Directive, which gave the armed forces the task of fighting drug trafficking and organized crime.[116] Growth in the number of drug cartels and in drug-related violence in Mexico prompted the government of President Vicente Fox to take a harder stance on security matters from 2005.[117] Among various approaches during recent years is the México Seguro (secure Mexico) operation, which began in

[109] Since 1997, 3 presidents have been removed from power after interventions by the military. Danopoulos, C. P. and Zirker, D., 'Governability and contemporary forms of military intervention: expanding Ecuadorian and Turkish models', *Journal of Security Sector Management*, vol. 4, no. 1 (Jan. 2006), p. 5.

[110] '$300 millones vinculan a Correa con las FF.AA.' [$300 million link Correa with the Armed Forces], *El Universo* (Guayaquil), 26 Aug. 2007.

[111] Baranauskas, T., 'New Ecuadorian government plans to modernize military equipment', Forecast International Government & Industry Group, 31 Jan. 2007.

[112] 'Defence minister says armed forces operating on a "tight" budget', 2 May 2007, *El Universo* (Guayaquil), World News Connection, NTIS; and 'Ecuador remains coy about new role regarding Colombia', *Latin America Weekly Report*, 29 Aug. 2006.

[113] 'Ecuador's defence spending increased', Forecast International, 6 Nov. 2007; and Vásquez, L., 'Ecuador eyes UAV for maritime surveillance', *Jane's Defence Weekly*, 16 Jan. 2008, p. 10.

[114] Military expenditure figures are not available for Belize, while both Costa Rica and Panama have no military expenditure since they have abolished their armed forces. See appendix 5A.

[115] 'When army and police become hard to tell apart', *Latin American Security & Strategic Review*, Nov. 2006.

[116] Díez, J. and Nicholls, I., *The Mexican Armed Forces in Transition* (US Army War College, Strategic Studies Institute: Carlisle, Pa., Jan. 2006), <http://www.strategicstudiesinstitute.army.mil/pubs/display.cfm?PubID=638>, p. 37; and Sánchez, A., 'Mexico's drug war: a society at risk—soldiers versus narco-soldiers', Council on Hemispheric Affairs, 22 May 2007, <http://www.coha.org/2007/05/22/>.

[117] Contreras, J., 'Losing the battle', *Newsweek International*, 11 July 2005.

June 2005 as an initiative to tackle drug crimes on the border with the USA.[118] The armed forces have also taken on public order tasks, for example in the 2006 civil protests in Oaxaca.[119]

Since President Felipe Calderón took office in December 2006, the role of the Mexican armed forces in domestic affairs has increased further, particularly in the fight against drug trafficking.[120] More troops have been mobilized to fight drug trafficking and organized crime, including 6000 troops in Tamaulipas state alone.[121] Calderón has also emphasized the need to produce better-trained troops with high morale in order to reduce the number of desertions—123 000 troops deserted between 2000 and 2006—and a large part of the military spending increase in 2007 was to improve the income and social benefits of military personnel.[122] In addition, Calderón aims to increase the effectiveness of the country's modestly sized forces by consolidating operational capabilities.[123] To finance the increasing expenditure on the military, Calderón excluded the armed forces from the Austerity Decree, a national economic strategy for reducing budget spending.[124]

The Middle East

Military expenditure in the Middle East was $91.5 billion in 2007.[125] It is estimated to have increased in real terms by 7 per cent in 2007 and by 62 per cent over the 10-year period 1998–2007. The estimates are uncertain, since data are not always available and some data are of uncertain reliability. The regional totals for recent years are based on rough estimates of some countries' spending, including for Iran, Iraq, Saudi Arabia and the United Arab Emirates. Data for Iraq and the UAE are not available for all years and no data are available for Qatar.

Oman, Saudi Arabia and Israel had the highest military burdens in the Middle East: they spent, respectively, 11.2, 8.5 and 8.0 per cent of their GDPs in 2006. The two highest spenders are Saudi Arabia (which accounted for 39 per cent of the regional total in 2007) and Israel (15 per cent of the regional

---

[118] 'Despite 'México Seguro', drug-related violence rises', *Latin American Security & Strategic Review*, July 2005; and 'As violence escalates, a new federal plan', *Latin American Security & Strategic Review*, Oct. 2005.

[119] 'When army and police become hard to tell apart' (note 115).

[120] Aguayo Quezada, S., 'Mexico: a war dispatch', Open Democracy, 25 June 2007, <http://www.opendemocracy.net/democracy_power/politics_protest/mexico_war_dispatch>; and 'Calderón signals tough stance on crime and unrest', *Latin American Security & Strategic Review*, Dec. 2006.

[121] McKinley, J. C., 'Mexico hits drugs gangs with full fury of war', *New York Times*, 22 Jan. 2008; and 'Mexican armed forces increase security, counternarcotic efforts in 2007', Notimex, Mexico City, 15 Dec. 2007, Translation from Spanish, World News Connection, NTIS.

[122] Guevara, I., 'Mexico charts new course for defence doctrine', *Jane's Defence Weekly*, 6 Feb. 2008; and 'Mexican armed forces increase security, counternarcotic efforts in 2007' (note 121).

[123] Guevara, I., 'Mexico's 2008 defence budget goes under review', *Jane's Defence Weekly*, 12 Dec. 2007, p. 8.

[124] Mexican Presidency of the Republic, 'President Calderón at presentation of evaluation of start of government', 15 Mar. 2007, <http://www.presidencia.gob.mx/en/press/?contenido=29477>.

[125] See appendix 5A, table 5A.1.

total). These two countries were also among those that increased their military budgets the most in 2007.

The official Iranian defence budget for 2007 of 79 871 billion rials ($8618 million) represents a decrease of 14 per cent in real terms over 2006.[126] Obtaining information on Iran's military expenditure is problematic. This official figure does not include spending on the Islamic Revolutionary Guards Corps, which consists of ground, air and naval forces. The Revolutionary Guards have 125 000 personnel, comparable to one-third of the regular armed forces, and are responsible for Iran's missile forces.[127] While the primary role of the Revolutionary Guards is internal security, they also have military functions and so part of the spending on the Revolutionary Guards should be included in total military spending. It has proven impossible to obtain this data. The Revolutionary Guards are also a major commercial enterprise, reportedly the third largest in the country. According to some sources they are financed through non-reported revenues from an array of activities such as petroleum production and construction work, with branches throughout the Middle East.[128]

Among the member states of the Gulf Cooperation Council, Saudi Arabia increased its military expenditure the most in 2007, facilitated by high oil revenues. Its budgeted military spending in 2007 was 133 billion rials ($35 billion), a 17 per cent real increase compared to 2006. Part of this increase was for a 20 per cent increase in ground forces.[129] The implementation of the major weapon acquisition programme initiated in 2007 will have a large impact on future levels of Saudi military expenditure. This includes the arms deal signed with the British Government in September 2007 for 72 Eurofighter Typhoon combat aircraft, the largest British–Saudi arms deal since the 1985 Al Yamamah arms deal; and other deals negotiated during 2007 with the USA and France.[130]

Israel's military budget for 2007 amounted to 56 billion shekels ($13.5 billion), including domestically funded military expenditure of 45.7 billion

---

[126] Iran does not report its military expenditure to SIPRI or to the UN, nor are data on overall military expenditure available in any official Iranian statistics. The source for the SIPRI figures for Iran is the IMF's *Government Finance Statistics Yearbook*. These figures are reported to the IMF by the Iranian Government according to the IMF's definition of defence. In previous editions of the SIPRI Yearbook, the figures for Iran included the figures provided under the heading 'public order and safety' as reported by Iran to the IMF. It was believed that this included spending on paramilitary forces. However, it now appears that this is not the case. Because the official Iranian Government figures do not include spending on the Revolutionary Guards (see below), the current SIPRI figures are likely to represents an underestimate of at least one-third. The inclusion of the figures for public order and safety may have given a closer estimate of Iran's total military expenditure, but it distorted the trend. See appendix 5A.

[127] Bruno, G., 'Iran's Revolutionary Guards', Council on Foreign Relations, 25 Oct. 2007, <http://www.cfr.org/publication/14324/>.

[128] One of the most significant companies is Khatam al-Anbya, which in 2006 had over $7 billion worth of deals in the oil, gas and transportation sectors. US Department of State, 'Briefing on Iran', 25 Oct. 2007, <http://www.state.gov/p/us/rm/2007/94178.htm>.

[129] 'Saudis launches $60b modernization plan', *Middle East Newsline*, 11 Nov. 2006; and 'Saudi military spending rising', *International Air Letter*, 27 July 2006, p. 5.

[130] 'Saudis launches $60b modernization plan' (note 129). See also chapter 7 in this volume, section III.

shekels ($11 billion) and $2.34 billion in military aid from the USA.[131] The 10 per cent real increase in Israel's military expenditure in 2007 was the second largest increase in 10 years. Military expenditure in Israel has increased in most years since 1998 and by 2007 it was 36 per cent higher in real terms than in 1998.

Israel's military operations against Hezbollah in Lebanon in July–August 2006 had a major impact on Israel's 2007 defence budget. The lessons drawn from this war may also have significant implications for Israel's future military strategy and spending. The costs of the war were substantial, both in terms of military expenditure and in economic damage. According to early estimates, there were direct costs to the Israeli Defence Forces (IDF) of 11.2 billion shekels ($2.7 billion). In addition, the cost of restoring military preparedness was estimated at 7–7.5 billion shekels ($1.7–1.8 billion) and the civilian costs (including physical damage, compensation payments to residents and lost income tax revenues) at 20–22 billion shekels ($4.8–5.3 billion).[132] The 2007 defence budget compensated the Ministry of Defence with 8.2 billion shekels ($2 billion) to cover the costs of the military operations in Lebanon.[133]

The Winograd Commission, the government appointed inquiry into the war in Lebanon which reported in January 2008, found that Israel's naval and air forces were inadequate to address the type of challenges posed by Hezbollah and that the ground forces were insufficiently prepared.[134] In anticipation of such a conclusion, the Tefen defence plan for 2008–12, which was finalized and approved in September 2007, is to raise investment in the ground forces, including plans to increase training and acquire armoured personnel carriers.[135]

---

[131] The domestically funded defence budget includes a direct budget of 35 billion shekels ($8.4 billion) and revenues from sales by the Ministry of Defence of 2.5 billion shekels ($0.6 billion). The remaining 8.2 billion shekels ($2 billion) is for the cost of the war in Lebanon (see below). Ben-David, A., 'Israel set for record defence spend in 2007', *Jane's Defence Weekly*, 3 Jan. 2007, p. 16. The US Government pledged in 2007 to increase military aid to Israel by 25% over 10 years, from $2.4 billion in 2008 to nearly $3 billion by 2018. Sharp, M. J., *US Foreign Assistance to Israel*, Congressional Research Service (CRS) Report for Congress RL33222 (US Congress, CRS: Washington, DC, 2 Jan. 2008), p. 2. See also chapter 7 in this volume, section III.

According to SIPRI's definition of military expenditure, foreign military aid should not be included in the recipient country's military expenditure. However, in the case of Israel, it has not been possible to separate foreign aid from the domestically funded military budget in a consistent manner over time. The figures for Israel in appendix 5A therefore include foreign military aid.

[132] Baranauskas, T., 'Recent fighting costs Israeli military $1.6 billion', Forecast International Government & Industry Group, 21 Aug. 2006; and 'Israeli military puts Lebanon war costs at ILS11.2 billion', *Haaretz*, 7 Sep. 2006.

[133] Opall-Rome, B., 'Lebanon war proves blessing for Israeli budget', *Defence News*, 11 Sep. 2006; and Ben-David (note 131).

[134] Israeli Ministry of Foreign Affairs, 'Winograd Committee submits final report', 30 Jan. 2008, <http://www.mfa.gov.il/MFA/MFAArchive/2000_2009/2008/>; and Boot, M., 'The second Lebanon war', *Weekly Standard* (Washington, DC), 4 Sep. 2006.

[135] Israel Defence Forces, 'IDF finalizes acquisition plans for coming years', 3 Sep. 2007, <http://dover.idf.il/IDF/English/News/today/2007/09/>; Israel Defence Forces, 'IDF response to the Winograd Committee report', 30 Jan. 2008, <http://dover.idf.il/IDF/English/News/today/2008n/01/>; and Eshel, D., 'Israel sets the stage for a massive, $60 billion buildup', *Defense Update*, 3 Sep. 2007. See also Krant, A., 'Multi-year plan to strengthen IDF conventional capabilities', Jewish Institute for National Security Affairs, 12 Nov. 2007, <http://www.jinsa.org/articles/view.html?documentid=3964>.

This is a reversal from the Kela defence plan for 2003–2008, which involved a 25 per cent cut in Israeli ground forces.[136]

VI. Conclusions

Global military spending increased by 45 per cent in real terms over the 10-year period 1998–2007 and by 6 per cent in 2007. Since 2001 growth in world military spending has accelerated to an annual average of 5.3 per cent from 2.2 per cent in the period 1998–2001. This is due primarily to US military spending, which accounts for 45 per cent of the world total and 63 per cent of the post-2001 increase in world military spending. Since 2001 US military spending has increased by 59 per cent in real terms, due mostly to spending on military operations in Afghanistan and Iraq, but also to increases in the base defence budget.

A large number of other countries have also increased their military spending since 2001. Of the 151 countries for which data were available for the entire period 2001–2007, the number that increased their military spending was 98–106 in the period 2001–2006, increasing to 117 countries in 2007.

The subregion with the highest increase in military expenditure over the decade 1998–2007 was Eastern Europe, with 162 per cent. Eastern Europe also had the highest increase in 2007, of 15 per cent, mostly accounted for by Russia. North America, the Middle East, South Asia, Africa and East Asia also had 10-year growth rates exceeding 50 per cent. Western Europe and Central America had the lowest growth in military spending, with 6 and 14 per cent growth respectively over the period 1998–2007.

The motivations for increases in military spending vary considerably between regions and countries and the diversity of these motivations has increased since 2001. They range from long-term, policy-based improvements in military capabilities in order to achieve certain objectives to urgent responses to immediate threats.

Aspirations to maintain, achieve or resume positions as a global or regional power are at play behind the military expenditure trends of the USA and such countries as Brazil, China, India and Russia. Another type of policy-related motivation is military reform or transformation. This can be as a result of shifting military allegiances, economic and political transition, aid-donor requirements or other factors. This type of motivation for increasing military spending is illustrated by the Central and East European countries that have joined or seek to join NATO and some countries in Africa. A third type of policy-related motivation is the desire to contribute to international peacekeeping operations. This is often associated with the build-up of new military capabilities with the goal of achieving interoperability with armed forces from other countries. While this motivation has contributed to increased military

---

[136] Ben-David, A., 'Israel cancels ground forces cuts', *Jane's Defence Weekly*, 17 Jan. 2007, p. 7. See also Omitoogun, W., 'Military expenditure in the Middle East after the Iraq war', *SIPRI Yearbook 2004: Armaments, Disarmament and International Security* (Oxford University Press: Oxford, 2004), p. 387.

expenditure in some developing countries, such as Ghana, the goals of the EU's European Security and Defence Policy have not yet led to a significant rising trend in the military spending of EU member states.

Affordability also plays a role in policy-related increases in military expenditure. In several of the countries with high military expenditure growth in 2007, the availability of economic resources was an important factor. Increased revenues from natural resources such as oil and gas made higher spending on the military possible in, for example, the Middle East and the South Caucasus. In other cases, increased military spending was facilitated by a large economy, as in the USA, or by economic growth, as in China, India and some countries in Africa and Latin America.

The more immediate security requirements that lead to increases in military spending include participation in armed conflicts and wars. For the USA, the conflicts in Afghanistan and Iraq have been key factors in obtaining congressional consent for massive increases in military expenditure. Similarly, Israeli military operations in the Palestinian territories and in Lebanon in 2006 have required increases in military spending. Involvement in actual or latent armed conflict is also the main reason for the rapid increases in military expenditure in the South Caucasus, South Asia and parts of East Asia. The risk that any of the dormant conflicts in Abkhazia, South Ossetia or Nagorno-Karabakh could reignite is clearly a factor behind increased military spending in the South Caucasus. The war in Afghanistan has created an unstable security environment in South Asia, particularly in Pakistan, in addition to the long-term conflicts in Kashmir and Sri Lanka. Several East Asian governments have reacted to internal rebel movements with military build-ups. Armed conflicts are also driving up military expenditure in Africa, both in countries directly involved in conflict and in their neighbours, although this is not fully reflected in military spending figures due to a lack of reliable data.

An uncertain external security environment short of conflict can also lead to increases in military spending. For example, although they are not directly involved in any of the conflicts in the Middle East, almost all members of the Gulf Cooperation Council have increased their military expenditure. Internal security problems and border security are other factors of an immediate nature that drive up military spending in some Latin American states and increasingly also in East Asia.

The factors driving increases in military spending in different countries since 2001 thus constitute a mixture of foreign policy objectives, real or perceived threats, armed conflict, and policies to contribute to international peacekeeping operations.

Appendix 5A. Tables of military expenditure

PETTER STÅLENHEIM, JAN GREBE, CATALINA PERDOMO
and ELISABETH SKÖNS*

Table 5A.1 presents military expenditure by region, by certain international organizations and by income group for the period 1998–2007 in US dollars at constant 2005 prices and exchange rates, and also for 2007 in current US dollars. Military expenditure by individual countries is presented in table 5A.2 in local currency and at current prices for the period 1998–2007 and in table 5A.3 in US dollars at constant 2005 prices and exchange rates for the period 1998–2007 and for 2007 in current US dollars. Table 5A.4 presents military expenditure for the period 1998–2007 as a percentage of countries' gross domestic product (GDP). Sources and methods are explained in appendix 5C. Notes and explanations of the conventions used appear below table 5A.4.

Military expenditure data from different editions of the SIPRI Yearbook should not be combined because of data revision between editions. Revisions can be significant; for example, when a better time series becomes available the entire SIPRI series is revised accordingly. Revisions in constant dollar series can also be caused by significant revisions in the economic statistics of the International Monetary Fund that are used for these calculations. When data are presented in local currency (in table 5A.2) but not in US dollars or as a share of GDP (in tables 5A.3 and 5A.4), this is due to a lack of economic data.

* Contribution of military expenditure data, estimates and advice are gratefully acknowledged from Julian Cooper (Centre for Russian and East European Studies, University of Birmingham), David Darchiashvili (Center for Civil–Military Relations and Security Studies, Tbilisi), Dimitar Dimitrov (University of National and World Economy, Sofia), Paul Dunne (University of the West of England, Bristol), Iñigo Guevara y Moyano (Colectivo de Análisis de la Seguridad con Democracia, Querétaro), Iduvina Hernández (Asociación para el estudio y la promoción de la seguridad en democracia, Guatemala City), Nazir Kamal (United Nations, New York), Armen Kouyoumdjian (country risk strategist, Valparaiso), Pavan Nair (Jagruti Seva Sanstha, Pune), Elina Noor (Institute of Strategic and International Studies Malaysia, Kuala Lumpur), Pere Ortega (Centre d'Estudis per la Pau J. M. Delàs, Barcelona), Tamara Pataraia (Caucasus Institute for Peace, Democracy and Development, Tbilisi), Thomas Scheetz (Lincoln University College, Buenos Aires), Ron Smith (Birkbeck College, London) and Ozren Zunec (University of Zagreb).

Table 5A.1. Military expenditure by region, by international organization and by income group, 1998–2007

Figures are in US $b. at constant 2005 prices and exchange rates for 1998–2007 and, in the right-most column, marked *, in current US$ b. for 2007. Figures do not always add up to totals because of the conventions of rounding.

	1998	1999	2000	2001	2002	2003	2004	2005	2006	2007	2007*
World total	**834**	**843**	**875**	**892**	**947**	**1 013**	**1 071**	**1 113**	**1 145**	**1 214**	**1 339**
Geographical regions											
Africa	11.1	11.9	12.3	13.5	14.3	14.1	15.8	16.0	15.8	16.8	18.5
North Africa	4.3	4.0	4.1	5.2	5.2	5.4	5.9	6.2	6.0	6.6	7.4
Sub-Saharan Africa	6.8	7.9	8.3	8.4	9.1	8.7	9.9	9.8	(9.7)	(10.1)	(11.2)
Americas	367	367	382	388	431	481	522	548	559	598	640
Caribbean	..	..	..	..	..	..	..	..	..	..	..
Central America	3.6	3.7	3.9	3.8	3.6	3.6	3.4	3.4	3.6	4.0	4.3
North America	340	341	354	357	399	453	493	516	525	562	596
South America	23.3	22.1	23.9	26.7	27.5	24.6	25.8	28.1	30.1	32.0	39.6
Asia and Oceania	132	135	139	146	153	160	166	176	186	200	219
Central Asia	(0.6)	0.5	..	(0.6)	..	(0.8)	..	..	..	..	..
East Asia	100	101	104	110	116	122	127	132	140	152	163
Oceania	11.4	11.9	11.8	12.2	12.7	13.2	13.8	14.3	15.1	16.4	18.7
South Asia	19.6	21.9	22.8	23.5	23.6	24.2	25.0	28.2	29.7	30.7	35.6
Europe	276	280	287	288	295	302	306	306	311	319	370
Central Europe	15.1	14.7	14.8	15.5	15.8	16.2	16.3	16.8	17.1	18.0	21.9
Eastern Europe	15.6	15.9	21.4	23.3	25.8	27.6	28.9	32.0	35.6	40.8	52.4
Western Europe	245	250	251	249	253	258	261	257	258	261	296
Middle East	48.8	48.1	54.3	56.7	54.3	56.0	60.3	67.2	73.9	79.0	91.5

MILITARY EXPENDITURE 209

Organizations

ASEAN	11.7	11.7	11.8	12.4	13.1	14.7	14.9	15.4	16.0	17.8	21.1
CIS	16.2	16.4	21.9	23.9	26.5	28.4	29.8	33.0	36.8	42.3	54.2
European Union	221	225	227	226	230	237	253	251	252	257	293
NATO	568	583	596	599	646	704	752	773	783	823	894
NATO Europe	228	242	243	242	247	252	259	256	258	261	298
OECD	666	673	689	692	740	800	844	866	876	920	994
OPEC	35.6	34.0	38.7	41.3	38.0	39.4	44.0	50.5	56.0	61.9	73.3
OSCE	615	621	641	645	695	755	800	823	837	883	968

Income group

Low	22.8	26.5	27.1	27.6	28.5	28.6	30.4	33.3	34.5	35.6	41.9
Lower middle	61.7	62.9	71.4	79.5	84.7	88.4	95.1	103	116	125	152
Upper middle	58.3	60.3	65.7	68.6	70.6	72.1	73.4	77.9	82.0	88.2	107
High	692	693	710	716	763	824	872	899	913	965	1 039

( ) = Total based on country data accounting for less than 90% of the regional total; . . = Available data account for less than 60% of the regional total; ASEAN = Association of Southeast Asian Nations; CIS = Commonwealth of Independent States; NATO = North Atlantic Treaty Organization; OECD = Organisation for Economic Co-operation and Development; OPEC = Organization of the Petroleum Exporting Countries; OSCE = Organization for Security and Co-operation in Europe.

Notes: The world total and the totals for regions, organizations and income groups in table 5A.1 are estimates, based on data in table 5A.3. When military expenditure data for a country are missing for a few years, estimates are made, most often on the assumption that the rate of change in that country's military expenditure is the same as that for the region to which it belongs. When no estimates can be made, countries are excluded from the totals. The countries excluded from all totals in table 5A.1 are Angola, Benin, Cuba, Equatorial Guinea, Guyana, Haiti, Iraq, North Korea, Myanmar (Burma), Qatar, Somalia, Trinidad and Tobago, and Viet Nam.

Totals for geographical regions add up to the world total and subregional totals add up to regional totals. Totals for regions and income groups cover the same groups of countries for all years. Totals for organizations cover only the member countries in the year given.

The country coverage of income groups is based on figures of 2005 gross national income (GNI) per capita as calculated in World Bank, *World Development Report 2007: Development and the Next Generation* (World Bank: Washington, DC, 2006), <http://www.worldbank.org/wdr2007/>.

Africa: Algeria, Angola, Benin, Botswana, Burkina Faso, Burundi, Cameroon, Cape Verde, Central African Republic, Chad, Congo (Republic of the), Congo (Democratic Republic of the, DRC), Côte d'Ivoire, Djibouti, Equatorial Guinea, Eritrea, Ethiopia, Gabon, Gambia, Ghana, Guinea, Guinea-Bissau, Kenya,

Lesotho, Liberia, Libya, Madagascar, Malawi, Mali, Mauritius, Mauritania, Morocco, Mozambique, Namibia, Niger, Nigeria, Rwanda, Senegal, Seychelles, Sierra Leone, Somalia, South Africa, Sudan, Swaziland, Tanzania, Togo, Tunisia, Uganda, Zambia, Zimbabwe. *North Africa*: Algeria, Libya, Morocco, Tunisia. *Sub-Saharan Africa*: Angola, Benin, Botswana, Burkina Faso, Burundi, Cameroon, Cape Verde, Central African Republic, Chad, Congo (Republic of the), Congo (Democratic Republic of the, DRC), Côte d'Ivoire, Djibouti, Equatorial Guinea, Eritrea, Ethiopia, Gabon, Gambia, Ghana, Guinea, Guinea-Bissau, Kenya, Lesotho, Liberia, Madagascar, Malawi, Mali, Mauritania, Mauritius, Mozambique, Namibia, Niger, Nigeria, Rwanda, Senegal, Seychelles, Sierra Leone, Somalia, South Africa, Sudan, Swaziland, Tanzania, Togo, Uganda, Zambia, Zimbabwe.

Americas: Argentina, Bahamas, Barbados, Belize, Bolivia, Brazil, Canada, Chile, Colombia, Costa Rica, Cuba, Dominican Republic, Ecuador, El Salvador, Guatemala, Guyana, Haiti, Honduras, Jamaica, Mexico, Nicaragua, Panama, Paraguay, Peru, Trinidad and Tobago, Uruguay, USA, Venezuela. *Caribbean*: Bahamas, Barbados, Cuba, Dominican Republic, Haiti, Jamaica and Trinidad and Tobago. *Central America*: Belize, Costa Rica, El Salvador, Guatemala, Honduras, Mexico, Nicaragua, Panama. *North America*: Canada, USA. *South America*: Argentina, Bolivia, Brazil, Chile, Colombia, Ecuador, Guyana, Paraguay, Peru, Uruguay, Venezuela.

Asia and Oceania: Afghanistan, Australia, Bangladesh, Brunei, Cambodia, China, Fiji, India, Indonesia, Japan, Kazakhstan, New Zealand, North Korea, South Korea, Kyrgyzstan, Laos, Malaysia, Mongolia, Myanmar (Burma), Nepal, Pakistan, Papua New Guinea, Philippines, Singapore, Sri Lanka, Taiwan, Tajikistan, Thailand, Tonga, Turkmenistan, Uzbekistan, Viet Nam. *Central Asia*: Kazakhstan, Kyrgyzstan, Tajikistan, Turkmenistan, Uzbekistan. *East Asia*: Brunei, Cambodia, China, Indonesia, Japan, North Korea, South Korea, Laos, Malaysia, Mongolia, Myanmar (Burma), Philippines, Singapore, Taiwan, Thailand, Viet Nam. *South Asia*: Afghanistan, Bangladesh, India, Nepal, Pakistan, Sri Lanka. *Oceania*: Australia, Fiji, New Zealand, Papua New Guinea, Tonga.

Europe: Albania, Armenia, Austria, Azerbaijan, Belarus, Belgium, Bosnia and Herzegovina, Bulgaria, Croatia, Cyprus, Czech Republic, Denmark, Estonia, Finland, France, Georgia, Germany, Greece, Hungary, Iceland, Ireland, Italy, Latvia, Lithuania, Luxembourg, Macedonia (Former Yugoslav Republic of, FYROM), Malta, Moldova, Montenegro, Netherlands, Norway, Poland, Portugal, Romania, Russia, Serbia, Slovakia, Slovenia, Spain, Sweden, Switzerland, Turkey, UK, Ukraine. *Central Europe*: Albania, Bosnia and Herzegovina, Bulgaria, Croatia, Czech Republic, Estonia, Hungary, Latvia, Lithuania, Macedonia (Former Yugoslav Republic of FYROM), Montenegro, Poland, Romania, Serbia, Slovakia, Slovenia. *Eastern Europe*: Armenia, Azerbaijan, Belarus, Georgia, Moldova, Russia, Ukraine. *Western Europe*: Austria, Belgium, Cyprus, Denmark, Finland, France, Germany, Greece, Iceland, Ireland, Italy, Luxembourg, Malta, Netherlands, Norway, Portugal, Spain, Sweden, Switzerland, Turkey, UK.

Middle East: Bahrain, Egypt, Iran, Iraq, Israel, Jordan, Kuwait, Lebanon, Oman, Qatar, Saudi Arabia, Syria, United Arab Emirates (UAE), Yemen. *ASEAN*: Brunei, Cambodia (1999–), Indonesia, Laos, Malaysia, Myanmar (Burma), Philippines, Singapore, Thailand, Viet Nam. *CIS*: Armenia, Azerbaijan, Belarus, Georgia, Kazakhstan, Kyrgyzstan, Moldova, Russia, Tajikistan, Turkmenistan, Ukraine, Uzbekistan.

European Union: Austria, Belgium, Bulgaria (2007–), Cyprus (2004–), Czech Republic (2004–), Denmark, Estonia (2004–), Finland, France, Germany, Greece, Hungary (2004–), Ireland, Italy, Latvia (2004–), Lithuania (2004–), Luxembourg, Malta (2004–), Netherlands, Poland (2004–), Portugal, Romania (2007–), Slovakia (2004–), Slovenia (2004–), Spain, Sweden, UK.

NATO: Belgium, Bulgaria (2004–), Canada, Czech Republic (1999–), Denmark, Estonia (2004–), France, Germany, Greece, Hungary (1999–), Iceland, Italy, Latvia (2004–), Lithuania (2004–), Luxembourg, Netherlands, Norway, Poland (1999–), Portugal, Romania (2004–), Slovakia (2004–), Slovenia

(2004–), Spain, Turkey, UK, USA. *NATO Europe:* Belgium, Bulgaria (2004–), Czech Republic (1999–), Denmark, Estonia (2004–), France, Germany, Greece, Hungary (1999–), Iceland, Italy, Latvia (2004–), Lithuania (2004–), Luxembourg, Netherlands, Norway, Poland (1999–), Portugal, Romania (2004–), Slovakia (2004–), Slovenia (2004–), Spain, Turkey, UK.

OECD: Australia, Austria, Belgium, Canada, Czech Republic, Denmark, Finland, France, Germany, Greece, Hungary, Iceland, Ireland, Italy, Japan, South Korea, Luxembourg, Mexico, Netherlands, New Zealand, Norway, Poland, Portugal, Slovakia (2000–), Spain, Sweden, Switzerland, Turkey, UK, USA.

OPEC: Algeria, Angola (2007–), Indonesia, Iran, Iraq, Kuwait, Libya, Nigeria, Qatar, Saudi Arabia, United Arab Emirates, Venezuela.

OSCE: Albania, Armenia, Austria, Azerbaijan, Belarus, Belgium, Bosnia and Herzegovina, Bulgaria, Canada, Croatia, Cyprus, Czech Republic, Denmark, Estonia, Finland, France, Georgia, Germany, Greece, Hungary, Iceland, Ireland, Italy, Kazakhstan, Kyrgyzstan, Latvia, Lithuania, Luxembourg, Macedonia (Former Yugoslav Republic of, FYROM), Malta, Moldova, Montenegro (2006–), Netherlands, Norway, Poland, Portugal, Romania, Russia, Serbia (2000–), Slovakia, Slovenia, Spain, Sweden, Switzerland, Tajikistan, Turkey, Turkmenistan, UK, Ukraine, USA, Uzbekistan.

Low-income countries (GNI/capita ≤$875 in 2005): Afghanistan, Bangladesh, Benin, Burkina Faso, Burundi, Cambodia, Central African Republic, Chad, Congo (Democratic Republic of the, DRC), Côte d'Ivoire, Eritrea, Ethiopia, Gambia, Ghana, Guinea, Guinea-Bissau, Haiti, India, Kenya, North Korea, Kyrgyzstan, Laos, Liberia, Madagascar, Malawi, Mali, Mauritania, Mongolia, Mozambique, Myanmar (Burma), Nepal, Niger, Nigeria, Pakistan, Papua New Guinea, Rwanda, Senegal, Sierra Leone, Somalia, Sudan, Tajikistan, Tanzania, Togo, Uganda, Uzbekistan, Viet Nam, Yemen, Zambia, Zimbabwe.

Lower-middle-income countries (GNI/capita $876–$3465 in 2005): Albania, Algeria, Angola, Armenia, Azerbaijan, Belarus, Bolivia, Bosnia and Herzegovina, Brazil, Bulgaria, Cameroon, Cape Verde, China, Colombia, Congo (Republic of the), Cuba, Djibouti, Dominican Republic, Ecuador, Egypt, El Salvador, Fiji, Georgia, Guatemala, Guyana, Honduras, Indonesia, Iran, Iraq, Jamaica, Jordan, Kazakhstan, Lesotho, Macedonia (Former Yugoslav Republic of, FYROM), Moldova, Morocco, Namibia, Nicaragua, Paraguay, Peru, Philippines, Serbia, Sri Lanka, Swaziland, Syria, Thailand, Tonga, Trinidad and Tobago, Turkmenistan, Tunisia, Ukraine.

Upper-middle-income countries (GNI/capita $3466–$10 725 in 2005): Argentina, Barbados, Belize, Botswana, Chile, Costa Rica, Croatia, Czech Republic, Equatorial Guinea, Estonia, Gabon, Hungary, Latvia, Lebanon, Lithuania, Libya, Malaysia, Mauritius, Mexico, Montenegro, Oman, Panama, Poland, Romania, Russia, Seychelles, Slovakia, South Africa, Turkey, Uruguay, Venezuela.

High-income countries (GNI/capita ≥$10 726 in 2005): Australia, Austria, Bahamas, Bahrain, Belgium, Brunei, Canada, Cyprus, Denmark, Finland, France, Germany, Greece, Iceland, Ireland, Israel, Italy, Japan, South Korea, Kuwait, Luxembourg, Malta, Netherlands, New Zealand, Norway, Portugal, Qatar, Saudi Arabia, Singapore, Slovenia, Spain, Sweden, Switzerland, Taiwan, United Arab Emirates, UK, USA.

Table 5A.2. Military expenditure by country, in local currency, 1998–2007

Figures are in local currency at current prices and are for calendar years, unless otherwise stated. Countries are grouped by region and subregion.

Country	Currency	1998	1999	2000	2001	2002	2003	2004	2005	2006	2007
Africa											
North Africa											
Algeria‡ [1]	m. dinars	112 248	121 597	141 576	161 505	167 380	170 764	201 930	214 320	224 767	273 415
Libya	m. dinars	675	535	556	496	575	700	894	981	769	807
Morocco	m. dirhams	13 878	11 569	9 129	16 619	16 254	17 418	17 182	18 006	18 775	19 730
Tunisia	m. dinars	417	424	456	483	491	525	554	608	574	..
Sub-Saharan											
Angola§‖ [2]	b. kwanzas	(0.1)	(0.6)	(2.2)	(5.7)	(17.9)	(27.3)	(80.0)	(104)	(127)	(172)
Benin	m. CFA francs	..	10 986	10 321	9 612	18 122	20 077	22 072	[24 677]	[25 601]	..
Botswana	m. pula	765	784	942	1 229	1 415	1 490	1 474	1 533	1 654	[1 945]
Burkina Faso†	m. CFA francs	[19 200]	[21 200]	[21 500]	22 259	24 666	25 571	30 289	33 649	37 081	45 448
Burundi	b. francs	26.3	28.5	30.5	44.2	41.8	47.0	49.4	53.6	46.0	50.1
Cameroon§	m. CFA francs	80 969	89 095	87 598	91 118	101 500	109 556	116 808	117 670	134 345	142 198
Cape Verde	m. escudos	443	518	814	572	530	565	573	636	626	640
Central Afr. Rep.‡ [3]	m. CFA francs	..	..	..	..	7 445	8 729	7 979	8 121	..	..
Chad	b. CFA francs	11.8	16.0	18.8	22.5	23.9	23.8	26.7	29.3	30.9	33.3
Congo, Republic of§	m. CFA francs	..	..	..	28 374	35 035	39 916	40 050	41 400	44 070	..
Congo, DRC[4]	m./b. francs	42.8	600	2 901	..	..	48.0	78.0	71.0	(76.0)	(85.4)
Côte d'Ivoire[5]	b. CFA francs	..	..	..	..	..	124	133	132	140	139
Djibouti	m. francs	4 042	4 053	3 979	4 045	4 500	..	..	..	..	..
Equatorial Guinea	CFA francs	..	..	..	..	..	..	..	..	..	..
Eritrea	m. nakfa	1 936	2 225	2 220	1 884	2 104	2 520	..	..	..	..
Ethiopia	m. birr	3 263	5 589	5 075	2 959	2 476	2 397	2 686	2 965	3 005	3 250
Gabon[6]	b. CFA francs	..	..	65.0	66.0	66.0	63.0	65.0	60.0	58.0	(59.0)
Gambia‡	m. dalasis	43.1	40.1	42.5	38.5	45.0	57.0	58.0	84.0	..	..
Ghana‖ [7]	m. cedis	13.3	15.8	27.7	23.2	29.3	46.2	50.7	58.2	69.4	106

Guinea[8]	b. francs	55.7	76.6	80.3	171	194	167	182	:	:	:
Guinea-Bissau[9]	m. CFA francs	1 711	:	6 786	4 533	4 435	4 362	:	6 391	:	:
Kenya	m. shillings	10 381	10 684	12 614	15 349	16 844	18 676	20 570	23 936	27 096	33 209
Lesotho	m. maloti	154	208	212	201	206	207	203	214	239	281
Liberia	m. dollars	:	:	:	:	:	:	252	361	[283]	[376]
Madagascar[|| 10]	b. ariary	54.9	56.6	63.9	85.7	78.9	89.8	102	108	116	154
Malawi	m. kwacha	450	635	698	916	1 136	1 278	2 391	4 027	[5 257]	[5 823]
Mali	b. CFA francs	32.2	36.0	41.4	43.8	45.8	51.6	54.5	63.2	68.9	[76.4]
Mauritania[‡]	b. ouguiyas	4.8	6.7	9.1	13.3	9.9	16.4	18.6	17.7	22.0	:
Mauritius	m. rupees	203	228	246	262	285	304	301	321	343	370
Mozambique[||]	m. new meticais	[585]	722	843	1 048	1 267	1 422	1 753	1 436	1 459	1 773
Namibia[11]	m. dollars	436	646	641	833	928	979	1 079	1 221	1 351	1 608
Niger	b. CFA francs	13.0	14.5	14.3	18.2	14.4	14.3	16.7	17.3	:	:
Nigeria[12]	m. naira	25 162	45 400	37 490	63 472	108 148	75 913	85 047	88 506	99 853	122 315
Rwanda[13]	b. francs	27.2	27.0	23.9	25.2	24.3	24.3	23.8	25.1	30.2	31.8
Senegal[§ ¶ 14]	m. CFA francs	44 300	48 200	44 400	50 500	51 829	56 293	56 819	65 619	77 678	92 557
Seychelles	m. rupees	55.5	59.3	59.0	64.8	64.1	66.1	87.6	81.0	80.0	77.0
Sierra Leone[15]	b. leones	:	:	48.8	59.4	57.0	66.8	62.0	68.1	[83.7]	[88.0]
Somalia	shillings	:	:	:	:	:	:	:	:	:	:
South Africa	m. rand	11 642	11 353	14 322	17 021	19 985	22 129	22 633	25 306	26 468	28 431
Sudan[‡ || 16]	m. dinars	522	1 085	1 510	1 004	1 276	1 039	3 200	2 838	:	:
Swaziland	m. emalangeni	[163]	[180]	[186]	[184]	[223]	[261]	[298]	:	:	:
Tanzania	b. shillings	89.3	95.7	108	132	136	130	139	157	184	202
Togo	m. CFA francs	:	:	:	:	:	16 757	16 757	17 532	:	:
Uganda	b. shillings	192	232	232	239	256	299	355	386	372	360
Zambia[|| 17]	b. kwacha	:	134	:	:	:	:	470	600	659	800
Zimbabwe[|| 18]	m. new dollars	3.7	10.1	15.4	15.8	37.3	136	1 300	2 942	(26 604)	(22 700)
Americas											
Caribbean											
Bahamas	m. dollars	33.4	34.1	28.6	28.1	30.2	32.9	34.9	38.7	48.2	58.3
Barbados	m. dollars	36.7	39.8	42.8	46.1	47.2	47.0	46.9	51.7	[52.8]	:

Country	Currency	1998	1999	2000	2001	2002	2003	2004	2005	2006	2007
Cuba	pesos	..	..	..	..	..	..	..	..	..	..
Dominican Rep.	m. pesos	1 818	2 005	2 872	3 742	4 440	3 578	4 093	6 687	6 339	[6 477]
Haiti	gourdes	..	..	..	..	..	..	..	..	..	..
Jamaica	m. dollars	1 741	1 762	1 873	2 133	2 755	3 167	3 337	3 695	4 776	5 302
Trinidad–Tobago	dollars	..	..	..	..	..	..	..	..	..	..
Central America											
Belize	dollars	..	..	..	..	..	..	..	..	..	..
Costa Rica[19]	colones	..	..	..	..	..	..	..	..	..	..
El Salvador	m. dollar	96.3	99.8	112	109	109	106	106	107	114	114
Guatemala	m. quetzales	894	914	1 225	1 546	1 239	1 420	913	798	1 111	1 274
Honduras[†][§][20]	m. lempiras	..	..	516	646	898	919	928	1 004	1 041	1 444
Mexico[†][21]	m. pesos	20 677	25 363	28 664	30 171	30 631	31 941	32 241	34 039	36 847	43 152
Nicaragua[22]	m. córdobas	278	318	390	389	460	537	527	568	614	705
Panama[23]	m. balboas	104	112	..	..	..	..	..	..	..	..
North America											
Canada	m. dollars	11 495	12 199	12 326	12 972	13 332	13 952	14 749	15 739	16 800	19 105
USA[24]	m. dollars	274 278	280 969	301 697	312 743	356 720	415 223	464 676	503 353	527 660	578 315
South America											
Argentina	m. pesos	3 782	3 852	3 739	3 638	3 784	4 433	4 803	5 553	5 719	[6 092]
Bolivia[25]	m. bolivianos	1 002	848	869	1 104	1 064	1 161	1 171	1 195	1 255	1 275
Brazil	m. reais	[16 960]	[16 408]	18 617	23 062	28 620	25 590	26 606	30 308	35 001	[40 123]
Chile[§][26]	b. pesos	1 249	1 367	1 502	1 615	1 765	1 743	2 216	2 463	2 809	2 882
Colombia[27]	b. pesos	[4 543]	[5 183]	[7 141]	[8 470]	7 524	8 996	10 139	11 446	12 684	13 574
Ecuador[||][28]	m. US dollars	549	296	266	384	505	739	710	954	950	1 253
Guyana	dollars	..	..	..	..	..	..	..	..	..	..
Paraguay[29]	b. guaranies	274	262	277	270	288	294	364	347	431	469
Peru[30]	m. soles	(2 671)	(2 773)	(3 228)	3 187	2 982	3 092	3 397	3 820	4 011	3 857

Uruguay	m. pesos	[3 815]	[4 174]	[3 663]	4 384	4 333	4 967	5 261	5 696	6 168	6 966
Venezuela[31]	b. bolivares	716	725	923	1 373	1 396	1 666	2 558	3 957	4 475	5 518
Asia											
Central Asia											
Kazakhstan	b. tenge	19.0	17.2	20.4	32.5	37.7	47.5	58.0	78.7	100	[155]
Kyrgyzstan[32]	m. soms	912	1 267	1 864	1 734	2 055	2 408	2 688	3 100	3 606	[4 635]
Tajikistan	m. somoni	17.6	18.7	21.5	29.6	70.7	107	134	..	..	..
Turkmenistan[33]	b. manats	436	582	..	..	..	..	..	..	..	..
Uzbekistan[34]	m. sum	..	34 860	41 115	..	..	53 018	..	..	..	..
East Asia											
Brunei	m. dollars	492	438	421	390	405	424	(337)	(414)	[433]	[447]
Cambodia	b. riel	312	336	309	280	265	270	272	289	328	[320]
China[35]	b. yuan	[149]	[165]	[182]	[216]	[253]	[283]	[324]	[363]	[431]	[506]
Indonesia	b. rupiahs	10 349	10 254	13 945	16 416	19 291	27 446	32 100	[34 658]	[41 735]	[48 256]
Japan[†][§][36]	b. yen	4 942	4 934	4 935	4 950	4 956	4 954	4 916	4 868	4 824	4 805
Korea, North	won	..	..	..	..	..	..	..	..	..	..
Korea, South[†][¶][37]	tr. won	13.6	13.3	14.5	15.5	16.4	17.5	18.9	21.1	21.5	24.2
Laos	b. kip	66.5	224	278	325	..	..	..	..	..	..
Malaysia	m. ringgits	4 547	6 321	5 826	7 351	8 504	10 950	10 728	11 817	11 981	13 791
Mongolia	m. tugriks	16 750	18 416	26 126	25 384	28 071	27 899	32 891	35 914	46 232	..
Myanmar[38]	b. kyats	37.3	43.7	58.8	63.9	73.1	..	..	..	..	..
Philippines	m. pesos	31 512	32 959	36 208	35 977	38 907	44 440	43 847	47 634	51 527	53 805
Singapore	m. dollars	7 475	7 616	7 466	7 721	8 108	8 230	8 525	9 094	9 848	10 445
Taiwan	b. dollars	299	258	243	248	225	228	249	250	241	312
Thailand	m. baht	86 133	74 809	71 268	75 413	76 724	77 027	[75 498]	[79 519]	[86 706]	[116 850]
Viet Nam	dong	..	..	..	..	..	..	..	..	..	..
South Asia											
Afghanistan[39]	m. afghani	..	..	..	..	..	..	5 440	5 521	6 223	10 255
Bangladesh	m. taka	28 436	31 277	33 377	34 020	34 105	36 150	39 630	43 005	46 950	..
India[40]	b. rupees	492	598	642	689	717	761	812	982	1 102	1 193

Country	Currency	1998	1999	2000	2001	2002	2003	2004	2005	2006	2007
Nepal¶41	m. rupees	2 789	3 239	3 648	4 837	6 621	7 951	9 756	11 153	[11 004]	[10 604]
Pakistan‡	b. rupees	140	147	154	170	188	207	232	263	287	[307]
Sri Lanka†‡42	b. rupees	42.5	40.1	56.9	54.2	49.2	47.0	56.3	61.5	81.4	105
Oceania											
Australia	m. dollars	10 799	11 496	11 975	12 995	14 077	14 965	16 119	17 184	18 826	20 949
Fiji†43	m. dollars	48.0	49.6	67.0	60.0	63.2	57.8	52.7	66.0	74.0	80.0
New Zealand	m. dollars	1 363	1 380	1 422	1 428	1 411	1 468	1 523	1 587	1 728	1 893
Papua New Guinea	m. kina	86.0	80.0	85.0	85.5	66.3	68.8	78.7	94.2	93.7	91.2
Tonga	th. pa'anga	3 693	3 535	3 837	4 211	4 319	4 560	4 366	5 119	6 878	7 566
Europe											
Albania¶44	m. leks	5 067	5 891	6 519	7 638	8 220	9 279	10 373	11 000	13 831	17 619
Armenia†45	b. drams	33.7	36.5	36.7	36.8	36.8	44.3	52.3	64.4	74.1	94.8
Austria	m. euros	[1 943]	[1 994]	[2 090]	[1 999]	1 999	2 111	2 158	2 160	2 105	2 629
Azerbaijan‖	m. new manat	[83.0]	[99.1]	[107]	[123]	[136]	[173]	[224]	288	640	797
Belarus	b. roubles	[10.5]	[41.4]	[123]	247	366	475	679	975	1 355	1 573
Belgium	m. euros	3 297	3 378	3 463	3 393	3 344	3 434	3 433	3 400	3 435	3 650
Bosnia–Herze.†¶46	m. marka	::	::	::	::	501	351	315	273	278	281
Bulgaria†	m. leva	512	595	677	805	859	895	930	1 006	1 116	1 132
Croatia	m. kunas	[9 082]	[7 367]	[5 461]	[5 251]	[5 775]	[4 757]	4 250	4 323	4 872	5 433
Cyprus†	m. pounds	169	106	118	142	100	101	107	109	114	::
Czech Republic47	m. koruny	37 643	41 688	44 670	44 978	48 924	53 194	52 481	58 445	55 358	53 906
Denmark	m. kroner	19 071	19 428	19 339	21 017	21 269	21 075	21 441	20 800	23 173	22 727
Estonia	m. krooni	843	1 083	1 329	1 640	2 028	2 376	2 581	2 890	3 307	4 568
Finland	m. euros	1 761	1 552	1 691	1 653	1 712	2 006	2 131	2 206	2 281	2 235
France48	m. euros	36 012	36 510	36 702	37 187	38 681	40 684	42 690	42 545	43 457	44 283
Georgia49	m. lari	[57.1]	[52.4]	[37.2]	[49.4]	74.6	91.5	135	388	716	1 271
Germany	m. euros	29 822	30 603	30 554	30 648	31 168	31 060	30 610	30 600	30 365	30 739
Greece	m. euros	5 061	5 439	5 921	5 986	6 085	[5 355]	[6 028]	[6 818]	[7 321]	[7 934]

Country	Currency										
Hungary	m. forint	151 215	191 485	226 041	272 426	279 569	314 380	310 731	318 552	277 804	279 953
Iceland	m. krónur	0	0	0	0	0	0	0	0	0	0
Ireland	m. euros	[662]	[696]	[754]	858	862	855	887	921	949	1 006
Italy[50]	m. euros	21 052	22 240	24 325	24 592	25 887	26 795	27 476	26 959	26 631	27 572
Latvia[51]	m. lats	24.8	33.1	42.4	54.6	91.0	108	124	154	206	254
Lithuania[¶][52]	m. litai	[448]	[388]	[644]	[652]	715	816	864	852	974	1 121
Luxembourg	m. euros	129	132	139	179	192	205	[213]	[238]	[263]	[268]
Macedonia, FYR[53]	m. denar	4 302	3 769	4 602	15 397	6 841	6 292	6 683	6 259	6 149	7 272
Malta[†]	th. liri	11 297	11 164	11 109	12 205	12 317	12 874	13 968	14 234	15 148	13 667
Moldova[†][¶][54]	m. lei	57.0	63.0	63.3	76.7	94.7	115	116	151	210	223
Montenegro[55]	m. euros	..	..	..	..	..	..	..	..	42.3	43.0
Netherlands	m. euros	6 154	6 595	6 482	6 929	7 149	7 404	7 552	7 693	8 145	8 133
Norway	m. kroner	25 087	25 809	25 722	26 669	32 461	31 985	32 945	31 471	31 805	32 502
Poland	m. złotys	12 170	12 852	13 871	15 695	16 220	17 215	18 842	20 259	21 282	23 254
Portugal	m. euros	2 098	2 259	2 393	2 598	2 765	2 792	[2 995]	[2 918]	[3 024]	[2 832]
Romania[||]	m. new lei	[1 113]	1 465	2 031	2 864	3 491	4 151	4 994	5 757	6 324	7 397
Russia[56]	b. roubles	[85.6]	[165]	[271]	[365]	[470]	[568]	[656]	[806]	[967]	[1 178]
Serbia[57]	m. dinars	6 441	8 600	21 292	33 060	43 695	42 070	43 154	41 996	47 342	55 912
Slovakia[†]	m. korunas	14 009	13 532	15 760	19 051	19 947	22 965	22 944	25 537	27 064	30 697
Slovenia[||]	m. euros	209	208	207	275	328	360	396	413	485	510
Spain	m. euros	6 756	7 092	7 599	7 972	8 414	8 587	9 132	9 508	11 506	12 432
Sweden[58]	m. kronor	40 801	42 541	44 542	42 639	42 401	42 903	40 527	41 240	41 150	40 595
Switzerland[†][¶][59]	m. francs	4 532	4 416	4 503	4 476	4 461	4 437	4 381	4 344	3 972	4 120
Turkey[¶][||]	m. new lira	2 289	4 168	6 248	8 844	12 108	13 553	13 386	13 840	16 451	17 736
UK[60]	m. pounds	22 261	22 530	23 301	24 230	25 725	29 683	32 102	33 002	33 825	35 188
Ukraine[§]	m. hryvnias	3 442	3 890	6 184	5 848	6 266	7 615	8 963	12 328	15 082	[20 685]
Middle East											
Bahrain[61]	m. dinars	111	123	121	126	126	176	180	183	203	[214]
Egypt	m. pounds	9 439	9 881	10 847	11 859	12 741	13 948	14 684	15 369	16 632	18 264
Iran[¶][62]	b. rials	7 744	12 992	21 984	26 996	23 211	31 633	45 960	64 655	78 164	79 871
Iraq[63]	b. dinars	..	..	..	..	..	..	..	(2 405)	(6 064)	(9 753)

Country	Currency	1998	1999	2000	2001	2002	2003	2004	2005	2006	2007
Israel[64]	m. shekels	34 901	38 016	39 587	41 788	48 957	46 350	43 988	46 240	50 757	[56 047]
Jordan	m. dinars	[352]	363	375	375	370	434	416	428	497	779
Kuwait	m. dinars	696	696	827	824	858	933	1 032	[1 142]	[1 177]	[1 378]
Lebanon	b. pounds	1 052	1 251	1 402	1 445	1 368	1 392	1 439	[1 463]	[1 590]	[2 114]
Oman‡	m. rials	676	687	809	933	958	1 010	1 144	1 404	1 550	[1 577]
Qatar	riyals	..	..	..	..	..	..	..	..	..	..
Saudi Arabia§ 65	m. rials	78 231	68 700	74 866	78 850	69 382	70 303	78 414	95 146	110 779	132 922
Syria	b. pounds	[40.4]	39.5	49.9	47.6	47.9	59.0	74.7	78.7	90.5	74.3
UAE[66]	m. dirhams	8 712	8 790	8 688	8 796	9 139	9 244	8 943	9 399	..	..
Yemen	b. riyals	52.2	61.5	76.6	[91.1]	130	148	136	156	162	209

Table 5A.3. Military expenditure by country, in constant US dollars for 1998–2007 and current US dollars for 2007

Figures are in US $m. at constant 2005 prices and exchange rates for 1998–2007 and, in the right-most column, marked *, in current US$ m. for 2007. Figures are for calendar years unless otherwise stated. Countries are grouped by region and subregion.

Country	1998	1999	2000	2001	2002	2003	2004	2005	2006	2007	2007*
Africa											
North Africa											
Algeria‡[1]	1 801	1 901	2 205	2 414	2 467	2 453	2 801	2 925	2 992	3 548	3 909
Libya	412	318	341	333	429	533	696	749	568	513	630
Morocco	1 721	1 425	1 104	1 997	1 900	2 013	1 956	2 030	2 049	2 118	2 376
Tunisia	386	382	400	415	411	428	436	469	423	:	:
Sub-Saharan											
Angola§||[2]	:	:	:	:	:	:	:	:	:	:	(2 226)
Benin	:	24.9	22.5	20.2	37.0	40.5	44.1	[46.8]	[46.8]	:	:
Botswana	256	243	269	329	351	339	313	300	290	[322]	[313]
Burkina Faso†	[41.7]	[46.5]	[47.3]	46.6	50.5	51.4	61.1	63.8	68.7	85.5	93.3
Burundi	45.7	47.9	41.2	54.7	52.4	53.2	51.6	49.6	41.4	42.5	47.5
Cameroon§	175	189	183	183	198	212	226	223	242	257	292
Cape Verde	5.3	6.0	9.6	6.5	6.0	6.3	6.5	7.2	6.7	6.6	7.8
Central African Republic‡[3]	:	:	:	:	14.8	16.7	15.6	15.4	:	:	:
Chad	25.3	37.4	42.3	45.0	45.5	46.1	54.6	55.5	54.2	56.7	68.4
Congo, Republic of§	:	:	:	60.7	72.3	80.5	79.9	78.5	80.8	:	:
Congo, DRC[4]	18.4	67.0	49.8	:	:	128	200	150	(142)	(135)	(198)
Côte d'Ivoire[5]	:	:	:	:	:	247	261	250	259	252	286
Djibouti	25.7	25.7	24.9	24.8	27.5	:	:	:	:	:	:
Equatorial Guinea	:	:	:	:	:	:	:	:	:	:	:
Eritrea	378	401	334	247	236	230	:	:	:	:	:
Ethiopia	518	822	741	471	387	319	346	342	263	242	367
Gabon[6]	:	:	129	128	128	120	123	114	106	(102)	(121)
Gambia‡	2.4	2.2	2.3	2.0	2.2	2.3	2.1	2.9	:	:	:

Country	1998	1999	2000	2001	2002	2003	2004	2005	2006	2007	2007*
Ghana‖7	51.6	54.7	76.6	48.2	53.0	65.9	64.3	64.1	69.0	118	114
Guinea8	32.2	42.4	41.6	84.2	92.6	70.7	65.5	:	:	:	:
Guinea-Bissau9	3.8	:	13.8	8.9	8.5	8.6	:	12.1	:	:	:
Kenya	233	227	243	280	301	304	300	317	313	354	488
Lesotho	38.0	48.7	46.7	49.1	37.6	35.4	33.0	33.6	35.4	39.0	39.1
Liberia	:	:	:	:	:	:	4.7	6.3	[4.6]	[5.5]	[6.1]
Madagascar‖10	55.8	52.3	52.7	66.1	52.5	60.5	60.2	54.0	52.1	62.9	80.5
Malawi	14.1	13.8	11.7	12.5	13.5	13.9	23.3	34.0	[38.9]	[39.6]	[41.5]
Mali	67.4	76.1	88.2	88.7	88.3	101	110	120	129	[142]	[157]
Mauritania	27.4	36.5	47.8	66.9	47.9	75.9	78.1	66.1	77.3	:	:
Mauritius	9.8	10.3	10.7	10.8	11.0	11.3	10.7	10.9	10.7	10.7	11.5
Mozambique	[51.3]	61.6	63.8	72.7	75.3	74.4	81.3	62.3	55.9	63.4	67.8
Namibia11	113	154	140	166	166	164	173	192	202	227	224
Niger	28.1	32.1	30.8	37.6	29.0	29.3	34.1	32.8	:	:	:
Nigeria12	453	780	592	844	1 273	783	764	674	703	825	960
Rwanda13	68.5	69.7	59.2	60.6	57.1	53.3	46.5	45.0	49.7	47.8	55.6
Senegal§¶14	91.9	99.1	90.6	100	100	109	110	124	144	164	190
Seychelles	13.1	13.2	12.3	12.8	12.6	12.6	16.1	14.7	14.6	13.8	12.4
Sierra Leone15	:	:	22.9	27.4	27.1	29.6	24.1	23.6	[26.4]	[25.5]	[29.4]
Somalia	:	:	:	:	:	:	:	:	:	:	:
South Africa	2 598	2 408	2 884	3 243	3 488	3 648	3 680	3 979	3 978	4 040	3 964
Sudan‡‖16	387	693	902	566	655	501	1 426	1 165	:	:	:
Swaziland	[41.8]	[43.5]	[40.1]	[37.5]	[40.5]	[44.2]	[48.8]	:	:	:	:
Tanzania	108	107	114	133	136	125	134	139	149	158	159
Togo	:	:	:	:	:	34.1	33.9	33.2	:	:	:
Uganda	145	164	160	161	173	188	216	217	196	182	210
Zambia‖17	:	95.1	:	:	:	:	125	134	135	149	195
Zimbabwe‖18	123	211	207	120	118	92.4	196	132	(107)	:	:

Americas

Caribbean											
Bahamas	37.6	37.8	31.4	30.0	31.9	33.6	35.4	38.7	47.1	55.8	58.3
Barbados	21.4	22.9	24.0	25.2	25.8	25.3	24.9	25.9	[24.6]	:	:
Cuba	:	:	:	:	:	:	:	:	:	:	:
Dominican Republic	158	164	218	261	294	186	140	220	194	[188]	[195]
Haiti	:	:	:	:	:	:	:	:	:	:	:
Jamaica	53.1	50.7	49.8	53.0	63.9	66.6	61.8	59.3	70.6	74.7	78.0
Trinidad and Tobago	:	:	:	:	:	:	:	:	:	:	:
Central America											
Belize	:	:	:	:	:	:	:	:	:	:	:
Costa Rica[19]	117	121	132	124	122	116	111	107	110	105	114
El Salvador	186	181	229	269	199	217	130	104	137	149	166
Guatemala	:	:	:	:	:	:	:	:	:	:	:
Honduras[†][§][20]	:	:	41.0	46.8	60.4	57.4	53.6	53.3	52.4	68.7	76.4
Mexico[†][21]	3 079	3 239	3 344	3 309	3 198	3 190	3 076	3 123	3 262	3 691	3 941
Nicaragua[22]	28.7	29.5	32.5	30.2	34.3	38.1	34.5	33.9	33.4	35.4	38.4
Panama[23]	112	119	:	:	:	:	:	:	:	:	:
North America											
Canada[24]	11 122	11 603	11 412	11 709	11 771	11 984	12 441	12 986	13 588	15 155	17 290
USA[24]	328 611	329 421	342 172	344 932	387 303	440 813	480 451	503 353	511 187	546 786	578 315
South America											
Argentina	2 062	2 125	2 082	2 048	1 692	1 748	1 813	1 912	1 776	[1 752]	[1 976]
Bolivia[25]	155	128	126	157	150	158	153	148	149	141	161
Brazil	[11 843]	[10 927]	11 582	13 427	15 367	11 977	11 682	12 452	13 803	[15 334]	[20 062]
Chile[§][26]	2 719	2 879	3 048	3 164	3 374	3 241	4 077	4 397	4 851	4 821	5 448
Colombia[27]	[3 244]	[3 338]	[4 211]	[4 626]	3 864	4 312	4 589	4 932	5 240	5 329	6 484
Ecuador[||][28]	688	353	317	439	578	783	727	954	922	1 196	1 253
Guyana	:	:	:	:	:	:	:	:	:	:	:
Paraguay[29]	77.8	69.7	67.6	61.5	59.3	53.0	62.9	56.2	63.7	65.0	92.9

Country	1998	1999	2000	2001	2002	2003	2004	2005	2006	2007	2007*
Peru[30]	(958)	(961)	(1 078)	1 043	975	988	1 047	1 159	1 193	1 133	1 217
Uruguay	[280]	[290]	[243]	278	241	232	225	233	219	249	289
Venezuela[31]	1 254	1 028	1 126	1 489	1 237	1 125	1 419	1 894	1 884	2 004	2 570
Asia											
Central Asia											
Kazakhstan	246	206	215	317	347	411	470	592	693	[996]	[1 258]
Kyrgyzstan[32]	44.2	44.8	55.5	48.3	56.1	63.8	68.4	75.6	83.3	[101]	[122]
Tajikistan	19.8	16.6	14.3	14.2	30.3	39.3	46.1	..	..	..	..
Turkmenistan[33]	168	182	..	70.7	..	..	..	..	..	..	..
Uzbekistan[34]	..	95.3	..	..	..	64.2	..	..	..	..	..
East Asia											
Brunei	301	269	254	234	249	260	(205)	(249)	[260]	[265]	[294]
Cambodia	89.7	92.8	86.0	78.4	71.9	72.3	70.1	70.6	76.5	72.4	78.7
China[35]	[19 300]	[21 600]	[23 800]	[28 000]	[33 100]	[36 600]	[40 300]	[44 300]	[51 900]	[58 300]	[66 100]
Indonesia	2 079	1 710	2 242	2 367	2 486	3 319	3 653	[3 571]	[3 802]	[4 160]	[5 314]
Japan[†][§][36]	43 405	43 483	43 802	44 275	44 725	44 814	44 473	44 165	43 666	43 557	40 244
Korea, North	..	..	..	..	..	..	..	..	..	..	..
Korea, South[†][¶][37]	16 127	15 689	16 652	17 133	17 605	18 203	19 003	20 603	20 533	22 623	25 996
Laos	29.1	42.9	42.5	46.1	..	..	..	..	..	..	..
Malaysia	1 365	1 847	1 677	2 087	2 370	3 020	2 917	3 120	3 054	3 455	3 988
Mongolia	22.9	23.5	29.8	27.3	29.9	28.2	30.8	29.8	36.5	..	..
Myanmar[38]	..	..	..	..	..	..	..	..	..	..	..
Philippines	818	807	853	794	833	920	857	865	880	899	1 142
Singapore	4 703	4 791	4 634	4 745	5 002	5 051	5 147	5 465	5 862	6 148	6 858
Taiwan	9 765	8 412	7 803	7 961	7 256	7 358	7 914	7 766	7 427	9 483	9 445
Thailand	2 440	2 113	1 982	2 063	2 087	2 058	[1 962]	[1 977]	[2 060]	[2 729]	[3 370]
Viet Nam	..	..	..	..	..	..	..	..	..	..	..

South Asia											
Afghanistan[39]	..	..	..	..	..	..	123	111	119	181	209
Bangladesh	624	647	675	675	655	657	659	669	684	..	..
India[40]	14 757	17 150	17 697	18 313	18 256	18 664	19 204	22 273	23 615	24 249	28 428
Nepal[¶][41]	52.9	57.1	62.8	81.1	108	122	146	156	[143]	[132]	[158]
Pakistan[‡]	3 281	3 311	3 320	3 553	3 819	4 077	4 248	4 412	4 465	[4 517]	[5 057]
Sri Lanka[†][‡][42]	751	676	904	755	625	562	626	612	713	804	949
Oceania											
Australia	10 150	10 648	10 617	11 038	11 609	12 008	12 638	13 122	13 885	15 097	17 214
Fiji[†][43]	33.7	34.2	45.7	39.2	41.0	36.0	31.9	39.1	42.7	44.1	49.1
New Zealand	1 112	1 127	1 131	1 107	1 066	1 089	1 105	1 117	1 177	1 259	1 377
Papua New Guinea	53.6	43.4	39.9	36.7	25.5	23.0	25.8	30.4	29.4	27.8	30.4
Tonga	3.4	3.1	3.2	3.2	3.0	2.8	2.4	2.6	3.3	3.5	3.8
Europe											
Albania[¶][44]	59.6	69.0	76.3	86.7	86.6	97.3	106	110	135	168	190
Armenia[†][45]	86.4	93.0	94.3	91.5	90.5	104	115	141	157	194	272
Austria	[2 751]	[2 807]	[2 875]	2 631	2 631	2 740	2 745	2 686	2 580	3 168	3 539
Azerbaijan[∥]	[102]	[133]	[141]	[160]	[172]	[215]	[260]	305	625	667	927
Belarus	[198]	[198]	[220]	274	284	287	348	453	588	631	734
Belgium	4 722	4 783	4 783	4 573	4 434	4 482	4 389	4 229	4 197	4 398	4 913
Bosnia–Herzegovina[†][¶][46]	..	..	..	..	333	231	208	173	165	162	193
Bulgaria[†]	478	542	559	619	624	637	622	641	663	631	779
Croatia	[1 901]	[1 490]	[1 050]	[963]	[1 042]	[857]	738	727	793	875	996
Cyprus[†]	441	273	291	344	235	228	237	234	239	..	..
Czech Republic[47]	1 862	2 019	2 082	2 003	2 140	2 325	2 231	2 439	2 253	2 144	2 587
Denmark	3 697	3 675	3 555	3 776	3 730	3 619	3 640	3 468	3 792	3 666	4 108
Estonia	85.6	106	126	147	175	202	213	229	251	329	393
Finland	2 434	2 120	2 234	2 129	2 171	2 521	2 673	2 744	2 793	2 677	3 008
France[48]	50 345	50 787	50 205	50 036	51 064	52 615	54 059	52 917	53 199	53 579	59 600
Georgia[49]	[51.7]	[39.8]	[27.2]	[34.5]	49.3	57.7	80.6	214	362	592	757

Country	1998	1999	2000	2001	2002	2003	2004	2005	2006	2007	2007*
Germany	40 993	41 822	41 147	40 474	40 604	40 044	38 816	38 060	37 133	36 929	41 371
Greece	7 876	8 246	8 701	8 508	8 350	[7 097]	[7 765]	[8 480]	[8 824]	[9 346]	[10 678]
Hungary	1 217	1 401	1 507	1 662	1 621	1 742	1 612	1 596	1 340	1 255	1 504
Iceland	0	0	0	0	0	0	0	0	0	0	0
Ireland	[1 050]	[1 086]	[1 115]	1 210	1 162	1 113	1 130	1 145	1 135	1 152	1 354
Italy[50]	30 763	31 969	34 102	33 543	34 459	34 739	34 853	33 531	32 445	33 086	37 109
Latvia[51]	56.2	73.3	91.6	115	188	217	234	272	342	390	487
Lithuania[¶][52]	[171]	[147]	[242]	[242]	264	305	319	308	338	372	436
Luxembourg	187	190	194	243	256	267	319	[296]	[319]	[319]	[361]
Macedonia, FYR[53]	101	88.8	102	325	142	129	136	127	121	140	160
Malta[†]	38.5	37.3	36.2	38.7	38.2	39.4	41.6	41.2	42.6	38.4	43.1
Moldova[†][¶][54]	13.6	10.8	8.3	9.1	10.7	11.6	10.4	12.0	14.9	14.9	18.0
Montenegro[55]	:	:	:	:	:	:	:	:	51.8	50.9	57.9
Netherlands	9 114	9 557	9 116	9 352	9 344	9 479	9 549	9 568	10 015	9 853	10 946
Norway	4 482	4 506	4 358	4 385	5 269	5 066	5 194	4 887	4 826	4 920	5 420
Poland	5 089	5 010	4 913	5 270	5 345	5 628	5 947	6 262	6 506	6 973	8 185
Portugal	3 210	3 378	3 479	3 617	3 719	3 636	[3 811]	[3 630]	[3 660]	[3 343]	[3 812]
Romania[‖]	[1 879]	1 696	1 614	1 693	1 684	1 737	1 868	1 976	2 036	2 303	3 019
Russia[56]	[13 600]	[14 000]	[19 100]	[21 200]	[23 600]	[25 100]	[26 100]	[28 500]	[31 200]	[35 400]	[45 600]
Serbia[57]	777	728	1 053	839	928	813	752	630	635	706	956
Slovakia[†]	744	650	676	761	771	818	760	823	835	925	1 222
Slovenia[‖]	392	369	336	412	457	476	505	514	589	602	694
Spain	10 419	10 691	11 074	11 216	11 485	11 375	11 741	11 826	13 825	14 628	16 732
Sweden[58]	5 954	6 178	6 411	5 993	5 833	5 791	5 450	5 521	5 435	5 272	5 924
Switzerland[†][¶][59]	3 888	3 757	3 773	3 714	3 678	3 635	3 560	3 489	3 157	3 262	3 385
Turkey[¶][‖]	14 865	16 414	15 885	14 562	13 752	12 286	10 973	10 301	11 080	11 066	13 508
UK[60]	47 691	47 542	47 778	48 786	50 963	57 140	60 018	60 003	59 595	59 705	70 096
Ukraine[§]	1 551	1 429	1 772	1 497	1 592	1 839	1 985	2 405	2 699	[3 321]	[4 096]

Middle East

Bahrain[61]	304	340	337	355	357	491	491	486	528	[543]	[570]
Egypt	2 215	2 250	2 405	2 571	2 689	2 816	2 665	2 659	2 674	2 706	3 212
Iran[62]	2 290	3 200	4 731	5 220	3 926	4 594	5 816	7 213	7 677	6 592	8 618
Iraq[63]	.	.	.	.	.	.	.	(1 634)	(2 783)	(3 313)	(7 649)
Israel[64]	8 981	9 299	9 574	9 996	11 087	10 421	9 931	10 303	11 076	[12 233]	[13 499]
Jordan	[567]	581	596	586	567	655	607	604	660	988	1 099
Kuwait	2 735	2 658	3 082	3 029	3 126	3 369	3 679	[3 909]	[3 909]	[4 400]	[4 801]
Lebanon	722	857	964	998	928	932	948	[970]	[999]	[1 284]	[1 402]
Oman‡	1 774	1 797	2 139	2 488	2 562	2 695	3 030	3 652	3 905	[3 813]	[4 101]
Qatar	.	.	.	.	.	.	.	.	.	.	.
Saudi Arabia§ [65]	20 513	18 260	20 125	21 434	18 817	18 956	21 074	25 393	28 926	33 793	35 484
Syria	[4 062]	4 124	5 418	5 018	5 056	5 887	7 137	7 011	7 328	5 703	6 619
United Arab Emirates[66]	2 986	2 950	2 876	2 836	2 862	2 807	2 585	2 559	.	.	.
Yemen	543	588	700	[744]	942	972	793	816	715	820	1 050

Table 5A.4. Military expenditure by country as percentage of gross domestic product, 1998–2006

Countries are grouped by region and subregion.

Country	1998	1999	2000	2001	2002	2003	2004	2005	2006
Africa									
North Africa									
Algeria‡1	4.0	3.8	3.4	3.8	3.7	3.2	3.3	2.9	2.7
Libya	5.3	3.8	3.1	2.7	2.2	2.2	2.2	1.8	1.1
Morocco	4.0	3.3	2.6	4.3	4.1	4.2	3.9	3.9	3.7
Tunisia	1.8	1.7	1.7	1.7	1.6	1.6	1.6	1.6	1.4
Sub-Saharan									
Angola§‖2	2.6	3.6	2.4	2.9	4.2	2.6	4.7	4.1	3.7
Benin	:	0.7	0.6	0.5	0.9	1.0	1.0	[1.1]	[1.0]
Botswana	3.5	3.0	3.0	3.5	3.8	3.6	3.2	2.9	2.7
Burkina Faso†	[1.1]	[1.2]	[1.2]	1.1	1.1	1.0	1.1	1.1	1.2
Burundi	6.6	6.3	6.0	8.0	7.2	7.3	6.6	6.2	4.7
Cameroon§	1.4	1.4	1.3	1.3	1.3	1.4	1.4	1.3	1.4
Cape Verde	0.9	0.8	1.3	0.8	0.7	0.7	0.7	0.7	0.6
Central African Republic‡3	:	:	:	:	1.1	1.3	1.2	1.1	:
Chad	1.2	1.7	1.9	1.8	1.7	1.5	1.1	0.9	0.9
Congo, Republic of the§	:	:	:	1.4	1.7	1.9	1.7	1.4	1.2
Congo, DRC4	0.4	1.2	1.0	:	:	2.1	3.0	2.1	(1.9)
Côte d'Ivoire5	:	:	:	:	:	1.5	1.6	1.5	1.5
Djibouti	4.4	4.2	4.0	3.9	4.2	:	:	:	:
Equatorial Guinea	:	:	:	:	:	:	:	:	:
Eritrea	35.1	37.4	36.2	24.7	23.7	24.1	:	:	:
Ethiopia	6.7	10.7	9.6	4.7	3.6	2.9	2.8	2.6	2.1
Gabon6	:	:	1.8	1.9	2.0	1.8	1.7	1.3	1.1
Gambia‡	0.9	0.8	0.7	0.6	0.5	0.5	0.5	0.6	:
Ghana‖7	0.8	0.8	1.0	0.6	0.6	0.7	0.6	0.6	0.6

Guinea[8]	1.3	1.6	1.5	2.9	3.1	2.3	2.0	:	:
Guinea-Bissau[9]	1.4	:	4.4	3.1	3.1	3.1	:	3.9	:
Kenya	1.2	1.2	1.3	1.5	1.6	1.6	1.6	1.7	1.6
Lesotho	3.2	3.8	3.6	3.1	2.8	2.6	2.4	2.3	2.4
Liberia	:	:	:	:	:	:	1.0	1.2	[0.8]
Madagascar[||] [10]	1.3	1.2	1.2	1.4	1.3	1.3	1.2	1.1	1.0
Malawi	0.8	0.8	0.7	0.7	0.8	0.7	1.2	1.6	[1.7]
Mali	1.9	2.0	2.2	2.0	2.0	2.1	2.1	2.3	2.2
Mauritania[‡]	2.1	2.7	3.5	4.6	3.2	4.9	4.7	3.6	3.0
Mauritius	0.2	0.2	0.2	0.2	0.2	0.2	0.2	0.2	0.2
Mozambique[||]	[1.2]	1.4	1.5	1.4	1.3	1.2	1.3	0.9	0.8
Namibia11	2.3	3.1	2.7	2.2	2.8	2.9	2.9	3.1	3.1
Niger	1.1	1.2	1.2	1.4	1.0	0.9	1.1	1.0	:
Nigeria[12]	0.9	1.4	0.8	1.3	1.9	1.1	1.0	0.6	0.6
Rwanda[13]	4.4	4.2	3.4	3.4	3.1	2.5	2.1	1.9	1.9
Senegal[§] [¶] [14]	1.5	1.5	1.3	1.4	1.4	1.4	1.3	1.4	1.6
Seychelles	1.7	1.8	1.7	1.8	1.7	1.7	2.3	2.1	1.9
Sierra Leone[15]	:	:	3.7	3.7	2.9	2.9	2.1	2.0	[2.1]
Somalia									
South Africa	1.6	1.4	1.6	1.7	1.7	1.8	1.6	1.6	1.5
Sudan[‡] [||] [16]	2.4	4.1	4.8	2.9	3.2	2.3	5.8	4.4	:
Swaziland	[2.1]	[2.0]	[1.8]	[1.6]	[1.7]	[1.7]	[1.8]	:	:
Tanzania	1.6	1.5	1.5	1.6	1.4	1.2	1.1	1.1	1.1
Togo	:	:	:	:	:	1.6	1.6	1.6	:
Uganda	2.4	2.7	2.5	2.4	2.4	2.3	2.5	2.4	2.0
Zambia[||] [17]	:	1.8	:	:	:	:	1.8	1.8	1.7
Zimbabwe[||] [18]	2.6	4.4	4.7	2.2	2.2	2.5	5.5	2.3	(1.9)
Americas									
Caribbean									
Bahamas	0.8	0.7	0.6	0.5	0.6	0.6	0.6	0.6	0.8
Barbados	0.8	0.8	0.8	0.9	1.0	0.9	0.8	0.8	[0.8]

Country	1998	1999	2000	2001	2002	2003	2004	2005	2006
Cuba	. .	. .	. .	. .	. .	. .	. .	. .	. .
Dominican Republic	0.6	0.6	0.7	0.9	1.0	0.6	0.4	0.6	0.5
Haiti	. .	. .	. .	. .	. .	. .	. .	. .	. .
Jamaica	0.6	0.6	0.6	0.6	0.7	0.7	0.6	0.6	0.7
Trinidad and Tobago	. .	. .	. .	. .	. .	. .	. .	. .	. .
Central America									
Belize	. .	. .	. .	. .	. .	. .	. .	. .	. .
Costa Rica[19]	0.0	0.0	0.0	0.0	0.0	0.0	0.0	0.0	0.0
El Salvador	0.8	0.8	0.9	0.8	0.8	0.7	0.7	0.6	0.6
Guatemala	0.7	0.7	0.8	0.9	0.7	0.7	0.4	0.3	0.4
Honduras[† § 20]	. .	. .	0.6	0.7	0.8	0.8	0.7	0.6	0.6
Mexico[† 21]	0.5	0.6	0.5	0.5	0.5	0.5	0.4	0.4	0.4
Nicaragua[22]	0.7	0.7	0.8	0.7	0.8	0.9	0.7	0.7	0.7
Panama[23]	1.0	1.0	. .	. .	. .	. .	. .	. .	. .
North America									
Canada	1.3	1.2	1.1	1.2	1.2	1.1	1.1	1.1	1.2
USA[24]	3.1	3.0	3.1	3.1	3.4	3.8	4.0	4.0	4.0
South America									
Argentina	1.3	1.4	1.3	1.4	1.2	1.2	1.1	1.0	0.9
Bolivia[25]	2.1	1.8	1.7	2.1	1.9	1.9	1.7	1.6	1.4
Brazil	[1.7]	[1.5]	1.6	1.8	1.9	1.5	1.4	1.4	1.5
Chile[§ 26]	3.4	3.7	3.7	3.7	3.8	3.4	3.8	3.7	3.6
Colombia[27]	[3.2]	[3.4]	[4.1]	[4.5]	3.7	3.9	3.9	4.0	4.0
Ecuador[‖ 28]	2.4	1.8	1.7	1.8	2.0	2.6	2.2	2.6	2.3
Guyana	. .	. .	. .	. .	. .	. .	. .	. .	. .
Paraguay[29]	1.3	1.2	1.1	1.0	1.0	0.8	0.9	0.8	0.8
Peru[30]	(1.6)	(1.6)	(1.7)	1.7	1.5	1.5	1.4	1.5	1.3

Uruguay	1.3	1.4	1.4	1.6	1.7	1.8	[1.5]	[1.8]	[1.6]
Venezuela³¹	1.2	1.3	1.2	1.2	1.3	1.5	1.2	1.2	1.4
Asia									
Central Asia									
Kazakhstan	1.0	1.0	1.0	1.1	1.1	1.0	0.8	0.8	1.1
Kyrgyzstan³²	3.2	3.1	2.8	2.9	2.7	2.3	2.9	2.6	2.7
Tajikistan	:	:	2.2	2.2	2.1	1.2	1.2	1.4	1.7
Turkmenistan³³	:	:	:	:	:	:	:	2.9	3.1
Uzbekistan³⁴	:	:	:	0.5	:	0.8	:	1.6	:
East Asia									
Brunei	[3.5]	(3.9)	(3.6)	5.1	5.3	5.2	5.7	6.1	7.5
Cambodia	1.1	1.1	1.3	1.5	1.6	1.8	2.2	2.5	2.7
China³⁵	[2.1]	[1.9]	[2.0]	[2.1]	[2.1]	[2.0]	[1.8]	[1.8]	[1.7]
Indonesia	[1.3]	[1.2]	1.4	1.3	1.0	1.0	1.0	0.9	1.1
Japan† § ³⁶	1.0	1.0	1.0	1.0	1.0	1.0	1.0	1.0	1.0
Korea, North	:	:	:	:	:	:	:	:	:
Korea, South† ¶ ³⁷	2.5	2.6	2.4	2.4	2.4	2.5	2.5	2.5	2.8
Laos	:	:	:	:	:	2.1	2.0	2.2	1.6
Malaysia	2.2	2.4	2.4	2.8	2.3	2.2	1.7	2.1	1.6
Mongolia	1.5	1.6	1.7	1.8	2.1	2.0	2.4	1.8	1.9
Myanmar³⁸	:	:	:	:	1.3	1.8	2.3	2.0	2.3
Philippines	0.9	0.9	0.9	1.0	1.0	1.0	1.1	1.1	1.2
Singapore	4.7	4.7	4.7	5.1	5.1	5.0	4.7	5.4	5.4
Taiwan	2.0	2.2	2.2	2.2	2.2	2.5	2.4	2.7	3.2
Thailand	[1.1]	[1.1]	[1.2]	1.3	1.4	1.5	1.4	1.6	1.9
Viet Nam	:	:	:	:	:	:	:	:	:
South Asia									
Afghanistan³⁹	1.5	1.5	1.9	:	:	:	:	:	:
Bangladesh	1.0	1.0	1.1	1.1	1.1	1.2	1.3	1.3	1.3
India⁴⁰	2.7	2.8	2.6	2.8	2.9	3.0	3.1	3.1	2.8

Country	1998	1999	2000	2001	2002	2003	2004	2005	2006
Nepal¶41	0.8	0.9	0.9	1.1	1.5	1.6	1.8	1.9	[1.7]
Pakistan‡	4.8	3.9	3.7	3.9	3.9	3.7	3.5	3.4	3.2
Sri Lanka†‡42	4.1	3.6	4.5	3.9	3.1	2.7	2.8	2.6	2.9
Oceania									
Australia	1.8	1.8	1.8	1.8	1.9	1.8	1.9	1.8	1.9
Fiji†43	1.5	1.3	1.9	1.6	1.6	1.3	1.1	1.3	1.4
New Zealand	1.3	1.3	1.3	1.2	1.1	1.1	1.1	1.1	1.1
Papua New Guinea	1.1	0.9	0.9	0.8	0.6	0.5	0.6	0.6	0.5
Tonga	1.5	1.4	1.4	1.4	1.2	1.2	1.0	1.1	1.4
Europe									
Albania¶44	1.2	1.2	1.2	1.3	1.3	1.3	1.4	1.3	1.6
Armenia†45	3.5	3.7	3.6	3.1	2.7	2.7	2.7	2.9	2.8
Austria	[1.0]	[1.0]	[1.0]	[0.9]	0.9	0.9	0.9	0.9	0.8
Azerbaijan‖	[2.4]	[2.6]	[2.3]	[2.3]	[2.2]	[2.4]	[2.6]	2.3	3.6
Belarus	[1.5]	[1.4]	[1.3]	1.4	1.4	1.3	1.4	1.5	1.7
Belgium	1.5	1.4	1.4	1.3	1.2	1.3	1.2	1.1	1.1
Bosnia and Herzegovina†¶46	..	..	..	..	4.3	2.8	2.3	1.8	1.7
Bulgaria†	2.3	2.5	2.5	2.7	2.7	2.6	2.4	2.4	2.3
Croatia	[6.6]	[5.2]	[3.6]	[3.2]	[3.2]	[2.4]	2.0	1.9	1.9
Cyprus†	3.4	2.0	2.0	2.3	1.6	1.5	1.4	1.4	1.4
Czech Republic47	1.9	2.0	2.0	1.9	2.0	2.1	1.9	2.0	1.7
Denmark	1.6	1.6	1.5	1.6	1.5	1.5	1.5	1.3	1.4
Estonia	1.1	1.3	1.4	1.5	1.7	1.7	1.7	1.6	1.6
Finland	1.5	1.3	1.3	1.2	1.2	1.4	1.4	1.4	1.4
France48	2.7	2.7	2.5	2.5	2.5	2.6	2.6	2.5	2.4
Georgia49	[1.1]	[0.9]	[0.6]	[0.7]	1.0	1.1	1.4	3.3	5.2
Germany	1.5	1.5	1.5	1.5	1.5	1.4	1.4	1.4	1.3
Greece	4.8	4.8	4.8	4.5	4.2	[3.4]	[3.6]	[3.8]	[3.8]

Hungary	1.5	1.7	1.7	1.8	1.6	1.7	1.5	1.4	1.2
Iceland	0.0	0.0	0.0	0.0	0.0	0.0	0.0	0.0	0.0
Ireland	[0.9]	[0.8]	[0.7]	0.7	0.7	0.6	0.6	0.6	0.5
Italy50	1.9	2.0	2.0	2.0	2.0	2.0	2.0	1.9	1.8
Latvia51	0.6	0.8	0.9	1.0	1.6	1.7	1.7	1.7	1.8
Lithuania¶52	[1.0]	[0.9]	[1.4]	[1.3]	1.4	1.4	1.4	1.2	1.2
Luxembourg	0.7	0.7	0.6	0.8	0.8	0.8	[0.8]	[0.8]	[0.8]
Macedonia, FYR53	2.2	1.8	1.9	6.6	2.8	2.5	2.5	2.2	2.0
Malta†	0.8	0.7	0.7	0.7	0.7	0.7	0.7	0.7	0.7
Moldova†¶54	0.6	0.5	0.4	0.4	0.4	0.4	0.4	0.4	0.5
Montenegro55	:	:	:	:	:	:	:	:	2.3
Netherlands	1.7	1.7	1.6	1.5	1.5	1.6	1.5	1.5	1.5
Norway	2.2	2.1	1.7	1.7	2.1	2.0	1.9	1.6	1.5
Poland	2.0	1.9	1.9	2.0	2.0	2.0	2.0	2.1	2.0
Portugal	2.2	2.0	2.0	2.0	2.0	2.0	[2.1]	[2.0]	[1.9]
Romania‖	[3.0]	2.7	2.5	2.5	2.3	2.1	2.0	2.0	1.8
Russia56	[3.3]	[3.4]	[3.7]	[4.1]	[4.3]	[4.3]	[3.8]	[3.7]	[3.6]
Serbia57	4.4	4.5	6.0	4.7	4.8	3.8	3.3	2.6	2.8
Slovakia†	1.8	1.6	1.7	1.9	1.8	1.9	1.7	1.7	1.7
Slovenia‖	1.4	1.3	1.2	1.4	1.5	1.5	1.5	1.5	1.6
Spain	1.3	1.2	1.2	1.2	1.2	1.1	1.1	1.0	1.2
Sweden58	2.1	2.0	2.0	1.9	1.8	1.7	1.6	1.5	1.5
Switzerland†¶59	1.2	1.1	1.1	1.1	1.0	1.0	1.0	1.0	0.8
Turkey¶‖	4.4	5.4	5.0	5.0	4.4	3.8	3.1	2.8	2.9
UK60	2.6	2.5	2.4	2.4	2.4	2.7	2.7	2.7	2.6
Ukraine§	3.4	3.0	3.6	2.9	2.8	2.8	2.6	2.8	2.8
Middle East									
Bahrain61	4.8	4.9	4.0	4.2	4.0	4.8	4.3	3.6	3.5
Egypt	3.3	3.2	3.2	3.3	3.4	3.3	3.0	2.9	2.7
Iran¶62	2.4	3.0	3.8	4.0	2.5	2.9	3.3	4.6	4.6
Iraq63	:	:	:	:	:	:	:	(3.8)	(7.8)

Country	1998	1999	2000	2001	2002	2003	2004	2005	2006
Israel[64]	8.6	8.5	8.0	8.4	9.5	8.8	7.9	7.9	8.0
Jordan	[6.3]	6.3	6.3	5.9	5.4	6.0	5.1	4.8	5.0
Kuwait	8.8	7.6	7.2	7.7	7.4	6.5	5.9	[4.7]	[4.0]
Lebanon	4.1	4.9	5.5	5.6	4.8	4.7	4.4	[4.5]	[4.6]
Oman‡	12.5	11.4	10.6	12.2	12.3	12.1	12.0	11.8	11.2
Qatar	..	..	..	..	..	..	..	..	..
Saudi Arabia§ 65	14.3	11.4	10.6	11.5	9.8	8.7	8.4	8.0	8.5
Syria	[5.1]	4.8	5.5	4.9	4.7	5.5	6.0	5.3	5.1
United Arab Emirates[66]	5.1	4.3	3.4	3.4	3.3	2.8	2.3	1.9	..
Yemen	6.2	5.2	5.0	[5.6]	7.2	7.1	5.5	5.1	4.3

( ) = uncertain figure; [ ] = SIPRI estimate; | = change of multiple of currency; † = all figures exclude military pensions; ‡ = all figures are for current spending only (i.e. exclude capital spending); § = all figures are for the adopted budget, rather than actual expenditure; ¶ = all figures exclude spending on paramilitary forces; ‖ = this country changed or redenominated its currency during the period; all figures have been converted to the latest currency.

[1] In July 2006 the Algerian Government issued supplementary budgets increasing total expenditure by 35%. It is not clear if any of these extra funds were allocated to the military.

[2] The rate of implementation of Angola's budget can vary considerably. The military expenditure for Angola should be seen in the context of highly uncertain economic statistics due to the impact of war on the Angolan economy.

[3] The Central African Republic's investment expenditure for 2005 amounted to an additional 775 000 CFA francs .

[4] The figures for the Democratic Republic of the Congo (DRC) in 2006 and 2007 are a forward estimate by the International Monetary Fund (IMF) and are probably underestimates due to the country's high rate of inflation.

[5] The figures for Côte d'Ivoire in 2003 are for budgeted spending rather than actual expenditure.

[6] The figures for Gabon exclude off-budget spending financed by the Provisions pour Investissements Hydrocarbures (PIH), an investment fund based on tax revenues from foreign oil companies active in Gabon.

[7] The figures for Ghana in 2001 are for the adopted budget rather than actual spending.

[8] The figures for Guinea might be an underestimate as the IMF reports large extra-budgetary spending for the military.

[9] An armed conflict broke out in Guinea-Bissau in 1998, which led to a substantial increase in military expenditure, especially in 2000. According to the IMF, the increase was financed by a credit from the banking system and by promissory notes. Due to the conflict, no data are available for 1999 and the consistency before and after this year is uncertain.

[10] The figures for Madagascar include expenditure for the gendarmerie and the National Police.

[11] The figures for Namibia for 1999 refer to the budget of the Ministry of Defence only. In addition to this the 1999 budget of the Ministry of Finance includes a contingency provision of N$104 million for the Namibian military presence in the Democratic Republic of the Congo (DRC). The figures for 2002 include a supplementary allocation of N$78.5 million.

[12] The figures for Nigeria before 1999 are understated because of the use by the military of a favourable dollar exchange rate.

[13] The figures for Rwanda for 1998 are from the official defence budget. According to the IMF there are additional sources for funding for military activities, both within the budget and extra-budgetary. The figures for 2005 and 2006 include allocations for African Union peacekeeping missions.

[14] In 1998 Senegal's additional expenditure on paramilitary forces was 21 100 million CFA francs.

[15] The figures for Sierra Leone in 1998 and 1999 are not available due to the coup d'etat and subsequent civil war.

[16] The figures for Sudan are for current spending on defence and security.

[17] The figures for Zambia are uncertain, especially those in constant dollars and shares of GDP, because of very rapid inflation and several changes of currency. Data are for adopted budget rather than actual expenditure for the period 2004 onwards.

[18] The figures for Zimbabwe should be used with caution because of extremely high inflation.

[19] Costa Rica has no armed forces. Expenditure for paramilitary forces, border guard, and maritime and air surveillance is less than 0.05% of GDP.

[20] The figures for Honduras do not include spending on arms imports. For the years 2005, 2006 and 2007 spending on military pensions was budgeted at an additional 58.9, 73.6 and 107.4 million lempiras, respectively.

[21] Mexico's spending on military pensions was roughly 3 billion pesos extra annually during the years 2004–2007.

[22] The figures for Nicaragua include military aid from the USA and Taiwan, which for the years 2002, 2003, 2004, 2005, 2006 and 2007 amounted to 12.5, 16.9, 13.6, 11.1, 7.3 and 28.8 million córdobas, respectively.

[23] The Panamanian Defence Forces were abolished in 1990 and replaced by a paramilitary force, consisting of the national police and air and maritime services.

[24] The figures for the USA are for financial year (1 Oct.–30 Sep.) rather than calendar year.

[25] The figures for Bolivia include some expenditure for civil defence.

[26] The figures for Chile include direct transfers from the state-owned copper company Corporación Nacional del Cobre (CODELCO) for military purchases. Since 2005 these transfers have increased rapidly due to rising copper prices.

[27] The figures for Colombia in 2002–2004 include a special allocation of 2.6 billion pesos from a war tax decree of 12 August 2002.

[28] Ecuador changed its currency from the sucre to the US dollar on 13 March 2000. The current price figures for each year represent the dollar value of military expenditure at the market exchange rate for that year.

[29] The figures for Paraguay in 2003 are for the modified budget, rather than actual expenditure.

[30] The figures for Peru before 2001 are based on data from the Peruvian Ministry of Defence and are suspected to come from different stages of the budget process. The figures for Peru in 2005 do not include the transfer of 20% of gas production revenues from the state-owned company CAMISEA to the armed forces and national police.

[31] The figures for Venezuela for 1998, 2006 and 2007are for the adopted budget rather than for actual expenditure.

[32] The figures for Kyrgyzstan include spending on internal security, accounting for a substantial part of total military spending.

[33] The coverage of the series for Turkmenistan varies over time due to classification changes in the Turkmen system of public accounts.

[34] The figures for Uzbekistan expressed in constant US dollars should be seen in the light of considerable difference between the official and the unofficial exchange rates.

[35] The figures for China are for estimated total military expenditure. On the estimates in local currency and as a share of GDP for the period 1989–98, see Wang, S., 'The military expenditure of China, 1989–98', *SIPRI Yearbook 1999: Armaments, Disarmament and International Security* (Oxford University Press: Oxford, 1999), pp. 334–49. The estimates for the years 1999–2002 are based on the percentage change in official military expenditure and on the assumption of a gradual decrease in the commercial earnings of the People's Liberation Army (PLA).

[36] The figures for Japan include spending on the activities of the Special Action Committee on Okinawa (SACO).

[37] The figures for South Korea do not include spending on arms imports.

[38] The figures for Myanmar (Burma) are not presented in US dollar terms owing to the extreme variation in stated exchange rate between the kyat and the US dollar.

[39] The figures for Afghanistan are for core budget expenditure on the Afghan National Army. If spending in the external budget, paid for directly by military aid, were included, then total military spending would be more than 6 times higher.

[40] The figures for India include expenditure on the paramilitary forces of the Border Security Force, the Central Reserve Police Force, the Assam Rifles and the Indo-Tibetan Border Police but do not include spending on military nuclear activities.

[41] In financial year 1998/99 Nepal's additional expenditure on paramilitary forces was 3315 million rupees.

[42] The figures for Sri Lanka for 2000 do not fully reflect a special allocation of 28 billion rupees for war-related expenditure.

[43] For the years 1998–2002 Fiji's spending on military pensions amounted to roughly an additional 3.5% of annual military spending.

[44] The figures for Albania from 2001 onwards are for budgeted rather than actual expenditure. The figures prior to 2006 do not fully include pensions.

[45] If the figures for Armenia were to include spending on military pensions they would be 15–20% higher.

[46] The figures for Bosnia and Herzegovina from 2005 onwards are for the Armed Forces of Bosnia and Herzegovina, which was formed in 2005 from the Croat–Bosniak Army of the Federation of Bosnia and Herzegovina and the Bosnian Serb Army of Republika Srpska. The figures prior to 2005 include expenditure for both the Army of the Federation of Bosnia and Herzegovina and the Army of Republika Srpska. The figures do not include expenditure on arms imports.

[47] The figures for the Czech Republic do not include military aid to Afghanistan or Iraq. Aid to Afghanistan was 18.7 million koruny in 2004 and 612.6 million koruny in 2005. Aid to Afghanistan was 1.1 million koruny in the first seven months of 2007. Aid to Iraq was 1.1 million koruny in 2005.

[48] The figures for France from 2006 are calculated with a new methodology due to a change in the French budgetary system and financial law.

[49] The figures for Georgia from 2002 are for the budgeted expenditure. The budget figures for 2003 are believed to be an underestimation of actual spending because of the political turmoil during the year.

[50] The figures for Italy include spending on civil defence, which typically accounts for about 4.5% of the total.

[51] The figures for Latvia do not include allocations for military pensions paid by Russia, which averaged 27 million lats annually over the years 1996–98.

[52] The figures for Lithuania exclude most expenditure on paramilitary forces.

[53] The definition of military expenditure for FYROM changed from 2006. Border troops were transferred from the Ministry of Defence to the Ministry of Interior Affairs and part of the military pensions, previously entirely excluded, are now included.

[54] Adding all military items in Moldova's budget, including expenditure on military pensions and paramilitary forces, would give total military expenditure for 2005, 2006 and 2007 of 343, 457 and 530 million lei, respectively.

[55] Montenegro declared its independence from the State Union of Serbia and Montenegro on 3 June 2006.

[56] For the sources and methods of the military expenditure figures for Russia see Cooper, J., 'The military expenditure of the USSR and the Russian Federation, 1987–97', *SIPRI Yearbook 1998: Armaments, Disarmament and International Security* (Oxford University Press: Oxford, 1998), pp. 243–59.

[57] Montenegro seceded from the State Union of Serbia and Montenegro on 3 June 2006. The figures for Serbia up to 2005 are for the State Union of Serbia and Montenegro (known as the Federal Republic of Yugoslavia until February 2003) and for 2006 onwards for Serbia alone.

[58] Sweden changed its accounting system in 2001, giving rise to a series break between 2000 and 2001. This break means that the decrease in military expenditure between 2000 and 2001 is overestimated by 1.4 percentage points.

[59] Because of a change in Switzerland's accounting systems, the decrease in spending between 2005 and 2006 might be overestimated.

[60] The series for the UK has a break between 2000 and 2001 because in 2001 the UK changed its accounting system for military expenditure from a 'cash basis' to a 'resource basis'. It is not clear what impact this change had on the trend in British military expenditure.

[61] The figures for Bahrain for the years 2002–2004 are for the adopted budget rather than the actual expenditure.

[62] The figures for Iran do not include spending on paramilitary forces such as the Islamic Revolutionary Guards Corps.

[63] The figures for Iraq are for security spending. The data should be seen in the light of the unstable security situation and high rate of inflation.

[64] The figures for Israel include military aid from the USA, which in 2007 was $2.34 billion.

[65] The figures for Saudi Arabia are for defence and security.

[66] The figures for the United Arab Emirates (UAE) exclude the military expenditure of its 7 constituent emirates. If their spending were included, the UAE's total military expenditure would be considerably higher.

Appendix 5B. NATO military expenditure by category

PETTER STÅLENHEIM and JAN GREBE

Table 5B.1. NATO military expenditure on personnel and equipment, 1998–2007

Figures are in US$ m. at 2005 prices and exchange rates. Figures in italics are percentage changes from previous year. Iceland, which has no military expenditure, is omitted.

Country	Item	1998	1999	2000	2001	2002	2003	2004	2005	2006	2007
North America											
Canada	Personnel	4 896	4 945	5 000	5 104	5 329	5 458	5 784	6 103	6 433	6 545
	Personnel change	*8.9*	*1.0*	*1.1*	*2.1*	*4.4*	*2.4*	*6.0*	*5.5*	*5.4*	*1.7*
	Equipment	1 247	960	1 413	1 320	1 642	1 651	1 732	1 563	1 629	2 668
	Equipment change	*8.6*	*–23.0*	*47.2*	*–6.5*	*24.4*	*0.6*	*4.9*	*–9.7*	*4.2*	*63.8*
USA	Personnel	128 080	125 401	129 085	124 894	139 629	159 029	165 465	175 384	171 754	157 770
	Personnel change	*–2.6*	*–2.1*	*2.9*	*–3.2*	*11.8*	*13.9*	*4.0*	*6.0*	*–2.1*	*–8.1*
	Equipment	84 035	82 072	74 988	88 547	106 232	108 017	118 266	123 491	128 304	136 630
	Equipment change	*–3.8*	*–2.3*	*–8.6*	*18.1*	*20.0*	*1.7*	*9.5*	*4.4*	*3.9*	*6.5*
Europe											
Belgium	Personnel	3 233	3 274	3 148	3 143	3 168	3 261	3 230	3 174	3 160	3 258
	Personnel change	*–1.3*	*1.3*	*–3.9*	*–0.1*	*0.8*	*2.9*	*–1.0*	*–1.7*	*–0.4*	*3.1*
	Equipment	278	313	277	327	314	239	241	269	248	290
	Equipment change	*–5.3*	*12.6*	*–11.4*	*17.9*	*–3.8*	*–24.0*	*1.1*	*11.3*	*–7.8*	*17.2*
Bulgaria	Personnel	..	..	..	..	..	..	349	335	326	344
	Personnel change	..	..	..	..	..	..		*–3.9*	*–2.7*	*5.6*
	Equipment	..	..	..	..	..	..	115	111	104	129
	Equipment change	..	..	..	..	..	..		*–3.6*	*–6.3*	*23.9*

Czech Rep.	Personnel	: :	885	928	965	961	1 108	1 043	1 050	1 038
	Personnel change	: :		4.9	4.0	-0.5	15.3	-5.8	0.6	-1.1
	Equipment	: :	464	410	370	447	334	206	323	313
	Equipment change	: :		-11.6	-9.7	20.7	-25.3	-38.4	57.3	-3.2
Denmark	Personnel	2 220	1 940	1 975	1 940	1 865	1 945	1 908	1 847	1 898
	Personnel change	3.2	-12.0	1.8	-1.8	-3.9	4.3	-2.0	-3.1	2.8
	Equipment	512	525	633	503	583	698	388	584	509
	Equipment change	1.9	25.3	20.6	-20.6	15.9	19.8	-44.5	50.6	-12.8
Estonia	Personnel	: :					62.5	59.6	58.2	74.2
	Personnel change	: :						-4.6	-2.3	27.5
	Equipment	: :					24.0	24.3	32.4	49.8
	Equipment change	: :						1.3	33.3	53.6
France	Personnel	30 515	30 315	30 287	30 999	31 001	31 016	30 704	30 053	29 946
	Personnel change	3.3	-1.1	-0.1	2.3	0.0	0.0	-1.0	-2.1	-0.4
	Equipment	9 745	9 466	9 700	9 761	10 795	11 322	11 284	12 340	12 000
	Equipment change	-14.4	-3.9	2.5	0.6	10.6	4.9	-0.3	9.4	-2.8
Germany	Personnel	25 061	24 959	24 408	24 127	24 065	23 006	22 168	21 200	20 935
	Personnel change	-2.2	-0.2	-2.2	-1.2	-0.3	-4.4	-3.6	-4.4	-1.2
	Equipment	5 200	5 559	5 677	5 706	5 505	5 743	5 395	5 571	5 659
	Equipment change	18.3	0.7	2.1	0.5	-3.5	4.3	-6.1	3.3	1.6
Greece	Personnel	4 758	5 502	5 506	4 493	4 211	4 781	5 005	5 186	5 469
	Personnel change	5.8	8.7	0.1	-18.4	-6.3	13.5	4.7	3.6	5.5
	Equipment	1 625	1 569	1 308	870	603	454	1 032	1 047	1 205
	Equipment change	15.8	-1.7	-16.6	-33.5	-30.6	-24.8	127.4	1.4	15.2
Hungary	Personnel	641	736	796	798	849	797	768	745	660
	Personnel change	: :	14.8	8.2	0.2	6.4	-6.2	-3.6	-3.0	-11.4
	Equipment	288	187	175	180	179	191	135	129	166
	Equipment change	: :	-35.2	-6.6	3.1	-0.4	6.6	-29.6	-4.3	28.9

Country	Item	1998	1999	2000	2001	2002	2003	2004	2005	2006	2007
Italy	Personnel	22 559	23 662	24 334	24 263	25 500	25 250	26241	25 849	26 568	26 332
	Personnel change	0.5	4.9	2.8	-0.3	5.1	-1.0	3.9	-1.5	2.8	-0.9
	Equipment	3 824	3 737	4 890	3 459	4 268	4 489	4 075	3 049	2 336	3606
	Equipment change	13.2	-2.3	30.8	-29.3	23.4	5.2	-9.2	-25.2	-23.4	54.4
Latvia	Personnel	:	:	:	:	:	:	78.5	101	115	118
	Personnel change	:	:	:	:	:	:	:	29.2	13.1	2.8
	Equipment	:	:	:	:	:	:	13.3	17.7	36.0	44.7
	Equipment change	:	:	:	:	:	:	:	32.9	103	24.3
Lithuania	Personnel	:	:	:	:	:	:	163	177	185	204
	Personnel change	:	:	:	:	:	:	:	8.7	4.2	10.3
	Equipment	:	:	:	:	:	:	39.2	46.5	57.4	71.5
	Equipment change	:	:	:	:	:	:	:	18.8	23.3	24.6
Luxembourg	Personnel	144	145	147	166	173	180	187	184	188	191
	Personnel change	5.1	0.2	1.9	12.9	3.9	4.3	3.9	-1.8	2.3	1.6
	Equipment	12.1	9.6	9.0	29.4	14.7	16.8	19.7	27.9	21.3	83.5
	Equipment change	101	-21.4	-5.7	227	-50.1	14.7	16.8	41.9	-23.5	291
Netherlands	Personnel	4 764	4 759	4 635	4 491	4 788	4 990	4 823	4 830	4 787	4 720
	Personnel change	-6.9	-0.1	-2.6	-3.1	6.6	4.2	-3.3	0.1	-0.9	-1.4
	Equipment	1 399	1 614	1 554	1 559	1 484	1 416	1 595	1 528	1 638	1 852
	Equipment change	-2.9	15.4	-3.7	0.4	-4.9	-4.5	12.6	-4.2	10.1	10.1
Norway	Personnel	1 689	1 755	1 776	1 712	1 996	2 038	2 144	2 092	2 190	2 085
	Personnel change	4.5	3.9	1.2	-3.6	16.6	2.1	5.2	-2.4	4.7	-4.8
	Equipment	1 120	1 017	846	928	1 248	1 105	1 188	1 029	936	1 185
	Equipment change	8.3	-9.1	-16.8	9.7	34.5	-11.5	7.5	-13.4	-9.0	26.6
Poland	Personnel	:	3 064	2 959	3 121	3 119	3 258	3 233	3 173	3 128	3 442
	Personnel change	:	:	-3.4	5.5	-0.1	4.5	-0.8	-1.9	-1.4	10.0
	Equipment	:	546	416	428	534	624	776	808	1 058	1 585
	Equipment change	:	:	-23.7	3.0	24.7	16.9	24.4	4.0	31.0	49.8

Portugal	Personnel	2 657	2 809	2 846	2 924	2 356	2 144	2 165	2 381	2 319	2 137
	Personnel change	*1.3*	*5.7*	*1.3*	*2.7*	*-19.4*	*-9.0*	*1.0*	*9.9*	*-2.6*	*-7.8*
	Equipment	123	141	223	192	115	202	222	280	271	342
	Equipment change	*-54.6*	*15.2*	*57.9*	*-13.8*	*-40.0*	*74.9*	*10.0*	*25.9*	*-3.1*	*26.2*
Romania	Personnel	:	:	:	:	:	:	944	1 126	1 218	1 483
	Personnel change	:	:	:	:	:	:	:	*19.2*	*8.2*	*21.8*
	Equipment	:	:	:	:	:	:	477	394	489	456
	Equipment change	:	:	:	:	:	:	:	*-17.4*	*23.9*	*-6.7*
Slovakia	Personnel	:	:	:	:	:	:	384	384	410	452
	Personnel change	:	:	:	:	:	:	*0.0*	*0.0*	*6.8*	*10.3*
	Equipment	:	:	:	:	:	:		122	106	161
	Equipment change	:	:	:	:	:	:	*79.0*	*53.8*	*-12.7*	*51.7*
Slovenia	Personnel	:	:	:	:	:	:	311	329	366	367
	Personnel change	:	:	:	:	:	:	:	*5.9*	*11.2*	*0.3*
	Equipment	:	:	:	:	:	:		48.6	74.3	43.5
	Equipment change	:	:	:	:	:	:	*93.4*	*-48.0*	*52.8*	*-41.4*
Spain	Personnel	7 028	7 050	7 079	7 112	7 168	7 062	7 064	7 124	7 395	7 858
	Personnel change	*0.3*	*0.3*	*0.4*	*0.5*	*0.8*	*-1.5*	*0.0*	*0.8*	*3.8*	*6.3*
	Equipment	1 248	1 232	1 433	1 419	3 035	2 815	2 993	2 879	3 000	3 305
	Equipment change	*-13.4*	*-1.3*	*16.3*	*-1.0*	*114*	*-7.3*	*6.3*	*-3.8*	*4.2*	*10.2*
Turkey	Personnel	7 203	7 718	7 161	6 504	6 305	5 605	5 452	5 374	5 384	5 434
	Personnel change	*4.8*	*7.2*	*-7.2*	*-9.2*	*-3.1*	*-11.1*	*-2.7*	*-1.4*	*0.2*	*0.9*
	Equipment	3 069	4 187	4 495	4 798	4 333	4 700	3 605	3 074	3 828	3 785
	Equipment change	*-19.9*	*36.4*	*7.4*	*6.8*	*-9.7*	*8.5*	*-23.3*	*-14.7*	*24.5*	*-1.1*
UK	Personnel	18 301	18 048	18 436	19 408	19 866	20 127	19 931	23 249	23 034	22 111
	Personnel change	*-2.9*	*-1.4*	*2.1*	*5.3*	*2.4*	*1.3*	*-1.0*	*16.6*	*-0.9*	*-4.0*
	Equipment	12 741	12 776	12 416	11 871	11 797	11 505	11 439	12 910	12 087	12 988
	Equipment change	*6.7*	*0.3*	*-2.8*	*-4.4*	*-0.6*	*-2.5*	*-0.6*	*12.9*	*-6.4*	*7.4*

Country	Item	1998	1999	2000	2001	2002	2003	2004	2005	2006	2007
NATO Europe (23 countries)											
	Personnel	130 132	135 834	136 857	136 764	137 762	136 867	139 415	141 537	140 911	140 558
	Personnel change	0.3	4.4	0.8	-0.1	0.7	-0.6	1.9	1.5	-0.4	-0.3
	Equipment	40 895	43 247	44 328	42 914	44 535	45 226	45 737	45 055	46 360	49 830
	Equipment change	-1.1	5.8	2.5	-3.2	3.8	1.6	1.1	-1.5	2.9	7.5
NATO Europe (pre-2004 members; 16 countries)											
	Personnel	130 132	135 834	136 857	136 746	137 762	136 867	137 123	139 024	138 234	137 515
	Personnel change	0.3	4.4	0.8	-0.1	0.7	-0.6	0.2	1.4	-0.6	-0.5
	Equipment	40 895	43 247	44 328	42 914	44 535	45 226	44 896	44 291	45 461	48 874
	Equipment change	-1.1	5.8	2.5	-3.2	3.8	1.6	-0.7	-1.3	2.6	7.5
NATO Europe (pre-1999 members; 13 countries)											
	Personnel	130 132	132 129	132 227	131 900	132 879	131 799	131 985	134 040	133 311	132 375
	Personnel change	0.3	1.5	0.1	-0.3	0.7	-0.8	0.1	1.6	-0.5	-0.7
	Equipment	40 895	42 413	43 261	41 901	43 450	43 975	43 594	43 144	43 951	46 810
	Equipment change	-1.1	3.7	2.0	-3.1	3.7	1.2	-0.9	-1.0	1.9	6.5
NATO total (25 countries)											
	Personnel	263 107	266 181	270 942	266 743	282 719	301 354	310 664	323 023	319 098	304 872
	Personnel change	-1.0	1.2	1.8	-1.5	6.0	6.6	3.1	4.0	-1.2	-4.5
	Equipment	126 177	126 279	120 729	132 781	152 409	154 894	165 735	170 109	176 293	189 128
	Equipment change	-3.0	0.1	-4.4	10.0	14.8	1.6	7.0	2.6	3.6	7.3
NATO total (pre-2004 members; 18 countries)											
	Personnel	263 107	266 181	270 942	266 743	282 719	301 354	308 372	320 511	316 421	301 829
	Personnel change	-1.0	1.2	1.8	-1.5	6.0	6.6	2.3	3.9	-1.3	-4.6
	Equipment	126 177	126 279	120 729	132 781	152 409	154 894	164 893	169 345	175 394	188 173
	Equipment change	-3.0	0.1	-4.4	10.0	14.8	1.6	6.5	2.7	3.6	7.3

NATO total (pre-1999 members; 15 countries)

Personnel	263 107	262 475	266 362	261 898	277 837	296 285	303 234	315 526	311 498	296 689
Personnel change	–1.0	–0.2	1.5	–1.7	6.1	6.6	2.3	4.1	–1.3	–4.8
Equipment	126 177	125 445	119 662	131 768	151 324	153 643	163 592	168 198	173 884	186 108
Equipment change	–3.0	–0.6	–4.6	10.1	14.8	1.5	6.5	2.8	3.4	7.0

Notes: The figures in this table are based on NATO statistics on the distribution of total military expenditure by category. The figures here are calculated by applying the shares for personnel and equipment to the figures for total military expenditure converted to constant 2005 US dollars using consumer price indices and market exchange rates from the IMF International Financial Statistics database, <http://www.imfstatistics.org/imf/>.

Data are included in the totals for NATO and NATO Europe from the year of accession (1999 for Hungary, Poland and Romania; 2004 for Bulgaria, Estonia, Latvia, Lithuania, Slovakia and Slovenia). Additional series are provided for total spending of the states that have been members throughout the period 1998–2007 (15 in NATO and 13 in NATO Europe; Belgium, Canada, Denmark, France, Germany, Greece, Italy, Luxembourg, Netherlands, Norway, Portugal, Spain, Turkey, UK, USA) and for those that have been members throughout the period 1999–2007 (18 in NATO and 16 in NATO Europe) in order to show the trend for a consistent group of countries.

In 2004 NATO member states agreed on a change in the definition of military expenditure. For all countries except France, Italy, Luxembourg and the Netherlands, figures from 2002 are reported according to the new definition (i.e. excluding 'Other Forces' that are not 'realistically deployable'). Data reported by France, Italy, Luxembourg and the Netherlands do not entirely conform with the new definition. For Greece, Hungary, Portugal and Turkey the change in definitions has made a big difference. All data are reported according the old definition up to and including 2002 and for personnel up to 2003, creating two breaks in all series except for the countries that have not changed definitions—one between 2001 and 2002 and one between 2002 and 2003.

Sources: NATO, 'Financial and economic data relating to NATO defence: defence expenditures of NATO countries (1980–2002)', Press Release M-DPC-2(2002)139, 20 Dec. 2002; NATO, 'Financial and economic data relating to NATO defence: defence expenditures of NATO countries (1980–2003)', Press Release (2003)146, 1 Dec. 2003; NATO, 'NATO–Russia compendium of financial and economic data relating to defence', Information for the press, 9 June 2005; NATO, 'NATO–Russia compendium of financial and economic data relating to defence: defence expenditures of NRC countries (1985–2005)', Press Release (2005)161, 9 Dec. 2005; NATO, 'NATO–Russia compendium of financial and economic data relating to defence: defence expenditures of NRC countries (1985–2006)', Press Release (2006)159, 18 Dec. 2006; and NATO, 'NATO–Russia compendium of financial and economic data relating to defence', Information for the press, 18 Dec. 2007—all available from <http://www.nato.int/issues/defence_expenditures/>.

Appendix 5C. Sources and methods for military expenditure data

ELISABETH SKÖNS and PETTER STÅLENHEIM

I. Introduction

This appendix describes the sources and methods for the SIPRI military expenditure data provided in chapter 5 and appendices 5A and 5B, and on the SIPRI Military Expenditure Project website, <http://www.sipri.org/contents/milap/>.

The data in this edition of the SIPRI Yearbook should not be linked to the military expenditure data published in previous editions because the data series are continuously revised and updated. This is true in particular for the most recent years as figures for budget allocations are replaced by figures for actual expenditure. In some cases entire series are revised as new and better data become available. The SIPRI Military Expenditure Database includes consistent series dating back to 1988 for most countries.[1] Data for the years 1950–87—published in previous editions of the SIPRI Yearbook—cannot always be combined with the post-1987 data since SIPRI conducted a major review of the data for many countries for the period beginning in 1988. Changes in base years and method of currency conversion also hinder comparison between editions of the SIPRI Yearbook. In this edition, the base year for the constant dollar series (table 5A.3) is 2005. Conversion to constant US dollars has been made using market exchange rates (MERs) for all countries.

II. The purpose of the data

The main purpose of the data on military expenditure is to provide an easily identifiable measure of the scale of resources absorbed by the military. Military expenditure is an input measure, which is not directly related to the 'output' of military activities, such as military capability or military security. Long-term trends in military expenditure and sudden changes in trend may be signs of a change in military output, but interpretations of this type should be made with caution.

The purpose of the specific tables are as follows. Data in constant dollars for world military expenditure and military expenditure by region, organization and income group are provided (in table 5A.1) to enable assessments of trends in these aggregates. Country data on military expenditure in local currency at current prices (in table 5A.2) are the original data for all the other tables. These are provided to contribute to transparency and to enable comparison with data reported in government sources and elsewhere. Country data in constant dollars are provided (in table 5A.3) to allow for comparison over time for individual countries. In addition, data in current dollars for 2007 are provided for regions (in table 5A.1) and for countries (in table 5A.3). The current dollar figures give a better basis for international comparisons than the constant dollar data—although international comparisons of expend-

---

[1] The SIPRI Military Expenditure Database can be accessed at <http://www.sipri.org/contents/milap/milex/mex_database1.html>.

iture are conceptually problematic (see section IV below). The current dollar figures also facilitate comparison with other economic indicators, which are often expressed in current dollar terms. Data on military expenditure as a share of gross domestic product (GDP) are provided (in table 5A.4) as an indicator of the proportion of a country's resources used for military activities, that is, as an indicator of the economic burden of military expenditure, also called the defence burden or the military burden.

III. The coverage of the data

The military expenditure tables in appendix 5A cover 168 countries for the 10-year period 1998–2007. Total military expenditure figures are calculated for three types of country groupings—geographical region, international organization and country income group (categorized by gross national income per capita). The coverage of each of these groupings is provided in the notes to table 5A.1.

The definition of military expenditure

The guideline definition of military expenditure used by SIPRI includes expenditure on the following actors and activities: (*a*) the armed forces, including peacekeeping forces; (*b*) defence ministries and other government agencies engaged in defence projects; (*c*) paramilitary forces, when judged to be trained and equipped for military operations; and (*d*) military space activities. It includes all current and capital expenditure on: (*a*) military and civil personnel, including retirement pensions of military personnel and social services for personnel; (*b*) operations and maintenance; (*c*) procurement; (*d*) military research and development; and (*e*) military aid (in the military expenditure of the donor country). It does not include civil defence and current expenditure for past military activities, such as for veterans' benefits, demobilization, conversion and weapon destruction.

IV. The limitations of the data

A number of limitations are associated with the data on military expenditure. They are of three main types: reliability, validity and comparability.

The main problems of reliability are due to the less than comprehensive coverage of official military expenditure data, the lack of detailed information on military expenditure and the lack of data on actual, rather than budgeted, military expenditure. In many countries the official data cover only a part of total military expenditure. Important items can be hidden under non-military budget headings or can even be financed entirely outside the government budget. Many such off-budget mechanisms are employed in practice.[2] For a more comprehensive overview of the conceptual problems and sources of uncertainty involved in all sets of military expenditure data, the reader is referred to other sources.[3]

[2] For an overview of such mechanisms see Hendrickson, D. and Ball, N., 'Off-budget military expenditure and revenue: issues and policy perspectives for donors', Conflict, Security and Development Group (CSDG) Occasional Papers no. 1, CSDG, King's College London, Jan. 2002.

[3] Such overviews include Brzoska, M., 'World military expenditures', eds K. Hartley and T. Sandler, *Handbook of Defense Economics*, vol. 1 (Elsevier: Amsterdam, 1995); and Ball, N., 'Measuring third world security expenditure: a research note', *World Development*, vol. 12, no. 2 (Feb. 1984), pp. 157–64.

The validity of expenditure data depends on the purpose for which they are used. Since expenditure data are a measure of monetary input, their most valid use is as an indicator of the economic resources consumed for military purposes. For the same reason, their utility as an indicator of military strength or capability is limited. While military expenditure does have an impact on military capability, so do many other factors such as the balance between personnel and equipment, the technological level of military equipment, and the state of maintenance and repair, as well as the overall security environment in which the armed forces are to be employed.

The comparability of the data is limited by two different types of factor: the varying coverage (or definition) of the data and the method of currency conversion. The coverage of official data on military expenditure varies significantly between countries and over time for the same country. For the conversion into a common currency, as discussed below, the choice of exchange rate makes a great difference in cross-country comparisons. This is a general problem in international comparisons of economic data and is not specific to military expenditure. However, since international comparison of military expenditure is often a sensitive issue, it is important to bear in mind that the interpretation of cross-country comparisons of military expenditure is greatly influenced by the choice of exchange rate.

V. Methods

SIPRI data are based on open sources and reflect the official data reported by governments. In practice, it is impossible to apply the SIPRI definition of military expenditure to all countries, since this would require detailed information about what is included in military budgets and about off-budget military expenditure items, and an extensive process of recalculation. In many cases SIPRI is confined to using the official data provided by governments, regardless of definition. In these cases, SIPRI chooses the data series that corresponds most closely to the SIPRI definition of military expenditure. Priority is given to choosing a uniform time series for each country, in order to achieve consistency over time, rather than to adjusting the figures for individual years according to a common definition.

Estimation

Estimates of military expenditure are predominantly made either when the coverage of official data diverges significantly from the SIPRI definition or when no consistent time series is available. In the first case, estimates are made on the basis of an analysis of primarily official government budget and expenditure accounts. The most comprehensive estimates of this type—those for China and Russia—have been presented in detail in previous editions of the Yearbook.[4] In the second case, when only incomplete times series are available, the figures from the data series which corres-

For African countries see Omitoogun, W., *Military Expenditure Data in Africa: A Survey of Cameroon, Ethiopia, Ghana, Kenya, Nigeria and Uganda*, SIPRI Research Report no. 17 (Oxford University Press: Oxford, 2003).

[4] Cooper, J., 'The military expenditure of the USSR and the Russian Federation, 1987–97', *SIPRI Yearbook 1998: Armaments, Disarmament and International Security* (Oxford University Press: Oxford, 1998), pp. 243–59; and Wang, S., 'The military expenditure of China, 1989–98', *SIPRI Yearbook 1999: Armaments, Disarmament and International Security* (Oxford University Press: Oxford, 1999), pp. 334–49.

ponds most closely to the SIPRI definition are used for the years covered by that series. Figures for the missing years are then estimated by applying the percentage change between years in an alternative series to the data in the first series. These difficulties mean that the military expenditure data cannot be accurately compared between countries. They are more appropriately used for comparisons over time.

All estimates are based on official government data or other empirical evidence from open sources. This avoids the introduction of assumptions or extrapolations into the military expenditure statistics. Thus, no estimates are made for countries that do not release any official data, and no figures are displayed for these countries. SIPRI estimates are presented in square brackets in the tables. Round brackets are used when data are uncertain for other reasons, for example, when the data are based on a source of uncertain reliability and in cases when data expressed in constant dollars or as shares of GDP are uncertain due to a lack of reliable economic data.

Data for the most recent years include two types of estimate, which apply to all countries. First, figures for the most recent years are for adopted budget, budget estimates or revised estimates, the majority of which are revised in subsequent years. Second, in table 5A.3 the deflator used for the final year in the series is an estimate based on part of a year or as provided by the International Monetary Fund (IMF). Unless exceptional uncertainty is involved, these estimates are not bracketed.

The totals for the world, regions, organizations and income groups in table 5A.1 are estimates because data are not available for all countries in all years. These estimates are most often made on the assumption that the rate of change for an individual country for which data are missing is the same as the average for the region to which it belongs. When no estimate can be made, countries are excluded from all totals.

Calculations

With one exception, the SIPRI military expenditure figures are presented on a calendar-year basis on the assumption of an even rate of expenditure throughout the financial year. The exception is for the United States, for which SIPRI follows the reporting format of the source—a financial-year basis.

The original data are provided in local currency at current prices (table 5A.2). The only calculation made on these data is to convert to calendar year figures the figures for those countries that have a financial year that differs from the calendar year. These data are converted to US dollars at constant prices and exchange rates with 2005 as the base year (table 5A.3). Country data on military expenditure as a share of GDP (table 5A.4) are calculated in domestic currency at current prices and for calendar years.

The choice of base year for data expressed in constant dollars has an impact on cross-country expenditure comparisons because variations in prices and currencies differ between countries. For conversion from current to constant prices, SIPRI uses the national consumer prices indexes as the deflator. This means that the trend in the SIPRI military expenditure data in constant dollars reflects the real change in their equivalent purchasing power for civilian consumption.[5] Conversion to dollars is then made by use of the annual average market exchange rate of each country.

---

[5] A military-specific deflator is a more appropriate choice for the purpose of measuring purchasing power in terms of the amount of military personnel, goods and services that could be bought for the monetary allocations for military purposes. However, military-specific deflators are not available for most countries.

Purchasing power parity versus market exchange rates

An alternative to using market exchange rates for currency conversion is to use purchasing power parity (PPP) conversion factors (also called PPP exchange rates). The PPP dollar rate of a country's currency is defined by the World Bank as 'the number of units of a country's currency required to buy the same amount of goods and services in the domestic market as a U.S. dollar would buy in the United States'.[6]

The only PPP rates available for all countries are those estimated by the International Comparison Program (ICP), coordinated by the World Bank.[7] These PPP rates are designed to make it possible to determine and make international comparisons between the real value of a country's economic output (GDP) and the standard of living of its residents. Since MERs are determined by the supply and demand of currencies used in international transactions, they do not necessarily reflect differences in price levels between countries. However, the prices of many goods and services on domestic markets are determined in partial or complete isolation from the rest of the world. PPP rates are developed to control for such differences in price levels in order to provide a measure of the real purchasing power of the GDP of each country.

Using PPP rates instead of MERs results in much higher output and expenditure figures for many countries.[8] The difference is greatest for developing countries since they have relatively low prices for non-traded goods and services. This means that a unit of local currency has greater purchasing power within a developing country (which is better reflected by using PPP rates) than it has internationally (which is what is reflected by using MERs).[9]

PPP rates are statistical estimates, calculated on the basis of collected price data for a basket of goods and services for benchmark years. Between benchmark years, the PPP rates are extrapolated forward using ratios of prices indexes, either GDP deflators or consumer price indexes. Like all statistics, they are point estimates that fall within some margin of error of the unknown, true values. In February 2008 the ICP released the final results of a new round of PPP estimation for the benchmark year 2005.[10] These results date back to at least 1993 for most emerging markets and developing countries. The new PPP rates for 2005 are based on price surveys for more than 1000 goods and services conducted during 2005 and 2006. They include ICP estimates of PPP rates for 100 developing countries and PPP estimates for another 46 countries provided by the joint Eurostat–Organisation for Economic Co-operation and Development PPP programme.

The 2005 round of PPP estimates includes about 40 more countries than the previous, 1993 round. New methods have also been developed to overcome shortcomings in previous price data collection and estimation processes. The 2005 ICP round has resulted in a significant revision of the PPP for developing countries. The 2005 data

---

[6] World Bank, *World Development Indicators 2007* (World Bank: Washington, DC, 2007), p. 245.

[7] On the International Comparison Program see its website at <http://go.worldbank.org/X3R0INNH80>.

[8] See table 5.2 in chapter 5.

[9] On the issues involved in international comparison and currency conversion and the use of PPP rates see Ward, M., 'International comparisons of military expenditures: issues and challenges of using purchasing power parities', *SIPRI Yearbook 2006: Armaments, Disarmament and International Security* (Oxford University Press: Oxford, 2006), pp. 369–86.

[10] International Comparison Program (ICP), *2005 International Comparison Program: Tables of Final Results* (World Bank: Washington, DC, Feb. 2008), <http://www.worldbank.org/data/icp/>.

involved a reduction in the PPP rates of developing countries (and thus a downward revision of their GDPs expressed in PPP dollars) and an upward revision in other countries, including those for all oil-exporting countries. The revision has been particularly large for some key emerging market countries, especially China, which participated in the 2005 ICP survey for the first time. The new PPP rate for China is around 40 per cent lower than the previous estimates, which were extrapolated from a bilateral comparison of 1986 prices between China and the USA, which proved to be an inaccurate guide.[11] As a result of these improvements, the new PPP data cannot be combined with the ICP's previous PPP rate estimates.[12]

For the conversion of military expenditure data into US dollars, the relevance of GDP-based PPP rates is limited. The PPP rates produced by the ICP are estimates based on statistical surveys of price data for a basket of goods and services that are major components of the gross domestic product, including both traded and non-traded items. The intention is that the PPP rates should reflect the prices of goods and services that are representative of consumption patterns in each country. This means that purchasing power is determined primarily for civilian goods and services. The interpretation of military expenditure data converted using GDP-based PPP rates therefore reflects the amount of civilian goods and services that could be bought for the amount of money devoted to the military sector. The extent to which these data reflect the amount of military goods and services that the military budget can buy is not known.

The ICP notes that PPP rates should not be used for all international comparisons and that MERs should be used to measure such things as international trade, capital flows and the value of foreign debt.[13] Military expenditure is used to purchase a number of goods and services which are not typical of national consumption patterns. For example, the price of conscripts can be assumed to be lower than the price of a typical basket of goods and services, while the prices of advanced weapon systems and of their maintenance and repair services can be assumed to be much higher. Due to these uncertainties, and despite the limitations of MERs, SIPRI uses market exchange rates to convert military expenditure data into US dollars.

VI. Sources

The sources for military expenditure data are, in order of priority: (a) primary sources, that is, official data provided by national governments, either in their official publications or in response to questionnaires; (b) secondary sources which quote primary data; and (c) other secondary sources.

The first category consists of national budget documents, defence White Papers and public finance statistics as well as responses to a SIPRI questionnaire which is sent out annually to the finance and defence ministries, central banks, and national statistical offices of the countries in the SIPRI Military Expenditure Database (see appendix 5D). It also includes government responses to questionnaires about military

---

[11] Elekdag, S. and Lall, S., 'Global growth estimates trimmed after PPP revisions', *IMF Survey Magazine*, 8 Jan. 2008.

[12] International Comparison Program (ICP), *2005 International Comparison Program: Preliminary Results* (World Bank: Washington, DC, Dec. 2007), pp. 11–13.

[13] International Comparison Program (note 12), p. 10.

expenditure sent out by the United Nations and, if made available by the countries themselves, the Organization for Security and Co-operation in Europe.

The second category includes international statistics, such as those of the North Atlantic Treaty Organization (NATO) and the IMF. Data for the 16 pre-1999 NATO member states have traditionally been taken from military expenditure statistics published in a number of NATO sources. The introduction by NATO of a new definition of military expenditure in 2005 has made it necessary to rely on other sources for some NATO countries for the most recent years. Data for many developing countries are taken from the IMF's *Government Finance Statistics Yearbook*, which provides a defence heading for most IMF member countries, and from country reports by IMF staff. This category also includes publications of other organizations that provide proper references to the primary sources used, such as the Country Reports of the Economist Intelligence Unit.

The third category of sources consists of specialist journals and newspapers.

The main sources for economic data are the publications of the IMF: *International Financial Statistics*, *World Economic Outlook* and country reports by IMF staff. The source for PPP rates in this volume is the preliminary results of the 2005 International Comparison Program.[14]

---

[14] International Comparison Program (note 12).

Appendix 5D. The reporting of military expenditure data

CATALINA PERDOMO and ÅSA BLOMSTRÖM

I. Introduction

An important source of official data on military expenditure is the annual government reporting within the framework of the United Nations Standardized Instrument for Reporting Military Expenditures. Governments also report such data to SIPRI in response to SIPRI's annual requests. This appendix provides information on the reporting of military expenditure data to the UN and SIPRI. The systems of reporting are described in section II. The levels of reporting in 2007 are given in section III and the trends in reporting for the period 2001–2007 in section IV.

II. The reporting systems

The United Nations reporting system

Each year the UN Secretary-General invites all member states (currently 192) through a *note verbale* to report their military expenditure for the most recent financial year. The basis for this request is a UN General Assembly resolution adopted in 1980.[1] Successive biennial General Assembly resolutions have called for the continued reporting of military expenditure by member states.[2]

The justification for this request has changed over the years. The initial purpose was to use the reporting system as a step on the road to gradual reductions in military budgets.[3] The justification stated in the latest resolution is that 'a better flow of objective information on military matters can help to relieve international tension and is therefore an important contribution to conflict prevention' and that transparency in military issues is an essential element for building trust among countries.[4]

Countries are requested to report (preferably and to the extent possible) using the reporting instrument developed for this purpose—the UN Standardized Instrument for Reporting Military Expenditures—or in any other format for reporting military expenditure developed by other international or regional organizations. The instrument is in the form of a matrix with fields for the reporting of disaggregated data by function (aggregate personnel, operations and maintenance, procurement, construction, and research and development) and by military service (e.g. air force, army and navy) and to give aggregated totals. In the belief that some countries found this

---

[1] UN General Assembly Resolution A/RES/35/142 B, 12 Dec. 1980. The texts of UN General Assembly resolutions are available at <http://www.un.org/documents/resga.htm>.

[2] The most recent such resolution is UN General Assembly Resolution A/RES/62/13, 5 Dec. 2007.

[3] See Omitoogun, W. and Sköns, E., 'Military expenditure data: a 40-year overview', *SIPRI Yearbook 2006: Armaments, Disarmament and International Security* (Oxford University Press: Oxford: 2006), pp. 276–77, 286, 291.

[4] UN General Assembly Resolution A/RES/62/13 (note 2).

Table 5D.1. Reporting of military expenditure data to SIPRI and the United Nations, by region, 2007

Figures are numbers of countries. Nil reports to the UN are not included.[a]

Region/subregion[b]	Reporting to the UN			Reporting to SIPRI			Total SIPRI and UN reports[c]
	Requests	Countries reporting data	Total	Requests	Countries reporting data	Total	
Africa	50	Burkina Faso, Namibia[e]	2	49[d]	Burkina Faso, Mauritius, Seychelles, South Africa, Uganda[f], Zimbabwe	6	7
Americas							
North America	2	Canada, USA	2	2	Canada[f], USA	2	2
Central America	7	El Salvador[e], Guatemala[g], Mexico[g], Nicaragua	4	7	Guatemala, Honduras, Mexico	3	5
South America	11	Argentina, Bolivia[e], Brazil, Ecuador, Paraguay	5	11	Bolivia, Brazil[f]	2	5
Caribbean	8	Jamaica[g]	1	8	–	0	1
Asia and Oceania							
Central Asia	5	Kazakhstan	1	5	–	0	1
East Asia	17	Cambodia[e], China[e], Japan[g], Malaysia[e], Mongolia[e], South Korea[e]	6	16	China[f], Indonesia, Japan, South Korea, Thailand	5	8
South Asia	6	Bangladesh[e], Nepal[g]	2	6	Sri Lanka	1	3
Oceania	4	Australia, New Zealand	2	4[h]	Australia	1	2
Europe							
Western Europe	21	Belgium, Cyprus[e], Denmark, Finland, France[e], Germany, Greece, Ireland, Italy, Luxembourg, Malta, Netherlands, Norway, Portugal, Spain, Sweden, Switzerland, Turkey, UK	19	21	Austria, Denmark, Finland, France, Greece, Ireland[f], Italy, Malta, Netherlands, Norway, Portugal, Sweden, Switzerland, Turkey	14	20

Region							
Central Europe	16	Albania, Bosnia and Herzegovina[e], Bulgaria, Croatia, Czech Republic, Estonia, Hungary[e], Latvia, Lithuania, FYROM[g], Poland, Romania, Slovakia	13	16	Albania, Bosnia and Herzegovina, Bulgaria, Croatia, Czech Republic, Hungary, Latvia, Lithuania, FYROM, Poland, Romania, Serbia, Slovakia, Slovenia	14	15
Eastern Europe	7	Armenia[e], Belarus, Georgia[g], Moldova[e], Russia, Ukraine	6	7	Armenia, Belarus, Georgia, Moldova, Ukraine	5	6
Middle East	14	Israel[e], Jordan, Lebanon[e]	3	14	Jordan[f], Lebanon	2	3
Total	168[i]		66	166		55	78

FYROM = Former Yugoslav Republic of Macedonia.

[a] Twelve UN member states submitted nil reports to the UN: Andorra, Grenada, Iceland, Liechtenstein, Marshall Islands, Monaco, Nauru, Panama, Saint Lucia, Saint Vincent and the Grenadines, Samoa, and Solomon Islands. In addition, 1 non-UN member submitted a nil report: Cook Islands.

[b] In order to make the SIPRI and UN reporting systems comparable, countries are grouped according to the geographical regions in the SIPRI Military Expenditure Database. See appendix 5A.

[c] This column shows the total number of countries that submitted reports with military expenditure data to either SIPRI or the UN (excluding nil reports). Totals may be smaller than the sums of reports to the UN and SIPRI because the same country may report to both organizations.

[d] There are 50 African countries in the SIPRI Military Expenditure Database, but SIPRI is unable to send requests to Somalia because of a lack of contact details.

[e] These 18 countries reported their data using a simplified UN form.

[f] These 6 countries did not use the SIPRI questionnaire in their report to SIPRI.

[g] These countries used both the simplified and standardized forms when reporting to the UN. In this table they are counted as standardized form responses.

[h] There are 5 Oceanian countries in the SIPRI Military Expenditure Database, but SIPRI did not send a request to Tonga in 2007.

[i] In addition, the UN sent requests to 24 very small states.

Sources: United Nations, 'Objective information on military matters, including transparency of military expenditures', Report of the UN Secretary-General, UN documents A/62/158, 26 July 2007, A/62/158/Add. 1, 14 Sep. 2007, and A/62/158/Add. 2, 15 Oct. 2007, <http://disarmament2.un.org/cab/milex.html>; and submitted filled-in SIPRI questionnaires.

matrix too complicated and in order to encourage reporting by more countries, in 2002 the UN introduced an alternative, simplified reporting form.[5]

The UN Office for Disarmament Affairs (ODA, formerly the Department for Disarmament Affairs) manages the system. The reported data are included in an annual report by the UN Secretary-General to the General Assembly and are published in appropriate UN media.[6] In addition, the ODA periodically publishes documents analysing the reporting trends to the UN. The most recent example is the 2007 ODA report on world and regional military expenditure reporting, by country, for the period 1996–2007.[7]

The SIPRI reporting system

SIPRI has sent requests for data on military expenditure to governments on an annual basis since 1993. Such requests are sent to all countries that are included in the SIPRI Military Expenditure Database (currently 168 countries).[8] The reported data are one source of information used in preparing SIPRI's tables of military expenditure.[9]

The SIPRI request for data is sent to various national government offices and embassies of the respective countries. The SIPRI questionnaire is a simplified version of the UN instrument, with fields for data on spending on military and civilian personnel, operations and maintenance, procurement, military construction, military research and development, paramilitary forces, and military aid provided and received. Data are requested for the five most recent years in order to ensure consistency over time.

III. Reporting of military expenditure data in 2007

Table 5D.1 lists the countries (by region) that reported data on military expenditure to the United Nations and SIPRI in 2007. It also gives the number of reports submitted to each of these organizations and the overall number of countries requested to report (i.e. the number of UN member states and the number of requests sent out by SIPRI) by region. Finally, the table gives the number of countries that reported either to the UN or to SIPRI. All figures in table 5D.1 exclude 'nil reports'.[10]

---

[5] United Nations, Department for Disarmament Affairs, *Transparency in Armaments: United Nations Instrument for Reporting Military Expenditures—Global and Regional Participation 1981–2002* (United Nations: New York, 2003), <http://disarmament.un.org/cab/Bk2-TransArms.pdf>, p. 3; see also the UN's standardized instrument and simplified form on pp. 12–14.

[6] United Nations, Department for Disarmament Affairs, *Transparency in Armaments: United Nations Standardized Instrument for Reporting Military Expenditures—Guidelines* (United Nations: New York, [n.d.]), <http://disarmament2.un.org/cab/milex>, p. 1; and UN General Assembly Resolution A/RES/ 62/13 (note 2).

[7] United Nations, Office for Disarmament Affairs, *United Nations Standardized Instrument for Reporting Military Expenditures: Pattern of Global and Regional Participation by States 1996–2007* (United Nations: New York, [n.d.]), <http://disarmament2.un.org/cab/milex>.

[8] There were 2 exceptions in 2007: SIPRI did not send requests to Somalia or to Tonga.

[9] See appendix 5A. The SIPRI Military Expenditure Database is available at <http://www.sipri.org/ contents/milap/milex/mex_database1.html>.

[10] A nil report is a questionnaire returned to the UN with no data entered, submitted by a country that does not maintain regular armed forces. Most of the countries submitting nil reports are very small states. The exceptions in 2007 were Iceland and Panama.

In 2007 a total of 78 countries reported data on military spending to either the UN or SIPRI. The 66 countries that reported to the UN account for 39 per cent of UN member states (excluding the 24 very small states). Twelve of the 24 very small states also submitted reports, all of which were nil reports. The 55 countries reporting military expenditure data to SIPRI in 2007 represent a reporting rate of 33 per cent.

On a regional basis the best reporting rates in 2007 were for Europe and the Americas, where most countries submitted reports to both the UN and SIPRI. In Western Europe 19 out of 20 countries reported to either the UN or SIPRI, excluding the nil report submitted by Iceland. In Central Europe all but one country reported data, the exception being Montenegro. Similarly, all East European states (the European members of the Commonwealth of Independent States) except one, Azerbaijan, reported to either the UN or SIPRI.

In North America, both countries reported military expenditure data to the UN and SIPRI. In Central America, five out of seven countries reported, and in South America five out of 11 countries submitted reports. None of the eight Caribbean countries reported to SIPRI and only one, Jamaica, reported to the UN.

Half of the six South Asian countries and eight of the 17 East Asian states reported to the UN or SIPRI, while one Central Asian country, Kazakhstan, reported. Of the four countries in Oceania, two reported to either the UN or SIPRI.

In Africa and the Middle East the response rate was very low in 2007, as it has been in previous years. Of the 50 states in Africa only 7 (14 per cent) reported to the UN or SIPRI, while only 3 of the 14 Middle Eastern countries reported, a reporting rate of just 21 per cent.

IV. Trends in reporting of military expenditure, 2001–2007

Government reporting to the UN and SIPRI dropped significantly in 2007 (see table 5D.2). In the period 2001–2007 the reporting rate to the UN has fluctuated. The number of countries reporting data to the UN decreased to 66 in 2007 from its high point of 70 in 2002. Including nil reports, the total number of reports to the UN was 78 in 2007, representing a decrease compared to the 80 reports in 2006.

Reporting to SIPRI was at its highest in 2005, at 67 countries. It decreased to 60 countries in 2006 and again to 55 in 2007. The total number of requests sent by SIPRI has increased from 158 requests in 2001 to 166 in 2007. With a higher number of requests sent and a decreasing number of reports received by SIPRI, the rate of response has decreased over the period 2001–2007 from 40 per cent to 33 per cent.

Overall, the number of countries reporting to either the UN or SIPRI decreased from 85 in 2006 to 78 in 2007.

According to the latest ODA report on participation in the UN reporting system, the total number of countries reporting at any time during the period 1996–2006 has increased. Most countries have participated at least once in the UN reporting system. The regions with the lowest reporting rates were Africa and the Middle East.[11] The countries in these regions have consistently fail to report data, whereas countries in other regions have reported on an irregular basis.[12]

The need to improve the participation in the UN reporting system has resulted in a decision by the UN General Assembly, at the suggestion of the ODA, to increase its

[11] United Nations (note 7), pp. 5–6.
[12] United Nations (note 7), pp. 5–9.

Table 5D.2. Number of countries reporting their military expenditure to SIPRI and the United Nations, 2001–2007

	2001	2002	2003	2004	2005	2006	2007
UN reporting system[a]							
Number of UN member states	189	191	191	191	191	192	192
UN members excluding very small states	165	167	167	167	167	168	168
Number of reports to the UN[b]	56	70	64	68	62	69	66
Standardized reports	56	70	54	54	55	54	48
Simplified reports	..	..	10	14	7	15	18
Nil reports[c]	5	11	11	10	12	11	12
SIPRI reporting system							
Number of SIPRI requests	158	158	158	159	167	166	166
Number of reports to SIPRI	63	61	64	62	67	60	55
Total number of reports to the UN or SIPRI[d]	..	..	..	..	..	85	78

[a] The figures for 2001–2003 and 2005–2006 include some late submissions of data to the UN and are therefore slightly higher than those presented in previous editions of the SIPRI Yearbook. The data for 2007 include late submissions up to 15 Oct. 2007, but some countries may report after this date.

[b] These figures exclude nil reports.

[c] A nil report is a questionnaire returned to the UN with no data entered, submitted by a country that does not maintain regular armed forces.

[d] These figures are for the total number of countries that submitted reports with military expenditure data (excluding nil reports) to either the UN or SIPRI. Totals may be smaller than the sums of reports to the UN and SIPRI because the same country may report to both organizations. Totals before 2006 are not available because of changes in the way responses to the UN and SIPRI are counted.

Sources: United Nations, 'Objective information on military matters, including transparency of military expenditures', Reports of the Secretary-General, various dates, 2001–2007, <http://disarmament2.un.org/cab/milex.html>; and submitted filled-in SIPRI questionnaires.

efforts in that regard. Thus, the 2007 UN General Assembly resolution on transparency of military expenditures noted the need to review the operation of the reporting system and to improve and broaden participation. For this purpose, it requested the creation of a group of governmental experts, to begin work in 2010.[13]

[13] UN General Assembly Resolution A/RES/62/13 (note 2), paragraph 5.

6. Arms production

SAM PERLO-FREEMAN and ELISABETH SKÖNS

I. Introduction

Global arms production is increasing. Arms sales by the 100 largest arms-producing companies (the 'SIPRI Top 100') amounted to $315 billion in 2006, an increase of 9 per cent in nominal terms and 5 per cent in real terms over 2005. This is a similar rate of increase to the previous year but is considerably lower than the high growth rates in 2003 and 2004. These 100 companies represent a large part of the global arms industry's output of military goods and services, in particular the high-technology output.[1]

The main centre of arms production that is not reflected in the SIPRI Top 100 is China. While the Chinese arms industry is developing rapidly, in size as well as technological level, it is not possible to include Chinese arms-producing enterprises in the Top 100 because of a lack of comparable financial data.[2] The lack of readily accessible information about the Chinese arms industry also makes it difficult to monitor its general development. In addition, there may be companies in other countries that have high arms sales but do not appear in the Top 100 since this information is not readily available. Nevertheless, an analysis of the companies in the SIPRI Top 100 is sufficient to capture the major trends in the modern global arms industry outside China.

US companies dominate the Top 100 list, both numerically and financially, with West European companies some way behind. The highest growth rates have been experienced by companies that focus on the markets generated by rapid technological development and outsourcing, while the ongoing conflict in Iraq has increased the demand for armoured vehicles and other equipment

[1] A rough estimate suggests that the arms sales of the SIPRI Top 100 companies in 1995 accounted for about three-quarters of global arms production. This share is likely to have increased since then because of the concentration process that has taken place since the end of the cold war. Sköns, E. and Dunne, J. P., 'Economics of arms production', ed. L. Kurtz, *Encyclopedia of Violence, Peace and Conflict,* 2nd edition (Elsevier: Oxford, forthcoming 2008).

[2] According to rough estimates, the arms sales of the 11 largest arms-producing enterprises in China accounted for 3.2–5.6% of the SIPRI Top 100 in 2003. This is based on estimated total sales for these companies of 315 billion yuan ($38 billion), and assuming that arms sales account for 20–35% of total sales. The assumed arms sales shares are based on a statement in China's 2004 Defence White Paper, saying that civilian products accounted for more than 65% of the total output of the Chinese arms industry, and a study concluding that the estimated amount of civilian production in each of the 11 enterprises was in the range 65–90%. Surry, E., 'An estimate of the value of Chinese arms production', Paper presented at the 11th Annual Conference on Economics and Security, University of the West of England, 5–7 July 2007, <http://www.sipri.org/contents/milap/milex/publications/unpublished.html>. See also Chinese State Council, *China's National Defence in 2004* (Information Office of the State Council of the People's Republic of China: Beijing, Dec. 2004), <http://www.china.org.cn/e-white/20041227/>; and Medeiros, E., 'Analyzing China's defense industries and the implications for Chinese military modernization', Testimony presented to the US–China Economic and Security Review Commission, 6 Feb. 2004, RAND Corporation, Santa Monica, Calif., <http://rand.org/pubs/testimonies/CT217/>.

Table 6.1. Regional and national shares of arms sales for the SIPRI Top 100 arms-producing companies in the world excluding China,[a] 2006 compared to 2005

Arms sales figures are in US$ b., at current prices and exchange rates. Figures do not always add up to totals because of the conventions of rounding.

Number of companies	Region/ country[b]	Arms sales[c] ($ b.)		Change in arms sales, 2005–06 (%)		Share of total Top 100 arms sales, 2006 (%)
		2005[d]	2006	Nominal[e]	Real[f]	
42	**North America**	**184.1**	**200.7**	*9*	*6*	*63.6*
41	USA	183.6	200.2	*9*	*6*	*63.5*
1	Canada	0.4	0.5	*14*	*4*	*0.2*
34	**Western Europe**	**85.6**	**92.1**	*8*	*4*	*29.2*
11	United Kingdom	35.2	37.3	*6*	*2*	*11.8*
6	France	19.9	19.5	*–2*	*–5*	*6.2*
1	Trans-European[g]	9.6	12.6	*32*	*28*	*4.0*
5	Italy	10.6	11.0	*4*	*1*	*3.5*
5	Germany[h]	5.2	6.1	*17*	*14*	*1.9*
1	Sweden	2.1	2.3	*7*	*4*	*0.7*
2	Spain	1.6	1.9	*13*	*8*	*0.6*
1	Switzerland	0.5	0.6	*–8*	*–9*	*0.2*
1	Finland	0.3	0.5	*41*	*38*	*0.2*
1	Norway	0.4	0.5	*22*	*18*	*0.1*
8	**Eastern Europe**	**4.6**	**6.1**	*32*	*15*	*1.9*
8	Russia	4.6	6.1	*32*	*15*	*1.9*
8	**Other OECD**	**7.6**	**7.5**	*–1*	*0*	*2.4*
4	Japan[i]	5.4	5.2	*–2*	*2*	*1.7*
3	South Korea[j]	1.7	1.8	*4*	*–5*	*0.6*
1	Australia	0.5	0.5	*2*	*0*	*0.2*
8	**Other non-OECD**	**7.6**	**9.0**	*19*	*15*	*2.9*
4	Israel	3.7	4.6	*26*	*22*	*1.5*
3	India[k]	3.0	3.5	*19*	*15*	*1.1*
1	Singapore	0.9	0.9	*–6*	*–11*	*0.3*
100	**Total**	**289.4**	**315.3**	*9*	*5*	*100.0*

OECD = Organisation for Economic Co-operation and Development.

[a] Although it is known that several Chinese arms-producing enterprises are large enough to rank among the SIPRI Top 100, it has not been possible to include them because of lack of comparable and sufficiently accurate data. In addition, there are companies in other countries, such as Kazakhstan and Ukraine, that could also be large enough to appear in the SIPRI Top 100 list if data were available, but this is less certain.

[b] Figures for a country or region refer to the arms sales of Top 100 companies headquartered in that country or region, including those in its foreign subsidiaries, and thus do not reflect the sales of arms actually produced in that country or region.

[c] Arms sales include all company arms sales, both domestic and export.

[d] Arms sales figures for 2005 refer to companies in the SIPRI Top 100 for 2006, and not to companies in the Top 100 for 2005.

[e] This column gives the change in arms sales 2005–2006 in current US dollars.

[f] This column gives the change in arms sales 2005–2006 in constant (2006) US dollars.

[g] The company classified as trans-European is EADS. See appendix 6A.

^h Figures for Germany include a rough estimate for ThyssenKrupp.

ⁱ Arms sales data for Japanese companies represent new military contracts awarded by the Japan Defense Agency (JDA) in 2006, rather than actual arms sales for the year. The JDA became the Ministry of Defense in Jan. 2007.

^j Figures for South Korean companies are uncertain.

^k Figures for India are based on a rough estimate for Indian Ordnance Factories.

Source: Appendix 6A, table 6A.

required by the US armed forces. Russian companies also experienced high growth rates during 2006—although from a low initial level—primarily in aerospace and air defence.

Merger and acquisition activity continues to lead to further concentration in the arms industry. Transatlantic mergers and acquisitions during 2007 involved almost exclusively British acquisitions in the United States. In Western Europe the two main developments in 2007 were the policy-driven naval consolidations in France and the United Kingdom and further political moves to procurement cooperation and arms industry integration within the European Union (EU). In Russia the government moved to consolidate some sectors of the arms industry under large state-owned holding companies in order to permit more direct central government involvement and to promote private investment in the industry.

Section II of this chapter presents and analyses the main trends in the SIPRI Top 100 companies. Section III discusses merger and acquisition deals in the North American and European arms industries during 2007, and developments in the restructuring of the West European and Russian arms industries. Section IV presents the conclusions. Appendix 6A lists the SIPRI Top 100 arms-producing companies in 2006, and appendix 6B lists the major acquisitions in the North American and West European arms industries in 2007.

II. The SIPRI Top 100 arms-producing companies

The growth of the world's largest arms-producing companies showed no signs of slowing in 2006. The value of the combined arms sales of the 100 largest arms-producing companies in the world apart from China was $315 billion in 2006 compared to $289 billion for the same companies in 2005 (see table 6.1). The SIPRI Top 100 is dominated by companies based in the USA, with 41 US companies accounting for 63 per cent of the Top 100's arms sales in 2006. Thirty-four West European companies accounted for 29 per cent. These shares are almost identical to those for 2005. Of the remainder, the countries with the highest company arms sales in the Top 100 were Russia with eight companies (1.9 per cent of Top 100 arms sales), Japan with four (1.7 per cent), Israel with four (1.5 per cent) and India with three (1.1 per cent). Twelve companies entered the Top 100 list in 2006, six of them for the first time.[3]

---

[3] These 12 companies appear in the Top 100 for 2006 but did not appear in the Top 100 for 2005 as published in *SIPRI Yearbook 2007*. The 6 companies listed in a Top 100 list for the first time include 1 newly identified company, Chugach Alaska Corporation. See appendix 6A.

Table 6.2. Trends in arms sales of companies in the SIPRI Top 100 arms-producing companies in the world excluding China, 2002–2006

	2002	2003	2004	2005	2006	2002–2006
Arms sales at current prices and exchange rates						
Total ($ b.)	197	236	275	292	315	
Change (%)		20	16	6	8	60
Arms sales at constant (2006) prices and exchange rates						
Total ($ b.)	240	268	292	302	315	
Change (%)		12	9	3	4	32

Note: The data in this table refer to the companies in the SIPRI Top 100 in each year, which means that they refer to a different set of companies each year, as ranked from a consistent set of data. The figure for 2005 is thus different from the figure for 2005 in table 6.1.

Source: Appendix 6A; and the SIPRI Arms Industry Database.

The companies in the SIPRI Top 100 for 2006 increased their combined arms sales by 9 per cent in nominal terms and 5 per cent in real terms, a slightly lower rate of growth than in 2005. However, comparing the Top 100 companies in 2006 with the set of companies included in the Top 100 for 2005, the combined arms sales increased by 8 per cent in nominal terms and by 4 per cent in real terms (see table 6.2).[4]

Companies that increased their arms sales the most in 2006

Eight companies increased their arms sales by more than $1 billion in 2006 (see table 6.3). Sixteen companies increased their sales by more than 30 per cent (including three that also increased sales by more than $1 billion). Some of these increases are the result of mergers and acquisitions and some appear to be the result of organic growth, particularly in the areas of armoured vehicles and high-technology electronics and communications.

Six companies in the top 10 increased their arms sales by more than $1 billion, and one of these—EADS—also increased its arms sales by more than 30 per cent. Three companies in the top 10—Boeing, Lockheed Martin and Raytheon—had large absolute increases that represented only single-figure

[4] The 5% real-terms growth rate compares the sales of the Top 100 companies for 2006 with the *same* companies' arms sales in 2005. The 4% figure compares the Top 100 for 2006 with the *different* group of companies that formed the Top 100 for 2005. The first figure will almost always be higher, as new entrants to the Top 100 must have grown faster than those companies that left the Top 100. If the companies in the Top 100 had not changed, the 2 figures would be identical.

The SIPRI data on arms-producing companies are continuously revised, which means that they are not strictly comparable between editions of the SIPRI Yearbook. Not only are some figures for individual companies revised when improved data are obtained, but the coverage may also differ due to problems of obtaining data or making good enough estimates for all companies every year. Thus, the data used here on the SIPRI Top 100 for 2005 may differ from those published in *SIPRI Yearbook 2007*. However, the data set used for each edition of the Yearbook is consistent as far as possible across countries and over time.

percentage increases. The increase in the sales of L-3 Communications was mostly due to a continued strategy of acquiring operations that provide 'key capabilities, technologies and customers', with 14 acquisitions in 2006.[5] The growth rates of BAE Systems, Finmeccanica and Northrop Grumman slowed following rapid expansion in 2005, while Thales's arms sales fell in 2006.

US companies

For the second consecutive year, several US companies involved in military vehicle production showed strong increases in their arms sales in 2006, including General Dynamics, Armor Holdings,[6] AM General and Oshkosh Truck. Much of this increase is due to the high and increasing demand generated by the conflict in Iraq, in particular by the US Army's requirement for the rapid delivery of mine-resistant ambush protected (MRAP) vehicles.[7] Force Protection, a company outside the SIPRI Top 100 that manufactures the Cougar and Buffalo MRAP vehicles, which are increasingly used by US forces in Iraq, also increased its sales almost fourfold in 2006.[8] Another company that has benefited from immediate wartime requirements is Ceradyne, which manufactures body armour.

Three other US companies increased their revenues from arms sales in 2006 by over 30 per cent: the military electronics firm DRS Technologies; ARINC, a military services company providing engineering, maintenance and upgrading, logistics, systems integration, computing and simulation services; and EDS, which provides information technology (IT) services to many governments, including to the US Department of Defense (DOD) and the British Ministry of Defence (MOD). This was the second consecutive year in which the arms sales of DRS Technologies and EDS grew by more than 30 per cent.[9] DRS Technologies' sales growth in 2006 is largely attributable to its takeover in January 2006 of Engineering Support Systems, as well as organic sales growth of 13.9 per cent.[10]

Other companies—from the USA and elsewhere—in the areas of high-technology electronics and communications and of military services also had significant arms sales increases, reflecting the continued focus by military planners on 'network-centric warfare' alongside the more immediate require-

[5] L-3, *Annual Report 2006* (L-3 Communications: New York, 2007), <http://www.l-3com.com/investor-relations/financialreports.aspx>, p. 4.

[6] Armor Holdings was acquired by BAE Systems in May 2007.

[7] On the increase in US military expenditure due to the conflict in Iraq see chapter 5 in this volume, section III.

[8] 'Force Protection gears up new factory in NYC', *Defense Industry Daily*, 18 July 2007; and Force Protection, *Form 10-K Annual Report under Section 13 or 15(d) of the Securities Exchange Act of 1934 for the Fiscal Year ended December 31, 2006* (US Securities and Exchange Commission: Washington, DC, 16 Mar. 2007), <http://www.sec.gov/edgar.shtml>.

[9] On EDS's role in outsourcing and network-centric IT see Sköns, E. and Surry, E., 'Arms production', *SIPRI Yearbook 2007: Armaments, Disarmament and International Security* (Oxford University Press: Oxford, 2007), pp. 353–54.

[10] Anderson, G., 'DRS declares "best ever year"', *Jane's Defence Industry*, June 2007, p. 12.

Table 6.3. Companies in the SIPRI Top 100 with the largest increase in arms sales in 2006

Figures are in US$ m., at current prices and exchange rates.

Rank 2006	Company	Country	Sector	Arms sales ($ m.) 2005	Arms sales ($ m.) 2006	Change 2005–06 $ m.	Change 2005–06 %
Companies with the largest absolute increase in arms sales (by more than $1 b.)							
7	EADS	W. Eur.	Ac El Mi Sp	9 580	12 600	3 020	*31.5*
6	General Dynamics	USA	A El MV Sh	16 570	18 770	2 200	*13.3*
2	Lockheed Martin	USA	Ac El Mi Sp	26 200	28 120	1 920	*7.3*
8	L-3 Communications	USA	El	8 470	9 980	1 510	*17.8*
18	SAFRAN	France	Comp (Ac El Eng)	2 630	3 780	1 150	*43.7*
1	Boeing	USA	Ac El Mi Sp	29 590	30 690	1 100	*3.7*
22	DRS Technologies	USA	El	1 670	2 740	1 070	*64.1*
5	Raytheon	USA	El Mi	18 500	19 530	1 030	*5.6*
Companies with the largest relative increase in arms sales (by more than 30%)							
75	MiG	Russia	Ac	240	570	330	*137.5*
89	Ceradyne	USA	Comp (Oth)	240	510	270	*112.5*
22	DRS Technologies	USA	El	1 670	2 740	1 070	*64.1*
82	ARINC	USA	Comp (El)	330	540	210	*63.6*
30	Armor Holdings	USA	Comp (MV Oth)	1 190	1 930	740	*62.2*
48	Krauss-Maffei Wegmann	Germany	MV	750	1 190	440	*58.7*
85	Ufimskoe MPO	Russia	Eng	350	530	180	*51.4*
69	TRV Corporation	Russia	Mi	430	650	220	*51.2*
100	Elettronica	Italy	El	300	440	140	*46.7*
18	SAFRAN	France	Comp (Ac El Eng)	2 630	3 780	1 150	*43.7*
93	Patria Industries	Finland	Ac MV SA/A	340	480	140	*41.0*
39	Hindustan Aeronautics	India	Ac Mi	1 100	1 550	450	*40.1*
43	Elbit Systems	Israel	El	1 000	1 400	400	*40.0*
27	EDS	USA	Comp (Oth)	1 570	2 170	600	*38.2*
33	AM General	USA	MV	1 280	1 700	420	*32.8*
7	EADS	W. Eur.	Ac El Mi Sp	9 580	12 600	3 020	*31.5*

A = artillery; Ac = aircraft; El = electronics; Eng = engines; Mi = missiles; MV = military vehicles; SA/A = small arms/ammunition; Sh = ships; Sp = space; Oth = other; Comp (. . .) = components, services or anything other than final systems in the sectors in parentheses.

Source: Appendix 6A.

ments of US forces in Afghanistan and Iraq, and the long-term trend towards more outsourcing of military services.[11]

---

[11] On the trend towards outsourcing military functions see Perlo-Freeman, S. and Sköns, E., 'The private military services industry', SIPRI Research Paper, June 2008, <http://books.sipri.org/product_info?c_product_id=361>.

European companies

Despite continued management woes and programme delays, EADS expanded its arms sales by $3 billion in 2006, the largest absolute increase. While part of this increase is due to the strength of the euro against the dollar, the company also enjoyed increased revenues. Much of this increase was from sales of military transport aircraft, as the Airbus A400M aircraft passed several industrial and contractual milestones,[12] but there were also smaller increases in EADS's Eurocopter, military space (Astrium) and Eurofighter Typhoon sales.[13]

The other European companies that increased their arms sales by 30 per cent or more in 2006 were those operating in the sectors of the arms industry that have also seen most growth in other regions of the world: two in the high-tech areas of military electronics and communications—SAFRAN (France) and Elettronica (Italy)—and two armoured-vehicle manufacturers—Krauss-Maffei Wegmann (Germany) and Patria (Finland). BAE Systems saw smaller, but still substantial, increases in its Electronics, Information and Support and Land Systems businesses.

Russian companies

Three Russian companies had large increases in arms sales in 2006—the aircraft manufacturer MiG, the missile maker TRV and the engine producer Ufimskoe MPO. MiG more than doubled its arms sales. These increases come in the context of increasing Russian arms exports over recent years, with particularly strong orders for combat aircraft, missiles and air defence systems.[14]

Other major Russian companies had smaller, but still substantial, increases. These include the air defence systems company Almaz-Antei, the avionics company Aerokosmicheskoe Oborudovanie, and the aircraft manufacturers Irkut (due partly to increased sales of Su-30 MKI aircraft kits to India) and Sukhoi (which delivered Su-30 MK2 fighter aircraft to Venezuela).[15] In financial terms, Almaz-Antei was the largest Russian arms exporter in 2006, with major sales of air defence systems to Algeria and Iran.[16] In contrast, two Rus-

---

[12] However, in Nov. 2007 EADS announced a 6–12 month delay to the A400M programme, postponing first deliveries to 2010–11. This led the company to place a €1.2–1.4 billion ($1.6–1.9 billion) charge against its 2007 earnings. 'Airbus A400M program delayed 6–12 months', *Defense Industry Daily*, 5 Nov. 2007; and EADS, 'EDS announces charge estimate for revised A400M delivery schedule', Press release, Amsterdam, 5 Nov. 2007, <http://www.eads.com/1024/en/investor/News_and_Events/news_ir/2007.html>.

[13] EADS, *Annual Review 2006* (EADS: Schipol-Rijk, 2007), pp. III, 41, <http://www.reports.eads.net/2006/>. The Eurofighter Typhoon is produced by a consortium of 3 companies: Alenia Aeronautica, BAE Systems and EADS.

[14] See Wezeman, S. et al., 'International arms transfers', *SIPRI Yearbook 2007* (note 9), pp. 392–96; and chapter 7 in this volume, section III. As Russian state-owned companies do not produce publicly available annual reports, it is difficult to analyse the sources of these companies' revenue increases. This is particularly the case for export sales, where the relationship between orders, deliveries and company revenues is not clear.

[15] On the aircraft exports see Wezeman et al. (note 14), p. 394.

[16] Anderson, G., 'Almaz-Antei lead Russian exports', *Jane's Defence Industry*, July 2007, p. 10.

Table 6.4. Companies in the SIPRI Top 100 specializing in military services[a]

Companies are US-based unless otherwise stated.

Rank 2006	Company (country)	Arms sales, 2006 (US $m.)	Service sectors
8	L-3 Communications	9 980	IT, systems support, MRO, training
12	Halliburton	6 630	Logistics, facilities management
13	Computer Sciences Corporation	6 300	IT, training, systems support, intelligence
14	SAIC	5 800	R&D, IT, systems support, training, logistics, intelligence
27	EDS	2 170	IT
36	QinetiQ (UK)	1 610	R&D, IT, systems support, training
40	URS Corporation	1 530	Systems support, logistics
44	VT Group (UK)	1 400	MRO, facilities management, logistics, IT, training
47	CACI International	1 280	R&D, IT, logistics, systems support, intelligence
49	Serco (UK)	1 170	Facilities management, training, logistics, systems support, MRO
53	ManTech International	1 080	IT, systems support,
57	DynCorp	900	MRO, logistics, facilities management, systems support, armed security, intelligence
60	Babcock International Group (UK)	760	Facilities management, MRO, systems support
75	Cubic Corp.	560	Training, systems support
79	Chugach Alaska Corp.	550	Facilities management
82	ARINC	540	IT, systems support, training
83	Mitre	540	R&D, IT, systems support
97	Jacobs Engineering Group	460	R&D, IT, systems support

IT = information technology; MRO = maintenance, repairs and overhaul; R&D = research and development.

[a] US companies are listed as specializing in military services if more than 50% of their prime (direct) contract awards from the US Department of Defense in 2006 (2005 in the case of Cubic Corporation) were in the 'Other services' category. British companies are classified as specializing in military services based on the description of their activities in their annual reports, including divisional breakdowns of their sales.

Source: Appendix 6A; and Perlo-Freeman, S. and Sköns, E., 'The private military services industry', SIPRI Research Paper, June 2008, <http://books.sipri.org/product_info?c_product_id=361>.

sian shipbuilders—Admiralteiskie Verfi and Sevmash—saw their arms sales fall by more than half in 2006, dropping out of the Top 100 list.

Overall, the Russian arms industry remained heavily export dependent in 2006.[17] This may change with the implementation of the State Armaments Programme for 2007–15. This 5000 billion roubles ($189 billion) rearmament

[17] On changes in the Russian export market see chapter 7 in this volume, section III.

programme for the Russian armed forces aims to replace 45 per cent of their equipment by 2015. In 2007, 300 billion roubles ($11.3 billion) was allocated for procurement.[18]

Other countries

Indian companies in the SIPRI Top 100 increased their arms sales significantly in 2006, benefiting from rising military spending.[19] Hindustan Aeronautics had the highest percentage increase, and now ranks at number 38 in the Top 100, its highest ranking ever.[20] Israeli companies also had substantial increases in revenue. Most notable was the increase in the arms sales of the military electronics company Elbit Systems. The main components of this increase were sales of land systems to the US Marine Corps and revenues from the British Watchkeeper unmanned aerial vehicle (UAV) programme.[21]

Military services companies in the SIPRI Top 100

Companies providing military services, rather than military goods, constitute an increasing proportion of the arms industry. The companies specializing in sales of military services are often called private military companies, private military firms or private security companies.[22] The rapid growth of this industry segment in recent decades is due to the trend for outsourcing a range of military activities that were previously performed by the armed forces or by defence ministry employees. This trend has been most significant in the USA and the UK, but it is emerging in many other countries. While outsourcing has been increasing since at least the 1980s, the conflict in Iraq has accelerated the trend. This is reflected in the composition of the SIPRI Top 100: 18 of the companies in the Top 100 for 2006 operated primarily in the military services sector (see table 6.4), compared with a fairly stable level of 11–13 for most of the period 1996–2002.[23]

[18] Gavrilov, Yu., 'Armiya sdelala zakaz: Sergei Ivanov vybral prioritetnoe oruzhie na blizhaishie tri goda [The army has made the order: Sergei Ivanov has selected priority weapon for the next three years], *Rossiiskaya gazeta*, 12 Sep. 2007; and Saradzhyan, S., 'Russia prepares for "wars of the future"', *ISN Security Watch*, 12 Feb 2007, <http://www.isn.ethz.ch/news/sw/details.cfm?ID=17240>.

[19] See chapter 5 in this volume, section V.

[20] Hindustan Aeronautics attributes the rise specifically to the MiG-27 Mk 1 and Jaguar combat aircraft licensed production programmes, the Dhruv Advanced Light Helicopter programme, and DO-228 transport aircraft upgrades. Hindustan Aeronautics, 'HAL turnover soars to R7,505 Crores', Press release, 5 Apr. 2007, <http://www.hal-india.com/press.asp>.

[21] Elbit Systems, *Management's Report for the Year ended December 31, 2006* (Elbit Systems: Haifa, 2007), <http://www.elbitsystems.com/investors.asp?id=953>, pp. 16–17.

[22] On this phenomenon see e.g. Holmqvist, C., *Private Security Companies: The Case for Regulation*, SIPRI Policy Paper no. 9 (SIPRI: Stockholm, 2005), <hrrp://books.sipri.org/>; Singer, P. W., *Corporate Warriors: The Rise of the Privatized Military Industry* (Cornell University Press: Ithaca, N.Y., 2003); and Wulf, H., *Internationalizing and Privatizing War and Peace: The Bumpy Ride to Peace Building* (Palgrave Macmillan: Houndmills, 2005), pp. 169–70.

[23] SIPRI Arms Industry Database. The figures for previous years may not correspond to the figures published in previous editions of the SIPRI Yearbook; see note 4.

Military services include a range of activities of a military-specific nature, including IT, equipment support and maintenance, base management, logistics, training, intelligence services and armed security in conflict zones. Military services do not include services of a purely civilian nature (such as health care) provided to a military customer.[24] Military services such as armed security in conflict zones may also be procured from private companies by civilian branches of government, multinational companies, non-governmental organizations and intergovernmental organizations.

The trend for military outsourcing has generated considerable controversy both from an economic viewpoint and regarding the accountability of the use of force. These concerns have become particularly acute with the extensive use of private contractors by the USA and its allies in Afghanistan and Iraq. This use has encompassed both companies providing private armed force, such as Blackwater, and those providing support services, such as the former Halliburton subsidiary KBR.[25]

Chinese companies

Chinese arms-producing companies, some of which would be included in the SIPRI Top 100 if sufficient data were available, produce across the full spectrum of equipment, at an increasing level of technological sophistication. They are, however, still some way behind the most advanced producers and—to a decreasing extent—are still dependent on Russian technology.[26]

Evidence of technological developments in the Chinese arms industry includes the apparent entry into service of the J-11B fourth-generation combat aircraft. It was designed by the Shenyang Aircraft Company, based on the Russian Su-27 SK aircraft and is armed with indigenously designed PL-12 beyond-visual-range air-to-air missiles (BVRAAMs). China has also developed new artillery and precision missiles and bombs and has a developing command, control, communications, computers, intelligence, surveillance and reconnaissance (C4ISR) network aided by new reconnaissance satellite launches.[27] During 2007 there were continuing moves to restructure the Chinese arms industry along corporate lines, transforming the state-owned enterprises that make up the industry into shareholding companies and permitting

[24] For a list of military services provided by private companies see appendix 6A, table 6A.1.

[25] On the military services segment of the arms industry and the companies involved in it see Perlo-Freeman and Sköns (note 11). See also Holmqvist (note 22); Singer (note 22); and Wulf (note 22).

[26] See Medeiros, E. S. et al., *A New Direction for China's Defense Industry* (Rand Corporation: Santa Monica, Calif., 2005); and Cordesman, A. H. and Kleiber, M., *Chinese Military Modernization: Force Development and Strategic Capabilities* (Center for Strategic and International Studies: Washington, DC, 2007).

[27] Minnick, W., 'China heightens Pacific challenge to U.S. forces', *Defense News*, 17 Sep. 2007, p. 18; Wen, J., 'Details emerge of China's J-11B heavy fighter', *Jane's Defence Weekly*, 9 May 2007, p. 38; and Hewson, R., 'China unveils recent weapons developments', *Jane's Defence Weekly*, 16 May 2007, p. 6.

some foreign investment, although with the Chinese Government retaining a controlling stake.[28]

III. Restructuring of the arms industry in 2007

There were considerably more large merger and acquisition deals in the arms industry in 2007 than in 2006, with at least seven mega-deals (i.e. acquisitions with a value of over $1 billion; see table 6.5 and appendix 6B).[29] There was only one such deal in 2006 and five in 2005.[30] Three of the mega-deals in 2007 were transatlantic acquisitions and at least four were domestic US deals. The size of these deals varied between $1.1 billion and $4.8 billion.

Among the companies that were bought in 2007 are four that rank among the SIPRI Top 100 arms-producing companies for 2006: Armor Holdings, EDO Corporation, United Industrial Corporation and ARINC. In addition, three former subsidiaries bought in 2007 had arms sales large enough to rank them among the Top 100: Devonport Management Ltd (DML, with arms sales of $780 million in 2006), Smiths Aerospace (sales of $1.3 billion) and Thales's naval operations (sales of $1.6 billion).

All but one of the companies acquired in large-scale deals are US-based. The exception is the British company Smiths Aerospace, which was acquired by the US company General Electric (GE). Indeed, of the 53 deals recorded in appendix 6B, 34 involve the acquisition of a US-based company.

The overall trends in arms industry mergers and acquisitions and the drivers of those trends have changed over time. In the early post-cold war period, when a significant fall in military expenditure led to a reduction in the size of the arms industry, mergers and acquisitions were one of several company strategies to cope with this change. It was paralleled by other strategies, such as exiting the arms industry, diversification into civilian production, internal company rationalization and, although often unsuccessfully, efforts to increase arms exports.[31] During the late 1990s there was a rapid concentration process in the US arms industry, largely driven by investment firms and other actors in the financial sector.[32] At the same time in Western Europe, cross-border acquisitions of arms-producing operations faced various legal, political and economic barriers.

[28] Chen, S.-C. J., 'China to unleash market forces in arms sector', Forbes.com, 26 June 2007, <http://www.forbes.com/2007/06/26/china-defense-stocks-markets-equity-cx_jc_0626markets1.html>.

[29] The total number of cross-border mega-deals in all industries worldwide in 2006 was 172. United Nations Conference on Trade and Development (UNCTAD), *World Investment Report 2007: Transnational Corporations, Extractive Industries and Development* (UNCTAD: New York, 2007), pp. 5–6.

[30] Surry, E., 'Major arms industry acquisitions, 2006', *SIPRI Yearbook 2007* (note 9), pp. 383–85; and Surry, E., 'Table of acquisitions, 2005', *SIPRI Yearbook 2005: Armaments, Disarmament and International Security* (Oxford University Press: Oxford, 2005), pp. 428–30.

[31] See e.g. Sköns, E. and Weidacher, R., 'Arms production', *SIPRI Yearbook 2000: Armaments, Disarmament and International Security* (Oxford University Press: Oxford, 2000), pp. 314–20.

[32] Markusen, A. R. and Costigan, S. S., 'The military industrial challenge', and Oden, M., 'Cashing in, cashing out, and converting: restructuring of the defence industrial base in the 1990s', eds A. R. Markusen and S. S. Costigan, *Arming the Future: A Defense Industry for the 21st Century* (Council on Foreign Relations Press: New York, 1999).

Table 6.5. The largest acquisitions in the West European and North American arms industry, 2007

Figures are in US $m., at current prices.

Buyer company (country)	Acquired company (country)	Seller company (country)	Deal value ($ m.)
General Electric (USA)	Smiths Aerospace (UK)	Smiths Group (UK)	4 800
BAE Systems (UK)	Armor Holdings (USA)	Publicly listed	4 532
URS Corporation (USA)	Washington Group International (USA)	Publicly listed	3 100
Carlyle Group (USA)	ARINC (USA)	Privately owned	. .
ITT Corporation (USA)	EDO Corporation (USA)	Publicly listed	1 700
Meggitt (UK)	K&F Industries (USA)	Publicly listed	1 300
Veritas Capital (USA)	Aeroflex (USA)	Publicly listed	1 300
Textron (USA)	United Industrial Corporation (USA)	Publicly listed	1 100
Thales (France)	67% of Alcatel Alenia Space (France) and 33% of Telespazio (Italy)	Alcatel-Lucent (France)	895
DCN (France)	Thales's naval operations (France)	Thales (France)	714[a]
Babcock International (UK)	Devonport Management Ltd (UK)	KBR (USA)	699

[a] This deal value refers to the implicit valuation of DCN's stake. See appendix 6B.

Source: Appendix 6B.

The current trend in mergers and acquisitions has somewhat different drivers. In the US arms industry, acquisition activity is concentrated in expanding sectors, where the large bulk of new contracts are to be won. Such targets include companies specializing in communications and IT related to network-centric programmes. Other companies with strong prospects are the private security companies that are benefiting from the outsourcing and privatization of traditionally military functions such as logistics and IT (as discussed above). Companies in the traditional arms industry are acquiring companies that have strong capabilities in these types of service, and new companies are emerging that specialize in this field.[33]

Another important driver is the increase in US military expenditure. The resulting increase in military contracts from the US Government means that non-US companies want to access the US market by acquiring companies located in the USA. The effect of this driver is limited by strict US regulations and policies on foreign acquisitions. As a result, most of the resulting acquisitions have been by British companies, because of the close long-term military–industrial relationship between the UK and the USA, but some other

[33] Perlo-Freeman and Sköns (note 11).

European companies, such as EADS, have also made significant US investments.

A new but growing phenomenon in the restructuring of the arms industry is the active role of private equity and investment firms. These make investments primarily to raise the value to their shareholders of their investment portfolios. This trend began in the USA in the mid-1990s and then spread to Europe. It indicates that there is much to gain in the buying and selling of arms industry stocks.

Governments also have a role in the restructuring of the arms industry. Not only are they the major customers for arms, but they also provide the legal frameworks that allow anti-competitive or, in some cases, foreign acquisitions to be blocked. Governments have sometimes actively promoted individual mergers and acquisitions, as was the case in 2007 with major naval restructuring deals in France and the UK (see below). However, most governments do not actively engage in individual cases on a systematic basis. The main exception in recent years has been the Russian Government. The Russian arms industry experienced a virtual collapse after the end of the cold war due to the sharp cuts in Russian military expenditure and the consequent near cessation of domestic orders from the arms industry. However, since the late 1990s there has been a gradual recovery of the Russian arms industry, primarily due to the growth in domestic orders, but also because of a radical restructuring and consolidation of the industry.[34] The Russian Government, under President Vladimir Putin, has assumed an increasingly active role in this process.

The main mergers and acquisitions in 2007 are described in more detail in the following sections.

Mergers and acquisitions within the United States

The largest merger and acquisition deal within the US arms industry in 2007 was the acquisition of Washington Group International by URS Corporation in November 2007. Both are engineering services companies with military customers representing relatively small shares of their total sales—36 per cent in the case of URS and 17 per cent in the case of Washington Group in 2006.[35] URS Corporation provides engineering, construction and technical services to public sector customers worldwide, while Washington Group—now the

[34] Cooper, J., 'Developments in the Russian arms industry', *SIPRI Yearbook 2006 Armaments, Disarmament and International Security* (Oxford University Press: Oxford, 2006).

[35] URS Corporation, 'URS Corporation completes acquisition of Washington Group International', Press release, 15 Nov. 2007, <http://www.urs-wng.com/pressReleases/>. Washington Group's defence division had sales of $576 million in 2006. However, Washington Group is not included in the SIPRI Top 100 because the majority of the defence division's activities appears to consist of 'demilitarization' or 'threat reduction' services—including its role in safeguarding former Soviet nuclear weapons, and destroying stocks of chemical and biological weapons—which SIPRI does not classify as arms sales. Other activities of the division, including military base management services, are classed as arms sales. Washington Group International, *Form 10-K Annual Report under Section 13 or 15(d) of the Securities Exchange Act of 1934 for the Fiscal Year ended December 29, 2006* (US Securities and Exchange Commission: Washington, DC, 26 Feb. 2007), <http://www.sec.gov/edgar.shtml>.

Washington Division of URS—provides a similar set of services, in particular to the mining and energy industries as well as to the military.

Two major acquisitions were made in 2007 by private equity firms with a history of arms industry investments. The Carlyle Group agreed in July to purchase the military services company ARINC for an undisclosed sum.[36] In August Veritas Capital completed the $1.1 billion acquisition of Aeroflex, a fast-growing microelectronics and test and measuring equipment company, whose revenues have increased by approximately 175 per cent since 2002.[37] URS, Washington Group and ARINC were all major services providers to the US DOD in 2006.

The other two very large-scale US deals in 2007 were in the field of military electronics and UAVs. ITT Corporation agreed to acquire EDO Corporation, thereby obtaining a role in the F-35 Joint Strike Fighter and Littoral Combat Ship programmes.[38] Textron's acquisition of United Industrial Corporation expanded its product range into the UAV sector.[39]

The above deals reflect the increased business activity and financial interest in military services prime contractors (i.e. companies contracting directly with the US DOD) and in major suppliers (second-tier or sub-prime contractors) in certain areas, such as military electronics and aerospace subsystems. In addition, many larger companies, especially those that focus on high-tech electronics and communications, continued strategies of acquiring small- or medium-sized operations that offered particular niche capabilities and technologies—in some cases firms with as few as a dozen employees. Compared to the 1990s, the consolidation process in the US arms industry has shifted from mergers and acquisitions among major platform producers to these second-tier and service sectors.

Transatlantic mergers and acquisitions

The two largest acquisitions in 2007 involved deals between British and US companies. These were the $4.8 billion acquisition by General Electric (USA) of Smiths Aerospace from Smiths Group (UK), completed in May 2007, and the $4.5 billion purchase by BAE Systems (UK) of Armor Holdings (USA), completed in July 2007. The first of these deals represents a significant consolidation in the aerospace industry at the sub-prime level. The combined arms sales of GE and Smiths Aerospace in 2006 were $4.5 billion, which would have been enough to put the joint company in 15th place in the SIPRI Top 100

[36] Anderson, G., 'Carlyle reveals ARINC purchase', *Jane's Defence Industry*, Aug. 2007, p. 15.

[37] Aeroflex, 'Acquisition of Aeroflex Incorporated completed', News release, 15 Aug. 2007, <http://www.aeroflex.com/aboutus/investor/investor.cfm>; and 'Fast Track 50', *Defense News*, 20 Aug. 2007, p. 14.

[38] Anderson, G., 'ITT enters into definitive agreement to purchase EDO', *Jane's Defence Industry*, Nov. 2007, p. 13.

[39] Anderson, G., 'Textron enters accord to buy AAI Corporation', *Jane's Defence Industry*, Nov. 2007, p. 13.

for 2006.[40] The deal expands GE's engine and services business for military and civil aerospace, adding Smiths Aerospace's various avionics and electronic systems. Armor Holdings makes armour plating for military vehicles much in demand for the Iraq conflict. Its 2006 arms sales of $1930 million represent an astonishing 32-fold increase on pre-invasion arms sales. Its acquisition by BAE Systems will greatly expand the latter's Land and Armaments Group in the USA as part of its US subsidiary, BAE Systems Inc. The acquisition makes BAE Systems a key supplier of certain classes of armoured vehicles to the US Army, and is likely to increase its share of revenues from the USA from one-third to 45 per cent.[41] BAE Systems' Land and Armaments Group is now of comparable size to the land systems operations of General Dynamics.[42]

Meggitt, a British aerospace components and military services company, acquired the US-based K&F Industries for $1.8 billion in June 2007.[43] K&F Industries also produces aerospace components, in particular wheels, brakes, braking control systems and fuel tanks. In 2006, 29 per cent of its revenues of $424 million were military related.[44]

Although it is at a smaller scale, it is also worth noting QinetiQ's high level of acquisition activity in the USA, with five such deals completed or agreed in 2007, with a total value of $333 million (as well as one British acquisition worth $40 million). The largest purchase was that of Analex for $173 million. Analex, which had revenues of $150 million in 2006, provides IT, aerospace engineering and security, and intelligence support services for military, intelligence and space programmes.[45]

The high level of transatlantic merger and acquisition activity reflects the increasing interconnections between the British and US arms industries and in particular the privileged position of British arms-producing companies as regards acquisitions in the US arms industry compared with other European companies. This process was furthered by the 2007 Defense Trade Cooperation Treaty. If it is approved and enters into force, the treaty will make it easier for some US military equipment and technology to be transferred to the

---

[40] Smiths Aerospace had sales of £1.3 billion ($2.4 billion) in 2006, of which 54% (£702 million; $1.3 billion) was military related. Smiths Group, *Annual Report and Accounts 2006* (Smiths Group: London, 2006), <http://reports.smiths.com/annualreport2006/>, pp. 13, 16.

[41] Anderson, G., 'Unique fit justifies Armor pricing', *Jane's Defence Industry*, July 2007, p. 15.

[42] The combined sales of BAE Systems' Land and Armaments Group and Armor Holdings were $5.8 billion in 2006, while General Dynamics' Combat Systems division had sales of $6 billion. BAE Systems, *Annual Report 2006* (BAE Systems: London, 2007), <http://production.investis.com/investors/rs/>; and General Dynamics, *United States Securities and Exchange Commission Form 10-K for the Fiscal Year ended December 31, 2006* (US Securities and Exchange Commission: Washington, DC, 23 Feb. 2007), <http://www.sec.gov/edgar.shtml>.

[43] K&F Industries, 'Meggitt-USA Inc. completes acquisition of K&F Industries', Press release, 22 June 2007, <http://www.kandfindustries.com/press/>.

[44] K&F Industries Holdings, *Form 10-K Annual Report under Section 13 or 15(d) of the Securities Exchange Act of 1934 for the Fiscal Year ended December 31, 2006* (US Securities and Exchange Commission: Washington, DC, 2 Mar. 2007), <http://www.sec.gov/edgar.shtml>.

[45] 'QinetiQ buys Analex Corp., extends US footprint', *Defence Industry Daily*, 22 Jan. 2007.

UK by a waiver to the USA's International Traffic in Arms Regulations, which normally require a separate export licence for each transaction.[46]

Naval restructuring within Western Europe

While there were few large cross-border merger and acquisition deals within Western Europe during 2007, both France and the UK saw major government-promoted consolidations in their naval industries.

In the UK, BAE Systems and VT Group agreed in July to form a joint venture merging all their surface warship activities. The two companies account for 85 per cent of British naval shipbuilding, and the deal was actively encouraged by the British Government in line with its Maritime Industrial Strategy, which promotes consolidation.[47] Indeed, the Defence Procurement Minister, Paul Drayson, had explicitly declared such consolidation to be a condition of the government granting approval to commence production of ('main gate') the UK's new aircraft carrier programme (the Carrier Vessel Future, CVF), in which BAE and VT are major partners. The British Government confirmed that the CVF programme would go ahead on 25 July 2007, the same day as the joint venture was announced. Under the terms of the deal, BAE Systems will own 55 per cent of the joint venture and VT Group 45 per cent, with BAE possessing an option to buy out VT after 3 years.[48]

Another agreement in 2007 linked to the CVF programme was the acquisition by Babcock International, a naval and general military services company, of Devonport Management Ltd, the owner of the Devonport naval dockyard. DML, the sole supplier of submarine refitting and deep maintenance of submarines for the British MOD, was bought from a joint venture in which the US company KBR had a 51 per cent stake. Its sale was in part the result of British MOD concerns regarding the flotation of KBR by Halliburton in December 2006. The British Government warned that it might use its 'special share' in DML to seize KBR's stake in the joint venture if it felt that British

---

[46] The Treaty between the Government of the United States of America and the Government of the United Kingdom of Great Britain and Northern Ireland concerning Defense Trade Cooperation was signed on 21 and 26 June 2007; its text is available at <http://www.state.gov/t/pm/rls/othr/misc/92770.htm>. See also Smith, K., 'US and UK reach defence accord', *Jane's Defence Weekly*, 27 June 2007, p. 18. The current version of the International Traffic in Arms Regulations, issued under the 1976 Arms Export Control Act, is available at <http://pmddtc.state.gov/itar_index.htm>.

[47] The Maritime Industrial Strategy forms part of the Defence Industrial Strategy. British Ministry of Defence (MOD), *Defence Industrial Strategy: Defence White Paper*, Cm 6697 (MOD: London, Dec. 2005), pp. 68–77.

[48] VT Group, 'VT Group and BAE Systems to create a world-class provider of naval ships and through-life support', Press release, 25 July 2007, <http://www.vtplc.com/newsandevents/newsdetails.asp?ItemID=709>; Anderson, G., 'VT, BAE confirm alliance as UK approves carrier', *Jane's Defence Weekly*, 1 Aug. 2007, p. 22; and Anderson, G., 'Drayson stalls CVF Main Gate until industry consolidation occurs', *Jane's Defence Weekly*, 3 Jan. 2007, p. 19. There are reports that the CVF programme may be delayed by 18 months or more due to defence budget shortages, possibly throwing this merger into doubt. Chuter, A., 'U.K. may delay carrier 18 months', *Defense News*, 10 Jan. 2008.

security interests would be jeopardized by the flotation of KBR.[49] On the basis of 2006 figures, the acquisition will double Babcock's arms sales.

In France, the state-owned shipbuilders DCN and Thales finalized a long-negotiated tie-up of their naval activities, following approval from the European Commission. Under the terms of the deal, DCN acquired Thales's naval activities in France, but none of Thales's operations in other countries.[50] In return, Thales acquired a 25 per cent stake in DCN, with an option to increase this stake to 35 per cent in 2009. The operations acquired by DCN were valued at €514 million ($645 million), and Thales also paid €55 million ($69 million) as part of the deal to acquire the stake in DCN. DCN will henceforth be known as DCNS.[51]

The French Government welcomed the transaction not only as a major consolidation of the French naval industry but also as a step towards broader European naval integration. However, according to DCN's Chief Executive, Jean-Marie Poimbœuf, this latter goal is likely to be 3–5 years away. Despite a picture of 'duplication and fragmentation' in the industry, Poimbœuf believes that the differing requirements among buyer governments combined with current high levels of naval construction mean that there are doubts as to whether the political will to undertake integration exists.[52]

Developments in EU military–industrial policy

During 2007 there was a continued political push within the EU for cross-border integration of national arms industries and for open and cooperative intra-EU arms procurement. This has been driven by doubts about the long-term viability of maintaining parallel national capabilities in military research, technology and production given the flat military budgets in EU countries.

The defence ministers of the participating member states of the European Defence Agency (EDA) agreed two policy documents in 2007: one on a strategy to build a European defence-technological and -industrial base and the other on a framework for a European strategy on military research and technology (R&T).[53]

---

[49] British Office of Fair Trading, 'Completed acquisition by Babcock International Group plc of Devonport Management Limited', Decision, 3 Sep. 2007, <http://www.oft.gov.uk/advice_and_resources/resource_base/Mergers_home/decisions/2007/Babcock>; Anderson, G., Hammick, D. and Smith, K., 'Babcock agrees to purchase DML', Jane's Defence Industry, June 2007, p. 13; and 'In brief: mergers and acquisitions', Jane's Defence Industry, Aug. 2007, p. 14.

[50] The acquired units are Thales Naval France, a 50% stake in the Armaris naval company and a 35% stake in MOPA2, the prime contractor for PA2, France's planned new aircraft carrier. This makes DCN the sole shareholder of Armaris and MOPA2. DCN, 'The consolidation of naval activities in France between Thales and DCN is operational', Press release, 29 Mar. 2007, <http://www.dcn.fr/us/medias/popup.php?id=148>.

[51] Tran, P., 'Thales pays less than expected for DCN stake', Defense News, 2 Apr. 2007; and Lewis, J. A. C., 'Thales acquires 25% slice of DCN', Jane's Defence Weekly, 11 Apr. 2007, p. 18.

[52] Smith, K., 'DCN, Thales and the French government sign naval accord', Jane's Defence Industry, May 2007, p. 16; and Smith, K., 'Consolidation: no plain sailing', Jane's Defence Weekly, 21 Feb. 2007, p. 23.

[53] The participating member states are the EU member states other than Denmark. For a full list and a brief description of the EDA see annex B in this volume.

The defence-technological and -industrial base strategy calls for a 'more integrated, less duplicative, and more interdependent' European military-technological and -industrial base.[54] Among other measures to be taken to achieve this, EU states will consolidate demand by adhering to a Capability Development Plan,[55] coordinate national equipment requirements, make procurement processes more transparent and open to intra-EU competition, and increase collaborative arms procurement. The strategy also calls for collaboration to start early, at the requirement specification and R&T stages, and to move away from *juste retour* policies, whereby each country's arms industry receives work from a project in proportion to its government's financial contribution to the project.

The EDA framework for an R&T strategy proposes the development of a prioritized list of technologies on which to focus R&T efforts.[56] It also proposes the means to achieve this, including increasing integration of the military and civilian R&T bases, improvements in the effectiveness of R&T collaboration and setting R&T and procurement expenditure targets.[57] The latter targets were spelled out as being: to raise the shares of military expenditure spent on procurement (including research and development, R&D) to 20 per cent (from 19.4 per cent in 2006) and on R&T to 2 per cent (from 1.4 per cent); to raise the share of arms procurement expenditure spent on collaborative European armament programmes to 35 per cent (from 21 per cent in 2006); and to raise the share of defence R&T expenditure spent on collaborative European programmes to 20 per cent (from 10 per cent).[58] One motivation for this is the comparison with the USA: according to EDA statistics, in 2006 combined EU military R&D spending was one-sixth of the US level and military R&T spending was less than one-fifth of the US level.[59]

---

[54] European Defence Agency, 'A strategy for a European defence technological and industrial base', Brussels, 14 May 2007, <http://eda.europa.eu/genericitem.aspx?id=211>, p. 2.

[55] Key EU documents on capabilities include the 1999 Helsinki Headline Goal, the 2001 European Capabilities Action Plan and the 2004 Headline Goal 2010. Helsinki European Council, Presidency Conclusions, 10–11 Dec. 1999, <http://europa.eu/european_council/conclusions/>, Annex 1 to Annex IV; Council of the European Union, General Affairs, Statement on improving European military capabilities, 2386th Council meeting, Brussels, 19–20 Nov. 2001, <http://europa.eu/rapid/pressReleasesAction.do?reference=PRES/01/414>; and Council of the European Union, General Affairs, Headline Goal 2010, 17 May 2004. On the EDA's work on a Capability Development Plan see <http://eda.europa.eu/generic item.aspx?area=Organisation&id=115>.

[56] European Defence Agency, 'Framework for a European defence research & technology strategy', 19 Nov. 2007, <http://eda.europa.eu/newsitem.aspx?id=287>, p. 3.

[57] European Defence Agency (note 56), pp. 4–7.

[58] European Defence Agency, 'EU ministers adopt framework for joint European strategy in defence R&T', Press release, 19 Nov. 2007, <http://eda.europa.eu/newsitem.aspx?id=287>.

[59] In 2006 EDA participating member states spent €9.7 billion ($12.2 billion) on military R&D, compared with US spending of €58 billion ($73 billion). For the R&T subcategory, EDA participating member states' spending was €2.5 billion ($3.1 billion) compared to US spending of €13.6 billion ($17.1 billion). European Defence Agency, 'European–United States defence expenditure in 2006', Brussels, 21 Dec. 2007, <http://eda.europa.eu/facts.aspx>. The EDA defines R&T as 'expenditure for basic research, applied research and technology demonstration for defence purposes', while the broader category of R&D covers all 'programmes up to the point where expenditure for production of equipment starts to be incurred'.

The European Commission—with its focus on promoting a competitive intra-EU market—presented in 2007 two proposals for new directives to further that goal in the arms industry. The first proposed directive sets out a common set of rules for public procurement in the military and security sectors.[60] If adopted, it would allow for a flexible set of procedures that takes account of the specific nature of these markets and addresses concerns such as security of information and security of supply. By removing the justification that general EU procurement rules are unsuitable for arms procurement, the Commission aims to reduce the number of times that member states invoke Article 296 of the 1957 Treaty of Rome—which allows a country to exempt arms procurement contracts from EU competition rules in order to protect 'essential interests of its security'.[61] The objective of the second proposed directive is to relax export control regulations for intra-EU transfers of military equipment and services.[62]

The EDA has made some progress in facilitating collaborative EU projects, although so far only for contracts with a low value. By December 2007, eight cross-border contracts worth €44 million ($55 million) had been awarded by being advertised on the EDA Electronic Bulletin Board on Defence Contracts Opportunities (EBB).[63] Collaborative research programmes have also been initiated under EDA auspices for Software Defined Radio (SDR) and for the Joint Investment Programme on Force Protection (JIP-FP). The first contracts for the JIP-FP—which is worth €55 million over three years—were signed in December 2007 and do not involve *juste retour* arrangements.[64]

However, doubts remain, including among senior EU defence officials, as to how extensive changes in the European arms industry will actually be. The outgoing EDA Chief Executive, Nick Witney, spoke in November 2007 of 'massive inertia' and risk-aversion in the military sector, and a failure of

[60] European Commission, Proposal for a Directive of the European Parliament and of the Council on the coordination of procedures for the award of certain public works contracts, public supply contracts and public service contracts in the fields of defence and security, COM(2007) 766 final, Brussels, 5 Dec. 2007.

[61] An earlier interpretative communication had clarified the limits for the application of Article 296. European Commission, Interpretative Communication on the application of Article 296 of the Treaty in the field of defence procurement, COM(2006) 779 final, Brussels, 7 Dec. 2006. The Treaty Establishing the European Economic Community (Treaty of Rome) was signed on 25 Mar. 1957 and entered into force on 1 Jan. 1958. The formal title was changed in 1992 to the Treaty Establishing the European Community. The original text and the current text as amended are available at <http://eur-lex.europa.eu/en/treaties/index.htm>. Article 296 of the current treaty was Article 223 of the original treaty. See also Sköns and Surry (note 9), pp. 371–72.

[62] European Commission, Proposal for a Directive of the European Parliament and of the Council on simplifying terms and conditions of transfers of defence-related products within the Community, COM(2007) 765 final, Brussels, 5 Dec. 2007. See also chapter 11 in this volume, section III.

[63] European Defence Agency, 'EDA welcomes Commission communication on EU defence industry and market', Press release, 5 Dec. 2007, <http://eda.europa.eu/newsitem.aspx?id=299>. The EBB is at <http://eda.europa.eu/ebbweb/>.

[64] The specific contracts are for individual protective armour, a multi-sensor anti-sniper system and stand-off detection of chemical, biological, radiological, nuclear and explosive (CBRNE) devices. European Defence Agency, 'EDA signs first contracts under R&T Joint Investment Programme on Force Protection', Press release, 14 Dec. 2007, <http://eda.europa.eu/newsitem.aspx?id=301>.

leadership in translating policy agreements into practical changes.[65] A recent report by the EU Institute for Security Studies sets out many of the problems in achieving successful collaborative arms projects.[66] This includes a lack of coordination of capability requirements—even within the shared 2010 Head-line Goal states often have varying requirements based on their differing military strategies or force structures, and there are difficulties in synchronizing timescales for delivery of new systems. Another major problem highlighted in the report is the continued attachment of producer countries to maintaining their own domestic military–industrial bases and the promotion of 'national champions', which are often reinforced by the close links between government and industry. This can undermine nominal commitments to more open competition—for example, the precise demands of a government procurement contract can be worded to favour domestic industry. *Juste retour* is also cited by the report as a major obstacle to efficient collaboration.

There has also been negative reaction to the EU integration and competition agenda from some of the new EU member states—in particular Poland—amid fears that their industries would be unable to compete with those of Western Europe in an open EU arms market.[67] This has been reinforced by the pressure from the European Commission on the Polish Government to cease subsidizing its shipbuilding industry.[68] Given the increasing integration between the British and US arms industries and the implications of closer European cooperation for the privileged access of British companies to US markets and technologies, the UK may lose interest in increasing European cooperation. For example, the UK is not taking part in the SDR or JIP-FP programmes.[69]

Thus, despite the policy push by EU institutions and the economic and technological imperatives towards integration in order to maintain viable European industries in the face of US competition, there is little evidence that this will be sufficient to overcome traditional commitments to national arms industries on the part of European governments.

Concerns remain among some critics that the push for EU armaments cooperation is part of an increasingly military-oriented agenda on the part of the EU. One element of the European military-technological and -industrial base strategy that will cause particular concern in some circles is the call for

[65] See e.g. Anderson, G., 'Departing Witney refers to "massive inertia" in Europe's defence industry', *Jane's Defence Industry*, Nov. 2007, p. 4.

[66] Darnis, J.-P. et al., *Lessons Learned from European Defence Equipment Programmes*, Occasional Paper no. 69 (EU Institute for Security Studies: Paris, Oct. 2007).

[67] E.g. Lentowicz, Z, 'Polish labor unionist expresses concern about EU's single arms production market', *Rzeczpospolita*, 18 Dec. 2007, English translation in International Security & Counter Terrorism Reference Center, World News Connection, National Technical Information Service (NTIS), US Department of Commerce.

[68] Thorpe, N., 'Solidarity runs dry', *From Our Own Correspondent*, BBC Radio 4, 28 July 2007, Transcript available at <http://news.bbc.co.uk/2/6919518.stm>.

[69] Graham Jordan and Tim Williams have argued that the differences between national visions of the EDA's purpose is one cause of worsening relations between the UK and the EDA: the UK saw the EDA as a means of identifying and finding solutions to military capability gaps, while other countries saw it as a means of promoting armaments cooperation. Jordan, G. and Williams, T., 'Hope deferred? The European Defence Agency after three years', *RUSI Journal*, vol. 152, no. 3 (June 2007).

armaments research to make increased use of resources from beyond the military establishments and the arms industry—including from universities—which could create ethical concerns for researchers and academic institutions.[70]

State-led arms industry consolidation in Russia

Among other moves towards more centralized state control in the Russian arms industry, in 2007 the Russian Government took further steps to consolidate the aircraft- and shipbuilding industries under large state-owned holding companies.

The United Aircraft Corporation (UAC), which consolidates most of Russia's civil and military fixed-wing aircraft design and production assets, began operation in 2007.[71] The company, which is majority-owned by the Russian state, will include 20 companies. The largest component of UAC is Sukhoi, which contributed 54 per cent of the company's initial assets of 96 billion roubles ($3.5 billion). The UAC also has a 38 per cent stake in the Irkut Corporation, 86 per cent of Ilyushin, 91 per cent of Tupolev and 26 per cent of each of the KnAAPO and NAPO aircraft production plants.[72] Although delayed, MiG and Kazan Aviation (KAPO) are also due to be incorporated into UAC.[73]

There appear to be several goals behind the creation of UAC. One is for the state to take a more direct management role in the industry. This has been underlined by the choice of Sergei Ivanov, First Deputy Prime Minister and former defence minister, as Chairman of the Board of Directors.[74] Another goal is to achieve cost savings. There is chronic overcapacity in the sector, which is described by Irkut as being 'overcrowded with design bureaus, production plants and entities'.[75] A third goal is to channel investment into an industry struggling with ageing infrastructure and machinery. In March 2007 Ivanov announced plans for $7.7 billion of state investment in arms industry

---

[70] See e.g. Hagelin, B., 'Science- and technology-based military innovation: the United States and Europe', *SIPRI Yearbook 2004: Armaments, Disarmament and International Security* (Oxford University Press: Oxford, 2004), pp. 300–303. Another study describes the increasing use of university science and engineering departments for military research, especially in the UK, with potentially negative consequences for academic freedom. Langley, C., Parkinson, S. and Webber, P., *More Scientists in The Laboratory: The Militarisation of Science and Technology—An Update* (Scientists for Global Responsibility: Folkestone, Aug. 2007).

[71] UAC was officially registered as a joint stock company in Nov. 2006, following a Feb. 2006 decree by President Putin. The Presidential Decree 'on the joint stock company "the United Aircraft Construction Corporation"', Decree no. 140, was signed on 20 Feb. 2006. The text of the decree is available at <http://document.kremlin.ru/doc.asp?ID=032432> (in Russian).

[72] United Aircraft Corporation, 'About UAC', <http://www.uacrussia.ru/en/corporation/>; and Abdullaev, N., 'A new Russian aerospace giant?', *Defense News*, 20 Nov. 2006.

[73] Komarov, M. and Barrie, D., 'Revolution deferred', *Aviation Week & Space Technology*, 24–31 Dec. 2007, p. 28.

[74] Abdullaev (note 72).

[75] Irkut Corporation, *Annual Report 2006* (Irkut Corporation: Moscow, 2007), p. 23.

restructuring.[76] In addition, an initial public offering is expected in 2008 to attract private investment in UAC, although the Russian Government will keep at least a 51 per cent stake.[77]

The United Shipbuilding Corporation (USC) was established as an entirely state-owned company by a presidential decree of March 2007 and was formally registered in November 2007.[78] USC amalgamates all wholly or partially state-owned shipyards and design bureaus for surface ships. Decision-making responsibility, which is currently dispersed through several agencies in the sector, will be centralized.[79]

A third state-owned conglomerate, Rostekhnologii, was established by an act of parliament of November 2007.[80] It combines Rosoboronexport, the state arms export company, with several military and civilian production operations, including Oboronprom (itself a holding company for Russia's helicopter industry), Defensive Systems (an air defence and military electronics company), Oboronpromlizing (an engineering equipment supplier), AvtoVAZ (a car maker) and VSMPO-AVISMA (a titanium producer).[81] Rostekhnologii's Director General, Sergei Chemezov (formerly head of Rosoboronexport), aims to use the new structure to boost R&D and attract private capital (although the state will retain a controlling interest of at least 25 per cent plus one share), and to coordinate Russia's arms export activities with the industrial supply chain.[82]

Some observers are concerned that all these moves towards more centralized state control, combined with new regulations designating a large number of 'strategic enterprises' in which foreign ownership will be restricted, will make it harder to attract private investment.[83]

In parallel with this process of consolidation and centralization within the Russian arms industry, industrial and technological cooperation is beginning to be pursued with other countries' industries. In 2007 the Indian and Russian governments signed agreements for the joint development of a fifth generation

[76] Anderson, G., 'Ivanov reveals extent of Russian defence industrial restructuring', *Jane's Defence Weekly*, 21 Mar. 2007, p. 20.

[77] Smith, K., 'Russian UABC reveals scheme for IPO in 2008', *Jane's Defence Weekly*, 7 Mar. 2007, p. 22.

[78] The Presidential Decree 'on the joint stock company "the United Shipbuilding Corporation"', Decree no. 394, was signed on 21 Mar. 2007. The text of the decree is available at <http://document. kremlin.ru/doc.asp?ID=038538> (in Russian).

[79] Alyakrinskaya, N., 'Big & bad boats are back', *Moscow News Weekly*, 13 Apr. 2007; REGNUM News Agency, 'Registratsiya Ob"edinennoi sudostroitel'noi korporatsii zavershilas' (Sankt-Peterburg)' [Registration of the United Shipbuilding Corporation completed (St Petersburg)], 19 Nov. 2007, <http:// www.regnum.ru/news/917314.html>; and Abdullaev, N., 'Shipyards next in line for Russian consolidation', *Defense News*, 2 Apr. 2007.

[80] The Russian Federal Law 'on the state corporation "Rostekhnologii"', Law no. 270 of 23 Nov. 2007, is available at <http://document.kremlin.ru/doc.asp?ID=042960> (in Russian).

[81] 'Rostekhnologii brings together Russia's best defence assets', ITAR-TASS, 26 Nov. 2007.

[82] 'Russian official talks about new state corporation dealing with arms exports', *Nezavisimaya gazeta*, 29 Nov. 2007, English translation in International Security & Counter Terrorism Reference Center, World News Connection, NTIS; and Petrov, N., 'Rostekhnologii: defense industry super-corporation', RIA Novosti, 4 Dec. 2007, <http://en.rian.ru/analysis/20071204/90845337.html>.

[83] Anderson, G., 'Russia's defence and aerospace industries and the new era of nationalisation', *RUSI Defence Systems*, vol. 9, no. 3 (spring 2007).

combat aircraft and a multi-role transport aircraft.[84] Moves were also made towards cooperation with West European companies: Rosoboronexport and Thales signed a memorandum of understanding in June 2007 on technical, industrial and commercial cooperation in the naval sector;[85] and Rosoboronexport and the shipbuilding company DCNS (formerly DCN) signed a contract in November 2007 for joint research projects between DCNS and the Krylov Shipbuilding Research Institute, St Petersburg.[86]

IV. Conclusions

The trend of increasing arms sales in the SIPRI Top 100 companies continued in 2006, with the majority of the growth coming from US companies that have benefited from the continuing rise in US military spending, including for the conflicts in Afghanistan and Iraq. These foreign military operations have not only generated increased demand for specific requirements, such as armoured vehicles, body armour and military consumables, but have also involved an overall increase in the USA's core military budget, to the benefit of the arms industry.[87] A few major West European companies also increased their arms sales, with the majority of the increase accounted for by three companies: EADS, BAE Systems and SAFRAN. Strong export orders meant that Russian aircraft and missile companies also increased their arms sales.

The number of major merger and acquisition deals increased in 2007, with the great majority of activity—including at least six of the largest deals—focused on the growing US arms industry. Of non-US companies, generally only those from the UK have been allowed to take advantage of this by acquiring US companies. The two largest acquisitions in 2007 were transatlantic deals between US and British companies: the takeover of the US company Armor Holdings by BAE Systems and the acquisition by General Electric of the British company Smiths Aerospace.

In the European Union, there was continued activity on the policy front to promote intra-European integration, driven by actual and foreseen difficulties in competing with US companies. However, doubts remain as to the degree to which governments will be willing to move away from protecting their national military–industrial bases to promote integration. In Russia, two new giant state-owned holding companies were created in the arms industry: Rostekhnologii and the United Shipbuilding Corporation. A third, the United Aircraft Corporation, began operations. The new conglomerates represent a more direct state role in the management of the arms industry, the practical consequences of which have yet to become clear.

---

[84] See chapter 7 in this volume, section III.

[85] Thales, 'Thales and Rosoboronexport signed a memorandum of understanding for cooperation in the naval field', Press release, 29 June 2007.

[86] DCNS, 'Rosoboronexport and DCNS sign a purchase general contract for R&D', Press release, 25 Oct. 2007.

[87] See chapter 5 in this volume, section III.

Appendix 6A. The SIPRI Top 100 arms-producing companies, 2006

SAM PERLO-FREEMAN and THE SIPRI ARMS INDUSTRY NETWORK*

I. Selection criteria and sources of data

Table 6A.2 lists the world's 100 largest arms-producing companies (excluding Chinese companies), ranked by their arms sales in 2006 (the SIPRI Top 100 for 2006). The table contains information on the companies' arms sales in 2005 and 2006 and their total sales, profit and employment in 2006. It includes public and private companies, but excludes manufacturing or maintenance units of the armed services. Only companies with operational activities in the field of military goods and services are listed, not holding or investment companies. Chinese companies are excluded because of the lack of data. Companies from other countries might also have been included at the lower end of the list had sufficient data been available.

Publicly available information on arms sales and other financial and employment data on the arms industry worldwide are limited. The sources of data for table 6A.2 include: company annual reports and websites, a SIPRI questionnaire, and news published in the business sections of newspapers, in military journals and by Internet news services specializing in military matters. Press releases, marketing reports, government publications of prime contract awards and country surveys were also consulted. Where no data are available from these sources, estimates have been made by SIPRI. The scope of the data and the geographical coverage are largely determined by the availability of information. All data are continuously revised and updated and may change between different editions of the SIPRI Yearbook.

II. Definitions

Arms sales are defined by SIPRI as sales of military goods and services to military customers, including both sales for domestic procurement and sales for export. Military goods and services are those which are designed specifically for military purposes and the technologies related to such goods and services. Military goods are military-specific equipment, and do not include general purpose goods, such as oil, electricity, office computers, uniforms and boots. Military services are also military-specific. They include: technical services such as information technology, maintenance, repair and overhaul, and operational support; services related to the oper-

* Participants in the network for 2006 were: Ken Epps (Project Ploughshares, Waterloo, Ontario), Giovanni Gasparini (Istituto Affari Internazionali, Rome), Gülay Günlük-Şenesen (Istanbul University), Jean-Paul Hébert (Centre Interdisciplinaire de Recherches sur la Paix et d'Etudes Stratégiques, Paris), Shinichi Kohno (Mitsubishi Research Institute, Tokyo), Christos Kollias (University of Thessaly, Volos), Pere Ortega (Centre d'Estudis per la Pau J. M. Delàs, Barcelona) and Ruslan Pukhov (Centre for Analysis of Strategies and Technologies, Moscow)

Table 6A.1. Types of military services provided by private companies

Service	Description	Example companies
Research and analysis		
Research and development	Basic research and technology development	SAIC, CACI, Battelle, Mitre
Analysis and planning	Strategic research and consulting, threat analysis, war gaming, etc.	SAIC, Booz Allen Hamilton
Technical services		
Information technology services	Software development, IT systems support, infrastructure development simulation, etc.	EDS, Computer Sciences Corp., most major prime contractors
System support	Supporting operation of military equipment and systems	Prime contractors, research companies
Equipment maintenance, repair and overhaul		Most major prime contractors
Facilities management	Integrated management of military bases	Babcock, Serco, Northrop Grumman, Chugach Alaska Corp.
Operational support		
Logistics	Supply to armed forces in operational conditions	Halliburton
Training	Simulation, managing firing ranges, weapons systems training	L-3 Communications, Northrop Grumman, Lockheed Martin, DynCorp
Intelligence services	Intelligence gathering, surveillance, interrogation, counterterrorism, interpretation	CACI, SAIC, Booz Allen Hamilton
Weapon destruction and disposal	Unexploded ordnance clearance, clearing of firing ranges, weapons collection and destruction, demining	Washington Group, Parsons, Shaw Group
Armed force		
Armed security	Protection of diplomats and civilian convoys in conflict zones	Blackwater, DynCorp, Armor Group

Source: Perlo-Freeman, S. and Sköns, E., 'The private military services industry', SIPRI Research Paper, June 2008, <http://books.sipri.org/product_info?c_product_id=361>.

ation of the armed forces, such as intelligence, training, logistics and facilities management; and armed security in conflict zones. They do not include the peacetime provision of purely civilian services, such as health care, cleaning and catering, and transportation, but supply services to operationally deployed forces are included. The SIPRI Arms Industry Database, from which the SIPRI Top 100 is drawn, has been updated to include a more systematic coverage of the military services segment of the arms industry, in accordance with the definition given above.[1] Table 6A.1 lists the

[1] See also Perlo-Freeman, S. and Sköns, E., 'The private military services industry', SIPRI Research Paper, June 2008, <http://books.sipri.org/product_info?c_product_id=361>.

main types of military service activities performed by companies in the SIPRI database, illustrating the application of the arms sales definition in relation to military services.

This definition of arms sales serves as a guideline; in practice it is difficult to apply. Nor is there any good alternative, since no generally agreed standard definition exists. The data on arms sales in table 6A.2 often reflect only what each company considers to be the defence share of its total sales. The comparability of the company arms sales figures given in table 6A.2 is therefore limited.

Data on total sales, profit and employment are for entire companies, not for arms-producing divisions alone. All data are for consolidated sales, including those of national and foreign subsidiaries. The profit data represent profit after taxes. Employment data are year-end figures, except for those companies that publish only a yearly average. All data are presented on the financial year basis reported by the company in its annual report.

III. Calculations

Arms sales are sometimes estimated by SIPRI. In some cases SIPRI uses the figure for the total sales of a 'defence' division, although the division may also have some, unspecified, civil sales. When the company does not report a sales figure for a defence division or similar entity, estimates can sometimes be made based on data on contract awards, information on the company's current arms production programmes and figures provided by company officials in media or other reports.

The data for arms sales are used as an approximation of the annual value of arms production. For most companies this is realistic. The main exception is shipbuilding companies. For these companies there is a significant discrepancy between the value of annual production and annual sales because of the long lead (production) time of ships and the low production run (number). Some shipbuilding companies provide estimates of the value of their annual production. These data are then used by SIPRI for those companies.

All data are collected in local currency and at current prices. For conversion from local currencies to US dollars, SIPRI uses the International Monetary Fund (IMF) annual average of market exchange rates (as provided in *International Financial Statistics*). The data in table 6A.2 are provided in current dollars. Changes between years in these data are difficult to interpret because the change in dollar values is made up of several components: the change in arms sales, the rate of inflation and, for sales conducted in local currency, fluctuations in the exchange rate. Sales on the international arms market are often conducted in dollars. Fluctuations in exchange rates then do not have an impact on the dollar values but affect instead the value in local currency. If the value of the dollar declines, then the company's revenue in local currency falls and, if its production inputs are paid for in local currency—which most often is the case—this has a negative impact on the company's profit margins. Calculations in constant dollar terms are difficult to interpret for the same reasons. Without knowing the relative shares of arms sales derived from domestic procurement and from arms exports, it is impossible to interpret the exact meaning and implications of the arms sales data. These data should therefore be used with caution. This is particularly true for countries with strongly fluctuating exchange rates.

Table 6A.2. The SIPRI Top 100 arms-producing companies in the world excluding China, 2006[a]

Figures for sales and profits are in US$ m., at current prices and exchange rates.

Rank[b] 2006	Rank[b] 2005	Company (parent company)	Country	Sector[c]	Arms sales 2006	Arms sales 2005	Total sales, 2006	Arms sales as % of total sales, 2006	Profit, 2006	Employment, 2006
1	1	Boeing	USA	Ac El Mi Sp	30 690	29 590	61 530	50	2 215	154 000
2	2	Lockheed Martin	USA	Ac El Mi Sp	28 120	26 200	39 620	71	2 529	140 000
3	4	BAE Systems[d]	UK	A Ac El Mi MV SA/A Sh	24 060	23 230	25 327	95	1 189	88 600
4	3	Northrop Grumman[e]	USA	Ac El Mi Sh Sp	23 650	23 330	30 148	78	1 542	122 200
5	5	Raytheon	USA	El Mi	19 530	18 500	20 291	96	1 283	80 000
6	6	General Dynamics	USA	A El MV Sh	18 770	16 570	24 063	78	1 856	81 000
7	7	EADS[f]	W. Eur.	Ac El Mi Sp	12 600	9 580	49 478	25	124	116 810
S	–	BAE Systems Inc. (BAE Systems, UK)	USA	A El MV SA/A	11 280	..	11 283	100	..	51 700
8	10	L-3 Communications	USA	El	9 980	8 470	12 477	80	526	63 700
9	9	Finmeccanica	Italy	A Ac El Mi MV SA/A	8 990	8 770	15 649	57	1 280	58 060
10	8	Thales	France	El Mi SA/A	8 240	8 940	12 878	64	487	52 160
11	11	United Technologies	USA	El Eng	7 650	6 840	47 829	16	3 732	214 500
12	13	Halliburton[g]	USA	Comp (Oth)	6 630	6 040	22 576	29	2 348	104 000
S	S	KBR (Halliburton)[g]	USA	Comp (Oth)	6 630	6 040	9 633	69	168	56 000
13	12	Computer Sciences Corp.	USA	Comp (Oth)	6 300	6 100	14 857	42	..	79 000
14	14	SAIC[h]	USA	Comp (Oth)	5 800	5 060	8 294	70	391	44 000
15	15	Honeywell	USA	El	4 400	4 300	31 367	14	2 083	118 000
S	S	MBDA (BAE Systems, UK/ EADS, W. Europe/ Finmeccanica, Italy)[i]	W. Eur.	Mi	4 140	4 080	4 141	100	..	10 400
16	17	Rolls-Royce[j]	UK	Eng	3 960	3 470	13 167	30	1 829	38 000
17	20	SAFRAN	France	Comp (Ac El Eng)	3 780	2 630	13 602	28	222	61 360

Rank[b] 2006	Rank[b] 2005	Company (parent company)	Country	Sector[c]	Arms sales 2006	Arms sales 2005	Total sales, 2006	Arms sales as % of total sales, 2006	Profit, 2006	Employment, 2006
S	S	Pratt & Whitney (United Technologies)	USA	Eng	3 650	3 280	11 100	33	..	38 420
18	16	DCN[k]	France	Sh	3 400	3 520	3 396	100	279	12 460
19	18	ITT	USA	El	3 290	3 190	7 808	42	581	37 500
20	19	General Electric	USA	Eng	3 260	3 000	163 000	2	20 829	319 000
S	S	AgustaWestland (Finmeccanica)	Italy	Ac	2 820	2 560	3 422	82	213	8 900
21	29	DRS Technologies[l]	USA	El	2 740	1 670	2 821	97	127	9 670
S	S	Eurocopter (EADS, W. Europe)	France	Ac	2 580	2 120	4 772	54	0	13 420
22	22	Mitsubishi Heavy Industries[m]	Japan	Ac Mi MV Sh	2 390	2 190	26 376	9	420	62 200
23	24	Alliant Techsystems	USA	SA/A	2 350	2 060	3 565	66	184	16 000
S	S	MBDA France (MBDA, W. Eur.)	France	Mi	2 260	2 040	2 265	100	124	4 420
24	23	Saab	Sweden	Ac El Mi	2 250	2 110	2 855	79	..	13 560
25	26	Textron	USA	Ac El Eng MV	2 180	1 800	11 490	19	706	40 000
26	31	EDS[n]	USA	Comp (Oth)	2 170	1 570	21 268	10	470	131 000
S	S	Selex Sensors and Airborne Systems (Finmeccanica)	Italy	Comp (El)	2 060	1 580	2 183	94	98	7 170
27	25	Rockwell Collins	USA	El	2 040	1 810	3 863	53	477	19 000
28	30	Almaz-Antei[o]	Russia	Mi	1 960	1 590	2 287	86	181	82 790
29	42	Armor Holdings	USA	Comp (MV Oth)	1 930	1 190	2 361	82	134 562	8 150
30	33	Israel Aerospace Industries[p]	Israel	Ac El Mi	1 820	1 520	2 800	65	130	15 000
S	S	Sikorsky (United Technologies)	USA	Ac	1 820	1 550	3 200	57	..	11 420
31	27	Rheinmetall	Germany	A El MV SA/A	1 810	1 740	4 553	40	154	18 800
32	41	AM General[q]	USA	MV	1 700	1 280		..	..	..
33	37	Harris	USA	El	1 660	1 440	3 475	48	238	13 900
34	39	ThyssenKrupp[r]	Germany	Sh	1 620	1 390	59 128	3	2 138	187 590
35	32	QinetiQ	UK	Comp (Oth)	1 610	1 550	2 115	76	127	13 500
36	28	CEA	France	Oth	1 590	1 710	4 141	38	..	15 330

Rank 2008	Rank 2007	Company	Country	Sector	Arms sales 2008	Arms sales 2007	Total sales 2008	Arms sales as % of total	Profit	Employment
37	21	Dassault Aviation	France	Ac	1 570	2 210	4 143	38	353	11 930
38	46	Hindustan Aeronautics[s]	India	Ac Mi	1 550	1 100	1 717	90	385	..
39	38	URS Corp.	USA	El	1 530	1 410	4 240	36	113	26 000
40	36	Smiths Group	UK	El	1 480	1 450	6 482	23	45	31 320
41	35	Goodrich Corp.	USA	Comp (Ac)	1 470	1 510	5 878	25	482	23 400
S	S	Alenia Aeronautica (Finmeccanica)	Italy	Ac	1 450	1 390	2 394	60	65	12 140
42	51	Elbit Systems[t]	Israel	El	1 400	1 000	1 523	92	72	8 030
43	45	VT Group[u]	UK	Sh	1 400	1 170	1 848	76	93	12 900
44	47	Oshkosh Truck	USA	MV	1 320	1 060	3 427	38	326	9 390
45	40	Indian Ordnance Factories[v]	India	A SA/A	1 300	1 300	1 589	82	..	116 910
S	S	EADS Astrium (EADS, W. Eur.)[w]	France	Sp	1 290	960	4 030	32	..	11 930
46	43	CACI International	USA	Comp (Oth)	1 280	1 190	1 755	73	85	10 400
47	60	Krauss-Maffei Wegmann[x]	Germany	MV	1 190	750	1 255	95	..	2 800
48	49	Serco[y]	UK	Oth	1 170	1 030	4 688	25	146	40 090
49	50	Cobham	UK	Comp (Ac El)	1 140	1 010	1 869	61	273	9 510
50	44	Kawasaki Heavy Industries[m]	Japan	Ac Eng Mi Sh	1 120	1 180	12 366	9	256	29 210
51	53	Navantia	Spain	Sh	1 110	970	1 404	79	-44	5 560
52	56	ManTech International Corp.[z]	USA	Comp (Oth)	1 080	930	1 137	95	51	5 600
53	48	Mitsubishi Electric[m]	Japan	El Mi	1 010	1 040	33 143	3	1 058	102 840
54	59	Rafael[aa]	Israel	Ac Mi SA/A Oth	950	800	1 001	95	26	..
55	57	Nexter[bb]	France	A MV SA/A	900	910	903	100	98	2 490
56	58	DynCorp International[cc]	USA	Comp (Oth)	900	870	2 082	43	27	14 000
57	55	ST Engineering	Singapore	Ac El MV SA/A Sh	880	940	2 822	31	280	17 000
58	62	Diehl	Germany	Mi SA/A	850	720	2 669	32	..	10 440
S	S	General Dynamics Land Systems Canada (General Dynamics, USA)	Canada	MV	820	420	..	..	..	1 700
S	S	Devonport Management Ltd (KBR, USA)[dd]	UK	Sh	780	800	835	94	59	5 190
59	70	Babcock International Group[ee]	UK	Sh Oth	760	610	1 818	42	83	9 640
60	66	Irkut Corp.[o]	Russia	Ac	740	630	832	89	44	17 620

Rank[b] 2006	2005	Company (parent company)	Country	Sector[c]	Arms sales 2006	Arms sales 2005	Total sales, 2006	Arms sales as % of total sales, 2006	Profit, 2006	Employment, 2006
61	64	Indra	Spain	El	740	670	2 447	30	143	19 500
62	61	GKN	UK	Comp (Ac)	740	740	7 069	10	326	36 120
63	63	Samsung[ff]	S. Korea	A El MV Sh	720	710	87 841	1	8 150	222 000
64	52	NEC[m]	Japan	El	710	980	42 377	2	-86	154 180
65	76	Bharat Electronics	India	El	660	560	872	76	158	. .
66	69	Fincantieri	Italy	Sh	660	610	3 051	22	74	9 400
67	71	EDO Corp.[gg]	USA	El	660	600	715	92	12	4 000
68	95	TRV Corp.[o]	Russia	Mi	650	430	688	95	55	21 360
69	74	Aerospace Corp.[hh]	USA	Comp (Oth)	640	580	720	89	. .	3 500
S	S	Selex Communications (Finmeccanica)	Italy	Comp (El Oth)	630	680	788	80	. .	4 910
70	68	MTU Aero Engines	Germany	Eng	610	610	3 032	20	112	7 080
71	80	Sukhoi Co.[o]	Russia	Ac	600	520	717	84	12	27 700
72	75	Curtiss-Wright Corp.	USA	Comp (Ac Sh)	580	570	1 282	45	81	6 230
73	88	SRA International	USA	El	580	470	1 179	49	63	4 960
74	–	MiG[o]	Russia	Ac	570	240	577	99	30	24 830
75	78	Cubic Corp.	USA	Comp (El Oth)	560	540	821	69	24	6 000
76	86	Moog	USA	Comp (El Mi)	560	480	1 306	43	81	7 270
77	72	Korea Aerospace Industries[ii]	S. Korea	Ac	550	590	725	76	-114	2 720
78	81	Chugach Alaska Corp.[jj]	USA	Comp (Oth)	550	520	890	62	. .	6 300
79	87	United Industrial Corp.	USA	Ac	550	480	564	97	47	2 320
80	73	RUAG	Switzerl.	A Ac Eng SA/A	540	590	995	55	55	5 680
81	–	ARINC[kk]	USA	Comp (El)	540	330	919	58	10	3 200
82	83	Mitre	USA	Oth	540	500	1 025	53	. .	6 310
83	89	Teledyne Technologies	USA	El	540	470	1 433	38	80	7 700
84	–	Ufimskoe MPO[o]	Russia	Eng	530	350	552	96	55	18 670
85	84	Ultra Electronics	UK	El	530	490	694	76	73	2 990

		Company	Country	Sector						
S		Thales Australia (Thales, France)	Australia	A El Mi MV SA/A Sh	530	500	625	*85*	..	3 340
86	82	Tenix[ll]	Australia	El SA/A Sh	510	500	753	*68*	..	4 000
87	94	Severnaya Verf[o]	Russia	Sh	510	440	637	*80*	1	3 330
88	—	Ceradyne Inc.	USA	Comp (Oth)	510	240	663	*76*	128	2 210
S		Samsung Techwin (Samsung)	S. Korea	A El Eng MV	510	510	2 950	*17*	162	4 830
89	93	CAE	Canada	El	500	440	1 102	*45*	112	5 000
90	79	Avio	Italy	Eng	500	530	1 757	*28*	−29	4 840
91	97	Korp. Aerokosmicheskoe Oborudovanie[o]	Russia	El	500	400	707	*71*	104	37 600
S		Thales Nederland (Thales, France)	Netherl.	El	500	430	498	*100*	..	..
S		Santa Bárbara Sistemas (General Dynamics, USA)	Spain	A MV SA/A	500	480	502	*100*	..	1 980
92	—	Patria	Finland	Ac MV SA/A	480	340	562	*85*	32	2 450
93	—	Doosan[mm]	S. Korea		480	380	14 564	*3*	..	29 800
94	91	Meggitt	UK	Oth	480	460	1 233	*39*	178	6 400
95	—	Gencorp	USA	El Eng	480	380	621	*77*	−39	3 140
S		Doosan Infracore (Doosan Group)	S. Korea	A Mi MV	480	380	3 376	*14*	140	..
96	85	Jacobs Engineering Group[m]	USA	Comp (Oth)	460	480	7 421	*6*	197	43 800
97	—	Kongsberg Gruppen	Norway	El Mi SA/A	450	370	1 047	*43*	39	3 650
98	—	Israel Military Industries[oo]	Israel	A MV SA/A	440	340	460	*95*	..	3 080
99	—	Elettronica	Italy	El	440	300	439	*100*	13	800
S		General Dynamics Canada (General Dynamics, USA)	Canada		440	250	437	*100*	0	2 100
S		Selex Sistemi Integrati (Finmeccanica)	Italy	Comp (El)	440	470	748	*59*	78	2 880
100	99	MBDA Italia (MBDA, W. Europe) (Finmeccanica)	Italy	Mi	440	410	437	*100*	56	1 410
S		Fiat[pp]	Italy	MV	430	390	64 994	*1*	1 444	172 010
S		Iveco (Fiat)	Italy	MV	430	390	11 463	*4*	685	24 530
S		Oto Melara (Finmeccanica)	Italy	A MV Mi	430	380	427	*100*	4	1 360
S		Samsung Thales[qq] (Thales, France/Samsung)	S. Korea	El	430	400	475	*90*	23	1 000

[a] Although it is known that several Chinese arms-producing enterprises are large enough to rank among the SIPRI Top 100, it has not been possible to include them because of lack of comparable and sufficiently accurate data. In addition, there are companies in other countries, such as Kazakhstan and Ukraine, that could also be large enough to appear in the SIPRI Top 100 list if data were available, but this is less certain.

[b] Companies are ranked according to the value of their arms sales in 2006. Companies with the designation S are subsidiaries. A dash (–) indicates either that the company did not make arms sales in 2005, that it did not rank among the SIPRI Top 100 for 2005 or that data for 2005 are not available. Company names and structures are listed as they were on 31 Dec. 2006. Information about subsequent changes is provided in these footnotes. The 2005 ranks may differ from those published in *SIPRI Yearbook 2007* owing to the continual revision of data, most often because of changes reported by the company itself and sometimes because of improved estimations. Major revisions are explained in these footnotes.

[c] Key to abbreviations: A = artillery; Ac = aircraft; El = electronics; Eng = engines; Mi = missiles; MV = military vehicles; SA/A = small arms/ammunition; Sh = ships; Sp = space; Oth = other; Comp (. . .) = components, services or anything less than final systems in the sectors within the parentheses—used only for companies that do not produce final systems.

[d] BAE Systems completed the divestment of its 20% stake in Airbus in Oct. 2006. Figures for Airbus are excluded from its published financial statements and from SIPRI data. BAE Systems undertakes a small amount of civilian work. The 95% arms sales share is an estimate.

[e] The arms sales share of total sales for Northrop Grumman is taken from the *Defense News* Top 100 for 2006.

[f] As of 31 Dec. 2007 EADS (European Aeronautic Defence and Space Company) was 22.52% owned by DaimlerChrysler (Germany), 27.53% by SOGEADE (whose share capital is held by Lagardère and the French State) and 5.49% by SEPI, a Spanish state holding company. EADS is registered in the Netherlands. On 9 Feb. 2007 DaimlerChrysler reached an agreement with a consortium of private and public-sector investors by which it will reduce its shareholding in EADS by 7.5 percentage points.

[g] The arms sales figures for Halliburton are for its KBR subsidiary, which was floated as an independent company in Apr. 2007. Halliburton is included in the Top 100 for 2006 as it still owned KBR on 31 Dec. 2006. The arms sales figures for KBR are an estimate based on US Department of Defense (DOD) prime contract awards, the revenues of KBR's subsidiary Devonport Management Ltd (DML) and payments by the British Ministry of Defence (MOD) to other divisions of KBR, less an estimate for civilian contracts with the US Army for restoring Iraqi oilfields. KBR sold DML to Babcock in June 2007.

[h] The arms sales figures for SAIC are based on the arms sales share in the *Defense News* Top 100 for 2006.

[i] MBDA is 37.5% owned by each of BAE Systems and EADS and 25% by Finmeccanica.

[j] The arms sales figures for Rolls-Royce are an estimate, as the company does not publish information on the civil–military breakdown of its Marine Division's sales and has not responded to requests for this information.

[k] DCN was renamed DCNS following its acquisition of Thales's naval operations in Apr. 2007.

[l] The arms sales figures for DRS Technologies are based on a small estimate of the company's non-military sales.

[m] For Japanese companies figures in the arms sales column represent new military contracts rather than arms sales.

[n] The arms sales figures for EDS are based on US DOD prime contract awards and a conservative estimate of £500 m. for sales to the British MOD. *UK Defence Statistics* lists EDS as a company paid £500 m. or more by the MOD in 2006.

[o] This is the fifth year in which Russian companies have been covered by the SIPRI Top 100. There may be other Russian companies that should be in the list, but for which insufficient data are available. The situation in the Russian arms industry is still very fluid, and company names are likely to change as they are restructured. In particular, many Russian arms-producing companies are now subsidiaries of large, state-controlled conglomerates; see chapter 6, section III. Irkut and Sukhoi provide detailed financial information on their websites. All data for Irkut are from its own consolidated financial statements. For all other Russian companies in the list, figures for total sales and profits in 2006 are from Expert RA, the Russian rating agency, while figures for arms sales share estimates and employment are from the Centre for Analysis of Strategies and Technologies, Moscow.

[p] The arms sales share of total sales for Israel Aerospace Industries is based on data from 2005.

[q] Limited financial data are publicly available for AM General. The SIPRI estimate of arms sales is based on a 3-year average of US DOD prime contract awards plus an estimate of its exports.

[r] The arms sales figures for ThyssenKrupp are a rough estimate, based on two-thirds of its Marine Division revenues. The company does not publish information on the civil–military breakdown of this division and has not responded to SIPRI requests for this information.

[s] The arms sales share of total sales for Hindustan Aeronautics is taken from the *Defense News* Top 100 for 2006.

[t] The arms sales figures for Elbit Systems are based on a small estimate of the company's non-military sales.

[u] The arms sales figures for VT Group are a rough estimate, as the company does not publish information on the civil–military breakdown of its revenues and has not responded to SIPRI requests for this information.

[v] The arms sales share for Indian Ordnance Factories is based on 2005 data. The total sales figure is expected sales.

[w] EADS Astrium was previously known as EADS Space.

[x] The arms sales figures for Krauss-Maffei Wegmann are based on a small estimate of the company's non-military sales.

[y] Serco has been reincluded in the SIPRI Top 100 following several years absence, as its military outsourcing activities have been reclassified as 'arms sales' under the SIPRI definition following a review.

[z] The arms sales figures for ManTech are based on a small estimate of the company's non-military sales.

[aa] The arms sales figures for Rafael are based on a small estimate of the company's non-military sales.

[bb] Nexter is a wholly owned subsidiary of the French state-owned land systems company GIAT Industries. Nexter was created in the restructuring of GIAT in Sep. 2006 and includes all the former operational activities of GIAT, which remains as a holding company.

[cc] DynCorp was floated as an independent company by Veritas Capital in May 2006. The arms sales figures are revenues from the US DOD. This is probably an underestimate, as some security contracts with the US State Department should probably be classified as military business, and thus are 'arms sales' under the SIPRI definition.

[dd] KBR sold Devonport Management Ltd to Babcock in June 2007. See note g.

[ee] The arms sales figures for Babcock were kindly provided by the company by special request.

[ff] Data for Samsung arms sales are somewhat uncertain. The estimate is based on the approximate arms sales of Samsung Techwin plus 50% of the estimated arms sales of Samsung Thales, which is 50% owned by Samsung.

gg The arms sales figures for EDO are based on a small estimate of the company's non-military sales.

hh The Aerospace Corporation operates a US Government-funded research and development centre for the US Air Force.

ii The arms sales share of total sales for Korea Aerospace Industries is taken from the *Defense News* Top 100 for 2006.

jj The arms sales figures for Chugach Alaska are based on US DOD prime contract awards.

kk The arms sales share of total sales for ARINC is taken from the *Defense News* Top 100 for 2006.

ll The arms sales share of total sales for Tenix is taken from the *Australian Defence Magazine* Top 40 Australian Defence Contractors for 2006.

mm Arms sales for Doosan are those of its Doosan Infracore subsidiary, the new name given to Daewoo Heavy Industries & Machinery following its purchase by Doosan in 2005.

nn The arms sales figures for Jacobs Engineering Group represent US DOD prime contract awards.

oo The arms sales figures for Israel Military Industries are based on a small estimate of its non-military Homeland Security business.

pp The arms sales of Fiat are those of its Iveco trucks and commercial vehicles division, which sells some military vehicles.

qq The arms sales figures for Samsung Thales are based on a small estimate of its non-military business.

Appendix 6B. Major arms industry acquisitions, 2007

SAM PERLO-FREEMAN

Table 6B.1 lists major acquisitions in the North American and West European arms industry that were announced or completed between 1 January and 31 December 2007. It is not an exhaustive list of all acquisition activity but gives a general overview of strategically significant and financially noteworthy transactions.

Table 6B.1. Major acquisitions in the North American and West European arms industry, 2007

Figures are in US $m., at current prices. North American companies are US-based unless indicated otherwise.

Buyer company (country)	Acquired company (country)	Seller (country)[a]	Deal value ($ m.)[b]	Revenue/employees[c]
Within North America				
URS Corp.	Washington Group International	Publicly listed	3 100	$3398 m.
Carlyle Group	ARINC	Privately owned	..	$918 m.
ITT	EDO Corp.	Publicly listed	1 700	$715 m.
Veritas Capital	Aeroflex	Publicly listed	1 300	$552 m.
Textron	United Industrial Corp.	Publicly listed	1 100	$564 m.
Harris	Multimax	Privately owned	400	$315 m.
Esterline Technologies	CMC Electronics (Canada)	ONCAP	335	$295 m.
General Dynamics	SNC Technologies (Canada)	SNC Lavalin (Canada)	275	..
Alliant Techsystems	Swales Aerospace	Employee-owned	..	$193 m.
Honeywell	Dimensions International	Privately owned	230	$173.5 m.
ManTech International Corp.	SRS Technologies	Privately owned	>170[d]	$175 m.
CACI	Athena Innovative Solutions	Veritas Capital	..	$110 m.
CACI	Wexford Group International	Employee-owned	..	$100 m.
L-3 Communications	Global Communications Solutions	Privately owned	..	$90 m.

Buyer company (country)	Acquired company (country)	Seller (country)[a]	Deal value ($ m.)[b]	Revenue/employees[c]
Lockheed Martin	Management Systems	Employee-owned	..	600 employees
ManTech International Corp.	McDonald Bradley	Privately owned	76	$50 m.
ViaSat	Intelligent Compression Technologies	Privately owned	54.6	..
Raytheon	Oakley Networks	Privately owned	41	200 employees
Moog	Quickset International	Privately owned	38	$27 m.
Rockwell Collins	ITAC	Privately owned	36	..
Teledyne Technologies	D. G. O'Brien	Privately owned	36	$26.2 m.
CAE (Canada)	Engenuity Technologies (Canada)	Publicly listed	20	$15 m.
ITT	Dolphin Technology	Privately owned	..	$12 m.
L-3 Communications	Geneva Aerospace	Privately owned	..	..
Transatlantic: West European acquisitions of companies based in North America				
BAE Systems (UK)[e]	Armor Holdings	Publicly listed	4 532	$2 361 m.
Meggitt (UK)[f]	K&F Industries	Publicly listed	1 300	$424 m.
Qinetiq (UK)[g]	Analex	Publicly listed	173	$150.3 m.
GKN (UK)	TAMG	Teleflex Inc.	..	$135 m.
Qinetiq (UK)[g]	ITS Corp.	Riordan, Lewis & Hayden	90	$77 m.
Qinetiq (UK)[g]	3H Technologies	Privately owned	52	$33 m.
Qinetiq (UK)[g]	Patriot Antenna Systems	Privately owned	45	..
Cobham (UK)	Milcom	Privately owned	42.5	$100 m.
VT Group (UK)[h]	Talley Defense Systems	Privately owned	..	$60 m.
Nammo (Norway)	Criticom	Privately owned	33	$19 m.
Ultra Electronics (UK)	Allied Perception	Privately owned	9.2	..
Qinetiq (UK)[g]	Automatika	Privately owned	9.2	..
Rolls-Royce (UK)	Seaworthy Systems	Privately owned	..	58 employees

Transatlantic:: North American acquisitions of companies based in Western Europe

General Electric	Smiths Aerospace (UK)	Smiths Group (UK)	4 800	$2400 m.
United Technologies[i]	PZL Mielic (Poland)	Polish Government	84.1	..
ViaSat	JAST Antenna Systems (Switzerland)	Privately owned	6.5	..

Within Western Europe

Thales (France)	67% of Alcatel Alenia Space (France) and 33% of Telespazio (Italy)[j]	Alcatel-Lucent (France)	895	$841 m.
DCN (France)	Thales's naval operations (France)	Thales (France)	714[k]	$2000 m.
Babcock International Group (UK)	Devonport Management Ltd (UK)	KBR (USA)	699	$835 m.
KH Finance (UK)	Smiths Marine Systems business (UK)	Smiths Group (UK)	109.4	..
Chemring Group (UK)	Simmel Difesa (Italy)	Publicly listed	102	$53 m.
MBDA (W. Europe)	Bayern-Chemie (Germany)	EADS (W. Europe, 50%) and Thales (France, 50%)	66	$53 m.
Cohort (UK)	Sea Group (UK)	Privately owned	51.7	$33 m.
Qinetiq (UK)	Bolden James Holdings (UK)	ISIS Equity Partners (UK)	40	$36 m.
Finmeccanica (Italy)	Datamat (Italy)	Publicly listed	30	$28 m.
Mazel Group (Spain)	Engineering Services & Design Tehnology (Spain)	ITP Group (Spain)	..	$28 m.
Saab (Sweden)	Seaeye (UK)	Privately owned	25.6	$22 m.
Chemring Group (UK)	Richmond Electronics & Engineering (UK)	Privately owned	23	$11 m.
Ultra Electroncs (UK)	Atkins & Partners (UK)	Privately owned	8	$7 m.

[a] 'Publicly listed' means the company's shares were publicly traded on a stock exchange of its home country, with no single majority shareholder. 'Privately owned' means the company was owned by one or more private shareholders, with its shares not traded on any stock exchange.

[b] In cases where the deal value was not available in US dollars, currency conversion has been made using the International Monetary Fund average exchange rate for the calendar month in which the transaction was made. Companies do not always disclose the values of transactions.

[c] Where deal values are not known, the acquired company's annual revenue is listed where known (either actual revenue for 2006 or expected revenue for 2007). Where revenue is not available in US dollars, currency conversion has been made using the International Monetary Fund average exchange rate for the appropriate year. Where information is not available for either the deal value or the acquired company's revenue, the acquired company's number of employees

is shown, where known. Within each regional category, acquisitions are listed first in order of deal size where known, then in order of the acquired company's revenue where known. Where only employee numbers are known, the acquisitions are listed according to a conservative estimate of the likely range of revenues of the acquired company.

[d] According to ManTech, 'The Company used cash available and $170 million in borrowings from its new senior secured $300 million credit facility to finance the acquisition.' ManTech, 'ManTech completes the acquisition of SRS Technologies, Inc.', Press release, 8 May, 2007, <http://www.mantech.com/news/>.

[e] BAE Systems completed its acquisition of Armor Holdings through its US subsidiary BAE Systems Inc. Armor Group was merged with BAE's Land Systems and Armaments division, based in Arlington, Virginia.

[f] Meggitt completed its acquisition of K&F Industries through its US subsidiary Meggitt USA Inc.

[g] QinetiQ completed its US acquisitions through its US subsidiary QinetiQ North America and its subsidiaries.

[h] VT completed its acquisition of Milcom through its US subsidiary VT Services Inc.

[i] United Technologies acquired PZL Mielic through its Sikorsky subsidiary.

[j] Alcatel Alenia Space and Telespazio were joint ventures between Alcatel-Lucent and Finmecannica, who own the remainder of the shares (i.e. 33% of Alcatel Alenia Space and 67% of Telespazio). Together they now form the 'New Space Alliance' between Thales and Finmecannica. Alcatel Alenia Space has been renamed Thales Alenia Space.

[k] DCN acquired the following operations from Thales: Thales Naval France, a 50% stake in the Armaris naval company and a 35% stake in MOPA2, the prime contractor for PA2, France's planned new aircraft carrier. These operations were valued at €514 million ($645 million). In return for these companies and a payment to DCN of €55 million ($69 million), Thales acquired a 25% stake in DCN. DCN is now known as DCNS.

7. International arms transfers

PAUL HOLTOM, MARK BROMLEY and PIETER D. WEZEMAN

I. Introduction

Although the volume of deliveries of major conventional weapons dropped in 2007 compared to 2006, the long-term upward trend in transfers that began in 2003–2004 continues—transfers over the period 2003–2007 were 7 per cent higher than in 2002–2006. The five largest suppliers for the period 2003–2007—the USA, Russia, Germany, France and the UK—accounted for approximately 80 per cent of all deliveries. Among the major recipients during this period were regional powers in Asia, such as India, China and South Korea; North Atlantic Treaty Organization (NATO) member states Greece and Turkey; and US allies in the 'global war on terrorism' and beneficiaries of US military aid in Asia and the Middle East. Both supplier and recipient states cited a number of political, financial and security related objectives to justify the transfers that support the upward trend. For a number of states in Africa, the Middle East and South America, resource revenues fuelled rising military budgets, which in turn financed significant increases in the volume of orders for, and deliveries of, arms.[1]

Section II of this chapter presents the major trends in global arms transfers for the period 2003–2007 and an estimate of the financial value of the global arms trade in 2006. Section III details significant developments in the transfers of the five largest suppliers of arms in 2007. Section IV examines the increasing volume of arms transferred to South America in the period 2003–2007, with a particular focus on Chile, Venezuela and Brazil. Section V outlines international transfers to the conflict zones of Afghanistan and Darfur, Sudan. Section VI presents a summary of the chapter's conclusions.

Appendix 7A presents data on the recipients and suppliers of major conventional weapons in 2003–2007. Appendix 7B presents official data on the financial value of the arms trade in 1998–2006. Appendix 7C outlines the methodology of the data collection, the calculation of the SIPRI trend-indicator value (TIV) and the coverage of the SIPRI Arms Transfers Database. Information on deliveries and contracts for major conventional weapons referred to in this chapter are taken from the SIPRI Arms Transfers Database.[2]

---

[1] See chapter 5 in this volume, section V. On military budgets in South America see also Stålenheim, P., Perdomo, C. and Sköns, E., 'Military expenditure', *SIPRI Yearbook 2007: Armaments, Disarmament and International Security* (Oxford University Press: Oxford, 2007), pp. 285–88.

[2] The SIPRI Arms Transfers Database is available at <http://armstrade.sipri.org/>. The data on which this chapter is based are given in the 'Register of major conventional weapon transfers, 2007', which can be accessed via this URL. Data in the register are valid as of 13 Feb. 2008.

Table 7.1. The five largest suppliers of major conventional weapons and their main recipients, 2003–2007

Supplier	Share of global arms transfers (%)	No. of recipients	Main recipients (share of supplier's transfers, %)
USA	*31*	71	South Korea (*12*), Israel (*12*), UAE (*9*), Greece (*8*)
Russia	*25*	45	China (*45*), India (*22*), Venezuela (*5*), Algeria (*4*)
Germany	*10*	49	Turkey (*15*), Greece (*14*), South Africa (*12*), Australia (*9*)
France	*9*	43	UAE (*41*), Greece (*12*), Saudi Arabia (*9*), Singapore (*7*)
UK	*4*	38	USA (*17*), Romania (*9*), Chile (*9*), India (*8*)

UAE = United Arab Emirates.

Source: SIPRI Arms Transfers Database, <http://armstrade.sipri.org/>.

II. Major trends in international arms transfers

The SIPRI Arms Transfers Project maintains the SIPRI Arms Transfers Database, which contains information on deliveries of major conventional weapons to states, international organizations and non-state armed groups since 1950.[3] SIPRI ascribes a trend-indicator value to each weapon or subsystem included in the database. SIPRI then calculates the volume of transfers to, from and between all of the above-listed entities using the TIV and the number of weapon systems or subsystems delivered in a given year.[4] TIV figures do not represent financial values for weapon transfers; they are an indicator of the volume of transfers. Therefore, TIV figures should not be cited directly. They are best used as the raw data for calculating trends in international arms transfers over periods of time, global percentages for suppliers and recipients, and percentages for the volume of transfers to or from particular states.

The trends in international arms transfers, 2003–2007

For the period 2003–2007 the five largest suppliers of major conventional weapons were the USA, Russia, Germany, France and the UK (see table 7.1). The main recipients were China (which received 12 per cent of all international transfers), India (8 per cent), the United Arab Emirates (UAE; 7 per cent), Greece (6 per cent) and South Korea (5 per cent). The main recipient regions were Asia (37 per cent), Europe (23 per cent) and the Middle East (22 per cent). (On recipients and suppliers, see appendix 7A.) While the volume of international transfers of major conventional weapons for the

---

[3] The SIPRI Arms Transfers Database does not document international transfers of nuclear, biological and chemical weapons or of small arms, although some light weapons are included.

[4] The method used to calculate the TIV is described in appendix 7C and a more detailed description is available on the SIPRI Arms Transfers Project website at <http://www.sipri.org/contents/armstrad/at methods.html>. The figures in this chapter may differ from those in previous editions of the SIPRI Yearbook because the Arms Transfers Database is constantly updated.

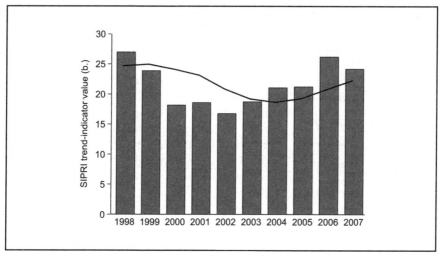

Figure 7.1. The trend in transfers of major conventional weapons, 1998–2007

Notes: See appendix 7C for an explanation of the SIPRI trend-indicator value. The bar graph shows annual totals and the line graph shows the five-year moving average. Five-year averages are plotted at the last year of each five-year period.

Source: SIPRI Arms Transfers Database, <http://armstrade.sipri.org/>.

period 2003–2007 has continued the increase since 2000–2004, the volume transferred in 2007 alone was 8 per cent lower than in 2006 (see figure 7.1). This is largely because deliveries to two of the three largest recipients decreased significantly in 2007 in comparison with 2006: deliveries to China were 62 per cent lower and deliveries to the UAE were 50 per cent lower.[5]

Despite decreased deliveries to and orders by China, Asia will continue to remain a major recipient region, with India, Indonesia, South Korea, Taiwan and a number of other Asian states embarking on ambitious arms acquisition programmes that will require imported weapon systems and subsystems. The major suppliers will continue to engage in intense competition for export orders to Asia and the Middle East. Libya and Saudi Arabia are likely to become major recipients once again.

The financial value of the international arms trade in 2006

It is not possible to ascribe a precise financial value to the international arms trade. However, by aggregating financial data on the value of their arms exports released by the main suppliers, it is possible to make an indicative estimate. The estimated financial value of the international arms trade in 2006 is $45.6 billion, which represents 0.4 per cent of world trade.[6] In financial

---

[5] Because year-on-year deliveries can fluctuate significantly, a 5-year moving average is used to provide a more stable measure for trends in international transfers of major conventional weapons.

[6] This figure is likely to be below the true figure since a number of significant exporters, including China, do not release data on the financial value of their arms exports. Total world trade in 2006

terms, the USA was the largest arms exporter in 2006, with exports worth $14 billion; Russia is in second place, with $6.5 billion of exports; France is in third place, with $5.1 billion of exports; the UK is in fourth place, with $3.8 billion of exports; and Israel is in fifth place, with $3 billion of exports.[7]

SIPRI bases the estimated financial value of the international arms trade on official government data published in either national reports on arms exports or public statements by government officials.[8] There are significant limitations on using official national data for assessing the financial value of the inter-national arms trade. First, there is no internationally agreed definition of what constitutes 'arms' and so governments use different lists when collecting and reporting data on the financial value of their arms exports. Second, there is no standardized methodology concerning how to collect and report such data, with some states reporting on licences issued or used and other states using data collected from customs agencies. Third, a number of states produce more than one data set based on different lists of goods or different methodologies.

III. Major supplier developments, 2007

There were noteworthy changes in a number of significant major supplier–recipient relationships in 2007 due to a range of domestic and international political concerns over transfers to particular recipients, changing procurement plans, and competition for orders between the major five suppliers in Asia, the Middle East and North Africa.

The United States

In the period 2003–2007 three regions received the bulk of US arms transfers: the Middle East (32 per cent), Asia (31 per cent) and Europe (27 per cent). Concerns were expressed in the US Congress about proposed arms sales and military aid to states in both Asia and the Middle East.[9] Additionally, as of January 2008 the USA had imposed arms export restrictions—including par-tial and blanket arms embargoes—on 25 countries.[10] Despite these circum-

---

amounted to $12 029 billion. International Monetary Fund, International Financial Statistics online, <http://www.imfstatistics.org/imf/>.

[7] See appendix 7B.

[8] As of Jan. 2008, 31 states had published a national report on arms exports, compared with 6 states as of Jan. 1998. See appendix 7B for available national data on the financial value of their arms exports. In addition to financial data, certain of these reports contain information on the type of arms exported, the number of items involved and, in some cases, the type of end-user. In 2007 national reports on arms exports were published for the first time by Bulgaria, Montenegro and Serbia. All available official reports on arms exports are available at <http://www.sipri.org/contents/armstrad/atlinks_gov.html>.

[9] E.g. US Congress, Senate Resolution 372 expressing the concerns of the Senate on the declaration of a state of emergency in Pakistan, 8 Nov. 2007, <http://www.govtrack.us/congress/bill.xpd?tab=main&bill=sr110-372>.

[10] US Department of State, Directorate of Defense Trade Controls, 'Embargoed countries', Dec. 2007, <http://pmddtc.state.gov/country.htm>. Of the 26 US embargoes, 11 were imposed by the United Nations. On the impact of UN arms embargoes see Fruchart, D. et al., *United Nations Arms Embargoes: Their Impact on Arms Flows and Target Behaviour* (SIPRI/Uppsala University: Stockholm, 2007).

stances, the USA was the largest supplier of major conventional weapons in 2007.

In Asia, transfers to Taiwan and Pakistan were under particular scrutiny. Taiwan—the seventh largest recipient (5 per cent) of US transfers during 2003–2007—announced in 2007 that it was allocating initial funding for 30 AH-64D combat helicopters, 12 P-3CUP maritime patrol aircraft, 4 Patriot Advanced Capability-3 (PAC-3) surface-to-air missile (SAM) systems and 66 F-16C combat aircraft.[11] The helicopters, patrol aircraft and SAMs were offered to Taiwan by the USA, but the US Government appeared reluctant to supply Taiwan with additional F-16 aircraft for fear of provoking China.[12] Over the period 2003–2007, the USA accounted for about 97 per cent of transfers to Taiwan, with France accounting for the remaining 3 per cent.

Pakistan was the 13th largest recipient (2 per cent) of US transfers in the period 2003–2007. Pakistan's share of US transfers is likely to increase significantly in the future, as the USA agreed in 2006 to provide 26 F-16 combat aircraft (second-hand, but modernized to F-16C standards) and 20 AH-1F combat helicopters as military aid. The USA has also authorized the sale of 18 new F-16C combat aircraft (with an option on 18 more). However, these transfers are contingent on political developments in Pakistan. In response to Pakistani President Pervez Musharraf's declaration of emergency rule in November 2007, several members of the US Congress called for a careful review of Pakistan's US military aid package and the suspension of transfers that were not directly related to the fight against al-Qaeda and the Taliban.[13] Over the period 2003–2007, China and France accounted for about 27 per cent and 16 per cent, respectively, of transfers to Pakistan, compared to a US share of 36 per cent.

In the Middle East, Israel, the UAE and Egypt were the largest recipients of US transfers for the period 2003–2007.[14] For the same period, Iraq was the seventh largest recipient of US transfers in the region. Supplies to Israel and Egypt were primarily funded by US military aid. In July 2007 the US Secretary of State, Condoleezza Rice, announced that the US Government plans to increase military aid for Israel and Egypt: to $30 billion to Israel for the 10-year period 2009–2018 (an increase of 25 per cent) and to $13 billion to Egypt over the decade.[15] Rice also announced plans to negotiate the sale of an

---

[11] Minnick, W., 'Taiwan to purchase Patriots, Apaches', *Defense News*, 7 Jan. 2008, p. 4; and Griffin, C., 'Boom and bust: the strengths and weaknesses of Taiwan's defense strategy emerge', *Armed Forces Journal*, Jan. 2008.

[12] Although the USA continues to supply arms to Taiwan, it does not report these transfers to the UN Register of Conventional Arms (UNROCA). UNROCA submission rules changed in 2006, requesting only submissions between UN member states. As a consequence of these rule changes, in 2007 China made its first submission to UNROCA since 1997.

[13] US Congress (note 9).

[14] Egypt received 7% of US transfers. For Israel and the UAE see table 7.1.

[15] US military aid for Israel was $2.2 billion in 2005 and $2.26 billion in 2006. The requested levels of funding were $2.34 billion for 2007 and $2.4 billion for 2008. US military aid for Egypt was approximately $1.3 billion in 2005 and 2006, with the same sum requested for 2007 and 2008. US Department of State, 'Foreign military financing account summaries', <http://www.state.gov/t/pm/ppa/sat/c14560.

estimated $20 billion worth of foreign military assets to member states of the Gulf Cooperation Council (GCC) to 'help bolster forces of moderation and support a broader strategy to counter the negative influences of al-Qaeda, Hizballah, Syria and Iran'.[16] The proposed arms sales to the GCC states include PAC-3 SAM systems to Kuwait and the UAE, improved airborne early warning capabilities to Saudi Arabia and the UAE, and advanced air-to-surface weapons to Saudi Arabia and the UAE, for use with previously supplied combat aircraft from the USA.[17] While not strongly objecting to most of the proposed deals, Democratic and Republican members of the US Congress expressed concern at plans to sell 900 JDAM guided bombs to Saudi Arabia for an estimated $123 million. They demanded that the sale should only take place if US President George W. Bush could guarantee that the bombs would not be used against the USA or Israel.[18] Deliveries of these systems would maintain future US transfers to the Middle East at the current high volume. In addition to the USA, the other four largest suppliers are also targeting the Middle East for transfers (see below).[19]

Despite generally large US military aid programmes in the Middle East, Iraq accounted for less than 1 per cent of total US transfers during 2003–2007. The USA accounted for 25 per cent of Iraqi imports of major conventional weapons during this period, supplying an estimated 398 Badger armoured personnel carriers (APCs) and 16 UH-1H transport helicopters. The USA also funded transfers of military equipment to Iraq from Central and Eastern Europe. For example, in September 2007 the US Government announced plans to purchase 336 new BTR-3E1 infantry fighting vehicles (IFVs) from Ukraine for the Iraqi armed forces.[20] However, US-funded transfers of surplus military equipment from Central and Eastern Europe to Iraqi forces have been delivered late and have been of poor quality. The transfers have also been poorly controlled; for example, it was announced in 2007 that an estimated 110 000 Kalashnikov rifles and 80 000 pistols purchased by the USA and supplied to the Iraqi security forces were unaccounted for.[21] US-funded transfers

htm>; and AFX News Limited, 'Israeli PM announces 30 billion US dollar US defence aid', Forbes. com, 29 July 2007, <http://www.forbes.com/markets/feeds/afx/2007/07/29/afx3963706.html>.

[16] US Department of State, 'Assistance agreements with Gulf states, Israel and Egypt', 30 July 2007, <http://www.state.gov/secretary/rm/2007/89600.htm>; and Miles, D., 'Arms sale to help bolster long-term Gulf security', US Department of Defense, American Forces Press Service, 30 July 2007, <http://www.defenselink.mil/news/newsarticle.aspx?id=46882>. For a list of members and a brief description of the GCC see annex B in this volume.

[17] Blanchard, C. M. and Grimmett, R. F., *The Gulf Security Dialogue and Related Arms Sale Proposals*, Congressional Research Service (CRS) Report for Congress RL34322 (US Congress, CRS: Washington, DC, 14 Jan. 2008).

[18] Matthews, W., 'Lawmakers caution White House on proposed JDAM sale to Saudi Arabia', *Defense News*, 19 Nov. 2007.

[19] On arms procurement by the GCC states and Iran see Wezeman, S. T. et al., 'International arms transfers', *SIPRI Yearbook 2007* (note 1), pp. 396–402.

[20] US Department of Defense, Defense Security Cooperation Agency, 'Iraq: various vehicles, small arms ammunition, explosives and communications equipment', News release, 25 Sep. 2007.

[21] US Government Accountability Office (GAO), *Stabilizing Iraq: DOD Cannot Ensure that US-Funded Equipment Has Reached Iraqi Security Forces*, GAO-07-711 (GAO: Washington, DC, 31 July 2007), p. 11.

to Afghan security forces have suffered from similar problems (see section V below).

Russia

Russia transferred its largest volume of major conventional weapons to Asia: 74 per cent of total deliveries for the period 2003–2007. With its abilities to offer a broad range of weapon systems at lower prices than other suppliers and to sell to countries that are subject to arms export control restrictions by the USA and European Union (EU) member states,[22] Russia has marketed itself as a reliable supplier for established and new markets in Asia, the Middle East, North Africa and South America. Concerns that have been expressed by Russian officials with regard to the Russian arms industry's poor quality controls and defective products are now also being voiced by major recipients of Russian arms: China, India and Algeria.[23] For example, Algeria, which concluded a $8 billion arms deal with Russia in March 2006, halted deliveries of MiG-29SMT combat aircraft and discussed the possibility of returning the first deliveries to Russia because of its dissatisfaction with the quality.[24]

EU and US restrictions on exports of arms and related technologies and the USA's willingness to impose sanctions against countries that supply arms and related technologies to China have limited China's range of suppliers.[25] Although Russia continues to meet this need—with China receiving 94 per cent of its major conventional weapons from Russia for the period 2003–2007—no new contracts for aircraft or ships were signed in 2007. Explanations for the lack of new orders from China include its efforts to further develop its domestic arms industry and its dissatisfaction with delays in outstanding orders and the poor quality of the equipment delivered.[26] Despite these factors, it was reported in late 2006 that China was planning to buy up to 50 Su-33 combat aircraft and more ships.[27] There are divisions among Russian officials regarding such transfers, for reasons relating to future security scenarios and concerns that China will buy limited numbers of advanced systems

[22] Wezeman et al. (note 19), pp. 394–96.

[23] Russian Defence Minister Ivan Ivanov, the Russian Ministry of Defence's Armaments Directorate and Rosoboronzakaz have all highlighted these problems in recent years. See Cooper, J., 'Development in the Russian arms industry', *SIPRI Yearbook 2006: Armaments, Disarmament and International Security* (Oxford University Press: Oxford, 2006), p. 444; and '"Russians need to improve the quality of their weapons", says expert', *Jane's Defence Industry*, Apr. 2005, p. 4. The formation of Rostekhnologii is intended to help remedy quality problems in the Russian arms industry, as well as strengthen supply chains and boost research and development. See chapter 6 in this volume, section III.

[24] Gritskova, A., Kiseleva, E. and Lantratov, K., 'Algeria lays down Russian arms', *Kommersant*, 18 Feb. 2008.

[25] SIPRI Arms Transfers Project, 'EU and other multilateral arms embargoes', <http://www.sipri.org/contents/armstrad/embargoes.html>; and US Department of State (note 10). E.g. in 2005 the USA imposed sanctions on Israel's arms industry following Israeli sales of Harpy unmanned aerial vehicles and spare parts to China in 2000 and 2002. Hagelin, B., Bromley, M. and Wezeman, S. T., 'International arms transfers', *SIPRI Yearbook 2006* (note 23), p. 457.

[26] Petrov, N., 'Problems in Russian–Chinese military-technical cooperation', RIA Novosti, 25 Sep. 2007, <http://en.rian.ru/analysis/20070925/80780903.html>.

[27] Wezeman et al. (note 19), p. 393.

with the intention of copying them.[28] However, this concern has not yet been borne out in several arms industry sectors, as China relies on Russian licensed production and components for combat aircraft and missiles, such as AL-31FN engines for the J-10 combat aircraft. China has also formally sought and received permission from Russia to re-export the Russian-produced RD-93 engines, which are integral to China's JF-17 combat aircraft, to several African and Asian states.[29]

India is an example of a country for which, despite competition from Western suppliers, Russia remains the dominant supplier. Russia accounted for 70 per cent of transfers to India for 2003–2007, compared with 14 per cent from EU member states, 6 per cent from Israel and 2 per cent from the USA. In 2007 India echoed Algerian and Chinese complaints regarding Russian transfers. Russia announced delays in the delivery of the *Admiral Gorshkov* aircraft carrier and three Talwar Class frigates, while India suspended payment for the modernization of Il-38 maritime patrol aircraft due to 'substandard' work and refused to accept delivery of a Kilo Class submarine due to technical problems with the Klub land-attack missiles carried on this submarine.[30] Despite these setbacks, new deals were announced in 2007 for the transfer or licensed production of 40 Su-30MKI combat aircraft, 24 Smerch multiple rocket launchers, 347 T-90S tanks and 80 Mi-17 helicopters, as well as upgrades for 172 Mi-8/Mi-17 helicopters and 67 MiG-29 combat aircraft. An agreement to exchange 18 Su-30s for Su-30MKIs was also concluded. These arrangements, in particular those for combat aircraft, have buoyed Russian hopes that the MiG-35 combat aircraft will win the $10 billion Indian tender for 126 multi-role combat aircraft.[31] The MiG-35 faces competition from the Swedish JAS-39 Gripen, the French Rafale, the pan-European (British, German, Italian and Spanish) Eurofighter Typhoon and the US F-16 and F/A-18.[32] The delivery of the first BrahMos cruise missiles to the Indian Army in 2007 represents one of the most prominent examples of Russian willingness to transfer technology and engage in joint production with India.[33] India expects the first Indian export contracts for BrahMos missiles to be signed in 2008, with Malaysia cited as one of the most interested states.[34] The Indian–Russian intergovernmental military-technical cooperation (MTC) agreements

[28] Litovkin, V., 'Voenno-exportnyi tupik' [Military exports dead end], *Nezavisimaya gazeta*, 29 Jan. 2008.

[29] 'China to re-export Russian jet engine', *Kommersant*, 20 Nov. 2007. At the beginning of 2008, Pakistan was the only state to have ordered the JF-17.

[30] Unnithan, S., 'Dud missile', *India Today*, 10 Jan. 2008.

[31] 'Korporatsiya "MiG" uverena v pobede v indiiskom tendere na postavku 126 srednikh mnogotse-levykh istrebitelei' [MiG corporation believes in victory in Indian tender for 126 medium multi-role combat aircraft], ARMS-TASS, 11 Nov. 2007, <http://arms-tass.su/?page=article&aid=47669&cid=43>.

[32] Government of India Press Information Bureau, 'Request for proposal for 126 medium multi-role combat aircraft issued', 28 Aug. 2007, <http://pib.nic.in/release/release.asp?relid=30522&kwd=>.

[33] 'Address of the President of India, H. E. Dr. A. P. J. Abdul Kalam, during the commencement of the delivery of BRAHMOS missile systems to the Indian army', Embassy of the Russian Federation in India, New Delhi, 21 June 2007, <http://www.india.mid.ru/sp_84_e.html>.

[34] 'Indiya gotova postavit' rakety "BrahMos" Malaizii' [India ready to sell BrahMos missiles to Malaysia], ARMS-TASS, 8 Oct. 2007, <http://arms-tass.su/?page=article&aid=46024&cid=25>.

on the joint design and development of a fifth-generation combat aircraft and a multi-role transport aircraft were signed in October and November 2007, respectively, signalling further cooperation in the arms sphere.[35]

Another significant agreement on transfers to Asia was concluded with the granting of a $1 billion credit arrangement with Indonesia for arms purchases.[36] The proposed transfers to Indonesia—as with those for Algeria, Iran, Malaysia and Venezuela—are one element of intergovernmental trade relationships that include agreements on joint resource exploration and energy development projects. The most controversial of these relationships is with Iran, as United Nations Security Council Resolution 1747 calls for 'vigilance and restraint' with regard to major conventional weapons transfers, associated services and manufacturing assistance to Iran.[37] Following a Iranian–Russian intergovernmental MTC committee meeting in December 2007, the Iranian Defence Minister, Mustapha Mohammad Najjar, announced that Russia would deliver an undisclosed number of S-300PMU-1 (SA-10) SAM systems to Iran in 2008.[38] However, Russia immediately denied the reports, stating that the issue was 'not on the agenda, is not being considered and is not being discussed with Iran at the moment'.[39] Despite media rumours throughout 2007 that Iran planned to acquire combat aircraft and other weapons systems from Russia, Iran and Russia did not reveal new contracts for major conventional weapons in 2007.[40]

Germany, France and the United Kingdom

After the dominant arms exporters—the USA and Russia—EU member states Germany, France and the UK represent the next tier of suppliers. As a group, their largest recipient regions for the period 2003–2007 were Europe (39 per cent), the Middle East (22 per cent) and Asia (17 per cent). There are two EU

[35] Government of India Press Information Bureau, 'India and Russia sign landmark agreement for joint development and production of fifth generation fighter aircraft', 18 Oct. 2007, <http://pib.nic.in/release/rel_print_page.asp?relid=32016>; and 'List of agreements signed between India and Russia during Prime Minister's visit to Moscow', Government of India Press Information Bureau, 12 Nov. 2007, <http://pib.nic.in/release/rel_print_page.asp?relid=32746>.

[36] This credit arrangement is reportedly to be used for the acquisition of 10 Mi-17 and 5 Mi-35 helicopters, 20 BMP-3 IFVs and 2 submarines. In Aug. 2007, Indonesia signed a contract for 3 Su-27SKM and 3 Su-30MK2 aircraft, which will not be paid for by the $1 billion credit. 'Atom, turizm, oruzhie' [Atom, tourism, weapons], *Nezavisimaya gazeta*, 5 Sep. 2007.

[37] UN Security Council Resolution 1747, 24 Mar. 2007. UN documents on the Iran embargo are available at <http://www.un.org/sc/committees/1737/>. See also chapter 8 in this volume, section II.

[38] 'Rossiya postavit Iranu kompleksy S-300' [Russia to deliver S-300s to Iran], *Kommersant*, 26 Dec. 2007.

[39] Russian Federal Service on Military-Technical Cooperation, 'O postavkakh iranu ZRS S-300: po povodu soobshchenii v presse o VTC Rossii i Irana' [Regarding deliveries of S300 air defence systems to Iran: In connection with media reports on MTC of Russia and Iran], 27 Dec. 2007, <http://www.fsvts.gov.ru/db/kvts-portal/CDA393755C69C872C32573BE004E3240/ddb/heap/doc.html>. It has been suggested that Belarus is negotiating the sale of 2 surplus S-300PT (SA-10A) SAM systems to Iran. Harrington, M., 'Iran set to acquire S-300PTs from Belarus', *Jane's International Defence Review*, Feb. 2008, p. 6.

[40] Hughes, R., 'Iran set to obtain Pantsyr via Syria', *Jane's Defence Weekly*, 23 May 2007, p. 5; and Lantratov, K. et al., 'MiGs will defend Syria and Iran', *Kommersant*, 19 June 2007.

mechanisms that can influence transfers by EU member states. First, the Council of the EU can call for the imposition of arms embargoes. As of January 2008, 14 countries were subject to EU arms embargoes, with Iran the latest addition to the list.[41] Second, the EU Code of Conduct on Arms Exports can inform member state decisions to license applications.[42] However, national governments continue to make the final decisions on transfers and promote their domestic arms companies' exports.[43] There are differences in the restrictiveness of the export policies of the governments and EU member states compete for orders.

For the period 2003–2007 Germany was the third largest supplier of major conventional weapons. Sixty-two per cent of its transfers went to EU or NATO recipient states. Germany also competes for export orders against other EU member states in other regions of the world—for example, against France for a contract to supply Pakistan with three submarines worth around $1.5 billion.[44] However, in November 2007 the German Foreign Minister, Frank-Walter Steinmeier, announced that the German Government was to reconsider ongoing arms deliveries to Pakistan in response to President Musharraf's decision to impose a state of emergency.[45] As a result, deliveries of M-113 APCs and Luna unmanned aerial vehicles (UAVs) to Pakistan were temporarily halted.[46] Steinmeier has also expressed a negative opinion of the proposed US arms packages to the Middle East announced in July 2007, stating that 'a military buildup is hardly the best solution to the unstable situation in the Middle East'.[47] Additionally, members of the German Government coalition opposed the French arms deals with Libya. However, German companies are part of the Eurofighter consortium that will provide 72 Eurofighter Typhoon combat aircraft to Saudi Arabia via the UK and will also co-produce the Milan missiles to be supplied to Libya via France (see below).[48]

France—the fourth largest supplier of major conventional weapons for the period 2003–2007—took significant steps in 2007 to promote its arms exports. The French Defence Minister, Hervé Morin, identified the strengthening of French arms export efforts as a top priority after taking office in June 2007;

[41] Council Common Position 2007/246/CFSP of 23 April 2007 amending Common Position 2007/140/CFSP concerning restrictive measures against Iran, *Official Journal of the European Union*, L106 (24 Apr. 2007). Developments in EU arms embargoes can be found on the SIPRI Arms Transfers Project website (note 25).

[42] Council of the European Union, 'European Union Code of Conduct on Arms Exports', document 8675/2/98, Rev. 2, Brussels, 5 June 1998. See chapter 11 in this volume, section III.

[43] Bromley, M., *The Impact on Domestic Policy of the EU Code of Conduct on Arms Export: The Czech Republic, the Netherlands and Spain*, SIPRI Policy Paper no. 21 (SIPRI: Stockholm, 2008).

[44] Grevast, J. and Lewis A. C., 'Pakistan delays sub design selection, says source', *Jane's Defence Industry*, July 2007, p. 4.

[45] Steinmeier, F.-W., German Minister of Foreign Affairs, Speech concerning recent developments in Pakistan, German Bundestag, Berlin, 8 Nov. 2007, *Die Bundesregierung*, Bulletin no. 123-3 <http://www.bundesregierung.de/nn_1514/Content/DE/Bulletin/2007/11/123-3-bmaa-bt-pakistan.html>.

[46] Lurz, A., 'Gefährliche militärhilfe? Deutsche Rüstungsexporte nach Pakistan' [Dangerous military assistance? German arms exports to Pakistan], *Streitkräfte und Strategien*, 12 Jan. 2008.

[47] Reuters, 'German FM criticizes proposed U.S. arms sale to Middle East', *Haaretz*, 1 Aug. 2007.

[48] 'Germany knew of Libya arms deal, says spokesman', *Deutsche Welle*, 7 Aug. 2007; and Lewis, J. A. C., 'Dassault holds talks with Libya over Rafale sale', *Jane's Defence Weekly*, 5 Sep. 2007, p. 9.

and in September 2007 a special task force was established within the presidential office to promote arms exports.[49] On the assumption that arms export efforts were underperforming, the French Government announced its intention to increase arms exports to a value similar to that of domestic arms procurement—€8–10 billion ($11–14 billion).[50] This was followed in December 2007 by a government announcement that France's arms export licensing system would be simplified and modernized to support the arms industry's export efforts.[51]

French President Nicolas Sarkozy has played a prominent role in promoting the country's arms exports in the Middle East and North Africa since entering office. He met Libyan leader Muammar Qadhafi twice during 2007 to discuss potential sales of 14 Rafale combat aircraft, eight Tiger combat helicopters, two Gowind corvettes and Milan anti-tank missiles.[52] In January 2008 Sarkozy visited Saudi Arabia to support efforts to secure contracts to supply naval vessels and border security systems.[53] Saudi Arabia accounted for 9 per cent of French arms exports during 2003–2007, and France obtained Saudi orders for artillery, SAMs and tanker aircraft during 2006 and 2007. Traditionally, France faces tough competition from the USA and other EU member states for Saudi arms orders, with Russia also emerging as a potential competitor for Saudi orders in 2007.[54] Although at the end of 2007 there were fairly significant orders for frigates, helicopters, missiles and submarines, the French arms export portfolio did not include any orders for new combat aircraft. While France delivered 87 combat aircraft during the period 2003–2007, Morocco selected the US F-16 combat aircraft rather than the French Rafale, and Saudi Arabia opted for the UK-assembled Eurofighter Typhoon in 2007.

The UK—the fifth largest supplier of major conventional weapons for the period 2003–2007—also reformed its export promotion department in 2007. In December 2007 the British Secretary of State for Business, Enterprise and Regulatory Reform, John Hutton, revealed that the national arms export promotion agency, the Defence Export Services Organization, would, as of 1 April 2008, become the Defence and Security Group within the British Department of Enterprise, Trade and Investment.[55] Another similarity with

[49] Tran, P., 'France works to revive flagging arms exports', *Defense News*, 17 Dec. 2007, p. 9; and Agence France-Presse, 'France sets up special arms sales task force', ABCmoney.co.uk, 24 Oct. 2007, <http://www.abcmoney.co.uk/news/242007151151.htm>.

[50] Cabirol, M., 'La Défense vise 8 à 10 milliards d'euros d'exportations' [Defence aims at 8 to 10 billion euros' worth of exports], *La Tribune*, 3 Sep. 2007.

[51] French Ministry of Defence, 'La stratégie de relance des exportations du Ministere de la Défense' [The strategy for the relaunch of exports of Ministry of Defense], Press Dossier, 13 Dec. 2007, <http://www.defense.gouv.fr/ministre/prises_de_parole/dossier_de_presse/la_strategie_de_relance_des_exporta tions_du_ministere_de_la_defense>.

[52] Hall, B., 'Gadaffi's visit to France sparks protests', *Financial Times*, 10 Dec. 2007.

[53] Pirot, L., 'French offer Saudi nuclear energy help', Associated Press, 13 Jan 2008, <http://abcnews.go.com/print?id=4128864>.

[54] E.g. France reportedly lost a deal to supply Saudi Arabia with 150 helicopters, worth $2.2 billion, to Russia. Kahwaji, R., 'Saudis to buy 150 Russian Helos', *Defense News*, 5 Nov. 2007.

[55] Hutton, J., Secretary of State for Business, Enterprise and Regulatory Reform, 'Defence exports', Statement to the British House of Commons, *Commons Hansard*, Column 16WS–17WS, 11 Dec. 2007, <http://www.publications.parliament.uk/pa/cm200708/cmhansrd/cm071211/wmsindx/71211-x.htm>.

France has been the way in which British leaders have also played an active role in promoting arms exports to Libya and Saudi Arabia—two countries that have previously been lucrative markets for arms exports.[56] In May 2007 the British Prime Minister, Tony Blair, also met with Qadhafi to discuss the possible sale of SAM systems and the conclusion of a $900 million exploration deal between energy company BP and Libya.[57] In September 2007 the UK announced an agreement to supply 72 Eurofighter Typhoon combat aircraft to Saudi Arabia in a deal called 'Project Al Salam'. The agreement could be worth up to £20 billion ($40 billion) if all options are exercised over a 25-year period.[58]

IV. Arms transfers to South America

Over the period 2003–2007 South America accounted for only 5 per cent of the volume of international arms transfers; however, the volume transferred to this region during this period was 47 per cent higher than in 1998–2002. This section gives a brief overview of recent and upcoming arms transfers to Chile and Venezuela (two countries that have seen a significant increase in arms imports in recent years) and Brazil (which made a number of major arms procurement related announcements during 2007) and assesses speculation of an arms race in the region.

In September 2006 Óscar Arias Sánchez, President of Costa Rica, citing recent purchases by Chile, Venezuela and others, declared that the region 'has begun a new arms race'.[59] While there is some evidence of competitive behaviour—for example, in Brazil's apparent desire to keep pace with Venezuela's modernizations—and of potential increases in tension—particularly in Colombia's response to Venezuela's acquisitions—it is doubtful that events in the region can be accurately described as an 'arms race' in classical terms.[60] Acquisitions have been primarily motivated by efforts to replace or upgrade military inventories in order to maintain existing capabilities; respond to predominantly domestic security threats; strengthen ties with supplier governments; boost domestic arms industries; participate in peacekeeping missions; or bolster each country's regional or international profile. Meanwhile, formal

---

[56] SIPRI Arms Transfers Project (note 25), 'International arms embargoes'.

[57] Chuter, A., 'Libya buys U.K. firm's communication system', *Defense News*, 4 June 2007.

[58] Ripley, T., 'Typhoon: deal of the decade', *Jane's Defence Weekly*, 26 Sep. 2007, p. 23.

[59] Oppenheimer, A., 'Just what Latin America needed—a new arms race', *Miami Herald*, 17 Sep. 2007, p. 16A. These concerns have been echoed elsewhere. E.g. see Malamud, C. and García Encina, C., 'Rearmament or renovation of military equipment in Latin America', Working Paper 31/2006, Real Instituto Elcano, 1 Feb. 2007, <http://www.realinstitutoelcano.org/documentos/283.asp>; and Downie, A., 'A South American arms race?', *Time*, 21 Dec. 2007.

[60] The classic arms race model defines an arms race as a situation in which a state's build-up of weaponry is positively related to the amount of weaponry its rival has and to the grievance felt towards the rival and negatively related to the amount of arms it has already. Richardson, L. F., *Arms and Insecurity: A Mathematical Study of Causes and Origins of War* (Boxwood Press: Pittsburgh, Pa., 1960). However, this model is designed for situations in which 20–30 years of time series data are available. For situations that are developing as the analysis is undertaken, the only approach is to analyse the motivations behind specific arms acquisitions and look for evidence of competitive behaviour.

and informal confidence-building measures (CBMs) have played a positive role in offsetting the negative impact of arms acquisitions. However, levels of adoption and application are uneven, with participation in CBMs stronger in the Southern Cone than the Andean region.[61]

Recent purchases by Chile

Chile's military budget has increased in recent years, largely due to a continued rise in the value of copper.[62] Increased arms transfers have seen Chile rise from the 38th largest recipient of military equipment for the period 1998–2002 to the 12th largest recipient for the period 2003–2007 and the largest in South America.[63] During this period, 82 per cent of transfers of major conventional weapons to Chile came from EU member states, 15 per cent came from the USA and 3 per cent came from Israel. During 2006 and 2007, Chile took delivery of 10 new F-16C combat aircraft from the USA; 18 second-hand F-16AM combat aircraft, 2 second-hand Doorman frigates and 2 second-hand Van Heemskerck frigates from the Netherlands; 3 second-hand Type-23 frigates from the UK; 24 second-hand M-109 155-mm self-propelled guns from Switzerland; the first 5 of 136 second-hand Leopard-2 tanks from Germany; the second of 2 Scorpene submarines built by France and Spain; and a number of Derby and Python-4 air-to-air missiles from Israel.

Chile's acquisitions replace mostly ageing or decommissioned systems. For example, the F-16 aircraft replaced Mirage-series combat aircraft, while the Scorpene submarines replaced two Oberon submarines commissioned in 1976. However, the purchases of F-16 aircraft, Scorpene submarines and Leopard-2 tanks indicate a significant qualitative advance, particularly in comparison with the armed forces of other countries in the region. Chile may become the first country in South America to possess 'NATO-standard' military forces.[64]

Chile's arms purchases have sparked some concern in the region, particularly in Bolivia and Peru, both of which have long-standing border disputes with Chile.[65] In response to regional tensions, Chile, together with its neighbours, has developed a range of CBMs relating to defence and security issues. Defence and foreign ministers from Argentina, Chile and Peru meet for bilateral exchanges of information.[66] Relations between Bolivia and Chile,

---

[61] See Bromley, M. and Perdomo, C., 'CBMs in Latin America and the effect of arms acquisitions by Venezuela', Working Paper 41/2005, Real Instituto Elcano, 22 Sep. 2005, <http://www.realinstituto elcano.org/documentos/216.asp>.

[62] According to the Restricted law on copper, Law no. 13 196 of 29 Oct. 1958 (most recently modified in 1987), 10% of total revenue from copper exports is set aside to finance military acquisitions.

[63] Nonetheless, Chile accounted for just 2% of global transfers of major conventional weapons for the period 2003–2007.

[64] Gonzalez Cabrera, P., 'Chilean military plans to be NATO-standard force by 2010', El Mercurio, 18 July 2005.

[65] Higuera, J., 'Chile confirms plans to buy second-hand F-16s', Jane's Defence Weekly, 6 July 2005, p. 8.

[66] 'Thawing relations with Peru', Latin American Security & Strategic Review, Sep. 2007, p. 9; and 'Defence agreements with Argentina and China', Latin American Security & Strategic Review, Sep. 2006, p. 8.

frozen for several years, also improved during 2007.[67] Cooperation between Chile and Argentina is particularly strong, encompassing cooperation on the procurement of new frigates and the development of a joint battalion for deployment in UN peacekeeping operations.[68] Argentina, Bolivia and Peru have recently announced their own force modernization programmes. Their programmes are mainly aimed at restoring the operational condition of their military equipment, rather than seeking to match Chilean acquisitions.[69]

Recent purchases by Venezuela

Venezuela's military budget was $2.57 billion in 2007, an increase of 78 per cent over 2003, the largest rise in South America.[70] Venezuela has also moved from being the 56th largest recipient of major conventional weapons for the period 1998–2002 to 24th place for 2003–2007. For the latter period, 92 per cent of transfers of major conventional weapons to Venezuela came from Russia, 3 per cent from China and 2 per cent from Israel.

The budget increase, made possible by rising international oil prices, supported significant arms purchases by Venezuela between 2005 and 2007, including $4 billion worth of agreements with Russia.[71] These include deals for 10 Mi-35 combat helicopters, 3 Mi-26 heavy transport helicopters, 40 Mi-17 multi-role helicopters, 100 000 AK-103 rifles, 24 Su-30MK combat aircraft and, possibly, a number of TOR-M1 SAM systems. Venezuela is also acquiring four patrol boats and four corvettes from Spain and three JY-1 radars from China. Weapon systems delivered by the end of the 2007 included all of the Mi-35 and Mi-26 helicopters, half of the Mi-17 helicopters and 18 of the 24 Su-30MK aircraft. Throughout 2007 there were persistent rumours of a raft of new purchases from Russia, including Su-35 and Su-39 combat aircraft, An-74 and Il-76 transport aircraft, Mi-28 combat helicopters and Kilo Class submarines. However, no new contracts were signed, leading some to question Venezuela's ability to fund further large acquisitions.[72]

Venezuela's arms purchases are geared towards a number of different goals. As in Chile, many of the items purchased are replacements for outdated or obsolete weapon systems. Venezuelan President Hugo Chávez has also spoken repeatedly of the supposed threat posed by the USA and its plans to overthrow

---

[67] 'Rapprochement with Bolivia', *Latin American Security & Strategic Review*, Sep. 2007, p. 9.

[68] Cavas, C. P., 'Leading Latin nations share budget data, costs', *Defense News*, 25 Apr. 2005, p. 1; and Higuera, J., 'Turning up the heat', *Jane's Defence Weekly*, 9 Jan. 2008, p. 26.

[69] Baranauskas, T., 'Bolivian air force to get various aircraft', Forecast International Government & Industry Group, 26 Feb. 2007; Cruz Tantalean, C., 'Peru's upgrade plan shifts focus', *Jane's Defence Weekly*, 10 Oct. 2007, p. 31; Barragán, J. M. and Higuera, J., 'Buenos Aires announces forces funding boost', *Jane's Defence Weekly*, 31 Oct. 2007, p. 32; and Baranauskas, T., 'New Peruvian government will not try to match Chilean arms upgrades', Forecast International Government & Industry Group, 13 Sep. 2006.

[70] See chapter 5 and appendix 5A in this volume.

[71] 'Russia plans to double the volume of arms deliveries to Venezuela', ARMS-TASS, 30 Oct. 2007, <http://arms-tass.su/?page=article&aid=47060&cid=43>.

[72] Abdullaev, N. and Cavas, C. P., 'Russia, Venezuela hint at submarine deal', *Defence News*, 16 July 2007.

his government. This motivated Venezuela's announcement of the creation of a large reserve force armed with AK-103 rifles for conducting guerrilla-style operations in case of invasion.[73] The threat of a US invasion has also been used to justify purchases of combat aircraft and SAMs.[74] Meanwhile, the helicopter acquisitions are aimed at extending the military's presence along Venezuela's 2000 kilometre-long border with Colombia.[75] Other Venezuelan goals cited by commentators include the consolidation of the government's standing with the military; intimidating or impressing its neighbours; and strengthening ties with Russia.[76] Venezuelan's purchasing and supply options have been strongly shaped by a US embargo on arms transfers in place since August 2006.[77]

Particular attention has been paid to Venezuela's purchase of Su-30MK combat aircraft, especially by Colombia. Colombia and Venezuela have frequently been at odds over a number issues, including a long-running dispute over territorial waters and Colombia's armed conflict with the FARC guerrilla movement. Relations between Colombian President Álvaro Uribe and President Chávez have been frosty for several years and took a sharp turn for the worse in 2007.[78] In August 2007 the Colombian Government announced plans to raise military expenditure to its highest level in 30 years.[79] Colombian officials have denied that the move is a response to Venezuela's acquisitions, consistently emphasizing that tackling the guerrilla-led insurgency is the sole motivation.[80] Informal exchanges of information and other CBMs have taken place between Colombia and Venezuela, helping to allay suspicions, although these mechanisms are less developed than those put in place by Chile and its neighbours.[81]

[73] 'Russian rifles for snipers', *Latin American Security & Strategic Review*, Sep. 2007, p. 17.

[74] 'Defending Venezuela', *Jane's Intelligence Review*, Jan. 2007, p. 66.

[75] 'Venezuela reportedly finalizes $1B deal for helicopters, SU-30s', *Defense Industry Daily*, 27 July 2006.

[76] De Franceschi, J., 'Russia arms Latin America', *VOA News Now*, Voice of America, 27 Apr. 2007, Transcript <http://www.voanews.com/english/archive/2007-04/2007-05-02-voa4.cfm>; and 'Venezuela reportedly finalizes $1B deal for helicopters, SU-30s' (note 75).

[77] Murphy, J., 'US extends arms embargo on Venezuela', *Jane's Defence Weekly*, 30 Aug. 2006, p. 19. US export restrictions and political pressure have also blocked Venezuelan attempts to purchase military equipment from other suppliers, including Brazil, Israel, Spain and Sweden.

[78] Mander, B. and Lapper, R., 'Chávez puts Colombia relations in "freezer"', *Financial Times*, 26 Nov. 2007.

[79] Bedoya, J., 'Movilidad de las tropas sera prioridad en gasto de $8,2 billiones recogidos por impuestode guerra' [Troop mobility will be the priority in the allocation of $8.2 billion collected under war tax], *El Tiempo* (Bogota), 6 Aug. 2007.

[80] 'Colombia aprueba plan de 3.370 mln dlr para gasto militar' [Colombia approves request of $3370 million for military spending], Reuters América Latina, 27 Feb. 2007.

[81] 'Caracas to deploy troops & new radar on the border', *Latin American Security & Strategic Review*, June 2006, p. 9; and 'US intelligence chiefs see no major security threat from Latin America', *Latin American Security & Strategic Review*, Mar. 2007, p. 1.

Recent purchases by Brazil

Brazil fell from being the 21st largest recipient of military equipment for the period 1998–2002 to 32nd place for 2003–2007. During the period 2003–2007, 64 per cent of transfers of major conventional weapons to Brazil came from EU member states, 17 per cent from the USA and 7 per cent from Canada. Deliveries of major conventional weapons systems to Brazil during 2006 and 2007 were far more limited than transfers to Chile or Venezuela. Transfers included 8 of a planned 12 second-hand Mirage-2000C combat aircraft from France; 7 of 12 C-295M transport aircraft from Spain; and 6 S-70 Blackhawk helicopters from the USA. Brazil is also modernizing its fleet of F-5E combat aircraft, equipping them with Derby air-to-air missiles from Israel. By the end of 2007, the Brazilian Air Force had also received 50 of the 99 EMB-314 Super Tucano trainer and combat aircraft procured from the Brazilian company Embraer.[82]

Two announcements in 2007 have the potential to have a significant impact on both Brazil's military capabilities and its global ranking as a recipient of military goods. First, in July the government revived a long-standing project to build a nuclear-powered submarine. Brazil plans to invest 1 billion reais ($560 million) over eight years to purchase French or German technology to build the submarine and to develop a nuclear reactor to power the boat.[83] Second, in November the government announced the relaunch of the 'F-X' combat aircraft programme, giving the green light for a selection process beginning in January 2008 and providing $2.2 billion for the procurement of up to 36 aircraft.[84] These purchases will be backed up by an increase in Brazil's military budget, set to rise from 6.5 billion reais ($3.64 billion) in 2007 to 10 billion reais ($5.6 billion) in 2008.[85]

In justifying the new acquisitions, officials have cited the needs to: reverse a series of defence budget cuts that have sharply reduced the capabilities of

---

[82] Embraer, 'Embraer delivers 50th A-29 Super Tucano to Brazilian air force', Press release, 19 Sep. 2007, <http://www.embraer.com/english/content/imprensa/press_releases_detalhe.asp?id=1670>; and 'Brazil confirms Derby BVR AAM procurement', *Jane's Missiles and Rockets*, Jan. 2007, p. 16.

[83] Reuters, 'Brazil to build $500m nuclear sub', 11 July 2007, <http://www.news.com.au/story/0,235 99,22054761-23109,00.html>. Brazil first raised the prospect of building a nuclear powered submarine in 1979 and the plan has since been subject to frequent policy reversals. E.g. in Nov. 2006 it was announced that the plan was being postponed indefinitely in favour of the licensed construction of a Type-214 submarine from Germany and the modernization of 5 existing Type-209 submarines for a total cost of 2.71 billion reais ($1.24 billion). How these plans will be affected by the Brazilian Government's July 2007 announcement remains unclear. Squassoni, S. and Fite, D., 'Brazil as litmus test: resende and restrictions on uranium enrichment', *Arms Control Today*, Oct. 2005; 'Brazilian navy postpones indefinitely its nuclear submarine construction program', *O Estado de S. Paulo*, 15 Nov. 2006, Translation from Portuguese, Forecast International Market Alert News Center; and 'Brazil's navy wants to buy at least 33 ships', *O Estado de S. Paulo*, 13 May 2007, Translation from Portuguese, Forecast International Market Alert News Center.

[84] 'Fighter deal green light to update Brazilian air force', *Flight International*, 12 Nov. 2007. The original F-X programme was cancelled in 2005 to redirect funds to the 'Fome Zero' (zero hunger) plan. Stålenheim et al. (note 1), p. 286.

[85] 'Brazil denies "arms race" with Venezuela', Xinhua, 31 Oct. 2007, <http://news.xinhuanet.com/english/2007-11/01/content_6988196.htm>.

Brazil's armed forces; reinvigorate the domestic defence industry; and boost arms exports. In September 2007 Brazilian President Lula da Silva announced the creation of a working party to draft a National Defence Strategy to hasten the recovery of the 'capability of our armed forces and the technological edge we once had in certain fields'. The working party was given 12 months to devise a 10–15 year defence development plan.[86] In reversing previous cuts Brazilian officials have focused on the need to improve capabilities in order to better police the country's vast coastline and remote border areas, particularly the Amazon region.[87] As of November 2007, only 267 of the Brazilian Air Force's 719 aircraft were deemed airworthy.[88]

To strengthen Brazil's defence industry, the government has stated that the arms procurement deals announced in 2007 will include production in Brazil and significant levels of technology transfer.[89] Brazil was a significant arms exporter in the 1980s and the government is keen to increase the value of its arms exports.[90] The attempt to reinvigorate a domestic arms industry via purchases of advanced military technology from abroad is a policy that Brazil and other countries in the developing world have tried in the past, with mixed levels of success.[91]

The 2007 procurement announcements came in the wake of a string of commentaries by Brazilian analysts and former government officials raising questions about Venezuela's arms purchases.[92] Relations between Brazil's President da Silva and Venezuela's President Chávez have been warm, but tensions have increased following Venezuela's support for Bolivia's nationalization of its hydrocarbon industry in May 2006.[93] In announcing the new procurement plans, Brazilian officials have been at pains to stress that they were not motivated by the Venezuelan purchases.[94]

---

[86] 'Brazil to boost defense industry and acquire 36 fighter jets', *Mercopress*, 6 Nov. 2007; and Guevara, I., 'Brazil eyes new defence doctrine', *Jane's Defence Weekly*, 26 Sep. 2007, p. 7.

[87] 'Brazil to boost defense industry and acquire 36 fighter jets' (note 86).

[88] 'Fighter deal green light to update Brazilian air force' (note 84).

[89] 'Brazil to boost defense industry and acquire 36 fighter jets' (note 86).

[90] Lehman, S., 'Brazil plans comeback of its once-lucrative defense industry', Associated Press, 7 Mar. 2005; and 'Brazil looks for weapons export gains', *Jane's Defence Weekly*, 4 May 2005, p. 10. During the period 1984–88, Brazil was the 11th largest arms exporter with 41% of its transfers going to Iraq. Following the end of the 1980–88 Iran–Iraq War Brazil's arms exports declined significantly and, despite retaining significant market shares in sections of the aerospace and small arms markets, it has never regained the level of exports it had in the mid-1980s.

[91] Brauer J. and Dunne, J. P. (eds), *Arms Trade and Economic Development: Theory, Policy, and Cases in Arms Trade Offsets* (Routledge: London, 2004).

[92] Former Brazilian Foreign Minister Celso Lafer and former Brazilian President José Sarney both voiced concerns over Venezuela's arms purchases in 2006 and the need for Brazil to respond in kind. 'Latin America: press sees Chavez's arms deals as potential threat', *World News Connection*, 18 Aug. 2006; and 'No arms race, no response to Venezuela', *Latin American Security & Strategic Review*, Nov. 2007, p. 11.

[93] 'How gas is realigning South America', *Latin American Security & Strategic Review*, Aug. 2006, p. 12. Also see 'Lula and Chávez compete for alliances across the region', *Latin American Security & Strategic Review*, Aug. 2007, pp. 1–2; and 'Brazil and Chile lead strategies to contain Chávez without isolating him', *Latin American Security & Strategic Review*, Sep. 2007, pp. 1–2.

[94] 'Brazil rules out Venezuelan arms race', *El Universal*, 4 July 2007.

V. International arms transfers to conflict zones: Afghanistan and Sudan

The first edition of the SIPRI Yearbook gave three reasons for arms suppliers to meet the demand for weapons created by conflict: (*a*) to gain political influence; (*b*) as a substitute for an interested external party's direct military presence; (*c*) and powerful economic pressures to sell arms.[95] Arms, other military equipment and 'training' can also be supplied to gain or secure access to, or transit for, natural resources.[96] Meanwhile, for a variety of economic or ideological reasons, governments continue to overtly and covertly supply arms to warring parties, while international peacekeepers often struggle to obtain sufficient arms and military equipment.[97] This section addresses the questions 'Who supplies the arms, how and why?', with reference to arms transfers to Afghanistan and Sudan.

Afghanistan

Following the Soviet invasion of 1979, Afghanistan became an international 'arms warehouse', as large quantities of major conventional weapons and small arms and light weapons (SALW) flowed to the various forces fighting there throughout the 1980s and 1990s. While Afghanistan was the 79th largest recipient of transfers of major conventional weapons for the period 2003–2007, for the period 1988–1992 Afghanistan was the fifth largest recipient. This section considers significant developments in 2007 with regard to international arms transfers to armed non-state actors, the Afghan National Army (ANA) and the national armed forces participating in the multinational International Security Assistance Force (ISAF) in Afghanistan.[98]

Armed non-state actors

Since 2005 there has been a dramatic increase in armed violence by non-state actors in Afghanistan.[99] The Afghan Government's Disbandment of Illegal Armed Groups programme estimates that there are more than 1800 illegal armed groups operating in Afghanistan, including insurgents, such as the Tali-

---

[95] 'The third world: military expenditure and the trade in major weapons', *SIPRI Yearbook of World Armaments and Disarmament 1968/69* (Almqvist and Wiksell: Stockholm, 1969), pp. 53–55.

[96] Klare, M. T., *Blood and Oil: The Dangers and Consequences of America's Growing Petroleum Dependency* (Penguin: London, 2005); and Stokes, D., '"Blood for oil?" global capital, counter-insurgency and the dual logic of American energy security', *Review of International Studies*, vol. 22, no. 2 (2007), pp. 245–64.

[97] See chapter 3 in this volume.

[98] The section on armed non-state actors discusses allegations regarding international SALW transfers, which are not contained in the SIPRI Arms Transfers Database. The international transfers of major conventional weapons discussed in the sections on the ANA and ISAF can be found in the SIPRI Arms Transfers Database (note 2).

[99] Lindberg, S. and Melvin, N. J., 'Major armed conflicts', *SIPRI Yearbook 2007* (note 1), pp. 61–66.

ban and Gulbuddin Hekmatyar's Hizb i-Islami forces, local militias and narco-criminal groups.[100] However, the Taliban is the only group operating in Afghanistan that is currently the target of a mandatory UN arms embargo.[101] Despite the embargo and the efforts of the Afghan Government, access to weapons does not appear to have diminished in 2007.

In February 2007 Mullah Dadullah, a senior Taliban commander, announced that the upward trend in armed violence would continue as 'extra weapons' had been supplied to the Taliban, including arms that would be able to bring down helicopters.[102] Although Dadullah's threat implicitly referred to man-portable air defence systems (MANPADS), the main weapons used by insurgent forces in 2007 appear to be small arms, mortars, rocket-propelled grenades and improvised explosive devices.[103] It is assumed that the territory of the Federally Administered Tribal Areas of Pakistan has served as the main conduit, stockpile and supplier of arms to the Taliban.[104] Reports in 2007 suggested that the Afghan–Iranian border had grown in significance. The British and US governments highlighted Iran as a source and transit state for arms seized by the ANA and ISAF and accused Iran of covertly supplying arms to the Taliban.[105] The British Government also approached China regarding suspected trafficking to the Taliban of Chinese-made arms via Iran.[106] In response, Iran denied involvement in arming the Taliban,[107] and China officially stated that it had not exported arms to Afghanistan.[108] This difficulty in identifying the origins of many of the arms found in, or trafficked into,

[100] Government of Afghanistan, Disbandment of Illegal Armed Groups, <http://www.diag.gov.af/>.

[101] An UN arms embargo was imposed on Taliban-controlled Afghanistan on 19 Dec. 2000. On 16 Jan. 2002, a mandatory UN arms embargo was imposed on the Taliban, wherever located. UN Security Council resolutions 1333, 19 Dec. 2000, and 1367, 16 Jan. 2002. See also Fruchart et al. (note 10); and Holtom, P., 'United Nations arms embargoes: their impact on arms flows and target behaviour—Case study: The Taliban', SIPRI, Stockholm, 2007, <http://books.sipri.org/product_info?c_product_id=356>.

[102] Achakzai, S. A., 'Afghan Taliban say rearmed, ready for war', Reuters, 23 Feb. 2007, <http://www.reuters.com/article/featuredCrisis/idUSSP100413>.

[103] This statement is based on reports of engagements with insurgents from the website of the Combined Joint Task Force 82, Operation Enduring Freedom, <http://www.cjtf82.com/>; and United Nations, Sixth Report of the Analytical Support and Sanctions Monitoring Team appointed pursuant to Security Council resolution 1526 (2004) and 1617 (2005) concerning Al-Qaida and the Taliban and associated individuals and entities, UN Document S/2007/132, 8 Mar. 2007, p. 32.

[104] Norell, M., *The Taliban and the Muttahida Majlis-e-Amal (MMA)*, Memo 2021 (Swedish Defence Agency: Stockholm, Mar. 2007), p. 37; Rashid, A., 'Dangerous neighbours', *Far Eastern Economic Review*, 9 Jan. 2003, p. 19; and United Nations, Second report of the Analytical Support and Sanctions Monitoring Team appointed pursuant to resolution 1526 (2004) concerning Al-Qaida and the Taliban and associated individuals and entities, UN Document S/2005/83, 15 Feb. 2003, p. 32.

[105] 'Audio: Des Browne on Afghanistan and Iraq', Podcast, *The Guardian*, 16 Aug. 2007, <http://blogs.guardian.co.uk/podcasts/2007/08/des_browne_on_afghanistan_and.html>; and Miles, D., 'Gates, Karzai share optimism about Afghanistan's course', US Department of Defense, American Forces Press Service, 4 June 2007, <http://www.defenselink.mil/news/newsarticle.aspx?id=46276>.

[106] Danahar, P., 'Taleban "getting Chinese weapons"', BBC News, 3 Sep. 2007, <http://news.bbc.co.uk/2/6975934.stm>.

[107] Khilwatgar, N., 'No evidence of arms supply from other countries: ISAF', *Pajhwok Afghan News*, 18 July 2007.

[108] Chinese Ministry of Foreign Affairs, 'Foreign Ministry spokesman Qin Gang's regular press conference on 10 July 2007', 11 July 2007, <http://www.fmprc.gov.cn/eng/xwfw/s2510/2511/t339160.htm>.

Afghanistan today is further complicated by the difficulty in identifying the intended recipients of the arms—a point raised by a number of commentators in response to the British and US governments' allegations that arms seized were intended for the Taliban.[109]

The Afghan National Army

The US Department of Defense (DOD), which has been responsible for over-seeing the training and equipping of the ANA, initially decided that the ANA should be equipped with Soviet-designed arms from Afghanistan's Dis-armament, Demobilization and Reintegration and Heavy Weapons Canton-ment projects, as well as Soviet-designed surplus from coalition allies.[110] The DOD adopted this approach because (a) this equipment was familiar to recruits and (b) several coalition allies were willing to provide such surplus.[111] As in Iraq, official US reports have highlighted that deliveries of military equipment were late and that supplies were often old, faulty and overpriced.[112] In an effort to help modernize the ANA, DOD deliveries of $2 billion worth of US military surplus equipment, arms and infrastructure—including 2500 high mobility multipurpose military vehicles and 'tens of thousands' of M-16 rifles—began in 2007.[113] The US budget for 2008 provides a further $2.7 bil-lion to train and equip the ANA and Afghan National Police.[114]

In November 2006 the Afghan Defence Minister, Abdul Rahim Wardak, announced his desire for the ANA 'to have equipment which can be interoper-able with the [ISAF] units and also NATO'.[115] Turkey provided the ANA's first batch of NATO standard-calibre artillery with a donation of 24 155-mm howitzers in 2007. Greece announced in 2007 that it would supply the ANA with 13 Leopard-1 tanks; Australia, Canada and Norway are potential candi-dates for providing additional second-hand Leopard tanks in the future.[116] The

[109] Wright, J., 'Outside assistance: is Iran supporting the Afghan insurgency', Jane's Intelligence Review, Sep. 2007, pp. 38–43.

[110] US Government Accountability Office (GAO), Afghanistan Security: Efforts to Establish Army and Police Have Made Progress, But Future Plans Need to be Better Defined, GAO-05-575 (GAO: Washington, DC, June 2005), pp. 15–16.

[111] US Government Accountability Office (note 110), p. 16.

[112] Garamone, J., 'Justice, defense agencies examine contracting problems', US Department of Defense, American Forces Press Service, 28 Aug. 2007, <http://www.defenselink.mil/news/newsarticle. aspx?id=47209>; and McCaffrey, B. R., 'Academic report—trip to Afghanistan and Pakistan', 3 June 2006, <http://www.washingtonspeakers.com/prod_images/pdfs/McCaffreyBarry.VisitToAfghanistan.05. 06.pdf>, pp. 6–7.

[113] Tran, T., 'Afghanistan to get $2 billion in US gear', Associated Press, 4 July 2006, <http://www. afghannews.net/index.php?action=show&type=news&id=844.com>.

[114] US Office of Management and Budget, Budget of the United States Government, Fiscal Year 2008, Appendix, Detailed Budget Estimates (Government Printing Office: Washington, DC, 2007), <http://www.whitehouse.gov/omb/budget/fy2008/appendix.html>, pp. 247–48.

[115] US Department of Defense, 'DoD news briefing with LTG Eikenberry and Minister of Defense Wardak at the Pentagon', 21 Nov. 2006, <http://www.defenselink.mil/transcripts/transcript.aspx? transcriptid=3816>.

[116] 'Afghanistan may get Norwegian tanks', Norway Post, 25 Oct. 2006; NATO, 'Fact sheet: NATO support to Afghan national army (ANA)', Oct. 2007, <http://www.nato.int/isaf/topics/factsheets/nato-

USA will also arrange for the transfer of reconnaissance and transport planes, transport and combat helicopters and light combat aircraft, enabling the Afghan Air Force to have 112 operational aircraft by 2015.[117] It is envisaged that Soviet-designed helicopters will continue to form the bulk of helicopter transfers, with three Mi-17 helicopters transferred from the Czech Republic in 2007. In 2008 the USA is funding the transfer of a further three Mi-17 and six Mi-35 helicopters from the Czech Republic, one Mi-17 from Slovakia, nine Mi-17 via the UAE and four modernized An-32 transport aircraft from Ukraine. The USA is also expected to supply the Afghan Air Force with 20 C-27 transport aircraft purchased from Italy, with deliveries scheduled to begin in 2009.[118]

The International Security Assistance Force

Experiences on the ground have influenced procurement plans for the national armed forces that contribute to ISAF in Afghanistan, with significant acquisitions shifting toward strategic airlift capabilities, helicopters, armoured vehicles and UAVs. This is in line with the NATO 2006 Riga Summit Declaration's recognition of the need to increase strategic airlift capabilities 'to conduct and support multinational joint expeditionary operations far from home territory'.[119] As a result, orders for C-17 transport aircraft from the USA by NATO member states increased in 2006–2007.[120] Heavy transport helicopters were also in demand: the Netherlands announced in February 2007 plans to acquire six US-produced CH-47F helicopters and upgrade a further 11 Dutch CH-47D helicopters to CH-47F standard, and the UK announced the upgrade of eight CH-47 helicopters in December 2007. The situation is so desperate regarding tactical air transport capacities that NATO has awarded a $37 million contract to a privately owned US company to provide fixed- and rotary-wing aircraft for airlift duties in Afghanistan.[121]

National forces operating in Afghanistan were also seeking heavier armoured vehicles, with Canada shelving its plans to acquire 66 Stryker/LAV-III 105-mm mobile gun systems and opting instead to replace 114 old Leopard-C2 tanks with 20 leased Leopard-2A6M tanks from Germany and 100 second-hand Leopard-2A4/6 tanks from the Netherlands. Conditions in

support-to-ana-factsheet.pdf>; and Pugliese, D., 'Canada may supply Afghan military with Leopard tanks', CanWest News Service, 21 May 2007.

[117] US Department of Defense, 'DoD Press Briefing with Brig. Gen. Lindell at the Pentagon, Arlington, Va.', 24 Jan. 2008, <http://www.defenselink.mil/transcripts/transcript.aspx?transcriptid=4126>.

[118] Khilwatgar, N., 'AAF to get 26 aircraft this year', Pajhwok Afghan News, 17 Jan. 2008, <http://www.pajhwok.com/viewstory.asp?lng=eng&id=48767>; and US Department of Defense (note 117).

[119] NATO, 'Riga Summit Declaration', Press Release (2006)150, 29 Nov. 2006, <http://www.nato.int/docu/pr/2006/p06-150e.htm>.

[120] In 2007 the UK ordered and received its fifth and sixth C-17s and Canada received the first 2 of 4 C-17s. A consortium of 15 NATO members plus Finland and Sweden sought to acquire 3 or 4 C-17s. NATO, 'Allies agree on Strategic Airlift Capability initiative', Press Release (2007)075, 20 June 2007, <http://www.nato.int/docu/pr/2007/p07-075e.html>.

[121] Fiorenza, N., 'NATO outsources additional airlift for Afghanistan', Jane's Defence Weekly, 2 Jan. 2008, p. 6.

Afghanistan have also seen increased use of, and demand for, a range of UAV systems, with Israel emerging alongside the USA as one of the main suppliers to ISAF forces. In 2007 Israel supplied large Hermes-450 UAVs to British forces in Afghanistan. The UK also deployed its first US-supplied armed M-Q9 UAV to Afghanistan in October 2007, while Denmark acquired the US-built Raven-B mini-UAV in 2007. The deployment of new generations of UAVs, of varying sizes, in Afghanistan is perhaps one of the most striking examples of the theatre's use as a test ground for new weapons.

Sudan

Since the beginning of the conflict in Darfur, armed non-state actors have relied primarily on SALW, while the Sudanese armed forces have used major conventional weapons in the region. For the period 1998–2002 Sudan was ranked the 66th largest recipient of transfers of major conventional weapons and was 44th for the period 2003–2007. This section considers significant developments in 2007 with regard to international arms transfers to armed non-state actors, the Sudanese Government's armed forces and the African Union/United Nations Hybrid Operation in Darfur (UNAMID).[122]

Armed non-state actors

In reaction to the conflict in the Darfur region of Sudan, on 30 July 2004 UN Security Council Resolution 1556 imposed an embargo on supplies of arms and military equipment to armed non-state actors operating in Darfur.[123] In 2007 a UN panel of experts concluded that the Government of Eritrea directly supplied arms and military equipment to armed non-state actors in Darfur.[124] It also suspected that high-level government officials from Chad and Libya arranged for military support to armed non-state actors in Darfur. Armed non-state actors in Darfur have also equipped themselves with arms and military equipment stolen from Sudanese Government armed forces and small arms trafficked into Darfur from neighbouring countries.[125] There is also strong evidence that the Sudanese Government used Arab tribesmen in Darfur, known as the Janjaweed, as a militia—organizing, financing and arming them.[126]

[122] The international transfers of SALW to non-state actors and the Sudanese Government discussed here are not contained in the SIPRI Arms Transfers Database. The international transfers of major conventional weapons discussed in the section on the Sudanese Government's armed forces can be found in the SIPRI Arms Transfers Database.

[123] UN Security Council Resolution 1556, 30 July 2004. For an analysis of the conflict in Darfur see chapter 2 in this volume, section IV. For a more in-depth study of arms transfers to Sudan before and during the UN arms embargoes see Wezeman, P., 'United Nations arms embargoes: their impact on arms flows and target behaviour—Case study: Darfur (Sudan)', SIPRI, Stockholm, 2007, <http://books.sipri.org/product_info?c_product_id=356>.

[124] United Nations, Final report of the panel of experts as requested by the Security Council in paragraph 2 of resolution 1665 (2006), UN Document S/2007/584, 3 Oct. 2007, pp. 27–28.

[125] Amnesty International, 'Sudan: arming the perpetrators of grave abuses in Darfur', 16 Nov. 2004, <http://www.amnesty.org/en/library/info/AFR54/139/2004>, p. 26.

[126] United Nations (note 124), p. 56.

Sudanese Government armed forces

In 2005 UN Security Council Resolution 1591 expanded the coverage of the arms embargo on Darfur, prohibiting the movement of military equipment to all belligerents in Darfur, including Sudanese Government forces based in Darfur.[127] In the period 2003–2007 the Government of Sudan accounted for a negligible share of the global volume of transfers. The Sudanese Government's main supplier of major conventional weapons in this period was Russia, which accounted for an estimated 87 per cent of the transfers, while China accounted for 8 per cent. During this period, Russia supplied 20 combat helicopters and 12 MiG-29S combat aircraft, while China supplied at least six K-8 and three A-5 light combat aircraft. Since the 1990s, Chinese, Iranian and Russian companies have also supported the expansion of Sudan's own capabilities to assemble and produce small arms, artillery and armoured vehicles.[128] Available data suggest that China and Iran accounted for over 95 per cent of all small arms and related ammunition supplied to Sudan in the period 1992–2005.[129] Other arms suppliers are likely to include India and Turkey, as Sudan signed military agreements with these countries in 2003 and 2006, respectively.[130]

The Sudanese Government has ignored the UN arms embargo imposed by Resolution 1591, deploying Chinese and Russian arms and military equipment to government forces in Darfur without the prior consent of the UN Sanctions Committee appointed to monitor the resolution.[131] Despite the Sudanese Government's contravention of the resolution, China and Russia have opposed calls to impose a blanket UN arms embargo on Sudan.[132] There are several possible motives for the Chinese and Russian positions. First, China and Russia have opposed the imposition of UN arms embargoes on governments condemned for violence against their civilians—most recently Myanmar (Burma)—by citing the importance of the principle of non-interference in the internal affairs of sovereign states.[133] Second, transfers strengthen ties between the Sudanese Government and the Chinese and Russian governments. They are therefore considered one of the ways in which China in particular has sought to gain access to Sudanese oil reserves and other economic opportunities. Access to the Sudanese oil industry is a significant element of China's

[127] UN Security Council Resolution 1591, 29 Mar. 2005.

[128] A list of Chinese-, Iranian- and Russian-designed weapons produced in Sudan can be found at the website of the Sudanese Military Industry Corporation, <http://mic.sd/english/abouten.htm>.

[129] Small Arms Survey, 'The militarization of Sudan', Sudan Issue Brief: Human Security Baseline Assessment no. 6 (Apr. 2007).

[130] 'Sudan, Turkey ink military cooperation accord', *Sudan Tribune*, 1 Aug. 2006; and 'India offers defence help to Sudan', *The Hindu*, 15 Dec. 2003.

[131] United Nations (note 124), pp. 28–42, 60–64.

[132] E.g. China and Russia abstained from the vote on UN Security Council Resolution 1591. China also abstained from the vote on Resolution 1556. For UN Security Council voting records see the UN Bibliographic Information System (UBISNET), <http://unbisnet.un.org/>.

[133] China and Russia have repeatedly announced their shared view on this principle in joint statements since 1997. A recent example is see Joint statement of the Russian Federation and People's Republic of Chinese on international order in the 21st century, 1 July 2005, available from the Russian Ministry of Foreign Affairs website, <http://www.mid.ru/>.

energy policy and China has made major investments in oil exploration in Sudan.[134] Third, an embargo would mean the loss of revenues from arms sales, although this is likely to be a minor consideration as arms transfers to Sudan represented only about 2 per cent of Chinese and Russian major conventional weapons transfers in the period 2003–2007.

African Union/United Nations Hybrid Operation in Darfur

In contrast to the continuing flow of arms to the belligerents in Darfur, African armed forces deployed as part of international peacekeeping operations in the region report significant shortages in essential military equipment. In November 2007 UNAMID lacked two medium transport aircraft, three medium utility helicopter units and a light tactical helicopter unit. The UN Secretary-General, Ban Ki-Moon, appealed to 'Member States which are in a position to provide these capabilities to do so'.[135] UNAMID illustrates the problem of the international community encouraging African countries to provide a significant proportion of the peacekeeping forces deployed in Africa, while most sub-Saharan countries are poorly equipped for such missions.[136] The EU, its member states and Canada have provided some military aid—including training, helicopters for non-combat transport roles and some armoured vehicles to help improve African peacekeeping capabilities.[137] US military aid, aimed primarily at strengthening African military forces as part of the US 'global war on terrorism', also contributes to African peacekeeping capabilities.[138] However, sub-Saharan African countries remain dependent on limited financial means to procure most of their weapons, which continue to be supplied mainly by China and East European states.

VI. Conclusions

For the past 15 years (1993–2007) the five largest suppliers of major conventional weapons have remained the same: the USA, Russia, Germany, France and the UK. Although these suppliers are likely to continue to account for the largest shares of the volume of international arms transfers, concerns were

---

[134] Small Arms Survey, 'Arms, oil and Darfur', Sudan Issue Brief: Human Security Baseline Assessment no. 7 (July 2007); and Taylor, I., 'China's oil diplomacy in Africa', *International Affairs*, vol. 82, no. 5 (2006), pp. 937–59.

[135] United Nations, Report of the Secretary-General on the deployment of the African Union–United Nations Hybrid operation in Darfur, UN Document S/2007/653, 5 Nov. 2007, p. 3. The UNAMID commander stated that UNAMID forces required at least 12 combat helicopters, 18 military transport helicopters and a considerable number of armoured vehicles, with developed countries targeted as potential donors. 'Darfur peacekeeper warns of high expectations', allAfrica.com, 6 Nov. 2007, <http://all africa.com/stories/200711060094.html>.

[136] See chapter 3 in this volume.

[137] Canadian Ministry of National Defence, 'Operation AUGURAL', 16 Apr. 2007, <http://www. mdn.ca/site/Operations/augural/index_e.asp; and EU Council Secretariat, 'EU support to the African Union Mission in Darfur-AMIS', Fact sheet, May 2007, <http://www.consilium.europa.eu/cms3_fo/ showPage.asp?id=1087&lang=en>.

[138] 'The doves of war', *The Economist*, 24 Nov. 2007, pp. 52–53.

expressed in 2007 regarding the export prospects for French and Russian weapons. Nevertheless, orders for major conventional arms announced in 2007 indicate that the volume of international arms transfers will continue to grow. Developments in 2007 suggest that there could be a change in the composition of the largest recipients in the next 5–15 years, with Saudi Arabia, Libya and Taiwan significantly increasing their ranking.

Despite attention-grabbing headlines, it seems unlikely that South America is in the midst of a classically defined arms race. There is some evidence that the arms acquisition programmes of Brazil, Chile and Venezuela have been influenced by the actions of their neighbours and have themselves had an impact on the procurement decisions of other states in the region. Nonetheless, other domestic factors, such as the need to replace and modernize inventories for new missions, peacekeeping and traditional national defence, appear to be the main explanation for increasing arms transfers. In addition, improved systems of information exchange and other CBMs have helped to limit the negative fallout created by arms acquisitions. Finally, few countries have either the desire or ability to compete with the resource-fuelled acquisitions of Chile or Venezuela, or with the economically powerful Brazil.

The international transfer of arms to conflict zones in Afghanistan and Sudan illustrates a number of tendencies. First, UN arms embargoes imposed on armed non-state actors in Afghanistan and Sudan have thus far failed to stop their arms acquisitions. Second, major arms suppliers have been willing to show their support for the Afghan and Sudanese governments by directly supplying them with arms. In the Afghan case, the shift from Soviet to US and other Western equipment is a significant change in US arms supplies to the ANA. China and Russia continue to support Sudan with arms supplies and to block a blanket UN arms embargo on Sudan. Third, although both ISAF and UNAMID forces lament shortages of suitable combat and transport helicopters, UNAMID's equipment concerns are of a different order of magnitude to those of ISAF.

Appendix 7A. The suppliers and recipients of major conventional weapons

THE SIPRI ARMS TRANSFERS PROJECT

The SIPRI Arms Transfers Project maintains the SIPRI Arms Transfers Database, which contains information on deliveries of major conventional weapons to states, international organizations and non-state armed groups since 1950 (see <http://arms trade.sipri.org/>). SIPRI ascribes a trend-indicator value (TIV) to each weapon or subsystem included in the database. SIPRI then calculates the volume of transfers to, from and between all of the above-listed entities using the TIV and the number of weapon systems or subsystems delivered in a given year. TIV figures do not represent financial values for weapon transfers; they are an indicator of the volume of transfers. Therefore, TIV figures should not be cited directly. They are best used as the raw data for calculating trends in international arms transfers over periods of time, global percentages for suppliers and recipients, and percentages for the volume of transfers to or from particular states.

Table 7A.1 presents the sources of the weapons transferred to the 10 largest recipients of major conventional weapons in the period 2003–2007. Table 7A.2 shows the regional distribution of the exports of the 10 largest suppliers of major conventional weapons for the period 2003–2007. Table 7A.3 presents the SIPRI TIV for all recipients of major conventional weapons for the period 2003–2007. Table 7A.4 presents the SIPRI TIV for all suppliers of major conventional weapons for the period 2003–2007.

Table 7A.1. The 10 largest recipients of major conventional weapons and their suppliers, 2003–2007

Figures are the supplier's share, as a percentage, of the total volume of imports per recipient. Only suppliers with a share of 1 per cent or more of total imports of any of the 10 largest recipients are listed. Smaller suppliers are grouped together as 'other'. Figures may not add up because of the conventions of rounding.

Supplier	\ Recipient \ China	India	UAE	Greece	South Korea	Israel	Egypt	Australia	Turkey	USA
Australia	—	—	—	—	—	—	—	—	—	1
Canada	—	—	—	<1	<1	—	—	2	—	28
China	—	—	—	—	—	—	4	—	<1	—
Denmark	—	—	—	3	—	—	—	—	—	—
France	2	4	52	18	9	—	—	6	1	1
Finland	—	—	—	<1	—	—	—	1	—	1
Germany	1	1	1	17	6	6	2	28	56	2
Israel	—	6	—	2	—	—	3	2	4	6
Italy	—	<1	<1	5	—	—	—	1	4	<1
South Korea	—	—	—	—	—	—	—	—	4	—
Montenegro	—	—	—	—	—	—	—	—	—	—
Netherlands	—	<1	—	6	2	—	6	—	2	—
Poland	—	4	—	—	—	—	4	—	—	—
Russia	94	70	<1	6	5	—	20	—	—	—
South Africa	—	—	<1	—	—	—	—	—	—	—
Spain	—	—	—	—	—	—	—	—	2	2
Switzerland	<1	—	<1	—	—	—	—	—	—	1
Sweden	—	—	—	<1	—	—	—	8	2	23
UK	1	4	—	3	—	—	1	2	—	<1
Ukraine	2	2	2	—	—	—	—	2	2	31
USA	—	2	43	40	77	94	60	50	25	3
Uzbekistan	—	5	—	—	—	—	—	—	—	—
Other	—	1	1	—	—	—	—	1	—	<1
Total	**100**	**100**	**100**	**100**	**100**	**100**	**100**	**100**	**100**	**100**

Table 7A.2. The 10 largest suppliers of major conventional weapons and their destination, by region, 2003–2007

Figures are the supplier's share, as a percentage, of the total volume of exports per recipient region. Figures may not add up because of the conventions of rounding. For the states in each region see appendix 5A in this volume.

Recipient region	Supplier									
	USA	Russia	Germany	France	UK	Netherlands	Italy	Sweden	China	Ukraine
Africa	<1	10	13	1	6	<1	5	–	14	17
North Africa	<1	5	1	<1	<1	–	<1	–	–	13
Sub-Saharan Africa	<1	5	12	1	6	<1	5	–	14	4
Americas	5	5	4	5	32	27	35	3	2	5
South America	2	5	3	4	9	21	33	2	2	–
Asia and Oceania	36	74	17	28	23	13	14	16	52	35
Central Asia	<1	<1	–	–	–	–	–	–	–	2
East Asia	27	51	8	18	13	9	6	1	8	21
Oceania	5	–	8	2	1	3	–	14	–	–
South Asia	3	23	1	8	9	1	8	1	44	12
Europe	27	3	62	16	33	55	46	81	1	16
Central Europe	4	<1	7	1	10	7	10	40	–	<1
Eastern Europe	–	1	–	<1	<1	–	–	–	–	16
Western Europe	23	1	55	15	23	49	36	41	1	<1
Middle East	32	8	4	50	6	5	<1	–	31	24
Total	**100**	**100**	**100**	**100**	**100**	**100**	**100**	**100**	**100**	**100**

Notes for tables 7A.1 and 7A.2: – = nil or negligible; <1 = 0.5 or more, but less than 1.

Source for tables 7A.1 and 7A.2: SIPRI Arms Transfers Database, <http://armstrade.sipri.org/>.

Table 7A.3. The recipients of major conventional weapons, 2003–2007

The table includes all countries and non-state actors that imported major conventional weapons in the five-year period 2003–2007. The ranking is according to 2003–2007 total imports. Figures for the volume of imports are SIPRI trend-indicator values (TIV) expressed in US$ m. at constant (1990) prices (see the note below). The right-hand column shows the recipient state's share of global arms imports for 2003–2007. Figures may not add up to totals because of the conventions of rounding.

Rank 2003–2007	Rank 2002–2006[a]	Recipient	Volume of imports (TIV)						% share, 2003–2007
			2003	2004	2005	2006	2007	03–07	2007
1	1	China	2 068	2 906	3 346	3 719	1 424	13 463	*12*
2	2	India	2 870	2 331	1 182	1 404	1 318	9 105	*8*
3	3	UAE	700	1 436	2 224	2 067	1 040	7 467	*7*
4	4	Greece	2 226	1 498	540	817	2 089	7 170	*6*
5	6	South Korea	575	967	661	1 527	1 807	5 536	*5*
6	7	Israel	292	845	1 108	1 102	891	4 239	*4*
7	5	Egypt	816	752	736	1 020	418	3 743	*3*
8	8	Australia	864	558	560	765	685	3 432	*3*
9	9	Turkey	433	174	984	317	944	2 853	*3*
10	10	USA	501	523	476	514	587	2 601	*2*
11	11	Pakistan	592	385	333	321	715	2 347	*2*
12	17	Chile	175	57	403	1 034	615	2 283	*2*
13	13	Japan	465	412	299	477	519	2 171	*2*
14	19	Poland	376	242	97	424	985	2 123	*2*
15	15	UK	787	135	16	332	698	1 969	*2*
16	16	Italy	516	434	136	702	176	1 965	*2*
17	12	Taiwan	101	341	794	608	3	1 846	*2*
18	21	Singapore	70	384	543	47	707	1 751	*2*
19	30	South Africa	2	2	187	689	855	1 734	*2*
20	18	Spain	110	245	391	537	385	1 669	*2*
21	14	Saudi Arabia	159	952	148	185	72	1 517	*1*
22	27	Algeria	197	272	152	125	700	1 446	*1*
23	26	Malaysia	137	81	16	646	550	1 429	*1*
24	39	Venezuela	13	13	27	477	887	1 417	*1*
25	24	Canada	127	317	110	120	623	1 296	*1*
26	22	Germany	62	254	248	560	85	1 209	*1*
27	23	Iran	198	136	86	450	297	1 168	*1*
28	25	Romania	25	292	553	140	70	1 081	*<1*
29	38	Indonesia	358	101	27	46	475	1 007	*<1*
30	40	Norway	4	6	4	457	483	953	*<1*
31	28	Portugal	57	43	391	429	2	922	*<1*
32	33	Brazil	71	118	277	177	175	818	*<1*
33	32	Czech Republic	104	7	622	65	15	813	*<1*
34	35	Peru	22	47	368	193	172	801	*<1*
35	29	Viet Nam	32	259	336	152	1	779	*<1*
36	31	Netherlands	172	151	119	90	210	742	*<1*
37	20	Yemen	40	314	308	57	–	720	*<1*
38	44	Denmark	46	216	103	141	201	708	*<1*
39	46	Iraq	–	46	152	254	244	695	*<1*
40	34	Jordan	300	203	32	76	83	695	*<1*
41	42	Finland	231	76	96	130	110	642	*<1*

Rank 2003– 2007	Rank 2002– 2006[a]	Recipient	Volume of imports (TIV)						% share, 2003– 2007
			2003	2004	2005	2006	2007	03–07	
42	43	Switzerland	91	175	159	70	126	621	<1
43	37	Oman	32	41	100	415	4	591	<1
44	36	Sudan	140	299	81	49	–	569	<1
45	41	Eritrea	–	280	271	–	–	551	<1
46	56	Hungary	–	3	13	277	192	485	–
47	64	Austria	43	55	21	–	335	455	–
48	48	Ethiopia	193	199	–	–	–	392	–
49	50	Sweden	63	48	62	125	85	383	–
50	45	Thailand	153	117	58	38	9	375	–
51	47	Mexico	9	253	36	53	11	362	–
52	55	France	57	93	–	121	63	334	–
53	51	Bangladesh	9	33	29	240	17	329	–
54	58	Belarus	–	–	6	254	–	260	–
55	61	New Zealand	108	50	8	8	70	244	–
56	59	Argentina	12	162	4	17	41	236	–
57	60	Bulgaria	2	12	158	20	38	231	–
58	77	Belgium	27	18	–	4	171	220	–
59	54	Azerbaijan	–	3	45	142	27	218	–
60	52	Morocco	7	–	96	65	44	212	–
61	53	Colombia	128	11	10	22	38	210	–
62	63	Libya	145	–	–	45	3	192	–
63	76	Kuwait	49	1	19	–	117	186	–
64	57	Tunisia	–	–	168	18	–	186	–
65	65	Georgia	1	45	70	62	4	183	–
66	75	Namibia	–	13	–	72	72	157	–
67	66	Armenia	–	151	–	–	–	151	–
68	62	Bahrain	6	10	57	60	15	149	–
69	67	Kazakhstan	–	46	32	42	21	142	–
70	49	Myanmar (Burma)	71	11	25	20	–	126	–
71	68	Lithuania	1	58	14	45	4	122	–
72	72	Syria	46	19	7	18	30	119	–
73	70	NATO	–	–	–	116	–	116	–
74	83	Latvia	28	15	7	11	51	111	–
75	78	Philippines	8	37	14	20	28	108	–
76	69	Sri Lanka	12	26	25	42	1	107	–
77	73	Ecuador	–	9	45	45	–	99	–
78	79	Afghanistan	17	–	31	3	37	88	–
79	80	Nigeria	54	10	–	9	15	88	–
80	71	Côte d'Ivoire	68	14	–	–	–	82	–
81	90	Estonia	15	7	16	6	30	75	–
82	81	Tanzania	56	–	9	9	–	73	–
83	86	Zimbabwe	23	–	20	20	–	63	–
84	106	Cambodia	–	–	24	–	36	60	–
85	94	Uruguay	–	–	20	7	33	60	–
86	87	African Union	–	–	49	8	–	57	–
87	84	Ireland	–	28	4	11	13	55	–
88	92	Ghana	6	33	–	–	13	53	–
89	85	Cyprus	6	–	20	26	–	52	–

Rank 2003–2007	Rank 2002–2006[a]	Recipient	Volume of imports (TIV)						% share, 2003–2007
			2003	2004	2005	2006	2007	03–07	2003–2007
90	102	Gabon	–	5	–	23	21	49	–
91	91	Albania	2	–	42	–	5	49	–
92	82	Uganda	19	8	17	5	–	48	–
93	97	Croatia	24	8	–	–	14	46	–
94	88	Nepal	9	32	5	–	–	46	–
95	74	Angola	3	8	26	4	–	41	–
96	95	Jamaica	–	–	13	25	1	39	–
97	93	North Korea	10	9	5	5	9	38	–
98	96	Slovenia	15	15	2	2	2	38	–
99	89	DR Congo	–	15	–	17	–	32	–
100	98	Dominican Rep.	3	27	2	–	–	32	–
101	100	Turkmenistan	20	10	–	–	–	30	–
102	105	Zambia	–	–	–	23	3	26	–
103	103	Kenya	–	–	25	–	–	25	–
104	109	Burkina Faso	–	–	19	1	4	24	–
105	122	Equatorial Guinea	–	8	–	–	15	22	–
106	108	Senegal	–	–	6	15	–	22	–
107	110	Chad	–	–	–	18	3	21	–
108	114	Bolivia	–	1	9	5	5	21	–
109	116	Mali	–	–	13	–	7	20	–
110	111	Kyrgyzstan	9	5	3	1	–	18	–
111	113	Malta	–	–	18	–	–	18	–
112	112	Botswana	7	9	–	–	–	16	–
113	117	Niger	14	–	–	–	–	14	–
114	118	Tajikistan	–	–	–	13	–	13	–
115	115	Lebanon /Hezbollah[b]	–	1	–	11	–	13	–
116	107	Qatar	12	–	–	–	–	12	–
117	121	CAR	–	–	–	9	–	9	–
118	104	El Salvador	9	–	–	–	–	9	–
119	120	Djibouti	–	–	8	–	–	8	–
120	123	Gambia	–	7	–	–	–	7	–
121	101	Mauritania	7	–	–	–	–	7	–
122	119	Cameroon	–	–	5	–	–	5	–
123	126	Congo, Rep. of	–	–	4	1	–	5	–
124	127	Laos	–	–	4	–	–	4	–
125	128	Paraguay	–	4	1	–	–	4	–
126	99	Slovakia	–	–	4	–	–	4	–
127	129	Russia	–	–	–	4	–	4	–
128	131	Mauritius	–	–	–	4	–	4	–
129	139	Lebanon	–	–	1	–	3	4	–
130	125	Benin	–	–	–	–	3	3	–
131	133	Rwanda	–	–	–	3	–	3	–
132	132	Brunei	–	–	1	2	–	3	–
133	134	United Nations	–	1	1	1	–	3	–
134	135	Lesotho	–	1	–	1	–	2	–
135	147	Palestinian Authority	–	–	–	–	2	2	–
136	136	Guinea	1	–	–	–	–	1	–

Rank 2003–2007	Rank 2002–2006[a]	Recipient	Volume of imports (TIV)						% share, 2003–2007
			2003	2004	2005	2006	2007	03–07	2007
137	137	Luxembourg	1	–	–	–	–	1	–
138	146	Bahamas	–	–	–	–	1	1	–
139	138	Mozambique	1	–	–	–	–	1	–
140	141	Somalia/UIC[b]	–	–	–	–	–	–	–
141	143	Macedonia	–	–	–	–	–	–	–
142	144	Sri Lanka/LTTE[b]	–	–	–	–	–	–	–
143	145	Bhutan	–	–	–	–	–	–	–
144	140	Panama	–	–	–	–	–	–	–
146	142	Uganda/LRA[b]	–	–	–	–	–	–	–
147	124	Uzbekistan	–	–	–	–	–	–	–
148	130	Burundi	–	–	–	–	–	–	–
–	–	Unknown countries[c]	–	–	–	–	–	–	–
–	–	Unknown rebel groups[c]	–	–	–	–	–	–	–
		Total	**18 750**	**21 089**	**21 256**	**26 223**	**24 210**	**111 528**	*100*

– = nil or negligible; <1 = 0.5 or more, but less than 1; CAR = Central African Republic; UAE = United Arab Emirates.

Note: The SIPRI data on arms transfers relate to actual deliveries of major conventional weapons. To permit comparison between the data on such deliveries of different weapons and to identify general trends, SIPRI uses a trend-indicator value. This value is only an indicator of the volume of international arms transfers and not of the financial values of such transfers. Thus, it is not comparable to economic statistics such as gross domestic product or export/import figures. The method for calculating the trend-indicator value is described in appendix 7C and on the SIPRI Arms Transfers Project website, <http://www.sipri.org/contents/armstrad/atmethods.html>.

[a] The rank order for recipients in 2002–2006 differs from that published in *SIPRI Yearbook 2007* because of subsequent revision of figures for these years.

[b] Deliveries to this country include arms received by a non-state actor or rebel group: LRA = Lord's Resistance Army; LTTE = Liberation Tigers of Tamil Eelam; UIC = Union of Islamic Courts.

[c] This represents one or more unknown country or rebel group.

Source: SIPRI Arms Transfers Database, <http://armstrade.sipri.org/>.

Table 7A.4. The suppliers of major conventional weapons, 2003–2007

The table includes all countries and non-state actors that exported major conventional weapons in the five-year period 2003–2007. The ranking is according to 2003–2007 total exports. Figures for the volume of imports are SIPRI trend-indicator values (TIV) expressed in US$ m. at constant (1990) prices (see the note below). The right-hand column shows the supplier state's share of global arms exports for 2003–2007. Figures may not add up to totals because of the conventions of rounding.

Rank 2003–2007	Rank 2002–2006[a]	Supplier	Volume of exports (TIV)						% share, 2003–2007
			2003	2004	2005	2006	2007	03–07	
1	1	USA	5 581	6 616	7 026	7 821	7 454	34 499	*31*
2	2	Russia	5 355	6 400	5 576	6 463	4 588	28 382	*25*
3	3	Germany	1 706	1 017	1 879	2 891	3 395	10 889	*10*
4	4	France	1 313	2 267	1 688	1 586	2 690	9 544	*9*
5	5	UK	624	1 143	871	978	1 151	4 766	*4*
6	6	Netherlands	342	218	611	1 575	1 355	4 101	*4*
7	7	Italy	311	210	818	694	562	2 596	*2*
8	10	Sweden	468	287	536	437	413	2 141	*2*
9	8	China	580	288	271	562	355	2 057	*2*
10	9	Ukraine	397	354	308	563	109	1 731	*2*
11	12	Spain	158	56	133	825	529	1 701	*2*
12	11	Israel	309	561	280	246	238	1 635	*1*
13	13	Canada	276	302	206	210	343	1 337	*1*
14	14	Switzerland	120	217	196	208	211	952	*<1*
15	16	Poland	72	43	17	255	135	522	*<1*
16	15	Uzbekistan	340	170	4	–	–	514	*<1*
17	22	South Korea	104	20	32	80	214	450	–
18	18	South Africa	43	71	24	140	80	358	–
19	17	Belgium	15	47	171	58	10	301	–
20	21	Denmark	59	173	1	1	5	238	–
21	30	Montenegro[b]	..	..	..	126	85	211	–
22	24	Turkey	38	20	51	56	33	198	–
23	25	Finland	23	21	27	97	24	192	–
24	20	Belarus	80	50	24	35	–	190	–
25	19	Norway	83	79	12	14	–	187	–
26	23	Czech Republic	64	1	68	38	13	183	–
27	27	Libya	23	60	45	21	9	158	–
28	28	Austria	3	3	3	62	86	156	–
29	26	Bulgaria	48	16	66	5	7	141	–
30	33	Brazil	–	44	10	32	24	110	–
31	31	Australia	40	2	50	4	1	97	–
32	34	Kyrgyzstan	92	–	–	–	–	92	–
33	29	Slovakia	–	79	–	7	–	86	–
34	36	Greece	6	32	13	23	–	74	–
35	39	Hungary	–	–	68	–	6	74	–
36	40	Jordan	–	42	17	–	13	71	–
37	37	Singapore	–	66	3	–	–	70	–
38	45	Romania	24	–	2	8	16	50	–
39	43	India	4	22	4	14	–	43	–
40	35	Indonesia	–	25	8	8	–	41	–
41	41	Pakistan	9	9	11	9	–	37	–

Rank 2003–2007	Rank 2002–2006[a]	Supplier	Volume of exports (TIV)						% share, 2003–2007
			2003	2004	2005	2006	2007	03–07	2007
42	44	Saudi Arabia	–	–	36	–	–	36	–
43	46	UAE	–	2	25	7	3	36	–
44	64	Portugal	–	–	–	–	30	30	–
45	38	North Korea	13	13	–	–	–	26	–
46	47	Iran	9	1	–	10	–	21	–
47	48	Kazakhstan	–	5	–	12	–	18	–
48	49	Malta	–	10	–	–	–	10	–
49	50	Thailand	5	5	–	–	–	10	–
50	51	Serbia[b]	–	4	–	5	–	9	–
52	32	Georgia	–	7	–	–	–	7	–
52	52	Venezuela	–	1	–	5	1	7	–
53	53	Qatar	–	–	–	6	–	6	–
54	54	Peru	–	5	–	–	–	5	–
55	56	Moldova	–	–	4	–	–	4	–
56	63	Philippines	–	–	–	–	4	4	–
57	57	Syria	–	–	–	3	–	3	–
58	59	New Zealand	–	1	–	–	–	1	–
59	62	Oman	–	–	1	–	–	1	–
60	60	Chile	–	–	–	–	–	–	–
61	42	Lebanon	–	–	–	–	–	–	–
62	58	Lithuania	–	–	–	–	–	–	–
63	61	Angola	–	–	–	–	–	–	–
64	55	Bosnia and Herzegovina	–	–	–	–	–	–	–
–	–	Unknown countries[c]	14	4	61	25	18	121	–
		Total	**18 750**	**21 089**	**21 256**	**26 223**	**24 210**	**111 528**	*100*

– = nil or negligible; <1 = 0.5 or more, but less than 1; UAE = United Arab Emirates.

Note: The SIPRI data on arms transfers relate to actual deliveries of major conventional weapons. To permit comparison between the data on such deliveries of different weapons and to identify general trends, SIPRI uses a trend-indicator value. This value is only an indicator of the volume of international arms transfers and not of the financial values of such transfers. Thus, it is not comparable to economic statistics such as gross domestic product or export/import figures. The method for calculating the trend-indicator value is described in appendix 7C and on the SIPRI Arms Transfers Project website, <http://www.sipri.org/contents/armstrad/atmethods.html>.

[a] The rank order for suppliers in 2002–2006 differs from that published in *SIPRI Yearbook 2007* because of subsequent revision of figures for these years.

[b] Montenegro seceded from the State Union of Serbia and Montenegro on 3 June 2006. The figures for Serbia up to 2005 are for the State Union of Serbia and Montenegro (known as the Federal Republic of Yugoslavia until February 2003) and for 2006 onwards for Serbia alone.

[c] This represents one or more unknown countries.

Source: SIPRI Arms Transfers Database, <http://armstrade.sipri.org/>.

Appendix 7B. The financial value of the arms trade

MARK BROMLEY

Table 7B.1. The financial value of global arms exports according to national government and industry sources, 1998–2006

Figures are in US$ m. at constant (2006) prices. Conversion to constant (2006) US dollars is made using the market exchange rates of the reporting year and the US consumer price index (CPI).

	1998	1999	2000	2001	2002	2003	2004	2005	2006	Stated data coverage
World total[a]	**43 803**	**41 510**	**33 660**	**28 796**	**31 626**	**37 716**	**43 037**	**39 704**	**45 628**	
Australia	11	403	25	58	276	421	..	..	..	Arms exports (the figure for 2003 covers 1 July 2003–30 June 2004)
Austria	287	509	607	393	247	304	21	329	384	Licences for arms exports
Belgium	893	802	840	865	1 209	824	721	329	1 103	Licences for arms exports
Brazil	87	483	210	330	187	54	304	294	..	Arms exports
Canada	351	354	377	435	484	566	528	274	..	Arms exports (excludes exports to the USA)
Czech Republic	126	116	94	61	81	103	119	113	117	Arms exports
Denmark	..	..	..	78	120	99	135	113	164	Licences for arms exports
Finland	43	52	25	41	57	61	56	132	67	Arms exports
France	7 715	4 708	2 820	3 114	4 494	5 127	9 150	4 819	5 061	Arms exports
Germany	856	1 875	733	374	335	1 649	1 496	2 092	1 724	Arms exports (only covers exports of 'weapons of war')
Greece	..	58	23	52	55	139	20	37	110	Licences for arms exports
Hungary	..	..	20	10	8	14	12	15	20	Arms exports
India	41	21	..	..	53	103	75	59	95	Arms exports (the figure for 2006 covers 1 Apr. 2006–31 Mar. 2007)
Ireland	28	77	33	55	38	43	36	39	58	Licences for arms exports
Israel	2 324	1 944	2 065	2 277	2 241	2 575	2 775	2 864	3 000	Arms exports

	1998	1999	2000	2001	2002	2003	2004	2005	2006	Stated data coverage
Italy	1 385	1 142	651	564	514	779	636	1 067	1 217	Arms exports
Korea, South	182	238	64	228	157	263	448	268	250	Arms exports
Netherlands	593	472	450	663	475	1 423	827	1 508	1 411	Licences for arms exports
Norway	170	190	141	203	322	468	319	394	455	Arms exports
Pakistan	..	36	47	91	112	110	107	206	..	Arms exports
Poland	..	..	47	57	90	226	349	372	345	Licences for arms exports
Portugal	21	14	14	11	6	31	16	9	1	Arms exports
Romania	69	81	44	28	49	77	45	37	..	Arms exports
Russia	3 215	4 103	4 308	4 218	5 402	5 918	6 169	6 323	6 500	Arms exports
Slovakia	45	67	52	106	35	47	86	64	80	Arms exports
South Africa	145	217	234	230	273	449	452	..	..	Licences for arms exports
Spain	225	182	149	235	290	474	538	538	1 060	Arms exports
Sweden[b]	547	535	559	337	396	878	1 059	1 192	1 406	Arms exports
Switzerland	182	187	148	174	200	308	345	214	317	Arms exports
Turkey	99	102	144	153	278	363	209	348	..	Arms exports
UK[b]	4 030	1 921	3 048	2 511	1 583	1 776	2 719	2 609	3 792	Arms exports
Ukraine	371	..	585	569	560	548	..	..	..	Arms exports
USA[b]	19 265	20 265	14 809	10 274	11 141	11 584	12 239	11 865	14 008	Arms exports

Note: The countries included in this table are those that provide official financial data on their arms exports for at least 5 of the 9 years covered and where values given exceed $5 million for a majority of the years reported on. For certain countries, data on the value of arms export licences have been used because these are the only figures available. SIPRI estimates that together the countries in the table account for over 90% of exports of conventional arms. By totalling the financial value of these exports it is possible to estimate the value of the global arms trade. The national arms export data in this table are not entirely reliable or comparable between years.

[a] When calculating annual totals, national figures are converted to calendar years, assuming equal distribution over the range of years. Where data are unavailable, totals include estimates based on the average rate of change in the sample as a whole.

[b] These states release additional, higher figures. These are available at <http://www.sipri.org/contents/armstrad/at_gov_ind_data.html>.

Sources: Data are based on published information or direct communication with governments or official industry bodies. For a full list of sources and all available financial data on arms exports see <http://www.sipri.org/contents/armstrad/at_gov_ind_data.html>.

Appendix 7C. Sources and methods for arms transfers data

THE SIPRI ARMS TRANSFERS PROJECT

The SIPRI Arms Transfers Project reports on international flows of conventional weapons. Since publicly available information is inadequate for the tracking of all weapons and other military equipment, SIPRI covers only what it terms major conventional weapons. Data are collected from open sources for the SIPRI Arms Transfers Database and presented in a register that identifies the suppliers, recipients and the weapons delivered,[1] and in tables that provide a measure of the trends in the total flow of major weapons and its geographical pattern. SIPRI has developed a unique trend-indicator value (TIV) system. This value is not comparable to financial data such as gross domestic product, public expenditure, or export or import figures.

The database covers the period from 1950. Data collection and analysis are continuous processes. As new data become available the database is updated for all years covered.[2]

I. Revision of methods in 2007

New published technical information on individual weapons may necessitate a recalculation of their TIV. From time to time, however, more significant and generic modifications are introduced to reflect the changing reality of arms transfers or to make use of new sources of information. For example, in 2006 turrets for armoured vehicles and ships were added to the database, and the calculation of the SIPRI TIV for production under licence was reviewed and modified. Such changes are made retroactively for the entire database in order to preserve a meaningful time series.

In 2007 the coverage of the database was expanded to include guided but unpowered bombs and shells. These weapons have become widespread in recent years and are as important as other, guided short-range missiles in terms of technology, price and influence on military doctrine.

II. Selection criteria and coverage

Selection criteria

SIPRI uses the term 'arms transfer' rather than 'arms trade' or 'arms sale'. SIPRI covers not only sales of weapons, including manufacturing licences, but also other forms of weapon supply, such as aid and gifts.

---

[1] The register of transfers of major conventional weapons, which appeared in previous editions of the SIPRI Yearbook, is now available on the SIPRI website in 2 formats: a register with the data used for the analysis presented in this chapter, and a more flexible searchable database with the most recent data. SIPRI's online database is continually updated. See <http://armstrade.sipri.org/>.

[2] Thus, data from different editions of the SIPRI Yearbook or other SIPRI publications cannot be combined or compared. Full, up-to-date data are available in the SIPRI Arms Transfers Database (note 1).

The weapons transferred must be destined for the armed forces, paramilitary forces or intelligence agencies of another country. Weapons supplied to or from armed non-state actor in an armed conflict are included as deliveries to or from the individual armed non-state actor, identified under separate 'recipient' or 'supplier' headings. Supplies to or from international organizations are also included and categorized in the same fashion. In cases where deliveries are identified but it is impossible to identify either the supplier or the recipient with an acceptable degree of certainty, transfers are registered as coming from 'unknown' suppliers or going to 'unknown' recipients. Suppliers are termed 'multiple' only if there is a transfer agreement for weapons produced by two or more cooperating countries and if it is not clear which country will make the delivery.

Weapons must be transferred voluntarily by the supplier. This includes weapons delivered illegally—without proper authorization by the government of the supplier or the recipient country—but excludes captured weapons and weapons obtained from defectors. Finally, the weapons must have a military purpose. Systems such as aircraft used mainly for other branches of government but registered with and operated by the armed forces are excluded. Weapons supplied for technical or arms procurement evaluation purposes only are not included.

Major conventional weapons: the coverage

SIPRI covers only what it terms major conventional weapons, defined as follows.

1. *Aircraft*: all fixed-wing aircraft and helicopters, including unmanned reconnaissance/surveillance aircraft, with the exception of microlight aircraft, powered and unpowered gliders and target drones.

2. *Armoured vehicles*: all vehicles with integral armour protection, including all types of tank, tank destroyer, armoured car, armoured personnel carrier, armoured support vehicle and infantry fighting vehicle. Only vehicles with very light armour protection (such as trucks with an integral but lightly armoured cabin) are excluded.

3. *Artillery*: naval, fixed, self-propelled and towed guns, howitzers, multiple rocket launchers and mortars, with a calibre equal to or above 100 millimetres.

4. *Sensors*: (a) all land-, aircraft- and ship-based active (radar) and passive (e.g. electro-optical) surveillance systems with a range of at least 25 kilometres, with the exception of navigation and weather radars, (b) all fire-control radars, with the exception of range-only radars, and (c) anti-submarine warfare and anti-ship sonar systems for ships and helicopters. In cases where the system is fitted on a platform (vehicle, aircraft or ship), the register only notes those systems that come from a different supplier from that of the platform.

5. *Air defence systems*: (a) all land-based surface-to-air missile (SAM) systems, and (b) all anti-aircraft guns with a calibre of more than 40 mm. This includes self-propelled systems on armoured or unarmoured chassis.

6. *Missiles*: (a) all powered, guided missiles and torpedoes with conventional warheads, and (b) all unpowered but guided bombs and shells. Unguided rockets, free-fall aerial munitions, anti-submarine rockets and target drones are excluded.

7. *Ships*: (a) all ships with a standard tonnage of 100 tonnes or more, and (b) all ships armed with artillery of 100-mm calibre or more, torpedoes or guided missiles, with the exception of most survey ships, tugs and some transport ships.

8. *Engines*: (*a*) engines for military aircraft, for example, combat-capable aircraft, larger military transport and support aircraft, including helicopters; (*b*) engines for combat ships, such as fast attack craft, corvettes, frigates, destroyers, cruisers, aircraft carriers and submarines; (*c*) engines for most armoured vehicles—generally engines of more than 200 horsepower output. In cases where the system is fitted on a platform (vehicle, aircraft or ship), the register only notes those systems that come from a different supplier from the supplier of the platform.

9. *Other*: (*a*) all turrets for armoured vehicles fitted with a gun of at least 20-mm calibre or with guided anti-tank missiles, (*b*) all turrets for ships fitted with a gun of at least 57-mm calibre, and (*c*) all turrets for ships fitted with multiple guns with a combined calibre of at least 57 mm. In cases where the system is fitted on a platform (vehicle or ship), the register only notes those systems that come from a different supplier from the supplier of the platform.

The statistics presented refer to transfers of weapons in these nine categories only. Transfers of other military equipment—such as small arms and light weapons, nuclear, biological or chemical weapons, trucks, artillery under 100-mm calibre, ammunition, support equipment and components, as well as services or technology transfers—are not included.

III. The SIPRI trend indicator

The SIPRI system for the valuation of arms transfers is designed as a trend-measuring device. It allows the measurement of changes in the total flow of major weapons and its geographical pattern. The trends presented in the tables of SIPRI trend-indicator values are based only on actual deliveries during the year or years covered in the relevant tables and figures, not on orders signed in a year.

The TIV system, in which similar weapons have similar values, shows both the quantity and quality of the weapons transferred—in other words, it describes the transfer of military resources. It does not reflect the financial value of (or payments for) weapons transferred. This is impossible for three reasons. First, in many cases no reliable data on the value of a transfer are available. Second, even if the value of a transfer is known, in almost every case it is the total value of a deal, which may include not only the weapons themselves but also other items related to these weapons (e.g. spare parts, armament or ammunition) as well as support systems (e.g. specialized vehicles) and items related to the integration of the weapon in the armed forces (e.g. training, or software changes to existing systems). Third, even if the value of a transfer is known, important details about the financial arrangements of the transfer (e.g. credit or loan conditions and discounts) are often unavailable.[3]

Measuring the military implications of transfers would require a concentration on the value of the weapons as a military resource. Again, this could be done from the actual money values of the weapons transferred, assuming that these values generally reflect the military capability of the weapon. However, the problems listed above would still apply. For example, a very expensive weapon may be transferred as aid at a 'zero' price; although it will therefore not show up in financial statistics, it will still

---

[3] It is possible to present a very rough idea of the economic factors from the financial statistics now available from most arms-exporting countries. However, most of these statistics lack sufficient detail. Such data are available from the SIPRI Arms Transfers Project via <http://www.sipri.org/contents/arms trad/>.

be a significant transfer of military resources. The SIPRI solution is a system in which military resources are measured by including an evaluation of the technical parameters of weapons. The purpose and performance of a weapon are evaluated, and it is assigned a value in an index that reflects its value as a military resource in relation to other weapons. This can be done under the condition that a number of benchmarks or reference points are established by assigning some weapons a fixed place in the index, thus forming its core. All other weapons are compared to these core weapons.

In short, the process of calculating the SIPRI TIV for individual weapons is as follows. For a number of weapon types it is possible to find the average unit acquisition price in open sources. It is assumed that such real prices roughly reflect the military resource value of a system. For example, a combat aircraft bought for $10 million may be assumed to be a resource twice as great as one bought for $5 million, and a submarine bought for $100 million may be assumed to be 10 times the resource that a $10 million combat aircraft would represent. Weapons with a real price are used as the core weapons of the valuation. Weapons for which a price is not known are compared with core weapons in the following steps.

1. The description of a weapon is compared with the description of the core weapon. In cases where no core weapon exactly matches the description of the weapon for which a price is to be found, the closest match is sought.

2. Standard characteristics of size and performance (weight, speed, range and payload) are compared with those of a core weapon of a similar description. For example, a 15 000-kilogram combat aircraft would be compared with a combat aircraft of similar size.

3. Other characteristics, such as the type of electronics, loading or unloading arrangements, engine, tracks or wheels, armament and materials, are compared.

4. Weapons are compared with a core weapon from the same period.

Weapons in a 'used' condition are given a value 40 per cent of that of a new weapon. Used weapons that have been significantly refurbished or modified by the supplier before delivery (and have thereby become a greater military resource) are given a value of 66 per cent of the value when new. In reality there may be huge differences in the military resource value of a used weapon depending on its condition and the modifications during the years of use.

The SIPRI trend indicator does not take into account the conditions under which a weapon is operated (e.g. an F-16 combat aircraft operated by well-balanced, well-trained and well-integrated armed forces has a much greater military value than the same aircraft operated by a developing country; the resource is the same but the effect is very different). The trend indicator also accepts the prices of the core weapons as genuine rather than reflecting costs that, even if officially part of the programme, are not exclusively related to the weapon itself. For example, funds that appear to be allocated to a particular weapon programme could be related to optional add-ons and armament or to the development of basic technology that will be included (free of cost) in other programmes. Such funds could also act, in effect, as government subsidies to keep industry in business by paying more than the weapon is worth.

In cases where subsystems, such as sensors and engines, are produced and delivered by suppliers other than the supplier of the platform on which the subsystems are fitted, the TIV calculation of the platform would be reduced by the value of components. The TIV of the components would be listed as coming from a supplier different than the supplier of the platform.

IV. Sources

The Arms Transfers Project uses a variety of sources to collect data: newspapers; periodicals and journals; books, monographs and annual reference works; and official national and international documents. The common criterion for all these sources is that they are open, that is, published and available to the public.

Such open information cannot, however, provide a comprehensive picture of world arms transfers. Published reports often provide only partial information, and substantial disagreement between them is common. Order and delivery dates and exact numbers (or even types) of weapons ordered and delivered, or the identity of suppliers or recipients, may not always be clear. Exercising judgement and making informed estimates are therefore important elements in compiling the SIPRI Arms Transfers Database. Estimates are conservative and may be underestimates.

All sources of data as well as calculations of estimates are documented in the SIPRI Arms Transfers Database.

Part III. Non-proliferation, arms control and disarmament, 2007

8. Nuclear arms control and non-proliferation

SHANNON N. KILE

I. Introduction

In 2007 the nuclear programmes of two states, Iran and North Korea, remained at the centre of international controversies about the proliferation of nuclear weapons. The International Atomic Energy Agency (IAEA) made some progress towards resolving issues related to the history of Iran's sensitive nuclear fuel cycle activities, including uranium enrichment, that had called into question the peaceful nature of those activities. At the same time, Iran continued to refuse to comply with United Nations Security Council resolutions demanding that it suspend its enrichment programme. In East Asia, there was a breakthrough in the multilateral negotiations on the fate of the nuclear programme of the Democratic People's Republic of Korea (DPRK, or North Korea), which in February 2007 agreed to an Action Plan for disabling and eventually eliminating its nuclear infrastructure. Elsewhere, controversy continued over the Indian–United States Civil Nuclear Cooperation Initiative (CNCI) and its proposed exemption of India from US and multilateral nuclear supplier restrictions. In Geneva there were renewed but ultimately unsuccessful efforts at the Conference on Disarmament (CD) to open negotiations on a global fissile material cut-off treaty (FMCT).

This chapter reviews the main developments in nuclear arms control and non-proliferation in 2007. Section II describes developments related to Iran's nuclear programme and summarizes the IAEA's findings about the country's past and current nuclear activities. Section III describes the diplomatic deal reached in the Six-Party Talks in which North Korea pledged to give up its nuclear infrastructure in return for economic and security benefits. Section IV examines the controversy over the Indian–US nuclear deal, focusing on the obstacles to its implementation. Section V summarizes the efforts at the CD to resolve the impasse that has blocked for more than a decade the opening of negotiations on an FMCT. Section VI summarizes international initiatives aimed at enhancing nuclear security and the safe disposal of surplus fissile material, while section VII presents the conclusions.

Appendix 8A provides tables of data on the nuclear forces or capabilities of the USA, Russia, the United Kingdom, France, China, India, Pakistan, Israel and North Korea. Appendix 8B provides details of global inventories of fissile material. Appendix 8C surveys the main ballistic missile defence programmes under development in the USA. Appendix 8D describes the techniques used in nuclear forensics analysis and their application in verifying treaty compliance.

II. Iran and nuclear proliferation concerns

In 2007 the international controversy over the scope and nature of Iran's nuclear programme intensified as Iran proceeded apace with its uranium enrichment activities. The controversy emerged at the end of 2002 and centred on findings by the IAEA that Iran had failed, over a period of two decades, to declare important nuclear activities in contravention of its comprehensive safeguards agreement with the agency mandated by the 1968 Treaty on the Non-Proliferation of Nuclear Weapons (Non-Proliferation Treaty, NPT).[1] It was heightened by revelations, in 2004, that Iran had procured nuclear technology and equipment through the smuggling network organized by Pakistan's chief nuclear engineer, Abdul Qadeer Khan.[2] Iran maintains that its nuclear programme is intended solely for peaceful purposes and that any safeguards violations were inadvertent and minor in nature. However, in Europe, the USA and elsewhere, there is concern that Iran is attempting to put into place, under the cover of a civilian nuclear energy programme, the sensitive fuel cycle facilities needed to produce plutonium and highly enriched uranium (HEU) for nuclear weapons. Since October 2003, three European Union (EU) member states—France, Germany and the UK, the 'E3'—have taken the lead in attempting to resolve the controversy through negotiations with Iran. These negotiations have also involved the participation of the High Representative for the EU's Common Foreign and Security Policy, Javier Solana.[3]

Iran's defiance of UN Security Council resolutions

The year 2007 opened with Iran continuing to defy UN Security Council resolutions 1696 and 1737, which demand that Iran immediately suspend all uranium enrichment-related and plutonium reprocessing activities.[4] Resolution 1737 imposed a limited set of economic and political sanctions on Iran under Article 41 of Chapter VII of the UN Charter.[5] Iran had promptly rejected that resolution as 'invalid' and 'illegal' and vowed to review its cooperation with the IAEA.[6]

---

[1] Iran acceded to the NPT as a non-nuclear weapon state on 2 Feb. 1970. Its comprehensive safeguards agreement with the International Atomic Energy Agency (INFCIRC/214) entered into force on 15 May 1974. For a summary of the NPT see annex A in this volume.

[2] On the Khan network see International Institute for Strategic Studies (IISS), *Nuclear Black Markets: Pakistan, A. Q. Khan and the Rise of Proliferation Networks*, IISS Strategic Dossier (Routledge: Abingdon, 2007).

[3] For European and Iranian views on the nuclear issue see Kile, S. N. (ed.), *Europe and Iran: Perspectives on Non-proliferation*, SIPRI Research Report no. 21 (Oxford University Press: Oxford, 2005).

[4] On the UN Security Council's deliberations on the Iranian nuclear issue see Kile, S. N., 'Nuclear arms control and non-proliferation', *SIPRI Yearbook 2007: Armaments, Disarmament and International Security* (Oxford University Press: Oxford, 2003), pp. 488–93.

[5] UN Security Council Resolution 1737, 23 Dec. 2006. The UN documents cited here are available from <http://documents.un.org/>.

[6] 'UN votes for Iran nuclear sanctions', Al Jazeera, 23 Dec. 2006, <http://english.aljazeera.net/NR/exeres/A742D5DB-379A-4A0F-8DFA-40213800A37C.htm>. In Jan. 2007 Iran reportedly sought to deny visas to IAEA inspectors who were citizens of countries that voted in favour of Resolution 1737.

In February 2007 the IAEA Director General, Mohamed ElBaradei, reported to the IAEA Board of Governors that Iran had not suspended its enrichment or other sensitive nuclear fuel cycle activities.[7] He noted that the Atomic Energy Organization of Iran (AEOI) had installed additional P-1 gas centrifuges at both the Pilot Fuel Enrichment Plant (PFEP) and the Fuel Enrichment Plant (FEP) near Natanz. Iranian technicians at the PFEP continued to operate single centrifuges as well as 10-, 24- and 164-machine cascades, into which uranium hexafluoride (UF_6) was being fed 'intermittently'.[8] Iran had informed the IAEA that it would install additional centrifuge cascades at the FEP and planned to feed UF_6 into the cascades already in place there. The report also noted that Iran had increased the production of UF_6 at the Uranium Conversion Facility (UCF) in Esfahan. In addition, it continued to build a 40-megawatt-thermal ($MW(t)$) heavy water-moderated IR-40 reactor near Arak.[9] Following the report, the IAEA Board voted to partially or completely suspend 22 of the agency's 55 technical cooperation projects with Iran.[10]

On 24 March 2007 the UN Security Council unanimously adopted Resolution 1747, which tightened the sanctions on Iran and reaffirmed that it must 'comply without further delay' with the steps required by the IAEA Board of Governors, including a full and sustained suspension of all enrichment-related and reprocessing activities as well as the ratification and implementation of the Additional Protocol.[11] The Security Council asked the IAEA Director General to issue a new report within 60 days. It promised to suspend the sanctions 'if and for so long as Iran suspends all enrichment-related and reprocessing activities, including research and development, as verified by the IAEA, to allow for negotiations in good faith'.[12]

Iranian officials sharply criticized Resolution 1747 as overstepping the Security Council's legal authority and warned that the country would curtail

'Iran bars 38 IAEA inspectors from entering country for nuke check', RIA Novosti, 22 Jan. 2007, <http://en.rian.ru/world/20070122/59499341.html>.

[7] IAEA, Board of Governors, 'Implementation of the NPT safeguards agreement and relevant provisions of Security Council Resolution 1737 (2006) in the Islamic Republic of Iran', Report by the Director General, GOV/2007/8, 22 Feb. 2007, pp. 1, 5. Most of the IAEA documents and publications cited here are available from the IAEA's website, <http://www.iaea.org/>.

[8] Uranium hexafluoride is the feedstock used in most uranium enrichment processes, including gas centrifuges. See Krass, A. et al., SIPRI, *Uranium Enrichment and Nuclear Weapon Proliferation* (Taylor & Francis: London, 1983), <http://books.sipri.org/product_info?c_product_id=286>.

[9] IAEA (note 7), p. 1. This type of reactor is well suited for producing weapon-grade plutonium. When completed in 2010, it is estimated that the reactor will be able to produce spent fuel with enough plutonium for *c*. 2 weapons each year.

[10] 'IAEA cuts technical aid to Iran', Radio Free Europe/Radio Liberty, 8 Mar. 2007, <http://www.rferl.org/featuresarticle/2007/3/66AACED3-C509-4233-AC46-EE1E61911F8B.html>. See also Boureston, J. and Lacey, J., 'Nuclear technical cooperation: a right or privilege?', *Arms Control Today*, vol. 37, no. 7 (Sep. 2007).

[11] UN Security Council Resolution 1747, 24 Mar. 2007. For a description of the sanctions, see chapter 11 in this volume, section II. In Dec. 2003 Iran signed an Additional Protocol to its comprehensive safeguards agreement with the IAEA granting agency inspectors enhanced powers to investigate possible undeclared nuclear activities. In Feb. 2006 Iran announced that it would no longer act in accordance with the provisions of the protocol, which had yet to be ratified by the Majlis (parliament), in protest of the IAEA Board of Governors' decision to report the Iranian nuclear file to the UN Security Council.

[12] UN Security Council Resolution 1747 (note 11).

cooperation with the IAEA in the face of Security Council-imposed sanctions.[13] The Iranian Foreign Minister, Manouchehr Mottaki, complained that the Security Council was 'being abused to take an unlawful, unnecessary and unjustifiable action' against Iran's peaceful nuclear programme, which 'presents no threat to international peace and security and falls, therefore, outside the Council's Charter-based mandate'.[14]

On 29 March Iran informed the IAEA that it had suspended implementation of the modified text of its Subsidiary Arrangements General Part, Code 3.1, concerning the early provision of design information and would instead implement the original text, agreed in 1976, which required Iran to submit design information for new facilities 'not later than 180 days before the facility is scheduled to receive nuclear material for the first time'.[15] Iran also informed the IAEA that it would no longer allow agency inspectors to verify the design information for the IR-40 reactor that had been provided by Iran pursuant to the modified Code 3.1.[16]

The Iranian decision was challenged on both legal and political grounds. The IAEA stated that there was no mechanism in Iran's safeguards agreement (INFCIRC/214) for the unilateral suspension of provisions agreed to in subsidiary arrangements and that the agency's right to verify design information provided to it was a 'continuing right' which was not dependent on the stage of construction of a facility.[17] The USA complained that the move further undermined confidence in the Iranian leadership's intentions and raised 'serious concern' about 'the possibility of Iran building new and sensitive nuclear facilities in secret and only informing the IAEA just before operations begin'.[18]

Diplomatic impasse over new sanctions

On 25 April 2007 Solana met Ali Larijani, Secretary of Iran's Supreme National Security Council, to discuss modalities for resuming negotiations on

[13] Islamic Republic News Agency, 'Leader warns of consequences of illegal actions against Iran', 22 Mar. 2007, <http://www2.irna.ir/en/news/view/line-17/0703225333091859.htm>.

[14] Quoted in UN Security Council, 'Security Council toughens sanctions against Iran, adds arms embargo with unanimous adoption of Resolution 1747 (2007)', Press release, 24 Mar. 2007, <http://www.un.org/News/Press/docs/2007/sc8980.doc.htm>.

[15] Iran's response is reported in IAEA, Board of Governors, 'Implementation of the NPT safeguards agreement and relevant provisions of Security Council Resolutions in the Islamic Republic of Iran', Report by the Director General, GOV/2007/22, 23 May 2007, p. 3. The modified text of Code 3.1, agreed between Iran and the IAEA in Feb. 2003 after the existence of the Natanz enrichment plants had been revealed, required Iran to provide the IAEA with design information for new nuclear facilities 'as soon as the decision to construct, or to authorize construction, of such a facility has been taken, whichever is earlier'. On the declaration requirements see appendix 8D, section III.

[16] IAEA (note 15). Iran argued that under the 1976 version of Code 3.1, to which it had 'reverted', the verification of such information was not justified, given the preliminary construction stage of the facility.

[17] IAEA (note 15).

[18] US Mission to International Organizations in Vienna, 'Iran's denials of design information and verification: more cause for international concern', June 2007, <http://vienna.usmission.gov/_unvie/speeches_and_related_documents/Anti-Narcotics-Trafficking-Programs-and-Initiatives/1698.php>.

the nuclear issue.[19] The meeting had been preceded by the decision of the Council of the European Union to impose additional sanctions on Iran going beyond those mandated in resolutions 1737 and 1747, including a total arms embargo.[20] Solana reportedly proposed a 'double suspension', whereby Iran would agree to halt its uranium enrichment activities and the EU and the Security Council would suspend their sanctions, pending the negotiation of a long-term settlement.[21] However, the talks ended inconclusively. The Iranian President, Mahmoud Ahmadinejad, rejected the 'double suspension' idea, insisting that Iran would not halt what were legitimate nuclear activities.[22]

Iran's defiance of resolutions 1737 and 1747 led to protracted discussions between China, France, Germany, Russia, the UK and the USA (the 'P5 + 1 states') about how to induce or compel the Iranian leadership to comply with the Security Council's demands. The discussions took place against the background of ElBaradei's May report to the IAEA Board, which stated that Iran had increased its enrichment activities and continued work on the IR-40 reactor in defiance of the resolutions.[23] During a press conference prior to the report's release, ElBaradei had sparked a controversy by stating that 'from a proliferation perspective, the fact of the matter is that one of the purposes of suspension'—to prevent the Iranians from mastering centrifuge technology—had been 'overtaken by events' in Iran.[24]

While there was a general consensus that the Security Council had to take action to enforce its authority, disagreements persisted over the measures to be included in any new resolution. The E3 and the USA urged the Security Council to impose additional sanctions on Iran. However, they also reiterated the offer of the package of political and economic incentives that was offered by the P5 + 1 in June 2006.[25] In contrast, China and Russia continued to resist US-led calls for a third round of sanctions, arguing that diplomacy should be given more time to work. On 20 June the Russian Foreign Minister, Sergei Lavrov, stated that a new Security Council resolution would be 'adopted only after the [IAEA] Director General reports that the possibility of resolving some of the remaining issues has been exhausted'.[26] Lavrov emphasized that the nuclear controversy should be resolved in the framework of IAEA–Iranian cooperation.

---

[19] Islamic Republic News Agency, 'Iran welcomes correct, precise talks: Larijani', 25 Apr. 2007, <http://www.globalsecurity.org/wmd/library/news/iran/2007/iran-070425-irna02.htm>.

[20] Council Common Position 2007/246/CFSP of 23 April 2007 amending Common Position 2007/140/CFSP concerning restrictive measures against Iran, *Official Journal of the European Union*, L106 (24 Apr. 2007), pp. 67–75.

[21] Weitz, R., 'European Union–Iranian negotiations: what's next?', *WMD Insights*, May 2007.

[22] Hafezi, P., 'Ahmadinejad says Iran won't back down in atom row', Reuters, 23 Apr. 2007, <http://uk.reuters.com/article/oilRpt/idUKDAH34040120070423>.

[23] IAEA (note 15), pp. 2, 4.

[24] Heinrich, M., 'World should adapt to Iran atom advances: ElBaradei', Reuters, 15 May 2007, <http://www.reuters.com/article/worldNews/idUSL1544636620070515>.

[25] Kerr, P., 'U.S. allies await Iran's response to nuclear offer', *Arms Control Today*, vol. 36, no. 6 (July/Aug. 2006).

[26] 'Lavrov sets condition for new UN move', Reuters, 20 June 2007, <http://www.reuters.com/article/topNews/idUSL2092290920070620>.

In October 2007 the USA announced a comprehensive package of sanctions aimed at curtailing international commercial and banking activities in Iran. It also designated the Islamic Revolutionary Guard Corps as a proliferator of weapons of mass destruction (WMD), thereby making it subject to wide-ranging sanctions.[27] The announcement came as the US Administration continued to press the European Union to adopt rules to prevent EU companies from trading with or investing in Iran, similar to the restrictions already codified in US legislation.[28] The newly elected French President, Nicolas Sarkozy, shifted France's position towards the tougher approach advocated by the USA, warning that Iran's nuclear ambitions would otherwise lead to 'an Iranian bomb or the bombing of Iran'.[29] However, Germany and other EU member states with significant trade ties to Iran remained reluctant to impose unilateral sanctions against it.[30] They were supported by some smaller member states which were concerned that unilateral EU sanctions would undermine the role of the Security Council.

Russia continued to be generally supportive of Iran, where it was completing construction of a 1000-megawatt-electric (MW(e)) light-water nuclear power reactor near Bushehr, on the Gulf coast. Russia had previously insisted—over US objections—that any Security Council sanctions resolution include an exemption for the Bushehr nuclear power plant project. On 16 December 2007 Russia delivered to Iran the first shipment of nuclear fuel for the reactor at Bushehr.[31] Iran and Russia had reached agreement the previous week on a schedule to finish building the plant after years of delays, which Russian officials attributed to Iran's payment arrears in the $1 billion deal.[32] The fuel was to be delivered in several batches, with the whole operation scheduled to take two months.[33] The main Russian contractor, Atomstroyexport, stated that the plant would be ready to operate no sooner than six months after all the fuel rods for the reactor had been delivered.[34] US Administration officials reportedly complained that the delivery agreement, coming shortly after the release of a new US intelligence estimate on Iran's nuclear

[27] Wright, R., 'U.S. to impose new sanctions targeting Iran's military', *Washington Post*, 25 Oct. 2007. In addition, the USA designated the Revolutionary Guards' Quds Force as a terrorist organization.

[28] MacAskill, E., 'US steps up effort to stop EU firms trading with Iran', *The Guardian*, 20 July 2007.

[29] Samuel, H., 'Nicolas Sarkozy warns of Iran's nuclear crisis', *Daily Telegraph*, 31 Aug. 2007; and 'France fails to sell EU sanctions against Iran', Global Security Newswire, 16 Oct. 2007, <http://www.nti.org/d_newswire/issues/2007_10_16.html>.

[30] 'Berlin says US and France guilty of hypocrisy', *Der Spiegel*, 24 Sep. 2007. In 2006 Germany was the largest exporter to Iran, with total exports exceeding €4.1 billion ($5.1 billion). Jones, G., 'Germany's pivotal role in the Iranian nuclear standoff', *Proliferation Analysis*, Carnegie Endowment for International Peace, 20 Nov. 2007, <http://www.carnegieendowment.org/npp/publications/index.cfm?fa=view&id=19720>.

[31] 'Russia ships nuclear fuel to Iran', BBC News, 17 Dec. 2007 <http://news.bbc.co.uk/2/7147463.stm>.

[32] 'Bushehr nuclear plant launch delayed over new crisis in Russia-Iran relations', *Pravda*, 27 July 2007.

[33] 'Bushehr received second N-fuel batch from Russia', Nuclear.ru, 28 Dec. 2007, <http://www.nuclear.ru/eng/press/nuclear_power/2108595>.

[34] Cooper, H., 'Iran receives nuclear fuel in blow to U.S.', *New York Times*, 18 Dec. 2007.

programme (see below), would encourage Iranian intransigence at the Security Council.[35]

Following the first shipment, Lavrov, the Russian Foreign Minister, said that there was no longer any economic rationale for Iran to proceed with its uranium enrichment programme now that Russia was delivering the fuel for the Bushehr reactor.[36] However, according to Gholamreza Aghazadeh, the head of the AEOI, Iran needed to produce fuel at Natanz for a 360-MW(e) indigenous power plant to be built at Darkhovin, in south-western Khuzestan province.[37] The AEOI has begun construction work on the Darkhovin plant, but it is not expected to be completed for a decade.[38]

The IAEA–Iranian work plan

On 21 August 2007 Iran and the IAEA finalized a work plan for answering all outstanding safeguards compliance issues in Iran. The plan was prepared following a series of discussions in Tehran led by ElBaradei and Iran's chief nuclear negotiator, Ali Larijani.[39] It set out the modalities and a timeline for the IAEA and Iran to resolve all remaining issues related to the IAEA's investigation into Iran's past nuclear activities. The IAEA agreed to submit in writing all of its questions by 15 September 2007 and Iran agreed to provide the 'required clarifications and information' by specified dates.[40]

The timeline called for the IAEA and Iran to conclude and close, in an agreed order, the files on six outstanding issues. The IAEA stated that there were 'no other remaining issues and ambiguities regarding Iran's past nuclear program and activities'.[41] The first of these issues, which had to do with the dates of undeclared plutonium separation experiments carried out by Iran, was declared closed on 20 August, when the IAEA confirmed that earlier statements made by Iran were consistent with the agency's findings.[42] To resolve the other issues, the IAEA agreed to submit to Iran its questions about: (*a*) the origins of enriched uranium particles discovered in environmental samples

---

[35] Daragahi, B. and Stack, M., 'Russian nuclear fuel lands in Iran', *Los Angeles Times*, 18 Dec. 2007.

[36] 'Russia sees no need for Iran to continue with uranium enrichment', RIA Novosti, 26 Dec. 2007, <http://en.rian.ru/russia/20071226/94168822.html>.

[37] Cooper (note 34). The location is sometimes referred to by other nearby place names, including Ahvaz, Darkhouin, Esteghlal and Karun.

[38] 'Iran's first home-made nuclear power plant to be operational in 9 years', Xinhua, 24 Dec. 2007, <http://news.xinhuanet.com/english/2007-12/25/content_7306339.htm>; and 'Iran starts second atomic power plant: report', Reuters, 8 Feb. 2008, <http://www.reuters.com/article/topNews/idUSL0812863720 080208>.

[39] Communication dated 27 August 2007 from the Permanent Mission of the Islamic Republic of Iran to the Agency concerning the text of the Understandings of the Islamic Republic of Iran and the IAEA on the Modalities of Resolution of the Outstanding Issues, available in IAEA, INFCIRC/711, 27 Aug. 2007.

[40] INFCIRC/711 (note 39), p. 6. See also Squassoni, S. and Gerami, N., 'Iran's plan for nuclear compliance', Carnegie Endowment for International Peace, 6 Sep. 2007 <http://www.carnegieendowment. org/files/iran_timeline4.pdf>.

[41] INFCIRC/711 (note 39), p. 6.

[42] INFCIRC/711 (note 39), p. 2.

taken at a 'technical university in Iran';[43] (b) Iranian statements about the procurement of P-1 and P-2 centrifuge design information, components and related equipment through a network of foreign intermediaries, and the scope and timelines of Iran's centrifuge research and development (R&D) activities;[44] (c) a document, discovered in Iran by IAEA inspectors in 2005, that described 'procedures for the reduction of [UF_6] to uranium metal in small quantities, and for the casting of enriched and depleted uranium metal into hemispheres';[45] (d) the purpose of Iran's experiments involving the isotope polonium-210; and (e) certain Iranian activities at the Gchine uranium mine. The IAEA also agreed to provide Iran with documentation it had been given by the USA pertaining to the so-called Green Salt Project, which allegedly involved work on the conversion of uranium dioxide into uranium tetrafluoride ('green salt'), and tests related to high explosives and the design of a missile re-entry vehicle. Iran continued to dismiss these allegations as baseless and politically motivated but agreed to review this evidence as a goodwill gesture.[46]

In addition to the work plan, Iran agreed to cooperate with the IAEA on preparing a safeguards approach and a facility attachment for the FEP at Natanz, which subsequently entered into force on 30 September 2007.[47] Iran also agreed to allow the IAEA to resume on-site inspections of the IR-40 reactor under construction near Arak, which Iran had halted in response to the Security Council's adoption of Resolution 1747.

The announcement of the work plan was received unenthusiastically in the USA and many EU countries, where it was portrayed as a capitulation to Iranian pressure.[48] It led to a wave of criticism directed against ElBaradei for allegedly having exceeded his statutory authority as IAEA Director General by independently negotiating a political deal with Iran.[49] While accepting the work plan's goals, Western diplomats expressed dismay that it had ignored the Security Council's demands that Iran immediately suspend its enrichment pro-

---

[43] On the contamination issue see IAEA, Board of Governors, 'Implementation of the NPT safeguards agreement in the Islamic Republic of Iran', Report by the Director General, GOV/2004/83, Vienna, 15 Nov. 2004, pp. 8–10.

[44] For a description of Iran's centrifuge enrichment programmes see International Institute for Strategic Studies (IISS), *Iran's Strategic Weapons Programme: A Net Assessment* (Routledge: Abingdon, 2005), pp. 45–56.

[45] The work plan did not set a time frame for resolving this issue. The existence of the document has been a matter of international concern, since the uranium metal hemispheres could be used to form the core of an implosion-type nuclear weapon.

[46] INFCIRC/711 (note 39), p. 7.

[47] The safeguards approach outlines the types of inspection mechanisms that may be used at Natanz. The facility attachment specifies how these mechanisms are to be implemented. IAEA, Board of Governors, 'Implementation of the NPT safeguards agreement and relevant provisions of Security Council resolutions 1737 (2006) and 1747 (2007) in the Islamic Republic of Iran', Report by the Director General, GOV/2007/58, 15 Nov. 2007, p. 6.

[48] Heinrich, M., 'Developing states rap "interference" in Iran deal', Reuters, 11 Sep. 2007, <http://www.reuters.com/article/worldNews/idUSL1154089720070911>. On 11 Sep. 2007 an EU statement to the IAEA Board 'took note' of the work plan but stopped short of endorsing it or expressing approval.

[49] See e.g. 'Rogue regulator', *Washington Post*, 5 Sep. 2007.

gramme and re-implement the Additional Protocol.[50] Diplomats and leading non-governmental experts also expressed concern about the sequential nature of the plan, in particular the possibility that Iran could use it to buy time to continue its enrichment activities by delaying the resolution of outstanding questions.[51] They pointed out that the work plan's language seemed to violate a fundamental safeguards principle in that it precluded the IAEA or its member states from raising these issues again, even if new information were to emerge, once the files on them had been closed.[52]

Impasse in E3–EU–Iranian negotiations

As the positions of Iran and the USA on the suspension issue hardened in the summer of 2007, the E3 reportedly began to consider proposals for a compromise deal that would involve a less-than-complete suspension by Iran of its enrichment programme.[53] On 23 October 2007 Solana met in Rome with Iran's new chief nuclear negotiator, Saeed Jalili, who had succeeded Larijani following the latter's resignation several days earlier.[54] Solana put forward a 'double freeze' proposal, under which the UN Security Council would stop consideration of further sanctions if Iran agreed, as a confidence-building measure, to temporarily halt the expansion of its enrichment programme.[55] This would be followed by a full suspension of Iran's enrichment programme and the simultaneous suspension of the existing sanctions. The diplomatic sequence envisioned by Solana's proposal was a departure from previous E3 proposals, which had stated that negotiations could begin only after Iran completely suspended all uranium enrichment activities. It appeared to reflect a new European approach that accepted the reality of Iran's enrichment capability but sought to constrain it as much as possible. However, Jalili ruled out making any concession on Iran's enrichment programme. A joint statement issued by the E3 following the meeting complained that 'Iran made no gesture of goodwill in Rome, refusing both the double freeze and the double suspen-

[50] Webb, G., 'Iran–IAEA nuclear plan receives qualified Western support', Global Security Newswire, 12 Sep. 2007, <http://www.nti.org/d_newswire/issues/2007/9/12/4f722640-1feb-401d-bcc9-2d876f8433fe.html>.

[51] Albright, D. and Shire, J., 'A flawed IAEA–Iran agreement on resolving outstanding issues', ISIS Report on Iran, 28 Aug. 2007, <http://www.isis-online.org/publications/iran/flawedagreement.pdf>.

[52] Albright and Shire (note 51).

[53] 'Key U.S. allies exploring compromise enrichment suspension deal with Iran', *International Herald Tribune*, 22 June 2007.

[54] The appointment of Jalili, a close supporter of President Ahmadinejad, was interpreted by some observers as reflecting Ahmadinejad's increased influence in foreign policy decision making within the Iranian leadership. See Posch, W., 'Only personal? The Larijani crisis revisited', Policy Brief no. 3, Centre for Iranian Studies, Durham University, <http://www.dur.ac.uk/resources/iranian.studies/larijani_final01.pdf>.

[55] Walker, S., 'Iran and EU face tough nuclear talks', Reuters, 29 Nov. 2007, <http://www.reuters.com/article/worldNews/idUSL2735773820071129>.

sion'.[56] On 30 November Solana and Jalili met for another round of talks that ended inconclusively.[57]

The IAEA Director General's assessment of Iran's nuclear programme

On 15 November ElBaradei issued the latest in a series of reports to the IAEA Board that painted a mixed picture of the agency's progress in clarifying Iran's past and current nuclear activities. The report was generally positive about Iran's cooperation with the IAEA in implementing the August 2007 work plan, stating that Iran 'has provided sufficient access to individuals and has responded in a timely manner to questions and provided clarifications and amplifications on issues raised in the context of the work plan'.[58] As a result, the IAEA had been able to conclude that Iran's answers about the histories of the P-1 and P-2 centrifuge programmes were consistent with the agency's findings about those programmes. The report noted that the IAEA had submitted to Iran its questions about the other outstanding issues, in accordance with the work plan, and was awaiting Iran's answers and clarifications. More generally, the report stated that Iran had provided safeguards inspectors with access to declared nuclear materials, and provided the required material accountancy reports, to enable the agency to verify that none of the declared nuclear materials inside Iran had been diverted to prohibited activities.[59] Iran's ambassador to the IAEA, Ali-Asghar Soltanieh, hailed the findings as evidence that Iran had shown 'good will in clearing up ambiguities in its peaceful nuclear activities' and argued that the IAEA Board no longer had any justification for referring Iran's nuclear file to the Security Council.[60]

At the same time, ElBaradei's report stated that Iran's cooperation in answering the IAEA's questions had been 'reactive rather than proactive' and emphasized that 'Iran's active cooperation and full transparency are indispensable for full and prompt implementation of the work plan'.[61] Moreover, it cautioned that the IAEA was still not in a position to provide credible assurances about the absence of undeclared nuclear materials or activities in the country. The report noted that 'since early 2006, the Agency has not received the type of information that Iran had previously been providing, pursuant to the Additional Protocol', which meant that the IAEA's knowledge about Iran's current nuclear programme was 'diminishing'.[62]

The US Administration seized on the latter findings to renew its push for new sanctions against Iran.[63] Gregory Schulte, the US ambassador to the

[56] Quoted in Walker (note 55).

[57] 'Iran rejects EU "disappointment"', BBC News, 1 Dec. 2007, <http://news.bbc.co.uk/2/7122440.stm>.

[58] IAEA (note 47), p. 8.

[59] IAEA (note 47), p. 8.

[60] 'Iran showed goodwill in clearing up ambiguities', *Tehran Times*, 24 Nov. 2007, pp. 1, 15.

[61] IAEA (note 47), p. 8.

[62] IAEA (note 47), p. 9.

[63] Wright, R., 'US to seek new sanctions against Iran', *Washington Post*, 16 Nov. 2007.

IAEA, said that the report showed that Iran's cooperation with the IAEA remained 'selective and incomplete' and that Iran had not met 'the world's expectation of full disclosure'.[64] In addition, the E3 and the USA argued that ElBaradei's report did not alter the fundamental issue at the centre of the dispute, namely, Iran's non-compliance with two legally binding Security Council resolutions.

ElBaradei reported that Iran had not suspended its enrichment-related activities, including R&D work on the P-2 centrifuge design, and was continuing the operation of the PFEP and FEP.[65] Iran had achieved its stated objective of installing a complete centrifuge 'module', consisting of 18 164-centrifuge cascades (or 2952 centrifuges), at the FEP.[66] This in effect made the FEP a pilot plant, since Iran had installed the 18-cascade module there before demonstrating that it could operate the single cascade at the PFEP.[67]

The report also noted that Iran had introduced UF_6 into all of the cascades, but that the UF_6 feed rate had 'remained below the expected quantity for a facility of this design'.[68] The feed rate had risen incrementally in the period 13 August–3 November 2007, when the number of operating cascades increased from 12 to 18.[69] According to one estimate, the FEP produced an average of 22 kilograms of fuel-grade low-enriched uranium per month during this period.[70] This amount was well below the full potential of the module and was an indication that Iran still faced technical problems in operating a large number of cascades at the same time in parallel. ElBaradei's report noted that IAEA inspectors had not observed preparations at the FEP for installing centrifuges or centrifuge pipe work outside the original 18-cascade module.[71] This suggested that Iran may have decided to temporarily stop at the single module, although it remained committed to the goal of a 54 000-centrifuge plant. A key question for many analysts was whether Iran had halted installation work because it lacked the capacity to manufacture significantly more

---

[64] Schulte, G., US Permanent Representative to the United Nations and International Organizations in Vienna, 'Failing the test of full disclosure', 15 Nov. 2007, <http://vienna.usmission.gov/_unvie/speeches_and_related_documents/Iran/1723.php>.

[65] IAEA (note 47), p. 8. Iran was also continuing construction of the IR-40 reactor near Arak.

[66] IAEA (note 47), p. 6. This marked a tenfold increase in the number of centrifuges compared with Nov. 2006.

[67] International Institute for Strategic Studies, 'Nuclear Iran: how close is it?', *IISS Strategic Comments*, vol. 13, no. 7 (Sep. 2007), p. 2. President Ahmadinejad was widely believed to have made a political decision to put as many centrifuges in place as possible in order to improve Iran's diplomatic bargaining position.

[68] IAEA (note 47), p. 6.

[69] IAEA (note 47), p. 6. During this period, Iran consumed 550 kg of UF_6, nearly as much as the 690 kg consumed during the period Feb.–Aug. 2007.

[70] Albright, D. and Shire, J., 'November IAEA report: centrifuge file not closed; Natanz enrichment expands', ISIS Issue Brief, 15 Nov. 2007, <http://www.isis-online.org/publications/iran/ISISIssueBrief Iran15Nov2007.pdf>.

[71] IAEA (note 47), p. 6.

than the 3000 centrifuges already in place or had done so for political and diplomatic reasons.[72]

The US National Intelligence Estimate on Iran

On 3 December 2007 the US Director of National Intelligence, Mike McConnell, released an unclassified summary of a new National Intelligence Estimate (NIE) of Iran's nuclear intentions and capabilities. The NIE, which reflected the consensus views of 16 US intelligence agencies, concluded 'with high confidence' that Iran had halted its nuclear weapon programme four years earlier, in the autumn of 2003, and had not resumed work on nuclear weapons as of mid-2007.[73] The conclusion was reportedly based on Iranian military communications intercepted by the USA, among other sources.[74] It marked a major departure from the previous NIE on Iran, completed in May 2005, which had concluded that Iran had a clandestine programme under way to develop nuclear weapons. The new estimate stated that Iran's decision to halt its nuclear weapon programme suggested that it was 'less determined to develop nuclear weapons than we have been judging since 2005'. It also concluded 'with high confidence that the halt was directed primarily in response to increasing international scrutiny and pressure resulting from the exposure of Iran's previously undeclared nuclear work', which in turn suggested that 'Iran may be more vulnerable to influence' than had been previously judged.[75]

The 2007 NIE acknowledged that the US intelligence community did not know whether Iran intended to develop nuclear weapons but implied that it was pursuing the option to do so in the future. The report noted that 'Iranian entities' were continuing 'to develop a range of technical capabilities that could be applied to producing nuclear weapons', if a decision to do so were made. However, it was unclear whether the Iranian leadership was 'willing to maintain the halt of its nuclear weapon program indefinitely' or whether it would or already had 'set specific criteria that will prompt it to restart the program'. The report also warned that 'convincing the Iranian leadership to forgo the eventual development of nuclear weapons' would be difficult 'given the linkage many within the leadership probably see between nuclear weapons development and Iran's key national security and foreign policy objectives'.[76]

The new NIE did not substantially revise recent assessments made by US intelligence agencies about when Iran might be able to produce a nuclear weapon. It judged 'with moderate confidence' that the earliest date that Iran

---

[72] Fitzpatrick, M., 'Can Iran's nuclear capability be kept latent?, *Survival*, vol. 49, no. 1 (spring 2007), pp. 50–51; and Albright, D. and Shirer, J., 'A witch's brew? Evaluating Iran's uranium-enrichment progress', *Arms Control Today*, vol. 37, no. 9 (Nov. 2007).

[73] See 'key judgments' in US Director of National Intelligence, 'National Intelligence Estimate—Iran: nuclear intentions and capabilities', Nov. 2007, <http://www.dni.gov/press_releases/20071203_release.pdf>, p. 8.

[74] Linzer, D. and Warrick, J., 'U.S. finds that Iran halted nuclear arms bid in 2003', *Washington Post*, 4 Dec. 2007.

[75] US Director of National Intelligence (note 73), p. 5.

[76] US Director of National Intelligence (note 73), p. 6.

would be 'technically capable' of producing enough HEU for a nuclear weapon was 2009. However, Iran was more likely to achieve this capability in 2010–15, or possibly later, in light of the ongoing technical problems in its enrichment programme.[77]

The release of the 2007 NIE elicited mixed international reactions. Some governments disputed its main conclusion. In a rare public rift with the USA on intelligence matters, Israeli officials cited 'clear and solid intelligence' that Iran was continuing to develop nuclear weapons.[78] In contrast, the Russian Foreign Minister, Lavrov, said there was no proof that Iran ever had a nuclear weapon programme. He praised the Iranian leadership for its readiness to cooperate with the IAEA in resolving the outstanding questions about its past nuclear activities.[79] Iranian President Ahmadinejad hailed the report as a 'victory' for Iran and claimed that it undermined the legal basis for the UN Security Council's consideration of the nuclear file.[80]

The release of the updated NIE immediately changed the political dynamics of the debate in Europe and the USA about how to address concerns about Iran's nuclear programme. In the USA the report's finding that Iran was not currently pursuing a dedicated nuclear weapon programme was widely seen as having undercut political support for US military action against Iran. In October 2007 President George W. Bush had warned that a nuclear-armed Iran could lead to 'World War III', a comment that fuelled speculation that the USA was prepared to take military action against Iranian nuclear facilities and other targets if diplomatic efforts proved fruitless.[81] The NIE's conclusions were also seen as complicating efforts by the USA and some European countries at the UN Security Council to impose a further round of sanctions on Iran. Chinese and Russian officials said that the report raised questions about the need for a new Security Council resolution imposing additional sanctions.[82]

III. North Korea's nuclear programme and the Six-Party Talks

In 2007 some progress was made towards resolving the international confrontation over North Korea's nuclear weapon programme. The dispute arose in 2002, when a series of tit-for-tat moves by North Korea and the USA resulted in the collapse of the 1994 Agreed Framework and the expulsion of IAEA

---

[77] US Director of National Intelligence (note 73), pp. 6, 8. The NIE assessed that 'Iran would probably use covert facilities—rather than its declared nuclear sites—for the production of highly enriched uranium for a weapon'.

[78] Mitnik, J., 'Israel challenges report on nukes', *Washington Times*, 5 Dec. 2007.

[79] Associated Press, 'Lavrov: "No proof Iran had nuke program"', *Jerusalem Post*, 5 Dec. 2007.

[80] Dareini, A. A., 'Ahmadinejad: report a "victory"', *Washington Times*, 5 Dec. 2007.

[81] Spetalnick, M., 'Bush: threat of World War III if Iran goes nuclear', Reuters, 17 Oct. 2007, <http://www.reuters.com/article/newsOne/idUSN1732974320071017>.

[82] Sciolino, E., 'Europeans see murkier case for sanctions', *New York Times*, 4 Dec. 2007; 'China questions UN Iran sanctions', BBC News, 5 Dec. 2007, <http://news.bbc.co.uk/2/7128183.stm>; and Dareini (note 80).

monitors from North Korea.[83] This was followed in 2003 by North Korea's formal withdrawal from the NPT.[84] On 9 October 2006 North Korea further raised the stakes when it carried out an underground nuclear test explosion.[85] The test led the UN Security Council to unanimously adopt Resolution 1718, demanding that North Korea verifiably abandon all WMD and ballistic missile programmes.[86] It also required all UN member states to take a variety of measures to restrict certain conventional weapon systems and dual-use goods and materials from entering North Korea.[87]

Progress in the Six-Party Talks

The year 2007 opened with uncertain prospects for progress in the Six-Party Talks between China, Japan, North Korea, the Republic of Korea (ROK, or South Korea), Russia and the USA. The talks began in August 2003 and aimed at resolving the diplomatic impasse over North Korea's nuclear programme.[88] On 19 September 2005 they achieved an apparent breakthrough when the parties reached agreement on a Joint Statement on principles guiding future talks aimed at the 'verifiable denuclearization of the Korean Peninsula in a peaceful manner'.[89] Immediately after the Joint Statement was issued, however, the two main antagonists—North Korea and the USA—presented conflicting versions of what had actually been agreed, especially with regard to the sequencing of a possible deal on dismantling North Korea's nuclear infrastructure.[90] The prospects for resolving the disagreement were complicated by the USA's imposition, in September 2005, of new restrictions on North Korea's trading and financial activities. The US Administration claimed that the measures were motivated by North Korean money laundering activities unrelated to the nuclear issue. The move prompted North Korea to stage a year-long boycott of the Six-Party Talks. It returned to the talks, reportedly under Chinese pressure, in December 2006 but insisted that the USA had to remove the financial sanctions before it would consider a new US denuclearization proposal.[91]

[83] On the breakdown of the North Korean–US Agreed Framework see Kile, S. N., 'Nuclear arms control, non-proliferation and missile defence', *SIPRI Yearbook 2003: Armaments, Disarmament and International Security* (Oxford University Press: Oxford, 2003), pp. 578–92.

[84] North Korea acceded to the NPT as a non-nuclear weapon state party on 12 Dec. 1985. Its withdrawal from the treaty took effect on 10 Apr. 2003. North Korea's comprehensive safeguards agreement with the IAEA (INFCIRC/403) was considered also to have lapsed on that date.

[85] On the test and the methods used to determine whether a nuclear explosion had occurred see Fedchenko, V. and Ferm Helgren, R., 'Nuclear explosions, 1945–2006', *SIPRI Yearbook 2007* (note 4), pp. 552–53; and appendix 8D, section III.

[86] UN Security Council Resolution 1718, 14 Oct. 2006.

[87] See Anthony, I. and Bauer, S., 'Controls on security-related international transfers', *SIPRI Yearbook 2007* (note 4), pp. 658–63.

[88] Zissis, C., 'The Six-Party Talks on North Korea's nuclear program', *Backgrounder*, US Council on Foreign Relations, updated 4 Dec. 2007, <http://www.cfr.org/publication/13593>.

[89] US Department of State, Office of the Spokesman, 'Joint Statement of the Fourth Round of the Six-Party Talks', Washington, DC, 19 Sep. 2005, <http://www.state.gov/r/pa/prs/ps/2005/53490.htm>.

[90] See Kile, S. N., 'Nuclear arms control and non-proliferation', *SIPRI Yearbook 2006: Armaments, Disarmament and International Security* (Oxford University Press: Oxford, 2003), pp. 632–33.

[91] Kerr, P. 'No progress at North Korea talks', *Arms Control Today*, vol. 37, no. 1 (Jan./Feb. 2007).

In January 2007 North Korea and the USA resumed direct contact, fuelling speculation that a thaw in their relations could pave the way for progress in the Six-Party Talks. Officials from the US Treasury Department met with North Korean foreign trade representatives to discuss a partial lifting of the US financial sanctions that would unfreeze North Korean assets held in the Banco Delta Asia in Macao.[92] In addition, the US Assistant Secretary of State for East Asian and Pacific Affairs, Christopher R. Hill, and the North Korean Vice Minister of Foreign Affairs, Kim Gye Gwan, held talks during which North Korea reportedly showed a greater willingness to resume discussions about shutting down its nuclear programme in exchange for economic and energy assistance.[93] The talks were held against the background of warnings from UN and other aid agencies of growing food and energy shortages in North Korea.[94]

The February 2007 Action Plan

On 13 February 2007 the fifth round of the Six-Party Talks ended with agreement on an Action Plan containing a series of steps for beginning the implementation of the September 2005 Joint Statement.[95] During a 60-day 'initial actions period', North Korea pledged to shut down and seal the 5-MW(e) graphite-moderated research reactor and reprocessing facility located at Yongbyon, 'for the purpose of eventual abandonment'.[96] IAEA inspectors would conduct the 'necessary monitoring and verifications' of the shutdown. North Korea also agreed to provide the other parties with a list of all its nuclear programmes, 'including plutonium extracted from used fuel rods', that were to be 'abandoned' pursuant to the Joint Statement.

In return, the other parties agreed to provide emergency energy assistance to North Korea equivalent to 50 000 tonnes of heavy fuel oil (HFO).[97] The Action Plan had stipulated that this assistance would begin to be delivered during the initial 60-day period, but US officials insisted that North Korea must shut down its nuclear facilities before receiving it.[98] The Action Plan also specified that North Korea and the USA would start bilateral talks aimed at

---

[92] Associated Press, 'Glaser to meet with N.Korean officials', *Washington Post*, 28 Jan. 2007.

[93] Lee, J., 'N.K. shows flexibility at talks', *Korea Herald*, 9 Feb. 2007.

[94] 'Food aid key to N Korea talks', BBC News, 7 Feb. 2007, <http://news.bbc.co.uk/2/6338941.stm>; and Fifield, A., 'Ailing power grid puts Nkoreans in the dark', *Financial Times*, 13 Feb. 2007, p. 3.

[95] The first round of the Six-Party Talks was held on 27–29 Aug. 2003; the second round on 25–28 Feb. 2004; the third round on 23–26 June 2004; the fourth round on 26 July–7 Aug. and 13–19 Sep. 2005; and the fifth round on 9–11 Nov. 2004, 18–22 Dec. 2006 and 8–13 Feb. 2007. In 2007 a sixth round was held on 19–22 Mar., 18–20 July and 27–30 Sep. 2007. Chinese Ministry of Foreign Affairs, 'Initial actions for the implementation of the Joint Statement', 13 Feb. 2007, <http://www.fmprc.gov.cn/eng/zxxx/t297463.htm>.

[96] Chinese Ministry of Foreign Affairs (note 95). The first draft reportedly stipulated that North Korea abandon its nuclear weapons as part of the initial phase—a demand that North Korean negotiators rejected. 'Negotiators watered down North Korea nuclear stand', Global Security Newswire, 26 Feb. 2007, <http://www.nti.org/d_newswire/issues/2007_2_26.html>.

[97] Chinese Ministry of Foreign Affairs (note 95).

[98] Yardley, J. and Sanger, D., 'Nuclear talks on North Korea hit roadblock', *New York Times*, 12 Feb. 2007. South Korea agreed to provide the energy assistance.

resolving pending bilateral issues and moving towards full diplomatic relations.[99] It also established five working groups, which were to begin meeting within 30 days, to 'discuss and formulate specific plans' for implementing the 2005 Joint Statement. The six parties agreed to reconvene the following month to hear reports from the working groups and to discuss 'actions for the next phase'.[100]

The Action Plan described the second, follow-on phase in general terms. North Korea would provide a 'complete and correct declaration' of all of its nuclear programmes and 'disable' all existing nuclear facilities.[101] In return, the other parties would provide 'economic, energy and humanitarian assistance up to the equivalent' of 1 million tonnes of heavy fuel oil, including the initial shipment equivalent to 50 000 tonnes of HFO.[102] The modalities of this assistance were to be determined 'through consultations and appropriate assessments' of the working group on economic and energy cooperation.

While the Action Plan was hailed as a breakthrough, a number of key issues were unresolved. It did not specify the methods by which North Korea's nuclear facilities at Yongbyon were to be disabled or how these measures would be verified.[103] The plan also did not specify whether North Korea would 'abandon' its existing stocks of separated plutonium and nuclear weapons as well as its nuclear facilities.

In addition, the Action Plan did not address the controversial issue of North Korea's suspected work on uranium enrichment.[104] It was US allegations in October 2002 that North Korea had a secret centrifuge uranium enrichment programme under way, in contravention of the Agreed Framework, which led directly to the breakdown of the deal. These were based in part on evidence that the nuclear smuggling network centred around the Pakistani nuclear scientist A. Q. Khan had given centrifuge designs and a small number of complete P-1 centrifuges to North Korea.[105] However, in early 2007 the US intelli-

---

[99] Chinese Ministry of Foreign Affairs (note 95). The USA undertook to begin the process of removing the designation of North Korea as a state sponsor of terrorism and ending trade sanctions imposed under the US 1917 Trading with the Enemy Act.

[100] Chinese Ministry of Foreign Affairs (note 95). The working groups addressed: (a) denuclearization of the Korean peninsula, (b) normalization of North Korean–US relations, (c) normalization of North Korean–Japanese relations, (d) economic and energy cooperation, and (e) a North East Asia peace and security mechanism.

[101] According to 2 non-governmental experts, 'disablement' has come to mean 'a deliberate, mutually agreed action or set of actions taken to make it relatively more difficult and time-consuming to restart a facility after it is shut down', while terms are being worked out for its eventual dismantlement. Albright, D. and Brannan, P., 'Disabling DPRK nuclear facilities', Working paper, United States Institute of Peace, 23 Oct. 2007, <http://www.usip.org/pubs/working_papers/wp5_dprk.pdf>.

[102] Chinese Ministry of Foreign Affairs (note 95). Japan refused to contribute to the assistance to North Korea until North Korea fully accounted for the Japanese citizens it had admitted abducting in the 1970s.

[103] Klingner, B., 'North Korea: worrisome gaps in Six-Party Talks' joint statement', Web Memo no. 1655, Heritage Foundation, 4 Oct. 2007, <http://www.heritage.org/Research/AsiaandthePacific/wm1655.cfm>.

[104] Pinkston, D. and Spector, L., 'Six-parties adopt steps for North Korean denuclearization but uranium enrichment controversy looms as major obstacle', WMD Insights, Apr. 2007.

[105] International Institute for Strategic Studies (note 2), pp. 72–76.

gence community publicly backed away from claims that North Korea was developing a significant uranium enrichment capability.[106]

Implementation of the Action Plan

The implementation of the initial phase of the Action Plan, which was to be completed within 60 days of the announcement of the agreement, immediately fell behind schedule due primarily to procedural obstacles connected with the repatriation of North Korean funds frozen in the Banco Delta Asia. North Korea refused to begin shutting down its nuclear facilities until it had received all of the estimated $25 million in the account.[107]

Following a Russian-mediated deal to complete the money transfer, the implementation of the Action Plan got under way in the summer of 2007. During a visit to North Korea on 14–17 July 2007 IAEA inspectors verified that North Korea had shut down the 5-MW(e) research reactor, the radiochemical laboratory and the nuclear fuel fabrication plant at the Yongbyon complex.[108] They also confirmed that no new construction had been carried out at the 50-MW(e) reactor at Yongbyon and the 200-MW(e) reactor at Taechon, both of which remained unfinished. In addition to verifying the shutdown of the Yongbyon facilities, the inspectors installed seals and surveillance equipment to allow the IAEA to remotely monitor the status of the complex. The IAEA and North Korea had agreed on the modalities for new monitoring and containment measures during a visit to Pyongyang by an agency team on 26–29 June 2007.[109]

Disablement of North Korean nuclear facilities

On 3 October 2007 the six parties issued a statement on 'second-phase actions' in which North Korea agreed to disable the nuclear facilities at Yongbyon and provide a 'complete and correct declaration of all of its nuclear programs' by 31 December 2007.[110] The parties established an expert group to recommend specific disablement measures that would be 'safe, verifiable, and consistent with international standards'. The USA was asked to lead the disablement activities and provide the initial funding for them.[111]

---

[106] Kerr, P., 'Doubts rise on North Korea's uranium-enrichment program', *Arms Control Today*, vol. 37, no. 3 (Apr. 2007); and Gumbel, A., 'CIA blunder "prompted Korean nuclear race"', *Independent on Sunday*, 2 Mar. 2007.

[107] 'N. Korea nuclear deadline in doubt', BBC News, 4 Apr. 2007, <http://news.bbc.co.uk/2/6525145.stm>.

[108] IAEA, Board of Governors and General Conference, 'Application of safeguards in the Democratic People's Republic of Korea (DPRK)', Report by the Director General, GOV/2007/45–GC(51)/19, 17 Aug. 2007.

[109] IAEA, Board of Governors, 'Monitoring and verification in the Democratic People's Republic of Korea', Report by the Director General, GOV/2007/36, 3 July 2007.

[110] Chinese Ministry of Foreign Affairs, 'Second-phase actions for the implementation of the Joint Statement', 3 Oct. 2007, <http://wcm.fmprc.gov.cn/ce/cgsf/eng/xw/t369084.htm>.

[111] Chinese Ministry of Foreign Affairs (note 110).

A US Government team arrived in Pyongyang in mid-October 2007 to continue discussions on a disablement plan with North Korean technical experts. A key issue in the discussions had been how reversible the proposed disablement measures would be. North Korea favoured non-destructive measures, such as the physical deactivation of facilities, that could be reversed in a matter of weeks or a few months. In contrast, US Assistant Secretary of State Hill indicated that US experts favoured more destructive measures that would require at least 12 months to reverse.[112] Some non-governmental analysts cautioned that the disablement steps needed to be carefully chosen, since more destructive measure could damage North Korean components needed for future verification activities, in particular verifying the correctness and completeness of North Korea's declaration of its fissile material stocks.[113]

The two sides eventually agreed on a disablement plan that reportedly included 10 separate steps to disable the three facilities at Yongbyon and the process began in early November 2007. The first step towards disabling the 5-MW(e) reactor at Yongbyon, removing all 8000 irradiated fuel rods and transferring them to an adjacent storage pond for cooling, proved to be more time-consuming than expected because the storage pond was contaminated with radioactive debris and had a water chemistry that was unsuited for long-term storage.[114] It was not immediately clear what the other steps would involve, since the two sides agreed not to disclose them until after they had been carried out.[115]

On 1 December 2007 US President Bush wrote a personal letter to North Korea's leader, Kim Jong Il. US commentators noted that the collegial tone of the letter differed dramatically from Bush's previous comments about Kim.[116] Bush reportedly held out the prospect of normalized relations with the USA if North Korea fully disclosed its nuclear programmes and began to eliminate them.[117] He emphasized that it was essential for North Korea to declare the number of warheads it had built as well as the amount of weapon-grade fissile material it had produced. Bush also called for North Korea to disclose any nuclear material, equipment or expertise that it may have transferred to other countries.

The latter issue had taken on new importance following revelations about an Israeli air strike inside Syria on 6 September 2007.[118] Israeli and US officials revealed few details but stated that the air strike was conducted against a

[112] US State Department, 'On-the-record briefing: Assistant Secretary of State for East Asian and Pacific Affairs and Head of the U.S. Delegation to the Six-Party Talks Christopher R. Hill', Washington, DC, 3 Oct. 2007, <http://www.state.gov/p/eap/rls/rm/2007/93234.htm>.

[113] Albright and Brannan (note 101), p. 19.

[114] Crail, P., 'Disablement begins but process unclear', Arms Control Today, vol. 37 no. 10 (Dec. 2007); and Lewis, J., 'It's all about water chemistry', Arms Control Wonk, 14 Jan. 2008, <http://www.armscontrolwonk.com/1767/its-all-about-water-chemistry>.

[115] Crail (note 114).

[116] 'Bush's secret letter to Kim', Washington Post, 7 Dec. 2007.

[117] Cooper, H., 'A new Bush tack on North Korea', New York Times, 6 Dec. 2007.

[118] Israel admits air strike on Syria', BBC News, 2 Oct. 2007, <http://news.bbc.co.uk/2/7024287.stm>. See also Hersch, S., 'A strike in the dark', New Yorker, 11 Feb. 2008.

partly constructed undeclared nuclear reactor, located at a site near the Euphrates River and allegedly modelled on the 5-MW(e) graphite-moderated reactor that North Korea had used to produce plutonium for nuclear weapons.[119] Syria confirmed Israel's air attack but denied that it had struck a nuclear plant or had killed North Korean personnel at the site.[120] North Korea denied reports that it had secret nuclear cooperation with Syria and strongly condemned the attack.[121]

North Korean failure to meet deadline

The year 2007 ended with North Korea missing the 31 December deadline to disable all of its nuclear facilities at Yongbyon. The delay in disabling the 5-MW(e) reactor had been expected because of the safety concerns about discharging the irradiated fuel rods.[122] However, the US State Department reported that North Korea had also slowed the pace of disablement work.[123] A foreign ministry spokesman confirmed that North Korea had been forced to 'adjust the tempo of the disablement of some nuclear facilities', as an 'action-for-action' response to delays in the delivery of heavy fuel oil and energy-related equipment to North Korea. He added that the unloading of the spent fuel rods would be completed in 'about 100 days'.[124]

North Korea also failed to submit to the other parties a comprehensive declaration of its nuclear programmes by the year-end deadline. According to the foreign ministry spokesman, North Korea had 'worked out a report on the nuclear declaration' in November 2007 and 'notified the US side of its contents', but the USA insisted on 'further consultations'.[125] The main sticking point was that North Korea continued to deny that it had a clandestine uranium enrichment programme.[126] This denial was apparently contradicted when US scientists discovered traces of enriched uranium on smelted aluminium tubing provided by North Korea.[127] North Korea acknowledged that it had imported

[119] 'Report: IDF raid seized nuclear material before Syria air strike', *Haaretz*, 23 Sep. 2007; and Sanger, D. and Mazzetti, M., 'Israel struck Syrian nuclear project, analysts say', *New York Times*, 14 Oct. 2007.

[120] 'Syria says Israeli air raid aimed at justifying attack', Agence France-Presse, 29 Sep. 2007, <http://afp.google.com/article/ALeqM5hcd8yNVwB0Z6ZOjoi1YKbiWIremw>.

[121] Korean Central News Agency, 'Israel condemned for intrusion into Syria's territorial air', 11 Sep. 2007, <http://www.kcna.co.jp/item/2007/200709/news09/12.htm>; and Korean Central News Agency, 'Rumor about "secret nuclear cooperation" between DPRK and Syria dismissed', 18 Sep. 2007, <http://www.kcna.co.jp/item/2007/200709/news09/19.htm>.

[122] Mohammed, A. and Plemming, S., 'North Korea resists Dec 31 declaration deadline', Reuters, 20 Dec. 2007, <http://www.alertnet.org/thenews/newsdesk/N20203654.htm>.

[123] Casey, T., Deputy Spokesman, US State Department, 'North Korea declaration', Press statement, Washington, DC, 30 Dec. 2007, <http://www.state.gov/r/pa/prs/ps/2007/dec/98147.htm>.

[124] Korean Central News Agency, 'DPRK Foreign Ministry spokesman on issue of implementation of October 3 agreement', 4 Jan 2008, <http://www.kcna.co.jp/item/2008/200801/news01/05.htm>. The spokesman also claimed that the USA had not honoured its promise to remove North Korea from the US list of state sponsors of terrorism.

[125] Korean Central News Agency (note 124).

[126] 'North Korea again denies uranium enrichment program', Yonhap, 27 Dec. 2007.

[127] Kessler, G., 'Uranium traces found on N. Korean tubes', *Washington Post*, 21 Dec. 2007.

tonnes of high-strength aluminium tubes from Russia in June 2002 but stated that the tubes had nothing to do with uranium enrichment.[128] In addition to the dispute over alleged uranium enrichment activities, North Korea reportedly intended to declare that it had 30 kg of separated plutonium, considerably less than the US estimate of more than 50 kg.[129]

The governments of Japan, South Korea and the USA expressed disappointment that North Korea had missed the deadline. However, US State Department officials counselled patience and stressed a comprehensive and accurate declaration was more important than one delivered on time.[130]

IV. The Indian–US Civil Nuclear Cooperation Initiative

In 2007 India and the USA took steps to implement the Civil Nuclear Cooperation Initiative that was launched in July 2005.[131] The CNCI's goal is the resumption of 'full civil nuclear cooperation' between India and the USA. This represents a reversal of three decades of US non-proliferation policy, which had been aimed at preventing India from obtaining nuclear fuel and advanced reactors from the USA and other suppliers following India's nuclear test explosion in 1974.[132] The US Administration argued that the growing strategic importance of India, and its rapidly improving relations with the USA, warranted making a one-time exception to nuclear non-proliferation rules and regulatory arrangements.[133] However, the proposed deal has been criticized in the USA for implicitly endorsing, if not actually assisting, the further growth of India's nuclear arsenal and undermining US non-proliferation objectives. It has been widely criticized in India for constraining the country's military nuclear programme and compromising its sovereignty.

In December 2006 the US Congress approved legislation, the Henry J. Hyde US–India Peaceful Atomic Energy Cooperation Act (after the bill's chief sponsor in the House of Representatives), amending the Atomic Energy Act of 1954 by creating an India-specific exemption from certain provisions of the act.[134] The amendment was a prerequisite for US negotiators to be able to con-

---

[128] Korean Central News Agency (note 124); and Kessler (note 127).

[129] Choe, S., 'North Korea may miss nuclear deadline', *International Herald Tribune*, 20 Dec. 2007.

[130] 'NKorea says it declared nuclear programmes', Agence France-Presse, 4 Jan. 2008; and Choe (note 129).

[131] The White House, 'Joint statement between US President George W. Bush and Indian Prime Minister Manmohan Singh', News release, Washington, DC, 18 July 2005, <http://www.whitehouse.gov/news/releases/2005/07/20050718-6.html>. On the origins of the CNCI see Ahlström, C., 'Legal aspects of the Indian–US Civil Nuclear Cooperation Initiative', *SIPRI Yearbook 2006* (note 90), pp. 669–85.

[132] The Indian nuclear explosive device was widely believed to have used US and other foreign-supplied nuclear technology provided for peaceful purposes. For a comprehensive history of India's nuclear programme see Perkovich, G., *India's Nuclear Bomb: The Impact on Global Proliferation* (University of California Press: Berkeley, Calif., 1999).

[133] See e.g. Burns, N., 'America's strategic opportunity with India', *Foreign Affairs*, vol. 86, no. 6 (Nov./Dec. 2007).

[134] The Henry J. Hyde United States–India Peaceful Atomic Energy Act of 2006, US public law 109-401, was signed into law on 18 Dec. 2006. Its text is available at <http://thomas.loc.gov/cgi-bin/bdquery/z?d109:HR05682:>. See also Kile (note 4), pp. 498–501.

clude with India a so-called 123 agreement that would specify the terms governing the resumption of trade in nuclear material and technology envisioned in the CNCI.[135] The Hyde Act imposed a number of conditions aimed at ensuring that a 123 agreement with India complied with the Atomic Energy Act and related legislation.[136]

The agreement negotiated by the Indian and US governments must be approved by the US Congress before it can enter into force. However, the Hyde Act stipulates that before the Congress would formally consider a 123 agreement, two additional steps had to be completed. First, the IAEA and India had to negotiate, and the IAEA Board of Governors had to approve, a safeguards agreement covering India's civil nuclear reactors.[137] Second, the Nuclear Suppliers Group (NSG) needs to reach a consensus agreement to exempt India from the rule, adopted by the NSG in 1992, that prohibits nuclear exports to states that have not concluded a comprehensive safeguards agreement (INFCIRC/153) with the IAEA covering all of their nuclear facilities.[138] In the NSG, the proposed deal has been supported by France, Russia and the UK, in addition to the USA.[139] At the same time, the idea of making an exemption for India has been sharply criticized by several NSG participants, notably Ireland and Sweden. The NSG, which operates on the basis of the consensus principle, reportedly decided not to take up the US request until India has completed the parallel negotiations on the 123 agreement with the USA and on a new safeguards agreement with the IAEA.[140]

These requirements complicated the prospects for rapidly implementing the CNCI, even if all the substantive issues raised in India and the USA were to be resolved in a 123 agreement. Many supporters and opponents of the deal believed that its chances for success were linked to an expedited timetable. The increasing focus on presidential politics in the USA in 2008 was widely seen as making congressional action on a 123 agreement less likely later in the year and the deal might not survive the change in US administrations.[141]

---

[135] McGoldrick, F., Bengelsdorf, H. and Scheinman, L., 'The U.S.–India nuclear deal: taking stock', *Arms Control Today*, vol. 35, no. 8 (Oct. 2005). Section 123 of the 1954 Atomic Energy Act (42 USC 2153) requires the US Government to conclude an agreement containing a number of binding conditions and assurances, including full-scope safeguards, as a prerequisite for any significant peaceful nuclear cooperation with any state not legally recognized under the NPT as a nuclear weapon state.

[136] See Kile (note 4), pp. 498–501.

[137] In Mar. 2006 India and the USA agreed on a plan for separating India's nuclear programme into civilian and military components. India designated 14 of its 22 nuclear reactors as being civilian. Kile (note 4), pp. 496–97.

[138] For discussion of the NSG's structure and activities see Anthony, I., Ahlström, C. and Fedchenko, V., *Reforming Nuclear Export Controls: The Future of the Nuclear Suppliers Group*, SIPRI Research Report no. 22 (Oxford University Press: Oxford, 2007). For a list of the 45 participants in the NSG see annex B in this volume.

[139] 'China not to oppose nuclear deal: US', *Dawn*, 20 Dec. 2006.

[140] Hibbs, M., 'More delays loom over NSG trade sanctions and India', *Nuclear Fuel*, vol. 32, no. 1 (1 Jan. 2007), pp. 11–12.

[141] Horner, D., 'Singh's pullback sparks speculation on prospects of US–India nuclear deal', *Nuclear Fuel*, vol. 32, no. 22 (22 Oct. 2007), pp. 1, 9–10.

The Indian–US 123 agreement

On 27 July 2007 India and the USA announced that they had concluded a draft 123 agreement, following more than a year of negotiations, to establish a framework for civil nuclear cooperation between them, including fuel assurances, technology transfers and safeguards arrangements.[142] In response to concerns raised in both countries about these issues, the two governments sought to highlight how the agreement promoted their respective interests.[143] These efforts led some critics to warn that the parties appeared to have different interpretations of several key provisions of the 123 agreement that invited future disputes in Indian–US relations.[144] Other critics charged that the US Administration's eagerness to move ahead with the deal had led it to capitulate to Indian demands on most points of contention and to conclude an agreement that disregarded conditions established by the Hyde Act which India had deemed to be 'deal-killers'.[145]

The key provisions of the proposed US–India 123 agreement reflected the outcome of negotiations on four main points of contention.[146]

Cessation and termination in the event of an Indian nuclear test. At the insistence of the Indian Government, the text did not explicitly provide for the right of the USA to halt nuclear cooperation and require India to return US-supplied material, components and equipment if India were to conduct a nuclear explosive test.[147] The agreement does provide, in generic terms in Article 14(2), for the right of termination and for the so-called right of return. It stipulates that the party seeking termination has to give one year's notice to the other party, but that before doing so both would 'consider carefully' whether the circumstances leading to termination resulted from a changed security environment or 'as a response to similar actions by other States which could impact national security'—an apparent reference to a nuclear test by Pakistan. This suggested to some observers that in some circumstances, for

---

[142] 'India and US confirm nuclear pact', BBC News, 27 July 2007, <http://news.bbc.co.uk/2/6919 552.stm>.

[143] See US Department of State, Office of the Spokesman, 'U.S.–India Civil Nuclear Cooperation Initiative: bilateral agreement on peaceful nuclear cooperation', Fact sheet, Washington, DC, 27 July 2007, <http://www.state.gov/r/pa/prs/ps/2007/89552.htm>; and Indian Ministry of External Affairs, 'Fact sheet on the India–US civil nuclear energy co-operation: conclusion of the "123" Agreement', New Delhi, 27 July 2007, <http://www.meaindia.nic.in/pressrelease/2007/07/27pr01.htm>.

[144] Krepon, M. and Stolar, A., 'The US–India 123 Agreement: from bad to worse', Henry L. Stimson Center, 23 Aug. 2007, <http://www.stimson.org/print.cfm?SN=SA200708221446>.

[145] See 'Courses of action for Congress and the Nuclear Suppliers Group: a conversation with the Hon. Edward J. Markey on nuclear cooperation between the United States and India', Council on Foreign Relations, Washington, DC, 13 Sep. 2007, <http://www.cfr.org/publication/14213/courses_of_action_for_congress_and_the_nuclear_suppliers_group.html>.

[146] Agreement for cooperation between the Government of India and the Government of the United States of America concerning peaceful uses of nuclear energy, 3 Aug. 2007, <http://www.state.gov/documents/organization/90157.pdf>.

[147] Section 123a(4) of the 1954 Atomic Energy Act stipulates that any nuclear cooperation agreement between the USA and a foreign government must provide for a US right to require the return of nuclear material and equipment subject to the agreement, including any special fissionable material produced through their use, if the recipient country conducts a nuclear test.

example in response to a Pakistani test, India's resumption of nuclear testing would not necessarily be grounds for the USA to terminate nuclear cooperation with it or require the return of US-supplied equipment and material, as mandated by the Hyde Act.[148] In addition, the agreement sets out elsewhere in Article 14 a potentially onerous series of legal requirements, including agreements on compensation and safety issues, that had to be met before the right of return could be exercised.[149]

Nuclear fuel supply guarantees for India. One of the Indian Government's paramount objectives in the negotiations on the 123 agreement was to guarantee the 'uninterrupted operation' of the country's civil nuclear reactors by obtaining lifetime fuel supply assurances for those reactors.[150] In Article 5(6)b of the proposed agreement, the USA undertakes to 'support an a Indian effort to develop a strategic reserve of nuclear fuel to guard against any disruption of supply over the lifetime of India's reactors'. It also pledges to help India find alternative sources of nuclear fuel in the event of a supply interruption by convening 'a group of friendly supplier countries such as Russia, France and the United Kingdom'. These guarantees were understood in India as having been offered unconditionally by the USA. In the USA, however, there was criticism that this provision appeared to contradicted the Hyde Act, which specifies that the assurance of supply arrangements to which the USA had agreed covered only the disruption of fuel supplies 'due to market failures or similar reasons and not due to Indian actions, such as a nuclear explosive test'.[151]

Safeguards. In Article 5(6)c India pledges to place its civilian nuclear facilities under 'India-specific safeguards in perpetuity' and to negotiate an 'appropriate safeguards agreement to this end with the IAEA'.[152] The safeguards agreement would presumably cover the 14 nuclear reactors designated by India as being 'civilian'.[153] At the same time, India reserves the right to take 'corrective measures' to ensure the 'uninterrupted operation of its civilian nuclear reactors'. While the agreement did not define what was meant by 'India-specific or 'corrective measures', many observers suggested that India

---

[148] Kimball, D. and McGoldrick, F., 'U.S.–Indian nuclear agreement: a bad deal gets worse', *Arms Control Today*, vol. 37, no. 6 (Aug. 2007). Section 104(a) of the Hyde Act stipulates that, in the event of an Indian nuclear test, US nuclear cooperation be terminated and India would be required to return all US-origin equipment and materials that it may have received under the deal as well as any material produced by India with these items.

[149] Varadarajan, S., 'Insulating India's reactors from fuel disruption reality check', *The Hindu*, 8 Aug. 2007.

[150] Varadarajan, S., 'Lifetime fuel guarantee remains a sticking point in "123" talks with U.S.', *The Hindu*, 13 Dec. 2006. Some Indian officials cited as a precedent the Kudankulam reactor deal with Russia, in which India had received sovereign and unqualified Russian guarantees for the lifetime supply of fuel for the reactors being imported from Russia.

[151] Kimball and McGoldrick (note 148).

[152] On 21 Nov. 2007 the IAEA Director General, ElBaradei, and the Chairman of the Indian Atomic Energy Commission (AEC), Anil Kakodkar, met to initiate consultations on an India-specific safeguards agreement. IAEA, 'IAEA–India to launch consultations for India-specific safeguards agreement', Press release 2007/21, 21 Nov. 2007, <http://www.iaea.org/NewsCenter/PressReleases/2007/prn200721.html>.

[153] This number includes 6 foreign-supplied power reactors which India had already agreed would be subject to IAEA facility-specific (INFCIRC/66) safeguards.

was seeking a safeguards arrangement that would allow for the suspension of 'permanent' safeguards in the event that foreign fuel supplies were interrupted.[154]

Reprocessing by India of US-origin spent fuel. The proposed agreement grants India long-term consent to reprocess US-origin spent nuclear fuel. This marks a significant departure from the long-standing US policy to deny other countries advance reprocessing rights: in the past the USA had only given pro-grammatic consent to the European Atomic Energy Community (Euratom) and Japan as part of their 123 agreements.[155] As part of the agreement India will have to construct a new reprocessing facility under IAEA safeguards to handle US-origin spent fuel. In addition, the two governments must agree on 'arrangements and procedures' under which any Indian reprocessing of US-origin spent fuel could occur.

The agreement also provides the option for the two countries to conclude future arrangements to trade reprocessing and enrichment technologies. The Hyde Act limits such transfers to scenarios involving a multinational facility in an IAEA-approved project or a facility involved in a multinational project to develop a proliferation-resistant fuel cycle.

Political opposition in India

The announcement of the 123 agreement led to renewed opposition to the nuclear deal at both ends of the Indian political spectrum. The leader of the Hindu nationalist Bharatiya Janata Party (BJP), India's main opposition party, called for a renegotiation of the agreement, arguing that it would constrain India's nuclear testing option and would lead to 'strategic subservience to the USA'.[156] More crucially, four communist parties (known as the Left parties), which were not a part of the governing coalition but which supported it in the parliament, threatened to withdraw their support for the United Progressive Alliance (UPA)-led government if the latter proceeded with the nuclear deal—a move that would raise the possibility of early elections. The Left parties said they were 'unable to accept' the 123 agreement in the context of the 'bur-geoning strategic alliance' with the USA, and asked the government not to implement it, pending a parliamentary review.[157] The largest of these parties, the Communist Party of India (Marxist), adopted a resolution on 23 August warning that that the agreement would 'bind India into a strategic alliance with the United States with long-term consequences' for the country's inde-pendent foreign policy and called for the government to reconsider the deal.[158]

In October the Left parties' opposition appeared to have effectively killed the nuclear deal, after the Indian Prime Minister, Manmohan Singh,

[154] Kimball and McGoldrick (note 148); and Varadarajan (note 150).
[155] The consent for reprocessing in Europe and Japan preceded the US policy of restriction on repro-cessing in nuclear agreements that were put into law by the 1978 Nuclear Non-proliferation Act.
[156] George, V., 'Renegotiate 123: Advani gives in to pressure from party', *Indian Express*, 31 Aug. 2007.
[157] 'Left "unable to accept" 123 agreement', *The Hindu*, 8 Aug. 2007.
[158] 'CPI(M) Central Committee resolution on nuclear deal', *The Hindu*, 23 Aug. 2007.

announced that he would not risk a no-confidence vote by initiating talks with the IAEA on a safeguards agreement.[159] However, on 17 November the four Left parties provisionally agreed to let the government begin talks with the IAEA Secretariat. They stipulated that any draft safeguards agreement would not be signed by either the IAEA or India before being presented to the UPA–Left Committee on India–US Civil Nuclear Cooperation.[160] This committee, which had been established in September by the leaders of the Left parties and the UPA to find a way out of the political impasse over the nuclear deal, would consider the 'impact of the provisions of the Hyde Act and the 123 agreement on the IAEA Safeguards Agreement' and take this into account before 'finalizing its findings'. Some Indian observers believed that the most likely outcome was that the safeguards agreement would be allowed to die in the committee in order to sustain the minority UPA-led government.[161]

V. The fissile material cut-off treaty

In 2007 the 65-member Conference on Disarmament failed for the eleventh consecutive year to open negotiations on a 'non-discriminatory, multilateral and effectively verifiable treaty banning the production of fissile material for nuclear weapons or other nuclear explosive devices', as called for by the mandate adopted by the CD in 1995 (the so-called Shannon mandate).[162] The CD's first session in 2007 was marked by renewed efforts to break the impasse over the work programme, following on the progress made in 2006.[163] On 23 March the P6 (the ambassadors of South Africa, Sri Lanka, Spain, Sweden, Switzerland and Syria, who served as the six presidents of the CD sessions in 2007) put forward a draft decision document proposing that the CD agree to appoint, 'without prejudice to future work and negotiations on its agenda items', four 'coordinators' who would 'preside over' negotiations on a fissile material production ban as well as three other issues on the CD's agenda.[164] The P6 proposal called for the commencement of negotiations on an FMCT without addressing the contentious question of whether the ban should apply only to the future production of fissile material for weapon purposes or should also prevent existing stocks of such material from being used to manufacture new weapons. It also avoided addressing the question of whether the proposed treaty should contain a formal verification regime, which was opposed by the

---

[159] Page, J., 'Phone call derails controversial deal to attract India into nuclear fold', *The Times*, 16 Oct. 2007.

[160] Kumar, V., 'Government can go to IAEA', *The Hindu*, 17 Nov. 2007.

[161] Kumar (note 160).

[162] Conference on Disarmament, Report of Ambassador Gerald E. Shannon of Canada on consultations on the most appropriate arrangement to negotiate a treaty banning the production of fissile material for nuclear weapons or other nuclear explosive devices, CD/1299, 24 Mar. 1995, <http://www.reaching criticalwill.org/political/cd/shannon.html>. For a brief description and list of members of the CD see annex B in this volume.

[163] See Kile (note 4), pp. 509–10.

[164] Conference on Disarmament, Presidential Draft Decision, CD/2007/L.1, 23 Mar. 2007; and 'CD edges closer to a work programme', *Disarmament Diplomacy*, no. 84 (spring 2007).

USA.[165] Instead, by calling for negotiations 'without any preconditions', the P6 proposal suggested that the disputes over verification and the scope of the treaty should be settled in the course of the negotiations.[166]

The P6 proposal appeared to enjoy widespread support in the CD but failed to produce a breakthrough. India and other Group of 21 (G21) non-aligned states expressed a number of substantive and procedural concerns about it but stated that they would not block its adoption by consensus.[167] However, China, Iran and Pakistan raised objections to the proposal which the P6 were unable to accommodate in a complementary statement.[168] The main objection of all three countries was that any negotiations on a treaty banning the production of fissile material for military purposed had to be conducted explicitly under the 1995 Shannon mandate. They emphasized that this mandate had clearly provided for a formal verification mechanism. Pakistan and Iran also insisted that the negotiating mandate for the scope of the treaty ban should go beyond mandating stopping fissile material production and should cover existing stocks.[169] China's unwillingness to embrace the P6 proposal was consistent with its general lack of enthusiasm for concluding a ban, at least in the near term, on producing fissile material for weapon purposes.[170]

VI. International cooperation to improve nuclear security[171]

In 2007 investment in international non-proliferation and disarmament assistance (INDA) programmes, primarily in Russia, remained at roughly the same level as in previous years.[172] The most important INDA initiative, the Group of

---

[165] The Bush Administration had concluded in 2004 that an FMCT was not 'effectively verifiable', as called for in the 1995 mandate and therefore should not include a formal verification mechanism. US Department of State, 'US proposal to the Conference on Disarmament', Remarks by Jackie W. Sanders, Permanent Representative to the Conference on Disarmament and Special Representative of the President for the Nonproliferation of Nuclear Weapons, Geneva, 29 July 2004, <http://www.state.gov/t/ac/rls/rm/2004/34929.htm>.

[166] Meyer, P., 'Is there any fizz left in the fissban? Prospects for a fissile material cut-off treaty', Arms Control Today, vol. 37, no. 10 (Dec. 2007).

[167] Conference on Disarmament, 'Presidential report to the Conference on Disarmament on part III of the 2007 session', CD/1828*, 30 Aug. 2007, p. 2; and Varadarajan, S., 'Fissile material ban talks inch towards consensus', The Hindu, 2 July 2007.

[168] Conference on Disarmament, 'Complementary presidential statement reflecting an understanding of the Conference on the implementation of CD/2007/L.1**', CD/2007/CRP5*, 29 June 2007.

[169] Statement by Ambassador Seyed Mohammad Kazem Sajjadpour, Iran's Permanent Representative at the Conference on Disarmament, Geneva, 21 June 2007, <http://www.reachingcriticalwill.org/political/cd/speeches07/2session/June21Iran.html>; and Statement by Ambassador Masood Khan, Pakistan's Permanent Representative at the Conference on Disarmament, Geneva, 13 Sep. 2007, <http://www.reachingcriticalwill.org/political/cd/speeches07/3session/Sept13Pakistan.pdf>.

[170] See e.g. Meyer (note 166).

[171] Vitaly Fedchenko, SIPRI Researcher, wrote this section of the chapter with contributions from Ekaterina Khudina, SIPRI Intern. See also Feiveson, H. et al., 'Fissile materials: global stocks, production and elimination', SIPRI Yearbook 2007 (note 4), pp. 558–76; Fedchenko, V., 'Multilateral control of the nuclear fuel cycle', SIPRI Yearbook 2006 (note 90), pp. 686–705; and chapter 9 in this volume, section V.

[172] The major INDA donor, the USA, budgeted $1.91 billion for financial year (FY) 2008, slightly more than the $1.86 billion it budgeted in FY 2007. Project on Managing the Atom, Interactive Threat Reduction Budget database, <http://www.nti.org/e_research/cnwm/charts/cnm_funding_interactive.asp>.

Eight (G8) Global Partnership against the Spread of Weapons and Materials of Mass Destruction, reached the halfway point of its agreed 10-year duration.[173] At the 2007 annual G8 summit meeting, held at Heligendamm, Germany, the member states reaffirmed their commitment under the Global Partnership to raise up to $20 billion by 2012 to support priority projects.[174] They reported having made significant progress over the previous five years in the destruction of chemical weapons, dismantlement of nuclear submarines, employment of former weapon scientists and the physical protection of nuclear materials.[175] The least successful Global Partnership priority area was identified as the permanent disposition of fissile materials, in particular plutonium.

Russian–US cooperation on the disposition of nuclear materials

After the end of the cold war the disposition of weapon-grade plutonium and HEU became a high priority for both Russia and the USA, with both countries holding stocks of these materials in excess of their defence requirements. The disposition of 500 tonnes of HEU from Russian nuclear weapons was effectively addressed by the 1993 Russian–US HEU purchase agreement.[176] As of 30 September 2007, 315 tonnes of HEU (equal to approximately 12 615 nuclear warheads) had been blended down into 9200 tonnes of low-enriched uranium for use as nuclear reactor fuel.[177]

The disposition of excess weapon-grade plutonium has been more problematic. In 2000 Russia and the USA signed a Plutonium Management and Disposition Agreement (PMDA), in which the two countries agreed to each eliminate 34 tonnes of surplus weapon-grade plutonium.[178] Under the PMDA, the parties could use two methods for disposing of the plutonium: converting it to

[173] The G8 Global Partnership was established at the 2002 G8 Summit in Kananaskis, Canada, to support cooperative projects, initially in Russia, aimed at addressing non-proliferation, disarmament, counterterrorism and nuclear safety issues. G8 Kananaskis Summit 2002, 'The G8 Global Partnership against the Spread of Weapons and Materials of Mass Destruction', 27 June 2002, <http://www.g8.gc.ca/2002Kananaskis/globpart-en.asp>. See also Anthony, I. and Fedchenko, V., 'International non-proliferation and disarmament assistance', *SIPRI Yearbook 2005: Armaments, Disarmament and International Security* (Oxford University Press: Oxford, 2005), pp. 675–98.

[174] The Global Partnership programme identified 4 main priorities: the destruction of chemical weapons, the dismantlement of decommissioned nuclear submarines, the permanent disposition of fissile materials, and the employment of former weapon scientists in non-military activities.

[175] G8 Heiligendamm Summit 2007, 'Report on the G8 Global Partnership' and annex A, 'Consolidated report data', 8 June 2007, <http://www.g-8.de/Webs/G8/EN/G8Summit/SummitDocuments/summit-documents.html>.

[176] The Agreement between the Government of the United States of America and the Government of the Russian Federation concerning the Disposition of Highly Enriched Uranium from Nuclear Weapons was signed on 18 Feb. 1993. The text of the agreement is available at <http://www.nti.org/db/nisprofs/russia/fulltext/heudeal/heufull.htm>. See also Timbie, J., 'Energy from bombs: problems and solutions in the implementation of a high-priority nonproliferation project', *Science and Global Security*, vol. 12, no. 3 (2004), pp. 165–92.

[177] United States Enrichment Corporation, 'US–Russian Megatons to Megawatts Program status report', 30 Sep. 2007, <http://www.usec.com/v2001_02/HTML/megatons_howitworks.asp>.

[178] The Agreement between the Government of the United States of America and the Government of the Russian Federation concerning the Management and Disposition of Plutonium Designated as No Longer Required for Defense Purposes and Related Cooperation was signed on 1 Sep. 2000. The text of the agreement is available at <http://www.state.gov/documents/organization/18557.pdf>.

mixed oxide (MOX) fuel for use in nuclear power reactors; or immobilizing it and putting it in long-term storage in a manner that precluded its use in nuclear weapons. Russia chose the MOX fuel option.[179] The USA initially intended to pursue both options but, after reviewing US non-proliferation policies in 2001, the Bush Administration deemed this to be too costly and outlined a plan to convert almost all of the USA's surplus plutonium to MOX fuel.[180] The US Department of Energy started construction of the MOX Fuel Fabrication Facility at the Savannah River Site near Aiken, South Carolina, on 1 August 2007.[181]

Initially, the PMDA envisaged disposing of the plutonium within 20 years (at a rate of at least 2 tonnes per year), beginning no later than 31 December 2007. However, the disposal programme did not start in 2007 because of disputes over two issues. The first had to with the liability protection of individuals employed by the USA for project implementation and claims for damages caused by their actions.[182] This was resolved when a new liability agreement was signed as a protocol to the PMDA on 15 September 2006.[183]

The second dispute related to Russia's plans to irradiate the MOX fuel in so-called fast reactors, rather than the light-water reactors (LWRs) envisaged in the PMDA. Russia's view has been that its plutonium stockpiles should be used to produce energy as part of its long-term strategy to create a closed nuclear fuel cycle based on fast-neutron breeder reactors.[184] Russia thus has been reluctant to use LWRs for plutonium disposition, suggesting instead that MOX fuel be irradiated in its current BOR-60 and BN-600 fast reactors and the planned BN-800 fast reactor. The USA, a major donor to plutonium disposal efforts in Russia, has opposed this option on the grounds that it is more expensive (the projected cost of the BN-800 reactor is $1.3 billion) and less proliferation-resistant.

In March 2007 the head of the Russian Federal Atomic Energy Agency (Rosatom), Sergei Kirienko, proposed a new approach to plutonium disposal that would abandon the irradiation of MOX fuel in LWRs in favour of the use of three fast reactors. In addition, Russia would not request US funding for

[179] Russia has an estimated stockpile of *c*. 145 tonnes of separated weapon-grade plutonium. See appendix 8B.

[180] Wolf, A., US Congress, Congressional Research Service (CRS), *Nonproliferation and Threat Reduction Assistance: U.S. Programs in the Former Soviet Union*, CRS Report for Congress RL31957 (CRS: Washington, DC, 28 Nov. 2007), pp. 43–44.

[181] US Department of Energy, National Nuclear Security Administration, 'NNSA starts construction on MOX fuel fabrication facility in South Carolina', Press release, Washington, DC, 1 Aug. 2007, <http://nnsa.energy.gov/news/1016.htm>.

[182] On the liability issue see Kile (note 90), p. 635.

[183] US Department of Energy, 'U.S. and Russia sign liability protocol', Press release, Washington, DC, 15 Sep. 2006, <http://www.energy.gov/print/4160.htm>.

[184] A closed nuclear fuel cycle is one in which spent nuclear fuel is reprocessed after irradiation in a reactor in order to recover uranium or plutonium for refabrication back into nuclear fuel. The fuel cycle can be 'closed' in various ways, e.g. by using plutonium in a fast breeder reactor, as Russia plans to do. Fast reactors are generally designed to use plutonium fuels and may be set up to operate in 'breeder' or 'burner' modes. In breeder mode, a fast reactor produces, through the transmutation of uranium-238, more plutonium than it consumes. In burner mode, the reactor consumes plutonium by converting it into short-lived isotopes.

construction of the BN-800 reactor.[185] On 19 November 2007 Kirienko and the US Secretary of Energy, Samuel W. Bodman, signed a joint statement outlining and endorsing the proposed plan: Rosatom will dispose of plutonium by irradiating the MOX fuel in the BN-600 and BN-800 reactors as soon as all technical modifications and the construction of necessary facilities are finished.[186] The reactors will be able to dispose of at least 1.5 tonnes of plutonium annually. Plutonium disposal in the BN-600 will begin 'in the 2012 timeframe', with disposal in the BN-800 starting 'soon thereafter'. US officials emphasized that, in the PMDA framework, the two reactors would operate as burners rather than breeders and would not create new stocks of separated plutonium.[187]

VII. Conclusions

In 2007 the nuclear programmes of Iran and North Korea remained at the forefront of international concerns about the proliferation of nuclear weapons. In the case of Iran, the urgency of these concerns was diminished somewhat by the US intelligence community's conclusion that Iran had halted its clandestine nuclear weapon programme in 2003 and had not resumed weaponization research and development activities as of mid-2007. This conclusion effectively undercut political support for the US Administration to take military action against Iran's nuclear facilities. At the same time, it underscored that there is a pressing need to rewrite non-proliferation rules to address what many believe is an inherent structural weakness in the NPT: namely, that non-nuclear weapon states can covertly develop a nuclear weapon capability by putting in place, under the cover of a civil nuclear energy programme, the fuel cycle facilities needed to produce weapon-usable nuclear material.

In this context, the Iranian and North Korean cases have led to calls for the adoption of a permanent ban on the construction of new nationally controlled facilities for producing fissile material. The ban would be accompanied by the establishment of nuclear fuel banks, of the type currently envisioned by the IAEA, and other fuel supply assurances. In the view of many non-proliferation specialists, the long-term goal should be to establish multinational or international arrangements for controlling the nuclear fuel cycle activities of greatest proliferation concern—uranium enrichment and plutonium reprocessing— as well as spent fuel management and waste disposal. Although the latter is by no means a new idea, it is one for which the time is increasingly ripe in terms of strengthening and extending the nuclear non-proliferation regime.

[185] MacLachlan, A., 'Russia, US could take decisive step in plutonium disposition program', *Nuclear Fuel*, 21 May 2007, pp. 1, 5–6. In 2006 the Russian Government resumed financing construction of the BN-800 reactor from the federal budget. 'Correction: nuclear power future lies in fast neutron reactors– Kiriyenko', RIA Novosti, 14 Dec. 2005, <http://en.rian.ru/russia/20051214/42490704.html>.

[186] US Department of Energy, 'US and Russia sign plan for Russian plutonium disposition', Press release, 19 Nov. 2007, <http://www.energy.gov/nationalsecurity/5742.htm>. The US Department of Energy will contribute $400 million for this work

[187] Horner, D., 'US officials provide details on plutonium disposition pact with Russia', *Nuclear Fuel*, 17 Dec. 2007, pp. 1, 17–18.

Appendix 8A. World nuclear forces, 2008

SHANNON N. KILE, VITALY FEDCHENKO and
HANS M. KRISTENSEN

I. Introduction

While world attention in 2007 focused on the nuclear test by the Democratic People's Republic of Korea (DPRK, or North Korea) and Iran's uranium enrichment programme, eight nuclear weapon states possess almost 10 200 operational nuclear weapons (see table 8A.1). Several thousand of these nuclear weapons are kept on high alert, ready to be launched within minutes. If all nuclear warheads are counted—operational warheads, spares, those in both active and inactive storage, and intact warheads scheduled for later dismantlement—the United States, Russia, the United Kingdom, France, China, India, Pakistan and Israel together possess a total of more than 25 000 warheads.

All of the five legally recognized nuclear weapon states, as defined by the 1968 Treaty on the Non-Proliferation of Nuclear Weapons (Non-Proliferation Treaty, NPT),[1] appear determined to remain nuclear powers for the foreseeable future and are in the midst or on the verge of modernizing their nuclear forces. At the same time, Russia and the USA are in the process of reducing their operational nuclear forces from cold war levels as a result of two bilateral treaties—the 1991 Treaty on the Reduction and Limitation of Strategic Offensive Arms (START I Treaty) and the 2002 Strategic Offensive Reductions Treaty (SORT).[2] Sections II and III of this appendix discuss the composition of the deployed nuclear forces of the USA and Russia, respectively. The nuclear arsenals of the UK, France and China are considerably smaller than those of the USA and Russia, but those three lesser nuclear powers are either deploying new nuclear weapons or have announced their intention to do so in the future. Data on their delivery vehicles and warhead stockpiles are presented in sections IV–VI.

Reliable information about the operational status of the nuclear arsenals of the three states that are not parties to the NPT—India, Pakistan and Israel—is difficult to find. In the absence of official declarations, the information that is available is often contradictory or incorrect. India and Pakistan are expanding their nuclear strike capabilities, while Israel appears to be waiting to see how the situation in Iran develops. Sections VII–IX provide information about the status of the Indian, Pakistani and Israeli nuclear arsenals. North Korea's military nuclear capabilities are discussed in section X.

The figures presented here are estimates based on public information and contain some uncertainties, as reflected in the notes to the tables.

---

[1] According to the NPT, only states that manufactured and exploded a nuclear device prior to 1 Jan. 1967 are recognized as nuclear weapon states. By this definition, China, France, Russia, the UK and the USA are the nuclear weapon states parties to the NPT. For a summary of the NPT see annex A in this volume.

[2] For summaries of the START I and SORT treaties see annex A in this volume.

Table 8A.1. World nuclear forces, January 2008

All figures are approximate.

Country[a]	Strategic warheads	Non-strategic warheads	Total number of warheads
USA	3 575	500	4 075[b]
Russia	3 113	2 076	5 189[c]
UK	185[d]	–	185
France	348	–	348
China	161	15	176
India	–	–	60–70[e]
Pakistan	–	–	60[e]
Israel	–	–	80[e]
Total			**10 183**

[a] North Korea claimed in 2005 that it had developed nuclear weapons and conducted a nuclear test in 2006, but there is no public information to verify that North Korea has weaponized its nuclear capability.

[b] The total US stockpile, including reserves, contains c. 5300 warheads. Another 5100 warheads are scheduled to be dismantled between now and 2023.

[c] The total Russian stockpile contains c. 14 000 warheads, of which c. 8800 are in reserve or awaiting dismantlement.

[d] Some warheads on British strategic submarines have sub-strategic missions previously covered by tactical nuclear weapons.

[e] The stockpiles of India, Pakistan and Israel are thought to be only partly deployed.

II. US nuclear forces

As of January 2008, the USA maintained an estimated arsenal of approximately 4075 operational nuclear warheads, consisting of roughly 3575 strategic and 500 non-strategic warheads (see table 8A.2).[3] In addition to this operational arsenal, approximately 1260 warheads are held in reserve, for a total stockpile of approximately 5300 warheads. Over 5100 other warheads were removed from the US Department of Defense (DOD) stockpile at the end of 2007, destined to be dismantled by 2023.

This force level is a significant change compared with the estimate presented in *SIPRI Yearbook 2006*, and is precipitated by the announcement by the administration of President George W. Bush on 18 December 2007 that it would meet the goal of the 2004 Nuclear Weapons Stockpile Plan of reducing the total stockpile 'by nearly 50 percent from the 2001 level' five years early, in 2007 instead of 2012.[4] The

[3] According to the US Department of State, 'the number of U.S. operationally deployed strategic nuclear warheads was 3,696 as of December 31, 2006'. US Department of State, Bureau of Verification, Compliance, and Implementation, '2007 Annual report on implementation of the Moscow Treaty', 12 July 2007, <http://www.state.gov/t/vci/rls/rpt/88187.htm>, p. 1.

[4] See The White House, 'President Bush approves significant reduction in nuclear weapons stockpile', Press release, 18 Dec. 2007, <http://www.whitehouse.gov/news/releases/2007/12/20071218-3.html>; US Department of Energy, National Nuclear Security Administration, 'NNSA releases draft plan to transform nuclear weapons complex', 18 Dec. 2007, <http://nnsa.energy.gov/news/print/1463.htm>; and Agence France-Presse, 'US accelerates nuclear stockpile cuts: White House', GlobalSecurity.org, 18 Dec. 2007, <http://www.globalsecurity.org/org/news/2007/071218-stockpile-cuts.htm>. The classified Nuclear Weapons Stockpile Plan was submitted to the US Congress on 3 June 2004. US Department of Energy,

Table 8A.2. US nuclear forces, January 2008

Type	Designation	No. deployed	Year first deployed	Range (km)[a]	Warhead loading	No. of warheads
Strategic forces						**3 575**
Bombers[b]		*104/72*				*1 083*
B-52H	Stratofortress	94/56	1961	16 000	ALCM 5–150 kt	528[c]
B-2	Spirit	20/16	1994	11 000	B61-7, -11, B83-1 bombs	555[d]
ICBMs[e]		*488*				*764*
LGM-30G	Minuteman III					
	Mk-12	138	1970	13 000	1–3 x 170 kt	214
	Mk-12A	250	1979	13 000	1–3 x 335 kt	450
	Mk-21 SERV	100	2006	13 000	1 x 300 kt	100
SSBNs/SLBMs[f]		*228*				*1 728*
UGM-133A	Trident II (D-5)					
	Mk-4	..	1992	>7 400	6 x 100 kt	1 344
	Mk-5	..	1990	>7 400	6 x 475 kt	384
Non-strategic forces						**500**
B61-3, -4 bombs		..	1979	..	0.3–170 kt	400[g]
Tomahawk SLCM		320	1984	2 500	1 x 5–150 kt	100[h]
Total						**4 075[i]**

.. = not applicable; ALCM = air-launched cruise missile; ICBM = intercontinental ballistic missile; kt = kiloton; SERV = security-enhanced re-entry vehicle; SLBM = submarine-launched ballistic missile; SLCM = sea-launched cruise missile; SSBN = nuclear-powered ballistic missile submarine.

[a] Aircraft range is given for illustrative purposes only; actual mission range will vary according to flight profile and weapon loading.

[b] The first figure in the *No. deployed* column is the total number of B-52Hs in the inventory, including those for training, test and reserve. The second figure is for primary mission inventory aircraft, i.e. the number of operational aircraft assigned for nuclear and conventional wartime missions.

[c] Approximately 860 ALCMs may have been withdrawn in 2007 due to early implementation of the 2004 Nuclear Weapons Stockpile Plan. All advanced cruise missiles have also been retired.

[d] These warheads are available for both the B-52H and the B-2A, but the B-2A is thought to be the main bomb delivery vehicle.

[e] The 2006 Quadrennial Defense Review decided to reduce the ICBM force to 450 missiles by 2008. The download of most Minuteman ICBMs to 1 warhead to meet the warhead ceiling mandated by the 2002 Strategic Offensive Reductions Treaty (SORT) is under way, but c. 25 missiles will continue to carry 3 warheads each.

[f] Although D-5 missiles are counted under the 1991 Treaty on the Reduction and Limitation of Strategic Offensive Arms (START I Treaty) as carrying 8 warheads each, the US Navy completed a preliminary download in 2005 (to an average of 6 warheads per missile) and will conduct an additional download to an average of 4 warheads per missile to meet the SORT-mandated warhead ceiling by 2012.

[g] Approximately 350 B61 bombs are deployed in Europe at 7 airbases in 6 NATO countries.

[h] Another 190 W80-0s are in inactive storage. The Tomahawk cruise missile (TLAM/N, from Tomahawk land attack missile, nuclear) is no longer deployed at sea but is stored on land.

[j] Approximately 1260 additional warheads are in reserve, for a total stockpile of *c.* 5300 warheads. Nearly 5100 warheads are awaiting dismantlement. In addition, *c.* 15 000 plutonium pits are stored at the Pantex Plant in Texas.

Sources: US Department of Defense, various budget reports and press releases; US Department of Energy, various budget reports and plans; US Department of State, START I Treaty Memoranda of Understanding, 1990–Jan. 2008; US Department of Defense, various documents obtained under the Freedom of Information Act; US Air Force, US Navy and US Department of Energy, personal communication; 'Nuclear notebook', *Bulletin of the Atomic Scientists*, various issues; US Naval Institute, *Proceedings*, various issues; and Authors' estimates.

stockpile reduction has so far occurred largely on paper, because it consists of transferring ownership of the warheads from the DOD to the Department of Energy (DOE). In practical terms, the weapons will mostly remain at their bases for several years because the DOE does not have capacity to store them.

The stockpile announcement accompanied the National Nuclear Security Administration's publication of the *Draft Complex Transformation Supplemental Programmatic Environmental Impact Statement* (SPEIS) for modernizing the US nuclear weapon complex.[5] Complex Transformation, a scaled-down version of the 2006 plan known as Complex 2030,[6] evaluates how the nuclear weapon complex should be structured to meet nuclear weapon production and maintenance requirements at force levels below those imposed by SORT. The plan proposes consolidating the complex and increasing the capacity to produce plutonium 'pits' (cores) from the current 10 annually to up to 200.

The Bush Administration's proposal to begin production, in 2014, of the first of a series of Reliable Replacement Warheads (RRWs) ran into opposition in the US Congress, which rejected the administration's funding request for 2008. Instead, the Congress delayed a decision on RRW funding until after the completion of a new assessment of future US strategic nuclear deterrence requirements.

In an effort to 'ensure that stockpile and infrastructure transformation is not misperceived by other nations as "restarting the arms race"', the Bush Administration announced in 2007 that dismantlement of retired warheads had increased by 146 per cent.[7] Although the percentage increase looks impressive, the actual number of warheads dismantled appears to be modest compared with the rate of dismantlement during the 1990s. On the basis of previously declassified or released dismantlement information, it is possible to estimate that the 146 per cent increase means roughly 260 warheads. For comparison, the average number of warheads dismantled per year

National Nuclear Security Administration, 'Administration plans significant reduction in nuclear weapons stockpile', News release, Washington, DC, 3 June 2004, <http://www.nnsa.doe.gov/news releases.htm>.

[5] US Department of Energy (DOE), National Nuclear Security Administration, *Draft Complex Transformation Supplemental Programmatic Environmental Impact Statement* (DOE: Washington, DC, Dec. 2007), <http://www.complextransformationspeis.com/>.

[6] US Department of Energy (DOE), National Nuclear Security Administration, *Complex 2030: An Infrastructure Planning Scenario for a Nuclear Weapons Complex Able to Meet the Threat of the 21st Century*, DOE/NA-0013 (DOE: Washington, DC, Oct. 2006).

[7] US Department of Energy, National Nuclear Security Administration (NNSA), 'Nuclear weapons dismantlements up 146 percent', *NNSA Monthly News*, Nov./Dec. 2007, p. 1.

during the 1990s was nearly 1200. Dismantlement is not currently a priority at the Pantex Plant in Texas, where the focus is on life extension of the warheads that are slated to remain in the enduring stockpile. As a result, dismantling the current back-log of retired warheads will not be completed until 2023.[8]

In parallel with reducing the nuclear arsenal, the DOD has upgraded its nuclear strike plans to reflect new presidential guidance and a transition in war planning from the Single Integrated Operational Plan (SIOP) of the cold war to a set of smaller and more flexible strike plans designed to defeat today's adversaries. In March 2003 a new series of executable scenario-based strike options against regional states armed with weapons of mass destruction (WMD) was added to the strategic war plan, which is now known as OPLAN (Operations Plan) 8044. This was refined in October 2004 and resulted in an updated war plan known as OPLAN 8044 Revision 05. In February 2005 General Richard B. Meyers, chairman of the Joint Chiefs of Staff, described some of the characteristics of the plan: '[US Strategic Command] has revised our strategic deterrence and response plan that became effective in the fall of 2004. This revised, detailed plan provides more flexible options to assure allies, and dissuade, deter, and if necessary, defeat adversaries in a wider range of contingencies'.[9]

In mid-2004 a controversial plan for striking regional adversaries pre-emptively with conventional and nuclear weapons, called CONPLAN (Concept Plan) 8022, entered into effect as the combat employment part of a new Global Strike mission. The plan was withdrawn in the fall of 2004, however, and the strike options incorporated into OPLAN 8044.

Land-based ballistic missiles

The US intercontinental ballistic missile (ICBM) force is undergoing significant change as part of the USA's implementation of SORT. Approximately 764 warheads were deployed on 488 ICBMs as of January 2008, a reduction of 136 warheads compared with 2007 due to offloading of W62 warheads and downloading of W78 warheads. The last W62 is scheduled to be offloaded in 2009, and additional download-ing of W78s will reduce the total loading to 500 warheads in 2011. As the 170-kiloton W62 is removed from the missiles, the modern 300-kt Mk-21/W87 security-enhanced re-entry vehicle (SERV) is being installed. The increased power of the W87 will broaden the range of targets of the Minuteman force. A previous plan to convert the ICBM force to single-warhead configuration has been modified: 25 mis-siles will continue to carry three warheads. Several hundred additional warheads will be kept in storage for upload to increase the warheads on the ICBM force if necessary in the future. Work is continuing on designing a new ICBM to begin replacing the Minuteman III missile from 2018.

Only one Minuteman III missile flight test was launched in 2007, compared to four in 2006. That missile was launched from Vandenberg Air Force Base (AFB) in Calif-ornia on 7 February and delivered a single, unarmed warhead approximately 6760 kilometres, with impact on a water target east of Kwajalein in the Marshall Islands.

[8] US Department of Energy (note 6), p. 8.

[9] Myers, R. B., General, US Air Force, Chairman of the Joint Chiefs of Staff, Posture statement before the Senate Armed Services Committee, 17 Feb. 2005, <http://www.senate.gov/~armed_services/statemnt/2005/February/Myers%2002-17-05.pdf>, p. 32.

Ballistic missile submarines

The conversion of Pacific-based nuclear-powered ballistic missile submarines (SSBNs, from 'ship submersible ballistic nuclear') from Trident I C-4 missiles to the longer-range and more accurate Trident II D-5 missile is nearing completion with the USS *Alabama* scheduled to complete conversion in 2008. Twelve operational Ohio Class SSBNs carry a total of 228 D-5 submarine-launched ballistic missiles (SLBMs), each of which is estimated to be armed with an average of six warheads. Two additional SSBNs are undergoing overhaul at any given time, and their 48 missiles and 288 warheads are not included in the total. In the future, eight SSBNs will be based in the Pacific and six in the Atlantic, focusing the US sea-based deterrent against targets in China and elsewhere in the Pacific region.

In 2008 the US Navy will begin production of a modified D-5 missile. A total of 108 missiles are planned by 2011, at a cost of more than $4 billion, with initial deployment scheduled for 2013. The modified D-5 SLBM will arm the Ohio Class SSBNs for the rest of their service lives, which have been extended from 30 to 44 years. The oldest submarine is scheduled to retire in 2029, at which point a new SSBN class is planned to become operational. Development studies for the new class, known as SSBN(X), have begun.

Three Trident II D-5 missiles were test-launched during 2007 in two events. The USS *Tennessee* launched two missiles from the eastern test range off the Florida coast on 15 May. The missiles were the first to carry the new Lockheed low-cost test missile kit, which converts an operational missile into test configuration and contains range safety devices and flight telemetry instrumentation. On 29 November the USS *Henry M. Jackson* test-launched a single missile from the western test range in an operation to certify the submarine for deployment after a lengthy retrofit from C-4 to D-5 SLBMs.

The deployment of the W76-1/Mk4A warhead, a modernized version of the existing W76/Mk4, was scheduled to begin in March 2008, but owing to a technical production problem the programme has been delayed. The programme involves production of approximately 2000 W76-1 warheads up to 2021.[10] The W76-1/Mk4 is equipped with a new fuse that will give military planners more flexibility in setting the height of burst to 'enable W76 to take advantage of [the] higher accuracy of the D-5 missile'[11] and hold at risk a wider range of targets including hard targets. The increased lethality of the W76-1 warhead may also permit a reduction of the explosive yield.

Another potential upgrade, proposed by the US Strategic Command (STRATCOM), involves the 'accuracy adjunct', a manoeuvring attachment that was developed for the Mk4 re-entry vehicle to give the weapon 'GPS-life accuracy'. The US Congress has refused to approve the upgrade, which would enable STRATCOM to deploy conventional warheads on the D-5 SLBM.[12]

---

[10] Kristensen, H. M., 'Administration increases submarine nuclear warhead production plan', FAS Strategic Security Blog, 30 Aug. 2007, <http://www.fas.org/blog/ssp/2007/08/us_triples_submarine_war head.php>.

[11] US Department of Energy (DOE), Office of Defense Programs, *Stockpile Stewardship and Management Plan: First Annual Update, October 1997* (DOE: Washington, DC, Oct. 2006), pp. 1–14. This document was partially declassified and released under the Freedom of Information Act.

[12] The 2006 Quadrennial Defense Review directed STRATCOM to replace nuclear warheads on 24 Trident II (D-5) missiles with 96 conventional warheads for deployment in 2008. The Congress has

The first of a series of RRWs is designed to replace a portion of the W76 warheads currently deployed on the D-5 missiles. The Nuclear Weapons Council has approved a preliminary RRW-1 design, which is based on the two-stage thermonuclear SKUA-9 design developed by Lawrence Livermore National Laboratory. The high-yield design was tested several times during the early 1970s, prior to the 1974 Threshold Test-Ban Treaty (TTBT).[13] If funded by the Congress, the warhead would be incorporated into the Mk5 re-entry body originally designed for the W88 warhead.

Long-range bombers

A B-2 bomber crashed on Guam on 23 February 2008, the first loss of the $1.2 billion stealth bomber. Of the remaining 20 B-2s, 16 have nuclear missions. Both the bomber fleet and their nuclear weapons continued to be upgraded. Approximately 1000 nuclear warheads are earmarked for delivery by B-52H and B-2 bombers, including W80-1 warheads on air-launched cruise missiles and B61-7, B61-11, and B83-1 gravity bombs. The US Air Force is studying options for a new long-range strike aircraft to begin replacing the current bomber force from 2018.

The advanced cruise missile (ACM) was retired in 2007, and approximately half of the air-launched cruise missiles (ALCMs) were withdrawn from the stockpile as part of a plan to reduce by nearly 50 per cent the size of the stockpile by the end of 2007. The life extension of the W80-1 warhead has been put on hold and the Air Force is designing a next-generation nuclear-armed cruise missile known as the enhanced cruise missile.

Non-strategic nuclear weapons[14]

As of January 2008, the USA retained approximately 500 active non-strategic nuclear warheads. These consisted of 400 B61 gravity bombs and 100 W80-0 warheads for Tomahawk cruise missiles (TLAM/Ns, from Tomahawk land attack missiles, nuclear). Another 800 non-strategic warheads are in inactive storage. Approximately 350 B61 bombs are deployed in Europe at seven airbases in six North Atlantic Treaty Organization (NATO) member states (Belgium, Germany, Italy, the Netherlands, Turkey and the UK). The bombs were apparently withdrawn from Ramstein Air Base, Germany, in 2005.[15] The aircraft of non-nuclear weapon NATO countries that are assigned nuclear strike missions with US nuclear weapons include Belgian and Dutch F-16 and German and Italian Tornado combat aircraft.[16] The US arsenal in Europe may include inactive bombs. A portion of the new Joint Strike Fighter force will be nuclear-capable.

---

been unwilling to fund the programme and has expressed concern about the implications for crisis stability of mixing nuclear- and conventionally armed ballistic missiles.

[13] For a summary of the Treaty on the Limitation of Underground Nuclear Weapon Tests see annex A in this volume.

[14] Neither START nor SORT place limits on Russian and US inventories of non-strategic nuclear weapons. The US Nuclear Posture Review also did not address this category of weapons.

[15] On the history and status of US nuclear weapons in Europe see Kristensen, H. M., 'United States removes nuclear weapons from German Base, documents indicate', FAS Strategic Security Blog, 9 July 2007, <http://www.fas.org/blog/ssp/2007/07/united_states_removes_nuclear.php>.

[16] See Kristensen, H. M., *US Nuclear Weapons in Europe* (Natural Resources Defense Council: Washington, DC, 2005), <http://www.nrdc.org/nuclear/euro.contents.asp>.

Only 100 W80-0 warheads for the TLAM/N are active; another 200 are in inactive storage. TLAM/Ns are earmarked for deployment on selected Los Angeles, Improved Los Angeles and Virginia Class nuclear-powered attack submarines (SSNs, from ship submersible nuclear). TLAM/Ns are not deployed at sea under normal circumstances but can be redeployed within 30 days of a decision to do so. All are stored at strategic weapon facilities at Bangor, Washington, and Kings Bay, Georgia. The W80-0 may be retired in the near future.

Nuclear warhead stockpile management and modernization

The total US stockpile of roughly 5300 warheads is organized in two categories: active and inactive warheads. The active category includes intact warheads with all components that are either deployed on operational delivery systems, are part of the 'responsive force' of reserve warheads that can be deployed on operational delivery systems in a relatively short time, or are spare warheads. The inactive category includes warheads that are held in long-term storage as a reserve with their limited life components (tritium) removed. In addition to these warheads, more than 5100 other warheads are awaiting dismantling.

The USA keeps nearly 5000 plutonium pits in storage at the Pantex Plant in Texas as a strategic reserve. Another 10 000 pits at Pantex make up most of the 43 tonnes of weapon-grade plutonium previously declared in excess of military needs by the administrations of President Bill Clinton and President George W. Bush. All of these nearly 15 000 pits come from retired warheads. Approximately 5000 canned assemblies (thermonuclear secondaries) are kept at the Oak Ridge Y-12 Plant in Tennessee.

III. Russian nuclear forces

As of January 2008, Russia had an estimated 5189 nuclear warheads (see table 8A.3). In 2007 Russia continued to reduce its strategic nuclear forces in accordance with its commitments under SORT and as part of a doctrinal shift away from a 'substantially redundant' (*suschestvenno izbytochnyi*) and towards a 'minimally sufficient' (*garantirovanno dostatochnyi*) deterrence posture. According to a senior Russian military planner, Russia's strategic nuclear forces can still guarantee 'minimally sufficient' deterrence until 2015–20 within the force ceilings imposed by SORT, even if the USA develops a ballistic missile defence (BMD) system.[17] However, he said that the strategic forces would need qualitative improvements to enhance their survivability and ability to penetrate missile defences in the futute. Russia has prioritized the procurement of the land-based SS-27 (RS12-M2/1 Topol-M) ICBMs and the development of sea-launched SS-NX-30 Bulava missile systems, while continuing to extend the service lives of older missiles as an interim measure. In 2007 Russia began flight tests of a new road-mobile missile with multiple independently targetable re-entry vehicles (MIRVs) and missile defence penetration aids, continued to upgrade its sea-based strategic force and resumed regular long-range patrols of strategic aviation.

---

[17] Umnov, S., 'SYaS Rossii: naraschivaniye vozmozhnostey po preodoleniyu protivoraketnoy oborony' [Russia's SNF: building up ballistic missile defence penetration capacities], *Voenno-Promyshlennyi Kur'er*, 8–14 Mar. 2006. On US BMD programmes see appendix 8C.

Table 8A.3. Russian nuclear forces, January 2008

Type and Russian designation (NATO designation)	No. deployed	Year first deployed	Range (km)[a]	Warhead loading	No. of warheads
Strategic offensive forces	**685**				**3 113**
Bombers	*79*				*884*
Tu-95MS6 (Bear-H6)	32	1981	6 500–10 500	6 x AS-15A ALCMs, bombs	192
Tu-95MS16 (Bear-H16)	32	1981	6 500–10 500	16 x AS-15A ALCMs, bombs	512
Tu-160 (Blackjack)	15	1987	10 500–13 200	12 x AS-15B ALCMs or AS-16 SRAMs, bombs	180
ICBMs[b]	*430*				*1 605*
RS-20 B/V (SS-18 Satan)	75	1979	11 000–15 000	10 x 500–750 kt	750
RS-18 (SS-19 Stiletto)	100	1980	10 000	6 x 500–750 kt	600
RS-12M (SS-25 Sickle)	201	1985	10 500	1 x 550 kt	201
RS-12M2 Topol-M (SS-27)	48	1997	10 500	1 x 550 kt	48
RS-12M1 Topol-M (SS-27)	6	2006	10 500	1 x 550 kt	6
SLBMs	*176*				*624*
RSM-50 (SS-N-18 M1 Stingray)	80	1978	6 500	3 x 200 kt	240
RSM-54 (SS-N-23 Skiff/Sineva)	96	1986	9 000	4 x 100 kt	384
Strategic defensive forces	**2 000**				**733**
Anti-ballistic missiles[b]					
51T6 (SH-11 Gorgon)	32	1989		1 x 1000 kt	32
53T6 (SH-08 Gazelle)	68	1986		1 x 10 kt	68
S-300 (SA-10/20 Grumble)	1 900	1980		low kt	633
Non-strategic forces					**1 343**
Land-based non-strategic bombers	*524*				*524[c]*
Tu-22M Backfire	124	1974		2 x AS-4 ASM, bombs	124[c]
Su-24 Fencer	400	1974		2 x bombs	400[c]
Naval non-strategic attack aircraft	*179*				*295*
Tu-22M Backfire	58	1974		2 x AS-4 ASM, bombs	116
Su-24 Fencer	58	1974		2 x bombs	116
Be-12 Mail/Il-38 May	63	1967/68		1 x depth bomb	63
Sea-launched cruise missiles SS-N-9, SS-N-12, SS-N-19, SS-N-21, SS-N-22					*276*
Anti-submarine warfare and surface-to-air missile weapons SS-N-15/16, SA-N-1/3/6, depth bombs, torpedoes[c]					*248*
Total strategic defensive and non-strategic forces					**2 076**
Total					**5 189[d]**

ALCM = air-launched cruise missile; ASM = air-to-surface missile; kt = kiloton; ICBM = intercontinental ballistic missile; NATO = North Atlantic Treaty Organization; SLBM = Submarine-launched ballistic missile; SRAM = short-range attack missile.

[a] Aircraft range is given for illustrative purposes only; actual mission range will vary.

b The SH-11 Gorgon may not be operational. The SA-10 Grumble, SA-12A Gladiator, SA-12B Giant and S-400 Triumf may have some capability against some ballistic missiles. Only a third of 1900 deployed SA-10s are counted as having nuclear capability.

c These figures assume that only half of land-based strike aircraft have a nuclear mission. Surface ships are not estimated to be assigned nuclear torpedoes.

d An additional *c*. 8800 warheads are estimated to be in reserve or awaiting dismantlement for a total stockpile of *c*. 14 000 warheads.

Sources: US Department of State, START I Treaty Memoranda of Understanding, 1990–Jan. 2008; US Air Force, National Air and Space Intelligence Center (NASIC), *Ballistic and Cruise Missile Threat* (NASIC: Wright-Patterson Air Force Base, Ohio, Mar. 2006), <http://www.nukestrat.com/us/afn/NASIC2006.pdf>; US Central Intelligence Agency, National Intelligence Council, 'Foreign missile developments and the ballistic missile threat through 2015' (unclassified summary), Dec. 2001 <http://www.fas.org/spp/starwars/CIA-NIE.htm>; US Department of Defense, 'Proliferation: threat and response', Washington, DC, Jan. 2001, <http://www.fas.org/irp/threat/prolif00.pdf>; World News Connection, National Technical Information Service (NTIS), US Department of Commerce, various issues; Russianforces.org; International Institute for Strategic Studies, *The Military Balance 2007* (Routledge: London, 2007); Cochran, T. B. et al., *Nuclear Weapons Databook Volume IV: Soviet Nuclear* Weapons (Harper & Row: New York, 1989); *Proceedings*, US Naval Institute, various issues; 'Nuclear notebook', *Bulletin of the Atomic Scientists*, various issues; and Authors' estimates.

Land-based ballistic missiles

The Russian Strategic Rocket Forces (SRF) consist of three missile armies: the 27th Guards Missile Army (Vladimir, five divisions), the 31st Missile Army (Orenburg, three divisions) and the 33rd Guards Missile Army (Omsk, five divisions).[18]

As of January 2008, Russia had on combat duty 75 SS-18 Satan (R-36M) heavy ICBMs in two versions: the R-36MUTTKh (RS-20B) and the R-36M2 Voevoda (RS-20V), deployed in Dombarovsky (41 missiles) and Uzhur (34 missiles).[19] The RS-20B was first deployed in 1979–83 and the RS-20V in 1988–92. Both are silo-based, two-stage, liquid-propellant ICBMs designed and produced in Ukraine.[20]

Russia intends to keep RS-20V missiles in service until 2016–18, but the RS-20B missiles are being gradually retired from service.[21] Instead of dismantlement, the SRF sometimes refurbishes them as Dnepr space launch vehicles (SLVs). In 2007 Russia conducted three successful launches of Dnepr SLVs: on 17 April and 15 June from Baikonur, Kazakhstan, and on 28 June from Yasnyi launch site in Orenburg region.[22]

As of January 2008, Russia had a total of 100 SS-19 Stiletto (RS-18) missiles deployed at Kozelsk (50 missiles) and Tatischevo (50 missiles).[23] The SS-19 is a silo-

[18] US Department of State, START I Memorandum of Understanding, Jan. 2008. On Russian missile deployments see also 'Russian strategic nuclear forces', <http://russianforces.org/missiles/>.

[19] US Department of State (note 18), pp. 13, 17.

[20] Lennox, D. (ed.), *Jane's Strategic Weapon Systems* (Jane's Information Group: Coulsdon, July 2006), pp. 128–30.

[21] Russian Strategic Rocket Forces, Information and Public Relations Service, 'Pusk mezhkontinental'noy ballisticheskoy rakety RS-20V ("Voevoda")' [Launch of the intercontinental ballistic missile RS-20V ('Voevoda')], 21 Dec. 2006, <http://www.mil.ru/848/1045/1275/rvsn/19220/index.shtml?id=19753>.

[22] Russian Strategic Rocket Forces, Information and Public Relations Service, 'Pusk rakety RS-20B' [Lauch of an RS-20B missile], 15 June 2007, <http://www.mil.ru/848/1045/1275/rvsn/19220/index.shtml?id=25678>; and 'Russia launches SS-18 "Satan" ICBM with U.S. satellite', RIA Novosti, 28 June 2007, <http://en.rian.ru/world/20070628/68007073.html>.

[23] US Department of State (note 18), pp. 20, 24.

based, two-stage, liquid-propellant ICBM capable of carrying up to six warheads, which entered into service in 1980.[24] On 29 October 2007 the SS-19 missile was successfully test-launched from Baikonur to its target at the Kura test range. As a result of the test, the SS-19's service life was extended to 31 years.[25]

Russia has 201 SS-25 Sickle (RS-12M Topol) ICBMs deployed in eight missile divisions across the country.[26] The SS-25 is a road-mobile, three-stage solid-propellant ICBM that carries a single warhead. It was first deployed in 1985.[27] According to Russian press reports, the SS-25 is expected to be in service until 2015.[28] On 18 October and 8 December 2007 the SRF successfully launched SS-25 missiles from the Plesetsk and the Kapustin Yar test site launch sites, respectively. The service life of the weapon was reported to have been extended to 21 years.[29]

The SS-27 Topol-M missile is a three-stage solid-propellant ICBM that has been developed in both road-mobile (RS-12M1) and silo-based (RS-12M2) versions, which the missile's designers say use standardized and interoperable components. Russia plans to deploy 40 RS-12M1 and 114 RS-12M2 missiles by 2015.[30] As of January 2008 Russia had 48 RS-12M2 missiles at the 60th Missile Division in Tatischevo, Saratov oblast, and 6 RS-12M1 missiles at the 54th Missile Division in Teikovo, Ivanovo region.[31] Deployment of the silo-based RS-12M2 will be completed in 2010.[32]

On 7 May 2007 the SRF Commander, Nikolai Solovtsov, announced that Russia will start to install MIRVs on SS-27 Topol-M missiles 'in two or three years', probably referring to the expiry of START I in December 2009.[33] The treaty prohibits the installation of MIRVs on existing missiles but does not restrict the development of new ones.[34]

On 29 May 2007 a MIRVed missile, designated the 'RS-24', was test-fired for the first time. It was launched from a specially modified transporter-erector-launcher (TEL) vehicle at the Plesetsk launch site and successfully hit its target at the Kura test range.[35] On 25 December 2007 the second launch of the RS-24 was conducted at

---

[24] ed. Lennox (note 20), pp. 130–32.

[25] 'Russia launches RS-18 ICBM from Baikonur in Kazakhstan-1', RIA Novosti, 29 Oct. 2007, <http://en.rian.ru/russia/20071029/85783408.html>.

[26] US Department of State (note 18).

[27] ed. Lennnox (note 20), pp. 136–39.

[28] 'Russia fires intercontinental ballistic missile', ITAR-TASS, 18 Oct. 2007.

[29] Russian Strategic Rocket Forces, Information and Public Relations Service, 'Pusk rakety RS-12M "Topol"' [The launch of the missile RS-12M 'Topol'], 18 Oct. 2007, <http://www.mil.ru/848/1045/1275/rvsn/19220/index.shtml?id=32232>; and 'Russia test-fires RS-12M ballistic missile', RIA Novosti, 8 Dec. 2007, <http://en.rian.ru/russia/20071208/91500297.html>.

[30] Nikol'skii, A., 'Mutatsiya "Topolya"' [Topol's mutation], Vedomosti, 8 May 2007; and Isachenkov, V., 'Russia plans new ICBMs, nuclear subs', Washington Post, 7 Feb. 2007.

[31] Russian Ministry of Defence, '"Topol-M" missile system is on duty', 10 Jan. 2008, <http://www.mil.ru/eng/1866/12078/details/index.shtml?id=35978>.

[32] 'Russia to deploy fixed-site Topol-M ICBMs by 2010-SMF cmdr', RIA Novosti, 8 May 2007, <http://en.rian.ru/russia/20070508/65086382.html>.

[33] Nikol'skii, A. (note 30).

[34] On legal issues concerning MIRVs see Sokov, N., 'Russia tests a new ground-launched cruise missile and a new strategic missile on the same day', Monterey Institute of International Studies, James Martin Center for Nonproliferation Studies, 1 June 2007, <http://cns.miis.edu/pubs/week/070601.htm>.

[35] 'Pervyi start' [First start], Krasnaya Zvezda, 30 May 2007; and Richardson, D., 'Russia tests a new ICBM', Jane's Missiles and Rockets, vol. 11, no. 7 (July 2007), pp. 1–2.

Plesetsk, with three test warheads successfully reaching the Kura range.[36] Russian officials stated that the RS-24 is not an entirely new missile but a 'new version' of the SS-27 Topol-M, with the MIRVs as the main difference from the SS-27 Topol-M.[37] In order to declare the missile as a new type under START I, Russia will have to make other treaty-specified modifications, such as altering the diameter or length of the missile's first stage or changing the launch weight. Alternatively, the missile could be maintained as a 'prototype' (not accountable under START I) until the treaty's expiry date.[38]

After the first launch Solovtsov announced that the RS-24 test programme would require no more than five additional launches, and the missile could be placed in service by 2010. He also stated that advanced missile defence penetration capability would be added to the RS-24 and probably to the single-warhead SS-27 Topol-Ms as well.[39] In February 2008, however, Solovtsov declared that the RS-24 would enter service in 2009 and that two flight tests were planned in 2008.[40]

Ballistic missile submarines and sea-launched ballistic missiles

The Russian Navy operates 14 SSBNs in its Northern and Pacific fleets. Of these, six are Delta III Class (Project 667BDR Kalmar) submarines. The *Petropavlovsk-Kamchatskii*, the *Svyatoi Georgii Pobedonosets*, the *Zelenograd* and the *Podol'sk* are deployed with the Pacific Fleet, and the *Ryazan'* and the *Borisoglebsk* with the Northern Fleet. On 21 September 2007 the *Ryazan'* completed a two-year overhaul at the Zvezdochka shipyard in Severodvinsk, and it began sea trials in December 2007.[41]

The Russian Navy also operates six Delta IV Class (Project 667BDRM Delfin) submarines, all part of the Northern Fleet. Four of them—the *Bryansk*, the *Tula*, the *Verkhotur'e* and the *Yekaterinburg*—are currently in service after returning from an overhaul.[42] In November 2006 two Delta IV submarines—the *Kareliya* and the *Novo-*

---

[36] 'Putin: puski raket—eto prazdnichnyi feierverk' [Putin: missile launches are festive fireworks], Rosbalt News Agency, 26 Dec. 2007, <http://www.rosbalt.ru/2007/12/26/443915.html>.

[37] Richardson (note 35), p. 1; and Gertsev, O., 'Rabota po "Bulave" idet po planu' [Development of 'Bulava' is proceeding according to plan], *Voenno-Promyshlennyi Kurier*, 5–11 Sep. 2007.

[38] For more discussion see Sokov (note 34).

[39] Isby, D., 'RS-24s set to receive penetration aids, MIRVs', *Jane's Missiles and Rockets*, vol. 11, no. 11 (Nov. 2007), p. 4.

[40] 'Russia's RS-24 ICBM to enter service in 2009—SMF commander', RIA Novosti, 27 Feb. 2008, <http://en.rian.ru/russia/20080227/100186909.html>.

[41] 'V Severodvinske spushchena na vodu posle planovogo remonta strategicheskaya atomnaya podlodka Severnogo flota "Ryazan"' [Northern Fleet's SSBN 'Ryazan' was launched in Severodvinsk after a planned overhaul], ARMS-TASS, 21 Sep. 2007, <http://armstass.su/?page=article&aid=45389&cid=25>; and 'PLARB Severnogo flota "Ryazan" vyshla na hodovye ispytaniya posle remonta v Severodvinske' [Northern Fleet's SSBN 'Ryazan' has started sea trials after an overhaul in Severodvinsk], ARMS-TASS, 13 Dec. 2007, <http://www.armstass.su/?page=article&aid=49071& cid=25>.

[42] 'PLARB Severnogo flota "Bryansk" ushla na bazu v Zapolyar'e posle modernizatsii v Severodvinske' [Northern Fleet's PLARB 'Bryansk' sailed to its base beyond the Arctic Circle after an overhaul in Severodvinsk], ARMS-TASS, 23 Jan. 2008, <http://www.armstass.su/?page=article&aid=50377&cid =25>; and Kile, S. N., Fedchenko, V. and Kristensen, H. M., 'World nuclear forces, 2007', *SIPRI Yearbook 2007: Armaments, Disarmament and International Security* (Oxford University Press: Oxford, 2007), p. 528.

moskovsk—started service life-extension overhauls.[43] The Delta IV submarines are scheduled to remain in service for 10 years after these overhauls.[44]

The Soviet Union built six Typhoon Class (Project 941 Akula) SSBNs in 1976–89. Russia decommissioned three of them in 1996. One of them, renamed the *Dmitrii Donskoi,* was relaunched in June 2002 after an overhaul and is used as a test platform for the new SS-NX-30 Bulava (RSM-56) missile, which is under development. Russian military officials have indicated that in future the *Dmitrii Donskoi* may be equipped with the full complement of Bulava missiles. The two remaining submarines—the *Arkhangel'sk* and the *Severstal'*—were withdrawn from service in 2004 for financial reasons, and a decision on their future was not taken in 2007.[45]

Russia is building three SSBNs of a new class, the Project 955 Borei. The first in the class, the *Yurii Dolgorukii,* was launched on 15 April 2007 and is expected to enter service in 2008.[46] The second and third submarines, the *Aleksandr Nevskii* (to enter service in 2009) and the *Vladimir Monomakh* (to enter service in 2011) were laid down at the Sevmash shipyard in March 2004 and March 2006, respectively.[47] Each Borei SSBN is equipped with 16 RSM-56 missiles.[48] The Russian Government plans to have eight Borei SSBNs by 2015.[49] In July 2007 the Russian Navy announced plans to build a new submarine base for Borei Class submarines at Viluchinsk on the Kamchatka peninsula.[50]

Russia's SLBM force currently consists of two types of missile—the SS-N-18 M1 Stingray (RSM-50) and the SS-N-23 Skiff (RSM-54). The SS-N-18 M1 first entered service in 1978 and is deployed on Delta III Class submarines. It has two liquid-fuelled stages and carries three warheads.[51] On 7 August 2007 a Delta III Class SSBN, the *Petropavlovsk-Kamchatskii,* launched an SS-N-18 M1 SLBM from the Pacific that successfully hit the target at the Chizha test range.[52]

The SS-N-23 Skiff SLBM, a successor to the SS-N-18, was first test-launched in 1983 and is deployed on Delta IV Class submarines.[53] It has since been modified twice. In 1996–2002 an improved re-entry vehicle was added,[54] and in 2002–2005, the missile was modernized to extend its service life and a new satellite guidance

[43] 'SSBN Kareliya enters Zvezdochka yard for medium repair', Interfax-AVN, 2 Nov. 2006; and Popov, A., ' "Begemot" ego proslavil' ['Begemot' made him famous], *Severnyi Rabochii*, 30 Nov. 2006, <http://www.nworker.ru/article.phtml?id=4616>.

[44] ARMS-TASS (note 42).

[45] '"Taifuny" ne budut pereoborudovat'sya pod "Bulavu-M"' ['Typhoons' will not be re-equipped with 'Bulava-Ms'], Vesti.Ru, 5 Aug. 2007, <http://www.vesti.ru/doc.html?id=133340>.

[46] Nikol'skii, A., 'Podlodka na polveka' [Submarine for 50 years], *Vedomosti*, 16 Apr. 2007; and Richardson, D., 'Bulava SLBM makes successful flight', *Jane's Missiles and Rockets*, vol. 11, no. 8 (Aug. 2006), p. 3.

[47] 'Iz-pod vody dostali' [Reached from under water], *Kommersant Business Guide*, 4 July 2006.

[48] US Department of State (note 18), p. 55.

[49] Isachenkov, V., 'Russia plans new ICBMs, nuclear subs', *Washington Post*, 7 Feb. 2007.

[50] 'Rossiya postroit novuyu bazu atomnykh podlodok' [Russia will build a new nuclear submarine base], BBC News, 9 July 2007, <http://news.bbc.co.uk/hi/russian/russia/newsid_6283000/6283024.stm>.

[51] ed. Lennox (note 20), pp. 149–50.

[52] 'Russia test launches sea-based ballistic missile in Pacific-1', RIA Novosti, 7 Aug. 2007, <http://en.rian.ru/russia/20070807/70528653.html>.

[53] ed. Lennox (note 20), pp. 155–56.

[54] Kontareva, E., 'Gosudarstvo vysoko otsenilo vklad yuzhnoural'tsev v modernizatsiyu odnogo iz luchshikh strategicheskikh kompleksov Voenno-Morskogo Flota Rossii' [The state highly appreciated the contribution of the people of the South Urals to modernization of one of the best strategic missile complexes of the Russian Navy], Ural-Press-Inform News Agency, 23 Sep. 2005, <http://uralpress.ru/show_article.php?id=82055>.

system was added.[55] The upgraded version of the missile is called the Sineva ('the Blue') in Russian. According to the US Air Force, the Sineva has the same range as the SS-N-23 Skiff but can carry up to 10 warheads.[56] However, the START I information exchange memorandum does not make a distinction between the two versions.[57]

On 9 July 2007 President Vladimir Putin signed a decree accepting the Sineva SLBM into service.[58] Serial production of the missile is under way.[59] Four Sineva SLBMs were delivered in 2006 and another 12 were procured in 2007.[60] On 25 December 2007 a Delta IV SSBN, the *Tula*, test launched a Sineva from an underwater position in the Barents Sea that hit a simulated target at the Kura test range.[61] Russia also continues to test the SS-N-23 Skiff. On 17 December the *Tula* launched an 18-year-old SS-N-23 missile, whose service life certification was set to expire shortly thereafter, from a submerged position in the Barents Sea.[62]

Russia is giving high priority to the development of the SS-NX-30 Bulava, a new three-stage, solid-propellant SLBM. President Putin has declared that Borei Class SSBNs, equipped with the new Bulava SLBM, will form the backbone of Russia's strategic deterrent force together with the Topol-M ICBM.[63] The missile will reportedly have a maximum range of 8300 km.[64] Russia has declared that the Bulava will be attributed under START I counting rules as carrying six warheads,[65] although some of the capacity may instead be used for carrying missile-defence penetration aids or for other purposes.

As of December 2007 six Bulava test launches had been conducted. Two tests in 2005 were successful, but the three in 2006 ended in failure.[66] On 28 June 2007 the *Dmitrii Donskoi* SSBN fired a Bulava missile from a location in the White Sea, and

---

[55] 'Atomnyi podvodnyi raketnyi kreiser "Tula" Severnogo flota osushchestvil uchebno-boevoi pusk mezhkontinentalnoy ballisticheskoy raketi' [SSBN 'Tula' has launched an intercontinental ballistic missile], ARMS-TASS, 17 Dec. 2007, <http://armstass.su/?page=article&aid=49154 &cid=25>.

[56] US Air Force, National Air and Space Intelligence Center (NASIC), *Ballistic and Cruise Missile Threat* (NASIC: Wright-Patterson Air Force Base, Ohio, Mar. 2006), <http://www.nukestrat.com/us/afn/NASIC2006.pdf>.

[57] US Department of State (note 18), p. 1.

[58] Makeyev Design Bureau, 'President RF V. V. Putin podpisal ukaz o prinyatii na vooruzheniye VMF raketnogo kompleksa "Sineva"' [Russian President V. V. Putin has signed a decree accepting the missile complex 'Sineva' into the Navy's arsenal], News release, 16 July 2007, <http://www.makeyev.ru/news.php?extend.27>.

[59] Richardson, D., 'Russian SLBMs should see out 2030', *Jane's Missiles and Rockets*, vol. 11, no. 5 (May 2007), p. 10.

[60] Barabanov, M., 'I tselogo flota malo' [The fleet is not enough], Rosbalt News Agency, 18 Sep. 2007, <http://www.rosbalt.ru/2007/09/17/413702.html>. On the Russian fleet see <http://www.kommersant.com/p856120/russian_naval_fleet_directory/>.

[61] Makeyev Design Bureau, 'Soobscheniye o puske RSM-54 "Sineva"' [Report on the launch of the RSM-54 'Sineva'], 26 Dec. 2007, <http://www.makeyev.ru/comment.php?comment.news.47>.

[62] Makeyev Design Bureau, 'Uspeshnyi pusk ballisticheskoy rakety RSM-54' [Successful launch of the ballistic missile RSM-54], 26 Dec. 2007, <http://www.makeyev.ru/comment.php?comment.news.44>.

[63] Putin, V., President of the Russian Federation, Annual Address to the Federal Assembly of the Russian Federation, 10 May 2006, <http://www.kremlin.ru/eng/speeches/2006/05/10/1823_type70029type 82912_105566.shtml>.

[64] ed. Lennox (note 20), p. 166.

[65] US Department of State (note 18), p. 1.

[66] Kile, Fedchenko and Kristensen (note 42), p. 529; and Kile, S. N., Fedchenko, V. and Kristensen, H. M., 'World nuclear forces, 2006', *SIPRI Yearbook 2006: Armaments, Disarmament and International Security* (Oxford University Press: Oxford, 2006), p. 652.

the simulated warhead hit the target at the Kura test range.[67] Shortly after the test Russian military officials announced plans to start large-scale production of Bulava components and to complete missile testing in 2008 after conducting launches to determine the maximum range of the missile.[68]

In November and December 2007 the Russian press reported that another test launch of Bulava had been conducted on 10 November. The missile reportedly failed immediately after launch.[69]

Strategic aviation

Russia's strategic aviation units are grouped under the 37th Air Army of the Supreme High Command (Strategic) of the Russian Air Force. They include the 22nd Guards Heavy Bomber Division based in Engels and Ryazan, with 14 Blackjack (Tu-160), 17 Bear-H16 (Tu-95MS16) and 7 Bear-H6 (Tu-95MS6) aircraft; and the 326th Heavy Bomber Division based in Ukrainka, Khabarovsk kray, with 15 Tu-95MS16 and 25 Tu-95MS6 aircraft.[70] The 37th Air Army also comprises four divisions of Backfire C (Tu-22M3) bombers.[71] The Russian Minister of Defence, Sergei Ivanov, announced in February 2007 that Russia plans to have a total of 50 Tu-160 and Tu-95MS bombers in service by 2015.[72] This would probably be accomplished by retiring some Tu-95MSs and completing the production of a limited number of Tu-160s. In 2007 the Kazan Aviation Plant completed the production of a new Tu-160 bomber, which began flight testing on 28 December 2007 and is expected to enter service in 2008.[73]

In 2007 Russia's decision to resume regular long-range strategic bomber patrols resulted in several encounters with British, Norwegian and US fighter aircraft.[74]

Non-strategic nuclear weapons

There is considerable uncertainty in estimates of Russia's inventory of non-strategic nuclear weapons, which continues to be characterized by a high degree of secrecy and a lack of transparency. Since the end of the cold war, Russia has significantly reduced this inventory pursuant to President Boris Yeltsin's 1992 unilateral initiative on non-strategic nuclear weapons.[75] In 2007 the top Ministry of Defence official responsible

---

[67] 'Russia test launches sea-based ballistic missile—Navy-1', RIA Novosti, 28 June 2007, <http://en.rian.ru/russia/20070628/68009320.html>.

[68] Isby, D., 'Bulava-M SLBM looks set to enter production', *Jane's Missiles and Rockets*, vol. 11, no. 10 (Oct. 2007), p. 3.

[69] Lantratov, K. and Gritskova, A., 'Den'gi est', oruzhiya net' [There is money, but no weapon], *Kommersant*, 21 Nov. 2007.

[70] US Department of State (note 18), pp. 62–63.

[71] Khudoleev, V., '37-ya derzhit kurs' [37th Army is following the course], *Krasnaya Zvezda*, 23 Dec. 2005.

[72] Russian State Duma, Transcript of the Plenary Session, 7 Feb. 2007, <http://wbase.duma.gov.ru/steno/nph-sdb.exe>.

[73] 'New serial Tu-160 Blackjack bomber undergoes flight test', RIA Novosti, 10 Jan. 2008, <http://en.rian.ru/russia/20080110/96102740.html>.

[74] Putin, V., President of the Russian Federation, Press Statement and Responses to Media Questions following the Peace Mission 2007 Counterterrorism Exercises and the Shanghai Cooperation Organisation Summit, General Forces Training Ground 225, Chebarkul, Chelyabinsk Region, 17 Aug. 2007, <http://president.kremlin.ru/eng/speeches/2007/08/17/2033_type82915_141812.shtml>.

[75] As part of a series of reciprocal unilateral presidential initiatives on nuclear weapons between the Soviet Union or Russia and the USA, Yeltsin announced on 29 Jan. 1992 that the production of nuclear

for nuclear weapon custody, Colonel General Vladimir Verkhovtsev, reported on the progress made in reducing this inventory but did not give specific numbers of warheads.[76] On the basis of the number of available delivery platforms, it can be estimated that Russia has approximately 2100 warheads that are operational for delivery by anti-ballistic missiles, air-defence missiles, tactical aircraft and naval cruise missiles, depth bombs and torpedoes.[77] In addition, Russia is believed to have up to several thousand non-strategic warheads held in reserve or awaiting dismantlement.

IV. British nuclear forces

The United Kingdom's nuclear deterrent consists of a sea-based component only, namely, Vanguard Class Trident SSBNs, Trident II (D-5) SLBMs and associated warheads (see table 8A.4). The UK possesses an operational stockpile of about 185 nuclear warheads available for use by a fleet of four Vanguard Class Trident SSBNs. All British nuclear warheads are designed and manufactured at the Atomic Weapons Establishment, Aldermaston, Berkshire. The UK leases 58 Trident II (D-5) SLBMs, including spares, from the US Navy. Under a system of 'mingled asset ownership' Trident II (D-5) missiles to be loaded onto British submarines are randomly selected from the stockpile at the US Navy's Trident facility in Kings Bay, Georgia. The submarines then go to the Royal Naval Armaments Depot at Coulport, Argyll and Bute, where the missiles are fitted with warheads that are designed and manufactured at the Atomic Weapons Establishment.

Each SSBN is equipped with 16 Trident II (D-5) missiles carrying up to 48 warheads. The warhead is similar to the US W76 warhead and has an explosive yield of about 100 kt. As part of a reduced force-loading option, it is believed that a number of the Trident II (D-5) missiles are deployed with only one warhead instead of three; this warhead may also have a greatly reduced explosive yield, possibly produced by the detonation of only the fission primary.[78]

The British Ministry of Defence's 1998 Strategic Defence Review added a 'sub-strategic' role to the Trident fleet. The review states that 'the credibility of deterrence also depends on retaining an option for a limited strike that would not automatically lead to a full scale nuclear exchange' as a means of demonstrating resolve or conveying a political message.[79] A 2002 addendum to the Strategic Defence Review

warheads for land-based tactical missiles, artillery shells and landmines had ceased and that Russia had begun eliminating one-third of its naval non-strategic warheads and one-half of its nuclear surface-to-air missile warheads. He stated that tactical air force weapons would be reduced by one-half and proposed placing the remaining weapons in centralized storage bases on a reciprocal basis with the USA. Excerpts from the text of Yeltsin's statement are reproduced in *SIPRI Yearbook 1992: World Armaments and Disarmament* (Oxford University Press: Oxford, 1992), pp. 89–92.

[76] Volgin, V., 'Strategicheskii monitoring' [Strategic monitoring], *Rossiiskaya Gazeta*, 31 Oct. 2007. According to Verkhovtsev, in 2007 Russia had eliminated the following percentages of its non-strategic nuclear warheads compared with 1992: 100% of the ground forces' warheads, 60% of surface-to air missile warheads, 50% of the Air Force's warheads, 30% of the Navy's warheads.

[77] Warheads for ships and submarines are stored on land in depots and can be deployed if necessary.

[78] Quinlan, M., 'The future of United Kingdom nuclear weapons: shaping the debate', *International Affairs*, vol. 82, no. 4 (July 2006).

[79] British Ministry of Defence (MOD), *The Strategic Defence Review: Modern Forces for the Modern World*, Cm 3999 (MOD: London, July 1998), p. 63.

Table 8A.4. British nuclear forces, January 2008

Type	Designation	No. deployed	Year first deployed	Range (km)[a]	Warhead loading	No. of warheads
Submarine-launched ballistic missiles						
D-5	Trident II	48	1994	>7 400	1–3 x 100 kt	185[b]

kt = kiloton.

[a] Range is given for illustrative purposes only; actual mission range will vary according to flight profile and weapon loading.

[b] Fewer than 160 warheads are operationally available, *c.* 144 to arm 48 missiles on 3 of 4 nuclear-powered ballistic missile submarines. The operational stockpile may consist of *c.* 185 warheads, with additional warheads in reserve. Only 1 boat is on patrol at any time, with up to 48 warheads.

Sources: British Ministry of Defence (MOD), White Papers, press releases and the MOD website, <http://www.mod.uk/>; British House of Commons, *Parliamentary Debates* (*Hansard*); Norris, R. S. et al., *Nuclear Weapons Databook*, vol. 5, *British, French, and Chinese Nuclear Weapons* (Westview: Boulder, Colo., 1994), p. 9; 'Nuclear notebook', *Bulletin of the Atomic Scientists*, various issues; and Authors' estimate.

extendes the role of nuclear weapons to include deterring 'leaders of states of concern and terrorist organizations'.[80]

In a posture known as continuous at sea deterrence (CASD), one British SSBN is on patrol at all times. The second and third SSBNs can be put to sea fairly rapidly, but there are not enough missiles in the British inventory to arm the fourth submarine. Since the end of the cold war, the SSBN on patrol has been kept at a level of reduced readiness with a 'notice to fire' measured in days and its missiles de-targeted. Some patrol coordination may take place with France. The 300th British deterrent patrol was completed in 2007.

The four Vanguard Class SSBNs were each designed to reach the end of their nominal service lives from the early 2020s. The British Government concluded in its December 2006 White Paper, after 'an exhaustive review of possible future threats and deterrent options' that 'renewing the Trident system, by replacing the existing submarines and extending the life of the Trident missiles, is the best and most cost effective way to maintain our ability to deter future threats to the UK'.[81] It also proposed starting, in the near future, the design and construction work on a successor SSBN to the Vanguard Class that would enter service in the 2020s. On 14 March 2007 the British House of Commons approved the government's plan to replace the Vanguard SSBNs with a fleet of new Trident submarines.[82]

The 2006 White Paper also proposed that the new SSBN might be equipped with the modified Trident II D5LE SLBMs that the USA is building, thereby keeping the Trident II (D-5) missile in service until the early 2040s.[83] To assuage concerns that

[80] British Ministry of Defence, *The Strategic Defence Review: A New Chapter*, Cm 5566, vol. 1 (Stationery Office: London, July 2002), p. 12.

[81] British Ministry of Defence and British Foreign and Commonwealth Office, *The Future of the United Kingdom's Nuclear Deterrent*, Cm 6994 (Stationery Office: London, Dec. 2006).

[82] 'Trident plan wins Commons support', BBC News, 15 Mar. 2007, <http://news.bbc.co.uk/2/6448173.stm>.

[83] British Ministry of Defence and British Foreign and Commonwealth Office (note 81).

the UK was not complying with its commitment under Article VI of the NPT to work in good faith towards nuclear disarmament, the government proposed a small reduction in the British nuclear stockpile. It deferred a decision until the next parliament (due to be elected by 2010) on whether to refurbish or replace the current warheads. On 15 November 2007 in a written answer to a parliamentary question, the Secretary of State for Defence, Des Browne, confirmed that the UK's inventory of 'operationally available warheads' had been reduced 'from fewer than 200 to fewer than 160'.[84] A small inventory of non-operational reserve warheads presumably also exists.

According to the 2006 White Paper, the procurement costs of the new submarines and associated infrastructure would be about £15–20 billion ($28.5–38 billion), at 2006 prices, for a four-boat fleet. Most of this cost (c. £1 billion, or $1.9 billion, per annum) would be incurred during the period 2012–27.[85]

V. French nuclear forces

There has been a gradual evolution in France's nuclear doctrine since the end of the cold war. French officials have emphasized the need for greater flexibility in meeting a widening range of plausible deterrence scenarios. In 2006 President Jacques Chirac stated that France's nuclear deterrent remained the fundamental guarantor of its security, including against the dangers of regional instability growing extremism and the proliferation of WMD. Chirac threatened to retaliate with nuclear weapons against any state found to be supporting terrorism against France or considering the use of WMD and revealed that French nuclear forces had already been reconfigured accordingly (see table 8A.5). This involved reducing the number of nuclear warheads on SLBMs to allow more precisely targeted strikes.[86]

France's sea-based strategic force consists of a fleet of four operational SSBNs, of which three are of the new Triomphant Class and one is of the L'Inflexible Class. The remaining L'Inflexible Class SSBN will be retired when the fourth and final vessel of the Triomphant Class, Le Terrible, enters service in 2010. Laid down in 2002, Le Terrible is due to be launched in 2008, beginning sea trials in 2009.[87]

All French SSBNs are armed with 16 Aérospatiale M45 missiles, which carry up to six TN-75 warheads.[88] In 2010–15, beginning with the Le Terrible, the Triomphant Class SSBNs will be retrofitted with the longer-range M51.1 SLBM, which is a three-stage solid-propellant missile armed with up to six TN-75 warheads. It is estimated to have a maximum range of 6000–8000 km.[89]

[84] British House of Commons, 'Trident missiles', Hansard, 15 Nov. 2007, C363W <http://www.publications.parliament.uk/pa/cm200708/cmhansrd/cm071115/text/71115w0007.htm#07111542000024>.

[85] British Ministry of Defence and British Foreign and Commonwealth Office (note 81).

[86] Chirac, J., 'Speech by Jacques Chirac, President of the French Republic, during his visit to the Strategic Air and Maritime Forces at Landivisiau/L'Ile Longue', 19 Jan. 2006, <http://www.elysee.fr/elysee/elysee.fr/anglais/speeches_and_documents/2006/speech_by_jacques_chirac_president_of_the_french_republic_during_his_visit_to_the_stategic_forces.38447.html>.

[87] Richardson, D., 'M51 ballistic missile proves itself in a full-range test flight', Jane's Missiles & Rockets, vol. 11, no. 1 (Jan. 2007), pp. 1–2.

[88] Norris, R. S. and Kristensen, H. M., 'French nuclear forces, 2005', Bulletin of the Atomic Scientists, vol. 61, no. 4 (July/Aug. 2005), pp. 73–75.

[89] Lennox, D. (ed.), Jane's Strategic Weapon Systems (Jane's Information Group: Coulsdon, July 2007), pp. 44–45; and 'France's nuclear-powered Le Vigilant prepares for patrol', Jane's Missiles & Rockets, vol. 9, no. 2 (Feb. 2005), p. 5.

Table 8A.5. French nuclear forces, January 2008

Type	No. deployed	Year first deployed	Range (km)[a]	Warhead loading	No. of warheads
Land-based aircraft					
Mirage 2000N	60	1988	2 750	1 x 300 kt ASMP	50
Carrier-based aircraft					
Super Étendard	24	1978	650	1 x 300 kt ASMP	10
Submarine-launched ballistic missiles					
M45	48	1996	6 000[b]	6 x 100 kt	288
Total					**348[c]**

ASMP = Air–Sol Moyenne Portée; kt = kiloton.

[a] Aircraft range is given for illustrative purposes only; actual mission range will vary according to flight profile and weapon loading.

[b] The range of the M45 submarine-launched ballistic missile is listed as only 4000 km in a 2001 report from the National Defence Commission of the French National Assembly.

[c] France may also have a small inventory of reserve warheads.

Sources: French Ministry of Defense website, <http://www.defense.gouv.fr/>, various policy papers, press releases and force profiles; French National Assembly, various defence bills; Norris, R. S. et al., *Nuclear Weapons Databook*, vol. 5, *British, French, and Chinese Nuclear Weapons* (Westview: Boulder, Colo., 1994), p. 10; *Air Actualités*, various issues; *Aviation Week & Space Technology*, various issues; 'Nuclear notebook', *Bulletin of the Atomic Scientists*, various issues; and Authors' estimates.

As of January 2008 the M51.1 missile had been flight-tested twice, on 9 November 2006 and 21 June 2007. Both times an unarmed M51.1 missile was launched from the Landes Missile Launch Test Centre at Biscarosse, Aquitaine.[90] Simulated underwater launches are due to start in late 2008 at Toulon, Provence-Alpes-Côte d'Azur. The first underwater launch from a submarine is planned for 2010. A total of 10 test launches are planned.[91] A follow-on version of the missile, the M51.2, may be under development for possible deployment in 2015–17.

The air component of the French nuclear force consists of two types of aircraft: approximately 60 Mirage 2000N aircraft, equipping three Air Force squadrons with nuclear strike roles; and about 24 Super Étendard aircraft deployed on the aircraft carrier *Charles de Gaulle*. Both types of aircraft carry the Air–Sol Moyenne Portée (ASMP) cruise missile. A total of 90 ASMP missiles were produced, along with 80 TN81 300-kt warheads for them. France may have about 60 operational ASMP missiles with nuclear warheads deployed, with additional missiles in storage.[92]

---

[90] Richardson (note 87); 'France tests strategic missile', Global Security Newswire, 10 Nov. 2006, <http://www.nti.org/d_newswire/issues/2006_11_10.html >; Agence France-Presse, 'France tests ballistic missile for nuclear deployment', Spacewar.com, 9 Nov. 2006, <http://www.spacewar.com/reports/France_Tests_Ballistic_Missile_For_Nuclear_Deployment_999.html>; and 'Second M51 SLBM flight test hits target', *Jane's Missiles & Rockets*, vol. 12, no. 8 (Aug. 2008), p. 8.

[91] Isby, D., 'M51 tests set to begin on schedule', *Jane's Missiles & Rockets*, vol. 10, no. 12 (Dec. 2006), p. 10.

[92] Fiszer, M., 'French MoD to develop nuclear missile', *Journal of Electronic Defense*, vol. 26, no. 12 (Dec. 2003), p. 21.

A follow-on cruise missile, the ASMP-A (Air–Sol Moyenne Portée Améliorée), is planned to gradually replace the ASMP.[93] The ASMP-A is expected to enter service in 2008. The nuclear-capable missile will initially equip one Mirage 2000N squadron, and then a second squadron in September 2010. An Air Force Rafale F3 squadron is reportedly scheduled to receive the ASMP-A in December 2009, and the Navy's Rafale F3 combat aircraft will receive the missile in 2010.[94]

VI. Chinese nuclear forces

According to its 2006 Defence White Paper, China 'upholds the principles of counter-attack in self-defence and limited development of nuclear weapons, and aims at building a lean and effective nuclear force'. Chinese nuclear forces are stated to have the purpose of deterring 'other countries from using or threatening to use nuclear weapons against China'.[95] The 2006 White Paper reiterates commitment to 'the policy of no first use of nuclear weapons at any time and under any circumstances'.

China is estimated to have an arsenal of approximately 176 operational nuclear weapons for delivery mainly by ballistic missiles and aircraft (see table 8A.6). Additional warheads may be in reserve, giving a total stockpile of about 240 warheads.[96] The Chinese Foreign Ministry stated in 2004 that China possessed 'the smallest nuclear arsenal' among the nuclear weapon states.[97] China has a long-term nuclear force modernization programme under way. It is still unclear whether China intends to significantly expand its ballistic missile force or to deploy newer, more survivable missiles in approximately the same numbers as today.[98]

As of early 2008, China had four types of deployed ICBMs: the solid-fuel mobile DF-31 and DF-31A; the silo-based, liquid fuel DF-5A (CSS-4); and the smaller liquid-fuel DF-4 (CSS-3).[99] A 2007 US DOD report suggested that the DF-31 achieved 'initial threat availability' in 2006 and probably had achieved 'operational

[93] Norris, R. S., and Kristensen, H. M., 'Nuclear notebook: nuclear cruise missiles', *Bulletin of the Atomic Scientists*, vol. 63, no. 6 (Nov./Dec. 2007), p. 61.

[94] Isby (note 91).

[95] Chinese State Council, *China's National Defense in 2006* (Information Office of the State Council of the People's Republic of China: Beijing, Dec. 2006), <http://www.china.org.cn/english/features/book/194421.htm>.

[96] In 2006 the US Defense Intelligence Agency repeated an estimate that China has over 100 nuclear warheads deployed on ballistic missiles and some additional warheads in storage. Maples, M. D., Director, US Defense Intelligence Agency, 'Current and projected national security threats to the United States', Statement for the record, US Senate Armed Services Committee, 28 Feb. 2006, <http://www.dia.mil/publicaffairs/Testimonies/statement24.html>. The 2008 DOD report on China's military forces lists approximately 138 nuclear ballistic missiles. US Department of Defense, *Military Power of the People's Republic of China 2008* (DOD: Washington, DC, 3 Mar. 2008), <http://www.defenselink.mil/pubs/china.html>, p. 56. In 2005 a US non-governmental analyst calculated that China's operational arsenal might be as small as 80 warheads. Lewis, J., 'The ambiguous arsenal', *Bulletin of the Atomic Scientists*, vol. 61, no. 3 (May/June 2005), pp. 52–59.

[97] Chinese Ministry of Foreign Affairs, 'Fact sheet: China: nuclear disarmament and reduction of [sic]', Beijing, 27 Apr. 2004, <http://www.fmprc.gov.cn/eng/wjb/zzjg/jks/cjjk/2622/t93539.htm>.

[98] Kristensen, H. M., Norris, R. S. and McKinzie, M. G., *Chinese Nuclear Forces and U.S. Nuclear War Planning* (Federation of American Scientists and Natural Resources Defense Council: Washington, DC, Nov. 2006), p. 43, <http://www.fas.org/nuke/guide/china/Book2006.pdf>.

[99] US Department of Defense (note 96), pp. 3, 5, 23, 24–27, 30, 56.

Table 8A.6. Chinese nuclear forces, January 2008

Type and Chinese designation (US designation)	No. deployed	Year first deployed	Range (km)[a]	Warhead loading	No. of warheads
Strategic weapons					**~161**
Land-based missiles[b]	*~121*				*~121*
DF-3A (CSS-2)	17	1971	3 100[c]	1 x 3.3 Mt	17
DF-4 (CSS-3)	17	1980	5 500	1 x 3.3 Mt	17
DF-5A (CSS-4)	20	1981	13 000	1 x 4–5 Mt	20
DF-21 (CSS-5)	~55	1991	2 100[c]	1 x 200–300 kt	~55
DF-31 (CSS-X-10)	<10	2007	>7 200	1 x . .	<10
DF-31A (?)	<10	(2008–10)	>11 200	1 x . .	<10
SLBMs	*0*				*0*
JL-1 (CSS-N-3)	(12)	1986	>1 770	1 x 200–300 kt	(12)
JL-2 (CSS-NX-5)	(24)	(2008–10)	>7 200	1 x ?	(24)
Aircraft[d]	*>20*				*~40*
H-6 (B-6)	20	1965	3 100	1 x bomb	~20
Attack (Qian-5, others?)	. .	1972–?	. .	1 x bomb	~20
Non-strategic weapons[e]					
Cruise missiles (DH-10)	50–250	2007	>2000	1 x . .	~15[f]
Short-range ballistic missiles (DF-15 and DF-11)					. .
Total					**~176**[g]

( ) = not fully operational; kt = kiloton; Mt = megaton; SLBM = submarine-launched ballistic missile; . . = unknown.

[a] Aircraft range is given for illustrative purposes only; actual mission range will vary.

[b] China defines missile ranges as short-range <1000 km; medium-range 1000–3000 km; long-range 3000–8000 km; and intercontinental range >8000 km.

[c] The range of the DF-3A and the DF-21A may be longer than is normally reported.

[d] The figures for aircraft are for nuclear-configured versions only.

[e] Other than the DH-10, the existence of tactical warheads is uncertain but possible.

[f] Can be delivered from H-6 bomber and ground-based launcher.

[g] Additional warheads are thought to be in storage. The total stockpile is believed to comprise *c*. 240 warheads.

Sources: US Department of Defense (DOD), Office of the Secretary of Defense, *Military Power of the People's Republic of China*, Annual Report to Congress, various years (DOD: Washington, DC), <http://www.defenselink.mil/pubs/china.html>; US Air Force, National Air and Space Intelligence Center (NASIC), various documents; US Central Intelligence Agency, various documents; US DOD, Office of the Secretary of Defense, 'Proliferation: threat and response', Washington, DC, Jan. 2001, <http://www.defenselink.mil/pubs/archive.html>; Kristensen, H. M., Norris, R. S. and McKinzie, M. G., *Chinese Nuclear Forces and U.S. Nuclear War Planning* (Federation of American Scientists and Natural Resources Defense Council: Washington, DC, Nov. 2006), <http://www.fas.org/nuke/guide/china/Book2006. pdf>; Norris, R. S. et al., *Nuclear Weapons Databook*, vol. 5, *British, French, and Chinese Nuclear Weapons* (Westview: Boulder, Colo., 1994); 'Nuclear notebook', *Bulletin of the Atomic Scientists*, various issues; Google Earth; and Authors' estimates.

status' by May 2007.[100] China deploys one type of medium-range ballistic missile (MRBM)[101]—the solid-fuel, road-mobile DF-21 (CSS-5)—and one type of intermediate-range ballistic missile (IRBM)—the liquid-fuel DF-3A (CSS-2). The DF-3A and the DF-4 are expected to be completely replaced by the DF-21 and DF-31.

China operates a single Type 092 (Xia Class) SSBN armed with 12 intermediate-range solid-fuel, single-warhead JL-1 (CSS-N-3) SLBMs. The submarine has never conducted a deterrent patrol and is not thought to be fully operational.[102] The 2006 White Paper states that the Chinese Navy 'aims at . . . enhancing its capabilities in integrated maritime operations and nuclear counterattacks'.[103] To this end, China is developing the Type 094 (Jin Class) SSBN. It will carry the intercontinental-range JL-2 SLBM with a range of more than 7200 km. The US DOD estimates that the JL-2 will reach an 'initial operational capability' in 2009–2010.[104]

Commercial satellite imagery analysed by the Federation of American Scientists in 2007 showed the existence of at least two Type 094 submarines and confirms that each has 12 launch tubes for JL-2 SLBMs.[105] The US Office of Naval Intelligence projected in December 2006 that 'a fleet of probably five TYPE 094 SSBNs will be built in order to provide more redundancy and capacity for a near-continuous at-sea SSBN presence'.[106] This projection was somewhat confirmed by the DOD in 2008, which stated that 'by 2010, China's nuclear forces will likely comprise . . . up to five Jin-class SSBNs'.[107] The first Jin (Type 094) Class SSBN was launched in 2004 and is currently being fitted out. A second vessel was launched in 2006,[108] and a third vessel may be under construction.

It is thought that China has a small stockpile of nuclear bombs earmarked for delivery by aircraft as a contingency mission. The most likely aircraft to have a nuclear role today are the H-6 bombers. China has also started deploying the DH-10 land-attack cruise missile, which exists in a nuclear and conventional version for delivery by the H-6 and ground forces.

VII. Indian nuclear forces

Most published estimates of the size of the Indian nuclear stockpile are based on calculations of the total amount of weapon-grade plutonium that India has produced. There is considerable uncertainty in these calculations. There have also been numer-

[100] US Department of Defense (note 96), p. 56; and US Department of Defense (DOD), *Military Power of the People's Republic of China 2007* (DOD: Washington, DC, 25 May 2007), <http://www.defenselink.mil/pubs/china.html>, p. 42.

[101] Although China has its own system for defining missile ranges, the US DOD definitions are used here: short-range = <1100 km; medium-range = 1100–2750 km; intermediate-range = 2750–5500 km; and intercontinental range = >5500 km. See Kristensen, Norris and McKinzie (note 98), p. 218.

[102] Kristensen, Norris and McKinzie (note 98), pp. 77–80.

[103] Chinese State Council (note 95).

[104] US Department of Defense (note 96), p. 3.

[105] Kristensen, H. M., 'A closer look at China's new SSBNs', FAS Strategic Security Blog, 15 Oct. 2007, <http://www.fas.org/blog/ssp/2007/10/post_4.php>; and Kristensen, H. M., 'Two more Chinese SSBNs spotted', FAS Strategic Security Blog, 4 Oct. 2007, <http://www.fas.org/blog/ssp/2007/10/two_more_chinese_ssbns_spotted.php>.

[106] US Navy, Office of Naval Intelligence, Answers to questions obtained by Hans M. Kristensen under the Freedom of Information Act, 20 Dec. 2006, <http://www.fas.org/nuke/guide/china/ONI2006.pdf>.

[107] US Department of Defense (note 96), p. 25.

[108] Saunders, S. (ed.), *Jane's Fighting Ships 2006–2007* (Jane's Information Group: Coulsdon, 2006), p. 120.

Table 8A.7. Indian nuclear forces, January 2008

Type	Range $(km)^a$	Payload (kg)	Status
Land-based ballistic missiles			
Prithvi I (P-I)	150	800	Entered service in 1994; widely believed to have a nuclear delivery role; fewer than 50 launchers have been deployed; most recent flight test on 9 May 2007
Agni I^b	>700	1 000	Test-launched on 5 Oct and 24 Oct. 2007^c
Agni II	>2 000	1 000	Last test-launched on 29 Oct. 2004^c
Agni III	>3 500	1 500	Under development; test-launched on 12 Apr. 2007
Sea-based ballistic missiles			
Danush	400	1 000	Last test-launched on 30 Mar. 2007; induction under way
K-15	700	. .	Launched from a submerged pontoon on 26 Feb. 2008
Aircraft^d			
Mirage 2000H Vajra	1 850	6 300	Has reportedly been certified for delivery of nuclear gravity bomb
Jaguar IS Shamsher	1 400	4 760	Some of 4 squadrons may have a nuclear delivery role

^{a} Missile payloads may have to be reduced in order to achieve maximum range. Aircraft range is given for illustrative purposes only; actual mission range will vary according to flight profile and weapon loading.

^{b} The original Agni I, now known as the Agni, was a technology demonstrator programme that ended in 1996.

^{c} Media reports in late 2007 and early 2008 indicated that the Agni I and the Agni II had achieved operational status.

^{d} Other aircraft in the Indian Air Force's inventory that are potentially suitable for a nuclear role are the MiG-27 (Bahadur) and the Su-30MKI. The Su-30MKI can be refuelled in-flight by the IL-78 aerial tanker.

Sources: Indian Ministry of Defence, annual reports and press releases; International Institute for Strategic Studies (IISS), *The Military Balance 2005–2006* (Routledge: Abingdon, 2006); US Air Force, National Air and Space Intelligence Center (NASIC), *Ballistic and Cruise Missile Threat* (NASIC: Wright-Patterson Air Force Base, Ohio, Mar. 2006), <http://www.nukestrat.com/us/afn/threat.htm>; US Central Intelligence Agency, 'Unclassified report to Congress on the acquisition of technology relating to weapons of mass destruction and advanced conventional munitions, 1 January through 30 June 2002', Apr. 2003, <http://www.nti.org/e_research/official_docs/cia/cia.html>; US Central Intelligence Agency, National Intelligence Council, 'Foreign missile developments and the ballistic missile threat through 2015' (unclassified summary), Dec. 2001, <http://www.dni.gov/nic/PDF_GIF_otherprod/missilethreat2001.pdf>; Lennox, D. (ed.), *Jane's Strategic Weapon Systems* (Jane's Information Group: Coulsdon, 2004); Bharat Rakshak, Consortium of Indian military websites <http://www.bharat-rakshak.com>; 'Nuclear notebook', *Bulletin of the Atomic Scientists*, various issues; and Authors' estimates.

ous media and government reports suggesting that India has not manufactured as many nuclear weapons as it otherwise could owing to material constraints. On the basis of an upper bound estimate of its inventory of weapon-grade plutonium— 650 kg as of December 2006—India would have the material capacity to build an arsenal exceeding 100 nuclear weapons.[109] The conservative estimate presented here is that the Indian arsenal holds about 60–70 nuclear weapons. The figure is based on the lower range of a widely-cited estimate of India's military plutonium inventory as well as on unclassified assessments made by the US intelligence community.[110] It is not publicly known whether India has produced high enriched uranium (HEU) for weapon purposes, in particular for thermonuclear devices.

India's nuclear doctrine, which was published as a draft document in 1999, is 'based on the principle of a minimum credible deterrent and no-first-use'.[111] However, additional guidelines published in January 2003 stated that India would use nuclear weapons to deter or retaliate against the use of chemical or biological weapons.[112] There have been no official statements specifying the size of the arsenal required for 'minimum credible deterrence' but, according to the Indian Ministry of Defence, it involves 'a mix of land-based, maritime and air capabilities'.[113]

Strike aircraft

At present, aircraft are the core of India's nuclear strike capabilities (see table 8A.7). The Indian Air Force (IAF) has reportedly certified the Mirage 2000H Vajra ('Divine Thunder') multi-role aircraft for delivery of nuclear gravity bombs. The IAF deploys two squadrons of Mirage 2000H aircraft at the Gwalior Air Force Station in north-central India. In addition to the Mirage 2000H, some of the IAF's four squadrons of Jaguar IS Shamsher ('Sword') fighter-bombers may have a nuclear delivery role.[114] Other aircraft which are suitable for a nuclear role are the MiG-27 and the Su-30MKI.

Land-based ballistic missiles

The Prithvi ('Earth') was India's sole operational ballistic missile for many years. A number of Prithvi I missiles are widely believed to have been modified to deliver nuclear warheads, although this has not been officially confirmed. The Prithvi I (SS-150) is a single-stage, road-mobile ballistic missile capable of delivering a 1000-kg warhead to a maximum range of 150 km. The missile was first flight-tested in 1988 and entered service with the Indian Army in 1994. It is currently deployed

[109] See appendix 8B, table 8B.2.

[110] Albright, D., 'India's military plutonium inventory, end of 2004', *Global Stocks of Nuclear Explosive Materials*, Institute for Science and International Security <http://www.isis-online.org/global_stocks/end2003/india_military_plutonium.pdf>. The estimate assumes that each warhead would require at least 5 kg of plutonium.

[111] Indian Ministry of External Affairs, 'Draft report of National Security Advisory Board on Indian Nuclear Doctrine', 17 Aug. 1999, <http://meaindia.nic.in/disarmament/dm17Aug99.htm>.

[112] Indian Ministry of External Affairs, 'The Cabinet Committee on Security reviews operationalization of India's nuclear doctrine', Press release, 4 Jan. 2003, <http://meaindia.nic.in/pressrelease/2003/01/04pr01.htm>.

[113] Indian Ministry of Defence (MOD), *Annual Report 2004–05* (MOD: New Delhi, 2005), <http://mod.nic.in/reports/report05.htm>, p. 14.

[114] Norris, R. and Kristensen, H., 'India's nuclear forces', *Bulletin of the Atomic Scientists*, vol. 61, no. 5 (Sep./Oct. 2005), pp. 73–75.

with the Army's 333, 444 and 555 missile groups. On 9 May 2007 a Prithvi I missile was successfully test-launched at the Integrated Test Range (ITR) at Chandipur-on-Sea, Orissa, on the Bay of Bengal. Officials at India's Defence Research and Development Organisation (DRDO) described the test as a 'user trial' for production quality control involving a missile selected at random from the Army's inventory.[115]

There are two newer versions of the Prithvi missile—the Prithvi II (SS-250), which has entered into service with the Air Force, and the Prithvi III (SS-350)—with improved range, accuracy and handling characteristics. Both are capable of carrying nuclear warheads but are not believed to be assigned a nuclear delivery role.

Indian defence sources indicate that the family of longer-range Agni ('Fire') ballistic missiles, which are designed to provide a short reaction time nuclear capability, has largely taken over the Prithvi's nuclear role.[116] The short-range Agni I is a single-stage solid-fuel missile that can deliver a 1000-kg warhead to a maximum range of 700–800 km. The two-stage Agni II can deliver a similar payload to a range of up to 2000–2500 km. The missiles are road and rail mobile, and both can carry nuclear as well as conventional warheads. In April 2007 the Indian Defence Minister, A. K. Antony, indicated that the Agni I and the Agni II missiles had yet to be inducted into the armed forces but stated that this would be done in a 'reasonable time' and without 'unnecessary delay'.[117] On 4 February 2008, however, three days after Pakistan launched an IRBM, the Indian Government reportedly announced that the Agni I and the Agni II were operationally deployed with India's Strategic Forces Command's 334th and 335th rocket regiments.[118]

On 5 October 2007, army personnel from the Strategic Forces Command successfully test-launched an Agni I missile at the Chandipur-on-Sea facility. The test was described as a 'training trial' for the Indian Army.[119] It was followed, on 24 October, by the test launch of an Agni I missile equipped with improved re-entry technology.[120] The Agni II has not been test-launched since October 2004.

On 12 April 2007 the DRDO conducted the second test flight of the intermediate-range Agni III. The missile was launched from a fixed platform at the ITR on Wheelers Islands in the Bay of Bengal.[121] The first flight test, in July 2006, failed after the missile crashed into the sea reportedly due to problems with its heat shield.[122] The missile is expected to be able to deliver a 1500-kg payload to a range of up to 3500 km. This would put large areas of China within range of launch points in eastern India, although Indian defence officials have denied that the missile was

[115] 'Prithvi missile to test-fired again', Rediff News,5 May 2007, <http://www.rediff.com/news/2007/may/05prithvi.htm>; and 'India tests nuclear-capable surface missile', Agence France-Presse, 9 May 2007, <http://www.spacewar.com/reports/India_Tests_Nuclear_Capable_Surface_Missile_999.html>.

[116] 'Prithvi SRBM', Bharat Rakshak: consortium of Indian military websites, 28 Dec. 2005, <http://www.bharat-rakshak.com/MISSILES/Prithvi.html>.

[117] 'Agni-III missile tests will continue: Antony', Rediff News, 14 Apr. 2007, <http://www.rediff.com/news/2007/apr/14agni.htm>.

[118] Bermudez, J. S., Jr., 'Pakistan carries our successful Ghauri launch', Jane's Defence Weekly, 13 Feb. 2008, p. 18.

[119] Pubby, M., 'Nuclear-capable Agni-I missile is all set for army's first training trial', India Express, 2 Oct. 2007.

[120] 'India test-fires nuclear capable missile', Agence France-Presse, 24 Oct. 2007, <http://www.spacewar.com/reports/India_test_fires_nuclear-capable_missile_999.html>.

[121] 'India successfully test fires Agni III test ballistic missile', The Hindu, 12 Apr. 2007; and Srivastava, S., 'India has China in its range', Asia Times, 14 Apr. 2007.

[122] 'India demonstrates Agni 3 with "textbook precision"', Jane's Missiles & Rockets, vol. 11, no. 6 (June 2007), p. 2.

designed with China in mind. The DRDO is developing a longer-range version of the Agni III missile, sometimes referred to as Agni III* (Agni Three Star), which may begin flight tests in 2009.[123]

In June 2007 there were unconfirmed media reports that the Indian Government had decided not to proceed with the development of an ICBM with a range exceeding 5000 km.[124] The decision to impose a 5000-km range limit, or 'cap', on strategic missiles was reportedly intended as a 'goodwill gesture' aimed at facilitating implementation of the Indian–US Civil Nuclear Cooperation Initiative (CNCI) as well as an effort to forestall additional sanctions on exports of critical material for India's missile programme.[125] However, in December 2007 DRDO officials stated that design work was under way on a three-stage, nuclear-capable Agni missile with a range of up to 6000 km.[126]

There has been speculation in recent years that India is developing a 10 000 km-range ICBM, known as the Surya ('Sun'), based on India's Polar Space-Launch Vehicle (PSLV).[127]. In 2007 there were no authoritative statements indicating that India is actively pursuing such a programme.

Sea-launched ballistic missiles

India continues efforts to develop the naval component of its planned 'triad' of nuclear forces. The converted Prithvi II missile, the Dhanush ('Bow'), was test-launched on 30 March 2007 from the Indian Navy ship *Rajput*. This was the fourth flight test of the Dhanush, which the Indian Ministry of Defence (MOD) has stated will be capable of carrying both conventional and nuclear warheads.[128] The MOD stated in 2006 that the 'process of weaponisation of INS *Suvarna* and *Subhadra* with the Dhanush missile is under progress'.[129]

India's first test launch of an SLBM occurred on 26 February 2008, when the K-15 was launched from a submerged pontoon near Visakhapatnam on India's east coast. An MOD spokesperson said that the test 'was successful', and the media reported that the missile has a range of 700 km, similar to that of the Agni I.[130] MOD officials disclosed in 2007 that the DRDO had tested components of an underwater missile

---

[123] Joseph, J., 'Missile programmes disappoint scientists', *Daily News & Analysis* (Mumbai), 14 Apr. 2007; and 'India to test Agni III+ ballistic missile in 2009', *Express India*, 7 Jan. 2008.

[124] Thapar, V., 'Missile capped: govt under fire', CNN-IBN News, 19 June 2007, <http://www. ibnlive.com/news/india-softens-missile-power-for-us/43179-11.html>; and 'Thinking cap', *Daily News & Analysis* (Mumbai), 18 June 2007.

[125] See Joshi, S., 'India and Pakistan missile race surges on', *WMD Insights*, Oct. 2007. After the flight test of the Agni III in Apr. 2007, the USA and a number of other exporters suspended the sale to India of polyacrylonitrile (PAN) carbon fibre, which is used to make missile engine casings. On the CNCI see chapter 8, section IV.

[126] 'India building 6,000 km nuclear-capable missile', Agence France-Presse, 12 Dec. 2007, <http:// www.spacewar.com/reports/India_building_6000km_nuclear-capable_missile_999.html>; and Dikshit, S., 'Range of ballistic missiles to be improved', *The Hindu*, 13 Dec. 2007.

[127] 'Indian press reports potential for ICBM development', *Jane's Missiles & Rockets*, vol. 9, no. 10 (Oct. 2005), pp. 10–11.

[128] Indian Ministry of Defence, 'Dhanush successfully test fired', Press release, New Delhi, 8 Nov. 2004, <http://mod.nic.in/pressreleases/content.asp?id=853>.

[129] Indian Ministry of Defence (MOD), *Annual Report 2006* (MOD: New Delhi, 2006), <http://mod. nic.in/reports/ebody.htm>, p. 88.

[130] 'India successfully tests submarine-based missile', Reuters, 26 Feb. 2008; and 'India test-fires sea-based nuclear-capable missile: ministry', Agence France-Presse, 26 Feb. 2008.

launch system and was developing a two-stage ballistic missile, designated the K-15, to be launched from a submerged submarine using a gas booster.[131] The K-15 is expected to be deployed on an indigenous nuclear-powered submarine, the Advanced Technology Vessel (ATV), which has been under development since the 1970s. Government officials have stated the ATV is scheduled to be launched in the spring of 2009 and to begin sea trials.[132] There has been considerable speculation that India was developing an SLBM known as the Sagarika ('Oceanic'), and some reports of the K-15 launch also called it the Sagarika. However, the Indian MOD stated in 2006 that 'There is no missile project by the name "Sagarika"'.[133]

VIII. Pakistani nuclear forces

The estimate presented here—that Pakistan possesses approximately 60 nuclear weapons—is conservative. On the basis of recent estimates of the size of Pakistan's military inventory of HEU and separated plutonium, the country could theoretically produce 70–100 nuclear weapons.[134] However, Pakistan is believed to have used only part of this inventory to manufacture warheads, and thus the actual number of warheads is likely to be lower than this. Pakistani officials claim that the country has already produced more warheads than needed to satisfy its current 'minimum deterrence requirement' but note that this requirement is subject to review 'according to situation'.[135] Pakistan's Prime Minister, Shaukat Aziz, asserted in January 2007 that since the Indian–US CNCI could result in more fissile material becoming available for India's military stockpile, and since India has expressed interest in acquiring missile defences, Pakistan 'would need to take measures to ensure the credibility of our deterrence'.[136]

Pakistan's current nuclear arsenal is based primarily on HEU, which is produced by a gas centrifuge uranium enrichment facility at the Kahuta Research Laboratories (also called the A. Q. Khan Research Laboratories). There is evidence that Pakistan is moving towards a plutonium-based arsenal.[137] Pakistan is currently operating the 50-megawatt thermal (MW(t)) Khushab I reactor, completed in 1998, which is cap-

---

[131] Associated Press, 'India developing submarine launched ballistic missiles', *International Herald Tribune*, 11 Sep. 2007; and Unnithan, S., 'The secret undersea weapon', *India Today*, 28 Jan. 2008.

[132] Raghuvanshi, R., 'India working on sea-based nuclear missiles', *Defense News*, 15 Oct. 2007; and Joseph, J., 'Sea trials of nuke submarine in 2 yrs', *Daily News & Analysis* (Mumbai), 4 Dec. 2007.

[133] Indian Ministry of Defence, 'Development and trials-missiles', Press release, New Delhi, 2 Aug. 2006, <http://pib.nic.in/release/rel_print_page1.asp?relid=19395>.

[134] Pakistan possessed an estimated 1.4 ± 0.3 tonnes of HEU and about 80 kg of separated plutonium as of 2007. See also appendix 8B. It is assumed that Pakistan's HEU weapons are of solid core, implosion-type designs requiring 15–20 kg of HEU each, and its plutonium weapons require at the very least c. 4–5 kg of plutonium.

[135] Interview with Gen. Ehsanul Haq, Chairman of Joint Chiefs of Staff Committee, Today with Kamran Khan, Karachi Geo News TV, 24 Nov. 2006, Translation from Urdu, World News Connection, National Technical Information Service (NTIS), US Department of Commerce.

[136] Press Trust India, 'Pak apprehensive about Indo-US nuclear deal: Aziz', *Economic Times* (Mumbai), 31 Jan. 2007.

[137] Plutonium-based nuclear warheads would normally be lighter and more compact than those using HEU to achieve the same yield. Such warheads could either be fitted onto smaller missiles, possibly including cruise missiles, or give already deployed ballistic missiles longer ranges.

able of producing about 10–12 kg of weapon-grade plutonium annually.[138] It is building a second heavy-water reactor at the Khushab nuclear complex, Punjab. According
to one estimate by non-governmental experts, the new reactor is likely to be in the
'40 to 100 MWt range'.[139] In 2007 commercial satellite images indicated that Pakistan had begun construction of a new reactor, identical to the second, at Khushab.[140]
This would enable Pakistan to significantly increase its plutonium production capability, provided that the country has sufficient spent fuel-reprocessing capacity. Plutonium separation takes place at the pilot-scale New Labs reprocessing plant at Rawalpindi, Punjab. A new chemical separation facility appears to be nearing completion at
Chashma, Punjab.[141]

Strike aircraft

The aircraft of the Pakistani Air Force that is most likely to be used in the nuclear
weapon delivery role is the F-16 (see table 8A.8). Other aircraft, such as the
Mirage V or the Chinese-produced A-5, could also be used. Pakistan currently maintains 32 F-16 aircraft in service, deployed in three squadrons. In September 2006
Pakistan signed a deal with the USA, worth $5.1 billion, to buy 18 Block 52 F-16C/D
aircraft, with an option for 18 more. Pakistan will also receive 24 used USAF F-16s at
a later date.[142] As part of the agreement, the 32 F-16A/Bs already in Pakistani service
are to receive a midlife update.[143] The USA delivered the first two F-16s in July
2007.[144]

Ballistic missiles

Pakistan has begun deployment of two types of short-range ballistic missiles
(SRBMs) which are believed to have nuclear delivery roles. The Ghaznavi (Hatf-3) is
a single-stage, solid-propellant, road-mobile SRBM which was formally inducted into
service in 2004. It is believed to be a domestically produced copy of the M-11 missile
that was acquired from China in the 1990s. The Pakistani Army test-launched a
Ghaznavi missile on 13 February 2008.[145] The other short-range ballistic missile, the

[138] Mian, Z. et al., International Panel on Fissile Materials (IPFM), *Fissile Materials in South Asia:
The Implications of the U.S.–India Nuclear Deal*, IPFM Research Report no. 1 (IPFM: Princeton, N.J.,
Sep. 2006), <http://www.fissilematerials.org/ipfm/site_down/ipfmresearchreport01.pdf>.

[139] Cochran, T. B., Natural Resources Defense Council, 'What is the size of Khushab II?', 8 Sep.
2006, <http://docs.nrdc.org/nuclear/nuc_06090801A.pdf>.

[140] Albright, D. and Brannan, P., 'Pakistan appears to be building a third putonium production reactor
at Khushab nuclear site', Institute for Science and International Security Report, 21 June 2007,
<http://www.isis-online.org/publications/southasia/ThirdKhushabReactor.pdf>.

[141] Albright, D. and Brannan, P., 'Chashma nuclear site in Pakistan with possible reprocessing plant',
Institute for Science and International Security Report, 18 Jan. 2007, <http://www.isis-online.org/
publications/southasia/chashma.pdf>.

[142] Schanz, M., 'US and Pakistan hammer out new F-16 deal', *Air Force Magazine*, vol. 90, no. 12
(Dec. 2006), p. 12; and 'Pakistan agrees deal with US for F-16s', *Jane's Defense Weekly*, 11 Oct. 2006,
p. 16. The agreement stipulated that Pakistan would not equip the F-16s with systems to penetrate air
defences and would seek in advance US approval for any F-16 flights out of Pakistani airspace.

[143] Schanz (note 142).

[144] US Embassy in Pakistan, 'U.S. delivers two F-16 fighters to Pakistan Air Force', Press release,
Islamabad, 11 July 2007, <http://islamabad.usembassy.gov/pakistan/h07071101.html>.

[145] 'Ghaznavi missile launched', *Dawn*, 14 Feb. 2008. See also President of the Islamic Republic of
Pakistan, Office of the Press Secretary, 'Pakistan successfully test fires short range ballistic missile',

Table 8A.8. Pakistani nuclear forces, January 2008

Type	Range (km)[a]	Payload (kg)	Status
Aircraft			
F-16A/B	1 600	4 500	32 aircraft, deployed in 3 squadrons; most likely aircraft to have a nuclear delivery role
Ballistic missiles			
Ghaznavi (Hatf-3)	~400	500	Entered service with the Pakistani Army in 2004; fewer than 50 launchers have been deployed; last test-launched on 13 Feb. 2008
Shaheen I (Hatf-4)	>450[b]	750–1 000	Entered service with the Pakistani Army in 2003; fewer than 50 launchers deployed; last test-launched on 25 Jan. 2008
Shaheen II (Hatf-6)	>2 000	~1 000	Under development; fourth test launch on 23 Feb. 2007
Ghauri I (Hatf-5)	>1 200	700–1 000	Entered service with the Pakistani Army in 2003; fewer than 50 launchers deployed; test-launched on 1 Feb. 2008
Ghauri II	2 300	. .	Under development; status uncertain
Cruise missiles			
Babur (Haft 7)	700[c]	. .	Under development; ground-launched version tested 3 times in 2007 (Mar., June and Dec.); sea- and air-launched versions also under development

[a] Missile payloads may have to be reduced in order to achieve maximum range. Aircraft range is given for illustrative purposes only; actual mission range will vary according to flight profile and weapon loading.

[b] Some unofficial sources claim a range of 600–1500 km.

[c] Since 2006 the range of flight tests have been increased from 500 to 700 km.

Sources: US Air Force, National Air and Space Intelligence Center (NASIC), *Ballistic and Cruise Missile Threat* (NASIC: Wright-Patterson Air Force Base, Ohio, Aug. 2003), <http://www.nukestrat.com/us/afn/NAIC2003rev.pdf>; US Central Intelligence Agency, Unclassified report to Congress on the acquisition of technology relating to weapons of mass destruction and advanced conventional munitions, 1 January through 30 June 2002', Apr. 2003, <http://www.nti.org/e_research/official_docs/cia/cia.html>; US Central Intelligence Agency, National Intelligence Council, 'Foreign missile developments and the ballistic missile threat through 2015' (unclassified summary), Dec. 2001, <http://www.dni.gov/nic/PDF_GIF_other prod/missilethreat2001.pdf>; International Institute for Strategic Studies, *The Military Balance 2005–2006* (Routledge: London, 2004); 'Nuclear notebook', *Bulletin of the Atomic Scientists*, various issues; and Authors' estimates.

Shaheen I (Hatf-4), entered into service with the Pakistani Army in 2003. It was most recently test-launched on 25 January 2008 during a troop training exercise.[146] There are rumors that the short-range Abdali may also be nuclear-capable. After a test launch in March 2007, the president's office stated in a press release that the missile 'can carry all types of warheads'.

Pakistan's only MRBM currently in service is the Ghauri I (Hatf-5), which is a road-mobile, liquid-propellant, single-warhead missile. Pakistani defence officials have declared it to have a nuclear delivery role. In addition to the Ghauri MRBM, Pakistan continues to develop the two-stage road-mobile solid-propellant Shaheen II (Hatf-6) MRBM. On 23 February 2007 the Pakistani military announced that an upgraded Shaheen II missile had been successfully test-launched to a range of 2000 km.[147] The launch, which was described as being 'part of a continuous process of validation and technical improvement',[148] was the fourth test of the Shaheen II, which may soon become operational. The Shaheen II's range of 2000–2500 km means that it can reach targets across India. Pakistani military officials have denied that the country was seeking to develop long-range ballistic missiles that could strike targets outside the region.[149]

Pakistan is continuing to develop its arsenal of cruise missiles. On 11 December 2007, Pakistan test-fired a nuclear-capable cruise missile, designated the Babur (Hatf-7), from a ground launcher This marked the missile's fourth ground-launched test flight since 2005. According to a statement issued by the military, the range of the low-flying, subsonic cruise missile had been increased from 500 to 700 km, and efforts are under way to increase the range further to 1000 km.[150] Pakistan is developing an air-launched version of the Babur, which will reportedly be carried by F-16 and JF-17 aircraft.[151] It is also developing a sea-launched version, to be deployed on the Agosta Class attack submarine, that is intended to give Pakistan a second-strike capability.[152] Pakistani officials have insisted that the Babur is an entirely indigenous programme. However, some non-governmental analysts have noted that the missile appears to be similar to the new Chinese DH-10 air-launched cruise missile, which is suspected to be a reverse-engineered US Tomahawk cruise missile.[153]

Press release, 31 Mar. 2007, <http://www.presidentofpakistan.gov.pk/NewsEventsDetail.aspx?News EventID=3617>.

[146] 'Pakistan tests ballistic missile', BBC News, 25 Jan. 2008, <http://news.bbc.co.uk/2/7208416.stm>; and President of the Islamic Republic of Pakistan, Office of the Press Secretary, 'Pakistan successfully launches Shaheen-1 missile', Press release, 29 Nov. 2006, <http://www.presidentofpakistan.gov.pk/ NewsEventsDetail.aspx?NewsEventID=3411>.

[147] 'Pakistan test-fires long-range missile', *PakTribune*, 23 Feb. 2007.

[148] Iqbal, T., 'Pakistan tests upgraded Shaheen II', Pakistan Defence, 22 Feb. 2007, <http://www. defence.pk/news/publish/article73.php>.

[149] Interview with Gen. Ehsanul Haq (note 135).

[150] President of the Islamic Republic of Pakistan, Office of the Press Secretary, 'Government has prepared comprehensive plan to equip armed forces: Musharraf', Press release, 30 May 2007, <http://www. presidentofpakistan.gov.pk/NewsEventsDetail.aspx?NewsEventID=3713>.

[151] 'Pakistan successfully test-fires Hataf-VII missile', *PakTribune*, 26 July 2007.

[152] Hali, S., 'Second strike capability', *The Nation* (Islamabad), 16 Aug. 2006.

[153] Norris, R. S. and Kristensen, H. M., 'Pakistan's nuclear forces, 2007', *Bulletin of the Atomic Scientists*, vol. 63, no. 3 (May/June 2007).

Table 8A.9. Israeli nuclear forces, January 2008

Type	Range (km)^a	Payload (kg)	Status
Aircraft^b			
F-16A/B/C/ D/I Falcon	1 600	5 400	205 aircraft in the inventory; some are believed to be certified for nuclear weapon delivery
Ballistic missiles^c			
Jericho II	1 500–1 800	750–1 000	*c.* 50 missiles; first deployed in 1990; test-launched on 27 June 2001
Jericho III	>4 800	. .	Test launched on 17 Jan. 2008
Submarines			
Dolphin			Rumoured to be equipped with nuclear-capable cruise missiles; denied by Israel

^{a} Missile payloads may have to be reduced in order to achieve maximum range. Aircraft range is given for illustrative purposes only; actual mission range will vary.

^{b} Some of Israel's 25 F-15I aircraft may also have a long-range nuclear delivery role.

^{c} The Shavit space launch vehicle, if converted to a ballistic missile, could deliver a 775-kg payload a distance of 4000 km. The Jericho I, first deployed in 1973, is no longer operational.

Sources: Cohen, A. and Burr, W., 'Israel crosses the threshold', *Bulletin of the Atomic Scientists*, May/June 2006, pp. 22–30; Cohen, A., *Israel and the Bomb* (Columbia University Press: New York, 1998); Albright, D., Berkhout, F. and Walker, W., SIPRI, *Plutonium and Highly Enriched Uranium 1996: World Inventories, Capabilities and Policies* (Oxford University Press: Oxford, 1997); Lennox, D. (ed.), *Jane's Strategic Weapon Systems* (Jane's Information Group, Ltd: Coulsdon, 2003); Fetter, S., 'Israeli ballistic missile capabilities', *Physics and Society,* vol. 19, no. 3 (July 1990), pp. 3–4 (see unpublished 'Ballistic missile primer' for an updated analysis, <http://www.puaf.umd.edu/Fetter/1990-MissilePrimer.pdf>); 'Nuclear notebook', *Bulletin of the Atomic Scientists*, various issues; and Authors' estimates.

IX. Israeli nuclear forces

Israel continues to maintain its long-standing policy of nuclear ambiguity, neither officially confirming nor denying that it possesses nuclear weapons. However, in December 2006 the Israeli Prime Minister, Ehud Olmert, made a statement that was widely interpreted as tacitly acknowledging that Israel possessed a nuclear arsenal. Speaking to German television, Olmert included Israel in a list of countries that possess nuclear weapons.[154] Olmert and other Israeli officials quickly disavowed the remark and reiterated that Israel 'will not be the first country that introduces nuclear weapons to the Middle East'.[155]

The size of the Israeli nuclear weapon stockpile is unknown but is widely believed to consist of roughly 100 plutonium warheads. According to one estimate, Israel possessed 340–560 kg of military plutonium as of December 2006, or the equivalent

[154] 'Was Olmert über Atomwaffen sagte' [What Olmert said about nuclear weapons], N24 television channel, 12 Dec. 2006.

[155] Boudreaux, R., 'Fallout rains on Israel's Olmert after nuclear remark', *Los Angeles Times*, 13 Dec. 2006.

of up to 110 warheads, assuming that each contains 5 kg of plutonium.[156] Only part of this plutonium may have been used to produce warheads. It is estimated here that Israel may have approximately 80 intact warheads, of which 50 are re-entry vehicles for delivery by ballistic missiles and the rest bombs for delivery by aircraft (see table 8A.9). Many analysts believe that Israel has a recessed nuclear arsenal (i.e. one that is stored but not fully armed, requiring some preparation before use). There has been speculation that Israel may have produced non-strategic nuclear weapons, including artillery shells and atomic demolition munitions, but this has never been confirmed.

On 17 January 2008 Israel conducted a test launch reportedly of a long-range ballistic missile from the Palmahim AFB. The Israeli Ministry of Defence did not provide details of the type or purpose of the missile but stated that the experiment tested the missile's rocket propulsion system and was successful.[157] Israeli radio speculated that the missile was a Jericho III IRBM.[158] The Jericho III is believed to be a three-stage solid-propellant missile, with a probable maximum range of 4800–6500 km and an estimated payload of 1000–1300 kg. It is reported to be in development, with an estimated in-service date in 2008.[159]

X. North Korea's military nuclear capabilities

North Korea demonstrated a nuclear weapon capability in October 2006 by carrying out an underground nuclear test explosion.[160] However, the unexpectedly low explosion yield led many experts to believe that it had been a 'fizzle' (an inefficient detonation releasing less explosive energy than expected). This has raised doubts about whether North Korea has mastered the design and engineering skills needed to manufacture an operational nuclear weapon.[161] On 28 March 2007 the US Central Intelligence Agency Director, Michael Hayden, stated that the North Korean nuclear test was a 'failure'.[162]

North Korea is believed to have produced and separated enough plutonium from the spent fuel of its 5-megawatt-electric graphite-moderated research reactor at Yongbyon to be able to build a small number of nuclear warheads. In December 2007, as part of its 'complete and correct' declaration of past and present nuclear activities, North Korea reportedly informed the United States that it had a separated a total of 30 kg of plutonium; of this, it had used 6 kg for its nuclear test in October 2006.[163] The declared amount was at the lower end of estimates by US Government experts of how much plutonium North Korea could have separated and has raised

[156] See appendix 8B, table 8B.2.

[157] Katz, Y., 'Israel test-fires long-range ballistic missile', *Jerusalem Post*, 17 Jan. 2008.

[158] 'Israel says carries out missile launching test', Reuters, 17 Jan. 2008, <http://www.reuters.com/article/worldNews/idUSL175785020080117>.

[159] ed. Lennox (note 20), pp. 81–83.

[160] Fedchenko, V. and Ferm Hellgren, R., 'Nuclear explosions, 1945–2006', *SIPRI Yearbook 2007* (note 42), pp. 552–57.

[161] Sanger, D. E. and Broad, W. J., 'Small blast, or "big deal"? U.S. experts look for clues', *New York Times*, 11 Oct. 2006.

[162] 'CIA says North Korea nuclear test a failure: report', Reuters, 28 Mar. 2007, <http://www.reuters.com/article/topNews/idUSSEO15521620070328>.

[163] 'North Korea produced 30 kg of plutonium–newspaper', Reuters, 21 Apr. 2008, <http://in.reuters.com/article/worldNews/idINIndia-33143320080421>; and Kessler, G., 'N. Korea agrees to blow up its tower at its nuclear facility', *Washington Post*, 2 May 2008, p. A13.

doubts about the correctness of North Korea's declaration. These estimates are based on calculations of how long the Yongbyon reactor operated to build up plutonium in the fuel rods and how much plutonium was chemically extracted from the spent fuel at the adjacent reprocessing plant. Two US non-governmental experts estimated that, as of February 2007, North Korea had a total plutonium stock of 46–64 kg of plutonium, of which about 28–50 kg was in separated form and usable in nuclear weapons.[164] This would be sufficient to produce 6–10 nuclear weapons, assuming that each weapon used 4.5–5.0 kg of weapon-grade plutonium

North Korea deploys approximately 500–600 road-mobile SRBMs of three types—Hwasong-5 (Scud B), Hwasong-6 (Scud Mod-C) and Hwasong-7 (Scud Mod-D)—and 50–200 road-mobile Nodong MRBMs.[165] It is also developing the longer-range Taepodong-1 and Taepodong-2 missiles. On 25 April 2007 North Korea held a large military parade in Pyongyang featuring ballistic missiles, reportedly including the Hwasong-6 (Scud C), Hwasong-7 (Scud D) and a new short-range KN-02, a North Korean version of the Russian 9K79 Tochka (SS-21 'Scarab') surface-to-surface missile.[166] Most analysts consider it unlikely that North Korea has developed a nuclear warhead that is light and compact enough to fit onto a ballistic missile.[167]

[164] Albright, D. and Brannan, P., 'The North Korean plutonium stock, February 2007', Institute for Science and International Security (ISIS), 20 Feb. 2007, <http://www.isis-online.org/publications/dprk/DPRKplutoniumFEB.pdf>.

[165] US Air Force (note 56); ed. Lennox (note 20), pp. 90–96; and Nuclear Threat Initiative, 'North Korea Profile: missile capabilities', Dec. 2006, <http://www.nti.org/e_research/profiles/NK/Missile/62.html>.

[166] Isby, D. C., 'N Korea parades latest missiles', Jane's Missiles and Rockets, June 2007, p. 2; and Bermudez, J. S., 'North Korea takes wraps off the KN-02', Jane's Defence Weekly, 9 May 2007, p. 25.

[167] See e.g. Hecker, S., 'Report on North Korean nuclear program', Nautilus Institute, Policy Forum Online, 06-97A, 15 Nov. 2006, <http://www.nautilus.org/fora/security/0697Hecker.html>.

Appendix 8B. Global stocks of fissile materials, 2007

HAROLD FEIVESON, ALEXANDER GLASER, ZIA MIAN and
FRANK VON HIPPEL*

Table 8B.1. Global stocks of highly enriched uranium (HEU), 2007[a]

Country	National stockpiles (93% enriched equivalent, tonnes)	Production status	Comments
China	20 ± 4	Stopped 1987–89	
France[b]	36.4 ± 6	Stopped early 1996	Includes 6.4 tonnes declared civilian
India[c]	0.2 ± 0.1	Continuing	
Pakistan[d]	1.4 ± 0.3	Continuing	
Russia[e]	770 ± 300	Stopped 1987 or 1988	Includes 100 tonnes assumed to be reserved for naval and other reactor fuel; does not include 200 tonnes to be blended down
UK[f]	23.4 (declared)	Stopped 1963	
USA[g]	508 (declared)	Stopped 1992	Includes 128 tonnes reserved for naval fuel and 20 tonnes for other HEU reactor fuel; Does not include 146 tonnes to be blended down or for disposition as waste.
Non-nuclear weapon states[h]	~10		
Total	**~1370**		**Not including 346 tonnes to be blended down**

[a] Totals are rounded to nearest 5 tonnes. Blending down of excess Russian and US weapon HEU up to early and mid-2007, respectively, has been taken into account. A 20% uncertainty is assumed in the figures for China, France and Pakistan, and 50% for India.

[b] France declared 6.4 tonnes of civilian HEU to the International Atomic Energy Agency (IAEA) as of the end of 2006; it is assumed here to be weapon grade, 93% enriched HEU.

[c] It is believed that India is producing HEU (93% enriched equivalent) at a rate of less than 0.1 tonnes each year for use as naval reactor fuel.

[d] This figure assumes production at a rate of 0.1 tonnes per year between 2003 and 2007.

[e] As of 16 Apr. 2007, 300 tonnes of Russia's weapon-grade HEU had been blended down. The estimate shown for the Russian reserve for naval reactors is not based on any public information.

[f] This figure includes 22.9 tonnes of HEU as of 31 Mar. 2002, the average enrichments of which were not given. The UK declared 1.4 tonnes of civilian HEU to the IAEA as of the end of 2006.

* International Panel on Fissile Materials, Princeton University.

g The amount of US HEU is given in actual tonnes, not 93% enriched equivalent. As of 30 Sep. 1996 the USA had an inventory of 740.7 tonnes of HEU containing 620.3 tonnes of uranium-235 and had declared 177.8 tonnes containing 122 tonnes of uranium-235 to be excess. An additional 20 tonnes were declared excess in 2005, an amount that was increased to 60 tonnes in 2006. The same average enrichment as the material previously declared excess is assumed. This would leave a residual stockpile equivalent (in terms of uranium-235 content) of 491 tonnes of 93% enriched HEU. It is assumed that, during the subsequent decade, *c.* 20 tonnes were consumed for naval reactor fuel and *c.* 5 tonnes for research reactor fuel. As of mid-2007 the USA had blended down 87 tonnes of HEU.

h This figure does not include HEU originally enriched to 20–26% in spent fast-reactor fuel in Kazakhstan.

Table 8B.2. Global stocks of separated plutonium, 2007

Country	Military stocks as of December 2006 (tonnes)	Military production status	Civilian stocks as of December 2006, unless indicated (tonnes)
Belgium*a*	0		3.7 (includes 0.4 abroad)
China	4 ± 0.8	Stopped in 1991	0
France	5 ± 1.0	Stopped in 1994	52.4 (does not include 29.7 foreign owned)
Germany	0		15 in France, Germany and the UK
India*b*	0.65 ± 0.13	Continuing	5.4
Israel*c*	0.45 ± 0.11	Continuing	0
Japan	0		6.7 in Japan + a total of 38 in France and the UK
North Korea	0.035 ± 0.018	Stopped in 2007	0
Pakistan*d*	0.08 ± 0.016	Continuing	0
Russia*e*	145 ± 25 (34–50 declared excess)	Effectively stopped in 1997	42.4
Switzerland	0		0 (does not include 0.7 foreign owned)
UK	7.9 (4.4 declared excess)	Stopped in 1989	81.3 (includes 0.9 abroad, but not 26.5 foreign owned)
USA*f*	92 (53.9 declared excess)	Stopped in 1988	0
Totals	**~255 ± 27 (up to 100 declared excess)**		**244.9**

a This figure is as of the end of 2004.

b As part of the Indian–US Civil Nuclear Cooperation Initiative, India has proposed to include in the military sector much of the plutonium separated from India's spent power-reactor fuel that is labelled civilian here. India is estimated to be producing *c.* 30 kg a year of weapons plutonium from the CIRUS and Dhruva reactors. The estimate is based on an assumption that 50% of India's accumulated heavy-water reactor spent fuel has been reprocessed. An uncertainty of 20% for military plutonium production is assumed.

c Israel is believed to still be operating the Dimona plutonium production reactor, but may be using it primarily for tritium production.

d Pakistan is estimated to be producing *c.* 10 kg a year of weapon plutonium from its Khushab-1 reactor. Two additional plutonium production reactors are under construction at the same site. An uncertainty of 20% for military plutonium production is assumed.

e Russia is producing *c.* 1.2 tonnes of weapon-grade plutonium annually in 3 production reactors that continue to operate because they also produce heat and electricity for nearby communities. Russia has committed itself not to use this material for weapons. The military plutonium holdings of the other Non-Proliferation Treaty-signatory nuclear weapon states were unchanged between 2003 and 2007.

f In its IAEA INFCIRC/549 statement of 30 Nov. 2007, the USA declared as civilian stocks (as of Dec. 2006) a total of 44.9 tonnes of material described as plutonium contained in unirradiated MOX fuel or other forms, and unirradiated separated plutonium held elsewhere. On 17 Sep. 2007, the Secretary of Energy, Samuel W. Bodman, announced the removal of a further 9 tonnes of plutonium from the US weapon stockpile.

Sources for table 8B.1: Institute for Science and International Security (ISIS), *Global Stocks of Nuclear Explosive Materials* (ISIS: Washington, DC, Dec. 2003), <http://www.isisonline. org/global_stocks/end2003/tableofcontents.html>; Albright, D., Berkhout, F. and Walker, W., SIPRI, *Plutonium and Highly Enriched Uranium 1996: World Inventories, Capabilities and Policies* (Oxford University Press: Oxford, 1997), p. 80, table 4.1; *Russia*: United States Enrichment Corporation, 'Megaton to megawatts', <http://www.usec.com>; *UK*: British Ministry of Defence, 'Historical accounting for UK defence highly enriched uranium', London, Mar. 2006, <http://www.mod.uk/DefenceInternet/AboutDefence/CorporatePublica tions/HealthandSafetyPublications/Uranium/>; International Atomic Energy Agency (IAEA), Communication received from the United Kingdom of Great Britain and Northern Ireland concerning its policies regarding the management of plutonium, INFCIRC/549/Add.8/9, 15 Sep. 2006; *USA*: US Department of Energy (DOE), *Highly Enriched Uranium, Striking a Balance: A Historical Report on the United States Highly Enriched Uranium Production, Acquisition, and Utilization Activities from 1945 through September 30, 1996* (DOE: Washington, DC, 2001); George, R. and Tousley, D., DOE, 'US highly enriched uranium disposition', Presentation to the Nuclear Energy Institute Fuel Supply Forum, 24 Jan. 2006; Tobey, W., Deputy Administrator for Defence Nuclear Nonproliferation, National Nuclear Security Administration, DOE, Statement before the House Government Reform Committee Subcommittee on National Security, Emerging Threats, and International Relations, 26 Sep. 2006; Vogler, K., 'The U.S. highly enriched uranium (HEU) disposition program', 48th Annual INMM Meeting, Tucson, Ariz., 8–12 July 2007; *Non-nuclear weapon states*: IAEA, *Annual Report 2005* (IAEA: Vienna, 2006), table A20.

Sources for table 8B.2: Institute for Science and International Security (ISIS), *Global Stocks of Nuclear Explosive Materials* (ISIS: Washington, DC, Dec. 2003), <http://www.isisonline. org/global_stocks/end2003/tableofcontents.html>; *Military production status*: Albright, D., Berkhout, F. and Walker, W., SIPRI, *Plutonium and Highly Enriched Uranium 1996: World Inventories, Capabilities and Policies* (Oxford University Press: Oxford, 1997); US Department of Energy (DOE), 'U.S. removes nine metric tons of plutonium from nuclear weapons stockpile', Press release, 17 Sep. 2007, <http://www.energy.gov/nationalsecurity/5500.htm>; *Civilian stocks (except for India)*: declarations by country to the International Atomic Energy Agency (IAEA) under INFCIRC/549, <http://www.iaea.org/Publications/Documents/>; *India*: Mian, Z. et al., *Fissile Materials in South Asia and the Implications of the U.S.–India Nuclear Deal*, International Panel on Fissile Materials (IPFM) Research Report no. 1 (IPFM: Princeton, N.J., Sep. 2006), <http://www.ipfmlibrary.org/rr01.pdf>; *North Korea*: Albright, D. and Brannan P., 'The North Korean plutonium stock mid-2006', Institute for Science and International Security (ISIS), Washington, DC, 26 June 2006; *Russia*: Agreement between the Government of the United States of America and the Government of the Russian Federation concerning the Management and Disposition of Plutonium Designated as No Longer Required for Defense Purposes and Related Cooperation (Russian–US Plutonium Management and Disposition Agreement), signed on 1 Sep. 2000.

Appendix 8C. A survey of US ballistic missile defence programmes

SHANNON N. KILE

I. Introduction

The United States continues to pursue an expansive array of programmes for active defence against perceived emerging threats from ballistic missiles, including missiles potentially carrying nuclear warheads. This appendix surveys the main US ballistic missile defence (BMD) programmes. It focuses on the weapon and sensor technologies being developed for defence systems designed to counter short-, medium- and long-range ballistic missiles. Section II summarizes the evolving plans of the US Department of Defense (DOD) for building an integrated BMD architecture to protect US territory and allies from missile attack. It highlights concerns about the technological readiness of individual programme elements and the likely effectiveness of the proposed system in realistic missile engagement scenarios. Section III looks at the international dimension of US missile defence activities. It describes joint BMD development programmes under way with Israel and Japan, which involve significant defence-industrial cooperation, and cooperation in the framework of the North Atlantic Treaty Organization (NATO). Section IV presents the conclusions.

II. US ballistic missile defence programmes

The US Administration of President George W. Bush entered office in 2001 committed to developing a robust missile defence system to protect the USA.[1] One argument put forward by senior administration officials was that a nationwide missile defence system would usefully supplement nuclear deterrence; this supplement was increasingly needed in the light of the emergence of states armed with long-range ballistic missiles—possibly armed with nuclear, biological or chemical weapons—which might not be deterred by threats of devastating retaliation.[2] Other arguments focused on the prospect that a state might initiate a regional conflict involving US allies and important US national interests in the mistaken belief that its missiles might deter the USA from intervening in the conflict. In the US Administration's view, the deployment of a nationwide missile defence system—even one using unproven technologies—would force potential adversaries to reassess the risks that they would face by confronting the USA, thereby enhancing US freedom of action when responding to regional crises.[3]

---

[1] The National 1999 Missile Defense Act had already committed the USA 'to deploy as soon as is technologically possible an effective National Missile Defense system capable of defending the territory of the United States against limited ballistic missile attack (whether accidental, unauthorized, or deliberate)'. The National Missile Defense Act of 1999, US Public Law 106-38, was signed into law on 22 July 1999.

[2] Wolfowitz, P., US Deputy Secretary of Defense, Prepared Statement before the Armed Services Committee, US Senate, 12 July 2001, <http://armed-services.senate.gov/hearings/2001/c010712a.htm>.

[3] Wolfowitz (note 2).

In January 2002, the Secretary of Defense, Donald Rumsfeld, identified four main missile defence priorities: (*a*) 'to defend the U.S., deployed forces, allies, and friends'; (*b*) 'to employ a Ballistic Missile Defense System (BMDS) that layers defenses to intercept missiles in all phases of their flight'; (*c*) 'to enable the Services to field elements of the overall BMDS as soon as practicable'; and (*d*) 'to develop and test technologies' and 'improve the effectiveness of deployed capability by inserting new technologies as they become available or when the threat warrants an accelerated capability'.[4] National Security Presidential Directive 23, signed by Bush in December 2002, mandated the deployment of an initial defence capability, beginning in 2004, 'as a starting point for fielding improved and expanded missile defenses later'.[5]

In order to accelerate the deployment of an initial defence capability, the US Missile Defense Agency (MDA)—the main body within the DOD responsible for missile defence activities—has adopted an 'evolutionary approach' to the development of key elements of the BMDS.[6] Rather than settling on a final missile defence architecture, the MDA decided to deploy an initial set of capabilities that would evolve over time to take advantage of technological developments. This capabilities-based acquisition process, also called 'spiral development', departs from the traditional US approach to weapon procurement in that the MDA cannot estimate the overall cost of the missile defence system or determine its final capabilities because the system's baseline architecture changes over time.[7] Spiral development also departs from usual DOD practice, to 'fly before buy', in that the MDA can procure individual systems before they are fully tested and certified as meeting established performance goals.[8]

As part of the spiral development process, the MDA has organized missile defence programme activities into two-year time periods, or 'blocks', consisting of specified capabilities (e.g. Block 2006 represents capability goals to be achieved in 2006–2007, Block 2008 represents 2008–2009 etc.). Each successive block is designed to build on the capabilities previously acquired. In the first block—Block 2004—the MDA began to deploy an integrated BMDS, which incorporated both theatre missile defences (those designed to intercept short- to medium-range ballistic missiles) and strategic defences (those designed to intercept long-range missiles) in a single 'layered' defence architecture.[9]

The MDA has focused its activities in blocks 2006 and 2008 on maintaining and sustaining the defence capability initiated in 2004 by completing the planned deployments of interceptors, sensors and command systems.[10] Over the same period, it is pursuing research, development, testing and evaluation (RDT&E) programmes aimed

[4] Rumsfeld, D., US Secretary of Defense, 'Missile defense program direction', Memorandum, 2 Jan. 2002, <http://www.defenselink.mil/releases/release.aspx?releaseid=3203>.

[5] The White House, 'National policy on ballistic missile defense', National Security Presidential Directive 23, 16 Dec. 2002. The text is available at <http://www.fas.org/irp/offdocs/nspd/>.

[6] Prior to Jan. 2002 the MDA was known as the Ballistic Missile Defense Organization (BMDO).

[7] The spiral development approach has been criticized for limiting the US Congress's ability to oversee spending on missile defence by 'making it difficult to reconcile outcomes with original expectations and to determine the actual cost . . . of individual operational assets'. US Government Accountability Office (GAO), *Defense Acquisitions: Missile Defense Agency's Flexibility Reduces Transparency of Program*, GAO-07-799T (GAO: Washington, DC, 30 Apr. 2007), <http://www.gao.gov/>, p. 9.

[8] Coyle, P., 'Is missile defense on target?', *Arms Control Today*, vol. 33, no. 8 (Oct. 2003), p. 9.

[9] US Missile Defense Agency, 'The Ballistic Missile Defense System', Fact sheet, Aug. 2007, <http://www.mda.mil/mdalink/html/factsheet.html>.

[10] US Missile Defense Agency, 'Fiscal year 2008 (FY08) budget estimates: overview', 31 Jan. 2007, <http://www.mda.mil/mdalink/pdf/budgetfy08.pdf>, p. 4.

Table 8C.1. Summary of principal US missile defence programmes, December 2007

Programme	System	Status
Interceptors		
Terminal phase		
Patriot Advanced Capability-3 (PAC-3)	Land-based, air-transportable launcher, single-stage Extended Range Interceptor (ERINT) missile armed with explosive warhead, phased array radar and engagement control station (ECS)[a]	Most technologically mature BMD system, in US Army service since 2003; a total of 712 missiles to be in US inventory at end of 2008
Terminal High Altitude Area Defence (THAAD)[b]	Truck-mounted launchers equipped with hit-to-kill interceptor missiles, mobile X-band radar, and battle management command and control (BMC2) system	Resumed flight tests in 2005, after major design changes; successful interception tests in Jan. and Oct. 2007; first unit to be deployed in 2009
Mid-course phase		
Ground-based Midcourse Defense (GMD)	Long-range, multi-stage Ground-Based Interceptor (GBI) missile carrying an EKV for intercepting ICBMs; land- and sea-based tracking radars; and a GMD Fire Control and Communications (GFC/C) system	GBI and GMD radar network used in successful interception test in Sep. 2007; 40 GBI missiles to be based at Fort Greely, Alaska, 4 at Vandenberg AFB, California, and 10 in Poland by 2011
Aegis Ballistic Missile Defense	Aegis ships equipped with AN/SPY-1 radar reconfigured for a long-range surveillance and track (LRS&T) capability and Block 1A SM-3 hit-to-kill interceptors for engaging short- and medium-range ballistic missiles	3 Aegis BMD cruisers and 13 destroyers to be in US Navy service at end of 2008 with c. 40 SM-3s; the Block 2 SM-3 to be fielded in 2013 will have capability to intercept ICBMs
Multiple Kill Vehicle (MKV)	Long-range interceptor carrying 8–20 miniaturized EKVs which can independently track and target multiple warheads and mid-course countermeasures, such as decoy re-entry vehicles	Control system of payload carrier vehicle tested in 2006; testing of EKVs to begin in 2009; initial operational capability in 2014
Boost phase		
Airborne Laser (ABL)	Modified Boeing 747 aircraft carrying a modular, megawatt-class chemical oxygen iodine laser (COIL), beam control optics, infrared sensors, and target acquisition and tracking lasers	Continuing systems-integration problems; successful in-flight test of target tracking laser in Mar. 2007; first 'lethality test' of laser in 2009
Kinetic Energy Interceptor (KEI)	A fast-burn, high-velocity interceptor missile to be deployed on mobile land launchers or on sea-based platforms near an enemy launch site; may replace ABL as main boost-phase defence system	Land-based booster flight to be tested in 2008; sea-based platform to be selected in 2008; initial operational capability to be determined

Programme	System	Status
Sensors		
Sea-Based X-band (SBX) radar	High resolution radar based on manoeuvrable offshore platform for acquisition, tracking and discrimination of target missiles	Completed sea trials in 2007; used in successful test of GMD elements in Sep. 2007; to be based at Adak Island, Alaska
AN/TPY-2 radar[c]	Transportable high-resolution radar for detecting, tracking and discriminating missile threats; designed as part of the THAAD system	First radar activated in Oct. 2006 by US Army unit at Japanese airbase in Shariki, Japan
Space Tracking and Surveillance System (STSS)[d]	Constellation of low-earth orbit satellites designed to detect and track missiles in all phases of flight; size of constellation to be determined	Two satellites to be launched in 2008
Space-Based Infrared System– High (SBIRS-High)[e]	USAF procurement plan is for 3 satellites in geosynchronous orbit, and 2 satellites with infrared sensors in highly elliptical orbit, to provide early warning of ballistic missile launches	Programme beset by technical delays and cost overruns; restructured in 2002, 2004 and 2005; launch of first satellite scheduled for 2008
Upgraded Early-Warning Radar (UEWR)	Modified early-warning radar (EWR) for detection and tracking of post-boost and mid-course re-entry vehicles; data transmitted to 2 GMD Fire Control Centres, in Alaska and Colorado	Upgrade of US EWR at RAF Fylingdales, UK, completed in Aug. 2007; upgrade of US EWR at Thule, Greenland to be completed in 2009

AFB = Air Force Base; BMD = ballistic missile defence; EKV = exoatmospheric kill vehicle; ICBM = intercontinental ballistic missile; SM-3 = Standard Missile-3; USAF = US Air Force.

[a] US missile defence programmes are organized according to the 3 phases of a ballistic missile's flight: 'boost' (the powered ascent phase, from launch to booster-engine burnout), 'midcourse' (the exoatmospheric phase, between booster burnout and re-entry into the atmosphere), and 'terminal' (the re-entry phase, ending with the missile warhead's impact).

The PAC-3 system is designed to provide point defence against short-range ballistic missiles but can also engage aircraft and cruise missiles.

[b] THAAD has an 'endo-/exoatmospheric capability' to intercept medium-range ballistic missiles above the earth's atmosphere as well as inside the atmosphere.

[c] This was formerly known as Forward-Based X-band (FBX) radar.

[d] This was formerly known as Space-Based Infrared System–Low (SBIRS-Low).

[e] Because of continuing problems with SBIRS-High, the USAF began a parallel programme in 2006 known as the Alternative Infrared Satellite System (AIRSS).

Sources: Obering, H. A. (Lieut. Gen.), Director, US Missile Defense Agency, 'Fiscal year 2008 defense authorization ballistic missile defense', Statement before the US Senate Armed Services Committee, Strategic Forces Subcommittee, 11 Apr. 2007, <http://armed-services. senate.gov/testimony.cfm?wit_id=4103&id=2675>; US Missile Defense Agency, 'Fiscal Year 2008 (FY08) budget estimate: overview', 31 Jan. 2007, <http://www.mda.mil/mdalink/pdf/ budgetfy08.pdf>; US Missile Defense Agency, Fact Sheets (various), <http://www.mda.mil/ mdalink/html/factsheet.html>; Jane's Missiles & Rockets (various issues); and Boese, W., 'Missile defense remains budget priority', Arms Control Today, vol. 37, no. 2 (Mar. 2007).

Table 8C.2. Funding for the US Missile Defense Agency, financial years 2003–13

Figures are for requested funds, in US $m. at current prices. Years are financial years (1 Oct.–
30 Sep.). Figures do not include Defense-Wide Resources funding for missile defence programmes.

Year	2003	2004	2005	2006	2007	2008	2008–13[a]
Funding	6 714	7 674	9 169	7 695	9 388	8 899	56 666

[a] This is a projected figure.

Sources: US Department of Defense (DOD), *Fiscal Year (FY) 2008 Budget Estimates: Research, Development, Test and Evaluation, Defense-Wide*, vol. 2, *Missile Defense Agency* (DOD: Washington, DC, 2007), <http://www.defenselink.mil/comptroller/defbudget/fy2008/budget_justification/>; US Missile Defense Agency, 'FY 2005 budget estimates overview', 2 Feb. 2004, <http://www.cdi.org/news/missile-defense/mdafy05.pdf>; and Kadish, R. (Lieut. Gen.), Director, Missile Defense Agency, 'Missile defense program and fiscal year 2004 budget', Statement before the US Senate Armed Services Committee, 18 Mar. 2003, <http://armed-services.senate.gov/testimony.cfm?wit_id=1708&id=646>.

at filling gaps in capabilities and improving the initial defence capability by adding new systems. These latter include boost-phase interceptors (the Airborne Laser and the Kinetic Energy Interceptor), a terminal-phase interceptor (Terminal High Altitude Area Defense, THAAD) and a 'volume kill capability' (the Multiple Kill Vehicle). In the longer term, beyond 2012, the MDA is making 'capabilities investments' in new space-based sensors (the Space Tracking and Surveillance System) and in advanced technologies in order to be able to defend against more sophisticated or unexpected missile threats.[11] The principal US missile defence programmes are summarized in table 8C.1.

The US Administration requested $8.9 billion in financial year 2008 for all of the programme elements of the Missile Defense Agency (see table 8C.2).[12] In 2007, the US Government Accountability Office (GAO) estimated that the USA had spent $107 billion on missile defence since the mid-1980s.[13]

The initial defence capability

At the end of 2007 the USA's deployed missile defence capability consisted of the following elements: Ground-based Midcourse Defense (GMD), Aegis Ballistic Missile Defense, Patriot Advanced Capability-3 (PAC-3) and the Command, Control, Battle Management and Communications (C2BMC) system (see table 8C.3).

The centrepiece of the MDA's initial defence capability against long-range ballistic missiles threats is the Ground-based Midcourse Defense system. The GMD system consists of a 'hit-to-kill' interceptor missile and a network of land- and sea-based radars. The three-stage Ground-Based Interceptor (GBI) missile carries an exoatmospheric kill vehicle (EKV), which is designed to collide with and destroy intermediate-

[11] US Missile Defense Agency (note 10), p. 5.
[12] The request did not include funds for missile defence programmes managed by the armed services, such as the US Air Force's Space-Based Infrared System (SBIRS) satellite network and the US Army's Patriot missile defence system.
[13] US Government Accountability Office (note 7), p. 4.

and intercontinental-range ballistic missiles in the mid-course phase of flight. A series of technical problems and accidents in developing the GBI significantly delayed the selection and flight testing of the booster vehicle. Despite these setbacks, the MDA began to deploy the interceptor missiles at the end of 2004.[14] A GAO report in March 2007 noted that the GBI programme continued to face technical challenges with the EKV's infrared seeker as well as with the redesign and testing of the booster's guidance, navigation and control subsystems.[15]

The MDA's Block 2006 programme has also focused on deploying GMD sensor elements. These are land- and sea-based radars for detecting and tracking long-range ballistic missiles and transmitting targeting information though the C^2BMC system. In June 2006 the US Army deployed a transportable AN/TPY-2 X-band radar at a Japan Air Self-Defense Force airbase in north-eastern Japan.[16] The Sea-Based X-band (SBX) radar completed calibration tests while undergoing sea trials in 2007 and was expected to be fully integrated into the GMD system after reaching its homeport in the Aleutian Islands.[17] In addition, the upgrading of the 1960s-era Ballistic Missile Early Warning System (BMEWS) radar at Royal Air Force (RAF) Fylingdales base in the United Kingdom was completed in August 2007, pursuant to a 2003 British–US agreement to allow the DOD to use the US radar at the base for missile defence purposes.[18] In June 2007 the US Air Force began work on upgrading its early-warning radar at Thule, Greenland, which was scheduled to be completed in the autumn of 2009.[19]

The GMD test programme was restructured in 2005 because of flight-test failures and quality-control problems. After a lengthy hiatus, the MDA conducted two successful flight tests in 2006 using interceptors; the second was an 'end-to-end' test of an engagement scenario and resulted in a target intercept.[20] In September 2007 the MDA conducted a flight test involving a successful intercept by a GBI missile. The test evaluated the performance of the interceptor missile's rocket motor system and the EKV. It was also designed to evaluate the performance of several elements of the BMDS.[21] This included demonstrating the ability of the upgraded early-warning radar at Beale Air Force Base, California, and the SBX radar to acquire and track a target missile and transmit the data through the C^2BMC system. The target missile was also successfully tracked by an Aegis cruiser using the AN/SPY-1 radar.

The Aegis BMD test programme reached another milestone in 2007. On 6 November an Aegis cruiser in the Pacific Ocean, USS *Lake Erie*, successfully intercepted two target missiles launched from Hawaii with two Standard Missile-3 (SM-3) Block

---

[14] Graham, B., 'Missile defense testing may be inadequate', *Washington Post*, 22 Jan. 2004.

[15] US Government Accountability Office (GAO), '*Defense Acquisitions: Assessments of Selected Weapon Programs*, GAO-07-406SP (GAO: Washington, DC, Mar. 2007), pp. 83–84.

[16] Coleman, J., 'U.S., Japan expand missile-defense plan', *Washington Post*, 23 June 2006.

[17] US Missile Defense Agency, 'Sea-based X-band radar (SBX)', Fact sheet, Aug. 2007, <http://www.mda.mil/mdalink/html/factsheet.html>; and 'Sea-Based X-band radar completes fine calibration testing', *Space War*, 15 Mar. 2007, <http://www.spacewar.com/pageone/spacewar-2007-03-15.html>.

[18] 'Upgrade to the early warning radar at Fylingdales', *Royal Air Force News*, 26 July 2007; and British Ministry of Defence, 'MOD replies to US request to upgrade RAF Fylingdales', Press release, 5 Feb. 2003, <http://www.gnn.gov.uk/content/detail.asp?ReleaseID=28649&NewsAreaID=2>.

[19] 'Thule EWR upgrade begins', *CDI Missile Defense Update*, no. 6 (11 July 2007), <http://www.cdi.org/program/document.cfm?documentid=4011>.

[20] Samson, V. and Black, S., 'Flight tests for Ground-based Midcourse Defense (GMD) system', Center for Defense Information, 18 June 2007, <http://www.cdi.org/pdfs/gmd ift2.pdf>.

[21] US Missile Defense Agency, 'Missile defense exercise and flight test successfully completed', News release, 28 Sep. 2007, <http://www.mda.mil/mdalink/html/newsrel.html>.

Table 8C.3. Deployed US Ballistic Missile Defense System (BMDS) elements, December 2007

Category	BMDS element	Location
Silo-based interceptors	22 GBI missiles	Fort Greely, Alaska
	3 GBI missiles	Vandenberg AFB, Calif.
Mobile interceptors	3 Aegis BMD engagement cruisers[a]	US Pacific Fleet
	7 Aegis BMD engagement destroyers[a]	US Pacific Fleet
	546 PAC-3 missiles	US Army worldwide
Fixed site sensors	Cobra Dane radar[b]	Shemya Island, Alaska
	2 upgraded early-warning radar	Beale AFB, Calif., and RAF Fylingdales, UK
Transportable/ mobile sensors	Sea-based X-band radar	Adak Island, Alaska
	AN/TPY-2 X-Band radar	Shariki AFB, Japan
	7 Aegis Long-range Surveillance and Track (LRS&T) destroyers[c]	US Pacific Fleet

AFB = Air Force Base; BMD = ballistic missile defence; GBI = Ground-Based Interceptor; PAC-3 = Patriot Advanced Capability-3

[a] At the end of 2007 the US Navy had 21 Standard Missile-3 (SM-3) missile interceptors available for deployment on Aegis BMD engagement ships

[b] The modified Cobra Dane phased-array radar, which was originally designed to track missiles launched from the Soviet Union, has a limited capability to detect missiles launched towards the USA from North Korea.

[c] The destroyers are to be refitted with a BMD engagement capability by the end of 2008.

Sources: Obering, H. A. (Lieut. Gen.), Director, US Missile Defense Agency, 'Fiscal year 2008 defense authorization ballistic missile defense', Statement before the US Senate Armed Services Committee, Strategic Forces Subcommittee, 11 Apr. 2007, <http://armed-services.senate.gov/testimony.cfm?wit_id=4103&id=2675>; and US Missile Defense Agency, 'Fiscal year 2008 (FY08) budget estimate: overview', 31 Jan. 2007, <http://www.mda.mil/mdalink/pdf/budgetfy08.pdf>.

IA interceptor missiles. This was the sea-based system's first test involving the simultaneous engagement of multiple targets. According to the MDA's criteria, these were the tenth and eleventh successful intercepts, of 13 targets in 12 flight tests for the Aegis BMD programme.[22]

Concerns about technology readiness

In July 2006 the Department of Defense placed the BMDS on limited operational alert for the first time in response to North Korea's resumption of long-range ballistic missile flight tests.[23] President Bush's statement that US missile defences would have had 'a reasonable chance' of shooting down a North Korean test missile was disputed by Philip Coyle, who was the DOD's director of Operational Test and Evaluation

[22] US Missile Defense Agency, 'Sea-based missile defense "hit to kill" intercept achieved', News release, 6 Nov. 2007, <http://www.mda.mil/mdalink/html/newsrel.html>.

[23] Shanker, T., 'Missile defense system is up and running, military says', *New York Times*, 3 Oct. 2007.

from 1994 to 2001. Coyle said that the system had 'no demonstrated capability to defend the United States against enemy attack under realistic conditions'.[24] Critics inside and outside the US Government have long complained that the MDA did not subject key weapon systems and sensors to operational tests designed to simulate real-world conditions.[25] In particular, they have charged that the tests to date have been highly orchestrated and failed to include even simple countermeasures, such as warhead decoys, that an adversary would be likely to use.[26] This led the DOD's Defense Science Board to warn at the end of 2006 that 'Fielding the current systems in larger numbers will not lead to a robust system'.[27] In response to these complaints, the director of the MDA told the US Congress in 2007 that, as part of its Block 2008 activities, the agency would conduct increasingly realistic operational tests, including adding countermeasures to a GMD system test scheduled for 2008.[28]

III. International missile defence cooperation

Proposed US missile defence deployments in Europe

In 2007 the USA began negotiations with the Czech Republic and Poland on a US proposal to deploy on their territories missile interceptors and a tracking radar developed as part of its GMD system. The US Government claims that the proposed deployments are needed to counter threats posed by Iran's emerging long-range ballistic missile capabilities.[29] However, they have sparked a public debate about the feasibility and desirability of missile defences in Europe. The USA's plan has also faced strenuous objections from the Russian Government.[30]

The US proposal involves the deployment of US BMDS assets at two sites in Europe. The first is an airbase near Koszalin, in northern Poland, where 'up to ten' silo-based interceptor missiles will be deployed in 2011–13.[31] The interceptors will be a two-stage variant of the GBI missile and will consist of a booster stage and an EKV attached to the second rather than the third stage. They will have greater acceleration but a shorter range than the three-stage missiles being deployed on US territory. According to the MDA, the two-stage GBI missile will be 'better suited for

[24] Center for Defense Information, 'Former and current officials skeptical of missile defense efficacy', *CDI Missile Defense Update*, no. 7 (10 Aug. 2006), <http://www.cdi.org/program/document.cfm?documentid=3620>.

[25] Boese, W., 'More testing urged for missile defense', *Arms Control Today*, vol. 35, no. 6 (July/Aug 2005); and Thompson, M., 'Can America's missile defense handle North Korea?', *Time*, 3 July 2006.

[26] See e.g. Cloud, D. S., 'Missile Defense System intercepts rocket in test', *New York Times*, 2 Sep. 2006; and Watson, R., 'Physicist blows whistle on US missile defence', *The Times*, 3 Jan. 2003.

[27] US Department of Defense (DOD), Defense Science Board Task Force, *Nuclear Capabilities*, Report summary (DOD: Washington, DC, Dec. 2006), <http://www.acq.osd.mil/dsb/reports.htm>, p. 7.

[28] Obering, H. A. (Lieut. Gen.), Director, US Missile Defense Agency, 'Fiscal year 2008 defense authorization ballistic missile defense', Statement before the US Senate Armed Services Committee, Strategic Forces Subcommittee, 11 Apr. 2007, <http://armed-services.senate.gov/testimony.cfm?wit_id=4103&id=2675>, pp. 21–26.

[29] Rood, J., US Assistant Secretary for International Security and Non-Proliferation, 'International missile defence: challenges for Europe', Remarks to the 8th Royal United Services Institute (RUSI) Missile Defence Conference, London, 27 Feb. 2007, <http://www.state.gov/t/isn/rls/rm/81242.htm>.

[30] See chapter 1 in this volume, section III.

[31] US departments of State and Defense, *Proposed U.S. Missile Defense Assets in Europe* (Missile Defense Agency: Washington, DC, June 2007), <http://www.mda.mil/mdaLink/html/thirdsite.html>, p. 3.

the engagement ranges and timelines for Europe', since the three-stage interceptor's minimum flight range is too long for it to be able to engage missiles launched from Iran.[32]

The second site is in the Brdy district of the Czech Republic and would host a large X-band radar called the European Midcourse Radar (EMR). The radar equipment is currently deployed at Kwajalein atoll in the Marshall Islands, central Pacific Ocean, in support of the MDA's BMDS test programme and would be upgraded and moved to Europe in 2011.[33] This narrow-beam, high-resolution radar will allow its US operators to discriminate target clusters (i.e. distinguish the missile warhead from other missile parts and potential countermeasures) travelling above the atmosphere. The EMR will also provide precision tracking and guidance information (known as 'cueing' data) to the interceptor missiles, thereby significantly expanding the latter's area of defensive coverage. In addition, the MDA may deploy an X-band radar at a site closer to Iran, such as in Turkey or the Caucasus, to provide early detection and enhanced tracking information to the EMR.[34]

According to a DOD analysis, the Czech Republic and Poland are the 'optimal' locations for the interceptors and the radar in terms of maximizing defensive coverage of European territory against intermediate-range ballistic missiles launched from the Middle East.[35] However, in 2007 some observers disputed the MDA's claim, noting that the current plan left south-eastern Europe unprotected.[36] In addition, two prominent non-governmental experts concluded that the proposed US missile defence deployments in the Czech Republic and Poland would be capable of engaging all Russian intercontinental ballistic missiles (ICBMs) launched from sites west of the Urals and flying towards the east coast of the USA.[37] They argued that positioning the interceptors and radar closer to Iran would better defend Europe from Iranian missiles while being too far away from Russia to pose a threat to its ICBM force.

The North Atlantic Treaty Organization[38]

As part of its 1999 Strategic Concept, NATO is developing a theatre missile defence system: the Active Layered Theatre Ballistic Missile Defence (ALTBMD) programme to protect its deployed forces within or outside its territory against short- and medium-range ballistic missiles.[39] ALTBMD is a multi-layered 'system of systems' consisting of low- and high-altitude defences, communications, command and control

---

[32] US departments of State and Defense (note 31), p. 4.

[33] US departments of State and Defense (note 31), p. 4.

[34] US departments of State and Defense (note 31), p. 5.

[35] US departments of State and Defense (note 31), p. 6. The deployments will also provide 'redundant coverage' for the continental USA against intercontinental ballistic missiles launched from the Middle East.

[36] See e.g. Tauscher, E., 'European missile defense: a congressional perspective', *Arms Control Today*, vol. 37, no. 8 (Oct. 2007).

[37] Lewis, G. N. and Postol, T. A., 'European missile defense: the technological basis of Russian concerns', *Arms Control Today*, vol. 37, no. 8 (Oct. 2007).

[38] For more on NATO's consideration of missile defences see chapter 1 in this volume, section V.

[39] See NATO, Active Layered Theatre Ballistic Missile Defence Programme Office, 'The ALTBMD system', 6 Nov. 2007, <http://www.tmd.nato.int/system.html>; and Yost, D. S., 'Missile defence on NATO's agenda', *NATO Review*, no. 3/2006 (autumn 2006), <http://www.nato.int/docu/review/2006/issue3/english/analysis1.html>; and NATO, 'The alliance's strategic concept', Press Release NAC-S(99)65, 24 Apr. 1999, <http://www.nato.int/docu/pr/1999/>.

systems, early-warning sensors, radar and various interceptors.[40] It will integrate into a single NATO command and control network the sensors and interceptors provided by member states, such as the Franco-Italian Surface Air Moyenne Portée/Terre (SAMP/T) system and the US Patriot anti-missile missile system. In September 2006 the first contract for the development of a key component of the system, the NATO Battlefield Management Command, Control, Communication and Intelligence (BMC³I) capability, was awarded. ALTBMD is scheduled to achieve an initial operational capability by 2010 and to be fully operational by 2016.[41]

The Medium Extended Air Defense System (MEADS) continues to be developed under a NATO contract awarded in 2004. MEADS is a joint German–Italian–US air defence programme designed to defend against short-range ballistic missiles, cruise missiles and aircraft.[42] The system consists of a lightweight launcher, 360-degree fire control and surveillance radars, and a battle management command and control (BMC²) system designed to be interoperable within NATO forces. When it enters into service in 2014, MEADS will initially use the current PAC-3 interceptor missile, augmented by Missile Segment Enhancement (MSE) technologies that will give it greater range and performance.[43] In 2003 the MEADS development programme was combined with the US Army's PAC-3 programme in order to create an integrated PAC-3–MEADS capability.[44]

Japan

Japan's interest in missile defence intensified in the wake of North Korea's unexpected test-firing in 1998 of a long-range Taepodong ballistic missile over the main Japanese island of Honshu. Japanese missile defence plans are predicated on close cooperation with the USA. In December 2004 the Japanese cabinet approved its National Defense Program Guidelines, which inter alia envisioned increased Japanese–US 'cooperation on ballistic missile defense' and 'equipment and technology exchange'.[45] The two countries subsequently concluded a deal to allow Japan's licensed production of the US PAC-3 missile and also undertook to jointly develop the Standard Missile-3 interceptor.[46] In June 2006 Japan and the USA followed up these ventures with a new cooperation agreement under which missile defence tech-

[40] NATO, 'Missile defence: what does this mean in practice?', Topics, 13 June 2007, <http://www.nato.int/issues/missile_defence/practice.html>.

[41] NATO, Active Layered Theatre Ballistic Missile Defence Programme Office, 'NATO missile defence–evolution', 6 Nov. 2007, <http://www.tmd.nato.int/mdevolution.html>.

[42] The USA has a 58% share in the programme, Germany 25% and Italy 17%. 'Beyond Patriot: the MEADS program SD&D phase', Defense Industry Daily, 14 Aug. 2007. The USA is expected to procure 48 MEADS firing units, Germany 24 units and Italy 9 units. Six launchers with up to 12 missiles each make up a firing unit.

[43] 'Beyond Patriot' (note 42).

[44] Kingston, T. and Ratnam, G., 'Europe wary of U.S. missile defense promises', Defense News, 13 Oct. 2003, pp. 1, 8.

[45] Japanese Ministry of Defense (MOD), Defense of Japan 2007, White Paper (MOD: Tokyo, 2007), <http://www.mod.go.jp/e/publ/w_paper/>, 'National Defense Program Guidelines, FY 2005–', pp. 462—69.

[46] 'Japan licensed to produce Patriot PAC-3s', Defense Industry Daily, 19 July 2005, <http://www.defenseindustrydaily.com/japan-licensed-to-produce-patriot-pac3s-0876>; and Japan Defense Agency (JDA), Defense of Japan 2006, White Paper (JDA: Tokyo, 2006), <http://www.mod.go.jp/e/publ/w_paper/>, 'Statement by the Chief Cabinet Secretary "Japan–U.S. cooperative development of advanced SM-3 missile for ballistic missile defense"', p. 459.

nology developed by Japanese defence contractors could be shared with US partners.[47] The technology transfer issue was a politically sensitive one in Japan, which had long adhered to a self-imposed ban on arms exports in line with its pacifist constitution.

Japan is developing a high-altitude, exoatmospheric anti-missile capability that will consist of six Japan Maritime Self-Defense Force (JMSDF) destroyers equipped with the Aegis BMD radar and weapon control system and SM-3 missiles. These will be fitted on two new Aegis destroyers currently under construction in Nagasaki. The JMSDF is also refitting four Kongo Class Aegis destroyers with the upgraded radar as well as with Block 1A SM-3 missiles and associated launch canisters.[48] Japan and the USA are proceeding with development work on a Block 2 SM-3 missile which will have an enhanced capability for engaging ICBMs.

The Japanese Government's concern about North Korea's intentions and missile capabilities led to the deployment to Japan, in August 2006, of one of the US Navy's Aegis cruisers. The arrival of the USS *Shiloh* at the US Navy base in Yokosuka sparked public protests over Japan's integration into US missile defence plans.[49]

Japan's low-altitude anti-missile capability will initially consist of 16 land-based PAC-3 missile batteries.[50] In 2006 the Japan Defense Agency (JDA, which became the Ministry of Defense in January 2007) announced plans to buy 124 Patriot surface-to-air missiles by 2010.[51] It ordered a total of 36 interceptors from the USA, with the remainder to be produced in Japan beginning in 2008. The JDA subsequently announced that it intended to purchase additional US-built Patriot missiles.[52] In March 2007, approximately one year ahead of schedule, the Japan Self-Defense Forces (JSDF) deployed its first Patriot missile battery at the Iruma base near Tokyo.[53] In addition to the deployments by the JSDF, in October 2006 the first PAC-3 battalion was deployed at the US Air Force's Kadena Air Base on Okinawa.[54]

Israel

The Israeli–US Arrow Weapon System (AWS) is the most technologically mature of the USA's collaborative missile defence development programmes.[55] The AWS was designed to track and destroy Scud-type ballistic missiles in the terminal phase of their flight trajectory. The centrepiece of the system is the Arrow 2 interceptor mis-

---

[47] Coleman (note 16).

[48] This work is being done in cooperation with Lockheed Martin under a 3-year, $124 million contract. Wolf, J., 'Experimental U.S.-Japan missile tip passes first test', *Defense News*, 8 Mar. 2006.

[49] Kyodo News Agency, 'U.S. deploys missile-intercept ship here', *Japan Times*, 30 Aug. 2006.

[50] Japanese Ministry of Defense (note 45), p. 171.

[51] Yamaguchi, M., Associated Press, 'U.S. to put Patriot interceptors in Japan', *Washington Post*, 26 June 2006.

[52] Agence France-Presse, 'US offers Japan 80 Patriot missiles', *Space Daily,* 24 Aug. 2006; and Obering (note 28), p. 26.

[53] Hogg, C., 'Japan mounts missile self-defence', BBC News, 30 Mar 2007, <http://news.bbc.co.uk/2/6509211.stm>.

[54] Associated Press, 'U.S. Patriot missile parts arrive on Okinawa, sparking local protest', *International Herald Tribune*, 3 Oct. 2006.

[55] Israel Aerospace Industries (IAI) is the prime contractor and lead system integrator for the AWS. A US consortium led by the Boeing Company produces nearly 40% of the components for the Arrow 2 interceptor missile. Lennox, D. (ed.), *Jane's Strategic Weapon Systems* (Jane's Information Group: Coulsdon, 2007), p. 248; and Sampson, V., 'Israel's Arrow missile defense: not ready for prime time', Center for Defense Information, 9 Oct. 2002, <http://www.cdi.org/missile-defense/arrow.cfm>.

sile, which is equipped with both infrared and active radar sensors and a blast-fragmentation warhead. The Israeli Air Force (IAF) currently deploys two Arrow 2 batteries, one located at an airbase near Tel Aviv, which became operational in 2000, and the other at an undisclosed site in northern Israel. Each battery is believed to consist of four to eight mobile launchers, one Green Pine multifunction phased-array radar, one Citron Tree fire-control centre, one launch-control centre and approximately 50 Arrow 2 interceptor missiles.[56] The IAF has reportedly decided to augment this 'thin deployment', which was intended primarily to counter Scud missiles launched from Iraq, with additional Arrow 2 batteries in northern Israel. The goal is to enhance Israel's ability in a future conflict to defend against potential barrage attacks by the growing ballistic missile forces of Iran and Syria.[57]

In 2007 US and Israeli concern about Iran's development of longer-range variants of its Shahab missile led the two countries to extend by five years the Arrow System Improvement Program (ASIP), which had been scheduled to conclude in 2008. The US Missile Defence Agency also significantly increased funding for Arrow upgrades and interoperability testing as well as for future joint missile projects.[58] As part of ASIP activities in 2007, the Israel Missile Defense Organization (IMDO) conducted the first flight tests of a Block 3 Arrow 2 interceptor missile.[59] The upgraded missile is designed to intercept target missiles at higher altitudes and longer ranges, so that the debris from possible nuclear, biological or chemical warheads will fall farther away from Israeli territory. The tests also employed the Block 3 Green Pine radar, which has improved resolution for identifying decoys and other penetration aids that Iran may be developing to defeat missile defences.[60]

Israeli defence officials are studying a new exoatmospheric interceptor missile—designated Arrow 3—capable of defending against attacks by ballistic missiles with ranges in excess of 2000 kilometres and possibly carrying nuclear, biological or chemical warheads. The IMDO's preliminary plans envision the Arrow 3 as being the first line in a layered missile defence architecture; current and improved versions of the Arrow 2 would be deployed as a second-echelon guard against target missiles that 'leak' through the initial defence as well as against lesser missile threats.[61] Israel may supplement the lower defence tier with the US-built PAC-3 system.[62]

There is intense interest in Israel in developing an affordable system capable of intercepting artillery rockets and short-range ballistic missiles (SRBMs).[63] In October 2007 the US and Israeli defence ministers agreed to establish a panel to examine an Israeli proposal to augment their countries' missile defence cooperation to include short-range rockets and missiles.[64] Israel is currently developing a system, known as Iron Dome, to address the threat of short-range rockets, including Qassam improvised

[56] ed. Lennox (note 55), p. 248;

[57] Katz, Y., 'IDF modifying Arrow deployment in the north', *Jerusalem Post*, 23 Aug. 2007.

[58] Opall-Rome, B., 'Pentagon extends Arrow funding through 2013', *Defense News*, 15 Feb. 2007.

[59] Hughes, R. and Ben-David, A., 'Arrow 2 test exceeds Israeli expectations', *Jane's Defence Weekly*, 24 Dec. 2003, p. 17.

[60] Isby, D. C., 'Israel upgrades Green Pine', *Jane's Missiles & Rockets*, vol. 10, no. 6 (Mar. 2006), p. 12.

[61] Opall-Rome, B., 'Israel to develop top-tier missile interceptor,' *Defense News*, 22 Oct. 2007.

[62] Katz, Y., 'Air force might buy latest Patriot missile systems', *Jerusalem Post*, 20 Aug. 2007.

[63] Associated Press, 'Israel: Hezbollah militants in Lebanon have new rockets that can hit Tel Aviv, UN chief says', *International Herald Tribune*, 31 Oct. 2007.

[64] Roberts, K. and Williams, D., 'U.S., Israel to study layered missile defenses', Reuters, 10 Oct. 2007, <http://www.reuters.com/article/topNews/idUSN1645256320071017>.

rockets and the 122-mm Katyusha artillery rockets fired into Israel from the Gaza Strip and southern Lebanon by Palestinian and Hezbollah guerrillas.[65] Israel's defence minister has indicated that the system could be ready for deployment by 2010.[66] In addition, in 2006 the IMDO and the US MDA awarded a multi-year contract to an Israeli–US consortium to develop a new Short Range Missile Defense (SRMD) system, which is known as David's Sling, capable of defeating a variety of short-range ballistic missile threats, such as the Iranian-produced Fajr and Zelzal SRBMs deployed by Hezbollah forces in southern Lebanon.[67]

IV. Conclusions

Missile defence remains a high priority for the United States. The DOD's Missile Defense Agency is pursuing a phased set of research and development and procurement programmes for weapon and sensor systems that will be integrated, over time, into a single, multi-layered Ballistic Missile Defence System. The US Administration accelerated key weapon system and sensor programmes in order to begin deploying an initial set of missile defence capabilities by the end of 2004. This has raised concerns about the maturity of the missile defence technologies being developed and about the cost and likely effectiveness of the systems to be deployed.

There are signs of growing interest in missile defence systems in countries other than the USA. This marks a departure from the cold war era, when interest in missile defence was limited primarily to the superpowers. The new interest has been motivated in part by the desire of some countries to promote their defence-industrial cooperation with the USA. More importantly, it has been motivated by the proliferation of short- and medium-range ballistic missiles in specific regional settings, namely East Asia, South Asia and the Middle East.

[65] On Hezbollah's supplies of arms see Wezeman, S. T. et al., 'International arms transfers', *SIPRI Yearbook 2007: Armaments, Disarmament and International Security* (Oxford University Press: Oxford, 2007), pp. 409–11.

[66] Reuters, 'Barak: system for shooting down short-range rockets to be ready by 2010', *Haaretz*, 18 Oct. 2007.

[67] 'Rafael, Raytheon win contract for Israeli defence system', *Jane's Missiles & Rockets*, vol. 10, no. 7 (July 2006), p. 13. The system will reportedly consist of a hit-to-kill interceptor equipped with an infrared sensor

Appendix 8D. Nuclear forensic analysis

VITALY FEDCHENKO

I. Introduction

Like many international treaties and national laws, the 1968 Treaty on the Non-Proliferation of Nuclear Weapons (Non-Proliferation Treaty, NPT) requires mechanisms to verify compliance.[1] The International Atomic Energy Agency (IAEA) has a specific system of safeguards to verify compliance with the treaty's prohibitions on the manufacture of a nuclear weapon by a non-nuclear weapon state. Individual states also have regulatory and law-enforcement agencies whose tasks are to enforce controls on the transfer of nuclear material and to prevent or prosecute the illicit trafficking of nuclear materials. Should the 1996 Comprehensive Nuclear Test-Ban Treaty (CTBT) come into force, the compliance verification mechanism currently being worked on by the Preparatory Commission for the Comprehensive Nuclear Test-Ban Treaty Organization (CTBTO Preparatory Commission, or CTBTO) would apply.[2] Other examples include verification of the proposed fissile material cut-off treaty.[3]

The practical implementation of these verification mechanisms requires the application of appropriate technologies; these verification mechanisms and technologies influence each other. On the one hand, the application of verification arrangements must rely on technology. As technology advances, it provides better means for verification arrangements to pursue their goals. On the other hand, the goals or working conditions of verification mechanisms may change with time, creating a demand for new technologies and even new scientific disciplines. Nuclear forensic analysis (or nuclear forensics) is an example of such a new discipline. Certain nuclear forensic techniques have been used for many years in isolated applications. However, the maturity and popularity of the technologies involved have recently increased to the point where nuclear forensics should be treated as a separate scientific discipline. This appendix explains its importance for the verification and law enforcement applications mentioned above.

Section II of this appendix outlines the definition, major features, applications and some technologies employed by nuclear forensics analysis. Section III gives some examples of the use of nuclear forensic analysis in specific cases. Section IV concludes by discussing the advantages and limitations of nuclear forensics.

II. The definitions, process and technologies of nuclear forensics

The terms 'nuclear forensic analysis' and 'nuclear forensics' were probably first coined in the context of combating nuclear smuggling, a problem that emerged in the

---

[1] For a summary of the NPT and a list of its 190 parties see annex A in this volume.

[2] For a summary and list of signatories of the CTBT, which has yet to enter into force, see annex A in this volume.

[3] On the negotiation of a fissile material cut-off treaty see chapter 8, section V.

early 1990s.[4] The investigations and prosecutions of the first such cases called for the development and application of techniques to analyse the nuclear materials involved in order to produce evidence for use in courts of law—hence the term 'nuclear forensics'.

The *Oxford English Dictionary* defines 'forensic' as 'Pertaining to, connected with, or used in courts of law; suitable or analogous to pleadings in court'.[5] More broadly, the term is understood in the specialized literature as 'the application of science to law'.[6] Although such definitions probably refer mostly to national laws, they could be interpreted as including international laws, regulations and, in particular, treaties.

The IAEA defines *nuclear forensics* as 'the analysis of intercepted illicit nuclear or radioactive material and any associated material to provide evidence for nuclear attribution', where *attribution* refers to 'the process of identifying the source of nuclear or radioactive material used in illegal activities, to determine the point of origin and routes of transit involving such material, and ultimately to contribute to the prosecution of those responsible'.[7]

These IAEA definitions are based on the work of the US Department of Energy's National Laboratories community involved in combating nuclear smuggling.[8] The definitions are used in the context of the IAEA's work on nuclear security, which is separate from the IAEA's safeguards activities.[9] However, the analytical techniques used in the combating of illicit trafficking of nuclear materials have much greater potential and, in fact, have been extensively used for many years in other fields. In order to capture all possible applications of the techniques in question, this appendix uses the following broad definitions.[10]

Nuclear forensic analysis (nuclear forensics) is the analysis of a sample of nuclear or radioactive material and any associated information to provide evidence for determining the history of the sample material. Nuclear forensic analysis includes characterization, nuclear forensic interpretation and reconstruction.

Characterization is the determination of a sample's characteristics. It typically involves an elemental analysis of the sample, most often including isotopic analysis of nuclear materials—uranium (U) or plutonium (Pu)—and selected minor constituents—e.g. lead. It also includes physical characterization, for example, measuring the key dimensions of solid samples or determining the particle size and shape distributions of powder samples.

---

[4] Moody, K. J., Hutcheon, I. D. and Grant, P. M., *Nuclear Forensic Analysis* (CRC Press: Boca Raton, Fla., 2005), pp. vi–vii.

[5] *The Oxford English Dictionary*, vol. IV (Oxford University Press: Oxford, 1978), p. F-438.

[6] Saferstein, R., *Criminalistics: An Introduction to Forensic Science*, 4th edn (Prentice Hall: Englewood Cliffs, N.J., 1990), p. 1, quoted in Moody, Hutcheon and Grant (note 4), p. vi.

[7] International Atomic Energy Agency (IAEA), *Nuclear Forensics Support: Reference Manual*, IAEA Nuclear Security Series no. 2, Technical Guidance (IAEA: Vienna, 2006), pp. 2–3. Most of the IAEA documents and publications cited here are available from the IAEA's website, <http://www.iaea.org/>.

[8] Kristo, M. J. et. al., 'Model action plan for nuclear forensics and nuclear attribution', UCRL-TR-202675, US Department of Energy, Lawrence Livermore National Laboratory, 5 Mar. 2004, <http://www.osti.gov/energycitations/product.biblio.jsp?osti_id=15009803>.

[9] IAEA, 'Nuclear security', <http://www-ns.iaea.org/security/>.

[10] These definitions of 'nuclear forensic analysis', 'characterization', 'nuclear forensic interpretation' and 'reconstruction' were developed on the basis of the IAEA definitions (note 7) in close cooperation with Dr James Acton of King's College London.

Nuclear forensic interpretation is the process of correlating the characteristics of the sample with information on known methods of material production and handling to produce endogenic information about a sample.[11]

Reconstruction is the process of combining the endogenic information obtained by nuclear forensic interpretation with exogenic information to determine as full a history as possible of the nuclear or radioactive material or an event. This phase is called *attribution* in the narrower contexts of investigations of illicit nuclear materials trafficking and nuclear terrorism events.

Usually there are specific features that interest a researcher in the material's history, such as its origin and producer, point of diversion, age, routes of transit and planned end use. The goal of nuclear forensics—to reconstruct the history of the material or an event—makes it a technique of choice in a number of applications. The specific application defines what is required to be found out from the material in the sample. For example, investigators of a nuclear smuggling case would want to determine the source of the material, at which point it was diverted from legitimate uses, what its possible illegitimate use could be, and so on. Investigators of a nuclear or radiological terrorism incident would look for the material's origin in order to ensure a correctly targeted response. IAEA safeguards inspectors may want to know if the isotopic composition and production date of sample material gathered from a state's nuclear facilities correspond to the state's declared inventory. The CTBTO collects air samples in order to verify the nuclear nature of suspected explosions. Verification procedures of a fissile material cut-off treaty, if and when negotiated, would probably include determination of the age of nuclear materials and might include some kind of environmental sampling to ensure that production of new nuclear materials subject to the treaty does not continue.

Analytical processes and technologies

Following the way in which the IAEA analyses the samples collected in the framework of its safeguards activities both illustrates the process of nuclear forensic analysis and allows the most popular technologies involved to be described.[12]

There are two types of samples: samples of nuclear materials and environmental samples (such as swipes from various surfaces of equipment or buildings, or some volume of air, water, sediments, vegetation, soil or biota). The IAEA operates a nuclear material analysis system consisting of two distinct networks of analytical laboratories (NWAL), a Network of Analytical Laboratories for Nuclear Samples and a Network of Analytical Laboratories for Environmental Samples (with 13 active laboratories in seven member states).[13] These laboratories, which are nominated by

---

[11] Endogenic information is information derived from the analysis of the sample material and interpretation of the resulting data. In contrast, exogenic information—e.g. archive material or historical databases—is external to the analysis of the material and interpretation of the results of that analysis. IAEA (note 7), p. 31; and Mayer, K., Wallenius, M. and Ray, I., 'Tracing the origin of diverted or stolen nuclear material through nuclear forensic investigations', eds R. Avenhaus et al., *Verifying Treaty Compliance: Limiting Weapons of Mass Destruction and Monitoring Kyoto Protocol Provisions* (Springer: Heidelberg, 2006), p. 402.

[12] On the use of nuclear forensics for IAEA safeguards see also Fedchenko, V., 'Weapons of mass analysis', *Jane's Intelligence Review*, vol. 19, no. 11 (Nov. 2007), pp. 48–51.

[13] Information on the number of active laboratories was provided by Dr Klaus Mayer. For the formal list, which may also include laboratories that are temporarily uninvolved in the network, see IAEA,

IAEA member states, provide the IAEA with highly specialized measurement capabilities which it could not afford to establish for itself. The IAEA inspectors collect 600–1200 samples every year. In 2006, for example, 756 nuclear samples were collected, 760 were analysed and 1664 verification results were generated. An additional 492 environmental samples were processed as described below.[14]

The first step in sample analysis is characterization. Once collected, environmental samples are shipped to the Clean Laboratory for Safeguards of the IAEA's Safeguards Analytical Laboratory (SAL) in Seibersdorf, Austria. These samples typically contain six cotton swipes, four of which are archived for reference purposes and two of which are analysed.[15] The samples are assigned code numbers to conceal their origin before being screened at SAL for the presence of radioactive isotopes by high-resolution gamma spectrometry (HRGS) and for the presence of uranium and plutonium by X-ray fluorescence analysis (XRF).[16] On the basis of the screening results and according to the IAEA inspectors' requirements, the IAEA identifies methods and laboratories for further sample analysis. These subsequent measurements are conducted by either bulk or particle analysis techniques.

The IAEA Department of Safeguards requests 200–400 bulk analyses of environmental samples each year, which are conducted by about seven members of the NWAL (other than SAL). No information concerning origin is attached to any sample, so bias from laboratory personnel is normally ruled out. Traditionally, bulk analyses are conducted by various mass spectrometry methods, most importantly thermal ionization mass spectrometry (TIMS) and inductively coupled plasma mass spectrometry (ICP-MS).[17]

'Safeguards Analytical Laboratory: IAEA Network of Analytical Laboratories for Safeguards', <http://www.iaea.org/OurWork/ST/NA/NAAL/sal/salCLnwal.php>.

[14] Schmitzer, C. et al., 'The Safeguards Analytical Laboratory and the future of nuclear materials analysis for the IAEA', European Safeguards Research and Development Association (ESARDA), *29th Annual Meeting: Symposium on Safeguards and Nuclear Material Management* (Office for Official Publications of the European Communities: Luxembourg, 2007), p. 1.

[15] Bevaart, L., Donohue, D. and Fuhr, W., 'Future requirements for the analysis of environmental samples and the evaluation of the results', ESARDA (note 14), p. 2.

[16] HRGS is a technique making use of the fact that most radioactive isotopes emit characteristic gamma rays, thus determining the energy and count rate of gamma rays emitted by the material may provide information on its isotopic contents. HRGS is capable of detecting as little as 5 micrograms of uranium, down to tens of nanograms of plutonium, and in some cases, of estimating uranium enrichment. A microgram (μg) is 1×10^{-6} grams; a nanogram (ng) is 1×10^{-9} g.

XRF exploits the fact that, if X-rays bombard a material, they can expel electrons from the inner orbitals of the atoms. Electrons at higher orbitals will 'fall' into the vacant places in lower orbitals and emit X-rays in the process. The energy of such X-rays is characteristic to the element emitting it, and the count rate is proportional to the amount of the element present. The XRF system installed at SAL is reported to have a detection limit for uranium on a swipe of 35 ng per square centimetre. Bevaart, Donohue and Fuhr (note 15), pp. 2–3; and Piksaikin, V. M., Pshakin, G. M. and Roshchenko, V. A., 'Review of methods and instruments for determining undeclared nuclear materials and activities', *Science and Global Security*, vol. 14, no. 1 (Jan.–Apr. 2006), pp. 49–72.

[17] Mass spectrometric techniques utilize the difference in masses of nuclides. The atoms contained in a sample are transformed into ions, separated by an electromagnetic field and counted according to their mass and charge. Mass spectrometric methods differ in the way the sample material is ionized (e.g. thermal ionization or ionization by plasma) and in the type of mass analyser. For TIMS, the entire swipe is ashed and dissolved in acid, then uranium and plutonium are chemically separated, placed on a metallic filament and ionized by heating. For ICP-MS the sample is also dissolved and chemically purified, then it is nebulized in a spray chamber and aspirated into an argon plasma. Moody, Hutcheon and Grant (note 4), pp. 350–54.

TIMS analysis conducted in SAL reportedly allows for detection limits of 70 femtograms of plutonium-239 and 1 nanogram of natural uranium.[18] Much better TIMS uranium detection limits, also down to the femtogram range, have been reported elsewhere.[19] In 2007 SAL was in the process of acquiring ICP-MS equipment, which would allow for less stringent chemical separation procedures and thus decrease the time needed for analysis. ICP-MS detection limits are generally comparable to or better than those of TIMS.[20]

Some samples contain just a few useful particles and so cannot be analysed in bulk. The IAEA normally issues 500–800 requests for analysis of particles in environmental samples each year. Of these, about 40 per cent are analysed using secondary ion mass spectrometry (SIMS) and about 60 per cent using fission track thermal ionization mass spectrometry (FT-TIMS).[21] SIMS is usually used for uranium isotope measurements, while FT-TIMS is used for both uranium and plutonium measurements. FT-TIMS has a lower detection limit, in a pico- and femtogram range, compared with a nano- and picogram range for SIMS.[22] For this reason, in 2007 the IAEA explored the possibilities of installing more FT-TIMS or equivalent capacity, such as ultra-high sensitivity SIMS (UHS-SIMS).[23] Much can be learned by examining the particle visually using optical or electron microscopy, and thus collecting information on its morphology.[24]

Once the characterization of the sample is finished, the IAEA interprets the information produced. For instance, the information on the isotopic composition of plutonium in a collected sample could be used to calculate the date when it was separated from the spent fuel or otherwise chemically purified. As another example, the details of a uranium particle's morphology can yield information on the temperature at which it was formed and thus indicate the production process. All information analysed at this second step is endogenic. Sometimes certain parameters obtained during the characterization and interpretation processes can be combined into a 'nuclear fingerprint'—the combination characteristic for the mode of production of the material.[25]

During the third step—reconstruction—the endogenic information is fed into a broader analysis, which employs all relevant data that is available. In order to reconstruct the history of the material or the facility under consideration, the IAEA Department of Safeguards can use satellite imagery analysis, open source information ana-

---

[18] Bevaart, Donohue and Fuhr (note 15), p. 4. A femtogram (fg) is 1 x 10^{-15} g.

[19] Piksaikin, Pshakin and Roshchenko (note 16), p. 71.

[20] Bevaart, Donohue and Fuhr (note 15), p. 4; and Moody, Hutcheon and Grant (note 4), p. 357.

[21] In SIMS the individual particles in the sample are found and bombarded by a high-energy, finely focused primary ion beam, usually O_2^+, Cs^+, or O^-. The beam penetrates a few nanometers into the particle and causes secondary ions to be 'sputtered' out, making them available for separation according to their mass and analysis.

In FT-TIMS the particles are removed from the swipe, attached to a fission-track plastic (Lexan), and irradiated in a nuclear reactor with thermal neutrons. Fissile isotopes fission during the irradiation and leave tracks in the plastic, which permits the particles containing them to be located under an optical microscope. These particles are then picked out, loaded onto a heating filament and then ionized and analysed by a TIMS instrument. Bevaart, Donohue and Fuhr (note 15), p. 4; and Moody, Hutcheon and Grant (note 4), pp. 354–56.

[22] Piksaikin, Pshakin and Roshchenko (note 16), pp. 71–72. A picogram (pg) is 1 x 10^{-12} g.

[23] Bevaart, Donohue and Fuhr (note 15), p.5.

[24] US Congress, Office of Technology Assessment, *Environmental Monitoring for Nuclear Safeguards*, OTA-BP-ISS-168 (Government Printing Office: Washington, DC, Sep. 1995), p. 26.

[25] Mayer, K. et al., 'Recent advances in nuclear forensic science', ESARDA (note 14), pp. 1–2.

lysis, data on the facility design and associated nuclear trade, as well as other information provided by the member states. At this stage the nuclear fingerprint can be compared against the IAEA's nuclear fingerprint database and other sets of nuclear fingerprints collected elsewhere. The process may be iterative; that is, the results of the reconstruction process may call for additional measurements of the collected samples or for the collection of new samples.

III. Examples of applications of nuclear forensic analysis

The first applications of nuclear forensic analysis took place during and in the aftermath of World War II as the United States and its allies investigated first the German and then the Soviet nuclear programmes. Nuclear forensic techniques were expanded and refined in the subsequent decades as more states developed nuclear capabilities. The entry into force of the NPT created a much greater need for nuclear forensic techniques as the IAEA implemented its comprehensive safeguards agreements (CSAs), most recently in the cases of Iran and North Korea. Demand for nuclear forensic analysis began to grow from the early 1990s partly due to the emergence of nuclear material smuggling and the need to investigate and prosecute such cases.

Examples of the use of nuclear forensics in these varying cases are given below. However, although nuclear smuggling is by far the best known application of nuclear forensics, in both the scientific and popular literature,[26] the examples below focus on less publicized applications.

Analysis of airborne debris to verify nuclear reactor operation[27]

The demand for what have since been named nuclear forensic analysis techniques was probably first recognized and formulated by the head of the British–US Manhattan Project, Brigadier General Leslie R. Groves, in 1943. Finding that the information produced by the US intelligence community was not sufficient to provide an adequate picture of the German nuclear weapon programme, Groves introduced the innovative concept of radiological intelligence.[28] He assigned Luis W. Alvarez, a future Nobel laureate for physics, to develop a method for detecting operating nuclear reactors on German territory.[29]

Alvarez's method involved detecting the radioactive gases that reactors emit during their normal operation, in particular the radioactive isotope xenon-133 (Xe-133). It is generated at a high rate during fission of uranium-235, uranium-238 and plutonium-239, which means that it is produced in significant quantities by any reactor. Xenon is a noble gas, so it escapes a reactor in detectable quantities instead of chemically reacting with other elements. The half-life of Xe-133 is 5.243 days, which means that it does not appear in the atmosphere naturally. It is also relatively easy to separate

---

[26] Moody, Hutcheon and Grant (note 4), pp. 401–20; and e.g. Clancy, T., *The Sum of All Fears* (Putnam: New York, 1991).

[27] The term debris can be applied to all sizes of particles resulting from a nuclear reaction, including gases.

[28] Ziegler, C. A. and Jacobson, D., *Spying without Spies: Origins of America's Secret Nuclear Surveillance System* (Praeger Publishers: Westport, Conn., 1995), pp. 3–9. Groves is also famous for leading the Alsos mission. See Hart, J. D., 'The ALSOS mission, 1943–1945: a secret U.S. scientific intelligence unit', *International Journal of Intelligence*, vol. 18, no. 3 (Oct. 2005).

[29] Alvarez, L. W., *Alvarez: Adventures of a Physicist* (Basic Books: New York, 1989), pp. 119–22.

from the nitrogen and oxygen in the air. All these qualities make Xe-133 perfect for detection as a 'signature' of an operating nuclear facility.[30]

A xenon-detection system consisting of air-sampling equipment and a ground-based laboratory for sample analysis was developed by the summer of 1944. A few Douglas A-26 Invader aircraft collected air samples over Germany in the autumn of 1944, but no Xe-133 was found.[31] This confirmed that Germany did not have any nuclear reactors in operation and initiated a new form of intelligence gathering.

Analysis of airborne debris to verify nuclear weapon tests

Similar equipment designed to filter out airborne radioactive particles was later mounted on Boeing WB-29 aircraft and used to detect the first Soviet nuclear weapon tests. The first such test, designated RDS-1 in the Soviet Union, was conducted on 29 August 1949 at the Semipalatinsk test site, which is now within the territory of Kazakhstan. By the spring of 1949 the US radiological intelligence agency, AFOAT-1 (Air Force, deputy chief of staff for Operations, Atomic Energy Office, Section 1), had established routine airborne dust collection flights along two routes— from Fairbanks, Alaska, to the North Pole and from Fairbanks to Yokota, Japan—in order to analyse air masses travelling eastward from Soviet territory.[32]

On 3 September 1949 the WB-29 aircraft returning to Fairbanks from Japan collected the first traces of radioactive particles, which were presumably carried to the Pacific from the Semipalatinsk nuclear test site in an air mass. During the following days an all-out effort was made to collect as many samples as possible. Since the air mass containing particles had moved on over the territory of North America to the northern regions of the Atlantic, the USA also enlisted the help of the British atomic energy authorities and the British Royal Air Force.[33]

Analysis of the particles collected revealed the presence of fission products, mostly isotopes of barium, cerium, iodine and molybdenum. The radioactive isotopes all had the same age, indicating that their probable origin was a bomb explosion rather than a nuclear reactor accident. Also, the fission product yield curve was more consistent with the fission of plutonium than of highly enriched uranium (HEU), so the US scientists guessed that the Soviet nuclear weapon was plutonium-based and was therefore an implosion-type bomb.[34] In addition, US scientists tested the particles for traces of neptunium-237, an isotope produced from U-238 in nuclear reactions involving energetic neutrons. The test allowed the conclusion that the RDS-1 bomb probably had a layer of natural uranium as a tamper and reflector.[35]

---

[30] Saey, P. R. J., 'Ultra-low-level measurements of argon, krypton and radioxenon for treaty verification purposes', *ESARDA Bulletin*, no. 36 (July 2007), p. 44; and Kalinowski, M. B. et al., 'Environmental sample analysis', eds Avenhaus et al. (note 11), pp. 376–77.

[31] Ziegler and Jacobson (note 28), pp.7–8.

[32] Ziegler and Jacobson (note 28), p. 201.

[33] Ziegler and Jacobson (note 28), pp. 204–11.

[34] The fission product yield curve, sometimes referred to as the 'Mae West curve' due to its characteristic 2-peak form, is a graph of the mass or mole yield of fission products against their atomic number. Its shape depends on the fissile isotope and the energy of the neutrons inducing fission. See e.g. Saey (note 30), p. 43.

[35] A tamper is a layer of a dense material that surrounds the fissile material in a nuclear weapon. The tamper lengthens the short time for which the material holds together under the extreme pressures of the explosion and thereby increases the efficiency of the weapon by increasing the proportion of the fissile material that undergoes fission. A neutron reflector is a layer of material immediately surrounding the

Analysing the known meteorological data, meteorologists made backward projections of the trajectories of the air masses. The calculated age of the radioactive isotopes in the samples gave an estimate of the time of the event: sometime between 26 and 29 August 1949. This provided the cut-off time at which to stop the backward projection of air mass trajectories and thus defined, accurately but not precisely, the area where the test was conducted.[36]

It is important to note that all this information was obtained using the radio-chemical analysis methods available at the time. Contemporary analysis methodologies and equipment are reported to be much more advanced and sensitive and to be capable of providing more data on a weapon's design, yield and other parameters.[37] The same or similar techniques could also be employed to provide information on the origin of the nuclear material used in a nuclear explosive device set off in an act of terrorism. For instance, post-explosion analysis of the fission products may provide estimates of the pre-explosion isotopic content of the fuel.[38] This, in turn, may provide a nuclear fingerprint which can be used to identify the source of the material and, perhaps, to ensure correctly targeted retribution.

The successful detection of the RDS-1 test spurred the rapid development of the USA's global nuclear explosion monitoring infrastructure. The monitoring is performed by the US Atomic Energy Detection System (USAEDS), operated by AFOAT-1's successor, the US Air Force Technical Applications Center (AFTAC). In addition to national intelligence activities, AFTAC monitors compliance with the 1963 Partial Test-Ban Treaty (PTBT), the 1974 Threshold Test-Ban Treaty and the 1976 Peaceful Nuclear Explosions Treaty.[39] In 1998 USAEDS detected and confirmed the nuclear nature of explosions in India and Pakistan.

USAEDS was also involved in investigating the so-called Vela incident in 1979. On 21 September 1979 AFTAC personnel conducting a routine readout of the Vela 6911 monitoring satellite received sensor readings very similar to the 'double flash' that is characteristic of an atmospheric nuclear weapon test.[40] The US Government launched an extensive investigation, including a massive air sampling operation by AFTAC aircraft and the collection of environmental samples by Central Intelligence Agency (CIA) personnel. No traces of radioactive debris relevant to the event were found.[41]

Following North Korea's announcement in October 2006 that it had conducted an underground nuclear test, the US Air Force dispatched its WC-135W Constant Phoenix atmospheric collection aircraft, which is normally used for verification of the PTBT. It collected useful samples starting from two days after the event. Based on the analysis of collected radioactive debris, AFTAC was able to verify to US national

---

fissile material which reflects neutrons back to the core and thus reduces the critical mass of the missile material and increases the weapon's efficiency.

[36] Ziegler and Jacobson (note 28), pp. 204–11.

[37] Moody, Hutcheon and Grant (note 4), pp. 203–205.

[38] Moody, Hutcheon and Grant (note 4), p. 205.

[39] For summaries of these treaties and lists of their parties see annex A in this volume.

[40] The nature of a double flash produced by a nuclear explosion in the atmosphere is explained in Barasch, G. E., 'Light flash produced by an atmospheric nuclear explosion', LASL-79-84, Los Alamos Scientific Laboratory, Nov. 1979, <http://www.gwu.edu/~nsarchiv/NSAEBB/NSAEBB190/>.

[41] Richelson, J. T., Spying on the Bomb: American Nuclear Intelligence from Nazi Germany to Iran and North Korea (W. W. Norton & Company: New York, 2006), pp. 288, 315.

authorities that 'the event was nuclear in nature'.[42] The governments of the USA and other states that had investigated North Korea's claim and, later, the CTBTO independently concluded that the event had been a nuclear explosion.[43]

The US Government did not provide details of the radioactive sample collection and analysis that followed North Korea's announcement. A non-governmental researcher has concluded that the aircraft was probably able to collect only two fission products in detectable quantities: Xe-133 and Xe-135.[44] The same study concluded that the activity ratio of these two isotopes could be used to confirm that the test was nuclear, although the samples were probably not sufficient to 'determine the fissile material used . . . , particularly if detected as much as two days after a test'.[45] Much less information could have been derived from collected debris in the case of the 2006 North Korea test than that of the 1949 RDS-1 test because the former explosion was underground, concealing almost all isotopes.

The same capacities employed by AFTAC in nuclear test verification are also used to help with the IAEA's safeguards work. AFTAC is a member of the IAEA's NWAL, specializing in analysing environmental samples.[46] As of 2007, AFTAC is one of three organizations in the world providing the IAEA with the capacity to analyse the isotopic composition of particles in swipe samples using one of the most sensitive techniques available, FT-TIMS.[47]

Uranium particle analysis to verify Iran's declaration to the IAEA

Media reports published in August 2002 prompted the IAEA to investigate the existence of undeclared uranium enrichment facilities in Iran.[48] During the visit of a high-level IAEA delegation to Iran in February 2003, Iranian authorities acknowledged the construction of two centrifuge enrichment plants at Natanz, the Pilot Fuel Enrichment Plant (PFEP) and the large Fuel Enrichment Plant (FEP), as well as the existence of a workshop of the Kalaye Electric Company (KEC) in Tehran used for production of centrifuge components. Iran stated that its enrichment programme was indigenous

---

[42] US Air Force Intelligence, Surveillance and Reconnaissance Agency, 'Air Force Technical Applications Center', Fact sheet, June 2007, <http://www.afisr.af.mil/library/factsheets/factsheet.asp?id= 10309>.

[43] US Office of the Director of National Intelligence, 'Statement by the Office of the Director of National Intelligence on the North Korea nuclear test', News release, 16 Oct. 2006, <http://www.dni. gov/announcements/announcements.htm>; Fedchenko, V. and Ferm Hellgren, R., 'Nuclear explosions, 1945–2006', *SIPRI Yearbook 2007: Armaments, Disarmament and International Security* (Oxford University Press: Oxford, 2007), pp. 552–57; and CTBTO, 'The CTBT verification regime put to the test: the event in the DPRK on 9 October 2006', Featured article, 4 Sep. 2007, <http://www.ctbto.org/press_centre/featured_articles/2007/2007_0409_dprk.htm>. Among the other states that investigated the event, Sweden collected and analysed air samples from South Korea. Swedish Defence Research Agency (FOI), 'FOI found radioactive xenon following explosion in North Korea', Press release, 19 Dec. 2006, <http://www.foi.se/FOI/Templates/NewsPage____5412.aspx>.

[44] Zhang, H., 'Off-site air sampling analysis and North Korean nuclear test', Proceedings of the Institute for Nuclear Materials Management 48th Annual Meeting, Tucson, Ariz., 8–12 July 2007, <http://www.belfercenter.org/publication/17537/>.

[45] Zhang (note 44), p. 6.

[46] IAEA (note 13).

[47] US Congress (note 24), p. 26; IAEA (note 13); and Bevaart, Donohue and Fuhr (note 15).

[48] For a detailed account of the disclosure of Iran's pursuit of sensitive nuclear fuel cycle technologies see Kile, S. N., 'Nuclear arms control and non-proliferation', *SIPRI Yearbook 2004: Armaments, Disarmament and International Security* (Oxford University Press: Oxford, 2004), pp. 604–12.

and that no enrichment activities involving actual nuclear material were being conducted at those or other locations at that time.[49]

That was a claim of a considerable significance because Iran—like any other nonnuclear weapon state party to the NPT which has in force a CSA with the IAEA—is required to declare any new nuclear facility before it commences operation and to provide the IAEA with specific information on its design.[50] States do so by completing a design information questionnaire (DIQ). The specific details of the DIQ submission are defined in an annex to the safeguards agreement that describes subsidiary arrangements. Such subsidiary arrangements are negotiated by the IAEA separately with each state.

Since 1976 all states have been required to complete a DIQ for any new installation no later than 180 days before the introduction of nuclear material to the facility. In the aftermath of the 1991 Gulf War the IAEA Board of Governors decided to change the subsidiary arrangements in subsequently negotiated CSAs so that the states would have to 'provide design information to the Agency at the time of the decision to construct, or to authorize the construction of, any nuclear facility (i.e. well before construction actually begins) in order to create confidence in the peaceful purpose of the facility'.[51] However, Iran did not accede to these new rules until 26 February 2003, after the existence of enrichment facilities had been discovered.[52]

Thus, if no nuclear material had been introduced to those facilities before they were discovered, Iran had not committed an act of non-compliance with its CSA. If the material had been introduced, then the failure to declare such a facility would be in contravention of Iran's CSA.[53]

In order to determine whether nuclear material had been introduced into the facilities, the IAEA began to take environmental samples at the Natanz plants in March and at the Tehran workshop in August 2003.[54] The IAEA inspectors noted that there had been 'considerable modification' of the KEC site before they could take samples and that this 'may impact on the accuracy of the environmental sampling and the Agency's ability to verify Iran's declarations'.[55] Despite the interference, samples revealed the presence of uranium particles at both sites that were not consistent with the material in the inventory declared by Iran to the IAEA.

In total, discoveries of particles of natural uranium, low-enriched uranium (LEU) and HEU particles of up to 70 per cent enrichment (with the majority of the HEU being enriched to 36–54 per cent of U-235) were reported by the IAEA. This pro-

[49] IAEA, Board of Governors, 'Implementation of the NPT safeguards agreement in the Islamic Republic of Iran', Report by the Director General, GOV/2003/40, 6 June 2003, p. 2.

[50] 'Design information' is defined by the IAEA as 'information concerning nuclear material subject to safeguards . . . and the features of facilities relevant to safeguarding such material'. IAEA, *IAEA Safeguards Glossary*, International Nuclear Verification Series no. 3, 2001 edn (IAEA: Vienna, 2002), p. 26.

[51] IAEA, Board of Governors, 'Strengthening of agency safeguards: the provision and use of design information', GOV/2554/Attachment 2/Rev.2, 1 Apr. 1992, p. 1. See also Hibbs, M., 'Safeguards agreement required early completion of DIQ by Syria', *Nuclear Fuel*, vol. 32, no. 23 (5 Nov. 2007), p. 9; and Schriefer, D., 'The international level', eds Avenhaus et al. (note 11), pp. 437, 452.

[52] IAEA (note 49), p. 4.

[53] In fact, if Iran had intended to introduce nuclear material into the facilities within 180 days of their discovery, then, technically, Iran would have been in contravention of its CSA. However, there is no way in which such a supposition could be proved.

[54] IAEA, Board of Governors, 'Implementation of the NPT Safeguards Agreement in the Islamic Republic of Iran', Report by the Director General, GOV/2003/75, 10 Nov. 2003, annex 1, pp. 7–8.

[55] IAEA, Board of Governors, 'Implementation of the NPT Safeguards Agreement in the Islamic Republic of Iran', Report by the Director General, GOV/2003/63, 26 Aug. 2003, p. 7.

vided conclusive evidence of undeclared activity: either enriched uranium had been imported or enrichment experiments had taken place in Iran. Many of the LEU and HEU particles also had an elevated U-236 content, suggesting the use of uranium extracted from spent nuclear fuel. This again pointed to either unknown reprocessing activities or an import of enriched material.[56]

Confronted with the evidence, Iran admitted its involvement in both undeclared domestic enrichment experiments and a covert international nuclear trade. In a letter of 21 October 2003 Iran admitted that, contrary to its earlier statements, it had conducted small-scale enrichment experiments between 1999 and 2002. These experiments achieved an enrichment level of no more than 1.2 per cent U-235.[57] More importantly, in August 2003 Iran officially admitted that it had in fact imported some centrifuge parts. It suggested that the HEU contamination originated from imported parts and identified Pakistan as a supplier.[58] Pakistan eventually agreed to hand over centrifuge components requested by the IAEA to allow comparison of uranium particles.[59] The IAEA received components on 21 May 2005, took swipe samples and analysed them at SAL. The results confirmed that most of the contamination was probably of Pakistani origin, as stated by Iran.[60]

The experience in Iran has demonstrated that, although nuclear forensic techniques may be useful for safeguards implementation, they must be complemented with other sources of data, such as open source analysis, satellite imagery and information from IAEA member states. The discovery of enriched uranium in Iran was possible only after the IAEA learned about the Natanz plants from elsewhere.

Plutonium age determination to verify North Korea's initial declaration

North Korea acceded to the NPT in 1985 and, after a significant delay, signed a comprehensive safeguards agreement with the IAEA on 30 January 1992.[61] As required by Article 62 of the CSA, on 4 May 1992 North Korea submitted to the IAEA 'an initial report on all nuclear material subject to safeguards'.[62]

The report contained a declaration that North Korea had conducted a single experiment in March 1990 at the Radiochemical Laboratory in Yongbyon on separating less than 100 grams of plutonium from the damaged spent fuel rods removed from the

---

[56] IAEA, Board of Governors, 'Implementation of the NPT Safeguards Agreement in the Islamic Republic of Iran', Report by the Director General, GOV/2004/83, 15 Nov. 2004, p. 9.

[57] IAEA (note 54), pp. 6–7.

[58] Kile, S. N., 'Nuclear arms control and non-proliferation', *SIPRI Yearbook 2005: Armaments, Disarmament and International Security* (Oxford University Press: Oxford, 2005), pp. 558–59.

[59] Bokhari, F., 'Pakistan may hand over nuclear centrifuges', *Financial Times*, 25 Mar. 2005; and 'Centrifuge parts sent to IAEA', *Dawn* (Karachi), 27 May 2005.

[60] IAEA, Board of Governors, 'Implementation of the NPT Safeguards Agreement in the Islamic Republic of Iran', Report by the Director General, GOV/2005/67, 2 Sep. 2005, p. 4.

[61] The Agreement of 30 January 1992 between the Government of the Democratic People's Republic of Korea and the International Atomic Energy Agency for the Application of Safeguards in Connection with the Treaty on the Non-Proliferation of Nuclear Weapons entered into force on 10 Apr. 1992; its text is published in IAEA, INFCIRC/403, May 1992. See also Lockwood, D. and Wolfsthal, J. B., 'Nuclear weapon developments and proliferation', *SIPRI Yearbook 1993: World Armaments and Disarmament* (Oxford University Press: Oxford, 1993), p. 244.

[62] An 'initial report' is defined by the IAEA as a document required under the CSA containing 'an official statement by the State on all nuclear material subject to safeguards', from which the IAEA 'establishes a unified inventory of all nuclear material . . . for the State'. IAEA (note 50), p. 94.

adjacent 25 megawatt-thermal gas-graphite reactor. In the summer of 1992 the IAEA conducted initial inspections in order to verify this and other declared information.

Inspectors took swipe samples from inside and outside glove boxes at the end of the reprocessing line at Yongbyon, where freshly separated plutonium is converted from liquid form into oxide compound. Inspectors also took samples of separated plutonium and the nuclear waste from which it was said to have been separated. The samples were sent to SAL and US laboratories to determine their elemental and isotopic composition. These data could then be used for calculating the 'age' of the material.[63]

The 'age' of nuclear material is defined as the time elapsed since its last separation or latest chemical purification. Plutonium isotopes undergo various types of radioactive decay, producing so-called daughter nuclides. The greater is the age of the material, the more the 'parent' isotope decays, to be replaced by daughter nuclides. In other words, 'the disintegration of a radioactive (parent-) isotope and the build up of a corresponding amount of daughter nuclide serve as built-in chronometer'.[64] The ratios of some parent–daughter pairs can therefore be useful to calculate the material's age. For plutonium such pairs are: Pu-238–U-234, Pu-239–U-235, Pu-240–U-236 and Pu-241–americium-241.

The age of the plutonium in the North Korean swipe samples should have been the time since it was separated from the spent fuel, which was declared as being slightly more than two years by the time of the analysis in the summer of 1992. The analysis of the plutonium decay products by the IAEA suggested that North Korea separated plutonium not once, as declared, but three times—in 1989, 1990 and 1991. The analysis could not determine the amount of separated plutonium that had been produced, but it did provide yet more evidence that the North Korean declaration to the IAEA was not entirely correct.[65]

Age determination techniques could also form part of the verification processes of the proposed fissile material cut-off treaty. In this context, samples of both plutonium and uranium could be analysed in order to establish if they were produced before or after a certain cut-off date.

IV. Conclusions

Developments in technology offer continual improvements in the tools for verification and enforcement of national and global non-proliferation mechanisms. One of those tools, nuclear forensic analysis, was invented in its earliest form even before the first nuclear weapon was tested. For decades it developed in the context of cold war arms control treaty verification, until its utility for other important applications—such as nuclear smuggling investigations, IAEA safeguards and CTBT verification—was demonstrated during the 1990s. The anti-terrorism capability of nuclear forensics has been emphasized since the terrorist attacks of 11 September 2001 on the USA.

Nuclear forensic analysis is an impressive tool that is capable of extracting useful information from minute traces of material. It is most productive if used in con-

[63] Fischer, D., *History of the International Atomic Energy Agency: The First Forty Years* (IAEA: Vienna, 1997), p. 289; and Albright, D., 'North Korean plutonium production', *Science & Global Security*, vol. 5, no. 1 (Dec. 1994), pp. 66–67.

[64] Mayer, Wallenius and Ray (note 11), p. 401.

[65] Albright (note 63), p. 66.

nection with other techniques: nuclear weapon test analysis is more precise if examination of airborne radioactive debris is complemented with seismological, hydro-acoustic and infrasound monitoring; and environmental sampling is most useful for IAEA safeguards verification if complemented with input from open source and overhead imagery analysis and improved provision of design information.

There are also legal and political constraints. Nuclear forensics is most useful if applied quickly and as close to the event as possible. The denial of timely access to the location or the material can diminish accuracy or, in extreme cases, prevent useful information from being obtained by nuclear forensics. Although often designed specifically to deal with the lack of access, the technology is still limited by the external conditions determining when and how it can be applied. Thus, while of increasing importance, nuclear forensics remains just one tool in the verification and enforcement toolbox.

9. Reducing security threats from chemical and biological materials

JOHN HART and PETER CLEVESTIG

I. Introduction

Chemical and biological warfare (CBW) prevention and response measures are evolving away from state-based CBW programmes to encompass more diffuse, less quantifiable, non-state and sometimes speculative threat scenarios—such as those involving improvised devices that contain toxic chemicals or pathogens. Actors that were traditionally on the periphery of efforts to prohibit CBW, such as public health providers, are now routinely included in threat perceptions and risk analyses.

The increasing involvement of the security sector in scientific research into the prevention of CBW has also continued to raise concern about the free pursuit and dissemination of peaceful scientific research. In the absence of effective security (e.g. bio-security) the expanded bio-preparedness research in some states may also pose an inherent threat.[1] The growing number of high-level containment laboratories and the greater range of pathogens studied are promoting the spread of potentially sensitive data and expertise. This is exacerbating the dilemma posed by the dual-purpose nature of the biological and chemical materials handled.

Section II of this chapter discusses the assessment and control of the security threats posed by chemical and biological material, the meeting of the states parties to the 1972 Biological and Toxin Weapons Convention (BTWC) and the 12th Conference of the States Parties (CSP) to the 1993 Chemical Weapons Convention (CWC).[2] Allegations of violations of these treaties and of past CBW programmes are described in section III. Past CBW activities in Iraq and the disbanding of the United Nations Special Commission on Iraq (UNMOVIC) are discussed in section IV. Developments in CBW prevention, response and remediation—including international non-proliferation and dis-

---

[1] This chapter uses the World Health Organization definition of bio-security: 'the principles, technologies and practices implemented to secure pathogens, toxins and sensitive technology from unauthorized access, loss, theft, misuse, diversion or intentional release'. World Health Organization (WHO), *Biorisk Management: Laboratory Biosecurity Guidance* (WHO: Geneva, Sep. 2006), <http://www.who.int/resources/publications/biosafety/WHO_CDS_EPR_2006_6/en/>.

[2] For summaries of the Convention on the Prohibition of the Development, Production and Stockpiling of Bacteriological (Biological) and Toxin Weapons and on Their Destruction and of the Convention on the Prohibition of the Development, Production, Stockpiling and Use of Chemical Weapons and on Their Destruction see annex A in this volume.

armament assistance, bio-security and bio-safety,[3] chemical security and scientific and technological developments—are analysed in section V. The conclusions are presented in section VI. Appendix 9A addresses international public health diplomacy and the global surveillance of avian influenza.

II. The assessment and control of security threats posed by chemical and biological material

Arms control and disarmament regimes have traditionally addressed threats posed by state-run CBW programmes. Despite some uncertainty about the evaluations, the number of known and suspected programmes listed in major 'status of proliferation' reports has fallen in recent years.[4] Much of the uncertainty is due to a lack of agreement on the dividing line between offensive and defensive work and concern that offensive CBW standby capacities might be maintained under the guise of so-called protective or defence research programmes, including counterterrorism and peacekeeping programmes.[5] The difficulties in determining the difference between offensive and defensive work are also at the centre of discussions to implement effective oversight of scientific research and development (R&D) work.

Since the 11 September 2001 terrorist attacks in the United States, defence planners and analysts have placed greater emphasis on the development of threat scenarios involving non-state actors. The number of publications and reports on these threats, particularly those concerning bioterrorism (some of which are repetitive and use secondary sources), continues to rise. Some are based on information that considers specific events and developments, while others are more general, open-ended vulnerability assessments. Information on the effects of a release of pathogens is inadequate (mainly due to the limited number of cases of the accidental release of pathogens or bioterrorism), and it is difficult to predict whether a given bioterrorism incident would cause numerous casualties and deaths.

---

[3] Bio-safety is safety while working with pathogens. See Kuhlau, F., *Countering Bio-threats: EU Instruments for Managing Biological Materials, Technology and Knowledge*, SIPRI Policy Paper no. 19 (SIPRI: Stockholm, Aug. 2007), <http://books.sipri.org/>.

[4] E.g. Milton Leitenberg observes that, although it can be argued that the number of states claimed by the USA to possess biological weapons (BWs) has (since the mid-1980s) remained more or less stable at 12–13, there has been a notable reduction of states cited since the mid-1990s. Leitenberg, M., 'Evolution of the current threat', eds A. Wenger and R. Wollenmann, *Bioterrorism: Confronting a Complex Threat* (Lynne Rienner: London, 2007), pp. 39–76. A comparative analysis of US 'status of proliferation' assessments is difficult partly because they are not consistently made public; the agencies involved sometimes arrive at differing conclusions; and the assessments that are made public generally contain caveats that leave open the possibility that the state does not possess BWs or an offensive BW programme, but rather a 'BW-capability'.

[5] See Hart, J. D., 'The ALSOS Mission, 1943–1945: a secret US scientific intelligence unit', *International Journal of Intelligence and CounterIntelligence*, vol. 18, no. 3 (fall 2005), pp. 508–37; Leitenberg, M., 'Biological weapons arms control', *Contemporary Security Policy*, vol. 17, no. 1 (Apr. 1996), pp. 1–79; and Roffey, R., 'Biological weapons and potential indicators of offensive biological weapon activities', *SIPRI Yearbook 2004: Armaments, Disarmament and International Security* (Oxford University Press: Oxford, 2004), pp. 557–71.

Much of the current focus on efforts to evaluate and meet possible security threats posed by chemical and biological material deals with disparate possibilities concerning actors and institutions that have traditionally not been directly involved in CBW arms control and disarmament efforts. Some efforts encompass the chemical industry; the possible challenges posed to the BTWC and the CWC by biological and chemical incapacitants; the monitoring and oversight of scientific research, material and equipment; effectively extending state-based legal obligations to individuals and groups;[6] disease surveillance and response; and the consideration of ethics and codes of conduct for life science and chemistry practitioners, including researchers and students.[7] Various procedural and legal aspects of the implementation of arms control regimes also continue to be addressed.

Biological weapon arms control and disarmament

International biological warfare prevention efforts in 2007 included consideration of effective national implementing legislation, codes of conduct and ethics, disease surveillance and response, and bio-safety and bio-security.

In 2007 the UN Office for Disarmament Affairs (ODA) started to develop a Bio-incident Database, as called for by the 2006 UN Global Counter-Terrorism Strategy.[8] The ODA requested that the UN member states provide an updated list—last compiled in 1989—of qualified experts and laboratories to support the UN Secretary-General's authority to investigate alleged chemical and biological weapon use.[9] The ODA also organized two meetings of technical experts to review the technical guidelines and procedures for carrying out such inspections.[10] The groups of experts updated the technical part of the guidelines in order to ensure that scientific and technological changes are reflected, including an increased focus on the biological field.

The International Criminal Police Organization (Interpol) continued to implement a Biocriminalization Project, an initiative launched by its Bioterrorism Prevention Program in September 2006, which includes the development of a Biocriminalization Database.[11]

---

[6] This is required by Article IV of the BTWC and Article VII of the CWC.

[7] E.g. Miller, S. and Selgelid, M. J., 'Ethical and philosophical consideration of the dual-use dilemma in the biological sciences', *Science and Engineering Ethics*, vol. 13, no. 4 (Dec. 2007), pp. 523–80.

[8] UN Global Counter-Terrorism Strategy, <http://www.un.org/terrorism/>.

[9] UN General Assembly, 'Chemical and bacteriological (biological) weapons', Report of the Secretary-General, UN document A/44/561, 4 Oct. 1989. The UN documents cited here are available from <http://documents.un.org/>.

[10] United Nations, 'UN action to counter terrorism, implementing the Global Counter-Terrorism strategy', Fact sheet, Dec. 2007, p. 3. See also Littlewood, J., *Investigating Allegations of CBW Use: Reviving the UN Secretary-General's Mechanism*, Compliance Chronicles, no. 3 (Canada Centre for Treaty Compliance: Ottawa, Dec. 2006). The current ODA activities focus primarily on the requirements to support investigations of alleged biological weapon use because the Organisation for the Prohibition of Chemical Weapons would have primary responsibility for investigation of alleged chemical weapon use.

[11] Interpol, 'Bioterrorism, biocriminalization', Public information sheet, <http://www.interpol.int/Public/BioTerrorism/bioC/default.asp>.

In 2007 states considered further the appropriate division of responsibility for bioterrorism efforts. This included discussion of how the Interpol and ODA database projects relate to each other. The ODA database is meant to operate in nearly real time and the data sets would be provided directly from governments. If a bio-incident were determined to be hoax, the incident would be deleted from the ODA database. Interpol's database, in contrast, is a criminal police data set that cannot be fully released until or unless a prosecution is final or the member state providing the information allows it to be shared with the public. Such efforts are meant to assist capacity building by states to meet bio-threats.[12]

The importance has also been noted of distinguishing at least eight categories of biological weapon-related events: hoaxes, threats, the consideration or discussion of use, product tampering, the purchase of material, attacks on facilities, attempts to produce agents or to use them, and actual use.[13]

Implementation of the BTWC

As of 31 December 2007, 159 states had ratified or acceded to the BTWC.[14] In December 2006 the Sixth Review Conference to the convention agreed an inter-sessional process for 2007–10 which consists of four annual meetings to 'discuss, and promote common understanding and effective action' on four areas.[15] Of these, the inter-sessional—one expert, one political—meetings in 2007 considered: (a) ways and means to enhance national implementation, including enforcement of national legislation, strengthening of national institutions and coordination among national law enforcement institutions; and (b) regional and subregional cooperation on BTWC implementation.[16]

In 2007 the temporary three-person Implementation Support Unit (ISU), established by the Sixth Review Conference, also began to operate. The ISU, which became fully operational on 2 August and is located at the UN Office at Geneva, provides support for inter-sessional meetings and receives and distributes politically binding information exchanges meant to serve as confidence-building measures (CBMs) among the BTWC parties.[17] In 2007 it

---

[12] See Kellman, B., *Bioviolence: Preventing Biological Terror and Crime* (Cambridge University Press: New York, 2007).

[13] Leitenberg (note 4), p. 48.

[14] The states that had signed but not ratified the BTWC were Burundi, Central African Republic, Côte d'Ivoire, Egypt, Guyana, Haiti, Liberia, Madagascar, Malawi, Myanmar (Burma), Nepal, Somalia, Syria, Tanzania and United Arab Emerates. The UN member states that had neither signed nor ratified the convention were Angola, Cameroon, Chad, Comoros, Cook Islands, Djibouti, Eritrea, Guinea, Israel, Kiribati, Marshall Islands, Mauritania, Micronesia, Mozambique, Namibia, Nauru, Niue, Samoa, Tuvalu and Zambia. For a list of signatories see annex A in this volume.

[15] For information on the Sixth Review Conference see Hart, J. and Kuhlau, F., 'Chemical and biological weapon developments and arms control', *SIPRI Yearbook 2007: Armaments, Disarmament and International Security* (Oxford University Press: Oxford, 2007), pp. 578–83.

[16] Sixth BTWC Review Conference, 'Final document', document BWC/CONF.VI/6, Dec. 2006, p. 21.

[17] UN Office at Geneva, Disarmament, restricted area for States Parties [to the BTWC], <http://www.unog.ch/bwc/restricted>. The annual, politically binding information exchanges are meant to serve as CBMs to help strengthen the treaty regime.

produced a CD-ROM containing all CBM returns for the period 1987–2007 (available to BTWC parties only) and established a website (only accessible to BTWC parties) as the principal method for the dissemination of BTWC-related information and access to a National Implementation Database.[18]

A 2007 study of CBM returns from 10 states from three geographic group-ings concluded that there is great variation between states in terms of their authority to obtain required information due to differences in respective levels of available resources and type of legal authority. The study also found that there was uncertainty among the parties on the type of information to be declared between and within states, and that a subjective element is present in the evaluation of what information is relevant and should therefore be declared.[19]

The European Union (EU) extended until April 2008 the implementation of a Council joint action to support the BTWC by promoting universal member-ship to the convention and national implementation of its provisions. It did so partly by convening five regional workshops in 2006–2007 to explain the benefits of joining the convention to non-parties and offering states technical assistance to join and implement the treaty. A survey of national legislation and the extent to which the convention is effectively implemented was also carried out.[20] A number of the parties, including Australia, Indonesia and the USA, continued to host and carry out regional activities on BTWC implemen-tation, bio-safety and bio-security.

More specific information on the status of achieving universal membership to the BTWC also became available. An Israeli government representative stated in 2007 that Israel agrees that 'the threat of biological warfare is indeed an ominous one' but that 'regional circumstances . . . cannot be overlooked' and 'it is our sincere hope that the future will yield improved regional circum-stances which would allow a renewed consideration of this issue'.[21] According to Masood Khan, the chairman of the 2007 inter-sessional meetings of BTWC states parties, the preparations to accede to or ratify the BTWC in five states were 'well advanced',[22] while efforts to do the same in a further eight states,

---

[18] The database is password accessible at <http://www.unog.ch/bwc/NID>. See UN Office at Geneva, Implementation Support Unit, Report of the Implementation Support Unit, document BWC/MSP/2007/3*, 4 Dec. 2007.

[19] Lentzos, F. and Woodward, A., *National Data Collection Processes for CBM Submissions: Revisit-ing the Confidence Building Measures (CBM) of the Biological and Toxin Weapons Convention (BTWC) after Twenty Years of CBM Submissions* (London School of Economics and Verification Research, Training and Information Centre: London, Dec. 2007). On CBM-related issues see also the publications of the Hamburg Research Group for Biological Arms Control, <http://www.biological-arms-control.org/Publications.htm>.

[20] Council of the European Union, 'EU Joint Action in support of the Biological and Toxin Weapons Convention', <http://www.euja-btwc.eu/euja>; and Council Joint Action 2006/184/CFSP of 27 February 2006 in support of the Biological and Toxin Weapons Convention, in the framework of the EU Strategy against the Proliferation of Weapons of Mass Destruction, *Official Journal of the European Union*, L65 (7 Mar. 2006), pp. 51–55.

[21] Khan, M., 'Biological Weapons Convention: Meeting of Experts 2007, interim report by the Chair-man, Ambassador Masood Khan (Pakistan), on universalization activities', 24 Aug. 2007, Geneva, docu-ment circulated to Meeting of Expert participants.

[22] The states were Burundi, Comoros, Madagascar, Mozambique and Myanmar (Burma).

while positive, were at an earlier stage.[23] He also listed states for which he had little indication about the time frame for their joining the BTWC,[24] while three states indicated that they did not intend to join the regime in the near future because of 'regional security circumstances'.[25] An additional eight states provided no feedback to his request for information.[26]

The 2007 meetings of the parties to the BTWC

The Meeting of Experts took place on 20–24 August 2007, and the Meeting of States Parties was held on 10–14 December.[27] Both were conducted under the chairmanship of Masood Khan of Pakistan and consisted of exchanges of information, views and consideration of offers for cooperation and assistance.

The Meeting of Experts circulated and considered papers describing the parties' experiences in implementing the BTWC and measures to improve cooperation among national agencies. A consolidated list of the BTWC parties' key texts from national papers and statements was also produced.[28] Khan identified the following themes of the meeting: (a) approaches to national implementation should be tailored to meet the specific cases (i.e. to avoid the 'one size fits all' approach),[29] (b) the ISU should be used as 'a catalyst in better coordinating and managing activities', and (c) the parties need to assist each other with building capacity to better implement the convention. He also thanked the EU, India, Pakistan and the USA for their readiness to provide national implementation assistance.[30] The parties considered information on broad approaches to national implementation as well as detailed descriptions of such issues as law enforcement and cooperation between and within states.

[23] The states were Cameroon, Côte d'Ivoire, Guinea, Namibia, Nepal, Tanzania, United Arab Emirates and Zambia.

[24] The states were Angola, Central African Republic, Chad, Cook Islands, Guyana, Liberia, Malawi, Marshall Islands, Micronesia, Nauru and Nieue.

[25] The states were Egypt, Israel and Syria.

[26] The states were Djibouti, Eritrea, Haiti, Kiribati, Mauritania, Samoa, Somalia and Tuvalu. BTWC Meeting of States Parties, 'Obtaining universality for the Biological Weapons Convention, introducing the Report of the Chairman', 11 Dec. 2007, Geneva; and BTWC Meeting of States Parties, 'Report of the Chairman on universalization activities, submitted by the Chairman', document BWC/MSP/2007/4, 11 Dec. 2007.

[27] The BioWeapons Prevention Project (BWPP) produced daily briefing papers on the work of the meetings. See the BWPP website <http://www.bwpp.org/>. See also the UN Office at Geneva website, <http://www.unog.ch/bwc/>; and the 'Biological and Toxin Weapons Convention' website <http://www.opbw.org/>.

[28] BTWC Meeting of Experts, 'Considerations, lessons, perspectives, recommendations, conclusions and proposals from the presentations, conclusions and proposals drawn form the presentations, statements, working papers and interventions on the topics under discussion at the meeting (as of 15:30 on 23 August)', document BWC/MSP/2007/MX/CRP.2, 24 Aug. 2007.

[29] This point was also made in 2005 regional BTWC implementation workshops and the 2005 meetings of BTWC parties in Geneva.

[30] BTWC Meeting of Experts, 'Biological Weapons Convention: Meeting of Experts 2007, closing remarks of the Chairman, Ambassador Masood Khan (Pakistan)', 24 Aug. 2007, Geneva. National legislation can be divided into 3 types of activity: (a) legislation to transpose convention obligations into national law, (b) methods for monitoring relevant work with biological agents and toxins under the jurisdiction or territory of a state, and (c) the means for enforcing legislation once a violation is suspected. Lentzos, F., 'Representation from the trenches: ongoing monitoring for implementing the BWC', *Disarmament Diplomacy*, no. 85 (summer 2007), p. 54.

The meeting of experts also produced a concluding draft factual report for possible inclusion in the final document of the Meeting of States Parties.[31]

At the start of the Meeting of States Parties Khan tabled a synthesis paper which itemized measures developed by the Meeting of Experts to implement the 2007 mandate. The measures were organized as lists of steps to: (*a*) translate BTWC obligations into effective national measures, (*b*) manage and coordinate the operation of national measures, (*c*) enforce national measures, and (*d*) review the efficacy and efficiency of national measures. Khan also listed measures that could be taken to maximize the effectiveness of efforts to implement regional and subregional cooperation on BTWC implementation.[32] Although the parties expressed positive views of the work and importance of the ISU, the USA sounded a note of diplomatic caution when it expressed 'deep concern over recommendations encouraging support for increased responsibilities' for the ISU and emphasized that voluntary contributions by BTWC parties 'must not in any way undermine the strict delineation of the ISU operations that was the basis for the compromise text [agreed by the 2006 Sixth Review Conference] of the mandate'.[33] This statement was prompted by a working paper tabled by the Netherlands on behalf of the EU which listed measures that could be taken to support the ISU.[34] For example, one measure proposed that the ISU could be provided with additional financial resources to organize a forum similar to the Organisation for the Prohibition of Chemical Weapons (OPCW) Academic Forum, but to do so would be difficult given that the ISU's staff is currently limited to three people.[35] An underlying US concern was that the ISU not evolve towards becoming a de facto permanent institutional structure.[36]

The Meeting of States Parties issued a final report that provides factual information about the agenda, the organization of the meeting, a list of participants, and the statements and measures considered.[37] In closing the meeting,

[31] BTWC Meeting of Experts, 'Draft report of meeting of experts', document BWC/MSP/2007/MX/CRP.1, 24 Aug. 2007.

[32] BTWC Meeting of States Parties, 'Synthesis of considerations, lessons, perspectives, recommendations, conclusions and proposals drawn from the presentations, statements, working papers and interventions on the topics under discussion at the Meeting of Experts', document BWC/MSP/2007/L.1, 9 Nov. 2007.

[33] US Mission to International Organizations, Geneva Switzerland, 'Statement by H. E. Ambassador Christina Rocca, U.S. representative, Biological Weapons Convention, 2007 Meeting of States Parties', Geneva, 10 Dec. 2007. On the institutional issue see Hart, J., Kuhlau, F. and Simon, J., 'Chemical and biological weapon developments and arms control', *SIPRI Yearbook 2003: Armaments, Disarmament and International Security* (Oxford University Press: Oxford, 2003), pp. 646–50.

[34] BTWC Meeting of Experts, 'Netherlands: supporting the BTWC Implementation Support Unit', document BWC/MSP/2007/WP.3, 7 Dec. 2007.

[35] BioWeapons Prevention Project, 'The Meeting of States Parties: the opening day', MSP report no. 2, 11 Dec. 2007.

[36] For background on the question of whether an institutionalized body should be established to oversee BTWC implementation see Zanders, J. P., 'Verification of the BTWC: seeking the impossible or impossible to seek?', ed. G. Lindstrom, *Enforcing Non-Proliferation: The European Union and the 2006 BTWC Review Conference*, Chaillot Paper no. 93 (EU Institute for Security Studies: Paris, Nov. 2006), pp. 50–54.

[37] BTWC Meeting of States Parties, 'Report of the Meeting of States Parties', 14 Dec. 2007, advance copy.

Khan stated that the conference had been productive and represented a 'good start on our goal of moving from adjacency to synergy' in the parties' efforts to strengthen the convention.[38]

Chemical weapon arms control and disarmament

As of 31 December 2007, 183 states had ratified or acceded to the CWC, the principal international legal instrument against chemical warfare; an additional six states had signed but not ratified the convention, and seven states had neither signed nor ratified it.[39]

The Conference of the States Parties

The 12th Session of the Conference of the States Parties to the CWC met on 5–9 November 2007. The ability of the OPCW to fulfil its mandate depends on its receiving funds from the states parties in a timely manner. A number of adjustments were made by the CSP to regularize the payment status of those parties in arrears and to improve the organization's captial flow. The CSP approved the OPCW's programme and budget of €75 025 734 ($109 million) for 2008.[40] It is the third consecutive 'zero nominal growth' budget. The CSP also approved, for the first time, a multi-year payment plan for two parties that were in arrears in their payments to the OPCW and authorized the Executive Council to approve similar payment plans for other parties in 2008. The mechanism is meant to permit parties with unpaid advances to the OPCW Working Capital Fund (WCF) or annual contributions to regularize their payment status over periods of more than one year. It is another in a series of adjustments the parties have taken to improve capital flow so as to avoid situations, such as that which occurred in 2001, when some scheduled inspections were cancelled for lack of funding.[41] A number of the parties have not paid their annual contributions in full for several years.[42] The underpay-

[38] BTWC Meeting of States Parties, 'Biological Weapons Convention: Meeting of States Parties 2007, Chairman's closing remarks', 14 Dec. 2007, Geneva.

[39] Barbados and the Republic of the Congo became parties to the CWC in 2007. The states that have signed, but not ratified the CWC are Bahamas, Dominican Republic, Guinea-Bissau, Israel and Myanmar (Burma). The states that had not signed or acceded to the CWC as of Dec. 2007 were Angola, Egypt, Iraq, North Korea, Lebanon, Somalia and Syria.

[40] OPCW, 'Decision, programme and budget of the OPCW for 2007', document C-12/DEC.4, 7 Nov. 2007, para. 3.

[41] OPCW, 'Decision, proposals for a multi-year payment plan to regularise the payment of outstanding annual contributions', document C-12/DEC.7. For a discussion of previous OPCW budgetary and planning challenges see Zanders, J. P., Hart, J. and Kuhlau, F., 'Chemical and biological weapon developments and arms control', *SIPRI Yearbook 2002: Armaments, Disarmament and International Security* (Oxford University Press: Oxford, 2002), pp. 683–85.

[42] As of Oct. 2007, the OPCW was owed €36 034 468 ($52 million) in unpaid annual contributions for the period 1993–2007. As of Nov. 2007, the OPCW had received approximately 80% of the 2007 assessed contributions from member states. OPCW, 'Report of the Director-General, OPCW income and expenditure for the financial year to 30 June 2007', document C-12/DG.8, 17 Oct. 2007; and OPCW, 'Opening statement by the Director-General to the Conference of the States Parties at its Twelfth Session', document C-12/DG.11, 5 Nov. 2007, p. 7, para. 98. As of early 2008 about half of the total shortfall had been paid.

ment or non-payment of annual dues and contributions to the WCF has the potential to undermine programme delivery and to reduce the influence of such parties on OPCW policy- and decision making.[43]

The CSP also stressed that it was 'imperative' that further efforts be made to ensure that all the parties fully implement the provisions of Article VII of the CWC (National Implementation Measures) and that the parties should notify the OPCW of the designation or establishment of a national authority and inform the OPCW of steps they have taken to enact legislation and administrative measures to implement the convention.[44]

The CSP also extended the OPCW Plan of Action on universality of the CWC until 2009.[45] The OPCW's Director-General summarized, by region, the status of efforts to achieve universality in which he noted that Iraq and Lebanon have completed the necessary parliamentary procedures to accede to the CWC.[46] He also stated that the OPCW had engaged in dialogue with Egypt, Israel and Syria to discuss their possible accession to the convention and that North Korea had not responded to any of the OPCW's initiatives.[47] As of August 2007, 173 parties (95 per cent) had established or designated a national authority; 120 parties (66 per cent) had reported to the Technical Secretariat the adoption of legislative and administrative measures to implement the CWC; and 77 parties (42 per cent) had adopted and reported on national legislation covering all key areas required by the CWC.[48]

A broader consideration of the appropriate measures that the OPCW should take in the field of economic and technological cooperation, including the balance of organizational resources that should be devoted to implementing the various parts of the OPCW's programme and budget. Some parties wish to conclude Article X and Article XI 'action plans',[49] but the parties have not been able to agree the specific measures to be included in such plans.

---

[43] For provisions on voting rights in case of non-payment of dues see CWC, Article VIII, para. 8.

[44] OPCW, 'Decision, regarding the implementation of Article VII obligations', documentC-12/DEC.9, 9 Nov. 2007.

[45] OPCW, 'Decision, universality of the Chemical Weapons Convention and the further implementation of the universality action plan', document C-12/DEC.11, 9 Nov. 2007.

[46] OPCW, 'Opening statement by the Director-General to the Conference of the States Parties at its Twelfth Session', document C-12/DG.11, 5 Nov. 2007, p. 14, para. 84.

[47] OPCW (note 46), pp. 14–15, paras 87–88. A number of states in the Middle East have indicated that they are not willing to accede to the CWC unless Israel accedes to the 1968 Treaty on the Non-proliferation of Nuclear Weapons (Non-Proliferation Treaty, NPT). Israel, a signatory to the CWC, has indicated a need to agree other regional political and security concerns before a Middle East free of weapons of mass destruction can be achieved. UN Security Council Resolution 1718, 14 Oct. 2006, decided that North Korea must verifiably abandon all of its WMD programmes.

[48] OPCW, 'Note by the Director-General, Report to the Conference of the States Parties at its Twelfth Session on the status of implementation of article VII of the Chemical Weapons Convention as at 22 August 2007', document C-12/DG.6, 9 Oct. 2007, p. 6.

[49] E.g. OPCW, 'Delegation of South Africa, Statement on behalf of the African States Parties to the CWC during the Twelfth session of the Conference of States Parties, 5 to 9 November 2007', The Hague, 5 Nov. 2007. The OPCW has 7 programmes on cooperation in the peaceful uses of chemistry: (a) associate programme, (b) analytical skills development course, (c) conference support programme, (d) research projects programme, (e) internship support programme, (f) laboratory assistance programme, and (g) equipment exchange programme.

The CSP also considered site-selection methodologies for chemical industry inspections and related matters such as the appropriate geographic distribution of such inspections, particularly for 'other chemical production facilities'.[50] The outcome of such considerations—both in terms of specific decisions taken and CWC implementation practice—will increasingly shape the future CWC regime as chemical weapon stockpiles are eliminated and OPCW resources and political attention are increasingly directed towards other 'core' CWC objectives.[51]

In 2007 the EU agreed a Joint Action of €1.7 million ($2.4 million) for seven projects to support OPCW activities to implement the 2003 EU Strategy against Proliferation of Weapons of Mass Destruction (WMD): (*a*) universality of the CWC, (*b*) national implementation of the CWC, (*c*) international cooperation in the field of chemical activities, (*d*) assistance and protection against chemical weapons, (*e*) the update of the OPCW's scheduled chemicals database for verification purposes, (*f*) the OPCW Industry and Protection Forum, and (*g*) provision of financial support to OPCW visit teams to chemical weapon destruction facilities.[52] The OPCW also organized a number of regional workshops and visits to support universalization and effective national implementation.[53]

Essentially all CWC implementation issues have been considered in some form since the 1993–97 Preparatory Commission which elaborated the specific procedures and structures to allow the OPCW to implement the CWC immediately once it entered into force.[54] As the destruction of chemical weapon stockpiles approaches completion, the OPCW will increasingly become more of a non-proliferation and technical assistance organization (rather than a disarmament organization).[55] This shift in focus will include further attention to verify that chemical weapons are not produced (including by the chemical industry). This implies improving implementation of the CWC's provisions on chemical transfers. There is also a growing expectation that further steps will be taken to ensure effective verification, including through comprehensive national implementation. Given the fact that chemical

---

[50] As of 19 Dec. 2007, 5177 industrial facilities were liable to OPCW inspection.

[51] For background on CWC chemical industry verification see Hart, J. and Sutherland, R. G., 'Chemical industry verification under the CWC: scientific and technological developments and diplomatic practice', Paper presented at OPCW Academic Forum, The Hague, 18–19 Sep. 2007, <http://www.opcw academicforum.org/>.

[52] Council Joint Action 2007/185/CFSP of 19 March 2007 on support for OPCW activities in the framework of the implementation of the EU Strategy against Proliferation of Weapons of Mass Destruction, *Official Journal of the European Union*, L85 (27 Mar. 2007), pp. 13–21. The visits were agreed by the 11th Conference of the States Parties to the OPCW. See Hart and Kuhlau (note 15), p. 586.

[53] E.g. on 14–15 Apr. the OPCW organized a subregional workshop for customs authorities in South East Europe on technical aspects of the CWC's chemical transfers regime in Croatia.

[54] See Kenyon, I. R. and Feakes, D. (eds), *The Creation of the Organisation for the Prohibition of Chemical Weapons: A Case Study in the Birth of an Intergovernmental Organisation* (TMC Asser Press: The Hague, 2007). See also proceedings of the IUPAC/OPCW International Workshop: Impact of Advances in Science and Technology on the Chemical Weapons Convention, 22–25 Apr. 2007, Zagreb, Croatia, <http://www7.nationalacademies.org/IUPAC-OPCW_Workshop/>.

[55] Some parties object to the term 'non-proliferation', although it does appear in official OPCW documentation.

weapons produced before 1 January 1946 will continue to be recovered, the OPCW Working Group for the Preparation of the Second Review Conference has suggested that the Second Review Conference might consider the practicality of setting a deadline for the destruction of such weapons as they are recovered over the coming decades. In order to consider such issues and help mark the 10th anniversary of the entry into force of the CWC, a series of meetings were held in a number of CWC member states and at the UN. Academics, policymakers, diplomats and industry officials attended the OPCW Academic Forum 2007 and the OPCW Industry Protection Forum 2007. Both are intended to function as ongoing open-ended mechanisms to facilitate the exchange of information and views on CWC implementation through dedicated websites.[56]

Destruction of chemical weapons[57]

As of 19 December 2007, of approximately 71 330 agent tonnes of declared chemical weapons, about 26 296 agent tonnes had been verifiably destroyed; of approximately 8.67 million declared items, about 2.85 million munitions and containers had been destroyed.[58] As of the same date, 12 states had declared 65 chemical weapon production facilities of which 42 had been destroyed and 19 converted for peaceful purposes not prohibited under the CWC.[59] The declared possessors of chemical weapons are Albania, India, South Korea, Libya, Russia and the USA. On 22–23 October 2007 the first of the special visits to Russia and the USA that were agreed by the 11th CSP were conducted when the chairman of the Executive Council, the Director-General and designated Executive Council representatives visited the Anniston Chemical Agent Disposal Facility.[60] A similar visit is planned to be carried out in Russia in 2008. These visits reflect the concern of the parties that destruction deadlines should be met and allow Russia and the USA to signal the seriousness with which they will attempt to meet these deadlines.

On 11 July the OPCW confirmed that Albania had completed the destruction of its chemical weapon stockpile (totalling 16 678 kilograms of mostly sulphur mustard)—the first possessor of stockpiled chemical weapons to do

[56] Papers and presentations from the forums are available at <http://www.opcwacademicforum.org/> and <http://www.opcwipf.org/>.

[57] For further information on chemical weapon stockpiles (e.g. cost, type and quantity) see previous SIPRI CBW Yearbook chapters.

[58] OPCW, 'The chemical weapons ban: facts and figures', <http://www.opcw.org/factsandfigures/>.

[59] OPCW (note 58). The states are Bosnia and Herzegovina, China, France, India, Iran, Japan, South Korea, Libya, Russia, Serbia, the UK and the USA. The CWC defines a chemical weapon production facility as a facility that has produced chemical weapons at any time since 1 Jan. 1946. CWC, Article II, para. 8. For quantity and type of chemical weapon stockpiles and associated destruction programmes see CBW chapters in previous SIPRI Yearbooks.

[60] OPCW (note 46), para. 15.

so.[61] In 2007 Albania provided details of its destruction programme, including outside assistance, and publicly described the composition of its stockpile.[62]

India received an extension to 28 April 2009 of the deadline by which it must destroy all of its Category 1 chemical weapons.[63] As of 30 September 2007, India had destroyed 86.03 per cent of its Category 1 chemical weapon stockpile and all of its declared Category 2 and 3 chemical weapons.[64]

Libya received an extension of the deadline by which it must destroy all of its Category 1 chemical weapons to 31 December 2010.[65] As of 30 September 2007, Libya had destroyed all of its Category 3 chemical weapons and 39 per cent of its Category 2 chemical weapons.[66] Libya is obligated to destroy all of the Category 2 chemical weapons by 31 December 2011. On 18 June 2007 Libya withdrew from an agreement with the USA to share the costs of destroying its chemical weapon stockpile. Among the possible reasons cited for this were that Libya wanted the USA to pay more than $45 million (of a total estimated cost of $60 million), to cover liability for damage or destruction of US-provided equipment and to retain US-provided equipment.[67]

The Russian chemical weapon stockpile is stored at six locations.[68] Russian officials continued to indicate that they receive less destruction assistance than promised and that a lack of multi-year funding commitments is complicating its destruction planning. Russia has received an extension of the deadline by which it must complete the destruction of its Category 1 stockpile to 29 April 2012. As of 30 September 2007, Russia had destroyed more than 8000 tonnes (more than 23 per cent) of its Category 1 stockpiles. Russia has also completed the destruction of all of its Category 2 and 3 chemical weapons.[69] France pledged support through the British chemical weapon destruction

---

[61] 'Verification, Albania [is] the first country to destroy all of its chemical weapons', *Chemical Disarmament*, vol. 5, no. 3 (Sep. 2007), p. 9.

[62] Albania declared to the OPCW 580 canisters of sulphur mustard (HD) weighing 13.71 tonnes, 49 canisters or glass containers of lewisite (L) weighing 0.97 tonnes, 4 canisters of sulphur mustard/lewisite (HD-L) mixture weighing 0.4 tonnes, 33 canisters of adamsite (DM) weighing 0.33 tonnes, and 80 canisters of chloroacetophenone (CN) weighing 1.04 tonnes. Vucaj, F., 'Albania, Republic of Albania: world leader in chemical disarmament', *Chemical Disarmament*, vol. 5, 10th anniversary special edition (May 2007), pp. 6–10.

[63] The definition of chemical weapon categories, which is partly based on what schedule a chemical may be listed under in the CWC's Annex of Chemicals, is given in CWC, Verification Annex, Part IV(A), para. 16.

[64] OPCW (note 46), p. 4, para. 19.

[65] For information on Libya's stockpile and background on its accession to the CWC see Hart, J. and Kile, S. N., 'Libya's renunciation of NBC weapons and longer-range missile programmes', *SIPRI Yearbook 2005: Armaments, Disarmament and International Security* (Oxford University Press: Oxford, 2005), pp. 629–48.

[66] OPCW (note 46), p. 4, para. 20.

[67] Bollfrass, A., 'Libya backs out of CW destruction agreement', *Arms Control Today*, vol. 37, no. 6 (July/Aug. 2007), p. 29.

[68] The locations are Kambarka, Udmurtia Republic; Kizner, Udmurtia Republic; Maradikovsky, Kirov oblast; Pochep, Bryansk oblast; Leonidovka, Penza oblast; and Shchuchye, Kurgan oblast. For background on Russian chemical weapon destruction see 'Unichtozhenie khimicheskogo oruzhiya v R.F.' [Destruction of chemical weapons in the R[ussian] F[ederation]], *Rossiiskaya Gazeta*, <http://www.rg.ru/ximiya.html>; and *Khimicheskoe Razoruzhenie: Otkrity Elektronny Zhurnal* [Chemical Disarmament: Open Electronic Journal], <http://www.chemicaldisarmament.ru/>.

[69] OPCW (note 46), p. 3, para. 17.

assistance framework with an offer (of approximately €6 million) being allocated to the stockpile at Shchuchye. Italy has bilaterally offered up to €360 million to Pochep.

One party to the CWC, widely understood to be South Korea, has declared possessing a chemical weapon stockpile but has declined to identify itself publicly. It has received an extension to 31 December 2008 of the deadline to complete the destruction of its chemical weapon stockpiles. As of 30 September 2007 it had destroyed over 85 per cent of its Category 1 chemical weapons and all of its Category 2 and 3 chemical weapons.[70]

As of 10 December the USA had destroyed 50 per cent of its stockpiled chemical weapons, currently stored at five locations.[71] There was further concern about the transport and off-site treatment of caustic VX—an organophosphorus nerve agent—hydrolysate from the Newport chemical weapon destruction facility.[72] The USA has received an extension for the completion of the destruction of its Category 1 stockpile to 29 April 2012. As of 19 December 2007, the USA had destroyed more than 45 per cent of its Category 1 chemical weapons and had destroyed 100 per cent of its Category 3 chemical weapons.[73]

As of 19 December 2007, three countries had declared that abandoned chemical weapons (ACWs) are present on their territories, and 13 countries had declared that they posses old chemical weapons (OCWs).[74] Starting in 2010, Nord Stream, a German–Russian business consortium, plans to operate a 1200-kilometre gas pipeline that will link Viborg, Russia, and Greifswald, Germany, and pass through the Swedish economic zone east of the Swedish island of Gotland. Some European and Swedish officials and environmentalists have expressed concern that the pipeline could disturb World War II-era munition dump sites in the Baltic Sea, including chemical weapons.[75]

China and Japan have until 2012 to complete the destruction of recovered chemical weapons abandoned by Japan in China during World War II. In 2007

[70] OPCW (note 46), p. 4, para. 19. In this speech the Director-General refers to the country as 'a state party'.

[71] US Army Chemical Materials Agency, 'U.S. Army destroys 50 percent of U.S. chemical agent stockpile', Press release, 10 Dec. 2007. The stockpile locations are Alabama, Arkansas, Indiana, Oregon and Utah.

[72] For background see US Government Accountability Office (GAO), *Chemical Demilitarization: Actions Needed to Improve the Reliability of the Army's Cost Comparison Analysis for Treatment and Disposal Options for Newport's VX Hydrolysate*, GAO-070240R (GAO: Washington, DC, 26 Jan. 2007).

[73] OPCW (note 58).

[74] The countries that have declared ACWs to the OPCW are China, Italy and Panama. The countries that have declared OCWs to the OPCW are Austria, Australia, Belgium, Canada, France, Germany, Italy, Japan, Russia, Slovenia, Solomon Islands, the UK and the USA. ACWs are defined as chemical weapons that were abandoned by a state after 1 Jan. 1925 on the territory of another state without the permission of the latter. CWC, Article II, para. 6. OCWs are defined as chemical weapons that were produced before 1925 or chemical weapons produced between 1925 and 1946 that have deteriorated to such an extent that they are no longer usable in the manner in which they were designed. CWC, Article II, para. 5. For information on countries not discussed in this chapter see CBW chapters in previous editions of the SIPRI Yearbook.

[75] 'Nord Stream reviderar gasledning' [North Stream modifies gas line], *Svenska Dagbladet*, 9 Nov. 2007. See also Nord Stream's website, <http://www.nord-stream.com/>.

Japan announced its intention to introduce a mobile destruction system (probably an explosive containment chamber) to complement the planned construction of a fixed chemical weapon destruction facility in Haerbaling, Jilin Province in north-east China. Approximately 300 000–400 000 ACWs are estimated to be located in the province, of which approximately 38 000 have been recovered and are awaiting destruction. Since 1991 the two countries have jointly conducted approximately 75 fact-finding missions or site investigations of suspected ACW sites and, since 2000, have carried out 16 excavation and recovery operations.[76]

In March 2007 the United Kingdom completed the destruction of all of its OCWs, totalling 3812 munitions, at a cost of £10 million ($20 million).[77]

III. Violations and past programmes

No major 'status of proliferation' reports on CBW activities appear to have been released in 2007. Such reports all tend to list similar states, and it is generally not possible to evaluate their accuracy since the information on which they are based is classified. They also usually contain caveats that leave open the possibility that a state is not developing or seeking to acquire CBW. When asked whether any states were currently developing biological weapons, the head of Russia's Radiation, Chemical and Biological Defence Troops, Colonel-General Vladimir Ivanovich Filippov, replied: 'At the current time there is no available official evidence that any country is developing biological weapons'.[78]

One of the few official public indications that al-Qaeda is seeking to acquire chemical or biological weapons is contained in a partial transcript released by the US Department of Defense of a tribunal hearing that was conducted at the US Naval Base at Guantánamo Bay, Cuba. Khalid Sheikh Muhammed, a US-designated enemy combatant accused of having served as the head of al-Qaeda's military committee and of being Osama bin Laden's principal operative responsible for directing the 11 September 2001 attacks on the USA, is quoted as stating: 'I was directly in charge, after the death of Sheikh Abu Hafs Al-Masri Subhi Abu Sittah, of managing and following up on the Cell for the Production of Biological Weapons, such as anthrax and others, and following up on Dirty Bomb Operations on American soil'.[79]

[76] Nishi, M., 'Abandoned chemical weapons in China: efforts for early destruction', Presentation at 10th International Chemical Weapons Demilitarisation Conference: CWD2007, Brussels, 14–18 May 2007.

[77] British Ministry of Defence, 'Britain completes destruction of old chemical weapons', *Defence News*, 27 Mar. 2007, <http://www.mod.uk/DefenceInternet/DefenceNews/DefencePolicyAndBusiness/BritainCompletesDestructionOfOldChemicalWeaponHoldings.htm>.

[78] Tikhonov, A., 'Voiska vysokikh tekhnologii' [High technology forces], *Krasnaya Zvezda*, 13 Nov. 2007.

[79] US Department of Defence, 'Unclassified, verbatim transcript of combatant status review tribunal hearing for ISN 10024', 2007, <http://www.defenselink.mil/news/transcript_ISN10024.pdf>, p. 17. Muhammed also admitted responsibility for decapitating US journalist Daniel Pearl in Pakistan.

In 2007 a series of chlorine attacks occurred in Iraq which caused many of those who were not injured or killed by the associated explosives to become ill. Some attacks appear to have been designed to cause harm through both explosives and the chemical, while other attacks were attempts to explosively disseminate chlorine. There was concern that insurgents might refine their dispersal techniques. The OPCW and the UN issued statements condemning the attacks. The use of chlorine was also a factor in discussions in the USA on how to protect its municipal water supplies and whether to replace chlorine with other chemicals.[80]

In June 2007 an Iraqi court sentenced Ali Hassan al-Majid ('Chemical Ali') and two associates to death for their role in the 1988 Anfal campaign against the Kurdish population in northern Iraq, including the town of Halabja, in which Iraqi military units employed chemical weapons.[81]

IV. Iraq: closing the file?

On 29 June 2007 the UN Monitoring, Verification and Inspection Commission was disbanded when the UN Security Council adopted Resolution 1762. This immediately ended the mandates of UNMOVIC and the International Atomic Energy Agency (IAEA) under relevant UN resolutions concerning Iraq that were passed following Iraq's 1990 invasion of Kuwait. Resolution 1762, which was passed by a vote of 14–0 with Russia abstaining, requested the UN Secretary-General to 'take all necessary measures' to provide for the 'appropriate disposition' of UNMOVIC's archives and other property under arrangements that ensure that 'sensitive proliferation information' and information provided in confidence by UN member states are 'kept under strict control'.[82] UN member states had, since the 2003 US–British-led attack on Iraq, periodically considered whether and how to dismantle UNMOVIC or transform it.[83] For example, Iraq wished to recover the remaining funds in the UNMOVIC account, while some states, including Russia, argued that UNMOVIC should formally assess whether Iraq was free of weapons of mass destruction and WMD programmes. These states expressed concern that, without such confirmation within the UN framework, uncertainty would remain on whether remnants of Iraq's WMD programmes posed a continuing threat to international peace and security.[84]

---

[80] The New Jersey District Water Commission switched from using chlorine to sodium hypochlorite. Wright, J., 'Plant hit for use of chlorine', *The Record* (Hackensack), 28 May 2007.

[81] See Hiltermann, J. R., *A Poisonous Affair: America, Iraq, and the Gassing of Halabja* (Cambridge University Press: New York, 2007).

[82] UN Security Council Resolution 1762, 29 June 2007, paras 1, 5.

[83] E.g. it has been proposed that UNMOVIC's assets be transferred to support the UN Secretary-General's mechanism to investigate alleged CBW use.

[84] UNMOVIC was not allowed to operate in Iraq and the USA did not brief UNMOVIC on its classified findings of its WMD survey work in Iraq. Kerr, P., 'Security Council ends UNMOVIC', *Arms Control Today*, vol. 37, no. 7 (Sep. 2007), pp. 40–41; and Kerr, P., 'Security Council may close Iraq inspection unit', *Arms Control Today*, vol. 37, no. 5 (June 2007), pp. 27–28.

In a letter to the Security Council, the UK and the USA stated that the coalition occupying Iraq had taken 'all appropriate steps' to 'secure, remove, disable, render harmless, eliminate or destroy' all of Iraq's known WMD and ballistic missiles with a range greater than 150 km, as well as 'all known elements of Iraq's programmes established to research, develop, design, manufacture, produce, support, assemble and employ such weapons and delivery systems, subsystems and components thereof'.[85] Iraq's constitution obligates it to 'respect and implement' its international obligations in the field of nuclear, biological and chemical (NBC) weapons.[86] The Iraqi Monitoring Directorate, which oversees the transfer of dual-use substances, is also working to harmonize its export control legislation according to international standards, including within the framework of UN Security Council Resolution 1540.[87]

The UNMOVIC Acting Executive Chairman, Dimitri Perricos, presented to the Security Council UNMOVIC's 29th (and final) quarterly report of its activities. He also briefed the Security Council on the work of UNMOVIC and its predecessor body (the UN Special Commission on Iraq, UNSCOM), in part by referring to an unclassified compendium report totalling more than 1000 pages on Iraq's WMD programmes that UNMOVIC released on 27 June.[88] UNMOVIC also included a special appendix in its final quarterly report describing the challenges associated with verifying small quantities of CBW agents, partly in order to inform consideration of the issue of non-state actors seeking to acquire toxic chemical agents or their precursors—a matter of some concern for UN member states because of the 2007 use of toxic industrial chemicals by insurgents in Iraq.[89]

UNMOVIC's 'substantive' records have been transferred to the UN archive with restricted access until further notice. According to an UNMOVIC spokesman, Ewen Buchanen, most of the documents are 'sprinkled in some way'

[85] Letter from the Secretary of State for Foreign and Commonwealth Affairs of the United Kingdom of Great Britain and Northern Ireland and Secretary of State of the United States of America to the United Nations addressed to the President of the Security Council, Appendix I, United Nations Security Council Resolution 1762, 29 June 2007, p. 3.

[86] The Iraqi constitution states: 'The Iraqi Government shall respect and implement Iraq's international obligations regarding the non-proliferation, non-development, non-production and non-utilization of nuclear, chemical and biological weapons, and shall prohibit associated equipment, materiel, technologies and communications systems for use in the development, manufacture, production and utilization of such weapons'. Letter dated 8 April 2007 from the Minister for Foreign Affairs of Iraq addressed to the President of the Security Council [original in Arabic], UN Security Council Resolution 1762, 29 June 2007, para. 2.

[87] UN Security Council Resolution 1540, 28 Apr. 2004; and Letter dated 8 April 2007 from the Minister for Foreign Affairs of Iraq addressed to the President of the Security Council (note 86), appendix II, paras 5, 7. See also the 1540 Committee website, <http://disarmament2.un.org/Committee1540/>.

[88] The compendium was divided into: (a) building a UN verification system, (b) the structure of Iraq's proscribed weapon programmes, (c) chemical weapon programme, (d) missile programme, (e) biological weapon programme, (f) procurement issues, (g) the interconnections between Iraq's weapon programmes, and (h) observations and lessons learned. UNMOVIC, 'Twenty-ninth quarterly report on the activities of the United Nations Monitoring, Verification and Inspection Commission in accordance with paragraph 12 of Security Council Resolution 1284 (1999)', UN document S/2007/314, 29 May 2007; and UNMOVIC, Compendium [Report] (United Nations: New York, June 2007).

[89] Perricos, D., 'Acting Executive Chairman's speaking notes—Security Council, 29 June 2007', <http://www.unmovic.org/>.

with proliferation sensitive information.[90] Part of the archive, which reportedly has just under 460 metres of paper files and 1 terabyte (1 million megabytes) of electronic data, would also be of interest to those wishing to keep NBC weapon programmes secret.[91] The UN ODA has hired a number of former UNSCOM and UNMOVIC staff. UNMOVIC's material and residual expertise could also be used to further develop an authoritative record to help inform future analyses of arms control and disarmament issues or to support the UN Secretary-General's authority to investigate allegations of chemical and biological weapon use.

Concern about bioterrorism was highlighted on 29 August when gram quantities of phosgene in metal and glass containers placed in sealed plastic bags were found in an UNMOVIC office in New York when staff were packing material for long-term storage. The samples probably originated from an analytical laboratory at the al-Muthanna Chemical Weapons Complex and had been removed by inspectors in 1996.[92]

The 2003 attack against Iraq was justified partly on the basis of discredited information provided by a then anonymous Iraqi engineer named Rafid Ahmed Alwan living in Germany (codenamed 'Curveball'), who maintained that Iraq possessed mobile biological weapon production facilities. Despite suspicion by Germany's Federal Intelligence Service (Bundesnachrichtendienst) and other analysts, including in the USA, regarding Curveball's credibility, US officials decided to use his information to support the case for attacking Iraq in 2003.[93] Subsequent investigations, including by the Iraq Survey Group,[94] failed to uncover any such facilities.[95] In 2007 a US investigative news agency broadcast a segment devoted to Curveball,[96] and the National Security Archive—an independent non-governmental research institute and library located at George Washington University—published collected pri-

---

[90] Kerr, P., 'Security Council ends UNMOVIC', *Arms Control Today*, vol. 37, no. 7 (Sep. 2007), pp. 40–1.

[91] Kulish, N., 'End looms for Iraq arms inspection unit', *New York Times*, 18 June 2007.

[92] United Nations, 'Daily press briefing by the Office of the Spokesperson for the Secretary-General', 30 Aug. 2007, <http://www.un.org/News/briefings/docs/2007/db070830.doc.htm>.

[93] The White House, 'Iraq, denial and deception, US Secretary of State Colin Powell addresses the UN Security Council', New York, 5 Feb. 2003, <http://www.whitehouse.gov/news/releases/2003/02/print/20030205-1.html>.

[94] The ISG was a fact-finding mission sent to the country by the US–British-led coalition forces that attacked Iraq in order to find UN-prohibited NBC weapons and ballistic missiles having a range of more than 150 km.

[95] Guthrie, R., Hart, J., Kuhlau, F. and Simon, J., 'Chemical and biological warfare developments and arms control', *SIPRI Yearbook 2004* (note 5), pp. 683–91; Guthrie, R., Hart, J. and Kuhlau, F., 'Chemical and biological warfare developments and arms control', *SIPRI Yearbook 2005* (note 65), pp. 616–26; and Guthrie, R., Hart, J. and Kuhlau, F., 'Chemical and biological warfare developments and arms control', *SIPRI Yearbook 2006: Armaments, Disarmament and International Security* (Oxford University Press: Oxford, 2006), pp. 724–25.

[96] CBS News, *Sixty Minutes*, 'Faulty intel source "Curve Ball" revealed', 4 Nov. 2007, transcript available at <http://www.cbsnews.com/stories/2007/11/01/60minutes/main3440577.shtml>. See also Drogin, B., *Curveball: Spies, Lies and the Con Man Who Caused a War* (Random House: New York, 2007).

mary documents about Curveball.[97] It is not possible to remove all uncertainty regarding the fate of Iraq's former WMD programmes, but the case can be said to be closed.

V. CBW prevention, response and remediation

Governments and various international institutions continued to consider and develop a variety of overlapping initiatives in the field of CBW prevention and remediation in 2007.[98] Security specialists and governments also evaluated whether and how such initiatives and measures should be implemented, both in terms of general policy and in terms of specific technical or operational-level challenges. Much of the focus of these efforts has been on how to prevent and respond to acts of bioterrorism, bio-crimes, and chemical terrorism by non-state actors or attacks carried out without claims of responsibility, including with possible clandestine state involvement.[99]

The threat analyses and risk assessments associated with CBW terrorism prevention, response and remediation and their effective implementation are inherently more diffuse, uncertain and open-ended than for 'traditional' state-based military threats involving conventional weapons. This is partly because of the variety and type of actors involved in such activities (e.g. the public health and security sectors), and partly because of the lack of clear, quantifiable or otherwise 'objective' criteria to assess such threats and of operationally meaningful criteria with which to evaluate the effective implementation of measures to address them. These efforts are further complicated by a lack of authoritative public information with which to carry out such analyses. Finally, many states do not feel directly threatened by CBW terrorism and some of the consideration of measures to meet CBW terrorism threats can lack resonance with them especially when limited resources must be prioritized and implemented.

Efforts to identify and mitigate perceived CBW threats were carried out in such areas as: (*a*) scientific R&D to support response capabilities; (*b*) the consideration of measures to restrict 'sensitive' research or its public dissemination; (*c*) the improvement of disease surveillance and response; (*d*) the development of inventories of sensitive materials and high-level containment facilities—bio-safety level (BSL)-3 and BSL-4 level—and the implementation of measures to more safely secure them (e.g. through enhancing awareness of bio-security); (*e*) the improvement and expansion of infrastructure and other capacity to respond to CBW attacks, including the role of microbial forensics

[97] Prados, J. (ed.), *The Record on Curveball: Declassified Documents and Key Participants Show the Importance of Phony Intelligence in the Origins of the Iraq War*, National Security Archive Electronic Briefing Book no. 234 (George Washington University, National Security Archive: Washington, DC, 5 Nov. 2007), <http://www.gwu.edu/~nsarchiv/NSAEBB/NSAEBB234/>.

[98] E.g. Bonin, S., *International Biodefense Handbook 2007: An Inventory of National and International Biodefense Practices and Policies* (Swiss Federal Institute of Technology, Center for Security Studies: Zurich, 2007), <http://www.crn.ethz.ch/publications/crn_team/detail.cfm?id=31124>.

[99] For a review of the concept of bio-crimes or bio-incidents see Kellman (note 12).

(discussed below); (*f*) awareness raising; (*g*) generic scientific and technological developments; and (*h*) linking these factors with policymaking and implementation.

International non-proliferation and disarmament assistance

Some cooperative threat reduction activities involve the sharing of biological materials, including sample strains. In Russia the ability to do this was put in doubt when, on 28 May 2007, it was reported that the Russian Federal Customs Service had stopped the export of all human medical biological material from the country in accordance with Russia's export control regulations. The decision was reportedly the result of a Federal Security Service report to Russian President Vladimir Putin on bioterrorism which alleged that the West was developing genetic weapons against Russia. Concern was expressed that clinical trials of drugs involving international pharmaceutical companies would be ended.[100]

Other cooperative threat reduction measures have been directed towards facilities that were formerly part of the Soviet Anti-Plague System (APS), many focusing on the cataloguing and safe storage of pathogen strains. A report by the Monterey Institute describes the status of the facilities in 10 of the former Soviet republics and the effects of the economic crises that occurred following the dissolution of the Soviet Union.[101] To varying degrees, the administration of APS facilities was merged by the national authorities into their respective sanitary epidemiological system structures.[102] However, the APS was dismantled in Moldova, while it maintained its independence in Georgia. Continuing challenges face APS facilities, including a need to: improve safety conditions, research capacity, disease surveillance and response capacity; replace obsolete equipment, ensuring that pathogen strains are secure; and retain staff expertise.[103] A compendium of biological weapon-related studies written by Chinese biological weapon arms control and disarmament specialists, including a review of Chinese bio-safety and biosecurity laws and regulations (e.g. for the shipment of pathogens), measures to strengthen bio-safety and bio-security in China, and Chinese views of biological weapon arms control and disarmament, was also published in 2007.[104] One analyst observed that while China has 'ample' regulatory rules

[100] 'Russia warily eyes human samples: in the name of fighting bioterrorism, export of biological materials prohibited', *Kommersant*, 30 May 2007.

[101] The 2 states with APS facilities not covered by the study are Russia and Turkmenistan (Estonia, Latvia and Lithuania were also not included because they did not possess such facilities).

[102] The sanitary epidemiological system was a Soviet-era organization with public health responsibilities but generally lacking experience with highly dangerous pathogens.

[103] Ouagrham-Gormley, S. B., Melikishvili, A. and Zilinskas, R., *The Anti-plague System in the Newly Independent States, 1992 and Onwards: Assessing Proliferation Risks and Potential for Enhanced Public Health in Central Asia and the Caucasus* (Monterey Institute, James Martin Center for Nonproliferation Studies: Monterey, Calif., 3 Jan. 2008), <http://cns.miis.edu/research/antiplague/>.

[104] Smithson, A. (ed.), *Beijing on Biohazards: Chinese Experts on Bioweapons Nonproliferation Issues* (Monterey Institute, James Martin Center for Nonproliferation Studies: Monterey, Calif., Aug. 2007), <http://cns.miis.edu/pubs/week/070917.htm>.

and laws dealing with bio-safety and bio-security, the country has 'a consistent problem of implementation' which may, in turn, be partly caused by a 'normative "top-down"' approach together with inadequate resources and training at the operational level.[105]

Biological security

Many countries, including the members of the EU, continued to consider critical infrastructure vulnerabilities partly in light of the terrorist attacks in Madrid in 2004 and London in 2005 and placed greater focus on the threat of bioterrorism and efforts to counter it. In July the European Commission issued a draft Green Paper on bio-preparedness in order to initiate a consultative process throughout Europe on how to reduce biological risks and enhance Europe's bio-preparedness capacity, including via proactive measures, emergency management of bio-related events and establishing investigative capabilities.[106] It also posed the question of whether publication restrictions should be applied when sensitive biological research with a dual use is concerned.[107]

The European Committee for Standardization (Comité Européen de Normalisation, CEN) organized an international bio-safety and bio-security laboratory workshop in association with the EBSA, the American Biological Safety Association and Det Norske Veritas, a consultancy firm. The meeting's objective was to draft a CEN agreement for internationally recognized bio-safety and bio-security management standards.[108] This was done because of concern over the international expansion of biological laboratories. These efforts complement the 2006 World Health Organization bio-safety and bio-security guidelines and existing national regulatory requirements.[109]

Following an endorsement by its member states, the Organisation for Economic Co-operation and Development (OECD) published best practice guidelines on bio-security for biological resource centres, irrespective of the types of materials in custody, use or transfer.[110] At the request of the Dutch Ministry of Education, *A Code of Conduct for Biosecurity* for life-science researchers was published as part of Dutch efforts to further implement the BTWC and as

---

[105] Gill, B., 'Reading the nonproliferation tea leaves from *Beijing on Biohazards* essays', ed. Smithson (note 104), pp. 137–41.

[106] European Commission, 'Green Paper on bio-prepardness', 11 July 2007, COM(2007) 399 final, p. 13 (draft).

[107] E.g. it asked whether research should be published in 2 versions: a public one with no sensitive content and a restricted one containing 'sensitive parts of the research with access only for relevant bio-stakeholders'. How and who would define and implement terms such as 'sensitive' and 'relevant' remains unclear. European Commission (note 106), p. 13. For information on EU instruments with possible application in the biological security field see Kuhlau (note 3).

[108] European Biosafety Association, American Biological Safety Association and Det Norske Veritas, 'Laboratory biorisk management standard: international biorisk standard development initiative', 25 July 2007. The working draft document is available at <http://www.biorisk.eu/>.

[109] World Health Organization (WHO), *Biorisk Management: Laboratory Biosecurity Guidance* (WHO: Geneva).

[110] Organisation for Economic Co-operation and Development (OECD), *OECD Best Practice Guidelines for Biological Resource Centres* (OECD: Paris, 2007).

a means to reduce the likelihood of bioterrorism.[111] The document was the result of surveys of measures already in place at governmental and academic institutions, including some in other countries, and of existing legislation and codes of conduct for biotechnology and microbiology. A follow-up workshop, attended mostly by the stakeholders, led to the release of an initial draft document.[112]

Chemical security

Some states continued to implement various critical infrastructure protection programmes in 2007, including through the identification of potential human and physical weaknesses at chemical facilities in order to 'harden' them against possible attack. Such programmes may include the adoption of alternate production routes that do not require the delivery of toxic chemicals from off-site or the longer-term storage of such chemicals on-site. Efforts may also be undertaken to modify production routes to ensure that any dangerous starter or intermediate chemicals are, where possible, consumed as rapidly as possible. Further consideration has been given to replacing toxic chemicals with others that are less risky if used in a chemical attack. For example, in the USA, policymakers further considered the risks associated with the continuing use of chlorine at water purification plants.[113]

In 2007 the US Department of Homeland Security (DHS) also began implementing the Chemical Facility Anti-Terrorism Standards (CFATS), which impose comprehensive security regulations for 'high-risk' chemical facilities. CFATS requires all chemical facilities to prepare security vulnerability assessments and to develop and implement site security plans according to DHS risk-based performance standards.[114] The DHS estimates that there are approximately 7000 high-risk chemical facilities in the USA. Facilities that do not comply with the regulations can be forcibly closed or fined up to $25 000 per day.[115]

Disease surveillance and response[116]

Disease surveillance and response is important to biological security partly in order to determine whether a disease outbreak is deliberate. In 2007 measures continued to be developed to assist in the evaluation, gathering and integration of information to improve international disease surveillance and response.

[111] Royal Netherlands Academy of Arts and Sciences (KNAW), *A Code of Conduct for Biosecurity: Report by the Biosecurity Working Group* (KNAW: Amsterdam, Aug. 2007).
[112] See Royal Netherlands Academy of Arts and Sciences (note 111).
[113] See Hart and Sutherland (note 51).
[114] See US Department of Homeland Security, 'Chemical facility anti-terrorism standards', 20 Nov. 2007, <http://www.dhs.gov/xprevprot/laws/gc_1166796969417.shtm>.
[115] Ember, L., 'Chemical plant security', *Chemical & Engineering News*, vol. 85, no. 15 (9 Apr. 2007), p. 13.
[116] On work by the World Health Organization (WHO) see appendix 9A.

There were further indications that global warming will have to be increasingly taken into consideration when assessing whether disease outbreaks are naturally occurring or deliberate.

Work continued under the EU's Project BIOSAFE to establish a European-wide disease surveillance network and database information system. The project is intended to strengthen the ability of public health and civil protection authorities to respond to both accidental and deliberate releases of biological agents.

In 2007 a US citizen flew from Atlanta to Paris and back again while knowing that he was infected with a multi-drug-resistant strain of tuberculosis. Because he had travelled against medical instructions and had placed the health of fellow travellers in jeopardy, the US Centers for Disease Control and Prevention (CDC) placed him in involuntary isolation, the first time the CDC had issued an isolation order since 1963. The incident sparked debate in the US Congress and elsewhere about domestic health and safety regulations, including how they may not take into account the speed of international travel. The case also highlighted the confusion over quarantine procedures and the authority of when and how to enforce them.[117]

Bio-incidents

Failures in bio-containment and bio-security received wide publicity in 2007, including at facilities where awareness and compliance with procedures were thought to be high. One such breach occurred on 3 August at a farm near Pirbright in Surrey, UK, where an outbreak of foot-and-mouth disease (FMD) was discovered. Pirbright houses the Institute of Animal Health (IAH), which uses small quantities of live FMD virus for experimentation, as well as two private biotechnology companies: Merial Animal Health Ltd and Stabilitech Ltd. The Merial facility was producing large quantities of FMD vaccine, while Stabilitech used only small quantities of live FMD virus—comparable to those used by the IAH. The initial outbreak at a neighbouring farm led to a rapid investigation on 5 August by the Department for Environment, Food and Rural Affairs, the Veterinary Medicines Directorate and the Environment Agency, headed by the Health and Safety Executive with support from local and governmental agencies.

On 7 August a second farm was infected with FMD. The strain of FMD was identified as an FMD reference strain that had been obtained from the 1967 FMD epidemic in the UK and is commonly used at reference laboratories and in the production of pharmaceuticals, as at the Pirbright site. The strain does not occur naturally. The investigation focused on the Pirbright facilities and the IAH's final report was submitted four weeks after the first confirmation of

---

[117] For legal background see Swendiman, K. S. and Elsea, J. K., US Congress, Congressional Research Service (CRS), *Federal and State Quarantine and Isolation Authority*, CRS Report for Congress RL33201 (CRS: Washington, DC, 23 Jan. 2007); and Jones, N. L. and Shimabukuro, J. O., US Congress, Congressional Research Service (CRS), *Quarantine and Isolation: Selected Legal Issues Relating to Employment*, CRS Report for Congress RL33609 (CRS: Washington, DC, 28 Feb. 2007).

an FMD outbreak.[118] It stated that breaches in bio-security procedures, recent high precipitation in the area and lack of maintenance (i.e. cracked wastewater piping due to tree root ingress) contributed to the release of live FMD virus, which subsequently led to the infection of animals at nearby farms. The bio-security breaches included: the incomplete inactivation of live virus through insufficient chemical effluent filtering; allowing some live virus to reach the public sewer system, and eventually the surrounding soil, through unsealed manholes; the lack of standard operating procedures for handling blockages in effluent drains; and the lack of control over human and vehicle movement in and around the facility premises because construction work was being performed at the time of the outbreak. The dissemination of the FMD virus to neighbouring farms occurred because the soil around the facility was contaminated by the overflowing sewer system and spread by vehicles entering and exiting the area.

In testimony before the US House of Representatives Committee on Energy and Commerce Subcommittee on Oversight and Investigations, Keith Rhodes, the chief technologist at the Center for Technology and Engineering, noted the increasing number of BSL-3 and BSL-4 laboratories in the USA.[119] Incidents at high-containment laboratories were cited to highlight the lessons learned, including the importance of good bio-safety and bio-security practices in conjunction with the expansion of such facilities. The British FMD outbreak illustrated the importance of continued financial commitment to ensure adequate maintenance. In 2007 several potential exposures to *Coxiella burnetii* (the causative agent of Q fever) also occurred at Texas A&M University but were not reported to the CDC, as required by law.[120] Among the lessons learned in these instances was the need for specialized training for staff working with 'select agents', and making the necessary adaptations of BSL level-specific procedures when working in these laboratories.[121] An additional incident cited in the testimony involved a one-hour power outage at the new CDC BSL-4 facility in June 2007, following lightning strikes that rendered both primary

---

[118] British Health and Safety Executive (HSE), *Final Report on Potential Breaches of Biosecurity at the Pirbright Site 2007* (HSE: 2007).

[119] See Government Accountability Office (GAO), *High-Containment Biosafety Laboratories; Preliminary Observations on the Oversight of the Proliferation of BSL-3 and BSL-4 Laboratories in the United States, Statement of Keith Rhodes, Chief Technologist, Center for Technology and Engineering, Applied Research and Methods*, GAO-08-108T (GAO: Washington, DC, 4 Oct. 2007).

[120] See the Public Health Security and Bioterrorism Preparedness and Response Act of 2002, US public law 107-188, <http://www.fda.gov/oc/bioterrorism/bioact.html>, including its subpart, the Agricultural Bioterrorism Protection Act of 2002, <http://www.aphis.usda.gov/programs/ag_selectagent/ag_bioterr_Q&A.html>, and Title 42 Code of Federal Regulations, part 73.19, available at Centers for Disease Control and Prevention, Select Agent Program, <http://www.cdc.gov/od/sap>.

[121] Select agents are designated hazardous microorganisms or toxins that pose high risk to human, animal or plant health. Select agents have been identified as such because of their potential use as biological weapons, and their transfer and use in the scientific and medical community is regulated. For information and lists of pathogens see the websites of the Centers for Disease Control and Prevention (CDC), Select Agent Program (note 120); the CDC's National Select Agent Registry, <http://www.selectagents.gov/>; the US Department of Agriculture, Animal and Plant Health Inspection Service, <http://www.aphis.usda.gov/programs/ag_selectagent/>; and the Australia Group, 'Common control lists', <http://www.australiagroup.net/en/controllists.html>.

and backup power unavailable. This incident caused concern because it occurred at a top US laboratory facility operated by noted national experts. The event could have compromised the integrity of containment and could theoretically occur at other existing or planned high-containment facilities. It also demonstrated the need for redundant backup-to-backup power systems when building such facilities.

Scientific research

The scientific community and those involved in international security continue to consider possible CBW threats posed by scientific research and what measures should be taken to implement a reasonable, effective and balanced approach to bio-safety and bio-security. There is a widespread feeling among scientists that scientific research and information is 'value-free' (i.e. neither inherently harmful nor beneficial) and that any attempts to restrict their dissemination would damage scientific progress and, in any case, would be problematic because the work would be carried out elsewhere. Some researchers are also concerned that implementing restrictions will create another hurdle in the process of applying for grants and that their scientific work might not be published if deemed to be 'sensitive'. Partly for these reasons, some researchers are attempting to identify such research proposals and modify them before they are carried out in order to avoid attempts to classify or modify publication of the results.[122]

In 2007 the J. Craig Venter Institute, the Center for Strategic and International Studies and the Massachusetts Institute of Technology's Biological Engineering Department issued a report examining the safety and security concerns posed by synthetic genomics.[123] It identified three main points for possible policy intervention: (a) commercial firms that sell synthetic DNA (oligonucleotides, genes or genomes) to users; (b) owners of laboratory 'bench-top' DNA synthesizers, with which users can produce DNA; and (c) the users (consumers) of synthetic DNA and the institutions that support and oversee their work.[124]

To address the first point, the report suggests the following requirements: commercial firms must use approved software to screen orders; an institutional bio-safety officer or similar 'responsible official' must verify that those who order synthetic DNA from commercial firms are legitimate users; and commercial firms must store information about customers and their orders. In order to implement the second point, the report provides the following options: owners of DNA synthesizers must register their machines; owners of

---

[122] It may be possible, to an extent, to modify the parameters of the research proposal, perhaps informally, without undermining the integrity of the research objectives.

[123] Garfinkel, M. S. et al., 'Synthetic genomics: options for governance', Massachusetts Institute of Technology Department of Biological Engineering, J. Craig Venter Institute, Center for Strategic and International Studies, Oct. 2007, <http://www.jcvi.org/research/synthetic-genomics-report/>.

[124] Garfinkel et al. (note 123), p. ii.

DNA synthesizers must be licensed; and a licence must be required to own DNA synthesizers and buy reagents and services.[125]

Finally, the report suggests measures to address legitimate users of synthetic genomic technology. Education about risks and best practices should be incorporated in university curricula; a bio-safety manual for synthetic biology laboratories should be compiled;[126] a clearing house for best practices should be established; the responsibility of institutional biosafety committees (IBCs) should include evaluating 'risky' experiments; and, in order to evaluate such experiments, IBC review responsibilities should be broadened and combined with oversight by a national advisory group and enhanced enforcement of compliance with bio-safety guidelines.[127] The report presents a wide scope for interpreting and implementing the options identified.

On 1 November the UK introduced the Academic Technology Approval Scheme, which requires all postgraduate students from outside the European Economic Area and Switzerland who intend to study natural sciences to complete a questionnaire that is then vetted by British security services. The questionnaire is being used to assist with implementation of a programme to prevent the spread of sensitive knowledge.[128]

Scientific developments having implications for the prevention of CBW

Some scientific and technological developments can readily be incorporated into efforts to prevent CBW, while others suggest possibilities for carrying out CBW or defeating existing methods for detecting and treating those affected by CBW agents.

Microbial forensics is a developing field with some parallels to nuclear forensics.[129] It can be defined as 'a scientific discipline dedicated to analyzing evidence from a bioterrorism act, biocrime, or inadvertent microorganism/ toxin release for attribution purposes'.[130] The related technical and political challenges include developing the parameters for sharing strains and database access. Health care providers are interested in treating the victims, not preserving the crime scene to support a prosecution. The importance of biological forensics was also illustrated during the 2007 outbreak of FMD in the UK.

In the arms control and disarmament context, synthetic biology increasingly appears to symbolize the difficulty of effective international control and over-

[125] Garfinkel et al. (note 123), p. ii.

[126] E.g. see International Biorisk Standard Development Initiative, 'Laboratory biorisk management standard', draft, 25 July 2007, <http://www.biorisk.eu/documents/draft_document.PDF>; and Clevestig, P., *Biosecurity Handbook: A Guide to Assessing and Managing Biorisks in a Laboratory Setting* (SIPRI: Stockholm, forthcoming 2008).

[127] Garfinkel et al. (note 123), p. ii.

[128] Brumfiel, G., 'Foreign students face extra UK security checks', *Nature*, 7 Nov. 2007. See also British Foreign and Commonwealth Office, 'Counter-proliferation: Academic Technology Approval Scheme (ATAS)', <http://www.fco.gov.uk/atas/>.

[129] See appendix 8D in this volume.

[130] Budowle, B. et al., 'Microbial forensics', eds R. G. Breeze, B. Budowle and S. E. Schutzer, *Microbial Forensics* (Elsevier: London, 2005), p. 9. See also Emanuel, P. et al. (eds), *Sampling for Biological Agents in the Environment* (ASM Press: Washington, DC, 2007).

sight over scientific and technological developments to ensure that they are not misused for CBW purposes. It has been defined as 'the design and construction of new biological parts, devices, and systems; and the re-design of existing, natural biological systems for useful purposes'. For example, a 2006 British Royal Society report notes that synthetic biology technology is available worldwide; genetic material can be ordered through the post; and DNA synthesis can be ordered over the Internet.[131] The Massachusetts Institute of Technology currently operates a 'Registry of standard biological parts' to further the development of synthetic biology.[132]

In 2007 the J. Craig Venter Institute succeeded for the first time in transplanting the genome of naked DNA from *Mycoplasma mycoides* (the causative agent for bovine contagious pleuropneumonia) into *Mycoplasma capricolum* cells, another known animal pathogen that can cause severe arthritis in cattle, goats and sheep.[133] Such developments represent potential bio-security and dual-use risks as there is insufficient understanding of the consequences under relevant national and international laws and regulations. The Australia Group, an informal arrangement of states that meets periodically to harmonize national export controls, is discussing how to capture synthetic biology in its guidelines.[134] A major related consideration is how best to confirm the identity and intention of the end-user.

If it becomes feasible, using bioinformatics to determine the morphology and behaviour of an organism that does not exist in nature would have security implications. In principle, this development would be possible provided that such efforts are able to account for the presence and absence of genes, their mutations and epigenetic factors and the function of non-encoding DNA that is associated with each gene.

Legal and regulatory implications of scientific developments

There are two broad aspects of scientific developments with legal and regulatory implications: physical materials and intangible technology. The legal implications of synthetic biology also remain uncertain and include how to establish and maintain effective oversight of the transfer of DNA segments that can be sent by post. Other difficulties include agreeing a usable legal definition of a pathogen, such as agreeing how much of a polynucleotide

---

[131] British Royal Society, *Report of the RS-IAP-ICSU International Workshop on Science and Technology Developments Relevant to the Biological and Toxin Weapons Convention* (Royal Society: London, Nov. 2006), pp. 3–4.

[132] Massachusetts Institute of Technology, 'Registry of standard biological parts', <http://parts.mit.edu/registry/>.

[133] J. Craig Venter Institute, 'JCVI scientists publish first bacterial genome transplantation changing one species to another', Press release, 28 June 2007, <http://www.jcvi.org/>; and Lartigue, C. et al., 'Genome transplantation in bacteria: changing one species to another', *Science*, 3 Aug. 2007, pp. 632–38.

[134] 'In recognition of rapid international developments in the field of synthetic biology, Australia Group members agreed to pay particular attention to synthetic biological agents with a view towards formulating an appropriate Group response'. Australia Group, 'Media release, 2007 Australia Group plenary', Press release, June 2007, <http://www.australiagroup.net/en/releases/press_2007.htm>. On the Australia Group see chapter 11 in this volume.

sequence should be present in order for it to meet the legal definition of a select agent or its equivalent. Other developments with policy implications for the prevention of CBW include how to achieve a better understanding and oversight of the international sale of turnkey (i.e. ready for immediate use) biological and chemical facilities and the outsourcing of biological and chemical R&D and production.

The increasing difficulty of maintaining oversight of transfers of knowledge and expertise was highlighted by a US report on 'deemed exports'.[135] The USA's long-term interest is to participate in the 'global creation of knowledge' rather than to take measures to 'protect the lesser body of knowledge' that it produces domestically. Otherwise, with overly restrictive controls, the USA risks being unable to participate in the 'body of scientific and technical knowledge' about which it is not aware. This, in turn, should therefore be the principal US concern. It also stated that researchers may be required to obtain an export licence before they can be authorized to share equipment when conducting a project that includes international students and the equipment being used is judged to have a 'military application'. Biological 'laboratory equipment designed to be used to produce various toxins' could therefore fall under the military application guideline if it is determined that terrorists could use the equipment for hostile purposes. Such an interpretation, if strictly and universally applied, could undermine research.

VI. Conclusions

Efforts to reduce the possible security threats posed by chemical and biological material continued in 2007. However, further steps will be needed to maintain and strengthen the international prohibition against CBW. For example, studies bridging the gap between political and technical issues should continue to be carried out. Such work would inform analyses of how dual-use technologies and equipment are handled in practice and would also promote better understanding of the derivation and use of information.

Advances in science and technology and their impact on CBW proliferation and control remain poorly understood. The developing field of microbial forensics is integral to national and international bio-preparedness planning. It is important that cooperation between a range of agencies, including law enforcement and public health authorities, is established and maintained (e.g. when identifying and responding to deliberate use of biological agents) and to facilitate prosecutions.[136]

---

[135] A deemed export is the release to a foreign national within the USA of technology or source code having both military and civilian applications. Deemed Export Advisory Committee, *The Deemed Export Rule in the Era of Globalization* (US Department of Commerce: Washington, DC, 20 Dec. 2007), pp. 3–5.

[136] See Mathews, R. J., 'WMD arms control agreements in the post-September 11 security environment: part of the "counter-terrorism toolbox"', *Melbourne Journal of International Law*, vol. 8 (2007), pp. 292–310.

Appendix 9A. International public health diplomacy and the global surveillance of avian influenza

BERNICE RAVECHÉ

I. Introduction

Experts widely agree that another influenza pandemic is on the horizon. The pressing questions are when, where and in which form a strain of avian influenza, a variation of the H5N1 virus, will cause a pandemic in humans. Influenza has caused some of the most devastating epidemics in human history. The influenza pandemic between 1918 and 1919, known as the Spanish flu, claimed an estimated 40–100 million lives and was the result of a strain of avian influenza, H1N1, in the same family of viruses as H5N1.[1] Scientists state that an avian influenza pandemic could be a precursor to a 1918-like pandemic, which could seriously affect the world's population. According to mathematical models based on the lack of human immunity to the H5N1 virus and the current mortality rate of the virus, an avian influenza pandemic could claim more than 100 million lives.[2] Although vaccines can combat seasonal influenza outbreaks and more advanced disease surveillance systems exist now than in 1918, an avian influenza pandemic presents enormous potential challenges to global health and security.

The process of globalization has multiplied the quantity and types of international flows of people and goods. The recognition that globalization can have negative as well as positive effects is contributing to an evolving approach to security that emphasizes the role of governance in safeguarding the basic functions of modern societies against a variety of potential threats. These threats are not limited to deliberate and malicious acts. This approach has not been fully conceptualized, but it is described and analysed in an emerging literature under various headings such as 'functional security', 'societal security' or 'human security'. According to this approach, security policy consists of marshalling the resources available to prevent or, if prevention fails, to respond effectively to events that jeopardize the safety of people and the areas where they live. This requires many public agencies as well as private actors to cooperate in new configurations to create and maintain the safety of these areas, which need not necessarily coincide with national borders.

Globalization has already had an impact on the nature and spread of infectious diseases, as reflected in the outbreak of severe acute respiratory syndrome (SARS) in 2003.[3] This impact is likely to grow as more and more parts of the world are drawn into transnational cooperation networks. The SARS outbreak underlined the need for international collaboration and communication between different parts of the global

---

[1] Thomas, J. K. and Noppenberger, J., 'Avian influenza: a review', *American Journal of Health-System Pharmacy*, 15 Jan. 2007, pp. 149–65.

[2] Thomas and Noppenberger (note 1).

[3] Njuguna, J. T., 'The SARS epidemic: the control of infectious disease and biological weapon threats', *SIPRI Yearbook 2004: Armaments, Disarmament and International Security* (Oxford University Press: Oxford, 2004), pp. 697–712.

public health community as well as the need for political cooperation. While the SARS outbreak was contained relatively quickly, the initial response of governments showed that international cooperation cannot be taken for granted.

Given the potential for globalization to cause or exacerbate public health problems in different parts of the world, the World Health Organization (WHO) is likely to play an important role in any collective effort to build societal security. The WHO's role in governing global health is changing, as evidenced by the revised International Health Regulations (IHR) that were adopted in 2005 and began to be implemented in June 2007.[4] The revised IHR give the organization a historically unprecedented degree of authority over member states and their disease surveillance, response and reporting systems. The new IHR have serious implications for the actions required of countries with cases of SARS and H5N1. This appendix explores the political and economic issues associated with the prevention and control strategies for avian influenza, primarily addressing the issues related to vaccine research and development. It uses Indonesia as an example of a developing country's reluctance to adhere to WHO guidelines and recommended actions.

Section II provides a brief background of the WHO and discusses its changing role in governing global health in accordance with the revised IHR. Section III briefly describes influenza, its epidemiology and the global outbreak situation since 2003. It also outlines the current primary and secondary prevention strategies to control an avian influenza outbreak in poultry, which have been gathered from a review of literature from scientific journals, the WHO, the United Nations Food and Agriculture Organization (FAO), the World Organization for Animal Health (Office International des Epizooties, OIE) and the United States Centers for Disease Control and Prevention (CDC). Section IV is a case study of Indonesia that discusses the current outbreak situation, past and present strategies implemented by the Indonesian Government to control and prevent an avian influenza outbreak in animals and humans, and the associated challenges. The case study also provides a timeline of events, from the Government of Indonesia's initial refusal to send virus samples to the WHO up to its decision in early 2008 to send avian influenza samples to a WHO laboratory. The conclusions are presented in section V.

II. The changing role of the World Health Organization

The WHO's primary roles and responsibilities include 'providing leadership on matters critical to health ... shaping the research agenda ... setting norms and standards and promoting and monitoring their implementation, articulating ethical and evidence-based policy options; providing technical support ... and monitoring the health situation'.[5] Established in 1946 as a specialized UN agency, the WHO is undergoing an identity crisis because of its drastically changing role, the increased authority granted to it by the IHR and, most importantly, the increasing influence of global health trends on domestic and foreign policy. The WHO is not the only international organization that is dedicated to global health security, but it is the only such organization that is well connected with the ministries of health of almost every

[4] World Health Organization (WHO), Fifty-eighth World Health Assembly, Resolution WHA58.3: Revision of the International Health Regulations, 23 May 2005, <http://www.who.int/csr/ihr/IHRWHA 58_3-en.pdf>.

[5] WHO, 'The role of the WHO in public health', <http://www.who.int/about/role/en/>.

country, making it a crucial stakeholder in protecting and enhancing global public health security.

The WHO was established on the principle that 'the health of all peoples is fundamental to the attainment of peace and security and is dependent upon the fullest co-operation of individuals and States'.[6] In its early history the WHO primarily focused on improving the health of people in developing countries in order to facilitate commerce and economic growth in both the developing and developed world. The predecessor to the IHR was created in 1903 in order to control diseases spread in ports and by ships engaged in international trade. In their earliest form the IHR only applied to cholera and the plague but in 1912 and 1926 yellow fever, typhus, relapsing fever and smallpox were added to the list of reportable diseases.[7] After the WHO was created, the IHR fell under the WHO's mandate, and it gained the sole right to modify and implement them. Except for the WHO's massive campaign to eradicate smallpox in the late 1960s and early 1970s, the IHR have never been fully implemented or adopted by states because of the fear of economic retribution or embargo on a country's goods and services if it reported an outbreak of smallpox or another of the deadly diseases listed in the IHR. The 2003 SARS outbreak, the HIV/AIDS pandemic and avian influenza have prompted the WHO to revise the IHR again in the hope that states will implement them in a timely manner and abide by this legal framework in order to increase global public health security.

The revised International Health Regulations

The revised International Health Regulations were adopted on 23 May 2005 and implemented on 15 June 2007. Because of the IHR's long history of ineffectiveness and non-compliance by a minority of member states, the WHO revised the IHR using a legal framework that gives the WHO an unprecedented legal authority over the global disease surveillance and reporting requirements of the member states. The revised IHR take an all-risks approach to diseases. States are to report all events that could result in public health emergencies of international concern, including those caused by chemical agents, contaminated food and radioactive material. The revised IHR also give the director-general of the WHO the authority to ascertain when a disease is considered a global public health threat or emergency.

Under the revised IHR, states are required to notify the WHO within 24 hours of an emerging global health threat that has not been encountered previously. This rapid notification system is intended to promote timely information sharing among member states in the event of an infectious disease outbreak. When Indonesia refused to send samples to the WHO in 2003, the revised IHR had not yet begun to be implemented, but the revised notification system was designed to protect the health of the global population by preventing states from taking similar actions. Furthermore, each state is required to 'develop, strengthen and maintain core national public health capacities', with the additional creation of a national IHR focal point, which is designed to assess, report and respond promptly to public health risks and emergencies. The revised IHR also require the WHO to share non-governmental data sources with member states and related international organizations to enable a coordinated and appropriate

---

[6] WHO, Constitution of the World Health Organization, Oct. 2006, <http://www.who.int/governance/eb/constitution/en/>, preamble.

[7] Zacher, M., 'The transformation in global health collaboration since the 1990s', eds F. C. Cooper, J. J. Kirton and T. Schrecker, *Governing Global Health* (Ashgate: Burlington, Vt., 2007), pp. 16–27.

response to an emerging public health risk. Utilizing non-governmental sources of data was useful to the WHO during the SARS outbreak.[8] Recognizing the importance of non-governmental sources of data in the revised IHR will help to promote the WHO's Global Outbreak Alert and Response Network (GOARN) and encourage international scientists and researchers to share valuable information.[9]

The revised IHR reflect a shifting paradigm in global health as well as the changing role of the WHO. In the WHO's *World Health Report 2007* global public health is discussed solely in terms of a securitization paradigm.[10] The driving motivation for the revision of the IHR was to strengthen international public health security which, according to the WHO, is contingent upon strengthening countries' disease surveillance and response systems to ensure timely management of public health risks.[11] In June 2007, in order to guide the implementation of the revised IHR, the WHO published a strategy for implementation and identified four strategic actions that countries must complete: action 1, to 'strengthen national disease surveillance, prevention, control and response systems'; action 2, to 'strengthen public health security in travel and transport'; action 3, to 'strengthen WHO global alert and response systems'; and action 4, to 'strengthen the management of specific risks'.[12]

This implementation plan for the revised IHR relies on a coordinated and established public health infrastructure that many developing countries still lack. The WHO dealt sparingly with incentives or sanctions that countries will receive if they follow the revised IHR or choose not to adhere to this action plan. More importantly, it does not address how countries are to fund the required projects. In a 2007 article, Phillipe Calain discusses the barriers to implementation of the revised IHR on the grounds that they threaten state sovereignty. He argues that international political commitment to comply with the revised IHR is negatively affected by 'perceived threats to sovereignty, blurred international health agendas, lack of internationally recognized codes of conduct for outbreak investigations and erosion of the impartiality and independence of international agencies' (mainly referring to the WHO).[13]

III. Background on avian influenza

Influenza viruses are categorized into three types: A, B and C.[14] Only influenza A and B viruses can cause disease in humans. Influenza A is the type that causes seasonal

---

[8] Fidler, D. P. and Gostin, L. P., 'The new international health regulations: an historic development for international law and public health', *Journal of Law, Medicine & Ethics*, vol. 34, no. 1 (spring 2006), pp. 85–96.

[9] The WHO created GOARN in Apr. 2000. It provides an international network for the technical coordination of international alert and response activities for both governmental and non-governmental data sources.

[10] WHO, *World Health Report 2007—A Safer Future: Global Public Health Security in the 21st Century* (WHO: Geneva, 2007), <http://www.who.int/whr/2007/en>.

[11] WHO, *Global Collaboration to Meet Threats to Public Health Security* (WHO: Geneva, 2007), <http://www.who.int/whr/2007/overview/en/index2.html>.

[12] WHO, *International Health Regulations (2005): Areas of Work for Implementation* (WHO: Geneva, June 2007), <http://www.who.int/csr/ihr/area_of_work/en>.

[13] Calain, P., 'Exploring the international arena of global public health surveillance', *Health Policy and Planning*, vol. 22 (2007), pp. 13–20.

[14] Influenza viruses belong to the orthomyxovirus family and are spherical or tubular enveloped viruses containing an 8-segmented negative sense RNA genome within a matrix (M_1) and membrane (M_2) protein shell. The RNA genome is associated with a nucleoprotein and a transcriptase protein. Influenza types A, B and C are differentiated by their M_1 and M_2 proteins and nucleoproteins.

Table 9A.1. H5N1 human cases globally, 2003–2007

Country	2003 C	2003 D	2004 C	2004 D	2005 C	2005 D	2006 C	2006 D	2007 C	2007 D	Total C	Total D
Azerbaijan	0	0	0	0	0	0	8	5	0	0	8	5
Cambodia	0	0	0	0	4	4	2	2	1	1	7	7
China	1	1	0	0	8	5	13	8	5	3	27	17
Djibouti	0	0	0	0	0	0	1	0	0	0	1	0
Egypt	0	0	0	0	0	0	18	10	23	6	41	16
Indonesia	0	0	0	0	20	13	55	45	41	36	116	94
Iraq	0	0	0	0	0	0	3	2	0	0	3	2
Laos	0	0	0	0	0	0	0	0	2	2	2	2
Myanmar	0	0	0	0	0	0	0	0	1	0	1	0
Nigeria	0	0	0	0	0	0	0	0	1	1	1	1
Pakistan	0	0	0	0	0	0	0	0	1	1	1	1
Thailand	0	0	17	12	5	2	3	3	0	0	25	17
Turkey	0	0	0	0	0	0	12	4	0	0	12	4
Viet Nam	3	3	29	20	61	19	0	0	8	5	101	47
Total	**4**	**4**	**46**	**32**	**98**	**43**	**115**	**79**	**83**	**55**	**346**	**213**

C= cases; D = deaths.

Source: World Health Organization, 'Cumulative number of confirmed human cases of avian influenza reported to WHO', 28 Dec. 2007, <http://www.who.int/csr/disease/avian_influenza/country/cases_table_2007_12_28/en>.

influenza, which affects approximately 10–20 per cent of the world's population each year, and can also infect other animal species.[15] It is divided into subtypes, based on the two surface proteins, hemagglutinin (HA) and neuraminidase (NA).[16] These surface proteins are responsible for the infectious capacity of the virus by direct interaction with host cell proteins. Thus, HA and NA govern the host range and specificity of the virus as well as the degree of immune evasion.[17] Using this classification, influenza A strains are named according to their HA subtype followed by their NA subtype, as is the case with the highly pathogenic avian influenza strain H5N1. Currently, 16 HA subtypes and 9 NA subtypes are known. The global human population has no immunity to H5N1 because this strain was previously only present in wild fowl and poultry populations. Humans are therefore susceptible to infection.

Wild fowl are the main reservoir for influenza A viruses. While wild fowl mainly carry influenza A asymptomatically, domesticated birds such as chickens, turkeys and ducks are highly susceptible to the viruses and will develop severe symptoms following infection and have a high mortality rate. The disease caused by H5N1 in humans

[15] WHO, 'Avian influenza: food safety issues', 27 Apr. 2007, <http://www.who.int/foodsafety/micro/avian/en/>.

[16] Influenza B viruses are subdivided into strains, not subtypes, on the basis of the HA and NA composition because influenza B viruses do not cause severe pandemics similar to influenza A. Furthermore, influenza B does not undergo the process of antigenic shift. However, influenza B can cause severe human disease and death. HA and NA are both glyocproteins (proteins carrying large sugar residues with sialic acids) and are anchored to the virus surface membrane.

[17] The term 'host range' refers to the range of species in which a pathogen can cause infections and disease. 'Immune evasion' refers to the lack of specific antibodies towards a novel antigen (i.e. from a new influenza strain carrying mutations).

is clinically more aggressive than seasonal influenza. According to the WHO, there have been 346 human cases of H5N1, of which 213 were fatal (see table 9A.1).[18] The overall case fatality rate thus far has been roughly 60 per cent, with the 10–19 age group suffering the most fatalities. This epidemiological pattern is consistent with the morbidity and mortality trends of the 1918 pandemic, where influenza mostly claimed the lives of young adults ranging in age from 20 to 44.[19] Because the case fatality rate is dependent on the number of H5N1 cases reported, and not all cases are reported, the true case fatality rate of H5N1 will never be known.

The main concern related to human and avian influenza A viruses is their ability to quickly change and adapt their genomes, and hence widen their host ranges. This occurs in two different ways. First, the accumulation of mutations over time that facilitates the evasion of host immune responses through selection is referred to as 'antigenic drift'.[20] Second, genetic reassortment (antigenic shift) between human and animal influenza viruses can occur in an intermediate host.[21] Influenza viruses can infect a wide variety of species, including humans, fowl, swine, horses and sea mammals (e.g. seals). Such infections, in turn, provide ample subtype combinations for novel influenza strains to develop if the opportunity arises. Such a situation is common in many parts of Asia, where domestic poultry and swine may reside in close proximity and be exposed to the excrement of wild migratory birds carrying H5N1 and to human handlers carrying the human subtypes. It is believed that swine are the intermediary reservoir from which aggressive influenza strains emerge. Emerging influenza strains warrant close observation, rapid disease surveillance and reporting because such a reassortment might occur and result in a new strain with high pathogenicity in humans and the capability for rapid human-to-human transmission.

The first documented human cases of H5N1 occurred in 1997 in Hong Kong, where 18 individuals were infected.[22] This outbreak was caused by direct contact with infected poultry. In response to the outbreak in humans and poultry, 1.5 million birds were culled within three days in order to prevent further human infection. This drastic strategy quelled the outbreak in Hong Kong until the surge of H5N1 cases in South East Asia in 2003. The incubation period for seasonal influenza in humans is roughly 2 to 3 days. However, current data suggest that the incubation period for humans infected with H5N1 ranges from 2 to 16 days. Because H5N1 is an emerging infectious disease, there is still a paucity of data and limited evidence about its manifestation in humans and other animal species. This complicates the diagnosis of an individual with H5N1 because symptoms in past patients have ranged from high fever, diarrhoea, vomiting and influenza-like symptoms to acute encephalitis. The efficacy of antivirals like oseltamivir to reduce viral replication and improve survival is

[18] These numbers are taken from the last WHO report released in 2007. WHO, 'Cumulative number of confirmed human cases of avian influenza reported to WHO', 28 Dec. 2007, <http://www.who.int/csr/disease/avian_influenza/country/cases_table_2007_12_28/en>.

[19] Taubenberger J. K., and Morens D. M., '1918 influenza: the mother of all pandemics', *Emerging Infectious Disease*, vol. 12, no. 1 (Jan. 2006), pp. 15–22.

[20] Mutations are common, and random, mis-incorporations of nucleotides during the replication of genomes. They are more prevalent in viruses with RNA genomes. Selection refers to Darwinian natural selection where inefficient virus particles will be selected and removed by host immune response or through the creation of defective particles.

[21] Reassortment in influenza viruses occurs as a result of the genomes segmented nature: the segments can combine with similar segments—even segments from influenza viruses of different origin or host species—thereby producing novel variants of varying HA and NA subtypes.

[22] WHO (note 10), p. 46.

limited because this drug needs to be administered within 48 hours of the onset of the illness and, in most cases, the disease is detected and diagnosed in its later stages.

Primary and secondary prevention strategies

In its 2005 Recommended Strategic Action Plan for responding to the avian influenza pandemic threat, the WHO stated that all of the necessary criteria in order for an avian influenza pandemic to occur had been met—with the exception of the ability for H5N1 to transfer efficiently from person to person.[23] Although there has been one known case of human-to-human transmission among a family in Indonesia, human-to-human transmission has not been sustained in the current strain of the virus. The human transmissibility of H5N1 could be increased through a reassortment event in which genetic material is exchanged between humans and birds during co-infection or through a gradual adaptive mutation process. In order to prevent human exposure to H5N1, countries should primarily focus on controlling the disease in animals and then prevent human behaviour that would expose them to the disease.

However, the main strategies to minimize human contact with birds and excrement are difficult to implement in developing countries with weak public health infrastructure and disease surveillance systems. Additionally, many of the prevention strategies designed to control the H5N1 virus call for dramatic changes in farming strategies and the culling of large numbers of domestic poultry. This has been very difficult to institute in rural South East Asian communities, where poultry is the main source of income as well as food. South East Asian governments, particularly Indonesia, have been unable to compensate farmers for culled poultry. This financial challenge is a major barrier to animal disease prevention strategies. Consequently, farmers have often been reluctant to report sick poultry to government officials. Furthermore, the H5N1 virus has been manifesting itself among domestic ducks that show no signs or symptoms of carrying the illness.

The resistance to culling poultry has, in some cases, been overcome by force, with the military and police carrying out the culling process. As a result, when villagers are aware of a local mandate to cull poultry some have hidden their chickens or quickly sold them at market to avoid loss. At the root of the problem of stopping the spread of infection is simply that many districts lack knowledge about H5N1 and how to prevent infection.

An established public health infrastructure that adheres to current bio-safety and bio-security measures to block the introduction of the virus is necessary to prevent avian influenza from affecting domestic poultry.[24] Primary prevention strategies encompass all levels of domestic poultry production from large, so called sector 1 corporations to smaller sector 4 backyard farms and 'wet markets' (i.e. open food markets). These strategies include routine monitoring of poultry for signs of illness, hygienic poultry butchering practices, routine cleaning of faecal matter from storage and transport facilities as well as mass education to promote bio-safety measures. Once the virus has been identified, the 'stampede method' is recommended during

[23] WHO, *Responding to the Avian Influenza Threat: Recommended Strategic Actions* (WHO: Geneva, 2005), <http://www.who.int/csr/resources/publications/influenza/WHO_CDS_CSR_GIP_2005_8/en>.

[24] See Kuhlau, F., *Countering Bio-threats: EU Instruments for Managing Biological Materials, Technology and Knowledge*, SIPRI Policy Paper no. 19 (SIPRI: Stockholm, Aug. 2007), <http://books.sipri.org/>. Bio-safety is safety while working with pathogens. Bio-security is security at facilities containing pathogens and other sensitive materials.

the early stages of infection among domestic poultry. This method includes creating three zones surrounding the infected poultry and culling all poultry in zones 1 and 2 (those closest to the detection site). In order to be effective, the stampede method must be complemented by a compensation package for owners of the culled poultry. These established best practice guidelines to prevent and control avian influenza outbreaks are applicable to developed countries but are not necessarily appropriate for developing countries.

However, according to the updated *Global Strategy for Prevention and Control of H5N1 Highly Pathogenic Avian Influenza* developed by the FAO and the OIE, in countries where H5N1 is endemic, experience indicates that eliminating infected flocks only provides short-term mitigation.[25] Appropriate changes need to be made in disease management practices on farms and in high-risk marketing practices to regulate the uncontrolled movement of poultry through live bird markets.

Vaccination is an alternative secondary prevention strategy to control the number of poultry that are infected with H5N1, but there have been recent debates over the efficacy of this strategy. On 22 March 2007 in Verona, Italy, 400 experts from the OIE, the FAO and the Istituto Zooprofilattico Sperimentale delle Venezie (IZSVe) with the support of the European Commission attended a conference to review the current vaccination programmes of various countries in order to provide best practice guidelines. The conference recommended that poultry should be vaccinated against avian influenza in Egypt, Indonesia and Nigeria, where the disease has become endemic. The OIE stated that a 'successful vaccination campaign depends mainly on the use of high quality vaccines complying with OIE standards, appropriate infrastructure to ensure the rapid and safe delivery of vaccines (cold chain), monitoring of vaccinated flocks, movement control of poultry, and adequate financial resources'.[26] In addition to the enormous economic costs of a mass vaccination programme for infected or possibly infected animals, a successful vaccination programme requires a strong public health infrastructure and veterinary personnel, elements which are not present in Indonesia and other countries to which avian influenza is endemic.

Regardless of the lack of data verifying its efficiency, vaccinating poultry is highly recommended by developed countries because it produces more numerical evaluation data. In addition, it is a more tangible proactive strategy than emphasizing long-term behaviour change that does not produce quantifiable results. Avian influenza cannot be controlled or prevented by relying solely on the 'quick fix' that vaccines provide. If vaccination programmes are not implemented properly with the most up-to-date quality of vaccine and are not aggressively monitored, they can actually accelerate the mutation of the virus. According to the WHO's Manila spokesman, Peter Cordingley, 'vaccination can sometimes cause silent transmission of infection from asymptomatic birds. Mass vaccination programmes entail people tramping around the countryside from farm to farm and they can spread the disease with them. The first response must be culling.'[27] Furthermore, such programmes can complicate the current veterinary monitoring systems of healthy and sick poultry by masking symptoms

[25] UN Food and Agriculture Organization (FAO) and World Organization for Animal Health (OIE), *Global Strategy for Prevention and Control of H5N1 Highly Pathogenic Avian Influenza* (FAO: Rome, Mar. 2007), <http://www.fao.org/avianflu/en/>.

[26] Zampaglipone, M., 'Combining poultry vaccination with other disease control measures to combat H5N1: international conference in Verona reviews vaccination methods', World Organization for Animal Health, Press release, Verona, 22 Mar. 2007, <http://www.oie.int/eng/press/en_070322.htm>.

[27] Parry, J., 'Vaccinating poultry against avian flu is contributing to spread', *British Medical Journal*, vol. 331 (26 Nov. 2005), p. 1223.

in infected animals. Because vaccination does not completely eradicate the virus from a flock and therefore a region or country, some countries have even banned vaccination because it interferes with the stampede method of totally eliminating the disease from an infected region.[28]

IV. Case study: Indonesia

Indonesia is currently the 'hot zone' of the H5N1 outbreak in both humans and poultry. As of December 2007, Indonesia has had the most human cases of H5N1 and the highest case fatality rate, approximately 81 per cent, of any country with human cases of H5N1.[29] International scientists and epidemiologists are still trying to determine why the case fatality rate is so high in Indonesia compared to other countries like China, where it is 63 per cent, Thailand, where it is 68 per cent, and Viet Nam, where it is only 47 per cent. More puzzling than the high fatality rate is that several cases of family clusters of H5N1 have been reported. On 18 May 2006 the WHO documented the largest family cluster of H5N1 cases—an Indonesian family where seven people were infected, spanning four households—suggesting evidence of human-to-human transmission. It is believed that the first victim became infected through contact with infected poultry and then proceeded to infect six other family members.[30] The WHO and the international community have been very concerned about the situation in Indonesia because of these scientific anomalies and the hypothesis that, if the virus were to mutate, Indonesia is likely to be the location for a reassortment event. In addition to being the epicentre of the avian influenza global epidemic, Indonesia was selected as a case study for this appendix because of its government's vocal disapproval of the WHO's current virus sharing programme due to perceived unequal access to influenza vaccines between developed and developing countries.

The H5N1 outbreak in Indonesia started in mid-2003, originally in the provinces of Banten and Kava. The disease spread rapidly to all provinces of Java and the Ministry of Agriculture internationally declared the H5N1 outbreak in January 2004. Although the WHO, the OIE and the FAO recommend that culling be the first response to an outbreak, that method was not an option for the Indonesian Government because Java (containing 60 per cent of the country's birds) is the centre of the Indonesian poultry production and farmers could not be compensated for their economic losses. The Indonesian Government therefore initiated a mass vaccination programme in early 2004 for all sector 4 farms as an attempt to control the disease. However, this programme failed because of the limited amount of vaccine available, the lack of appropriate equipment, facilities and personnel to transport and administer the vaccine, and the low operating budget. It is possible that this rushed vaccination programme further exacerbated the outbreak, which is now endemic in 30 of Indonesia's 33 provinces.[31]

---

[28] Saad, M. Z., 'Opinion: doing the thing to do away with bird flu', *New Straits Times*, 9 July 2007.

[29] The data in this section are based on table 9A.1.

[30] WHO, 'H5N1 avian influenza: timeline of major events', 28 Jan. 2008, <http://www.who.int/csr/disease/avian_influenza/timeline2008_01_30.pdf>.

[31] FAO, 'Tapping local knowledge in Indonesia to battle avian influenza', 26 July 2007, <http://www.fao.org/newsroom/en/news/2007/1000631>.

Indonesia is an archipelago consisting of over 6000 inhabited islands with a population of 220 million people,[32] over half of whom reside in Java, which was hardest hit by H5N1. The Indonesian poultry sector employs roughly 10 million people who care for over 1.3 billion chickens that are spread throughout 30 million backyard farms and are sold or traded in 13 000 daily wet markets.[33] This extensive poultry production and trading system provides a perfect breeding ground for H5N1. The health care sector, both human and animal, is highly decentralized with little national control. Over 400 local districts independently address health and agricultural needs. After the Asian financial crisis in 1997–98, the national veterinary services were drastically downsized, leaving some islands and provinces without any trained government veterinarians. The decentralization of the public health infrastructure in Indonesia has severely affected the national disease surveillance and reporting systems and has serious implications for the health of Indonesians. Many local districts lack the capacity and capability for disease reporting and surveillance, and the current epidemiological detection systems are costly to implement. Peter Roeder, a field consultant for the UN in Indonesia, has stated that there is no on-the-ground systematic programme in Indonesia and the situation is 'a bloody mess'.[34] Furthermore, case detection is often imprecise because of the high prevalence of other respiratory illnesses in areas endemic for H5N1 that present similar initial symptoms to avian influenza.

On 7 March 2006 the Indonesian National Committee for Avian Influenza Control and Pandemic Influenza Preparedness education campaign was instituted in order to provide massive public health education about avian influenza. This educational campaign stressed the effective steps that individuals can take to reduce the risk of contracting the H5N1 virus through limiting their contact with infected species, practicing hygienic and appropriate slaughtering practices as well as routine cleaning of storage and market facilities. There has been no formal evaluation of this education campaign, but there is limited anecdotal evidence of a persistent lack of knowledge among the Indonesian public about H5N1 and how to prevent human infection.[35]

Since mid-2006 there has been progress in utilizing local knowledge and community capacity to compensate for the lack of national and local veterinary services available as a result of decentralization. Participatory epidemiology and participatory surveillance are two methods developed by FAO epidemiologists that enlist local farmers to help in disease tracking and surveillance. Formally known as participatory disease surveillance and response (PDS/R), this method was successful in the FAO's Global Rinderpest Eradication programme in Africa in the early 1990s, where there was also an underdeveloped veterinary system. Including community members in disease surveillance methods helps build local sustainable capacity and knowledge about H5N1 and ways to control the virus in poultry. Veterinarians in Indonesia welcome this programme because there are too many backyard farms and districts to

[32] UN Population Fund (UNFPA), 'Indonesia', <http://www.unfpa.org/profile/indonesia.cfm>.

[33] Butler, D., 'Indonesia struggles to control bid flu outbreak', *Nature,* 13 Oct. 2007, p. 937.

[34] Butler, D., 'Disease surveillance needs a revolution', *Nature,* 2 Mar. 2006, pp. 6–7.

[35] Thieme, O., Background paper presented at the Technical Meeting on Highly Pathogenic Avian Influenza and Human H5N1 Infection, Rome, 27–29 June 2007. Basic public education about H5N1 should be the first and main focus of the Indonesian Government, yet on 14 June 2007 the Indonesian national committee for avian influenza announced that it recommended a more robust vaccination programme be implemented to control the H5N1 outbreak. Indonesian National Committee for Avian Influenza Control and Pandemic Influenza Preparedness, Press release, 14 June 2007, <http://www.komnasfbpi.go.id/news_june14_07.html>.

monitor given the limited personnel. It is impossible for any highly technologically advanced disease surveillance system to work efficiently without a developed fundamental public health infrastructure. Indonesia is a prime example of the difficulty that scientists face in accessing the more than 6000 inhabited islands to monitor over 1.3 billion chickens, retrieving accurate data and reporting. Once appropriately evaluated, the PDR/S technique should be a valuable tool for both developed and developing countries, enabling them to improve their disease surveillance systems by collaborating with their citizens.

The US Agency for International Development (USAID), the Australian Agency for International Development (AusAID) and the Government of Japan have contributed over $10 million to support the PDS/R initiative in Indonesia.[36] However, a large portion of international funding has been allocated to modern disease surveillance technology and high-level laboratories in developing countries. The US Department of Defense has proposed setting up high-tech labs modelled on the US network of infectious disease laboratories. The motivation behind such laboratories is to improve the US early-warning system. Mark Savey, the head epidemiologist directing France's food safety agency, cautions against relying on modern disease surveillance technology to track and control infectious diseases: 'You don't need satellites, PCR and geographic information systems to fight outbreaks. The lab's top priority should be building large teams of local staff, who are familiar with the region and its practice. If you do not have that, then surveillance will stay in the Middle Ages.'[37] International aid comes coupled with considerable pressure on the receiving country to cooperate with outside agendas that might not correspond with the receiving country's priorities.

The avian influenza virus sharing debate

In December 2006 the Indonesian Government withheld samples from the WHO because of uneven distribution of influenza vaccines, especially those made from virus samples collected in Indonesia. For more than 50 years the Global Influenza Surveillance Network has collected virus samples that enable international scientists to monitor the evolution of the virus and determine the risk of a pandemic. The Indonesian Government has demanded that prior approval be obtained for the development of a vaccine from a virus found in the country and that a discount price for such a vaccine be negotiated for countries where the H5N1 virus is endemic. The Indonesian Government referred to the 1992 Convention on Biological Diversity, which stipulates that a country has to share the benefits if others make use of its genetic resources.[38] To provide an incentive for Indonesia to resume sharing samples with it, the WHO has facilitated several proposals to improve access to vaccines and has awarded six countries (Brazil, India, Indonesia, Mexico, Thailand and Viet Nam) grants donated by Japan and the USA for a total of $18 million to develop their own vaccine manufacturing capacities; this, in turn, promotes the development of domes-

---

[36] FAO (note 31).

[37] Butler (note 34).

[38] Enserink, M., 'Indonesia earns flu accord at World Health Assembly', *Science*, 25 May 2007, p. 1108. The Convention on Biological Diversity was signed on 5 June 1992 and entered into force on 29 Dec. 1993. On the convention see <http://www.cbd.int/convention>.

tic capacity.[39] Pharmaceutical companies are not the only parties to recognize the possibility of making a large profit from vaccine development. Researchers and governments worldwide are also well aware of this lucrative possibility, which is an incentive to demanding ready access to virus genome sharing from all countries affected by H5N1. Professor Sangokt Marzuki of the Indonesian Academy of Sciences has stated that the academy had considered the potential financial benefits of developing vaccines and drugs while not sharing their data and accruing royalties from intellectual rights but that it ultimately gave in to international pressure and 'for the sake of basic human interests'.[40]

After a two-day meeting with top WHO officials about international protocols for virus sample sharing programmes, the Indonesian Minister of Health, Siti Fadillah Supari, agreed to resume sharing virus samples with the WHO on 26 March 2007.[41] In her closing remarks at the 60th annual meeting of the World Health Assembly, on 15 May 2007, the WHO Director-General, Dr Margaret Chan, acknowledged her increased role in protecting international health security as a result of the revised IHR and reminded member states of their obligations under the adopted resolution on sharing influenza viruses.[42] The Indonesian influenza virus sharing stalemate prompted the 'Global pandemic influenza action plan to increase vaccine supply' document on the sharing of influenza vaccines and a plan to guarantee the equitable and affordable sharing of the vaccine in the event of a pandemic.[43] However, this draft proposal is vague and lacks a definitive action plan to enable the WHO to meet its stated aims. As a result of this ambiguity and the lack of measurable objectives, in August 2007 Indonesian officials announced that they would again withhold virus samples unless a formal system is established that guarantees equitable access to vaccines developed from shared samples. David Heymann, the assistant WHO Director-General, stated on 6 August 2007 that 'Indonesia is putting the public health security of the whole world at risk because they're not sharing viruses'.[44] After an unsuccessful meeting on 23 November, WHO and Indonesian officials had still not come to an agreement over an acceptable avian influenza virus sharing programme.[45] However, in early 2008, after 'receiving assurances its rights to any vaccines produced from them would be recognized', Indonesia sent 12 avian influenza samples to the WHO.[46]

Although there are major differences between AIDS and H5N1, both diseases have initiated heated debates concerning ethical issues related to vaccine research and development. AIDS has forced the WHO to address public health, diseases and vaccines using the legal framework of intellectual property rights and trade, more for-

[39] WHO, 'WHO facilitates influenza vaccine technology transfer to developing countries', 24 Apr. 2007, <http://www.who.int/mediacentre/news/notes/2007/np18/en>.

[40] Rukmantara, A., 'Bird flu data now open to all', *Jakarta Post*, 13 July 2007.

[41] 'Bird flu sample row ends with agreement', *Jakarta Post*, 28 Mar. 2007.

[42] WHO, 'Closing remarks to the 60th World Health Assembly', 23 May 2007, <http://www.who.int/dg/speeches/2007/230507_closing/en/>.

[43] Centre for Infectious Disease Research and Policy, 'Indonesia to keep withholding virus samples for now', 9 Aug 2007, <http://www.cidrap.umn.edu/cidrap/content/influenza/panflu/news/aug0907indonesia.html>.

[44] Centre for Infectious Disease Research and Policy (note 43).

[45] Centre for Infectious Disease Research and Policy, 'Virus-sharing pact eludes WHO group, but work will continue', 26 Nov. 2007, <http://www.cidrap.umn.edu/cidrap/content/influenza/avianflu/news/nov2607pact.html>.

[46] 'Indonesia resumes bird flu samples to WHO: official', Agence France-Presse, 23 Feb. 2008.

468 NON-PROLIFERATION, ARMS CONTROL, DISARMAMENT, 2007

mally governed by the World Trade Organization. Indonesia's rejection of the normative system of influenza virus sharing has further forced the WHO to address the intellectual property rights issue, which is a very uncomfortable position for it and further blurs its primary mission of ensuring the highest level of health for all people.

Pharmaceutical companies and independent scientists are very interested and willing to invest in Indonesia in order to gain access to the most current version of the virus. In order for a vaccine to successfully produce immunity in a given human population, it must be developed using the most current strain of the influenza virus. Baxter Healthcare SA, a Swiss-based subsidiary of the US pharmaceutical company Baxter Healthcare International Inc., began clinical trials in Singapore and Hong Kong in July 2007 of a vaccine that was created with strains from Indonesia. These clinical trials are part of an agreement reached in February 2007 between Baxter Healthcare and the Indonesian Government according to which Baxter Healthcare will provide technical equipment and assistance to develop the vaccine in exchange for up-to-date virus specimens from infected poultry and humans within Indonesia's borders.[47] Siti stated that the agreement was made with Baxter Healthcare because it was the 'only company offering to produce human vaccines for the specific Indonesian bird flu strain'.[48] This agreement between Baxter Healthcare and the Indonesian Government is controversial and further increased tensions between the WHO, manufacturers, government and researchers over preserving intellectual property rights.

V. Conclusions

The public health sector and the WHO are continually influenced by the growing national and international interest and investment in enhancing bio-security and bio-safety. Global public health has been increasingly discussed using security rhetoric, and infectious diseases, such as avian influenza and SARS, were labelled a 'threat to global health security' by the UN Security Council in 2004. Public health and national security have a reciprocal relationship because public health can be improved through increased security, and security can likewise be improved by incorporating public health concerns. Globalization has changed the structure of global health governance by introducing new actors and interested parties due to the rise of health as a foreign policy concern. This has drastic implications for the WHO, which was the original governing body of global health and was created as a specialized agency associated with the United Nations. The WHO has felt increased pressure from governments and international organizations to securitize global public health by increasing early-warning systems and disease surveillance systems to protect the world's population from feared infectious disease outbreaks like SARS and the looming threat of avian influenza.

Countries cannot rely solely on stamping out, culling or vaccinating poultry; there must be a comprehensive H5N1 prevention plan that includes evidence-based prevention strategies to address the problem. Improving bio-safety measures is less expensive than a mass vaccination programme, although it requires changing human behaviour, which is much more time consuming, and does not provide immediate or easily measurable results for evaluation.

[47] 'Baxter to develop bird flu vaccine for Indonesia', *Jakarta Post*, 8 Feb. 2007.
[48] 'Baxter to develop bird flu vaccine for Indonesia' (note 47).

However, it must be asked whether this securitization paradigm is the best way to conceptualize global public health because countries have differing opinions on security priorities, as exemplified by the influenza virus sharing debate between Indonesia and the WHO. The revised IHR mandate member states to drastically increase their disease surveillance systems, and they thus reflect the securitization of global public health. The WHO has not addressed or given any formal guidance to countries on how they should prioritize their public health funding between current health threats while simultaneously strengthening technical disease surveillance capacities for potential pandemics like avian influenza. The future will show if the WHO can maintain impartiality and neutrality throughout the implementation of the revised IHR. If the WHO cannot prove its credibility to both developing and developed countries, it will lose its place as the leading international global health organization and global public health will further be dictated by individual countries' foreign policy.

10. Conventional arms control

ZDZISLAW LACHOWSKI

I. Introduction

There were many troubling developments for conventional arms control in 2007, although there was positive progress in some areas. In the biggest challenge yet to the 1990 Treaty on Conventional Armed Forces in Europe (CFE Treaty) the Russian Federation 'suspended' its participation in the regime.[1] This gave rise to more energetic consideration of the current status of conventional arms control in Europe. The weakening of the CFE arms control regime led to some disquieting reactions in the South Caucasus, while in Moldova the deadlock persisted over Russia's removal of personnel and equipment. In contrast, there was further implementation of the 2005 Georgia–Russia agreement on the closure of Russian military bases and other facilities in Georgia and the subregional arms control regime in the Balkans continued to operate smoothly. Outside Europe, North and South Korea restarted talks in 2007 on building confidence on their mutual border.[2]

The states participating in the Organization for Security and Co-operation in Europe (OSCE) continued to develop confidence- and security-building measures (CSBMs) and other arms control-related arrangements in 2007, with the aim of better meeting Europe's regional and subregional risks and challenges. Globally, there was progress in dealing with 'inhumane weapons', and the international Oslo process on cluster munitions, which was launched in 2006, gained momentum.

In reviewing these and other issues, this chapter assesses the major developments relating to conventional arms control in 2007. Section II gives a brief overview of the gathering crisis over the CFE Treaty, an analysis of the critical events during the year, the status of Russia's commitments made in Istanbul in 1999 and the impact of the crisis on low-intensity conflicts in Europe. Developments in subregional arms control in the former Yugoslavia are also reviewed. Arms control-related efforts to promote confidence, render assistance and foster predictability in the OSCE area are addressed in section III. The issue of mines and cluster munitions is dealt with in section IV. Section V presents the conclusions.

---

[1] On conventional arms control in Europe before 2006 see the relevant chapters in previous editions of the SIPRI Yearbook.

[2] During the Oct. 2007 visit by South Korean President Roh Moon-hyun to North Korea, he and North Korean leader Kim Jong Il signed a statement containing a section devoted to confidence-building measures (CBMs) which pledged to terminate military hostilities and reduce military tension and conflict through dialogue and negotiation. For discussion of CBMs in the Korean context see Lachowski, Z. et al., *Tools for Building Confidence on the Korean Peninsula* (SIPRI/Center for Security Studies, ETH Zurich: Stockholm/Zurich, 2007), <http://www.korea-cbms.ethz.ch/>.

Table 10.1. Major developments related to the 1990 Treaty on Conventional Armed Forces in Europe, 1999–2006

Date	Event
1999	The Agreement on Adaptation of the CFE Treaty is signed.
2000	Belarus and Ukraine ratify the Agreement on Adaptation.
	Beyond-the-Urals equipment. Russia formally complies with the pledge of 14 June 1991 to destroy or convert 14 500 TLE items east of the Urals. In 1996 Russia had been allowed to substitute armoured combat vehicles for a number of battle tanks scheduled for destruction and later to eliminate the shortfall with regard to tanks. Together with Kazakhstan, Russia completes the destruction of the remaining excess of tanks in mid-2003.
2001	The second CFE Review Conference takes place. Special emphasis is put on the issue of unaccounted TLE.
	Withdrawal from Georgia. After Russia's initial pullout from its military bases, Georgia and Russia fall out over the remaining bases; an impasse follows.
	Withdrawal from Moldova. Russia pulls out its TLE. It fails to withdraw its military personnel and dispose of its stockpiled ammunition and equipment by the end of 2002. No withdrawals have taken place since 2004.
2002	*Flank dispute.* Russia presents data indicating that it has decreased the quantity of its TLE (raised in 1999 to strengthen its forces in Chechnya) and is now in compliance with the relevant provisions of the adapted (but not yet in force) treaty. Formally, however, Russia has been in breach of the 1996 Flank Document since 31 May 1999.
2003	Kazakhstan ratifies the Agreement on Adaptation.
2004	*New NATO members.* Estonia, Latvia, Lithuania and Slovenia, none of which is party to the CFE Treaty, join NATO. Russia denounces 'a legal black hole' along its borders with the Baltic states. NATO pledges not to deploy substantial numbers of TLE in its new member states. With Bulgaria and Romania also joining NATO, Russia feels at a growing disadvantage vis-à-vis the enlarged NATO in conventional armaments terms.
	Russia ratifies the Agreement on Adaptation.
2005	*Withdrawal from Georgia.* Georgia and Russia reach agreement that Russia will withdraw its troops and close its bases during 2008.
2006	The third CFE Review Conference takes place. Russia's proposal for provisional application of the Agreement on Adaptation fails.

CFE = Conventional Armed Forces in Europe (Treaty); NATO = North Atlantic Treaty Organization; TLE = treaty-limited equipment.

Source: SIPRI Yearbook, 2000–2007.

II. European arms control

The 1990 CFE Treaty regime remains by far the most elaborate conventional arms control regime worldwide.[3] Acclaimed as the cornerstone of European security, it has contributed significantly to removing the threat of large-scale military attack from Europe and has enhanced confidence, openness and

[3] For a brief summary of the Treaty on Conventional Armed Forces in Europe and a list of its parties see annex A in this volume. The text of the treaty and protocols is available at <http://www.osce.org/item/13752.html?html=1>.

mutual reassurance in the region. The CFE Treaty process has also inspired regional arms control solutions in the Balkans and Central Asia.

The CFE Treaty was built on a bipolar concept of an equilibrium of forces between the North Atlantic Treaty Organization (NATO) and the now defunct Warsaw Treaty Organization in its Atlantic-to-the-Urals (ATTU) zone of application. It sets equal ceilings on major categories of heavy conventional armaments and equipment (the treaty-limited equipment, TLE) of the two groups of states. The 1999 Agreement on Adaptation of the CFE Treaty discards the bipolar concept.[4] On entry into force it will (a) introduce a new regime of arms control based on national and territorial ceilings, codified in the agreement's protocols as binding limits; (b) increase the verifiability of its provisions; and (c) open the adapted treaty regime to European states which were not yet parties to the CFE Treaty in 1999. The agreement has not entered into force because of the refusal of the NATO members and other states parties to ratify it until Russia complies with the commitments it made at the 1999 OSCE Istanbul Summit.[5] Of the 30 signatories of the CFE Treaty, only Belarus, Kazakhstan, Russia and Ukraine have ratified the Agreement on Adaptation.[6] The original CFE Treaty and the associated agreed documents and decisions therefore continue to be binding on all parties.

The CFE Treaty regime at a crossroads

In the first seven years after the signing of the 1999 Agreement on Adaptation, there was little progress towards its entry into force. Both NATO and Russia have repeatedly pledged to 'work cooperatively' towards ratification. Agreement was reached on several sticking points (see table 10.1), but major disagreements remained over the implementation of the Istanbul commitments, especially those related to Georgia and Moldova. As a result, the CFE process stalled.

The showdown

In 2006 Russia adopted a new approach in its relations with NATO. Having made many unsuccessful exhortations for the NATO member states to ratify

---

[4] For a brief summary of the agreement and a list of its signatories see annex A in this volume. The text of the agreement is available at <http://www.osce.org/item/13760.html?html=1>. For the text of the CFE Treaty as amended by the Agreement on Adaptation see *SIPRI Yearbook 2000: Armaments, Disarmament and International Security* (Oxford University Press: Oxford, 2000), pp. 627–42.

[5] Istanbul Summit Declaration, Istanbul, 17 Nov. 1999, paragraphs 15–19; and Final Act of the Conference of the States Parties to the Treaty on Conventional Armed Forces in Europe, Istanbul, 17 Nov. 1999, Annex 14. These texts are reproduced in *SIPRI Yearbook 2000* (note 4), pp. 642–46; and OSCE, *Istanbul Document 1999* (OSCE: Vienna, 2000), <http://www.osce.org/item/15853.html>, pp. 46–54, 236–59. So far Russia has failed to implement the following Istanbul commitments: (a) to close the Gudauta base in Abkhazia, Georgia; (b) to withdraw all Russian troops and ammunition from Moldova's Trans-Dniester region; and (c) to eliminate the stocks of ammunition and military equipment in the Trans-Dniester region. In addition, the states parties to the CFE Treaty are not agreed on how to treat the Russian peacekeepers in Georgia and Moldova.

[6] However, Ukraine has not deposited its instruments of ratification with the treaty depositary.

the Agreement on Adaptation, Russia resorted to alternative arguments demonstrating the growing incompatibility of the original treaty regime with political and strategic reality. These claims were echoed by some NATO states' concerns about US intransigence. In addition, Russia threw the extraneous issue of US missile defence in the Czech Republic and Poland into the conventional arms control debate.[7]

In 2007, reassured by its resurgent economic performance, frustrated by the West's continuing refusals to address its security concerns, and with the forthcoming elections in mind, Russia became more assertive in its relations with the United States and the other NATO allies. In February 2007, speaking on the CFE Treaty at the annual Munich Conference on Security Policy, Russian President Vladimir Putin warned the West against imposing 'new dividing lines and walls' on Russia.[8] Statements by the Russian foreign and defence ministers and by the Russian representatives in the CFE Treaty's Joint Consultative Group (JCG) and the NATO–Russia Council (NRC) claimed that the treaty regime was increasingly 'outdated' and 'degraded and withered', especially in the light of the alleged build-up of a system of military bases along Russia's borders.[9] In March the Russian delegation to the JCG presented the results of its 'comprehensive analysis' of the CFE-related situation.[10] Russia proposed that the following issues be addressed.

1. The 'absurdity' of the cold war bloc-related limits means that new members of NATO continue to be counted as belonging to the Eastern (i.e. former Warsaw Treaty Organization) group of states parties. Russia suggested that the new NATO states should be transferred to the Western group.

2. As the result of Bulgaria and Romania joining NATO in 2004, the Western group has vastly exceeded the flank limitations agreed in 1996.[11] The USA's planned deployments of TLE would further exacerbate these violations. Russia asked the USA to provide a legal justification of this deployment.[12]

---

[7] On US ballistic missile defence plans see chapter 1 and appendix 8C in this volume.

[8] Putin, V. V., President of the Russian Federation, Speech at the 43rd Munich Conference on Security Policy, English translation, 10 Feb. 2007, <http://www.securityconference.de/konferenzen/rede.php?sprache=en&id=179>.

[9] Joint Consultative Group, Statement by the delegation of the Russian Federation, document JCG.JOUR/625, 27 Mar. 2007, annex. On post-cold war changes in basing policy see Lachowski, Z., *Foreign Military Bases in Eurasia*, SIPRI Policy Paper no. 18 (SIPRI: Stockholm, 2007), <http://books.sipri.org/>.

[10] Joint Consultative Group (note 9).

[11] These limitations are included in the Flank Document, Annex A of the Final Document of the First Conference to Review the Operation of the Treaty on Conventional Armed Forces in Europe and the Concluding Act of the Negotiation on Personnel Strength, Vienna, 15–31 May 1996. For the text of these documents see *SIPRI Yearbook 1997: Armaments, Disarmament and International Security* (Oxford University Press: Oxford, 1997), pp. 511–14, or <http://www.osce.org/item/13755.html?html=1>.

[12] In response, in May 2007 the US delegation to the JCG presented a legal analysis of cross-group stationing (i.e. the stationing of troops from a member of one group of states on the territory of a member of the other group of states). Its main thesis was that no provision of the CFE Treaty prohibits cross-group stationing as long as the group ceilings are not violated and the host state consents to the stationing. The only restriction that applies is in Article V, which allows the temporary deployment of TLE on the territory of a member of the *same* group of states parties. Joint Consultative Group, 'Legal ana-

3. Estonia, Latvia and Lithuania have been members of NATO since 2004 but are not parties to the CFE Treaty. As a goodwill gesture to alleviate the uncertainty and unpredictability in that region, Russia proposes that the Baltic states accede to the existing CFE Treaty.[13]

4. NATO should clarify what it means by 'full implementation' of the Istanbul commitments to prevent it from making more and more demands on Russia. NATO should also clarify the meaning of the term 'substantial combat forces', as contained in its 1997 pledge not to undertake 'additional permanent stationing of substantial combat forces'.[14]

In addition, Russia reserved the right to make further requests with the aim of 'restoring the balances' in the treaty regime. These issues constituted the basis for further elaboration of Russia's stance during 2007 as the crisis developed.

On 26 April, in response to the growing dispute over the US plans to deploy missile defences in the Czech Republic and Poland and to establish military installations ('bases') in Bulgaria and Romania for use by US troops,[15] President Putin proposed to 'examine the possibility of suspending' Russia's commitments under the CFE Treaty 'until such time as all NATO members without exception ratify it and start strictly observing its provisions, as Russia has been doing so far on a unilateral basis'.[16] Subsequently, Russia stated that it would suspend inspections, notifications and data exchanges, although it did not immediately put this into effect pending further developments.[17] The suspension of observance of the CFE Treaty is not provided for in the treaty, and so lacks a legal footing.[18] The NATO states parties to the CFE Treaty

lysis of cross-group stationing', Statement by the delegation of the United States of America, document JCG.JOUR/627, 8 May 2007, Annex 3.

[13] The 3 Baltic states and Slovenia, all NATO members, have repeatedly declared their readiness to accede to the Adapted CFE Treaty once it has entered into force.

[14] The pledge was made in NATO, Statement by the North Atlantic Council, 14 Mar. 1997, <http://www.nato.int/docu/pr/1997/>; and reiterated and amplified in the Founding Act on Mutual Relations, Cooperation and Security between NATO and the Russian Federation, which was signed on 27 May 1997, <http://www.nato.int/docu/basictxt/fndact-a.htm>.

[15] Russia has persistently claimed that the USA will station 5000 troops in each of Bulgaria and Romania. See e.g. Putin (note 8); and Litovkin, V., 'Byt' ili ne byt'? Vot v chem vopros' [To be or not be? That is the question], *Nezavisimoe voennoe obozrenie*, 22 June 2007. The USA has said that it will deploy in Bulgaria and Romania combat elements of a brigade, stationed in Germany, on a rotational basis. Since these deployments will be below brigade level, the USA claims that they do not constitute 'substantial combat forces'. Russia also drew attention to the USA's reluctance to accept the Russian proposals on new CSBMs regarding the foreign stationing of forces. On Russia's proposed CSBMs see Lachowski, Z. and Sjögren, M., 'Conventional arms control', *SIPRI Yearbook 2007: Armaments, Disarmament and International Security* (Oxford University Press: Oxford, 2007), pp. 613–14.

[16] Putin, V. V., President of the Russian Federation, Annual Address to the Federal Assembly, Moscow, 26 Apr. 2007, <http://www.kremlin.ru/eng/sdocs/speeches.shtml?stype=70029>. Russian officials later sought to sever the direct linkage between the US missile defence plans and CFE issues. See e.g. 'Baluyevskiy addresses CFE, NMD issues on eve of Russia–NATO meeting', World News Connection, National Technical Information Service (NTIS), US Department of Commerce, 9 May 2007.

[17] 'DOVSE: nikakikh inspektsii v Rossii i uvedomlenii bol'she ne budet' [CFE: there will be no more inspections in Russia and no notifications], *Nezavisimaya gazeta*, 23 May 2007.

[18] Russia claims that its unilateral suspension is in conformity with international law. Article 57 of the 1969 Vienna Convention on the Law of Treaties, to which Russia is a party, provides that 'The operation of a treaty in regard . . . to a particular party may be suspended: (a) in conformity with the provisions of

'noted with concern' President Putin's remarks and requested further clarifications while declaring their willingness to engage in discussions in 'a positive spirit'.[19] In a series of talks in the JCG and the NRC, NATO declared its openness to discuss all issues of mutual concern.

Disappointed by the West's response to its suggestions, on 28 May 2007 Russia requested that an extraordinary conference of the states parties be convened in accordance with Article XXI of the CFE Treaty. Russia presented a number of 'exceptional circumstances' to justify its demand for the meeting, in particular, the serious consequences of NATO enlargement for the implementation of the treaty, NATO's foot-dragging on ratification of the Agreement on the Adaptation, and the USA's plans to deploy conventional armaments in Bulgaria and Romania.[20] However, the Russian Foreign Minister, Sergei Lavrov, made it clear that Russia was not going to withdraw from the treaty but simply wanted to spell out its concerns.[21]

The Extraordinary Conference of the States Parties to the CFE Treaty was held in Vienna on 12–15 June. Russia elaborated on the 'failures', numerical superiority and other 'negative effects' of the conduct of NATO states.

1. Bulgaria, the Czech Republic, Hungary, Poland, Romania and Slovakia have failed to formalize their move from one group of states parties to the other.

2. In the wake of the enlargement of NATO ('the group of States Parties that signed or acceded to the Treaty of Brussels of 1948 or the Treaty of Washington of 1949', in the wording of the CFE Treaty), its members exceed both the aggregate and flank limits.

3. The US deployments on the territories of Bulgaria and Romania violate not only Article V's provisions on temporary deployment, but also NATO's commitment regarding permanent deployments as set forth in its 1997 pledge.[22]

4. States parties have failed to 'expeditiously' ratify the Agreement on Adaptation so that it could enter into force as soon as possible, as was pledged in the Final Act of the 1999 Istanbul CFE conference.[23] This is despite Russia's claimed constructive approach within and outside the CFE regime.

the treaty; or (b) at any time by consent of all the parties'. The CFE Treaty provides for withdrawal but does not explicitly provide for suspension, so it is difficult to legally justify doing so using the content of the treaty itself. NATO and the USA have thus far opted for expressing 'disappointment', stopping short of challenging Russia's right to suspend the treaty. For more detailed discussion of the legal implications of Russia's move see Hollis, D. B., 'Russia suspends CFE Treaty participation', *ASIL Insight*, vol. 11, issue 19 (23 July 2007).

[19] Joint Consultative Group, Statement by the delegation of Canada, document JCG.JOUR/627, 27 Mar. 2007, Annex 1.

[20] Dutch Ministry of Foreign Affairs, Notification pursuant to Article XXII of the Treaty on Conventional Armed Forces in Europe, Request for Extraordinary Conference, Russian Federation, 28 May 2007.

[21] Dempsey, J., 'Russia and U.S. back away from confrontation', *International Herald Tribune*, 6 June 2007.

[22] NATO (note 14). See also note 15.

[23] Final Act of the Conference of the States Parties to the Treaty on Conventional Armed Forces in Europe (note 5).

5. The Czech Republic, Hungary, Poland and Slovakia have failed to have their territorial ceilings adjusted, as promised in March 1999.[24]

Accordingly, Russia proposed a schedule to 'restore the viability' of the treaty.[25] The deadlines are listed in table 10.2.

Some of Russia's concerns would be easily resolved by the entry into force of the Agreement on Adaptation, but Russia's failure to comply with its Istanbul commitments remains an obstacle. NATO has rejected Russia's successive attempts to de-link its CFE Treaty obligations and the political commitments made in Istanbul.[26] The claim that US deployments in Bulgaria and Romania would violate the treaty provisions was denied by both the USA and the two states concerned.[27]

The differences proved irreconcilable and the Extraordinary Conference ended in failure, unable to agree on a final document. However, the NATO states and Russia left the conference declaring their openness to further talks.[28] European Union (EU) member states voiced disappointment over Russia's move and the OSCE Chairman-in-Office called on the states parties to overcome their differences.[29] Belarus shared Russia's concerns but stopped short of withdrawal from or suspension of the CFE regime. Instead, it proposed a provisional application of the adapted treaty until it enters into force. NATO's draft final document suggested that three forums be convened following the Extraordinary Conference: an informal meeting in the autumn of 2007 to examine the future of the CFE Treaty regime and potential accession procedures; another Extraordinary Conference prior to the November 2007 OSCE Ministerial Council; and a seminar in the winter of 2008 to pursue cooperative planning for the implementation of the adapted treaty. In addition, NATO encouraged a high-level dialogue on security and arms control in Europe.[30]

[24] Joint Consultative Group, Decision on CFE Treaty Adaptation, document JCG.DD/4/99, 30 Mar. 1999, chart 2. See also Lachowski, Z., 'Conventional arms control', *SIPRI Yearbook 1999: Armaments, Disarmament and International Security* (Oxford University Press: Oxford, 1999), pp. 622–23. These 4 countries have lowered their TLE holdings well below the declared national ceilings under the Agreement on Adaptation (equal to their respective territorial ceilings) and have promised to meet their territorial ceiling commitments as soon as the adapted treaty enters into force. At the end of 2007 Russia quietly dropped its demand vis-à-vis these countries.

[25] CFE Extraordinary Conference, Delegation of Russia, Draft basic provisions of the Final Document of the Extraordinary Conference of the States Parties to the Treaty on Conventional Armed Forces in Europe, document CFE-EC(07).JOUR, 11–15 June 2007, Annex 33, attachment 2.

[26] See CFE Extraordinary Conference, Delegation of Italy, Statement, 15 June 2007, available at <http://www.nato.int/docu/update/2007/06-june/e0615a.html>.

[27] CFE Extraordinary Conference, Delegation of the United States of America, Statement, document CFE-EC(07).JOUR, 12 June 2007, Annex 4; and Joint Consultative Group, Delegation of Bulgaria, Statement, document JCG.JOUR/627, 8 May 2007, Annex 4.

[28] NATO, 'NATO response to Russian announcement of intent to suspend obligations under the CFE Treaty', Press Release (2007)085, 16 July 2007, <http://www.nato.int/docu/pr/2007/>.

[29] 'EU states join criticism of Putin's arms-treaty withdrawal', EurActiv.com, 16 July 2007, <http://www.euractiv.com/en/security/article-165543>; and OSCE, 'OSCE Chairman issues statement after CFE treaty conference ends in Vienna', Press release, 15 June 2007, <http://www.osce.org/item/25158.html>.

[30] CFE Extraordinary Conference, Delegation of Italy, Proposed Extraordinary Conference final document, document CFE-EC(07).JOUR, 11–15 June 2007, Annex 31, attachment.

Table 10.2. Russia's proposed schedule for restoring the viability of the Treaty on Conventional Armed Forces in Europe

Date	Event
1 October 2007	Bulgaria, the Czech Republic, Hungary, Poland, Romania and Slovakia transfer to the Western group of states. Estonia, Latvia and Lithuania participate in the treaty as members of the Western group. The ratification processes of the Agreement on Adaptation start.
1 January 2008	The states of the Western group adjust their MLHs of TLE and undertake to provide headroom for the MLHs of the 3 Baltic states within the group's aggregate limits.
1 March 2008	Estonia, Latvia and Lithuania accede to the treaty.
15 June 2008	The national and territorial ceilings of the Western group of states under the Agreement on Adaptation are adjusted. The Czech Republic, Hungary, Poland and Slovakia do not exceed their territorial ceiling parameters adopted under the 1999 CFE Final Act. A decision on non-application of provisions relating to territorial sub-ceilings (i.e. abolition of the flank regime) is adopted. Depositing of the instruments of ratification ends.
1 July 2008	If the Agreement on Adaptation does not enter into force by 25 June, provisional application begins until the official entry into force. Consultations in the JCG on the terms of accession of new states and negotiations on further modernization of the adapted treaty start.
1 October 2008	A draft common understanding of the term 'substantial combat forces' is submitted by Russia and the Western group of states to the JCG. The states parties refrain from additional 'substantial' deployments outside their territory.

CFE = Conventional Armed Forces in Europe (Treaty); JCG = Joint Consultative Group; MLH = maximum level for holdings; TLE = treaty-limited equipment.

Source: CFE Extraordinary Conference, Delegation of Russia, Draft basic provisions of the Final Document of the Extraordinary Conference of the States Parties to the Treaty on Conventional Armed Forces in Europe, document CFE-EC(07).JOUR, 15 June 2007, annex 33, attachment 2.

Soon after the Extraordinary Conference ended, Russia began to refuse inspections from NATO states, referring to the *force majeure* clauses of the CFE Treaty, and later stopped the provision of CFE-related information. However, on-site inspections were permitted again after a few days. On 13 July President Putin signed a decree on Russia's suspension (which was not meant to amount to withdrawal) of the operation of the CFE Treaty and associated international agreements, valid from 12 December 2007.[31] In a legal sense,

---

[31] The Presidential Decree 'on the suspension by the Russian Federation of the Treaty on Conventional Armed Forces in Europe and associated international agreements', Decree no. 872, was signed on 13 July 2007. The text of the decree is available at <http://document.kremlin.ru/doc.asp?ID=040713> (in Russian). The associated international agreements specifically mentioned include the Budapest Agreement of 3 Nov. 1990 on maximum levels for holdings of conventional armaments and equipment of the Warsaw Treaty Organization members (Bulgaria, Czechoslovakia, Hungary, Poland, Romania and the Soviet Union) and the 1996 Flank Document (note 11). The suspension also implicitly applies to other CFE-related documents.

Russia thereby risked placing itself in violation of the treaty.[32] Russia's move was motivated by the 'exceptional circumstances' that it presented at the Extraordinary Conference. As conditions for resuming the operation of the treaty and related documents Russia demanded that 'concrete steps' be taken according to its proposals to 'eliminate Russian apprehensions and to restore the viability of the Treaty regime'.[33] Russia hinted that, if the CFE regime could not be adapted, then a new system of arms control and confidence-building measures should be developed.[34] The Russian threat caused Armenia, Azerbaijan, Georgia and Ukraine to consider the impact of such a change on their respective security situations.[35]

Russia's tough rhetoric and the Presidential Decree of 13 July prompted negotiations in the following months. In July–September, the USA, in consultations with its allies and Russia, developed a plan for a set of 'parallel actions' that would lead to the Agreement on Adaptation entering into force by the summer of 2008 and the Istanbul commitments being met. An informal brainstorming session devoted to the future of the CFE Treaty was held on 30 September–3 October at Bad Saarow, Germany, which gathered delegations from the 30 states parties to the CFE Treaty and the four other NATO member states. The US plan—entitled 'CFE: a timeline for achieving Adapted CFE ratification and fulfilling the Istanbul commitments'—was presented.[36] In addition to a number of issues raised by Russia, two major obstacles to ratification turned out to be insurmountable: agreeing on the nature and substance of the Istanbul commitments and Russia's demand that the flank limitations be lifted.[37]

During the autumn of 2007 the USA, in consultation with Georgia, Moldova and NATO allies, enhanced its diplomatic activity vis-à-vis Russia. 'New

[32] See note 18.

[33] Joint Consultative Group, Memorandum, document JCG.JOUR/635, 17 July 2007, Annex 1, attachment 1.

[34] See e.g. Lavrov, S., 'Containing Russia: back to the future?', Russian Ministry of Foreign Affairs, 19 July 2007, <http://www.ln.mid.ru/brp_4.nsf/sps/8F8005F0C5CA3710C325731D0022E227>. This article was originally intended to be published in *Foreign Affairs*. In this context, an article by a Russian analyst compared the original and current CFE entitlements and the actual ratio of US/NATO and Russian armed forces. Going against the Russian mainstream view of the CFE situation, he concluded that: (*a*) Russia cannot complain that is constrained by the treaty when it does not make full use of its quotas; (*b*) NATO and the USA are not building up their strength in Europe but have both considerably reduced their armed forces; and (*c*) Russia's claims for military equality are misled—the end of the CFE regime could result, if NATO so wished, in a NATO superiority of 10–15 times over Russia instead of the current 2–3 times. He also argues that talk in Russia about the creation of 'a potential for a surprise attack' is unrealistic. Even the problem of 'grey zones'—states that are not party to the CFE Treaty but are members of NATO (the Baltic states and Slovenia) or could join NATO (Albania, Croatia, Georgia, the Former Yugoslav Republic of Macedonia and Ukraine) is not serious enough to be worth abandoning the CFE regime. Khramchikhin, A. A., 'Kop'ya lomat' ne stoit' [It is not worth breaking lances], *Nezavisimoe voennoe obozrenie*, 31 Aug. 2007.

[35] On the reactions in the South Caucasus see below. See also Joint Consultative Group, Statement by Ukraine, document JCG.DEL/28/07, 9 Nov. 2007

[36] Socor, V., '"Action for action" on the CFE Treaty: opportunity and risk', *Eurasia Daily Monitor*, 9 Oct. 2007.

[37] Joint Consultative Group, Chairperson's summary of the informal meeting on the future of the CFE regime, held from 30 September to 3 October 2007, in Bad Saarow, Germany, document JCG.JOUR/640, 9 Oct. 2007, annex.

ideas' presented during the visit to Moscow of the US secretaries of State and Defense on 12 October resulted in little progress on missile defence and arms control in Europe.[38] Later that month a complex package of inducements on the CFE Treaty, Kosovo and Iran issues was reported to have been offered by the USA.[39] A challenge for the USA was to find ways to persuade Russia to fulfil its commitments while maintaining unity in NATO, some of whose members—such as Germany and France[40]—sought to placate Russia with concessions while others insisted on the strong linkage between the Istanbul commitments and treaty ratification. By November the USA was 'rather encouraged' by the progress made.[41] The US diplomacy pursued three goals: 'to maintain a common NATO approach; to identify ways forward to achieve fulfillment of remaining Istanbul commitments; and to establish conditions that will make it possible for Russia to continue full implementation of the current CFE Treaty, and allow NATO Allies, including the United States, to move forward to seek ratification of the Adapted CFE Treaty'.

A follow-up seminar to the Bad Saarow dialogue on the future of the CFE regime took place on 5–6 November in Paris and reportedly helped to promote further thinking on the sticking points.[42] Another informal meeting of this type was held on the margins of the Madrid OSCE Ministerial Council in late November. Meanwhile, the two houses of the Russian Parliament voted unanimously in support of a law to suspend Russia's participation in the CFE Treaty, which was signed by President Putin on 29 November.[43]

On 12 December, the day on which the suspension took effect, the Russian Ministry of Foreign Affairs issued a statement declaring that Russia will not be bound by restrictions on the number of its TLE.[44] However, it reiterated the assurance earlier made by Russian officials that Russia did not have plans for the massive build-up or concentration of treaty-related armaments and equip-

[38] Shanker, T. and Myers, S. L., 'Putin spars with top U.S. officials visiting Moscow', *International Herald Tribune*, 12 Oct. 2007.

[39] Dempsey, J., 'U.S. pushes to get Russia on its side', *International Herald Tribune*, 29 Oct. 2007.

[40] In a joint article the foreign ministers of France and Germany declared that the CFE Treaty must remain the anchor of European stability and that they were open to further changes and amendments. Steinmeier, F.-W. and Kouchner, B., 'Europa und seine Sicherheit' [Europe and its security], *Frankfurter Allgemeine Zeitung*, 29 Oct. 2007; and Kouchner, B. and Steinmeier, F.-W., 'L'Europe et sa sécurité' [Europe and its security], *Le Figaro*, 29 Oct. 2007.

[41] Kramer, D. J., US Deputy Assistant Secretary of State for European and Eurasian Affairs, 'Twenty-first century security in the OSCE region', Testimony before the Commission on Security and Cooperation in Europe, Washington, DC, 5 Nov. 2007, <http://www.state.gov/p/eur/rls/rm/94654.htm>.

[42] Joint Consultative Group, Declaration by France, document JCG.DEL/30/07, 13 Nov. 2007.

[43] The Russian Federal Law 'on the suspension by the Russian Federation of the effect of the Treaty on Conventional Armed Forces in Europe', Law no. 276 of 29 Nov. 2007, is available at <http://document.kremlin.ru/doc.asp?ID=043061> (in Russian). The Duma, the lower house of the Russian Parliament, voted on 7 Nov. and the Federation Council, the upper house, on 16 Nov. It is telling that, following the votes in the Russian Parliament, it emerged that the US Defense Secretary, Robert Gates, had decided to freeze plans to reduce the number of US troops stationed in Europe. Shanker, T., 'Gates halts cut in army force in Europe', *New York Times*, 21 Nov. 2007.

[44] Russian Ministry of Foreign Affairs, Statement regarding suspension by Russian Federation of Treaty on Conventional Armed Forces in Europe (CFE Treaty), 12 Dec. 2007. In a 'goodwill' gesture, in Dec. Russia circulated in the JCG 'summarized information' on the quantities of its TLE.

ment on its borders. At the same time, Russia expressed its readiness to continue a 'result-oriented' dialogue on the CFE Treaty.

Russian withdrawal from Georgia and Moldova

In 2005 Georgia and Russia agreed on the closure of the Russian military bases and other military facilities and withdrawal of Russian forces from Georgia by the end of 2008.[45] In March 2006 the two countries signed further agreements on the temporary operation of the Russian bases and the withdrawal and transit through Georgia of Russian troops and equipment. Despite all regional problems and disagreements between the two countries (including the crisis over the dropping of a Russian missile on Georgian territory on 6 August 2007), the pullout of Russian armaments and troops continued in 2007. Having withdrawn from the Russian headquarters in Tbilisi at the end of 2006, in 2007 Russia handed over its remaining principal military bases and installations in Akhalkalaki (on 27 June) and Batumi (on 15 November).[46]

With some progress in Georgia, international attention has turned to Moldova, where Russian troops remain in the secessionist region of Trans-Dniester. Withdrawal of Russian TLE was completed in 2001, but the lack of a political settlement over Trans-Dniester caused Russia to delay the withdrawal of its troops and the disposal or withdrawal of its remaining 20 000 tonnes of stockpiled ammunition and non-CFE-limited equipment, part of its Istanbul commitments.

For some time during 2007 Moldova sought bilateral agreement with Russia on the settlement of the Trans-Dniester and related issues. In June the USA unsuccessfully sounded out the possibility—which was supported by Moldova—of creating an alternative multilateral peacekeeping force, with Russian participation.[47] In the autumn of 2007, Moldovan President Vladimir Voronin proposed 'full demilitarization' of Moldova on both banks of the Dniester River and the replacement of the existing military peacekeeping mechanism with an entirely civilian operation under an OSCE mandate.[48] Russia continued to make the withdrawal of its forces and ammunition contingent on a

---

[45] Joint Statement by the Ministers of Foreign Affairs of the Russian Federation and Georgia, Russian Ministry of Foreign Affairs, 30 May 2005. On the accord see Lachowski, Z., 'Conventional arms control', *SIPRI Yearbook 2006: Armaments, Disarmament and International Security* (Oxford University Press: Oxford, 2006), pp. 758–60.

[46] Once again, Azerbaijan criticized the transfer of Russian equipment to the Russian base in Gyumri, Armenia, alleging that it is being handed over to rebels in Nagorno-Karabakh. Russia strongly rejected these charges. Mamedov, S., Litovkin, V. and Simonyan, Yu., 'Baku zhdet ob'yasnenii Moskvy' [Baku expects explanations from Moscow], *Nezavisimaya gazeta*, 12 Sep. 2007.

[47] Associated Press, 'U.S. pushes for peace force in Moldova', *International Herald Tribune*, 5 June 2007. In a possible sequence, Russia would withdraw its troops from Trans-Dniester and Gudauta, Georgia, and would join an international peacekeeping force. The NATO member states would then expeditiously ratify and bring into force the Agreement on Adaptation, whereupon the Baltic states could join the adapted treaty. In the final stage, NATO could favourably consider Russian demands to raise the flank limits, especially those in North Caucasus. See Socor, V., 'Solution in Moldova—"key to Russia–West dispute" at CFE Treaty conference', *Eurasia Daily Monitor*, 14 June 2007.

[48] Socor, V., 'Voronin proposes full demilitarization of Moldova', *Eurasia Daily Monitor*, 16 Oct. 2007. On the peacekeeping operation in Trans-Dniester see appendix 3A in this volume.

'political settlement' over Trans-Dniester—a settlement which Russia itself makes impossible by supporting the Trans-Dniester authorities. The '5 + 2' format talks, which were launched in 2005 in an attempt to reach a political agreement concerning Moldova, did not resume in 2007.[49]

The Armenia–Azerbaijan conflict

In the context of continuing tensions in their relations, until 2000–2001 Armenia and Azerbaijan both exceeded their maximum levels of TLE under the CFE Treaty.[50] The USA has also pointed to other improprieties by these countries in their compliance with the treaty,[51] and both states have traded accusations of non-compliance by the other side.

In 2006 Azerbaijan notified the other states parties that it had exceeded its national maximum levels of holdings in battle tanks and heavy artillery pieces.[52] Alongside sharp increases in military expenditure and accompanying militarization in the South Caucasian countries, this gave rise to international concerns.[53] The spectre of an accelerating arms race in the region coincided with the NATO–Russia crisis over the CFE Treaty. Azerbaijan initially argued that the increase in its holdings of TLE resulted from its armaments modernization process and delays in the removal of old equipment. At the same time it accused Armenia of keeping substantial amounts of TLE in the occupied territory of Nagorno-Karabakh—amounts higher than its entire national entitlements.[54]

The mutual accusations were nothing new. Russia's move to 'suspend' its CFE compliance was used as a pretext by Azerbaijan to declare itself as being in a *force majeure* situation followed by an indirect suggestion that it would increase its national quotas.[55] Armenia immediately warned of a 'domino

---

[49] The talks involve 5 parties—Moldova, the OSCE, Russia, Trans-Dniester and Ukraine—plus 2 observers—the EU and the USA.

[50] Azerbaijan had fully met the CFE limits by 1 Jan. 2000. Armenia complied with its limits a year later.

[51] See US Department of State, Bureau of Verification and Compliance, *Adherence to and Compliance with Arms Control, Nonproliferation, and Disarmament Agreements and Commitments* (Department of State: Washington, DC, Aug. 2005), <http://www.state.gov/t/vci/rls/rpt/51977.htm>, pp. 34–38.

[52] Ukraine notified the other states parties of the transfer of these weapons to Azerbaijan under an information exchange on arms transfers in 2005. Reportedly, Azerbaijan exceeded its tank quota by 41 units and the artillery quota by 58. Later these numbers grew to 99 and 71 units, respectively. CFE Extraordinary Conference, document CFE-EC-(07).JOUR, 13 June 2007, Annex 26. See also chapter 5 in this volume, section IV.

[53] Mamedov, J., 'Azerbaijan flexes military muscles', Caucasian Reporting Service no. 402, Institute for War & Peace Reporting, 19 July 2007, <http://www.iwpr.net/?s=f&o=337254>; and Petrosian, D., 'Armenia concerned at Caucasus arms race', Caucasian Reporting Service no. 402, Institute for War & Peace Reporting, 19 July 2007, <http://www.iwpr.net/?s=f&o=337252>. On military expenditure in the South Caucasus see chapter 5 in this volume, section IV.

[54] According to Azerbaijani estimates, Armenia is 'hiding' up to 316 tanks, 324 armoured combat vehicles (ACVs) and 322 artillery pieces in Nagorno-Karabakh. The CFE entitlements of Armenia and Azerbaijan are 220 tanks, 220 ACVs and 285 artillery pieces each. CFE Extraordinary Conference, document CFE-EC-(07).JOUR, 13 June 2007, Annex 28.

[55] CFE Extraordinary Conference, document CFE-EC-(07).JOUR, 15 June 2007, Annex 35.

effect'.[56] Eventually, in one of the few political statements that came out of the Madrid OSCE Ministerial Meeting in November, the two states agreed to continue the ongoing negotiation on the settlement of the Nagorno-Karabakh conflict.[57]

Subregional arms control in the former Yugoslavia

According to the Personal Representative of the OSCE Chairperson-in-Office for Article IV, the implementation of the 1996 Agreement on Sub-Regional Arms Control (Florence Agreement) is working very well in its two major dimensions: the exchange of information and notifications (which is being advanced) and the verification regime.[58] Armaments have been destroyed voluntarily since the end of the official reduction period on 31 October 1997, and by 2007 the parties had scrapped nearly 8900 items of heavy weapons.[59] In January 2007 the OSCE approved the use of its Communication Network in implementing the Dayton Agreement and tasked its Communication Group with the technical implementation of the decision.[60]

Montenegro became a party to the Florence Agreement as of 16 January 2007 and in July the governments of Montenegro and Serbia agreed that the numerical limitations for both parties will not exceed the total limitations that held for the Federal Republic of Yugoslavia.[61] A formal amendment to the agreement will be signed by the four parties—Bosnia and Herzegovina, Croatia, Montenegro and Serbia. In the meantime, Montenegro and Serbia will comply with the limitations contained in the bilateral agreement.

It is likely that an updated version of the Florence Agreement that incorporates all the amendments and changes will be finalized during its sixth review conference, to be held in June 2008. Given the positive developments in the region, more 'ownership' of implementation could be transferred from the international community and the OSCE to the parties to the agreement.

[56] CFE Extraordinary Conference, document CFE-EC-(07).JOUR, 15 June 2007, Annex 38.

[57] OSCE, Ministerial Council, Madrid, Ministerial statement, document MC.DOC/2/07, 30 Nov. 2007.

[58] Periotto, C. (Brig. Gen.), Personal Representative of the OSCE Chairperson-in-Office for Article IV, Report to the Fifteenth Meeting of the OSCE Ministerial Council on the Implementation of the Agreement on Sub-Regional Arms Control (Article IV, Annex 1-B, Dayton Peace Accords), document MC.GAL/4/07, 13 Nov. 2007. The Florence Agreement was agreed under Article IV of Annex 1B of the 1995 General Framework for Peace in Bosnia and Herzegovina (Dayton Agreement), which was signed on 14 Dec. 1995. The text of the Dayton Agreement is available at <http://www.oscebih.org/overview/gfap/eng/> and the text of the Florence Agreement at <http://www.oscebih.org/public/document.asp?dep=4>. For a summary of the Florence Agreement see annex A in this volume.

[59] Periotto (note 58).

[60] OSCE, Forum for Security Co-operation (FCS), 'Use of the OSCE communications network to support the implementation of Article IV of the Dayton Peace Accords', Decision no. 1/07, document FSC.DEC/1/07, 31 Jan. 2007. Many of the FSC documents cited in this chapter are available at <http://www.osce.org/fsc/documents.html>.

[61] Periotto (note 58).

III. Building confidence and security in the OSCE area[62]

For some time the focus of the OSCE community has remained on its unique dimension—military confidence and security building, in particular CSBMs, control, management and reduction of small arms and light weapons (SALW) and stockpiles of conventional ammunition, including rocket fuel components, and the 1994 Code of Conduct on Politico-Military Aspects of Security.[63]

Alongside these central areas, the OSCE's Forum for Security Co-operation (FSC) has worked to support United Nations Security Council Resolution 1540 on non-proliferation of weapons of mass destruction by developing a best practice guide, with Canada and the USA as the lead countries;[64] explored a possible role for the OSCE in the area of civil–military emergency prepared-ness (CMEP); and decided to enhance the OSCE's role in combating anti-personnel mines (APMs) by holding a special meeting early in 2008.[65] In October 2007 a special FSC meeting on existing and future arms control and CSBMs in the OSCE area was held.

During 2007 Russia actively proposed several confidence-building measures relating to the Vienna Document 1999.[66] However, no CSBM was agreed during 2007 because many participating states considered that introducing new measures without first ensuring the effectiveness of existing CSBMs might weaken rather than strengthen the Vienna Document regime. In add-ition, the developing CFE crisis was not conducive to new agreements, but it did give a stimulus to consideration of enhancing arms control and CSBM efforts in 2008.[67]

---

[62] For a list of the states participating on the OSCE see annex B in this volume.

[63] OSCE, Code of Conduct on Politico-Military Aspects of Security, document DOC.FSC/1/95, 3 Dec. 1994, <http://www.osce.org/fsc/22158.html>.

[64] UN Security Council Resolution 1540, 28 Apr. 2004. See also Anthony, I., 'Arms control and non-proliferation: the role of international organizations', *SIPRI Yearbook 2005: Armaments, Disarmament and International Security* (Oxford University Press: Oxford, 2005), pp. 542–47; and Ahlström, C., 'United Nations Security Council Resolution 1540: non-proliferation by means of international legisla-tion', *SIPRI Yearbook 2007* (note 15), pp. 460–73.

[65] OSCE, Forum for Security Co-operation, Danish Chairmanship, Letter from the Chairperson of the Forum for Security Co-operation to the Minister for Foreign Affairs of Spain, Chairperson of the Fif-teenth Meeting of the OSCE Ministerial Council, document MC.GAL/5/07/REV. 1, 21 Nov. 2007.

[66] OSCE, Vienna Document 1999 of the Negotiations on Confidence- and Security-Building Meas-ures, document FSC.DOC/1/99, 16 Nov. 1999, <http://www.osce.org/fsc/22154.html>. Russia's pro-posals included: prior notification of deployment of foreign military forces on the territory of an OSCE participating state in the CSBM zone of application; exchange of information on multinational rapid reaction forces (also proposed by Belarus); 'reopening' (i.e. updating) the Vienna Document 1999; prior notification of large-scale military transits in the CSBM zone of application; a single deadline for sub-mission of information on defence planning; definition of the 'specified area' and the duration of evalu-ation visits under the terms of the Vienna Document; and prior notification of major military activities that are below the Vienna Document thresholds.

[67] OSCE, Ministerial Council, 'Issues relevant to the Forum on Security Co-operation', Decision no. 3/07, document MC.DEC/3/07, 20 Nov. 2007, <http://www.osce.org/conferences/mc_2007.html? page=documents&session_id=203>.

Small arms and light weapons

The 2000 OSCE Document on Small Arms and Light Weapons (SALW Document) and the other relevant documents remain an effective instrument for addressing the substance of SALW problems, fostering transparency and confidence among the participating states, and helping to combat terrorism and organized crime.[68] The OSCE *Handbook of Best Practices on Small Arms and Light Weapons* has been translated into several languages and is also being disseminated and promoted outside the OSCE area. In 2001–2006 OSCE participating states destroyed 6.4 million small arms, 5.2 million of which had been deemed as surplus and 1.2 million of which had been seized from illegal possession and trafficking.[69]

In March 2007 the FSC held a special meeting in Vienna on combating the illicit trafficking of SALW by air. Presentations showed the close relationship between illicit trafficking in SALW and security threats, such as terrorism and regional conflicts. Experts and delegates from the participating states and representatives of the air transport sector and international, governmental and non-governmental organizations discussed ways of improving controls over the air-cargo sector through enhanced national implementation of international regulations.[70] A mechanism for exchanging information on national legislation and regulatory frameworks for import and export controls relating to the air transport sector as well as enhanced dialogue and increased synergy between states and the private sector were supported by participants.[71] The meeting recommended that a best practice guide on combating illicit trafficking in SALW be developed.[72] The initiative on reviewing the implementation of existing commitments on SALW export control resulted in the FSC adopting a decision in October on information exchange with regard to the 2004 OSCE

[68] OSCE, Forum for Security Co-operation, Document on Small Arms and Light Weapons, 24 Nov. 2000, <http://www.osce.org/fsc/13281.html>. The other documents include: OSCE, *Handbook of Best Practices on Small Arms and Light Weapons* (OSCE: Vienna, 2003), <http://www.osce.org/fsc/item_11_ 13550.html>; OSCE, Forum for Security Co-operation, 'Standard elements of end-user certificates and verification procedures for SALW exports', Decision no. 5/04, document FSC/DEC/5/04, 17 Nov. 2004, <http://www.osce.org/item/1699.html?html=1>; OSCE, Forum for Security Co-operation, 'Principles on the control of brokering in small arms and light weapons', Decision no. 8/04, document FSC/DEC/8/04, 24 Nov. 2004; and OSCE, Ministerial Council, 'OSCE principles for export controls of man-portable air defence systems', Decision no. 8/04, document MC.DEC/8/04, 7 Dec. 2004, <http://www.osce.org/atu/ 13364.html>. On these documents see Lachowski, Z. and Sjögren, M., 'Conventional arms control' and Anthony, I. and Bauer, S., 'Transfer controls and destruction programmes', *SIPRI Yearbook 2004: Armaments, Disarmament and International Security* (Oxford University Press: Oxford, 2004), pp. 726, 751–53; and Lachowski, Z. and Dunay, P., 'Conventional arms control and military confidence building', *SIPRI Yearbook 2005* (note 64), pp. 659–61.

[69] OSCE, 'Further implementation of the OSCE Document on Small Arms and Light Weapons', FSC Chairperson's Progress Report to the 15th Ministerial Council, Madrid, document MC.GAL/7/07, 14 Nov. 2007, <http://www.osce.org/item/28669.html?html=1>, p. 5.

[70] OSCE (note 69), p. 10.

[71] See OSCE, Forum for Security Co-operation, 'Closing remarks made by the FSC Chairperson at the closing session of the Special FSC Meeting on combating the illicit trafficking of small arms and light weapons by air', 21 Mar. 2007, document FSC.DEL/101/07, 22 Mar. 2007.

[72] OSCE, Forum for Security Co-operation, 'OSCE focuses on combating illicit trafficking of small arms, light weapons by air', Press release, 21 Mar. 2007, <http://www.osce.org/fsc/item_1_23696.html>.

Principles on the control and brokering in SALW.[73] The decision requests participating states to exchange information on their current regulations concerning brokering activities, with the OSCE's Conflict Prevention Centre to provide a summary report of the replies from participating states.

Section V of the SALW Document concerns requests for assistance from the OSCE states in the field of destruction, stockpile management and security. SALW projects for 2006–2008 in Tajikistan (phase II, on stockpile physical security and training outside Dushanbe) and for 2007–2008 in Belarus (on destruction) are being carried out.[74]

Despite these achievements, SALW endeavours face considerable obstacles. The rate of implementation of information exchanges has decreased and the implementation of FSC decisions on export controls of SALW, including man-portable air defence systems (MANPADS), remains unclear. The total amount of money pledged for SALW projects declined considerably in 2007 compared with 2006 and only 18 of the 56 OSCE states donated or contributed to an SALW or conventional ammunition project in 2005–2007.[75] More cooperation and coordination within the OSCE as well as between the OSCE and other international organizations are needed. In addition, the potential of the OSCE field missions could be exploited more effectively.

Destruction of stockpiles of ammunition and toxic rocket fuel

Insecure or uncontrolled stockpiles of conventional ammunition and toxic liquid rocket fuel components pose cross-dimensional security, humanitarian, economic and environmental risks. Under the 2003 OSCE Document on Stockpiles of Conventional Ammunition (SCA Document), any OSCE state that has identified a security risk to its surplus stockpiles and needs assistance to address such a risk may request the assistance of the international community through the OSCE.[76]

Up to the end of 2006, five requests had been submitted to the OSCE for assistance in disposal of conventional ammunition (by Belarus, Kazakhstan, Russia, Tajikistan and Ukraine) and five for assistance in the elimination of the rocket fuel components mélange and samine (by Armenia, Afghanistan, Kazakhstan, Ukraine and Uzbekistan). In 2007 new requests under the SCA Document were submitted by Georgia, Moldova, Montenegro and Ukraine, bringing the total number of requests to 14. The Ukrainian project, to overcome the consequences of the May 2004 explosion at the ammunition depot in Novobohdanivka, was successfully completed in August 2007. The project to eliminate mélange in Armenia was completed in September. Russia, which

---

[73] OSCE, Forum for Security Co-operation, 'An information exchange with regard to OSCE principles on the control of brokering in small arms and light weapons', Decision no. 11/07, document FSC.DEC/11/07, 17 Oct. 2007.

[74] OSCE (note 71), pp. 6–8.

[75] OSCE (note 71), pp. 9, 18–19.

[76] OSCE Document on Stockpiles of Conventional Ammunition, document FSC.DOC/1/03, 19 Nov. 2003, <http://www.osce.org/fsc/13282.html>.

had requested assistance in dealing with the disposal of obsolete ammunition, withdrew its request in March 2007. Phase I of the SALW and conventional ammunition project (on conventional armaments destruction) in Tajikistan was successfully completed in November 2006; phase II is ongoing (see above).[77]

In 2007 the FSC Editorial Review Board completed its work on a best practice guide on ammunition marking, tracing and record-keeping (drafted by Germany) and worked on two more guides—on destruction and physical security of conventional ammunition—with the aim of finalizing the work in 2008.[78]

The Code of Conduct on Politico-Military Aspects of Security

The 1994 Code of Conduct on Politico-Military Aspects of Security (COC) remains the normative document on the cooperative behaviour and mutual responsibilities of states in the OSCE region and the democratic control of their armed forces.[79] It also addresses politico-military relations within states. In 2007 several food-for-thought papers and draft decisions were presented on such issues as: updating the COC questionnaire, promoting public awareness of the COC and additional steps to implement the COC.

On 23 May, as a follow-up to the special meeting on the COC of 26 September 2006, a meeting of the FSC Working Group A on the Code was held. The debate was structured in three parts: (a) how to strengthen the implementation of the COC; (b) how to promote public awareness, publication and outreach of the COC; and (c) how to determine which supplementary measures could improve the implementation of the COC.[80]

Following the May meeting, an FSC coordinator was appointed to collate ideas, views, proposals and input by delegations of OSCE participating states with regard to the COC, and to assist the FSC chairperson and the FSC Troika in developing modalities for various steps towards a better implementation of the Code.[81] The drafting of an updated COC questionnaire and the consolidation of a register of proposals have progressed. In addition, the OSCE and its Conflict Prevention Centre organized a number of workshops and seminars during 2007—in Armenia (Yerevan), Azerbaijan (Baku), Bosnia and Herzegovina (Sarajevo) and Montenegro (Podgorica)—to support the operation of the Code of Conduct.

[77] OSCE, 'Further implementation of the OSCE Document on Stockpiles of Conventional Ammunition', FSC Chairperson's Progress Report to the 15th Ministerial Council, Madrid, document MC.GAL/6/07, 14 Nov. 2007, <http://www.osce.org/item/28668.html?html=1>, pp. 8–17.

[78] OSCE (note 77), p. 19.

[79] OSCE (note 63).

[80] OSCE, Forum for Security Co-operation, Chair's perception/Summary, 347th (Special) meeting of Working Group A on the Code of Conduct on Politico-Military Aspects of Security, 23 May 2007, document FSC.DEL/319/07, 21 June 2007.

[81] The FSC Troika consists of the current, previous and next chairpersons of the FSC.

IV. Global efforts to counter inhumane weapons

Anti-personnel mines

The 1997 APM Convention commits states parties to destroy their stockpiles of anti-personnel mines and to clear them from their territories.[82] The list of states committed to banning APMs is growing on all continents. In 2007 Indonesia ratified the convention and Iraq, Kuwait and Palau acceded to it, bringing the number of parties to 156. Two signatory states—Marshall Islands and Poland—have not yet ratified the APM Convention.[83] In addition, 35 non-state armed groups have fulfilled their pledge to observe the ban on APMs.[84]

Under the APM Convention, states parties agree to destroy their existing stockpiles within four years of ratification, and to clear deployed anti-personnel mines from their territory within 10 years. Of the 156 states parties to the APM Convention, 146 do not have stockpiles of APMs.[85] According to Landmine Monitor, 41.8 million stockpiled mines had been destroyed as of August 2007 while 46 states have 176 million APMs stockpiled. The vast majority of these stockpiles belong to China (*c.* 110 million), Russia (26.5 million), the USA (10.4 million), Pakistan (*c.* 6 million) and India (*c.* 4–5 million), which are not party to the convention.[86]

Cluster munitions

During 2007 international action against cluster munitions gained momentum, comparable with the Ottawa process to ban landmines launched a decade before. Thirty-four countries are known to have produced more than 210 types

---

[82] For a summary of the Convention on the Prohibition of the Use, Stockpiling, Production and Transfer of Anti-Personnel Mines and on their Destruction and a list of its parties see annex A in this volume.

[83] Having declared almost 1 million APMs at the end of 2006, Poland has announced that it will not join until 2015. International Campaign to Ban Landmines, *Landmine Monitor Report 2007: Toward a Mine-Free World* (Mines Action Canada: Ottawa, 2007), <http://www.icbl.org/lm/2007/>, 'Country and area reports'. The Marshall Islands gave a positive signal by voting in favour of UN General Assembly Resolution 61/84, 18 Dec. 2006, which calls for universalization of the convention. No state opposed the resolution but 17 abstained: Cuba, Egypt, India, Iran, Israel, Kazakhstan, South Korea, Kyrgyzstan, Lebanon, Libya, Myanmar (Burma), Pakistan, Russia, Syria, the USA, Uzbekistan and Viet Nam.

[84] These are the 35 groups that have signed the Deed of Commitment under Geneva Call for adherence to a total ban on anti-personnel mines and for cooperation in mine action, which was opened for signature on 4 Oct. 2001. The text of the deed and the list of its signatories are available at <http://www.genevacall.org/>. See also Geneva Call and Graduate Institute of International and Development Studies, Program for the Study of International Organization(s), *Armed Non-state Actors and Landmines*, vol. 3, *Towards a Holistic Approach to Armed Non-state Actors?* (Geneva Call: Geneva, 2007).

[85] The states parties destroying their stockpiles as at Aug. 2007 were Afghanistan, Belarus, Burundi, Greece, Indonesia, Sudan, Turkey and Ukraine. Ethiopia and Iraq are also thought to have stockpiles of APMs. Landmine Monitor estimates that 14 million APMs remain to be eliminated by these 10 countries. International Campaign to Ban Landmines (note 83), Executive summary, p. 15.

[86] International Campaign to Ban Landmines (note 83), Executive summary, pp. 15–16. Two countries—Myanmar (Burma) and Russia—actively deploy APMs. Most major producers of landmines refrain from exporting APMs. International Campaign to Ban Landmines (note 83), Executive summary, pp. 1, 14–15.

of cluster munitions and it is estimated that at least 75 countries stockpile these weapons.[87]

In November 2006 the Third Review Conference of the 1981 Certain Conventional Weapons (CCW) Convention devoted a significant amount of time to addressing cluster munitions.[88] Twenty-seven states supported a proposal for a mandate to begin negotiations under the convention on a legally binding instrument addressing the humanitarian concerns posed by such munitions. The proposal was rejected by a number of states (including China, Russia, the United Kingdom and the USA) in favour of a weak mandate to continue discussions on explosive remnants of war, including cluster munitions. However, 25 states which advocated a strong negotiating mandate issued a declaration calling for an agreement that would prohibit the use of cluster munitions that 'pose serious humanitarian hazards because they are for example unreliable and/or inaccurate' and would require destruction of stockpiles of such weapons.[89] Norway, one of the leading states of this group, called for an independent process outside the CCW Convention to negotiate a treaty banning cluster munitions that have unacceptable humanitarian consequences.[90]

The first meeting of the 'Oslo process' was held on 22–23 February 2007 in Oslo, Norway. At the meeting 46 states committed themselves in the Oslo Declaration to conclude a new international treaty banning cluster munitions 'that cause unacceptable harm to civilians' by 2008 and to establish a framework for cooperation and assistance to victims, clearance of contaminated areas, risk education, and destruction of stockpiles of prohibited cluster munitions.[91] A draft treaty text was distributed and discussed at the first follow-up meeting, in Lima, Peru, on 23–25 May 2007, which gathered states and international and non-governmental organizations (such as the UN, the International Committee of the Red Cross and the Cluster Munitions Coalition).[92] By that point, a total of 74 states had joined the Oslo process (i.e. stated support for the objectives of the Oslo Declaration).

The CCW Convention's Group of Governmental Experts (GGE) met in June 2007 with the sole substantive topic being action on cluster munitions. However, the outcome was modest.[93] At this meeting, the USA announced that

---

[87] Goose, S. D., 'Cluster munitions: ban them', *Arms Control Today*, vol. 38, no. 1 (Jan./Feb. 2008).

[88] For a summary of the Convention on Prohibitions or Restrictions on the Use of Certain Conventional Weapons which may be Deemed to be Excessively Injurious or to have Indiscriminate Effects (also known as the 'Inhumane Weapons' Convention) and a list of its parties see annex A in this volume.

[89] CCW Convention, Third Review Conference, 'Declaration on cluster munitions', CCW/CONF.III/WP.18, 20 Nov. 2006.

[90] Cluster Munitions Coalition, RevCon Daily Updates no. 9, 17 Nov. 2006, <http://www.stopclustermunitions.org/news.asp?id=39>.

[91] Oslo Conference on Cluster Munitions, Declaration, 23 Feb. 2007, <http://www.regjeringen.no/templates/RedaksjonellArtikkel.aspx?id=449312>. Of the 49 states meeting in Oslo, only Japan, Poland and Romania did not support the Oslo Declaration.

[92] Lima Conference on Cluster Munitions, Chair's discussion text, 23–25 May 2007, <http://www.clusterprocess.org/limatext>.

[93] United Nations Office at Geneva, 'CCW governmental experts recommend action on cluster munitions', Press release, 26 June 2007.

it would back negotiations on cluster munitions under the CCW Convention.[94] The EU also supported the adoption by the GGE of a negotiating mandate to conclude a 'legally-binding instrument that addresses the humanitarian concerns of cluster munitions in all their aspects' by the end of 2008.[95] On 13 November, acting on an EU–Germany initiative,[96] a meeting of the parties to the CCW Convention adopted a mandate that tasked the GGE to 'negotiate a proposal to address urgently the humanitarian impact of cluster munitions, while striking a balance between military and humanitarian considerations'. The meeting decided that the GGE should 'make every effort' to negotiate the proposal as rapidly as possible and to report on the progress made to the next meeting, in November 2008.[97] Not surprisingly, the modest outcome of the CCW meeting met with criticism from the Oslo process participants. However, proponents of a CCW protocol on cluster munitions claim that, if agreed, it would include more major powers, producers and users of cluster munitions.

On 5–7 December, 138 states and 140 representatives of advocacy groups from 50 countries gathered in Vienna for the third Oslo process conference.[98] The most contentious issues at the conference were the definition and prohibition of cluster munitions. Some countries demanded exemptions for munitions with characteristics such as self-destruct mechanisms or a supposed 1 per cent failure rate. There was also a call for a transition period during which the banned weapons could be used until alternative weapons become available. A meeting to develop the treaty was scheduled for Wellington, New Zealand, in February 2008, with a final conference for formal negotiations in Dublin, Ireland, in May 2008.

V. Conclusions

In 2007 conventional arms control in Europe fell victim to deepening disagreements between Russia and the other states parties to the CFE Treaty. Although disturbing, the brinkmanship over the CFE Treaty is simply a reflection of the wider spectrum of strategic, political, military and other issues that divide the OSCE community of states rather than a conflict in its own right.

[94] Boese, W., 'Cluster munitions control efforts make gains', *Arms Control Today*, vol. 37, no. 6 (July/Aug. 2007).

[95] German Presidency of the European Union, 'CCW-GGE on ERW and cluster munitions: EU statement', 19 June 2007, Geneva, <http://www.eu2007.de/en/News/Statements_in_International_Organisations/>.

[96] See German Presidency of the European Union (note 95).

[97] Meeting of the High Contracting Parties to the CCW Convention, Report, document CCW/MSP/2007/5, Geneva, 7–13 Nov. 2007, paragraph 37.

[98] Cluster Munitions Coalition, 'CMC report on the Vienna Conference on Cluster Munitions', 21 Dec. 2007, <http://www.stopclustermunitions.org/news.asp?id=107>. Following the example set by Belgium, which banned cluster munitions in Feb. 2006, and Norway, which announced a moratorium on use of cluster munitions in 2006, in early Dec. 2007 Austria passed a law banning these weapons. The Federal law on the ban on cluster munitions was promulgated in *Bundesgesetzblatt I*, no. 12/2008 (7 Jan. 2008). See also Cumming-Bruce, N., 'Austria bans cluster munitions', *International Herald Tribune*, 7 Dec. 2007.

With regard to the treaty regime itself, Russia's separation of its legal arms control obligations and its political commitments put it at loggerheads with states parties who insist on treating the CFE process as a whole. The 'suspension' of the implementation of the CFE Treaty in December effectively placed Russia in breach of critical disarmament-related obligations. The NATO states, wishing to cooperatively engage Russia, chose not to challenge it on the grounds of international law.

In the absence of a political compromise, the CFE Treaty is likely to remain in limbo. Two key issues dominate the CFE agenda: the nature and substance of the 1999 Istanbul commitments and the flank limitations dispute. The USA and other NATO member states have belatedly acknowledged the need to pay more serious attention to Russia's CFE-related concerns, both for the sake of the viability of the regime and for intra-NATO cohesion. However, if Russia hopes to disrupt NATO or weaken its stance, it risks miscalculation and overplaying its hand; prolonging the crisis may well result in the opposite outcome—solidifying NATO's ranks. The principal Russian demand—that flank limits be removed—would require a huge concession on the part of the two most interested NATO states, Norway and Turkey, not to mention the concerns of other flank countries and their neighbours. Given Russia's current behaviour and its own non-observance of the flank restrictions, agreement does not seem likely to be forthcoming. In addition, both the NATO members and states that are poised to join the agreed adapted CFE regime will be unwilling to accede to a treaty that is to be substantially changed to accommodate the demands of one party, at the apparent expense of others' sense of security.

The suspension of CFE implementation has already had a damaging effect on the adherence of other states parties. Some have begun to reassess their security position in the event that the CFE regime should collapse, while an arms race is already gaining momentum in the South Caucasus.

Paradoxically, the current crisis creates an opportunity to seriously rethink the current relevance of the CFE regime. Despite—or because of—the crisis, arms control has risen on the European security agenda. With the 'hard' arms control regime deadlocked, some OSCE states and experts suggest a 'soft' arms control regime of confidence- and security-building measures. However, with confidence being undermined in one place, it is difficult to restore and develop it in another. Nevertheless, the norm-setting Code of Conduct on Politico-Military Aspects of Security retains its relevance and importance, and other confidence- and stability-enhancing steps in the OSCE area continue to focus on the multiple dangers created by surplus stockpiles of small arms and light weapons, ammunition and toxic fuel.

In developments beyond Europe, the number of states adhering to the APM Convention rose to 156, thus taking it further towards universalization. Similar humanitarian concerns are drawing increasing interest in efforts to eliminate cluster munitions worldwide.

11. Controls on security-related international transfers

IAN ANTHONY, SIBYLLE BAUER and ANNA WETTER

I. Introduction

Export controls are preventive measures intended to help ensure that exported goods do not contribute to activities in other countries that are either illegal or undesirable from the perspective of the authorities in the exporting state. Historically, defence items—those items that were specifically designed, developed or modified for military use—have usually been held under careful control. However, in recent years export controls have been extended to many dual-use items—those items that were neither specifically designed nor developed for military application but can be used in weapon programmes. Many countries updated their export control laws in the 1990s following the discovery that Iraq and other countries had supported clandestine weapon programmes by purchasing dual-use equipment, materials and technology. The effective enforcement of these laws requires the active, competent and cooperative involvement of a range of national actors—including customs, police, intelligence and prosecution services—and an appropriate legal framework, including penalties for export control violations.

This chapter highlights the efforts of multilateral cooperation regimes, the European Union (EU) and the United Nations to control international transfers of proliferation-sensitive items by developing, implementing and enforcing export control laws. Section II examines recent developments in multilateral cooperation arrangements that attempt to improve the effectiveness of the participating states' national export controls. Section III discusses developments in EU export control policies for defence articles and dual-use items. Section IV examines the investigation and prosecution of suspected violations of export control laws. The conclusions are presented in section V.

II. Developments in multilateral export control regimes

Four informal multilateral cooperation regimes worked in their specific fields to strengthen export control cooperation in 2007: the Australia Group (AG), the Nuclear Suppliers Group (NSG), the Wassenaar Arrangement on Export Controls for Conventional Arms and Dual-Use Goods and Technologies (WA) and the Missile Technology Control Regime (MTCR). The states participating in these cooperation regimes and in the Zangger Committee are listed in

Table 11.1. Membership of multilateral weapon and technology transfer control regimes, as of 1 January 2008

State	Zangger Committee 1974	NSG 1978	Australia Group 1985	MTCR 1987	Wassenaar Arrangement 1996
Argentina	x	x	x	x	x
Australia	x	x	x	x	x
Austria	x	x	x	x	x
Belarus		x			
Belgium	x	x	x	x	x
Brazil		x		x	
Bulgaria	x	x	x	x	x
Canada	x	x	x	x	x
China	x	x			
Croatia	x	x	x*		x
Cyprus		x	x		
Czech Republic	x	x	x	x	x
Denmark	x	x	x	x	x
Estonia		x	x		x
Finland	x	x	x	x	x
France	x	x	x	x	x
Germany	x	x	x	x	x
Greece	x	x	x	x	x
Hungary	x	x	x	x	x
Iceland			x	x	
Ireland	x	x	x	x	x
Italy	x	x	x	x	x
Japan	x	x	x	x	x
Kazakhstan		x			
Korea, South	x	x	x	x	x
Latvia		x	x		x
Lithuania		x	x		x
Luxembourg	x	x	x	x	x
Malta		x	x		x
Netherlands	x	x	x	x	x
New Zealand		x	x	x	x
Norway	x	x	x	x	x
Poland	x	x	x	x	x
Portugal	x	x	x	x	x
Romania	x	x	x		x
Russia	x	x		x	x
Slovakia	x	x	x		x
Slovenia	x	x	x		x
South Africa	x	x		x	x
Spain	x	x	x	x	x
Sweden	x	x	x	x	x
Switzerland	x	x	x	x	x
Turkey	x	x	x	x	x
UK	x	x	x	x	x
Ukraine	x	x	x	x	x
USA	x	x	x	x	x
European Commission	o	o	x		
Total membership	**36**	**45**	**41**	**34**	**40**

NSG = Nuclear Suppliers Group; MTCR = Missile Technology Control Regime; o = observer; x = member or participant; * = joined in 2007.

Note: The years in the column headings indicate when each export control regime was formally established, although the groups may have met on an informal basis before then.

table 11.1.[1] In addition to information exchange, all four multilateral arrangements conduct outreach efforts to non-participating states that emphasize increased transparency and the importance of modern and effective export controls. These efforts can help non-participating states to apply the guidelines, control lists, standards and procedures developed by regime partners.

The Australia Group

The AG was established in 1985 in the light of international concern about the use of chemical weapons in the 1980–88 Iran–Iraq War. Initially, the members cooperated to maintain and develop their national export controls to prevent the export of chemicals that might be used for, or diverted to, chemical weapon programmes. Participating states now seek to prevent the intentional or inadvertent supply of materials or equipment to chemical or biological weapon programmes by sharing information on proliferation cases and strategies to manage them.[2]

Insights from previous proliferation cases along with relevant developments in science and technology can lead to revisions of the lists of items subject to national export control by AG members. For example, in 2007 Australia Group members agreed to pay particular attention to synthetic biological agents.[3] Following this decision, the AG agreed to amend its animal pathogens list to clarify the coverage of controls on *Mycoplasma mycoides*—a bacterium that causes a severe and contagious respiratory disease in cattle.[4] As the bacterium's genome had been sequenced, the AG believed that *M. mycoides* could be synthetically reproduced and pose a potential proliferation threat.[5]

The Nuclear Suppliers Group

Created in 1975, the aim of the NSG is to prevent the proliferation of nuclear weapons through export controls on nuclear and nuclear-related material, equipment, software and technology.[6] The export controls, which are implemented by the participating states through national legislation and procedures, are not intended to prevent or hinder international cooperation on peaceful

---

[1] The Zangger Committee participants seek to take account of the effect of 'changing security aspects' on the 1968 Treaty on the Non-proliferation of Nuclear Weapons (Non-Proliferation Treaty, NPT) and to 'adapt export control conditions and criteria' in that light, although it is not formally part of the NPT regime. See also annex B in this volume.

[2] See the AG website at <http://www.australiagroup.net/>.

[3] On synthetic biology see chapter 9 this volume, section V.

[4] Australia Group, 'Media release: 2007 Australia Group plenary', Press release, Paris, 12–15 June 2007, <http://www.australiagroup.net/en/agm_2007.htm/>.

[5] The disease, which is endemic in most of Africa and a problem for agriculture in parts of Asia, has occurred in cattle in the past decade in Italy, Portugal and Spain. Additional information can be found in the online database of the European Bioinformatics Institute of the European Molecular Biology Laboratory, <http://www.ebi.ac.uk/>.

[6] On the NSG see Anthony, I., Ahlström, C. and Fedchenko, V., *Reforming Nuclear Export Controls: The Future of the Nuclear Suppliers Group*, SIPRI Research Report no. 22 (Oxford University Press: Oxford, 2007); see also the NSG website at <http://www.nuclearsuppliersgroup.org/>.

uses of nuclear energy. NSG-participating states exchange information related to cases where their authorities deny licences to export nuclear or nuclear-related dual-use items for reasons related to the NSG guidelines, which in turn helps countries to assess export applications.[7]

In 2007 the exchange of information on current proliferation challenges in the framework of the NSG included the implementation of two UN Security Council resolutions on Iran. In Resolution 1737 the Security Council decided that all states should block Iranian access to equipment and technology if the items could contribute to activities related to uranium enrichment, nuclear waste reprocessing or heavy water.[8] The resolution also instructs states to freeze the funds and financial assets of a designated list of Iranian entities and people associated with proliferation-sensitive activities. In March 2007 the latter list was revised in Resolution 1747.[9]

Iran depends on international trade to supply its nuclear and nuclear-related industries with equipment, technology and materials. Iran has also sought to buy dual-use items to support its engineering and petrochemical industries as well as for use in mineral research and specialized technical universities and research centres. These items can be legally supplied to Iran (which is a party to the 1968 Non-Proliferation Treaty, NPT[10]) for legitimate, peaceful purposes—including for use in the nuclear industry. However, such transfers must be authorized, and licence assessments depend on access to information that allows national export authorities to determine (a) the end-use of a requested item and (b) the risk that an item will be diverted to an illegitimate end-use. Based on the interventions of the NSG, it has been reported that applications to export dual-use items to Iran were denied on 75 occasions between 2002 and 2007.[11]

It is a fundamental principle of the NSG that suppliers should only authorize transfers of control-listed items when they are satisfied that the transfers would not contribute to the proliferation of nuclear weapons or other nuclear explosive devices. According to NSG guidelines, suppliers should only transfer control-listed items and technology to a non-nuclear weapon state after the importing state has brought into force an agreement with the International Atomic Energy Agency (IAEA) requiring the application of safeguards on all source and special fissionable material in its current and future peaceful activities. Moreover, the NSG requires that the importing state must apply com-

---

[7] For the NSG guidelines on nuclear transfers and transfers of nuclear-related dual-use equipment, materials, software and related technology see <http://www.nuclearsuppliersgroup.org/guide.htm>.

[8] UN Security Council Resolution 1737, 23 Dec. 2006. The resolution also required states to block access to items that would assist the development of nuclear weapon delivery systems (see below).

[9] UN Security Council Resolution 1747, 24 Mar. 2007.

[10] For a brief summary of and list of the parties to the Treaty on the Non-Proliferation of Nuclear Weapons see annex A in this volume.

[11] Hoge, W., 'Iran was blocked from buying nuclear materials at least 75 times, group says', *New York Times*, 16 Nov. 2007.

prehensive IAEA safeguards before any new nuclear supply agreements are concluded.[12]

India has posed a specific challenge to the application of NSG guidelines. As India is a country with nuclear weapons but is not a nuclear weapon state from a legal perspective within the scope of the NPT, the transfer of control-listed items to India is not addressed in the NSG guidelines. As cooperation with India's military nuclear programme is prevented under the provisions of the NPT, the NSG guidelines on exports of nuclear and nuclear-related dual-use items would either need to be modified to permit civil cooperation with India or some kind of exemption from several provisions would need to be granted.

In the light of the commitment to expand bilateral activities in the field of civil nuclear energy contained in the July 2005 Indian–US Civil Nuclear Cooperation Initiative (CNCI), the United States circulated a 'pre-decision' draft of how civil nuclear cooperation could be facilitated prior to the 2006 NSG plenary meeting.[13] However, the issue was not formally presented at the meeting and no decision on how to proceed was sought at that time. Indian Government officials are reported to have given informal briefings to NSG participating states on the sidelines of the 2007 plenary meeting. A special envoy of the Indian Prime Minister, Shyam Saran, visited some NSG participating states during 2007 to seek their support.[14] The USA convened a special meeting of NSG participating states in September 2007 to give a briefing on the current status of various elements of the CNCI.[15] A number of NSG participating states were reported to have opposed any decision by the NSG until a bilateral safeguards agreement has been concluded between India and the IAEA.[16] As of January 2008 the NSG had not taken a position on either the need for, or the form of, its relationship with India but was reported to be discussing the conditions that could attend a modification of the guidelines.[17]

Several countries have explored civil nuclear cooperation with India since the CNCI was announced in 2005, including Australia, France and Russia. In August 2007 the Australian Prime Minister, John Howard, informed the Indian Prime Minister, Manmohan Singh, that Australia was willing to open dis-

---

[12] Comprehensive safeguards are based on a combination of nuclear material accountancy, complemented by containment and surveillance techniques, such as tamper-proof seals and cameras that the IAEA installs at facilities to monitor activities on a continuous basis.

[13] Vishwanathan, A., *The Nuclear Suppliers Group and the Indo–US Nuclear Deal*, IDSA Strategic Comments (Institute for Defence Studies & Analyses: New Delhi, 26 Sep. 2007).

[14] 'EU says "closely watching" India's talk with UN nuclear body', PTI News Agency, 26 Nov. 2007.

[15] On the CNCI see US Department of State, 'Joint statement by President George W. Bush and Prime Minister Manmohan Singh', Washington, DC, 18 July 2005, <http://www.state.gov/p/sca/rls/pr/2005/49763.htm/>; Ahlström, C., 'Legal aspects of the Indian–US Civil Nuclear Cooperation Initiative', *SIPRI Yearbook 2006: Armaments, Disarmament and International Security* (Oxford University Press: Oxford, 2006), pp. 669–85; and chapter 8 this volume, section IV.

[16] Hibbs, M., 'Approval in 2007 of US–India deal may hinge on Infcirc-66 safeguards', *Nuclear Fuel*, vol. 32, no. 21 (8 Oct. 2007), pp. 4–5. Discussions on a bilateral safeguards agreement opened in Nov. 2007. International Atomic Energy Agency, 'IAEA–India to launch consultations for India-specific safeguards agreement', Press release, 21 Nov. 2007. See also chapter 8 this volume, section IV.

[17] Hibbs, M., 'NSG prepares to set specific conditions for lifting sanctions against India', *Nuclear Fuel*, vol. 33, no. 2 (14 Jan. 2008), pp. 1, 10.

cussions about the supply of natural uranium to India.[18] Following the December 2007 election of Kevin Rudd as Australian Prime Minister, the new Australian Foreign Minister, Stephen Smith, reversed this decision, referring to the 'long standing commitment of the Australian Labor Party that we don't authorize the export of uranium to countries who are not parties to the Nuclear Nonproliferation Treaty'.[19]

The Wassenaar Arrangement

Agreement to establish the WA was made in 1995 at a meeting in Wassenaar, the Netherlands. Its objective is to promote transparency and the exchange of information and views on transfers of an agreed range of items. The WA encourages responsibility in transfers of conventional arms and related dual-use goods and technologies and seeks to prevent 'destabilizing accumulations' of such items.[20]

Every four years the WA undertakes a review and evaluation of its overall performance. For the WA's third assessment in 2007, working groups on the following areas were established: Best Practices of Export Control Regulations, Re-export Control of Conventional Weapons Systems, Transparency and Outreach. The WA's subsidiary bodies (the General Working Group, the Experts Group, and the Licensing and Enforcement Officers Meeting) met during the year to exchange information and to prepare decisions prior to the plenary meeting in December 2007.[21] The meeting agreed to continue to conduct outreach through dialogue with non-participating states and international organizations to promote best practices related to export controls, among others for man-portable air defence systems (MANPADS); however, no consensus could be reached on expanding membership.

WA participating states made modifications to the export control lists, with a particular focus on devices used to initiate explosions and equipment for the disposal of improvised explosive devices (IEDs). For the first time, the WA also undertook a major editorial review of the control list. Roughly 2500 editorial changes were made to improve consistency and to increase the list's usability for licensing authorities and industry; the changes do not materially affect the scope of the controls.[22] The Experts Group and the MTCR began a dialogue in 2007 to develop a common understanding of terminology and technical parameters on certain navigation equipment given the overlap between the regime lists.

[18] High Commission of India in Australia, 'In response to a question regarding Australian Prime Minister's telephone call to PM', 16 Aug. 2007, <http://www.hcindia-au.org/pr_132.html/>.

[19] Bowden, R., 'Australia rules out Uranium sales to India', Worldpress.org, 20 Jan. 2008, <http://www.worldpress.org/Asia/3047.cfm/>.

[20] See the WA website at <http://www.wassenaar.org/index.html/>.

[21] Wassenaar Arrangement, 'Public statement 2007 plenary meeting of the Wassenaar Arrangement on Export Controls for Conventional Arms and Dual-Use Goods and Technologies', Vienna, 6 Dec. 2007. All public WA documents are available at <http://www.wassenaar.org/>.

[22] For updated control lists and a summary of changes adopted at the December 2007 plenary see <http://www.wassenaar.org/controllists/index.html/>.

The WA plenary meeting approved amendments to the 2003 elements for export controls of MANPADS.[23] The amendments strengthened language about production equipment and training. They also added requirements for end-use assurances and the possibility of post-shipment checks in recipient countries. A provision was added that non-participating states could be provided with technical and expert support in developing and implementing their legislation to control MANPADS transfers. The 2002 'Best practices for exports of small arms and light weapons' were also amended 'to bring them in line with language adopted by the UN in 2005 on marking and tracing of small arms and light weapons'.[24]

The plenary also approved two new documents: 'Statement of understanding on implementation of end-use controls for dual use items' and 'Best practices to prevent destabilising transfers of small arms and light weapons (SALW) through air transport'.[25] The end-use statement recommends that both the respective competent authorities and the exporter apply risk-management principles to the three phases of end-use controls.[26] For the competent authorities, this translates into a risk-based approach during the pre-licence phase (e.g. through awareness raising with industry), the application procedure (e.g. plausibility checks, inter-agency consultations) and after the licence is granted (e.g. information exchange between governments, 'proportionate and dissuasive penalties' to deter violations, monitoring end-use obligations, post-shipment controls and reporting). On the exporter side, responsibilities during the three phases include internal compliance programmes; physical and technical security arrangements and a two-way information exchange with authorities on sensitive end-users and business contacts; presentation of appropriate documents and further explanations during the application procedure; and record-keeping and post-shipment controls once a transfer is completed. The best practices document contains a series of measures to be taken at the national level to prevent the undesirable and illegal transport of SALW by non-state actors and to support the work of enforcement officers. These measures include the provision of specific transport details in advance of granting an export licence, which can in turn be used in a prosecution should those terms be violated, and exchange of information that could be fed into a national risk assessment in the licensing and enforcement process.

---

[23] Wassenaar Arrangement, 'Elements for export controls of man-portable air defence systems (MANPADS)', Vienna, Dec. 2007, <http://www.wassenaar.org/publicdocuments/index.html/>.

[24] Wassenaar Arrangement, 'Updated best practice guidelines for exports of small arms and light weapons (SALW)', Vienna, Dec. 2007, <http://www.wassenaar.org/publicdocuments/index.html/>.

[25] Wassenaar Arrangement, 'Statement of understanding on implementation of end-use controls for dual use items', Vienna, Dec. 2007, <http://www.wassenaar.org/publicdocuments/index.html/>; and Wassenaar Arrangement, 'Best practices to prevent destabilising transfers of small arms and light weapons (SALW) through air transport', Vienna, Dec. 2007, <http://www.wassenaar.org/public documents/index.html/>.

[26] The term 'exporter' refers to the legal or physical person who has the authority to determine and control the sending of items outside the physical jurisdiction or customs boundary of a state. For a glossary of terms used in this chapter see SIRPI Non-proliferation and Export Control Project, 'Glossary of terms used in arms and dual-use export control', <http://www.sipri.org/contents/expcon/eglossa.html>.

The Missile Technology Control Regime

Established in 1987, the MTCR is an informal arrangement in which countries that share the goal of non-proliferation of unmanned delivery systems for nuclear, biological or chemical weapons cooperate to exchange information and coordinate their national export licensing processes.[27]

The MTCR undertakes outreach activities to inform non-participating states about the regime's activities and to provide practical assistance regarding efforts to prevent the proliferation of missile delivery systems. At the plenary meeting in early November 2007, MTCR partners proposed outreach to Belarus, China, Croatia, Egypt, Jordan, India, Israel, Kazakhstan, Libya, Panama, Singapore, Syria, the United Arab Emirates and Yemen and agreed that explanations of the rationale behind changes to the list of controlled goods could be taken up in outreach meetings. The MTCR considered new membership applications from a number of countries, but no consensus was reached on any of the applications, which are evaluated on a case-by-case basis and on both political and technical grounds.[28] The MTCR has yet to consider Russia's proposal for a comprehensive review of the regime's work pending details of what such a review might encompass.

The electronic point of contact (ePOC) database that MTCR partners use to facilitate the secure exchange of documents and to notify each other when they deny an export licence was under further development in 2007. Revisions will allow partners to renew notifications online with the date of the most recent renewal appearing in the database with the relevant notification. The ePOC database will also be able to trace revoked denials for up to five years following the revocation.

The MTCR and regional missile developments

MTCR partners have drawn attention to the significant number of ballistic missile tests that have been carried out by India, Iran, North Korea and Pakistan recently.[29] During their information exchange at the plenary meeting, MTCR partners considered and expressed concern over regional missile developments, in particular in Iran and North Korea.[30] Iran continued to test ballistic missiles during 2007, and in November the Iranian Minister of Defence, Mostafa Mohammad Najjar, made reference to the test-firing of a missile with a range of 2000 kilometres which he called the Ashura, said to

---

[27] See the MTCR website at <http://www.mtcr.info/>.

[28] China, Croatia, Cyprus, Estonia, Kazakhstan, Latvia, Libya, Lithuania, Malta, Romania, Slovakia and Slovenia all sought to participate in the MTCR.

[29] See Anthony, I. and Bauer, S., 'Controls on security-related international transfers', *SIPRI Yearbook 2007: Armaments, Disarmament and International Security* (Oxford University Press: Oxford, 2007), p. 645.

[30] 'Opening Statement by the Secretary General for European Affairs, Mr. Dimitrios K. Katsoudas', 22nd MTCR Plenary, Athens, 7 Nov. 2007, <http://www.mfa.gr/www.mfa.gr/Articles/en-US/141107_F 1551.htm/>.

have been developed and produced by the Iranian Ministry of Defence.[31] US officials subsequently informed General Yury Baluyevsky, the Chief of General Staff of the Russian armed forces, that an Iranian missile test had taken place on 20 November.[32] MTCR partners emphasized the need to support the implementation of decisions by the UN Security Council. The plenary reiterated its support for UN Security Council Resolution 1540, which declares proliferation of weapons of mass destruction (WMD) and their means of delivery a threat to international peace and security and obliges all UN member states to exercise effective export controls over such weapons and related materials.[33] The partners also noted the direct relevance of a number of UN Security Council resolutions (specifically resolutions 1718, 1737 and 1747, see below) to MTCR export controls and expressed their determination to implement these resolutions.

UN Security Council Resolution 1718 was agreed after the test of a nuclear explosive device by North Korea in October 2006.[34] The resolution requires UN member states to 'prevent the direct or indirect supply, sale or transfer to North Korea, through their territories or by their nationals, or using their flag vessels or aircraft, and whether or not originating in their territories' of certain specific items. The items subject to the embargo include missiles and missile systems 'as defined for the purpose of the United Nations Register of Conventional Arms' as well as 'additional items, materials, equipment, goods and technology' as determined by a Security Council committee set up for the purpose of overseeing implementation of the resolution.[35]

While the UN has not imposed an arms embargo on Iran, both resolutions 1737 and 1747 include certain provisions with direct relevance to missile-related export controls. UN Security Council Resolution 1737 adopted in December 2006 includes a provision that member states should supply items listed in UN Security Council document S/2006/815 to Iran only under specific circumstances.[36] This document contains a list of items, materials, equipment, goods and technology related to ballistic missile programmes derived directly from the MTCR control list. Transfer of the listed items to Iran is prohibited if the authorities of the exporting state find that they would contribute to the development of nuclear weapon delivery systems.

In all other cases the export of listed items should only take place on three conditions. First, the authorities in the exporting state must apply the guidelines set out in another Security Council document, S/2006/985, which con-

[31] 'Iran's new ballistic missile "Ashura"', Agence France-Presse, 27 Nov. 2007.

[32] 'Russian general says no evidence that Iran tested new missile', ITAR-TASS, 7 Dec. 2007.

[33] UN Security Council Resolution 1540, 28 Apr. 2004; Anthony, I., 'Reducing security risks by controlling possession and use of civil materials', *SIPRI Yearbook 2007* (note 29); and Ahlström, C., 'United Nations Security Council Resolution 1540: non-proliferation by means of international legislation', *SIPRI Yearbook 2007* (note 29).

[34] UN Security Council Resolution 1718, 14 Oct. 2006.

[35] The list of items can be found on the website of the committee at <http://www.un.org/sc/committees/1718/>.

[36] United Nations, List of items, materials, equipment, goods and technology related to ballistic missile programmes, attached to S/2006/815, 13 Oct 2006.

tains the MTCR guidelines.[37] Second, the authorities in the exporting state must obtain and be in a position to effectively exercise a right to verify the end-use and end-use location of any supplied item. Third, the authorities must notify the relevant UN Security Council committee within 10 days of the supply, sale or transfer.

Resolution 1747 amplifies Resolution 1737 and calls on all states to 'exercise vigilance and restraint in the supply, sale or transfer directly or indirectly from their territories or by their nationals or using their flag vessels or aircraft' to Iran of a range of items, missiles or missile systems as defined for the purpose of the UN Register of Conventional Arms (UNROCA). Similar vigilance and restraint should also be shown in regard to any 'technical assistance or training, financial assistance, investment, brokering or other services, and the transfer of financial resources or services, related to the supply, sale, transfer, manufacture or use of such items'.[38]

The MTCR and other missile-control mechanisms

The UN High Representative for Disarmament Affairs, Serge Duarte, has concluded that the manufacture and proliferation of delivery systems 'remain difficult problems, and there is no multilateral missiles treaty or even signs of one arising anytime soon'.[39] In October 2007 Russia and the USA circulated a joint statement on the 1987 Treaty on the Elimination of Intermediate-Range and Shorter-Range Missiles (INF Treaty) at the UN General Assembly First Committee on disarmament and international security. The statement calls on all interested countries to 'discuss the possibility of imparting a global character to this important regime through the renunciation of ground-launched ballistic and cruise missiles with ranges between 500 and 5500 kilometres, leading to destruction of any such missiles and the cessation of associated programmes'.[40] Russia introduced a similar proposal at a meeting of the foreign ministers of the Organization for Security and Co-operation in Europe (OSCE) in November 2007. Russia had hoped for this to be a joint proposal with the USA, but the USA did not support the discussion of a missile treaty in a Euro-

---

[37] United Nations, Guidelines for sensitive missile-relevant transfers, annex to S/2006/985, 15 Dec. 2006.

[38] The UNROCA defines missiles as '(a) Guided or unguided rockets, ballistic or cruise missiles capable of delivering a warhead or weapon of destruction to a range of at least 25 kilometers, and means designed or modified specifically for launching such missiles or rockets . . . this subcategory includes remotely piloted vehicles with the characteristics for missiles as defined above but does not include ground-to-air missiles (b) Man-Portable Air-Defence Systems (MANPADS).' United Nations Register of Conventional Arms, *Information Booklet 2007* (UN Department for Disarmament Affairs: New York, 2007), <http://disarmament.un.org/cab/register.html>, p. 6.

[39] Duarte, S., 'Current state of affairs in the field of arms control and disarmament and the role of the respective organizations', Statement before the First Committee of the UN General Assembly, 8 Oct. 2007. Since Nov. 2000 the UN General Assembly has engaged a Panel of Government Experts to consider 'the issue of missiles in all its aspects'. In 2002 the panel produced its first report which contained no actionable proposals other than a recommendation to continue discussions. It has not subsequently been possible to achieve the necessary consensus within the group to produce any further reports.

[40] United Nations, Joint United States–Russian statement on the treaty on the elimination of intermediate-range and shorter-range missiles, A/C.1/62/3, 1 Nov. 2007.

pean regional forum. The proposal, when introduced, did not attract the support of all OSCE foreign ministers.[41]

The Hague Code of Conduct against the Proliferation of Ballistic Missiles (HCOC), which was opened for signature at the Hague in November 2002, was developed by MTCR participating states.[42] The HCOC contains transparency and confidence-building measures that are intended to reduce mistrust by explaining how missile technology is being applied by states with legitimate missile programmes. These measures include pre-launch notifications, which contain advance information on rocket, ballistic missile and space launch vehicles, and annual declarations on relevant national policies. When the HCOC was launched 93 countries signed on as subscribing states. By December 2007 the number of subscribing states had grown to 127.[43]

The extent to which the HCOC has achieved its objectives is difficult to establish and paradoxically, given its focus on transparency, public information about the activities of the HCOC is scarce. The expansion in participation has largely reflected decisions by countries that have no ballistic missile programmes.[44] Most countries with emerging ballistic missile programmes have refused to participate, as have China, India and Pakistan—although China is willing to maintain engagement and exchange information with HCOC members without subscribing to the code.[45] Public reports suggest that a significant number of the states that subscribe to the HCOC do not file annual declarations of their ballistic missile and space launch vehicle-related policies.[46] In many cases the states concerned would have nothing to report and may be reluctant to carry the cost of filing blank or 'nil' reports.

III. Supply-side measures in the European Union

During 2007 the complex system that the European Union has developed to control exports of military and dual-use items continued to evolve. In December 2006 the European Commission proposed revisions to the EU dual-use

---

[41] 'US stance on making INF Treaty universal looks strange—Lavrov', ITAR-TASS, 5 Dec. 2007.

[42] At the 1999 plenary meeting of the MTCR at Noordwijk, the Netherlands, the participating states agreed that additional steps would be needed to control missile proliferation beyond export control coordination. During discussions in 2000 it became clear that participating states preferred to seek a relatively quick process resulting in a political code of conduct rather than a legal agreement. By 2001 participating states had agreed on the text of a draft code of conduct and had begun to discuss its content with non-MTCR states.

[43] For a list of subscribing states see annex B in this volume.

[44] Philippine Department of Foreign Affairs, 'Philippines concludes productive chairmanship of Hague Code of Conduct (HCOC) against ballistic missile proliferation', Press release SFA-AGR-540-06, 27 June 2006.

[45] Chinese Ministry for Foreign Affairs, 'The Hague Code of Conduct against the Proliferation of Ballistic Missiles (HCOC)', Press release, 21 May 2007, <http://www.fmprc.gov.cn/eng/wjb/zzjg/jks/kjlc/wkdd/t410752.htm>.

[46] Keohane, D., 'Challenges in missile non-proliferation—multilateral approaches: the Hague Code of Conduct against Ballistic Missile Proliferation', Report on the International Conference organized by the European Union Institute for Security Studies, Vienna, 30 May 2007.

export control regime, including amendments to the legal framework.[47] Although member states considered the proposals, no agreement on how to modify the current system was reached during 2007.

In their national export licence assessments, EU member states take into account the eight criteria of the EU Code of Conduct on Arms Exports, which also includes reporting, information exchange and consultation obligations.[48] The Council of the EU's Working Party on Conventional Arms Exports (COARM) plays a central role in facilitating discussion of arms transfer issues within the EU. COARM publishes a user's guide that is intended to help EU member states apply the Code of Conduct and that includes best practice guidelines for the interpretation of the code's criteria. In 2007 COARM published best practice guidelines for the remaining three of the eight criteria.[49] COARM also added a chapter to the user's guide on post-shipment controls, which encourages information exchange on the national measures that member states use in order to ensure that end-use agreements are respected. The user's guide also recommends that member states inform each other when brokering registration requests are denied.

Implementing UN Security Council sanctions in EU law

As reported in section II, the UN Security Council adopted several resolutions restricting or prohibiting transfers of a range of items to Iran, including UN Security Council Resolution 1737. Article 8 of EU Council Regulation 1334/2000—the primary legislation which governs the export of dual-use items from the EU—underlines that in making licensing decisions member states must take into account their obligations under sanctions imposed by a binding resolution of the UN Security Council.[50] However, Article 3 makes clear that the law does not apply to items that only pass through the EU and does not create any licensing requirement for items in transit or trans-shipment on the way to Iran. Article 3 also makes clear that the regulation does not apply to transfers of technology which take place through contact between people—either inside the EU during visits by foreign nationals or outside the EU during visits by EU nationals to other countries.[51] Therefore, Regulation

---

[47] European Commission, Proposal for a Council Regulation setting up a Community regime for the control of exports of dual-use items and technology, COM(2006) 829 Final, Brussels, 18 Dec. 2006.

[48] Council of the European Union, EU Code of Conduct on Arms Exports, 8675/2/98 Rev. 2, Brussels, 5 June 1998. On the impact of the code over its first 10 years see Bromley, M., *The Impact on Domestic Policy of the EU Code of Conduct on Arms Exports: the Czech Republic, the Netherlands and Spain*, SIPRI Policy Paper no. 21 (SIPRI: Stockholm, Apr. 2008).

[49] Council of the European Union, 'User's guide to the European Union Code of Conduct on Arms Exports', 10684/1/07 Rev. 1, Brussels, 3 July 2007. The new additions were for criterion 1, related to international obligations of member states, criterion 5, related to the security of friends and allies of EU member states, and criterion 6, on the attitude of the buyer country to terrorism.

[50] Council Regulation (EC) No. 1334/2000 of 22 June 2000 setting up a Community regime for the control of exports of dual-use items and technology, *Official Journal of the European Communities*, L159 (30 June 2000), p. 5.

[51] While there is no primary legislation at European level, EU member states have agreed that they will control such transfers through national legislation. To that end, the Council adopted Council Joint

1334/2000 by itself cannot be an adequate basis to implement the UN decisions.[52] In general member states have adopted the practice of first stating the measures that are needed to meet the objectives of any UN resolution as part of the EU's Common Foreign and Security Policy, usually in the form of a common position. A Council regulation will then provide the basis for action to interrupt or reduce economic or financial relations with the country in question.

In February 2007 the EU Council adopted a common position identifying the particular restrictive measures to be applied to Iran in order to achieve the objectives of UN Security Council Resolution 1737.[53] In April 2007 Regulation 423/2007 concerning restrictive measures against Iran put these restrictive measures into a law that is binding on all EU member states.[54] Regulation 423/2007 prohibits the supply to Iran of all goods and technology listed in an annex to the regulation; this annex is identical to the NSG and MTCR lists. The regulation also provides legal authority to stop these same items in transit through the EU and to control technical assistance and services not covered by Regulation 1334/2000. In addition, the regulation defines a list of goods and technologies that are not usually controlled but that could contribute to enrichment-related, reprocessing or heavy water-related activities, to the development of nuclear weapon delivery systems, or to the pursuit of activities related to other topics about which the IAEA has expressed concerns or identified as outstanding.[55] The regulation requires exporters to seek authorization before exporting these items, which are listed in a separate annex to the EU law.[56] By this means the EU extended the scope of restrictions beyond those required to implement UN decisions.

In contrast to exports of dual-use items, exports of military items are controlled by the national legislation of member states and not by European law. While many missile-related dual-use items are controlled by Regulation 1334/2000, missiles themselves are not. Missiles and rockets as well as components specifically designed for them are on the national munitions list that forms part of the arms export control law in each member state. In February 2007 the EU prohibited the export of missiles and rockets to Iran.[57] Subsequent measures agreed by the EU go beyond the decisions taken in the UN

Action of 22 June 2000 concerning the control of technical assistance related to certain military end-uses (2000/401/CFSP), *Official Journal of the European Communities*, L159 (30 June 2000), pp. 216–17.

[52] One of the proposals put forward by the European Commission would create a legal basis to control items in transit through the EU, a modification that is also necessary to bring EU law into line with the requirements of UN Security Council Resolution 1540.

[53] Council Common Position 2007/140/CFSP of 27 February 2007 concerning restrictive measures against Iran, *Official Journal of the European Union*, L61 (28 Feb. 2007), pp. 49–55.

[54] Council Regulation (EC) No. 423/2007 of 19 April 2007 concerning restrictive measures against Iran, *Official Journal of the European Union*, L103 (20 Apr. 2007), pp. 1–23. This regulation was subsequently amended and updated by Council Regulation (EC) No. 618/2007 of 5 June 2007 amending Regulation (EC) No. 423/2007 concerning restrictive measures against Iran, *Official Journal of the European Union*, L143 (6 June 2007), pp. 1–2.

[55] As called for by the preamble, paragraph 5, of Council Common 2007/140/CFSP (note 53).

[56] Council Regulation No. 423/2007 (note 54), Article 3.

[57] Council Common Position 2007/140/CFSP (note 53).

Security Council in relation to conventional arms. Whereas the UN Security Council has called on states to exercise vigilance and restraint in the supply of conventional weapons to Iran, in April 2007 the EU prohibited the transfer, sale or supply to Iran of 'arms and related materiel of all types, including weapons and ammunition, military vehicles and equipment, paramilitary equipment and spare parts for the aforementioned'.[58]

Regulating intra-EU transfers of arms

As noted above, while the export of dual-use items is controlled by a single piece of EU legislation, exports of military articles and services are controlled by separate legislation in each of the 27 EU member states. Moreover, military items are not part of the single European market and member states apply their national laws and regulations when selling arms to one another. While member states apply the common criteria laid down in the Code of Conduct on arms exports when considering applications to export military articles, the scope for their interpretation still permits national policy differences. Through cooperation and reporting (including denial notification and regular consultations) the EU has promoted increasing convergence among national authorities in the application of export policies of military-related products to third countries.[59]

In December 2007 the European Commission proposed a piece of legislation intended to simplify national licensing procedures for transfers of certain items within the EU.[60] The proposal contained two main elements. First, member states would be required to grant general and global licences for intra-EU transfers of specified items. Individual licensing would not be prohibited, but would become exceptional. Second, member states would be obliged to create general licences for transfers of military-related products to governments in any other member state and for transfers to recipients in other member states certified in accordance with common criteria to be laid down in legislation.

Another significant aspect of the proposed legislation relates to the creation of an agreed list of export-controlled munitions. All EU member states have made a political commitment to control a list of items based on the Munitions List compiled by the Wassenaar Arrangement.[61] This list has been adopted by

---

[58] Council Common Position 2007/246/CFSP of 23 April 2007 amending Common Position 2007/140/CFSP concerning restrictive measures against Iran, *Official Journal of the European Union*, L106 (24 Apr. 2007), pp. 67–75.

[59] In EU terminology, a 'third-country' is any non-member of the EU.

[60] European Commission, Proposal for a directive of the European Parliament and of the Council on simplifying terms and conditions of transfers of defence-related products within the Community, COM(2007) 765 Final, Brussels, 5 Dec. 2007.

[61] Only 1 EU member state (Cyprus) does not participate in the WA. However, as the EU has adopted it as a reference list, Cyprus is politically bound to control WA Munitions List items through national legislation. The EU list, which is revised to reflect changes agreed in the Wassenaar Arrangement, was updated in Mar. 2007. Common Military List of the European Union, *Official Journal of the European Union*, L88 (29 Mar. 2007), pp. 58–89.

the EU as a reference list—called the Common Military List of the European Union—to which member states apply the Code of Conduct. There is no harmonized approach among member states regarding how the items on the Common Military List are incorporated into national laws and regulations. In some cases the list is adopted as a national control list without modification. In other cases the listed items are reworked into an existing national control list that is tailored to national guidelines and licensing systems. Working with the Common Military List for certain transactions and a national control list for others could undermine the objective of simplifying regulations and reducing transaction costs for exporting companies. If passed, the legislation would make the Common Military List a single, legally binding list of defence products, replacing the current national lists in cases of intra-EU transfers. Additionally, the European Commission has proposed applying the legislation to all military-related products that correspond to those listed in the Common Military List—including subsystems, components, spare parts, technology transfer, and maintenance and repair.

The Commission's proposal recognizes that reducing scrutiny of intra-EU transfers would require confidence between member states that there will be no retransfer that would not have been approved by the originating member state. To address this problem the proposal recommends a certification system. Member states would be required to certify companies wishing to make use of general licences according to common requirements. When applying for an export licence, certified companies would have to confirm to their national authorities that they understand and respect the export limitations issued by the originating member states. The incorporation of company certification and greater exchange of information between licensing officials and industry would add a new dimension to the process of converging of national export controls.

These proposed measures are intended to reduce what has been described by the Commission and the European Defence Agency as a fragmented European defence industry.[62] Simplification measures were also discussed in the 1990s but failed, not least because of EU member states' concerns that the measures would infringe on their sovereign powers regarding arms production and trade—concerns that are being voiced again in the current debate.[63] If adopted, the legislation would represent a significant change in EU export control.

The revised EU Customs Code

Since October 1992 the import and export of goods within the EU has been governed by the Community Customs Code.[64] Following the March 2004 bomb attacks on the train network in Madrid the European Council issued the

[62] See chapter 6 this volume, section III.

[63] See e.g. Ninth Annual Report according to Operative Provision 8 of the European Union Code of Conduct on Arms Exports, *Official Journal of the European Union*, C253 (26 Oct. 2007), p. 3.

[64] Council Regulation (EEC) No. 2913/92 of 12 October 1992 establishing the Community Customs Code, *Official Journal of the European Communities*, L302 (19 Oct. 1992), p. 1.

Declaration on Combating Terrorism.[65] One customs-related aspect of the declaration was a commitment to protect the security of international transport and ensure effective systems of border control. This commitment added a higher public security element to EU customs work and required the revision of the primary legislation governing customs procedures.

In April 2005 the European Parliament and the Council made security-related amendments to the customs code.[66] The amendments had three main elements. First, the status of Authorized Economic Operator (AEO) was created. Second, a common approach was laid down in relation to risk assessment of items of potential concern from a security perspective. Third, a requirement for advance notification of the arrival and departure of goods at the border of the EU customs boundary was introduced. The amendments also established a timetable for the strengthened security component in the customs code, with some of the key elements scheduled for introduction by the end of 2008 and the remaining elements to follow by July 2009. In December 2006 the Commission published detailed implementing regulations.[67]

Businesses involved in the international supply chain can apply to national customs services for the status of Authorized Economic Operator, which would be awarded to them if the national authorities certify that agreed standards have been met.[68] Businesses decide whether or not to apply for AEO status; they also decide whether or not to limit their trade activities to partners that have received AEO status. Customs authorities in EU member states assess the AEO applications using standards and criteria laid down at European level.[69] Once awarded, AEO status is recognized by national customs authorities across the EU. Businesses that receive the AEO certificate are considered by authorities to be reliable in implementing customs-related operations and, therefore, are entitled to enjoy certain benefits. The benefits include simplified procedures for clearing goods for import and export, fewer document and physical checks on goods, and a preferential status in regard to security- and safety-related inspections at premises. The certification scheme started to come into force in January 2008.

Combining trade facilitation with law enforcement is a problem faced by customs authorities around the world. The increased volume of international

[65] European Council, 'Declaration on Combating Terrorism', Brussels, 25 Mar. 2004, <http://www.ue.eu.int/ueDocs/cms_Data/docs/pressData/en/ec/79637.pdf/>.

[66] Regulation (EC) No. 648/2005 of the European Parliament and of the Council of 13 April 2005 amending Council Regulation (EEC) No. 2913/92 establishing the Community Customs Code, *Official Journal of the European Union*, L117 (4 May 2005), pp. 13–19.

[67] Commission Regulation (EC) No. 1875/2006 of 18 December 2006 amending Regulation (EEC) No. 2454/93 laying down provisions for the implementation of Council Regulation (EEC) No. 2913/92 establishing the Community Customs Code, *Official Journal of the European Union*, L360 (19 Dec. 2006), pp 64–125.

[68] An economic operator is a business or individual involved in activities covered by customs legislation. Manufacturers, exporters, freight forwarders, warehouse managers, customs agents and carriers are all examples of economic operators.

[69] The criteria include the record of compliance, the existence of a document management system, the financial solvency of the operator, and physical safety and security criteria (including access control, physical containment) used by the operator.

trade coupled with the need to remain competitive in the global marketplace has put pressure on operators managing seaports, airports and land crossings to move goods more quickly along the supply chain. These factors partly explain the low percentage of shipments that are physically inspected by customs authorities. Customs authorities have responded by trying to target particular shipments for inspection based on the result of an assessment of the risk posed by any given cargo. Targeted inspections have been under development for a considerable time to enforce laws related to, for example, the protection of endangered species of plants and animals. However, using this approach to combat terrorism and non-proliferation is a more recent development.

In 2003 the EU carried out a pilot action to create a common approach to risk assessment. A comprehensive catalogue of risk indicators and a detailed list of questions organized in distinct risk areas were developed to help to measure the threat that a particular shipment would not comply with EU legislation.[70] Information related to the goods being shipped into and out of the EU are compared with risk profiles for places, goods and operators. These profiles are compiled nationally using uniform criteria. This work has underpinned the legal requirement for all goods moving into and out of the EU to be subject to a common risk assessment by July 2009.[71] The risk assessment system being developed is a valuable tool, but it does not replace the need for well-trained and motivated customs officers. Although the system will flag shipments for selection, the decision about what to inspect will be made by a customs officer and is not automatic. To avoid any potential distortions arising from different levels of national enforcement, the customs code requires that, where the assessment returns a positive risk analysis, an equivalent level of preventive control must be applied by EU national authorities.[72]

The risk assessment system is possible because of the 2005 decision that the arrival and departure of goods must be notified in advance.[73] This decision will be fully implemented by 2009. At that time the advance notification of entry and exit of goods will become mandatory and, if operators do not submit the necessary information, they will find that their goods either cannot be loaded or will be stopped at the border.

As a practical matter, the security system must be supported by information technology, and the customs authorities of EU member states have been working on an electronic customs project. Currently all EU customs services can exchange information electronically. The project's final objective is that authorities will be able to exchange information in real time among the offices involved in a specific procedure, rather than between headquarters.[74]

---

[70] European Commission, 'Standardised framework for risk management in the customs administration of the EU', 17 Nov. 2004, <http://ec.europa.eu/taxation_customs/customs/customs_controls/risk_management/customs_eu/index_en.htm>.

[71] Regulation (EC) No. 648/2005 (note 66).

[72] Commission Regulation (EC) No. 1875/2006 (note 67).

[73] Regulation (EC) No. 648/2005 (note 66).

[74] European Commission, 'Electronic customs', 7 Dec. 2005, <http://ec.europa.eu/taxation_customs/customs/policy_issues/e-customs_initiative/index_en.htm>.

While these changes are needed to implement the revisions to the Community Customs Code, the revised system will also help the EU to meet its international obligations. For example, the new customs code will make the EU compliant with the World Customs Organization (WCO) SAFE Framework of Standards—which all EU member states have made a political commitment to support.[75] As a centre of global trade, the EU has a strong interest in ensuring that border controls do not introduce unnecessary complications in transactions with key trade partners. The EU has begun to discuss how the customs code can be harmonized with the systems being used in the USA that share certain features and objectives, in particular the US Customs–Trade Partnership Against Terrorism (US-CTPAT) and has also opened a dialogue on customs issues with China.[76]

IV. The role of investigation and prosecution in enforcing export controls of dual-use goods

Each year thousands of dual-use items are traded internationally. Generally, most exporters share the objectives that export controls try to achieve, such as preventing the proliferation of nuclear, biological or chemical weapons and their missile delivery systems. The main emphasis in enforcing export controls is usually placed on techniques that help exporters avoid the unauthorized export of controlled items. Ideally, export control enforcement agencies work together with exporters to reduce the risk that violations will occur because of negligence or a lack of understanding. For example, authorities can help exporters by offering advice on how to properly classify products, how to screen prospective customers and by pointing out indicators that suggest risks associated with a particular end-use, end-user or destination.

Nevertheless, dual-use items are sometimes transferred without the proper authorization. Typically, however, proliferators try to acquire weapons by using established trading routes and concealing the item's true end-use and final end-user. For example, Japan has modern and comprehensive laws to control exports of dual-use items. Nevertheless, in June 2007 four executives of the Mitutoyo Corporation were sentenced for their role in illegally exporting precision instruments that measure objects in three dimensions. Inspectors from the IAEA had found one of the Mitutoyo machines at a nuclear-related facility in Libya in 2003, causing Japanese investigators to launch an inquiry into exports by the company. This led to the charge that Mitutoyo had exported five machines to Malaysia and Singapore without the proper authorization—a charge that the company admitted.[77]

---

[75] World Customs Organization, 'WCO SAFE Framework of Standards', June 2007, <http://www.wcoomd.org/home.htm/>.

[76] In Jan. 2007 the EU and the USA set up a working group of customs specialists to examine how to achieve mutual recognition of their respective trade partnership programmes. European Commission, 'Customs and security', 5 Mar. 2008, <http://ec.europa.eu/taxation_customs/customs/policy_issues/customs_security/index_en.htm>.

[77] Hongo, J., 'Mitutoyo execs receive suspended terms', *Japan Times*, 26 June 2007.

Several recent international initiatives have emphasized the role of criminal law in enforcing export controls. For example, the US-led Proliferation Security Initiative (PSI) encourages the active use of law enforcement and criminal justice procedures to tackle illicit trafficking in proliferation-sensitive items. In addition, many of the multilateral export control regimes have also begun to pay closer attention to enforcement issues in general, including criminal sanctions.[78] UN Security Council Resolution 1540 of April 2004 requires states to establish and enforce 'appropriate criminal or civil penalties' for violations of export control laws and regulations.[79] EU Council Regulation 1334/2000 requires member states to lay down the penalties applicable to infringements of dual-use export control laws and regulations and stipulates that penalties must be 'effective, proportionate and dissuasive'.[80]

Criminal law could support effective enforcement of export controls either by general prevention (i.e. deterring violation of the laws by adopting an exemplary punishment system) or through special prevention (i.e. stopping an individual offender from committing further crimes, e.g. through imprisonment). However, the emphasis placed on these legal theories within the overall spectrum of enforcement options is not agreed. Discussions in Europe have underlined that whether or not penalties in general have a deterring function remains a controversial question, and one that is governed by domestic (rather than European) legislation that is guided by traditions relating to national penal laws.

While Regulation 1334/2000 leaves the specific penalties entirely to the discretion of member states, the European Commission has proposed a revision requiring the member states to have the option of criminal sanctions where serious export control offences are proved and to agree on a minimum tariff for sentencing.[81] In 2005 and 2006 the EU collected information on (*a*) the export control provisions that are in force in the member states, (*b*) the states' views on whether or not sanctions (administrative and criminal) should be harmonized within the EU, and (*c*) the type of sanctions that are currently applicable in the states for violation of export control laws and which could be made subject to EU harmonization. The results revealed variations in how offences are dealt with at the national level. A majority of the member states expressed a reluctance to harmonize sanctions in their replies.[82]

---

[78] On the potential expanded role for the PSI and the enforcement discussion in multilateral regimes see Anthony and Bauer (note 29), pp. 647–51. On the PSI see also Ahlström, C., 'The Proliferation Security Initiative: international law aspects of the Statement of Interdiction Principles', *SIPRI Yearbook 2005: Armaments, Disarmament and International Security* (Oxford University Press: Oxford, 2005).

[79] Examples of administrative penalties are financial penalties, the loss of export licences, the loss of right to privileges (e.g. to simplified procedures) and the loss of property rights through confiscation. Examples of criminal penalties are fines, imprisonment and suspended sentences.

[80] On the implication of effective, proportionate and dissuasive penalties see e.g. Court of Justice of the European Communities, *Commission of the European Communities v Hellenic Republic*, 'Failure of a member state to fulfil its obligations—failure to establish and make available the Community's own resources', Case 68/88, 21 Sep. 1989.

[81] European Commission (note 47).

[82] E.g. the maximum penalty for a serious breach of an export control law can result in 15 years in prison in Germany and Hungary whereas Ireland applies a maximum penalty of 12 months in prison.

There is an apparent gap between the number of suspected illegal activities and the number of prosecutions in the EU member states. Discussions have revealed that some member states maintain a policy of refraining from bringing suspected offences in front of a court, possibly to protect their dual-use industries. Most member states have either very limited or no experience of prosecuting export control-related cases.[83] National laws also diverge on the question of which actors should be held liable under the EU's export control legislation. The national legislation of member states is only obliged to hold the actual exporter liable. However, acknowledging that actors other than exporters could be responsible for the spread of WMD, Germany has gone a step further to include liability for brokers and shippers of dual-use goods in its national legislation.[84] In contrast, the United Kingdom remains reluctant to make other actors in the export chain liable under its export control legislation. In addition to their export control legislation, most states have laws that could deal with such actors. However, investigators and prosecutors must be familiar with export control issues in order to make use of that legislation to address suspected illegal exports of dual-use items in an effective way.

In addition to the variety of prosecution policies and applicable sanctions in the member states, there are also prosecution discrepancies. Some member states use a system in which prosecutors have a duty to prosecute whereas other systems require that the prosecutors assess the public interest before proceeding to trial. In practice, there is a risk that trial decisions are governed by aspects related primarily to time and resources. The complex and technical nature of the export control legislation may also deter a prosecutor who has some latitude as to whether or not to press charges.

In most EU member states, if a suspect is to be convicted of a serious export control-related offence, the prosecutor usually has to prove that the suspect, at least passively, has confirmed that the exported goods were destined for WMD proliferation uses. If intent cannot be proved, the prosecutor can use the option of subsidiary legislation, such as the submission of false documents to the licensing authority. However, acts of this kind are likely to be seen by a court as technical offences and carry low penalties. Proving intent requires law enforcement actors to collect adequate and sufficient evidence. Intelligence services often play a central role in detecting export-related offences, but the information that they hold may not be available to investigators and public prosecutors as evidence for trial purposes.[85] In contrast to the usually limited

---

[83] Realizing the need for coordination and exchange of experience in most of the member states, the European Commission's Directorate-General for Justice, Freedom and Security sponsored a seminar on investigating and prosecuting offences related to the illegal export of dual-use goods in EU member states in Stockholm on 10–12 Sep. 2007. The seminar was co-hosted by SIPRI and the Swedish Prosecution office for national security. Wetter, A., *Enforcing European Union Law on Exports of Dual-use Goods*, SIPRI Research Report no. 24 (Oxford University Press: Oxford, forthcoming 2008).

[84] Foreign Trade and Payments Act (Außenwirtschaftsgesetz, AWG) of 28 Apr. 1961, Article 34, as amended by the law of 28 Mar. 2006.

[85] The interests of intelligence services and the law enforcement community may not be aligned. E.g. an intelligence service may prefer to use information to better understand the proliferation activities of a particular country, rather than to prosecute a dealer or broker in dual-use items.

attention devoted to unauthorized exports of dual-use goods in many states, the illicit trafficking in nuclear and other radioactive material is given high priority by both law enforcement communities and the media.[86]

V. Conclusions

The role of export controls in supporting the implementation of the main multilateral non-proliferation treaties is now supplemented by the important role that they play in implementing decisions of the UN. One key challenge for export control authorities is how to implement and enforce the comprehensive export control and non-proliferation sanctions in place (including financial sanctions), which requires adapting legal bases and rethinking institutional set-ups and procedures. UN Security Council Resolution 1540 requires all UN member states to enforce effective penalties for export control violations of dual-use goods, but the debate about what constitutes such sanctions has yet to take place. The EU has initiated a debate about what constitutes dissuasive, effective and proportionate sanctions in export control.

The great majority of exporters understand and want to comply with the underlying objectives of export control. However, proven cases in which controlled items were exported without authorization underline that voluntary compliance with export controls cannot be assumed from all exporters. It is necessary to have mechanisms to enforce the controls. The need for enforcement agencies, in particular customs, to play an increased role in delivering security is gradually being acknowledged and reflected in recent initiatives in the context of EU, UN, WCO and national initiatives. However, this role is yet to be fully recognized and supported through the required personnel and financial allocations and underpinned through the appropriate strategies, laws and procedures.

Prevention is the overarching goal, meaning that enforcement tasks such as detection, disruption and interdiction are key components of law enforcement in preventing unauthorized exports. While the organizational distribution of legal powers to perform these tasks and their implementation vary, enforcement usually involves customs, border and other police forces, and intelligence services. Civil society has also played a role in collecting and distributing information about possible violations of export control laws. In addition to law enforcement tasks, prosecutors play an important role in giving effect to export control laws by bringing perpetrators to court. Cooperation between all of the listed actors is essential for the accomplishment of successful prevention. However, both prevention and effective enforcement first require establishing an export controls system based on a political-strategic mandate, clear procedures and allocation of responsibilities, a solid legal basis, and an institutional memory—each tailored to a country's specific situation.

---

[86] On the illicit trafficking in nuclear and other radioactive material see also International Atomic Energy Agency (IAEA), *Combating Illicit Trafficking in Nuclear and Other Radioactive Material*, IAEA Nuclear Security Series no. 6 (IAEA: Vienna, 2007); and appendix 8D in this volume.

Annexes

Annex A. Arms control and disarmament agreements

Annex B. International organizations and intergovernmental bodies

Annex C. Chronology 2007

Annex A. Arms control and disarmament agreements

NENNE BODELL

This annex lists multi- and bilateral treaties, conventions, protocols and agreements relating to arms control and disarmament. Agreements are listed in chronological order. The status of agreements and of their parties and signatories is as at 1 January 2008.

Notes

1. The agreements are listed in the order of the date on which they were adopted, signed or opened for signature (multilateral agreements) or signed (bilateral agreements). The date on which they entered into force and the depositary for multilateral treaties are also given.

2. The main source of information is the lists of signatories and parties provided by the depositaries of the treaties.

3. For a few major treaties, the substantive parts of the most important reservations, declarations or interpretive statements made in connection with a state's signature, ratification, accession or succession are given in notes below the entry. For the 1925 Geneva Protocol, only 'explicit reservations' are listed here.

4. States and organizations listed as parties have ratified, acceded or succeeded to the agreements. Former non-self-governing territories, upon attaining statehood, sometimes make general statements of continuity to all agreements concluded by the former governing power. This annex lists as parties only those new states that have made an uncontested declaration on continuity or have notified the depositary of their succession.

5. Unless stated otherwise, the multilateral agreements listed in this annex are open to all states or to all states in the respective zone (or region) for signature, ratification, accession or succession.

6. A complete list of UN member states, with the year in which they became members, appears in annex B in this volume. Not all the signatories and parties appearing in this annex are UN members.

7. Taiwan, while not recognized as a sovereign state by some countries, is listed as a party to the agreements that it has ratified.

8. The Russian Federation continues the international obligations that were assumed by the Soviet Union.

9. Serbia continues the international obligations of the former State Union of Serbia and Montenegro.

Protocol for the Prohibition of the Use in War of Asphyxiating, Poisonous or Other Gases, and of Bacteriological Methods of Warfare (1925 Geneva Protocol)

Signed at Geneva on 17 June 1925; entered into force on 8 February 1928; depositary French Government

The protocol declares that the parties agree to be bound by the prohibition on the use of these weapons in war.

Parties (135): Afghanistan, Albania, Algeria[1], Angola[1], Antigua and Barbuda, Argentina, Australia, Austria, Bahrain[1], Bangladesh[1], Barbados, Belgium, Benin, Bhutan, Bolivia, Brazil, Bulgaria, Burkina Faso, Cambodia[1], Cameroon, Canada, Cape Verde, Central African Republic, Chile, China[1], Côte d'Ivoire, Croatia, Cuba, Cyprus, Czech Republic, Denmark, Dominican Republic, Ecuador, Egypt, Equatorial Guinea, Estonia, Ethiopia, Fiji[1], Finland, France, Gambia, Germany, Ghana, Greece, Grenada, Guatemala, Guinea-Bissau, Holy See, Hungary, Iceland, India[1], Indonesia, Iran, Iraq[1], Ireland, Israel[2], Italy, Jamaica, Japan, Jordan[3], Kenya, Korea (North)[1], Korea (South)[5], Kuwait[1], Laos, Latvia, Lebanon, Lesotho, Liberia, Libya[1], Liechtenstein, Lithuania, Luxembourg, Madagascar, Malawi, Malaysia, Maldives, Malta, Mauritius, Mexico, Monaco, Mongolia, Morocco, Nepal, Netherlands, New Zealand, Nicaragua, Niger, Nigeria[1], Norway, Pakistan, Panama, Papua New Guinea[1], Paraguay, Peru, Philippines, Poland, Portugal, Qatar, Romania, Russia, Rwanda, Saint Kitts and Nevis, Saint Lucia, Saint Vincent and the Grenadines, Saudi Arabia, Senegal, Serbia[1], Sierra Leone, Slovakia, Solomon Islands[1], South Africa, Spain, Sri Lanka, Sudan, Swaziland, Sweden, Switzerland, Syria, Taiwan, Tanzania, Thailand[4], Togo, Tonga, Trinidad and Tobago, Tunisia, Turkey, Uganda, UK, Ukraine, Uruguay, USA[4], Venezuela, Viet Nam[1], Yemen

[1] The protocol is binding on this state only as regards states which have signed and ratified or acceded to it. The protocol will cease to be binding on this state in regard to any enemy state whose armed forces or whose allies fail to respect the prohibitions laid down in it.

[2] The protocol is binding on Israel only as regards states which have signed and ratified or acceded to it. The protocol shall cease to be binding on Israel in regard to any enemy state whose armed forces, or the armed forces of whose allies, or the regular or irregular forces, or groups or individuals operating from its territory, fail to respect the prohibitions which are the object of the protocol.

[3] Jordan undertakes to respect the obligations contained in the protocol with regard to states which have undertaken similar commitments. It is not bound by the protocol as regards states whose armed forces, regular or irregular, do not respect the provisions of the protocol.

[4] The protocol shall cease to be binding on this state with respect to use in war of asphyxiating, poisonous or other gases, and of all analogous liquids, materials or devices, in regard to any enemy state if such state or any of its allies fails to respect the prohibitions laid down in the protocol.

[5] South Korea withdrew its reservation concerning bacteriological and toxin weapons in 2002.

Signed but not ratified: El Salvador

Convention on the Prevention and Punishment of the Crime of Genocide (Genocide Convention)

Adopted at Paris by the UN General Assembly on 9 December 1948; entered into force on 12 January 1951; depositary UN Secretary-General

Under the convention any commission of acts intended to destroy, in whole or in part, a national, ethnic, racial or religious group as such is declared to be a crime punishable under international law.

Parties (140): Afghanistan, Albania*, Algeria*, Andorra, Antigua and Barbuda, Argentina*, Armenia, Australia, Austria, Azerbaijan, Bahamas, Bahrain*, Bangladesh*, Barbados,

Belarus*, Belgium, Belize, Bolivia, Bosnia and Herzegovina, Brazil, Bulgaria*, Burkina Faso, Burundi, Cambodia, Canada, Chile, China*, Colombia, Comoros, Congo (Democratic Republic of the), Costa Rica, Côte d'Ivoire, Croatia, Cuba, Cyprus, Czech Republic, Denmark, Ecuador, Egypt, El Salvador, Estonia, Ethiopia, Fiji, Finland, France, Gabon, Gambia, Georgia, Germany, Ghana, Greece, Guatemala, Guinea, Haiti, Honduras, Hungary*, Iceland, India*, Iran, Iraq, Ireland, Israel, Italy, Jamaica, Jordan, Kazakhstan, Korea (North), Korea (South), Kuwait, Kyrgyzstan, Laos, Latvia, Lebanon, Lesotho, Liberia, Libya, Liechtenstein, Lithuania, Luxembourg, Macedonia (Former Yugoslav Republic of), Malaysia*, Maldives, Mali, Mexico, Moldova, Monaco, Mongolia*, Montenegro*, Morocco*, Mozambique, Myanmar*, Namibia, Nepal, Netherlands, New Zealand, Nicaragua, Norway, Pakistan, Panama, Papua New Guinea, Paraguay, Peru, Philippines*, Poland*, Portugal*, Romania*, Russia*, Rwanda*, Saint Vincent and the Grenadines, Saudi Arabia, Senegal, Serbia*, Seychelles, Singapore*, Slovakia, Slovenia, South Africa, Spain*, Sri Lanka, Sudan, Sweden, Switzerland, Syria, Tanzania, Togo, Tonga, Trinidad and Tobago, Tunisia, Turkey, Uganda, UK, Ukraine*, United Arab Emirates, Uruguay, USA*, Uzbekistan, Venezuela*, Viet Nam*, Yemen*, Zimbabwe

* With reservation and/or declaration.

Signed but not ratified: Dominican Republic

Geneva Convention (IV) Relative to the Protection of Civilian Persons in Time of War

Signed at Geneva on 12 August 1949; entered into force on 21 October 1950; depositary Swiss Federal Council

Geneva Convention (IV) establishes rules for the protection of civilians in areas covered by war and in occupied territories. This convention was formulated at the Diplomatic Conference held from 21 April to 12 August 1949. (Other conventions adopted at the same time were: Convention (I) for the Amelioration of the Condition of the Wounded and Sick in Armed Forces in the Field; Convention (II) for the Amelioration of the Condition of the Wounded, Sick and Shipwrecked Members of Armed Forces at Sea; and Convention (III) Relative to the Treatment of Prisoners of War.)

Parties (194): Afghanistan, Albania*, Algeria, Andorra, Angola*, Antigua and Barbuda, Argentina, Armenia, Australia*, Austria, Azerbaijan, Bahamas, Bahrain, Bangladesh*, Barbados*, Belarus, Belgium, Belize, Benin, Bhutan, Bolivia, Bosnia and Herzegovina, Botswana, Brazil, Brunei Darussalam, Bulgaria, Burkina Faso, Burundi, Cambodia, Cameroon, Canada, Cape Verde, Central African Republic, Chad, Chile, China*, Colombia, Comoros, Congo (Democratic Republic of the), Congo (Republic of the), Cook Islands, Costa Rica, Côte d'Ivoire, Croatia, Cuba, Cyprus, Czech Republic*, Denmark, Djibouti, Dominica, Dominican Republic, Ecuador, Egypt, El Salvador, Equatorial Guinea, Estonia, Eritrea, Ethiopia, Fiji, Finland, France, Gabon, Gambia, Georgia, Germany*, Ghana, Greece, Grenada, Guatemala, Guinea, Guinea-Bissau*, Guyana, Haiti, Holy See, Honduras, Hungary, Iceland, India, Indonesia, Iran*, Iraq, Ireland, Israel*, Italy, Jamaica, Japan, Jordan, Kazakhstan, Kenya, Kiribati, Korea (North)*, Korea (South)*, Kuwait*, Kyrgyzstan, Laos, Latvia, Lebanon, Lesotho, Liberia, Libya, Liechtenstein, Lithuania, Luxembourg, Macedonia (Former Yugoslav Republic of)*, Madagascar, Malawi, Malaysia, Maldives, Mali, Malta, Marshall Islands, Mauritania, Mauritius, Mexico, Micronesia, Moldova, Monaco, Mongolia, Montenegro, Morocco, Mozambique, Myanmar, Namibia, Nauru, Nepal, Netherlands, New Zealand*, Nicaragua, Niger, Nigeria, Norway, Oman, Pakistan*, Palau, Panama, Papua New Guinea, Paraguay, Peru, Philippines, Poland, Portugal*, Qatar, Romania, Russia*, Rwanda,

Saint Kitts and Nevis, Saint Lucia, Saint Vincent and the Grenadines, Samoa, San Marino, Sao Tome and Principe, Saudi Arabia, Senegal, Serbia, Seychelles, Sierra Leone, Singapore, Slovakia, Slovenia, Solomon Islands, Somalia, South Africa, Spain, Sri Lanka, Sudan, Suriname*, Swaziland, Sweden, Switzerland, Syria, Tajikistan, Tanzania, Thailand, Timor-Leste, Togo, Tonga, Trinidad and Tobago, Tunisia, Turkey, Turkmenistan, Tuvalu, Uganda, UK*, Ukraine*, United Arab Emirates, Uruguay*, USA*, Uzbekistan, Vanuatu, Venezuela, Viet Nam*, Yemen*, Zambia, Zimbabwe

* With reservation and/or declaration.

In 1989 the Palestine Liberation Organization (PLO) informed the depositary that it had decided to adhere to the four Geneva conventions and the two protocols of 1977.

See also Protocols I and II of 1977.

Antarctic Treaty

Signed at Washington, DC, on 1 December 1959; entered into force on 23 June 1961; depositary US Government

The treaty declares the Antarctic an area to be used exclusively for peaceful purposes. It prohibits any measure of a military nature in the Antarctic, such as the establishment of military bases and fortifications, and the carrying out of military manoeuvres or the testing of any type of weapon. The treaty bans any nuclear explosion as well as the disposal of radioactive waste material in Antarctica.

In accordance with Article IX, consultative meetings are convened at regular intervals to exchange information and hold consultations on matters pertaining to Antarctica, as well as to recommend to the governments measures in furtherance of the principles and objectives of the treaty.

The treaty is open for accession by UN members or by other states invited to accede with the consent of all the parties entitled to participate in the consultative meetings provided for in Article IX. States demonstrating their interest in Antarctica by conducting substantial scientific research activity there, such as the establishment of a scientific station or the despatch of a scientific expedition, are entitled to become consultative members.

Parties (46): Argentina†, Australia†, Austria, Belarus, Belgium†, Brazil†, Bulgaria†, Canada, Chile†, China*, Colombia, Cuba, Czech Republic, Denmark, Ecuador†, Estonia, Finland†, France†, Germany†, Greece, Guatemala, Hungary, India†, Italy†, Japan†, Korea (North), Korea (South)†, Netherlands†, New Zealand†, Norway†, Papua New Guinea, Peru†, Poland†, Romania, Russia†, Slovakia, South Africa†, Spain†, Sweden†, Switzerland, Turkey, UK†, Ukraine†, Uruguay†, USA†, Venezuela

† This state is a consultative member under Article IX of the treaty.

The Protocol on Environmental Protection (**1991 Madrid Protocol**) entered into force on 14 January 1998.

Treaty Banning Nuclear Weapon Tests in the Atmosphere, in Outer Space and Under Water (Partial Test-Ban Treaty, PTBT)

Signed at Moscow by three original parties on 5 August 1963 and opened for signature by other states at London, Moscow and Washington, DC, on 8 August 1963; entered into force on 10 October 1963; depositaries British, Russian and US governments

The treaty prohibits the carrying out of any nuclear weapon test explosion or any other nuclear explosion: (*a*) in the atmosphere, beyond its limits, including outer space, or under water, including territorial waters or high seas; and (*b*) in any other environment if such explosion causes radioactive debris to be present outside the territorial limits of the state under whose jurisdiction or control the explosion is conducted.

Parties (125): Afghanistan, Antigua and Barbuda, Argentina, Armenia, Australia, Austria, Bahamas, Bangladesh, Belarus, Belgium, Benin, Bhutan, Bolivia, Bosnia and Herzegovina, Botswana, Brazil, Bulgaria, Canada, Cape Verde, Central African Republic, Chad, Chile, Colombia, Congo (Democratic Republic of the), Costa Rica, Côte d'Ivoire, Croatia, Cyprus, Czech Republic, Denmark, Dominican Republic, Ecuador, Egypt, El Salvador, Equatorial Guinea, Fiji, Finland, Gabon, Gambia, Germany, Ghana, Greece, Guatemala, Guinea-Bissau, Honduras, Hungary, Iceland, India, Indonesia, Iran, Iraq, Ireland, Israel, Italy, Jamaica, Japan, Jordan, Kenya, Korea (South), Kuwait, Laos, Lebanon, Liberia, Libya, Luxembourg, Madagascar, Malawi, Malaysia, Malta, Mauritania, Mauritius, Mexico, Mongolia, Morocco, Myanmar, Nepal, Netherlands, New Zealand, Nicaragua, Niger, Nigeria, Norway, Pakistan, Panama, Papua New Guinea, Peru, Philippines, Poland, Romania, Russia, Rwanda, Samoa, San Marino, Senegal, Serbia, Seychelles, Sierra Leone, Singapore, Slovakia, Slovenia, South Africa, Spain, Sri Lanka, Sudan, Suriname, Swaziland, Sweden, Switzerland, Syria, Taiwan, Tanzania, Thailand, Togo, Tonga, Trinidad and Tobago, Tunisia, Turkey, Uganda, UK, Ukraine, Uruguay, USA, Venezuela, Yemen, Zambia

Signed but not ratified: Algeria, Burkina Faso, Burundi, Cameroon, Ethiopia, Haiti, Mali, Paraguay, Portugal, Somalia, Viet Nam

Treaty on Principles Governing the Activities of States in the Exploration and Use of Outer Space, Including the Moon and Other Celestial Bodies (Outer Space Treaty)

Opened for signature at London, Moscow and Washington, DC, on 27 January 1967; entered into force on 10 October 1967; depositaries British, Russian and US governments

The treaty prohibits the placing into orbit around the earth of any object carrying nuclear weapons or any other kind of weapons of mass destruction, the installation of such weapons on celestial bodies, or the stationing of them in outer space in any other manner. The establishment of military bases, installations and fortifications, the testing of any type of weapons and the conduct of military manoeuvres on celestial bodies are also forbidden.

Parties (108): Afghanistan, Algeria, Antigua and Barbuda, Argentina, Australia, Austria, Bahamas, Bangladesh, Barbados, Belarus, Belgium, Benin, Brazil, Brunei Darussalam, Bulgaria, Burkina Faso, Canada, Chile, China, Cuba, Cyprus, Czech Republic, Denmark, Dominica, Dominican Republic, Ecuador, Egypt, El Salvador, Equatorial Guinea, Fiji,

Finland, France, Germany, Greece, Grenada, Guinea-Bissau, Hungary, Iceland, India, Indonesia, Iraq, Ireland, Israel, Italy, Jamaica, Japan, Kazakhstan, Kenya, Korea (South), Kuwait, Laos, Lebanon, Libya, Luxembourg, Madagascar, Mali, Mauritius, Mexico, Mongolia, Montenegro, Morocco, Myanmar, Nepal, Netherlands, New Zealand, Niger, Nigeria, Norway, Pakistan, Papua New Guinea, Peru, Poland, Portugal, Romania, Russia, Saint Kitts and Nevis, Saint Lucia, Saint Vincent and the Grenadines, San Marino, Saudi Arabia, Seychelles, Sierra Leone, Singapore, Slovakia, Solomon Islands, South Africa, Spain, Sri Lanka, Swaziland, Sweden, Switzerland, Syria, Taiwan, Thailand, Togo, Tonga, Tunisia, Turkey, Uganda, UK, Ukraine, United Arab Emirates, Uruguay, USA, Venezuela, Viet Nam, Yemen, Zambia

Signed but not ratified: Bolivia, Botswana, Burundi, Cameroon, Central African Republic, Colombia, Congo (Democratic Republic of the), Congo (Republic of the), Ethiopia, Gambia, Ghana, Guyana, Haiti, Holy See, Honduras, Iran, Jordan, Lesotho, Macedonia (Former Yugoslav Republic of), Malaysia, Nicaragua, Panama, Philippines, Rwanda, Serbia, Somalia, Trinidad and Tobago

Treaty for the Prohibition of Nuclear Weapons in Latin America and the Caribbean (Treaty of Tlatelolco)

Original treaty opened for signature at Mexico City on 14 February 1967; entered into force. The treaty was amended in 1990, 1991 and 1992; depositary Mexican Government

The treaty prohibits the testing, use, manufacture, production or acquisition by any means, as well as the receipt, storage, installation, deployment and any form of possession of any nuclear weapons by Latin American and Caribbean countries.

The parties should conclude agreements individually with the IAEA for the application of safeguards to their nuclear activities. The IAEA has the exclusive power to carry out special inspections.

The treaty is open for signature by all the independent states of the Latin American and Caribbean zone as defined in the treaty.

Under *Additional Protocol I* states with territories within the zone (France, the Netherlands, the UK and the USA) undertake to apply the statute of military denuclearization to these territories.

Under *Additional Protocol II* the recognized nuclear weapon states—China, France, Russia, the UK and the USA—undertake to respect the statute of military denuclearization of Latin America and the Caribbean and not to contribute to acts involving a violation of the treaty, nor to use or threaten to use nuclear weapons against the parties to the treaty.

Parties to the original treaty (33): Antigua and Barbuda, Argentina, Bahamas, Barbados, Belize, Bolivia, Brazil, Chile, Colombia, Costa Rica, Cuba, Dominica, Dominican Republic, Ecuador, El Salvador, Grenada, Guatemala, Guyana, Haiti, Honduras, Jamaica, Mexico, Nicaragua, Panama, Paraguay, Peru, Saint Kitts and Nevis, Saint Lucia, Saint Vincent and the Grenadines, Suriname, Trinidad and Tobago, Uruguay, Venezuela

Amendments ratified by: Argentina, Barbados, Belize, Brazil, Chile, Colombia, Costa Rica, Cuba, Dominican Republic, Ecuador, El Salvador, Grenada, Guatemala, Guyana, Jamaica, Mexico, Panama, Paraguay, Peru, Suriname, Uruguay, Venezuela
Note: Not all the countries listed have ratified all three amendments.

Parties to Additional Protocol I: France[1], Netherlands, UK[2], USA[3]

Parties to Additional Protocol II: China[4], France[5], Russia[6], UK[2], USA[7]

[1] France declared that Protocol I shall not apply to transit across French territories situated within the zone of the treaty, and destined for other French territories. The protocol shall not limit the participation of the populations of the French territories in the activities mentioned in Article 1 of the treaty, and in efforts connected with the national defence of France. France does not consider the zone defined in the treaty as established in accordance with international law; it cannot, therefore, agree that the treaty should apply to that zone.

[2] When signing and ratifying protocols I and II, the UK made the following declarations of understanding: The signing and ratification by the UK could not be regarded as affecting in any way the legal status of any territory for the international relations of which the UK is responsible, lying within the limits of the geographical zone established by the treaty. Should any party to the treaty carry out any act of aggression with the support of a nuclear weapon state, the UK would be free to reconsider the extent to which it could be regarded as bound by the provisions of Protocol II.

[3] The USA ratified Protocol I with the following understandings: The provisions of the treaty do not affect the exclusive power and legal competence under international law of a state adhering to this Protocol to grant or deny transit and transport privileges to its own or any other vessels or aircraft irrespective of cargo or armaments; the provisions do not affect rights under international law of a state adhering to this protocol regarding the exercise of the freedom of the seas, or regarding passage through or over waters subject to the sovereignty of a state. The declarations attached by the USA to its ratification of Protocol II apply also to Protocol I.

[4] China declared that it will never send its means of transportation and delivery carrying nuclear weapons into the territory, territorial sea or airspace of Latin American countries.

[5] France stated that it interprets the undertaking contained in Article 3 of Protocol II to mean that it presents no obstacle to the full exercise of the right of self-defence enshrined in Article 51 of the UN Charter; it takes note of the interpretation by the Preparatory Commission for the Denuclearization of Latin America according to which the treaty does not apply to transit, the granting or denying of which lies within the exclusive competence of each state party in accordance with international law. In 1974 France made a supplementary statement to the effect that it was prepared to consider its obligations under Protocol II as applying not only to the signatories of the treaty, but also to the territories for which the statute of denuclearization was in force in conformity with Protocol I.

[6] On signing and ratifying Protocol II, the USSR stated that it assumed that the effect of Article 1 of the treaty extends to any nuclear explosive device and that, accordingly, the carrying out by any party of nuclear explosions for peaceful purposes would be a violation of its obligations under Article 1 and would be incompatible with its non-nuclear weapon status. For states parties to the treaty, a solution to the problem of peaceful nuclear explosions can be found in accordance with the provisions of Article V of the NPT and within the framework of the international procedures of the IAEA. It declared that authorizing the transit of nuclear weapons in any form would be contrary to the objectives of the treaty.

Any actions undertaken by a state or states parties to the treaty which are not compatible with their non-nuclear weapon status, and also the commission by one or more states parties to the treaty of an act of aggression with the support of a state which is in possession of nuclear weapons or together with such a state, will be regarded by the USSR as incompatible with the obligations of those countries under the treaty. In such cases it would reserve the right to reconsider its obligations under Protocol II. It further reserves the right to reconsider its attitude to this protocol in the event of any actions on the part of other states possessing nuclear weapons which are incompatible with their obligations under the said protocol.

[7] The USA signed and ratified Protocol II with the following declarations and understandings: Each of the parties retains exclusive power and legal competence to grant or deny non-parties transit and transport privileges. As regards the undertaking not to use or threaten to use nuclear weapons against the parties, the USA would consider that an armed attack by a party, in which it was assisted by a nuclear weapon state, would be incompatible with the treaty.

Treaty on the Non-proliferation of Nuclear Weapons (Non-Proliferation Treaty, NPT)

Opened for signature at London, Moscow and Washington, DC, on 1 July 1968; entered into force on 5 March 1970; depositaries British, Russian and US governments

The treaty prohibits the transfer by a nuclear weapon state—defined in the treaty as those which have manufactured and exploded a nuclear weapon or other nuclear explosive device prior to 1 January 1967—to any recipient whatsoever of nuclear weapons or other nuclear explosive devices or of control over them, as well as the assistance, encouragement or inducement of any non-nuclear weapon state to manufacture or otherwise acquire such weapons or devices. It also prohibits the receipt by non-nuclear weapon states from any transferor whatsoever, as well as the manufacture or other acquisition by those states, of nuclear weapons or other nuclear explosive devices.

The parties undertake to facilitate the exchange of equipment, materials and scientific and technological information for the peaceful uses of nuclear energy and to ensure that potential benefits from peaceful applications of nuclear explosions will be made available to non-nuclear weapon parties to the treaty. They also undertake to pursue negotiations in good faith on effective measures relating to cessation of the nuclear arms race at an early date and to nuclear disarmament, and on a treaty on general and complete disarmament.

Non-nuclear weapon states undertake to conclude safeguard agreements with the International Atomic Energy Agency (IAEA) with a view to preventing diversion of nuclear energy from peaceful uses to nuclear weapons or other nuclear explosive devices. A Model Protocol Additional to the Safeguards Agreements, strengthening the measures, was approved in 1997; Additional Safeguards Protocols are signed by states individually with the IAEA.

A Review and Extension Conference, convened in 1995 in accordance with the treaty, decided that the treaty should remain in force indefinitely.

Parties (190): Afghanistan†, Albania†, Algeria†, Andorra, Angola, Antigua and Barbuda†, Argentina†, Armenia†, Australia†, Austria†, Azerbaijan†, Bahamas†, Bahrain, Bangladesh†, Barbados†, Belarus†, Belgium†, Belize†, Benin, Bhutan†, Bolivia†, Bosnia and Herzegovina†, Botswana, Brazil†, Brunei Darussalam†, Bulgaria†, Burkina Faso†, Burundi, Cambodia†, Cameroon†, Canada†, Cape Verde, Central African Republic, Chad, Chile†, China†, Colombia, Comoros, Congo (Democratic Republic of the)†, Congo (Republic of the), Costa Rica†, Côte d'Ivoire†, Croatia†, Cuba†, Cyprus†, Czech Republic†, Denmark†, Djibouti, Dominica†, Dominican Republic†, Ecuador†, Egypt†, El Salvador†, Equatorial Guinea, Eritrea, Estonia†, Ethiopia†, Fiji†, Finland†, France†, Gabon, Gambia†, Georgia, Germany†, Ghana†, Greece†, Grenada†, Guatemala†, Guinea, Guinea-Bissau, Guyana†, Haiti, Holy See†, Honduras†, Hungary†, Iceland†, Indonesia†, Iran†, Iraq†, Ireland†, Italy†, Jamaica†, Japan†, Jordan†, Kazakhstan†, Kenya, Kiribati†, Korea (South)†, Kuwait†, Kyrgyzstan†, Laos†, Latvia†, Lebanon†, Lesotho†, Liberia, Libya†, Liechtenstein†, Lithuania†, Luxembourg†, Macedonia† (Former Yugoslav Republic of), Madagascar†, Malawi†, Malaysia†, Maldives†, Mali†, Malta†, Marshall Islands, Mauritania, Mauritius†, Mexico†, Micronesia, Moldova, Monaco†, Mongolia†, Montenegro, Morocco†, Mozambique, Myanmar†, Namibia†, Nauru†, Nepal†, Netherlands†, New Zealand†, Nicaragua†, Niger, Nigeria†, Norway†, Oman, Palau, Panama, Papua New Guinea†, Paraguay†, Peru†, Philippines†, Poland†, Portugal†, Qatar, Romania†, Russia†, Rwanda, Saint Kitts and Nevis†, Saint Lucia†, Saint Vincent and the Grenadines†, Samoa†, San Marino†, Sao Tome and Principe, Saudi Arabia, Senegal†, Serbia†, Seychelles†, Sierra Leone, Singapore†, Slovakia†, Slovenia†, Solomon Islands†, Somalia, South Africa†, Spain†, Sri Lanka†, Sudan†, Suriname†, Swaziland†, Sweden†, Switzerland†, Syria†, Taiwan, Tajikistan†, Tanzania†, Thailand†, Togo, Timor-Leste, Tonga†, Trinidad and Tobago†, Tunisia†, Turkey†, Turkmenistan, Tuvalu†, Uganda, UK†, Ukraine†, United Arab Emirates†, Uruguay†, USA†, Uzbekistan†, Vanuatu, Venezuela†, Viet Nam†, Yemen†, Zambia†, Zimbabwe†

   † Party with safeguards agreements in force with the IAEA, as required by the treaty, or concluded by a nuclear weapon state, as defined in the treaty, on a voluntary basis.

85 Additional Safeguards Protocols in force: Afghanistan, Armenia, Australia, Austria, Azerbaijan, Bangladesh, Belgium, Botswana, Bulgaria, Burkina Faso, Burundi, Canada, Chile, China, Congo (Democratic Republic of the), Croatia, Cuba, Cyprus, Czech Republic, Denmark, Ecuador, El Salvador, Estonia, Fiji, Finland, France, Georgia, Germany, Ghana, Greece, Haiti, Holy See, Hungary, Iceland, Indonesia, Ireland, Italy, Jamaica, Japan, Jordan, Kazakhstan, Korea (South), Kuwait, Latvia, Libya, Lithuania, Luxembourg, Macedonia (Former Yugoslav Republic of), Madagascar, Malawi, Mali, Malta, Marshall Islands, Monaco, Mongolia, Netherlands, New Zealand, Nicaragua, Niger, Nigeria, Norway, Palau, Panama, Paraguay, Peru, Poland, Portugal, Romania, Russia, Seychelles, Slovakia, Slovenia, South Africa, Spain, Sweden, Switzerland, Tajikistan, Tanzania, Turkey, Turkmenistan, Uganda, UK, Ukraine, Uruguay, Uzbekistan

Notes: On 6 Feb. 2007 Iran informed the IAEA that it would no longer act in accordance with the provisions of its unratified Additional Safeguards Protocol. Taiwan, although it has not concluded a safeguards agreement, has agreed to apply the measures contained in the 1997 Model Additional Safeguards Protocol.

Treaty on the Prohibition of the Emplacement of Nuclear Weapons and other Weapons of Mass Destruction on the Seabed and the Ocean Floor and in the Subsoil thereof (Seabed Treaty)

Opened for signature at London, Moscow and Washington, DC, on 11 February 1971; entered into force on 18 May 1972; depositaries British, Russian and US governments

The treaty prohibits implanting or emplacing on the seabed and the ocean floor and in the subsoil thereof beyond the outer limit of a 12-mile (19-km) seabed zone any nuclear weapons or any other types of weapons of mass destruction as well as structures, launching installations or any other facilities specifically designed for storing, testing or using such weapons.

Parties (95): Afghanistan, Algeria, Antigua and Barbuda, Argentina, Australia, Austria, Bahamas, Belarus, Belgium, Benin, Bosnia and Herzegovina, Botswana, Brazil[1], Bulgaria, Canada[2], Cape Verde, Central African Republic, China, Congo (Republic of the), Côte d'Ivoire, Croatia, Cuba, Cyprus, Czech Republic, Denmark, Dominican Republic, Ethiopia, Finland, Germany, Ghana, Greece, Guatemala, Guinea-Bissau, Hungary, Iceland, India[3], Iran, Iraq, Ireland, Italy[4], Jamaica, Japan, Jordan, Korea (South), Laos, Latvia, Lesotho, Libya, Liechtenstein, Luxembourg, Malaysia, Malta, Mauritius, Mexico[5], Mongolia, Montenegro, Morocco, Nepal, Netherlands, New Zealand, Nicaragua, Niger, Norway, Panama, Philippines, Poland, Portugal, Qatar, Romania, Russia, Rwanda, Saint Vincent and the Grenadines, Sao Tome and Principe, Saudi Arabia, Serbia[6], Seychelles, Singapore, Slovakia, Slovenia, Solomon Islands, South Africa, Spain, Swaziland, Sweden, Switzerland, Taiwan, Togo, Tunisia, Turkey[7], UK, Ukraine, USA, Viet Nam[8], Yemen, Zambia

[1] It is the understanding of Brazil that the word 'observation', as it appears in para. 1 of Article III of the treaty, refers only to observation that is incidental to the normal course of navigation in accordance with international law.

[2] Canada declared that Article I, para. 1, cannot be interpreted as indicating that any state has a right to implant or emplace any weapons not prohibited under Article I, para. 1, on the seabed and ocean floor, and in the subsoil thereof, beyond the limits of national jurisdiction, or as constituting any limitation on the principle that this area of the seabed and ocean floor and the subsoil thereof shall be reserved for exclusively peaceful purposes. Articles I, II and III cannot be interpreted as indicating that any state but the coastal state has any right to implant or emplace any weapon not prohibited under Article I, para. 1 on the continental shelf, or the subsoil thereof, appertaining to that coastal state, beyond the outer limit of the seabed zone referred to in Article I and defined in Article II. Article III cannot be interpreted as indicating any restrictions or limitation upon the rights of the coastal state, consistent with its exclusive

sovereign rights with respect to the continental shelf, to verify, inspect or effect the removal of any weapon, structure, installation, facility or device implanted or emplaced on the continental shelf, or the subsoil thereof, appertaining to that coastal state, beyond the outer limit of the seabed zone referred to in Article I and defined in Article II.

3 The accession by India is based on its position that it has full and exclusive rights over the continental shelf adjoining its territory and beyond its territorial waters and the subsoil thereof. There cannot, therefore, be any restriction on, or limitation of, the sovereign right of India as a coastal state to verify, inspect, remove or destroy any weapon, device, structure, installation or facility, which might be implanted or emplaced on or beneath its continental shelf by any other country, or to take such other steps as may be considered necessary to safeguard its security.

4 Italy stated, inter alia, that in the case of agreements on further measures in the field of disarmament to prevent an arms race on the seabed and ocean floor and in their subsoil, the question of the delimitation of the area within which these measures would find application shall have to be examined and solved in each instance in accordance with the nature of the measures to be adopted.

5 Mexico declared that the treaty cannot be interpreted to mean that a state has the right to emplace weapons of mass destruction, or arms or military equipment of any type, on the continental shelf of Mexico. It reserves the right to verify, inspect, remove or destroy any weapon, structure, installation, device or equipment placed on its continental shelf, including nuclear weapons or other weapons of mass destruction.

6 In 1974 the Ambassador of Yugoslavia transmitted to the US Secretary of State a note stating that in the view of the Yugoslav Government, Article III, para. 1, of the treaty should be interpreted in such a way that a state exercising its right under this article shall be obliged to notify in advance the coastal state, in so far as its observations are to be carried out 'within the stretch of the sea extending above the continental shelf of the said state'. The USA objected to the Yugoslav reservation, which it considered incompatible with the object and purpose of the treaty.

7 Turkey declared that the provisions of Article II cannot be used by a state party in support of claims other than those related to disarmament. Hence, Article II cannot be interpreted as establishing a link with the UN Convention on the Law of the Sea. Furthermore, no provision of the Seabed Treaty confers on parties the right to militarize zones which have been demilitarized by other international instruments. Nor can it be interpreted as conferring on either the coastal states or other states the right to emplace nuclear weapons or other weapons of mass destruction on the continental shelf of a demilitarized territory.

8 Viet Nam stated that no provision of the treaty should be interpreted in a way that would contradict the rights of the coastal states with regard to their continental shelf, including the right to take measures to ensure their security.

Signed but not ratified: Bolivia, Burundi, Cambodia, Cameroon, Colombia, Costa Rica, Equatorial Guinea, Gambia, Guinea, Honduras, Lebanon, Liberia, Madagascar, Mali, Myanmar, Paraguay, Senegal, Sierra Leone, Sudan, Tanzania, Uruguay

Convention on the Prohibition of the Development, Production and Stockpiling of Bacteriological (Biological) and Toxin Weapons and on their Destruction (Biological and Toxin Weapons Convention, BTWC)

Opened for signature at London, Moscow and Washington, DC, on 10 April 1972; entered into force on 26 March 1975; depositaries British, Russian and US governments

The convention prohibits the development, production, stockpiling or acquisition by other means or retention of microbial or other biological agents or toxins whatever their origin or method of production of types and in quantities that have no justification of prophylactic, protective or other peaceful purposes, as well as weapons, equipment or means of delivery designed to use such agents or toxins for hostile purposes or in armed conflict. The destruction of the agents, toxins, weapons, equipment and means of delivery in the possession of the parties, or their diversion to peaceful purposes, should be effected not later than nine months after the entry into force of the convention for each country. According to a mandate from the 1996 BTWC

Review Conference, an ad hoc group is considering verification and other measures to strengthen the convention.

Parties (159): Afghanistan, Albania, Algeria, Antigua and Barbuda, Argentina, Armenia, Australia, Austria, Azerbaijan, Bahamas, Bahrain, Bangladesh, Barbados, Belarus, Belgium, Belize, Benin, Bhutan, Bolivia, Bosnia and Herzegovina, Botswana, Brazil, Brunei Darussalam, Bulgaria, Burkina Faso, Cambodia, Canada, Cape Verde, Chile, China, Colombia, Congo (Democratic Republic of the), Congo (Republic of the), Costa Rica, Croatia, Cuba, Cyprus, Czech Republic, Denmark, Dominica, Dominican Republic, Ecuador, El Salvador, Equatorial Guinea, Estonia, Ethiopia, Fiji, Finland, France, Gabon, Gambia, Georgia, Germany, Ghana, Greece, Grenada, Guatemala, Guinea-Bissau, Holy See, Honduras, Hungary, Iceland, India, Indonesia, Iran, Iraq, Ireland, Italy, Jamaica, Japan, Jordan, Kazakhstan, Kenya, Korea (North), Korea (South), Kuwait, Kyrgyzstan, Laos, Latvia, Lebanon, Lesotho, Libya, Liechtenstein, Lithuania, Luxembourg, Macedonia (Former Yugoslav Republic of), Malaysia, Maldives, Mali, Malta, Mauritius, Mexico, Moldova, Monaco, Mongolia, Montenegro, Morocco, Netherlands, New Zealand, Nicaragua, Niger, Nigeria, Norway, Oman, Pakistan, Palau, Panama, Papua New Guinea, Paraguay, Peru, Philippines, Poland, Portugal, Qatar, Romania, Russia, Rwanda, Saint Kitts and Nevis, Saint Lucia, Saint Vincent and the Grenadines, San Marino, Sao Tome and Principe, Saudi Arabia, Senegal, Serbia, Seychelles, Sierra Leone, Singapore, Slovakia, Slovenia, Solomon Islands, South Africa, Spain, Sri Lanka, Sudan, Suriname, Swaziland, Sweden, Switzerland*, Taiwan, Thailand, Timor-Leste, Togo, Tonga, Trinidad and Tobago, Tunisia, Turkey, Turkmenistan, Uganda, UK, Ukraine, Uruguay, USA, Uzbekistan, Vanuatu, Venezuela, Viet Nam, Yemen, Zimbabwe

* With reservation.

Signed but not ratified: Burundi, Central African Republic, Côte d'Ivoire, Egypt, Guyana, Haiti, Liberia, Madagascar, Malawi, Myanmar, Nepal, Somalia, Syria, Tanzania, United Arab Emirates

Treaty on the Limitation of Anti-Ballistic Missile Systems (ABM Treaty)

Signed by the USA and the USSR at Moscow on 26 May 1972; entered into force on 3 October 1972; not in force from 13 June 2002

The parties—Russia and the USA—undertook not to build nationwide defences against ballistic missile attack and to limit the development and deployment of permitted strategic missile defences. The treaty prohibited the parties from giving air defence missiles, radars or launchers the technical ability to counter strategic ballistic missiles and from testing them in a strategic ABM mode.

The **1974 Protocol** to the ABM Treaty introduced further numerical restrictions on permitted ballistic missile defences.

In 1997 Russia and the USA signed a set of Agreed Statements, specifying the demarcation line between strategic missile defences, which are not permitted under the treaty, and non-strategic or theatre missile defences (TMD), which are permitted under the treaty. The set of 1997 agreements on anti-missile defence were ratified by Russia in April 2000, but because the USA did not ratify them they did not enter into force. On 13 December 2001 the USA announced its withdrawal from the ABM Treaty, which came into effect on 13 June 2002.

Treaty on the Limitation of Underground Nuclear Weapon Tests (Threshold Test-Ban Treaty, TTBT)

Signed by the USA and the USSR at Moscow on 3 July 1974; entered into force on 11 December 1990

The parties—Russia and the USA—undertake not to carry out any underground nuclear weapon test having a yield exceeding 150 kilotons. The 1974 verification protocol was replaced in 1990 with a new protocol.

Treaty on Underground Nuclear Explosions for Peaceful Purposes (Peaceful Nuclear Explosions Treaty, PNET)

Signed by the USA and the USSR at Moscow and Washington, DC, on 28 May 1976; entered into force on 11 December 1990

The parties—Russia and the USA—undertake not to carry out any individual underground nuclear explosion for peaceful purposes having a yield exceeding 150 kilotons or any group explosion having an aggregate yield exceeding 150 kilotons; and not to carry out any group explosion having an aggregate yield exceeding 1500 kilotons unless the individual explosions in the group could be identified and measured by agreed verification procedures.

Convention on the Prohibition of Military or Any Other Hostile Use of Environmental Modification Techniques (Enmod Convention)

Opened for signature at Geneva on 18 May 1977; entered into force on 5 October 1978; depositary UN Secretary-General

The convention prohibits military or any other hostile use of environmental modification techniques having widespread, long-lasting or severe effects as the means of destruction, damage or injury to states party to the convention. The term 'environmental modification techniques' refers to any technique for changing—through the deliberate manipulation of natural processes—the dynamics, composition or structure of the earth, including its biota, lithosphere, hydrosphere and atmosphere, or of outer space. The understandings reached during the negotiations, but not written into the convention, define the terms 'widespread', 'long-lasting' and 'severe'.

Parties (73): Afghanistan, Algeria, Antigua and Barbuda, Argentina, Armenia, Australia, Austria, Bangladesh, Belarus, Belgium, Benin, Brazil, Bulgaria, Canada, Cape Verde, Chile, China*, Costa Rica, Cuba, Cyprus, Czech Republic, Denmark, Dominica, Egypt, Finland, Germany, Ghana, Greece, Guatemala, Hungary, India, Ireland, Italy, Japan, Kazakhstan, Korea (North), Korea (South)*, Kuwait, Lithuania, Laos, Malawi, Mauritius, Mongolia, Netherlands*, New Zealand, Nicaragua, Niger, Norway, Pakistan, Panama, Papua New Guinea, Poland, Romania, Russia, Saint Lucia, Saint Vincent and the Grenadines, Sao Tome and Principe, Slovakia, Slovenia, Solomon Islands, Spain, Sri Lanka, Sweden, Switzerland, Tajikistan, Tunisia, UK, Ukraine, Uruguay, USA, Uzbekistan, Viet Nam, Yemen

* With declaration.

Signed but not ratified: Bolivia, Congo (Democratic Republic of the), Ethiopia, Holy See, Iceland, Iran, Iraq, Lebanon, Liberia, Luxembourg, Morocco, Portugal, Sierra Leone, Syria, Turkey, Uganda

Protocol I Additional to the 1949 Geneva Conventions, and Relating to the Protection of Victims of International Armed Conflicts

Protocol II Additional to the 1949 Geneva Conventions, and Relating to the Protection of Victims of Non-International Armed Conflicts

Opened for signature at Bern on 12 December 1977; entered into force on 7 December 1978; depositary Swiss Federal Council

The protocols confirm that the right of parties that are engaged in international or non-international armed conflicts to choose methods or means of warfare is not unlimited and that it is prohibited to use weapons or means of warfare that cause superfluous injury or unnecessary suffering.

Parties to Protocol I (167) and Protocol II (163): Albania, Algeria*, Angola[1]*, Antigua and Barbuda, Argentina*, Armenia, Australia*, Austria*, Bahamas, Bahrain, Bangladesh, Barbados, Belarus*, Belgium*, Belize, Benin, Bolivia*, Bosnia and Herzegovina*, Botswana, Brazil*, Brunei Darussalam, Bulgaria*, Burkina Faso*, Burundi, Cambodia, Cameroon, Canada*, Cape Verde*, Central African Republic, Chad, Chile*, China*, Colombia*, Comoros, Congo (Democratic Republic of the)*, Congo (Republic of the), Cook Islands*, Costa Rica*, Côte d'Ivoire, Croatia, Cuba, Cyprus*, Czech Republic*, Denmark*, Djibouti, Dominica, Dominican Republic, Ecuador, Egypt*, El Salvador*, Equatorial Guinea, Estonia, Ethiopia, Finland*, France*, Gabon, Gambia, Georgia, Germany*, Ghana, Greece*, Grenada, Guatemala, Guinea*, Guinea-Bissau, Guyana, Haiti, Holy See, Honduras, Hungary*, Iceland*, Ireland*, Italy*, Jamaica, Japan*, Jordan, Kazakhstan, Kenya, Korea (North)[1], Korea (South)*, Kuwait, Kyrgyzstan, Laos*, Latvia, Lebanon, Lesotho, Liberia, Libya, Liechtenstein*, Lithuania*, Luxembourg*, Macedonia (Former Yugoslav Republic of)*, Madagascar*, Malawi, Maldives, Mali*, Malta*, Mauritania, Mauritius*, Mexico[1], Micronesia, Moldova, Monaco, Mongolia*, Montenegro, Mozambique, Namibia*, Nauru, Netherlands*, New Zealand*, Nicaragua, Niger, Nigeria, Norway*, Oman, Palau, Panama*, Paraguay*, Peru, Philippines[2], Poland*, Portugal*, Qatar*, Romania*, Russia*, Rwanda*, Saint Kitts and Nevis, Saint Lucia, Saint Vincent and the Grenadines, Samoa, San Marino, Sao Tome and Principe, Saudi Arabia*, Senegal, Serbia*, Seychelles*, Sierra Leone, Slovakia*, Slovenia*, Solomon Islands, South Africa, Spain*, Sudan, Suriname, Swaziland, Sweden*, Switzerland*, Syria*[1], Tajikistan*, Tanzania, Timor-Leste, Togo*, Tonga*, Trinidad and Tobago*, Tunisia, Turkmenistan, Uganda, UK*, Ukraine*, United Arab Emirates*, Uruguay*, Uzbekistan, Vanuatu, Venezuela, Viet Nam[1], Yemen, Zambia, Zimbabwe

* With reservation and/or declaration.
[1] Party only to Protocol I.
[2] Party only to Protocol II.

In 1989 the Palestine Liberation Organization (PLO) informed the depositary that it had decided to adhere to the four Geneva conventions and the two protocols.

Convention on the Physical Protection of Nuclear Material and Nuclear Facilities

Original convention opened for signature at New York and Vienna on 3 March 1980; entered into force on 8 February 1987. The convention was amended in 2005; depositary IAEA Director General

The amended convention obligates the parties to protect nuclear facilities and material used for peaceful purposes while in storage as well as transport. The amendments will take effect 30 days after they have been ratified, accepted or approved by two-thirds of the states parties to the convention.

Parties to the original convention (130): Afghanistan, Albania, Algeria*, Andorra*, Antigua and Barbuda, Argentina*, Armenia, Australia, Austria*, Azerbaijan*, Bangladesh, Belarus, Belgium*, Bolivia, Bosnia and Herzegovina, Botswana, Brazil, Bulgaria, Burkina Faso, Cambodia, Cameroon, Canada, Cape Verde, Chile, China*, Colombia, Comoros, Congo (Democratic Republic of the), Costa Rica, Croatia, Cuba*, Cyprus*, Czech Republic, Denmark, Djibouti, Dominica, Ecuador, El Salvador*, Equatorial Guinea, Estonia, Euratom*, Finland*, France*, Georgia, Germany, Ghana, Greece*, Grenada, Guatemala*, Guinea, Guyana, Honduras, Hungary, Iceland, India*, Indonesia*, Ireland*, Israel*, Italy*, Jamaica, Japan, Kazakhstan, Kenya, Korea (South)*, Kuwait*, Latvia, Lebanon, Libya, Liechtenstein, Lithuania, Luxembourg*, Macedonia (Former Yugoslav Republic of), Madagascar, Mali, Malta, Marshall Islands, Mexico, Moldova, Monaco, Mongolia, Montenegro, Morocco, Mozambique*, Namibia, Nauru, Netherlands*, New Zealand, Nicaragua, Niger, Nigeria, Norway*, Oman*, Panama, Pakistan*, Palau, Paraguay, Peru*, Philippines, Poland, Portugal*, Qatar*, Romania*, Russia*, Senegal, Serbia, Seychelles, Slovakia, Slovenia, South Africa*, Spain*, Sudan, Swaziland, Sweden*, Switzerland*, Tajikistan, Tanzania, Togo, Tonga, Trinidad and Tobago, Tunisia, Turkey*, Turkmenistan, Uganda, UK*, Ukraine, United Arab Emirates, Uruguay, USA, Uzbekistan, Yemen

  * With reservation and/or declaration.

Signed but not ratified: Dominican Republic, Haiti

13 ratifications, acceptances or approvals of the amended convention deposited: Algeria, Austria, Bulgaria, Croatia, India, Kenya, Libya, Nigeria, Poland, Romania, Seychelles, Spain, Turkmenistan

Convention on Prohibitions or Restrictions on the Use of Certain Conventional Weapons which may be Deemed to be Excessively Injurious or to have Indiscriminate Effects (CCW Convention, or 'Inhumane Weapons' Convention)

The convention, with protocols I, II and III, was opened for signature at New York on 10 April 1981; entered into force on 2 December 1983; depositary UN Secretary-General

The convention is an 'umbrella treaty', under which specific agreements can be concluded in the form of protocols. In order to become a party to the convention a state must ratify at least two of the protocols.

The amendment to Article I of the original convention was opened for signature at Geneva on 21 November 2001. It expands the scope of application to non-international armed conflicts. The amended convention entered into force on 18 May 2004.

Protocol I prohibits the use of weapons intended to injure by fragments which are not detectable in the human body by X-rays.

Protocol II prohibits or restricts the use of mines, booby-traps and other devices.

Amended Protocol II, which entered into force on 3 December 1998, reinforces the constraints regarding landmines.

Protocol III restricts the use of incendiary weapons.

Protocol IV, which entered into force on 30 July 1998, prohibits the employment of laser weapons specifically designed to cause permanent blindness to un-enhanced vision.

Protocol V, which entered into force on 12 November 2006, recognizes the need for measures of a generic nature to minimize the risks and effects of explosive remnants of war.

Parties to the original convention and protocols (103): Albania, Argentina*, Australia, Austria, Bangladesh, Belarus, Belgium, Benin[1], Bolivia, Bosnia and Herzegovina, Brazil, Bulgaria, Burkina Faso, Cambodia, Cameroon, Canada*, Cape Verde, Chile[1], China*, Colombia, Costa Rica, Croatia, Cuba, Cyprus*, Czech Republic, Denmark, Djibouti, Ecuador, El Salvador, Estonia[1], Finland, France*, Gabon, Georgia, Germany, Greece, Guatemala, Holy See*, Honduras, Hungary, India, Ireland, Israel*[2], Italy*, Japan, Jordan[1], Korea (South)[3], Laos, Latvia, Lesotho, Liberia, Liechtenstein, Lithuania[1], Luxembourg, Macedonia (Former Yugoslav Republic of), Maldives[1], Mali, Malta, Mauritius, Mexico, Moldova, Monaco[3], Mongolia, Montenegro, Morocco[4], Nauru, Netherlands*, New Zealand, Nicaragua[1], Niger, Norway, Pakistan, Panama, Paraguay, Peru[1], Philippines, Poland, Portugal, Romania*, Russia, Senegal[5], Serbia, Seychelles, Sierra Leone[1], Slovakia, Slovenia, South Africa, Spain, Sri Lanka, Sweden, Switzerland, Tajikistan, Togo, Tunisia, Turkey*[3], Turkmenistan[2], Uganda, UK*, Ukraine, Uruguay, USA*[2], Uzbekistan, Venezuela

* With reservation and/or declaration.
[1] Party only to 1981 Protocols I and III.
[2] Party only to 1981 Protocols I and II.
[3] Party only to 1981 Protocol I.
[4] Party only to 1981 Protocol II.
[5] Party only to 1981 Protocol III.

Signed but not ratified the original convention and protocols: Afghanistan, Egypt, Iceland, Nigeria, Sudan, Viet Nam

Parties to the amended convention and original protocols (56): Albania, Argentina, Australia, Austria, Belgium, Bulgaria, Burkina Faso, Canada, Chile, China, Croatia, Cuba, Czech Republic, Denmark, El Salvador, Estonia, Finland, France, Germany, Greece, Holy See*, Hungary, India, Ireland, Italy, Japan, Korea (South), Latvia, Liberia, Liechtenstein, Lithuania, Luxembourg, Macedonia (Former Yugoslav Republic of), Malta, Mexico*, Moldova, Montenegro, Netherlands, Nicaragua, Niger, Norway, Panama, Peru, Poland, Romania, Russia, Serbia, Sierra Leone, Slovakia, Spain, Sri Lanka, Sweden, Switzerland, Turkey, UK, Ukraine

* With reservation and/or declaration.

Parties to Amended Protocol II (88): Albania, Argentina, Australia, Austria, Bangladesh, Belarus, Belgium, Bolivia, Bosnia and Herzegovina, Brazil, Bulgaria, Burkina Faso, Cambodia, Cameroon, Canada, Cape Verde, Chile, China, Colombia, Costa Rica, Croatia, Cyprus, Czech Republic, Denmark, Ecuador, El Salvador, Estonia, Finland, France, Germany, Greece, Guatemala, Holy See, Honduras, Hungary, India, Ireland, Israel, Italy, Japan, Jordan, Korea (South), Latvia, Liberia, Liechtenstein, Lithuania, Luxembourg, Macedonia (Former Yugoslav Republic of), Maldives, Mali, Malta, Moldova, Monaco, Morocco, Nauru,

Netherlands, New Zealand, Nicaragua, Niger, Norway, Pakistan, Panama, Paraguay, Peru, Philippines, Poland, Portugal, Romania, Russia, Senegal, Seychelles, Sierra Leone, Slovakia, Slovenia, South Africa, Spain, Sri Lanka, Sweden, Switzerland, Tajikistan, Tunisia, Turkey, Turkmenistan, UK, Ukraine, Uruguay, USA, Venezuela

Parties to Protocol IV (87): Albania, Argentina, Australia*, Austria*, Bangladesh, Belarus, Belgium*, Bolivia, Bosnia and Herzegovina, Brazil, Bulgaria, Burkina Faso, Cambodia, Cameroon, Canada*, Cape Verde, Chile, China, Colombia, Costa Rica, Croatia, Cyprus, Czech Republic, Denmark, Ecuador, El Salvador, Estonia, Finland, France, Georgia, Germany*, Greece*, Guatemala, Holy See, Honduras, Hungary, India, Ireland*, Israel*, Italy*, Japan, Latvia, Liberia, Liechtenstein*, Lithuania, Luxembourg, Macedonia (Former Yugoslav Republic of), Maldives, Mali, Malta, Mauritius, Mexico, Moldova, Mongolia, Montenegro, Morocco, Nauru, Netherlands*, New Zealand, Nicaragua, Niger, Norway, Pakistan, Panama, Peru, Philippines, Poland*, Portugal, Romania, Russia, Serbia, Seychelles, Sierra Leone, Slovakia, Slovenia, South Africa*, Spain, Sri Lanka, Sweden*, Switzerland*, Tajikistan, Tunisia, Turkey, UK*, Ukraine, Uruguay, Uzbekistan

* With reservation and/or declaration.

Parties to Protocol V (35): Albania, Australia, Austria, Bulgaria, Croatia, Czech Republic, Denmark, El Salvador, Estonia, Finland, France, Germany, Holy See*, Hungary, India, Ireland, Liberia, Liechtenstein, Lithuania, Luxembourg, Macedonia (Former Yugoslav Republic of), Malta, Netherlands, New Zealand, Nicaragua, Norway, Sierra Leone, Slovakia, Slovenia, Spain, Sweden, Switzerland, Tajikistan, Ukraine, Uruguay

* With reservation and/or declaration.

South Pacific Nuclear Free Zone Treaty (Treaty of Rarotonga)

Opened for signature at Rarotonga, Cook Islands, on 6 August 1985; entered into force on 11 December 1986; depositary Director of the Pacific Islands Forum Secretariat

The treaty prohibits the manufacture or acquisition by other means of any nuclear explosive device, as well as possession or control over such device by the parties anywhere inside or outside the zone defined in an annex. The parties also undertake not to supply nuclear material or equipment, unless subject to IAEA safeguards, and to prevent in their territories the stationing as well as the testing of any nuclear explosive device and undertake not to dump, and to prevent the dumping of, radioactive wastes and other radioactive matter at sea anywhere within the zone. Each party remains free to allow visits, as well as transit, by foreign ships and aircraft.

The treaty is open for signature by the members of the Pacific Islands Forum.

Under *Protocol 1* France, the UK and the USA undertake to apply the treaty prohibitions relating to the manufacture, stationing and testing of nuclear explosive devices in the territories situated within the zone for which they are internationally responsible.

Under *Protocol 2* China, France, Russia, the UK and the USA undertake not to use or threaten to use a nuclear explosive device against the parties to the treaty or against any territory within the zone for which a party to Protocol 1 is internationally responsible.

Under *Protocol 3* China, France, Russia, the UK and the USA undertake not to test any nuclear explosive device anywhere within the zone.

Parties (13): Australia, Cook Islands, Fiji, Kiribati, Nauru, New Zealand, Niue, Papua New Guinea, Samoa, Solomon Islands, Tonga, Tuvalu, Vanuatu

Parties to Protocol 1: France, UK; *signed but not ratified*: USA

Parties to Protocol 2: China, France[1], Russia, UK[2]; *signed but not ratified*: USA

[1] France declared that the negative security guarantees set out in Protocol 2 are the same as the Conference on Disarmament declaration of 6 Apr. 1995 referred to in UN Security Council Resolution 984 of 11 Apr. 1995.

[2] On ratifying Protocol 2 in 1997, the UK declared that nothing in the treaty affects the rights under international law with regard to transit of the zone or visits to ports and airfields within the zone by ships and aircraft. The UK will not be bound by the undertakings in Protocol 2 in case of an invasion or any other attack on the UK, its territories, its armed forces or its allies, carried out or sustained by a party to the treaty in association or alliance with a nuclear weapon state or if a party violates its non-proliferation obligations under the treaty.

Parties to Protocol 3: China, France, Russia, UK; *signed but not ratified*: USA

Treaty on the Elimination of Intermediate-Range and Shorter-Range Missiles (INF Treaty)

Signed by the USA and the USSR at Washington, DC, on 8 December 1987; entered into force on 1 June 1988

The treaty obligated the original parties—the USA and the USSR—to destroy all ground-launched ballistic and cruise missiles with a range of 500–5500 km (intermediate-range, 1000–5500 km; and shorter-range, 500–1000 km) and their launchers by 1 June 1991. A total of 2692 missiles were eliminated by May 1991. In 1994 treaty membership was expanded to include Belarus, Kazakhstan and Ukraine. For 10 years after 1 June 1991 on-site inspections were conducted to verify compliance. The use of surveillance satellites for data collection has continued after the end of on-site inspections on 31 May 2001.

Treaty on Conventional Armed Forces in Europe (CFE Treaty)

Original treaty signed at Paris on 19 November 1990; entered into force on 9 November 1992; depositary Dutch Government

The treaty sets ceilings on five categories of treaty-limited equipment (TLE)—battle tanks, armoured combat vehicles, artillery of at least 100-mm calibre, combat aircraft and attack helicopters—in an area stretching from the Atlantic Ocean to the Ural Mountains (the Atlantic-to-the-Urals, ATTU, zone).

The treaty was negotiated and signed by the member states of the Warsaw Treaty Organization and NATO within the framework of the Conference on Security and Co-operation in Europe (from 1995 the Organization for Security and Co-operation in Europe, OSCE).

The **1992 Tashkent Agreement**, adopted by the former Soviet republics with territories within the ATTU zone (with the exception of Estonia, Latvia and Lithuania) and the **1992 Oslo Document** (Final Document of the Extraordinary Conference of the States Parties to the CFE Treaty) introduced modifications to the treaty required because of the emergence of new states after the break-up of the USSR.

Parties (30): Armenia, Azerbaijan, Belarus, Belgium, Bulgaria, Canada, Czech Republic, Denmark, France, Georgia, Germany, Greece, Hungary, Iceland, Italy, Kazakhstan,

Luxembourg, Moldova, Netherlands, Norway, Poland, Portugal, Romania, Russia[1], Slovakia, Spain, Turkey, UK, Ukraine, USA

The first Review Conference of the CFE Treaty adopted the **1996 Flank Document**, which reorganized the flank areas geographically and numerically, allowing Russia and Ukraine to deploy more TLE.

Concluding Act of the Negotiation on Personnel Strength of Conventional Armed Forces in Europe (CFE-1A Agreement)

Signed by the parties to the CFE Treaty at Helsinki on 10 July 1992; entered into force simultaneously with the CFE Treaty; depositary Dutch Government

The agreement sets ceilings on the number of personnel of the conventional land-based armed forces of the parties within the ATTU zone.

Agreement on Adaptation of the CFE Treaty

Signed by the parties to the CFE Treaty at Helsinki on 19 November 1999; not in force; depositary Dutch Government

The agreement replaces the CFE Treaty bloc-to-bloc military balance with individual state limits on TLE holdings and provides for a new structure of limitations and new military flexibility mechanisms, flank sub-limits and enhanced transparency. It opens the CFE regime to all the other European states. It will enter into force when it has been ratified by all the signatories. The **1999 Final Act**, with annexes, contains politically binding arrangements with regard to the North Caucasus and Central and Eastern Europe, and withdrawals of armed forces from foreign territories.

3 ratifications of the Agreement on Adaptation deposited: Belarus, Kazakhstan, Russia*[1]

* With reservation and/or declaration.
Note: Ukraine has ratified the 1999 Agreement on Adaptation of the CFE Treaty but has not deposited its instruments with the depositary.

[1] On 14 July 2007 Russia declared its intention to suspend its participation in the CFE Treaty, which took effect on 12 Dec. 2007.

Treaty on the Reduction and Limitation of Strategic Offensive Arms (START I Treaty)

Signed by the USA and the USSR at Moscow on 31 July 1991; entered into force on 5 December 1994

The treaty obligated the original parties—the USA and the USSR—to make phased reductions in their offensive strategic nuclear forces over a seven-year period. It sets numerical limits on deployed strategic nuclear delivery vehicles (SNDVs)—ICBMs, SLBMs and heavy bombers—and the nuclear warheads they carry. In the Protocol to Facilitate the Implementation of the START Treaty (**1992 Lisbon Protocol**), which entered into force on 5 December 1994, Belarus, Kazakhstan and Ukraine also assumed the obligations of the former USSR under the treaty.

Treaty on Open Skies

Opened for signature at Helsinki on 24 March 1992; entered into force on 1 January 2002; depositaries Canadian and Hungarian governments

The treaty obligates the parties to submit their territories to short-notice unarmed surveillance flights. The area of application stretches from Vancouver, Canada, eastward to Vladivostok, Russia.

The treaty was negotiated between the member states of the Warsaw Treaty Organization and NATO. It was opened for signature by the NATO member states, former member states of the Warsaw Treaty Organization and the states of the former Soviet Union (except for Estonia, Latvia and Lithuania). For six months after entry into force of the treaty, any other participating state of the Organization for Security and Co-operation in Europe could apply for accession to the treaty, and from 1 July 2002 any state can apply to accede to the treaty.

Parties (34): Belarus, Belgium, Bosnia and Herzegovina, Bulgaria, Canada, Croatia, Czech Republic, Denmark, Estonia, Finland, France, Georgia, Germany, Greece, Hungary, Iceland, Italy, Latvia, Lithuania, Luxembourg, Netherlands, Norway, Poland, Portugal, Romania, Russia, Slovakia, Slovenia, Spain, Sweden, Turkey, UK, Ukraine, USA

Signed but not ratified: Kyrgyzstan

Treaty on Further Reduction and Limitation of Strategic Offensive Arms (START II Treaty)

Signed by Russia and the USA at Moscow on 3 January 1993; not in force

The treaty obligated the parties to eliminate their MIRVed ICBMs and reduce the number of their deployed strategic nuclear warheads to no more than 3000–3500 each (of which no more than 1750 may be deployed on SLBMs) by 1 January 2003. On 26 September 1997 the two parties signed a *Protocol* to the treaty providing for the extension until the end of 2007 of the period of implementation of the treaty.

Note: The START II Treaty was ratified by the US Senate and the Russian Parliament, but the two parties never exchanged the instruments of ratification. The treaty thus never entered into force. On 14 June 2002, as a response to the taking effect on 13 June of the USA's withdrawal from the ABM Treaty, Russia declared that it would no longer be bound by the START II Treaty.

Convention on the Prohibition of the Development, Production, Stockpiling and Use of Chemical Weapons and on their Destruction (Chemical Weapons Convention, CWC)

Opened for signature at Paris on 13 January 1993; entered into force on 29 April 1997; depositary UN Secretary-General

The convention prohibits the use, development, production, acquisition, transfer and stockpiling of chemical weapons. Each party undertakes to destroy its chemical weapons and production facilities by 29 April 2012.

Parties (183): Afghanistan, Albania, Algeria, Andorra, Antigua and Barbuda, Argentina, Armenia, Australia, Austria, Azerbaijan, Bahrain, Bangladesh, Barbados, Belarus, Belgium, Belize, Benin, Bhutan, Bolivia, Bosnia and Herzegovina, Botswana, Brazil, Brunei Darussalam, Bulgaria, Burkina Faso, Burundi, Cambodia, Cameroon, Canada, Cape Verde,

Central African Republic, Chad, Chile, China, Colombia, Comoros, Congo (Democratic Republic of the), Congo (Republic of the), Cook Islands, Costa Rica, Côte d'Ivoire, Croatia, Cuba, Cyprus, Czech Republic, Denmark, Djibouti, Dominica, Ecuador, El Salvador, Equatorial Guinea, Eritrea, Estonia, Ethiopia, Fiji, Finland, France, Gabon, Gambia, Georgia, Germany, Ghana, Greece, Grenada, Guatemala, Guinea, Guyana, Haiti, Holy See, Honduras, Hungary, Iceland, India, Indonesia, Iran, Ireland, Italy, Jamaica, Japan, Jordan, Kazakhstan, Kenya, Kiribati, Korea (South), Kuwait, Kyrgyzstan, Laos, Latvia, Lesotho, Liberia, Libya, Liechtenstein, Lithuania, Luxembourg, Macedonia (Former Yugoslav Republic of), Madagascar, Malawi, Malaysia, Maldives, Mali, Malta, Marshall Islands, Mauritania, Mauritius, Mexico, Micronesia, Moldova, Monaco, Mongolia, Montenegro, Morocco, Mozambique, Namibia, Nauru, Nepal, Netherlands, New Zealand, Nicaragua, Niger, Nigeria, Niue, Norway, Oman, Pakistan, Palau, Panama, Papua New Guinea, Paraguay, Peru, Philippines, Poland, Portugal, Qatar, Romania, Russia, Rwanda, Saint Kitts and Nevis, Saint Lucia, Saint Vincent and the Grenadines, Samoa, San Marino, Sao Tome and Principe, Saudi Arabia, Senegal, Serbia, Seychelles, Sierra Leone, Singapore, Slovakia, Slovenia, Solomon Islands, South Africa, Spain, Sri Lanka, Sudan, Suriname, Swaziland, Sweden, Switzerland, Tajikistan, Tanzania, Thailand, Timor-Leste, Togo, Tonga, Trinidad and Tobago, Tunisia, Turkey, Turkmenistan, Tuvalu, Uganda, UK, Ukraine, United Arab Emirates, Uruguay, USA, Uzbekistan, Vanuatu, Venezuela, Viet Nam, Yemen, Zambia, Zimbabwe

Signed but not ratified: Bahamas, Dominican Republic, Guinea-Bissau, Israel, Myanmar

Treaty on the Southeast Asia Nuclear Weapon-Free Zone (Treaty of Bangkok)

Signed at Bangkok on 15 December 1995; entered into force on 27 March 1997; depositary Thai Government

The treaty prohibits the development, manufacture, acquisition or testing of nuclear weapons inside or outside the zone as well as the stationing and transport of nuclear weapons in or through the zone. Each state party may decide for itself whether to allow visits and transit by foreign ships and aircraft. The parties undertake not to dump at sea or discharge into the atmosphere anywhere within the zone any radio-active material or wastes or dispose of radioactive material on land. The parties should conclude an agreement with the IAEA for the application of full-scope safeguards to their peaceful nuclear activities.

The zone includes not only the territories but also the continental shelves and exclusive economic zones of the states parties.

The treaty is open for all states of South East Asia.

Under a *Protocol* to the treaty, China, France, Russia, the UK and the USA are to undertake not to use or threaten to use nuclear weapons against any state party to the treaty. They should further undertake not to use nuclear weapons within the South East Asia nuclear weapon-free zone. The protocol will enter into force for each state party on the date of its deposit of the instrument of ratification.

Parties (10): Brunei Darussalam, Cambodia, Indonesia, Laos, Malaysia, Myanmar, Philippines, Singapore, Thailand, Viet Nam

Protocol: no signatures, no parties

African Nuclear-Weapon-Free Zone Treaty (Treaty of Pelindaba)

Signed at Cairo on 11 April 1996; not in force; depositary Secretary-General of the African Union

The treaty prohibits the research, development, manufacture and acquisition of nuclear explosive devices and the testing or stationing of any nuclear explosive device. Each party remains free to allow visits and transit by foreign ships and air-craft. The treaty also prohibits any attack against nuclear installations. The parties undertake not to dump or permit the dumping of radioactive waste and other radioactive matter anywhere within the zone. Each party should individually conclude an agreement with the IAEA for the application of comprehensive safeguards to their peaceful nuclear activities.

The zone includes the territory of the continent of Africa, island states members of the African Union (AU) and all islands considered by the AU to be part of Africa.

The treaty is open for signature by all the states of Africa. It will enter into force upon the 28th ratification.

Under *Protocol I* China, France, Russia, the UK and the USA are to undertake not to use or threaten to use a nuclear explosive device against the parties to the treaty.

Under *Protocol II* China, France, Russia, the UK and the USA are to undertake not to test nuclear explosive devices anywhere within the zone.

Under *Protocol III* states with territories within the zone for which they are internationally responsible are to undertake to observe certain provisions of the treaty with respect to these territories. This protocol is open for signature by France and Spain.

The protocols will enter into force simultaneously with the treaty for those protocol signatories that have deposited their instruments of ratification.

23 ratifications deposited: Algeria, Botswana, Burkina Faso, Côte d'Ivoire, Equatorial Guinea, Gabon, Gambia, Guinea, Kenya, Lesotho, Libya, Madagascar, Mali, Mauritania, Mauritius, Nigeria, Rwanda, Senegal, South Africa, Swaziland, Tanzania, Togo, Zimbabwe

Signed but not ratified: Angola, Benin, Burundi, Cameroon, Cape Verde, Central African Republic, Chad, Comoros, Congo (Democratic Republic of the), Congo (Republic of the), Djibouti, Egypt, Eritrea, Ethiopia, Ghana, Guinea-Bissau, Liberia, Malawi, Morocco, Mozambique, Namibia, Niger, Sao Tome and Principe, Seychelles, Sierra Leone, Sudan, Tunisia, Uganda, Zambia

Protocol I, ratifications deposited: China, France[1], UK[2]; *signed but not ratified*: Russia[3], USA[4]

Protocol II, ratifications deposited: China, France, UK[2]; *signed but not ratified*: Russia[3], USA[4]

Protocol III, ratifications deposited: France

[1] France stated that the Protocols did not affect its right to self-defence, as stipulated in Article 51 of the UN Charter. It clarified that its commitment under Article 1 of Protocol I was equivalent to the negative security assurances given by France to non-nuclear weapon states parties to the NPT, as confirmed in its declaration made on 6 Apr. 1995 at the Conference on Disarmament, and as referred to in UN Security Council Resolution 984 of 11 Apr. 1995.

[2] The UK stated that it did not accept the inclusion of the British Indian Ocean Territory within the African nuclear-weapon-free zone without its consent, and did not accept, by its adherence to Protocols I and II, any legal obligations in respect of that territory. Moreover, it would not be bound by its undertaking under Article 1 of Protocol I in case of an invasion or any other attack on the UK, its dependent territories, its armed forces or other troops, or its allies or a state towards which it had a security commitment, carried out or sustained by a party to the treaty in association or alliance with a nuclear weapon

state, or if any party to the treaty was in material breach of its own non-proliferation obligations under the treaty.

3 Russia stated that as long as a military base of a nuclear state was located on the islands of the Chagos archipelago these islands could not be regarded as fulfilling the requirements put forward by the treaty for nuclear-weapon-free territories. Moreover, since certain states declared that they would consider themselves free from the obligations under the protocols with regard to the mentioned territories, Russia could not consider itself to be bound by the obligations under Protocol I in respect to the same territories. Russia interpreted its obligations under Article 1 of Protocol I as follows: It would not use nuclear weapons against a state party to the treaty, except in the case of invasion or any other armed attack on Russia, its territory, its armed forces or other troops, its allies or a state towards which it had a security commitment, carried out or sustained by a non-nuclear weapon state party to the treaty, in association or alliance with a nuclear weapon state.

4 The USA stated, with respect to Protocol I, that it would consider an invasion or any other attack on the USA, its territories, its armed forces or other troops, or its allies or on a state towards which it had a security commitment, carried out or sustained by a party to the treaty in association or alliance with a nuclear-weapon state, to be incompatible with the treaty party's corresponding obligations. The USA also stated that neither the treaty nor Protocol II would apply to the activities of the UK, the USA or any other state not party to the treaty on the island of Diego Garcia or elsewhere in the British Indian Ocean Territory. Therefore, no change was required in the operations of US armed forces in Diego Garcia and elsewhere in these territories.

Agreement on Sub-Regional Arms Control (Florence Agreement)

Adopted at Florence; entered into force on 14 June 1996

The agreement was negotiated under the auspices of the OSCE in accordance with the mandate in the 1995 General Framework Agreement for Peace in Bosnia and Herzegovina (Dayton Agreement). It sets numerical ceilings on armaments of the former warring parties, now Bosnia and Herzegovina, Croatia, Montenegro and Serbia. Five categories of heavy conventional weapons are included: battle tanks, armoured combat vehicles, heavy artillery (75 mm and above), combat aircraft and attack helicopters. The reductions were completed by 31 October 1997; 6580 weapon items were destroyed by that date. In March 2006 the parties agreed on six legally binding amendments to the agreement.

Comprehensive Nuclear Test-Ban Treaty (CTBT)

Opened for signature at New York on 24 September 1996; not in force; depositary UN Secretary-General

The treaty prohibits the carrying out of any nuclear weapon test explosion or any other nuclear explosion, and urges each party to prevent any such nuclear explosion at any place under its jurisdiction or control and refrain from causing, encouraging or in any way participating in the carrying out of any nuclear weapon test explosion or any other nuclear explosion.

The treaty will enter into force 180 days after the date of the deposit of the instruments of ratification of the 44 states listed in an annex to the treaty. All the 44 states possess nuclear power reactors and/or nuclear research reactors.

The 44 states whose ratification is required for entry into force are: Algeria, Argentina, Australia, Austria, Bangladesh, Belgium, Brazil, Bulgaria, Canada, Chile, China*, Colombia*, Congo (Democratic Republic of the), Egypt*, Finland, France, Germany, Hungary, India*, Indonesia*, Iran*, Israel*, Italy, Japan, Korea (North)*, Korea (South), Mexico, Netherlands,

Norway, Pakistan*, Peru, Poland, Romania, Russia, Slovakia, South Africa, Spain, Sweden, Switzerland, Turkey, UK, Ukraine, USA* and Viet Nam.

* States which have not ratified the treaty.

138 ratifications deposited: Afghanistan, Albania, Algeria, Andorra, Antigua and Barbuda, Argentina, Armenia, Australia, Austria, Azerbaijan, Bahrain, Bangladesh, Belarus, Belgium, Belize, Benin, Bolivia, Bosnia and Herzegovina, Botswana, Brazil, Bulgaria, Burkina Faso, Cambodia, Cameroon, Canada, Cape Verde, Chile, Congo (Democratic Republic of the), Cook Islands, Costa Rica, Côte d'Ivoire, Croatia, Cyprus, Czech Republic, Denmark, Djibouti, Ecuador, El Salvador, Eritrea, Estonia, Ethiopia, Fiji, Finland, France, Gabon, Georgia, Germany, Greece, Grenada, Guyana, Haiti, Holy See, Honduras, Hungary, Iceland, Ireland, Italy, Jamaica, Japan, Jordan, Kazakhstan, Kenya, Kiribati, Korea (South), Kuwait, Kyrgyzstan, Laos, Latvia, Lesotho, Libya, Liechtenstein, Lithuania, Luxembourg, Macedonia (Former Yugoslav Republic of), Madagascar, Maldives, Mali, Malta, Mauritania, Mexico, Micronesia, Moldova, Monaco, Mongolia, Montenegro, Morocco, Namibia, Nauru, Netherlands, New Zealand, Nicaragua, Niger, Nigeria, Norway, Oman, Panama, Paraguay, Peru, Philippines, Poland, Portugal, Qatar, Romania, Russia, Rwanda, Saint Kitts and Nevis, Saint Lucia, Samoa, San Marino, Senegal, Serbia, Seychelles, Sierra Leone, Singapore, Slovakia, Slovenia, South Africa, Spain, Sudan, Suriname, Sweden, Switzerland, Tajikistan, Tanzania, Togo, Tunisia, Turkey, Turkmenistan, Uganda, UK, Ukraine, United Arab Emirates, Uruguay, Uzbekistan, Vanuatu, Venezuela, Viet Nam, Zambia

Signed but not ratified: Angola, Bahamas, Brunei Darussalam, Burundi, Central African Republic, Chad, China, Colombia, Comoros, Congo (Republic of the), Dominican Republic, Egypt, Equatorial Guinea, Gambia, Ghana, Guatemala, Guinea, Guinea-Bissau, Indonesia, Iran, Israel, Lebanon, Liberia, Malawi, Malaysia, Marshall Islands, Mozambique, Myanmar, Nepal, Palau, Papua New Guinea, Sao Tome and Principe, Solomon Islands, Sri Lanka, Swaziland, Thailand, USA, Yemen, Zimbabwe

Inter-American Convention Against the Illicit Manufacturing of and Trafficking in Firearms, Ammunition, Explosives, and Other Related Materials

Adopted at Washington, DC, on 13 November 1997; opened for signature at Washington, DC, on 14 November 1997; entered into force on 1 July 1998; depositary General Secretariat of the Organization of American States

The purpose of the convention is to prevent, combat and eradicate the illicit manufacturing of and trafficking in firearms, ammunition, explosives and other related materials; and to promote and facilitate cooperation and the exchange of information and experience among the parties.

Parties (27): Antigua and Barbuda, Argentina*, Bahamas, Barbados, Belize, Bolivia, Brazil, Chile, Colombia, Costa Rica, Dominica, Ecuador, El Salvador, Grenada, Guatemala, Haiti, Honduras, Mexico, Nicaragua, Panama, Paraguay, Peru, Saint Kitts and Nevis, Saint Lucia, Trinidad and Tobago, Uruguay, Venezuela

* With reservation.

Signed but not ratified: Canada, Dominican Republic, Guyana, Jamaica, Saint Vincent and the Grenadines, Suriname, USA

Convention on the Prohibition of the Use, Stockpiling, Production and Transfer of Anti-Personnel Mines and on their Destruction (APM Convention)

Opened for signature at Ottawa on 3–4 December 1997 and at New York on 5 December 1997; entered into force on 1 March 1999; depositary UN Secretary-General

The convention prohibits anti-personnel mines (APMs), which are defined as mines designed to be exploded by the presence, proximity or contact of a person and which will incapacitate, injure or kill one or more persons.

Each party undertakes to destroy all its stockpiled APMs as soon as possible but not later that four years after the entry into force of the convention for that state party. Each party also undertakes to destroy all APMs in mined areas under its jurisdiction or control not later than 10 years after the entry into force of the convention for that state party.

Parties (156): Afghanistan, Albania, Algeria, Andorra, Angola, Antigua and Barbuda, Argentina*, Australia*, Austria*, Bahamas, Bangladesh, Barbados, Belarus, Belgium, Belize, Benin, Bhutan, Bolivia, Bosnia and Herzegovina, Botswana, Brazil, Brunei Darussalam, Bulgaria, Burkina Faso, Burundi, Cambodia, Cameroon, Canada*, Cape Verde, Central African Republic, Chad, Chile*, Colombia, Comoros, Congo (Democratic Republic of the), Congo (Republic of the), Cook Islands, Costa Rica, Côte d'Ivoire, Croatia, Cyprus, Czech Republic*, Denmark, Djibouti, Dominica, Dominican Republic, Ecuador, El Salvador, Equatorial Guinea, Eritrea, Estonia, Ethiopia, Fiji, France, Gabon, Gambia, Germany, Ghana, Greece*, Grenada, Guatemala, Guinea, Guinea-Bissau, Guyana, Haiti, Holy See, Honduras, Hungary, Iceland, Indonesia, Iraq, Ireland, Italy, Jamaica, Japan, Jordan, Kenya, Kiribati, Kuwait, Latvia, Lesotho, Liberia, Liechtenstein, Lithuania*, Luxembourg, Macedonia (Former Yugoslav Republic of), Madagascar, Malawi, Malaysia, Maldives, Mali, Malta, Mauritania, Mauritius*, Mexico, Moldova, Monaco, Montenegro*, Mozambique, Namibia, Nauru, Netherlands, New Zealand, Nicaragua, Niger, Nigeria, Niue, Norway, Palau, Panama, Papua New Guinea, Paraguay, Peru, Philippines, Portugal, Qatar, Romania, Rwanda, Saint Kitts and Nevis, Saint Lucia, Saint Vincent and the Grenadines, Samoa, San Marino, Sao Tome and Principe, Senegal, Serbia*, Seychelles, Sierra Leone, Slovakia, Slovenia, Solomon Islands, South Africa*, Spain, Sudan, Suriname, Swaziland, Sweden*, Switzerland*, Tajikistan, Tanzania, Thailand, Timor-Leste, Togo, Trinidad and Tobago, Tunisia, Turkey, Turkmenistan, Uganda, UK*, Ukraine, Uruguay, Vanuatu, Venezuela, Yemen, Zambia, Zimbabwe

* With reservation and/or declaration.

Signed but not ratified: Marshall Islands, Poland

Inter-American Convention on Transparency in Conventional Weapons Acquisitions

Adopted at Guatemala City on 7 June 1999; entered into force on 21 November 2002; depositary General Secretariat of the Organization of American States

The objective of the convention is to contribute more fully to regional openness and transparency in the acquisition of conventional weapons by exchanging information regarding such acquisitions, for the purpose of promoting confidence among states in the Americas.

Parties (12): Argentina, Brazil, Canada, Chile, Ecuador, El Salvador, Guatemala, Nicaragua, Paraguay, Peru, Uruguay, Venezuela

Signed but not ratified: Bolivia, Colombia, Costa Rica, Dominica, Haiti, Honduras, Mexico, USA

Vienna Document 1999 on Confidence- and Security-Building Measures

Adopted by the participating states of the Organization for Security and Co-operation in Europe at Istanbul on 16 November 1999; entered into force on 1 January 2000

The Vienna Document 1999 builds on the 1986 Stockholm Document on Confidence- and Security-Building Measures (CSBMs) and Disarmament in Europe and previous Vienna Documents (1990, 1992 and 1994). The Vienna Document 1990 provided for military budget exchange, risk reduction procedures, a communication network and an annual CSBM implementation assessment. The Vienna Document 1992 and the Vienna Document 1994 introduced new mechanisms and parameters for military activities, defence planning and military contacts.

The Vienna Document 1999 introduces regional measures aimed at increasing transparency and confidence in a bilateral, multilateral and regional context and some improvements, in particular regarding the constraining measures.

Treaty on Strategic Offensive Reductions (SORT)

Signed by Russia and the USA at Moscow on 24 May 2002; entered into force on 1 June 2003

The treaty obligates the parties to reduce the number of their operationally deployed strategic nuclear warheads so that the aggregate numbers do not exceed 1700–2200 for each party by 31 December 2012.

ECOWAS Convention on Small Arms, Light Weapons, their Ammunition and Other Related Materials

Adopted by the member states of the Economic Community of West African States (ECOWAS) at Abuja, on 14 June 2006; not in force; depositary Executive Secretary of ECOWAS

The convention obligates the parties to prevent and combat the excessive and destabilizing accumulation of small arms and light weapons in the 15 ECOWAS member states. The convention will enter into force on the date of deposit of the ninth instrument of ratification.

4 ratifications deposited: Burkina Faso, Mali, Niger, Sierra Leone

Treaty on a Nuclear-Weapon-Free Zone in Central Asia (Treaty of Semipalatinsk)

Signed at Semipalatinsk on 8 September 2006; not in force; depositary Kyrgyz Government

The treaty and its protocol obligate the parties not to conduct research on, develop, manufacture, stockpile or otherwise acquire, possess or have control over any nuclear weapons or other nuclear explosive device by any means anywhere. The treaty will enter into force on the date of deposit of the fifth instrument of ratification.

2 ratifications deposited: Kyrgyzstan, Uzbekistan

Signed but not ratified: Kazakhstan, Tajikistan, Turkmenistan

Annex B. International organizations and intergovernmental bodies

NENNE BODELL

This annex describes the main international organizations, intergovernmental bodies, treaty-implementing bodies and export control regimes whose aims include the promotion of security, stability, peace or arms control and lists their members or participants as of 1 January 2008.

The member states of the United Nations and organs within the UN system are listed first, followed by all other organizations in alphabetical order. Note that not all members or participants of these organizations are UN member states. The address of an Internet site with information about each organization is provided where available. On the arms control and disarmament agreements mentioned here, see annex A in this volume.

United Nations (UN)
<http://www.un.org/>

The UN, the world intergovernmental organization, was founded in 1945 through the adoption of its Charter. Its headquarters are in New York, USA. The six principal UN organs are the General Assembly, the Security Council, the Economic and Social Council (ECOSOC), the Trusteeship Council (which suspended operation in 1994), the International Court of Justice (ICJ) and the secretariat. The UN also has a large number of specialized agencies and other autonomous bodies.

UN member states (192) and year of membership

Afghanistan, 1946	Benin, 1960	Chile, 1945
Albania, 1955	Bhutan, 1971	China, 1945
Algeria, 1962	Bolivia, 1945	Colombia, 1945
Andorra, 1993	Bosnia and Herzegovina, 1992	Comoros, 1975
Angola, 1976		Congo, Democratic Republic
Antigua and Barbuda, 1981	Botswana, 1966	of the, 1960
Argentina, 1945	Brazil, 1945	Congo, Republic of the, 1960
Armenia, 1992	Brunei Darussalam, 1984	Costa Rica, 1945
Australia, 1945	Bulgaria, 1955	Côte d'Ivoire, 1960
Austria, 1955	Burkina Faso, 1960	Croatia, 1992
Azerbaijan, 1992	Burundi, 1962	Cuba, 1945
Bahamas, 1973	Cambodia, 1955	Cyprus, 1960
Bahrain, 1971	Cameroon, 1960	Czech Republic, 1993
Bangladesh, 1974	Canada, 1945	Denmark, 1945
Barbados, 1966	Cape Verde, 1975	Djibouti, 1977
Belarus, 1945	Central African Republic, 1960	Dominica, 1978
Belgium, 1945		Dominican Republic, 1945
Belize, 1981	Chad, 1960	Ecuador, 1945

Egypt, 1945
El Salvador, 1945
Equatorial Guinea, 1968
Eritrea, 1993
Estonia, 1991
Ethiopia, 1945
Fiji, 1970
Finland, 1955
France, 1945
Gabon, 1960
Gambia, 1965
Georgia, 1992
Germany, 1973
Ghana, 1957
Greece, 1945
Grenada, 1974
Guatemala, 1945
Guinea, 1958
Guinea-Bissau, 1974
Guyana, 1966
Haiti, 1945
Honduras, 1945
Hungary, 1955
Iceland, 1946
India, 1945
Indonesia, 1950
Iran, 1945
Iraq, 1945
Ireland, 1955
Israel, 1949
Italy, 1955
Jamaica, 1962
Japan, 1956
Jordan, 1955
Kazakhstan, 1992
Kenya, 1963
Kiribati, 1999
Korea, Democratic People's
  Republic of (North Korea),
  1991
Korea, Republic of (South
  Korea), 1991
Kuwait, 1963
Kyrgyzstan, 1992
Laos, 1955
Latvia, 1991
Lebanon, 1945
Lesotho, 1966
Liberia, 1945

Libya, 1955
Liechtenstein, 1990
Lithuania, 1991
Luxembourg, 1945
Macedonia, Former Yugoslav
  Republic of, 1993
Madagascar, 1960
Malawi, 1964
Malaysia, 1957
Maldives, 1965
Mali, 1960
Malta, 1964
Marshall Islands, 1991
Mauritania, 1961
Mauritius, 1968
Mexico, 1945
Micronesia, 1991
Moldova, 1992
Monaco, 1993
Mongolia, 1961
Montenegro, 2006
Morocco, 1956
Mozambique, 1975
Myanmar, 1948
Namibia, 1990
Nauru, 1999
Nepal, 1955
Netherlands, 1945
New Zealand, 1945
Nicaragua, 1945
Niger, 1960
Nigeria, 1960
Norway, 1945
Oman, 1971
Pakistan, 1947
Palau, 1994
Panama, 1945
Papua New Guinea, 1975
Paraguay, 1945
Peru, 1945
Philippines, 1945
Poland, 1945
Portugal, 1955
Qatar, 1971
Romania, 1955
Russia, 1945
Rwanda, 1962
Saint Kitts and Nevis, 1983
Saint Lucia, 1979

Saint Vincent and the
  Grenadines, 1980
Samoa, 1976
San Marino, 1992
Sao Tome and Principe, 1975
Saudi Arabia, 1945
Senegal, 1960
Serbia, 2000
Seychelles, 1976
Sierra Leone, 1961
Singapore, 1965
Slovakia, 1993
Slovenia, 1992
Solomon Islands, 1978
Somalia, 1960
South Africa, 1945
Spain, 1955
Sri Lanka, 1955
Sudan, 1956
Suriname, 1975
Swaziland, 1968
Sweden, 1946
Switzerland, 2002
Syria, 1945
Tajikistan, 1992
Tanzania, 1961
Thailand, 1946
Timor-Leste, 2002
Togo, 1960
Tonga, 1999
Trinidad and Tobago, 1962
Tunisia, 1956
Turkey, 1945
Turkmenistan, 1992
Tuvalu, 2000
Uganda, 1962
UK, 1945
Ukraine, 1945
United Arab Emirates, 1971
Uruguay, 1945
USA, 1945
Uzbekistan, 1992
Vanuatu, 1981
Venezuela, 1945
Viet Nam, 1977
Yemen, 1947
Zambia, 1964
Zimbabwe, 1980

UN Security Council
<http://www.un.org/sc/>

Permanent members (the P5): China, France, Russia, UK, USA

Non-permanent members in 2008 (elected by the UN General Assembly for two-year terms; the year in brackets is the year at the end of which the term expires): Belgium (2008), Burkina Faso (2009), Costa Rica (2009), Croatia (2009), Indonesia (2008), Italy (2008), Libya (2009), Panama (2008), South Africa (2008), Viet Nam (2009)

Conference on Disarmament (CD)
<http://www.unog.ch/>

The CD is a multilateral arms control negotiating body that has been enlarged and renamed several times since 1959 and has had its present name since 1984. It is not a UN body but reports to the UN General Assembly. It is based in Geneva, Switzerland.

Members: Algeria, Argentina, Australia, Austria, Bangladesh, Belarus, Belgium, Brazil, Bulgaria, Cameroon, Canada, Chile, China, Colombia, Congo (Democratic Republic of the), Cuba, Ecuador, Egypt, Ethiopia, Finland, France, Germany, Hungary, India, Indonesia, Iran, Iraq, Ireland, Israel, Italy, Japan, Kazakhstan, Kenya, Korea (North), Korea (South), Malaysia, Mexico, Mongolia, Morocco, Myanmar, Netherlands, New Zealand, Nigeria, Norway, Pakistan, Peru, Poland, Romania, Russia, Senegal, Slovakia, South Africa, Spain, Sri Lanka, Sweden, Switzerland, Syria, Tunisia, Turkey, UK, Ukraine, USA, Venezuela, Viet Nam, Zimbabwe

International Atomic Energy Agency (IAEA)
<http://www.iaea.org/>

The IAEA is an intergovernmental organization within the UN system. It is endowed by its Statute, which entered into force in 1957, to promote the peaceful uses of atomic energy and ensure that nuclear activities are not used to further any military purpose. Under the 1968 Non-Proliferation Treaty and the nuclear weapon-free zone treaties, non-nuclear weapon states must accept IAEA nuclear safeguards to demonstrate the fulfilment of their obligation not to manufacture nuclear weapons. Its headquarters are in Vienna, Austria.

Members: Afghanistan, Albania, Algeria, Angola, Argentina, Armenia, Australia, Austria, Azerbaijan, Bangladesh, Belarus, Belgium, Belize, Benin, Bolivia, Bosnia and Herzegovina, Botswana, Brazil, Bulgaria, Burkina Faso, Cameroon, Canada, Central African Republic, Chad, Chile, China, Colombia, Congo (Democratic Republic of the), Costa Rica, Côte d'Ivoire, Croatia, Cuba, Cyprus, Czech Republic, Denmark, Dominican Republic, Ecuador, Egypt, El Salvador, Eritrea, Estonia, Ethiopia, Finland, France, Gabon, Georgia, Germany, Ghana, Greece, Guatemala, Haiti, Holy See, Honduras, Hungary, Iceland, India, Indonesia, Iran, Iraq, Ireland, Israel, Italy, Jamaica, Japan, Jordan, Kazakhstan, Kenya, Korea (South), Kuwait, Kyrgyzstan, Latvia, Lebanon, Liberia, Libya, Liechtenstein, Lithuania, Luxembourg, Macedonia (Former Yugoslav Republic of), Madagascar, Malawi, Malaysia, Mali, Malta, Marshall Islands, Mauritania, Mauritius, Mexico, Moldova, Monaco, Mongolia, Montenegro, Morocco, Mozambique, Myanmar, Namibia, Netherlands, New Zealand, Nicaragua, Niger, Nigeria, Norway, Pakistan, Palau, Panama, Paraguay, Peru, Philippines, Poland, Portugal, Qatar, Romania, Russia, Saudi Arabia, Senegal,

Serbia, Seychelles, Sierra Leone, Singapore, Slovakia, Slovenia, South Africa, Spain, Sri Lanka, Sudan, Sweden, Switzerland, Syria, Tajikistan, Tanzania, Thailand, Tunisia, Turkey, Uganda, UK, Ukraine, United Arab Emirates, Uruguay, USA, Uzbekistan, Venezuela, Viet Nam, Yemen, Zambia, Zimbabwe

Note: North Korea was a member of the IAEA until June 1994 and Cambodia until March 2003.

African Union (AU)
<http://www.africa-union.org/>

The AU was formally established in 2001 when the Constitutive Act of the African Union entered into force. In 2002 it replaced the Organization for African Unity. Membership is open to all African states. The AU promotes unity, security and conflict resolution, democracy, human rights, and political, social and economic integration in Africa. Its headquarters are in Addis Ababa, Ethiopia.

Members: Algeria, Angola, Benin, Botswana, Burkina Faso, Burundi, Cameroon, Cape Verde, Central African Republic, Chad, Comoros, Congo (Democratic Republic of the), Congo (Republic of the), Côte d'Ivoire, Djibouti, Egypt, Equatorial Guinea, Eritrea, Ethiopia, Gabon, Gambia, Ghana, Guinea, Guinea-Bissau, Kenya, Lesotho, Liberia, Libya, Madagascar, Malawi, Mali, Mauritania, Mauritius, Mozambique, Namibia, Niger, Nigeria, Rwanda, Western Sahara (Sahrawi Arab Democratic Republic, SADR), Sao Tome and Principe, Senegal, Seychelles, Sierra Leone, Somalia, South Africa, Sudan, Swaziland, Tanzania, Togo, Tunisia, Uganda, Zambia, Zimbabwe

Asia–Pacific Economic Cooperation (APEC)
<http://www.apec.org/>

APEC was established in 1989 to enhance economic growth and security in the Asia–Pacific region. Its member economies engage in dialogue and enter into non-binding commitments on e.g. combating terrorism, non-proliferation of weapons of mass destruction and effective export control systems. Its seat is in Singapore.

Member economies: Australia, Brunei Darussalam, Canada, Chile, China, Hong Kong, Indonesia, Japan, Korea (South), Malaysia, Mexico, New Zealand, Papua New Guinea, Peru, Philippines, Russia, Singapore, Taiwan, Thailand, USA, Viet Nam

Association of Southeast Asian Nations (ASEAN)
<http://www.aseansec.org/>

ASEAN was established in 1967 to promote economic, social and cultural development as well as regional peace and security in South East Asia. The seat of the secretariat is in Jakarta, Indonesia.

Members: Brunei Darussalam, Cambodia, Indonesia, Laos, Malaysia, Myanmar, Philippines, Singapore, Thailand, Viet Nam

ASEAN Regional Forum (ARF)
<http://www.aseanregionalforum.org/>

The ARF was established in 1994 to address security issues.

Participants: The ASEAN member states plus Australia, Bangladesh, Canada, China, European Union, India, Japan, Korea (North), Korea (South), Mongolia, New Zealand, Pakistan, Papua New Guinea, Russia, Timor-Leste, USA

ASEAN Plus Three

<http://www.aseansec.org/4918.htm>

Cooperation on political and security issues in the ASEAN Plus Three forum started in 1997 and was institutionalized in 1999.

Participants: The ASEAN member states plus China, Japan and Korea (South)

Australia Group (AG)

<http://www.australiagroup.net/>

The AG is a group of states, formed in 1985, that meet informally each year to monitor the proliferation of chemical and biological products and to discuss chemical and biological weapon-related items that should be subject to national regulatory measures.

Participants: Argentina, Australia, Austria, Belgium, Bulgaria, Canada, Croatia, Cyprus, Czech Republic, Denmark, Estonia, European Commission, Finland, France, Germany, Greece, Hungary, Iceland, Ireland, Italy, Japan, Korea (South), Latvia, Lithuania, Luxembourg, Malta, Netherlands, New Zealand, Norway, Poland, Portugal, Romania, Slovakia, Slovenia, Spain, Sweden, Switzerland, Turkey, UK, Ukraine, USA

Central European Initiative (CEI)

<http://www.ceinet.org/>

The CEI was established in 1989 to promote cooperation among its members in the political and economic spheres. It provides support to its non-EU members in their process of accession to the EU. The seat of the executive secretariat is in Trieste, Italy.

Members: Albania, Austria, Belarus, Bosnia and Herzegovina, Bulgaria, Croatia, Czech Republic, Hungary, Italy, Macedonia (Former Yugoslav Republic of), Moldova, Montenegro, Poland, Romania, Serbia, Slovakia, Slovenia, Ukraine

Collective Security Treaty Organization (CSTO)

<http://www.dkb.gov.ru/>

The CSTO was formally established in 2002–2003 by six signatories of the 1992 Collective Security Treaty. It aims to promote cooperation among its members. An objective is to provide a more efficient response to strategic problems such as terrorism and narcotics trafficking. Its seat is in Moscow, Russia.

Members: Armenia, Belarus, Kazakhstan, Kyrgyzstan, Russia, Tajikistan, Uzbekistan

Commonwealth of Independent States (CIS)
<http://www.cis.minsk.by/>

The CIS was established in 1991 as a framework for multilateral cooperation among former Soviet republics. Its headquarters are in Minsk, Belarus.

Members: Armenia, Azerbaijan, Belarus, Georgia, Kazakhstan, Kyrgyzstan, Moldova, Russia, Tajikistan, Turkmenistan, Ukraine, Uzbekistan

Commonwealth of Nations
<http://www.thecommonwealth.org/>

Established in its current form in 1949, the Commonwealth is an organization of developed and developing countries whose aim is to advance democracy, human rights, and sustainable economic and social development within its member states and beyond. Its secretariat is in London, UK.

Members: Antigua and Barbuda, Australia, Bahamas, Bangladesh, Barbados, Belize, Botswana, Brunei Darussalam, Cameroon, Canada, Cyprus, Dominica, Fiji*, Gambia, Ghana, Grenada, Guyana, India, Jamaica, Kenya, Kiribati, Lesotho, Malawi, Malaysia, Maldives, Malta, Mauritius, Mozambique, Namibia, Nauru, New Zealand, Nigeria, Pakistan**, Papua New Guinea, Saint Kitts and Nevis, Saint Lucia, Saint Vincent and the Grenadines, Samoa, Seychelles, Sierra Leone, Singapore, Solomon Islands, South Africa, Sri Lanka, Swaziland, Tanzania, Tonga, Trinidad and Tobago, Tuvalu, Uganda, UK, Vanuatu, Zambia

* Fiji was suspended from the Councils of the Commonwealth in December 2006.
** Pakistan was suspended from the Councils of the Commonwealth in November 2007.

Comprehensive Nuclear-Test-Ban Treaty Organization (CTBTO)
<http://www.ctbto.org/>

The CTBTO was established by the 1996 Comprehensive Nuclear Test-Ban Treaty (CTBT) to resolve questions of compliance with the treaty and as a forum for consultation and cooperation among the states parties. The CTBTO will become operational when the CTBT has entered into force. A Preparatory Commission was established to prepare for the work of the CTBTO, in particular by establishing the International Monitoring System, consisting of seismic, hydro-acoustic, infrasound and radionuclide stations from which data are transmitted to the CTBTO International Data Centre. Its seat is in Vienna, Austria.

Parties to the CTBT: See annex A

Conference on Interaction and Confidence-building Measures in Asia (CICA)

Initiated in 1992, CICA was established by the 1999 Declaration on the Principles Guiding Relations among the CICA Member States, as a forum to enhance security cooperation and confidence-building measures among the member states. It also promotes economic, social and cultural cooperation.

Members: Afghanistan, Azerbaijan, China, Egypt, India, Iran, Israel, Kazakhstan, Kyrgyzstan, Mongolia, Pakistan, Palestine, Russia, Tajikistan, Thailand, Turkey, Uzbekistan

Council for Security Cooperation in the Asia Pacific (CSCAP)
<http://www.cscap.ca/>

CSCAP was established in 1993 as an informal, non-governmental process for regional confidence building and security cooperation through dialogue and consultation on security matters in the Asia–Pacific region.

Member committees: Australia, Brunei Darussalam, Cambodia, Canada, China, CSCAP Europe, India, Indonesia, Japan, Korea (North), Korea (South), Malaysia, Mongolia, New Zealand, Papua New Guinea, Philippines, Russia, Singapore, Thailand, USA, Viet Nam

Council of Europe (COE)
<http://www.coe.int/>

Established in 1949, the Council is open to membership of all the European states that accept the principle of the rule of law and guarantee their citizens' human rights and fundamental freedoms. Its seat is in Strasbourg, France, Among its organs are the European Court of Human Rights and the Council of Europe Development Bank.

Members: Albania, Andorra, Armenia, Austria, Azerbaijan, Belgium, Bosnia and Herzegovina, Bulgaria, Croatia, Cyprus, Czech Republic, Denmark, Estonia, Finland, France, Georgia, Germany, Greece, Hungary, Iceland, Ireland, Italy, Latvia, Liechtenstein, Lithuania, Luxembourg, Macedonia (Former Yugoslav Republic of), Malta, Moldova, Monaco, Montenegro, Netherlands, Norway, Poland, Portugal, Romania, Russia, San Marino, Serbia, Slovakia, Slovenia, Spain, Sweden, Switzerland, Turkey, UK, Ukraine

Council of the Baltic Sea States (CBSS)
<http://www.cbss.st/>

The CBSS was established in 1992 as a regional intergovernmental organization for cooperation among the states of the Baltic Sea region. Its secretariat is in Stockholm, Sweden.

Members: Denmark, Estonia, European Commission, Finland, Germany, Iceland, Latvia, Lithuania, Norway, Poland, Russia, Sweden

Developing Eight (D-8)
<http://www.developing8.org/>

The D-8 is a group that was established in 1997 to improve the developing countries' positions in the world economy and enhance participation in decision making at the international level. It holds summit meetings every two years. The Council is composed of ministers of foreign affairs and is the political decision-making body. The Commission is the executive body. The secretariat is in Istanbul, Turkey.

Members: Bangladesh, Egypt, Indonesia, Iran, Malaysia, Nigeria, Pakistan, Turkey

Economic Community of West African States (ECOWAS)
<http://www.ecowas.int/>

ECOWAS was established in 1975 to promote trade and cooperation and contribute to development in West Africa. In 1981 it adopted the Protocol on Mutual Assistance in Defence Matters. Its executive secretariat is in Lagos, Nigeria.

Members: Benin, Burkina Faso, Cape Verde, Côte d'Ivoire, Gambia, Ghana, Guinea, Guinea-Bissau, Liberia, Mali, Niger, Nigeria, Senegal, Sierra Leone, Togo

European Union (EU)
<http://europa.eu/>

The EU is an organization of European states with its headquarters in Brussels, Belgium. The three EU 'pillars' are: the Community dimension, including the Single European Market, the Economic and Monetary Union (EMU) and the Euratom Treaty; the Common Foreign and Security Policy (CFSP); and police and judicial cooperation in criminal matters. The 2000 Treaty of Nice entered into force on 1 February 2003. The Treaty of Lisbon was signed by the EU heads of state or government in December 2007, but it will not enter into force until all the EU governments have ratified it.

Members: Austria, Belgium, Bulgaria, Cyprus, Czech Republic, Denmark, Estonia, Finland, France, Germany, Greece, Hungary, Ireland, Italy, Latvia, Lithuania, Luxembourg, Malta, Netherlands, Poland, Portugal, Romania, Slovakia, Slovenia, Spain, Sweden, UK

European Atomic Energy Community (Euratom, or EAEC)
<http://ec.europa.eu/euratom/>

Euratom was created by the 1957 Treaty Establishing the European Atomic Energy Community (Euratom Treaty) to promote the development of nuclear energy for peaceful purposes and to administer the multinational regional safeguards system covering the EU member states. It is located in Brussels, Belgium.

Members: The EU member states

European Defence Agency (EDA)
<http://eda.europa.eu/>

The EDA is an agency of the EU, under the direction of the Council. It was established in 2004 to help develop European defence capabilities, to promote European armaments cooperation and to work for a strong European defence technological and industrial base. The Steering Board, composed of the defence ministers of the participating member states and the European Commission, is its decision-making body. The EDA is located in Brussels, Belgium.

Participating member states: Austria, Belgium, Bulgaria, Cyprus, Czech Republic, Estonia, Finland, France, Germany, Greece, Hungary, Ireland, Italy, Latvia, Lithuania, Luxembourg, Malta, Netherlands, Poland, Portugal, Romania, Slovakia, Slovenia, Spain, Sweden, UK

Group of Eight (G8)
<http://www.g8.gc.ca/>

The G8 is a group of (originally seven) leading industrialized nations that have met informally, at the level of heads of state or government, since the 1970s.

Members: Canada, France, Germany, Italy, Japan, Russia, UK, USA

Gulf Cooperation Council (GCC)
<http://www.gcc-sg.org/>

Formally called the Cooperation Council for the Arab States of the Gulf, the GCC was created in 1981 to promote regional integration in such areas as economy, finance, trade, administration and legislation and to foster scientific and technical progress. The members also cooperate in areas of foreign policy and military and security matters. The Supreme Council is the highest GCC authority. Its headquarters are in Riyadh, Saudi Arabia

Members: Bahrain, Kuwait, Oman, Qatar, Saudi Arabia, United Arab Emirates

Hague Code of Conduct against Ballistic Missile Proliferation (HCOC)
<http://www.bmeia.gv.at/index.php?id=64664&L=1>

The 2002 HCOC is subscribed to by a group of states that recognize its principles, primarily the need to prevent and curb the proliferation of ballistic missile systems capable of delivering weapons of mass destruction and the importance of strengthening multilateral disarmament and non-proliferation mechanisms. The Austrian Ministry of Foreign Affairs, Vienna, Austria, acts as the HCOC secretariat.

Subscribing states: Afghanistan, Albania, Andorra, Argentina, Armenia, Australia, Austria, Azerbaijan, Belarus, Belgium, Benin, Bosnia and Herzegovina, Bulgaria, Burkina Faso, Burundi, Cambodia, Cameroon, Canada, Cape Verde, Chad, Chile, Colombia, Comoros, Cook Islands, Costa Rica, Croatia, Cyprus, Czech Republic, Denmark, Dominican Republic, Ecuador, El Salvador, Eritrea, Estonia, Ethiopia, Fiji, Finland, France, Gabon, Gambia, Georgia, Germany, Ghana, Greece, Guatemala, Guinea, Guinea-Bissau, Guyana, Haiti, Holy See, Honduras, Hungary, Iceland, Ireland, Italy, Japan, Jordan, Kazakhstan, Kenya, Kiribati, Korea (South), Latvia, Liberia, Libya, Liechtenstein, Lithuania, Luxembourg, Macedonia (Former Yugoslav Republic of), Madagascar, Malawi, Mali, Malta, Marshall Islands, Mauritania, Micronesia, Moldova, Monaco, Mongolia, Montenegro, Morocco, Mozambique, Netherlands, New Zealand, Nicaragua, Niger, Nigeria, Norway, Palau, Panama, Papua New Guinea, Paraguay, Peru, Philippines, Poland, Portugal, Romania, Russia, Rwanda, Senegal, Serbia, Seychelles, Sierra Leone, Slovakia, Slovenia, South Africa, Spain, Sudan, Suriname, Sweden, Switzerland, Tajikistan, Tanzania, Timor-Leste, Tonga, Tunisia, Turkey, Turkmenistan, Tuvalu, Uganda, UK, Ukraine, Uruguay, USA, Uzbekistan, Vanuatu, Venezuela, Zambia

Intergovernmental Authority on Development (IGAD)
<http://www.igad.org/>

Initiated in 1986 as the Intergovernmental Authority on Drought and Development, IGAD was formally established in 1996 to promote peace and stability in the Horn of

Africa and to create mechanisms for conflict prevention, management and resolution. Its secretariat is in Djibouti.

Members: Djibouti, Eritrea, Ethiopia, Kenya, Somalia, Sudan, Uganda

Joint Compliance and Inspection Commission (JCIC)

JCIC is the forum established by the 1991 START I Treaty in which the parties exchange data, resolve questions of compliance, clarify ambiguities and discuss ways to improve implementation of the START treaties. It convenes at the request of at least one of the parties.

Parties to the START treaties: See annex A

Joint Consultative Group (JCG)
<http://www.osce.org/item/13517.html>

The JCG was established by the 1990 Treaty on Conventional Armed Forces in Europe (CFE Treaty) to promote the objectives and implementation of the treaty by reconciling ambiguities of interpretation and implementation. Its seat is in Vienna, Austria.

Parties to the CFE Treaty: See annex A

League of Arab States
<http://www.arableagueonline.org/>

Also known as the Arab League, it was established in 1945. Its principal objective is to form closer union among Arab states and foster political and economic cooperation. An agreement for collective defence and economic cooperation among the members was signed in 1950. Its Permanent Headquarters are in Cairo, Egypt.

Members: Algeria, Bahrain, Comoros, Djibouti, Egypt, Iraq, Jordan, Kuwait, Lebanon, Libya, Mauritania, Morocco, Oman, Palestine, Qatar, Saudi Arabia, Somalia, Sudan, Syria, Tunisia, United Arab Emirates, Yemen

Mercado Común del Sur (MERCOSUR, Southern Common Market)
<http://www.mercosur.int/>

MERCOSUR was established in 1991 to achieve economic integration between the South American states. In 1996 it adopted a decision that only countries with democratic, accountable institutions in place would be allowed to participate. The Common Market Council is the highest decision-making body, and the Common Market Group is the permanent executive body. The secretariat and parliament are located in Montevideo, Uruguay.

Members: Argentina, Brazil, Paraguay, Uruguay

Missile Technology Control Regime (MTCR)
<http://www.mtcr.info/>

The MTCR is an informal military-related export control regime which in 1987 produced the Guidelines for Sensitive Missile-Relevant Transfers (subsequently revised). Its goal is to limit the spread of weapons of mass destruction by controlling ballistic missile delivery systems.

Partners: Argentina, Australia, Austria, Belgium, Brazil, Bulgaria, Canada, Czech Republic, Denmark, Finland, France, Germany, Greece, Hungary, Iceland, Ireland, Italy, Japan, Korea (South), Luxembourg, Netherlands, New Zealand, Norway, Poland, Portugal, Russia, South Africa, Spain, Sweden, Switzerland, Turkey, UK, Ukraine, USA

Non-Aligned Movement (NAM)
<http://www.cubanoal.cu/>

NAM was established in 1961 as a forum for consultations and coordination of positions in the United Nations on political, economic and arms control issues among non-aligned states.

Members: Afghanistan, Algeria, Angola, Antigua and Barbuda, Bahamas, Bahrain, Bangladesh, Barbados, Belarus, Belize, Benin, Bhutan, Bolivia, Botswana, Brunei Darussalam, Burkina Faso, Burundi, Cambodia, Cameroon, Cape Verde, Central African Republic, Chad, Chile, Colombia, Comoros, Congo (Democratic Republic of the), Congo (Republic of the), Côte d'Ivoire, Cuba, Djibouti, Dominica, Dominican Republic, Ecuador, Egypt, Equatorial Guinea, Eritrea, Ethiopia, Gabon, Gambia, Ghana, Grenada, Guatemala, Guinea, Guinea-Bissau, Guyana, Haiti, Honduras, India, Indonesia, Iran, Iraq, Jamaica, Jordan, Kenya, Korea (North), Kuwait, Laos, Lebanon, Lesotho, Liberia, Libya, Madagascar, Malawi, Malaysia, Maldives, Mali, Mauritania, Mauritius, Mongolia, Morocco, Mozambique, Myanmar, Namibia, Nepal, Nicaragua, Niger, Nigeria, Oman, Pakistan, Palestine Liberation Organization, Panama, Papua New Guinea, Peru, Philippines, Qatar, Rwanda, Saint Kitts and Nevis, Saint Lucia, Saint Vincent and the Grenadines, Sao Tome and Principe, Saudi Arabia, Senegal, Seychelles, Sierra Leone, Singapore, Somalia, South Africa, Sri Lanka, Sudan, Suriname, Swaziland, Syria, Tanzania, Thailand, Timor-Leste, Togo, Trinidad and Tobago, Tunisia, Turkmenistan, Uganda, United Arab Emirates, Uzbekistan, Vanuatu, Venezuela, Viet Nam, Yemen, Zambia, Zimbabwe

North Atlantic Treaty Organization (NATO)
<http://www.nato.int/>

NATO was established in 1949 by the North Atlantic Treaty (Washington Treaty) as a Western defence alliance. Article 5 of the treaty defines the members' commitment to respond to an armed attack against any party to the treaty. Its institutional headquarters are in Brussels, Belgium.

Members: Belgium, Bulgaria, Canada, Czech Republic, Denmark, Estonia, France*, Germany, Greece, Hungary, Iceland, Italy, Latvia, Lithuania, Luxembourg, Netherlands, Norway, Poland, Portugal, Romania, Slovakia, Slovenia, Spain, Turkey, UK, USA

* France is not in the integrated military structures of NATO.

Euro-Atlantic Partnership Council (EAPC)
<http://www.nato.int/issues/eapc/>

The EAPC was established in 1997, as a forum for cooperation between NATO and its Partnership for Peace partners.

Members: The NATO member states and Albania, Armenia, Austria, Azerbaijan, Belarus, Bosnia and Herzegovina, Croatia, Finland, Georgia, Ireland, Kazakhstan, Kyrgyzstan, Macedonia (Former Yugoslav Republic of), Moldova, Montenegro, Russia, Serbia, Sweden, Switzerland, Tajikistan, Turkmenistan, Ukraine, Uzbekistan

NATO–Russia Council (NRC)
<http://www.nato-russia-council.info/>

The NRC was established in 2002 as a mechanism for consultation, consensus building, cooperation, and joint decisions and action on security issues, focusing on areas of mutual interest identified in the 1997 NATO–Russia Founding Act on Mutual Relations, Cooperation and Security and new areas, such as terrorism, crisis management and non-proliferation.

Participants: The NATO member states and Russia

NATO–Ukraine Commission (NUC)
<http://www.nato.int/issues/nuc/>

The NUC was established in 1997 for consultations on political and security issues, conflict prevention and resolution, non-proliferation, arms exports and technology transfers, and other subjects of common concern.

Participants: The NATO member states and Ukraine

Nuclear Suppliers Group (NSG)
<http://www.nuclearsuppliersgroup.org/>

The NSG, formerly also known as the London Club, was established in 1975. It coordinates national export controls on nuclear materials according to its Guidelines for Nuclear Transfers (London Guidelines, first agreed in 1978), which contain a 'trigger list' of materials that should trigger IAEA safeguards when they are to be exported for peaceful purposes to any non-nuclear weapon state, and the Guidelines for Transfers of Nuclear-Related Dual-Use Equipment, Materials, Software and Related Technology (Warsaw Guidelines).

Participants: Argentina, Australia, Austria, Belarus, Belgium, Brazil, Bulgaria, Canada, China, Croatia, Cyprus, Czech Republic, Denmark, Estonia, Finland, France, Germany, Greece, Hungary, Ireland, Italy, Japan, Kazakhstan, Korea (South), Latvia, Lithuania, Luxembourg, Malta, Netherlands, New Zealand, Norway, Poland, Portugal, Romania, Russia, Slovakia, Slovenia, South Africa, Spain, Sweden, Switzerland, Turkey, UK, Ukraine, USA

Open Skies Consultative Commission (OSCC)
<http://www.osce.org/item/13516.html>

The OSCC was established by the 1992 Open Skies Treaty to resolve questions of compliance with the treaty.

Parties to the Open Skies Treaty: See annex A

Organisation Conjointe de Coopération en matière d'Armement (OCCAR, Organisation for Joint Armament Cooperation)
<http://www.occar-ea.org/>

OCCAR was established in 1996, with legal status since 2001, by four European states. Its aim is to provide more effective and efficient arrangements for the management of specific collaborative armament programmes. Its headquarters are in Bonn, Germany.

Members: Belgium, France, Germany, Italy, Spain, UK

Organisation for Economic Co-operation and Development (OECD)
<http://www.oecd.org/>

Established in 1961, the OECD's objectives are to promote economic and social welfare by coordinating policies among the member states. Its headquarters are in Paris, France.

Members: Australia, Austria, Belgium, Canada, Czech Republic, Denmark, Finland, France, Germany, Greece, Hungary, Iceland, Ireland, Italy, Japan, Korea (South), Luxembourg, Mexico, Netherlands, New Zealand, Norway, Poland, Portugal, Slovakia, Spain, Sweden, Switzerland, Turkey, UK, USA

Organization for Democracy and Economic Development–GUAM
<http://www.guam.org.ua/>

GUAM is a group of four states, established to promote stability and strengthen security, whose history goes back to 1997. The Organization was established in 2006. The members cooperate to promote social and economic development and trade in seven working groups. Its Information Office, which functions as a secretariat, is in Kyiv, Ukraine.

Members: Azerbaijan, Georgia, Moldova, Ukraine

Organization for Security and Co-operation in Europe (OSCE)
<http://www.osce.org/>

The Conference on Security and Co-operation in Europe (CSCE), which had been initiated in 1973, was renamed the OSCE and transformed into an organization in 1995 as a primary instrument for early warning, conflict prevention and crisis management. Its headquarters are in Vienna, Austria. Its Forum for Security Co-operation (FSC), also in Vienna, deals with arms control and confidence- and security-building measures. The OSCE comprises several institutions, all located in Europe.

Participants: Albania, Andorra, Armenia, Austria, Azerbaijan, Belarus, Belgium, Bosnia and Herzegovina, Bulgaria, Canada, Croatia, Cyprus, Czech Republic, Denmark, Estonia, Finland, France, Georgia, Germany, Greece, Holy See, Hungary, Iceland, Ireland, Italy, Kazakhstan, Kyrgyzstan, Latvia, Liechtenstein, Lithuania, Luxembourg, Macedonia (Former Yugoslav Republic of), Malta, Moldova, Monaco, Montenegro, Netherlands, Norway, Poland, Portugal, Romania, Russia, San Marino, Serbia, Slovakia, Slovenia, Spain, Sweden, Switzerland, Tajikistan, Turkey, Turkmenistan, UK, Ukraine, USA, Uzbekistan

Organisation for the Prohibition of Chemical Weapons (OPCW)
<http://www.opcw.org/>

The OPCW was established by the 1993 Chemical Weapons Convention as a body for the parties to oversee implementation of the convention and resolve questions of compliance. Its seat is in The Hague, the Netherlands.

Parties to the Chemical Weapons Convention: See annex A

Organization of American States (OAS)
<http://www.oas.org/>

The OAS is a group of states in the Americas that adopted its charter in 1948, with the objective of strengthening peace and security in the western hemisphere. The general secretariat is in Washington, DC, USA.

Members: Antigua and Barbuda, Argentina, Bahamas, Barbados, Belize, Bolivia, Brazil, Canada, Chile, Colombia, Costa Rica, Cuba*, Dominica, Dominican Republic, Ecuador, El Salvador, Grenada, Guatemala, Guyana, Haiti, Honduras, Jamaica, Mexico, Nicaragua, Panama, Paraguay, Peru, Saint Kitts and Nevis, Saint Lucia, Saint Vincent and the Grenadines, Suriname, Trinidad and Tobago, Uruguay, USA, Venezuela

* Cuba has been excluded from participation in the OAS since 1962.

Organization of the Black Sea Economic Cooperation (BSEC)
<http://www.bsec-organization.org/>

BSEC was established in 1992. Its aims are to ensure peace, stability and prosperity and to promote and develop economic cooperation and progress in the Black Sea region. Its permanent secretariat is in Istanbul, Turkey.

Members: Albania, Armenia, Azerbaijan, Bulgaria, Georgia, Greece, Moldova, Romania, Russia, Serbia, Turkey, Ukraine

Organization of the Islamic Conference (OIC)
<http://www.oic-oci.org/>

The OIC was established in 1969 by Islamic states to promote cooperation among the members and to support peace, security and the struggle of the people of Palestine and all Muslim people. Its secretariat is in Jeddah, Saudi Arabia.

Members: Afghanistan, Albania, Algeria, Azerbaijan, Bahrain, Bangladesh, Benin, Brunei Darussalam, Burkina Faso, Cameroon, Chad, Comoros, Côte d'Ivoire, Djibouti, Egypt, Gabon, Gambia, Guinea, Guinea-Bissau, Guyana, Indonesia, Iran, Iraq, Jordan, Kazakhstan, Kuwait, Kyrgyzstan, Lebanon, Libya, Malaysia, Maldives, Mali, Mauritania, Morocco, Mozambique, Niger, Nigeria, Oman, Pakistan, Palestine, Qatar, Saudi Arabia, Senegal, Sierra Leone, Somalia, Sudan, Suriname, Syria, Tajikistan, Togo, Tunisia, Turkey, Turkmenistan, Uganda, United Arab Emirates, Uzbekistan, Yemen

Organismo para la Proscripción de las Armas Nucleares en la América Latina y el Caribe (OPANAL, Agency for the Prohibition of Nuclear Weapons in Latin America and the Caribbean)
<http://www.opanal.org/>

OPANAL was established by the 1967 Treaty of Tlatelolco to resolve, together with the IAEA, questions of compliance with the treaty. Its seat is in Mexico City, Mexico.

Parties to the Treaty of Tlatelolco: See annex A

Pacific Islands Forum
<http://www.forumsec.org/>

The Forum was founded in 1971 by a group of South Pacific states that proposed the South Pacific Nuclear Free Zone, embodied in the 1985 Treaty of Rarotonga, and contribute to monitoring implementation of the treaty. The secretariat is in Suva, Fiji.

Members: Australia, Cook Islands, Fiji, Kiribati, Marshall Islands, Micronesia, Nauru, New Zealand, Niue, Palau, Papua New Guinea, Samoa, Solomon Islands, Tonga, Tuvalu, Vanuatu

Shanghai Cooperation Organisation (SCO)
<http://www.sectsco.org/>

The SCO's predecessor group, the Shanghai Five, was founded in 1996; it was renamed the SCO in 2001 and opened for membership of all states that support its aims. The member states cooperate on confidence-building measures and regional security and in the economic sphere. The SCO secretariat is in Beijing, China.

Members: China, Kazakhstan, Kyrgyzstan, Russia, Tajikistan, Uzbekistan

South Asian Association for Regional Co-operation (SAARC)
<http://www.saarc-sec.org/>

SAARC was created in 1985 as an association of states to promote political and economic cooperation in South Asia. It secretariat is in Kathmandu, Nepal.

Members: Afghanistan, Bangladesh, Bhutan, India, Maldives, Nepal, Pakistan, Sri Lanka

Southeast European Cooperative Initiative (SECI)
<http://www.secinet.info/>

SECI was initiated by the USA in coordination with the EU in 1996 to promote cooperation and stability among the countries of South Eastern Europe and facilitate their accession into European structures. The SECI secretariat is located in the OSCE offices in Vienna.

Members: Albania, Bosnia and Herzegovina, Bulgaria, Croatia, Greece, Hungary, Macedonia (Former Yugoslav Republic of), Moldova, Romania, Serbia, Slovenia, Turkey

Southern African Development Community (SADC)
<http://www.sadc.int/>

SADC was established in 1992 to promote regional economic development and the fundamental principles of sovereignty, peace and security, human rights and democracy. The secretariat is in Gaborone, Botswana.

Members: Angola, Botswana, Congo (Democratic Republic of the), Lesotho, Madagascar, Malawi, Mauritius, Mozambique, Namibia, South Africa, Swaziland, Tanzania, Zambia, Zimbabwe

Special Verification Commission (SVC)

The Commission was established by the 1987 Treaty on the Elimination of Inter-mediate-Range and Shorter-Range Missiles (INF Treaty) as a forum to resolve compliance questions and measures necessary to improve the viability and effectiveness of the treaty.

Parties to the INF Treaty: See annex A

Stability Pact for South Eastern Europe
<http://www.stabilitypact.org/>

The Pact was initiated by the EU at the 1999 Conference on South Eastern Europe and subsequently placed under OSCE auspices. It was intended to provide the sub-region with a comprehensive, long-term conflict prevention strategy by promoting political and economic reforms, development and enhanced security, and integration of South East European countries into the Euro-Atlantic institutions. Its activities were coordinated by the South Eastern Europe Regional Table and chaired by the Special Co-ordinator of the Stability Pact. The seat of the Special Co-ordinator was in Brussels, Belgium. It was replaced by the Regional Cooperation Council (RCC) on 28 February 2008.

Country partners: Albania, Austria, Belgium, Bosnia and Herzegovina, Bulgaria, Canada, Croatia, Cyprus, Czech Republic, Denmark, Estonia, Finland, France, Germany, Greece, Hungary, Ireland, Italy, Japan, Latvia, Lithuania, Luxembourg, Macedonia (Former Yugoslav Republic of), Malta, Moldova, Montenegro, Netherlands, Norway, Poland, Portugal, Romania, Russia, Serbia, Slovakia, Slovenia, Spain, Sweden, Switzerland, Turkey, UK, USA

Other partners: Central European Initiative, Council of Europe (Council of Europe Development Bank), European Bank for Reconstruction and Development, European Investment Bank, European Union (Council of the European Union, European Agency for Reconstruction, European Commission, European Parliament, Office for South Eastern Europe), International Finance Corporation, International Monetary Fund, International Organization for Migration, North Atlantic Treaty Organization, Office of the High Representative in Bosnia and Herzegovina, Organisation for Economic Co-operation and Development, Organization for Security and Co-operation in Europe, Organization of the Black Sea Economic Cooperation, Southeast European Cooperative Initiative, South-East

European Cooperation Process, United Nations (UN Development Programme, UN High Commissioner for Refugees, UN Mission in Kosovo), World Bank

Sub-Regional Consultative Commission (SRCC)
<http://www.osce.org/item/13692.html>

The SRCC was established by the 1996 Agreement on Sub-Regional Arms Control (Florence Agreement) as the forum in which the parties resolve questions of compliance with the agreement.

Parties to the Florence Agreement: See annex A

Wassenaar Arrangement (WA)
<http://www.wassenaar.org/>

The Wassenaar Arrangement on Export Controls for Conventional Arms and Dual-Use Goods and Technologies was formally established in 1996. It aims to prevent the acquisition of armaments and sensitive dual-use goods and technologies for military uses by states whose behaviour is cause for concern to the member states. Its secretariat is in Vienna, Austria.

Participants: Argentina, Australia, Austria, Belgium, Bulgaria, Canada, Croatia, Czech Republic, Denmark, Estonia, Finland, France, Germany, Greece, Hungary, Ireland, Italy, Japan, Korea (South), Latvia, Lithuania, Luxembourg, Malta, Netherlands, New Zealand, Norway, Poland, Portugal, Romania, Russia, Slovakia, Slovenia, South Africa, Spain, Sweden, Switzerland, Turkey, UK, Ukraine, USA

Western European Union (WEU)
<http://www.weu.int/>

The WEU was established by the 1954 Modified Brussels Treaty. Its seat is in Brussels, Belgium. WEU operational activities (the Petersberg Tasks) were transferred to the EU in 2000. The Assembly of WEU, the Interparliamentary European Security and Defence Assembly, seated in Paris, France, scrutinizes intergovernmental cooperation in armaments and arms research and development.

Members: Belgium, France, Germany, Greece, Italy, Luxembourg, Netherlands, Portugal, Spain, UK

Zangger Committee
<http://www.zanggercommittee.org/>

Established in 1971–74, the Nuclear Exporters Committee, called the Zangger Committee, is a group of nuclear supplier countries that meets informally twice a year to coordinate export controls on nuclear materials according to its regularly updated trigger list of items which, when exported, must be subject to IAEA safeguards. It complements the work of the Nuclear Suppliers Group.

Members: Argentina, Australia, Austria, Belgium, Bulgaria, Canada, China, Croatia, Cyprus, Czech Republic, Denmark, Finland, France, Germany, Greece, Hungary, Ireland, Italy, Japan, Korea (South), Luxembourg, Netherlands, Norway, Poland, Portugal, Romania, Russia, Slovakia, Slovenia, South Africa, Spain, Sweden, Switzerland, Turkey, UK, Ukraine, USA

Annex C. Chronology 2007

NENNE BODELL

This chronology lists the significant events in 2007 related to armaments, disarmament and international security. The dates are according to local time. Keywords are indicated in the right-hand column. Definitions of the abbreviations can be found on pages xxi–xxiv.

1 Jan.	Bulgaria and Romania become new members of the European Union (EU).	EU
10 Jan.	US President George W. Bush outlines his new strategy for US policy in Iraq and in the fight against terrorism. The USA will deploy more than 20 000 additional troops in Iraq; improve Iraqi security forces' capacity to protect the civilian population; and set political benchmarks for the Iraqi Government.	USA; Iraq
11 Jan.	China launches, from Xichang Satellite Launch Centre, a medium-range ballistic missile to destroy a Chinese weather satellite. This is the first known satellite intercept launch for more than 20 years and is regarded as a demonstration of China's weapons capabilities. The destruction of the satellite causes heavy pollution of space.	China; ASAT
15 Jan.	Former Maoist rebels take their seats in the interim Nepalese Parliament under the comprehensive peace agreement signed on 21 Nov. 2006, ending a 10-year rebel insurgency.	Nepal
19 Jan.	Meeting in Addis Ababa, Ethiopia, the Peace and Security Council of the African Union (AU) decides to organize the deployment of the AU Mission in Somalia (AMISOM) for a period of six months. (See also *20 Feb.*)	AU; Somalia; Peacekeeping
2 Feb.	The UN Special Envoy for the Future Status Process for Kosovo, Martti Ahtisaari, presents, in Belgrade, Serbia, and in Pristina, Kosovo, a plan for resolving the question of Kosovo's status. Under the plan Kosovo would be allowed its own national symbols, including flag and anthem, and to apply for membership of international organizations such as the UN and the IMF; and EU and NATO forces would remain in military and policing roles. (See also *26 Mar.*)	UN; Kosovo
6 Feb.	US President George W. Bush announces the creation of Africa Command (AFRICOM), the sixth unified combatant command, to strengthen the USA's security cooperation with Africa.	USA; Africa

7–9 Feb. Meeting in Mecca, Saudi Arabia, leaders of the Palestinian   Palestinians
factions Fatah and Hamas hold talks on solving the crisis that
threatens to ignite a civil war in the Palestinian territories. On
9 Feb. an agreement is reached to form a national unity government. The agreement contains no explicit recognition of
Israel.

8–13 Feb. The fifth round of the Six-Party Talks on North Korea—   North Korea;
between China, Japan, North Korea, South Korea, Russia and   Nuclear
the USA—is held in Beijing, China. On 13 Feb. a Denuclear-   programme
ization Action Plan is agreed to implement the Sep. 2005
agreement, under which North Korea has agreed to abandon
all its nuclear weapons and existing nuclear programmes.

10 Feb. At the annual Munich Conference on Security Policy, Russian   Russia/USA
President Vladimir Putin accuses the USA of provoking a
new arms race, in particular by developing ballistic missile
defences.

15 Feb. Twenty-nine suspects go on trial in Madrid, Spain, over the   Spain;
11 Mar. 2004 bomb attacks on trains that killed 191 people. It   Terrorism
is the biggest trial of alleged Islamic militants in Europe.

15 Feb. General Yury Baluyevsky, Chief of the General Staff of Rus-   Russia; INF
sia, threatens Russia's unilateral withdrawal from the 1987   Treaty
Intermediate-range Nuclear Forces (INF) Treaty unless the
USA changes its plans to install parts of its missile defence
shield in Central Europe.

20 Feb. The UN Security Council unanimously adopts Resolution   UN; AU;
1744, authorizing the AU to establish the AU Mission in   Somalia
Somalia (AMISOM) for a period of six months. AMISOM is
authorized to support dialogue and reconciliation in Somalia;
to protect the Transitional Federal Institution (TFIs) and help
them to carry out their government functions; and to provide
security for key infrastructure. AMISOM replaces the IGAD
Peace Support Mission to Somalia (IGASOM), authorized by
Resolution 1725 (2006).

22–23 Feb. At the Oslo Conference on Cluster Munitions, a declaration is   Arms control;
adopted calling for governments to 'conclude by 2008 a   Cluster
legally binding international instrument that will . . . prohibit   munitions
the use, production, transfer and stockpiling of cluster munitions that cause unacceptable harm to civilians'. The final
declaration is signed by 46 states. Among the states not
attending the conference are Australia, China, India, Israel,
Pakistan, Russia and the USA. Japan, Poland and Romania
attend but refuse to endorse the declaration.

26 Feb. The International Court of Justice (ICJ) finds that Serbia has   Serbia; ICJ
violated its obligations under the 1948 Genocide Convention,
with respect to the 1995 massacre in Srebrenica, Bosnia and
Herzegovina.

4 Mar.	Meeting in Ouagadougou, Burkina Faso, Ivorian President Laurent Gbagbo and the leader of the rebel group Forces Nouvelles de Côte d'Ivoire (FNCI, New Forces), Guillaume Kigbafori Soro, sign a peace agreement. Under the agreement a power-sharing government will be formed, a joint army command will be set up and the North–South buffer zone will be removed. A timetable for disarmament, voter registration and elections is set.	Côte d'Ivoire
5 Mar.	The trial of Ramush Haradinaj, former prime minister of Kosovo and a former commander of the Kosovo Liberation Army (KLA), who is charged with war crimes in the 1998–99 Kosovo conflict, starts at the International Criminal Tribunal for the former Yugoslavia (ICTY) in The Hague, Netherlands. Haradinaj resigned as prime minister and surrendered to the ICTY in Mar. 2005.	Kosovo; ICTY
6 Mar.	At the request of the Afghan Government, the NATO-led International Security Assistance Force (ISAF) and the Afghan National Security Force launch Operation Achilles, the largest joint operation against the Taliban in Helmand province, southern Afghanistan. The operation involves more than 4500 NATO troops and nearly 1000 Afghan soldiers.	NATO; ISAF; Afghanistan
10 Mar.	At a conference held in Baghdad aiming at restoring stability in Iraq, representatives from Iran, Syria and the USA are brought together for the first time in years. Also attending the conference are representatives of the UN Security Council, the Arab League and the Gulf Cooperation Council (GCC). (The first time ministerial-level meeting involving Iran and Syria is held on *3–4 May*.)	Iraq
15 Mar.	The US Department of Defense states that the suspected planner of the 11 Sep. 2001 attacks on the USA, Khalid Sheikh Mohammed, in a hearing at Guantánamo Bay, Cuba, has confessed responsibility for the 2001 attacks and for 30 other terror plots, including the 2002 attack in Bali, Indonesia.	Terrorism
19–22 Mar.	The sixth round of the Six-Party Talks—between China, Japan, North Korea, South Korea, Russia and the USA—is held in Beijing, China. The talks are suspended on 22 Mar. without an agreement after North Korea refuses to continue negotiations until its frozen assets in a Macau bank are transferred to a bank in China.	North Korea; Nuclear programme
22 Mar.	Heavy fighting breaks out in Mogadishu, Somalia, between Somali Government and Ethiopian forces and forces of the Union of Islamic Courts (UIC). The International Committee of the Red Cross says that the fighting is the heaviest in Mogadishu since the overthrow of Siad Barre in 1991.	Somalia; Ethiopia

24 Mar.	The UN Security Council unanimously adopts Resolution 1747, reaffirming that Iran should without further delay take the steps required by the IAEA Board of Governors in its Resolution GOV/2006/14 and in UN Security Council Resolution 1737 (2006). The resolutions require that Iran does not supply, sell or transfer directly or indirectly any arms or related material and that all states prohibit the procurement of such items from Iran by their nationals.	UN; Iran; Sanctions
26 Mar.	The UN Special Envoy for the Future Status Process for Kosovo, Martti Ahtisaari, presents the Comprehensive Proposal for the Kosovo Status Settlement to the UN Security Council. Under the proposal the only viable option for Kosovo is independence, with an initial period of 120 days of supervision by the UN Interim Administration Mission in Kosovo (UNMIK). An International Civilian Representative will be appointed to work with the Kosovo Assembly.	UN; Kosovo
28 Mar.	Meeting in Riyadh, Saudi Arabia, the members of the Arab League decide to relaunch the Middle East peace plan adopted in 2002, the Beirut Declaration. Under the plan the Arab states would recognize Israel if it withdraws from land occupied in the 1967 war.	Arab League; Israel
11 Apr.	Two suicide bombs in Algiers, Algeria, kill at least 33 people and injure over 200. Responsibility for the attacks is claimed by the al-Qaeda Organization in the Islamic Maghreb rebel group.	Algeria
16 Apr.	After months of international pressure the Sudanese Foreign Minister, Lam Akol, states that Sudan fully accepts the entire 'heavy support package' of troops, police officers, civilian staff and equipment which the UN will provide in support of the AU Mission in Sudan (AMIS).	UN; AU; Sudan
18 Apr.	After a routine inspection mission to the nuclear facility at Natanz, Iran, the IAEA confirms that Iran has assembled 1300 centrifuges and has begun the uranium enrichment process.	IAEA; Iran; Nuclear programme
18 Apr.	Nearly 200 people are killed and hundreds are injured in terrorist bomb attacks across Baghdad, mostly in Shia areas, on the deadliest day in Iraq since the US-led invasion in Mar. 2003.	Iraq; Terrorism
23 Apr.	The Council of the European Union agrees to impose additional sanctions on Iran, including a total arms embargo. The EU sanctions go further than those already agreed by UN Security Council resolutions 1737 (2006) and 1747 (2007).	EU; Iran; Sanctions
26 Apr.	In his annual address to the Russian Parliament, President Vladimir Putin states that Russia will suspend its implementation of the 1990 Treaty on Conventional Armed Forces in Europe (CFE Treaty) until all member states of NATO have ratified the 1999 Agreement on Adaptation of the CFE Treaty. (See also *13 July* and *12 Dec.*)	Russia; CFE Treaty

3–4 May	Meeting in Sharm el-Sheikh, Egypt, ministers from the EU, the G8 and Iraq's neighbouring states, including Iran and Syria, hold talks on Iraqi security. On 3 May the International Compact for Iraq is endorsed, under which Iraq will institute reforms promoting national reconciliation and will receive financial assistance.	Iraq
20 May– *2 Sep.*	Following an attack by Lebanese security forces on a building in Tripoli, Lebanon, fighting erupts in the Palestinian refugee camp at Nahr al-Bared between Islamist militants from the Fatah al-Islam group and the Lebanese armed forces. The fighting is the bloodiest internal fighting since the civil war in Lebanon ended in 1990. Nearly 400 people are killed.	Lebanon
23 May	The IAEA Director General, Mohamed ElBaradei, releases his report on the implementation of the NPT Safeguards Agreement and relevant provisions of Security Council resolutions in Iran. The report states that Iran has not suspended its uranium enrichment-related activities or agreed to any of the required transparency measures.	IAEA; Iran
23–25 May	As a follow-up to the Feb. Oslo Conference, the Lima Conference on Cluster Munitions is held in Lima, Peru. A draft treaty text, largely modelled on the 1997 Anti-Personnel Mines (APM) Convention, is discussed.	Arms control; Cluster munitions
11–15 June	An Extraordinary Conference of the States Parties to the Treaty on Conventional Armed Forces in Europe (CFE Treaty) is held in Vienna, Austria, at the request of Russia. The participants fail to agree on a joint statement.	CFE Treaty
14 June	Following a week of factional fighting between Fatah and Hamas in the Gaza Strip, leaving more than 100 people dead, Hamas claims to have full control over the Gaza Strip after seizing the headquarters of Fatah's Preventative Security Force and the presidential compound in Gaza City. Palestinian President Mahmoud Abbas dismisses the Hamas-led government and declares a state of emergency.	Gaza Strip; Palestinians
17 June	A new emergency Palestinian Government, excluding Hamas, is sworn in by President Abbas, and a decree is issued enabling the new prime minister, Salam Fayyad, to rule without parliamentary approval and outlawing all of Hamas's armed forces. Hamas claims that the new government is illegal.	Palestinians
17 June	After meeting with a delegation of the UN Security Council in Khartoum, Sudan, the Sudanese Government agrees unconditionally to the deployment of a 19 000-strong joint UN–AU peacekeeping force in Darfur.	UN; AU; Sudan
19 June	US and Iraqi troops launch Operation Arrowhead Ripper, a major offensive against al-Qaeda networks in Baqubah and its surroundings. At least 75 people are killed and another 130 are injured in a car bomb attack near the al-Khilani Shia mosque in Baghdad.	Iraq

19 June	Meeting in Baku, Azerbaijan, the leaders of the Organization for Democracy and Economic Development–GUAM issue a joint declaration agreeing to form a peacekeeping force of 500 personnel and pledging to improve global energy security.	GUAM
20 June	In its first judgement, the Special Court for Sierra Leone, based in Freetown, convicts three former leaders of the Armed Forces Revolutionary Council of war crimes and crimes against humanity during Sierra Leone's 1991–2002 civil war.	Sierra Leone; Special Court for Sierra Leone; War crimes
24 June	Ali Hassan al-Majid ('Chemical Ali') and two other defendants are sentenced to death by an Iraqi court for genocide, war crimes and crimes against humanity during the 1988 Anfal Campaign, in which up to 180 000 civilian Kurds were killed.	Iraq
25 June	The North Korean Ministry of Foreign Affairs confirms that it has received the funds that had been frozen in a Macau bank and announces that the negotiations on the shutdown of the Yongbyon reactor are to start with the IAEA team of inspectors. The inspectors arrive in Pyongyang on 26 June, the first such visit since 2002. Following the statement, South Korea announces that it will resume its food aid to North Korea.	North Korea; Nuclear programme; IAEA; South Korea
29 June	The UN Security Council adopts, by a vote of 14–0, with Russia abstaining, Resolution 1762, immediately terminating the mandates of the UN Monitoring, Verification and Inspection Commission (UNMOVIC) and the IAEA Iraq Nuclear Verification Office. It also requests the UN Secretary-General to ensure that UNMOVIC's archives are kept under strict control and to transfer to the Iraqi Government all remaining unencumbered funds.	UN; Iraq; UNMOVIC
10 July– 8 Aug	Following clashes since 3 July between Pakistani security forces and radical Islamist students occupying the Lal Masjid (Red Mosque) in Islamabad, the security forces storm the mosque. More than 100 people are killed in the heavy fighting. Following the events in Islamabad, violence escalates in North and South Waziristan, killing more than 200 people. The ceasefire between government forces and pro-Taliban militants breaks down.	Pakistan
11 July	The Organisation for the Prohibition of Chemical Weapons (OPCW) confirms the destruction of the entire chemical weapon stockpile in Albania. Albania is the first country to completely and verifiably destroy its chemical weapons under the obligations of the Chemical Weapons Convention (CWC).	Albania; CWC
13 July	Russian President Vladimir Putin signs a decree on the suspension of the Treaty on Conventional Armed Forces in Europe (CFE Treaty), under which Russia will no longer permit inspections or exchange data on its deployments. The suspension will take effect 150 days after the notification date. (See also *12 Dec.*)	Russia; CFE Treaty

18–20 July	The sixth round of the Six-Party Talks—between China, Japan, North Korea, South Korea, Russia and the USA—continues in Beijing, China. North Korea offers to declare all its nuclear weapons programmes and to disable them by the end of 2007, in return for energy aid. On 18 July IAEA inspectors confirm that all five nuclear facilities at the Yongbyon complex have been shut down, the first steps taken under the Feb. 2007 Action Plan.	North Korea; Nuclear programme
27 July	India and the USA conclude the negotiations on the Agreement for Cooperation between the Government of the United States of America and the Government of India Concerning Peaceful Uses of Nuclear Energy (123 Agreement). This draft agreement, required under the provisions of the US Atomic Energy Act of 1954, specifies the terms governing the resumption of the trade between them in nuclear material and technology envisaged in the Indian–US Civil Nuclear Cooperation Initiative signed in Mar. 2006.	India; USA; Nuclear energy
30 July	Following meetings during July between officials from the Iranian Government and representatives of the IAEA, a team of IAEA inspectors visits the nuclear reactor in Arak, Iran.	IAEA; Iran
31 July	The UN Security Council unanimously adopts Resolution 1769, establishing a joint AU–UN operation in Darfur, Sudan. The AU/UN Hybrid Operation in Darfur (UNAMID) will consist of 19 000 military personnel and should be deployed in Dec. 2007 at the latest.	UN; Sudan; Peacekeeping
6 Aug.	Georgian President Mikhail Saakashvili accuses Russia of carrying out an air raid on Georgian territory, firing a missile near the village of Tsitelubani. The missile has not exploded. Russia denies violations of Georgia's borders. The EU condemns the incident on 10 Aug. On 18 Aug. the OSCE Presidency initiates an inconclusive investigation to clarify the circumstances behind the incident.	Russia; Georgia
14 Aug.	At least 175 people are killed and several hundred are injured in a series of suicide bomb attacks near Mosul, Iraq. The attacks are targeted at a Kurdish religious minority, the Yezidi sect.	Iraq; Terrorism
20 Aug.	The UN Security Council unanimously adopts Resolution 1772, extending the AU Mission in Somalia (AMISOM) for a period of six months, and calling on the UN Secretary-General, Ban Ki-moon, to continue planning for a the possible deployment of a UN peacekeeping operation to replace AMISOM.	UN; AU; Somalia
21 Aug.	Meeting in Tehran, representatives of the Iranian Government and the IAEA agree on a work plan to resolve all outstanding safeguards compliance issues in Iran.	IAEA; Iran; Nuclear programme

6 Sep.	The USA's Independent Commission on the Security Forces of Iraq, headed by General James L. Jones, releases its report stating that, despite measurable progress, the Iraqi Army will be unable to take over internal security from US forces in the next 12–18 months; that the Iraq Interior Ministry is 'dysfunctional'; and that the national police force should be disbanded. The Commission's report is one of several progress reports ordered by the US Congress.	Iraq
6 Sep.	Israeli aircraft carry out an air strike inside Syria on what is alleged to be a nuclear-related facility that North Korea is helping to equip. North Korea denies the allegations.	Israel; North Korea; Syria
6–8 Sep.	More than 50 people are killed in two suicide attacks in Algeria. The al-Qaeda Organization in the Islamic Maghreb claims responsibility for the attacks.	Algeria
10 Sep.	The US military commander in Iraq, General David H. Petraeus, gives testimony before the US House of Representatives Armed Services and Foreign Affairs committees, stating that the military objectives of the US military surge are in large measure being met and that 30 000 troops can be withdrawn from Iraq. On 13 Sep. US President George W. Bush announces plans for a withdrawal of around 30 000 US troops from Iraq by mid-2008 and the next phase of the US Iraq strategy that will start in Dec. 2008, with troops moving towards a support role for the Iraq Army.	Iraq; USA
16 Sep.	When escorting a diplomatic convoy in Baghdad, Iraq, employees from the US security firm Blackwater open fire, killing 17 Iraqi civilians and causing a major public scandal. The incident leads to the US Secretary of Defense, Robert Gates, ordering a review of the way private security firms operate in Iraq.	Iraq; USA
25 Sep.	The UN Security Council unanimously adopts Resolution 1778 establishing a UN-mandated 'multidimensional presence' in Chad and the Central African Republic (CAR), to protect civilians and facilitate humanitarian aid to people affected by the conflict in Darfur, Sudan. The UN Mission in the Central African Republic and Chad (MINURCAT) will include military forces from EU members.	UN; CAR; Chad; Sudan
27 Sep.	Security forces in Myanmar (Burma) raid six monasteries and arrest hundreds of monks in an attempt to stem the protests against the military regime in Yangon and other cities. The protests have started after a rise in fuel prices in Aug., and the injuring by troops of monks at a demonstration in Pakokku on 5 Sep. Since 17 Sep. there have been daily protest marches by the monks. On 26 Sep. riot police attacked the demonstrators at the Shwedagon Pagoda, Yangon, killing at least five people.	Myanmar (Burma)

27–30 Sep.	The sixth round of the Six-Party Talks—between China, Japan, North Korea, South Korea, Russia and the USA—is concluded in Beijing, China. The participants discuss a 'road map' for when and how North Korea will disclose and dismantle all its nuclear facilities.	North Korea; Nuclear programme
28 Sep.	The UN Security Council unanimously adopts Resolution 1779, extending until 15 Oct. 2008 the mandate of the four-member Panel of Experts appointed to monitor the arms embargo on Darfur, and requesting the panel to coordinate its activities with the AU/UN Hybrid Operation in Darfur (UNAMID). The panel was originally appointed pursuant to Resolution 1591 (2005).	UN; Sudan; Darfur; Arms embargoes
2–4 Oct.	North Korean leader Kim Jong Il and South Korean President Roh Moo-hyun meet in Pyongyang, North Korea, for what is only the second summit meeting between the two countries' leaders in more than 50 years. On 4 Oct. a joint declaration is signed calling for a permanent peace deal to replace the armistice that ended the 1950–53 Korean War.	North Korea; South Korea
3 Oct.	Following the Six-Party Talks—between China, Japan, North Korea, South Korea, Russia and the USA—held on 27–30 Sep., in Beijing, China, the Chinese Deputy Foreign Minister, Wu Dawei, announces that North Korea has agreed to disable its main nuclear reactor at Yongbyon and to give a full account of its nuclear programme by 31 Dec. 2007.	North Korea; Nuclear programme
15 Oct.	The Council of the European Union adopts Joint Action 2007/677/CFSP on the EU military operation in Chad and the Central African Republic (EUFOR TCHAD/RCA) in accordance with UN Security Council Resolution 1778 of 25 Sep. (The operation is finally approved on 28 Jan. 2008.)	EU; CAR; Chad; Sudan
17 Oct.	The Turkish Parliament backs, by a vote of 507–19, a motion by Prime Minister Tayyip Erdoğan permitting the government to launch military operations in northern Iraq to target Kurdistan Workers Party (PKK) rebel bases there.	Turkey; Iraq
18 Oct.	More than 140 people are killed when two bombs explode among crowds in Karachi, Pakistan, celebrating the return of former Prime Minister Benazir Bhutto. Several Islamist groups have threatened to attack Bhutto when she returns to Pakistan.	Pakistan; Terrorism
3 Nov.	Pakistani President Pervez Musharraf declares a state of emergency, claiming it is needed because of a crisis caused by militant violence and unruly judiciary. Hundreds of people protesting against the emergency rule are arrested as police crack down on demonstrations in Karachi. The state of emergency is lifted on 15 Dec.	Pakistan
5 Nov.	The defence ministers of China and the USA, Cao Gangchuan and Robert Gates, announce the establishment of a military hotline between their defence ministries in an effort to ease tensions between the two countries.	China; USA

6 Nov.	A suicide attack in Baghlan province, northern Afghanistan, kills at least 40 people and wounds many more. The attack is one of the worst since the ousting of the Taliban in 2001. A Taliban spokesman denies its involvement in the attack.	Afghanistan; Terrorism
15 Nov.	The last of the Russian troops withdraw from the military base in Batumi, Georgia. The military base at Gaduata, Abkhazia, remains disputed.	Russia; Georgia; Military bases
22 Nov.	Following the failure of Pakistan to fulfil its obligations in accordance with Commonwealth principles by lifting emergency rule and fully restoring the constitution, the Commonwealth of Nations suspends Pakistan from the councils of the organization.	Pakistan; Commonwealth of Nations
27–28 Nov.	Meeting in Annapolis, Maryland, USA, Israeli Prime Minister Ehud Olmert and Palestinian President Mahmoud Abbas agree to start negotiations on a treaty 'resolving all outstanding issues', including the future of Jerusalem, borders, water refugees and settlements. Under the agreement the negotiations will take place every second week, starting 12 Dec.	Israel/ Palestinians
28 Nov.	Following strong international and internal pressure, Pakistani President Pervez Musharraf resigns as Chief of Army Staff, but remains as President for a third term.	Pakistan
28 Nov.	At the last round of negotiations on the final status of Kosovo between Serbia and Kosovo, under the auspices of UN mediators, in Baden, Austria, the parties fail to reach an agreement. (Kosovo unilaterally declares its independence on 17 Feb. 2008.)	UN; Kosovo
3 Dec.	The US Director of National Intelligence releases 'Iran: nuclear intentions and capabilities', an assessment of the status of Iran's nuclear programme which concludes that Iran halted its nuclear weapons programme in 2003.	Iran; USA
5–7 Dec.	The third meeting of the Oslo Process, the Vienna Conference on Cluster Munitions, with 138 states represented, ends with a consensus on the inclusion in the draft treaty banning cluster munitions, of victim assistance, clearance, stockpile destruction, and international cooperation and assistance. (The next meeting will be held in Wellington, New Zealand, in Feb. 2008.)	Arms control; Cluster munitions
12 Dec.	Russian officially suspends participation in the Treaty on Conventional Armed Forces in Europe (CFE Treaty). Under the suspension, inspections and other transparency measures intended to strengthen mutual military trust between Russia and NATO will not take place.	Russia; CFE Treaty
13 Dec.	Meeting in Lisbon, Portugal, the heads of state or government of the EU member states sign the Treaty of Lisbon, which amends the current treaties and gives the EU a new legal framework. If ratified by all member states, it will come into force in 2009.	EU

16 Dec.	The Turkish military carries out air strikes on PKK rebel bases deep inside northern Iraq, targeting areas in the Kandil Mountains and in Zap, Hakurk and Avasin. Iraqi officials claim that bombs hit several villages, killing civilians. The USA denies giving its permission for the attacks.	Turkey; Iraq; Kurds
27 Dec.	Former Prime Minister Benazir Bhutto is assassinated at an election campaign rally in Rawalpindi, Pakistan. The assassination is followed by widespread violence throughout Pakistan.	Pakistan
27 Dec.	Following the national elections and with President Mwai Kibaki declared as the winner, allegations of election fraud are made by the opposition and heavy ethnic violence erupts throughout Kenya. Large crowds of demonstrators fight with heavy armoured soldiers and police in several cities across the country, and several people are killed.	Kenya
31 Dec.	North Korea fails to meet the deadline to submit to the other parties a 'complete and correct' declaration of its nuclear programmes, as it promised to do under the agreement reached on 3 Oct. at the Six-Party Talks held in Beijing, China.	North Korea; Nuclear programme

About the authors

Dr Ian Anthony (United Kingdom) is SIPRI Research Coordinator and Leader of the SIPRI Non-proliferation and Export Control Project. His SIPRI publications include *Reforming Nuclear Export Controls: The Future of the Nuclear Suppliers Group*, SIPRI Research Report no. 22 (2007, co-author), *Reducing Threats at the Source: A European Perspective on Cooperative Threat Reduction*, SIPRI Research Report no. 19 (2004), *Russia and the Arms Trade* (1998, editor) and *The Future of Defence Industries in Central and Eastern Europe*, SIPRI Research Report no. 7 (1994, editor). He has contributed to the SIPRI Yearbook since 1988.

Megan Bastick (Australia/United Kingdom) is Deputy Head of the Special Programmes Division at the Geneva Centre for the Democratic Control of Armed Forces (DCAF). She leads work on gender and security. She is co-editor of the *Gender and Security Sector Reform Toolkit* (DCAF, 2008) and co-author of *Sexual Violence in Armed Conflict: Global Overview and Implications for the Security Sector* (DCAF, 2007) and *Security Sector Responses to Trafficking in Human Beings* (DCAF, 2007). Prior to joining DCAF, she worked with the Quaker United Nations Office, Geneva, and with the Australian Red Cross.

Dr Sibylle Bauer (Germany) is Head of the Export Control Programme of the SIPRI Non-proliferation and Export Control Project. Previously, she was a Researcher with the Institute for European Studies in Brussels. She has published widely on European export control and armaments issues, including chapters in *The Restructuring of the European Defence Industry* (Office for Official Publications of the European Communities, 2001), *Annuaire français de relations internationales* [French yearbook of international relations] (Bruylant, 2001) and *The Path to European Defence* (Maklu, 2003). She is co-author of *The European Union Code of Conduct on Arms Exports: Improving the Annual Report*, SIPRI Policy Paper no. 8 (Nov. 2004). She has contributed to the SIPRI Yearbook since 2004.

Åsa Blomström (Sweden) was Project Secretary for the SIPRI Military Expenditure, Arms Production and Arms Transfers projects until 2007. She was responsible for the electronic archive common to these three research areas, and maintained the SIPRI reporting system for military expenditure. She has contributed to the SIPRI Yearbook since 2006.

Nenne Bodell (Sweden) is Head of the SIPRI Library and Documentation Department and of the SIPRI Arms Control and Disarmament Documentary Survey Project. She has contributed to the SIPRI Yearbook since 2003.

Mark Bromley (United Kingdom) is a Research Associate with the SIPRI Arms Transfers Project, where his research focuses on European arms exports, European arms export controls and South American arms acquisitions. Previously, he was a Policy Analyst for the British American Security Information Council (BASIC). His publications include *The European Union Code of Conduct on Arms Exports: Improving the Annual Report*, SIPRI Policy Paper no. 8 (Nov. 2004, co-author), 'The Europeanisation of arms export policy in the Czech Republic, Slovakia, and Poland',

European Security (June 2007), *The Impact on Domestic Policy of the EU Code of Conduct on Arms Exports: The Czech Republic, the Netherlands and Spain*, SIPRI Policy Paper no. 21 (May 2008). and 'Towards a common, restrictive EU arms export policy? The impact of the EU Code of Conduct on major conventional arms exports', *European Foreign Affairs Review* (forthcoming 2008, co-author). He has contributed to the SIPRI Yearbook since 2004.

Dr Peter Clevestig (Sweden) is a Researcher with the Chemical and Biological Warfare Programme of the SIPRI Non-proliferation and Export Control Project. He studies the role and responsibility of the Swedish medical research community in preventing acts of mass impact terrorism and develops tools for implementing bio-security. An active member of the Nordic Biosafety Network, he lectures on the subjects of bio-security, bioterrorism, microbial forensics and dual-use research and biotechnologies of concern. He is the author or co-author of several scientific publications primarily in the field of virology.

Vitaly Fedchenko (Russia) is a Researcher with the SIPRI Non-proliferation and Export Control Project, with responsibility for nuclear security issues and the political, technological and educational dimensions of nuclear arms control and non-proliferation. Previously, he was a visiting researcher at SIPRI, a Researcher and Project Coordinator at the Center for Policy Studies in Russia, and a Research Fellow at the Institute for Applied International Research in Moscow. He is the author or co-author of several publications on international non-proliferation and disarmament assistance, the international nuclear fuel cycle and Russian nuclear exports, including *Reforming Nuclear Export Controls: The Future of the Nuclear Suppliers Group*, SIPRI Research Report no. 22 (2007, co-author). He has contributed to the SIPRI Yearbook since 2005.

Harold A. Feiveson (United States) is a Senior Research Policy Scientist at Princeton University and a member of Princeton's Program on Science and Global Security of the Woodrow Wilson School of Public and International Affairs. He has taught regularly at the Woodrow Wilson School for the past 32 years on a range of topics, including arms control. From 1963 to 1967 he was a member of the Science Bureau of the US Arms Control and Disarmament Agency. His principal research interests are in the fields of nuclear weapons and nuclear-energy policy. He is editor and a principal author of *The Nuclear Turning Point: A Blueprint for Deep Cuts and De-alerting of Nuclear Weapons* (Brookings, 1999) and editor of the international journal *Science & Global Security*.

Dr Alexander Glaser (Germany) is a member of the research staff of Princeton University's Program on Science and Global Security. Since 2006, he has also worked with the International Panel on Fissile Materials (IPFM). Glaser received his PhD in physics in 2005 from Darmstadt University of Technology, Germany. Between 2001 and 2003 he was an SSRC/MacArthur Fellow with the Security Studies Program at the Massachusetts Institute of Technology. During 2000 and 2001 he was an adviser to the German Federal Ministry of Environment and Reactor Safety. Glaser is associate editor of *Science & Global Security*.

Bates Gill (United States) is the seventh Director of SIPRI. Before joining SIPRI in October 2007, he held the Freeman Chair in China Studies at the Center for Strategic and International Studies in Washington, DC. He previously served as a Senior Fellow in Foreign Policy Studies and inaugural Director of the Center for Northeast Asian Policy Studies at the Brookings Institution. He has a long record of research and publication on international and regional security issues, particularly regarding arms control, non-proliferation, strategic nuclear relations, peacekeeping and military-technical development, especially with regard to China and Asia. His most recent publications include *Rising Star: China's New Security Diplomacy* (Brookings, 2007) and *China: The Balance Sheet—What the World Needs to Know Now About the Emerging Superpower* (Public Affairs, 2006, co-author).

Jan Grebe (Germany) was an Intern with the SIPRI Military Expenditure and Arms Production projects in 2007–2008. He is completing his studies in political science, sociology, and economic and social history at Aachen University.

Dr Jean-Yves Haine (Belgium) is a Senior Researcher with the SIPRI Euro-Atlantic, Regional and Global Security Project and a Visiting Professor at the University of Toronto, where he studies European security and defence, transatlantic relations and the use of force. Previously, he was a Research Fellow with the Harvard University Department of Government, a Senior Research Fellow at the European Union Institute for Security Studies and a European Security Research Fellow at the International Institute for Strategic Studies. His publications include 'The European Security Strategy and threats: is Europe secure?' in *The EU and the European Security Strategy: Forging a Global Europe* (Routledge, 2007) and *Les Etats-Unis ont-ils besoin d'alliés?* [Does the United States need allies?] (Payot, 2004), which won the 2004 France-Amérique Prize.

Lotta Harbom (Sweden) is a Research Assistant with the Uppsala Conflict Data Program at the Department of Peace and Conflict Research, Uppsala University. She has contributed to the SIPRI Yearbook since 2005.

John Hart (United States) is the Head of the Chemical and Biological Warfare Programme of the SIPRI Non-proliferation and Export Control Project. His publications include *Chemical Weapon Destruction in Russia: Political, Legal and Technical Aspects*, SIPRI Chemical & Biological Warfare Studies no. 17 (1998, co-editor); 'The ALSOS Mission, 1943–1945: a secret U.S. scientific intelligence unit', *International Journal of Intelligence and Counter Intelligence* (autumn 2005), 'The Soviet biological weapons program' in *Deadly Cultures: Biological Weapons since 1945* (Harvard University Press, 2006); and *Historical Dictionary of Nuclear, Biological and Chemical Warfare* (Scarecrow Press, 2007, co-author). He has contributed to the SIPRI Yearbook in 1997, 1998 and since 2002.

Dr Gunilla Herolf (Sweden) is a Senior Guest Researcher with the SIPRI Euro-Atlantic, Regional and Global Security Project. Her fields of interest include transatlantic cooperation, Nordic and Swedish security, and security cooperation within the EU and NATO and among countries in Western Europe, with an emphasis on France, Germany and the UK. Previously, she worked at the Swedish Institute of

International Affairs. Her recent publications include *France, Germany and the UK: Cooperation in Times of Turbulence* (Stockholm University, 2004) and *The Nordic Countries and the European Security and Defence Policy* (2006, co-editor). She participates in several European networks, including the EU-CONSENT project, financed by the European Commission's Sixth Framework Programme.

Dr Paul Holtom (United Kingdom) is a Researcher with the SIPRI Arms Transfers Project. Previously, he was a Research Fellow with the University of Glamorgan Centre for Border Studies. He has also been an International Expert for the Council of Europe's Transfrontier Cooperation Programme on the Kaliningrad oblast and Lead Researcher on small arms and light weapons projects in north-eastern and south-eastern Europe for Saferworld. He is the author of several journal articles on the Baltic states, Kaliningrad and the Russian Federation, *Arms Transit Trade in the Baltic Sea Region* (Saferworld, 2003) and *Turning the Page: Small Arms and Light Weapons in Albania* (Saferworld, 2005). He was lead author of the joint SIPRI/ Uppsala University report *United Nations Arms Embargoes: Their Impact on Arms Flows and Target Behaviour* (2007).

Shannon N. Kile (USA) is a Senior Researcher with the SIPRI Non-proliferation and Export Control Project. His principal areas of research are nuclear arms control and non-proliferation with a special interest in Iran and North Korea. He has contributed to numerous SIPRI publications, including chapters on nuclear arms control and nuclear forces and weapon technology for the SIPRI Yearbook since 1995. His recent publications include, as editor, *Europe and Iran: Perspectives on Non-proliferation*, SIPRI Research Report no. 21 (2005).

Hans M. Kristensen (Denmark) is Director of the Nuclear Information Project at the Federation of American Scientists (FAS). He is co-author of the 'Nuclear notebook' column in the *Bulletin of the Atomic Scientists*. His recent publications include *Chinese Nuclear Forces and U.S. Nuclear War Planning* (FAS/NRDC, 2006), *Global Strike: A Chronology of the Pentagon's New Offensive Strike Plan* (FAS, 2006), 'Preparing for the failure of deterrence' *SITREP* (November/December 2005) and 'New doctrine falls short of Bush pledge', *Arms Control Today* (September 2005). He has contributed to the SIPRI Yearbook since 2001.

Dr Zdzislaw Lachowski (Poland) is a Senior Researcher with the SIPRI Euro-Atlantic, Regional and Global Security Project. He has published widely on the problems of European military security and arms control as well as on European politico-military integration. He is the co-editor of *International Security in a Time of Change: Threats–Concepts–Institutions* (Nomos, 2004) and author of *Confidence-and Security-Building Measures in the New Europe*, SIPRI Research Report no. 18 (2004) and *Foreign Military Bases in Eurasia*, SIPRI Policy Paper no. 18 (2007). In 2006 he led a project on confidence-building measures for North and South Korea. He has contributed to the SIPRI Yearbook since 1992.

Zia Mian (Pakistan/United Kingdom) is a physicist with the Program on Science and Global Security, Woodrow Wilson School of Public and International Affairs, at Princeton University, where he directs the Project on Peace and Security in South Asia. For the past decade his work has focused on nuclear weapons, arms control and disarmament, and nuclear energy issues in Pakistan and India. He has previously worked at the Union of Concerned Scientists, the Sustainable Development Policy Institute and Quaid-e-Azam University, Islamabad. He contributed to the SIPRI Yearbook in 2003 and 2007.

Catalina Perdomo (Colombia) is a Research Associate with the SIPRI Military Expenditure Project, responsible for monitoring military expenditure in Africa, Latin America and the Middle East. Previously, she worked at the Inter-American Development Bank (IADB), at the Washington, DC, office of the Fundación Ideas para la Paz of Colombia and at the Bogotá office of Management Sciences for Development. She is the author of several publications on security and development, including 'International assistance for security sector reform' in *Obsevatorio de Análisis de los Sistemas Internacionales 2007–2008* [Observatory for international systems analysis 2007–2008] (Universidad Externado de Colombia, 2007), and co-author of *Informe sobre la implementación de la estrategia de desarrollo subnacional* [Report on the implementation of subnational development strategy] (IADB, 2004). She has contributed to the SIPRI Yearbook since 2004.

Dr Sam Perlo-Freeman (United Kingdom) is a Researcher with the SIPRI Arms Production Project, responsible for monitoring data on the major arms producing companies worldwide. Previously he was a Senior Lecturer in Economics at the University of the West of England, working in the field of defence and peace economics. He is the author of a number of publications, including 'The demand for military expenditure in developing countries', *International Review of Applied Economics* (January 2003, co-author), and 'Offsets and development of the Brazilian armaments industry'. in *Arms Trade and Economic Development: Theory and Policy in Offsets* (Routledge, 2004). He contributed to the SIPRI Yearbook in 2003 and 2004.

Bernice Raveché (United States) was an Intern with the SIPRI Chemical and Biological Warfare Programme in the summer of 2007. She has a BA in International Health and Nutrition from the University of Pennsylvania and is currently completing her master's degree in Public Health at Columbia University. Her research at SIPRI was supported by the Council of Women World Leaders.

Dr Albrecht Schnabel (Germany) is a Senior Research Fellow at swisspeace and a Lecturer in International Organizations and Conflict Management at the University of Bern Institute of Political Science. Previously, he served as an Academic Officer in the Peace and Governance Programme of the United Nations University, Tokyo. His publications have focused on ethnic conflict, conflict prevention, peacekeeping, post-conflict peacebuilding, security sector reform and human security.

Elisabeth Sköns (Sweden) is Leader of the SIPRI Military Expenditure and Arms Production projects. Her recent publications include articles or chapters on defence offsets in *Arms Trade and Economic Development: Theory and Policy in Offsets* (Routledge, 2004), on the restructuring of the West European defence industry in *Mot et avnasjonalisert forsvar?* [Towards a denationalized defence?] (Abstrakt, 2005), on the costs of armed conflict in *Peace and Security*, Expert Papers Series no. 5 (Secretariat of the International Task Force on Global Public Goods, 2006), on financing security in *The Statesman's Yearbook 2007* (Palgrave Macmillan, 2006), on the challenges of globalization for the military industry in *Annuario Armi–Disarmo Giorgio La Pira* [Giorgio La Pira arms–disarmament yearbook] (Jaca Book, 2008), and on the economics of arms production in *Encyclopedia of Violence, Peace and Conflict*, 2nd edn (Academic Press, forthcoming 2008, co-author). She has contributed to the SIPRI Yearbook since 1983.

Kirsten Soder (Germany) is a Research Assistant with the SIPRI Armed Conflict and Conflict Management Project. She supports the research work of the programme and compiles data for the SIPRI Multilateral Peace Operations Database.

Dr Ekaterina Stepanova (Russia) is the Leader of the SIPRI Armed Conflicts and Conflict Management Project. Since 2001 she has led a research group on non-traditional security threats at the Institute of World Economy and International Relations (IMEMO), Moscow. In 2003, she worked at SIPRI as a Researcher on armed conflict and terrorism. She is the author of *Terrorism in Asymmetrical Conflict: Ideological and Structural Aspects*, SIPRI Research Report no. 23 (Oxford University Press, 2008) and *Anti-Terrorism and Peace-Building During and After Conflict*, SIPRI Policy Paper no. 2 (Stockholm, 1993). She serves on the editorial board of *Terrorism and Political Violence*.

Petter Stålenheim (Sweden) is a Researcher with the SIPRI Military Expenditure Project, responsible for monitoring data on military expenditure, with a special focus on Europe and Central Asia, and for the maintenance of the SIPRI Military Expenditure Database. He has previously worked as a consultant to the International Institute for Democracy and Electoral Assistance (IDEA) in Stockholm and lectured at the George C. Marshall Center in Germany. He is co-author of *Armament and Disarmament in the Caucasus and Central Asia*, SIPRI Policy Paper no. 3 (July 2003). He has contributed to the SIPRI Yearbook since 1998.

Frank von Hippel (United States) is a nuclear physicist and Professor of Public and International Affairs at Princeton University. He has worked for the past 30 years on fissile material policy issues, including those relating to commercialization of plutonium recycling, ending the production of plutonium and highly enriched uranium for weapons, and ending the use of highly enriched uranium as a reactor fuel. In 1993–94 he served as Assistant Director for National Security in the White House Office of Science and Technology Policy. He is currently Co-chair of the International Panel on Fissile Materials.

Professor Peter Wallensteen (Sweden) has held the Dag Hammarskjöld Chair in Peace and Conflict Research at Uppsala University since 1985 and has been the Richard G. Starmann Sr Research Professor of Peace Studies at the University of Notre Dame since 2006. He directs the Uppsala Conflict Data Program and the Special Program on the Implementation of Targeted Sanctions. The second, updated edition of his book *Understanding Conflict Resolution: War, Peace and the Global System* (Sage) was published in 2007. He is co-editor of *International Sanctions: Between Words and Wars in the Global System* (Frank Cass, 2005). He has contributed to the SIPRI Yearbook since 1988.

Anna Wetter (Sweden) is studying for a PhD in the Law Faculty of Uppsala University. Until December 2007 she was a Research Associate with the SIPRI Non-proliferation and Export Control Project, responsible mainly for SIPRI's conferences on how the effective investigation and prosecution of export-related offences can help prevent the proliferation of weapons of mass destruction. Her publications include 'Nordic nuclear non-proliferation policies: different traditions and common objectives' in *The Nordic Countries and the European Security and Defence Policy* (2006, co-author), 'EU–China security relations: the "softer" side' in *The International Politics of EU–China Relations* (OUP, 2007, co-author) and *Enforcing European Union Law on Exports of Dual-use Goods*, SIPRI Research Report no. 24 (forthcoming 2008).

Pieter D. Wezeman (Netherlands) is a Researcher with the SIPRI Arms Transfers Project. He rejoined SIPRI in 2006, having previously worked at the institute from 1994 to 2003. From 2003 to 2006 he was a Senior Analyst for the Dutch Ministry of Defence in the field of proliferation of conventional and nuclear weapon technology. He contributed to the SIPRI Yearbook in 1995–2003 and 2007.

Sharon Wiharta (Indonesia) is a Researcher with the SIPRI Armed Conflict and Conflict Management Project, working on peacekeeping and peacebuilding issues, particularly efforts to promote justice and to establish the rule of law in post-conflict situations. Prior to joining SIPRI in 2001 she worked at the Center for International Affairs of the University of Washington, Seattle, where she conducted research on sustainable development issues. Her publications on peacekeeping and peacebuilding include *The Transition to a Just Order: Establishing Local Ownership after Conflict* (Folke Bernadotte Academy, 2007, co-author) and *Prospects for Peace Operations: Regional and National Dimensions* (Georgetown University Press, 2008, co-editor). In 2007 she led a study on behalf of the UN Office for the Coordination of Humanitarian Affairs which reported in *The Effectiveness of Foreign Military Assets in Natural Disaster Response* (2007). She has contributed to the SIPRI Yearbook since 2002.

Errata

Errata for this edition of the SIPRI Yearbook will appear at <http://yearbook2008. sipri.org/errata/> and in *SIPRI Yearbook 2009*.

SIPRI Yearbook 2007: Armaments, Disarmament and International Security

Page 130, figure 3A.1	*In the graph of total personnel deployed to peace missions, the bar for 2003 should be shorter, showing approximately 107 000 troops.*
Page 360, table 9.4	*For* 'Total, top 10 61.42' *read* 'Total, top 10 65.71'.
Page 486, line 13	*For* 'Mohamad ElBaradei' *read* 'Mohamed ElBaradei'.
Page 524, table 12A.3	*Under the heading SLBMs, the number of warheads on RSM-50 missiles should read* '240', *not* '252'. *The subtotal for SLBMs should thus read* '624', *not* '636'. *The subtotal of SLBMs deployed should read* '176', *not* '180'. *No other figures are affected.*
Page 590, line 10	*For* 'In Germany a third CWDF began operation' *read* 'In Germany a third destruction unit began operation'.
Page 592, lines 13–15	*For* 'was also published (together with Wendy Orent) by Igor Domaradskiy, a scientist who worked in the system in Soviet times' *read* 'was published by *Critical Reviews in Microbiology*'. *Domaradskiy published (with Orent) a separate report (see footnote 89).*
Page 652, footnote 49	*For* '16 Oct. 2005' *read* '16 Oct. 2006'.

Index

Asia, East: military expenditure 177, 194,
195–97, 205, 206, 208, 215, 222, 229
Asia, South: military expenditure 177,
194–99, 205, 206, 215–16, 223, 229–30
Asia–Pacific Economic Cooperation 546
Atomstroyexport 342
Australia:
Agency for International Development
(AusAID) 466
India and 497–98
military expenditure 216, 223, 230
uranium exports 498
Australia Group 493, 494, 495, 547
Austria: military expenditure 197, 216, 223,
230
avian influenza 456–69:
background to 459–64
conference on, 2007 463
H1N1 virus 456
H5N1 virus 456, 457, 460, 461, 462, 464,
465, 467
human-to-human transmission 462, 464
Indonesia and 464–68
participatory disease surveillance and
response (PDS/R) 465, 466
prevention strategies 462–64
vaccination 463–64, 466, 467, 468
virus-sharing debate 466–68
wild fowl and 460
World Health Organization and 457–59,
461, 462, 464
Avio 285
AvtoVAZ 276
Azerbaijan:
Armenia, conflict with 25, 482–83
CFE Treaty and 482
energy and 188
military expenditure 185, 186, 187–89,
216, 223, 230
Nagorno-Karabakh and 25, 185, 186, 187
NATO and 188
Russia and 479
Aziz, Abdul 68
Aziz, Shaukat 392
Azraq, Idris 59

B-2 bomber 372
Babcock International 270, 271, 283, 291
Babur missile 395
Bacar, Mohamed 117
BAE Systems 259, 261, 268, 269, 270, 277,
281, 290

Bahamas: military expenditure 213, 221, 227
Bahrain: military expenditure 217, 225, 231
Balkans, Western 16:
EU and 27–28
ballistic missile defence (BMD) *see under*
United States of America
Baltic Sea, chemical weapons dumped in 441
Baluyevsky, Yury 501, 562
Ban Ki-moon 23, 101, 109, 112, 316, 567
Bangkok Treaty (1995) 536
Bangladesh: military expenditure 215, 223,
229
Barbados: military expenditure 213, 221, 227
barium 421
Baxter Healthcare SA 468
Beckett, Margaret 7
Beirut Declaration (2002) 564
Belarus 486:
CFE Treaty and 477
military expenditure 216, 223, 230
Belgium: military expenditure 216, 223, 230,
236
Belize: military expenditure 214, 221, 228
Benin: military expenditure 212, 219, 226
Berlin Plus Agreement (2003) 33
Bharat Electronics 284
Bhutto, Benazir 70, 569, 571
BINUB (UN Integrated Office in Burundi)
115, 129
Biocriminalization Project 431
bio-incidents 450–52
bioinformatics 454
Biological and Toxin Weapons Convention
(BTWC, 1972):
CBWs 432–33
challenges to 431
implementation of 432–34
Implementation Support Unit 432, 435
Meeting of Experts 434, 435
Meeting of States Parties 434, 435
parties to 8, 432, 433
provisions 526–27
Sixth Review Conference 432, 435
biological weapons:
disarmament 431–36
non-state actors 430
scientific research and 452–53, 454–55
threat reduction measures 446–47
transfers of knowledge and 455
biology, synthetic 453–54, 495
bio-safety 430, 446, 448, 452–53, 462, 468:
in China 447–48